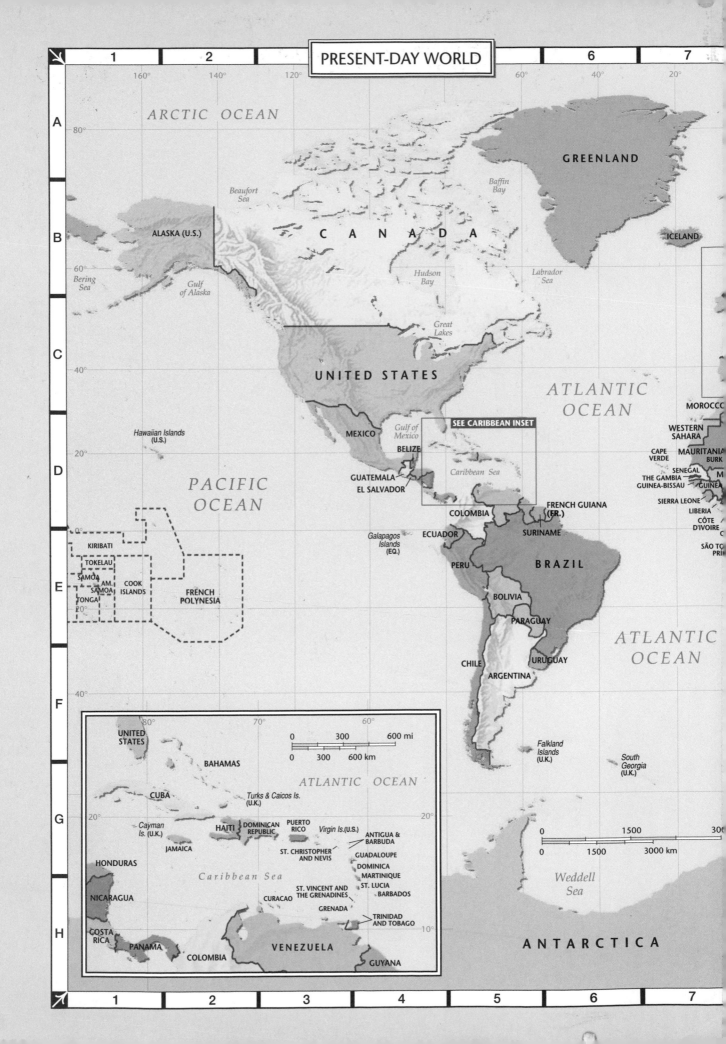

PRESENT-DAY WORLD

1   **2**   **6**   **7**

160°   140°   120°   60°   40°   20°

A

ARCTIC OCEAN

80°

GREENLAND

Baffin Bay

B

Beaufort Sea

ALASKA (U.S.)

C A N A D A

ICELAND

60°

Bering Sea

Gulf of Alaska

Hudson Bay

Labrador Sea

C

40°

Great Lakes

UNITED STATES

ATLANTIC OCEAN

MOROCCO

WESTERN SAHARA

D

20°

Hawaiian Islands (U.S.)

MEXICO

Gulf of Mexico

SEE CARIBBEAN INSET

CAPE VERDE   MAURITANIA
BURK

BELIZE

Caribbean Sea

SENEGAL

THE GAMBIA   M
GUINEA-BISSAU   GUINEA

GUATEMALA
EL SALVADOR

SIERRA LEONE
LIBERIA

PACIFIC OCEAN

COLOMBIA

FRENCH GUIANA
(FR.)

CÔTE
D'IVOIRE

0°

Galapagos Islands (EQ.)

ECUADOR

SURINAME

SÃO TO
PRIN

E

KIRIBATI

PERU

B R A Z I L

TOKELAU

SAMOA
AM.
SAMOA   COOK
ISLANDS

FRENCH
POLYNESIA

BOLIVIA

*ATLANTIC
OCEAN*

TONGA

20°

PARAGUAY

URUGUAY

CHILE

ARGENTINA

F

40°

Falkland Islands (U.K.)

South Georgia (U.K.)

80°   70°   60°

UNITED
STATES

0   300   600 mi

0   300   600 km

BAHAMAS

ATLANTIC OCEAN

G

CUBA

Turks & Caicos Is. (U.K.)

20°

Cayman Is. (U.K.)

HAITI   DOMINICAN
REPUBLIC

PUERTO
RICO

Virgin Is.(U.S.)

ANTIGUA &
BARBUDA

0   1500   300

JAMAICA

ST. CHRISTOPHER
AND NEVIS

GUADALOUPE

0   1500   3000 km

HONDURAS

Caribbean Sea

DOMINICA

MARTINIQUE

Weddell Sea

NICARAGUA

ST. VINCENT AND
THE GRENADINES

ST. LUCIA

BARBADOS

CURACAO

GRENADA

TRINIDAD
AND TOBAGO

H

COSTA
RICA

PANAMA

VENEZUELA

10°

A N T A R C T I C A

COLOMBIA

GUYANA

1   **2**   **5**   **6**   **7**

The Pathway to Success in Your College Courses

Your journey through college can be winding, filled with detours and potholes, or it can be relatively straight and smooth. The information below will help you have a pleasant experience along the way.

TIME MANAGEMENT

> *I am definitely going to take a course on time management . . . just as soon as I can work it into my schedule.*
>
> LOUIS E. BOONE

The time you spend preparing to study relates directly to a successful outcome. But time, or lack thereof, is a common complaint. How often do you comment that you don't have enough time to accomplish everything you wish to do?

How Do You Spend Your Time?

The first step in time management is to see how you currently spend your time. Have you ever taken the time to add up all of the hours you spend on your regular activities? Take a moment to write down everything you do during a seven-day period. These questions will help you consider all of the activities you do.

- You may spend 40 hours a week on your job, but what about commute time?
- You have to fuel your body. How many hours a week do you spend eating?
- Good grooming is essential. How many hours a week do you spend bathing and dressing?
- How much time do you give to your friends and family?

Remember, there are only 168 hours in a week. Is there any time left to sleep?

How Can I Make More Time?

You can't add hours to the day or days to the week, but if you learn to plan your time wisely, you should be able to make better use of the time you have. As an added bonus, you should feel less stress. Scheduling your time is a step in the right direction.

Develop schedules:

Long term

- Include fixed commitments only
- Include weekly obligations—job, classes, church, meetings, etc.
- Plan enough time for study—as a minimum, use two hours for every one hour in the classroom.
- Plan for weekly reviews—at least one hour each week for each class.

Intermediate

- One per week
- List major events and amount of work to be accomplished in each subject.
- Try to study at the same time every day.
- Make use of free hours between classes.
- Include non-study activities.

Short term

- Daily
- Use small note card you can carry with you.
- Write specifically what you need to accomplish that day.
- Mark out each item as it is completed.

STUDY ENVIRONMENT

Where you study and how you study is as important as how often you study.

- Identify a quiet place with a desk or table, a chair, and good lighting.
  - Your bed might be inviting, but remember your goal is to stay awake and concentrate.
- Although music or some type of background noise might be ok, avoid the TV.
  - It's too easy to get engrossed in a show rather than your course work.
  - Watching *CSI* can be interesting, but it probably won't help you with your *Introduction to Criminal Justice* final exam.
- Make sure you have everything you need: your textbooks, notes, paper and pencil, and a clock.
  - Why a clock? To help you manage your time.
- And, don't forget to take regular breaks.

LEARNING STYLES

- If you are assembling a toy or using a new computer program, do you put instructions aside and refer to them only when you run into trouble?
- Do you have to see a name or address in writing in order to remember it?
- Do you enjoy audio books, or do you find your mind wandering as you listen?

Your answers to these questions relate to your preferred learning style, and like clothing, one learning style doesn't fit all. If you have access to the Internet, you can take a learning style inventory at http://www.vark-learn.com/english/index.asp and then view helpsheets at http://www.vark-learn.com/english/page.asp?p=helpsheets related to your preferred learning style.

Visual Learners

- learn through seeing
- need to see the teacher's body language and facial expression to fully understand the content of a lesson.
- tend to prefer sitting at the front of the classroom to avoid visual obstructions (e.g. people's heads).
- may think in pictures and learn best from visual displays including: diagrams, illustrated text books, overhead transparencies, videos, flip charts and hand-outs.
- During a lecture or classroom discussion, visual learners often prefer to take detailed notes to absorb the information.

If you are a visual learner, here are some suggestions just for you:

- use visual materials such as pictures, charts, maps, graphs, etc.
- have a clear view of your teachers when they are speaking so you can see their body language and facial expression
- use color to highlight important points in text
- take notes or ask your teacher to provide handouts
- illustrate your ideas as a picture or brainstorming bubble before writing them down
- write a story and illustrate it
- use multi-media (e.g. computers, videos, and filmstrips)
- study in a quiet place away from verbal disturbances
- read illustrated books
- visualize information as a picture to aid memorization

Aural Learners

- learn through listening
- learn best through verbal lectures, discussions, talking things through and listening to what others have to say.
- interpret the underlying meanings of speech through listening to tone of voice, pitch, speed and other nuances. Written information may have little meaning until it is heard.
- often benefit from reading text aloud and using a tape recorder.

If you are an aural learner, here are some suggestions just for you:

- participate in class discussions/debates
- make speeches and presentations
- use a tape recorder during lectures instead of taking notes
- read text out aloud
- create musical jingles to aid memorization
- create mnemonics to aid memorization
- discuss your ideas verbally
- dictate to someone while they write down your thoughts
- use verbal analogies, and story telling to demonstrate your point

Read/Write Learners

- learn through reading and writing
- learn best by reading and re-reading the textbook and their notes, writing and rewriting their notes, and in general, organizing items into lists.

Kinesthetic Learners

- learn through moving, doing, and touching
- learn best through a hands-on approach, actively exploring the physical world around them.
- may find it hard to sit still for long periods and may become distracted by their need for activity and exploration.

If you are a tactile/kinesthetic learner, here are some suggestions just for you:

- take frequent study breaks
- move around to learn new things (e.g. read while on an exercise bike, mold a piece of clay to learn a new concept)
- work at a standing position
- chew gum while studying
- use bright colors to highlight reading material
- dress up your work space with posters
- if you wish, listen to music while you study
- skim through reading material to get a rough idea what it is about before settling down to read it in detail.

Multimodal Learners

- don't have a single preferred learning style.
- learn best through combinations.

If you have multiple preferences, you are in the majority as somewhere between fifty and seventy percent of any population seems to fit into that group.

READING SKILLS AND STRATEGIES

Good reading skills are essential to your success in your college-level classes. Here are a couple of reasons why:

- In high school, you may have been able to get good grades without reading much of the text. Now that you're in college, professors will expect you to read the textbook and they may test you on information not discussed in class but covered in the reading. In fact, many professors test on assigned readings as a check to make sure students are using their texts.
- The average freshman is assigned over 250 pages of reading each week, so clearly you're going to need to keep up with your reading assignments. If you do not read during week one, that means that you will need to read 500 pages the next week—just to stay caught up! If you choose not to read during the second week either . . . well, you can see how the work can just snowball.

Improving Your Reading Skills and Applying Reading Strategies

A good reader:

- seizes the main ideas.
- thinks about what the author is saying
- is active, not passive.
- concentrates on what is being read.
- remembers as much as possible.
- applies what is being read to personal experience.

Go to http://www.how-to-study.com/Improving%20Reading%20Skills.htm for more on reading skills.

SQ3R is one recommended method for improving your reading comprehension. The letters in the name stand for these five steps:

Survey: Before you read, scan the titles, headings, pictures, and summaries. Consider using the heading and subheadings as an outline for notes as you read.

Question: Ask yourself questions based on Step 1 and look for answers as you complete Step 3. For example, if a subheading is entitled "Basic Concepts of Reading," change it to read, "What are the Basic Concepts of Reading?"

Read: Read and take notes.

Recall: Without referring to the book or your notes, think about what you have read. See if your questions were answered. Could you explain the content to someone else? Try putting major concepts in your own words.

Review: Look at your questions, answers, notes and book to see how well you did recall. Observe carefully the points stated incorrectly or omitted. Fix carefully in mind the logical sequence of the entire idea, concepts, or problem. Finish up with a mental picture of the WHOLE.

Another method is **PQR3,** which stands for

Preview: Preview what you are going to read.

Question: Question what you are going to learn after the preview.

Read: Read the assignment.

Recite: Stop every once in a while, look up from the book, and put in your own words what you have just read.

Review: After you have finished, review the main points.

(Sounds similar to SQ3R, doesn't it?) Go to http://www.how-to-study.com/pqr.htm to learn more about this method.

There is even a related study method known as **M.U.R.D.E.R.**

Mood: Set a *positive* mood for yourself to study in.

Understand: Mark any information you don't understand in a particular unit and keep a focus on one unit or a manageable group of exercise.

Recall: After studying the unit, stop and put what you have learned into your own words.

Digest: Go back to what you did not understand and reconsider the information. Contact external expert sources (e.g., other books or an instructor) if you still cannot understand it.

Expand: ask three kinds of questions concerning the studied material:

- If I could speak to the author, what questions would I ask or what criticism would I offer?
- How could I apply this material to what I am interested in?
- How could I make this information interesting and understandable to other students?

Review: Go over the material you've covered. Review what strategies helped you understand and/or retain information in the past and apply these to your current studies.

Check this system out at http://www.studygs.net/murder.htm.

NOTE TAKING

Why take notes?

- It triggers basic lecturing processes and helps you to remember information.
- It helps you to concentrate in class.
- It helps you prepare for tests.
- Your notes are often a source of valuable clues for what information the instructor thinks most important (i.e., what will show up on the next test).
- Your notes often contain information that cannot be found elsewhere (i.e., in your textbook).

Evaluate your present note-taking system. Ask yourself:

- Did I use complete phrases or sentences that mean something to me later?
- Did I use any form at all?
- Are my notes clear or confusing?
- Did I capture main points and all subpoints?
- Did I streamline using abbreviations and shortcuts?

If you answered "no" to any of these questions, you may need to develop some new note-taking skills!

Guidelines for Taking Notes

- Concentrate on the lecture or on the reading material.
- Take notes consistently.
- Take notes selectively.
  - Do NOT try to write down every word.
  - Remember that the average lecturer speaks approximately 125–140 words per minute, and the average note-taker writes at a rate of about 25 words per minute.
- Translate ideas into your own words.
- Organize notes into some sort of logical form.
- Be brief. Write down only the major points and important information.
- Write legibly. Notes are useless if you cannot read them later!
- Don't be concerned with spelling and grammar.

There are many reasons for taking lecture notes.

- Making yourself take notes forces you to listen carefully and test your understanding of the material.
- When you are reviewing, notes provide a gauge to what is important in the text.
- Personal notes are usually easier to remember than the text.
- The writing down of important points helps you to remember then even before you have studied the material formally.

Instructors usually give clues to what is important to take down. Some of the more common clues are:

- Material written on the blackboard.
- Repetition
- Emphasis
  - Emphasis can be judged by tone of voice and gesture.
  - Emphasis can be judged by the amount of time the instructor spends on points and the number of examples he or she uses.
- Word signals (e.g. "There are **two points of view** on . . . " "The **third** reason is . . . " "In **conclusion** . . . ")
- Summaries given at the end of class.
- Reviews given at the beginning of class.

Each student should develop his or her own method of taking notes, but most students find the following suggestions helpful:

- Make your notes brief.
  - Never use a sentence where you can use a phrase. Never use a phrase where you can use a word.
  - Use abbreviations and symbols, but be consistent.

- Put most notes in your own words. However, the following should be noted exactly:
  - Formulas
  - Definitions
  - Specific facts
- Use outline form and/or a numbering system. Indention helps you distinguish major from minor points.
- Date your notes. Perhaps number the pages.
- If you miss a statement, write key words, skip a few spaces, and get the information later.
- Don't try to use every space on the page. Leave room for coordinating your notes with the text after the lecture. (You may want to list key terms in the margin or make a summary of the contents of the page.)

Here are some hints ("Do not's") regarding taking notes on classroom lectures that can save time for almost any student.

Do not plan to rewrite or type your notes later. To do so is to use a double amount of time; once to take the original notes a second to rewrite them. The advice is simple: DO IT RIGHT THE FIRST TIME!

Do not take notes in shorthand. Though shorthand is a valuable tool for a secretary, it is almost worthless for a student doing academic work. Here's why. Notes in shorthand cannot be studied in that form. They must first be transcribed. The act of transcribing notes takes an inordinate amount of time and energy but does not significantly contribute to their mastery. It is far better to have taken the notes originally in regular writing and then spend the time after that in direct study and recitation of the notes.

Do not record the lesson on a cassette tape or any other tape. The lecture on tape precludes flexibility. This statement can be better understood when seen in the light of a person who has taken his/her notes in regular writing. Immediately after taking the notes this person can study them in five minutes before the next class as s/he walks toward the next building, as s/he drinks his/her coffee, or whatever. Furthermore, this student, in looking over his/her notes, may decide that the notes contain only four worthwhile ideas which s/he can highlight, relegating the rest of the lecture to obscurity. Whereas the lecture on tape has to be listened to in its entirety including the worthwhile points as well as the "garbage," handwritten notes may be studied selectively. A student who takes the easy way out—recording the lecture on tape as he or she sits back doing nothing—will box him or herself into inflexibility.

Learning to make notes effectively will help you to improve your study and work habits and to remember important information. Often, students are deceived into thinking that because they **understand** everything that is said in class they will therefore remember it. This is dead wrong! Write it down.

As you make notes, you will develop skill in selecting important material and in discarding unimportant material. The secret to developing this skill is practice. Check your results constantly. Strive to improve. Notes enable you to retain important facts and data and to develop an accurate means of arranging necessary information.

Hints on Note Making

- Don't write down everything that you read or hear.
  - Be alert and attentive to the main points.
  - Concentrate on the "meat" of the subject and forget the trimmings.
- Notes should consist of key words or very short sentences. If a speaker gets sidetracked it is often possible to go back and add further information.
- Take accurate notes.
  - You should usually use your own words, but try not to change the meaning.
  - If you quote **directly** from an author, quote **correctly**.
- Think a minute about your material before you start making notes.
  - Don't take notes just to be taking notes!
  - Take notes that will be of real value to you when you look over them at a later date.
- Have a uniform system of punctuation and abbreviation that will make sense to you.
  - Use a skeleton outline and show importance by indenting.
  - Leave lots of white space for later additions.
- Omit descriptions and full explanations.
  - Keep your notes short and to the point.
  - Condense your material so you can grasp it rapidly.
- Don't worry about missing a point.
- Don't keep notes on oddly shaped pieces of paper.
  - Keep notes in order and in one place.
- Shortly after making your notes, go back and rework (not redo) your notes by adding extra points and spelling out unclear items.
  - Remember, we forget rapidly. Budget time for this vital step just as you do for the class itself.
- Review your notes regularly. This is the only way to achieve lasting memory.

These are only a few of the many methods for taking notes.

- the Cornell Method
- the Outline Method
- the Mapping Method (or Mindmapping)
- the Charting Method
- the Sentence Method

For details on these methods, go to http://www.sas.calpoly.edu/asc/ssl/notetaking.systems.html. Also check out this resource about note taking: http://www.how-to-study.com/Taking%20Notes%20in%20Class.htm

MEMORY TECHNIQUES

We hope that the information on preparing to study has been helpful, but do you feel that your real problem is remembering? Don't worry. There are ways to help you build your memory skills too.

Acronym

- An *acronym* is defined as "a word formed from the initial letters of a name," such as PCS for permanent change of station or SOC for Servicemembers Opportunity Colleges, "or by combining initial letters or parts of a series of words," as radar for radio detecting and ranging.
- Can you think of other acronyms?

Mnemonic

- A *mnemonic* is defined as "a device, such as a formula or rhyme, used as an aid in remembering."

Examples

As a child, you might have determined the number of days in a given month

- by reciting the rhyme "Thirty days hath September, April, June, and November . . ." or
- by using your knuckles ("peaks" have 31 days and "valleys" have 30, except February, of course).

If you have studied music, you might have used these techniques for remembering the names of the notes:

- FACE represents the names of the notes in the spaces on the staff.

- The first letters of the words in sentence "Every good boy does fine" represent the names of the notes on the lines on the staff.

A mnemonic used to recall the steps for simplifying algebraic expressions is "Please excuse my dear Aunt Sally."

- Perform operations within the innermost parentheses and work outward.
- Evaluate all exponential expressions.
- Perform multiplications and divisions as they occur, working from left to right.
- Perform additions and subtractions as they occur, working from left to right.

Use the sentence "My Very Educated Mother Just Served Us Nine Pizzas" to recall the order of the planets from the sun

- Mercury
- Venus
- Earth
- Mars
- Jupiter
- Neptune
- Pluto

Big Brown Rabbits Often Yield Great Big Vocal Groans When Gingerly Slapped for the color codes for resistors

- Black
- Brown
- Red
- Orange
- Yellow
- Green
- Blue
- Violet
- Gray
- White
- Gold
- Silver

PREPARING FOR AND TAKING TESTS

If you have practiced the strategies we have outlined in this orientation, you should be reviewing on a regular basis as you study rather than waiting to cram right before a test.

- Try to anticipate what is important and will be on the test, and use any review materials that are available, such as practice tests or review sheets.

Arkansas, Mississippi, Georgia, Florida, South Carolina, and North Carolina, fewer than 4 percent of black and white children attended school together.

More substantive progress had occurred in the border regions, where black and white students were far more likely to attend school together. In Kentucky, for example, 68 percent of the black students attended school with whites; figures in other southern states were Maryland 51 percent, West Virginia 63 percent, Missouri 42 percent, and Oklahoma 31 percent. Nearly 8 percent of black and white children in Texas also attended school together. But overall, compliance had been slow and incomplete.

The Struggle for School Desegregation in Little Rock, 1964–1980

The most celebrated resistance to *Brown* occurred in 1957 when Arkansas Governor Orval Faubus ordered state militia to prevent a handful of black students from being admitted to all-white Central High. After President Eisenhower sent the 101st Airborne Division to Little Rock to ensure admission of the black students, Faubus ordered the closing of both of Little Rock's high schools. In subsequent years, more subtle means were found to discourage the desegregation of Little Rock schools.

In 1964, all of the schools in Little Rock remained segregated (see the map at right, above). African Americans lived mostly in the eastern section of Little Rock, and their children attended all-black elementary schools and an all-black high school. White students attended all-white schools, including Central High.

By 1980, however, the schools of Little Rock had become fully desegregated (see the map at right, below). This map shows that not only did all schools include both white and black students, but that the proportion of black and white students varied little among the schools. The balance was achieved mostly by busing black students into formerly white schools. But the map also shows that Little Rock was itself becoming predominantly

black. Busing to achieve racial balance caused many whites to leave Little Rock and move to the mostly white suburbs. By 1980 Central High, which had been exclusively white in 1957, was two-thirds black. The same was true of most of the other schools in Little Rock. School officials worried that Little Rock schools would soon be nearly all black.

Similar patterns were evident in the North, too. Supreme Court rulings might change the law of the land, but the attitudes of the people were less malleable.

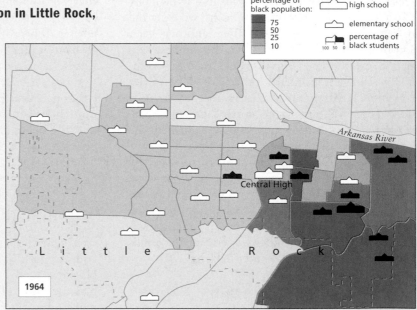

School segregation and residential pattern in Little Rock, Arkansas, 1964 and 1980

percentage of black population:
75
50
25
10

high school

elementary school

percentage of black students
100 50 0

1964

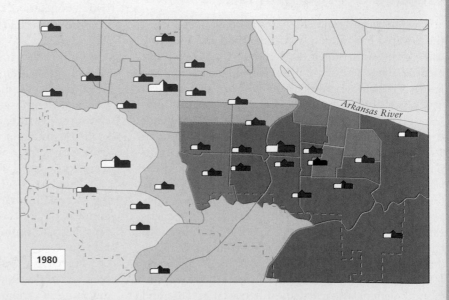

1980

In July 1965 Johnson raised the issue with his Cabinet. Undersecretary of State George Ball concurred with Bundy's assessment of the Vietcong as formidable adversaries but came up with an entirely different conclusion. "We cannot win," he said. "I truly have serious doubts that an army of Westerners can successfully fight Orientals in an Asian jungle." He proposed that the United States withdraw and accept the probable fall of South Vietnam. Defense Secretary McNamara, like every other member of the Cabinet, rejected Ball's views as defeatist. Johnson agreed. "If I got out of Vietnam," the President said, "I'd be doing exactly what [Neville] Chamberlain did in World War II. I'd be giving a big fat reward for aggression."

Johnson instead ordered the first of several huge increases in American ground forces in Vietnam. By the end of 1965, 184,000 Americans were in the field; a year later, 385,000; after another year, 485,000. By the middle of 1968 the number exceeded 538,000. Each increase was met by corresponding increases from the other side. The Soviet Union and China sent no combat troops, but stepped up their aid, and thousands of North Vietnamese regulars filtered across the 17th parallel to fight with the Vietcong guerrillas.

The new American strategy was not to seize any particular battlefield or terrain as in all previous wars, but to kill as many of the enemy as possible through bloody "search and destroy" operations. As the scope of the action broadened, the number of American casualties rose. The United States was engaged in a full-scale war, one that Congress never declared.

OPPOSITION TO THE WAR

Some Americans claimed that the struggle between the South Vietnamese government and the Vietcong was a civil war in which the United States should not meddle. They stressed the repressive character of the South Vietnamese government as proof that the war was not a contest between democracy and communism. They objected to the massive aerial bombings (more explosives were dropped on Vietnam between 1964 and 1968 than on Germany and Japan combined in World War II), to the use of napalm and defoliants such as Agent Orange that were sprayed on forests and crops and that wreaked havoc among noncombatants, and to the killing of civilians by American troops. As chairman of the Foreign Relations Committee, Senator William Fulbright had introduced the Gulf of Tonkin Resolution in 1964. By 1967 he was calling the war "unnecessary and immoral." American participation betrayed a "false and

dangerous dream of an imperial destiny." Above all, opponents of the war deplored the heavy loss of life—over 40,000 American dead by 1970, and hundreds of thousands of Vietnamese.

The cost of the war came to exceed $20 billion a year. But in large part because so many people objected to the war, Johnson refused to ask Congress to raise taxes to pay for it. The resulting deficits forced the government to borrow huge sums, caused interest rates to soar, and pushed prices higher.

Although Johnson's financial policies were short-sighted, if not blatantly irresponsible, and his statements about the war often disingenuous, he and his advisers believed they were defending freedom and democracy. As time passed and the human and financial costs mounted, it became clear that military victory was impossible. Yet American leaders were extraordinarily slow to grasp this fact. Repeatedly they advised the president that one more escalation (just so many more soldiers, just so many more air raids) would break the enemy's will. The arrogance bred by America's brief postwar monopoly of nuclear weapons persisted in some quarters long after the monopoly had been lost. This "superpower mentality," the belief that the United States was destined to be a kind of world policeman, was the cause of much future trouble.

THE ELECTION OF 1968

Gradually the opponents of the war gained numbers and strength. They began to include some of the president's advisers. By late 1967 McNamara, who had methodically tracked kill ratios, troop replacement rates, and nearly every other conceivable statistic, concluded that "the figures didn't add up" and the war could not be won. Deeply despondent, he resigned.

Opposition to the war was especially vehement on college campuses, some students objecting because they thought the United States had no business intervening in the Vietnam conflict, others because they feared being drafted, still others because so many students obtained educational deferments, while young men who were unable to attend college were conscripted.

Then, in November 1967, Eugene McCarthy, a low-keyed, introspective senator from Minnesota, announced his candidacy for the 1968 Democratic presidential nomination. Opposition to the war was his issue.

Preventing Johnson from being renominated seemed impossible. Aside from the difficulty of defeating a "reigning" president, there were the

DEBATING THE PAST

Would JFK have sent a half-million American troops to Vietnam? In the summer of 1963, Buddhist monks immolated themselves to protest Diem's repression. Several months later, Diem was ousted in a coup and JFK was assassinated. Within two years, President Johnson raised American troop levels in Vietnam to 300,000 and, by 1967, to half a million.

Many historians believe that if Kennedy had lived, he, too, would have sent more troops to Vietnam. Journalist David Halberstam (1969) emphasized that the same foreign policy advisers who guided Kennedy did so for Johnson, too. These men—Robert McNamara, McGeorge Bundy, and others—were, in Halberstam's mordantly ironic phrase, "the best and the brightest." Larry Berman (1982, 1989) showed that because Johnson was inexperienced in foreign policy, he had little choice but to listen to JFK's team. Lloyd C. Gardner (1995) and Brian Van De Mark (1991) emphasized the continuity—or rigidity—of American policymaking throughout the period. David Barrett (1993) described how Johnson wanted a way out of "that bitch of a war" but could not find one.

Those who have championed Kennedy's reputation insisted that JFK would have left Vietnam earlier. Arthur M. Schlesinger, Jr. (1978) explained that while Kennedy publicly endorsed the war, he was "secretly wondering how to get out." Schlesinger's thesis received unwanted support from filmmaker Oliver Stone's movie, *JFK* (1991). The movie hypothesized that Kennedy was assassinated by pro-war hawks in the military who feared the president would pull American troops out of Vietnam. The following year John M. Newman (1992) provided an historical brief for the movie.

But if Kennedy was looking for an excuse to get out of the war, why didn't he withdraw in response to Diem's persecution of the Buddhists? His decision to support a coup to replace Diem seemingly committed the United States to helping Diem's successors.

David Halberstam, *The Best and the Brightest* (1969), Larry Berman, *Planning a Tragedy* (1982) and *Lyndon Johnson's War* (1989), Brian Van De Mark, *Into the Quagmire* (1991), Lloyd C. Gardner, *Pay Any Price* (1995), David Barrett, *Uncertain Warriors* (1993), Arthur M. Schlesinger, Jr., *Robert Kennedy and His Times* (1978), John M. Newman, *JFK and Vietnam* (1992).

domestic achievements of Johnson's Great Society program: the health insurance program for retired people, greatly expanded federal funding of education and public housing, the Civil Rights Act. Even Senator McCarthy took his chances of being nominated so lightly that he did not trouble to set up a real organization. He entered the campaign only to "alleviate . . . this sense of political helplessness." Someone, he decided, must step forward to put the Vietnam question before the voters.

Stung by the critics, Johnson ordered General William C. Westmoreland, commander of American forces in Vietnam, to reassure the American people on the course of the war. The general obligingly returned to the United States in late 1967 and told the press that he could see "some light at the end of the tunnel."

Suddenly, early in 1968, on the heels of this announcement, North Vietnamese and Vietcong forces launched a general offensive to correspond with their Lunar New Year (called Tet). Striking 39 of the 44 provincial capitals, many other towns and cities, and every American base, they caused chaos throughout South Vietnam. They held Hué, the old capital of the country, for weeks. To root them out of Saigon the Americans had to level large sections of the city. Elsewhere the destruction was total, an irony highlighted by the remark of an American officer after the recapture of the village of Ben Tre: "It became necessary to destroy the town to save it."

The Tet offensive was essentially a series of raids; the communists did not expect to hold the cities indefinitely, and they did not. Their losses were enormous. Nevertheless the psychological impact in South Vietnam and in the United States made Tet a clear victory for the North. American pollsters reported an enormous shift of public opinion against further escalation of the fighting. When Westmoreland described Tet as a communist defeat and yet requested an additional 206,000 troops, McCarthy, who was campaigning in the New Hampshire primary, suddenly became a formidable figure. Thousands of students and other volunteers flocked to the state to ring doorbells on his behalf. On primary election day he polled 42 percent of the Democratic vote.

The political situation was confused. Before the primary, former attorney general Robert F. Kennedy, brother of the slain president, had refused either to seek the Democratic nomination or to support McCarthy, although he disliked Johnson intensely and was opposed to his policy in Vietnam. After McCarthy's success, he announced his candidacy.

Confronting this division in the ranks, President Johnson realized he could no longer hope to be an effective president. In a surprising televised announcement, he withdrew from the race. Vice President Hubert H. Humphrey then announced his candidacy, and Johnson threw the weight of his administration behind him.

Kennedy carried the primaries in Indiana and Nebraska. McCarthy won in Wisconsin and Oregon. In the climactic contest in California, Kennedy won by a small margin. However, immediately after his victory speech in a Los Angeles hotel, he was assassinated by Sirhan Sirhan, an Arab nationalist who had been incensed by Kennedy's support of Israel. In effect, Kennedy's death ensured the nomination of Humphrey.

The contest for the Republican nomination was far less dramatic, although its outcome, the nomination of Richard M. Nixon, would have been hard to predict a few years earlier. After his loss to Kennedy in 1960, Nixon ran unsuccessfully for governor of California in 1962, then moved to New York City and joined a prominent law firm. But he remained active in Republican affairs. In 1964 he had campaigned hard for Goldwater. When no other Republican developed extensive support as the 1968 election approached, Nixon entered the race, swept the primaries, and won an easy first-ballot victory at the Republican convention.

Nixon then astounded the country and dismayed liberals by choosing Governor Spiro T. Agnew of Maryland as his running mate. Agnew was a political unknown. ("Spiro who?" jokesters asked.) Nixon chose him primarily to attract southern votes.

Placating the South seemed necessary because Governor George C. Wallace of Alabama was making a determined bid to win enough electoral votes for his American Independent party to prevent any candidate from obtaining a majority. Wallace was flagrantly antiblack and anti-intellectual. (College professors were among his favorite targets. In attacking them he used such well-worn images as "ivory tower folks with pointed heads" and—more inventive—people without "sense enough to park a bicycle straight.") He seemed sure to attract substantial southern and conservative support. He denounced federal "meddling," the "coddling" of criminals, and the forced desegregation of schools. Nixon's choice of Agnew appeared to be an effort to contend with Wallace for conservative voters in the South.

This Republican strategy heightened the tension surrounding the Democratic convention, which met in Chicago in late August. Humphrey delegates controlled the convention. The vice president had a solid liberal record on domestic issues, but he had supported Johnson's Vietnam policy with equal solidity. Those who could not stomach the Nixon-Agnew ticket and who opposed the war faced a difficult choice. Several thousand activists, representing a dozen groups and advocating tactics ranging from orderly demonstrations to civil disobedience to indiscriminate violence, descended on Chicago to put pressure on the delegates to repudiate the Johnson Vietnam policy.

In the tense atmosphere that resulted, the party hierarchy overreacted. The mayor of Chicago, Richard J. Daley, whose ability to "influence" election results in a manner favorable to Democrats had often

▲ Alarmed by antiwar demonstrators at the 1968 Democratic national convention, Chicago Mayor Richard Daley ordered barbed wire fences erected in an attempt to control access to the convention hall. Protest demonstrations at the convention and Mayor Daley's heavy-handed response persuaded many voters that the fate of the republic would be safer in Republican hands.

been demonstrated, ringed the convention with policemen to protect it from disruption. This was a reasonable precaution in itself. Inside the building the delegates nominated Humphrey and adopted a war plank satisfactory to Johnson. Outside, however, provoked by the abusive language and violent behavior of radical demonstrators, the police tore into the protesters, in Norman Mailer's graphic phrase, "like a chain saw cutting into wood," while millions watched on television in fascinated horror.

At first the mayhem in Chicago seemed to benefit Nixon by strengthening the convictions of many voters that the tougher treatment of criminals and dissenters that he and Agnew were calling for was necessary. Those who were critical of the Chicago police tended to blame Humphrey, whom Mayor Daley supported.

Nixon campaigned at a deliberate, dignified pace. He made relatively few public appearances, relying instead on carefully arranged television interviews

and taped commercials. He stressed firm enforcement of the law and his desire "to bring us together." As for Vietnam, he would "end the war and win the peace," by just what means he did not say. Agnew, in his blunt, coarse way, assaulted Humphrey, the Democrats, and left-wing dissident groups. (Critics who remembered Nixon's own combative style in the era of Joseph McCarthy called Agnew "Nixon's Nixon.")

The Democratic campaign was badly organized. Humphrey was subjected to merciless heckling from antiwar audiences. He seemed far behind in the early stages. Shortly before election day, however, President Johnson helped him greatly by suspending air attacks on North Vietnam, and in the long run the Republican strategy helped increase his numbers, too. Black voters and the urban poor had no practical choice but to vote Democratic. Gradually Humphrey gained ground, and on election day the popular vote was close: Nixon slightly less than 31.8 million, Humphrey nearly 31.3 million. Nixon's Electoral College margin, however, was substantial—301 to 191. The remaining 46 electoral votes went to Wallace, whose 9.9 million votes came to 13.5 percent of the total. Together, Nixon and Wallace received 57 percent of the popular vote. Nevertheless, the Democrats retained control of both houses of Congress.

Nixon as President: "Vietnamizing" the War

When he took office in January 1969, Richard Nixon projected an image of calm and deliberate statesmanship; he introduced no startling changes, proposed no important new legislation. Indeed, he accepted more or less uncritically the New Deal approach to managing the economy. He considered the solution of the Vietnam problem his chief task. When the war in Southeast Asia first had burst on American consciousness in 1954, he had favored military intervention in keeping with the containment policy. As controversy over American policy developed, he had supported most of the actions of presidents Kennedy and Johnson. During the 1968 campaign he downplayed the Vietnam issue. Although he insisted he would end the war on "honorable" terms if elected, he suggested nothing very different from what Johnson was doing.

In office, Nixon first proposed a phased withdrawal of all non–South Vietnamese troops, to be followed by an internationally supervised election in South Vietnam. The North Vietnamese rejected this scheme and insisted that the United States withdraw its forces unconditionally. If the United States could

▲ The Viet Cong were initially terrified of what they called "angleworms," helicopters that swooped from the sky belching fire and rockets. The Viet Cong soon learned to aim two-thirds the distance of the fuselage ahead, so that the helicopter would fly into their bullets. Hundreds of helicopters were shot down by small arms fire.

number of American soldiers in Vietnam by 25,000. In September he promised that an additional 35,000 troops would be withdrawn.

These steps did not quiet American protesters. On October 15 an antiwar demonstration, Vietnam Moratorium Day, organized by students, produced an unprecedented outpouring of protest all over the country. Vice President Agnew famously retorted that the moratorium was an example of "national masochism" led by "an effete corps of impudent snobs who characterize themselves as intellectuals." A few days later he called on the country to "separate" radical students from society "with no more regret than we should feel over discarding rotten apples from a barrel," which at least had a quality of terseness that most of Agnew's pronouncements lacked.

A second Moratorium Day brought a crowd estimated at 250,000 to march past the White House. The president, unmoved, declared that a "silent majority" of the American people approved his course.

For a while, events appeared to vindicate Nixon's position. A gradual slowing of military activity in Vietnam had reduced American casualties. Troop withdrawals continued in an orderly fashion. A new lottery system for drafting men for military duty eliminated some of the inequities in the selective service law.

But the war continued. Early in 1970 reports that an American unit had massacred civilians, including dozens of women and children, in a Vietnamese hamlet known as My Lai revived the controversy over the purposes of the war and its corrosive effects on those who were fighting it. The American people, it seemed, were being torn apart by the war: one from another according to each one's interpretation of events; many within themselves as they tried to balance the war's horrors against their pride, their abhorrence of communism, and their unwillingness to turn their backs on their elected leader.

Nixon's most implacable enemy could have found no reason to think the president wished the war to go on. Its human, economic, and social costs could only vex his days and threaten his future reputation. When he reduced the level of the fighting, the communists merely waited for further reductions. When he raised it, many Americans denounced him. If he pulled out of Vietnam and the communists won, other Americans would be outraged.

Perhaps Nixon's error lay in his unwillingness to admit his own uncertainty, something the greatest presidents—one thinks immediately of Lincoln and Franklin Roosevelt—were never afraid to do. Facing a dilemma, he tried to convince the world that he was firmly in control of events, with the result that at

not prevail with a half million American troops, how, the North Vietnamese negotiator asked Henry Kissinger, the American negotiator, "can you succeed when you let your puppet troops do the fighting?" That question, Kissinger later admitted, "tormented" him.

The intransigence of the North Vietnamese left the president in a difficult position. Nixon could not compel the foe to end a war it had begun against the French nearly a quarter of a century earlier, and every passing day added to the strength of antiwar sentiment, which, as it expressed itself in ever more emphatic terms, in turn led to deeper divisions in the country. Yet Nixon could not face up to the consequences of ending the war on the communists' terms.

The president responded to the dilemma by trying to build up the South Vietnamese armed forces so that American troops could pull out without South Vietnam being overrun by the communists. He shipped so many planes to the Vietnamese that they came to have the fourth-largest air force in the world. The trouble with this strategy, called Vietnamization, was that for 15 years the United States had been trying without success to make the South Vietnamese capable of defending themselves. Nevertheless, efforts at Vietnamization were stepped up, and in June 1969 Nixon announced that he would soon reduce the

▲ South Vietnamese women and children were among those killed in the My Lai massacre in 1968. Some 300 apparently unarmed civilians were killed. Lieut. William Calley was convicted of murder and sentenced to life in prison. After many appeals, he was released in 1974.

times he seemed more like a high school valedictorian declaiming sententiously about the meaning of life than the mature statesman he so desperately wished to be. Thus he heightened the tensions he sought to relax—in America, in Vietnam, and elsewhere.

THE CAMBODIAN "INCURSION"

Late in April 1970 Nixon announced that Vietnamization was proceeding more rapidly than he had hoped, that communist power was weakening, and that within a year another 150,000 American soldiers would be extracted from Vietnam. A week later he announced that military intelligence had indicated that the enemy was consolidating its "sanctuaries" in neutral Cambodia and that he was therefore dispatching thousands of American troops to destroy these bases. (American planes had been bombing enemy sites in Cambodia for some time, although this fact was not revealed to the public until 1973.) Nixon even resumed bombing targets in North Vietnam.

"You've got to electrify people with bold decisions," he told the Joint Chiefs of Staff. "Let's go blow the hell out of them."

To foes of the war, Nixon's decision seemed so appallingly unwise that some of them began to fear that he had become mentally unbalanced. The contradictions between his confident statements about Vietnamization and his alarmist description of powerful enemy forces poised like a dagger 30-odd miles from Saigon did not seem the product of a reasoning mind. His failure to consult congressional leaders or many of his advisers before drastically altering his policy, the critics claimed, was unconstitutional and irresponsible. His insensitive response to the avalanche of criticism that descended on him further disturbed observers.

Nixon's shocking announcement triggered many campus demonstrations. One college where feeling ran high was Kent State University in Ohio. For several days students there clashed with local police; they broke windows and caused other damage to property. When the governor of Ohio called out the National

▲ National Guardsmen firing into a crowd of antiwar protesters at Kent State University killed 4 students and injured 11 others. The shootings triggered massive demonstrations and protests across the nation.

Guard, angry students showered the soldiers with stones. During a noontime protest on May 4 the guardsmen, who were poorly trained in crowd control, suddenly opened fire. Four students were killed, two of them women who were merely passing by on their way to class.

While the nation reeled from this shock, two students at Jackson State University were killed by Mississippi state policemen. A wave of student strikes followed, closing down hundreds of colleges, including many that had seen no previous unrest. Moderate students by the tens of thousands had joined with the radicals.

The almost universal condemnation of the invasion and of the way it had been planned shook Nixon hard. He backtracked, pulling American ground troops out of Cambodia quickly. But he did not change his Vietnam policy, and in fact Cambodia apparently stiffened his determination. As American ground troops were withdrawn, he stepped up air attacks.

The balance of forces remained in uneasy equilibrium through 1971. But late in March 1972 the North Vietnamese again mounted a series of assaults throughout South Vietnam. The president responded with heavier bombing, and he ordered the approaches to Haiphong and other North Vietnamese ports sown with mines to cut off the communists' supplies.

DÉTENTE WITH COMMUNISM

But in the midst of these aggressive actions, Nixon and his National Security Adviser, Henry Kissinger, devised a bold and ingenious diplomatic offensive, executed in nearly complete secrecy—from even the State and Defense departments! Nixon and Kissinger made an effective though not always harmonious team. They were both so self-centered that they did not always trust each other. Kissinger, who kept track of his own staff by bugging their phones, accused Nixon's top aides of doing the same to him. (Nixon did not tap Kissinger's phones, but he did secretly tape record their conversations along with those of nearly everyone else who entered the Oval Office—a revelation that subsequently enraged Kissinger, amazed the nation, and ended Nixon's presidency.)

Abandoning a lifetime of treating communism as a single worldwide conspiracy that had to be contained at all costs, Nixon decided to deal with China and the Soviet Union as separate powers and, as he put it, to "live together and work together" with both. Nixon and Kissinger called the new policy *détente,* a French term meaning "the relaxation of tensions between governments." But *détente* was not an expression of friendship so much as an acknowledgment that for decades the policy of containment had driven China and the Soviet Union closer together.

First Nixon sent Kissinger secretly to China and the Soviet Union to prepare the way for summit meetings with the communist leaders. Both the Chinese and the Soviets agreed to the meetings. Then, in February 1972, Nixon and Kissinger, accompanied by a small army of reporters and television crews, flew to Beijing. After much dining, sightseeing, posing for photographers, and consultation with Chinese officials, Nixon agreed to promote economic and cultural exchanges and supported the admission of communist China to the United Nations. (Since the founding of the United Nations, the United States had recognized only the Republic of China—Taiwan.) As a result, exports to communist China increased substantially, reaching $4 billion in 1980.

▲ President and Mrs. Nixon dining with Chinese communist officials in Beijing in February 1972. Even Nixon's harshest critics conceded that his initiative in reopening United States–China relations was a diplomatic master stroke.

Among other American products, the Chinese were introduced to Coca-Cola, marketed under a name meaning "tasty happiness," and other American products. Nixon's visit, ending more than 20 years of adamant American refusal to accept the reality of the Chinese revolution, marked a dramatic reversal; as such it was hailed throughout the world.

In May 1972 Nixon and Kissinger flew to Moscow. This trip also produced striking results. The mere fact that it took place while war still raged in Vietnam was remarkable. More important, however, the meeting resulted in a Strategic Arms Limitation Treaty (SALT). The two powers agreed to stop making nuclear ballistic missiles and to reduce the number of antiballistic missiles in their arsenals to 200. Nixon also agreed to permit large sales of American grain to the Soviet Union.

By the summer of 1972, with the presidential election looming in the fall, Kissinger redoubled his efforts to negotiate an end to the Vietnam war. By October he and the North Vietnamese had hammered

out a settlement calling for a cease-fire, the return of American prisoners of war, and the withdrawal of United States forces from Vietnam. Shortly before the presidential election Kissinger announced that peace was "at hand."

NIXON IN TRIUMPH

A few days later President Nixon was reelected, defeating the Democratic candidate, Senator George McGovern of South Dakota, in a landslide—521 electoral votes to 17. McGovern carried only Massachusetts and the District of Columbia. McGovern's campaign had been hampered by his tendency to advance poorly thought-out proposals, such as his scheme for funneling money directly to the poor, and by his rather bumbling, low-key oratorical style. The campaign marked the historical breakdown of the coalition that Franklin Roosevelt had fashioned and on which he and his Democratic successors,

particularly Truman and Johnson, had ridden to power. Of that coalition, only African Americans voted solidly for McGovern.

Nixon understandably interpreted his convincing triumph as an indication that the citizenry approved of everything he stood for. He had won over hundreds of thousands of voters who had supported Democrats in earlier elections. The "solid South" was again solid, but this time solidly Republican. Nixon's so-called southern strategy of reducing the pressure for school desegregation and otherwise restricting federal efforts on behalf of blacks had a powerful attraction to northern blue-collar workers as well.

Suddenly Nixon loomed as one of the most powerful and successful presidents in American history. His tough-minded but flexible handling of foreign policy questions, even his harsh Vietnamese policy, suggested decisiveness and self-confidence, qualities he had often seemed to lack in his earlier career. His willingness, despite his long history as a militant cold warrior, to negotiate with the communist nations indicated a new flexibility and creativity. His landslide victory appeared to demonstrate that a large majority of the people approved of his way of tackling the major problems of the times.

But Kissinger's agreement with the North Vietnamese came apart when Nguyen Van Thieu, the South Vietnamese president, refused to sign it. He claimed that the agreement, by permitting communist troops to remain in the south, would ensure his ultimate defeat. "Why," he asked Kissinger, "are you rushing to get the Nobel Prize?" To Kissinger's chagrin, Nixon sided with Thieu and resumed the bombing of North Vietnam in December 1972, this time sending the mighty B-52s directly over Hanoi and other cities. The destruction they caused was great, but their effectiveness as a means of forcing concessions from the North Vietnamese was at best debatable, and in these strikes for the first time the United States lost large numbers of the big strategic bombers.

In January 1973 a settlement was finally reached. As with the October "agreement," the North Vietnamese retained control of large sections of the south, and they promised to release American prisoners of war within 60 days. Thieu assented this time, largely because Nixon secretly pledged that the United States would "respond with full force" if North Vietnam resumed its offensive. Within several months most prisoners of war were released, and the last American troops were pulled out of Vietnam. More than 57,000 Americans had died in the long war, and over 300,000 more had been wounded. The cost had reached a staggering $150 billion. Nearly a

million communist soldiers and 185,000 South Vietnamese soldiers were reported killed.

In 1973, too, Kissinger was named Secretary of State; he shared the Nobel Prize for Peace with Le Duc Tho for negotiating an end to the Vietnam War

DOMESTIC POLICY UNDER NIXON

When Nixon became president in 1969, the major economic problem he faced was inflation. This was caused primarily by the heavy military expenditures and easy-money policies of the Johnson administration. Nixon cut federal spending and balanced the 1969 budget, while the Federal Reserve Board forced up interest rates to slow the expansion of the money supply. When prices continued to rise, uneasiness mounted and labor unions demanded large wage increases.

In 1970 Congress passed a law giving the president power to regulate prices and wages. Nixon originally opposed this legislation, but in the summer of 1971 he changed his mind and announced a 90-day price and wage freeze. Then he set up a pay board and a price commission with authority to limit wage and price increases when the freeze ended. These controls did not check inflation completely—and they angered union leaders, who felt that labor was being shortchanged—but they did slow the upward spiral.

In handling other domestic issues, the president was less firm. Like President Kennedy he was primarily interested in foreign affairs. He supported a bold plan for a "minimum income" for poor families, but dropped it when it alarmed his conservative supporters and got nowhere in Congress. But when a groundswell of public support for conserving natural resources and checking pollution led Congress to pass bills creating the Environmental Protection Agency (EPA) and the Clean Air Act of 1970, he signed them cheerfully.

Primarily he was concerned with his own political standing. Hoping to strengthen the Republican party in the South, he checked further federal efforts to force school desegregation on reluctant local districts, and he set out to add what he called "strict constructionists" to the Supreme Court, which he believed had swung too far to the left in such areas as race relations and the rights of persons accused of committing crimes. He also proposed mostly conservatives to fill vacancies in the Supreme Court.

After his triumphant reelection and the withdrawal of the last American troops from Vietnam, Nixon resolved to change the direction in which the nation had been moving for decades. He sought, on

the one hand, to strengthen the power of the presidency vis-à-vis Congress and, on the other, to decentralize the administration by encouraging state and local management of government programs. He announced that he intended to reduce the interference of the federal government in the affairs of individuals. People should be more self-reliant, he said, and he denounced what he called "permissiveness." Overconcern for the interests of blacks and other minorities must end. Criminals should be punished "without pity." No person or group should be coddled by the state.

These aims brought Nixon into conflict with liberals in both parties, with the leaders of minority groups, and with those alarmed by the increasing power of the executive. The conflict came to a head over the president's anti-inflation policy. After his second inauguration he ended price and wage controls and called for voluntary "restraints." This approach did not work. Prices soared in the most rapid inflation since the Korean War. In an effort to check the rise, Nixon set a rigid limit on federal expenditures. To keep within the limit, he cut back or abolished a large number of social welfare programs and reduced federal grants in support of science and education. He even impounded (refused to spend) funds already appropriated by Congress for purposes of which he disapproved.

The impoundment created a furor on Capitol Hill, but when Congress failed to override his vetoes of bills challenging this policy, it appeared that Nixon was in total command. The White House staff, headed by H. R. Haldeman (called "the Prussian") and John Ehrlichman, dominated the Washington bureaucracy like princes of the blood or oriental viziers and dealt with legislators as though they were lackeys or eunuchs. When asked to account for their actions they took refuge behind the shield of executive privilege—the doctrine, never before applied so broadly, that discussions and communications within the executive branch were confidential and therefore immune from congressional scrutiny. Critics began to grumble about a new "imperial presidency." No one seemed capable of checking Nixon.

THE WATERGATE BREAK-IN

On March 19, 1973, James McCord, a former agent of the Federal Bureau of Investigation accused of burglary, wrote a letter to the judge presiding at his trial. His act precipitated a series of disclosures that first disrupted and then destroyed the Nixon administration.

McCord had been employed during the 1972 presidential campaign as a security officer of the Committee to Re-elect the President (CREEP). At about 1 A.M. on June 17, 1972, he and four other men had broken into Democratic party headquarters at the Watergate, a complex of apartments and offices in Washington. The burglars were members of an unofficial CREEP surveillance group known as "the plumbers." Nixon, who was obsessed by a need to conceal information about his administration, had formed the group after the Pentagon Papers, a confidential report on government policy in Vietnam, had been leaked to the press. The "plumbers" had been caught rifling files and installing electronic eavesdropping devices.

Two other Republican campaign officials were soon implicated in the affair. Their arrest aroused suspicions that the Republican party was behind the break-in. Nixon denied it. "I can say categorically," he announced on June 22, "that no one on the White House staff, no one in this Administration presently employed, was involved in this very bizarre incident."

Most people evidently took the president at his word despite his well-known deviousness. (He had won the nickname "Tricky Dick" when he first ran for Congress in 1946.) He was far ahead in the polls and seemed so sure to win reelection that it was hard to believe he would stoop to burglary to discover what the Democrats were up to. In any case, the affair did not materially affect the election. When brought to trial early in 1973, most of the Watergate burglars pleaded guilty.

McCord, who did not, was convicted by the jury. Before Judge John J. Sirica imposed sentences on the culprits, however, McCord wrote his letter. High Republican officials had known about the burglary in advance and had paid the defendants "hush money" to keep their connection secret, McCord claimed. Perjury had been committed during the trial.

The truth of McCord's charges swiftly became apparent. The head of CREEP, Jeb Stuart Magruder, and President Nixon's lawyer, John W. Dean III, admitted their involvement. Among the disclosures that emerged over the following months were these:

- The acting director of the FBI, L. Patrick Gray, had destroyed documents related to the case.
- Large sums of money had been paid to the burglars at the instigation of the White House to ensure their silence.
- Agents of the Nixon administration had burglarized the office of a psychiatrist, seeking evidence against one of his patients, Daniel Ellsberg, who

had been charged with leaking the Pentagon Papers to the *New York Times*. (This disclosure led to the immediate dismissal of the charges against Ellsberg by the presiding judge.)

- CREEP officials had attempted to disrupt the campaigns of leading Democratic candidates during the 1972 primaries in a number of illegal ways.
- A number of corporations had made large contributions to the Nixon reelection campaign in violation of federal law.
- The Nixon administration had placed wiretaps on the telephones of some of its own officials as well as on those of journalists critical of its policies without first obtaining authorization from the courts.

These revelations led to the dismissal of John Dean and to the resignations of most of Nixon's closest advisers, including Haldeman, Ehrlichman, and Attorney General Richard Kleindienst. They also raised the question of the president's personal connection with the scandals. This he steadfastly denied. He insisted that he would investigate the Watergate

▲ "I am not a crook," Nixon famously declared, prompting this rebuttal by cartoonist Herblock of the *Washington Post* (May 24, 1974). It alludes to crucial missing sections of tape-recorded conversation in which Nixon allegedly authorized payment of money to the Watergate burglars to ensure their silence.

affair thoroughly and see that the guilty were punished. He refused, however, to allow investigators to examine White House documents, again on grounds of executive privilege, which he continued to assert in very broad terms.

In the teeth of Nixon's denials, John Dean, testifying under oath, stated flatly and in circumstantial detail that the president had been closely involved in the Watergate cover-up. (Before testifying, Dean consulted with the conservative Senator Barry Goldwater. When he explained what he was going to say, Goldwater replied: "Hell, I'm not surprised. That goddam Nixon has been lying all of his life.")

Dean had been a persuasive witness, but—unlike Goldwater—many people were reluctant to believe that a president could lie so cold-bloodedly to the entire country. Therefore, when it came out during later hearings of the Senate committee investigating the Watergate scandal that the president had systematically made secret tape recordings of White House conversations and telephone calls, the disclosure caused a sensation. It seemed obvious that these tapes would settle the question of Nixon's involvement once and for all. Again Nixon refused to allow access to the evidence.

One result of the scandals and of Nixon's attitude was a precipitous decline in his standing in public opinion polls. Calls for his resignation, even for impeachment, began to be heard. Yielding to pressure, he agreed to the appointment of an "independent" special prosecutor to investigate the Watergate affair, and he promised the appointee, Professor Archibald Cox of Harvard Law School, full cooperation.

Cox swiftly aroused the president's ire by seeking access to White House records, including the tapes. When Nixon refused to turn over the tapes, Cox obtained a subpoena from Judge Sirica ordering him to do so. The administration appealed this decision and lost in the appellate court. Then, while the case was headed for the Supreme Court, Nixon ordered the new attorney general, Elliot Richardson, to dismiss Cox. Both Richardson, who had promised the Senate during his confirmation hearings that the special prosecutor would have a free hand, and his chief assistant resigned rather than do as the president directed. The third-ranking officer of the Justice Department carried out Nixon's order.

These events of Saturday, October 20, promptly dubbed the Saturday Night Massacre, caused an outburst of public indignation. Congress was bombarded by thousands of letters and telegrams demanding the president's impeachment. The House Judiciary Committee began an investigation to see if enough evidence for impeachment existed. (The House of Representatives must vote to indict federal

officials for impeachment; the actual impeachment trial is conducted by the Senate.)

Once again Nixon backed down. He agreed to turn over the tapes to Judge Sirica with the understanding that relevant materials could be presented to the grand jury investigating the Watergate affair but that nothing would be revealed to the public. He then named a new special prosecutor, Leon Jaworski, and promised him access to whatever White House documents he needed. However, it soon came out that several tapes were missing and that an important section of another had been deliberately erased.

MORE TROUBLES FOR NIXON

The nation had never before experienced such a series of morale-shattering crises. While the seemingly unending complications of Watergate were unfolding during 1973, a number of unrelated disasters struck. First, pushed by a shortage of grain resulting from massive Soviet purchases authorized by détente policy, food prices shot up—wheat from $1.45 a bushel to over $5.00.

DOCUMENT

House Judiciary Committee's Conclusion on Impeachment

Then Vice President Agnew (defender of law and order, foe of permissiveness) was accused of income tax fraud and of having accepted bribes while serving as Baltimore county executive and governor of Maryland. To escape a jail term Agnew admitted in October that he had been guilty of tax evasion and resigned as vice president.

Acting according to the procedures for presidential and vice-presidential succession of the Twenty-fifth Amendment, adopted in 1967, President Nixon nominated Representative Gerald R. Ford of Michigan as vice president, and he was confirmed by Congress. Ford had served continuously in Congress since 1949 and as minority leader since 1964. His positions on public issues were close to Nixon's; he was an internationalist in foreign affairs and a conservative and convinced Republican partisan on domestic issues.

VIDEO

Richard Nixon, "I am not a crook"

Not long after the Agnew fiasco, Nixon, responding to charges that he had paid almost no income taxes during his presidency, published his 1969 to 1972 returns. They showed that he had paid only about $1600 in two years during which his income had exceeded half a million dollars. Although Nixon claimed that his returns were perfectly legal—he had taken huge deductions for the gift of some of his vice presidential papers to the National Archives—the legality, to say nothing of the propriety, of his actions was questionable. Combined

with charges that millions of dollars of public funds had been spent on improvements for his private residences in California and Florida, the tax issue further eroded his reputation, so much so that he felt obliged during a televised press conference to assure the audience: "I am not a crook."

THE JUDGMENT ON WATERGATE: "EXPLETIVE DELETED"

Meanwhile, special prosecutor Jaworski continued his investigation of the Watergate scandals. In March 1974 a grand jury indicted Haldeman; Ehrlichman; former attorney general John Mitchell, who had been head of CREEP at the time of the break-in; and four other White House aides for conspiring to block the Watergate investigation. The jurors also named Nixon an "unindicted co-conspirator," Jaworski having informed them that their power to indict a president was constitutionally questionable. Judge Sirica thereupon turned over the jury's evidence against Nixon to the House Judiciary Committee. Then both the Internal Revenue Service (IRS) and a joint congressional committee, announced that most of his deductions had been unjustified. The IRS assessed him nearly half a million dollars in taxes and interest, which he agreed to pay.

In an effort to check the mounting criticism, late in April Nixon released edited transcripts of the tapes he had turned over to the court the previous November. In addition to much incriminating evidence, the transcripts provided the public with a fascinating and shocking view of how the president conducted himself in private. In conversations he seemed confused, indecisive, and lacking in any concern for the public interest. His repeated use of foul language, so out of keeping with his public image, offended millions. The phrase "expletive deleted," inserted in place of words considered too vulgar for publication in family newspapers, overnight became a catchword.

The publication of the transcripts led even some of Nixon's strongest supporters to demand that he resign. And once the Judiciary Committee obtained the actual tapes, it became clear that the White House transcripts were in crucial respects inaccurate. Much material prejudicial to the president's case had been suppressed. Yet impeaching a president seemed so drastic a step that many people felt more direct proof of Nixon's involvement in the cover-up was necessary.

With the defendants in the Watergate case demanding access to tapes that they claimed would prove their innocence, Jaworski was compelled either

to obtain them or to risk having the charges dismissed on the grounds that the government was withholding evidence. He therefore subpoenaed 64 additional tapes. Nixon refused to obey the subpoena. Swiftly the case of *United States* v. *Richard M. Nixon* went to the Supreme Court.

In the summer of 1974—after so many months of alarms and crises—the Watergate drama reached its climax. The Judiciary Committee, following months of study of the evidence behind closed doors, decided to conduct its deliberations in open session. While millions watched on television, 38 members of the House of Representatives debated the charges. The discussions revealed both the thoroughness of the investigation and the soul-searching efforts of the representatives to render an impartial judgment. Three articles of impeachment were adopted. They charged the president with obstructing justice, misusing the powers of his office, and failing to obey the committee's subpoenas. Except in the case of the last article, many of the Republicans on the committee joined with the Democrats in voting aye, a clear indication that the full House would vote to impeach.

On the eve of the debates, the Supreme Court had ruled unanimously that the president must turn over the 64 subpoenaed tapes to the special prosecutor. Executive privilege had its place, the Court stated, but no person, not even a president, could "withhold evidence that is demonstrably relevant in a criminal trial." For reasons that soon became obvious, Nixon seriously considered defying the Court. Only when convinced that to do so would make his impeachment and conviction certain did he agree to comply.

He would not, however, resign. Even if the House impeached him, he was counting on his ability to hold the support of at least 34 senators (one-third plus one of the full Senate) to escape conviction. But events were passing beyond his control. The 64 subpoenaed tapes had to be transcribed and analyzed. When they were, Nixon's fate was sealed. Three recorded conversations between the president and H. R. Haldeman on June 23, 1972 (less than a week after the break-in and only one day after Nixon had assured the nation that no one in the White House had been involved in the affair), proved conclusively that Nixon had tried to obstruct justice by engaging the CIA in an effort to persuade the FBI not to follow up leads in the case on the spurious grounds that national security was involved.

When the House Judiciary Committee members read the new transcripts, all the Republican members who had voted against the impeachment articles reversed themselves. Republican leaders told the president categorically that the House would impeach him and that no more than a handful of senators would vote for acquittal.

THE MEANING OF WATERGATE

On August 8 Nixon announced his resignation. "Dear Mr. Secretary," his terse official letter to Secretary of State Kissinger ran, "I hereby resign the Office of President of the United States. Sincerely, Richard Nixon." The resignation took effect at noon on August 9, when Gerald Ford was sworn in as president. "Our long national nightmare is over," Ford declared.

Within weeks of taking office, Ford pardoned Nixon for whatever crimes he had committed in office, even any, if such existed, as had yet come to light. Not many Americans wanted to see the ex-president lodged in jail, but pardoning him seemed both illogical and incomprehensible when Nixon had admitted no guilt and had not yet been officially charged with any crime. (Nixon's instant acceptance of the pardon while claiming to have done no wrong was also illogical but not incomprehensible.)

The meaning of "Watergate" became the subject of much speculation. Whether Nixon's crude efforts to dominate Congress, to crush or inhibit dissent, and to subvert the electoral process would have permanently altered the American political system had they succeeded is beyond knowing. However, the orderly way in which these efforts were checked suggests that the system would have survived in any case.

Nixon's own drama is and must remain one of the most fascinating and enigmatic episodes in American history. Despite his fall from the heights because of personal flaws, his was not a tragedy in the Greek sense. When he finally yielded power he seemed without remorse or even awareness of his transgressions. Although he enjoyed the pomp and circumstance attendant on his high office and trumpeted his achievements to all the world, he was devoid of the classic hero's pride. Did he really intend to smash all opposition and rule like a tyrant, or was he driven by lack of confidence in himself? His stubborn aggressiveness and his overblown view of executive privilege may have reflected a need for constant reassurance that he was a mighty leader and that the nation accepted his right to exercise authority. One element in his downfall, preserved for posterity in videotapes of his television appearances, was that even while he was assuring the country of his innocence most vehemently, he did not look like an unsuspecting victim of the machinations of overzealous supporters. Perhaps at some profound level he did not want to be believed.

This explanation of Richard Nixon, however tentative, is at least comforting—it makes him appear less menacing. If it is correct, Americans can deplore the injuries he inflicted on society and still feel a certain compassion for him.

Whether Nixon's disgrace marked the end of one era or the beginning of another is a difficult question.

Like most critical moments in human history, it seems in retrospect to have been both. Nixon's détente with the Soviet Union and Red China was surely an early sign of the easing of Cold War tensions characteristic of the decades to follow. Yet the failure of Nixon's interventionist domestic policies, coming just as public disillusionment with the workings of many of the ambitious Great Society programs set in motion under Lyndon Johnson was mounting, put an end to the liberal era that had begun with the reforms of the New Deal.

MILESTONES

1942	Pacifists found Congress of Racial Equality (CORE)
1953	CIA backs coup in Iran
1955–1956	Martin Luther King, Jr. leads Montgomery, Alabama, bus boycott
1957	Southern Christian Leadership Conference (SCLC) is founded in Atlanta
1960	Black college students found Student Nonviolent Coordinating Committee (SNCC)
1961	CIA-trained Cuban exiles launch disastrous Bay of Pigs invasion
	Soviets build Berlin Wall
	John F. Kennedy founds Peace Corps
	Freedom riders integrate buses in South
1962	Soviet Premier Khrushchev precipitates Cuban Missile Crisis
1963	United States supports coup to oust President Ngo Dinh Diem of South Vietnam
	Martin Luther King, Jr. leads March on Washington
	Lee Harvey Oswald assassinates President Kennedy; Lyndon Johnson becomes president
1964	Congress endorses escalation of Vietnam War in Gulf of Tonkin Resolution
	Lyndon Johnson is elected president, begins Great Society program
	Congress passes historic Civil Rights Act
1965	Congress passes Immigration Act, ending national quota system
	Congress's Medicare Act pays some medical costs for senior citizens and the poor
	Congress funds education with Elementary and Secondary Education Act

1968	Communists strike all over South Vietnam in Tet Offensive
	Lyndon Johnson withdraws as candidate for reelection
	Richard Nixon is elected president
1969	Nixon announces "Vietnamization" of war
1970	Nixon announces "incursion" into Cambodia
	Antiwar student protesters are killed at Kent State and Jackson State universities
	Congress passes Clean Air Act and creates Environmental Protection Agency (EPA)
1972	Nixon's "plumbers" burglarize Democratic national headquarters at Watergate complex
	Nixon and Kissinger visit China and Soviet Union
	United States and Soviet Union sign Strategic Arms Limitation Treaty (SALT)
	Nixon is reelected in landslide
1973	House Judiciary Committee begins impeachment hearings against Nixon
	Vice President Spiro Agnew resigns; Gerald Ford is appointed vice president
	Last American troops leave Vietnam
	Nixon fires Watergate special prosecutor Archibald Cox (Saturday Night Massacre)
	Chilean socialist Salvador Allende is overthrown
1974	Supreme Court orders release of Nixon's White House tapes
	Nixon resigns; Gerald Ford becomes president and pardons Nixon

SUPPLEMENTARY READING

On Kennedy, consult Robert Dallek, *Unfinished Life: John F. Kennedy, 1917–1963* (2003), W. J. Rorabaugh, *Kennedy and the Promise of the Sixties* (2002), Richard Reeves, *President Kennedy* (1992), Herbert S. Parmet, *JFK: The Presidency of John F. Kennedy* (1983), and James Giglio, *The Presidency of John F. Kennedy* (1991). Arthur M. Schlesinger, Jr., *A Thousand Days* (1965) and Theodore Sorensen, *Kennedy* (1965) are rich in eyewitness detail but extremely pro-Kennedy. On Kennedy's foreign policy, see Lawrence Freedman, *Kennedy's Wars* (2000), and William Taubman, *Khrushchev* (2003). The Kennedy style can be "heard" in Ernest R. May and Philip D. Zelikow, eds., *The Kennedy Tapes: Inside the White House During the Cuban Missile Crisis* (1997). Also on the Cuban missile crisis, see Sheldon M. Stern, *Averting "The Final Failure": John F. Kennedy and the Secret Cuban Missile Crisis Meetings* (2003), Robert Weisbrot, *Maximum Danger* (2001), and Mark J. White, *The Cuban Missile Crisis* (1996). Gerald Posner, *Case Closed: Lee Harvey Oswald and the Assassination of JFK* (1994) debunks the conspriracy theorists.

Robert Caro, *The Years of Lyndon B. Johnson: The Path to Power* (1982) and *Means of Ascent* (1990) are extremely critical; Robert Dallek, *Lone Star Rising: Lyndon Johnson and His Times, 1908–1960* (1991) and *Flawed Giant: Lyndon B. Johnson, 1960–1973* (1998) are more balanced. Recent works include Irwin Unger, *LBJ: A Life* (1999), and H. W. Brands, *The Wages of Globalism: Lyndon Johnson and the Limits of American Power* (1995). See also Doris Kearns Goodwin, *Lyndon Johnson and the American Dream* (1976). Michael Beschloss, ed., *Taking Charge: The Johnson White House Tapes, 1963–1969* (1997) provides a verbatim, previously secret, account.

On Goldwater, see Robert A. Goldberg, *Barry Goldwater* (1995); Lisa McGirr, *Suburban Warriors: The Origins of the New American Right* (2001) examines the 1960s origins of a grassroots conservative movement.

For civil rights, in addition to works cited in the previous chapter, consult Taylor Branch's second volume in his biography of Martin Luther King, Jr., *Pillar of Fire* (1998). Diane McWhorter, *Carry Me Home* (2001) provides a gripping account of the civil rights struggle in Birmingham, Alabama. Nicholas Lemann, *The Promised Land: The Great Black Migration and How It Changed America* (1991) is also indispensable. Malcolm X, *Autobiography*, is a classic account of black alienation. See also Karl Evanzz, *The Messenger: The Rise and Fall of Elijah Muhammed* (1999) provides a detailed account of the founder of the Black Muslims; Michael E. Dyson's *Making Malcolm* (1995) is also

solid. James T. Patterson, *Brown v. Board of Education* (2001) has provided a thorough account of that Supreme Court decision.

On the election of 1968, Theodore H. White's *The Making of the President, 1968* (1969), is lively and entertaining. The best biography of Nixon is Stephen Ambrose, *Nixon* (1987–1991), but see also Richard Reeves, *Richard Nixon: Alone in the White House* (2001), Joan Hoff, *Nixon Reconsidered* (1994), and Herbert S. Parmet, *Richard Nixon and His America* (1990). Allen J. Matusow, *Nixon's Economy* (1998) is excellent. Dean J. Kotlowski, *Nixon's Civil Rights* (2001) argues that Nixon's actions—if not his rhetoric—were mostly supportive; J. Brooks Flippen, *Nixon and the Environment* (2000) makes a similar point about Nixon and environmental issues.

Henry Kissinger's memoirs, *White House Years* (1979) and *Years of Upheaval* (1982), are important though, like most such works, self-serving. Walter Isaacson's *Kissinger* (1992) is more balanced. See also Christopher Hitchens *The Trial of Henry Kissinger* (2001).

The literature on the war in Vietnam is enormous. Recent interpretations include David E. Kaiser, *American Tragedy: Kennedy, Johnson and the Origins of the Vietnam War* (2000), Lawrence Freedman, *Kennedy's Wars: Berlin, Cuba, Laos, and Vietnam* (2000), A. J. Langguth, *Our Vietnam: The War: 1954–1975* (2000), and Robert D. Schulzinger, *A Time for War* (1997). Neil Sheehan, *A Bright and Shining Lie* (1988), an account of the war from one American adviser's perspective, provides the best explanation of why the war could not be won. See also Lloyd C. Gardner, *Pay Any Price: Lyndon Johnson and the Wars for Vietnam* (1995). John Laurence, *The Cat from Hue: A Vietnam War Story* (2002) approaches the subject from a journalistic perspective.

For the antiwar movement, see Robert Buzzanco, *Masters of War: Military Dissent and Politics in the Vietnam Era* (1996), Rhodri Jeffreys-Jones, *Peace Now!* (1999), and Mary Hershberger, *Traveling to Vietnam: American Peace Activists and the War* (1998) on the ending of the war. See also Michael S. Foley, *Confronting the War Machine: Draft Resistance during the Vietnam War* (2003).

The best analysis of the Watergate affair is Stanley I. Kutler, *The Wars of Watergate* (1990) and *Abuse of Power* (1997), but see also Carl Bernstein and Robert Woodward, *All the President's Men* (1974) and *Final Days* (1976), John W. Dean, *Blind Ambition* (1976), and Leon Jaworski, *The Right and the Power* (1976). On Ford's elevation to the presidency, see James Cannon, *Time and Chance* (2001).

SUGGESTED WEBSITES

Presidents Kennedy, Johnson, Nixon, and Ford

http://www.ipl.org/div/POTUS/jfkennedy.html
http://www.ipl.org/div/POTUS/lbjohnson.html
http://www.ipl.org/div/POTUS/rmnixon.html
http://www.ipl.org/div/POTUS/grford/html

These sites contain basic data about each president's election, presidency, and speeches.

Vietnam Online

http://www.pbs.org/wgbh/pages/amex/vietnam/
From PBS and the American Experience, this site contains a detailed, interactive timeline of the war, interpretive essays, and autobiographical reflections.

My Lai Court Martial (1970)
http://www.law.umkc.edu/faculty/projects/ftrials/
mylai/mylai.htm
This site contains images, chronology, court and officials documents maintained by Dr. Douglas Linder at University of Missouri–Kansas City Law School.

***United States* v. *Cecil Price et al.* (The "Mississippi Burning" Trial), 1967**
http://www.law.umkc.edu/faculty/projects/ftrials/
price&bowers.html
This site contains images, chronology, and court and officials documents maintained by Dr. Doug Linder at the University of Missouri–Kansas City Law School.

Watergate
http://www.journale.com/watergate.html
This site contains primary and secondary sources relating to the event that forced Nixon's resignation.

Civil Rights Oral History Bibliography
http://www.usm.edu/crdp/html/dah.shtml
This University of Southern Mississippi site includes complete transcripts of the selected oral resources.

Society in Flux

▼ Roger Brown's *Tract Town* (1973) paints suburbia not as a rural utopia—see Chapter 11—but as a large prison, with each house a uniform, boxy cell.

CHAPTER CONTENTS

I n their inaugural addresses, the presidents of the postwar decades seemed preoccupied with change. In 1949 Truman described the nation as being at a "major turning point in the long history of the human race." Eight years later Eisenhower spoke of the need to lead the nation through "this tempest of change and turmoil." In 1961 Kennedy declared that the "torch had been passed to a new generation." In 1965 Lyndon Baines Johnson maintained that "ours is a time of change—rapid and fantastic change." Four years later Richard M. Nixon commented on the "spiralling pace of change."

This widespread perception of the decades after World War II as a time of change was everywhere apparent. The population was growing rapidly. People were on the move. And after the doom and gloom of the Great Depression and World War II, Americans were ready to relax and take advantage of all the goods and services that peace and prosperity made possible.

Yet the prosperity cast into sharper relief those excluded by race and gender from equal access to good education and jobs. Technological change also accelerated social change. By miniaturizing transistors, for example, the space program made it possible for teenagers to remain in continuous contact with popular music on their radios. The interpenetration of technology and popular culture was pervasive. In 1946, four days after an atomic bomb had been exploded on the Bikini atoll, a French fashion designer decided to call his skimpy bathing suit by the same name. During the 1960s wits observed that hemlines were going up faster than Saturn rockets.

A Society on the Move

One reason why Americans seemed constantly on the move was their devotion to automobiles. In the postwar decades the automobile entered its golden age. During the booming 1920s, when the car became an instrument of mass transportation, about 31 million autos were produced by American factories. During the 1950s, 58 million rolled off the assembly lines; during the 1960s, 77 million.

More people drove farther in more reliable and more comfortable vehicles over smoother if not always less congested highways. And the new cars were heavier and more powerful than their predecessors. Gasoline consumption first touched 15 billion gallons in 1931; it soared to 35 billion gallons in 1950 and to 92 billion in 1970. A new business, the motel industry (the word, typically American, was a combination of *motor* and *hotel*) developed to service the millions of tourists and business travelers who burned all this fuel.

The development of the interstate highway system, begun under Eisenhower in 1956, was a major cause of increased mobility. The new roads did far more than facilitate long-distance travel; they accelerated the shift of population to the suburbs and the consequent decline of inner-city districts.

Despite the speeds that cars maintained on them, the new highways were much safer than the old roads. The traffic death rate per mile driven fell steadily, almost entirely because of new interstates. On the other hand, the tremendous increase in automobiles led to an upsurge in traffic fatalities. In 1945, 27,000 people died in automobile accidents; in 1970, the number of fatalities approached 54,000, far more American deaths than in the Korean War. The environmental impact of the highway system was also severe. Elevated roads cut ugly swaths through cities, and the cars they carried released tons of noxious exhaust fumes into urban air. Hillsides were gashed, marshes filled in, forests felled—all in the name of speed and efficiency.

Although commercial air travel had existed in the 1930s and had profited from wartime technical advances in military aircraft, it truly came of age when the first jetliner—the Boeing 707, built in Seattle, Washington—went into service in 1958. Almost immediately jets came to dominate long-distance travel, while railroad passenger service and transatlantic liners declined in importance.

The Advent of Television

Another important postwar change was the advent of television as a means of mass communication. By 1961 there were 55 million sets in operation, and by the mid-1960s orbiting government and commercial satellites were relaying pictures from one continent to another instantly.

Television combined the immediacy of radio with the visual impact of films, and it displayed most of the strengths and weaknesses of both in exaggerated form. It swiftly became indispensable to the political system, both for its coverage of public events and as a vehicle for political advertising. Its handling of the events following President Kennedy's assassination and of other news developments made history come alive for tens of millions of viewers.

As for its influence on politics and political campaigning, as early as 1952 the Republicans made effective use of what came to be known as "spots," 20-second tapes of candidate Eisenhower responding to questions about his opinions on issues, important and trivial. In later campaigns candidates for state and local as well as national office spent millions to sell themselves or attack their opponents, often with little regard for the accuracy or relevance of their remarks.

Television also brought sports events before the viewer vividly, attracting enormous audiences and producing so much money in advertising revenue that the economics of professional sports was revolutionized. Team franchises were bought and sold for huge sums, and ordinary players commanded salaries in the hundreds of thousands, stars in the millions.

Some excellent drama was presented, especially on the National Educational Television network, along with many filmed documentaries. However, Newton Minow of the Federal Communications Commission (FCC) called the programming offered by most television stations a "vast wasteland." The lion's share of television time was devoted to uninspired and vulgar serials, routine variety shows, giveaway and quiz programs designed to reveal and revel in the ignorance of the average citizen, and reruns of old movies cut to fit rigid time periods and repeatedly interrupted at climactic points by commercials. Most sets had poor acoustic qualities, which made them inferior instruments for listening to music. Yet children found television fascinating, remaining transfixed before the screen when—their elders said—they should have been out of doors or curled up with a book.

Still another defect of television was its capacity for influencing the opinions and feelings of viewers. The insistent and strident claims of advertisers punctuated every program with monotonous regularity. Politicians discovered that no other device or method approached television as a means of reaching large numbers of voters with an illusion of intimacy. Because television time was expensive, candidates had to raise huge sums to use the medium—a dangerous

▲ Art historian Karal Ann Marling observed in *As Seen on TV* (1994) that the TV set originally functioned as a kind of picture, such as would be hung over the mantelpiece. This 1950s American living room illustrates the point, which has arranged pictures above the television. But the family is looking at the TV, riveted by the antics of a clown.

state of affairs in a democracy. In time Congress clamped a lid on campaign expenditures, but this action did not necessarily reduce the amounts spent on television, with its capacity to reach so many people.[1]

The importance of the national television networks, NBC, ABC, and CBS, was significantly modified in the 1980s by the rapid growth of cable television companies. Besides bringing the broadcasts of the networks to remote areas, cable made available large numbers of additional channels, thus greatly increasing the variety of materials offered to viewers. The introduction of video cassette recorders (VCRs) further increased the usefulness of television sets, which could be used to copy television programs and to view tapes of old and recent movies in private homes.

_____

[1]The government now provides substantial public funds to major candidates in presidential elections.

At Home and Work

Family life was changing in complicated ways. Sometimes men and women devised entirely new ways of raising families and reconciling the demands of work and marriage; at other times, they looked resolutely to the past for guidance as to their own lives.

In 1946, more than 10 percent of all single females over the age of 14 in the country got married. Government policies buttressed the inclinations of the people: to encourage taxpayers to have children, the federal government granted income tax deductions for dependents. The birthrate soared.

Most servicemen had idealized the joys of domesticity while abroad, and they and their wives were eager to concentrate on "making a home and raising a family" now that the war had ended. People sought security after the strains and dangers of the war years, but they faced the future hopefully, encouraged by

the booming economy and the sudden profusion of consumer goods. Satisfaction with the marital state was reflected in a slackening in the divorce rate. At the same time, perhaps because of the omnipresent signs of material progress and the confusion produced by rapid change, people tended to be conformists, looking over their shoulders, so to speak, rather than tackling life head on.

The period was marked by a cultural reaffirmation of domesticity. A 1947 survey by the *Woman's Home Companion* found that among possible careers, its readers favored nursing, clerical work, retailing, and teaching because these jobs offered the best preparation for women's "prime objective": marriage. Popular magazines like the *Ladies' Home Journal,* full of articles such as "Keep Those Home Fires Burning—With Hobbies" and "See How to Knit a Baby Blanket," showed college-educated women how to make a "career" of home management and child development.

Scholars mostly agreed that women belonged at home. In 1947 psychoanalyst Marynia Farnham explained that the female reproductive organs predisposed women to the protective and nurturing tasks of child rearing; women who pursued careers in the competitive world of business would forever be at odds with their bodies. Dr. Benjamin Spock, whose *Common Sense Guide to Baby and Child Care* first appeared in 1946 and sold 24 million copies during the next quarter century, insisted that a mother's most important job was to shore up her children's sense of self by providing continuous support and affection. Women who worked outside the home necessarily "neglected" their children. The child who was "mildly neglected," Spock added, was apt to grow up "mildly disturbed."

Harvard sociologist Talcott Parsons, the leading social scientist of the era, found a yet more compelling justification for female domesticity. The evolution of modern industrial society, he maintained, was linked to the specialization of gender roles. Advanced societies benefited from women performing the "expressive" tasks of family life, and men, the "instrumental" tasks of running economic and political systems. Women who worked outside the home not only endangered the mental well-being of themselves and their children but also retarded the progress of humanity.

Men were expected to cede management of the domestic sphere to women. Hollywood, its cameras pointed as ever directly at the concerns of audiences, underscored this point. In films such as *Life with Father* (1947), *Mr. Blandings Builds His Dream House* (1948), *Cheaper by the Dozen* (1950), and *Father of the Bride* (1950), irascible or befuddled patriarchs blunder into delicate family matters, only to be gently cased out of harm's way by their understanding and savvy wives. Television picked up on these and similar themes and hammered away at them each week in shows like Robert Young's ironically titled *Father Knows Best* (1954–1962) and Jackie Gleason's equally ironic take on working-class marriage, *The Honeymooners* (1953–1956). Even Lucille Ball and Vivian Vance, the screwball housewives in the popular sitcom *I Love Lucy* (1952–1957), had a better grasp of family dynamics than their stumblebum spouses.

Although men assumed prominent roles in some domestic rituals, such as presiding over the backyard barbecue or carving the holiday turkey, their chief responsibility was to earn enough money to sustain the family. This was considerably easier than in the past. From 1949 through 1975, unemployment never exceeded 7 percent, and during the mid–1960s it fell well below 4 percent. For those who had lived during the Depression the dominant social fact of the postwar era was the availability of work. As early as 1948, half the United Auto Workers questioned by Columbia sociologist C. Wright Mills told him that they "hardly ever" worried about losing their jobs.

But the *character* of work was changing in unsettling ways. The Second World War accelerated the growth of giant corporations, whose complex, global operations were built on mountains of paper. Regiments of managers ran the systems, and vast armies of clerical workers processed the expanded flow of information. In 1870, 1 in 160 workers was employed in clerical work; by 1950, that figure was 1 in 8. One-fifth of all employees of manufacturing firms worked in offices.

The shift in work patterns was reflected in the decline of sales as an occupation, and of the salesman as the exemplar of the entrepreneurial individualist. The moment was captured in Arthur Miller's *Death of a Salesman* (1949), a play that provided both the epitaph and explanation for the salesman's demise: Willy Loman (Low-man?) was a prickly loner, ill-equipped to take a place in the bland bureaucracies that were dominating the postwar economic landscape. Advertising departments made salesmen obsolete. They were increasingly replaced by the "organization man." The phrase came from sociologist William H. Whyte's 1956 best-selling book by that title. The "organization man" went to college, maintained a B average, joined sports teams and clubs, and found work in a large corporation. He subordinated his own interests, even his taste in clothes, to the requirements of the company. His wife was also affected by this pressure. In 1951 *Fortune* magazine cautioned her against drinking at company dinners because "it may go down in a dossier." "Be attractive," it added. "There is a strong correlation between executive success and the wife's appearance."

Blue-collar workers and clerical employees were not as subject to these pressures, but studies reveal

that they did not differ in their attitudes toward marriage and child rearing. "The vast changes . . . are pervasive," two demographers concluded. "Social and economic variables . . . such as race, ethnic status, education and residence, do not indicate differences with respect to trends in fertility."

The growth of suburbs gave a geographic dimension to the changing roles of husbands and wives. In the postwar years the federal government encouraged single-family home construction by allowing homeowners to deduct mortgage interest from their income taxes and by making low-cost mortgages available through the Federal Housing Administration.

New suburbs appeared almost like mushrooms after a spring rain. With their streets named after flowers or pleasant emotional states (the large postwar suburb of Levittown, near Philadelphia, featured Friendly Lane, Graceful Lane, Good Lane, and Shelter Lane), the suburbs were to function as havens for work-weary men.

This image, powerfully reiterated in television shows and films, sacrificed none of its allure for being unrealistic. Impressed as a child with the prim family life depicted in *Leave It to Beaver,* the poet Gary Soto, who grew up in the Mexican American barrio in Fresno, California, tried without success to persuade his family to dress for dinner.

In fact, the suburban world was unreal even for many of the women who inhabited it. More women were leaving the home during the day to find work in the burgeoning clerical and service sector. In 1940, only 1 in 4 civilian employees was female, one-third of them married. Three decades later, 4 in 10 paid employees were women, two-thirds of them married. Perhaps 20 million women—after returning home from work, fixing dinner, putting the children to bed, and doing a load of laundry—collapsed in front of the television set and watched domestic heroines such as Donna Reed vacuuming the house in high heels and pearls, making clothes and cakes from scratch, soothing the fragile psyches of her husband and children, and otherwise living a fantasy that accorded with the views of Farnham, Spock, and Parsons.

THE GROWING MIDDLE CLASS

Another postwar change was the marked broadening of the middle class. In 1947 only 5.7 million American families had what might be considered middle-class incomes—enough to provide something for leisure, entertainment, and cultural activities as well as for life's necessities. By the early 1960s more than 12 million families, about a third of the population, had such incomes.

The percentage of immigrants in the population declined steadily; in 1965 over 95 percent of all Americans were native-born. This trend contributed to social and cultural uniformity. So did the rising incomes of industrial workers and the changing character of their labor. By 1962 about 90 percent of all industrial workers enjoyed such fringe benefits as paid vacations and medical insurance at least partially financed by their employers, and nearly 70 percent participated in pension plans. The merger in 1955 of the two great labor federations, the AFL and the CIO, added to the prestige of all union labor as well as to the power of the new organization.

As blue-collar workers invaded the middle class by the tens of thousands, they moved to suburbs previously reserved for junior executives, shopkeepers, and the like. They shed their work clothes for business suits. They took up golf. In sum, they adopted values and attitudes commensurate with their new status—which helps explain the growing conservatism of labor unions. During the Great Depression, when they were underdogs of sorts, the unions fought for social justice. In the 1960s many union workers seemed more interested in preserving their gains against the ravages of inflation and taxation than in reforming society.

RELIGION IN CHANGING TIMES

Sociologists and other commentators on contemporary affairs found in the expansion of the middle class another explanation of the tendency of the country to glorify the conformist. They attributed to this expansion the blurring of party lines in politics, the national obsession with moderation and consensus, the complacency of so many Americans, and their tendency, for example, to be more interested in the social aspects of churchgoing than in the moral and philosophical aspects of religion.

Organized religion traditionally deals with eternal values, but it is always influenced by social, cultural, and economic developments. Never had this been truer in America than in the decades after World War II. All the major faiths, despite their differences, were affected. Immediately after the war the prosperity and buoyant optimism of the period led to an expansion of religious activity. The Catholic Church alone built over a thousand new schools and more than a hundred hospitals along with countless new churches. By 1950 the Southern Baptists had enrolled nearly 300,000 new members and built some 500 churches.

But while most faiths prospered materially, the faithful tended to accept the world as it was. In *Catholic, Protestant, Jew* (1955), Will Herberg argued that ethnic differences between people of different

▲ As a student at Crozer Theological Seminary, Martin Luther King, Jr. excelled at homiletics—the art of preaching. His deep, booming voice and pronounced gestures helped inspire the civil rights movement. "He's damn good," President Kennedy remarked after seeing him on television. King's powerful persona helped bring religion directly into public life.

dhism. Both these trends seemed alarming to the leaders of the established religious groups, in part because they reflected an "education gap" separating religious liberals from religious conservatives.

The civil rights movement and the war in Vietnam had important religious implications. Many militant blacks (Malcolm X is an early example) converted to the Muslim faith because of its lack of racial bias. Among those in the public eye who became Muslims were the heavyweight champion boxer Cassius Clay, who changed his name to Muhammad Ali, and Lew Alcindor, a basketball star who became Kareem Abdul Jabbar.

Nearly all religious groups played significant roles in the fight for racial justice that erupted after the Supreme Court outlawed segregation. Priests, ministers, and rabbis joined in antiwar demonstrations. The Reverend Martin Luther King, Jr.'s nonviolent approach was essentially religious, his oratory deeply felt, passionate, but always dignified and controlled.

The enormous outpouring produced by King's March on Washington in 1963 was swelled by many prominent religious leaders, and their example put pressure on both church hierarchies and ordinary members to become civil rights activists. Shocking photographs of police dogs being used to "subdue" demonstrating Catholic nuns in the Deep South converted uncounted thousands to the struggle.

All the social changes of the period had religious ramifications. Feminists objected to male domination of most Christian churches and called for the ordination of female ministers and priests; some religious leaders supported the feminists, but conservatives rejected their ideas out of hand. Every aspect of the sexual revolution, from the practice of couples living together openly outside of marriage to the tolerance of homosexuality and pornography to the legalization of contraception and abortion, caused shock waves in the religious community. The Roman Catholic insistence that the clergy remain celibate resulted in a decline in the number of young Catholics becoming priests and nuns. This dealt a crippling blow to the parochial school system, which depended heavily on the clergy for teachers.

Scientific and technological developments also affected both religious values and the way people wor-

backgrounds were becoming less important, and as a result, religious toleration was becoming routine. President Eisenhower lent authority to this argument when he said: "Our government makes no sense unless it is founded on a deeply felt religious faith—and I don't care what it is." According to a Gallup poll taken shortly after the war, 97 percent of Americans believed in God. However, another poll revealed that many people were woefully ignorant of religious history and doctrine. Large numbers of Christians, for example, were unable to tell pollsters the name of any of the four gospels.

Church and state were by law and the Constitution separate institutions, but on Flag Day in 1954 Eisenhower signed a law that added the phrase "one nation under God" to the Pledge of Allegiance. The next year, Congress added "In God We Trust" to the nation's currency. New Deal welfare legislation took on a large part of a burden previously borne by church groups. The expansion of higher education resulting from the GI Bill introduced millions of young adults to new ideas and appeared to make people somewhat more tolerant of the beliefs of others, religious beliefs included. On the other hand, studies showed that better-educated people tended to be less involved in the formal aspects of organized religion, and some became interested in non-Western faiths, such as Zen Bud-

shiped. Darwin's theory of evolution had social effects as well as directly religious ones in the nineteenth and early twentieth centuries, and these were to some extent still unresolved. Many religious groups still believed in the biblical explanation of creation and sought to have "creation theory" taught in the schools.

On another level, the prestige of secular science gave it a kind of religious aspect disturbing to some church leaders. Medical advances that some people marveled at, such as in vitro fertilization of human eggs, organ transplants, and the development of machines capable of keeping terminally ill people alive indefinitely, seemed to others to be "against nature" and indeed sacrilegious. More generally, the public was divided about the ultimate value of scientific progress. Controversies over the use of atomic energy in peace and war and over the conservation of natural resources all had religious aspects.

Radio and television had more direct effects on organized religion. The "Radio Priest" of the New Deal era, Father Charles Coughlin, was the prototype of a new kind of clergyman that flourished in the postwar period. The airwaves enabled rhetorically skilled preachers to reach millions with emotionally charged messages on religious topics and also on political and social questions. The most successful in the postwar years were the leaders of evangelical Protestant sects, and by the 1960s they had mastered television. Whereas most postwar revivalists, the most famous being Billy Graham, stressed interdenominational cooperation, in the 1970s a more militant, fundamentalist type emerged.

Television preachers tended to found churches and educational institutions of their own, and they used the airwaves to raise money to support them. They were extremely conservative both in their religious and in their political, social, and moral views. This brought them into conflict with many other developments of the period. However, in the mid-1980s a number of scandals caused disillusionment and widespread defections among their followers.

LITERATURE AND ART

For a time after World War II the nation seemed on the verge of a literary outburst comparable to that following World War I. A number of excellent novels based on the military experiences of young writers appeared, the most notable being Norman Mailer's *The Naked and the Dead* (1948) and James Jones's *From Here to Eternity* (1951). Unfortunately, a new renaissance did not develop. The most talented younger writers rejected materialist values but preferred to bewail their fate rather than rebel against it. In *On the*

▲ J. D. Salinger's best-seller *Catcher in the Rye* epitomized the troubled youth culture of the period. The book's main character, adolescent Holden Caulfield, is repulsed by the hypocrisy of the adult world and the emptiness of materialism.

Road (1957), Jack Kerouac, founder of the "beat" (for "beatific") school, reveled in the chaotic description of violence, perversion, and madness.

At the other extreme, J. D. Salinger, perhaps the most popular writer of the 1950s and the particular favorite of college students—*The Catcher in the Rye* (1951) sold nearly 2 million copies in hardcover and paperback editions—was an impeccable stylist, witty, and contemptuous of all pretense; but he too wrote about people entirely wrapped up in themselves. In *Catch–22* (1955), the book that replaced *The Catcher in the Rye* in the hearts of college students, Joseph Heller produced a war novel at once farcical and an indignant denunciation of the stupidity and waste of warfare.

The young writers' wariness toward the adult world reflected both the postwar idealization of adolescence and a widespread fear of the sober responsibilities of adulthood. Nowhere is this better described than in John Updike's Rabbit tetralogy. The precipitating scene in *Rabbit, Run* (1960), the first volume, occurs when young Harry Angstrom, a Magipeeler

salesman, returns from work to find his pregnant wife watching the *Mouseketeers* on TV. "We must work, boys and girls," says Jimmy, the oldest. "That's the way to be happy." Harry instead abandons his wife and son and flees in terror from adulthood. Updike resurrects the theme in *Rabbit at Rest* (1990), the final volume. Harry has retired as owner of a Toyota car dealership and his son, who has succeeded him, whines that the Japanese treat him like a robot. "Welcome to the real world, kid," Harry sniffs.

These novelists and a number of others whose books were of lesser quality were widely read. Year after year sales of books increased, despite much talk about how television and other diversions were undermining the public's interest in reading. Sales of paperbacks, first introduced in the United States in 1939 by Pocket Books, reached enormous proportions: by 1965 about 25,000 titles were in print and sales were approaching 1 million copies a day.

Cheapness and portability only partly accounted for the popularity of paperbacks. Readers could purchase them in drugstores, bus terminals, and supermarkets as well as in bookstores. The paperback became fashionable. People who rarely bought hardcover books purchased weighty volumes of literary criticism, translations of the works of obscure foreign novelists, specialized historical monographs, and difficult philosophical treatises now that they were available in paper covers.

The expansion of the book market, like so many other changes, was not an unalloyed benefit even for writers. It remained difficult for unknown authors to earn a decent living. Publishers tended to concentrate their interest and their money on authors already popular and on books aimed at a mass audience. Even among successful writers of unquestioned ability, the temptations involved in large advances and in book club contracts and movie rights diverted many from making the best use of their talents.

American painters were affected by many of the forces that influenced writers. The expansion of higher education, renewed affluence, and improvements in printing technology created a demand for works of art. Technology also enabled artists to experiment with new materials and styles. Leading artists became celebrities, some of them millionaires as well. Corporations increased their purchases of art, and museums attracted huge crowds by putting on "blockbuster" exhibitions of the work of famous painters and sculptors, living and dead. U.S. defense and intelligence agencies also funded expositions of American abstract painters because their aesthetic principles were diametrically opposed to the representational "realism" endorsed by Stalin and his ideologues in the Soviet Union.

▲ Andy Warhol, *Four Campbell's Soup Cans* (1965). Warhol was one of the most famous and influential of the Pop artists who, by using everyday objects in their works, attempted to close the gap between art and everyday existence.

The new American style was known as abstract expressionism, or action painting. This "New York school" was led by Jackson Pollock (1912–1956), who composed huge abstract designs by laying his canvas on the floor of his studio and squeezing paint on it directly from tube or pot in a wild tangle of color.

The abstract expressionists were utterly subjective in their approach to art. "The source of my painting is the Unconscious," Pollock explained. "I am not much aware of what is taking place; it is only after that I see what I have done." Pollock tried to produce not the representation of a landscape but, as the critic Harold Rosenberg put it, "an inner landscape that is part of himself."

The experimental spirit released by the abstract expressionists led to op art, which employed the physical impact of pure complementary colors to produce dynamic optical effects. Even within the rigid limitations of severely formal designs composed of concentric circles, stripes, squares, and rectangles, such paintings appeared to be constantly in motion, almost alive.

Op art was devoid of social connotations; another variant, pop art, playfully yet often with acid incisiveness satirized many aspects of American culture: its vapidity, its crudeness, its violence. The painters Jasper Johns, Roy Lichtenstein, and Andy Warhol created portraits of mundane objects such as flags, comic strips, soup cans, and packing cases. Op and pop art reflected the mechanized aspects of life; the painters made use of technology in their work—for example, they enhanced the shock of vibrating complementary colors by using fluorescent paints. Some artists imitated newspaper photograph techniques by fashioning their images of sharply defined dots of color. Others borrowed from contemporary commercial art, employing spray guns, stencils, and masking tape to produce flat, hard-edge effects. The line between op and pop was frequently crossed, as in Robert Indiana's *Love,* which was reproduced and imitated on posters, Christmas cards, book jackets, buttons, rings, and a postage stamp.

Color and shape as ends in themselves, stark and often on a heroic scale, typified the new styles. Color-field painters covered vast planes with flat, sometimes subtly shaded hues. Frank Stella, one of the most universally admired of the younger artists, composed complicated bands and curves of color on enormous, eccentrically shaped canvases. To an unprecedented degree, the artist's hand—the combination of patience and skill that had characterized traditional art—was removed from painting.

The pace of change in artistic fashion was dizzying—far more rapid than changes in literature. Awareness that their generation was leading European artists instead of following them gave both American artists and art lovers a sense of participating in events of historic importance.

As with literature, the effects of such success were not all healthy. Successful artists became national personalities, a few of them enormously rich. For these, each new work was exposed to the glare of publicity, sometimes with unfortunate results. Too much attention, like too much money, could be distracting, even corrupting, especially for young artists who needed time and obscurity to develop their talents. "Schools" rose and fell in rapid order, it seemed, at the whim of one or another influential critic or dealer. Being different was more highly valued than aesthetic quality or technical skill. No matter how outlandish, the newest thing attracted respectful attention. The idea of the avant-garde as a revolt of creative minds against the philistinism of the middle class no longer had meaning, despite the fact that the existence of an expanding middle class made the commercial success of modern art possible.

THE PERILS OF PROGRESS

The many changes of the era help explain why President Johnson warned in his inaugural address, "We have no promise from God that our greatness will endure." Looking at American society more broadly, two dilemmas seem to have emerged. One was that progress was often self-defeating. Reforms and innovations instituted with the best of motives often made things worse rather than better. Instances of this dilemma, large and small, are so numerous as to defy summary. DDT, a powerful chemical developed to kill insects that were spreading disease and destroying valuable food crops, proved to have lethal effects on birds and fish—and perhaps indirectly on human beings. Goods manufactured to make life fuller and happier (automobiles, detergents, electric power) produced waste products that disfigured the land and polluted air and water. Cities built to bring culture and employment to millions became pestholes of poverty and depravity.

Change occurred so fast that experience (the recollection of how things had been) tended to become less useful and sometimes even counterproductive as a guide for dealing with current problems. Foreign policies designed to prevent wars, based on knowledge of the causes of past wars, led, because the circumstances were different, to new wars. Parents who sought to transmit to their children the accumulated wisdom of their years found their advice rejected, often with good reason, because that wisdom had little application to the problems their children had to face.

The second dilemma was that modern industrial society placed an enormous premium on social cooperation, at the same time undermining the individual citizen's sense of being essential to the proper functioning of society. The economy was as complicated as a fine watch; a breakdown in any one sector swiftly spread to other sectors. Yet specialization had progressed so far that individual workers had little sense of the importance of their personal contributions and thus felt little responsibility for the smooth functioning of the whole. Effective democratic government required that all voters be knowledgeable and concerned, but few could feel that their individual voices had any effect on elections or public policies. The exhaust fumes of millions of automobiles poisoned the air, but it was difficult to expect the single motorist to inconvenience himself by leaving his car in the garage when his restraint would have no measurable effect on total pollution. "One person just can't feel that she's doing anything," a frustrated teenager wrote. "I can use soap instead of detergent . . . but what good do I feel I'm doing when there are people next door having a party with plastic spoons and paper plates?"

▲ This photograph shows an area of Vietnam defoliated by Agent Orange, a herbicide that killed plants by interfering with their metabolism. Nearly 4 million acres of Vietnam and Laos were sprayed with Agent Orange. Nearly 300,000 Americans, most of them soldiers who had complained that the chemical caused cancer and other ailments, received a total of $180 million in insurance payments from the companies that manufactured the herbicide.

People tried to deal with this dilemma by joining organizations dedicated to achieving particular goals, such as the American Association of Retired People (AARP), the conservationist Sierra Club, and the NAACP. But such groups often became so large that members felt almost as incapable of influencing them as they did of influencing the larger society. The groups were so numerous and had so many conflicting objectives that instead of making citizens more socially minded they often made them more self-centered. The organization—union, club, party, pressure group—was a potent force in society. Yet few organizations were primarily concerned with the common interest, although logic required that the common interest be regarded if individuals or groups were to achieve their special interests.

These dilemmas produced a paradox. The United States was the most powerful nation in the world, its people the best educated, the richest, and probably the most energetic. American society was technologically advanced and dynamic; American traditional values were idealistic, humane, democratic. Yet the nation seemed incapable of mobilizing its resources intelligently to confront the most obvious challenges, its citizens unable to achieve much personal happiness or identification with their fellows, the society helpless in trying to live up to its most universally accepted ideals.

In part the paradox was a product of the strengths of the society and the individuals who made it up. The populace as a whole was more sophisticated. People were more aware of their immediate interests, less willing to suspend judgment and follow leaders or to look on others as better qualified to decide what should be done. They belonged to the "me generation"; they knew that they lived in a society and that their lives were profoundly affected by that society, but they had trouble feeling that they were part of a society.

President Johnson recognized the problem. He hoped to solve it by establishing a "consensus" and building his Great Society. No real consensus emerged; American society remained fragmented, its members divided against themselves and often within themselves.

Awareness of the complexities and contradictions of life and human institutions was a mark of increasing maturity but also a source of uncertainty and insecurity.

THE COSTS OF PROSPERITY

The vexing character of modern conditions could be seen in every aspect of life. The gross national product approached and then swiftly passed a trillion dollars, but inflation was becoming increasingly serious. Workers constantly demanded raises—which only served to drive prices still higher.

Economic expansion resulted in large measure from technological advances, and these too proved to be mixed blessings. World War II stimulated the development of plastics, synthetic rubber, radar, television, and other electronic devices. After the war plastics invaded field after field—automobile parts, building materials, adhesives, packaging materials. In the 1950s public utility companies began to manufacture electricity from nuclear fuels because it was cheaper than that produced in coal- or oil-fired plants. But the possibility of catastrophic accidents and the problem of disposing of lethal radioactive waste products soon dampened public enthusiasm for nuclear power. Scientists insisted that the danger from radiation was insignificant, but the possibility of accidents could not be eliminated entirely.

Equally significant was the invention of the electronic computer, which revolutionized the collection and storage of records, solved mathematical problems beyond the scope of the most brilliant human minds, and speeded the work of bank tellers, librarians, billing clerks, statisticians—and income tax collectors. Computers lay at the heart of industrial automation, for they could control the integration and adjustment of the most complex machines. In automobile factories they made it possible to produce entire engine blocks automatically. In steel mills molten metal could be poured into molds, cooled, rolled, and cut into slabs without the intervention of a human hand, the computers locating defects and adjusting the machinery to correct them far more accurately than the most skilled steel worker, and in a matter of seconds. But the computerization of record-keeping and manufacturing raised the problem of how displaced clerks and automobile and steel workers were to find new jobs.

The vast outpouring of flimsy plastic products and the increased use of paper, metal foil, and other "disposable" packaging materials seemed about to bury the country beneath mountains of trash. Even an apparently ideal form of scientific advance, the use of commercial fertilizers to boost food output, had unfortunate side effects: phosphates washed from farmlands into streams sometimes upset the ecological balance and turned the streams into malodorous death traps for aquatic life. Above all, technology increased the capacity of the earth to support people. But as population increased, production and consumption increased, exhausting supplies of raw materials and speeding the pollution of air and water resources. And where would the process end? Viewed from a world perspective, it was obvious that the population explosion must be checked or it would check itself by pestilence, war, starvation, or some combination of these scourges. Yet how to check it?

NEW RACIAL TURMOIL

VIDEO

Malcolm X

President Johnson and most of those who supported his policies expected that the 1964 Civil Rights Act, the Economic Opportunity Act, Medicare and Medicaid, and the other elements in the war on poverty would produce an era of racial peace and genuine social harmony—the Great Society that everyone wanted. The change that occurred in the thinking of the black radical Malcolm X seemed a straw in the wind. In 1964 Malcolm left the Muslims and founded his own Organization of Afro-American Unity. While continuing to stress black self-help and the militant defense of black rights, he now saw the fight for racial equality as part of a larger struggle for all human rights. "What we do . . . helps all people everywhere who are fighting against oppression," he said. Yet as in so many other aspects of modern life, progress itself created new difficulties. Early in 1965 Black Muslim fanatics, furious at his defection, assassinated Malcolm X while he was making a speech in favor of racial harmony.

The assassination was an act of vengeance, not of social protest. More significant was the fact that official white recognition of past injustices was making blacks more insistent that all discrimination end. The very process of righting some past wrongs gave them the strength to fight more vigorously. Black militancy, building steadily during the war and the postwar years, had long been ignored by the white majority; in the mid-1960s it burst forth so powerfully that the most smug and obtuse white citizens had to accept its existence.

Even Martin Luther King, Jr., the herald of nonviolent resistance, became more aggressive. "We are not asking, we are demanding the ballot," he said in January 1965. A few weeks after Malcolm's death, King led a march from Selma, Alabama, to Montgomery as part of a campaign to force Alabama authorities to allow blacks to register to vote. King chose Selma because the county in which it was located had a black majority but only 325 registered black voters. He expected the authorities to react bru-

tally, thus attracting public sympathy for the marchers, and he was not disappointed. His marchers were assaulted by state policemen who wielded clubs and tossed canisters of tear gas. Liberal opinion was shocked as never before. Thousands of people descended on Selma to demonstrate their support for the black cause.

Charles Sherrod, SNCC Memorandum (1961)

The Student Nonviolent Coordinating Committee (SNCC), which had been born out of the struggle for racial integration, had become by the mid-1960s a radical organization openly scornful of integration and interracial cooperation. Many students had been radicalized by the threats and open violence they had experienced while trying to register rural blacks and organize schools for black children and by the foot-dragging of the Kennedy administration in working for racial justice. The slogan of the radicals was "Black Power," an expression that was given national currency by Stokely Carmichael, chairman of SNCC. Carmichael, a West Indian by birth, had grown up in Harlem. He had worked ceaselessly for black rights in the South, and as a result he had spent considerable time in southern jails, often on such trumped-up charges as pitching a tent on the grounds of a black school. Although willing to work with black moderates such as King, he was adamantly opposed to cooperating with whites of any stripe. "The time for white involvement in the fight for equality has ended," Carmichael announced in 1966. "If we are to proceed toward true liberation, we must set ourselves off from white people." "Integration is a subterfuge for the maintenance of white supremacy," Carmichael said on another occasion. Blacks should have their own schools, their own businesses, their own political parties, their own (African) culture.

Black Power caught on swiftly among militants. This troubled white liberals, who feared that Black Power would antagonize white conservatives. They argued that since blacks made up only about 11 percent of the population, any attempt to obtain racial justice through the use of naked power was sure to fail.

Watts Riots 1967

Meanwhile, black anger erupted in a series of destructive urban riots. The most important occurred in Watts, a ghetto of Los Angeles, in August 1965. A trivial incident brought thousands into the streets. The neighborhood almost literally exploded: For six days Watts was swept by fire, looting, and bloody fighting between local residents and nearly 15,000 National Guardsmen, called up to assist the police. The following two summers saw similar outbursts in scores of cities.

Then, in April 1968, Martin Luther King, Jr., was murdered in Memphis, Tennessee, by a white man, James Earl Ray. Blacks in more than a hundred cities unleashed their anger in outbursts of burning and looting. Whites were shocked and profoundly depressed. The death of King appeared to destroy the hope that his peaceful appeal to reason and right could solve the problems of racism.

Public fear and puzzlement led to many investigations of the causes of the riots, the most important being that of the commission headed by Governor Otto Kerner of Illinois, which President Johnson had appointed after the 1967 riots. The conclusions of most of the studies were complex but fairly clear. Race riots had a long history in the United States, but earlier troubles usually began with attacks by whites that led to black counterattacks. Riots of the Watts type were begun by blacks. Although much white-owned property was destroyed, the fighting was mostly between blacks and law enforcement officers trying to control them.

The rioters were expressing frustration and despair; their resentment was directed more at the social system than at individuals. As the Kerner Commission put it, the basic cause was the "white racism" that deprived blacks of access to good jobs, crowded them into slums, and eroded all hope of escape from such misery. Ghettoes bred crime and depravity—as slums always have—and the complacent refusal of whites to invest enough money and energy to help ghetto residents, or even to acknowledge that the black poor deserved help, made the modern slum unbearable.

▲ In July 1967 a race riot engulfed a 14-square-mile section of Detroit. Police watch for snipers as firefighters attempt to extinguish the flames. Forty-three people were killed, 1300 buildings were reduced to brick and ashes, and thousands were left homeless, most of them African Americans. While surveying the rubble, Mayor Jerome Cavanagh remarked: "It looks like Berlin in 1945."

While the ghettoes expanded, middle-class whites tended more and more to flee to the suburbs or to call on the police "to maintain law and order," a euphemism for cracking down hard on deviant black behavior no matter how obvious the connection between that behavior and the slum environment.

The victims of racism employed violence not so much to force change as to obtain psychic release; it was a way of getting rid of what they could not stomach, a kind of vomiting. Thus the riots concentrated in the ghettoes themselves, smashing, Samson-like, the source of degradation even when this meant self-destruction. When fires broke out in black districts, the firefighters who tried to extinguish them were often showered with bottles and bricks and sometimes shot at, while above the roar of the flames and the hiss of steam rose the apocalyptic chant, "Burn, baby, burn!"

DOCUMENT

Black Power
1967

The most frightening aspect of the riots was their tendency to polarize society on racial lines. Advocates of Black Power became more determined to separate themselves from white influence; they exasperated white supporters of school desegregation by demanding schools of their own. Extremists formed the Black Panther party and collected weapons to resist the police. "Shoot, don't loot," the radical H. Rap Brown advised all who would listen. The Panthers demanded public compensation for injustices done to blacks in the past, pointing out that following World War II, West Germany had made payments to Jews to make up for Hitler's persecutions. In 1968 they nominated Eldridge Cleaver for president. Although Cleaver was a convict on parole, he was an articulate and intelligent man whose autobiographical *Soul on Ice* (1967), written in prison, had attracted much praise.

Middle-class city residents often resented what seemed the "favoritism" of the federal government and state and local administrations, which sought through affirmative action to provide blacks with economic opportunities and social benefits. Efforts to desegregate ghetto schools by busing children out of their local neighborhoods were a particularly bitter cause of conflict. These developments caused a powerful white backlash. People already subjected to the pressures caused by inflation, specialization, and rapid change, and worried by rising urban crime rates and welfare costs, found black radicalism infuriating.

NATIVE-BORN ETHNICS

The struggles of blacks for equality went hand in hand with the struggles of those of Mexican descent, principally in the Southwest. After World War I, thousands of immigrants from Mexico flocked into that part of the country, mingling with the far larger native-born Hispanic population. They could do so legally because the restrictive immigration legislation of the 1920s did not apply to Western Hemisphere nations. When the Great Depression struck, Mexican Americans were the first to suffer—about half a million Hispanics who were not citizens were either deported or "persuaded" to return to Mexico. But during World War II and again between 1948 and 1965, federal legislation encouraged the importation of *braceros* (temporary farm workers). Many other Mexicans entered the country illegally. The latter were known as *mojados*, or "wetbacks," because they often slipped over the border by swimming across the Rio Grande.

Many of these Mexicans and other Spanish-speaking people, including the thousands from the territory of Puerto Rico who could immigrate to the mainland legally in unlimited numbers, settled in the big cities, where low-paying but usually steady work was available. They lived in slums called *barrios*, as segregated, crowded, and crime-ridden as the ghettoes of the blacks.

Spanish-speaking residents of the Southwest, native- and foreign-born, and to a lesser degree those in the big eastern cities, were for a time largely apolitical; they tended to remain close-knit and insular. But in the 1960s a new spirit of resistance arose. Leaders of the new movement called themselves Chicanos. The Chicanos demanded better schools for their children and easier access to higher education. They urged friends and relatives to take pride in their traditions and culture, to demand their rights, and to organize themselves politically. One Chicano nationalist group tried to secede from New Mexico, an act that brought it into confrontation with the army.

The Chicano leader with the widest influence was César Chávez, who concentrated on what superficially was a more limited goal—organizing migrant farm workers into unions. Chávez grew up in migrant camps in California; he had no schooling beyond the seventh grade. After serving in the navy during World War II, he went to work for the Community Service Organization (CSO), a group seeking to raise the political consciousness of the poor and to develop self-help programs for them. Chávez became general director of the CSO but resigned in 1962 because he felt it was not devoting enough attention to the plight of migrant workers. He then founded the National Farm Workers' Association, later known as the United Farm Workers' Organizing Committee.

In 1965 the grape pickers in his union in Delano, California, struck for higher wages and union recognition. Chávez, seeing in the strike an opportunity to attack the very structure of the migrant labor system, turned it into a countrywide crusade. Avoiding violence, he enlisted the support of church leaders; he organized sit-ins, a march on the state capital, and

▲ The Mexican American founder of the National Farm Workers Association and later head of the United Farm Workers Organizing Committee, César Chávez successfully organized migrant workers throughout California in the early 1960s and later led a nationwide boycott against California grape producers.

then a national consumer boycott of grapes that attracted the support of an estimated 17 million people. He demonstrated convincingly that migrant workers could be unionized and that the demands of minorities for equal treatment did not necessarily lead to separatism and class or racial antagonism.

Nevertheless, racial controversies continued. The struggles of black people for equal treatment in the 1950s and 1960s radicalized many Indians. These militants referred to themselves as Native Americans, not Indians. They used the term *Red Power* as blacks spoke of Black Power and called their more conservative colleagues "Uncle Tomahawks." The National Indian Youth Council and later the American Indian Movement (AIM) demanded the return of lands taken illegally from their ancestors. They called for self-determination and a concerted effort to revive tribal cultures, even the use of the mind-altering controlled substance peyote in religious ceremonies,[2] and they organized a Pan-Indian movement to advance the cause. Paradoxically, this policy brought them into conflict with traditionalist Indians devoted to local autonomy. (At least 40 Indian languages are still spoken.)

Some AIM leaders sought total separation from the United States; they envisaged setting up states within states, such as the Cherokees had established in Georgia in Jacksonian days. In 1973 radicals occupied the town of Wounded Knee, South Dakota (site of one of the most disgraceful massacres of Indians in the nineteenth century), and held it at gunpoint for weeks.

While traditionalists resisted the militants, liberal white opinion proved to be generally sympathetic. In 1975 Congress passed the Indian Self-Determination Act, which gave individual tribes much greater control over such matters as education, welfare programs, and law enforcement. The act specifically recognized the government's obligation to ensure "maximum Indian participation" in the management of federal policy in these areas.

Militant ethnic pride characterized the behavior of other racial minorities and of many white Americans too. Blacks donned dashikis and other African garments and wore their hair in natural "Afro" styles. Italian Americans, Polish Americans, and descendants of other "new immigrant" groups eagerly studied their history in order to preserve their culture and where necessary revive dying traditions. The American "melting pot," some historians now argued, had not amalgamated the immigrant strains as completely as had been thought. Ethnic diversity became for some an end to be desired, despite the possibility that differences might as easily inspire conflict as harmonious adjustment.

For all ethnics, the concern for origins was in part nostalgic and romantic. As the number of, say, Greek Americans who had ever seen Greece declined, the appeal of Greek culture and the sense that some Greek Americans had of belonging to a distinct cultural group increased. But for blacks, whose particular origins were obscured by the catastrophe of slavery, awareness of their distinctiveness was more important. Racial pride was a reflection of the new black militancy and the achievements that blacks had made in the postwar period. There was a black on the Supreme Court (Thurgood Marshall, tactician of the fight for school desegregation). President Johnson had named the first black to a Cabinet post (Robert Weaver, secretary of housing and urban development). The first black since Reconstruction (Edward W. Brooke of Massachusetts) was elected to the United States Senate in 1966. A number of large cities elected black mayors.

The color line was broken in major league baseball in 1947, and soon all professional sports were open to black athletes. Whereas the reign of black heavyweight boxing champion Jack Johnson (1908–1915) had inspired an open search for a "white hope" to depose him, and whereas the next black champion, Joe Louis (1937–1949), had been accepted by whites because he "knew his place" and was "well behaved," champion Muhammad Ali was a hero to both white and black boxing fans despite his often bizarre behavior, his militant advocacy of racial equality, and his adoption of the Muslim religion.

Their achievements and advances aside, African Americans had found real self-awareness. The attitude

---

[2]The California Supreme Court upheld the right to use peyote in this way in *People* v. *Woody* (1964).

of mind that ran from the lonely Denmark Vesey to Frederick Douglass and to W. E. B. Du Bois had become the black consensus.

RETHINKING PUBLIC EDUCATION

Young people were in the forefront of the fight for the rights of minorities. In a time of uncertainty and discontent, full of conflict and dilemma, youth was affected more strongly than the older generations, and it reacted more forcefully. No institution escaped its criticisms, not even the vaunted educational system, which many students claimed poorly suited their needs. This was still another paradox of modern life, for American public education was probably the most comprehensive in the world.

After World War I, under the impact of Freudian psychology, the emphasis in elementary education shifted from using the schools as instruments of social change, as John Dewey had recommended, to using them to promote the emotional development of the students. "Child-centered" educators played down academic achievement in favor of "adjustment." The change probably stimulated the students' imaginations and may possibly have improved their psychological well-being, but observers soon noted that the system produced poor work habits and fuzzy thinking and fostered plain ignorance. Although "educationists" insisted that they were not abandoning traditional academic subjects, they surely de-emphasized them.

The demands of society for rigorous intellectual achievement made this distortion of progressive education increasingly less satisfactory. Following World War II, critics began a concerted assault on the system. The leader of the attack was James B. Conant, former president of Harvard. His book *The American High School Today* (1959) sold nearly half a million copies, and his later studies of teacher education and the special problems of urban schools also attracted wide attention.

Conant flayed the schools for their failure to teach English grammar and composition effectively, for neglecting foreign languages, and for ignoring the needs of both the brightest and the dullest students. He insisted that teachers' colleges should place subject matter above educational methodology in their curricula.

The success of the Soviet Union in launching the first *Sputnik* in 1957 increased the influence of critics like Conant because it dealt a healthy blow to American overconfidence. To match the Soviet achievement, the United States needed thousands of engineers and scientists, and the schools were not turning out enough graduates prepared to study science and engineering at the college level. Suddenly the schools were under enormous pressure, for with more and more young people desiring to go to college, the colleges were raising their admission standards. The traditionalists thus gained the initiative, academic subjects a revived prestige. The National Defense Education Act of 1958 supplied a powerful stimulus by allocating funds for upgrading work in the sciences, foreign languages, and other subjects and for expanding guidance services and experimenting with television and other new teaching devices. States encouraged small schools to consolidate into larger units; high schools

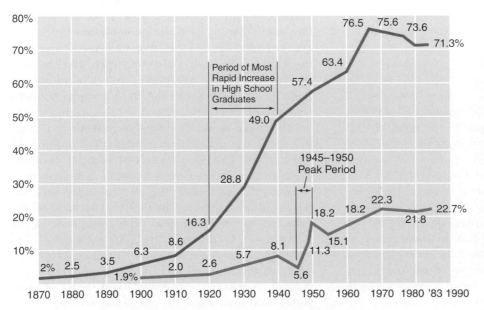

◄ **High School and College Graduates, 1870–1983**
Lyndon Johnson's Elementary and Secondary Education Act, passed in 1965, was a landmark in the century-long expansion of high school education and directly influenced college education in the United States. The most rapid increase in high school graduates occurred between 1920 and 1940, but the number of graduates as a percentage of all people aged 17 was greatest in 1967. The peak period for college graduates, 1945 to 1950, reflects the GI Bill after World War II.

became larger, as Conant proposed, allowing greater specialization among faculty and more college-level classes. Not until the large high schools were built did administrators perceive that many students, especially from disadvantaged minority groups, felt lost in them.

The post-*Sputnik* stress on academic achievement profoundly affected higher education too. Critics demanded that secondary schools and colleges raise their standards and place more stress on the sciences. Prestige institutions such as Harvard, Yale, Columbia, Stanford, and a dozen other colleges and universities, raised their entrance requirements. By the mid-1960s, the children of the baby boom generation were flocking to the nation's high schools and colleges. Population growth and the demands of society for specialized intellectual skills were causing educational institutions to burst at the seams. Enrollments had risen rapidly after World War II, mostly because of the GI Bill; by 1950 there were 2.6 million students in American colleges and universities. Thirty years later there were about 12 million. To bridge the gap between high school and college, two-year community colleges proliferated. Almost unknown before 1920, there were about 1300 two-year colleges by 1980, nearly all of them publicly financed. Enrollment in these institutions rose from 1.3 million in the mid-1960s to 6.4 million in the early 1990s.

The federal and state governments, together with private philanthropic institutions such as the Carnegie Corporation and the Ford Foundation, poured millions of dollars into education at every level—into preschool programs like Head Start, into dormitory and classroom construction, into teacher training, into scholarship funds. At the graduate level the federal government's research and development program provided billions of dollars for laboratories, equipment, professors' salaries, and student fellowships.

STUDENTS IN REVOLT

For a time after World War II, the expansion of higher education took place with remarkable smoothness. The veterans, more mature and eager to make up for lost time, concentrated on their studies, and younger students tended to follow their lead. But in the 1960s the mood changed. The members of this college generation had grown up during the postwar prosperity and had been trained by teachers who were, by and large, New Deal liberals. They had been told that government was supposed to regulate the economy in the general interest, help the weak against the strong, and protect the liberties of all. It seemed to many students not to be performing these functions.

Modern industrial society, with its "soul-less" corporations, its computers, and its almost equally

unfeeling human bureaucracies, provided these young people with material comforts and social advantages, but it made them feel insignificant and powerless. Their advantages also made them feel guilty when they thought about the millions of Americans who did not have them. The existence of poverty in a country as rich as the United States seemed intolerable, racial prejudice both stupid and evil. Yet the government seemed incapable of attacking these disgraceful conditions head-on. Still worse in their eyes, the response of their elders to McCarthyism appeared contemptible—craven cowardice of the worst sort—and dangerous. In the age of the atom, rabid anti-communism might end in nuclear war.

All these influences were encapsulated in a manifesto put forth by a small group of students at a meeting of Students for a Democratic Society (SDS), held at Port Huron, Michigan, in 1962. "We are the people of this generation . . . looking uncomfortably to the world we inherit," the Port Huron Statement began. Their main concerns were racial bigotry, the bomb, and the "disturbing paradoxes" associated with these concerns. How could an American reconcile the contradictions between the idea that "all men are created equal" with "the facts of Negro life in the South and the big cities of the North" and between the declared peaceful intentions of the government and its huge "economic and military investments in the Cold War?" Too many people and too many institutions, concentrating on preserving what they own and can command, "have closed their minds to the future."

SDS, Port Huron Statement (1962)

SDS grew rapidly, powered by rising college enrollments, protest against the escalation of the war in Vietnam, and a seemingly unending list of local campus issues. Radical students generally had little tolerance for injustice, and their dissatisfaction often found expression in public protests. The first great student outburst convulsed the University of California at Berkeley in the fall of 1964. Angry students, many veterans of the 1964 fight for black rights in the South, staged sit-down strikes in university buildings to protest the prohibition of political canvassing on the campus. This Free Speech Movement disrupted the institution over a period of weeks. Hundreds were arrested; the state legislature threatened reprisals; the faculty became involved in the controversy; and the crisis led to the resignation of the president of the University of California, Clark Kerr.

On campus after campus in the late 1960s students organized sit-ins and employed other disruptive tactics. Frequently professors and administrators played into the radicals' hands, being so offended by their methods and manners that they refused to recognize the legitimacy of some of their demands.

At Columbia in 1968, SDS and black students occupied university buildings and refused to leave unless a series of "nonnegotiable" demands (concerning such matters as the university's involvement in secret military research and its relations with minority groups living in the Columbia neighborhood) were met. When, after long delays, President Grayson Kirk called in the police to clear the buildings, a riot broke out in which dozens of students, some of them innocent bystanders, were clubbed and beaten. General student revulsion at the use of the police led to the resignation of Kirk and to the enactment of university reforms.

Equally significant in altering the students' mood was the frustration that so many of them felt with traditional aspects of college life. Regulations that students had formerly merely grumbled about evoked determined, even violent opposition. Dissidents denounced rules that restricted their personal lives, such as prohibitions on the use of alcohol and the banning of members of the opposite sex from dormitories. They complained that required courses inhibited their intellectual development. They demanded a share in the government of their institutions, long the private preserve of administrators and professors.

Beyond their specific complaints, the radicals refused to put up with anything they considered wrong. The knotty social problems that made their elders gravitate toward moderation led these students to become intransigent absolutists. The line between right and wrong became as sharply defined as the edge of a ruler. Racial prejudice was evil: it must be eradicated. War in a nuclear age was insane: armies must be disbanded. Poverty amid plenty was an abomination: end poverty now. To the counsel that evil can be eliminated only gradually, that misguided persons must be persuaded to mend their ways, that compromise was the path to true progress, they responded with scorn. Extremists among them, observing the weaknesses of American civilization, adopted a nihilistic position—the only way to deal with a "rotten" society was to destroy it.

Critics found the radical students infantile, old-fashioned, and authoritarian: infantile because they refused to tolerate frustration or delay, old-fashioned because their absolutist ideas had been exploded by several generations of philosophers and scientists, authoritarian because they rejected majority rule. As time passed, SDS was plagued by factional disputes. Radical women in the movement, for example, claimed that it was run by male chauvinists; women who sought some say in policy matters, one of them wrote, were met with "indifference, ridicule, and anger."

By the end of the 1960s, SDS had lost much of its influence with the general student body. Nevertheless, it had succeeded in focusing attention on genuine social and political weaknesses both on the campuses and in the larger world.

▲ "Alma mater," outside Low Memorial Hall of Columbia University, looks on sedately as SDS leader Mark Rudd denounces the school. Later, Rudd and other radicals climbed these stairs and ordered administrators to vacate the building. The students then occupied the buildings. New York City police subsequently threw the students out.

Black students influenced the academic world in a variety of ways. Almost without exception colleges tried to increase black enrollments through scholarship funds and by lowering academic entrance requirements when necessary to compensate for the poor preparation many black students had received in the schools. This did not mean that the black students were satisfied with college life. Most were not. They tended to keep to themselves and usually had little to do with the somewhat elitist SDS. But they demanded more control over all aspects of their education than did the typical white. They wanted black studies programs taught and administered by blacks. Achievement of these goals was difficult because of the shortage of black teachers and because professors—including most black professors—considered student control of appointments and curricula unwise

and in violation of the principles of academic freedom. Nevertheless the general academic response to black demands was accommodating; if confrontations occurred frequently, they were usually resolved by negotiation. Unlike white radical students, blacks tended to confine their demands to matters directly related to local conditions.

THE COUNTERCULTURE

Some young people, known generally as hippies, were so "turned off" by the modern world that they retreated from it, finding refuge in communes, drugs, and mystical religions, often wandering aimlessly from place to place. During the 1960s and 1970s groups of them could be found in every big city in the United States and Europe. Some hippies, like the poet Allen Ginsberg, one of their elder statesmen, and the novelist Ken Kesey, were genuinely creative people. Ginsberg's dark, desperate masterpiece "Howl," written apparently while under the influence of drugs in 1955, was perhaps the most widely read poem of the postwar era, certainly a work of major literary significance. "Howl" begins: "I saw the best minds of my generation destroyed by madness, starving hysterical naked," and goes on to describe the wanderings and searchings of these "angelheaded hipsters," a "lost battalion of platonic conversationalists . . . seeking jazz or sex or soup" in Houston, "whoring in Colorado," and "investigating the F.B.I. in beards and shorts" in California, all the while denouncing "the narcotic tobacco haze of Capitalism." "Howl" ends with Ginsberg's indignant, almost frantic assault on that "sphinx of cement and aluminum," the fire god Moloch, the devourer of children.

Others, however, such as the yippies Abbie Hoffman and Jerry Rubin, are best described as professional iconoclasts. (In 1968 yippies went through the motions of nominating a pig named Pigasus for president.) And most hippies were simply unwilling to confront the dilemmas of contemporary existence previously described.

The hippies developed a counterculture so directly opposite to the way of life of their parents' generation as to suggest to critics that they were still dominated by the culture they rejected. They wore old blue jeans and (it seemed) any nondescript garments they happened to find at hand. Male hippies wore their hair long and grew beards. Females avoided makeup, bras, and other devices more conventional women used to make themselves attractive to men. Both sexes rejected the old Protestant ethic; being part of the hippie world meant not caring about money or material goods or power over other

people. Love was more important than money or influence, feelings more significant than thought, natural things superior to anything manufactured.

Most hippies resembled the radicals in their political and social opinions. They were disgusted by the dishonesty and sordid antics of so many of the politicians, horrified by the brutality of Vietnam, appalled by racism, contemptuous of the smugness they encountered in colleges and universities. They believed in conservation, freedom of expression, tolerance, and peace.

But they rejected activism, being almost totally apolitical. Theirs was a world of folk songs and blaring acid rock music, of "be-ins," casual sex, and drugs. Their slogan, "Make love, not war" was more a general pacifist pronouncement than a specific criticism of events in Vietnam, although Vietnam surely had a great deal to do with their underlying pessimism. Indeed, with them passivity was a philosophy, almost a principle. At rock concerts they listened where earlier generations had danced. Hallucinogenic drugs heightened users' "experiences" while they were in fact in a stupor; a Harvard psychologist advised them to "Tune in, turn on, drop out." Another hippie slogan, "Do your own thing," will work in social situations only if no one does anything. Their communes were a far cry from the busy centers of social experimentation of the pre–Civil War Age of Reform.

THE SEXUAL REVOLUTION

Young people made the most striking contribution to the revolution that took place in the late 1960s in public attitudes toward sexual relationships. Here change came with startling swiftness. Almost overnight (it seemed in retrospect) conventional ideas about premarital sex, contraception and abortion, homosexuality, pornography, and a host of related matters were openly challenged. Probably the behavior of the majority of Americans did not alter radically, but the majority's beliefs and practices were no longer automatically acknowledged as the only valid ones. It became possible for individuals to espouse different values and to behave differently with at least relative impunity. Actions that in one decade would have led to social ostracism or even to imprisonment were in the next decade accepted almost as a matter of course.

The causes of this revolution were complex and interrelated; one change led to others. More efficient methods of contraception, especially the birth control pill, and antibiotics that cured venereal disease removed the two principal practical arguments against sex outside of marriage; with these barriers down, many people found their moral attitudes changing. Almost concurrently, Alfred C. Kinsey's *Sexual*

DEBATING THE PAST

Did mass culture make life shallow? At the 1969 Woodstock festival in New York, a half million young people came together to commune with each other through the medium of rock music. Did mass-produced culture—pop music, movies, TV, consumer products—render life superficial or did it deepen life by allowing many to share similar experiences?

For much of the twentieth century, intellectuals had sniffed at the low-brow cultural products of the mass media: Elvis Presley and rap, western films and fast-food restaurants, television sit-coms and Disneyland. A group of European Marxists known as the "Frankfurt school," many of whom had fled to the United States to escape Nazi persecution, maintained that when popular culture was transformed into a mass-marketed consumer item, it became debased. Worse, mass culture was a form of mindless escapism that distracted people from meaningful political action.

But during the 1960s and 1970s, historians began to look at mass culture and consumption in a different way. Historians of women, minorities, workers, and other marginalized groups decided that it was not enough to recount such peoples' struggles against oppression: it was equally important to explain how they lived and what they thought. Warren Susman (1984), Robin D. Kelley (1994), Kathy Peiss (1998), and others embraced popular culture—even mass culture—because the people they studied did so, too. Lizabeth Cohen (2003) added that the triumph of mass culture did not mean that Americans had abandoned politics. On the contrary, the United States became a "Consumer Republic" ruled by "citizen consumers."

Warren Susman, *Culture as History* (1984), Robin D. Kelley, *Race Rebels* (1994), Kathy Peiss, *Hope in a Jar* (1998), Lizabeth Cohen, *A Consumers' Republic* (2003). For the Frankfurt school, see Theodor Adorno, *Culture Industry* (1991) and Christopher Lasch, *The Culture of Narcissism* (1979). Walter Benjamin, *Complete Correspondence* (1999), argued in this correspondence with Adorno that mass-produced culture could free culture from the snob fetishism of high culture.

Behavior in the Human Male (1948), based on thousands of confidential interviews with persons from many walks of life, claimed that half of American men engaged in homosexual activities before adolescence; that 90 percent had masturbated; that between 30 and 45 percent had adulterous sexual relations; that 70 percent had patronized prostitutes; and that 17 percent of farm boys had had sexual relations with animals. Kinsey's data emphasized the diversity of sexual urges, and the foolishness of societal attempts to prescribe narrow standards of morality.

Sexual Behavior in the Human Male shocked many people, and many social scientists pointed out that a large sample was not necessarily representative. When he published *Sexual Behavior in the Human Female* in 1958, a book that demonstrated that the

▲ One of the major changes to occur in the 1970s and 1980s was the willingness of homosexuals to make public their sexual preference in the course of demanding full legal standing and equal rights.

sexual practices of women were as varied as those of men, Kinsey was subjected to a storm of abuse and deprived of the foundation support that had financed his research. (In 1997 historian James H. Jones challenged Kinsey's claims to scientific objectivity. Jones found that Kinsey and some of his researchers organized, participated in, and even filmed all manner of sexual activities involving interview subjects, prostitutes, colleagues, and spouses.)

Nevertheless, Kinsey was during his lifetime called "the Marx of the sexual revolution." Once it became possible to look at sex in primarily physical terms and to accept the idea that one's own urges might not be as uncommon as one had been led to believe, it became much more difficult to object to any sexual activity practiced in private by consenting adults. Homosexuals, for example, began openly to admit their feelings and to demand that the heterosexual society cease to harass and discriminate against them.

That the sexual revolution in its many aspects served useful functions was beyond dispute. Reducing irrational fears and inhibitions was liberating for many persons of both sexes, and it tended to help young people form permanent associations on the basis of deeper feelings than their sexual drives. Women surely profited from the new freedom, just as a greater sharing of family duties by husbands and fathers opened men's lives to many new satisfactions.

But like other changes, the revolution produced new problems, and some of its results were at best ambiguous. For young people, sexual freedom could be very unsettling; sometimes it generated social pressures that propelled them into relationships they were not yet prepared to handle, with grave psychological results. Equally perplexing was the rise in the number of illegitimate births. Easy cures did not eliminate venereal disease; on the contrary, the relaxation of sexual taboos produced what public health officials called a veritable epidemic of gonorrhea, a frightening increase in the incidence of syphilis, and the emergence of the new disease, acquired immune deficiency syndrome (AIDS).

Exercising the right to advocate and practice previously forbidden activities involved subjecting people who found those activities offensive—still a large proportion of the population—to embarrassment and even to acute emotional distress. To some people pornography seemed ethically wrong, and to most feminists it seemed degrading to women. Abortion raised difficult legal and moral questions, which exacerbated already serious social conflicts. Clearly, however, the sexual revolution was not about to end, nor the direction of change to be reversed.

WOMEN'S LIBERATION

Sexual freedom also contributed to the revival of the women's rights movement. For one thing, freedom involved a more drastic revolution for women than for men. Effective methods of contraception obviously affected women more directly than men, and the new attitudes heightened women's awareness of the way the old sexual standards and patterns of family living had restricted their entire existence. In fact the two movements interacted with each other in innumerable ways, some clear, others obscure. Concern for better job opportunities and for equal pay for equal work, for example, fed the demand for day-care centers for children.

Still another cause of the new drive for women's rights was concern for improving the treatment of minorities. Participation in and the mere observation of the civil rights movement encouraged American women—as it frequently had in earlier times—to speak out more forcefully for their own rights. Just as white people had callously demeaned and dominated black people until forced to desist by the victims of their prejudice, so, feminists argued, they were being demeaned and dominated by a male-oriented society and must fight back.

One of the leaders of the new women's movement was Betty Friedan. In *The Feminine Mystique* (1963), Friedan argued that advertisers, popular magazines, and other opinion-shaping forces were

undermining the capacity of women to use their intelligence and their talents creatively by a pervasive and not very subtle form of brainwashing designed to convince them of the virtues of domesticity. This Friedan deplored. She argued that without understanding why, thousands of women living supposedly happy lives were experiencing vague but persistent feelings of anger and discomfort. "The only way for a woman . . . to know herself as a person is by creative work of her own," she wrote. A "problem that had no name" was stifling women's potential.

The Feminine Mystique was what later came to be known as "consciousness raising" for thousands of women. Over a million copies were quickly sold. Back in 1922 a committee of physicians and social scientists had queried a thousand middle-class women about their personal lives. To the question: "Is your married life a happy one?" only 116 had answered no. But after her book came out, Friedan was deluged by hundreds of letters from women who had thought that their unease and depression despite their "happy" family life were both unique and unreasonable. Many now determined to expand their horizons by taking jobs or resuming their education.

Friedan had assumed that if able women acted with determination, employers would recognize their abilities and stop discriminating against them. This did not happen. In 1966 she and other feminists founded the National Organization for Women (NOW). Copying the tactics of black activists, NOW called for equal employment opportunities and equal pay as civil rights. "The time has come for a new movement toward true equality for all women in America and toward a fully equal partnership of the sexes," the leaders announced. "The silken curtain of prejudice and discrimination against women" in government, industry, the professions, religion, education, "and every other field of importance" must be drawn back. In 1967 NOW came out for an equal rights amendment to the Constitution, for changes in the divorce laws, and for the legalization of abortion, the right of "control of one's body."

By 1967, however, many younger feminists were arguing that NOW was not radical enough. They

▶ *text continues on page 848*

▲ Women marching on Fifth Avenue in New York City to demonstrate for equality. In 1968 the term "women's liberation movement" was used in the first issue of the crusade's national newsletter. Critics referred to its proponents as "libbers" and "libbies." The movement increasingly adopted as the preferred label, feminism, and "women's liberation" faded from use.

Mapping the Past

Roe v. *Wade* (1973) and the Abortion Controversy

In 1969, Norma McCorvey was twenty-five years old, unmarried, unemployed—and pregnant. When she requested an abortion, her doctor refused. Abortion, unless necessary to save the woman's life, was illegal in Texas. Her lawyer encouraged her to challenge the law. She consented, using the pseudonym "Jane Roe," and her lawyer filed suit against Henry Wade, the Dallas County prosecutor. In 1973, after McCorvey had delivered the baby, the U.S. Supreme Court rendered a decision in *Roe* v. *Wade*. Rejecting any "single" theory of life, the justices maintained that the "fetus" did not have a "right to life" until the final three months of pregnancy, when it was viable without the mother; until then, McCorvey's Fourteenth Amendment right to "privacy" took precedence. The state could not prevent her or any other woman from having an abortion in the first six months of pregnancy. With the possible exception of *Brown* v. *Board of Education* (1954), no Supreme Court decision had a more profound effect on American life in the twentieth century.

The Origins of Anti-Abortion Laws

In the colonial period, some women were executed for committing infanticide. The incidence of abortion then cannot be determined. But fragmentary sources indicate that abortion, though difficult to induce, was sometimes accomplished by ingesting toxic plants, such as foxglove, white hellebore, and mistletoe. The Puritans, who cited Biblical authority, criminalized abortion, though successful prosecutions were rare. Records for Middlesex County, Massachusetts, indicate only four convictions for attempted abortion from 1633 to 1699.

The Constitution made no reference to abortion. No state restricted the practice until 1821, when Connecticut prohibited the use of "deadly poisons" in the procedure. In 1829 New York prohibited anyone, including doctors, from attempting an abortion. By 1841, nine more states and the territory of Iowa imposed similar restrictions.

In 1859 the American Medical Association, in response to the number of deaths caused by surgical abortions, called for the "general suppression" of the practice. By 1900, every

state except Kentucky had passed anti-abortion laws. With minor modifications, these laws remained on the books well into the twentieth century. Most states allowed abortion when the woman had been impregnated by rape or incest or when a doctor thought it necessary to save the woman's life. In 1967, for example, Governor Ronald Reagan of California, an opponent of abortion, signed a law allowing doctors to perform abortions if the birth of a child would "gravely impair the physical or mental health of the mother." This gave doctors

Earliest State Restrictions on Abortion, 1821–1841

- states restricting abortion
- 1821 date of legislation

considerable discretion and pregnant women the option of finding a physician sympathetic to their concerns. The number of legal abortions in California increased from 5018 in 1968 to more than 100,000 by 1972. By then, only Louisiana, Pennsylvania, and New Hampshire outlawed all abortions. The *Roe* v. *Wade* ruling struck down the anti-abortion statute of every state in the nation except Hawaii, New York, and Alaska, which had already legalized most abortions.

Reagan and George H. W. Bush, whose Supreme Court appointments generally favored the right-to-life position. In *Webster* v. *Reproductive Health Services* (1989) and the *Planned Parenthood of Southeastern Pennsylvania* v. *Casey* (1992), the Supreme Court allowed states to impose certain conditions, such as tests of viability and waiting periods, before abortions could be performed. But well into the twenty-first century, *Roe* v. *Wade* still remained the law of the land.

Abortion Rates by State (2000)

The *Roe* v. *Wade* decision resulted in a rapid expansion of abortion facilities. From 1973 to 1980, the number of abortions performed annually increased from 745,000 to 1,500,000. In 2000, the most recent year for which reliable data is available, six million American women became pregnant. About 3.8 million (63 percent) gave birth to live infants, while 1.3 million (22 percent) ended in abortions and 900,000 (15 percent) in miscarriages. Because the rate of miscarriage varied little among states, the data for the map *(below right)* include only live births and abortions.

In Utah and Idaho, where Mormonism is strong, the abortion rate was 8 percent and 12 percent, respectively, among the lowest in the nation. Abortion rates were also low in predominantly rural states, such as South Dakota, Iowa, Nebraska, and Kentucky. The highest abortion rates were in New York, New Jersey, Nevada, and Maryland, where more than a third of all pregnancies were terminated. In the District of Columbia, 58 percent of pregnancies were aborted, the highest rate in the nation.

The *Roe* v. *Wade* decision energized a grass-roots right-to-life movement against abortion, often supported by Catholic and Protestant groups. The National Organization for Women took the lead in endorsing a woman's right to choose (pro-choice) whether to abort her pregnancy. The right-to-life movement provided indispensable organizational support to the presidential campaigns of Ronald

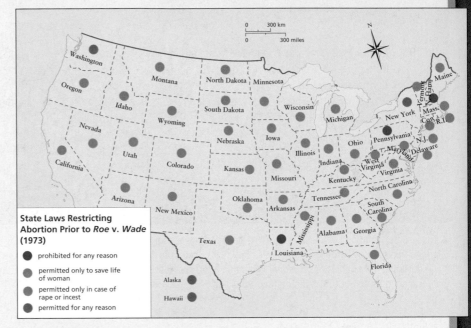

State Laws Restricting Abortion Prior to *Roe* v. *Wade* (1973)

- prohibited for any reason
- permitted only to save life of woman
- permitted only in case of rape or incest
- permitted for any reason

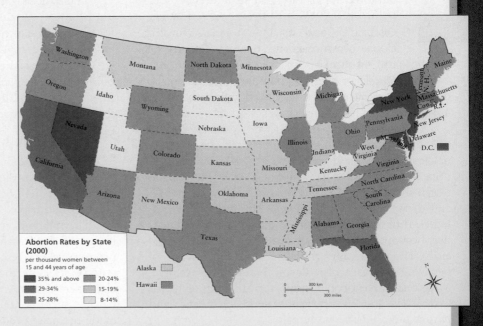

Abortion Rates by State (2000)
per thousand women between 15 and 44 years of age

- 35% and above
- 29-34%
- 25-28%
- 20-24%
- 15-19%
- 8-14%

▲ The issue of abortion continues to generate deep feelings among those on both sides of the 1973 Supreme Court *Roe* v. *Wade* decision. In this July 1992 photo, pro-choice adherents, who support the ruling declaring a woman's constitutional right to an abortion, clash with pro-lifers, who seek to overturn the decision, outside the U.S. Supreme Court building.

DOCUMENT

Chisholm, Equal Rights for Women (1969)

deplored its hierarchical structure, its lobbying activities, its stress on attracting celebrities, and its imitation of conventional pressure-group tactics. Equality of the two sexes smacked of "separate but equal" to these women, and indeed, many of them had been first radicalized by the struggle against racial segregation.

Typical was Kate Millett, whose *Sexual Politics* (1970) became a best-seller. Millett called for "a sexual revolution" to do away with "traditional inhibitions and taboos." She denounced male supremacy, which she described as "the institution of patriarchy," and drew a distinction between the immutable biological differences between men and women and gender, how men and women relate to one another socially and culturally, which are learned ways of behaving and thus capable of change. For example, Millett said that people must stop thinking of words like *violent* and *efficiency* as male characteristics and *passive* and *tenderness* as female.

The radicals gathered in small consciousness-raising groups to discuss questions as varied as the need for government-provided child-care centers, how best to denounce the annual Miss America contests, and lesbianism. They held conferences and seminars and published magazines, the most widely known being *Ms.*, edited by Gloria Steinem. Academics among them organized women's studies programs at dozens of colleges.

Some radical feminists advocated raising children in communal centers and doing away with marriage as a legal institution. Others described marriage as "legalized rape." Some rejected heterosexuality as a matter of principle.

The militants attacked all aspects of the standard image of the female sex. Avoiding the error of the progressive era reformers, who had fought for the vote by stressing the supposed purity and high moral character of women, they insisted on total equality. Clichés such as "the fair sex" and "the weaker sex" made them see red. They demanded that men bear as

much of the burden of caring for their children, cooking, and housework as women traditionally did. They took courses in self-defense to be able to protect themselves from muggers, rapists, and casual mashers. They denounced the use of masculine words like *chairman* (favoring *chairperson*) and of such terms as *mankind* and *men* to designate people in general. They substituted *Ms.* for both *Miss* and *Mrs.* on the grounds that the language drew no such distinction between unmarried and married men.

Few people escaped being affected by the women's movement. The presence of women in new roles—as television commentators, airline pilots, police officers—

did not prove that a large-scale shift in employment patterns had taken place. Yet even the most unregenerate male seemed to recognize that the balance of power and influence between the sexes had been altered. The sexual revolution was not about to end, the direction of change in gender relationships not to be reversed.

Many people in the vanguard of change thought they could catch a glimpse, in the not too distant future, of an egalitarian, tolerant, and fulfilling world. But it is hard to see clearly when one is moving, and American society in the 1960s was in flux. Many soon learned that change begets change, and not always what one expects.

MILESTONES

1946	Dr. Benjamin Spock publishes *Common Sense Guide to Baby and Child Care*
1947	Construction begins on Levittown, New York
1948	Norman Mailer publishes *The Naked and the Dead*
	Alfred C. Kinsey publishes *Sexual Behavior in the Human Male*
1951	J. D. Salinger publishes *Catcher in the Rye*
1955	Joseph Heller publishes *Catch-22*
	Allen Ginsberg publishes *Howl*
1956	AFL and CIO merge
	Federal Highway Act plans superhighway network
1957	Soviets launch *Sputnik*
	Jack Kerouac publishes *On the Road*
1958	Congress passes National Defense Education Act
	Alfred C. Kinsey publishes *Sexual Behavior in the Human Female*
1959	James B. Conant attacks American education system in *The American High School*
1960	FDA approves sale of birth control pills
1962	Students for a Democratic Society (SDS) issues Port Huron Statement
1963	Betty Friedan publishes *The Feminine Mystique*
	Martin Luther King, Jr. gives "I Have a Dream" speech during March on Washington

1964	Free Speech Movement disrupts University of California at Berkeley
1965	Black Muslim fanatics assassinate Malcolm X
	Cesar Chavez organizes boycott to support grape pickers
1965–1968	Riots rock black ghettoes
1966	National Organization for Women (NOW) is founded
1968	Police break student strike at Columbia University
	The Rev. Dr. Martin Luther King, Jr. is assassinated
1969	A half million attend Woodstock Festival in New York
	U.S. astronauts land on moon
1973	Supreme Court legalizes abortion in *Roe* v. *Wade*
1975	Congress gives tribes more autonomy in Indian Self-Determination Act
1989	Supreme Court limits abortion rights in *Webster* v. *Reproductive Health Services*
1992	Supreme Court further limits abortion rights in *Planned Parenthood* v. *Casey*

SUPPLEMENTARY READING

Kenneth T. Jackson, *Crabgrass Frontier* (1985) is indispensable on the evolution of the suburbs. On Jackson's argument that home ownership contributed to political conservativism, see Becky M. Nicolaides, *My Blue Heaven: Life and Politics in the Working-Class Suburbs of Los Angeles, 1920–1965* (2002). Elaine Tyler May, *Homeward Bound: American Families in the Cold War* (1988), locates the rise of a conservative ideological mindset within the home. The environmental consequences of suburbanization are the subject of Adam Rome, *The Bulldozer in the Countryside* (2001). For the cities, see Robert M. Fogelson, *Downtown: Its Rise and Fall, 1880–1950* (2001).

On the effects of the automobile, see Jane H. Kay's history/manifesto, *Asphalt Nation* (1997), and Virginia Scharff's *Taking the Wheel: Women and the Coming of the Motor Age* (1992).

For a favorable account of New Left of the 1960s, by a former leader of the SDS, see Todd Gitlin, *The Sixties: Years of Hope, Days of Rage* (1987). Maurice Isserman and Michael Kazin, *America Divided: The Civil War of the 1960s* (2000), though sympathetic to the New Left, note that conservatives emerged from the decade victorious. David Burner, *Making Peace with the Sixties* (1996) argues that the New Left unwisely abandoned its Old Left origins, and thus slipped into self-destructive hedonism. Peter Collier and David Horowitz, *Destructive Generation: Second Thoughts about the '60s* (1989) contend that the decade's "hedonism" and "revolutionary passion" culminated in "tragic consequences." See also Roger Kimball, *The Long March: How the Cultural Revolution of the 1960s Changed America* (2000), Dominick Cavallo, *A Faction of the Past: The Sixties in American History* (1999), and David Farber, *Chicago 68* (1988). Ellen Fitzpatrick, *History's Memory: Writing America's Past, 1880–1980* (2002) is especially critical of historians of this period for neglecting their scholarly forebears.

For television, see Mary Ann Watson, *The Expanding Vista: American Television in the Kennedy Years* (1994), James L. Baughman, *The Republic of Mass Culture: Journalism, Filmmaking, and Broadcasting in America Since 1941* (1991), Karal Ann Marling, *As Seen on TV: The Visual Culture of Everyday Life in the 1950s* (1994), and Josh Ozersky, *Archie Bunker's America: TV in an Era of Change* (2003). See also Glenn C. Altschuler, *All Shook Up: How Rock 'n' Roll Changed America* (2003).

On black radicalism, in addition to works cited in the previous chapter, see the first person accounts by Malcolm X, *Autobiography* (1966), Stokely Carmichael and C. V. Hamilton, *Black Power* (1967), and Eldridge Cleaver, *Soul on Ice* (1967). Other important books on race relations include Taylor Branch's multi-volume biography of Martin Luther King, Jr.: *Parting the Waters: 1954–1963* (1988), and *Pillar of Fire: America in the King Years, 1963–1965* (1998). On SNCC, see John Lewis's memoir, *Walking with the Wind* (1998), as well as Clayborne Carson, *In Struggle: SNCC and the Black Awakening of the 1960s* (1981). The neglected role of women in the movement is addressed in Chana Kai Lee, *For Freedom's Sake: The Life of Fannie Lou Hamer* (1999), and Carolyn Wedin, *Inheritors of the Spirit: Mary White Ovington and the Founding of NAACP* (1998).

Ronald Takaki, *A Different Mirror: A History of Multicultural History* (1993), provides an overview of the contemporary immigrant experience. Rodolfo Acuna, *Occupied America: A History of Chicanos* (2000), Manuel Gonzales, *Mexicanos: A History of Mexicans in the United States* (1999), and Ernesto Vigil, *The Crusade for Justice* (1999) provide surveys of broad trends of Chicano history in the United States. Biographies of César Chávez include, Richard Griswold del Castillo and Richard A. Garcia, *A Triumph of the Spirit* (1998), and Joan London and Henry Anderson, *So Shall Ye Reap: The Story of César Chávez and the Farm Workers Movement* (1970). James S. Olson and Raymond Wilson, *Native Americans in the Twentieth Century* (1984), is a good survey.

The literature on the women's movement is voluminous. Betty Friedan's *The Feminine Mystique* (1963), is essential, though her account must be modified in light of Daniel Horowitz, *Betty Friedan and the Making of The Feminine Mystique* (1998). Rosalind Rosenberg, *Divided Lives: American Women in the Twentieth Century* (1992) is a good introduction to women's history. See also Jo Freeman, *The Politics of Women's Liberation* (1975), and Susan M. Hartmann, *From Margin to Mainstream: Women and American Politics Since 1960* (1989). Narrower monographs include Dennis A. Deslippe, *"Rights, Not Roses": Unions and the Rise of Working-Class Feminism* (2000).

On abortion, Rickie Solinger, *Wake Up Little Suzie: Single Pregnancy and Race before* Roe v. Wade (1992), considers the situation before 1973. On the *Roe v. Wade* decision itself, see Laurence H. Tribe, *Abortion: The Clash of Absolutes* (1990), and Linda Gordon, *Moral Property of Women: A History of Birth Control Politics in America* (2002). Andrea Tone, *Devices and Desires: A History of Contraceptives in America* (2001) is useful on contraception more generally.

James H. Jones, *Alfred C. Kinsey: A Public/Private Life* (1997), finds that Kinsey's odd behavior discredits his scholarship; Jonathan Gathorne-Hardy, *Alfred C. Kinsey: Sex the Measure of All Things* (1998) is less critical. On sexual trends more generally, see Beth Bailey, *Sex in the Heartland* (1999) on Kansas in the 1960s and 1970s.

The early history of the AIDS crisis is movingly told in Randy Shilts, *And the Band Played On* (1987). See also Elizabeth Fee and Daniel M. Fox, eds., *AIDS: The Making of a Chronic Disease* (1992).

SUGGESTED WEBSITES

1950s America
http://www.writing.upenn.edu/~afilreis/50s/home.html
This site by University of Pennsylvania Professor Al Filreis contains a large array of 1950s literature and images in an alphabetical index.

Hollywood and the Movies During the 1950s
http://lib.berkeley.edu/MRC/50sbib.html
This site proves information on cinema and film during the 1950s.

Rock and Roll
http://www.rockhall.com/
By the late-1950s, rock and roll had become the music of the new generation.

Martin Luther King, Jr.
http://www.seattletimes.com/mlk/
This *Seattle Times* site has several articles about King and the Civil Rights Movement.

Martin Luther King, Jr. Papers Project
http://www.stanford.edu/group/King/
This Stanford University site has links and selected documents by and concerning Martin Luther King, Jr.

National Civil Rights Museum
http://www.civilrightsmuseum.org
This site allows a virtual tour of the museum with its interpretive exhibits.

The Diggers Archives
http://www.diggers.org/
This site provides information about The San Francisco Diggers, one of the legendary groups in the Haight-Ashbury from 1966–1968.

United States v. *Cecil Price et al.* (The "Mississippi Burning" Trial), 1967
http://www.law.umkc.edu/faculty/projects/ftrials/price&bowers.html
This site contains images, chronology, and court and official documents maintained by Dr. Doug Linder at the University of Missouri–Kansas City Law School.

The Sixties Project
http://lists.village.virginia.edu/sixties/
This University of Virginia site has extensive exhibits, documents, and personal narratives from the 1960s.

Civil Rights Oral History Bibliography
http://www.dept.usm.edu/crdp/html/dah.shtml
This University of Southern Mississippi site includes complete transcripts of the selected oral resources.

1969 Woodstock Festival and Concert
http://www.woodstock69.com
This site provides pictures and lists of songs from the famous rock festival.

Virtual Museum of Computing
http://vmoc.museophile.sbu.ac.uk
This site relates history of computing through a series of online exhibits.

The Computer Museum History Center
http://www.computerhistory.org
This site for the Computer Museum History Center features online archives and exhibits tracing decades of computer history.

Running on Empty: The Nation Transformed

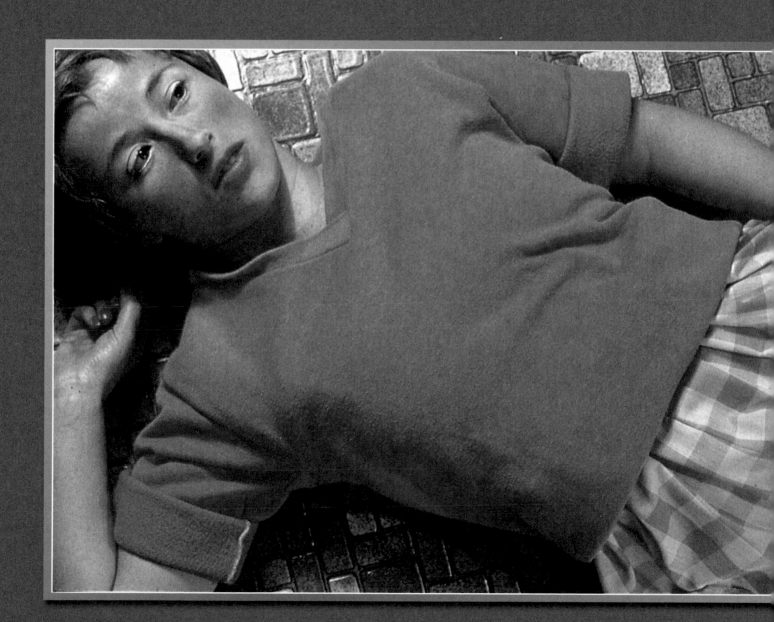

▼ Photographer Cindy Sherman's *Untitled No. 96* (1981), in which she poses as a vulnerable teenager, vacantly pondering a crumpled lonely hearts column. Did economic recession promote self-absorption?

CHAPTER CONTENTS

While most Americans watched, transfixed, as the events of Watergate interred the Nixon presidency, few were aware that a battle on the other side of the world was about to transform their lives. On October 6, 1973, the eve of Yom Kippur, the Jewish Day of Atonement, Egypt and Syria attacked the state of Israel. Six years earlier Israel had trounced the Egyptians with humiliating ease and taken possession of the Sinai peninsula, but now Egypt's armored divisions roared into the Sinai and threatened to slice Israel in half; Syrian troops advanced against Israel father north. Israeli Prime Minister Golda Meir pleaded with President Nixon for additional arms and aircraft. He ordered "every last goddamn airplane" be sent to Israel. "We are going to be condemned by the Arabs one way or the other," Nixon concluded. The United States immediately airlifted scores of fighter planes and other desperately needed matériel to Israel. The Israelis recrossed the Suez Canal, cut Egyptian supply lines, and forced Egypt's president, Anwar Sadat, to capitulate. But the Arab world then aimed its biggest weapon and aimed it squarely at the United States: It cut off oil shipments to the West.

THE OIL CRISIS

Deprived of Middle Eastern oil, the American economy sputtered. The price of oil rose to $12 a barrel, up from $3. This sent prices soaring for nearly everything else. Homes were heated with oil, factories were powered by it, utility plants used it to generate electricity, and farm produce was shipped to markets on gas-fueled trucks. Nylon and other synthetic fibers as well as paints, insecticides, fertilizers, and many plastic products were based on petrochemicals. Above all else, oil was refined into gasoline. By the time of the Yom Kippur War, American car owners were driving more than a trillion miles a year, the major reason why the United States, formerly a major oil exporter, imported one-third of its oil. The Arab oil embargo pushed up gas prices; service stations intermittently ran out of gasoline; long lines formed at those that remained open.

In the spring of 1974, Henry Kissinger negotiated an agreement that required Israel's withdrawal from some territory occupied since the 1967 war; the Arab nations then lifted the oil embargo. But the principal oil exporting nations—Venezuela, Saudi Arabia, Kuwait, Iraq, and Iran—had learned a valuable lesson: if they limited production, they could drive up the price of oil. After the embargo had ended, their cartel, the Organization of Petroleum Exporting Countries (OPEC), announced another price increase. Gasoline prices doubled overnight.

American automakers who had scoffed at bulbous Volkswagen "bugs" and tiny Japanese "boxes" now winced as these foreign competitors claimed the new market for small, fuel-efficient, front-wheel-drive cars. American auto companies were unable to respond to this challenge because their contracts with the United Automobile Workers (UAW) linked wages to consumer prices, which had floated upward with the price of oil. As production costs rose, manufacturers needed to sell more of their behemoth models, loaded with expensive options such as air conditioning, power windows, and stereo systems. They could not profitably sell the small cars the public craved. (In 1982, when Ford belatedly entered the front-wheel drive market, it lost $40 on each car sold.) By the end of the 1970s, Japanese automakers had captured 30 percent of the entire American automobile market.

FORD AS PRESIDENT

The country greeted the accession of Gerald Ford to the presidency with a collective sigh of relief. Most observers considered Ford unimaginative, certainly not brilliant. But he was hardworking, and—most important under the circumstances—his record was untouched by scandal. Although he was an almost automaton-like Republican partisan, nearly all the Democrats in Congress liked him. He was Nixon's opposite as a person, being gregarious and open, and he stated repeatedly that he took a dim view of Nixon's high-handed way of dealing with Congress. A most ordinary person, earnest but limited, Ford appeared unlikely to venture beyond conventional boundaries or to act rashly. This was what nearly everyone wanted of the president in the wake of Nixon.

Ford identified inflation as the chief economic culprit and asked patriotic citizens to signify their willingness to fight it by wearing WIN (Whip Inflation Now) buttons. Almost immediately the economy entered a precipitous slump. Production fell and the unemployment rate rose to above 9 percent, about twice the postwar average. The president was forced to ask for tax cuts and other measures aimed at stimulating business activity. This made inflation worse and did little to promote employment. The economic problems were difficult, and Ford was handicapped by the fact that the Democrats had solid control of Congress, but his performance was at best inept.

▲ Gas stations all over the country began running dry in 1973; the shortage worsened through the winter and into 1974.

▲ "My fellow Americans," Gerald Ford announced as he succeeded Richard Nixon in August, 1974, "our long national nightmare is over."

THE FALL OF SOUTH VIETNAM

Depressing news about the economy was compounded by unsettling events in Vietnam. In January 1975, after two years of a bloody "cease fire" (Hanoi charged Saigon with 301,000 violations; and Saigon charged its adversary with 35,673), North Vietnam initiated a two-year plan to conquer South Vietnam by striking just south of the 17th parallel. Dispirited and incompetently led, the South Vietnamese fell back, then fled headlong, and finally dissolved with a rapidity that astonished their attackers.

Ford had always supported the Vietnam war. As the military situation deteriorated, he urged Congress to pour more arms into the South to stem the North Vietnamese advance. The legislators flatly refused to do so, and on May 1, 1975 the Viet Cong and North Vietnamese entered Saigon, which they renamed Ho Chi Minh City. The long Vietnam war was finally over.

FORD VERSUS CARTER

Ford's uninspiring record on the economy and foreign policy suggested that he would be vulnerable in 1976. That year the Democrats chose James Earl Carter, a former governor of Georgia, as their candidate. Carter's rise from almost total obscurity was even more spectacular than that of George McGovern in 1972 and was made possible by the same forces: television, the democratization of the delegate-selection process, and the absence of a dominant leader among the Democrats.

Carter had been a naval officer and a substantial peanut farmer and warehouse owner before entering politics. He was elected governor of Georgia in 1970. While governor he won something of a reputation as a southern public official who treated black citizens fairly. (He hung a portrait of Martin Luther King, Jr., in his office.) Carter's political style was informal—he preferred to be called Jimmy. During the campaign for delegates he turned his inexperience in national politics to advantage, emphasizing his lack of connection with the Washington establishment rather than apologizing for it. He repeatedly called attention to his integrity and deep religious faith. "I'll never lie to you," he promised voters, a pledge that no candidate would have bothered to make before Nixon's disgrace. He won the Democratic nomination easily.

Carter sought to make the election a referendum on morality. After Watergate, an atmosphere of scandal permeated Washington, and aspiring journalists and congressmen trained their sights on Kissinger, who remained secretary of state after Nixon's resignation. The most significant of the allegations was his meddling in the affairs of Chile, which in 1970 was on the verge of electing Salvadore Allende, a Marxist, as president. "I don't see why we need to stand by and watch a country go communist due to the irresponsibility of its people," Kissinger had quipped. After Allende's election, Kissinger called on the CIA to "destabilize" Allende's regime. In 1973, Allende was murdered in a military coup and his government toppled. Carter promised an administration of "constant decency" in contrast to Kissinger's penchant for secret diplomacy and Machiavellian skullduggery.

Ford was opposed in the Republican campaign by ex-governor Ronald Reagan of California, a movie actor turned politician who was the darling of the Republican right wing. Reagan was an excellent speaker, whereas Ford proved somewhat bumbling on the stump. Reagan, too, hammered away at Kissinger, citing his "immoral" détente with Communist China. At Reagan's insistence, the Republican platform denounced "secret agreements, hidden from our people"—another jab at Kissinger.

Both Republican candidates gathered substantial blocs of delegates, but Ford staved off the Reagan challenge. That he did not win easily, possessed as he was of the advantage of incumbency, made his chances of election in November appear slim.

When the final contest began, both candidates were vague with respect to issues, a situation that hurt Carter particularly because he had made so much of honesty and straight talk. Ford stressed the need to control inflation, Carter to attack high unemployment. The election was memorable chiefly for its gaffes: Carter's admission to *Playboy* that he had "lusted after women in my heart" and Ford's declaration in a televised debate, "There is no Soviet domination in Eastern Europe." Voters were left to choose between Carter's seeming ignorance of human frailty and Ford's human frailty of seeming ignorant.

With both candidates stumbling toward the finish line, pundits predicted an extremely close contest, and they were right: Carter won, 297 electoral votes to 241, having carried most of the South, including Texas, and a few large industrial states. A key element in his victory was the fact that he got an overwhelming majority of the black vote (partly on his record in Georgia, partly because Ford had been unsympathetic toward the demands of the urban poor). He also ran well in districts dominated by labor union members. The wish of the public to punish the party of Richard Nixon probably was a further reason for his victory.

THE CARTER PRESIDENCY

Carter shone brightly in comparison with Nixon, and he seemed more forward-looking and imaginative than Ford. He tried to give a tone of democratic simplicity and moral fervor to his administration. After delivering his inaugural address he walked with his wife Rosalynn and their small daughter Amy in the parade from the Capitol to the White House instead of riding in a limousine. He enrolled Amy, a fourth-grader, in a largely black Washington public school. Soon after taking office he held a "call-in"; for two hours he answered questions phoned in by people from all over the country.

Carter's actual administration of his office did not go nearly so well. He put so many Georgians in important posts that his administration took on a parochial character. The administration developed a reputation for submitting complicated proposals to Congress with great fanfare and then failing to follow up on them. Whatever matter Carter was considering at the moment seemed to absorb him totally—other urgent matters were allowed to drift.

A NATIONAL MALAISE

To Carter, these difficulties were symptomatic of a more fundamental flaw in the nation's soul. In a heralded television speech he complained that "a moral and spiritual crisis" had sapped people's energies and undermined civic pride: "We've learned that piling up material goods cannot fill the emptiness of lives which have no confidence or purpose." Critics responded that the nation needed a president rather than a preacher, and that sermons on the emptiness of consumption rang hollow to those who had lost their jobs or whose paychecks had been shrunk by inflation.

The economic downturn, though triggered by the energy shortage, had more fundamental causes. In the prosperous postwar decades, many companies had become too big and complacent, more attuned to the demands of the corporate bureaucracy than the needs of customers. Workers' boredom lowered productivity. Absenteeism at General Motors and Ford doubled during the 1960s. On an average day in 1970, 5 percent of GM's workforce was missing without explanation, and on Mondays and Fridays ten percent failed to show up. That year Lee Iacocca, the president of Ford, was unnerved by employee attitudes during his visit to a plant at Wixcom, Indiana: "I see some young guy who's going full-time to school at Wayne State, his mind is elsewhere, and he doesn't give a shit what he builds, he doesn't care and he isn't involved in his job. We can't change a man like that anymore." Incapable of eliminating slipshod work in Ford plants, Iacocca recommended that dealers improve their repair shops.

Two years later simmering discontents among young workers boiled over at the GM assembly division at Lordstown, Ohio. GM had installed robotic welding machines, streamlined the workforce, and accelerated the assembly line: 100 cars passed through the line each hour—40 more than under the previous system. Without authorization from the national UAW, younger workers refused to work at the faster pace, allowing many chassis to pass through untouched and throwing the factory into chaos. "Significant numbers of American workers," the U.S. Department of Health, Education and Welfare concluded, had grown dissatisfied with the "dull, repetitive, seemingly meaningless tasks" of the postwar workplace.

Younger workers were growing impatient too with aging union leaders and a system that welded salary increases to seniority. Increasingly the young rejected the postwar accord in which organized labor essentially ceded control of the workplace in return for cost-of-living increases and job security.

Union membership slipped badly from the high point of the mid–1950s, when over one in three nonagricultural workers belonged to unions; by 1978, the

▲ An abandoned steel mill at Youngstown, Ohio, in 1986. The sign *(right)* reads: "Free Wood at Your Own Risk." The backbone of American industry throughout the twentieth century, midwestern steel sharply declined in the 1970s and all but collapsed during the 1980s.

proportion had declined to one in four, and by 1990, one in six. During the 1940s and 1950s, most workers voted to join a union, pay dues, and have the organization bargain for them. By 1978, however, union organizers were losing three-fourths of their campaigns to represent workers; and many workers who belonged to unions were opting to get out. Every year, 800 more union shops voted to rescind their affiliation.

STAGFLATION: THE WEIRD ECONOMY

Recessions are part of the natural business cycle: when economies overheat, they eventually cool down. But the economic crisis after 1973 was unsettling because, for the first time in the nation's history, the rising tide of unemployment had failed to extinguish inflation. Millions of workers lost their jobs, yet wages and prices continued to rise. The term "stagflation" (a combination of stagnation and inflation) was coined to describe this anomaly. In 1971 an inflation rate of 5 percent had so alarmed President Nixon that he had imposed a price freeze. By 1975 inflation had soared to 11 percent and by 1979, it peaked at a whopping 13 percent; unemployment ranged from 6 to 10 percent, nearly twice the usual postwar level.

Carter had promised to fight inflation by reducing government spending and balancing the budget and to stimulate the economy by cutting taxes, policies that were very much like those of Nixon and Ford. He advanced an admirable if complicated plan for conserving energy and reducing the dependence of the United States on OPEC oil. This plan would raise the tax on gasoline and impose a new tax on "gas guzzlers," cars that got relatively few miles per gallon. But in his typical fashion he did not press hard for these measures.

Congress raised the minimum wage to help low-paid workers cope with inflation. It pegged social security payments to the cost of living index in an effort to protect retirees. Thereafter, when prices rose, social security payments went up automatically. The poor and the pensioners got some immediate relief, but the laws made balancing the federal budget more difficult and the increased spending power of the recipients caused further upward pressure on prices. During the decade, social welfare spending more than doubled. The federal deficit soared from $8.7 billion in 1970 to $72.7 billion in 1980. The price spiral seemed unstoppable.

The federal government made matters worse in several ways. Wages and salaries rose in response to inflation, but taxes went up more rapidly because larger dollar incomes put people in higher tax brackets. This "bracket creep" caused resentment and

frustration among middle-class families. There were "taxpayer revolts" as many people turned against long-accepted but expensive government programs for aiding the poor. Federal borrowing to cover the deficit pushed up interest rates and increased the costs of all businesses that had to borrow.

Soaring mortgage rates made it more difficult to sell homes. The housing slump meant unemployment for thousands of carpenters, bricklayers, and other construction workers and bankruptcy for many builders. Double-digit interest rates also hurt small businesses seeking to expand. Savings and loan institutions were especially hard-hit because they were saddled with countless mortgages made when rates were as low as 4 and 5 percent. Now they had to pay much more than that to hold deposits and offer even higher rates to attract new money.

FAMILIES UNDER STRESS

Bad as inflation was in the mid–1970s, it got worse in 1979 when further instability in the Middle East nearly tripled the price of oil, which now reached $34 a barrel. This sent gasoline far over the $1 a gallon price barrier many had thought inconceivable. Within months Ford stock, at 32 in 1978, plummeted to 16; its credit rating with Standard and Poor's fell from AAA to an ignominious BBB. Chrysler, the third largest automaker, tottered near bankruptcy and then fell over the edge, saved in mid-fall only by a $1.2 billion federal loan guarantee. From 1978 to 1982, the jobs of one in three autoworkers were eliminated.

When workers—most of them men—lost relatively high-paying jobs in the automobile factories and steel mills, their spouses usually helped to make up for the loss in wages by taking low-paying jobs in restaurants, retail stores, and offices. In 1950, one in four married women had a job outside the home; by 1980, half did.

In 1976 Democratic Senator Lloyd Bentsen, while campaigning for vice president, observed that McDonald's fast-food chain employed more people than U.S. Steel. "There is something very wrong with a nation that is long on hamburgers and short on steel," he declared. In fact, the two phenomena went hand in hand. Overextended families had little time to shop for, prepare, and enjoy leisurely meals around the dinner table. Such families "deserved a break," according to the McDonald's jingle, and often bolted down fast food on the way to or from work or school.

▲ The National Organization for Women holds a rally in Illinois for the Equal Rights Amendment. In 1982, as the deadline for ratification was about to expire, a majority in the Illinois legislature approved ERA but not by sufficient margin. The defeat in Illinois meant that the ERA was dead.

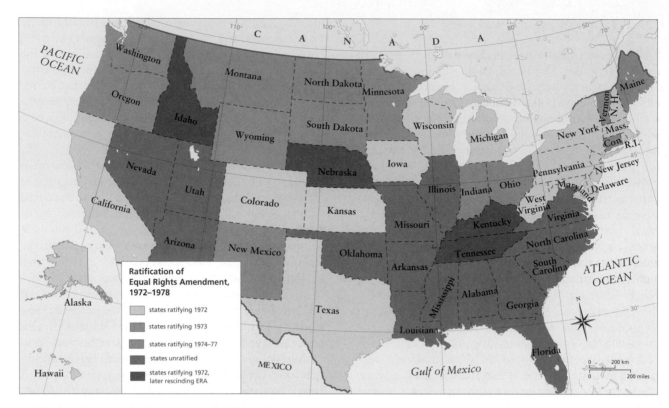

▲ **Failure of the Equal Rights Amendment, 1972–1982**

In 1972, Congress approved the Equal Rights Amendment. For it to become part of the Constitution, three-fourths of the states—38—had to ratify it. By the end of the year, 22 states had ratified. But then Phyllis Schlafly's campaign against ERA began to take hold. Only 8 ratified in 1973, and 3 in 1974. By the fall of 1978, only 35 states had ratified. Congress voted to extend the ratification deadline for four years, but failed to win enough states; in the meantime, some states that had ratified rescinded their vote, an action of uncertain legality. Opposition to ERA was focused in the South and in the Rocky Mountain states.

For the millions of young women whose gender consciousness had been shaped by Betty Friedan, Kate Millett, and other feminists, the recession struck at the worst possible time. Those who had anticipated a scamper up the corporate ladder discovered that the lower rungs were the first to be cut during recession. Many abandoned the idea of a career and settled for low-paying, dead-end jobs in the clerical or service sector. Yet some women, especially those who were well-educated, achieved strong gains during the 1970s: female lawyers jumped from 5 to 12 percent of the profession; and accountants, from 25 to 33 percent.

Just when the feminist movement required a united fight to gain legal parity with men, women increasingly were divided: into an intellectual and professional elite, eager to prove their merits on the job in fair competition with men; and an underpaid and ill-used underclass, vulnerable to the vagaries of a recessionary economy and to the dictates of (mostly male) bosses.

One casualty was the Equal Rights Amendment (ERA), which would make it unconstitutional to deny equal rights "on account of sex." First proposed by the National Woman's party in 1923, the ERA got nowhere. The National Organization for Women (NOW) revived the measure in the 1960s. The House of Representatives approved the ERA in 1971 and the Senate in 1972. By the end of 1972, 22 states had ratified the amendment, 16 short of the three-fourths needed for the ERA to become part of the constitution.

In 1973 Phyllis Schlafly, a former vice president of the National Federation of Republican Women and publisher of a conservative newsletter, spearheaded a nationwide campaign against the ERA. She argued that it would subject young women to the military draft, deprive divorced women of alimony and child custody, and make married women legally responsible for providing 50 percent of household income. Although most polls indicated that a majority of voters supported the ERA, Schlafly's words struck a responsive chord among anxious housewives and low-wage-earning women who doubted they could survive the recessionary economy on their own. The ratification campaign lost momentum and stalled, falling just three states short.

COLD WAR OR DÉTENTE?

"It is a new world," Carter declared in his first speech on foreign affairs. In contrast to the shadowy dealings and sly gambits of the Nixon-Kissinger years, he based his foreign policy on "constant decency." He announced that he would deal with other nations in a fair and humane way, putting the defense of "basic human rights" before all other concerns. He then cut off aid to Chile and Argentina because of human rights violations. He also negotiated treaties with Panama that provided for the gradual transfer of the Panama Canal to that nation and guaranteed the canal's neutrality. But he said little about what was going on in a long list of other nations whose citizens' rights were being repressed.

The president also intended to carry forward the Nixon-Kissinger policy of détente. In January 1979 the first exchange of ambassadors with the People's Republic of China took place. Maintaining good relations with the Soviet Union was more difficult, partly because while Secretary of State Cyrus Vance supported détente, Carter's national security adviser, Zbigniew Brzezinski, was strongly anti-Soviet. Carter fluctuated between the two approaches, yet seemed blissfully unaware of his ambivalence.

In 1979 another Strategic Arms Limitation Treaty (SALT II) was signed with the Soviet Union, but the following winter the Soviet Union sent troops into Afghanistan to overthrow the government there. Carter denounced the invasion and warned the Soviets that he would use force if they invaded any of the countries bordering the Persian Gulf. He withdrew the SALT treaty, which he had sent to the Senate for ratification. He also refused to allow American athletes to compete in the 1980 Olympic games, which were held in Moscow, and he began a new nuclear arms buildup.

Carter's one striking diplomatic achievement was the so-called Camp David Accords negotiated by Israel and Egypt. In September 1978 President Anwar Sadat of Egypt and Prime Minister Menachem Begin of Israel came to the United States at Carter's invitation to seek a peace treaty ending the state of war that had existed between their two countries for many years.

For two weeks they conferred at Camp David, the presidential retreat outside the capital, and Carter's mediation had much to do with their successful negotiations. In the treaty Israel promised to withdraw from territory captured from Egypt during the 1967 Israeli-Egypt war. Egypt in turn recognized Israel as a nation, the first Arab country to do so. Peace ensured an uninterrupted supply of Arab oil to the United States. The Camp David Accords were the first and, as it turned out, the last significant agreement of the twentieth century between Israel and a major Arab state.

▲ Anwar Sadat of Egypt, Jimmy Carter, and Menachem Begin of Israel agree to a peace settlement at Camp David in September, 1978. Sadat's concessions infuriated Arab extremists, who assassinated him three years later.

THE IRAN CRISIS: ORIGINS

At this point a dramatic shift in the Middle East thrust Carter into the spotlight as never before. On November 4, 1979, about 400 armed Muslim militants broke into the American embassy compound in Tehran, Iran, and took everyone within the walls captive.

The seizure had roots that ran far back in Iranian history. During World War II, Great Britain, the Soviet Union, and later the United States occupied Iran and forced its pro-German shah into exile, replacing him with his 22-year-old son, Muhammad Reza Pahlavi. But in the early 1950s power shifted to prime minister Muhammad Mossadegh, a leftist who sought to finance social reform by

▲ Iranian militants in Tehran burning the American flag. Such demonstrations attracted millions and helped establish the revolutionary regime's legitimacy among its own people. The alternative means of creating legitimacy, by holding elections, was often rejected on theological (and pragmatic) grounds by rulers in the Middle East.

nationalizing the mostly American-owned Anglo-Iranian Oil Company.

In 1953, the Iranian army, backed by the CIA, arrested Mossadegh and put the young Pahlavi in power. The fall of Mossadegh ensured a steady flow of cheap oil, but it turned most Iranians against the United States and Shah Pahlavi. His unpopularity led the shah to purchase enormous amounts of American arms. Over the years Iran became the most powerful military force in the region.

Although Iran was an enthusiastic member of the OPEC cartel, the shah was for obvious reasons a firm friend of the United States. In the troubled Middle East, Iran seemed "an island of stability," President Carter said.

The appearance of stability was deceptive. The shah's secret police, the Savak, brutally suppressed liberal opponents. At the same time, Muslim religious leaders were particularly offended by the shah's attempts to introduce Western ideas and technology into Iran. Because his American-supplied army and his American-trained secret police kept the shah in power, his opponents hated the United States almost as much as they hated their autocratic ruler.

Throughout 1977, riots and demonstrations convulsed Iran. When soldiers fired on protesters, the bloodshed caused more unrest, and that unrest, more bloodshed. Over 10,000 civilians were killed; many times that number were wounded. In 1978 the whole country seemed to rise against the shah. Finally, in January 1979, he was forced to flee. A revolutionary government headed by a religious leader, the Ayatollah Ruhollah Khomeini, assumed power.

Khomeini denounced the United States, the "Great Satan," whose support of the shah, he said, had caused the Iranian people untold suffering. When President Carter allowed the shah to come to the United States for medical treatment for cancer, militants in Tehran seized the American embassy.

THE IRAN CRISIS: CARTER'S DILEMMA

The militants announced that the Americans at the embassy would be held hostage until the United States returned the shah to Iran for trial as a traitor.

They also demanded that the shah's vast wealth be confiscated and surrendered to the Iranian government. President Carter rejected these demands. Instead Carter froze Iranian assets in the United States and banned trade with Iran until the hostages were freed.

A stalemate developed. Months passed. Even after the shah, who was terminally ill, left the United States for Panama, the Iranians remained adamant. The crisis produced a remarkable emotional response in the United States. For the first time since the Vietnam war the entire country agreed on something.

Nevertheless the hostages languished in Iran. In April 1980 Carter finally ordered a team of marine commandos flown into Iran in Sea Stallion helicopters in a desperate attempt to free the hostages. The raid was a fiasco. Several helicopters broke down when their rotors sucked sand into the engines. While the other helicopters were gathered at a desert rendezvous south of Tehran, Carter called off the attempt. In the confusion of a night departure there was a crash and eight commandos were killed. The Iranians made political capital of the incident, gleefully displaying on television the wrecked aircraft and captured American equipment. The stalemate continued. When the shah died in exile in Egypt in July 1980, the Iranians made no move to release the hostages.

THE ELECTION OF 1980

Despite the failure of the raid and the persistence of stagflation, Carter had more than enough delegates at the Democratic convention to win nomination on the first ballot. His Republican opponent in the campaign that followed was Ronald Reagan. At 69, Reagan was the oldest person ever nominated for president by a major party. However, his age was not a serious handicap in the campaign; he was physically trim and vigorous and seemed no older than most other prominent politicians.

Reagan had grown up a New Deal Democrat, but during and immediately after World War II he became disillusioned with liberalism. As president of the Screen Actors' Guild he attacked the influence of communists in the movie industry. After his movie career ended (he always insisted that he had not been typed as "the nice guy who didn't get the girl"), Reagan did publicity for General Electric until 1960, then worked for various conservative causes. He campaigned for Barry Goldwater during the 1964 presidential contest. Reagan won the undying loyalty of supporters of the Vietnam war, as well as the permanent enmity of the left, by proposing that the United

▲ Ronald Reagan astride a horse—a familiar photo-opportunity for presidents. (Recall the similar picture of LBJ, p. 803). But Reagan was an amiable cowboy; his smile and sense of humor were his most disarming weapons. In 1966 just after the election, when reporters asked him what sort of governor he would be, Reagan, a former actor, answered, "I don't know. I've never played a governor." Three months into his presidency, moments after he was seriously wounded in an assassination attempt, he took his wife's hand. "Honey," he said, "I forgot to duck." While being wheeled into the operating room, he quipped to the surgeons, "I hope you are all Republicans."

States "level North Vietnam, pave it, paint stripes on it, and make a parking lot out of it." In 1966 he ran for governor of California. "Hippies," he quipped, "act like Tarzan, look like Jane, and smell like Cheetah." He won the election.

Reagan was a controversial governor, in part because, despite his professed conservatism and his emphasis on economy, government spending in California increased dramatically during his term. Despite, or perhaps because of, this shift, he was easily reelected in 1970.

The 1980 presidential campaign ranks among the most curious in American history. One of Reagan's opponents at the Republican convention, Congressman John Anderson of Illinois, refused to accept defeat and ran for president as an independent because he thought both Carter and Reagan had little genuine popular support. But Anderson, too, inspired little enthusiasm.

Both Carter and Reagan spent much time explaining why the other was unsuited to be president. Carter defended his record, though without much conviction. Reagan denounced criminals, drug addicts, and all varieties of immorality and spoke in support of patriotism, religion, family life, and other "old-fashioned" virtues. This won him the enthusiastic backing of fundamentalist religious sects and other conservative groups. He also called for increased spending on defense, and he promised to transfer some functions of the federal government to the states and to cut taxes. He insisted at the same time that the budget could be balanced and inflation sharply reduced.

Reagan Presidential Campaign Ad: A Bear in the Woods

Reagan's tendency to depend on popular magazine articles, half-remembered conversations, and other informal sources for his economic "facts" reflected a mental imprecision that alarmed his critics, but his sunny disposition and his easygoing style compared favorably with Carter, who seemed tight-lipped and tense even when flashing his habitual toothy smile. A television debate between Carter and Reagan pointed up their personal differences, but Reagan's question to the audience: "Are you better off now than you were four years ago?" had more effect on the election than any policy he said he would pursue.

On election day the voting was light, but those who cast ballots gave Reagan over 43 million votes to Carter's 35 million and Anderson's 5.6 million. Dissatisfaction with the economy and the unresolved hostage crisis seem to have determined the result. The Republicans also gained control of the Senate and cut deeply into the Democratic majority in the House of Representatives.

Carter devoted his last weeks in office to the continuing hostage crisis. War had broken out between Iran and Iraq in September. The Iraqi president, Saddam Hussein, had hoped to exploit the chaos following the downfall of the shah to seize oil-rich territory in Iran. Early Iraqi victories prompted the Iranians to free the hostages in return for the release of Iranian assets that had been frozen in the United States. After 444 days in captivity, the 52 hostages were set free on January 20, the day Reagan was inaugurated.

REAGAN AS PRESIDENT

Despite his amiable, nonaggressive style, Reagan acted rapidly once in office. In August 1981 he displayed his determination in convincing fashion when the nation's air traffic controllers went on strike despite the fact that they were forbidden by law to do so. Reagan ordered them to return to work.

DOCUMENT

Reagan, Air Traffic Controllers Strike (1981)

Most refused; Reagan therefore discharged all 11,400 of them and began a hasty program to train replacements. Even after the strike collapsed, the president would not rehire the strikers. The air controllers' union was destroyed.

Reagan hoped to change the direction in which the country was moving. He demanded steep reductions in federal spending and the deficit, to be accomplished by cutting social welfare expenditures, such as welfare, food stamps and student loans, and by turning many functions of the federal government over to the states. The marketplace, not federal bureaucratic regulations, should govern most economic decisions.

He asked Congress to lower income taxes by 30 percent. When critics objected that this would increase the deficit, the president and his advisers reasoned that the tax cut would leave people with more money, which they would invest in productive ways. The new investment would generate more goods and jobs—and, ultimately, taxes for the federal government. This scheme became known as Reaganomics.

Helped by the votes of conservative Democrats, Reagan won congressional approval of the Budget Reconciliation Act, which reduced government expenditures on domestic programs by $39 billion. But Congress resisted reducing the politically popular "entitlement" programs, such as Social Security and Medicare, which accounted for about half of the budget.

Congress also enacted most of the tax cuts the president had asked for, lowering individual income taxes by 25 percent over three years. Because the percentage was the same for everyone, high-income taxpayers received a disproportionately large share of the savings. Business taxes were liberalized; capital gains, gift, and inheritance levies were reduced; and workers were given tax breaks to establish their own "individual" retirement accounts (IRAs).

Reagan also eliminated many government regulations affecting businesses. Long and complicated antitrust suits against International Business Machines and American Telephone and Telegraph, two of the largest corporations in the country, were dropped.

Many of Reagan's advisers urged him to reduce the military budget to bring the government's income more nearly in line with its outlays. Instead,

reviving the containment policy wholeheartedly, the president insisted that the military buildup was necessary because of the threat posed by the Soviet Union, which he called an "evil empire." In particular, he sought to expand and improve the nation's nuclear arsenal. He made no secret of his wish to create so formidable a nuclear force that the Soviets would have to back down in any confrontation.

In Central America he sought the overthrow of the left-wing government of Nicaragua and the defeat of communist rebels in El Salvador. He even used American troops to overthrow a Cuban-backed regime on the tiny Caribbean island of Grenada. When criticized for opposing leftist regimes while backing rightist dictators, Jeane Kirkpatrick, U.S. ambassador to the United Nations, explained "rightist authoritarian regimes can be transformed peacefully into democracies, but totalitarian Marxist ones cannot."

In 1982 the continuing turmoil in the Middle East plunged the Reagan administration into a new crisis. Israel had invaded Lebanon to destroy Palestine Liberation Organization units that were staging raids on northern Israeli settlements. Israeli troops easily overran much of the country, but in the process the Lebanese government disintegrated. Reagan agreed to commit American troops to an international peacekeeping force.

Tragedy resulted in October 1983 when a fanatical Muslim crashed a truck loaded with explosives into a building housing American marines. The building collapsed, killing 239 marines. Early the next year, Reagan removed the entire American peacekeeping force from Lebanon.

FOUR MORE YEARS

Being a sitting president with an extraordinarily high standing in public opinion polls, Reagan was nominated for a second term at the 1984 Republican convention without opposition. The Democratic nomination went to Walter Mondale of Minnesota, who had been vice president under Carter. Mondale electrified the country by choosing Representative Geraldine Ferraro of New York as his running mate. An Italian American and a Catholic, Ferraro was expected to appeal to conservative Democrats who had supported Reagan in 1980 and to win the votes of many Republican women.

Reagan began the campaign with several important advantages. He was especially popular among religious fundamentalists and other social conservatives, and these groups were increasingly vocal. President Nixon had spoken of a "silent majority." By 1980 the kind of people he was referring to were no longer

silent. Fundamentalist television preachers were almost all fervent Reaganites and the most successful of them were collecting tens of millions of dollars annually in contributions from viewers. One of these, the Reverend Jerry Falwell, founded the Moral Majority and set out to create a new political movement. "Americans are sick and tired of the way the amoral liberals are trying to corrupt our nation," Falwell announced in 1979.

During the first Reagan administration, the Moral Majority had become a powerful political force. Falwell was against drugs, the "coddling" of criminals, homosexuality, communism, and abortion, all things that Reagan also disliked. While not openly antiblack, Falwell disapproved of forced busing to integrate schools and a number of other government policies designed to help blacks and other minorities. Of course, Walter Mondale was also against many of the things that Falwell and his followers denounced, but Reagan was against them all. In addition, Reagan was in favor of government aid to private schools run by church groups, something dear to the Moral Majority despite the constitutional principle of separation of church and state.

But the Moral Majority, despite its name, was far from being an actual majority. Reagan's support was much more broadly based. Thousands of working people and an enormous percentage of white Southerners, types that had been solidly Democratic during the New Deal and beyond, now voted Republican. The president's personality was another important plus—voters continued to admire his informal yet firm style and his stress on patriotism and other "old-fashioned" virtues.

The tendency of voters to support a sitting president when the economy was on the rise was still another advantage. Unemployment fell to 7 percent, investment finally picked up, and inflation remained low. Interest rates were moving down slowly but steadily.

From the start Mondale emphasized the difficulties that he saw ahead for the nation. The president's economic policies, he said, hurt the poor, women, and minorities. Mondale also tried to focus attention on the huge increase in the federal deficit that Reagan's policies had produced. These were conventional campaign tactics. But Mondale, in a daring move, announced that he would *raise* taxes if elected. This promise, most unusual for a person running for office, was an attempt to counter his reputation for political caution.

Most polls showed Reagan far in the lead when the campaign began, and this remained true throughout the contest. Nothing Mondale or Ferraro did or said affected the president's popularity. Bad news,

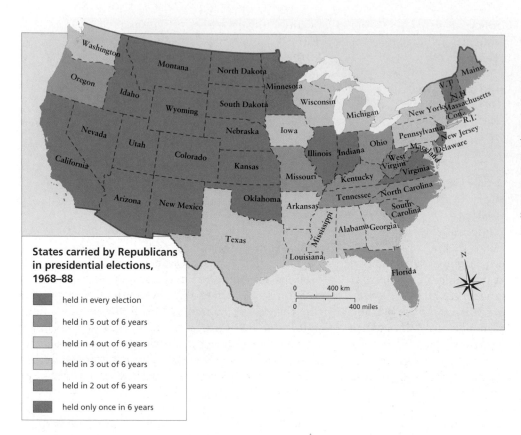

◀ **Success of the Republican "Southern Strategy"**
In 1968, Kevin M. Phillips, a key Nixon strategist, proposed a "southern strategy" to create an "emerging Republican majority." Many doubted that the South, which had long been opposed to the party of Lincoln, could be won over. But in presidential elections from 1968 to 1988, far more southern counties voted Republican than Democratic.

States carried by Republicans in presidential elections, 1968–88

- held in every election
- held in 5 out of 6 years
- held in 4 out of 6 years
- held in 3 out of 6 years
- held in 2 out of 6 years
- held only once in 6 years

even his own mistakes, had so little effect on Reagan's standing that people began to call him "the Teflon president." On election day he got nearly 60 percent of the popular vote and lost only in Minnesota, Mondale's home state, and in the District of Columbia. Reagan's Electoral College margin was overwhelming, 525 to 13.

Of all the elements in the Democratic New Deal coalition, only African Americans, who voted solidly for Mondale, remained loyal. The Democratic strategy of nominating a woman for vice president was a failure; far more women voted for Reagan than for the Mondale-Ferraro ticket.

Reagan's triumph, like the two landslide victories of Dwight Eisenhower in the 1950s, was a personal one. The Republicans made only minor gains in the House of Representatives and actually lost two seats in the Senate.

"THE REAGAN REVOLUTION"

Reagan's agenda for his second term closely resembled that of his first. In foreign affairs, he ran into continuing congressional resistance to his requests for military support for his anticommunist crusade. This was particularly true after Mikhail S. Gorbachev

became the Soviet premier in March 1985. Gorbachev seemed far more moderate and flexible than his predecessors. He began to encourage political debate and criticism in the Soviet Union—the policy known as *glasnost* (openness)—and he sought to stimulate the stagnant Soviet economy by decentralizing administration and rewarding individual enterprise *(perestroika)*.

Gorbachev also announced that he would continue to honor the unratified SALT II agreement, whereas Reagan, arguing that the Soviet Union had not respected the limits laid down in the pact, seemed bent on pushing ahead with the expansion and modernization of America's nuclear arsenal. Reagan sought funds to develop an elaborate system of missile defenses. He referred to it as the strategic defense initiative (SDI), although it was popularly known as Star Wars, a reference to the 1977 George Lucas film. SDI would consist of a network of computer-controlled space stations that would supposedly detect oncoming enemy missiles and destroy them.

When the president realized that the Soviets were eager for an agreement to limit nuclear weapons, he gradually abandoned his talk about Russia being an "evil empire." In October 1986 he met with Gorbachev in Iceland in search of an agreement

DOCUMENT

Reagan, "Evil Empire" Speech (1983)

DEBATING THE PAST

Did Reagan end the Cold War? In 1983 President Ronald Reagan denounced the Soviet Union as an "evil empire." In that same speech he made a prophecy that few took seriously at the time: The "last pages" in the history of communism "even now are being written." Six years later, when the Berlin wall came down (shown here), the Soviet empire was over. Within a few years, the Soviet Union itself had disintegrated.

Many credited Reagan with having won the Cold War. Caspar Weinberger, secretary of defense, explained that the Reagan administration had had a "secret campaign" to undermine the Soviet economy. Others credited Reagan's massive arms buildup with causing the Soviet economy to collapse from exhaustion. On the other hand, historian William Pemberton (1997) doubted whether Reagan had any coherent foreign policy at the outset; his chief contribution to winning the Cold War was resisting the advice of skeptical hardliners and accepting the conciliatory overtures of Mikhail Gorbachev, the Soviet premier.

Arthur M. Schlesinger, Jr. and John Lewis Gaddis (1992) saw the victory as a long-term and largely bipartisan team effort dating from the Truman presidency. Robert M. Gates (1996), Director of Central Intelligence under George H. W. Bush, said that Bush and his four predecessors in the presidency had ground down the Soviet opposition.

On the left, some scholars insisted that there had been no winner in a protracted dispute that had led to such chaos throughout the Third World. The United States, burdened with massive deficits, was not in much better shape. Others maintained that Reagan was fortunate to be the American president when a new generation of leaders, foremost among them Gorbachev, came to power in the Soviet Union.

For now, perhaps the last word can be that of George Smiley, the anti-Soviet spymaster created by novelist John le Carré (1991): "We won. Not that the victory matters a damn. And perhaps we didn't win anyway. Perhaps they just lost."

Peter Schweizer, *Victory* (1994), William E. Pemberton, *Exit with Honor* (1997), Robert M. Gates, *From the Shadows* (1996), Dana Allin, *Cold War Illusions* (1998); Schlesinger and Gaddis are cited in Michael J. Hogan, ed., *The End of the Cold War* (1992), and John le Carré, *The Secret Pilgrim* (1991).

on arms control. This summit went nowhere. The chief sticking point was SDI, which Gorbachev denounced as "space strike" weaponry that might be used to wipe out Soviet cities. Gorbachev proposed instead the elimination of all nuclear weapons. Reagan was determined to push Star Wars, partly because he apparently did not understand that the Europeans, fearing a conventional Soviet assault, were unsettled by the thought of *total* nuclear disarmament. The Iceland setback, however, proved to be temporary, and in 1988 at a second summit, Reagan and Gorbachev signed a treaty eliminating medium-range nuclear missiles.

Reagan nevertheless persisted in pressing for the Star Wars defense-in-space system. After NASA's spectacular Apollo program, which sent six expeditions to the moon between 1969 and 1972, the space agency's prestige was beyond measurement. The Skylab orbiting space station program (1973–1974) was equally successful. Next, shortly after the beginning of Reagan's first term, the manned space shuttle *Columbia,* launched by rocket power, was able, after orbiting for several days, to return to earth intact, gliding on its stubby, swept-back wings to an appointed landing strip. *Columbia* and other shuttles were soon transporting satellites into space for the government and private companies, and its astronauts were conducting military and scientific experiments of great importance.

Congress, however, balked at the enormous cost of Star Wars. Costs aside, the idea of relying for national defense on the complex technology involved in controlling machines in outer space suffered a further setback in 1986, when the space shuttle *Challenger* exploded shortly after takeoff, killing its seven-member crew. This disaster put a stop to the program until the cause had been discovered. In 1989 the shuttles began to fly again.

Reagan's basic domestic objectives—to reduce the scope of federal activity, particularly in the social welfare area; to lower income taxes; and to increase the strength of the armed forces—remained constant. Despite the tax cuts already made, congressional leaders of both parties agreed to the Income Tax Act of 1986, which reduced the top levy on personal incomes from 50 percent to 28 percent and the tax on corporate profits from 46 percent to 34 percent.

Liberal members of Congress, remembering how the voters had reacted to Mondale's talk about increasing taxes, found it politically difficult to oppose the measure. But the existing tax system was extremely complicated and full of loopholes benefiting particular interests. The new law did away with most of the tax shelters and special credits that corporations and well-to-do individuals had used to reduce their tax bills. The law also relieved 6 million low-income people from paying any federal income tax at all.

Reagan advanced another of his objectives more gradually. This was his appointment of conservatives to federal judgeships, including Sandra Day O'Connor, the first woman named to the Supreme Court. By 1988 Reagan had appointed three Supreme Court justices and well over half the members of the federal judiciary.

CHANGE AND UNCERTAINTY

But if the "Reagan revolution" seemed to have triumphed, powerful countering forces were at work that no individual or party could effectively control. For one thing, the makeup of the American people, always in a state of flux, was changing at a rate approaching that of the early 1900s when the "new" immigration had been at its peak. In the 1970s, after the Immigration Act of 1965 had put an end to the national-origins concept, more than 4 million immigrants entered the country, and the vast majority of these newcomers came from Asia and Latin America. This trend continued; of the 643,000 who arrived in 1988, more than 550,000 were from these two regions. More than 111,000 of the immigrants came from the Philippines, Korea, Vietnam, and other parts of the Pacific rim and East Asia. In addition, uncounted thousands entered the United States illegally, most crossing the long, sparsely settled border with Mexico. The nation's Hispanic population increased by 53 percent during the 1980s.

Some of the new immigrants were refugees from repressive regimes in Vietnam, Cuba, Haiti, and Central America, and nearly all were poor. Most tended, like their predecessors, to crowd together in ethnic neighborhoods. Spanish could be heard more often than English in large sections of Los Angeles, New York, Miami, and many other cities.

No strong demand for immigration restriction developed, perhaps because so many Americans were descendents of immigrants, and because the immigrants did work that needed to be done. However, conservatives found it appalling that so many people could enter the country illegally, and even Americans sympathetic to the so-called undocumented aliens agreed that control was desirable. Finally, in 1986, Congress passed a law offering amnesty to illegal immigrants long resident in the country and penalizing employers who hired illegal immigrants in the future. Many persons legalized their status under the new law, but the influx of illegal immigrants continued.

Problems developed because some employers refused to hire anyone with a foreign accent on the grounds that they might be "illegals" bearing false papers.

Other trends deeply disturbed thousands of Americans. The postwar population explosion and the following decline in the birthrate assured that great pressure on the Social Security system would be inevitable when the baby boomers born after World War II reached retirement age in the early twenty-first century. More immediately, the traditional family— long under stress—appeared to be weakening further. Year after year more than 1.1 million marriages ended in divorce. The tendency of couples to live together without getting married also continued, helping to explain why the number of illegitimate births rose steadily. So did the number of abortions—from 763,000 in 1974, right after abortion was legalized, to an average of 1.3 million a year in the 1980s. However, many women, married and unmarried, who had chosen careers over motherhood were having second thoughts as they approached the age when having children would no longer be possible.

In any case, more families were headed by single parents, in most cases, women. Between 1979 and 1987, the number of single-parent families living below the poverty line increased by 46 percent. A disproportionate number of these families were black, and many were poor, but the percentage of middle-class white women bearing children out of wedlock was also increasing.

AIDS

During the 1980s, the nation confronted its most serious health crisis in decades. In the late 1970s, world health officials had spotted the outbreak of yet another viral epidemic in central Africa; but no one noticed that this virus had mutated into a more lethal strain and was spreading to Europe and North America. On June 5, 1981, the Centers for Disease Control (CDC) alerted American health officials to an outbreak of a rare bacterial infection in Los Angeles. What made the outbreak distinctive was that this particular infection, usually found in infants or older people with fragile immune systems, had struck five healthy young men. All were homosexuals. Within months, all died.

By 1982 the CDC decided to call this new disease acquired immunodeficiency syndrome (AIDS). They learned that AIDS was caused by the human immunodeficiency virus (HIV), a lethal retro virus that destroys the body's defenses against infection, making victims susceptible to many diseases. HIV spreads when an infected person's body fluids come

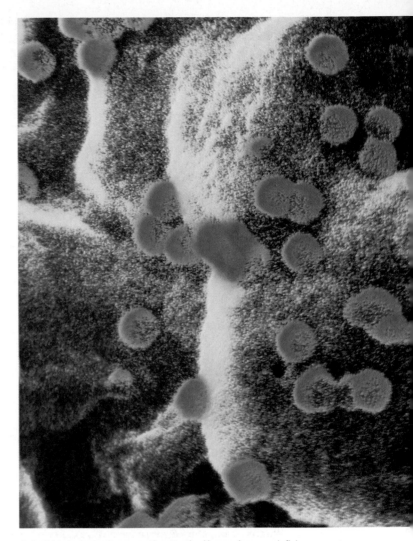

▲ In this electron microscope image, the Human Immunodeficiency Virus (HIV)—colored green—gloms onto a T-cell. The T-cell is a type of white blood cell that quarterbacks the body's defenses against infection. Many researchers looking for a cure for AIDS seek to prevent the HIV from glomming onto the T-cells.

in contact with someone else's. By the end of 1982, the CDC had documented 900 cases of AIDS; the disease was increasing exponentially. Soon HIV contaminated some of the nation's blood banks, and some recipients of transfusions came down with AIDS. In June 1983, when the federal budget approached $1 trillion, Congress finally voted $12 million for AIDS research and treatment.

Not until 1985, when the square-jawed romantic actor Rock Hudson confirmed that he was dying of AIDS, did the subject command widespread public attention. President Reagan, an old friend of Hudson's, publicly acknowledged that the disease constituted a grave health crisis. Congress approved

Reagan's call for a substantial increase in AIDS funding. But Reagan's appeal was belated and insufficient. By then, nearly 21,000 Americans had died; by 1999, the total number of AIDS-related deaths approached 400,000.

The AIDS epidemic affected public policy and private behavior. A nationwide educational campaign urged "safe" sex, especially the use of condoms, which by 1990 were distributed free in many high schools. Fear of the disease, and of those who suffered from it, exacerbated many people's homophobia. But the AIDS epidemic also forced most people to confront homosexuality directly and perhaps for the first time, and thus contributed to a deeper understanding of the complexity of human nature. After Hudson's revelation, for example, the *New York Times* commenced using "gay" and "lesbian," the terms then preferred by the people so identified, instead of "homosexual." Gay and lesbian organizations, the vanguard in the initial war against AIDS, continued to fight for social acceptance and legal rights.

THE NEW MERGER MOVEMENT

The Reagan years witnessed a mad frenzy of corporate mergers. The person most responsible was Michael Milken, a shrewd stockbroker of the firm of Drexel Burnham Lambert. Milken specialized in selling "junk bonds," the debt offerings of companies whose existing debts were already high. He persuaded hundreds of savings and loan associations, insurance companies, pension funds, and other big investors to buy these junk bonds, which, though risky, offered unusually high interest rates. The success of his initial ventures prompted Milken to approach smaller companies, invite them to issue huge numbers of junk bonds, and use the proceeds to acquire larger firms.

In 1985 Ronald Perelman, an aggressive entrepreneur, employed this strategy to perfection. He had recently obtained control of Pantry Pride, a small supermarket chain with a net worth of about $145 million, and sought to acquire Revlon, a $2 billion cosmetics and health care conglomerate. With Milken's help, he sold $1.5 billion in Pantry Pride bonds ("junk," because the debt so greatly exceeded the company's worth) and used that capital to buy Revlon. He then paid off the Pantry Pride bonds by selling huge chunks of Revlon and amalgamated the remainder of the company into Pantry Pride. The bond purchasers profited handsomely from the high return on the junk bonds, and Perelman made a fortune on the acquisition and reorganization of Revlon. That same year the R. J. Reynolds Tobacco Company purchased the food conglomerate Nabisco for $4.9

billion. Three years later this new giant, RJR Nabisco, was itself taken over by Kohlberg, Kravis, Roberts and Company for $24.9 billion.

During the frenzied decade of the 1980s, one-fifth of the Fortune 500 companies were taken over, merged, or forced to go private; in all, some 25,000 mergers and acquisitions were successfully undertaken; their total value was nearly a half-trillion dollars. To make their companies less tempting to cash-hungry raiders, many corporations took on whopping debts or acquired unprofitable companies. By the late 1980s, many American corporations were wallowing in red ink. Debt payments were gobbling up 50 percent of the nation's corporate pretax earnings.

"A JOB FOR LIFE": LAYOFFS HIT HOME

Most corporations coped with the debt in two ways: they sold assets, such as factories, offices, and warehouses; or they cut costs through layoffs. U.S. Steel, whose rusting mills desperately needed an infusion of capital, instead spent $5 billion to acquire Marathon Oil of Ohio; that decision meant that nearly 100,000 steelworkers lost their jobs. No firm was immune, nor any worker secure. "A job for life" had long been IBM's unofficial but endlessly repeated slogan. As late as 1985, it ran an advertisement to reassure employees: "Jobs may come and go—But people shouldn't." Yet during the next nine years a crippled IBM eliminated 80,000 jobs and more than a third of its workforce. During the 1980s, the total number of employees who worked for the Fortune 500 companies declined by three million; nearly one-third of all positions in middle management were eliminated. Millions of "organization men" (about one-third of whom now were women) were laid off as the organizations themselves "downsized," the corporate euphemism for wholesale firings.

Many of the jobs went abroad, where labor costs were lower and unions nonexistent. In 1980 Xerox of America, realizing that it could no longer compete with its more efficient Japanese subsidiary, transferred contracts to Japan and laid off tens of thousands of American workers. In 1984 Nike moved sewing operations to Indonesia, where it could hire female workers for a mere 14 cents an hour. In 1986 the chassis for the Mustang, the symbol of American automotive style, was built by Mazda in Hiroshima, Japan.

Towering mountains of private corporate debt nearly were overshadowed by the Everest of public

▶ *text continues on page 872*

American Lives

Bill Gates

"Project Breakthrough! World's First Minicomputer Kit to Rival Commercial Models." This headline in the January 1975 issue of *Popular Electronics* fired the neurons in Bill Gates's brain. The revolution had begun. Most earlier computers cost hundreds of thousands of dollars, filled room-sized air-conditioned vaults, and were found in university science centers, government agencies, and corporate headquarters. But this kit cost only $397. The computer (its name—*Altair*—came from a planet in the TV series *Star Trek),* could fit on a desktop. Gates believed that computers like this would soon be as much a part of life as telephones or automobiles. Armed with the slogan, "A computer on every desktop," he resolved to become the Henry Ford of the computer revolution (and to become, like Ford, immensely rich). He was twenty years old. The son of William Henry Gates, Jr., and Mary Maxwell Gates, William Henry Gates III was born in Seattle, Washington, on October 28, 1955.

Gates recognized Altair's fatal flaw: it did little more than cause a few lights to blink in complex ways. It lacked internal instructions to convert electrical signals into letters and numbers. He determined to write instructions—the software—to make the personal computer useful. Gates and Paul Allen, a school chum, telephoned Ed Roberts, the president of MITS, manufacturer of the Altair. They told him they had written operating software for the machine. Roberts was skeptical. Scores of programmers had made such claims, he said, but none had actually done it. He told them to bring their software to the company headquarters in Albuquerque, New Mexico within two months.

Allen and Gates were euphoric, but not for long: they had not even begun to write a program for the Altair. The challenge of doing so in five weeks would have been unimaginable but for one thing: the electronic core of the Altair was the Intel 8080 computer chip, and for years Allen and Gates had been devising machines and software based on the Intel 8008, whose logic was similar to the 8080.

The boys had met in 1967 at Lakeside, an elite private school, when Gates was in seventh grade, Allen in ninth. That year, the Lakeside Mothers Club had bought time on a digital

▲ Young Bill Gates

training terminal that connected by phone to a company that leased a mainframe computer. Within weeks of its installation, this computer had become Gates's life. He remained in the terminal room after school and late into the evenings, breaking only for Coke and pizza. Sometimes he conked out while staring at the screen; his clothes were perpetually wrinkled and spattered with pizza sauce. "He lived and breathed computers," a friend recalled.

Gates learned programming by writing programs and seeing what worked. His first was for playing tic-tac-toe. He also designed a program for student schedules at Lakeside. He placed "all the good girls in the school" (and very few males of any kind) in his own classes—an early manifestation of his penchant for defeating competitors by conniving to eliminate them.

Although his father was a wealthy corporate attorney and his mother a prominent socialite, Gates was preoccupied with making money. In high school he took a job tabulating automobile traffic data; this required that he count the holes in a roll of paper punched out when automobiles passed over a hose. He designed a computerized machine to count and analyze the data and he formed a company, Traf-O-Data, to build and market the device. However, Traf-O-Data failed to attract many customers—most municipalities and highway departments lost interest when they learned that the company was run by high school students.

Gates, who scored 800 on the math SATs (a perfect score), chose a complex strategy to gain admission to the most competitive colleges. In his application to Harvard, he emphasized his political involvement (he had worked one summer as a congressional page); to Yale, he cited his creativity (a starring role in a dramatic production) and character (a former Boy Scout); and to Princeton, "I positioned myself as a computer nerd." Admitted to all three, he went to Harvard. Allen went to work as a programmer for Honeywell. But when they began work on the Altair operating program, Allen moved into Gates's dormitory and Gates skipped most classes. To save time, they built a simulator based on the published specifications of the Altair and feverishly churned out the operating software.

They completed the program just hours before Allen boarded the plane to Albuquerque. (Allen went because he was older and presumably a more credible "corporate" spokesman.) The next morning, Allen fed long rolls of punched yellow paper tape—the software—into an Altair while company executives looked on skeptically. For fifteen minutes the machine clattered away. Misgivings mounted. Then the teletype printed the word, "READY." Allen typed: "PRINT 2 + 2." The teletype spat out: "4." The program worked. Gates and Allen had a deal.

Gates dropped out of Harvard and formed a partnership with Allen. They called their company Microsoft and moved to Albuquerque. They wrote operating programs for personal computers introduced by Apple, Commodore, and Radio Shack. Soon money was pouring into Microsoft. In 1979 they moved Microsoft to Bellevue, Washington, near Seattle. Then came the blockbuster.

In 1980 IBM, the nation's foremost manufacturer of mainframe computers, belatedly entered the burgeoning home computer market. IBM approached Gates to write the operating software for its new, state-of-the-art personal computer. IBM intended to keep the computer's specifications secret so that other manufacturers could not copy its design, but Gates shrewdly proposed that IBM make its specifications public. Doing so would allow the IBM personal computer to become the industry standard, giving IBM the edge in developing peripherals—printers, monitors, keyboards, and various applications. IBM agreed. Now Gates's software, called Microsoft-Disk Operating System (MS-DOS), would run every IBM personal computer as well as every IBM clone. In a single stroke, Gates had virtually monopolized the market for PC operating software.

After Allen was diagnosed with Hodgkin's disease in 1983, he briefly retired and purchased the Portland Trail Blazers basketball team; he became a billionaire. Microsoft's sales jumped from $7.5 million in 1980 to $140 million in 1985. Then Microsoft moved into software applications: word processing, accounting, and games. By 1991, Gates was the wealthiest man in the world.

debt held by the federal government itself. Reagan's insistence on a sharp cut in personal taxes and a substantial increase in military expenditures produced huge—and growing—annual federal deficits. When Reagan took office, the total federal debt was $900 million; eight years later, it exceeded $2.5 *trillion*. "No one imagined how bad the outcome would be," explained David Stockman, Reagan's budget director. "It got away from us."

A "BIPOLAR" ECONOMY, A FRACTURED SOCIETY

Although weighed down by debt, the economy did not crash through the floor, as many expected. In 1982 it began to gain strength and by the late 1980s it was growing at a rate unparalleled since the halcyon days of the 1960s. Despite the ominous, persistent increase in corporate layoffs, the stock market soared. Prices were coming down—traditionally evidence of slackening demand—yet the volume of business was growing!

Many economists and pundits warned that the run-up in stock prices was excessive; the bubble would surely burst. These misgivings were seemingly confirmed in 1987, when on a single day, the Dow-Jones industrial average fell 508 points to 1738. But stock prices quickly recovered and embarked on yet another long period of growth.

Although few perceived it at the time, the economy was undergoing a transformation of historic dimensions. Much as the depression after 1893 had strengthened the nation's economy by wiping out thousands of inefficient steel and machinery firms in New England and the Northeast, the seismic economic upheavals of the 20 years after 1973 toppled many of those same industries but thrust up new ones. As weeds grew in the parking lots of the factories of the "Rust Belt" of the Midwest, new companies and new technology industries sprouted in the "Silicon Valley" of California, along Route 128 outside of Boston, and in booming cities such as Seattle, Washington, and Austin, Texas.

By the end of the Reagan era, the economy consisted of two separate and increasingly unequal components: a battered sector of traditional heavy industry, characterized by declining wages and diminishing job opportunities; and an advancing high-tech and service sector dominated by aggressive, innovative, and individualistic entrepreneurs. The older corporations that survived the shakeout of the 1980s were leaner and better equipped to compete in expanding global markets.

Yet American society was becoming as fractured as the "bipolar" economy from which it drew sustenance. The Reagan tax cuts had disproportionately benefited the wealthy, as had the extraordinary rise of the stock market. Conversely, the economic transformation struck low- or semiskilled wage earners hardest; at the same time, the Reagan administration's shifting of much of the burden of social welfare onto state and local governments reduced benefits to those who lost jobs or could not find work in the strange new economy dominated by information services and bewildering new technologies. At the end of Reagan's second term the standard of living of the poorest fifth of the population (40 million people) was 9 percent lower than it had been in 1979, while that of the wealthiest fifth had risen about 20 percent

THE IRAN-CONTRA ARMS DEAL

The Reagan administration was generally credited with the nation's successes, and absolved of its failures. The effectiveness of the administration was finally compromised by two self-inflicted wounds involving American policy in Central America and the Middle East.

The Central American problem resulted from a revolution in Nicaragua, where in 1979 leftist rebels had overthrown the dictatorial regime of Anastasio Somoza. Because the victorious Sandinista government was supported by both Cuba and the Soviet Union, President Reagan was determined to force it from power. He backed anti-Sandinista elements in Nicaragua known as the Contras and in 1981 persuaded Congress to provide these "freedom fighters" with arms.

DOCUMENT

Reagan, Support for the Contras (1984)

But the Contras made little progress, and many Americans feared that aiding them would lead, as it had in Vietnam, to the use of American troops in the fighting. In October 1984 Congress banned further military aid to the rebels. The President then sought to persuade other countries and private American groups to help the Contras (as he put it) keep "body and soul together."

In the Middle East, the war between Iran and Iraq continued to rage. If either won decisively, it could control the flow of Middle Eastern oil. The United States therefore preferred a stalemate. Thus when Iran gained the advantage, Reagan provided $500 million a year in credits to Iraq. In early 1986, however, Reagan authorized the secret sale of American weapons directly to the Iranians in return for their help in releasing Americans held hostage to Islamic fundamentalists elsewhere in the Middle East.

The arms sale was arranged by Marine Colonel Oliver North, an aide of Reagan's national security adviser. North, who was already in charge of the administration's effort to supply the Nicaraguan Contras indirectly, used $12 million of the profit from the Iranian sales to provide weapons for the Contras, in plain violation of the Congressional ban on such aid.

News of the sales to Iran and of the use of the profits to supply the Contras came to light in November 1986 and of course caused a sensation. Colonel North was fired from his job with the security council, a special prosecutor was appointed to investigate the affair, and both a presidential committee and a joint congressional committee also began investigations. Reagan insisted that he knew nothing about the aid to the Contras. Critics pointed out that if he was telling the truth it was almost as bad since that meant that he had not been able to control his own administration.

Although he remained personally popular, President Reagan's influence with Congress and his reputation as a political leader plummeted. Comments by reporters ranged from "disengaged" and "gravely uninformed" to "out to lunch." Even earlier Martin Anderson, Reagan's chief economic adviser, had admitted that the president "made decisions like an ancient king or a Turkish pasha, passively letting his subjects serve him."

Reagan was not an able administrator; the Iran-Contra and financial scandals of his administration did not stick to him because he was seldom close enough to the action to get splattered by it. Reagan articulated, simply and persuasively, a handful of concepts—the "evil" character of Soviet communism, the need to get government off people's backs—and in so doing created a political climate conducive to change. Reagan was directly responsible for neither of the great transformations of the late twentieth century—the collapse of the Soviet Union and the restructuring of American corporations. Yet his actions and, indeed, his failures to act indisputably influenced them. His decision to increase military spending and undertake the fantastically expensive SDI ("Star Wars") forced Gorbachev to seek an accommodation with the United States. Reagan's tax cuts precipitated unimaginably large federal deficits, and deregulation unloosed a sordid pack of predators who preyed on the economy. Yet the ensuing Darwinian chaos strengthened those corporations that survived and gave them the muscle to prevail in emerging global markets. "We are the change," Reagan declared in his farewell address. What he had done, exactly, he did not say. Yet the statement, however roseate, vague, and self-congratulatory, was not untrue.

▲ "Mistakes were made," a cartoon in the *Washington Post*, 1986, which pointedly contrasts President Reagan with Teddy Roosevelt, Franklin D. Roosevelt, and Harry S Truman.

During the preceding 15 years, the American nation, like the automobiles that stretched for blocks in line to buy gasoline during the oil embargo, had been running on empty. The federal government was deeply in debt. Corporations had exhausted their cash reserves. Workers lived in fear of the layoff or bank foreclosure notice. Gone were the fanciful expressions of an earlier era—long and wide-bodied chassis, roaring V–8 engines, sweeping tail fins, chromium grills like the jaws of a barracuda. Most cars had become simple boxes, trimmed with plastic, whose efficient four-cylinder engines thrummed steadily.

The nation's aspirations, like its cars, had become smaller, more sensible. Politicians muted their rhetoric, rarely issuing grandiose declarations of war against some intractable foe of humanity. Corporate executives spoke of "downsizing" firms rather than building them into empires. And the American people increasingly hunkered down in their own private spaces, which they locked up and wired with alarms.

MILESTONES

1973	Israel, aided by United States, defeats Egypt and Syria	**1980s**	Enterpreneurs' merger movement leads to huge corporate debt
1973–1974	Arabs impose oil embagro	**1981**	Iran releases U.S. hostages
1974–1976	Gerald Ford serves as president after Nixon's resignation		Reagan appoints Sandra Day O'Connor to Supreme Court
1975	Vietnam War ends when South Vietnam falls		Reagan discharges striking air traffic controllers
1976	Jimmy Carter is elected president	**1981–1988**	War persists between Iran and Iraq
1978	Egypt and Israel sign Camp David Accords	**1982**	Centers for Disease Control identifies new disease, AIDS
1979	Jerry Falwell founds the Moral Majority	**1984**	Reagan is reelected president
	Muslim militants seize U.S. Embassy in Tehran, Iran	**1985**	Mikhail Gorbachev becomes premier of the Soviet Union
	United States recognizes People's Republic of China		Reagan secretly sells arms to Iran to finance Nicaraguan Contras
1980	Soviet troops invade Afghanistan	**1986**	Space shuttle *Challenger* explosion kills crew of seven
	U.S. rescue mission in Iran fails		
	Ronald Reagan is elected president		

SUPPLEMENTARY READING

Bruce J. Schulman, *The Seventies* (2001), surveys that decade, as Haynes Johnson, *Sleepwalking through History* (1992) does for the 1980s. On Gerald Ford, see James M. Cannon, *Time and Chance: Gerald Ford's Appointment with History* (1994), and John R. Greene, *The Presidency of Gerald R. Ford* (1995).

Peter G. Bourne, *Jimmy Carter* (1997), relates his subject's life and policies. Donald Spencer, *The Carter Implosion: Jimmy Carter and the Amateur Style of Diplomacy* (1988) contains its thesis in the title; Robert A. Strong, *Working the World: Jimmy Carter and the Making of American Foreign Policy* (2000), defends Carter's record.

On Reagan, in addition to the works cited in Debating the Past (p. 866), see Lou Cannon, *President Reagan* (1991) and *Governor Reagan* (2003), and Michael Schaller, *Reckoning with Reagan* (1992). Although Edmund Morris's *Dutch: A Memoir* (1999), which includes fictional characters and footnotes, is not what it purports to be, it nevertheless offers interesting observations. David A. Stockman, *The Triumph of Politics* (1986), contains a frank discussion of administration fiscal policies. Reagan's foreign policy remains controversial. Especially useful is Jack F. Matlock, *Reagan and Gorbachev* (2004). Peter Schweizer, *Victory: The Reagan Administration's Secret Strategy That Hastened the Collapse of the Soviet Union* (1994) summarizes its achievements; Frances FitzGerald, *Way Out There in the Blue: Reagan, Star Wars and the End of the Cold War* (2000), is sharply critical. See also Jay Winik, *On the Brink* (1996).

The early history of the AIDS crisis is movingly told in Randy Shilts, *And the Band Played On* (1987); see also Elizabeth Fee and Daniel M. Fox, eds., *AIDS: The Making of a Chronic Disease* (1992). John-Manual Andriote examines its impact on gays themselves in *Victory Deferred: How AIDS Changed Gay Life in America* (1999).

On the transformation of the economy, see Robert M. Collins, *More: The Politics of Economic Growth in Postwar America* (2000), Daniel Yergin, *The Prize: The Epic Quest for Oil, Money and Power* (1991), and Barry Bluestone and Bennett Harrison, *The Deindustrializing of America* (1982). On Michael Milken and junk bonds, see Harlan Platt, *The Predators Ball* (1988); also James B. Stewart, *Den of Thieves* (1991). On the United States and the global economy, see Robert Kuttner, *The End of Laissez Faire: National Purpose and the Global Economy After the Cold War* (1991), and Henry R. Nau, *The Myth of America's Decline: Leading the World Economy in the 1990s* (1990). On young Bill Gates, see James Wallace, *Hard Drive* (1992). David Bank offers a critical assessment of Gates's later period in *Breaking Windows* (2002).

SUGGESTED WEBSITES

Gerald Rudolph Ford
http://www.ipl.org/div/POTUS/grford.html

This site contains basic factual data about Ford's elections and presidency, speeches, and online bibliography.

James Earl Carter, Jr.
http://www.ipl.org/div/POTUS/jecarter.html

This site contains basic factual data about Carter's elections and presidency, speeches, and online bibliography.

The 80s Server
http://www.80s.com

Although the best parts of this site are restricted to members, it nonetheless has some great information about the 1980s.

Ronald Wilson Reagan
http://www.ipl.org/div/POTUS/rwreagan.html

This site contains basic factual data about Reagan's elections and presidency, speeches, and online biography.

Virtual Museum of Computing
http://vmoc.museophile.sbu.ac.uk

This site relates history of computing through a series of online exhibits.

The Computer Museum History Center
http://www.computerhistory.org

This site for the Computer Museum History Center features online archives and exhibits tracing decades of computer history.

Misdemeanors and High Crimes

▼ A solitary worker with a fire extinguisher approaches a six-story steel fragment of the World Trade Center, illuminated by a shaft of light. The morning sun imparts a soft blue tint to the smoke and dust. Americans searched, almost desperately, to find some redeeming purpose in the tragedy of September 11, 2001.

CHAPTER CONTENTS

During the final decade of the twentieth century and the opening years of the twenty-first, America was not so much stained by crime as saturated in it. Violent criminals and lesser miscreants held the spotlight partly because the dominant issues of the past were slipping from view. The Soviet Union was collapsing, burying communism in the rubble; and the American economy, after initial hesitation, was gaining momentum and surging forward at breakneck pace. Yet by the early years of the twenty-first century, victory on both fronts seemed hollow. The lifting of the iron curtain of Soviet domination allowed smoldering ethnic and religious tensions to flare up in former satellite states. And the superheated "new economy" of the 1990s bubbled with an insubstantial frothiness, as if its gains might evaporate at any moment. Through it all, the American people were so absorbed in

their own affairs—gruesome crimes and lurid scandals amid an exuberant and gaudy materialism—that they failed to perceive the new threat, from abroad and above, that was about to crash into their lives.

THE ELECTION OF 1988

In the absence of the issues of recent decades—the Soviet threat, the energy crisis, stagflation—the presidential election of 1988 might have easily been dominated by a compelling personality. But the candidates were anything but compelling. The selection of Vice President George H. W. Bush for the Republican nomination was a foregone conclusion. Bush, the son of a Connecticut senator, had attended an elite private school and Yale. He served as a pilot during World War II and then settled in Texas, where he worked in the family's oil business and became active in Republican politics. From 1971 to 1973 he served as ambassador to the UN and from 1976 to 1977 as director of the CIA. As Republican presidential hopeful, he trumpeted his experience as vice president; but when the Reagan administration was tarnished by the Iran-Contra scandal, Bush claimed that he had been "out of the loop" and thus free of the scandal. When testimony proved otherwise, he dithered.

The Democratic race was far more complicated but scarcely more inspiring. So many lackluster candidates entered the field that wits called them "the seven dwarfs." Governor Michael Dukakis of Massachusetts, stressing his record as an efficient manager, accumulated delegates steadily. During one debate, however, another Democratic hopeful, Senator Albert Gore of Tennessee, accused Dukakis of handing out "weekend passes for convicted criminals." This referred to a policy, adopted by Massachusetts and many other states, of granting brief furloughs to convicts with satisfactory prison records. Dukakis brushed aside the accusation and went on to win the nomination.

But Lee Atwater, campaign manager for Bush, discovered that during one such furlough Willie Horton, an African American who was serving time in a Massachusetts prison for rape and assault, had stabbed and raped a Maryland woman. "If I can make Willie Horton a household name," Atwater predicted, "we'll win the election." Atwater produced and aired a television advertisement showing prisoners, many of them black, streaming through a revolving door. After describing Horton's record, a voice intoned: "Dukakis wants to do for America what he's done for Massachusetts." The ad struck a responsive chord among white voters. Dukakis's attempts to shift the focus away from race and crime failed.

The presidential campaign became, in effect, a referendum on violent crime in which Dukakis failed the toughness test. Bush won 54 percent of the vote and carried the Electoral College, 426 to 112.

CRIME AND PUNISHMENT

The "law and order" movement had been initiated by Nixon in the late 1960s, but many of its goals were achieved during the next two decades. Responding to widespread calls for a crackdown on crime, elected officials hired more police, passed tougher laws, and built additional prisons.

The shift toward capital punishment was symptomatic. During the 1960s only a handful of criminals were executed. When the Supreme Court ruled in 1972 in the *Furman* decision that jury-imposed capital punishment was racially biased and thus unconstitutional, the matter seemed moot: no criminal had been executed since 1967. But many states, responding to a public demand for a crackdown on crime, rewrote capital punishment statutes in light of the *Furman* decision, depriving juries of discretion in sentencing. The Supreme Court upheld these laws and capital punishment resumed in 1976. Since then, nearly a thousand convicts have been executed.

State legislatures also imposed tougher sentences and made it more difficult for prisoners to obtain parole. In 1973 New York State passed laws that mandated harsh sentences for repeat drug offenders. In 1977 California replaced its parole system with mandatory sentencing, which denied convicts the prospect of early release. Ten other states adopted similar parole restrictions. Nationwide, the proportion of convicts serving long, mandatory sentences increased sharply. In 1993 Hayes Williams, a prisoner at the Louisiana State Penitentiary, commented on the effect of long, fixed sentences on young felons. "When this hits these little crackheads, these little rap-boogity youngsters, that their life been completely taken away from them and they're not going nowhere no more, they gonna go to killing themselves." From 1984 to 1995, more inmates died of suicide than in fights with other prisoners.

Another manifestation of the crackdown on crime was the increase in the nation's prison population. In 1973 the nation's prisons—state and federal—held about 10,000 convicts. By 1990 the number of prisoners exceeded 750,000, and by 2004, 2 million. This required the construction of a 1000-bed prison every week. In 1995, for the first time, states spent more on prisons than on higher education. Human Rights Watch reported that the United

▲ A teenage boy in a Texas jail; most prisons did not allow shoes or belts, which might be fashioned into weapons. During the 1990s, about 19 of 20 prison inmates were male. The great majority had been first arrested during their late teens and early twenties. In 1990 six in ten federal inmates had been convicted of drug charges.

States incarcerated more people than any country in the world, except perhaps Communist China, which did not disclose such information.

"CRACK" AND URBAN GANGS

Several factors intensified the problem of violent crime, especially in the inner cities. One was a shift in drug use. During the 1960s marijuana had become commonly available, especially on college campuses; this was followed by cocaine, which was far more powerful and addictive but so expensive that few could afford it.

During the 1980s growers of coca leaves in Peru and Bolivia greatly expanded production. Drug traffickers in Colombia devised sophisticated systems to transport cocaine to the United States. The price of cocaine dropped from $120 an ounce in 1981 to $50 in 1988.

Still more important was the proliferation of a cocaine-based compound called "crack" because it crackled when smoked. Crack was sold in $10 vials. Many users found that it gave an intense spasm of pleasure that overrode all other desires.

The lucrative crack trade led to bitter turf wars in the inner cities; dealers hired neighborhood youths, organized them into gangs, armed them with automatic weapons, and told them to drive competitors away. The term "drive-by shooting" entered the vocabulary. A survey of Los Angeles County in the early 1990s found that more than 150,000 young people belonged to 1000 gangs. Violence had become a fact of life. In 1985, before crack had seized hold of the inner city, there were 147 murders in Washington, D.C.; in 1991, the figure skyrocketed to 482.

Black on black murder had become an important cause of death for African Americans in their twenties. In 1988 Monsta' Kody Scott, who at age 11 pumped shotgun blasts into rival gang members, returned after prison to his Los Angeles neighborhood. He was horrified: gangs no longer merely shot their rivals but "sprayed" them with automatic weapons, 75 rounds to a clip, or blew them away with small rockets. By 2005, 30 percent of African American men in their twenties were in prison, or on probation or parole. The recurrent refrain of rap performers—that America was a prison—had become, for many, an everyday reality.

GEORGE H. W. BUSH AS PRESIDENT

In 1989 President Bush, having attacked Dukakis for being soft on crime, named a "drug czar" to coordinate various bureaucracies, increased federal funding of local police, and spent $2.5 billion to stop the flow of illegal drugs into the nation. Although the campaign generated plenty of arrests, drugs continued to pour in: as one dealer or trafficker was arrested, another took his place.

Bush also worked to shed the tough image he had cultivated during the campaign. In his inaugural address he said that he hoped to "make kinder the face of the nation and gentler the face of the world." He also displayed a more traditional command of the workings of government and the details of current events than his predecessor. At the same time he pleased right-wing Reagan loyalists by his opposition to abortion and gun control, and by calling for a constitutional amendment prohibiting the burning of the American flag. His standing in the polls soared.

THE COLLAPSE OF COMMUNISM IN EASTERN EUROPE

One important reason for this was the flood of good news from abroad. The reforms instituted in the Soviet Union by Gorbachev led to demands from its Eastern European satellites for similar liberalization. Gorbachev responded by announcing that the Soviet Union would not use force to keep communist governments in power in these nations. Swiftly the people of Poland, Hungary, Czechoslovakia, Bulgaria, Romania, East Germany, and the Baltics did away with the repressive regimes that had ruled them throughout the postwar era. Except in Romania, where the dictator Nicolae Ceausescu was executed, all these fundamental changes were carried out peacefully.

Almost overnight the international political climate changed. Soviet-style communism had been discredited. The Warsaw Pact was no longer a significant force. A Soviet attack anywhere was almost unthinkable. The Cold War was over at last.

President Bush profited from these developments immensely. He expressed moral support for the new governments (and in some cases provided modest financial assistance) but he refrained from embarrassing the Soviets. At a summit meeting in Washington in June 1990 Bush and Gorbachev signed agreements reducing American and Russian stockpiles of long-range nuclear missiles by 30 percent and eliminating chemical weapons.

In 1989 President Bush sent troops to Panama to overthrow General Manuel Noriega, who had refused to yield power when his figurehead presidential candidate lost a national election. Noriega was under indictment in the United States for drug trafficking. After temporarily seeking refuge in the Vatican embassy in Panama, he surrendered to the American forces and was taken to the United States, where he was tried, convicted, and imprisoned.

Bush thus accomplished the objective of the invasion. Latin Americans, however, were alarmed by the way the United States had used force in the region, and the fact that far more Panamanian civilians were killed and wounded in the affair than armed supporters of Noriega.

Meanwhile, in the summer of 1991, civil war broke out in Yugoslavia as Croatia and Slovenia sought independence from the Serbian-dominated central government. This conflict soon became a religious war, pitting Serb and Croatian Christians

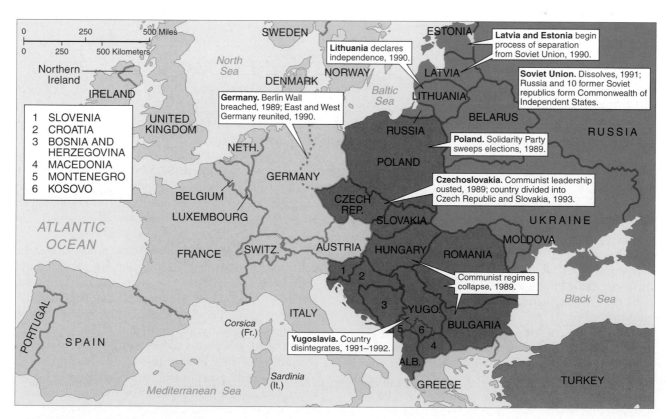

▲ **The Collapse of Communism in Eastern Europe**

against Bosnian Muslims. In the Soviet Union, nationalist and anticommunist groups demanded more local control of their affairs. President Gorbachev, who opposed this breakup, sought compromise, backing a draft treaty that would increase local autonomy and further privatize the Soviet economy.

In August, however, before this treaty could be ratified, hard-line communists attempted a coup. They arrested Gorbachev, who was vacationing in the Crimea, and ordered tanks into Moscow. But Boris Yeltsin, the anticommunist president of the Russian Republic, defied the rebels and roused the people of Moscow. The coup swiftly collapsed. Its leaders were arrested, the Communist party was officially disbanded, and the Soviet Union itself was replaced by a federation of states, of which Russia, led by Yeltsin, was the most important. Gorbachev, who had begun the process of liberation, found himself without a job.

THE WAR IN THE PERSIAN GULF

Although Reagan had provided economic assistance to Saddam Hussein of Iraq to prevent Iran from winning the Iran-Iraq war, few in the administration were enthusiastic about the Iraqi dictator. For years Saddam had been crushing the Kurds, an ethnic minority in northern Iraq that sought independence. In 1987 the U.S. State Department reported on his "widespread destruction and bulldozing of Kurdish villages." In March 1988, after Kurdish rebels had supported an Iranian advance into Iraq near Halabja, a mostly Kurdish city, Saddam's troops dropped mustard gas, sarin, and other chemical weapons on the city. Some 5000 civilians died. More chemical attacks followed. The United States protested the use of chemical weapons but said little about Saddam's relentless assault on the Kurds.

Worse was to come. In 1988, after the Iran-Iraq war had ended in a stalemate, Saddam intensified his war on the Kurds. Then, in August 1990, he launched an all-out attack on Iraq's tiny neighbor to the south, the oil-rich sheikdom of Kuwait. Saddam hoped to swallow up Kuwait, thus increasing Iraq's already large oil reserves to about 25 percent of the world's total. His soldiers overran Kuwait swiftly, then systematically carried off everything of value they could bring back to Iraq. Within a week Saddam annexed Kuwait and massed troops along the border of neighboring Saudi Arabia.

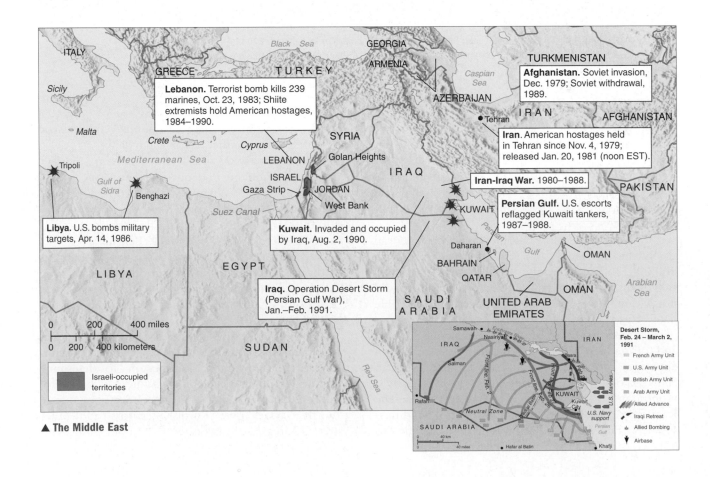

▲ **The Middle East**

▲ As the routed Iraqi army fled Kuwait, it ignited (literally) an ecological disaster by setting fire to the Kuwaiti oil fields. Here American soldiers advance past a burning oil well; it took many months before all the wells could be extinguished.

The Saudis and the Kuwaitis turned to the United States and other nations for help, and it was quickly given. In a matter of days the UN applied trade sanctions against Iraq, and at the invitation of Saudi Arabia, the United States (along with Great Britain, France, Italy, Egypt, and Syria) moved troops to Saudi bases.

By November, Bush had increased the American troops in the area from 180,000 to more than 500,000. In late November the UN took the fateful step of authorizing the use of this force if Saddam did not withdraw from Kuwait by January 15, 1991. He flatly refused to do so.

Congress voted to use force to dislodge Saddam and on January 17, the Americans unleashed an enormous air attack, directed by General Norman Schwarzkopf. This air assault went on for nearly a month, and it reduced much of Iraq to rubble. The Iraqi forces, aside from firing a number of Scud missiles at Israel and Saudi Arabia and setting fire to

hundreds of Kuwaiti oil wells, simply endured the rain of destruction that fell on them daily.

On February 23 Bush issued an ultimatum to Saddam: Pull out of Kuwait or face an invasion. When Saddam ignored the deadline, UN troops, more than 200,000 strong, struck. Bush called the assault "Desert Storm." Between February 24 and February 27 they retook Kuwait, killing tens of thousands of Iraqis in the process and capturing still larger numbers. Some 4000 Iraqi tanks and enormous quantities of other military equipment were destroyed.

President Bush on the Gulf War

Bush then stopped the attack, and Saddam agreed to UN terms that included paying reparations to Kuwait, allowing UN inspectors to determine whether Iraq was developing atomic and biological weapons, and agreeing to keep its airplanes out of "no-fly" zones over Kurdish territory and other strategic areas. Polls indicated that about 90 percent

of the American people approved both the president's management of the war and his overall performance as chief executive. These were the highest presidential approval ratings ever recorded.

President Bush and indeed most observers expected Saddam to be driven from power in disgrace by his own people. Indeed, Bush publicly urged the Iraqis to do so. The Kurds in northern Iraq and pro-Iranian Muslims in the south then took up arms, but Saddam used the remnants of his army to crush them. He also refused repeatedly to carry out the terms of the peace agreement, chiefly by hindering the UN inspections for weapons of mass destruction. This led critics to argue that Bush should not have stopped the fighting until Baghdad, the Iraqi capital, had been captured and Saddam's army destroyed.

THE DEFICIT WORSENS

The huge cost of the Persian Gulf War exacerbated the federal deficit. Candidate Bush had promised not to raise taxes, saying in a phrase he would later regret: "Read my lips: No new taxes." As President he recommitted himself to that objective; in fact he even proposed reducing the tax on capital gains. But like his conservative predecessor, Bush could not control the deficit. Congress obstinately resisted closing local military bases or cutting funding for favored defense contractors. Reducing nonmilitary expenditures, especially popular entitlement programs such as Medicare and Social Security, also proved nearly impossible.

The deficit for 1992 hit $290 billion. Bush had no choice but to join with Congress in raising the top income tax rate from 28 percent to 31 percent and levying higher taxes on gasoline, liquor, expensive automobiles, and certain other luxuries. This damaged his credibility and angered conservative Republicans. "Read my lips," critics muttered: "No more Bush."

LOOTING THE SAVINGS AND LOANS

Another drain on the federal treasury resulted from the demise of hundreds of federally insured savings and loan institutions (S&Ls). S&Ls had traditionally played an important role in nearly every community, and a secure if sleepy niche in the economy: home mortgages. In the 1980s Congress permitted S&Ls to enter the more lucrative but riskier business of commercial loans and stock investments. This attracted a swarm of aggressive investors who acquired

S&Ls and invested company assets in high-yield but risky junk bonds and real estate deals.

These speculations often failed to generate steady income. Worse, investments in junk bonds, untenanted office buildings and uninhabited planned communities were often worthless. In October 1987 the stock market crashed and hundreds of S&Ls were plunged into bankruptcy. In 1988 Michael Milken, the junk bond "guru," was indicted on 98 charges of fraud, stock manipulation, and insider trading. He pleaded guilty, agreed to pay $1.3 billion in compensation, and was sent to jail. Drexel Burnham Lambert, his investment firm, filed for bankruptcy. The junk bond market collapsed.

Still more S&Ls went under. Because their deposits were insured by the federal government, taxpayers were forced to cover the losses. The reserve fund for such purposes—$5 billion—was quickly exhausted. In 1991 Congress allocated $70 billion to close the failing S&Ls, liquidate their assets, and pay off depositors. The Justice Department charged nearly a thousand people for criminal involvement in a mess that, according to most estimates, would eventually cost taxpayers $500 billion. The destruction of the S&Ls was, arguably, the financial crime of the century. That it would spill into the political arena was inevitable.

WHITEWATER AND THE CLINTONS

William (Bill) Clinton was one of those who got caught up in the maelstrom. He was born William Jefferson Blythe IV, but his father died in a car accident before he was born. Though his stepfather was abusive and an alcoholic, at age 15 Bill legally took his stepfather's name. He graduated from Georgetown, won a Rhodes scholarship to study at Oxford University, and graduated from Yale Law school. He returned to Arkansas and was soon elected state attorney general.

In 1977 Clinton and his wife, Hillary Rodham, joined with James McDougal, a banker, to secure a loan to build vacation homes in the Ozarks. But the development, which they named Whitewater, eventually became insolvent. McDougal covered the debts with a loan from a savings and loan company he had acquired. In 1989 the savings and loan failed, costing the federal government $60 million to reimburse depositors. In 1992 federal investigators claimed that the Clintons had been "potential beneficiaries" of McDougal's illegal activities.

By this time Clinton, now governor of Arkansas, was campaigning in the New Hampshire primary for

the Democratic nomination for president. Few voters could make much sense of this tangled web of fiduciary finagling, nor did they have much opportunity to do so: another, far more explosive story threatened to sink the Clinton campaign. It came out that Clinton had for many years engaged in an extramarital affair with one Gennifer Flowers; Clinton's standing in the polls tumbled.

Hillary Rodham Clinton appeared with her husband on CBS's *60 Minutes* to address the allegations. Bill Clinton indignantly denied Flowers's statements but then issued an earnest if ambiguous appeal for forgiveness. "I have acknowledged causing pain in my marriage," he said. "I think most Americans will know what we're saying; they'll get it." Clinton was right, early evidence of his ability to address the American people directly, but on his own—carefully worded—terms. He finished second in New Hampshire, captured most of the remaining primaries, and won the Democratic nomination with ease. His choice of running mate—Senator Al Gore of Tennessee, a Vietnam veteran, family man, and environmentalist—helped the ticket considerably.

▲ Young Bill Clinton *(left)* shakes hands with President John F. Kennedy. "The torch has been passed to a new generation of Americans," Kennedy had declared in his inaugural. "Ask not what your country can do for you—ask what you can do for your country," JFK added. Thirty years later, Clinton's inaugural echoed Kennedy's: "Today, a generation raised in the shadows of the Cold War assumes new responsibilities," Clinton declared. "I challenge a new generation of young Americans to a season of service."

THE ELECTION OF 1992

While Clinton tiptoed through a minefield of personal scandal, President Bush rested secure in the belief that, after crushing Saddam's forces in the Gulf War, the 1992 election campaign would be little more than a victory lap. But he encountered unexpectedly stiff opposition within the Republican party. Patrick Buchanan, an outspoken conservative, did well enough to alarm White House strategists. Then Ross Perot, a billionaire Texan, announced his independent candidacy. Perot charged that both major parties were out of touch with "the people." He promised to spend $100 million of his own money on his campaign. Perot's platform had both conservative and liberal planks. He would "take the shackles

off of American business," avoid raising taxes, and cut government spending by "getting rid of waste." He also supported gun control, backed a woman's right to have an abortion, promised to get rid of political action committees, and called for an all-out effort to "restructure" the health care system.

Polls quickly revealed that Perot was popular in California, Texas, and other key states that Bush was counting on winning easily. For a time it seemed possible that in a three-way race no one would win a majority of the Electoral College and the election would be thrown into the House of Representatives for the first time since 1824. At the Republican convention in August, Bush was nominated without opposition.

Clinton accused Bush of failing to deal effectively with the lingering economic recession, which had worsened during the summer. He promised to undertake public works projects, to encourage private

investment, and to improve the nation's education and health insurance systems. Bush played down the seriousness of the recession, but his jaunty comments offended those who had lost their jobs.

On election day, more than 100 million citizens voted, a record. About 44 million voted for Clinton, 38 million for Bush, and 20 million for Perot. Clinton was elected with 370 electoral votes to Bush's 168. Perot did not win any electoral votes.

A New Start: Clinton

Clinton,
First Inaugural
Address

One reason for Clinton's success was his expressed intention to change health insurance and the welfare system, and to bring the budget deficit under control. His solid knowledge of public issues was impressive, and he created a general impression of mastery and self-confidence.

Another reason for Clinton's success was his willingness to reconcile differences. "Cooperation is better than conflict," he said on more than one occasion. But however valuable during a campaign, this reasonableness was sometimes a disadvantage once the power of the presidency was at Clinton's command. He set out to reverse many of the policies of the Reagan-Bush era, but when opposition developed, circumstances often persuaded him to retreat.

This led some critics to argue that Clinton was a poor leader. He had promised to end the ban on gays and lesbians in the armed services, but when the Joint Chiefs of the armed forces and a number of important members of Congress objected, he settled for a policy known as "don't ask, don't tell," meaning that such persons would be allowed to enlist only if they did not openly proclaim their sexual preferences. When relatively minor objections were raised to a number of his important appointments, he tended to back down rather than stand behind his choices.

In July 1993 Clinton used his executive authority to strengthen the Supreme Court majority in favor of upholding the landmark case of *Roe* v. *Wade*. (See the feature essay in Chapter 31, Mapping the Past: *"Roe v. Wade* (1973) and the Abortion Controversy," pp. 846–847.) The majority included three conservative justices who had been appointed by Reagan and Bush. Clinton appointed Ruth Bader Ginsberg, a judge known to believe that abortion was constitutional. Clinton also indicated that he would veto any bill limiting abortion rights. He also reversed important Bush policies by signing a revived family leave bill

into law and by authorizing the use of fetal tissue for research purposes.

The first major test of the president's will came when he submitted his first budget to Congress. He hoped to reduce the deficit by roughly $500 billion in five years, half by spending cuts, half by new taxes. The proposal for a tax increase roused a storm of protest. A number of congressional Democrats refused to go along with Clinton's budget, and since the Republicans in Congress voted solidly against any increase in taxes, the president was forced to accept major changes. Even so, the final bill passed by the narrowest of margins. Clinton rightly claimed a victory.

He then turned to his long-awaited proposal to reform the nation's expensive and incomplete health insurance system. A committee headed by his wife had been working for months with no indication that a plan acceptable to the medical profession, the health insurance industry, and ordinary citizens was likely to come from its deliberations. The plan that finally emerged seemed even more complicated and quite possibly more costly than the existing system. It never came to a vote in Congress.

Clinton Health
Care Reform
Proposals

Emergence of the Republican Majority

The Whitewater scandal, which Clinton had managed to brush aside during the campaign, gnawed at his presidency. Public pressure forced Attorney General Janet Reno to appoint a special prosecutor. She named Kenneth W. Starr, a Republican lawyer, to investigate Whitewater and other alleged misdeeds of the Clintons.

More troubles followed. Paula Corbin Jones, a State of Arkansas employee, charged that Clinton, while governor, had invited her to his hotel room and asked her to engage in oral sex. Clinton's attorney denied the accusation and sought to have the case dismissed on the grounds that a president could not be sued while in office. The case commenced a tortuous route through the courts.

Eager to take advantage of Clinton's troubles, Republicans looked to the 1994 congressional elections. Led by congressman Newt Gingrich of Georgia, they offered voters an ambitious program to stimulate the economy by reducing both the federal debt and the federal income tax. This would turn many of the functions of the federal government

over to the states or to private enterprise. Federally administered welfare programs were to be replaced by block grants to the states. Many measures protecting the environment, such as those making businesses responsible for cleaning up their waste, were to be repealed.

On election day, the Republicans gained control of both houses of Congress. Under the firm direction of Gingrich, now Speaker, the House approved nearly all of the provisions of this "contract with America." This appalled Clinton, who vetoed the 1995 budget drafted by the Republicans. When neither side agreed to a compromise, the government for a time ran out of money and shut down all but essential services.

THE ELECTION OF 1996

The public tended to blame Congress, and particularly Speaker Gingrich, for the shutdown. The president's approval rating rose. But the main issue of the day was the economy, and the upturn during and after 1991 benefited Clinton enormously. By the fall of 1996, unemployment had fallen well below 6 percent, and inflation below 3 percent. The Dow Jones industrial stock average of leading stocks soared past 6000, more than triple the average in 1987. Clinton was renominated for a second term without opposition.

A number of Republicans competed in their primaries, but after a slow start Bob Dole of Kansas, the Senate majority leader, won the nomination. Dole had been a senator for more than 30 years, but despite his experience he was a poor campaigner, stiff and monotone. His main proposal was a steep reduction of the deficit and a 15 percent income tax cut. Pressed to explain how this could be done without drastic cuts in popular social programs, especially Social Security and Medicare, he gave a distressingly vague reply. He captured headlines by criticizing popular music as "the leading edge of a culture becoming dangerously coarse" and denouncing Hollywood for making films that "revel in mindless violence and loveless sex."

Clinton, a charismatic campaigner, also promised to reduce the deficit, but by a lesser amount, so as to be able to spend more on education, the environment, and social welfare needs. He stressed preparing for the twenty-first century and took, in general, an optimistic view of the economy.

On election day Clinton won an impressive victory, sweeping the Northeast, all the Midwest except Indiana, the upper Mississippi Valley, and the Far West. He divided the South with Dole, who carried a band of states running north from Texas. Clinton's Electoral College margin was substantial, 379 to 159. The Republicans, however, retained control of both houses of Congress. Many retained, as well, an unquenchable hatred of Clinton.

A RACIAL DIVIDE

The decade of the 1990s had a hard edge, as political rhetoric was saturated by allegations of crimes and misdemeanors. Contributing to the harsh tone of the era was the arrest and spectacular murder trial of O. J. Simpson, a former star football running back for the University of Southern California and the Buffalo Bills. Simpson, who was black, was accused of stabbing his estranged wife and another man. Both of them were white. After a tempestuous nine-month trial, Simpson was acquitted.

To many whites, Simpson was another violent black male, while to many African Americans, he was another innocent black abused by a prejudiced criminal justice system. According to polls, 85 percent of blacks agreed with the "not guilty" verdict of the first Simpson trial, while only 34 percent of whites did. For the most part, neither race could understand the other's reasoning.

Many concluded that the cultural chasm between whites and blacks was widening. In 1992 Supreme Court justice Thurgood Marshall observed that educated Americans of each race appeared to have "given up on integration." After the Simpson trial Louis Farrakhan, leader of the black separatist Nation of Islam, called on African American men to express their solidarity by participating in a "Million Man March" on Washington, D.C. Many black leaders, including Jesse Jackson, embraced it. On October 16, 1995, the demonstration attracted perhaps a half million marchers, far more than had participated in Martin Luther King, Jr.'s "March on Washington" in 1963. But where King welcomed the whites in the audience and declared, "We cannot walk alone," Farrakhan called for "a more perfect union" of the multitude of black men gathered before him.

The persistence of inequality was one reason for the new separatism. In 1972 the incomes of black families were one-third less than those of white families; this was virtually unchanged 20 years later. The leading sectors of the post–1973 economy—technology and information services—placed a premium

on education, and here, too, the record in the late 1990s was unsettling. The math and reading scores of 17-year-old African American students rose relative to those of white students in the 1980s. But after 1988 black test scores fell sharply. The extent of the decline—it affected the children of the rich and poor alike, and the students of both public and parochial schools—suggests the importance of broader cultural factors.

A significant casualty of the changing tone of race relations was "affirmative action," which gave minorities preference in hiring and college admissions. Initially justified on the grounds that the legacy of slavery and the persistence of racism put blacks at an unfair disadvantage in finding jobs or gaining admission to college, affirmative action programs spread during the 1970s and 1980s. But in July 1995 the Regents of the University of California ordered an end to affirmative action. This decision touched off protests throughout the university system. The protests, however, drew attention to the issue and the following year California voters approved Proposition 209, which abolished racial and gender preferences in all government hiring and education. The U.S. Supreme Court let the law stand. Other states enacted similar laws.

The overt racism of an earlier era, enforced by custom and law, had become socially unacceptable and often explicitly illegal. But as the British writer Godfrey Hodgson observed, Americans in the 1990s appeared to be moving toward "a kind of voluntary apartheid" in which blacks and whites preferred to keep their distance In 1997, when President Clinton went to Little Rock to celebrate the fortieth anniversary of the desegregation of Central High School, he commented on the deterioration in race relations. The formerly all-white school was now mostly black, as were all public schools in Little Rock. "For the first time since the 1950s, our schools in America are resegregating," he noted.

As ever, race relations defied simple characterization. Opinion polls indicated that attitudes about race were becoming more complicated and ambivalent. By an overwhelming majority whites endorsed the accomplishments of the civil rights movement. Other polls revealed that in 1964 only 1 in 5 whites lived near a black neighbor; by 1994, 3 in 5 whites did so. In 1968 a Gallup poll found that only 17 percent of whites and 48 percent of blacks approved of marriages between blacks and whites; by 1994, the figures had increased to 45 percent of whites and 68 percent of blacks.

But many observed that even when white and black students attended the same schools, learned the same popular songs and rooted for the same teams, they often attended different classrooms, sat at separate tables in the cafeteria, and cheered from voluntarily segregated sections of the bleachers.

VIOLENCE AND POPULAR CULTURE

Popular culture, like athletics, often bridged the racial divide. But some observers took little solace in the broad appeal of youth-focused movies, pop songs, video and computer games, and TV shows. Such entertainment, they contended, romanticized an increasingly bloody culture of crime and violence. They cited as proof the intense violence of the movie industry, pointing out that in *Public Enemy,* reputedly the most violent film of the 1930s, and *Death Wish,* a controversial vigilante fantasy of 1974, the body count reached eight. But three movies released during the late 1980s—*Robocop, Die Hard,* and *Rambo III*—each produced a death tally of 60 or more, nearly one every two minutes. The trend culminated in *Natural Born Killers* (1994), director Oliver Stone's unimaginably violent "spoof" of media violence. Television imitated the movies as the networks crammed violent crime shows into prime time. In 1991 an exhaustive survey found that by the age of 18, the average viewer had witnessed some 40,000 murders on TV.

Popular music also acquired a new edge. In 1981 Warner Brothers launched a television channel featuring pop songs set to video. Music TV (MTV) was an instant success; within three years, some 24 million tuned in every day. Michael Jackson's video extravaganza, *Thriller* (1984), transformed the genre. Its surreal images, disjointed editing, and frenzied music set a new standard. Pop music acquired a harder beat and more explicit lyrics. In 1988 the American Academy of Pediatrics expressed concern that teen-agers on the average spent two hours a day watching rock videos. Over half featured violence and three-fourths contained sexually suggestive material.

A new sound called "rap" then emerged from the ghetto and spread by means of radio, cassettes, and CDs. Rap consisted of unpredictably metered lyrics set against an exaggeratedly heavy downbeat. Rap performers did not play musical instruments or sing songs so much as convey, in words and gestures, an attitude of defiant, raw rage against whatever challenged their sense of manhood: other young males; women, whom they derided in coarse sexual epithets; and the police. Predictably, raps such as "Cop Killer"

and "Illegal Search" contributed to the charge that rap condoned violence and crime.

"I call it crime rhyme," explained rapper Ice-T, "rhyme about actual street events." Some "gangsta" rappers dressed in stylized prison garb—beltless pants and "do-rags." Several major rappers were murdered, and others ran afoul of the law.

The appeal of rap quickly spread beyond black audiences. When Dr. Dre (Andrew Young), founder of a gangsta rap group and head of a record firm, discovered that whites bought more rap CDs than blacks, he promoted the career of a young white rapper, Eminem. Born Marshall Bruce Mathers III, Eminem attracted attention with songs such as "Murder, Murder," "Kill You," "Drug Ballad," and "Criminal." He bashed women, gays, his wife, and nearly everyone else. His lyrics were of such surpassing offensiveness that he became an overnight celebrity and instant millionaire. His fans, whom he treated with scorn, were delighted by the universality of his contempt. The list of those suing him included his mother.

The violation of social norms has long been part of adolescence. In the 1830s boys devoured "Davy Crockett" tales that championed sadistic violence and bawdy sexual antics; even during the presumably "conformist" decade of the 1950s young people enjoyed the scatological humor of *Mad Magazine*, the suggestive gyrations of Elvis Presley, and the rebellious sexual innuendo of nearly all types of popular music. Anthropologists have suggested that in Western societies adolescence is a transitional stage in which young people delight in "cultural inversions" that turn the social order upside down.

Most consumers of pop violence in the 1990s and early years of the 2000s, like the readers of the Crockett comics or *Mad Magazine*, had little difficulty distinguishing between cultural fantasies and everyday life. But for those who had grown up in ghettoes where gangs ruled the streets and where friends and relatives were commonly swallowed up by the criminal justice system, the culture of violence seemed to legitimate the meanness of everyday life. Moreover, violence and criminality were becoming so much a part of popular culture, and popular culture of adolescent life, that some retreated wholly to imaginative worlds conjured by movies, video and computer games, TV, and pop music. To them, the world of parents and teachers seemed duller and less responsive—less *real*—than the one inside their heads.

A few went so far as to act out destructive fantasies. On October 1, 1997, a 16-year-old boy stabbed his mother, shot and killed two students,

and wounded seven others at his high school in Pearl, Mississippi. Over the next 18 months a spate of similar shootings in West Paducah, Kentucky; Jonesboro, Arkansas; and Springfield, Oregon, left 5 more students dead and 23 wounded. On April 20, 1999, two teenagers, wearing trench coats and armed with automatic weapons, went on a rampage at Columbine High School in Littleton, Colorado. Before shooting themselves to death, they killed 12 students and a teacher and wounded more than 30. Their crime, previewed in a video prepared as a class project, turned out to be a replay of a 1995 movie, *The Basketball Diaries,* in which Leonardo DiCaprio, wearing a long, black coat and carrying a shotgun, bursts into school and shoots his classmates and teachers. A month after the Columbine shooting, a 15-year old shot six students at a high school in Conyers, Georgia.

CLINTON IMPEACHED

Although President Clinton steadfastly denied allegations of womanizing, in January 1998 a judge ordered Clinton to testify in the lawsuit Paula Corbin

▲ A seemingly anonymous well-wisher from the crowd greets President Bill Clinton. When Clinton was later investigated for having an affair with Monica Lewinsky, a former White House intern, this photograph of the two surfaced. Clinton's lack of discretion struck many as self-destructive.

Jones had filed against him. Jones, who sought to strengthen her suit by showing that Clinton had a history of propositioning women, also subpoenaed a former White House intern. Her name was Monica Lewinsky.

Lewinsky and Clinton were separately asked if they had had an affair, and each denied the charge. When word of their alleged relationship was leaked to the press, Clinton declared in a TV news conference: "I did not have sexual relations with that woman, Miss Lewinsky." Hillary Clinton denounced the allegations as part of a "vast right-wing conspiracy" against her husband.

Unbeknown to the Clintons, however, Lewinsky had been confiding to Linda Tripp, a former White House employee, and Tripp had secretly tape-recorded some 20 hours of their conversations. She turned these tapes over to special prosecutor Starr, whose investigations of the Clintons' roles in the Whitewater scandal had broadened into a more general inquiry. In the Tripp tapes Lewinsky provided intimate details of repeated sexual encounters with the president. Clinton and Lewinsky appeared to have lied under oath. Starr threatened to indict Lewinsky for perjury. In return for immunity from prosecution, she repudiated her earlier testimony and admitted that she had engaged in sexual relations with the president and that he and his aides had encouraged her to give misleading testimony in the Jones case.

When called in August to testify on videotape before the Starr grand jury, Clinton conceded that he had engaged in "inappropriate intimate contact" with Lewinsky. But he insisted, "I have not had sex with her as I defined it." When pressed to supply his own definition, he responded with legalistic obfuscation: "My understanding of this definition is it covers contact by the person being deposed with the enumerated areas, if the contact is done with an intent to arouse or gratify." Because Clinton had not intended to arouse or gratify Lewinsky, he had not "had sex" with her. He allowed that this definition was "rather strange."

More legalisms followed. When asked if he had ever been alone with her, he responded, "It depends on how you define alone." When asked if his lawyer had been correct when he had assured the judge in January that "there is absolutely no sex of any kind," Clinton said that the statement was not untrue because "it depends on what the meaning of the word 'is' is."

Clinton's testimony infuriated Starr, who made public Lewinsky's humiliatingly detailed testimony and announced that Clinton's deceptive testimony warranted consideration by the House of Representatives for impeachment.

But throughout Clinton's legal battles, opinion polls suggested that two in three Americans approved of his performance as president. Buoyed by the vibrant economy, most Americans blamed the scandal on the intrusive Starr nearly as much as the evasive Clinton. The November election proved disastrous for the Republicans, who nearly lost their majority in the House.

Clinton's troubles, however, were by no means over. Republican leaders in the House impeached Clinton on the grounds that he had committed perjury and had obstructed justice by inducing Lewinsky and others to give false testimony in the Jones case. The vote closely followed party lines.

The impeachment trial in the Senate began in January 1999. Chief Justice William Rehnquist presided. The Republicans numbered 55, enough to control the proceedings but twelve short of the two-thirds necessary to convict the president and remove him from office. Democrats, while publicly critical of Clinton's behavior, maintained that his indiscretions did not constitute "high crimes and misdemeanors" as specified in the Constitution for removal from office. They prevailed. The article accusing Clinton of perjury was defeated by a vote of 55 to 45; on the article alleging obstruction of justice, the vote was 50 to 50. Clinton remained president.

DOCUMENT

Articles of Impeachment Against Bill Clinton

CLINTON'S LEGACY

One reason why Clinton survived was the health of the economy. Few wanted to rock the ship of state when it was stuffed with cash. Until the final months, the Clinton years coincided with the longest economic boom in the nation's history. Clinton deserves considerable credit for the remarkable prosperity of the era. By reducing the federal deficit, interest rates came down, spurring investment and economic growth. By August 1998 unemployment had fallen to 4.5 percent, the lowest level since the 1960s; inflation had eased to a miniscule 1 percent, the lowest level since the 1950s. In 1998 the federal government operated at its first surplus since 1969. Then, as the economy soared during the next two years, so did government income. In the 2000 fiscal year, the surplus hit $237 billion.

Clinton also promoted globalization of the economy. He successfully promoted the North

American Free Trade Agreement to reduce tariff barriers; Congress approved NAFTA in 1993. During the last half of the 1990s, the United States led all industrial nations in the rate of growth of its real gross domestic product. But the new global economy harmed many. Some union leaders bitterly asked how their members could compete against convict labor in China or sweatshop workers in Indonesia or Malaysia. Others complained that the emphasis on worldwide economic growth was generating an environmental calamity. International protests against the World Trade Organization culminated in the disruption of its 2000 meeting in Seattle, when thousands of protesters went on a rampage, setting fires and looting stores.

Clinton's record in foreign affairs was mixed. In 1993 he failed in an effort to assemble an international force to prevent "ethnic cleansing" by Serbian troops against Muslims in Bosnia, formerly part of Yugoslavia. That same year a U.S. initiative to Somalia, an African nation wracked by civil war and famine, ended in failure when a Somali warlord ambushed and killed 15 American commandos. "Operation Restore Hope," as it was called, did not. In 1999 critics predicted another debacle when Clinton proposed a NATO effort to prevent General Slobodan Milosevic of Yugoslavia from crushing the predominantly Muslim province of Kosovo, which was attempting to secede. But after several months of intense NATO bombing of Serbia, Milosevic withdrew from Kosovo. Within a year, he was forced out of office and into prison, awaiting trial for war crimes before a UN tribunal.

The Balkan Proximity Peace Talks Agreement (1995)

Clinton labored, as had his predecessors in the White House, to broker peace between Israel and the Palestinians; like his predecessors, he failed. In 1993 Yitzhak Rabin, Israeli Prime Minister, and Yassir Arafat, leader of the Palestine Liberation Organization, signed an agreement preparing the groundwork for a Palestinian state. But extremists on both sides shattered the fragile accord. In 1995 Rabin was assassinated by a Jewish zealot. Palestinians, enraged by the construction of Israeli settlements in Palestinian territory, stepped up their campaign of suicide bombings. Israel retaliated with tank and helicopter attacks on suspected terrorist strongholds. In the fall of 2000, Clinton pressured the Israeli prime minister and Arafat to reach an accord. Despite some concessions on both sides, the talks collapsed. Arafat unleashed a new wave of uprisings, and hardliners, headed by Ariel Sharon, took charge of Israel. Violence intensified on both sides.

Whatever the successes and shortcomings of his administration, the Clinton presidency will always be linked to his relationship with a White House intern and the impeachment proceedings that ensued. Though by no means the first president to stray from matrimonial propriety, Clinton's behavior, in an era when the media thrived on scandal and crime, was symptomatic of an almost willful self-destructiveness.

THE ECONOMIC BOOM AND THE INTERNET

A significant part of the prosperity of the 1990s came from new technologies such as cellular phones and genetic engineering. But the most important was the development of a revolutionary form of communication: the Internet. Developed in the 1970s by U.S. military and academic institutions to coordinate research, the Internet initially proved an awkward means of linking information. Data in one computer did not readily relate to that elsewhere. The Internet was a communication system that lacked a common language.

That was remedied in the early 1990s by Tim Berners-Lee, a British physicist working at a research institute in Switzerland. He devised the software that became the grammar—the "protocols"—of the Internet "language." With this language, the internet became the World Wide Web (WWW), a conduit for a stream of electronic impulses flowing among hundreds of millions of computers.

The number of Websites increased exponentially. In 1995 Bill Gates's Microsoft entered the picture with its Windows operating system, which made the computer easy to use. Rather than drown in the coming deluge, Microsoft seized control of it. It competed with Netscape by creating a Web browser—Microsoft Internet Explorer—and embedded its software in the Windows 95 bundle. This provoked howls of protest from Netscape as well as from other service providers: America Online, CompuServe, and Prodigy. Microsoft, they complained, was threatening to monopolize access to and use of the Internet. (A federal judge concurred, ordering that Microsoft be broken up; his ruling was overturned on appeal in 2001.)

In the meantime, Jeff Bezos dreamed of using the Internet to sell books. In 1995 his company, Amazon.com, sold its first book. Within six years,

its annual sales approached $3 billion and its stock soared. Bezos became one of the richest men in the nation.

If Bezos could use the Web for selling books, others imagined they could sell everything from pet food to pornography. (eBay, an Internet auction house, had an online catalog consisting of three million items). Many start-up companies (dot-coms, in the argot of the day) consisted of little more than the hopes of the founders. "Venture capitalists," independent investors seeking to fund emerging "tech" companies, sensed a glittering new economic frontier somewhere down the Internet superhighway, and they poured billions into start-up dot-coms. In 1999 some 200 Internet compa-nies "went public," selling shares in the major stock exchanges. They raised $20 billion easily. NASDAQ, the exchange that specialized in tech companies, saw the value of its stocks skyrocket, its index more than doubling between October 1999 and March 2000. The prices of dot-com stocks kept on climbing though few generated profits; some lacked any revenue whatsoever.

In the spring of 2000, with the stock market still surging, a selling wave hit the tech stocks and spilled over to other companies. Stock prices plummeted. Within six months NASDAQ lost nearly half its value. In all, some $2 trillion in stocks and stock funds disappeared. As the 2000 election approached, many feared that the economy was nearing a recession.

THE 2000 ELECTION: GEORGE W. BUSH WINS BY ONE VOTE

During the 2000 campaign, Vice President Al Gore sought to prove his indispensability to President Clinton, whose administration was credited for the economic growth of the 1990s, as well as his distance from Bill Clinton, whose personal life was discredited by scandal. Gore showed his loyalty by raising money for the Democratic party, and his independence, by avoiding mention of Clinton. The strategy failed. Gore ran afoul of election laws when he solicited contributions too energetically and in inappropriate places, ranging from a Buddhist temple to the White House itself. And the president, irritated by Gore's refusal to champion the Clinton record, devoted his energies to his wife's successful campaign to represent New York in the Senate. Gore nevertheless secured the Democratic nomination and chose as running mate Senator Joseph Lieberman of Connecticut, an orthodox Jew and outspoken critic of Clinton during the impeachment proceedings.

The leading contender was George W. Bush, son of former President Bush. Like his father, Bush graduated from Yale and worked in the family oil business. He headed a group that bought the Texas Rangers baseball team. Although some doubted Bush's abilities, his visible success with the Rangers catapulted him into Texas politics. An effective and personable campaigner, he was elected governor in 1994. Six years later he defeated Senator John McCain of Arizona in a battle for the Republican nomination for president. Bush selected as running mate Richard Cheney, who had served as defense secretary in his father's administration.

Consumer activist and environmentalist Ralph Nader also entered the presidential race, running on the Green party ticket. This worried Gore, author of *Earth in the Balance;* he had hoped to carry the environmentalist vote.

The main issue was what to do with the federal surplus, which by some projections would reach over $1 trillion within five years. Bush called for a substantial tax cut; Gore wanted to increase spending on education and shore up the social security system.

Gore, though knowledgeable, seemed stiff, and he occasionally indulged in self-serving bombast, as when he claimed to have "invented" the Internet. Bush's principal offense was against the English language. "Rarely is the question asked," he once declaimed, "Is our children learning?" His poetic flights of fancy did not stay long aloft, as when he evoked American aspirations for "wings to take dream" and endorsed economic growth to "make the pie higher." However exaggerated or garbled their message, the candidates spent a record $1 billion in getting it to the voters.

Having been inundated with advertisements, many on election night breathed a sigh of relief that the election was finally over. They were wrong. By midnight it appeared that Bush had 246 electoral votes, and Gore, 267, with 270 necessary to win; but Florida, with 25 electoral votes, had not been decided. As returns trickled in, the television networks reversed themselves and declared Florida—and the election—"too close to call." Bush's lead there was 1784 out of nearly 6 million cast.

▶ *text continues on page 894*

Mapping the Past

Twenty Years of Terrorism

The past twenty years have witnessed increased terrorist attacks on Americans throughout the world. Most have been the work of Islamist radicals who opposed the strong American presence in the Middle East, U.S. support of Israel, or the secularism and modernism of the West. Because the attacks were not explicitly initiated by any state, they are termed acts of terrorism rather than of war.

The Middle East has a long history of terrorism, not always initiated by Islamist groups or supporters. In 1946, for example, Zionists seeking a Jewish state blew up the King David Hotel in Jerusalem, headquarters of the British command, killing 91.

The first major incident of anti-American terrorism in recent times occurred in 1983 when President Reagan sent an American peacekeeping force to Lebanon, whose government had disintegrated in the wake of an Israeli invasion. In several attacks, Islamic suicide bombers killed nearly 300 Americans, most of them soldiers.

In 1985 four Arabs seized control of the Italian cruise ship *Achille Lauro* in the eastern Mediterranean. After killing an elderly Jewish American tourist and tossing his body into the sea, they surrendered to Egyptian authorities on condition that they be allowed safe passage to Libya on an Egyptian airliner.

The terrorists chose Libya because the president of that nation, Muammar al-Qaddafi, was a bitter enemy of Israel and the United States and an open supporter of terrorist activities. To stop them, President Reagan ordered Navy F–14 jets to intercept the airliner. The jets forced the Egyptian pilot to land

▼ A gaping hole in the destroyer USS *Cole,* in the port of Aden, Yemen, caused by suicide bombers on October 12, 2000. The attack was linked to Osama bin Laden's al-Qaeda terrorist network, based in Afghanistan.

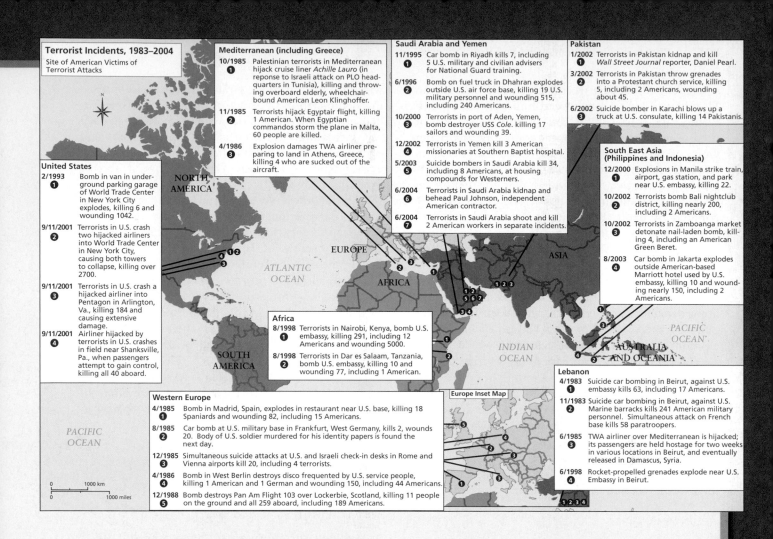

Terrorist Incidents, 1983–2004
Site of American Victims of Terrorist Attacks

Mediterranean (including Greece)

10/1985 ❶ Palestinian terrorists in Mediterranean hijack cruise liner *Achille Lauro* (in reponse to Israeli attack on PLO head-quarters in Tunisia), killing and throwing overboard elderly, wheelchair-bound American Leon Klinghoffer.

11/1985 ❷ Terrorists hijack Egyptair flight, killing 1 American. When Egyptian commandos storm the plane in Malta, 60 people are killed.

4/1986 ❸ Explosion damages TWA airliner preparing to land in Athens, Greece, killing 4 who are sucked out of the aircraft.

Saudi Arabia and Yemen

11/1995 ❶ Car bomb in Riyadh kills 7, including 5 U.S. military and civilian advisers for National Guard training.

6/1996 ❷ Bomb on fuel truck in Dhahran explodes outside U.S. air force base, killing 19 U.S. military personnel and wounding 515, including 240 Americans.

10/2000 ❸ Terrorists in port of Aden, Yemen, bomb destroyer USS *Cole*. killing 17 sailors and wounding 39.

12/2002 ❹ Terrorists in Yemen kill 3 American missionaries at Southern Baptist hospital.

5/2003 ❺ Suicide bombers in Saudi Arabia kill 34, including 8 Americans, at housing compounds for Westerners.

6/2004 ❻ Terrorists in Saudi Arabia kidnap and behead Paul Johnson, independent American contractor.

6/2004 ❼ Terrorists in Saudi Arabia shoot and kill 2 American workers in separate incidents.

Pakistan

1/2002 ❶ Terrorists in Pakistan kidnap and kill *Wall Street Journal* reporter, Daniel Pearl.

3/2002 ❷ Terrorists in Pakistan throw grenades into a Protestant church service, killing 5, including 2 Americans, wounding about 45.

6/2002 ❸ Suicide bomber in Karachi blows up a truck at U.S. consulate, killing 14 Pakistanis.

South East Asia (Philippines and Indonesia)

12/2000 ❶ Explosions in Manila strike train, airport, gas station, and park near U.S. embassy, killing 22.

10/2002 ❷ Terrorists bomb Bali nightclub district, killing nearly 200, including 2 Americans.

10/2002 ❸ Terrorists in Zamboanga market detonate nail-laden bomb, killing 4, including an American Green Beret.

8/2003 ❹ Car bomb in Jakarta explodes outside American-based Marriott hotel used by U.S. embassy, killing 10 and wounding nearly 150, including 2 Americans.

United States

2/1993 ❶ Bomb in van in underground parking garage of World Trade Center in New York City explodes, killing 6 and wounding 1042.

9/11/2001 ❷ Terrorists in U.S. crash two hijacked airliners into World Trade Center in New York City, causing both towers to collapse, killing over 2700.

9/11/2001 ❸ Terrorists in U.S. crash a hijacked airliner into Pentagon in Arlington, Va., killing 184 and causing extensive damage.

9/11/2001 ❹ Airliner hijacked by terrorists in U.S. crashes in field near Shanksville, Pa., when passengers attempt to gain control, killing all 40 aboard.

Africa

8/1998 ❶ Terrorists in Nairobi, Kenya, bomb U.S. embassy, killing 291, including 12 Americans and wounding 5000.

8/1998 ❷ Terrorists in Dar es Salaam, Tanzania, bomb U.S. embassy, killing 10 and wounding 77, including 1 American.

Western Europe

4/1985 ❶ Bomb in Madrid, Spain, explodes in restaurant near U.S. base, killing 18 Spaniards and wounding 82, including 15 Americans.

8/1985 ❷ Car bomb at U.S. military base in Frankfurt, West Germany, kills 2, wounds 20. Body of U.S. soldier murdered for his identity papers is found the next day.

12/1985 ❸ Simultaneous suicide attacks at U.S. and Israeli check-in desks in Rome and Vienna airports kill 20, including 4 terrorists.

4/1986 ❹ Bomb in West Berlin destroys disco frequented by U.S. service people, killing 1 American and 1 German and wounding 150, including 44 Americans.

12/1988 ❺ Bomb destroys Pan Am Flight 103 over Lockerbie, Scotland, killing 11 people on the ground and all 259 aboard, including 189 Americans.

Europe Inset Map

Lebanon

4/1983 ❶ Suicide car bombing in Beirut, against U.S. embassy kills 63, including 17 Americans.

11/1983 ❷ Suicide car bombing in Beirut, against U.S. Marine barracks kills 241 American military personnel. Simultaneous attack on French base kills 58 paratroopers.

6/1985 ❸ TWA airliner over Mediterranean is hijacked; its passengers are held hostage for two weeks in various locations in Beirut, and eventually released in Damascus, Syria.

6/1998 ❹ Rocket-propelled grenades explode near U.S. Embassy in Beirut.

---

in Italy instead of Libya, and the terrorists were taken into custody. Then, after a Libyan-planned bombing of a West German club frequented by American soldiers, Reagan launched an air strike against Libyan bases from airfields in Great Britain.

In December 1988 a bomb tore through the fuselage of a Pan Am 747 jetliner. The plane crashed in Lockerbie, Scotland, killing all 259 on board and 11 on the ground. A Scottish court convicted a Libyan intelligence officer and in 2003 Libya accepted responsibility for the crime.

On February 26, 1993, a tremendous explosion ripped through the parking garage of the World Trade Center in New York City. Smoke and flames engulfed the building. Six people were killed and more than 1000 injured. A serial number from a rented van, which had been packed with explosives, was found among the debris and traced to Islamic fundamentalists.

In February 1995 Ramzi Ahmed Yousef, accused of masterminding the bombing, was captured in Pakistan and returned to New York City for trial. While in custody, Yousef expressed his disappointment that the blast had failed to knock down one of the towers; he had hoped to kill 250,000 people. His action, he said, had been in retaliation for U.S. aid to Israel. Yousef and three accomplices were convicted and sentenced to life in prison.

In November 1995 a car bomb rocked an American military base in Riyadh, Saudi Arabia. Four Islamic militants, enraged that the American bases were supporting air attacks on Iraq, were convicted of the crime in Saudi Arabia and on May 31, 1996, they were publicly beheaded. In retaliation, a truck bomb destroyed another American military complex in Dhahran, also in Saudi Arabia. Nineteen servicemen were killed and 500 injured.

In August 1998 truck bombs tore through the American embassies in Nairobi, Kenya, and Dar Es Salaam, Tanzania. Nearly 300 died, including 12 Americans; 5000 were injured. Those arrested for the crime were Islamic extremists. On October 12, 2000, terrorists in a rubber boat laden with explosives rammed a U.S. destroyer, the USS *Cole,* docked in Yemen. The explosion ripped a hole in the ship, killing 17 American sailors and injuring dozens.

Then, on September 11, 2001, came the hijacking of four jetliners. Two were crashed into the World Trade Center towers in New York City, which collapsed. Another plunged into the Pentagon, near Washington. The fourth airliner went down in Pennsylvania after passengers attempted to retake it from the hijackers. These terrorist incidents killed more than 2700 people.

After a machine recount, Bush's margin in Florida was reduced to several hundred votes, with Democrats complaining that a punch-card ballot used in some communities was confusing, depriving Gore of thousands of votes; worse, the machines routinely failed to count incompletely punched ballots. Gore's lawyers demanded that the ballots in several predominantly Democratic counties be counted by hand. Republicans countered that Democrats had no right to change voting procedures after the election. They demanded that the hand recounts cease.

But when overseas absentee ballots began pouring in, many of them from military personnel, Republicans demanded that technical rules, such as those requiring that ballots be postmarked on or before the election, be waived. Gore objected.

The entire election ended up in the courts. On December 12, more than a month after the election, the Supreme Court ruled by a 5 to 4 vote that the selective hand recounts violated the Constitution's guarantee of equal protection. Bush's margin would stand.

Nationwide, Gore received 51 million votes, Bush, 50.5 million. Nader, who did not win any electoral votes, received nearly 3 million.

TERRORISM INTENSIFIES

After the fall of the Soviet Union, American military might seemed unassailable. Many foreign leaders, once valuable allies in the Cold War between the superpowers, bristled that that lucrative game had ended. Military dictators who been kept afloat by the Soviets or the Americans—and often from both simultaneously—now were obliged to seek the support of the people they had long ruled. This often proved to be destabilizing.

In many Arab nations, for example, rulers cultivated popular support by denouncing Israel, which refused to return Palestinian land seized in the 1967 war. The United States encouraged Israel to trade that land for peace. But few Israelis believed the promises of Arab leaders who had steadfastly called for the annihilation of Israel and had trained and funded terrorism. American diplomats called on Arab leaders to demonstrate their good faith by putting an end to terrorism; Israel would then return some of the Palestinian land. But Arab leaders, whose nations were often mired in poverty, knew that whenever their popularity waned, they could

win the approval of the Arab multitude with a rousing denunciation of Israel. And insofar as Israel relied ultimately on American support, the Arab rage was increasingly directed at the United States and American soldiers stationed abroad. (See the feature essay, Mapping the Past: "Twenty Years of Terrorism," pp. 892–893.)

During these years, several dozen separate terrorist organizations were behind the attacks on American targets. But in 1998 a new figure surfaced among the ranks of Islamist terrorists: Osama bin Laden, the son of a Saudi oil billionaire. In 1998, bin Laden published a *fatwa*—a religious edict—to Islamic peoples throughout the world: "To kill Americans and their allies, both civil and military, is an individual duty of every Muslim who is able . . ." By now, bin Laden was protected by an extremist Islamic group, the Taliban, which ruled Afghanistan. Six months later, bin Laden's terrorist organization—al-Qaeda—had perpetrated the bombings of the U.S. embassies in Nairobi and Dar es-Salaam in Africa. Worse was to follow.

SEPTEMBER 11, 2001

At 8:40 on the morning of September 11, 2001, Madeline Amy Sweeney, an attendant on American Airlines Flight 11, placed a cell phone call from the galley of the plane to her supervisor in Boston. In a whisper, she said that four Arab men had slashed the throats of two attendants, forced their way into the cockpit, and taken over the plane. She gave him their seat numbers so that their identities could be determined from the passenger log. The supervisor asked if she knew where the plane was headed. She looked out the window and noted that it was descending rapidly. "I see water and buildings." Then she paused: "Oh my God." The water was the Hudson River, and the buildings were the skyscrapers of lower Manhattan, foremost among them the 110-story twin towers of the World Trade Center.

The hijackers pushed the throttle to full, and the Boeing 767 was traveling at 500 miles per hour at 8:46 when it slammed into the 96th floor of the north tower. A fireball, fed by 10,000 gallons of jet fuel, instantly engulfed eight or nine stories.

Fifteen minutes later a second airliner came into view over Manhattan harbor, banked sharply, and plowed into the 80th floor of the south tower. New York mayor Rudolph Giuliani, who had raced to the

▲ A second jetliner approaches the South Tower of the World Trade Center on September 11, 2001. The North Tower had already been hit and was engulfed in flames and smoke.

scene, asked Fire Chief Peter Ganci, "What should I communicate to people?" "Tell them to get in the stairways," Ganci replied. "I think we can save everyone below the fire." The World Trade Center employed 50,000. As thousands fled the buildings, hundreds of firefighters, Ganci among them, charged up the stairs to rescue those who were trapped.

At 9:30 the White House received word that another hijacked airliner was barreling toward Washington, D.C. Secret Service agents rushed Vice President Richard Cheney to an emergency command bunker far below the White House. At 9:35 the airliner plunged into the Pentagon and burst into flames. Cheney telephoned President Bush, who was in Sarasota, Florida. The nation was under attack. Bush authorized the Air Force to shoot down any other hijacked airliners. A few minutes later a fourth hijacked airliner crashed into a field in Pennsylvania after passengers had declared their intention—again by cell phone—to retake the plane.

While television viewers absorbed these shocks, they watched as the upper floors of the World Trade Center towers blackened, like charred matches. At 9:59, the south tower collapsed, followed by the north tower a half hour later, pulverizing millions of tons of concrete and glass and enveloping lower Manhattan in choking dust. Nearly three thousand lay dead in the mountain of rubble, including Chief Ganci and 350 firemen; several hundred more perished at the Pentagon and in the crash of the airliner in Pennsylvania.

Teams of four or five Arabic-speaking men had hijacked each of the planes. Several of the hijackers were quickly linked to the al-Qaeda terrorist network run by Osama bin Laden, who had previously been indicted (but not captured) for the 1998 bombing of U.S. embassies in East Africa and the 2000 attack on the USS *Cole*. Bin Laden operated with impunity in Afghanistan, a nation governed by the Taliban, an extremist Islamic group.

That evening President Bush addressed the nation. He spoke simply and with force. "We will find these people," he said of the terrorists. "They will pay." Any government harboring the terrorists—an obvious reference to the Taliban—would be held equally responsible for the attack. Bin Laden, in a video recorded from an undisclosed location, denied involvement in the attack but praised those who carried it out.

Several weeks later, Bush declared that bin Laden would be taken "dead or alive." The president also offered a $25 million reward for his death or capture, an evocation of swift frontier justice that suited the national mood. Within the United States, thousands of Arabs were rounded up and detained; those with visa and immigration violations were imprisoned.

Then more trouble arrived at the capital, this time in the mail. Several letters addressed to government officials included threatening messages and a white powder consisting of billions of anthrax spores, which could prove fatal if touched or inhaled. Thousands of government employees took antibiotics as a precaution, but some spores had seeped out of the envelopes and killed a half dozen postal workers and mail recipients.

Bush responded to these multiple threats by creating a Cabinet position, the Office of Homeland Security, and naming Pennsylvania governor Tom Ridge to direct it. Repeatedly Ridge issued vague warnings of imminent terrorist attacks. How exactly Americans were to protect themselves, he did not say.

AMERICA FIGHTS BACK: WAR IN AFGHANISTAN

DOCUMENT

Bush, Address to Congress (September 20, 2001)

Bush had declared "war on terror," but it was to be a battle unlike any the nation had ever fought. Al-Qaeda had secret terrorist cells in many countries. Bin Laden was ensconced in remote Afghanistan, protected by thousands of Taliban soldiers who had inflicted heavy losses on Soviet invaders in the 1980s. (At the time, the United States had provided bin Laden and the Taliban with money and weapons.) The source of the anthrax letters proved even more problematic, because the spores resembled a strain developed in American military laboratories.

Bush's challenge was all the greater because of his own stated opposition to ill-defined and far-flung military operations. He had chastised the Clinton-Gore administration for "extending our troops all around the world." He underscored his reticence for such ventures by naming Colin Powell secretary of state. Powell, who had been sobered by his experiences in Vietnam, maintained that U.S. troops should only be deployed when their political objective was clear, military advantage overwhelming, and means of disengaging secure. This became known as the Powell doctrine, and Bush had endorsed it during the campaign. But the proposed war against terror adhered to none of its precepts. Now such scruples did not matter; the president had little choice but to fight.

Powell urged many European, Asian, and even Islamic states to crack down on terrorist cells in their countries and to provide assistance in the U.S. military campaign against the Taliban; he also persuaded anti-Taliban factions within Afghanistan to join forces to topple the regime. On September 20 Bush ordered the Taliban to surrender bin Laden and top al-Qaeda leaders; when the Taliban refused, Bush unloosed missiles and warplanes against Taliban installations and defenses, much like the campaign that had ended Serbian aggression against ethnic Muslims in Kosovo.

For several weeks, Taliban soldiers cowered in bunkers as bombs thudded nearby; but they defended their positions when anti-Taliban forces attacked. Then small teams of elite American soldiers, armed with hand-held computers and satellite-linked navigational devices, joined with anti-Taliban contingents, marking Taliban positions with laser spotters and communicating with high-altitude bombers. These planes, circling at 30,000 feet, dropped electronically guided bombs on Taliban troops with uncanny (but not infallible) accuracy. Now the Taliban soldiers fled; some switched allegiance and joined the anti-Taliban coalition. Within weeks the Taliban were driven from power. Only one American soldier was killed by hostile fire. (A few American soldiers and hundreds of non-combatants were killed by errant bombs.) The United States had won the first battles in the war against terror. But more were to come.

THE SECOND IRAQ WAR

In January 2002, after the Taliban had been crushed, President Bush declared that he would not "wait on events while dangers gather." The United States would take "preemptive actions" war—against regimes that threatened it. He identified Iran, North

Korea, and Iraq as an "axis of evil" that warranted special scrutiny. Immediately after September 11, he secretly initiated plans to attack Iraq, ruled by Saddam Hussein.

Secretary of State Colin Powell advised Bush not to attack Iraq. If Saddam were driven from power, Powell warned, Bush would become "the proud owner of 25 million people—you'll own it all." Vice President Dick Cheney, Defense Secretary Donald Rumsfeld, and others in the administration insisted that the Iraqis would welcome liberation and embrace democracy. A free Iraq, they added, would stimulate democratic reforms throughout the Middle East, as had happened in eastern Europe following the collapse of the Soviet Union. Bush agreed.

The Joint Chiefs of Staff proposed an invasion force numbering a half-million troops, as had been hurled against Saddam in 1991. Rumsfeld insisted on a smaller, faster, and cheaper force of 125,000. In the spring of 2002 CIA agents were spirited into Iraq and airplanes and soldiers were deployed to Kuwait. When reporters asked Bush if he was planning for war with

▲ President George W. Bush aboard the USS *Abraham Lincoln* on May 1, 2004. "Major combat operations in Iraq have ended," he declared. But in the months to come, American casualties mounted as some Iraqis resisted occupation by the United States. By that fall, more than 1000 United States servicemen had been killed in the Second Iraq War.

▲ On February 5, 2003 Secretary of State Colin Powell told the United Nations that the United States had no choice but to go to war against Iraq. "We know that Saddam Hussein is determined to keep his weapons of mass destruction; he's determined to make more." As of early 2005, no such weapons had been found.

Iraq, the famously tidy president replied, "I have no plans to attack on my desk."

In September, Bush sought congressional support. "The Iraqi regime possesses chemical and biological weapons," he declared, adding that Saddam also sought nuclear weapons. Congress voted overwhelmingly for the war appropriation.

Bush then called on the United Nations to join in the attack. That Saddam had used chemical weapons during the Iran-Iraq war and also against the Kurds was beyond dispute; but following Saddam's defeat in 1991, UN inspectors had destroyed thousands of tons of Iraqi chemical weapons. In recent years these inspectors had found little further evidence. Bush saw this as proof that Saddam had hoodwinked the inspectors. Then Powell, like Adlai Stevenson during the Cuban missile crisis in 1962,

▲ Marines bid farewell before departing for Iraq.

presented classified U.S. intelligence to the United Nations. Saddam, he said, had indeed been building and stockpiling weapons of mass destruction. The UN Security Council ordered Saddam to cooperate with UN inspectors and warned of "serious consequences" if he refused to do so.

After several months Bush grew impatient with the slow pace of the inspections. After the Security Council refused to take action, Bush formed a coalition to oust Saddam. The United States was joined by Great Britain, Italy, Spain, and a few other countries.

On March 20, 2003, American missiles and bombs pounded Saddam's defenses. The "Shock and Awe" campaign to liberate Iraq had begun. Two armored columns roared across the Kuwaiti

border into Iraq, passing burned-out Iraqi tanks from the first Gulf War. British forces moved along the coast toward the oil port of Basra. Television reporters, perched atop Humvees and armored personnel carriers, provided live coverage. Iraqi resistance was ineffective. The first night, American units had advanced half-way to Baghdad.

On April 4, the U.S. Army seized the Baghdad International Airport. That day, television footage aired on Al Jezeera, an Arab television network, showed a man—apparently Saddam—walking through Baghdad and exhorting the Iraqis: "Resist them, O courageous citizens of Baghdad. Our martyrs will go to paradise, and their dead will go to hell." The next morning, some 800 American soldiers in tanks and armored vehicles blasted their

way into down-town Baghdad. Some Iraqis poured into the streets to celebrate, but others looted offices, museums, stores, and hospitals. Saddam disappeared and his government evaporated. By mid-April, the Pentagon declared that major combat operations had come to an end.

But Iraq was in chaos. There were too few U.S. troops to preserve order. Islamist radicals, enraged by the American occupation, increasingly joined with Saddam's supporters in attacking occupation forces. The insurgents rammed trucks filled with explosives into police stations, wired cell phones to artillery shells and detonated them as Americans approached. Others sabotaged oil pipelines and power generators.

THE ELECTION OF 2004

The war became the main issue of the presidential campaign. Among Democratic candidates, Howard Dean, former governor of Vermont, zoomed ahead in the polls by denouncing the war. He also proved adept at using the Internet to raise funds and recruit supporters—"Deaniacs," as they were called. He endorsed national health insurance and legal recognition of marriage for gay and lesbian couples.

In December American soldiers captured Saddam in an underground bunker. Bush's approval rating soared. Many Democratic voters, worried that Bush would win in a landslide, looked for an alternative to the ultra-liberal Dean.

By January Senator John Kerry of Massachusetts was gaining in the polls. The son of a diplomat and a graduate of Yale, Kerry appeared accomplished and steady. He had commanded a patrol boat during the Vietnam War and was decorated for courage under fire. He won the Iowa caucuses and upset Dean in the New Hampshire primary. After the New Hampshire primary, Dean gave an over-the-top exhortation that culminated in a roar—"the scream," as pundits called it—that caused many to doubt his suitability. By April, Kerry had won the nomination. He chose Senator John Edwards of North Carolina, a wealthy trial lawyer, as his running mate.

In Iraq, the situation deteriorated further. In April the *60 Minutes* news program revealed that American captors had tortured Iraqi captives in the Abu Ghraib prison. Photographs of American soldiers, including women, taunting naked Muslim

▲ John Kerry, Democratic presidential candidate, campaigning in Philadelphia for "a stronger America."

men fueled the insurgency. Casualties mounted. The cost of the occupation was spiraling upward. More damaging politically was the failure to find any Iraqi weapons of mass destruction.

At the Democratic convention in July, Kerry emphasized his military service in Vietnam. "I am John Kerry, and I am reporting for duty," he said in his acceptance speech. This was an implicit contrast with Bush, who had served with the National Guard in Alabama and Texas during the Vietnam War. "As president," Kerry declared, "I will fight a smarter, more effective war on terror." He criticized Bush for attacking Iraq before capturing Osama bin Laden, who remained at large. He also chided the president for initiating war with insufficient international support, and not sending enough troops to preserve order and rebuild Iraq.

Bush mobilized conservatives and religious fundamentalists by proposing a constitutional amendment that would define marriage as the union between a man and a woman. Kerry endorsed gay

DEBATING THE PAST

Do historians ever get it right? The Debating the Past essays in previous chapters have offered hundreds of interpretations, many of them contradictory. Why, if historians are looking at the same past, do they see it so differently?

Consider the photograph above. It shows a cityscape as reflected on the many windows of a new skyscraper. Each pane of glass has its own angle of reflection, imposing unique distortions on the scene; note that one window—all black—is open, about to receive a pipe. Historians, too, look at the past from different perspectives, and sometimes crucial pieces of evidence are missing.

Well into the twentieth century, most historians believed that their collective labors—more research, more books—were leading to a composite picture that provided a fuller and clearer rendering of the past. But some recent historians have doubted whether their profession can sharpen the picture's focus, or whether a coherent vista of "the past" even existed. If our own lives are a jumble of motivations and confusions, how can one think it possible to paint a portrait of an entire people?

In an exhaustive study of the American Historical Association, Peter Novick (1988) further demonstrated that while historians have long championed objectivity in principle, their research has been riddled with bias. Ignorant of their cultural blinders, historians grope in search of historical truths they can never see.

By undercutting their profession's claims of "truth," Novick's book made historians more susceptible to an idea that was sweeping through literature departments. Known as "deconstruction" or "textualism" and derived from French philosopher Jacques Derrida, it held that "there is nothing outside the text." (Or, to use the metaphor of the photograph, there is nothing beyond the reflections.) No one could reasonably claim to know what a novelist meant by any novel, or what any statesman or historical figure meant by the words he or she spoke or wrote. By extension, no historian can explain what any historical record meant to the people of the times it reflected. Inspired by such observations, Robert F. Berkhofer (1995) repudiated the very idea of a grand historical narrative, partly because readers would interpret that narrative in their own ways.

Raising Berkhofer's contention at the end of a book that purports to provide just such a narrative may seem perverse. But his point contains an obvious truth: Readers of any work of history, this one included, will make of it what they will.

Peter Novick, *That Noble Dream* (1988), Robert F. Berkhofer, Jr., *Beyond the Great Story* (1995), Jacques Derrida, *Deconstruction in a Nutshell* (1997).

rights but endlessly qualified earlier statements in support of same-sex marriage.

Bush's campaign also pounced on Kerry's war record. Some Vietnam veterans seized on the fact that in 1971 Kerry had told a congressional committee that the Vietnam war was wrong and immoral. How, these veterans asked, could an antiwar activist lead the nation in time of war?

▲ A U.S. soldier taunting an Iraqi prisoner at Abu Ghraib prison. U.S. Major General Antonio M. Taguba reported on many such instances of "sadistic, blatant, and wanton criminal abuses." At least one prisoner died while being interrogated. The commander of the prison was dismissed and criminal charges were filed against some of the soldiers.

Republicans also portrayed Kerry as opportunistic. If Kerry and Edwards thought the war was a mistake, why did they vote for the original war resolution in the Senate? Kerry became entangled in long-winded explanations. "I actually voted for the $87 billion before I voted against it," he said on one occasion. Bush gleefully seized on this "flip-flop" and dubbed Kerry "Flipper." During a debate with Bush, Kerry conceded that he had "made a mistake" in explaining his position on Iraq. "But the president made a mistake in invading Iraq. Which is worse?"

"There's a mainstream in American politics," Bush told Kerry, "and you sit on the far left bank." The Democrat, Bush added, would likely raise taxes. Kerry, citing the huge federal deficit, replied: "Being lectured by the president on fiscal responsibility is a little bit like Tony Soprano talking to me about law and order."

The election, one of the most divisive in recent decades, brought 12 million more voters to the polls than in 2000. Kerry received 57 million votes, 3 million more than Ronald Reagan in his 1984 landslide. But Bush got over 60 million, a record. He also prevailed in the Electoral College, 286 to 252.

THE IMPONDERABLE FUTURE

No wartime president had ever lost a reelection campaign, and the pattern held true in 2004. As the situation in Iraq deteriorated, moreover, Bush's standing in the polls improved. Many voters preferred Bush's simple nostrums, even if flawed, to Kerry's complicated (and sometimes contradictory) approach.

"You know where I stand," Bush had declared at nearly every campaign stop, and in the end a majority of voters stood with him. But few took much solace from the view. In Iraq, bombings rocked police stations and public squares, and smoldering tensions between rival Muslim sects threatened to ignite a civil war. By early 2005, over 1400 American soldiers had been killed, ten times more than had died in the fighting that toppled Saddam. The federal deficit approached a half trillion dollars.

Would the defeat of Saddam discourage terrorists elsewhere and discourage rogue states such as Iran and North Korea from seeking nuclear weapons? Would a protracted U.S. military presence promote Iraqi democracy or generate resentment throughout the Arab world? Would the United States be able to find a way out of Iraq? If the specter of Vietnam haunted the 2004 election, it was because these questions echoed those that had been asked forty years earlier.

Historians are probably better than most other people at explaining how things got to be the way they are at any present moment. This is because events have causes and results, and these are things that historians are trained to study and understand. But historians are no better than anyone else at predicting the future.

In the modern world just about everything that happens is in some way related to everything else that is going on. Far too many things are happening for anyone to sort out which is going to have what effect on tomorrow's events, let alone those that occur a year from now. "Then" (whether tomorrow or next year) historians will be able to study those particular events and puzzle out their chief causes—but not "now."

Yet "now" is where we happen to be, and thus this book, so full of events and their causes and results, must end inconclusively. No one knows what will happen next. But not knowing what will happen is one reason why life is so interesting.

MILESTONES

1988	Republican George H. W. Bush elected president	**1998**	Clinton impeached by House of Representatives
1989	Gorbachev allows Eastern European nations to establish independent democratic governments	**1999**	Clinton acquitted by Senate; remains in office
1990	Iraq invades Kuwait		NATO troops, including Americans, sent to Kosovo to stop Serbian "ethnic cleansing"
	Germany is reunited		
1991	UN forces, led by the United States, drive Iraqi forces from Kuwait		Gun violence in schools escalates; 12 die at Columbine High School in Colorado
	Soviet Union is dissolved; Boris Yeltsin becomes president of Russia	**2000**	Republican George W. Bush elected president when Supreme Court halts Florida recounts
1992	Democrat Bill Clinton elected president		
1993	Ruth Bader Ginsberg becomes second woman associate justice of the Supreme Court	**2001**	Terrorists fly airliners into World Trade Center in New York, causing both towers to collapse, killing 3000
	Bomb explodes in parking garage of World Trade Center in New York, killing 6 and injuring 1000		United States attacks and defeats Taliban in Afghanistan
1994	Republicans win control of both houses of Congress	**2002**	President Bush prepares for war as he accuses Saddam Hussein of Iraq of developing weapons of mass destruction
	Congress defeats Clinton's health care reform plan		
1995	Terrorist bomb destroys Alfred P. Murrah Federal Building in Oklahoma City, killing 169	**2003**	U.S. and United Kingdom attack and defeat Iraq and capture Saddam Hussein
1996	Democrat Bill Clinton reelected president; Republicans retain control of Congress		Hostilities persist in Iraq
		2004	Republican George W. Bush reelected president
	Measure revamping federal welfare system passed by Congress and signed by President Clinton		

SUPPLEMENTARY READING

Haynes Johnson, *Divided We Fall: Gambling with History in the Nineties* (1994), notwithstanding its expansive title, discusses the first few years of the 1990s; for the end of the Cold War see Michael R. Beschloss and Strobe Talbot, *At the Highest Levels: The Inside Story of the End of the Cold War*, and John Lewis Gaddis, *The United States and the End of the Cold War* (1992).

Many scholars have attempted to fit the political developments of the era into a traditional framework: see Mary Jo Bane and David Ellwood, *Welfare Realities: From Rhetoric to Reform* (1994), Theodore J. Lowi, *The End of the Republican Era* (1995), and Robert S. McElvaine, *The End of the Conservative Era: Liberalism After Reagan* (1987).

For accounts of the George H. W. Bush administration, see Herbert Parmet, *George Bush: The Life of a Lone Star Yankee* (1997), and John R. Greene, *The Presidency of George Bush* (2000). Gary R. Hess provides a thoughtful comparison on war-making processes in *Presidential Decisions for War: Korea, Vietnam and the Persian Gulf* (2001). The Panama invasion is discussed in David Harris, *Shooting the Moon* (2001).

On Clinton prior to his move to the White House, see David Marannis, *First in His Class: A Biography of Bill Clinton* (1995). The *Starr Report* (1998), though hastily released and published, constituted the evidentiary base and set the tone for the subsequent impeachment debate. See also Richard A. Posner, *An Affair of State: The Investigation,*

Impeachment, and Trial of President Clinton (1999). On foreign policy, see David Halberstam, *War in a Time of Peace: Bush, Clinton and the Generals* (2001).

On the advance of conservatism, see Godfrey Hodgson, *The World Turned Rightside Up: A History of the Conservative Ascendancy in America* (1996). On the defeat of the ERA, see Mary Francis Berry, *Why ERA Failed* (1986), and Donald G. Mathews and Jane Sherron De Hart, *Sex, Gender, and the Politics of E.R.A.* (1990).

David Courtwright, *Violent Land: Single Men and Social Disorder from the Frontier to the Inner City* (1996) argues that much of the nation's crime has come from single males; for a cultural analysis of the infatuation with aggression, see Richard Slotkin, *Gunfighter Nation: The Myth of the Frontier in Twentieth-Century America* (1992). Bruce Jacobs, *Dealing Crack* (1999), provides a case study of the drug problem.

On race and ethnicity, see David A. Hollinger, *Postethnic America: Beyond Multiculturalism* (1995), Andrew Hacker, *Two Nations: Black and White, Separate, Hostile, Unequal* (1992), and Stephen Thernstrom and Abigail Thernstrom, *America in Black and White: One Nation, Indivisible* (1997).

John Cassidy, *Dot.con* (2002) surveys the Internet economy. For a history of the Internet, see Janet Abbate, *Inventing the Internet* (1999).

On the 2000 election, see David A. Kaplan, *The Accidental President* (2001), and Richard Posner, *Breaking the Deadlock* (2001).

The literature on terrorism is expanding rapidly. *The 9/11 Commission* Report (2004) is a detailed assessment of multiple failures in intelligence and security. Douglas Little, *American Orientalism: The United States and the Middle East since 1945* (2002) provides a useful overview of American policies, while Thomas L. Friedman, *From Beirut to Jerusalem* (1989) offers a thoughtful analysis of the complex problems of the region.

Bob Woodward's two books provide the best account of George W. Bush after the terrorist attack of September 11, 2001. *Bush at War* (2002) chronicles his leadership immediately after 9/11; *Plan of Attack* (2004), more critical, details Bush's campaign to oust Saddam Hussein of Iraq. Doug Brinkley, *Tour of Duty: John Kerry and the Vietnam War* (2004) is a solid narrative.

SUGGESTED WEBSITES

Desert Storm

http://www.desert-storm.com/

This site shows U.S. involvement in the Persian Gulf conflict.

Presidents George H. W. Bush and Bill Clinton

http://www.ipl.org/ref/POTUS/ghwbush.html

http://www.ipl.org/ref/POTUS/wjclinton.html

These sites contain basic data about each president's election, presidency, and speeches as well as an online biography of each.

Investigating the President: The Trial

http://www.cnn.com/ALLPOLITICS/resources/1998/lewinsky/

This CNN site provides information and documents about the scandals surrounding President Clinton and his impeachment.

Kosovo

http://www.cnn.com/SPECIALS/1998/10/kosovo/

This in-depth CNN Interactive site looks at the development and current resolution to the turmoil in Kosovo.

Oklahoma City Bombing

http://www.cnn.com/US/9703/okc.trial/

This CNN Interactive site has information about this terrorist act.

9/11 Attacks

http://911digitalarchives.org

This site preserves information about the terror attacks.

Appendix

The Declaration of Independence

The Articles of Confederation

The Constitution of the United States of America

Amendments to the Constitution

Presidential Election Maps, 1789–2004

For additional reference material, go to
www.ablongman.com/carnes12e/appendix

The online appendix includes the following:

The Declaration of Independence

In Congress, July 4, 1776

The Unanimous Declaration of the Thirteen United States of America,

When, in the course of human events, it becomes necessary for one people to dissolve the political bonds which have connected them with another, and to assume, among the powers of the earth, the separate and equal station to which the laws of nature and of nature's God entitle them, a decent respect to the opinions of mankind requires that they should declare the causes which impel them to the separation.

We hold these truths to be self-evident: That all men are created equal; that they are endowed by their Creator with certain unalienable rights; that among these are life, liberty, and the pursuit of happiness; that, to secure these rights, governments are instituted among men, deriving their just powers from the consent of the governed; that whenever any form of government becomes destructive of these ends, it is the right of the people to alter or to abolish it, and to institute new government, laying its foundation on such principles, and organizing its powers in such form, as to them shall seem most likely to effect their safety and happiness. Prudence, indeed, will dictate that governments long established should not be changed for light and transient causes; and accordingly all experience hath shown that mankind are more disposed to suffer, while evils are sufferable, than to right themselves by abolishing the forms to which they are accustomed. But when a long train of abuses and usurpations, pursuing invariably the same object, evinces a design to reduce them under absolute despotism, it is their right, it is their duty, to throw off such government, and to provide new guards for their future security. Such has been the patient sufferance of these colonies; and such is now the necessity which constrains them to alter their former systems of government. The history of the present King of Great Britain is a history of repeated injuries and usurpations, all having in direct object the establishment of an absolute tyranny over these states. To prove this, let facts be submitted to a candid world.

He has refused his assent to laws, the most wholesome and necessary for the public good.

He has forbidden his governors to pass laws of immediate and pressing importance, unless suspended in their operation till his assent should be obtained; and, when so suspended, he has utterly neglected to attend to them.

He has refused to pass other laws for the accommodation of large districts of people, unless those people would relinquish the right of representation in the legislature, a right inestimable to them, and formidable to tyrants only.

He has called together legislative bodies at places unusual, uncomfortable, and distant from the depository of their public records, for the sole purpose of fatiguing them into compliance with his measures.

He has dissolved representative houses repeatedly, for opposing, with manly firmness, his invasions on the rights of the people.

He has refused for a long time, after such dissolutions, to cause others to be elected; whereby the legislative powers, incapable of annihilation, have returned to the people at large for their exercise; the state remaining, in the mean time, exposed to all the dangers of invasions from without and convulsions within.

He has endeavored to prevent the population of these states; for that purpose obstructing the laws for naturalization of foreigners; refusing to pass others to encourage their migration hither, and raising the conditions of new appropriations of lands.

He has obstructed the administration of justice, by refusing his assent to laws for establishing judiciary powers.

He has made judges dependent on his will alone, for the tenure of their offices, and the amount and payment of their salaries.

He has erected a multitude of new offices, and sent hither swarms of officers to harass our people and eat out their substance.

He has kept among us, in times of peace, standing armies, without the consent of our legislatures.

He has affected to render the military independent of, and superior to, the civil power.

He has combined with others to subject us to a jurisdiction foreign to our constitution, and unacknowledged by our laws, giving his assent to their acts of pretended legislation:

For quartering large bodies of armed troops among us;

For protecting them, by a mock trial, from punishment for any murder which they should commit on the inhabitants of these states;

For cutting off our trade with all parts of the world;

For imposing taxes on us without our consent;

For depriving us, in many cases, of the benefits of trial by jury;

For transporting us beyond seas, to be tried for pretended offenses;

For abolishing the free system of English laws in a neighboring province, establishing therein an arbitrary government, and enlarging its boundaries, so as to render it at once an example and fit instrument for introducing the same absolute rule into these colonies;

For taking away our charters, abolishing our most valuable laws, and altering fundamentally the forms of our governments;

For suspending our own legislatures, and declaring themselves invested with power to legislate for us in all cases whatsoever.

He has abdicated government here, by declaring us out of his protection and waging war against us.

He has plundered our seas, ravaged our coasts, burned our towns, and destroyed the lives of our people.

He is at this time transporting large armies of foreign mercenaries to complete the works of death, desolation, and tyranny already begun with circumstances of cruelty and perfidy scarcely paralleled in the most barbarous ages, and totally unworthy the head of a civilized nation.

He has constrained our fellow-citizens, taken captive on the high seas, to bear arms against their country, to become the executioners of their friends and brethren, or to fall themselves by their hands.

He has excited domestic insurrection among us, and has endeavored to bring on the inhabitants of our frontiers the merciless Indian savages, whose known rule of warfare is an undistinguished destruction of all ages, sexes, and conditions.

In every stage of these oppressions we have petitioned for redress in the most humble terms; our repeated petitions have been answered only by repeated injury. A prince, whose character is thus marked by every act which may define a tyrant, is unfit to be the ruler of a free people.

Nor have we been wanting in our attentions to our British brethren. We have warned them, from time to time, of attempts by their legislature to extend an unwarrantable jurisdiction over us. We have reminded them of the circumstances of our emigration and settlement here. We have appealed to their native justice and magnanimity; and we have conjured them, by the ties of our common kindred, to disavow these usurpations, which would inevitably interrupt our connections and correspondence. They, too, have been deaf to the voice of justice and of consanguinity. We must, therefore, acquiesce in the necessity which denounces our separation, and hold them, as we hold the rest of mankind, enemies in war, in peace friends.

We, therefore, the representatives of the United States of America, in General Congress assembled, appealing to the Supreme Judge of the world for the rectitude of our intentions, do, in the name and by the authority of the good people of these colonies, solemnly publish and declare, that these United Colonies are, and of right ought to be, FREE AND INDEPENDENT STATES; that they are absolved from all allegiance to the British crown, and that all political connection between them and the state of Great Britain is, and ought to be, totally dissolved; and that, as free and independent states, they have full power to levy war, conclude peace, contract alliances, establish commerce, and do all other acts and things which independent states may of right do. And for the support of this declaration, with a firm reliance on the protection of Divine Providence, we mutually pledge to each other our lives, our fortunes, and our sacred honor.

JOHN HANCOCK

New Hampshire
Josiah Bartlett
William Whipple
Matthew Thornton

Massachusetts
John Adams
Samuel Adams
Robert Treat Paine
Elbridge Gerry

New York
William Floyd
Philip Livingston
Francis Lewis
Lewis Morris

Rhode Island
Stephen Hopkins
William Ellery

New Jersey
Richard Stockton
John Witherspoon
Francis Hopkinson
John Hart
Abraham Clark

Pennsylvania
Robert Morris
Benjamin Rush
Benjamin Franklin
John Morton
George Clymer
James Smith
George Taylor
James Wilson
George Ross

Delaware
Caeser Rodney
George Read
Thomas McKean

Maryland
Samuel Chase
William Paca
Thomas Stone
Charles Carroll
of Carrollton

North Carolina
William Hooper
Joseph Hewes
John Penn

Virginia
George Wythe
Richard Henry Lee
Thomas Jefferson
Benjamin Harrison
Thomas Nelson, Jr.
Francis Lightfoot Lee
Carter Braxton

South Carolina
Edward Rutledge
Thomas Heyward, Jr.
Thomas Lynch, Jr.
Arthur Middleton

Connecticut
Roger Sherman
Samuel Huntington
William Williams
Oliver Wolcott

Georgia
Button Gwinnett
Lyman Hall
George Walton

The Articles of Confederation

Between the States of New Hampshire, Massachusetts Bay, Rhode Island and Providence Plantations, Connecticut, New York, New Jersey, Pennsylvania, Delaware, Maryland, Virginia, North Carolina, South Carolina, Georgia

Article 1

The stile of this confederacy shall be "The United States of America."

Article 2

Each State retains its sovereignty, freedom and independence, and every power, jurisdiction, and right, which is not by this confederation expressly delegated to the United States, in Congress assembled.

Article 3

The said states hereby severally enter into a firm league of friendship with each other for their common defence, the security of their liberties and their mutual and general welfare; binding themselves to assist each other against all force offered to, or attacks made upon them, or any of them, on account of religion, sovereignty, trade, or any other pretence whatever.

Article 4

The better to secure and perpetuate mutual friendship and intercourse among the people of the different states in this union, the free inhabitants of each of these states, paupers, vagabonds, and fugitives from justice excepted, shall be entitled to all privileges and immunities of free citizens in the several states; and the people of each State shall have free ingress and regress to and from any other State, and shall enjoy therein all the privileges of trade and commerce, subject to the same duties, impositions, and restrictions, as the inhabitants thereof respectively; provided, that such restrictions shall not extend so far as to prevent the removal of property, imported into any State, to any other State of which the owner is an inhabitant; provided also, that no imposition, duties, or restriction, shall be laid by any State on the property of the United States, or either of them.

If any person guilty of, or charged with treason, felony, or other high misdemeanor in any State, shall flee from justice and be found in any of the United States, he shall, upon demand of the governor or executive power of the State from which he fled, be delivered up and removed to the State having jurisdiction of his offence.

Full faith and credit shall be given in each of these states to the records, acts, and judicial proceedings of the courts and magistrates of every other State.

Article 5

For the more convenient management of the general interests of the United States, delegates shall be annually appointed, in such manner as the legislature of each State shall direct, to meet in Congress, on the 1st Monday in November in every year, with a power reserved to each State to recall its delegates, or any of them, at any time within the year, and to send others in their stead for the remainder of the year.

No State shall be represented in Congress by less than two, nor by more than seven members; and no person shall be capable of being a delegate for more than three years in any term of six years; nor shall any person, being a delegate, be capable of holding any office under the United States, for which he, or any other for his benefit, receives any salary, fees, or emolument of any kind.

Each State shall maintain its own delegates in a meeting of the states, and while they act as members of the committee of the states.

In determining questions in the United States, in Congress assembled, each State shall have one vote.

Freedom of speech and debate in Congress shall not be impeached or questioned in any court or place out of Congress: and the members of Congress shall be protected in their persons from arrests and imprisonments, during the time of their going to and from, and attendance on Congress, except for treason, felony, or breach of the peace.

Article 6

No State, without the consent of the United States, in Congress assembled, shall send any embassy to, or receive any embassy from, or enter into any conference, agreement, alliance, or treaty with any king, prince, or state; nor shall any

person, holding any office of profit or trust under the United States, or any of them, accept of any present, emolument, office or title, of any kind whatever, from any king, prince, or foreign state; nor shall the United States, in Congress assembled, or any of them, grant any title of nobility.

No two or more states shall enter into any treaty, confederation, or alliance, whatever, between them, without the consent of the United States, in Congress assembled, specifying accurately the purposes for which the same is to be entered into, and how long it shall continue.

No State shall lay any imposts or duties which may interfere with any stipulations in treaties entered into by the United States, in Congress assembled, with any king, prince, or state, in pursuance of any treaties already proposed by Congress to the courts of France and Spain.

No vessels of war shall be kept up in time of peace by any State, except such number only as shall be deemed necessary by the United States, in Congress assembled, for the defence of such State or its trade; nor shall any body of forces be kept up by any State, in time of peace, except such number only as, in the judgment of the United States, in Congress assembled, shall be deemed requisite to garrison the forts necessary for the defence of such State; but every State shall always keep up a well regulated and disciplined militia, sufficiently armed and accoutred, and shall provide, and constantly have ready for use, in public stores, a due number of field pieces and tents, and a proper quantity of arms, ammunition and camp equipage.

No State shall engage in any war without the consent of the United States, in Congress assembled, unless such State be actually invaded by enemies, or shall have received certain advice of a resolution being formed by some nation of Indians to invade such State, and the danger is so imminent as not to admit of a delay till the United States, in Congress assembled, can be consulted; nor shall any State grant commissions to any ships or vessels of war, nor letters of marque or reprisal, except it be after a declaration of war by the United States, in Congress assembled, and then only against the kingdom or state, and the subjects thereof, against which war has been so declared, and under such regulations as shall be established by the United States, in Congress assembled, unless such States be infested by pirates, in which case vessels of war may be fitted out for that occasion, and kept so long as the danger shall continue, or until the United States, in Congress assembled, shall determine otherwise.

Article 7

When land forces are raised by any State for the common defence, all officers of or under the rank of colonel, shall be appointed by the legislature of each State respectively, by whom such forces shall be raised, or in such manner as such State shall direct; and all vacancies shall be filled up by the State which first made the appointment.

Article 8

All charges of war and all other expences, that shall be incurred for the common defence or general welfare, and allowed by the United States, in Congress assembled, shall be defrayed out of a common treasury, which shall be supplied by the several states, in proportion to the value of all land within each State, granted to or surveyed for any person, as such land and the buildings and improvements thereon shall be estimated according to such mode as the United States, in Congress assembled, shall, from time to time, direct and appoint.

The taxes for paying that proportion shall be laid and levied by the authority and direction of the legislatures of the several states, within the time agreed upon by the United States, in Congress assembled.

Article 9

The United States, in Congress assembled, shall have the sole and exclusive right and power of determining on peace and war, except in the cases mentioned in the 6th article; of sending and receiving ambassadors; entering into treaties and alliances, provided that no treaty of commerce shall be made, whereby the legislative power of the respective states shall be restrained from imposing such imposts and duties on foreigners as their own people are subjected to, or from prohibiting the exportation or importation of any species of goods or commodities whatsoever; of establishing rules for deciding, in all cases, what captures on land or water shall be legal, and in what manner prizes, taken by land or naval forces in the service of the United States, shall be divided or appropriated; of granting letters of marque and reprisal in times of peace; appointing courts for the trial of piracies and felonies committed on the high seas, and establishing courts for receiving and determining, finally, appeals in all cases of captures; provided, that no member of Congress shall be appointed a judge of any of the said courts.

The United States, in Congress assembled, shall also be the last resort on appeal in all disputes and differences now subsisting, or that hereafter may arise between two or more states sconcerning boundary, jurisdiction or any other cause whatever; which authority shall always be exercised in the manner following: whenever the legislative or executive authority, or lawful agent of any State, in controversy with another, shall present a petition to Congress, stating the matter in question, and praying for a hearing, notice thereof shall be given, by order of Congress, to the legislative or executive authority of the other State in controversy, and a day assigned for the appearance of the parties by their lawful agents, who shall then be directed to appoint, by joint consent, commissioners or judges to constitute a court for hearing and determining the matter in question; but, if they cannot agree, Congress shall name three persons out of each of the United States, and from the list of such persons each party shall alternately strike out one, in the petitioners beginning, until the number shall be reduced to thirteen; and from that number not less than seven, nor more than nine names, as Congress shall direct, shall, in the presence of Congress, be drawn out by lot; and the persons whose names shall be drawn, or any five of them, shall be commissioners or judges to hear and finally determine the controversy, so always as a major part of the judges who shall hear the cause shall agree in the determination; and if either party shall neglect to attend at the day appointed, without shewing reasons which Congress shall

judge sufficient, or, being present, shall refuse to strike, the Congress shall proceed to nominate three persons out of each State, and the secretary of Congress shall strike in behalf of such party absent or refusing; and the judgment and sentence of the court to be appointed, in the manner before prescribed, shall be final and conclusive; and if any of the parties shall refuse to submit to the authority of such court, or to appear or defend their claim or cause, the court shall nevertheless proceed to pronounce sentence or judgment, which shall, in like manner, be final and decisive, the judgment or sentence and other proceedings being, in either case, transmitted to Congress, and lodged among the acts of Congress for the security of the parties concerned: provided, that every commissioner, before he sits in judgment, shall take an oath, to be administered by one of the judges of the supreme or superior court of the State where the cause shall be tried, "well and truly to hear and determine the matter in question, according to the best of his judgment, without favour, affection, or hope of reward": provided, also, that no State shall be deprived of territory for the benefit of the United States.

All controversies concerning the private right of soil, claimed under different grants of two or more states, whose jurisdictions, as they may respect such lands and the states which passed such grants, are adjusted, the said grants, or either of them, being at the same time claimed to have originated antecedent to such settlement of jurisdiction, shall, on the petition of either party to the Congress of the United States, be finally determined, as near as may be, in the same manner as is before prescribed for deciding disputes respecting territorial jurisdiction between different states.

The United States, in Congress assembled, shall also have the sole and exclusive right and power of regulating the alloy and value of coin struck by their own authority, or by that of the respective states; fixing the standard of weights and measures throughout the United States; regulating the trade and managing all affairs with the Indians not members of any of the states; provided that the legislative right of any State within its own limits be not infringed or violated; establishing and regulating post offices from one State to another throughout all the United States, and exacting such postage on the papers passing through the same as may be requisite to defray the expences of the said office; appointing all officers of the land forces in the service of the United States, excepting regimental officers; appointing all the officers of the naval forces, and commissioning all officers whatever in the service of the United States; making rules for the government and regulation of the said land and naval forces, and directing their operations.

The United States, in Congress assembled, shall have authority to appoint a committee to sit in the recess of Congress, to be denominated "a Committee of the States," and to consist of one delegate from each State, and to appoint such other committees and civil officers as may be necessary for managing the general affairs of the United States, under their direction; to appoint one of their number to preside; provided that no person be allowed to serve in the office of president more than one year in any term of three years; to ascertain the necessary sums of money to be raised for the service of the United States, and to appropriate and apply the same for defraying the public expences; to borrow money or emit bills on the credit of the United States, transmitting, every half year, to the respective states, an account of the sums of money so borrowed or emitted; to build and equip a navy; to agree upon the number of land forces, and to make requisitions from each State for its quota, in proportion to the number of white inhabitants in such State; which requisitions shall be binding; and, thereupon, the legislature of each State shall appoint the regimental officers, raise the men, and cloathe, arm, and equip them in a soldierlike manner, at the expence of the United States; and the officers and men so cloathed, armed, and equipped, shall march to the place appointed and within the time agreed on by the United States, in Congress assembled; but if the United States, in Congress assembled, shall, on consideration of circumstances, judge proper that any State should not raise men, or should raise a smaller number than its quota, and that any other State should raise a greater number of men than the quota thereof, such extra number shall be raised, officered, cloathed, armed, and equipped in the same manner as the quota of such State, unless the legislature of such State shall judge that such extra number cannot be safely spared out of the same, in which case they shall raise, officer, cloathe, arm, and equip as many of such extra number as they judge can be safely spared. And the officers and men so cloathed, armed, and equipped, shall march to the place appointed and within the time agreed on by the United States, in Congress assembled.

The United States, in Congress assembled, shall never engage in a war, nor grant letters of marque and reprisal in time of peace, nor enter into any treaties or alliances, nor coin money, nor regulate the value thereof, nor ascertain the sums and expences necessary for the defence and welfare of the United States, or any of them: nor emit bills, nor borrow money on the credit of the United States, nor appropriate money, nor agree upon the number of vessels of war to be built or purchased, or the number of land or sea forces to be raised, nor appoint a commander in chief of the army or navy, unless nine states assent to the same; nor shall a question on any other point, except for adjourning from day to day, be determined, unless by the votes of a majority of the United States, in Congress assembled.

The Congress of the United States shall have power to adjourn to any time within the year, and to any place within the United States, so that no period of adjournment be for a longer duration than the space of six months, and shall publish the journal of their proceedings monthly, except such parts thereof, relating to treaties, alliances or military operations, as, in their judgment, require secrecy; and the yeas and nays of the delegates of each State on any question shall be entered on the journal, when it is desired by any delegate; and the delegates of a State, or any of them, at his, or their request, shall be furnished with a transcript of the said journal, except such parts as are above excepted, to lay before the legislatures of the several states.

Article 10

The committee of the states, or any nine of them, shall be authorized to execute, in the recess of Congress, such of the powers of Congress as the United States, in Congress

assembled, by the consent of nine states, shall, from time to time, think expedient to vest them with; provided, that no power be delegated to the said committee for the exercise of which, by the articles of confederation, the voice of nine states, in the Congress of the United States assembled, is requisite.

Article 11

Canada acceding to this confederation, and joining in the measures of the United States, shall be admitted into and entitled to all the advantages of this union; but no other colony shall be admitted into the same, unless such admission be agreed to by nine states.

Article 12

All bills of credit emitted, monies borrowed and debts contracted by, or under the authority of Congress before the assembling of the United States, in pursuance of the present confederation, shall be deemed and considered as a charge against the United States, for payment and satisfaction whereof the said United States and the public faith are hereby solemnly pledged.

Article 13

Every State shall abide by the determinations of the United States, in Congress assembled, on all questions which, by this confederation, are submitted to them. And the articles of this confederation shall be inviolably observed by every State, and the union shall be perpetual; nor shall any alteration at any time hereafter be made in any of them, unless such alteration be agreed to in a Congress of the United States, and be afterwards confirmed by the legislatures of every State.

These articles shall be proposed to the legislatures of all the United States, to be considered, and if approved of by them, they are advised to authorize their delegates to ratify the same in the Congress of the United States; which being done, the same shall become conclusive.

The Constitution of the United States of America

Preamble

We the People of the United States, in Order to form a more perfect Union, establish Justice, insure domestic Tranquility, provide for the common defence, promote the general Welfare, and secure the Blessings of Liberty to ourselves and our Posterity, do ordain and establish this Constitution for the United States of America.

Article I

Section 1

All legislative Powers herein granted shall be vested in a Congress of the United States, which shall consist of a Senate and House of Representatives.

Section 2

The House of Representatives shall be composed of Members chosen every second Year by the People of the several States, and the Electors in each State shall have the Qualifications requisite for Electors of the most numerous Branch of the State Legislature.

No Person shall be a Representative who shall not have attained to the Age of twenty five Years, and been seven Years a Citizen of the United States, and who shall not, when elected, be an inhabitant of that State in which he shall be chosen.

Representatives and direct Taxes shall be apportioned among the several States which may be included within this Union, according to their respective Numbers, *which shall be determined by adding to the whole Number of free Persons, including those bound to Service for a Term of Years, and excluding Indians not taxed, three fifths of all other Persons.* * The actual Enumeration shall be made within three Years after the first Meeting of the Congress of the United States, and within every subsequent Term of ten Years, in such Manner as they shall by Law direct. The Number of Representatives shall not exceed one for every thirty Thousand, but each State shall have at Least one Representative; *and until such enumeration shall be made, the State of New Hampshire shall be entitled to chuse three, Massachusetts eight, Rhode-Island and Providence Plantations one, Connecticut five, New York six, New Jersey four, Pennsylvania eight, Delaware one, Maryland six, Virginia ten, North Carolina five, South Carolina five, and Georgia three.*

When vacancies happen in the Representation from any State, the Executive Authority thereof shall issue Writs of Election to fill such Vacancies.

---

*Passages no longer in effect are printed in italic type.

The House of Representatives shall chuse their Speaker and other Officers; and shall have the sole Power of Impeachment.

Section 3

The Senate of the United States shall be composed of two Senators from each State, *chosen by the Legislature thereof,* for six Years; and each Senator shall have one Vote.

Immediately after they shall be assembled in Consequence of the first Election, they shall be divided as equally as may be into three Classes. The Seats of the Senators of the first Class shall be vacated at the Expiration of the second Year, of the second Class at the Expiration of the fourth Year, and of the third Class at the Expiration of the sixth Year so that one third may be chosen every second Year; and if Vacancies happen by Resignation, or otherwise, during the Recess of the Legislature of any state, the Executive thereof may make temporary Appointments until the next Meeting of the Legislature, which shall then fill such Vacancies.

No Person shall be a Senator who shall not have attained to the Age of thirty Years, and been nine Years a Citizen of the United States, and who shall not, when elected, be an Inhabitant of that State for which he shall be chosen.

The Vice President of the United States shall be President of the Senate, but shall have no Vote, unless they be equally divided.

The Senate shall chuse their other Officers, and also a President *pro tempore*, in the Absence of the Vice President, or when he shall exercise the Office of President of the United States.

The Senate shall have the sole Power to try all Impeachments. When sitting for that Purpose, they shall be on Oath or Affirmation. When the President of the United States is tried the Chief Justice shall preside: And no Person shall be convicted without the Concurrence of two thirds of the Members present.

Judgment in Cases of Impeachment shall not extend further than to removal from Office, and disqualification to hold and enjoy any Office of honor, Trust or Profit under the United States: but the Party convicted shall nevertheless be liable and subject to Indictment, Trial, Judgment and Punishment, according to Law.

Section 4

The Times, Places and Manner of holding Elections for Senators and Representatives, shall be prescribed in each State by the Legislature thereof; but the Congress may at

any time by Law make or alter such Regulations, except as to the Places of chusing Senators.

The Congress shall assemble at least once in every Year, *and such Meeting shall be on the first Monday in December, unless they shall by Law appoint a different Day.*

Section 5

Each House shall be the Judge of the Elections, Returns and Qualifications of its own Members, and a Majority of each shall constitute a Quorum to do Business; but a smaller Number may adjourn from day to day, and may be authorized to compel the Attendance of absent Members, in such Manner, and under such Penalties as each House may provide.

Each House may determine the Rules of its Proceedings, punish its Members for disorderly Behaviour, and, with the Concurrence of two thirds, expel a Member.

Each House shall keep a Journal of its Proceedings, and from time to time publish the same, excepting such Parts as may in their Judgment require Secrecy; and the Yeas and Nays of the Members of either House on any question shall, at the Desire of one fifth of those Present, be entered on the Journal.

Neither House, during the Session of Congress, shall, without the Consent of the other, adjourn for more than three days, nor to any other Place than that in which the two Houses shall be sitting.

Section 6

The Senators and Representatives shall receive a Compensation for their Services, to be ascertained by Law, and paid out of the Treasury of the United States. They shall in all Cases, except Treason, Felony and Breach of the Peace, be privileged from Arrest during their Attendance at the Session of their respective Houses, and in going to and returning from the same; and for any Speech or Debate in either House, they shall not be questioned in any other Place.

No Senator or Representative shall, during the Time for which he was elected, be appointed to any civil Office under the Authority of the United States, which shall have been created, or the Emoluments whereof shall have been encreased during such time, and no Person holding any Office under the United States, shall be a Member of either House during his Continuance in Office.

Section 7

All Bills for raising Revenue shall originate in the House of Representatives; but the Senate may propose or concur with Amendments as on other Bills.

Every Bill which shall have passed the House of Representatives and the Senate, shall, before it become a Law, be presented to the President of the United States; If he approve he shall sign it, but if not he shall return it, with his Objections to the House in which it shall have originated, who shall enter the Objections at large on their Journal, and proceed to reconsider it. If after such Reconsideration two thirds of that House shall agree to pass the Bill, it shall be sent, together with the Objections, to the other House, by which it shall likewise be reconsidered, and if approved by two thirds of that House, it shall become a Law. But in all such Cases the Votes of both Houses shall be determined by yeas and Nays, and the Names of the Persons voting for and against the Bill

shall be entered on the Journal of each House respectively. If any Bill shall not be returned by the President within ten Days (Sundays excepted) after it shall have been presented to him, the Same shall be a Law, in like Manner as if he had signed it, unless the Congress by their Adjournment prevent its Return, in which Case it shall not be a Law.

Every Order, Resolution, or Vote to which the Concurrence of the Senate and House of Representatives may be necessary (except on a question of Adjournment) shall be presented to the President of the United States; and before the Same shall take Effect, shall be approved by him, or being disapproved by him, shall be repassed by two thirds of the Senate and House of Representatives, according to the Rules and Limitations prescribed in the Case of a Bill.

Section 8

The Congress shall have Power To lay and collect Taxes, Duties, Imposts and Excises, to pay the Debts and provide for the common Defence and general Welfare of the United States; but all Duties, Imposts and Excises shall be uniform throughout the United States;

To borrow Money on the credit of the United States;

To regulate Commerce with foreign Nations, and among the several States, and with the Indian Tribes;

To establish an uniform Rule of Naturalization, and uniform Laws on the subject of Bankruptcies throughout the United States;

To coin Money, regulate the Value thereof, and of foreign Coin, and fix the Standard of Weights and Measures;

To provide for the Punishment of counterfeiting the Securities and current Coin of the United States;

To establish Post Offices and post Roads;

To promote the Progress of Science and useful Arts, by securing for limited Times to Authors and Inventors the exclusive Right to their respective Writings and Discoveries;

To constitute Tribunals inferior to the supreme Court;

To define and punish Piracies and Felonies committed on the high Seas, and Offences against the Law of Nations;

To declare War, grant Letters of Marque and Reprisal, and make Rules concerning Captures on Land and Water;

To raise and support Armies, but no Appropriation of Money to that Use shall be for a longer Term than two Years;

To provide and maintain a Navy;

To make Rules for the Government and Regulation of the land and naval Forces;

To provide for calling forth the Militia to execute the Laws of the Union, suppress Insurrections and repel Invasions;

To provide for organizing, arming, and disciplining, the Militia, and for governing such Part of them as may be employed in the Service of the United States, reserving to the States respectively, the Appointment of the Officers, and the Authority of training the Militia according to the discipline prescribed by Congress;

To exercise exclusive Legislation in all Cases whatsoever, over such District (not exceeding ten Miles square) as may, by Cession of particular States, and the Acceptance of Congress, become the Seat of the Government of the United States, and to exercise like Authority over all Places purchased by the Consent of the Legislature of the State in which the Same shall be, for the Erection of Forts, Magazines, Arsenals, dock-Yards, and other needful Buildings;—And

To make all Laws which shall be necessary and proper for carrying into Execution the foregoing Powers, and all other Powers vested by this Constitution in the Government of the United States, or in any Department of Officer thereof.

Section 9

The Migration or Importation of such Persons as any of the States now existing shall think proper to admit, shall not be prohibited by the Congress prior to the Year one thousand eight hundred and eight, but a Tax or duty may be imposed on such Importation, not exceeding ten dollars for each Person.

The Privilege of the Writ of Habeas Corpus shall not be suspended, unless when in Cases of Rebellion or Invasion the public Safety may require it.

No Bill of Attainder or ex post facto Law shall be passed.

No Capitation, or other direct, Tax shall be laid, unless in Proportion to the Census or Enumeration herein before directed to be taken.

No Tax or Duty shall be laid on Articles exported from any State.

No Preference shall be given by any Regulation of Commerce or Revenue to the Ports of one State over those of another: nor shall Vessels bound to, or from, one State, be obliged to enter, clear, or pay Duties in another.

No Money shall be drawn from the Treasury, but in Consequence of Appropriations made by Law; and a regular Statement and Account of the Receipts and Expenditures of all public Money shall be published from time to time.

No Title of Nobility shall be granted by the United States: And no Person holding any Office of Profit or Trust under them, shall, without the Consent of the Congress, accept of any present, Emolument, Office, or Title, of any kind whatever, from any King, Prince, or foreign State.

Section 10

No State shall enter into any Treaty, Alliance, or Confederation; grant Letters of Marque and Reprisal; coin Money; emit Bills of Credit; make any Thing but gold and silver Coin a Tender in Payment of Debts; pass any Bill of Attainder, ex post facto Law, or Law impairing the obligation of Contracts, or grant any Title of Nobility.

No State shall, without the Consent of the Congress, lay any Imposts or Duties on Imports or Exports, except what may be absolutely necessary for executing its inspection Laws: and the net Produce of all Duties and Imposts, laid by any State on Imports or Exports, shall be for the Use of the Treasury of the United States; and all such Laws shall be subject to the Revision and Controul of the Congress.

No State shall, without the Consent of Congress, lay any Duty of Tonnage, keep Troops, or Ships of War in time of Peace, enter into any Agreement or Compact with another State, or with a foreign Power, or engage in War, unless actually invaded, or in such imminent Danger as will not admit of delay.

Article II

Section 1

The executive Power shall be vested in a President of the United States of America. He shall hold his Office during the Term of four Years, and, together with the Vice President, chosen for the same Term, be elected, as follows:

Each State shall appoint, in such Manner as the Legislature thereof may direct, a Number of Electors, equal to the whole Number of Senators and Representatives to which the State may be entitled in the Congress: but no Senator or Representative, or Person holding an Office of Trust or Profit under the United States, shall be appointed an Elector.

The Electors shall meet in their respective States, and vote by Ballot for two Persons, of whom one at least shall not be an Inhabitant of the same State with themselves. And they shall make a List of all the Persons voted for, and of the Number of Votes for each; which List they shall sign and certify, and transmit sealed to the Seat of the Government of the United States, directed to the President of the Senate. The President of the Senate shall, in the Presence of the Senate and House of Representatives, open all the Certificates, and the Votes shall then be counted. The Person having the greatest Number of Votes shall be the President, if such Number be a Majority of the whole number of Electors appointed; and if there be more than one who have such Majority, and have an equal Number of Votes, then the House of Representatives shall immediately chuse by Ballot one of them for President; and if no Person have a Majority, then from the five highest on the List the said House shall in like Manner chuse the President. But in chusing the President, the Votes shall be taken by States, the Representation from each State having one Vote; A quorum for this Purpose shall consist of a Member or Members from two thirds of the States, and a Majority of all the States shall be necessary to a Choice. In every Case, after the Choice of the President, the Person having the greatest Number of Votes of the Electors shall be the Vice President. But if there should remain two or more who have equal Votes, the Senate shall chuse from them by Ballot the Vice President.

The Congress may determine the time of chusing the Electors, and the Day on which they shall give their Votes; which Day shall be the same throughout the United States.

No person except a natural born Citizen, *or a Citizen of the United States, at the time of the Adoption of this Constitution,* shall be eligible to the Office of President; neither shall any Person be eligible to that Office who shall not have attained to the Age of thirty five Years, and been fourteen Years a Resident within the United States.

In Case of the Removal of the President from Office, or of his Death, Resignation, or Inability to discharge the Powers and Duties of the said Office, the Same shall devolve on the Vice President, and the Congress may by Law provide for the Case of Removal, Death, Resignation or Inability, both of the President and Vice President, declaring what Officer shall then act as President, and such Officer shall act accordingly, until the Disability be removed, or a President shall be elected.

The President shall, at stated Times, receive for his Services, a Compensation, which shall neither be encreased nor diminished during the Period for which he shall have been elected, and he shall not receive within that period any other Emolument from the United States, or any of them.

Before he enter on the Execution of his Office, he shall take the following Oath or Affirmation:—"I do solemnly swear (or affirm) that I will faithfully execute the Office of President of the United States, and will to the best of my Ability, preserve, protect and defend the Constitution of the United States."

Section 2

The President shall be Commander in Chief of the Army and Navy of the United States, and of the Militia of the several States, when called into the actual Service of the United States; he may require the Opinion, in writing, of the principal Officer in each of the executive Departments, upon any Subject relating to the Duties of their respective Offices, and he shall have Power to grant Reprieves and Pardons for Offences against the United States, except in Cases of Impeachment.

He shall have Power, by and with the Advice and Consent of the Senate, to make Treaties, provided two thirds of the Senators present concur; and he shall nominate, and by and with the Advice and Consent of the Senate, shall appoint Ambassadors, other public Ministers and Consuls, Judges of the supreme Court, and all other Officers of the United States, whose Appointments are not herein otherwise provided for, and which shall be established by Law: but the Congress may by Law vest the Appointment of such inferior Officers, as they think proper in the President alone, in the Courts of Law, or in the Heads of Departments.

The President shall have Power to fill up all Vacancies that may happen during the Recess of the Senate, by granting Commissions which shall expire at the End of their next Session.

Section 3

He shall from time to time give to the Congress Information of the State of the Union, and recommend to their Consideration such Measures as he shall judge necessary and expedient; he may, on extraordinary Occasions, convene both Houses, or either of them, and in Case of disagreement between them, with Respect to the Time of Adjournment, he may adjourn them to such Time as he shall think proper; he shall receive Ambassadors and other public Ministers; he shall take Care that the Laws be faithfully executed, and shall Commission all the officers of the United States.

Section 4

The President, Vice President and all civil Officers of the United States, shall be removed from Office on Impeachment for, and Conviction of, Treason, Bribery or other high Crimes and Misdemeanors.

Article III

Section 1

The judicial Power of the United States, shall be vested in one supreme Court, and in such inferior Courts as the Congress may from time to time ordain and establish. The Judges, both of the supreme and inferior Courts, shall hold their offices during good Behaviour, and shall, at stated Times, receive for their Services, a Compensation, which shall not be diminished during their Continuance in Office.

Section 2

The judicial Power shall extend to all Cases, in Law and Equity, arising under this Constitution, the Laws of the United States, and Treaties made, or which shall be made, under their Authority;—to all Cases affecting Ambassadors, other public Ministers and Consuls;—to all Cases of admiralty and maritime Jurisdiction;—to Controversies to which the United States shall be a Party;—to Controversies between two or more States;—*between a State and Citizens of another State;*—between Citizens of different States;—between Citizens of the same State claiming Lands under Grants of different States, and between a State, or the Citizens thereof, and foreign States, Citizens or Subjects.

In all Cases affecting Ambassadors, other public Ministers and Consuls, and those in which a State shall be Party, the supreme Court shall have original Jurisdiction. In all the other Cases before mentioned, the supreme Court shall have appellate Jurisdiction, both as to Law and Fact, with such Exceptions, and under such Regulations as the Congress shall make.

The Trial of all Crimes, except in Cases of Impeachment, shall be by Jury; and such Trial shall be held in the State where the said Crimes shall have been committed, but when not committed within any State, the Trial shall be at such Place or Places as the Congress may by Law have directed.

Section 3

Treason against the United States, shall consist only in levying War against them, or in adhering to their Enemies, giving them Aid and Comfort. No person shall be convicted of Treason unless on the Testimony of two Witnesses to the same overt Act, or on Confession in open Court.

The Congress shall have Power to declare the Punishment of Treason, but no Attainder of Treason shall work Corruption of Blood, or Forfeiture except during the Life of the Person attainted.

Article IV

Section 1

Full Faith and Credit shall be given in each State to the public Acts, Records, and judicial Proceedings of every other State. And the Congress may by general Laws prescribe the Manner in which such Acts, Records and Proceedings shall be proved, and the Effect thereof.

Section 2

The Citizens of each State shall be entitled to all Privileges and Immunities of Citizens in the several States.

A Person charged in any State with Treason, Felony, or other Crime, who shall flee from Justice, and be found in another State, shall on Demand of the executive Authority of the State from which he fled, be delivered up, to be removed to the State having Jurisdiction of the Crime.

No Person held to Service or Labour in one State, under the Laws thereof, escaping into another, shall, in Consequence of any Law or Regulation therein, be discharged from such Service or Labour, but shall be delivered up on Claim of the Party to whom such Service or Labour may be due.

Section 3

New States may be admitted by the Congress into this Union; but no new State shall be formed or erected within the Jurisdiction of any other State; nor any State be formed by the Junction of two or more States, or Parts of States,

without the Consent of the Legislatures of the States concerned as well as of the Congress.

The Congress shall have Power to dispose of and make all needful Rules and Regulations respecting the Territory or other Property belonging to the United States; and nothing in this Constitution shall be so construed as to Prejudice any Claims of the United States, or of any particular States.

Section 4

The United States shall guarantee to every State in this Union a Republican Form of Government, and shall protect each of them against Invasion; and on Application of the Legislature, or of the Executive (when the Legislature cannot be convened) against domestic violence.

Article V

The Congress, whenever two thirds of both Houses shall deem it necessary, shall propose Amendments to this Constitution, or, on the Application of the Legislatures of two thirds of the several States, shall call a Convention for proposing Amendments, which, in either Case, shall be valid to all Intents and Purposes, as Part of this Constitution, when ratified by the Legislatures of three fourths of the several States, or by Conventions in three fourths thereof, as the one or the other Mode of Ratification may be proposed by the Congress; Provided *that no Amendment which may be made prior to the Year One thousand eight hundred and eight shall in any Manner affect the first and fourth Clauses in the Ninth Section of the first Article;* and that no State, without its Consent, shall be deprived of its equal Suffrage in the Senate.

Article VI

All Debts contracted and Engagements entered into, before the Adoption of this Constitution, shall be as valid against the United States under this Constitution, as under the Confederation.

This Constitution, and Laws of the United States which shall be made in Pursuance thereof; and all Treaties made, or which shall be made, under the Authority of the United States, shall be the supreme Law of the Land; and the Judges in every State shall be bound thereby, any Thing in the Constitution or Laws of any State to the Contrary notwithstanding.

The Senators and Representatives before mentioned, and the Members of the several State Legislatures, and all executive and Judicial Officers, both of the United States and of the several States, shall be bound by Oath or Affirmation, to support this Constitution; but no religious Test shall ever be required as a Qualification to any Office of public Trust under the United States.

Article VII

The Ratification of the Conventions of nine States, shall be sufficient for the Establishment of this Constitution between the States so ratifying the Same.

Done in Convention by the Unanimous Consent of the States present the Seventeenth Day of September in the Year of our Lord one thousand seven hundred and Eighty seven and of the Independence of the United States of America the Twelfth[†] IN WITNESS whereof We have hereunto subscribed our Names,

George Washington
President and Deputy from Virginia

Delaware
George Read
Gunning Bedford, Jr.
John Dickinson
Richard Bassett
Jacob Broom

Maryland
James McHenry
Daniel of St. Thomas Jenifer
Daniel Carroll

Virginia
John Blair
James Madison, Jr.

North Carolina
William Blount
Richard Dobbs Spraight
Hugh Williamson

South Carolina
John Rutledge
Charles Cotesworth Pinckney
Charles Pinckney
Pierce Butler

Georgia
William Paterson
William Few
Abraham Baldwin

New Hampshire
John Langdon
Nicholas Gilman

Massachusetts
Nathaniel Gorham
Rufus King

Connecticut
William Samuel Johnson
Roger Sherman

New York
Alexander Hamilton

New Jersey
William Livingston
David Brearley
Jonathan Dayton

Pennsylvania
Benjamin Franklin
Thomas Mifflin
Robert Morris
George Clymer
Thomas FitzSimons
Jared Ingersoll
James Wilson
Gouverneur Morris

[†]The Constitution was submitted on September 17, 1787, by the Constitutional Convention, was ratified by the Convention of several states at various dates up to May 29, 1790, and became effective on March 4, 1789.

Amendments to the Constitution

Amendment I

Congress shall make no law respecting an establishment of religion, or prohibiting the free exercise thereof; or abridging the freedom of speech, or of the press; or the right of the people peaceably to assemble, and to petition the Government for a redress of grievances.

Amendment II

A well regulated Militia being necessary to the security of a free State, the right of the people to keep and bear Arms, shall not be infringed.

Amendment III

No Soldier shall, in time of peace be quartered in any house, without the consent of the Owner, nor in time of war, but in a manner to be prescribed by law.

Amendment IV

The right of the people to be secure in their persons, houses, papers, and effects, against unreasonable searches and seizures, shall not be violated, and no Warrants shall issue, but upon probable cause, supported by Oath or affirmation, and particularly describing the place to be searched, and the persons or things to be seized.

Amendment V

No person shall be held to answer for a capital, or otherwise infamous crime, unless on a presentment or indictment of a Grand Jury, except in cases arising in the land or naval forces, or in the Militia, when in actual service in time of War or public danger; nor shall any person be subject for the same offense to be twice put in jeopardy of life or limb; nor shall be compelled in any criminal case to be a witness against himself, nor be deprived of life, liberty, or property, without due process of law; nor shall private property be taken for public use, without just compensation.

Amendment VI

In all criminal prosecutions, the accused shall enjoy the right to a speedy and public trial, by an impartial jury of the State and district wherein the crime shall have been committed, which district shall have been previously ascertained by law, and to be informed of the nature and cause of the accusation; to be confronted with the witnesses against him; to have compulsory process for obtaining witnesses in his favor, and to have the Assistance of Counsel for his defence.

Amendment VII

In Suits at common law, where the value in controversy shall exceed twenty dollars, the right of trial by jury shall be preserved, and no fact tried by a jury, shall be otherwise reexamined in any Court of the United States, than according to the rules of the common law.

Amendment VIII

Excessive bail shall not be required, nor excessive fines imposed, nor cruel and unusual punishments inflicted.

Amendment IX

The enumeration in the Constitution, of certain rights, shall not be construed to deny or disparage others retained by the people.

Amendment X*

The powers not delegated to the United States by the Constitution, nor prohibited by it to the States, are reserved to the States respectively, or to the people.

Amendment XI
[Adopted 1798]

The Judicial power of the United States shall not be construed to extend to any suit in law or equity, commenced or prosecuted against one of the United States by Citizens of another State, or by Citizens or Subjects of any Foreign State.

Amendment XII
[Adopted 1804]

The Electors shall meet in their respective states, and vote by ballot for President and Vice President, one of whom,

---

*The first ten amendments (the Bill of Rights) were ratified and their adoption was certified on December 15, 1791.

at least, shall not be an inhabitant of the same state with themselves; they shall name in their ballots the person voted for as President, and in distinct ballots the person voted for as Vice President, and they shall make distinct lists of all persons voted for as President, and of all persons voted for as Vice President, and of the number of votes for each, which lists they shall sign and certify, and transmit sealed to the seat of the government of the United States, directed to the President of the Senate;—The President of the Senate shall, in the presence of the Senate and House of Representatives, open all the certificates and the votes shall then be counted;—The person having the greatest number of votes for President, shall be the President, if such number be a majority of the whole number of Electors appointed; and if no person have such majority, then from the persons having the highest numbers not exceeding three on the list of those voted for as President, the House of Representatives shall choose immediately, by ballot, the President. But in choosing the President, the votes shall be taken by states, the representation from each state having one vote; a quorum for this purpose shall consist of a member or members from two-thirds of the states, and a majority of all the states shall be necessary to a choice. And if the House of Representatives shall not choose a President whenever the right of choice shall devolve upon them, before *the fourth day of March* next following, then the Vice President shall act as President, as in the case of the death or other constitutional disability of the President.— The person having the greatest number of votes as Vice President, shall be the Vice President, if such number be a majority of the whole number of Electors appointed, and if no person have a majority, then from the two highest numbers on the list, the Senate shall choose the Vice President; a quorum for the purpose shall consist of two-thirds of the whole number of Senators, and a majority of the whole number shall be necessary to a choice. But no person constitutionally ineligible to the office of President shall be eligible to that of Vice President of the United States.

Amendment XIII
[Adopted 1865]

Section 1

Neither slavery nor involuntary servitude, except as a punishment for crime whereof the party shall have been duly convicted, shall exist within the United States, or any place subject to their jurisdiction.

Section 2

Congress shall have power to enforce this article by appropriate legislation.

Amendment XIV
[Adopted 1868]

Section 1

All persons born or naturalized in the United States, and subject to the jurisdiction thereof, are citizens of the United States and of the State wherein they reside. No State shall make or enforce any law which shall abridge the privileges or immunities of citizens of the United States; nor shall any State deprive any person of life, liberty, or property, without due process of law; nor deny to any person within its jurisdiction the equal protection of the laws.

Section 2

Representatives shall be apportioned among the several States according to their respective numbers, counting the whole number of persons in each State, excluding Indians not taxed. But when the right to vote at any election for the choice of electors for President and Vice President of the United States, Representatives in Congress, the Executive and Judicial officers of a State, or the members of the Legislature thereof, is denied to any of the male inhabitants of such State, being twenty-one years of age, and citizens of the United States, or in any way abridged, except for participation in rebellion, or other crime, the basis of representation therein shall be reduced in the proportion which the number of such male citizens shall bear to the whole number of male citizens twenty-one years of age in such State.

Section 3

No person shall be a Senator or Representative in Congress, or elector of President and Vice President, or hold any office, civil or military, under the United States, or under any State, who, having previously taken an oath, as a member of Congress, or as an officer of the United States, or as a member of any State legislature, or as an executive or judicial officer of any State, to support the Constitution of the United States, shall have engaged in insurrection or rebellion against the same, or given aid or comfort to the enemies thereof. But Congress may by a vote of two-thirds of each House, remove such disability.

Section 4

The validity of the public debt of the United States, authorized by law, including debts incurred for payment of pensions and bounties for services in suppressing insurrection or rebellion, shall not be questioned. But neither the United States nor any State shall assume or pay any debt or obligation incurred in aid of insurrection or rebellion against the United States, or any claim for the loss or emancipation of any slave; but all such debts, obligations and claims shall be held illegal and void.

Section 5

The Congress shall have power to enforce, by appropriate legislation, the provisions of this article.

Amendment XV
[Adopted 1870]

Section 1

The right of citizens of the United States to vote shall not be denied or abridged by the United States or by any State on account of race, color, or previous condition of servitude.

Section 2

The Congress shall have power to enforce this article by appropriate legislation.

Amendment XVI

[Adopted 1913]

The Congress shall have power to lay and collect taxes on incomes, from whatever source derived, without apportionment among the several States, and without regard to any census or enumeration.

Amendment XVII

[Adopted 1913]

The Senate of the United States shall be composed of two Senators from each State, elected by the people thereof, for six years; and each Senator shall have one vote. The electors in each State shall have the qualifications requisite for electors of the most numerous branch of the State legislatures.

When vacancies happen in the representation of any State in the Senate, the executive authority of such State shall issue writs of election to fill such vacancies: *Provided,* That the legislature of any State may empower the executive thereof to make temporary appointments until the people fill the vacancies by election as the legislature may direct.

This amendment shall not be so construed as to affect the election or term of any Senator chosen before it becomes valid as part of the Constitution.

Amendment XVIII

[Adopted 1919, repealed 1933]

Section 1

After one year from the ratification of this article the manufacture, sale, or transportation of intoxicating liquors within, the importation thereof into, or the exportation thereof from the United States and all territory subject to the jurisdiction thereof for beverage purposes is hereby prohibited.

Section 2

The Congress and the several States shall have concurrent power to enforce this article by appropriate legislation.

Section 3

This article shall be inoperative unless it shall have been ratified as an amendment to the Constitution by the legislatures of the several States, as provided in the Constitution, within seven years from the date of the submission hereof to the States by the Congress.

Amendment XIX

[Adopted 1920]

The right of citizens of the United States to vote shall not be denied or abridged by the United States or by any State on account of sex.

Congress shall have power to enforce this article by appropriate legislation.

Amendment XX

[Adopted 1933]

Section 1

The terms of the President and Vice President shall end at noon on the 20th day of January, and the terms of Senators and Representatives at noon on the 3d day of January, of the years in which such terms would have ended if this article had not been ratified and the terms of their successors shall then begin.

Section 2

The Congress shall assemble at least once in every year, and such meeting shall begin at noon on the 3d day of January, unless they shall by law appoint a different day.

Section 3

If, at the time fixed for the beginning of the term of the President, the President elect shall have died, the Vice President elect shall become President. If a President shall not have been chosen before the time fixed for the beginning of his term, or if the President elect shall have failed to qualify, then the Vice President elect shall act as President until a President shall have qualified; and the Congress may by law provide for the case wherein neither a President elect nor a Vice President elect shall have qualified, declaring who shall then act as President, or the manner in which one who is to act shall be selected, and such person shall act accordingly until a President or Vice President shall have qualified.

Section 4

The Congress may by law provide for the case of the death of any of the persons from whom the House of Representatives may choose a President whenever the right of choice shall have devolved upon them, and for the case of the death of any of the persons from whom the Senate may choose a Vice President whenever the right of choice shall have devolved upon them.

Section 5

Sections 1 and 2 shall take effect on the 15th day of October following the ratification of this article.

Section 6

This article shall be inoperative unless it shall have been ratified as an amendment to the Constitution by the legislatures of three fourths of the several States within seven years from the date of its submission.

Amendment XXI

[Adopted 1933]

Section 1

The eighteenth article of amendment to the Constitution of the United States is hereby repealed.

Section 2

The transportation or importation into any State, Territory, or possession of the United States for delivery or use therein of intoxicating liquors in violation of the laws thereof, is hereby prohibited.

Section 3

This article shall be inoperative unless it shall have been ratified as an amendment to the Constitution by conventions in the several States, as provided in the Constitution, within seven years from the date of the submission hereof to the States by the Congress.

Amendment XXII
[Adopted 1951]
Section 1

No person shall be elected to the office of the President more than twice, and no person who has held the office of President, or acted as President, for more than two years of a term to which some other person was elected President shall be elected to the office of the President more than once. But this Article shall not apply to any person holding the office of President when this Article was proposed by the Congress, and shall not prevent any person who may be holding the office of President, or acting as President, during the term within which this Article becomes operative from holding the office of President or acting as President during the remainder of such term.

Section 2

This article shall be inoperative unless it shall have been ratified as an amendment to the Constitution by the legislatures of three-fourths of the several States within seven years from the date of its submission to the States by the Congress.

Amendment XXIII
[Adopted 1961]
Section 1

The District constituting the seat of Government of the United States shall appoint in such manner as the Congress shall direct:

A number of electors of President and Vice President equal to the whole number of Senators and Representatives in Congress to which the District would be entitled if it were a State, but in no event more than the least populous State; they shall be in addition to those appointed by the States, but they shall be considered, for the purposes of the election of President and Vice President, to be electors appointed by a State; and they shall meet in the District and perform such duties as provided by the twelfth article of amendment.

Section 2

The Congress shall have power to enforce this article by appropriate legislation.

Amendment XXIV
[Adopted 1964]
Section 1

The right of citizens of the United States to vote in any primary or other election for President or Vice President, for electors for President or Vice President, or for Senator or Representative in Congress, shall not be denied or abridged by the United States or any state by reason of failure to pay any poll tax or other tax.

Section 2

The Congress shall have the power to enforce this article by appropriate legislation.

Amendment XXV
[Adopted 1967]
Section 1

In case of the removal of the President from office or his death or resignation, the Vice President shall become President.

Section 2

Whenever there is a vacancy in the office of the Vice President, the President shall nominate a Vice President who shall take the office upon confirmation by a majority vote of both houses of Congress.

Section 3

Whenever the President transmits to the President pro tempore of the Senate and the Speaker of the House of Representatives his written declaration that he is unable to discharge the powers and duties of his office, and until he transmits to them a written declaration to the contrary, such powers and duties shall be discharged by the Vice President as Acting President.

Section 4

Whenever the Vice President and a majority of either the principal officers of the executive departments or of such other body as Congress may by law provide, transmit to the President pro tempore of the Senate and the Speaker of the House of Representatives their written declaration that the President is unable to discharge the powers and duties of his office, the Vice President shall immediately assume the powers and duties of the office as Acting President.

Thereafter, when the President transmits to the President pro tempore of the Senate and the Speaker of the House of Representatives his written declaration that no inability exists, he shall resume the powers and duties of his office unless the Vice President and a majority of either the principal officers of the executive department or of such other body as Congress may by law provide, transmit within four days to the President pro tempore of the Senate and the Speaker of the House of Representatives their written declaration that the President is unable to discharge the powers and duties of his office. Thereupon Congress shall decide the issue, assembling within 48 hours for that pur-

pose if not in session. If the Congress, within 21 days after receipt of the latter written declaration, or, if Congress is not in session, within 21 days after Congress is required to assemble, determines by two-thirds vote of both houses that the President is unable to discharge the powers and duties of his office, the Vice President shall continue to discharge the same as Acting President; otherwise, the President shall resume the powers and duties of his office.

Amendment XXVI
[Adopted 1971]

Section 1

The right of citizens of the United States, who are 18 years of age or older, to vote shall not be denied or abridged by the United States or any state on account of age.

Section 2

The Congress shall have the power to enforce this article by appropriate legislation.

Amendment XXVII
[Adopted 1992]

No law, varying the compensation for the services of the Senators and Representatives shall take effect, until an election of Representatives shall have intervened.

Presidential Election Maps, 1789–2004

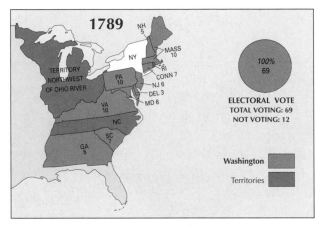

1789

ELECTORAL VOTE
TOTAL VOTING: 69
NOT VOTING: 12

100%
69

Washington

Territories

Each voting elector cast one of his two votes for Washington. New York failed to appoint its allotted eight electors in time and cast no electoral votes. North Carolina and Rhode Island did not vote because they had yet ratified the Constitution.

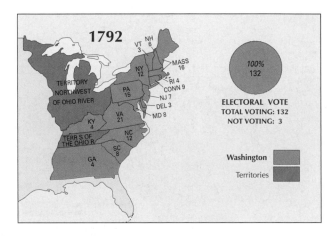

1792

ELECTORAL VOTE
TOTAL VOTING: 132
NOT VOTING: 3

100%
132

Washington

Territories

Each voting elector cast one of his two votes for Washington.

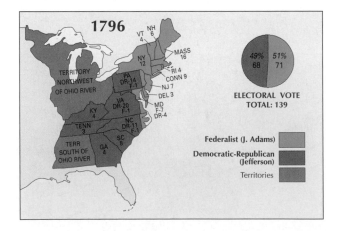

1796

ELECTORAL VOTE
TOTAL: 139

49%
68

51%
71

Federalist (J. Adams)

Democratic-Republican (Jefferson)

Territories

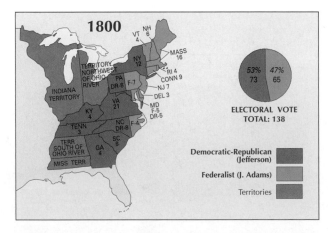

1800

ELECTORAL VOTE
TOTAL: 138

53%
73

47%
65

Democratic-Republican (Jefferson)

Federalist (J. Adams)

Territories

Democratic-Republican candidates Jefferson and Burr each received 73 electoral votes. The election was decided in the House of Representatives, where Jefferson was chosen President.

In the elections prior to 1804, each elector voted for two candidates for President. The candidate who received the largest number of votes, if that number was a majority, was declared President, and the candidate who received the second largest number of votes was declared Vice President.

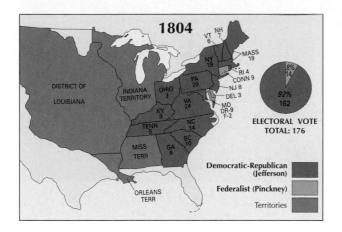

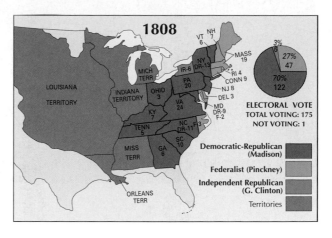

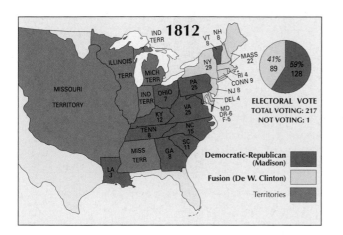

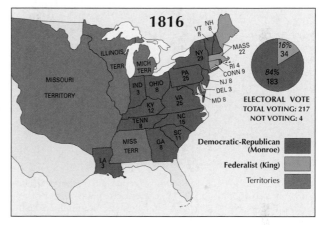

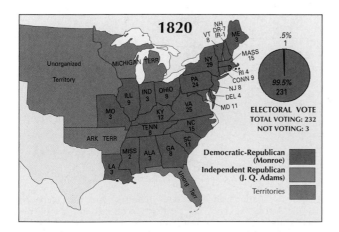

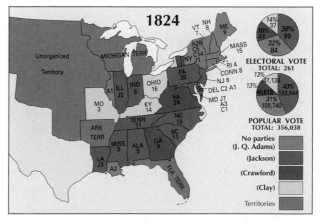

Because none of the candidates had a majority in the electoral college, the election was decided in the House of Representatives, where J.Q. Adams was chosen President.

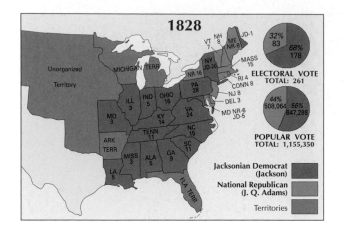

1828

Unorganized Territory

MICHIGAN TERR

VT 7
NH 8
ME NR-8
JD-1
MASS 15
NY JD-20 NR-16
RI 4
PA 28
CONN 8
NJ 8
DEL 3
MD NR-6 JD-5

ILL 3
IND 5
OHIO 16
VA 24
KY 14

MO 3
TENN 11
NC 15
SC 11

ARK TERR
MISS 3
ALA 5
GA 9

LA 5
FLA TERR

32% 83   68% 178

ELECTORAL VOTE
TOTAL: 261

44% 508,064   56% 647,286

POPULAR VOTE
TOTAL: 1,155,350

Jacksonian Democrat (Jackson)
National Republican (J. Q. Adams)
Territories

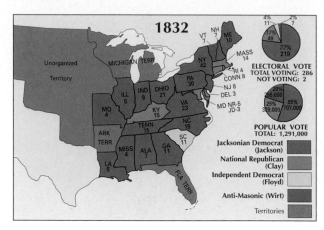

1832

Unorganized Territory

MICHIGAN TERR

VT 7
NH 7
ME 10
MASS 14
NY 42
RI 4
CONN 8
PA 30
NJ 8
DEL 3
MD NR-5 JD-3

ILL 5
IND 9
OHIO 21
VA 23
KY 15

MO 4
TENN 15
NC 15
SC 11

ARK TERR
MISS 4
ALA 7
GA 11

LA 6
FLA TERR

4% 11   2% 7
77% 49   27% 219

ELECTORAL VOTE
TOTAL VOTING: 286
NOT VOTING: 2

20% 265,000   55% 707,000
25% 329,000

POPULAR VOTE
TOTAL: 1,291,000

Jacksonian Democrat (Jackson)
National Republican (Clay)
Independent Democrat (Floyd)
Anti-Masonic (Wirt)
Territories

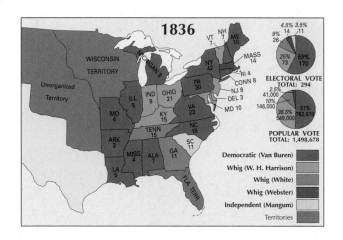

1836

WISCONSIN TERRITORY

MICHIGAN 3

Unorganized Territory

VT 7
NH 7
ME 10
MASS 14
NY 42
RI 4
CONN 8
PA 30
NJ 8
DEL 3
MD 10

ILL 5
IND 9
OHIO 21
VA 23
KY 15

MO 4
TENN 15
NC 15
SC 11

ARK 3
MISS 4
ALA 7
GA 11

LA 5
FLA TERR

4.5% 14   3.5% 11
9% 26
25% 73   58% 170

ELECTORAL VOTE
TOTAL: 294

2.5% 41,000
10% 146,000
36.5% 549,000   51% 762,678

POPULAR VOTE
TOTAL: 1,498,678

Democratic (Van Buren)
Whig (W. H. Harrison)
Whig (White)
Whig (Webster)
Independent (Mangum)
Territories

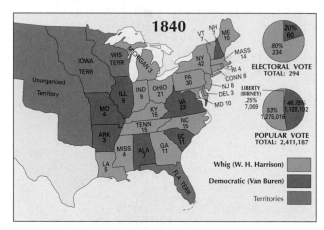

1840

IOWA TERR

WIS TERR

MICHIGAN 3

Unorganized Territory

VT 7
NH 7
ME 10
MASS 14
NY 42
RI 4
CONN 8
PA 30
NJ 8
DEL 3
MD 10

ILL 5
IND 9
OHIO 21
VA 23
KY 15

MO 4
TENN 15
NC 15
SC 11

ARK 3
MISS 4
ALA 7
GA 11

LA 5
FLA TERR

20% 60
80% 234

ELECTORAL VOTE
TOTAL: 294

LIBERTY (BIRNEY) .25% 7,069
53% 1,275,016   46.75% 1,128,102

POPULAR VOTE
TOTAL: 2,411,187

Whig (W. H. Harrison)
Democratic (Van Buren)
Territories

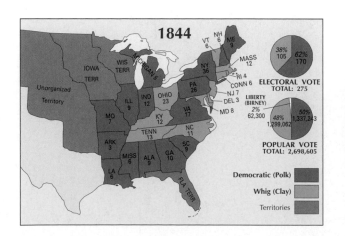

1844

IOWA TERR

WIS TERR

MICHIGAN 5

Unorganized Territory

VT 6
NH 6
ME 9
MASS 12
NY 36
RI 4
CONN 6
PA 26
NJ 7
DEL 3
MD 8

ILL 9
IND 12
OHIO 23
VA 17
KY 12

MO 7
TENN 13
NC 11
SC 9

ARK 3
MISS 6
ALA 9
GA 10

LA 6
FLA TERR

38% 105   62% 170

ELECTORAL VOTE
TOTAL: 275

LIBERTY (BIRNEY) 2% 62,300
48% 1,299,062   50% 1,337,243

POPULAR VOTE
TOTAL: 2,698,605

Democratic (Polk)
Whig (Clay)
Territories

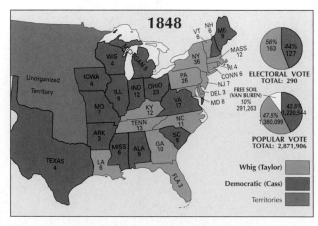

1848

IOWA 4

WIS 4

MICHIGAN 3

Unorganized Territory

VT 6
NH 6
ME 9
MASS 12
NY 36
RI 4
CONN 6
PA 26
NJ 7
DEL 3
MD 8

ILL 9
IND 12
OHIO 23
VA 17
KY 12

MO 7
TENN 13
NC 11
SC 9

ARK 3
MISS 6
ALA 9
GA 10

TEXAS 4
LA 6
FLA 3

56% 163   44% 127

ELECTORAL VOTE
TOTAL: 290

FREE SOIL (VAN BUREN) 10% 291,263
47.5% 1,360,099   42.5% 1,220,544

POPULAR VOTE
TOTAL: 2,871,906

Whig (Taylor)
Democratic (Cass)
Territories

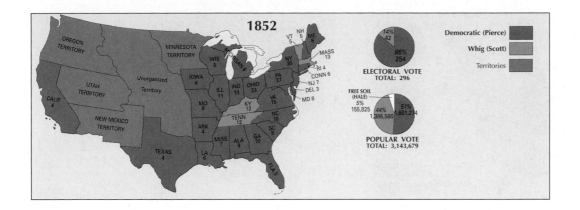

1852

Democratic (Pierce)
Whig (Scott)
Territories

ELECTORAL VOTE
TOTAL: 296

14%
42

86%
254

FREE SOIL (HALE)
5%
155,825

44%
1,386,580

51%
1,601,274

POPULAR VOTE
TOTAL: 3,143,679

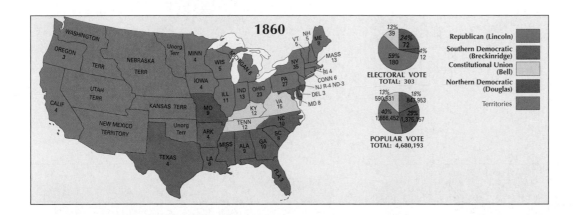

1856

Democratic (Buchanan)
Republican (Fremont)
American–Know Nothing–Whig (Fillmore)
Territories

ELECTORAL VOTE
TOTAL: 296

3%
8

38%
114

59%
174

POPULAR VOTE
TOTAL: 4,053,967

22%
874,534

33%
1,341,264

45%
1,838,169

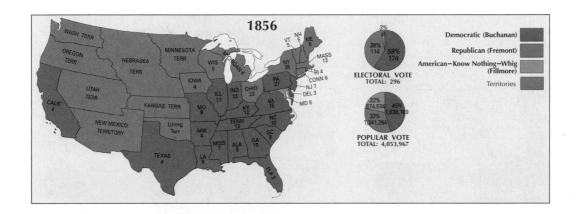

1860

Republican (Lincoln)
Southern Democratic (Breckinridge)
Constitutional Union (Bell)
Northern Democratic (Douglas)
Territories

ELECTORAL VOTE
TOTAL: 303

13%
39

24%
72

4%
12

59%
180

POPULAR VOTE
TOTAL: 4,680,193

13%
590,631

18%
848,953

40%
1,866,452

29%
1,375,157

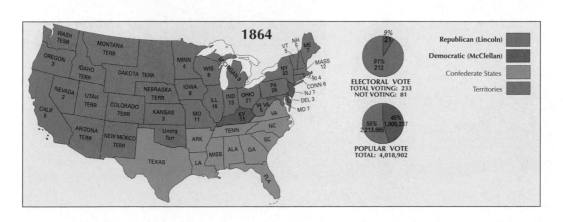

1864

Republican (Lincoln)
Democratic (McClellan)
Confederate States
Territories

ELECTORAL VOTE
TOTAL VOTING: 233
NOT VOTING: 81

9%
21

91%
212

POPULAR VOTE
TOTAL: 4,018,902

55%
2,213,665

45%
1,805,237

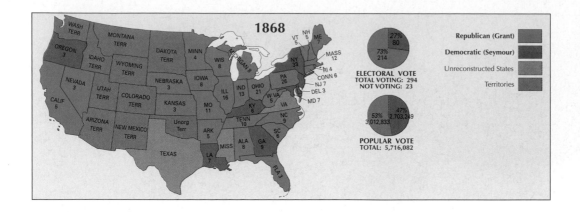

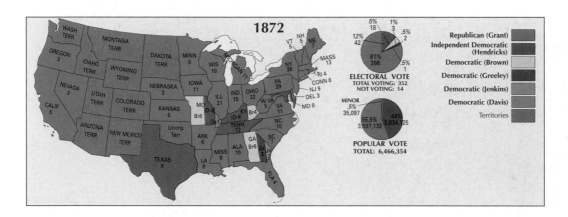

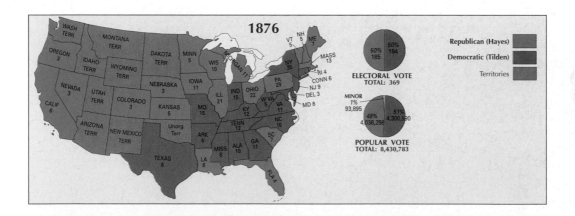

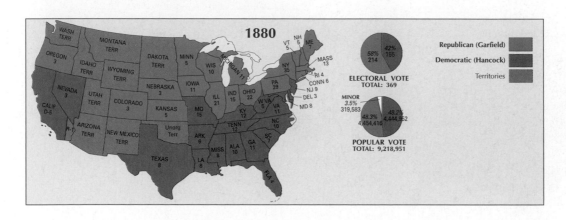

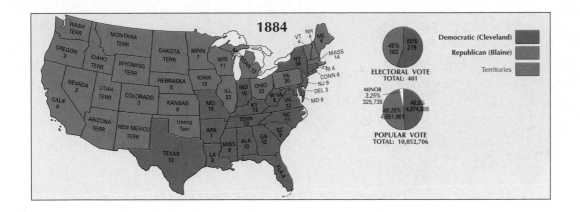

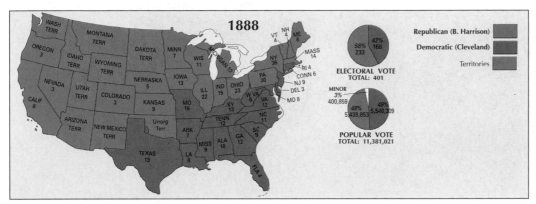

Republican candidate Harrison won the electoral vote but lost the popular vote to Democratic candidate Cleveland. Greer County (Oklahoma) voted as part of Texas.

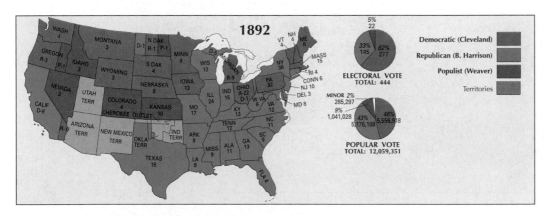

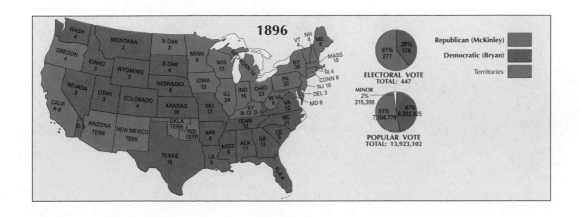

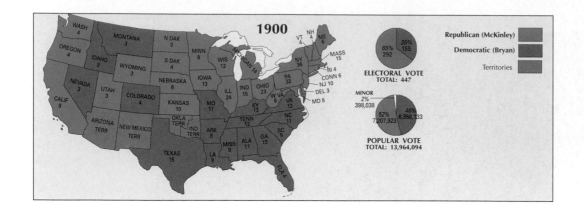

1900

Republican (McKinley)
Democratic (Bryan)
Territories

ELECTORAL VOTE
TOTAL: 447

65%
292

35%
155

MINOR
2%
398,038

52%
7,207,923

46%
6,358,133

POPULAR VOTE
TOTAL: 13,964,094

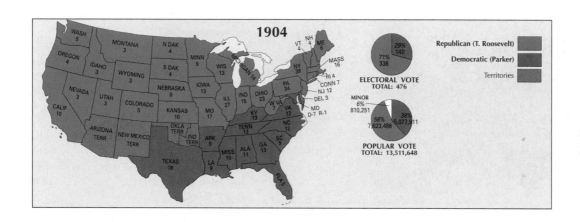

1904

Republican (T. Roosevelt)
Democratic (Parker)
Territories

ELECTORAL VOTE
TOTAL: 476

71%
336

29%
140

MINOR
6%
810,251

56%
7,623,486

38%
5,077,911

POPULAR VOTE
TOTAL: 13,511,648

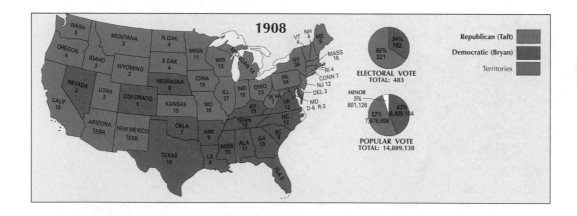

1908

Republican (Taft)
Democratic (Bryan)
Territories

ELECTORAL VOTE
TOTAL: 483

66%
321

34%
162

MINOR
5%
801,126

52%
7,678,908

43%
6,409,104

POPULAR VOTE
TOTAL: 14,889,138

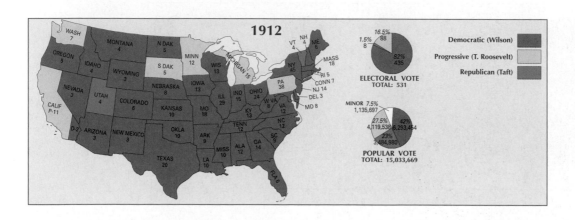

1912

Democratic (Wilson)
Progressive (T. Roosevelt)
Republican (Taft)

ELECTORAL VOTE
TOTAL: 531

82%
435

16.5%
88

1.5%
8

MINOR 7.5%
1,135,697

27.5%
4,119,538

42%
6,293,464

23%
3,484,980

POPULAR VOTE
TOTAL: 15,033,669

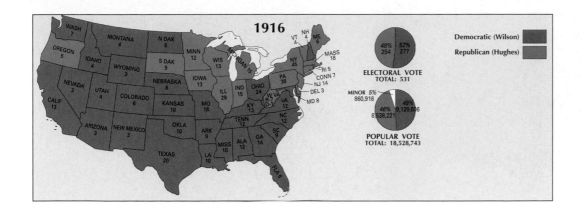

1916

Democratic (Wilson)
Republican (Hughes)

48% 254 | 52% 277

ELECTORAL VOTE
TOTAL: 531

MINOR 5%
860,916

46% 8,538,221 | 49% 9,129,606

POPULAR VOTE
TOTAL: 18,528,743

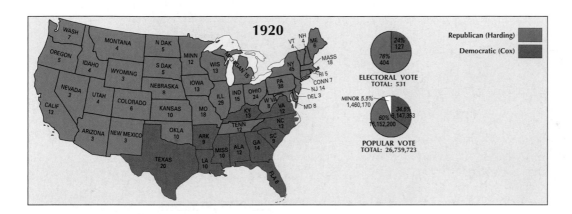

1920

Republican (Harding)
Democratic (Cox)

24% 127

76% 404

ELECTORAL VOTE
TOTAL: 531

MINOR 5.5%
1,460,170

60% 16,152,200 | 34.5% 9,147,353

POPULAR VOTE
TOTAL: 26,759,723

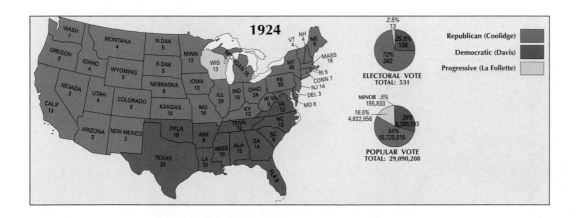

1924

Republican (Coolidge)
Democratic (Davis)
Progressive (La Follette)

2.5% 13

25.5% 136

72% 382

ELECTORAL VOTE
TOTAL: 531

MINOR .5%
155,833

16.5% 4,822,856 | 29% 8,386,503

54% 15,725,016

POPULAR VOTE
TOTAL: 29,090,208

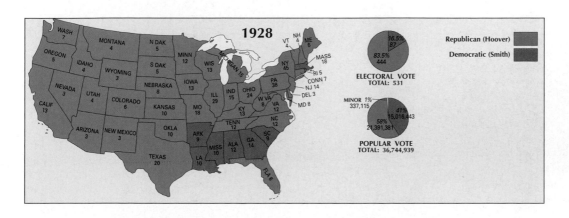

1928

Republican (Hoover)
Democratic (Smith)

16.5% 87

83.5% 444

ELECTORAL VOTE
TOTAL: 531

MINOR 1%
337,115

58% 21,391,381 | 41% 15,016,443

POPULAR VOTE
TOTAL: 36,744,939

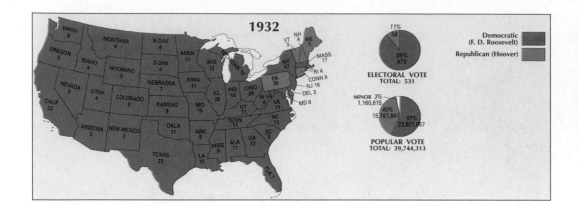

1932

11%
59

89%
472

ELECTORAL VOTE
TOTAL: 531

Democratic
(F. D. Roosevelt)
Republican (Hoover)

MINOR 3%
1,160,615

40%
15,761,841

57%
22,821,857

POPULAR VOTE
TOTAL: 39,744,313

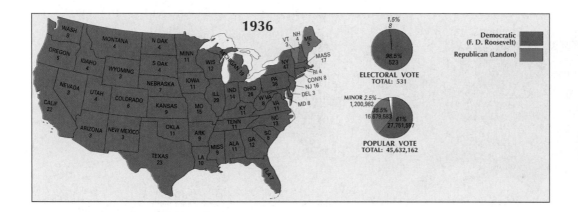

1936

1.5%
8

98.5%
523

ELECTORAL VOTE
TOTAL: 531

Democratic
(F. D. Roosevelt)
Republican (Landon)

MINOR 2.5%
1,200,982

36.5%
16,679,583

61%
27,751,597

POPULAR VOTE
TOTAL: 45,632,162

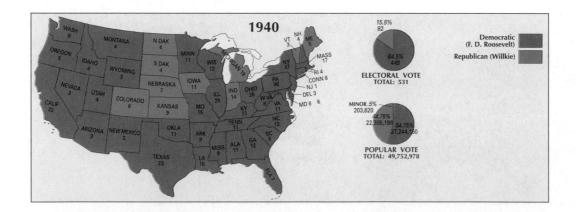

1940

15.5%
82

84.5%
449

ELECTORAL VOTE
TOTAL: 531

Democratic
(F. D. Roosevelt)
Republican (Willkie)

MINOR .5%
203,620

44.75%
22,305,198

54.75%
27,244,160

POPULAR VOTE
TOTAL: 49,752,978

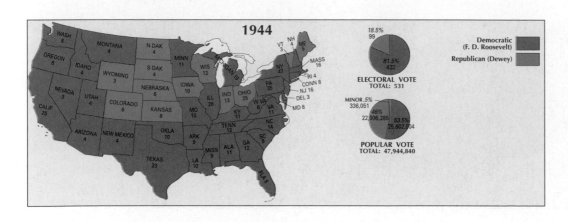

1944

18.5%
99

81.5%
432

ELECTORAL VOTE
TOTAL: 531

Democratic
(F. D. Roosevelt)
Republican (Dewey)

MINOR .5%
336,051

46%
22,006,285

53.5%
25,602,504

POPULAR VOTE
TOTAL: 47,944,840

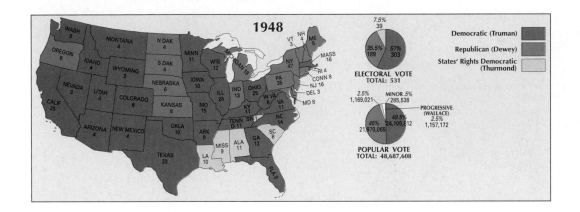

1948

ELECTORAL VOTE
TOTAL: 531

7.5%
39

35.5%
189

57%
303

POPULAR VOTE
TOTAL: 48,687,608

2.5%
1,169,021

MINOR .5%
285,538

45%
21,970,065

49.5%
24,105,812

PROGRESSIVE
(WALLACE)
2.5%
1,157,172

Democratic (Truman)
Republican (Dewey)
States' Rights Democratic
(Thurmond)

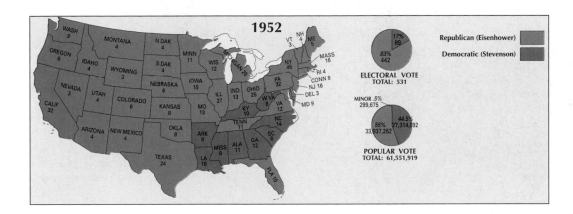

1952

ELECTORAL VOTE
TOTAL: 531

17%
89

83%
442

POPULAR VOTE
TOTAL: 61,551,919

MINOR .5%
299,675

55%
33,937,252

44.5%
27,314,992

Republican (Eisenhower)
Democratic (Stevenson)

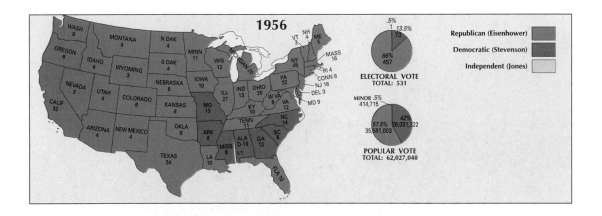

1956

ELECTORAL VOTE
TOTAL: 531

.5%
1

13.5%
73

86%
457

POPULAR VOTE
TOTAL: 62,027,040

MINOR .5%
414,715

57.5%
35,581,003

42%
26,031,322

Republican (Eisenhower)
Democratic (Stevenson)
Independent (Jones)

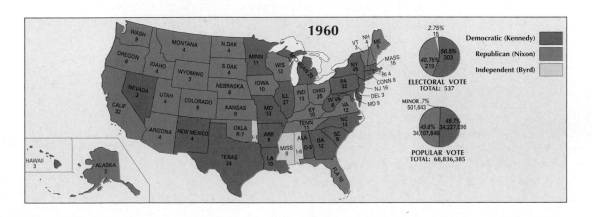

1960

ELECTORAL VOTE
TOTAL: 537

2.75%
15

40.75%
219

56.5%
303

POPULAR VOTE
TOTAL: 68,836,385

MINOR .7%
501,643

49.6%
34,107,646

49.7%
34,227,096

Democratic (Kennedy)
Republican (Nixon)
Independent (Byrd)

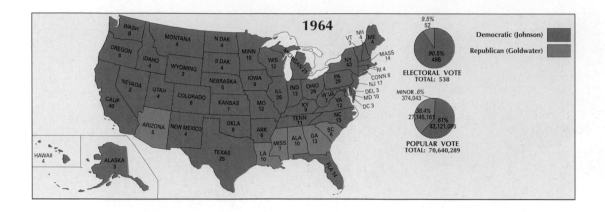

1964

9.5%
52

90.5%
486

ELECTORAL VOTE
TOTAL: 538

Democratic (Johnson)
Republican (Goldwater)

MINOR .6%
374,043

38.4%
27,145,161

61%
43,121,085

POPULAR VOTE
TOTAL: 70,640,289

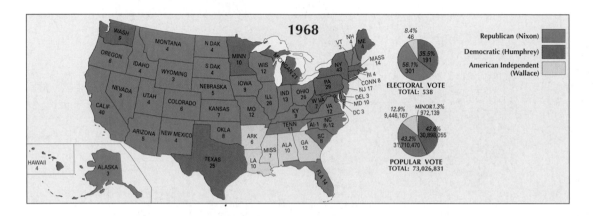

1968

8.4%
46

35.5%
191

56.1%
301

ELECTORAL VOTE
TOTAL: 538

Republican (Nixon)
Democratic (Humphrey)
American Independent (Wallace)

12.9%
9,446,167

MINOR 1.3%
972,139

42.6%
30,898,055

43.2%
31,710,470

POPULAR VOTE
TOTAL: 73,026,831

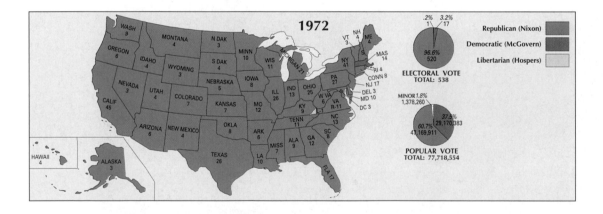

1972

.2%
1

3.2%
17

96.6%
520

ELECTORAL VOTE
TOTAL: 538

Republican (Nixon)
Democratic (McGovern)
Libertarian (Hospers)

MINOR 1.8%
1,378,260

37.5%
29,170,383

60.7%
47,169,911

POPULAR VOTE
TOTAL: 77,718,554

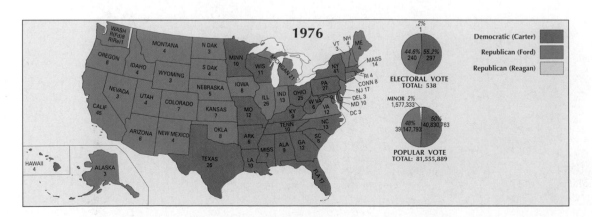

1976

.2%
1

44.6%
240

55.2%
297

ELECTORAL VOTE
TOTAL: 538

Democratic (Carter)
Republican (Ford)
Republican (Reagan)

MINOR 2%
1,577,333

48%
39,147,793

50%
40,830,763

POPULAR VOTE
TOTAL: 81,555,889

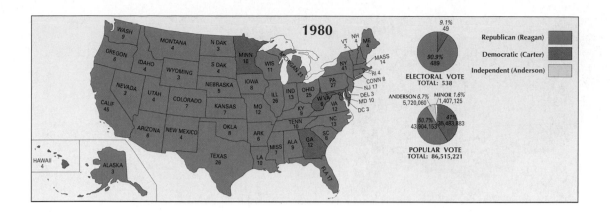

1980

ELECTORAL VOTE
TOTAL: 538

90.9%
489

9.1%
49

MINOR 1.6%
1,407,125

ANDERSON 6.7%
5,720,060

50.7%
43,904,153

41%
35,483,883

POPULAR VOTE
TOTAL: 86,515,221

Republican (Reagan)
Democratic (Carter)
Independent (Anderson)

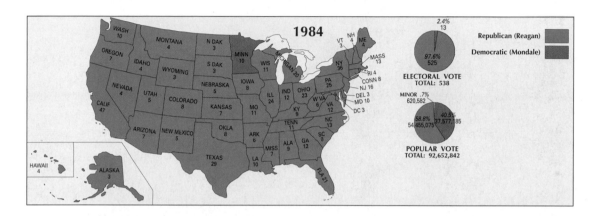

1984

ELECTORAL VOTE
TOTAL: 538

97.6%
525

2.4%
13

MINOR .7%
620,582

58.8%
54,455,075

40.5%
37,577,185

POPULAR VOTE
TOTAL: 92,652,842

Republican (Reagan)
Democratic (Mondale)

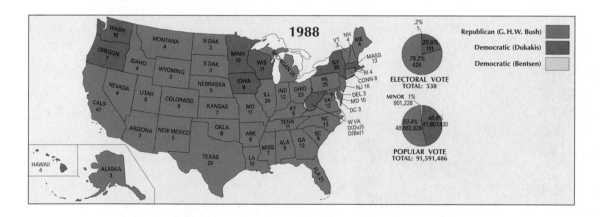

1988

ELECTORAL VOTE
TOTAL: 538

79.2%
426

20.6%
111

.2%
1

MINOR 1%
901,228

53.4%
48,882,828

45.6%
41,807,430

POPULAR VOTE
TOTAL: 91,591,486

Republican (G.H.W. Bush)
Democratic (Dukakis)
Democratic (Bentsen)

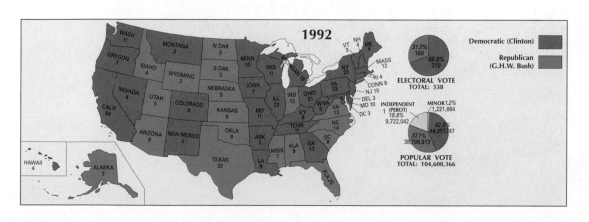

1992

ELECTORAL VOTE
TOTAL: 538

68.8%
370

31.2%
168

MINOR 1.2%
1,221,664

INDEPENDENT (PEROT)
18.8%
9,722,042

43%
44,857,747

37.1%
38,798,913

POPULAR VOTE
TOTAL: 104,600,366

Democratic (Clinton)
Republican (G.H.W. Bush)

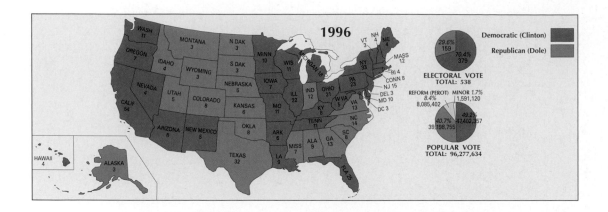

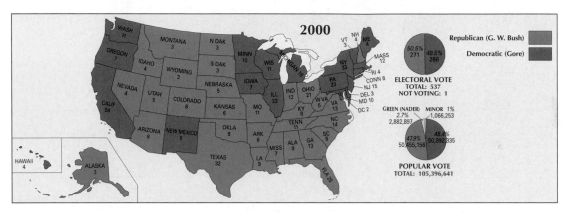

Republican candidate G. W. Bush won the electoral vote but lost the popular vote to Democratic candidate Gore. One elector from the District of Columbia abstained from voting.

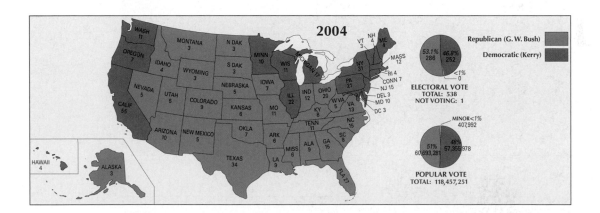

Picture Credits

Prologue: 2–3 Terrence Moore Photography. 5 Dorling Kindersely Media Library. 6 Jonathan Blair/Woodfin Camp & Associates. 7 © DD Bryant Photography. 9 Superstock, Florida. 10 © Jerry Jacka Photography. 12 Cahokia Mounds Historic Site. 14 © David Muench Photography. 15 Art Resource, NY.

Chapter 1: 18–19 Oroñoz Fotográfos. 22 The Bancroft Library, University of California. 24 Lee Bolton Picture Library/British Museum, London. 25 Oroñoz Fotográfos. 26 Dorling Kindersley Media Library. 28 Scala/Art Resource, NY. 29 National Trust/Art Resource, NY. 31 *Portrait of Pocahontas, Daughter of Powatan Chief* (detail), National Portrait Gallery, Smithsonian Institution/Art Resource, NY. 33 Plimoth Plantation/Courtesy of the Plimoth Plantation, Plymouth, MA. 35 Service Hydrographique de la Marine, Paris. 38 Farrell Grahan/National Geographic Images. 40 *Lord Baltimore with Grandson Cecilius Calvert* (detail), Enoch Pratt Free Library, Baltimore, MD. 41 *View of New Amsterdam (Hartger's View)*, Museum of the City of New York (29.100.792). 42 Benjamin West, *Penn's Treaty with the Indians* (detail), 1771–1772. Oil on canvas, 75-1/2 × 107-3/4". Courtesy of the Pennsylvania Academy of the Fine Arts, Philadelphia. Gift of Mrs. Sarah Harrison (The Joseph Harrison, Jr. Collection) (1878.1.10).

Chapter 2: 48–49 Eunice Bourne, *The Fishing Lady* (detail), Boston, Massachusetts, c. 1748. Embroidery, wool, silk and metallic yarns on linen, 20-1/2 × 43-1/2". Seth K. Sweester Fund (21.2233). Courtesy Musuem of Fine Arts, Boston. Reproduced with permission. © 2002 Museum of Fine Arts, Boston. All Rights Reserved. 50 Stone/Getty Images. 54 Werner Forman Archive/Art Resource, NY. 56 Library of Congress. 57 Library of Virginia. 59 Abby Aldrich Rockefeller Folk Art Museum, Williamsburg, VA. 61 Bishop Roberts, *Charleston Harbor*, Colonial Williamsburg Foundation. 63 Private Collection/Bridgeman Art Library. 64 Attributed to Freake-Gibbs, *The Mason Children— David, Joanna, & Abigail*, c. 1670, Fine Arts Museum of San Francisco. Gift of Mr. and Mrs. John D. Rockefeller 3rd (1979.7.3). 67 Photo by Mark Sexton/Peabody Essex Museum. 68 Unknown Boston painter, *Mrs. Elizabeth Freake and Baby Mary* (detail), c. 1670 Worcester Art Museum, Worcester, MA. Gift of Mr. and Mrs. Albert W. Rice. 69 Kobal Collection. 71 Unidentified artist, *Landscape (View of a Town)*, Worcester Art Museum, Worcester, MA. Gift of Dr. and Mrs. Kinnicut. 73 *Portrait of an Unidentified Woman (Formerly Edward Hyde, Viscount Cornbury)*, 18th century. © Collection of the New-York Historical Society (Acc. No. 1952.80).

Chapter 3: 78–79 *The Southeast Prospect of the City of New York* (detail), c. 1756–1757. © Collection of the New-York Historical Society (Acc. No. 904.1). 80 John Watson, *Portrait of Governor Lewis Morris*, Brooklyn Museum of Art, Dick S. Ramsay Fund and John Hill Morgan (43.196). 82 John Greenwood, *Sea Captains Carousing in Surinam*, 1758. St. Louis Art Museum, Purchase. 85 John Wallaston, *Portrait of George Whitfield*, c. 1742. The National Portrait Gallery, London. 87 Fenimore Art Museum, Cooperstown, NY. Richard Walker, photo. 88 White House Collection, © White House Historical Association. 91 John Vanderlyn, *Death of Jane McCrea*, 1803–1804. Wadsworth Athenaeum, CT. Purchase (1855.4). 93 *George Washington as Colonel of the Virginia Regiment*, 1772, by Charles Willson Peale, Washington-Curtis-Lee Collection, Washington and Lee University, Lexington, VA. 97 Getty Images. 99 Library of Congress. 100 Hartley Greens, England. 104 John Singleton Copley, *Samuel Adams* (detail), c. 1772. Oil on canvas, 49-1/2 × 39-1/2". Deposited by the City of Boston. Reproduced with permission. © 2002 Museum of Fine Arts, Boston. All Rights Reserved. 105 Courtesy of the Massachusetts Historical Society (MHS Image #: 67). 106 top, Library of Congress. 106 bottom, The Library Company of Philadelphia. 107 Thomas Birch, *Philadelphia: Second Street North from Market Street with Christ Church, 1799*. The Library Company of Philadelphia.

Chapter 4: 110–111 Winthrop Chandler, *The Battle of Bunker Hill* (detail), c. 1776–1777. Oil on canvas, 34-7/8 × 53-5/8". Gift of Mr. and Mrs. Gardner Richardson (1982.281). Courtesy Museum of Fine Arts, Boston. Reproduced with permission. © 2002 Museum of Fine Arts, Boston. All Rights Reserved. 112 Concord Museum, MA. 115 William Walcott, *Pulling Down the Statue of George III at Bowling Green* (detail), c. 1857. Lafayette College Art Collection, Pennsylvania. 117 Ganesvoort-Lansing Collection,

Collection, W. H. Jackson, WHJ-1410. 480 Tony Arruza/CORBIS. 484 Courtesy of Bethlehem Steel Corporation. 485 Library of Congress. 487 © Bettmannn/CORBIS. 489 © Collection of the New-York Historical Society. 492 The Biltmore Company. 492 Picture History. 493 © Bettmannn/CORBIS. 496 © Bettmannn/CORBIS. 497 © CORBIS. 499 North Wind Picture Archives.

Chapter 19: 502–503 Jacob Riis Collection/Museum of the City of New York. 506 Fred Hulstrand History in Pictures Collection, NDIRS-NDSU, Fargo, ND. 509 © Bettmannn/CORBIS. 511 The Granger Collection, New York. 513 National Park Service, Statue of Liberty Monument. 514 Library of Congress. 516–517 © Bettmannn/CORBIS. 518 Wisconsin Historical Society, Image ID: 26710. 519 Culver Pictures, Inc. 520 © Bettmannn/CORBIS. 521 Thomas Eakins, *Baseball Players Practicing* (detail), 1875. Watercolor; 10-7/8 × 12-7/8". Museum of Art, Rhode Island School of Design. Jesse Metcalf and Walter H. Kimball Funds. 523 Courtesy, Colorado Historical Society, F51020.

Chapter 20: 528–529 Winslow Homer, *Fox Hunt* (detail), 1893. Oil on canvas, 38 × 68-1/2". Pennsylvania Academy of Fine Arts, Philadelphia. Joseph E. Temple Fund (1894.4). 533 © Bettmann/Corbis. 535 Thomas Jefferson University, The Eakins Gallery. 537 Solomon D. Butcher Collection, Nebraska State Historical Society. 539 Library of Congress. 542 Philadelphia Museum of Art. Gift of Charles Bregler (1977-171-9). 542 *Swimming,* by Thomas Eakins, 1885. Oil on canvas. Purchased by the friends of Art, Forth Worth Art Association, 1925; acquired by the Amon Carter Museum, 1990, from the Modern Art Museum of Fort Worth through grants and donations from the Amon G. Carter Foundation, the Sid W. Richardson Foundation, and the Anne Burnett and Charles Tandy Foundation, Capital cities/ABC Foundation, Fort Worth Star-Telegram, The R. D. and Joan Dale Hubbard Foundation and the people of Fort Worth. Amon Carter Museum, Fort Worth, Texas. 544 Photofest. 545 Brown Brothers. 546 *Little Girl in a Blue Armchair,* 1878 (oil on canvas) (signature cropped), Cassatt, Mary Stevenson (1844–1926), Mellon College, National Gallery of Art, Washington, DC, USA, www.bridgeman.co.uk.

Chapter 21: 550–551 Library of Congress. 553 © CORBIS. 555 Brown Brothers. 556 The Granger Collection, New York. 557 Culver Pictures, Inc. 558 National Museum of American History, Smithsonian Institution. 559 Nebraska Historical Society, Solomon D. Butcher Collection [nbhips 10343]. 561 © CORBIS. 562 left, Kansas State Historical Society. 562 right, Kansas State Historical Society. 564 Culver Pictures, Inc. 568 The Granger Collection, New York.

Chapter 22: 572–573 Library of Congress. 574 Culver Pictures, Inc. 577 The New York Public Library, Astor, Lenox and Tilden Foundations. 579 Emma Goldman Papers/Library of Congress. 582 Courtesy of the Fogg Art Museum,

Harvard University Art Museums, on deposit from the Carpenter Center for the Visual Arts. 583 Culver Pictures, Inc. 584 The Schlesinger Library, Radcliffe Institute, Harvard University. 587 left, National Museum of American History, Smithsonian Institution. 587 right, Brown Brothers, Inc. 589 Library of Congress. 590 The Granger Collection, New York. 595 Brown Brothers, Inc. 597 Library of Congress. 599 National Portrait Gallery, Smithsonian Institution/Art Resource, NY.

Chapter 23: 602–603 Library of Congress. 605 left, *View of Canton,* c. 1860 (ink & w/c on paper), Tinqua (fl. 1860), Private Collection, www.bridgeman.co.uk. 605 right, Killie Family Papers/Presbyterian Historical Society, Presbyterian Church (USA) (Philadelphia). 607 Hawaii State Archives/Historical Records Branch. 610 The Granger Collection, New York. 611 Chicago Historical Society (ICHi-08428). 614 Vermont State House. 616 © Bettmann/CORBIS. 618 © Bettmann/CORBIS. 623 Dennis Kunkel/phototake. 625 Library of Congress.

Chapter 24: 628–629 The Art Archive/Imperial War Museum. 631 Imperial War Museum, London. 633 Brown Brothers, Inc. 634 Getty Images. 638 Culver Pictures, Inc. 639 Harry S Truman Library. 640 Library of Congress. 642 Photoworld/FPG International/Getty Images. 643 Courtesy of the Hagley Museum and Library. 644 © Bettmann/CORBIS. 645 Library of Congress. 648 © Bettmann/CORBIS. 649 The Granger Collection, New York. 652 left, Library of Congress. 652 right, Library of Congress. 655 Chicago Historical Society.

Chapter 25: 658–659 Jacob Lawrence, *Village Quartet* (detail), 1954. Courtesy of the artist and Francine Seders Gallery, Seattle, WA. © Gwendolyn Knight Lawrence, courtesy of Jacob and Gwendolyn Lawrence Foundation. 660 Culver Pictures, Inc. 662 Kobal Collection. 663 left, DN-0076798, Chicago Daily News negatives collection, Chicago Historical Society. 663 right, DN-0076751, Chicago Daily News negatives collection, Chicago Historical Society. 664 © Bettmann/CORBIS. 665 © Bettmann/CORBIS. 667 Getty Images. 668 Culver Pictures, Inc. 670 © Bettmann/CORBIS. 671 © Bettmann/CORBIS. 673 © Bettmann/CORBIS. 674 Kansas State Historical Society. 676 Photos12.com—Oasis. 678 Getty Images. 679 © Estate of Carl Van Vechten, Bruce Kellner. 681 Culver Pictures, Inc. 683 Courtesy of Special Collections and Archives, Wright State University.

Chapter 26: 686–687 Howard Thain, *The Great White Way—Times Square, New York City, 1925.* © The New-York Historical Society (Acc. No. 1963.150). 688 Library of Congress. 690 Library of Congress. 691 Getty Images. 694 AP/World Wide Photos. 698 © Bettmann/CORBIS. 701 © Bettmann/CORBIS. 702 University of Washington Libraries, Special Collections Division. 703 Library of Congress. 704 Library of Congress. 705 Franklin D. Roosevelt Library. 706 Library of Congress. 707 © Bettmann/CORBIS.

Chapter 27: 710–711 Isaac Soyer. *Employment Agency* (detail), 1937. Oil on canvas, 34-1/4 × 45" (87 × 114.3 cm). Whitney Museum of American Art. Purchase. Photography by Geoffrey Clements. 712 © Bettmann/CORBIS. 717 The Granger Collection, New York. 718 AP/Wide World Photos. 719 © Bettmann/CORBIS. 721 The Granger Collection, New York. 724 William C. Pryor/National Archives, Still Pictures Branch. 726 William Gropper/Vanity Fair, Condé Nast Publications, Inc. 727 © Bettmann/CORBIS. 728 Library of Congress. 729 Library of Congress, from *Cartoonist's Life* (Times Books, 1998). 730 Mandeville Special Collections Library, UCSD Libraries. 734 © Bettmann/CORBIS.

Chapter 28: 740–741 Library of Congress. 742 Superstock, New York. 744 Library of Congress. 745 Library of Congress. 746 Hulton/Archive/Getty Images. 747 Picture History. 749 National Archives. 750 Army Art Collection, U.S. Army Center of Military History. 752 © Bettmann/CORBIS. 753 Culver Pictures, Inc. 754 © Bettmann/CORBIS. 755 Photofest. 757 AP/Wide World Photos. 760 © Bettmann/CORBIS. 763 The Granger Collection, New York.

Chapter 29: 766–767 Edward Hopper, *Nighthawks* (detail), 1942. Oil on canvas, 84.1 × 152.4 cm. Friends of American Art Collection, 1942.51, © The Art Institute of Chicago. All Rights Reserved. 769 Getty Images. 773 AP/Wide World Photos. 776 © Bettmann/CORBIS. 777 Sovfoto/Eastfoto. 780 National Archives. 782 © Bettmann/CORBIS. 783 © Bettmann/CORBIS. 784 © CORBIS. 785 © Bettmann/CORBIS. 787 Elliot Erwitt/Magnum Photos, Inc. 789 © Bettmann/CORBIS.

Chapter 30: 794–795 CNAC/MNAM/Dist. Réunion des Musées Nationaux/Art Resource, NY. 796 Hulton/Archive/Getty Images. 797 akg-images. 798 © Bettmann/CORBIS. 800 AP/Wide World Photos. 802 © Bettmann/CORBIS. 803 © Bettmann/CORBIS. 809 AP/Wide World Photos. 811 © Bettmann/CORBIS. 812 Time Life Pictures/Getty Images. 813 Time Life Pictures/Getty Images. 814 © John Filo. 815 Magnum Photos, Inc. 818 Library of Congress, from Herblock: *A Cartoonist's Life* (Times Books, 1998).

Chapter 31: 824–825 © The School of the Art Institute of Chicago and the Brown Family. 827 © Harold M. Lambert/SuperStock. 830 Time Life Pictures/Getty Images. 831 © Bettmann/CORBIS. 832 © 2003 Andy Warhol Foundation for the Visual Arts/Artist Rights Society (ARS), NY. ™ Licensed by Campbell Soup Co. All Rights Reserved. 834 © Ian Berry/Magnum Photos. 836 AP/Wide World Photos. 838 Robert D./Black Star. 841 Getty Images. 843 © H. Diltz/CORBIS SYGMA. 844 © J. L. Atlan/CORBIS SYGMA. 845 © Bettmann/CORBIS. 848 Time Life Pictures/Getty Images.

Chapter 32: 852–853 Cindy Sherman, *Untitled* (detail), 1981. Courtesy the artist and Metro Pictures. 854 © S. Seitz/Woodfin Camp & Associates. 855 © Bettmann/CORBIS. 857 © Liaison/Getty Images. 858 © Charles Gatewood/The Image Works. 860 Courtesy: Jimmy Carter Library. 861 © Sipa Press. 862 Ronald Reagan Library. 866 AP/Wide World Photos. 868 SPL/Photoresearchers, Inc. 870 Getty Images. 873 Library of Congress/© 1986 by Herblock in *The Washington Post.*

Chapter 33: 876–877 © Sipa Press. 879 © Bob Daemmrich/The Image Works. 882 AP/Wide World Photos. 884 Getty Images. 888 Getty Images. 892 Getty Images. 895 AP/Wide World Photos. 897 left, © Reuters/CORBIS. 897 right, AP/Wide World Photos. 898 Hayne Palmour/Polaris Images. 899 LUKE FRAZZA/AFP/Getty Images. 900 Photodisc/Getty Images. 901 AFP/Getty Images.

INDEX

Note: Italicized letters *f, m,* and *n* following page numbers indicate figures (photos, illustrations, and graphs), maps, and footnotes, respectively.

Primary Source Documents

How to Analyze Primary Source Documents

Historians study sources to reconstruct the lifestyles and events of previous generations (what actually happened in the past), as well as to understand the past as the people who lived it did—to examine their ideas and thoughts about the world. By using sources, historians actually recreate history. They craft an understanding of the people, events, ideas, trends, and themes of the past based upon interpretation of those sources.

Primary sources are generally firsthand accounts or records. They may have been written or created during the time period under investigation, or perhaps were written by someone who lived then. Most crucially, they have not been interpreted by anyone else, though they may offer interpretations of the events they describe.

The primary source documents presented here give you the opportunity to put your investigative skills to the test by analyzing the sources yourself, rather than by reading others' interpretations.

WHEN ANALYZING A PRIMARY SOURCE, YOU SHOULD ASK SEVEN KEY QUESTIONS

1. **Who is the author?**
   Who wrote or created this? Is there a single or multiple authors? An author's identity sometimes helps you answer the later questions.

2. **What type of source is this?**
   All the sources here are documents, but what type? Is it a biography or a government document? This is a simple but crucial step because you must consider what you can expect to learn from the document.

3. **What is the message of this source?**
   What is the author describing? What is happening in the text? What is the story?

4. **Who is the intended audience?**
   Who is the author addressing? Was the source intended for private or public consumption? Identifying the audience will help you answer the next question.

5. **Why was this source created?**
   Does the author have an agenda, a larger purpose? Is the author trying to persuade the audience? Is the document or source simply a compilation of facts, or does it include opinion, inference, or interpretation?

6. **Is this source credible and accurate?**
   Historians must examine every source with a critical eye. What do you know about the author? Does the document make sense? Do the facts presented by the author or what you know about the time period support the thesis, statement, assertion, or story the author is conveying? Why should you trust, or distrust, this source?

7. **How is this source valuable to me?**
   How does the source relate to other sources from the time period or along the same issue or theme? Does it support or contradict them? Does it repeat information from other sources or add new information? How relevant is the source to your topic of inquiry? Does it extensively cover your topic, or only marginally or not at all? Remember, you should explore enough sources to obtain a variety of viewpoints.

Let's take a look at a portion of the document from Chapter 16 to see how this process works. Reading the full document selection, of course, provides even more clues to understanding this source.

DOCUMENT 16.1
Carl Schurz, *Report on the Condition of the South* (1865)

Carl Schurz was a German immigrant who rose to great political prominence in the United States. He was a leading member of the Republican Party from its founding and was a great supporter of Lincoln. During the Civil War he attained the rank of major general. After the war, Schurz continued to be active in politics, supporting many reform movements. In addition, he was writer and editor for several English- and German-language newspapers, and he wrote several books. In 1865 President Andrew Johnson sent Schurz to tour the South in order to report on its postwar status. An excerpt from Schurz's report appears below. The president was not pleased with the report.

We ought to keep in view, above all, the nature of the problem which is to be solved. As to what is commonly termed "reconstruction," it is not only the political machinery of the States and their constitutional relations to the general government, but the whole organism of southern society that must be reconstructed, or rather constructed anew, so as to bring it in harmony with the rest of American society. The difficulties of this task are not to be considered overcome when the people of the south take the oath of allegiance and elect governors and legislatures and members of Congress, and militia captains. That this would be done had become certain as soon as the surrenders of the southern armies had made further resistance impossible, and nothing in the world was left, even to the most uncompromising rebel, but to submit or to emigrate. It was also natural that they should avail themselves of every chance offered them to resume control of their home affairs and to regain their influence in the Union. But this can hardly be called the first step towards the solution of the true problem, and

it is a fair question to ask, whether the hasty gratification of their desire to resume such control would not create new embarrassments.

NOW LET'S LOOK AT WHAT WE CAN LEARN FROM THIS TEXT

1. **Who is the author?**

   From the head note, we know that Carl Schurz was a Republican politician, a Union officer in the Civil War, a German immigrant, and an author.

2. **What type of source is this?**

   This is an official government report commissioned by President Johnson.

3. **What is the message of this source?**

   In this first paragraph, Schurz is describing the potential difficulties of "reconstructing" the South after the Civil War. He is presenting what he perceives to be the goal of Reconstruction (to bring the South "in harmony with the rest of American society") as well as the potential pitfalls of quickly returning the southern states to the control of former Confederates ("creat[ing] new embarrassments").

4. **Who is the intended audience?**

   Schurz's primary audience is President Johnson, who commissioned the tour and report. You should consider, however, that since it was commissioned by a government official, other members of the government may have had access to it as well. The head note does not tell us if it was published for the public at large. Some minimal additional research, however, would confirm that it was published as a U.S. Senate Executive Document for the 1st session of the 39th Congress.

5. **Why was this source created?**

   In the very first sentence, Schurz presents Reconstruction as "the problem which is to be solved." From this statement we can infer that he felt his duty was not only to report on the "condition of the South," as described in the title, but to present his interpretation of the primary problems facing the nation as well as possible solutions.

6. **Is this source credible and accurate?**

   Though this is a government document, we must remember that Schurz likely could not be considered an impartial observer. He was from the North, was a Republican (the head note identifies him as "a great supporter of Lincoln"), and had fought in the Civil War. The overall tone of this paragraph, however, is very matter-of-fact. This may be attributable to Schurz's experience as a writer and editor. But we also know, from answering question 5, that Schurz felt his job was to do more than simply report. He framed his report in the form of problems and solutions. You must decide if these factors affected Schurz's credibility and accuracy as an observer of the conditions of the South in 1865. Here is the opportunity to begin to craft your interpretation of Reconstruction.

7. **How is this source valuable to you?**

   You must place the source within the context of your own research. Here are a few examples.

   This source would be an invaluable central component if you were researching:
   - firsthand accounts of the conditions in the South following the Civil War
   - a biographical paper on Carl Schurz

   It would be an important part of a paper on:
   - the various stages of Reconstruction
   - the disagreements between President Johnson and members of the Republican Party

   It would be crucial background information if you were researching:
   - Andrew Johnson's presidency
   - the return of Democratic rule in the former Confederacy

You now have the basic tools to begin analyzing historical documents yourself. As you apply these skills to the documents contained here, you will likely find that your skill level will rapidly increase. You may even find yourself reading others' interpretations of primary source documents with a more critical eye.

DOCUMENT P.1
Pima Creation Story (Traditional—Ancient)

The Pima lived in the Arizona Desert along the Gila and Salt Rivers, a remote location that helped them resist European influence. They were named "Pima" in the fifteenth century by the Spanish, who later recorded their first narratives. However, no creation stories were transcribed until the early twentieth century when a Pima named Edward H. Wood met J. W. Lloyd at the Pan-American Fair in Buffalo and asked his help in preserving the legends of Wood's grand-uncle, Thin Leather. The Pima creation story takes us to a landscape on the other side of the North American continent, to a people who favored stability, settlement, and peace and whose artistic traditions were long and rich.

In the beginning there was no earth, no water—nothing. There was only a Person, Juh-wert-a-Mah-kai, "The Doctor of the Earth."

He just floated, for there was no place for him to stand upon. There was no sun, no light, and he just floated about in the darkness, which was Darkness itself.

He wandered around in the nowhere till he thought he had wandered enough. Then he rubbed on his breast and rubbed out moah-haht-tack, that is, perspiration, or "greasy earth." This he rubbed out on the palm of his hand and held out. It tipped over three times, but the fourth time it stayed straight in the middle of the air and there it remains now as the world.

The first bush he created was the greasewood bush.

And he made ants, little tiny ants, to live on that bush, on its gum which comes out of its stem.

But these little ants did not do any good, so he created white ants, and these worked and enlarged the earth, and they kept on increasing it, larger and larger until it at last was big enough for himself to rest upon.

Then he created a Person. He made him out of his eye, out of the shadow of his eyes, to assist him, to be like him, and to help him in creating trees and human beings and everything that was to be on the earth.

The name of this being was Noo-ee—the buzzard.

Noo-ee was given all power, but he did not do the work he was created for. He did not care to help Juh-wert-a-Mah-kai, but let him go by himself.

And so The Doctor of the Earth himself created the mountains and everything that has seed and is good to eat. For if he had created human beings first they would have had nothing to live on.

DOCUMENT ANALYSIS

1. How does this creation story differ from the traditions of the Judeo-Christian experience?

_____

_____

_____

2. Does every society have a creation story/tradition? Give some examples.

_____

_____

_____

DOCUMENT P.2
Iroquois Creation Story (Traditional—Ancient)

The original homeland of the Iroquois was in upstate New York between the Adirondack Mountains and Niagara Falls. Through conquest and migration, the Iroquois gained control of most of the northeastern United States and eastern Canada. At its maximum in 1680, their empire extended west from the north shore of Chesapeake Bay through Kentucky to the junction of the Ohio and Mississippi Rivers. The following is an excerpt of the tribe's creation story.

Among the ancients there were two worlds in existence. The lower world was in great darkness—the possession of the great monster—but the upper world was inhabited by mankind; and there was a woman conceived who would have the twins born. When her travail drew near and her situation seemed to produce a great distress on her mind, she was induced by some of her relations to lay herself on a mattress which was prepared so as to gain refreshments for her wearied body. While she was asleep the very place sunk down towards the dark world.

The monsters of the great water were alarmed at her appearance of descending to the lower world. In consequence all the species of the creatures were immediately collected into where it was expected she would fall. When the monsters were assembled they made consultation, and one of them was appointed in haste to search the great deep in order to procure some earth, if it could be obtained. Accordingly the monster descends, succeeds, and returns to the place. Another requisition was presented: who would be capable to secure the woman from the terrors of the great water? None was able to comply until a great turtle came forward and proposed to endure her lasting weight. A small quantity of earth was varnished on the back part of the turtle. The woman alights on the seat prepared, and she receives a satisfaction.

While holding her, the turtle increased every moment and became a considerable island of earth, and apparently covered with great bushes. The woman remained in a state of unlimited darkness, and she was overtaken by her travail. While she was in the limits of distress one of the infants in her womb was moved by an evil opinion and he was determined to pass out under the side of the parent's arm, and the other infant in vain endeavored to prevent his design. The woman was in a painful condition during their disputes and the infants entered the dark world by compulsion, and their parent expired in a few moments. They had the power of sustenance without a nurse, and remained in the dark regions.

After a time the turtle increased to a great island and the infants were grown up, and one of them possessed a gentle disposition and was named Eni-gorio, or "the good mind." The other youth possessed an insolence of character and was named Enigon-ha-het-gea, or "the bad mind." The good mind was not content to remain in a dark situation and he was anxious to create a great light in the dark world; but the bad mind was desirous that the world should remain in a natural state. The good mind took the parent's head, of which he created an orb and established it in the center of the firmament, and it became of a very superior nature to bestow light to the new world—now, the sun. And again, he took the remnant of the body and formed another orb which was inferior to the light—now, the moon.

Whenever the light extended to the dark world the monsters were displeased and immediately concealed themselves in the deep places. The good mind continued the works of creation, and he formed numerous creeks and rivers on the Great Island, and then created numerous species of animals of the smallest and the greatest to inhabit the forests, and fishes of all kinds to inhabit the waters.

DOCUMENT ANALYSIS

1. Which sea animal was crucial to the creation of the world?

_____

_____

_____

2. From where does the sun come in the Iroquois legend?

_____

_____

_____

DOCUMENT 1.1
Captain John Smith, President in Virginia, to the Treasurer and Council of the Virginia Company, from Smith's *The Generall Historie of Virginia* (1624)

Virginia was the first and, for a time, the only English colony in the continental New World. Its boundaries spread as far to the north and west as its early explorers could imagine. In the document reproduced below, Virginia's president, John Smith, reports to the council of the underwriting Virginia Company to clarify some points and plead for a more rational approach to manpower and future shipments of provisions.

Right Honorable, &c.

I received your letter, wherein you write, that our minds are so set upon faction, and idle conceits in dividing the country without your consents, and that we feed you but with ifs and ands, hopes, and some few proofs; as if we would keep the mystery of the business to ourselves: and that we must expressly follow your instructions sent by Captain Newport: the charge of whose voyage amounts to near two thousand pounds, the which if we cannot defray by the ships' return, we are like to remain as banished men. To these particulars I humbly entreat your pardons if I offend you with my rude answer.

For our factions, unless you would have me run away and leave the country, I cannot prevent them: because I do make many stay that would else fly any whither. For the idle letter sent to my Lord of Salisbury, by the President and his confederates, for dividing the country &c. What it was I know not, for you saw no hand of mine to it; nor ever dreamed I of any such matter. That we feed you with hopes, &c. Though I be no scholar, I am past a school-boy; and I desire but to know, what either you, and these here, do know but that I have learned to tell you by the continual hazard of my life. I have not concealed from you anything I know; but I fear some cause you to believe much more than is true. . .

For the charge of this voyage of two or three thousand pounds, we have not received the value of a hundred pounds. And for the quartered boat to be borne by the soldiers over the falls, Newport had 120 of the best men he could choose. If he had burnt her to ashes, one might have carried her in a bag; but as she is, five hundred cannot, to a navigable place above the falls. And for him at that time to find in the South Sea, a mine of gold, or any of them sent by Sir Walter Raleigh; at our consultation I told them was as likely as the rest. But during this great discovery of thirty miles, (which might as well have been done by one man, and much more, for the value of a pound of copper at a seasonable time) they had the pinnace and all the boats with them, but one that remained with me to serve the fort.

In their absence I followed the new begun works of pitch and tar, glass, soap ashes, and clapboard; whereof some small quantities we have sent you. But if you rightly consider, what an infinite toil it is in Russia and Swethland [Sweden], where the woods are proper for naught else, and though there by the help both of man and beast in those ancient commonwealths, which many a hundred years have used it; yet thousands of those poor people can scarce get necessaries to live, but from hand to mouth. And though your factors there can buy as much in a week as will fraught you a ship, or as much as you please; you must not expect from us any such matter, which are but a many of ignorant, miserable souls, that are scarce able to get wherewith to live, and defend ourselves against the inconstant savages: finding but here and there a tree fit for the purpose, and want all things else the Russians have.

. . . From your ship we have not provision in victuals worth twenty pound, and we are more than two hundred to live upon this: the one half sick, the other little better. For the sailors (I confess) they daily make good cheer, but our diet is a little meal and water, and not sufficient of that. Though there be fish in the sea, fowls in the air, and beasts in the woods, their bounds are so large, they so wild, and we so weak and ignorant, we cannot much trouble them. . .

Now that you should know, I have made you as great a discovery as [Captain Newport], for less charge than he spendeth you every meal; I have sent you this map of the bay and rivers, with an annexed relation of the countries and nations that inhabit them, as you may see at large. Also two barrels of stones, and such as I take to be good iron ore at the least; so divided, as by their notes you may see in what places I found them.

. . . When you send again I entreat you rather send but thirty carpenters, husbandmen, gardners, fishermen, blacksmiths, masons, and diggers up of trees, roots, well provided; than a thousand of such as we have: for except we be able both to lodge them, and feed them, the most will consume with want of necessaries before they can be made good for anything.

Thus if you please to consider this account, and of the unnecessary wages to Captain Newport, or his ships so long lingering and staying here (for notwithstanding his boasting to leave us victuals for 12 months; though we had 89 by this discovery lame and sick, and but a pint of corn a day for a man, we were constrained to give him three hogsheads of that to victual him homeward) or yet to send into Germany or Poland for glassmen and the rest, till we be able to sustain ourselves and relieve them when they come. It were better to give five hundred pound a ton for those gross commodities in Denmark, than send for them hither, till more necessary things be provided. For in over-toiling our weak and unskillful bodies, to satisfy this desire of present profit, we can scarce ever recover ourselves from one supply to another.

And I humbly entreat you hereafter, let us know what we should receive, and not stand to the sailors' courtesy to leave us what they please; else you may charge us with what you will, but we not you with anything.

These are the causes that have kept us in Virginia, from laying such a foundation, that ere this might have given much better content and satisfaction; but as yet you must not look for any profitable returns: so I humbly rest.

DOCUMENT ANALYSIS

1. What was Smith's major complaint?

_____

_____

_____

2. Why were the colonists unable to fish and hunt for provisions?

_____

_____

_____

3. What general misconceptions did the treasury council seem to have concerning conditions in Virginia?

_____

_____

_____

DOCUMENT 1.2
John Winthrop, "A Model of Christian Charity" (1630)

When the first settlers came to Virginia they were faced with numerous hardships that nearly devastated their entire venture. In contrast, when the Puritans settled in Massachusetts in 1630 they experienced few major difficulties and grew into a thriving community. The major difference between these two colonies was in their leadership and organization. Specifically, the strict religious beliefs and firm authority of the Puritans' leader, John Winthrop, and the established order he created before arriving in America enabled the Puritans to meet the challenges of colonization better than the Virginia colonists did.

On board the ship Arabella, _Winthrop delivered the following sermon, entitled "A Model of Christian Charity." Notice how Winthrop portrayed their purpose in America as a divine mandate to serve as an example for the rest of the world._

God almighty in His most holy and wise providence hath so disposed of the condition of mankind, as in all times some must be rich, some poor, some high and eminent in power and dignity, others mean and in subjection.

Reason: First, to hold conformity with the rest of His works, being delighted to show forth the glory of His wisdom in the variety and difference of the creatures and the glory of His power, in ordering all these differences for the preservation and good of the whole.

Reason: Secondly, that He might have the more occasion to manifest the work of His spirit. First, upon the wicked in moderating and restraining them, so that the rich and mighty should not eat up the poor, nor the poor and despised rise up against their superiors and shake off their yoke. Secondly, in the regenerate in exercising His graces in them, as in the great ones, their love, mercy, gentleness, temperance, etc., in the poor and inferior sort, their faith, patience, obedience, etc.

Reason: Thirdly, that every man might have need of other, and from hence they might all be knit more nearly together in the bond of brotherly affection. From hence it appears plainly that no man is made more honorable than another, or more wealthy, etc., out of any particular and singular respect to himself, but for the glory of his creator and the common good of the creature, man.

Thus stands the cause between God and us. We are entered into covenant with Him for this work, we have taken out a commission, the Lord hath given us leave to draw our own articles, we have professed to enterprise these actions upon these and these ends, we have hereupon besought Him of favor and blessing. Now if the Lord shall please to hear us, and bring us in peace to the place we desire, then hath He ratified this covenant and sealed our commission, [and] will expect a strict performance of the articles contained in it, but if we shall neglect the observations of these articles which are the ends we have propounded, and dissembling with our God, shall fall to embrace this present world and prosecute our carnal intentions seeking great things for ourselves and our posterity, the Lord will surely break out in wrath against us, be revenged of such a perjured people, and make us know the price of the breach of such a covenant.

Now the only way to avoid this shipwreck and to provide for our posterity is to follow the counsel of Micah, to do justly, to love mercy, to walk humbly with our God. For this end we must be knit together in this work as one man, we must entertain each other in brotherly affection, we must be willing to abridge ourselves of our superfluities for the supply of others' necessities, we must uphold a familiar commerce together in all meekness, gentleness, patience, and liberality, we must delight in each other, make others' conditions our own, rejoice together, mourn together, labor and suffer together, always having before our eyes our commission and community in the work, our community as members of the same body. So shall we keep the unity of the spirit in the bond of peace.

The Lord will be our God and delight in all our ways, so that we shall see much more of His wisdom, power, goodness, and truth than formerly we have been acquainted with. We shall find that the God of Israel is among us, when ten of us shall be able to resist a thousand of our enemies, when He shall make us a praise and glory, that men shall say of succeeding plantations, the Lord make it like that of New England. For we must consider that we shall be as a city upon a hill, the eyes of all people are upon us. So that if we shall deal falsely with our God in this work we have undertaken and so cause Him to withdraw His present help from us, we shall be made a story and byword throughout the world, we shall open the mouths of enemies to speak evil of the ways of God and all professors for God's sake, we shall shame the faces of many of God's worthy servants, and cause their prayers to be turned into curses upon us till we be consumed out of the good land whither we are going.

And to shut up this discourse with that exhortation of Moses, that faithful servant of the Lord in His last farewell to Israel, Deut. 30., Beloved there is now set before us life and good, death and evil, in that we are commanded this day to love the Lord our God, and to love one another, to walk in His ways and to keep His commandments and His ordinance, and His laws, and the articles of our covenant with Him that we may live and be multiplied, and that the Lord our God my bless us in the land whither we go to possess it. But if our hearts shall turn away so that we will not obey, but shall be seduced and worship other Gods, our pleasures, our profits, and serve them, it is propounded unto us this day we shall surely perish out of the good land whither we pass over this vast sea to possess it. Therefore let us choose life, that we, and our seed, may live, and by obeying His voice, and cleaving to Him, for He is our life and our prosperity.

DOCUMENT ANALYSIS

1. To which biblical events did Winthrop compare the Puritan voyage? Why?

_____

_____

_____

2. What did Winthrop mean when he asserted that the new colony should be like a "city on a hill"? What, in his interpretation, was the duty of all the Puritan settlers?

_____

_____

_____

DOCUMENT 2.1
Alexander Falconbridge, The African Slave Trade (1788)

Alexander Falconbridge served as ship's surgeon on slaving ships during the latter half of the eighteenth century. During his voyages across the Atlantic, Falconbridge had occasion to observe the abhorrent treatment of the slaves at the hands of the crews. During one such voyage, Falconbridge wrote this account of the conditions on the ship, including his own views on the practice of slavery.

As soon as the wretched Africans, purchased at the fairs, fall into the hands of the black traders, they experience an earnest of those dreadful sufferings which they are doomed in future to undergo. And there is not the least room to doubt, but that even before they can reach the fairs, great numbers perish from cruel usage, want of food, travelling through inhospitable deserts, etc. They are brought from the places where they are purchased to Bonny, etc. in canoes; at the bottom of which they lie, having their hands tied with a kind of willow twigs, and a strict watch is kept over them. Their usage in other respects, during the time of passage, which generally lasts several days, is equally cruel. Their allowance of food is so scanty, that it is barely sufficient to support nature. They are, besides, much exposed to the violent rains which frequently fall here, being covered only with mats that afford but a slight defense; and as there is usually water at the bottom of the canoes, from their leaking, they are scarcely every dry.

Nor do these unhappying beings, after they become the property of the Europeans (from whom as a more civilized people, more humanity might naturally be expected), find their situation in the least amended. Their treatment is no less rigorous. The men Negroes, on being brought aboard the ship, are immediately fastened together, two and two, by handcuffs on their wrists, and irons riveted on their legs. They are then sent down between the decks, and placed in an apartment partitioned off for that purpose. The women likewise are placed in a separate room, on the same deck, but without being ironed. And an adjoining room, on the same deck is besides appointed for the boys. Thus are they placed in different apartments.

But at the same time, they are frequently stowed so close, as to admit of no other posture than lying on their sides. Neither will the height between decks, unless directly under the grating, permit them the indulgence of an erect posture; especially where there are platforms, which is generally the case. These platforms are a kind of shelf, about eight or nine feet in breadth, extending from the side of the ship towards the centre. They are placed nearly midway between the decks, at the distance of two or three feet from each deck. Upon these the Negroes are stowed in the same manner as they are on the deck underneath.

. . . About eight o'clock in the morning the Negroes are generally brought upon deck. Their irons being examined, a long chain, which is locked to a ring-bolt, fixed in the deck, is run through the rings of the shackles of the men, and then locked to another ring-bolt, fixed also in the deck. By this means fifty or sixty, and sometimes more, are fastened to one chain, in order to prevent them from rising, or endeavoring to escape. If the weather proves favorable, they are permitted to remain in that situation till four or five in the afternoon, when they are disengaged from the chain, and sent down.

. . . Upon the Negroes refusing to take sustenance, I have seen coals of fire, glowing hot, put on a shovel, and placed so near their lips, as to scorch and burn them. And this has been accompanied with threats, of forcing them to swallow the coals, if they any longer persisted in refusing to eat. These means have generally had the desired effect. I have also been credibly informed that a certain captain in the slave trade poured melted lead on such of the Negroes as obstinately refused their food.

Exercise being deemed necessary for the preservation of their health, they are sometimes obligated to dance, when the weather will permit their coming on deck. If they go about it reluctantly, or do not move with agility, they are flogged; a person standing by them all the time with a cat-o'-nine-tails in his hand for that purpose. Their music, upon these occasions, consists of a drum, sometimes with only one head; and when that is worn out, they do not scruple to make use of the bottom of one of the tubs before described. The poor wretches are frequently compelled to sing also; but when they do so, their songs are generally, as may naturally be expected, melancholy lamentations of their exile from their native country.

. . . On board some ships, the common sailors are allowed to have intercourse with such of the black women whose consent they can procure. And some of them have been known to take the inconstancy of their paramours so much to heart, as to leap overboard and drown themselves. The officers are permitted to indulge their passions among them at pleasure, and sometimes are guilty of such brutal excesses as disgrace human nature.

The hardships and inconveniences suffered by the Negroes during the passage are scarcely to be enumerated or conceived. They are far more violently affected by the seasickness than the Europeans. It frequently terminates in death, especially among the women. But the exclusion of the fresh air is among the most intolerable. For the purpose of admitting this needful refreshment, most of the ships in the slave trade are provided, between the decks, with five or six air-ports on each side of the ship, of about six inches in length, and four in breadth; in addition to which, some few ships, but not one in twenty, have what they denominate wind-sails. But whenever the sea is rough and the rain heavy, it becomes necessary to shut these, and every other conveyance by which the air is admitted. The fresh air being thus excluded, the Negroes' rooms very soon grow intolerably hot. The confined air, rendered noxious by the effluvia exhaled from their bodies, and by being repeatedly breathed, soon produces fevers and fluxes, which generally carries off great numbers of them.

. . . One morning, upon examining the place allotted for the sick Negroes, I perceived that one of them, who was so emaciated as scarcely to be able to walk, was missing, and was convinced that he must have gone overboard in the night, probably to put a more expeditious period to his sufferings. And, to conclude on this subject, I could not help being sensibly affected, on a former voyage, at observing with what apparent eagerness a black woman seized some dirt from off an African yam, and put it into her mouth, seeming to rejoice at the opportunity of possessing some of her native earth.

From these instances I think it may have been clearly deduced that the unhappy Africans are not bereft of the finer feelings, but have a strong attachment to their native country, together with a just sense of the value of liberty. And the situation of the miserable beings above described, more forcibly urges the necessity of abolishing a trade which is the source of such evils, than the most eloquent harangue, or persuasive arguments could do.

DOCUMENT ANALYSIS

1. What information does Falconbridge's account provide us about how Africans were taken into slavery, who participated in the African slave trade, and what role commerce and trade played in the slave trade system?

_____

_____

_____

2. How would Falconbridge's descriptions of the slave trade be of assistance to opponents of slavery?

_____

_____

_____

DOCUMENT 2.2
Gottlieb Mittelberger, On the Misfortune of Indentured Servants (1754)

Gottlieb Mittelberger emigrated to Pennsylvania from Germany in 1750 on a ship filled with poorer immigrants who would become indentured servants in Philadelphia. Mittelberger's own fortunes were not so bleak: he served as a schoolmaster and organist in Philadelphia for three years. He returned to Germany in 1754.

Both in Rotterdam and in Amsterdam the people are packed densely, like herrings so to say, in the large sea-vessels. One person receives a place of scarcely 2 feet width and 6 feet length in the bedstead, while many a ship carries four to six hundred souls; not to mention the innumerable implements, tools, provisions, water-barrels and other things which likewise occupy such space.

On account of contrary winds it takes the ships sometimes 2, 3, and 4 weeks to make the trip from Holland to England. But when the wind is good, they get there in 8 days or even sooner. Everything is examined there and the custom-duties paid, whence it comes that the ships ride there 8, 10 or 14 days and even longer at anchor, till they have taken in their full cargoes. During that time every one is compelled to spend his last remaining money and to consume his little stock of provisions which had been reserved for the sea; so that most passengers, finding themselves on the ocean where they would be in greater need of them, must greatly suffer from hunger and want. Many suffer want already on the water between Holland and Old England.

When the ships have for the last time weighed their anchors near the city of Kaupp [Cowes] in Old England, the real misery begins with the long voyage. For from there the ships, unless they have good wind, must often sail 8, 9, 10 to 12 weeks before they reach Philadelphia. But even with the best wind the voyage lasts 7 weeks.

But during the voyage there is on board these ships terrible misery, stench, fumes, horror, vomiting, many kinds of sea-sickness, fever, dysentery, headache, heat, constipation, boils, scurvy, cancer, mouth rot, and the like, all of which come from old and sharply salted food and meat, also from very bad and foul water, so that many die miserably.

Add to this want of provisions, hunger, thirst, frost, heat, dampness, anxiety, want, afflictions and lamentations, together with other trouble, as the lice abound so frightfully, especially on sick people, that they can be scraped off the body. The misery reaches the climax when a gale rages for 2 or 3 nights and days, so that every one believes that the ship will go to the bottom with all human beings on board. In such a visitation the people cry and pray most piteously.

Children from 1 to 7 years rarely survive the voyage. I witnessed misery in no less than 32 children in our ship, all of whom were thrown into the sea. The parents grieve all the more since their children find no resting-place in the earth, but are devoured by the monsters of the sea.

That most of the people get sick is not surprising, because, in addition to all other trials and hardships, warm food is served only three times a week, the rations being very poor and very little. Such meals can hardly be eaten, on account of being so unclean. The water which is served out of the ships is often very black, thick and full of worms, so that one cannot drink it without loathing, even with the greatest thirst. Toward the end we were compelled to eat the ship's biscuit which had been spoiled long ago; though in a whole biscuit there was scarcely a piece the size of a dollar that had not been full of red worms and spiders' nests.

At length, when, after a long and tedious voyage, the ships come in sight of land, so that the promontories can be seen, which the people were so eager and anxious to see, all creep from below on deck to see the land from afar, and they weep for joy, and pray and sing, thanking and praising God. The sight of the land makes the people on board the ship, especially the sick and the half-dead, alive again, so that their hearts leap within them; they shout and rejoice, and are content to bear their misery in patience, in the hope that they may soon reach the land in safety. But alas!

When the ships have landed at Philadelphia after their long voyage, no one is permitted to leave them except those who pay for their passage or can give good security; the others, who cannot pay, must remain on board the ships till they are purchased, and are released from the ships by their purchasers. The sick always fare the worst, for the healthy are naturally preferred and purchased first; and so the sick and wretched must often remain on board in front of the city for 2 or 3 weeks, and frequently die, whereas many a one, if he could pay his debt and were permitted to leave the ship immediately, might recover and remain alive.

The sale of human beings in the market on board the ship is carried out thus: Every day Englishmen, Dutchmen and High-German people come from the city of Philadelphia and other places, in part from a great distance, say 20, 30, or 40 hours away, and go on board the newly arrived ship that has brought and offers for sale passengers from Europe, and select among the healthy persons such as they deem suitable for their business, and bargain with them how long they will serve for their passage money, which most of them are still in debt for. When they have come to an agreement, it happens that adult persons bind themselves in writing to serve 3, 4, 5 or 6 years for the amount due by them, according to their age and strength. But very young people, from 10 to 15 years, must serve till they are 21 years old.

Many parents must sell and trade away their children like so many head of cattle; for if their children take the debt upon themselves, the parents can leave the ship free and unrestrained; but as the parents often do not know where and to what people their children are going, it often happens that such parents and children, after leaving the ship, do not see each other again for many years, perhaps no more in all their lives.

It often happens that whole families: husband, wife and children, are separated by being sold to different purchasers, especially when they have not paid any part of their passage money.

When a husband or wife has died at sea, when the ship has made more than half of her trip, the survivor must pay or serve not only for himself or herself but also for the deceased.

When both parents have died over half-way at sea, their children, especially when they are young and have nothing to pawn or pay, must stand for their own and their parents' passage, and serve till they are 21 years old. When one has served his or her term, he or she is entitled to a new suit of clothes at parting; and if it has been so stipulated, a man gets in addition a horse, a woman, or a cow. When a serf has an opportunity to marry in this country, he or she must pay for each year which he or she would have yet to serve, 5 or 6 pounds.

DOCUMENT ANALYSIS

1. What was indentured servitude like in the colonies? Was it much different from being a slave?

_____

_____

_____

DOCUMENT 3.1
Boston Gazette, Description of the Boston Massacre (1770)

The Boston Massacre took place on March 5, 1770, and was covered in detail by the Boston Gazette. *British troops had been stationed in the city since late 1768 to protect British customs officers and tensions between the soldiers and citizens of Boston had been building. The resulting clash between a group of citizens and soldiers on March 5 resulted in five civilian deaths, the removal of British troops from Boston, and trials for some of the soldiers involved. The Boston Massacre became a crucial element in anti-British propaganda in the colonies.*

. . . On the evening of Monday, being the fifth current, several soldiers of the 29th Regiment were seen parading the streets with their drawn cutlasses and bayonets, abusing and wounding numbers of the inhabitants.

A few minutes after nine o'clock four youths, named Edward Archbald, William Merchant, Francis Archbald, and John Leech, Jr., came down Cornhill together, and separating at Doctor Loring's corner, the two former were passing the narrow alley leading to Murray's barrack in which was a soldier brandishing a broad sword of an uncommon size against the walls, out of which he struck fire plentifully. A person of mean countenance armed with a large cudgel bore him company. Edward Archbald admonished Mr. Merchant to take care of the sword, on which the soldier turned round and struck Archbald on the arm, then pushed at Merchant and pierced through his clothes inside the arm close to the armpit and grazed the skin. Merchant then struck the soldier with a short stick he had; and the other person ran to the barrack and brought with him two soldiers, one armed with a pair of tongs, the other with a shovel. He with the tongs pursued Archbald back through the alley, collared and laid him over the head with the tongs. The noise brought people together; and John Hicks, a young lad, coming up, knocked the soldier down but let him get up again; and more lads gathering, drove them back to the barrack where the boys stood some time as it were to keep them in. In less than a minute ten or twelve of them came out with drawn cutlasses, clubs, and bayonets and set upon the unarmed boys and young folk who stood them a little while but, finding the inequality of their equipment, dis-

persed. On hearing the noise, one Samuel Atwood came up to see what was the matter; and entering the alley from dock square, heard the latter part of the combat; and when the boys had dispersed he met the ten or twelve soldiers aforesaid rushing down the alley towards the square and asked them if they intended to murder people? They answered "Yes, by God, root and branch!" With that one of them struck Mr. Atwood with a club which was repeated by another; and being unarmed, he turned to go off and received a wound on the left shoulder which reached the bone and gave him much pain. Retreating a few steps, Mr. Atwood met two officers and said, "Gentlemen, what is the matter?" They answered, "You'll see by and by." Immediately after, those heroes appeared in the square, asking "Where were the boogers? Where were the cowards?" But notwithstanding their fierceness to naked men, one of them advanced towards a youth who had a split of a raw stave in his hand and said, "Damn them, here is one of them." But the young man seeing a person near him with a drawn sword and good cane ready to support him, held up his stave in defiance; and they quietly passed by him up the little alley by Mr. Silsby's to King Street where they attacked single and unarmed persons till they raised much clamor, and then turned down Cornhill Street, insulting all they met in like manner and pursuing some to their very doors. Thirty or forty persons, mostly lads, being by this means gathered in King Street, Captain Preston with a party of men with charged bayonets, came from the main guard to the commissioner's house, the soldiers pushing their bayonets, crying, "Make way!" They took place by the custom house and, continuing to push to drive the people off, pricked some in several places, on which they were clamorous and, it is said, threw snowballs. On this, the Captain commanded them to fire; and more snowballs coming, he again said, "Damn you, fire, be the consequence what it will!" One soldier then fired, and a townsman with a cudgel struck him over the hands with such force that he dropped his firelock; and, rushing forward, aimed a blow at the Captain's head which grazed his hat and fell pretty heavy upon his arm. However, the soldiers continued the fire successively till seven or eight or, as some say, eleven guns were discharged.

DOCUMENT ANALYSIS

1. How does the author of this account describe the soldiers and pro-British persons? What adjectives does he use?

_____

_____

_____

2. Who are the "lads" in this account? How are they portrayed? What terms does the author use to describe them?

_____

_____

_____

3. Is the author of this account biased? If so, do his words and descriptions indicate that he is pro-British or anti-British?

_____

_____

_____

DOCUMENT 3.2
Benjamin Franklin on George Whitefield (1771)

Benjamin Franklin was one of America's foremost statesmen and scientists. A philosopher of the Enlightenment period, Franklin advocated the use of practical experimentation and reason in all areas of human existence. Despite this scientific orientation, Franklin found himself quite moved by the sermons of revivalist preacher George Whitefield, especially those that solicited funds for establishing an orphanage in the new colony of Georgia. This selection is excerpted from The Autobiography of Benjamin Franklin (1771).

In 1739 arriv'd among us from England the Rev. Mr. Whitefield, who had made himself remarkable there as an itinerant preacher. . . . The Multitudes of all Sects and Denominations that attended his Sermons were enormous, and it was matter of Speculation to me who was one of the Number, to observe the extraordinary Influence of his Oratory on his Hearers, and how much they admir'd & respected him, notwithstanding his common Abuse of them, by assuring them they were naturally half Beasts and half Devils. It was wonderful to see the Change soon made in the Manners of our Inhabitants; from being thoughtless or indifferent about Religion, it seem'd as if all the World were growing Religious; so that one could not walk thro' the Town in an Evening without Hearing Psalms sung in different Families of every Street. . . .

Mr. Whitefield, in leaving us, went preaching all the Way thro' the Colonies to Georgia. The Settlement of that Province had lately been begun; but instead of being made with hardy industrious Husbandmen accustomed to Labor, the only People fit for such an Enterprise, it was with Families of broken Shopkeepers and other insolvent Debtors, many of indolent & idle habits, taken out of the jails, who being set down in the Woods, unqualified for clearing Land, & unable to endure the Hardships of a new Settlement, perished in Numbers, leaving many helpless Children unprovided for. The Sight of their miserable Situation inspired the benevolent Heart of Mr. Whitefield with the idea of building an Orphan House there. . . .

Returning northward he preached up this Charity, & made large Collections; for his Eloquence had a wonderful Power over the Hearts and Purses of his Hearers, of which I myself was an Instance. I did not disapprove of the Design, but as Georgia was then destitute of Materials & Workmen, and it was propos'd to send them from Philadelphia at a great Expense, I thought it would have been better to have built the House here & Brought the Children to it. This I advis'd, but he was resolute in his first Project, and rejected my Counsel, and I thereupon refus'd to contribute. I happened soon after on one of his Sermons, in the Course of which I perceived he intended to finish with a Collection, & I silently resolved he should get nothing from me. I had in my Pocket a Handful of Copper Money, three or four silver Dollars, and five Pistoles in gold. As he proceeded I began to soften, and concluded to give the Coppers. Another Stroke of his Oratory made me asham'd of that, and determin'd me to give the Silver & he finished so admirably, that I empty'd my Pocket wholly into the Collector's Dish, Gold and all. At this Sermon there was also one of our Club, who being of my Sentiments respecting the Building in Georgia, and suspecting a Collection might be intended, had by Precaution emptied his Pockets before he came from home; towards the Conclusion of the Discourse, however, he felt a strong Desire to give, and apply'd to a Neighbor who stood near him to borrow some Money for the Purpose.

DOCUMENT ANALYSIS

1. How does Franklin explain the great impact that Whitefield's sermons had on him? How does Franklin fit his rational Enlightenment beliefs with Whitefield's evangelical religion of the Great Awakening?

_____

_____

_____

2. What kind of attitude does Franklin betray in his opinions of the new colony of Georgia?

_____

_____

_____

DOCUMENT 4.1
Joseph Warren, "Account of the Battle of Lexington" (1775)

In April 1775, following the battles at Lexington and Concord, Dr. Joseph Warren of Boston, a zealous champion of American liberty and president of the Massachusetts Provincial Congress, wrote an open letter to the British people giving the colonists' view of the events. It had been Warren who dispatched William Dawes and Paul Revere by separate routes to warn John Hancock, Samuel Adams, and other patriot leaders of the impending British march on Lexington.

MASSACHUSETTS.
IN PROVINCIAL CONGRESS
Watertown, April 26, 1775

TO THE INHABITANTS OF GREAT BRITAIN.

Friends and fellow subjects,

Hostilities are at length commenced in this colony, by the troops under command of general Gage; and it being of the greatest importance, that an early, true, and authentic account of this inhuman proceeding should be known to you, the congress of this colony have transmitted the same, and for want of a session of the hon. continental congress, think it proper to address you on this alarming occasion.

By the clearest depositions, relative to this transaction, it will appear, *that*, on the night preceding the 19th of April, instant, a body of the king's troops, under command of colonel Smith, were secretly landed at Cambridge, with an apparent design to take or destroy the military and other stores, provided for the defence of this colony, and deposited at Concord; that some inhabitants of the colony, on the night aforesaid whilst travelling peaceable on the road between Boston and Concord, were seized and greatly abused by armed men, who appeared to be officers of general Gage's army; that the town of Lexington, by these means, was alarmed, and a company of the inhabitants mustered on the occasion; that the regular troops, on their way to Concord, marched into the said town of Lexington, and the said company, on their approach, began to disperse; that notwithstanding this, the regulars rushed on with great violence, and first began hostilities, by firing on the said Lexington company, whereby, they killed eight, and wounded several others; that the regulars continued their fire until those of the said company, who were neither killed nor wounded, had made their escape; that colonel Smith, with the detachment, then marched to Concord, where a number of provincials were

again fired on by the troops, two of them killed and several wounded, before any of the provincials fired on them; and that these hostile measures of the troops produced an engagement that lasted through the day, in which many of he provincials, and more of the regular troops, were killed and wounded.

To give a particular account of the ravages of the troops, as they retreated from Concord to Charles Town, would be very difficult, if not impracticable; let it suffice to say, that a great number of the houses on the road were plundered, and rendered unfit for use; several were burnt; women in child-bed were driven by the soldiery naked into the streets; old men, peaceably in their houses, were shot dead, and such scenes exhibited, as would disgrace the annals of the most uncivilized nations.

These, brethren, are marks of ministerial vengeance against this colony, for refusing, with her sister colonies, a submission to slavery; but they have not yet detached us from our royal sovereign, we profess to be his loyal and dutiful subjects; and so hardly dealt with as we have been, are still ready, with our lives and fortunes, to defend his person, family, crown and dignity; nevertheless, to the persecution and tyranny of his cruel ministry, we will not tamely submit; appealing to Heaven for the justice of our cause, "we determine to die, or be free."

We cannot think that the honor, wisdom, and valor of Britons, will suffer them to be longer inactive spectators of *measures*, in which they themselves are so deeply interested; measures pursued in opposition to the solemn protests of many noble lords, and expressed sense of conspicuous commons, whose knowledge and virtue have long characterized them as some of the greatest men in the nation; *measures*, executing, contrary to the interest, petitions, and resolves of many large, respectable counties, cities, and boroughs, in Great Britain; measures highly incompatible with justice, but still pursued with a specious pretence of easing the nation of its burthens; *measures* which, if successful, must end in the ruin and slavery of Britain, as well as the persecuted American colonies.

We sincerely hope, that the Great Sovereign of the Universe, who hath so often appeared for the English nation, will support you in every rational and manly exertion with these colonies, for saving it from ruin, and that, in a constitutional connection with our mother country, we shall soon be altogether a free and happy people.

Signed by order,
JOS. WARREN, president

DOCUMENT ANALYSIS

1. Who are the primary aggressors according to this account? Describe some of the actions detailed in this account as evidence of this aggression.

_____

_____

_____

2. What appeal does Warren make to the people of Britain? What is the goal of this document?

_____

_____

_____

DOCUMENT 4.2
Slave Petition to the General Assembly in Connecticut (1779)

From Gary B. Nash, *Race and Revolution* (Madison, WI: Madison House, 1990), pp. 174–176.

The petition reproduced below was signed by two slaves, Prime and Prince, in Fairfield County, Connecticut, on behalf of all slaves in that county. Combining—as did other slave petitions—references to both the ongoing Revolutionary War and Christianity, their plea is representative of this particular era of U.S. history. The petition was denied, and Connecticut instead opted for a plan of gradual emancipation. In 1774 the legislature had outlawed the importation of slaves. In 1784 and 1797, the legislature passed additional laws that freed children born as slaves at ages 25 and 21, respectively. Slavery was not completely abolished in the state until 1848.

To the Honorable General Assembly of the State of Connecticut to be held at Hartford on the Second Thursday of Instant May [1779]—The Petition of the Negroes in the Towns of Stratford and Fairfield in the County of Fairfield who are held in a State of Slavery humbly showeth—

That many of your Petitioners, were (as they verily believe) most unjustly torn, from the Bosom of their dear Parents, and Friends, and without any Crime, by them committed, doomed, and bound down, to perpetual Slavery; and as if the Perpetrators of this horrid Wickedness, were conscious (that we poor Ignorant Africans, upon the least Glimmering Sight, derived from a Knowledge of the Sense and Practice of civilized Nations) should Convince them of their Sin, they have added another dreadful Evil, that of holding us in gross Ignorance, so as to render Our Subjection more easy and tolerable. May it please your Honors, we are most grievously affected, under the Consideration of the flagrant Injustice; Your Honors who are nobly contending, in the Cause of Liberty, whose Conduct excites the Admiration, and Reverence, of all the great Empires of the World; will not resent, our thus freely animadverting, on this detestable Practice; although our Skins are different in Color, from those whom we serve, Yet Reason & Revelation join to declare, that we are the Creatures of that God, who made of one Blood, and Kindred, all the Nations of the Earth; we perceive by our own Reflection, that we are endowed with the same Faculties with our masters, and there is nothing that leads us to a Belief, or Suspicion, that we are any more obliged to serve them, than they us, and the more we Consider of this matter, the more we are Convinced of our Right (by the Laws of Nature and by the whole Tenor of the Christian Religion, so far as we have been taught) to be free; we have endeavored rightly to understand what is our Right, and what is our Duty, and can never be convinced that we were made to be Slaves. Although God almighty may justly lay this, and more upon us, yet we deserve it not, from the hands of Men, we are impatient under the grievous Yoke, but our Reason teaches us that it is not best for us to use violent measures, to cast it off; we are also convinced, that we are unable to extricate ourselves from our abject State; but we think we may with the greatest Propriety look up to your Honors, (who are the fathers of the People) for Relief. And we not only groan under our own burden, but with concern, & Horror, look forward, & contemplate, the miserable Condition of our Children, who are training up, and kept in Preparation, for a like State of Bondage, and Servitude. We beg leave to submit, to your Honors serious Consideration, whether it is consistent with the present Claims, of the united States, to hold so many Thousands, of the Race of Adam, our Common Father, in perpetual Slavery. Can human Nature endure the Shocking Idea? can your Honors any longer Suffer this great Evil to prevail under your Government: we entreat your Honors, let no considerations of Public Inconvenience deter your Honors from interposing in behalf of your Petitioners; we ask for nothing, but what we are fully persuaded is ours to Claim. We beseech your Honors to weigh this matter in the Scale of Justice, and in your great Wisdom and goodness, apply such Remedy as the Evil does require; and let your Petitioners rejoice with your Honors in the Participation with your Honors of that inestimable Blessing, Freedom and your Humble Petitioners, as in Duty bound shall ever pray &c.

dated in Fairfield the 11th Day of May A D 1779—

Prime—a Negro man

servant to Mr. Vam A. Sturge of Fairfield

his mark

Prince—a Negro man

his mark

servant of Capt. Stephen Jenings of Fairfield—

in Behalf of themselves and the other Petitioners

DOCUMENT ANALYSIS

1. What religious argument did the petitioners offer?

_____

_____

_____

2. What did the petitioners describe as their greatest "horror" when contemplating the slave system?

_____

_____

_____

3. How did the petitioners place their argument within a global perspective? Which of their arguments referenced the Revolutionary War?

_____

_____

_____

DOCUMENT 5.1
George Washington, Sixth Annual Address to Congress (1794)

The Whiskey Rebellion of 1794 took place in western Pennsylvania. The reason for the rebellion was a federal tax on distilled spirits that had been levied in 1791. Producers resisted the tax, claiming that only the state had the right to impose such taxes. In a show of federal strength, President George Washington called up a militia to suppress the insurrection. The event was significant because it was the first challenge to federal authority in the United States and the first time a U.S. president called up state militias to enforce federal law. In this address Washington describes the rebellion and his decision to suppress it.

Fellow Citizens of the Senate and of the House of Representatives: When we call to mind the gracious indulgence of Heaven, by which the American People became a nation; when we survey the general prosperity of our country, and look forward to the riches, power, and happiness, to which it seems destined; with the deepest regret do I announce to you, that during your recess, some of the citizens of the United States have been found capable of an insurrection. It is due, however, to the character of our government, and to its stability, which cannot be shaken by the enemies of order, freely to unfold the course of this event.

During the session of the year one thousand seven hundred and ninety, it was expedient to exercise the legislative power, granted by the constitution of the United States, "to lay and collect excises." In a majority of the States, scarcely an objection was heard to this mode of taxation. In some, indeed, alarms were at first conceived, until they were banished by reason and patriotism. In the four western counties of Pennsylvania, a prejudice, fostered and embittered by the artifice of men, who labored for an ascendancy over the will of others, by the guidance of their passions, produced symptoms of riot and violence. It is well known, that Congress did not hesitate to examine the complaints which were presented, and to relieve them, as far as justice dictated, or general convenience would permit, but the impression, which this moderation made on the discontented, did not correspond, with what it deserved. The arts of delusion were no longer confined to the efforts of designing individuals.

The very forbearance to press prosecutions was misinterpreted into a fear of urging the execution of the laws; and associations of men began to denounce threats against the officers employed. From a belief, that by a more formal concert, their operation might be defeated, certain self-created societies assumed the tone of condemnation. Hence, while the greater part of Pennsylvania itself were conforming themselves to the acts of excise, a few counties were resolved to frustrate them. It was now perceived, that every expectation from the tenderness which had been hitherto pursued, was unavailing, and that further delay could only create an opinion of impotency or irresolution in the government. Legal process was, therefore, delivered to the marshal, against the rioters and delinquent distillers.

No sooner was he understood to be engaged in this duty, than the vengeance of armed men was aimed at his person, and the person and property of the inspector of the revenue. They fired upon the marshal, arrested him, and detained him for some time, as a prisoner. He was obliged, by the jeopardy of his life, to renounce the service of other process, on the west side of the Allegany mountain; and a deputation was afterwards sent to him to demand a surrender of that which he had served. A numerous body repeatedly attacked the house of the inspector, seized his papers of office, and finally destroyed by fire, his buildings, and whatsoever they contained. Both of these officers, from a just regard to their safety, fled to the seat of government; it being avowed, that the motives to such outrages were to compel the resignation of the inspector, to withstand by force of arms the authority of the United States, and thereby to extort a repeal of the laws of excise, and an alteration in the conduct of government.

Upon the testimony of these facts, an associate Justice of the Supreme Court of the United States notified to me, that "in the counties of Washington and Allegany, in Pennsylvania, laws of the United States were opposed, and the execution thereof obstructed by combinations, too powerful to be suppressed by the ordinary course of judicial proceedings, or by the powers vested in the marshal of that district." On this call, momentous in the extreme, I sought and weighed, what might best subdue the crisis. On the one hand, the judiciary was pronounced to be stripped of its capacity to enforce the laws; crimes, which reached the very existence of social order, were perpetrated without control, the friends of government were insulted, abused, and overawed into silence, or an apparent acquiescence; and the yield to the treasonable fury of so small a portion of the United States, would be to violate the fundamental principle of our constitution, which enjoins that the will of the majority shall prevail. On the other, to array citizen against citizen, to publish the dishonor of such excesses, to encounter the expense, and other embarrassments of so distant an expedition, were steps too delicate, too closely interwoven with many affecting considerations, to be lightly adopted. I postponed, therefore, the summoning of the militia immediately into the field. But I required them to be held in readiness, that if my anxious endeavors to reclaim the deluded, and to convince the malignant of their danger, should be fruitless, military force might be prepared to act, before the season should be too far advanced.

My Proclamation of the 7th of August last was accordingly issued, and accompanied by the appointment of Commissioners, who were charged to repair to the scene of insurrection. They were authorized to confer with any bodies of men, or individuals. They were instructed to be candid and explicit, in stating the sensations, which had been excited in the Executive, and his earnest wish to avoid a resort to coercion. To represent, however, that without submission, coercion must be the resort; but to invite them, at the same time, to return to the demeanor of faithful citizens, by such accommodations as lay within the sphere of the executive power. Pardon, too, was tendered to them by the government of the United States, and that of Pennsylvania, upon no other condition, than a satisfactory assurance of obedience to the laws.

Although the report of the commissioners marks their firmness and abilities, and must unite all virtuous men, by showing, that the means of conciliation have been exhausted, all of those who had committed or abetted the tumults, did not subscribe the mild form, which was proposed, as the atonement; and the indications of a peaceable temper were neither sufficiently general, nor conclusive, to recommend or warrant, a further suspension of the march of the militia.

Thus, the painful alternative could not be discarded. I ordered the militia to march, after once more admonishing the insurgents, in my proclamation of the 25th of September last. It was a task too difficult to ascertain with precision, the lowest degree of force, competent to the quelling of the insurrection. From a respect, indeed, to economy, and the ease of my fellow citizens belonging to the militia, it would have gratified me to accomplish such an estimate. My very reluctance to ascribe too much importance to the opposition, had its extent been accurately seen, would have been a decided inducement to the smallest efficient numbers.

In this uncertainty, therefore, I put in motion fifteen thousand men, as being an army, which according to all human calculation, would be prompt, and adequate in every view; and might perhaps, by rendering resistance desperate, prevent the effusion of blood. Quotas had been assigned to the states of New-Jersey, Pennsylvania, Maryland, and Virginia; the governor of Pennsylvania having declared on this occasion, an opinion which justified a requisition to the other states.

As commander in chief of the militia, when called into the actual service of the United States, I have visited the places of general rendezvous, to obtain more exact information, and to direct a plan for ulterior movements. Had there been room for a persuasion, that the laws were secure from obstruction; that the civil magistrate was able to bring to justice such of the most culpable, as have not embraced the proffered terms of amnesty, and may be deemed fit objects of example; that the friends to peace and good government were not in need of that aid and countenance, which they ought always to receive, and I trust, ever will receive, against the vicious and turbulent; I should have caught with avidity the opportunity of restoring the militia to their families and home. But succeeding intelligence has tended to manifest the necessity of what has

been done; it being now confessed by those who were not inclined to exaggerate the ill-conduct of the insurgents, that their malevolence was not pointed merely to a particular law; but that a spirit, inimical to all order, has actuated many of the offenders. If the state of things had afforded reason for the continuance of my presence with the army, it would not have been denied.

But every appearance assuring such an issue, as will redound to the reputation and strength of the United States, I have judged it most proper, to resume my duties at the seat of government, leaving the chief command with the governor of Virginia. Still, however, as it is probable, that in a commotion like the present, whatsoever may be the pretence, the purposes of mischief and revenge may not be laid aside; the stationing of a small force for a certain period in the four western counties of Pennsylvania will be indispensable; whether we contemplate the situation of those, who are connected with the execution of the laws; or of others who may have exposed themselves by an honorable attachment to them. . . .

While there is cause to lament, that occurrences of this nature should have disgraced the name, or interrupted the tranquility of any part of our community, or should have diverted to a new application, any portion of the public resources, there are not wanting real and substantial consolations for the misfortune. It has demonstrated, that our prosperity rests on solid foundations; by furnishing an additional proof, that my fellow citizens understand the true principles of government and liberty: that they feel their inseparable union: that notwithstanding all the devices which have been used to sway them from their interest and duty, they are now as ready to maintain the authority of the laws against licentious invasions, as they were to defend their rights against usurpation. It has been a spectacle, displaying to the highest advantage, the value of Republican Government, to behold the most and least wealthy of our citizens standing in the same ranks as private soldiers; pre-eminently distinguished by being the army of the constitution; undeterred by a march of three hundred miles over rugged mountains, by the approach of an inclement season, or by any other discouragement. Nor ought I to omit to acknowledge the efficacious and patriotic co-operation, which I have experienced from the chief magistrates of the states, to which my requisitions have been addressed.

To every description, indeed, of citizens let praise be given. But let them persevere in their affectionate vigilance over that precious depository of American happiness, the constitution of the United States. Let them cherish it too, for the sake of those, who from every clime are daily seeking a dwelling in our land. And when in the calm moments of reflection, they shall have retraced the origin and progress of the insurrection, let them determine whether it has not been fomented by combinations of men, who, careless of consequences, and disregarding the unerring truth, that those who rouse, cannot always appease a civil convulsion, have dis-

seminated, from an ignorance of perversion of facts, suspicions, jealousies, and accusations of the whole government.

Having thus fulfilled the engagement, which I took, when I entered this office, "to the best of my ability to preserve, protect, and defend the constitution of the United States," on you, Gentlemen, and the people by whom you are deputed, I rely for support. In the arrangements, to which the possibility of a similar contingency will naturally draw your attention, it ought not to be forgotten, that the militia laws have exhibited such striking defects, as could not have been supplied but by the zeal of our citizens. Besides the extraordinary expense and waste, which are not the least of the defects, every appeal to those laws is attended with a doubt of its success. The devising and establishing of a well regulated militia, would be a genuine source of legislative honor, and a perfect title to public gratitude. I, therefore, entertain a hope, that the present session will not pass, without carrying to its full energy the power of organizing, arming, and disciplining the militia; and thus providing, in the language of the constitution, for calling them forth to execute the laws of the union, suppress insurrections, and repel invasions. As auxiliary to the state of our defense, to which Congress can never too frequently recur, they will not omit to enquire whether the fortifications, which have been already licensed by law, be commensurate with our exigencies. . . .

An estimate of the necessary appropriations, including the expenditures into which we have been driven by the insurrection, will be submitted to Congress. Gentlemen of the Senate, and of the House of Representatives: The mint of the United States has entered upon the coinage of the precious metals; and considerable sums of defective coins and bullion have been lodged with the director by individuals. There is a pleasing prospect that the institution will, at no remote day, realize the expectation which was originally formed of its utility.

In subsequent communications, certain circumstances of our intercourse with foreign nations, will be transmitted to Congress. However, it may not be unseasonable to announce that my policy in our foreign transactions has been, to cultivate peace with all the world; to observe treaties with pure and absolute faith; to check every deviation from the line of impartiality; to explain what may have been misapprehended; and having thus acquired the right, to lose no time in acquiring the ability, to insist upon justice being done to ourselves.

Let us unite, therefore, in imploring the Supreme Ruler of nations, to spread his holy protection over these United States: to turn the machinations of the wicked to the confirming of our constitution: to enable us at all times to root out internal sedition, and put invasion to flight: to perpetuate to our country that prosperity, which his goodness has already conferred, and to verify the anticipations of this government being a safe guard to human rights.

DOCUMENT ANALYSIS

1. How did Washington defend his actions? What did he cite as the basis of his power to suppress the rebellion?

_____

_____

_____

2. What did Washington ask Congress to do in this address?

_____

_____

_____

3. How did Washington describe those who participated in the rebellion? In your opinion, was this a fair assessment? Why or why not?

_____

_____

_____

DOCUMENT 6.1
Opinion of the Supreme Court for *Marbury v. Madison* (1803)

Prior to leaving office, President Adams appointed several Federalist judges to the federal courts. Angered by these "midnight" appointments, Jefferson and his administration made several attempts to block the nominations and unseat the judges. The new administration failed to block any of the appointments except for that of William Marbury in the District of Columbia. Angered over the administration's actions, Marbury sued the new secretary of state, James Madison. This case, Marbury v. Madison, *failed to win Marbury his seat, but it officially established the Supreme Court's right to judicial review.*

In the order in which the Court has viewed this subject, the following questions have been considered and decided: 1st. Has the applicant a right to the commission he demands? 2nd. If he has a right, and that right has been violated, do the laws of this country afford him a remedy? 3rd. If they do afford him a remedy, is it a mandamus issuing from this court?. . .

It is . . . the opinion of the Court: 1st. That by signing the commission of Mr. Marbury, the President of the United States appointed him a justice of the peace for the county of Washington, in the District of Columbia; and that the seal of the United States, affixed thereto by the secretary of state, is conclusive testimony of the verity of the signature, and of the completion of the appointment; and that the appointment conferred on him a legal right to the office of the space of five years. 2nd. That, having this legal title to the office, he has a consequent right to the commission; a refusal to deliver which is a plain violation of that right, for which the laws of his country afford him a remedy. 3rd. It remains to be inquired whether he is entitled to the remedy for which he applies?. . .

This . . . is a plain case of a mandamus, either to deliver the commission, or a copy of it from the record; and it only remains to be inquired, whether it can issue from this court?

The act to establish the judicial courts of the United States authorizes the Supreme Court, "to issue writs of mandamus, in cases warranted by the principles and usages of law, to any courts appointed or persons holding office, under the authority of the United States." The secretary of state, being a person holding an office under the authority of the United States, is precisely within the letter of this description; and if this court is not authorized to issue a writ of mandamus to such an office, it must be because the law is unconstitutional. . .

The Constitution vests the whole judicial power of the United States in one Supreme Court, and such inferior courts as Congress shall, from time to time, ordain and establish. . .

In the distribution of this power, it is declared that "the Supreme Court shall have original jurisdiction in all cases affecting ambassadors, other public ministers and consuls, and those in which a state shall be a party. In all other cases, the Supreme Court shall have appellate jurisdiction.". . .

If it had been intended to leave it in the discretion of the legislature to apportion the judicial power between the supreme and inferior courts according to the will of that body, it would certainly have been useless to have proceeded further than to have defined the judicial power, and the tribunals in which it should be vested. The subsequent part of the section is mere surplus, is entirely without meaning,. . .

It cannot be presumed that any clause in the Constitution is intended to be without effect. . .

To enable this court, then, to issue a mandamus, it must be shown to be an exercise of appellate jurisdiction. . .

The authority, therefore, given to the Supreme Court, by the Act establishing the judicial courts of the United States, to issue writs of mandamus to public officers, appears not to be warranted by the Constitution. . .

DOCUMENT ANALYSIS

1. What role does Chief Justice Marshall hope the Supreme Court adopts in regards to the U.S. Constitution?

_____

_____

_____

2. Why was it important that the Chief Justice should be seen as speaking for all the members of the Supreme Court on this issue?

_____

_____

_____

DOCUMENT 6.2
Lewis and Clark Meet the Shoshone, August 17, 1805

Meriwether Lewis and William Clark were chosen by President Thomas Jefferson to survey the area known as Louisiana, purchased from France in 1803. Here, Lewis describes their first meeting with the Shoshone and the reunion of their guide Sacagawea with her people.

This morning I arose very early and dispatched Drewyer and the Indian down to the river. Sent Shields to hunt. I made McNeal cook the remainder of our meat which afforded a slight breakfast for ourselves and the chief. Drewyer had been gone about two hours when an Indian who had straggled some little distance down the river returned and reported that the white men were coming, that he had seen them just below. They all appeared transported with joy, and the chief repeated his fraternal hug. I felt quite as much gratified at this information as the Indians appeared to be. Shortly after Captain Clark arrived with the interpreter Charbono,

and the Indian woman, who proved to be a sister of the Chief Cameahwait. The meeting of those people was really affecting, particularly between Sah-cah-gar-we-ah [Sacagawea] and an Indian woman, who had been taken prisoner at the same time with her and who, had afterwards escaped from the Minnetares and rejoined her nation. At noon the canoes arrived, and we had the satisfaction once more to find ourselves all together, with a flattering prospect of being able to obtain as many horses shortly as would enable us to prosecute our voyage by land should that by water be deemed unadvisable.

We now formed our camp just below the junction of the forks on the larboard side in a level smooth bottom covered with a fine turf of greensward. Here we unloaded our canoes and arranged our baggage on shore; formed a canopy of one of our large sails and planted some willow brush in the ground to form a shade for the Indians to set under while we

spoke to them, which we thought it best to do this evening. Accordingly about 4 PM we called them together and through the medium of Labuish, Charbono and Sah-cah-gar-we-ah, we communicated to them fully the objects which had brought us into this distant part of the country, in which we took care to make them a conspicuous object of our own good wishes and the care of our government. We made them sensible of their dependence on the will of our government for every species of merchandise as well for their defense and comfort; and apprised them of the strength of our government and its friendly dispositions towards them. We also gave them as a reason why we wished to penetrate the country as far as the ocean to the west of them was to examine and find out a more direct way to bring merchandise to them. That as no trade could be carried on with them before our return to our homes that it was mutually advantageous to them as well as to ourselves, that they should render us such aids as they had it in their power to furnish in order to hasten our voyage and of course our return home, that such were their horses to transport our baggage without which we could not subsist, and that a pilot to conduct us through the mountains was also necessary if we could not descend the river by water, but that we did not ask either their horses or their services without giving a satisfactory compensation in return, that at present we wished them to collect as many horses as were necessary to transport our baggage to their village on the Columbia where we would then trade with them at our leisure for such horses as they could spare us.

They appeared well pleased with what had been said. The chief thanked us for friendship towards himself and nation and declared his wish to serve us in every respect, that he was sorry to find that it must yet be some time before they could be furnished with firearms but said they could live as they had done heretofore until we brought them as we had promised. He said they had not horses enough with them at present to remove our baggage to their village over the mountain, but that he would return to-morrow and encourage his people to come over with their horses and that he would bring his own and assist us. This was complying with all we wished at present. We next inquired who were chiefs among them. Cameahwait pointed out two others whom he said were chiefs. We gave him a medal of the small size with the likeness of Mr. Jefferson the President of the United States in relief on one side and clasp hands with a pipe and tomahawk on the other, to the other chiefs we gave each a small medal which were struck in the president of George Washington Esq. We also gave small medals of the last description to two young men whom the first chief informed us were good young men and much respected among them. We gave the first chief a uniform coat, shirt, a pair of scarlet leggings, a carrot of tobacco and some small articles. To each of the others we gave a shi[r]t, legging[s], handkerchief, a knife, some tobacco and a few small articles. We also distributed a good quantity paint, moccasins, awles, knives, beads, looking-glasses, &c. among the other Indians and gave them a plentiful meal of lyed corn which was the first they had ever eaten in their lives. They were much pleased with it. Every article about us appeared to excite astonishment in their minds; the appearance of the men, their arms, the canoes, our manner of working them, the black man York, and the sagacity of my dog were equally objects of admiration. I also shot my air-gun which was so perfectly incomprehensible that they immediately denominated it the great medicine. The idea which the Indians mean to convey by this appellation is something that emanates from or acts immediately by the influence or power of the Great Spirit; or that, in which, the power of God is manifest by its incomprehensible power of action. Our hunters killed four deer and an antelope this evening of which we also gave the Indians a good proportion. The ceremony of our council and smoking the pipe was in conformity of the custom of this nation performed barefoot. On those occasions points of etiquette are quite as much attended to by the Indians as among civilized nations. To keep Indians in a good humor you must not fatigue them with too much business at one time. Therefore after the council we gave them to eat and amused them a while by showing them such articles as we thought would be entertaining to them, and then renewed our inquiries with respect to the country. The information we derived was only a repetition of that they had given me before and in which they appeared to be so candid that I could not avoid yielding confidence to what they had said. Captain Clark and myself now concerted measures for our future operations, and it was mutually agreed that he should set out to-morrow morning with eleven men furnished with axes and other necessary tools for making canoes, their arms, accoutrements and as much of their baggage as they could carry; also to take the Indians, Charbono and the Indian woman with him; that on his arrival at the Shoshone camp he was to leave Charbono and the Indian woman to hasten the return of the Indians with their horses to this place, and to proceed himself with the eleven men down the Columbia in order to examine the river and if he found it navigable and could obtain timber to set about making canoes immediately. In the meantime I was to bring on the party and baggage to the Shoshone camp, calculating that by the time I should reach that place that he would have sufficiently informed himself with respect to the state of the river &c. as to determine us whether to prosecute our journey from thence by land or water. In the former case we should want all the horses which we could purchase, and in the latter only to hire the Indians to transport our baggage to the place at which we made the canoes. In order to inform me as early as possible of the state of the river he was to send back one of the men with the necessary information as soon as he should satisfy himself on this subject. This plan being settled we gave orders accordingly and the men prepared for an early march. The nights are very cold and the sun excessively hot in the day. We have no fuel here but a few dry willow brush and from the appearance of the country I am confident we shall not find game here to subsist us many days. These are additional reasons why I conceive it necessary to get under way as soon as possible. This morning Captain Clark had delayed until 7 A.M. before he set out just about which time Drewyer arrived with the Indian; he left the canoes to come on after him, and immediately set out and joined me as has been before mentioned. The spirits of the men were now much elated at the prospect of getting horses.

DOCUMENT ANALYSIS

1. In this excerpt, Lewis asserts that he and Clark "communicated to them fully the objects which had brought us into this distant part of the country." What messages did they attempt to convey to the Shoshone concerning the nature of their mission? How did they portray their country and its government? How do you think the Shoshone received these messages?

_____

_____

_____

2. How would you characterize Lewis's attitude toward the Shoshone?

_____

_____

_____

DOCUMENT 7.1
Pennsylvania Gazette, Letter Extract Concerning "Indian Hostilities" (1812)

Stories of the British inciting Native American groups to attack American settlers abounded in the days immediately preceding the War of 1812. The following excerpt from the Pennsylvania Gazette *blames the British for "Indian hostilities" in the Indiana and Illinois territories.*

The following is an extract of a letter from a gentleman at St. Charles, Louisiana Territory, dated Jan. 10, 1812.

In answer to your enquiry, respecting Indian hostilities in this quarter, I have to inform you, that some of the reports that have found their way into the public prints are much exaggerated, but are generally true. The depredations committed by them have been principally in Indiana and Illinois territories; some horses have been taken in this territory, but I believe no murders have been committed by them for the last ten or twelve months. I had flattered myself that the drubbing given them by the troops under the command of Gov. Harrison would have disposed them to return to order. In this it appears I was mistaken, for this day, by an express from Fort Madison, we are informed of cruel murders committed on some traders, about 100 miles above that Fort, by a party of the Pecant

nation. A Mr. Hunt, son of the late Col. Hunt, of the United States' army, and a Mr. Prior, were trading in that quarter—their houses about 3 miles distance from each other. The party of Indians came to Hunt's house, and appeared friendly until they obtained admittance into the house—they then shot down two men that Mr. Hunt had with him, seized him and a boy, who was his interpreter, tied them, and packed up the goods that were in the house, and carried them off. Mr. Hunt discovered that they believed him to be an Englishman, and on that account saved his life. They told him that they had sent another party to kill Prior, and carry off his goods, and that they intended in a short time to take the Fort—after which they would come on and kill every American they could find. They took Mr. Hunt and his boy with them some distance, but night came on, and proved extremely dark, which fortunately gave them an opportunity of escaping, and they arrived safe at Fort Madison on the sixth day.

The hostilities that have taken place, together with the mysterious conduct of the few Indians that are passing amongst us, lead me to believe they are determined for war, and that they are set on by British agents. If we go to war with England, I calculate on some very warm work in this quarter.

DOCUMENT ANALYSIS

1. What does the author of this letter foresee as the consequences of a war between England and the United States?

_____

_____

_____

2. Which historical event does "the drubbing given them by the troops under the command of Gov. Harrison" refer to?

_____

_____

_____

DOCUMENT 7.2
Letter from Dolley Payne Madison to Lucy Payne Todd (1814)
From Dolley Madison Papers, Library of Congress, Washington, DC.

The War of 1812 between the United States and Britain is often remembered for two particular events. One is the Battle of New Orleans, won by U.S. forces under Andrew Jackson after the Treaty of Ghent had already been signed. The other is the burning of Washington, D.C., including the White House. Dolley Madison, wife of President James Madison, famously saved the Gilbert Stuart portrait of George Washington as well as official state papers when she fled before British troops. The letter below is the document generally cited by historians to illustrate the event, although there is some suspicion that it might actually have been written years later.

Extract from a letter written to my sister published in the sketch of my life written for the "National Portrait Gallery."

Tuesday Augt. 23d. 1814

Dear Sister

My husband left me yesterday morng. to join Gen. Winder. He enquired anxiously whether I had courage, or firmness to remain in the President's house [White House] until his return, on the morrow, or succeeding day, and on my assurance that I had no fear but for him and the success of our army, he left me, beseeching me to take care of myself, and of the cabinet papers, public and private. I have since recd. two despatches

from him, written with a pencil; the last is alarming, because he desires I should be ready at a moment's warning to enter my carriage and leave the city; that the enemy seemed stronger than had been reported and that it might happen that they would reach the city, with intention to destroy it. . . . I am accordingly ready; I have pressed as many cabinet papers into trunks as to fill one carriage; our private property must be sacrificed, as it is impossible to procure wagons for its transportation. I am determined not to go myself until I see Mr. Madison safe, and he can accompany me, as I hear of much hostility towards him, . . . disaffection stalks around us. . . . My friends and acquaintances are all gone; Even Col. C with his hundred men, who were stationed as a guard in the enclosure . . . French John (a faithful domestic,) with his usual activity and resolution, offers to spike the cannon at the gate, and to lay a train of powder which would blow up the British, should they enter the house. To the last proposition I positively object, without being able, however, to make him understand why all advantages in war may not be taken.

Wednesday morng., twelve o'clock. Since sunrise I have been turning my spyglass in every direction and watching with unwearied anxiety, hoping to discern the approach of my dear husband and his friends, but, alas, I can descry only groups of military wandering in all directions, as if there was a lack of arms, or of spirit to fight for their own firesides!

Three O'clock. Will you believe it, my sister? We have had a battle or skirmish near Bladensburg, and I am still here within sound of the can-

non! Mr. Madison comes not; may God protect him! Two messengers covered with dust, come to bid me fly; but I wait for him. . . . At this late hour a wagon has been procured, I have had it filled with the plate and most valuable portable articles belonging to the house; whether it will reach its destination; the Bank of Maryland, or fall into the hands of British soldiery, events must determine.

Our kind friend, Mr. Carroll, has come to hasten my departure, and is in a very bad humor with me because I insist on waiting until the large picture of Gen. Washington is secured, and it requires to be unscrewed from the wall. This process was found too tedious for these perilous moments; I have ordered the frame to be broken, and the canvass taken out it is done, and the precious portrait placed in the hands of two gentlemen of New York, for safe keeping. And now, dear sister, I must leave this house, or t[he] retreating army will make me a prisoner in it, by filling up the road I am direc[ted] to take. When I shall again write you, or where I shall be tomorrow, I cannot tell!!

DOCUMENT ANALYSIS

1. What about this letter would make it such a popular historical artifact?

_____

_____

_____

2. If the letter was written at a later date with an eye toward documenting an historical event, would it be any less valuable as a primary source?

_____

_____

_____

DOCUMENT 8.1
Extract from the Albany *Daily Advertiser* (1819)

The Erie Canal was not completed until 1825, but the middle section, which ran from Utica to Rome, was completed in 1819. That opening is recounted in the excerpt below. The impact of the canal was immense. When completed, it traversed New York State and linked New York Harbor to the Great Lakes. It provided commercial transportation, encouraged westward expansion, and was the engineering marvel of its age. Cities and towns along its banks prospered, and New York City became the nation's shipping center.

The last two days have presented in this village, a scene of the liveliest interest; and I consider it among the privileges of my life to have been present to witness it. On Friday afternoon I walked to the head of the grand canal, the eastern extremity of which reaches within a very short distance of the village, and from one of the slight and airy bridges which crossed it, I had a sight that could not but exhilarate and elevate the mind. The waters were rushing in from the westward, and coming down their untried channel towards the sea. Their course, owing to the absorption of the new banks of the canal, and the distance they had to run from where the stream entered it, was much slower than I had anticipated; they continued gradually to steal along from bridge to bridge, and at first only spreading over the bed of the canal, imperceptibly rose and washed its sides with a gentle wave. It was dark before they reached the eastern extremity; but at sunrise next morning, they were on a level, two feet and a half deep throughout the whole distance of thirteen miles. The interest manifested by the whole country, as this new internal river rolled its first waves through the state, cannot be described. You might see the people running across the fields, climbing on trees and fences, and crowding the bank of the canal to gaze upon the welcome sight. A boat had been prepared at Rome, and as the waters came down the canal, you might mark their progress by that of this new Argo, which floated triumphantly along the Hellespont of the west, accompanied by the shouts of the peasantry, and having on her deck a military band. At nine the next morning, the bells began a merry peal, and the commissioners in carriages, proceeded from Bagg's hotel, to the place of embarkation.

The governor, accompanied by Gen. Van Rensselaer, Rev. Mr. Stansbury, of Albany, Rev. Dr. Blatchford, of Lansingburgh, Judge Miller, of Utica, Mr. Holly, Mr. Seymour, Judge Wright, Col. Lansing, Mr. Childs, Mr. Clark, Mr. Bunner, and a large company of their friends, embarked, at a quarter past nine, and were received with the roll of the drum, and the shouts of a large multitude of spectators. The boat, which received them, is built for passengers;—is sixty-one feet in length, and seven and an half feet in width;—having two rising cabins, of fourteen feet each, with a flat deck between them. In forty minutes the company reached Whitesborough, a distance of two miles and three quarters; the boat being drawn by a single horse, which walked on the towing path, attached to a tow rope, of about sixty feet long. The horse travelled, apparently, with the utmost ease. The boat, though literally loaded with passengers, drew but fourteen inches water. A military band played patriotic airs. From bridge to bridge, from village to village, the procession was saluted with cannon, and every bell whose sound could reach the canal, swung, as with instinctive life, as it passed by. At Whitesborough, a number of ladies embarked, and heightened, by their smiles, a scene which wanted but this to make it complete.

DOCUMENT ANALYSIS

1. How far did the boat travel on the canal in 40 minutes? How does this performance compare to modern means of transportation?

_____

_____

_____

2. Why was the canal such an innovation? How had goods and people been transported prior to its opening?

_____

_____

_____

2. Which transportation modes eventually replaced the canal system? Why?

_____

_____

_____

The Lowell Offering was a monthly literary magazine published (primarily between 1841 and 1845) by women factory workers in the textile mills of Lowell, Massachusetts. For many of the women and girls who worked in the factories, working at Lowell offered an opportunity to earn the highest wages of any women workers in America. Despite their long work hours, the Lowell workers could devote some of their time to attending evening classes and lectures, accessing Lowell's circulating library, or working on the magazine.

Much has been said of the factory girl and her employment. By some she has been represented as dwelling in a sort of brick-and-mortar paradise, having little to occupy thought save the weaving of gay and romantic fancies, while the spindle or the wheel flies obediently beneath her glance. Others have deemed her a mere servile drudge, chained to her labor by almost as strong a power as that which holds a bondman in his fetters; and, indeed, some have already given her the title of "the white slave of the North." Her real situation approaches neither one nor the other of these extremes. Her occupation is as laborious as that of almost any female who earns her own living, while it has also its sunny spots and its cheerful intervals, which make her hard labor seem comparatively pleasant and easy.

Look at her as she commences her weekly task. The rest of the Sabbath has made her heart and her step light, and she is early at her accustomed place, awaiting the starting of the machinery. Every thing having been cleaned and neatly arranged on the Saturday night, she has less to occupy her on Monday than on other days; and you may see her leaning from the window to watch the glitter of the sunrise on the water, or looking away at the distant forests and fields, while memory wanders to her beloved country home; or, it may be that she is conversing with a sister-laborer near; returning at regular intervals to see that her work is in order.

Soon the breakfast bell rings; in a moment the whirling wheels are stopped, and she hastens to join the throng which is pouring through the open gate. At the table she mingles with a various group. Each dispatches the meal hurriedly, though not often in silence; and if, as is sometimes the case, the rules of politeness are not punctiliously observed by all, the excuse of some lively country girl would be, "They don't give us time for manners."

The short half-hour is soon over; the bell rings again; and now our factory girl feels that she has commenced her day's work in earnest. The time is often apt to drag heavily till the dinner hour arrives. Perhaps some part of the work becomes deranged and stops; the constant friction causes a belt of leather to burst into a flame; a stranger visits the room, and scans the features and dress of its inmates inquiringly; and there is little else to break the monotony. The afternoon passes in much the same manner. Now and then she mingles with a knot of busy talkers who have collected to discuss some new occurrence, or holds pleasant converse with some intelligent and agreeable friend, whose acquaintance she has formed since her factory life commenced; but much of the time she is left to her own thoughts. While at her work, the clattering and rumbling around her prevent any other noise from attracting her attention, and she must think, or her life would be dull indeed.

Thus the day passes on, and evening comes; the time which she feels to be exclusively her own. How much is done in the three short hours from seven to ten o'clock. She has a new dress to finish; a call to make on some distant corporation; a meeting to attend; there is a lecture or a concert at some one of the public halls, and the attendance will be thin if she and her associates are not present; or, if nothing more imperative demands her time, she takes a stroll through the street or to the river with some of her mates, or sits down at home to peruse a new book. At ten o'clock all is still for the night.

The clang of the early bell awakes her to another day, very nearly the counterpart of the one which preceded it. And so the week rolls on, in the same routine, till Saturday comes. Saturday! the welcome sound! She busies herself to remove every particle of cotton and dust from her frame or looms, cheering herself meanwhile with sweet thoughts of the coming Sabbath; and when, at an earlier hour than usual, the mill is stopped, it looks almost beautiful in its neatness.

DOCUMENT ANALYSIS

1. Does this excerpt present an essentially positive or negative portrait of the Lowell factory system? Explain your answer.

_____

_____

_____

2. According to the excerpt, what resting period makes the balance of the working week endurable?

_____

_____

_____

3. Does the lifestyle of Lowell more clearly benefit the workers or the factory owners?

_____

_____

_____

DOCUMENT 9.1
Davy Crockett, Advice to Politicians (1833)

Davy Crockett had a great deal in common with Andrew Jackson. Both men were from Tennessee, both fought in the Indian wars (for a time Crockett even served under Jackson), and both used their military successes to propel their political careers. Crockett's advice to politicians reflects the new political culture that emerged in the so-called "Jacksonian Era." This era, characterized by the emergence of the "common man" in U.S. politics, was the ideal time for Crockett to pursue his career as a congressman.

"Attend all public meetings," says I, "and get some friend to move that you take the chair. If you fail in this attempt, make a push to be appointed secretary. The proceeding of course will be published, and your name is introduced to the public. But should you fail in both undertakings, get two or three acquaintances, over a bottle of whisky, to pass some resolutions, no matter on what subject. Publish them, even if you pay the printer. It will answer the purpose of breaking the ice, which is the main point in these matters.

"Intrigue until you are elected an officer of the militia. This is the second step toward promotion, and can be accomplished with ease, as I know an instance of an election being advertised, and no one attending, the innkeeper at whose house it was to be held, having a military turn, elected himself colonel of his regiment." Says I, "You may not accomplish your ends with as little difficulty, but do not be discouraged—Rome wasn't built in a day.

"If your ambition or circumstances compel you to serve your country and earn three dollars a day, by becoming a member of the legislature, you must first publicly avow that the constitution of the state is a shackle upon free and liberal legislation, and is, therefore, of as little use in the present enlightened age as an old almanac of the year in which the instrument was framed. There is policy in this measure, for by making the constitution a mere dead letter, your headlong proceedings will be attributed to a bold and unshackled mind; whereas, it might otherwise be thought they arose from sheer mulish ignorance. 'The Government' has set the example in his [Jackson's] attack upon the Constitution of the United States, and who should fear to follow where 'the Government' leads?

"When the day of election approaches, visit your constituents far and wide. Treat liberally, and drink freely, in order to rise in their estimation, though you fall in your own. True, you may be called a drunken dog by some of the clean-shirt and silk-stocking gentry, but the real roughnecks will style you a jovial fellow. Their votes are certain, and frequently count double.

"Do all you can to appear to advantage in the eyes of the women. That's easily done. You have but to kiss and slabber [slobber over] their children, wipe their noses, and pat them on the head. This cannot fail to please their mothers, and you may rely on your business being done in that quarter.

"Promise all that is asked," said I, "and more if you can think of anything. Offer to build a bridge or a church, to divide a county, create a batch of new offices, make a turnpike, or anything they like. Promises cost nothing; therefore, deny nobody who has a vote or sufficient influence to obtain one.

"Get up on all occasions, and sometimes on no occasion at all, and make long-winded speeches, though composed of nothing else than wind. Talk of your devotion to your country, your modesty and disinterestedness, or on any such fanciful subject. Rail against taxes of all kinds, officeholders, and bad harvest weather; and wind up with a flourish about the heroes who fought and bled for our liberties in the times that tried men's souls. To be sure, you run the risk of being considered a bladder of wind, or an empty barrel. But never mind that; you will find enough of the same fraternity to keep you in countenance.

"If any charity be going forward, be at the top of it, provided it is to be advertised publicly. If not, it isn't worth your while. None but a fool would place his candle under a bushel on such an occasion.

"These few directions." said I, "if properly attended to, will do your business. And when once elected—why, a fig for the dirty children, the promises, the bridges, the churches, the taxes, the offices, and the subscriptions. For it is absolutely necessary to forget all these before you can become a thoroughgoing politician, and a patriot of the first water."

DOCUMENT ANALYSIS

1. To whom does Crockett suggest a candidate should appeal for support?

_____

_____

_____

2. What does Crockett see as most important issues for politicians to consider?

_____

_____

_____

DOCUMENT 9.2
Black Hawk, Excerpt from "The Life of Black Hawk" (1833)

Sauk warrior Black Hawk led the Sauk and Fox peoples in their resistance against attempts by the U.S. government to take their lands. In 1804 a small group of tribal representatives supposedly conceded a vast amount of territory to the United States, much of it in present-day Illinois. Black Hawk eventually emerged as the leader of the Sauk and Fox peoples who refused to abandon these lands. This dispute culminated in the Black Hawk War of 1832 in which the Indians won a few initial battles but were ultimately defeated and lost their lands. Black Hawk was taken prisoner, and he wrote his autobiography the following year.

We generally paid a visit to St. Louis every summer; but, in consequence of the protracted war in which we had been engaged, I had not been there for some years. Our difficulties having all been settled, I concluded to take a small party, that summer, and go down to see our Spanish father. We went—and on our arrival, put up our lodges where the market-house now stands. After painting and dressing, we called to see our Spanish father, and were well received. He gave us a variety of presents, and plenty of provisions. We danced through the town as usual, and its inhabitants all seemed to be well pleased. They appeared to us like brothers and always gave us good advice.

On my next, and last, visit to my Spanish father, I discovered, on landing, that all was not right: every countenance seemed sad and gloomy! I inquired the cause, and was informed that the Americans were coming to take possession of the town and country! And that we should then lose our Spanish father! This news made myself and band sad—because we had always heard bad accounts of the Americans from Indians who had lived near them!—and we were sorry to lose our Spanish father, who had always treated us with great friendship.

A few days afterwards, the Americans arrived. I took my band, and went to take leave, for the last time, of our father. The Americans came to see him also. Seeing them approach, we passed out at one door, as they entered another—and immediately started, in canoes, for our village on Rock river—not liking the change any more than our friends appeared to, at St. Louis.

On arriving at our village, we gave the news, that strange people had taken St. Louis—and that we should never see our Spanish father again! This information made all our people sorry!

Some time afterwards, a boat came up the river, with a young American chief, and a small party of soldiers. We heard of them, (by runners,) soon after he had passed Salt river. Some of our young braves watched him every day, to see what sort of people he had on board! The boat, at length, arrived at Rock river, and the young chief came on shore with his interpreter, made a speech, and gave us some presents! We, in return, presented him with meat, and such provisions as we could spare.

We were all well pleased with the speech of the young chief. He gave us good advice; said our American father would treat us well. He presented us an American flag, which was hoisted. He then requested us to pull down our British flags—and give him our British medals promising to send us others on his return to St. Louis. This we declined, as we wished to have two Fathers!

When the young chief started, we sent runners to the Fox village, some miles distant, to direct them to treat him well as he passed—which they did. He went to the head of the Mississippi, and then returned to St. Louis. We did not see any Americans again for some time, being supplied with goods by British traders.

We were fortunate in not giving up our medals, for we learned afterwards, from our traders, that the chiefs high up on the Mississippi, who gave theirs, never received any in exchange for them. But the fault was not with the young American chief. He was a good man, and a great brave—and died in his country's service.

Some moons after this young chief descended the Mississippi, one of our people killed an American—and was confined, in the prison at St. Louis, for the offence. We held a council at our village to see what could be done for him,—which determined that Quàsh-quà-me, Pà-she-pa-ho, Oú-che-quà-ka, and Hà-she-quar-hi-qua, should go down to St. Louis, see our American father, and do all they could to have our friend released: by paying for the person killed—thus covering the blood, and satisfying the relations of the man murdered! This being the only means with us of saving a person who had killed another—and we then thought it was the same way with the whites!

The party started with the good wishes of the whole nation—hoping they would accomplish the object of their mission. The relatives of the prisoner blacked their faces, and fasted—hoping the Great Spirit would take pity on them, and return the husband and father to his wife and children.

Quàsh-quà-me and party remained a long time absent. They at length returned, and encamped a short distance below the village—but did not come up that day—nor did any person approach their camp! They appeared to be dressed in fine coats, and had medals! From these circumstances, we were in hopes that they had brought good news. Early the next morning, the Council Lodge was crowded—Quàsh-quà-me and party came up, and gave us the following account of their mission:

"On their arrival at St. Louis, they met their American father, and explained to him their business, and urged the release of their friend. The American chief told them he wanted land—and they had agreed to give him some on the west side of the Mississippi, and some on the Illinois side opposite the Jeffreon. When the business was all arranged, they expected to have their friend released to come home with them. But about the time they were ready to start, their friend was let out of prison, who ran a short distance, and was shot dead! This is all they could recollect of what was said and done. They had been drunk the greater part of the time they were in St. Louis."

This is all myself or nation knew of the treaty of 1804. It has been explained to me since. I find, by that treaty, all our country, east of the Mississippi, and south of the Jeffreon, was ceded to the United States for one thousand dollars a year! I will leave it to the people of the United States to say, whether our nation was properly represented in this treaty? or whether we received a fair compensation for the extent of country ceded by those four individuals? I could say much about this treaty, but I will not, at this time. It has been the origin of all our difficulties.

DOCUMENT ANALYSIS

1. What event did Black Hawk describe as "the origin of all our difficulties"?

_____

_____

_____

2. What were Black Hawk's initial impressions of the first Americans he encountered? Based on this account, could you have predicted his future conflicts with the United States?

_____

_____

_____

DOCUMENT 10.1
National Convention of Colored People, Report on Abolition (1847)

The National Convention of Colored People's Committee on Abolition included many runaway slaves who had become abolitionists, such as Frederick Douglass. Douglass and other African Americans advocated reform both on their own and through participation in organizations led by whites such as William Lloyd Garrison.

The Committee appointed to draft a Report respecting the best means of abolishing Slavery and destroying Caste in the United States, beg leave most respectfully to Report: That they have had the important subjects referred to them, under consideration, and have carefully endeavored to examine all their points and bearings to the best of their ability; and from every view they have been able to take they have arrived at the conclusion that the best means of abolishing slavery is proclamation of truth, and that the best means of destroying caste is the mental, moral and industrial improvement of our people.

First, as respects Slavery, Your Committee find this monstrous crime, this stupendous iniquity, closely interwoven with all the great interests, institutions and organizations of the country; pervading and influencing every class and grade of society, securing their support, obtaining their approbation, and commanding their homage. Availing itself of the advantage which age gives to crime, it has perverted the judgment, blunted the moral sense, blasted the sympathies, and created in the great mass,—the overwhelming majority of the people—a moral sentiment altogether favorable to its own character, and its own continuance. Press and pulpit are alike prostituted and made to serve the end of this infernal institution. The power of the government, and the sanctity of religion, church and state, are joined with the guilty oppressor against the oppressed-and the voice of this great nation is thundering in the ear of our enslaved fellow countrymen the terrible fiat, you shall be slaves or die!

The slave is in the minority, a small minority. The oppressors are an overwhelming majority. The oppressed are three millions, their oppressors are seventeen millions. The one is weak, the other is strong; the one is without arms, without means of concert, and without government; the other possess every advantage in these respects; and the deadly aim of their million of musketry, and loud-mouthed cannon tells the downtrodden slave in unmistakable language, he must be a slave or die.

In these circumstances, your committee are called upon to report as to the best means of abolishing slavery. And without pretending parties and factions, though did time permit, they would gladly do so, they beg at once to state their entire disapprobation of any plan of emancipation involving a resort to bloodshed. With the facts of our condition before us, it is impossible for us to contemplate any appeal to the slave to take vengeance on his guilty master, but with the utmost reprobation. Your Committee regards any counsel of this sort as the perfection of folly, suicidal in the extreme, and abominably wicked. We should utterly frown down and wholly discountenance any attempt to lead our people to confide in brute force as a reformatory instrumentality. All argument put forth in favor of insurrection and bloodshed, however well intended, is either the result of an unpardonable impatience or an atheistic want of faith in the power of truth as a means of regenerating and reforming the world.

Again we repeat, let us set our faces against all such absurd, unavailing, dangerous and mischievous ravings, emanating from what source they may. The voice of God and of common sense, equally point out a more excellent way, and that way is a faithful, earnest, and persevering enforcement of the great principles of justice and morality, religion and humanity. These are the only invincible and infallible means within our reach with which to overthrow this foul system of blood and ruin. Your Committee deem it susceptible of the clearest demonstration, that slavery exists in this country, because the people of this country WILL its existence. And they deem it equally clear, that no system or institution can exist for an hour against the earnestly-expressed WILL of the people. It were quite easy to bring to the support of the foregoing proposition powerful and conclusive illustrations from the history of reform in all ages, and especially in our own. But the palpable truths of the propositions, as well as the familiarity of the facts illustrating them, entirely obviate such a necessity.

Our age is an age of great discoveries; and one of the greatest is that which revealed that this world is to be ruled, shaped and guided by the marvelous might of mind. The human voice must supersede the roar of cannon. Truth alone is the legitimate antidote of falsehood. Liberty is always sufficient to grapple with tyranny. Free speech—free discussion—peaceful agitation, the foolishness of preaching these, under God, will subvert this giant crime, and send it reeling to its grave, as if smitten by a voice from the throne of God. Slavery exists because it is popular. It will cease to exist when it is made unpopular. Whatever therefore tends to make Slavery unpopular tends to its destruction. This every Slaveholder knows full well, and hence his opposition to all discussion of the subject. It is an evidence of intense feeling of alarm, when John C. Calhoun calls upon the North to put down what he is pleased to term "this plundering agitation." Let us give the Slaveholder what he most dislikes.

Let us expose his crimes and his foul abominations. He is reputable and must be made disreputable. He must be regarded as a moral leper—slummed as a loathsome wretch-outlawed from Christian communion, and from social respectability—an enemy of God and man, to be execrated by the community till he shall repent of his foul crimes, and give proof of his sincerity by breaking every chain and letting the oppressed go free. Let us invoke the Press and appeal to the pulpit to deal out the righteous denunciations of heaven against oppression, fraud and wrong, and the desire of our hearts will soon be given us in the triumph of Liberty throughout all the land. . .

DOCUMENT ANALYSIS

1. What are the principal ways the committee believed abolitionists could resist and overcome slavery? What means should be avoided? Why?

_____

_____

_____

2. How successful do you think the committee's strategy to abolish slavery would have been if the Civil War had not intervened?

_____

_____

_____

DOCUMENT 10.2
Mathew Carey, "Rules for Husbands and Wives" (1830)

Irish-born Mathew Carey eventually settled in Philadelphia, where he became a publisher, bookseller, and economist, with a special fondness for universal education. His Miscellaneous Essays *included the excerpt below, which outlined what he believed to be proper behavior between married persons. The United States was changing in the early 1830s, as recorded by Alexis de Tocqueville in* Democracy in America. *This period was marked by economic growth, westward expansion, expanding international and domestic markets, and scientific progress. The anti-slavery movement was gaining momentum, and from within that movement would emerge the women's rights movement. Carey's essay is an early reconsideration of proper gender roles in American society.*

Having seen various sets of maxims for the conduct of married life, which have appeared to me to contain some very injudicious items, degrading to wives, sinking them below the rank they ought to occupy, and reducing them in some degree to the level of mere housekeepers, and believing them radically erroneous, I annex a set which appear more rational and just than most of those which I have seen:

1. A good husband will always regard his wife as his equal; treat her with kindness, respect and attention; and never address her with an air of authority, as if she were, as some husbands appear to regard their wives, a mere housekeeper.
2. He will never interfere in her domestic concerns, hiring servants, &c.
3. He will always keep her liberally supplied with money for furnishing his table in a style proportioned to his means, and for the purchase of dress suitable to her station in life.
4. He will cheerfully and promptly comply with all her reasonable requests, when it can be done, without loss, or great inconvenience.
5. He will never allow himself to lose his temper towards her, by indifferent cookery, or irregularity in the hours of meals, or any other mismanagement of her servants, knowing the difficulty of making them do their duty.
6. If she have prudence and good sense, he will consult her on all great operations, involving the risk of ruin, or serious injury in case of failure. Many a man has been rescued from destruction by the wise counsels of his wife. Many a foolish husband has most seriously injured himself and family by the rejection of the advice of his wife, fearing, lest, if he followed it, he would be regarded as ruled by her! A husband can never procure a counselor more deeply interested in his welfare than his wife.
7. If distressed, or embarrassed in his circumstances, he will communicate his situation to her with candor, that she may bear his difficulties in mind, in her expenditures. Women sometimes, believing their husband's circumstances to be far better than they really are, expend money which cannot well be afforded, and which, if they knew their real situation, they would shrink from expending.

1. A good wife will always receive her husband with smiles,—leave nothing undone to render home agreeable—and gratefully reciprocate his kindness and attention.
2. She will study to discover means to gratify his inclinations, in regard to food and cookery; in the management of her family; in her dress, manners and deportment.
3. She will never attempt to rule, or appear to rule her husband. Such conduct degrades husbands—and wives always partake largely of the degradation of their husbands.
4. She will, in every thing reasonable, comply with his wishes—and, as far as possible, anticipate them.
5. She will avoid all altercations or arguments leading to ill-humor—and more especially before company.
6. She will never attempt to interfere in his business, unless he ask her advice or counsel, and will never attempt to control him in the management of it.

Should differences arise between husband and wife, the contest ought to be, not who will display the most spirit, but who will make the first advances. There is scarcely a more prolific source of unhappiness in the married state, than this "spirit," the legitimate offspring of pride and want of feeling.

Perhaps the whole art of happiness in the married state, might be compressed into these two maxims—"Bear and forbear"—and "let the husband treat his wife, and the wife treat her husband with as much respect and attention, as he would a strange lady, and she a strange gentleman." And surely this is not an extravagant requisition.

DOCUMENT ANALYSIS

1. Would any aspects of this essay have been considered radical in 1830? If so, then which ones?

_____

_____

_____

2. Why did Carey feel he is qualified to write such an essay? Upon what did he base his authority?

_____

_____

_____

3. In what ways did Carey's maxims challenge traditional gender roles, and in what ways did they reinforce them?

_____

_____

_____

DOCUMENT 11.1
O. A. Brownson, "Brook Farm," *United States Magazine and Democratic Review* 11 (November 1842)

Transcendentalism was a literary and philosophical movement that was popular in New England from the 1830s to the 1860s. It gained a wide audience thanks to works such as Henry David Thoreau's Walden. *Among its founders were some of the nation's most famous intellectuals and writers, including Nathaniel Hawthorne, Charles A. Dana, Ralph Waldo Emerson, Margaret Fuller, and Horace Greeley. Transcendentalism never included a strict religious philosophy, but most of its adherents believed in the divinity of humanity and the natural world and focused on the importance of intuition. Individualism and the satisfaction gained from physical work were central to transcendentalism, and Brook Farm, a utopian community in Massachusetts that existed from 1841 until 1847, attempted to transform those ideas into reality. In its last years Brook Farm was also greatly influenced by Fourierism, a utopian socialist philosophy named for its founder, the French philosopher Charles Fourier. The author of the excerpt below, O. A. Brownson, served as editor of the* United States Magazine and Democratic Review *from 1842 to 1844. Brownson was such an admirer of Brook Farm and its members that he sent his son there and he worked with community members on various publications.*

With respect to the labor, which is the material wealth of the establishment, and the body of its life, they intend to have all trades and occupations which contribute to necessities and healthy elegancies, within their own borders, so as not to buy them from without, which is too expensive; but at present their labor is agriculture, and the simplest housekeeping. . . .

Every one prescribes his own hours of labor, controlled only by his conscience, and the spirit of place, which tends to great industry, and almost to too much exertion. A drone would soon find himself isolated and neglected, and could not live there. The new comers, especially if they come from the city, have to begin gradually, but soon learn to increase the labor of one hour a day in the field, to six or seven hours, and some work all day long; but there can be no drudgery where there is no constraint. As all eat together, they change their dress for their meals; and so after tea they are all ready for grouping, in the parlors of the ladies, or in the library, or in the music-room, or they can go to their private rooms, or into the woods, or anywhere. They visit a good deal; and when they have business out of the community, nothing seems more easy than for them to arrange with others of their own number, to take their work or teaching for the time being; so that while they may work more than people out of the community, none seem such prisoners of their duties. The association of labor makes distribution according to taste and ability easy, and this takes the sting out of fatigue. . . .

For the women, there is, besides many branches of teaching, washing and ironing, housekeeping, sewing for the other sex, and for the children, and conducting all the social life. They have to hire one washerwoman now, but hope, bye and bye, to do all the washing within themselves. By the wide distribution of these labors, no one has any great weight of any one thing. They iron every forenoon but one; but they take turns, and each irons as long as she thinks right. The care of the houses is also distributed among those who are most active, in a way mutually satisfactory. . . .

. . . It is truly a most religious life, and does it not realize in miniature that identity of church and state which you think is the deepest idea of our American government? It seems to me that this community, point by point, corresponds with the great community of the Republic, whose divine lineaments are so much obscured by the rubbish of reported abuses (that, however, only lie on the surface, and may be shaken off, "like dewdrops from the lion's mane";) and whose divine proportions are now lost to our sight by the majestic grandeur with which they tower beyond the apprehension of our time-bound senses. For the theory of our government also proposes education (the freest development of the individual, according to the law of God) as its main end; an equal distribution of the results of labor among the laborers, as its means; and a mutual respect of each man by his neighbor as the basis. Only in America, I think, could such a community have so succeeded as I have described, composed of persons coming by chance, as it were, from all circumstances of life, and united only by a common idea and plan of life. They have succeeded, because they are the children of a government the ideal of which is the same as their own, although, as a mass, we are unconscious of it; so little do we understand our high vocation, and act up to it. But these miniatures of the great original shall educate us to the apprehension and realization of it, as a nation.

DOCUMENT ANALYSIS

1. In the final paragraph, what is the meaning of the phrase "in miniature that identity of church and state which you think is the deepest idea of our American government"?

_____

_____

_____

2. How was labor divided at Brook Farm? What restrictions, if any, were imposed on members of the community?

_____

_____

_____

3. Explain, in your own words, Brownson's reasoning that such a community could succeed only in America.

_____

_____

_____

DOCUMENT 11.2
Ralph Waldo Emerson, "The Concord Hymn" (1837)

The great resurgence of national pride that characterized Jackson's rise to the presidency touched every aspect of American life. One of the most evident manifestations of this national pride came in the form of a re-newed interest in commemorating the accomplishments of the nation's forefathers, who liberated the nation and provided for the prosperity at the time. "The Concord Hymn" by Ralph Waldo Emerson is an excellent example of the nationalistic pride felt by many Americans in the early nineteenth century. Emerson describes in great detail the sacrifices made by the men who fought at Concord, a great testament to the strength and will of the American nation.

By the rude bridge that arched the flood,
Their flag to April's breeze unfurled,
Here once the embattled farmers stood,
And fired the shot heard round the world.

The foe long since in silence slept;
Alike the conqueror silent sleeps;
And Time the ruined bridge has swept
Down the dark stream which seaward creeps.

On this green bank, by this soft stream,
We set to-day a votive stone;
That memory may their deed redeem,
When, like our sires, our sons are gone.

Spirit, that made those heroes dare
To die, or leave their children free,
Bid Time and Nature gently spare
The shaft we raise to them and thee.

DOCUMENT ANALYSIS

1. How do you think this poem was received by the American people? Would Americans from every part of the country have appreciated it for the same reasons? Why or why not?

_____

_____

_____

2. Why did Emerson describe the battle of Concord as "the shot heard round the world"?

_____

_____

_____

DOCUMENT 12.1
Richard Henry Dana, Jr., Assesses California in *Two Years Before the Mast* (1840)

Richard Henry Dana, Jr., distinguished himself as a Harvard graduate and an eminent lawyer who argued on behalf of slaves prosecuted under the Fugitive Slave Law and ultimately served in the Lincoln administration as U.S. attorney for Massachusetts. In addition, Dana enjoyed a literary career, based in large part upon the novel Two Years Before the Mast, *his account of the time he spent as a sailor aboard the* Pilgrim. *Dana undertook this adventure after an attack of measles had left his eyesight too poor to pursue his studies. The book was widely hailed in the United States and England as an excellent account of life at sea. Dana's voyage took him to California, and his observations offer a valuable glimpse of the region when it was still a part of Mexico, before the Mexican-American War and the Gold Rush.*

The Californians are an idle, thriftless people, and can make nothing for themselves. The country abounds in grapes, yet they buy bad wine made in Boston and brought round by us, at an immense price, and retail it among themselves at a real [a Spanish coin then worth 12 1/2 cents] by the small wine-glass. Their hides, too, which they value at two dollars in money, they give for something which costs seventy-five cents in Boston; and buy shoes (as like as not, made of their own hides, which have been carried twice round Cape Horn) at three and four dollars, and "chicken-skin" boots at fifteen dollars apiece. Things sell, on an average, at an advance of nearly three hundred per cent upon the Boston prices. . . .

Their complexions are various, depending—as well as their dress and manner—upon their rank; or, in other words, upon the amount of Spanish blood they can lay claim to. Those who are of pure Spanish blood, having never intermarried with the aborigines, have clear brunette complexions, and sometimes, even as fair as those of English women. There are but few of these families in California. . . . These form the aristocracy; intermarrying, and keeping up an exclusive system in every respect. They can be told by their complexions, dress, manner, and also by their speech. . . . From this upper class, they go down by regular shades, growing more and more dark and muddy, until you come to the pure Indian, who runs about with nothing upon him but a small piece of cloth, kept up by a wide leather strap drawn round his waist. Generally speaking, each person's caste is decided by the quality of the blood, which shows itself, too plainly to be concealed, at first sight. Yet the least drop of Spanish blood . . . is sufficient to raise them from the rank of slaves, and entitle them to a suit of clothes—boots, hat, cloak, spurs, long knife, and all complete, though coarse and dirty as may be—and to call themselves Espanolos, and to hold property, if they can get any. . . .

Another thing that surprised me was the quantity of silver that was in circulation. . . . The truth is, they have no credit system, no banks, and no way of investing money but in cattle. They have no circulating medium but silver and hides—which the sailors call "California bank notes." . . . Everything that they buy they must pay for in one or the other of these things. The hides they bring down dried and doubled, in clumsy ox-carts, or upon mules' backs, and the money they carry tied up in a handkerchief;—fifty, eighty, or an hundred dollars and half dollars. . . .

No Protestant has any civil rights, nor can he hold any property, or, indeed, remain more than a few weeks on shore, unless he belongs to some vessel. Consequently, the Americans and English who intend to reside here become Catholics, to a man; the current phrase among them being—"A man must leave his conscience at Cape Horn." . . .

The government of the country is an arbitrary democracy; having no common law, and no judiciary. Their only laws are made and unmade at the caprice of the legislature, and are as variable as the legislature itself. . . . Revolutions are matters of constant occurrence in California. They are got up by men who are at the foot of the ladder and in desperate circumstances, just as a new political party is started by such men in our own country. The only object, of course, is the loaves and fishes; and instead of caucusing, paragraphing, libelling, feasting, promising, and lying, as with us, they take muskets and bayonets, seizing upon the presidio and custom-house, divide the spoils, and declare a new dynasty. As for justice, they know no law but will and fear . . . .

Such are the people who inhabit a country embracing four or five hundred miles of sea-coast, with several good harbors; with fine forests in the north; the waters filled with fish, and the plains covered with thousands of herds of cattle; blessed with a climate, than which there can be no better in the world; free from all manner of diseases . . . ; and with a soil which corn yields from seventy to eighty fold. In the hands of an enterprising people, what a country this might be! we are ready to say. Yet how long would a people remain so, in such a country? The Americans (as those from the United States are called) and Englishmen, who are fast filling up the principal towns, and getting the trade into their hands, are indeed more industrious and effective than the Spaniards; yet their children are brought up Spaniards, in every respect, and if the "California fever" (laziness) spares the first generation, it always attacks the second.

DOCUMENT ANALYSIS

1. How does Dana's assessment of California's people compare to his assessment of the physical terrain and resources?

_____

_____

_____

2. Why did residents have to convert to Catholicism?

_____

_____

_____

3. What are Dana's feelings regarding California's political system? Does it compare favorably with the U.S. system, in his opinion?

_____

_____

_____

DOCUMENT 12.2
John C. Calhoun, Proposal to Preserve the Union (1850)

In the antebellum period, Senator John C. Calhoun was an ardent advocate of states' rights. In the great debates of the Jacksonian era, Calhoun combated federal tariff legislation by arguing that the states enjoyed the right to nullify certain pieces of federal legislation. In the ensuing years, Calhoun became increasingly strident in his defense of southern particularity. In this 1850 speech, Calhoun summarized his views on the present condition of the Union and his fears for the future.

I have, Senators, believed from the first that the agitation of the subject of slavery would, if not prevented by some timely and effective measure, end in disunion. . . . The agitation has been permitted to proceed, with almost no attempt to resist it, until it has reached a period when it can no longer be disguised or denied that the Union is in danger. You have thus had forced upon you the greatest and the gravest question that can ever come under your consideration: How can the Union be preserved?

. . . The first question, then, presented for consideration, in the investigation I propose to make, in order to obtain such knowledge, is: What is it that has endangered the Union?

To this question there can be but one answer: That the immediate cause is the almost universal discontent which pervades all the States composing the southern section of the Union. . . .

It is a great mistake to suppose, as is by some, that it originated with demagogues. . . . No; some cause, far deeper and more powerful than the one supposed must exist to account for discontent so wide and deep. The question, then, recurs: What is the cause of this discontent? It will be found in the belief of the people of the southern States, as prevalent as the discontent itself, that they cannot remain, as things now are, consistently with honor and safety, in the Union. The next question to be considered is: What has caused this belief?

One of the causes is, undoubtedly, to be traced to the long-continued agitation of the slave question on the part of the North, and the many aggressions which they have made on the rights of the South during the time. . . .

There is another, lying back of it, with which this is intimately connected, that may be regarded as the great and primary cause. That is to be found in the fact that the equilibrium between the two sections in the Government, as it stood when the Constitution was ratified and the Government put in action has been destroyed. At that time there was nearly a perfect equilibrium between the two, which afforded ample means to each to protect itself against the aggression of the other; but, as it now stands, one section has the exclusive power of controlling the Government, which leaves the other without any adequate means of protecting itself against its encroachment and oppression. . . .

[The] great increase of Senators, added to the great increase of the House of Representatives and the electoral college on the part of the North, which must take place under the next decade, will effectually and irretrievably destroy the equilibrium which existed when the Government commenced. . . .

What was once a constitutional federal republic is now converted, in reality, into one as absolute as that of the Autocrat of Russia, and as despotic in its tendency as any absolute Government that ever existed.

As, then, the North has the absolute control over the Government, it is manifest that on all questions between it and the South, where there is a diversity of interests, the interests of the latter will be sacrificed to the former, however oppressive the effects may be. . . . But if there was no question of vital importance to the South, in reference to which there was a diversity of views between the two sections, this state of things might be endured without the hazard of destruction to the South. But such is not the fact. . . .

I refer to the relation between the two races in the southern section, which constitutes a vital portion of her social organization. Every portion of the North entertains views and feelings more or less hostile to it. . . .

If the agitation goes on, the same force, acting with increased intensity, as has been shown, will finally snap every cord, when nothing will be left to bind the States together except force. . . .

How can the Union be saved? To this I answer, there is but one way by which it can be, and that is by adopting such measures as will satisfy the States belonging to the southern section that they can remain in the Union consistently with their honor and their safety.

DOCUMENT ANALYSIS

1. What presumptions do you think underlay Calhoun's thinking?

_____

_____

_____

2. Judging by this document, was it likely that a peaceful solution could have been found to the nation's sectional crisis in the 1850s, or was war inevitable?

_____

_____

_____

DOCUMENT 13.1
Nat Turner, *The Confession of Nat Turner* (1831)

In 1831 Nat Turner, a literate slave who had gained a considerable following among the slaves in Virginia, led an insurrection of slaves against their masters. Fifty-five whites were killed in the revolt, and at least that many African Americans were killed in immediate and delayed retaliation. The slave owners suspected a much wider conspiracy, however, and they responded with increasingly restrictive legal codes to prevent another uprising. Turner addressed his confession, which is excerpted below, to his white lawyer, Thomas R. Gray.

. . . To a mind like mine, restless, inquisitive and observant of every thing that was passing, it is easy to suppose that religion was the subject to which it would be directed, and although this subject principally occupied my thoughts—there was nothing that I saw or heard of to which my attention was not directed—The manner in which I learned to read and write, not only had great influence on my own mind, as I acquired it with the most perfect ease, so much so, that I have no recollection whatever of learning the alphabet—but to the astonishment of the family, one day, when a book was shewn to me to keep me from crying, I began spelling the names of different objects—this was a source of wonder to all in the neighborhood, particularly the blacks—and this learning was constantly improved at all opportunities—when I got large enough to go to work, while employed, I was reflecting on many things that would present themselves to my imagination, and whenever an opportunity occurred of looking at a book, when the school children were getting their lessons, I would find many things that the fertility of my own imagination had depicted to me before. . . .

[A]ll my time, not devoted to my master's service, was spent either in prayer, or in making experiments in casting different things in moulds made of earth, in attempting to make paper, gun-powder, and many other experiments, that although I could not perfect, yet convinced me of its practicability if I had the means.

I was not addicted to stealing in my youth, nor have ever been—Yet such was the confidence of the negroes in the neighborhood, even at this early period of my life, in my superior judgment, that they would often carry me with them when they were going on any roguery, to plan for them. Growing up among them, with this confidence in my superior judgment, and when this, in their opinions, was perfected by Divine inspiration, from the circumstances already alluded to in my infancy, and which belief was ever afterwards zealously inculcated by the austerity of my life and manners, which became the subject of remark by white and black.

Having soon discovered to be great, I must appear so, and therefore studiously avoided mixing in society, and wrapped myself in mystery, devoting my time to fasting and prayer—by this time, having arrived to man's estate, and hearing the scriptures commented on at meetings, I was struck with that particular passage which says: "Seek ye the kingdom of Heaven and all things shall be added unto you." I reflected much on this passage, and prayed daily for light on this subject—As I was praying one day at my plough, the spirit spoke to me, saying "Seek ye the kingdom of Heaven and all things shall be added unto you."

Question—what do you mean by the Spirit? Ans.—The Spirit that spoke to the prophets in former days—and I was greatly astonished, and for two years prayed continually, whenever my duty would permit—and then again I had the same revelation, which fully confirmed me in the impression that I was ordained for some great purpose in the hands of the Almighty.

Several years rolled round, in which many events occurred to strengthen me in this my belief. At this time I reverted in my mind to the remarks made of me in my childhood, and the things that had been shewn me—and as it had been said of me in my childhood by those by whom I had been taught to pray, both white and black, and in whom I had the greatest confidence, that I had too much sense to be raised, and if I was, I would never be of any use to any one as a slave. Now finding I had arrived to man's estate, and was a slave, and these revelations being made known to me, I began to direct my attention to this great object, to fulfil the purpose for which, by this time, I felt assured I was intended.

Knowing the influence I had obtained over the minds of my fellow servants (not by the means of conjuring and such like tricks—for to them I always spoke of such things with contempt) but by the communion of the Spirit whose revelations I often communicated to them, and they believed and said my wisdom came from God. I now began to prepare them for my purpose, by telling them something was about to happen that would terminate in fulfilling the great promise that had been made to me— . . .

DOCUMENT ANALYSIS

1. Ultimately, what did Nat Turner and his followers lack that was necessary for a successful uprising?

_____

_____

_____

2. Although the rebellion failed, what effect did it have on both slave owners and slaves?

_____

_____

_____

DOCUMENT 13.2
Horace Greeley, "An Overland Journey" (1860)

Horace Greeley was the editor of the New York Tribune *from 1841 to 1872. An outspoken reformer, Greeley championed such causes as temperance, public education, and abolition. Greeley is also associated with the westward migration of the nineteenth century and in this document argues in favor of a railroad connecting the Atlantic and Pacific coasts. The first transcontinental railroad was completed on May 10, 1869.*

The social, moral, and intellectual blessings of a Pacific railroad can hardly be glanced at within the limits of an article. Suffice it for the present that I merely suggest them.

1. Our mails are now carried to and from California by steamships, via Panama, in twenty to thirty days, starting once a fortnight. The average time of transit from writers throughout the Atlantic states to their correspondents on the Pacific exceeds thirty days. With a Pacific railroad, this would be reduced to ten; for the letters written in Illinois or Michigan would reach their destinations in the mining counties of California quicker than letters sent from New York or Philadelphia would reach San Francisco. With a daily mail by railroad from each of our Atlantic cities to and from California, it is hardly possible that the amount of both letters and printed matter transmitted, and consequently of postage, should not be speedily quadrupled.

2. The first need of California today is a large influx of intelligent, capable, virtuous women. With a railroad to the Pacific, avoiding the miseries and perils of six thousand miles of ocean transportation, and making the transit a pleasant and interesting overland journey of ten days, at a reduced cost, the migration of this class would be immensely accelerated and increased. With wages for all kinds of women's work at least thrice as high on the Pacific as in this quarter, and with larger opportunities for honorable and fit settlement in life, I cannot doubt that tens of thousands would annually cross the Plains, to the signal benefit of California and of the whole country, as well as the improvement of their own fortunes and the profit of the railroad.

3. Thousands now staying in California, expecting to "go home" so soon as they shall have somewhat improved their circumstances, would send or come for their families and settle on the Pacific for life, if a railroad were opened. Tens of thousands who have been to California and come back, unwilling either to live away from their families or to expose them to the present hardships of migration thither, would return with all they have, prepared to spend their remaining days in the land of gold, if there were a Pacific railroad.

4. Education is the vital want of California, second to its need of true women. School-books, and all the material of education, are now scarce and dear there. Almost all books sell there twice as high as here, and many of the best are scarcely attainable at any rate. With the Pacific railroad, all this would be changed for the better. The proportion of school-houses to grogshops would rapidly increase. All the elements of moral and religious melioration would be multiplied. Tens of thousands of our best citizens would visit the Pacific coast, receiving novel ideas and impressions, to their own profit and that of the people thus visited. Civilization, intelligence, refinement, on both sides of the mountain—still more, in the Great Basin enclosed by them—would receive a new and immense impulse, and the Union would acquire a greater accession of strength, power, endurance, and true glory, than it would from the acquisition of the whole continent down to Cape Horn.

The only points of view in which a railroad from the Missouri to the Pacific remains to be considered are those of its practicability, cost, location, and the ways and means. Let us look at them:

As to practicability, there is no room for hesitation or doubt. The Massachusetts Western, the Erie, the Pennsylvania, and the Baltimore and Ohio, have each encountered difficulties as formidable as any to be overcome by a Pacific railroad this side of the Sierra Nevada. Were the railroad simply to follow the principal emigrant trail up the Platte and down the Snake and Columbia to Oregon, or south-westwardly from the South Pass to the foot of the Sierra, it would encounter no serious obstacle. . . .

But let that government simply resolve that the Pacific road shall be built—let Congress enact that sealed proposals for its construction shall be invited, and that whichever responsible company or corporation shall offer adequate security for that construction, to be completed within ten years, on the lowest terms, shall have public aid, provided the amount required do not exceed fifty millions of dollars, and the work will be done, certainly for fifty millions' bonus, probably for much less. The government on its part should concede to the company a mile in width, according to the section lines, of the public lands on either side of the road as built, with the right to take timber, stone and earth from any public lands without charge; and should require of said company that it carry a daily through-mail each way at the price paid other roads for conveying mails on first-class routes; and should moreover stipulate for the conveyance at all times of troops, arms, munitions, provisions, etc., for the public service, at the lowest rates, with a right to the exclusive possession and use of the road whenever a national exigency shall seem to require it. The government should leave the choice of route entirely to the company, only stipulating that it shall connect the navigable waters of the Mississippi with those of the Pacific Ocean, and that it shall be constructed wholly through our own territory. . . .

By adopting this plan, the rivalries of routes will be made to work for, instead of working against, the construction of the road. Strenuous efforts will be made by the friends of each to put themselves in position to bid low enough to secure the location; and the lowest rate at which the work can safely be undertaken will unquestionably be bid. The road will be the property of the company constructing it, subject only to the rights of use, stipulated and paid for by the government. And, even were it to cost the latter a bonus of fully fifty millions, I feel certain that every farthing of that large sum will have been reimbursed to the treasury within five years after the completion of the work in the proceeds of land sales, in increased postages, and in duties on goods imported, sold, and consumed because of this railroad—not to speak of the annual saving of millions in the cost of transporting and supplying troops.

Men and brethren! let us resolve to have a railroad to the Pacific—to have it soon. It will add more to the strength and wealth of our country than would the acquisition of a dozen Cubas. It will prove a bond of union not easily broken, and a new spring to our national industry, prosperity and wealth. It will call new manufactures into existence, and increase the demand for the products of those already existing. It will open new vistas to national and to individual aspiration, and crush out filibusterism by giving a new and wholesome direction to the public mind. My long, fatiguing journey was undertaken in the hope that I might do something toward the early construction of the Pacific Railroad; and I trust that it has not been made wholly in vain.

DOCUMENT ANALYSIS

1. What were Greeley's major arguments in support of constructing a Pacific railroad?

_____

_____

2. Greeley asserted that constructing a Pacific railroad would contribute more to the nation's prosperity "than would the acquisition of a dozen Cubas." What is the significance of this observation, especially considering the year in which Greeley composed this piece?

_____

DOCUMENT 14.1
Opinion of the Supreme Court for *Dred Scott v. Sanford* (1857)

Dred Scott was a slave whose master had taken him to Illinois and the Wisconsin Territory, both of which prohibited slavery, before moving to Missouri, a slave state. In Missouri, Scott sued to gain his freedom. He argued that because his master had taken him to free states, he was no longer a slave. Scott fought his case all the way to the U.S. Supreme Court, where he ultimately lost. Beyond Scott's individual fate, the Court's decision had serious consequences for the fate of slaves, free African Americans, and the abolitionist cause in general. Not only the Court's judgment, but also the opinions of each of the justices, damaged the abolitionist cause. Particularly damning was the decision of Chief Justice Roger Taney, excerpted below.

Chief Justice Roger B. Taney: The Question is simply this: Can a negro, whose ancestors were imported into this country, and sold as slaves, become a member of the political community formed and brought into existence by the Constitution of the United States, and as such become entitled to all the rights, and privileges, and immunities, guarantied [sic] by that instrument to the citizen? One of which rights is the privilege of suing in a court of the United States in the cases specified in the constitution.

. . . The only matter in issue before the Court, therefore, is, whether the descendants of such slaves, when they shall be emancipated, or who are born of parents who had become free before their birth, are citizens of a State, in the sense which the word citizen is used in the Constitution.

. . .The words "people of the United States" and "citizens" are synonymous terms. . . . They both describe the political body who, according to our republican institutions, form the sovereignty, and who hold the power and conduct the government through their representatives. . . . The question before us is, whether the class of persons described in the plea in abatement compose a portion of this people, and are constituent members of this sovereignty? We think they are not, under the word "cit-izens" in the Constitution, and can therefore claim none of the rights and privileges which that instrument provides for and secures to citizens of the United States. On the contrary, they were at that time considered as a subordinate and inferior class of beings, who had been subjugated by the dominant race, and whether emancipated or not, yet remained subject to their authority, and had no rights or privileges but such as those who held the power and the government might choose to grant them. . . .

In discussing the question, we must not confound the rights of citizenship which a State may confer within its own limits, and the rights of citizenship as a member of the Union. It does not by any means follow, because he has all the rights and privileges of a citizen of a State, that he must be a citizen of the United States. . . .

In the opinion of the court, the legislation and histories of the times, and the language used in the Declaration of Independence, show, that neither the class of persons who had been imported as slaves, nor their descendants, whether they had become free or not, were then acknowledged as a part of the people, nor intended to be included in the general words used in that memorable instrument. . . .

They had for more than a century before been regarded as beings of an inferior order, and altogether unfit to associate with the white race, either in social or political relations, and so far inferior, that they had no rights which the white man was bound to respect; and that the negro might justly and lawfully be reduced to slavery for his benefit. . . .

. . . there are two clauses in the constitution which point directly and specifically to the negro race as a separate class of persons, and show clearly that they were not regarded as a portion of the people or citizens of the government then formed.

. . . upon full and careful consideration of the subject, the court is of opinion, that, upon the facts stated. . . , Dred Scott was not a citizen of Missouri within the meaning of the constitution of the United States and not entitled as such to sue in its courts. . . .

DOCUMENT ANALYSIS

1. Why did the language of this case so upset Northerners who were not necessarily in favor of abolishing slavery in the South?

_____

_____

_____

2. What effect did this ruling have on the status of free African Americans? How might this ruling have strengthened the abolitionist cause among Americans who did not consider African Americans their equals?

_____

_____

_____

DOCUMENT 14.2
Levi Coffin, Reminiscences of the Underground Railroad in the 1850s

Levi Coffin and his wife, Catherine, are remembered for their tireless work in assisting slaves to reach the safety of Canada via the Underground Railroad, a series of safe havens between the South and Montreal. Though originally from North Carolina, the Coffins were Quakers who adamantly opposed slavery. After moving to Indiana, they began working with the Underground Railroad in 1826. They continued their efforts after moving to Cincinnati in the 1840s. Eventually they helped more than 3,000 slaves to escape the South. Levi and Catherine were ostensibly the models for the characters Simeon and Rachel Halliday in Harriet Beecher Stowe's classic novel, Uncle Tom's Cabin. *Levi's memoirs were published in 1876.*

I was personally acquainted with all the active and reliable workers on the Underground Railroad in the city, both colored and white. There were a few wise and careful managers among the colored people, but it was not safe to trust all of them with the affairs of our work. Most of them were too careless, and a few were unworthy—they could be bribed by the slave hunters to betray the hiding places of the fugitives. We soon found it to be the best policy to confine our affairs to a few persons and to let the whereabouts of the slaves be known to as few people as possible.

When slave hunters were prowling around the city we found it necessary to use every precaution. We were soon fully initiated into the management of Underground Railroad matters in Cincinnati, and did not lack for work. Our willingness to aid the slaves was soon known, and hardly a fugitive came to the city without applying to us for assistance. There seemed to be a continual increase of runaways, and such was the vigilance of the pursuers that I was obliged to devote a large share of time from my business to making arrangements for their concealment and safe conveyance of the fugitives.

They sometimes came to our door frightened and panting and in a destitute condition, having fled in such haste and fear that they had no time to bring any clothing except what they had on, and that was often very scant. The expense of providing suitable clothing for them when it was necessary for them to go on immediately, or of feeding them when they were obliged to be concealed for days or weeks, was very heavy. . . .

Our house was large and well adapted for secreting fugitives. Very often slaves would lie concealed in upper chambers for weeks without the boarders or frequent visitors at the house knowing anything about it. My wife had a quiet unconcerned way of going about her work as if nothing unusual was on hand, which was calculated to lull every suspicion of those who might be watching, and who would have been at once aroused by any sign of secrecy or mystery. Even the intimate friends of the family did not know when there were slaves hidden in the house. . . .

The fugitives generally arrived in the night and were secreted among the friendly colored people or hidden in the upper room of our house. They came alone or in companies, and in a few instances had a white guide to direct them. . . .

DOCUMENT ANALYSIS

1. According to Coffin, what precautions or tactics did the Coffins employ to conceal fugitive slaves?

_____

_____

_____

2. Why did Coffin feel that he and his wife were successful conductors on the Underground Railroad?

_____

_____

_____

3. How did Coffin describe the plight of the fugitive slaves who fled to Cincinnati?

_____

_____

_____

DOCUMENT 15.1
Letter from H. Ford Douglas to Frederick Douglass's *Monthly* (January 8, 1863)

From: Edwin S. Redkey, ed., *A Grand Army of Black Men* (1992), pp. 24–25.

Edwin S. Redkey's book is a collection of more than 150 letters from African American soldiers to various newspapers and journals. The excerpt below was written just days after the Emancipation Proclamation was issued on January 1, 1863. At that point the Union decided to accept, and in fact encourage, black enlistment in the army and navy. Although enlistment was slow at first, black leaders such as Frederick Douglass openly encouraged enlistment because they believed it would help assure black citizenship when the war was over. By May 1863 the U.S. government had established the Bureau of Colored Troops. Eventually, 179,000 black men served in the army, and another 19,000 in the navy.

My wife sent me this morning the *Monthly* for December containing your appeal to England to "hands off" in this fearful conflict for freedom. It was indeed gratifying to me who have always felt more than a friendly interest in you and yours to read your eloquent and manly words of admonition to the Old Saxon mother States to give no moral or legal countenance to the claims of the impious Confederate States of America in their attempt to set up a Government established upon the idea of the perpetual bondage of the Negro. England has wisely withstood every temptation to do so—Abraham Lincoln has crossed the Rubicon and by one simple act of Justice to the slave links his memory with immortality.

The slaves are free! How can I write these precious words? And yet it is so unless twenty millions of people cradled in Christianity and civilization for a thousand years commit the foulest perjury that ever blackened the pages of history. In anticipation of this result I enlisted six months ago in order to be better prepared to play my part in the great drama of the Negro's redemption. I wanted its drill, its practical details, for mere theory does not make a good soldier. I have learned something of war, for I have seen war in its brightest as well as its bloodiest phase, and yet I have

nothing to regret. For since the stern necessities of this struggle have laid bare the naked issue of freedom on one side and slavery on the other—freedom shall have, in the future of this conflict if necessary, my blood as it has had in the past my earnest and best words. It seems to me that you can have no good reason for withholding from the government your hearty cooperation. This war will educate Mr. Lincoln out of his idea of the deportation of the Negro quite as fast as it has some of his other pro-slavery ideas with respect to employing them as soldiers.

Hitherto they have been socially and politically ignored by this government, but now by the fortunes of war they are cast morally and mentally helpless (so to speak) into the broad sunlight of our Republican civilization there to be educated and lifted to a higher and nobler life. National duties and responsibilities are not to be colonized, they must be heroically met and religiously performed. This mighty waste of manhood resulting from the dehumanizing character of slave institutions of America is now to be given back to the world through the patient toil and self-denial of this proud and haughty race. They must now pay back the negro in Spiritual culture in opportunities for self-improvement what they have taken from him for two hundred years by the constant over-taxing of his physical nature. This law of supply and demand regulates itself. And so this question of the colonization of the negro; it will be settled by laws over which war has no control. Now is the time for you to finish the crowning work of your life. Go to work at once and raise a Regiment and offer your services to the government, and I am confident they will be accepted. They say we will not fight. I want to see it tried on. You are the one to me of all others, to demonstrate this fact.

I belong to company G, 95th Regiment Illinois Volunteers—Captain Eliot N. Bush—a Christian and a gentleman. . . .

DOCUMENT ANALYSIS

1. Why did Douglas enlist in the army? What did he hope to gain from his enlistment?

_____

_____

_____

2. What was his opinion of the idea that African Americans should be colonized?

_____

_____

_____

3. What did he mean by the phrase "Abraham Lincoln has crossed the Rubicon"?

_____

_____

_____

DOCUMENT 15.2
Clara Barton, Memoirs of Medical Life at the Battlefield (1862)

Clara Barton was one of many women who supported the war effort by nursing troops, raising funds, and making clothes and bandages. This selection from her memoirs describes her initial ambivalence about exposing herself to the horrors of combat and the nightmarish conditions she found on the battlefields at Cedar Mountain and Second Manassas (Bull Run) during the summer of 1862.

I was strong and thought I might go to the rescue of the men who fell. . . What could I do but go with them, or work for them and my country? The patriot blood of my father was warm in my veins. The country which he had fought for, I might at least work for. . .

But I struggled long and hard with my sense of propriety—with the appalling fact that I was only a woman whispering in one ear, and

thundering in the other the groans of suffering men dying like dogs—unfed and unsheltered, for the life of every institution which had protected and educated me!

I said that I struggled long and hard with my sense of propriety and I say it with humiliation and shame. I am ashamed that I thought of such a thing.

When our armies fought on Cedar Mountain, I broke the shackles and went to the field. . .

Five days and nights with three hours sleep—a narrow escape from capture—and some days of getting the wounded into hospitals at Washington, brought Saturday, August 30. And if you chance to feel, that the positions I occupied were rough and unseemly for a woman—I can only reply that they were rough and unseemly for men. But under all, lay the life of the nation. I had inherited the rich blessing of health and strength of constitution—such as are seldom given to woman—and I felt that some return was due from me and that I ought to be there. . .

. . .Our coaches were not elegant or commodious; they had no seats, no platforms, no steps, a slide door on the side the only entrance, and this higher than my head. For my man attaining my elevated position, I must beg of you to draw on your imaginations and spare me the labor of reproducing the boxes, boards, and rails, which in those days, seemed to help me up and down the world. We did not criticize the unsightly helpers and were thankful that the stiff springs did not quite jostle us out. This need not be limited to this particular trip or train, but will for all that I have known in Army life. This is the kind of conveyance which your tons of generous gifts have reached the field with the freights. These trains through day and night, sunshine and heat and cold, have thundered over heights, across plains, the ravines, and over hastily built army bridges 90 feet across the stream beneath.

At 10 o'clock Sunday (August 31) our train drew up at Fairfax Station. The ground, for acres, was a thinly wooded slope—and among the trees on the leaves and grass, were laid the wounded who pouring in by scores of wagon loads, as picked up on the field the flag of truce. All day they came and the whole hillside was red. Bales of hay were broken open and scattered over the ground littering of cattle, and the sore, famishing men were laid upon it.

And when the night shut in, in the mist and darkness about us, we knew that standing apart from the world of anxious hearts, throbbing over the whole country, we were a little band of almost empty handed workers literally by ourselves in the wild woods of Virginia, with 3,000 suffering men crowded upon the few acres within our reach.

After gathering up every available implement or convenience for our work, our domestic inventory stood 2 water buckets, 5 tin cups, 1 camp kettle, 1 stew pan, 2 lanterns, 4 bread knives, 3 plates, and a 2-quart tin dish, and 3,000 guests to serve.

You will perceive by this, that I had not yet learned to equip myself, for I was no Pallas, ready armed, but grew into my work by hard thinking and sad experience. It may serve to relieve your apprehension for the future of my labors if I assure you that I was never caught so again.

But the most fearful scene was reserved for the night. I have said that the ground was littered with dry hay and that we had only two lanterns, but there were plenty of candles. The wounded were laid so close that it was impossible to move about in the dark. The slightest misstep brought a torrent of groans from some poor mangled fellow in your path.

Consequently here were seen persons of all grades from the careful man of God who walked with a prayer upon his lips to the careless driver hunting for his lost whip—each wandering about among this hay with an open flaming candle in his hands.

The slightest accident, the mere dropping of a light could have enveloped in flames this whole mass of helpless men.

How we watched and pleaded and cautioned as we worked and wept that night! How we put socks and slippers upon their cold feet, wrapped your blankets and quilts about them, and when we no longer these to give, how we covered them in the hay and left them to their rest!. . .

The slight, naked chest of a fair-haired lad caught my eye. Dropping down beside him, I bent low to draw the remnant of his blouse about him, when with a quick cry he threw his left arm across my neck and, burying his face in the folds of my dress, wept like a child at his mother's knee. I took his head in my hands and held it until great burst of grief passed away. "And do you know me?" he asked at length, "I am Charley Hamilton, we used to carry your satchel home from school!" My faithful pupil, poor Charley. That mangled right hand would never carry a satchel again.

About three o'clock in the morning I observed a surgeon with a little flickering candle in hand approaching me with cautious step up in the wood. "Lady," he said as he drew near, "will you go with me? Out on the hills is a poor distressed lad, mortally wounded, and dying. His piteous cries for his sister have touched all our hearts; none of us can relieve him but rather seem to distress him by presence."

By this time I was following him back over the bloody track, with great beseeching eyes of anguish on every side looking up into our faces, saying so plainly "Don't step on us."

DOCUMENT ANALYSIS

1. What conditions did Barton face when she reached the hospital in Fairfax? How did she cope with them?

_____

_____

_____

2. Women traditionally did not serve as nurses at this time period. How did that reality affect Barton's efforts at helping the men? How did the soldiers react to her assistance?

_____

_____

_____

DOCUMENT 16.1
Carl Schurz, *Report on the Condition of the South* (1865)

Carl Schurz was a German immigrant who rose to great political promi-
nence in the United States. He was a leading member of the Republican
Party and a great supporter of Lincoln. During the Civil War he attained
the rank of major general. After the war, Schurz continued to be active in
politics, supporting many reform movements. He was writer and editor
for several English- and German-language newspapers, and he published
several books. In 1865 President Andrew Johnson sent Schurz to tour the
South and to report on its postwar status. An excerpt from Schurz's report
appears below. The president was not pleased with the report.

We ought to keep in view, above all, the nature of the problem which
is to be solved. As to what is commonly termed "reconstruction," it is not
only the political machinery of the States and their constitutional relations
to the general government, but the whole organism of southern society
that must be reconstructed, or rather constructed anew, so as to bring it in
harmony with the rest of American society. The difficulties of this task are
not to be considered overcome when the people of the south take the oath
of allegiance and elect governors and legislatures and members of Congress, and militia captains. That this would be done had become certain as
soon as the surrenders of the southern armies had made further resistance
impossible, and nothing in the world was left, even to the most uncompromising rebel, but to submit or to emigrate. It was also natural that they
should avail themselves of every chance offered them to resume control of
their home affairs and to regain their influence in the Union. But this can
hardly be called the first step towards the solution of the true problem,
and it is a fair question to ask, whether the hasty gratification of their desire to resume such control would not create new embarrassments.

The true nature of the difficulties of the situation is this: The general
government of the republic has, by proclaiming the emancipation of the
slaves, commenced a great social revolution in the south, but has, as yet,
not completed it. Only the negative part of it is accomplished. The slaves
are emancipated in point of form, but free labor has not yet been put in
the place of slavery in point of fact. And now, in the midst of this critical
period of transition, the power which originated the revolution is expected to turn over its whole future development to another power which
from the beginning was hostile to it and has never yet entered into its
spirit, leaving the class in whose favor it was made completely without
power to protect itself and to take an influential part in that development.
The history of the world will be searched in vain for a proceeding similar
to this which did not lead either to a rapid and violent reaction, or to the
most serious trouble and civil disorder. It cannot be said that the conduct
of the southern people since the close of the war has exhibited such extraordinary wisdom and self-abnegation as to make them an exception to
the rule. In my dispatches from the south I repeatedly expressed the opinion that the people were not yet in a frame of mind to legislate calmly and
understandingly upon the subject of free negro labor. And this I reported
to be the opinion of some of our most prominent military commanders
and other observing men.

It is, indeed, difficult to imagine circumstances more unfavorable for
the development of a calm and unprejudiced public opinion than those
under which the southern people are at present laboring. The war has not
only defeated their political aspirations, but it has broken up their whole
social organization. When the rebellion was put down they found themselves not only conquered in a political and military sense, but economically ruined. The planters, who represented the wealth of the southern
country, are partly laboring under the severest embarrassments, partly reduced to absolute poverty. Many who are stripped of all available means,
and have nothing but their land, cross their arms in gloomy despondency,
incapable of rising to a manly resolution. Others, who still possess means,
are at a loss how to use them, as their old way of doing things is, by the
abolition of slavery, rendered impracticable, at least where the military
arm of the government has enforced emancipation. Others are still trying
to go on in the old way, and that old way is in fact the only one they understand, and in which they have any confidence. Only a minority is try-

ing to adopt the new order of things. A large number of the plantations,
probably a considerable majority of the more valuable estates, is under
heavy mortgages, and the owners know that, unless they retrieve their fortunes in a comparatively short space of time, their property will pass out
of their hands. Almost all are, to some extent, embarrassed.

The nervous anxiety which such a state of things produces extends
also to those classes of society which, although not composed of planters,
were always in close business connection with the planting interest, and
there was hardly a branch of commerce or industry in the south which
was not directly or indirectly so connected. Besides, the southern soldiers,
when returning from the war, did not, like the northern soldiers, find a
prosperous community which merely waited for their arrival to give them
remunerative employment. They found, many of them, their homesteads
destroyed, their farms devastated, their families in distress; and those that
were less unfortunate found, at all events, an impoverished and exhausted
community which had but little to offer them. Thus a great many have
been thrown upon the world to shift as best they can. They must do
something honest or dishonest, and must do it soon, to make a living,
and their prospects are, at present, not very bright. Thus that nervous
anxiety to hastily repair broken fortunes, and to prevent still greater ruin
and distress, embraces nearly all classes, and imprints upon all the movements of the social body a morbid character. In which direction will these
people be most apt to turn their eyes? Leaving the prejudice of race out of
the question, from early youth they have been acquainted with but one
system of labor, and with that one system they have been in the habit of
identifying all their interests. They know of no way to help themselves but
the one they are accustomed to. Another system of labor is presented to
them, which, however, owing to circumstances which they do not appreciate, appears at first in an unpromising light. To try it they consider an
experiment which they cannot afford to make while their wants are urgent. They have not reasoned calmly enough to convince themselves that
the trial must be made. It is, indeed, not wonderful that, under such circumstances, they should study, not how to introduce and develop free labor, but how to avoid its introduction, and how to return as much and as
quickly as possible to something like the old order of things. Nor is it
wonderful that such studies should find an expression in their attempts at
legislation. But the circumstance that this tendency is natural does not
render it less dangerous and objectionable.

The practical question presents itself: Is the immediate restoration
of the late rebel States to absolute self-control so necessary that it must be
done even at the risk of endangering one of the great results of the war,
and of bringing on in those States insurrection or anarchy, or would it
not be better to postpone that restoration until such dangers are passed?
If, as long as the change from slavery to free labor is known to the southern people only by its destructive results, these people must be expected
to throw obstacles in its way, would it not seem necessary that the movement of social "reconstruction" be kept in the right channel by the hand
of the power which originated the change, until that change can have dis-
closed some of its beneficial effects? It is certain that every success of free
negro labor will augment the number of its friends, and disarm some of
the prejudices and assumptions of its opponents. I am convinced one
good harvest made by unadulterated free labor in the south would have a
far better effect than all the oaths that have been taken, and all the ordinances that have as yet been passed by southern conventions. But how
can such a result be attained?

The facts enumerated in this report, as well as the news we receive
from the south from day to day, must make it evident to every unbiased
observer that unadulterated free labor cannot be had at present, unless
the national government holds its protective and controlling hand over it.
It appears, also, that the more efficient this protection of free labor against
all disturbing and reactionary influences, the sooner may such a satisfactory result be looked for. One reason why the southern people are so slow
in accommodating themselves to the new order of things is, that they
confidently expect soon to be permitted to regulate matters according to

their own notions. Every concession made to them by the government has been taken as an encouragement to persevere in this hope, and, unfortunately for them, this hope is nourished by influences from other parts of the country. Hence their anxiety to have their State governments restored at once, to have the troops withdrawn, and the Freedmen's Bureau abolished, although a good many discerning men know well that, in view of the lawless spirit still prevailing, it would be far better for them to have the general order of society firmly maintained by the federal power until things have arrived at a final settlement. Had, from the beginning, the conviction been forced upon them that the adulteration of the new order of things by the admixture of elements belonging to the system of slavery would under no circumstances be permitted, a much larger number would have launched their energies into the new channel, and, seeing that they could do "no better," faithfully co-operated with the government. It is hope which fixes them in their perverse notions. That hope nourished or fully gratified, they will persevere in the same direction. That hope destroyed, a great many will, by the force of necessity, at once accommodate themselves to the logic of the change.

If, therefore, the national government firmly and unequivocally announces its policy not to give up the control of the free-labor reform until it is finally accomplished, the progress of that reform will undoubtedly be far more rapid and far less difficult than it will be if the attitude of the government is such as to permit contrary hopes to be indulged in. The machinery by which the government has so far exercised its protection of the negro and of free labor in the south—the Freedmen's Bureau—is very unpopular in that part of the country, as every institution placed there as a barrier to reactionary aspirations would be. That abuses were committed with the management of freedmen's affairs; that some of the officers of the bureau were men of more enthusiasm than discretion, and in many cases went beyond their authority: all this is certainly true. But, while the southern people are always ready to expatiate upon the shortcomings of the Freedmen's Bureau, they are not so ready to recognize the services it has rendered. I feel warranted in saying that not half of the labor that has been done in the south this year, or will be done there next year, would have been or would be done but for the exertions of the Freedmen's Bureau. The confusion and disorder of the transition period would have been infinitely greater had not an agency interfered which possessed the confidence of the emancipated slaves; which could disabuse them of any extravagant notions and expectations and be trusted; which could administer to them good advice and be voluntarily obeyed. No other agency, except one placed there by the national government, could have wielded that moral power whose interposition was so necessary to prevent southern society from falling at once into the chaos of a general collision between its different elements. That the success achieved by the Freedmen's Bureau is as yet very incomplete cannot be disputed. A more perfect organization and a more carefully selected personnel may be desirable; but it is doubtful whether a more suitable machinery can be devised to secure to free labor in the south that protection against disturbing influences which the nature of the situation still imperatively demands.

DOCUMENT ANALYSIS

1. Was Schurz hopeful about the situation in the South in 1865?

_____

_____

_____

2. What did Schurz predict would happen in the South? Was he correct?

_____

_____

_____

3. What was Schurz's opinion of the Freedmen's Bureau? Did he recommend that it continue to operate?

_____

_____

_____

DOCUMENT 17.1
Accounts of the Wounded Knee Massacre (1890s)

In late 1890 troops of the U.S. Seventh Cavalry killed more than 200 Native American men, women, and children at Pine Ridge reservation located along Wounded Knee Creek in South Dakota. A number of long-standing issues on the reservations contributed to the tension prior to the massacre. In the bad crop years of 1889 and 1890, the U.S. government failed to provide the full amount of food, agricultural implements and seeds, clothing, and supplies mandated by its treaty with the Lakota Nation. Many Lakota, including Black Elk, criticized the violent reactions of the Indian agents, many of whom were inexperienced and some of whom were remnants of Custer's Seventh Cavalry, which had been crushed by Sitting Bull just 14 years before at the Little Big Horn. Black Elk, a veteran of the Battle of the Little Big Horn, describes the tragedy at Wounded Knee in this excerpt from his autobiography, Black Elk Speaks. *The second document is an excerpt from President Benjamin Harrison's annual message, delivered December 9, 1891. Harrison describes the conflict and the progress of the program to decrease Native American landholdings. Many years later, Flying Hawk recollected the events.*

Black Elk

It was about this time that bad news came to us from the north. We heard that some policemen from Standing Rock had gone to arrest Sitting Bull on Grand River, and that he would not let them take him; so there was a fight, and they killed him.

It was not near the end of the Moon of Popping Trees, and I was twenty-seven years old [December 1890]. We heard that Big Foot was coming down from the Badlands with nearly four hundred people. Some of these were from Sitting Bull's band. They had run away when Sitting Bull was killed, and joined Big Foot on Good River. There were only about a hundred warriors in this band, and all the others were women and children and some old men. They were all starving and freezing, and Big Foot was so sick that they had to bring him along in a pony drag. They had all run away to hide in the Badlands, and they were coming in now because they were starving and freezing. Soldiers were over there looking for them. The soldiers had everything and were not freezing and starving. Near Porcupine Butte the soldiers came up to the Big Foots, and they surrendered and went along with the soldiers to Wounded Knee Creek.

It was in the evening when we heard that the Big Foots were camped over there with the soldiers, about fifteen miles by the old road from where we were. It was the next morning [December 29, 1890] that something terrible happened.

That evening before it happened, I went in to Pine Ridge and heard these things, and while I was there, soldiers started for where the Big Foots were. These made about five hundred soldiers that were there next morning. When I saw them starting I felt that something terrible was going to happen. That night I could hardly sleep at all. I walked around most of the night.

In the morning I went out after my horses, and while I was out I heard shooting off toward the east, and I knew from the sound that it must be wagon-guns [cannon] going off. The sounds went right through my body, and I felt that something terrible would happen. . . . [He donned his ghost shirt, and armed only with a bow, mounted his pony and rode in the direction of the shooting, and was joined on the way by others.]

In a little while we had come to the top of the ridge where, looking to the east, you can see for the first time the monument and the burying ground on the little hill where the church is. That is where the terrible thing started. Just south of the burying ground on the little hill a deep dry gulch runs about east and west, very crooked, and it rises westward to nearly the top of the ridge where we were. It had no name, but the Wasichus [white men] sometimes call it Battle Creek now. We stopped on the ridge not far from the head of the dry gulch. Wagon-guns were still going off over there on the little hill, and they were going off again where they hit among the gulch. There was much shooting down yonder, and there were many cries, and we could see cavalrymen scattered over the hills ahead of us. Cavalrymen were riding along the gulch and shooting into it, where the women and children were running away and trying to hide in the gullies and the stunted pines. . . .

We followed down along the dry gulch, and what we saw was terrible. Dead and wounded women and children and little babies were scattered all along there where they had been trying to run away. The soldiers had followed along the gulch, as they ran, and murdered them in there. Sometimes they were in heaps because they had huddled together, and some were scattering all along. Sometimes bunches of them had been killed and torn to pieces where the wagon guns hit them. I saw a little baby trying to suck its mother, but she was bloody and dead.

There were two little boys at one place in this gulch. They had guns and they had been killing soldiers all by themselves. We could see the soldiers they had killed. The boys were all alone there, and they were not hurt. These were very brave little boys.

When we drove the soldiers back, they dug themselves in, and we were not enough people to drive them out from there. In the evening they marched off up Wounded Knee Creek, and then we saw all that they had done there.

Men and women and children were heaped and scattered all over the flat at the bottom of the little hill where the soldiers had their wagon-guns, and westward up the dry gulch all the way to the high ridge, the dead women and children and babies were scattered.

When I saw this I wished that I had died too, but I was not sorry for the women and children. It was better for them to be happy in the other world, and I wanted to be there too. But before I went there I wanted to have revenge. I thought there might be a day, and we should have revenge.

In the morning the soldiers began to take all the guns away from the Big Foots, who were camped in the flat below the little hill where the monument and burying ground are now. The people had stacked most of their guns, and even their knives, by the teepee where Big Foot was lying sick. Soldiers were on the little hill and all around, and there were soldiers across the dry gulch to the south and over east along Wounded Knee Creek too. The people were nearly surrounded, and the wagon-guns were pointed at them.

It was a good winter day when all this happened. The sun was shining. But after the soldiers marched away from their dirty work, a heavy snow began to fall. The wind came up in the night. There was a big blizzard, and it grew very cold. The snow drifted deep in the crooked gulch, and it was one long grave of butchered women and children and babies, who had never done any harm and were only trying to run away.

Benjamin Harrison, Report on Wounded Knee Massacre and the Decrease in Indian Land Acreage, 1891

The outbreak among the Sioux which occurred in December last is as to its causes and incidents fully reported upon by the War Department and the Department of the Interior. That these Indians had some just complaints, especially in the matter of the reduction of the appropriation for rations and in the delays attending the enactment of laws to enable the Department to perform the engagements entered into with them, is probably true; but the Sioux tribes are naturally warlike and turbulent, and their warriors were excited by their medicine men and chiefs, who preached the coming of an Indian messiah who was to give them power to destroy their enemies. In view of the alarm that prevailed among the white settlers near the reservation and of the fatal consequences that would have resulted from an Indian incursion, I placed at the disposal of General Miles, commanding the Division of the Missouri, all such forces that we thought by him to be required. He is entitled to the credit of having given thorough protection to the settlers and of bringing the hostiles into subjection with the least possible loss of life. . . .

Since March 4, 1889, about 23,000,000 acres have been separated from Indian reservations and added to the public domain for the use of those who desired to secure free homes under our beneficent laws. It is difficult to estimate the increase of wealth which will result from the conversion of these waste lands into farms, but it is more difficult to estimate

the betterment which will result to the families that have found renewed hope and courage in the ownership of a home and the assurance of a comfortable subsistence under free and healthful conditions. It is also gratifying to be able to feel, as we may, that his work has proceeded upon lines of justice toward the Indian, and that he may now, if he will, secure to himself the good influences of a settled habitation, the fruits of industry, and the security of citizenship.

Flying Hawk's Recollections of Wounded Knee (1936)

This was the last big trouble with the Indians and soldiers and was in the winter in 1890. When the Indians would not come in from the Bad Lands, they got a big army together with plenty of clothing and supplies and camp-and-wagon equipment for a big campaign; they had enough soldiers to make a round-up of all the Indians they called hostiles.

The Government army, after many fights and loss of lives, succeeded in driving these starving Indians, with their families of women and gaunt-faced children, into a trap, where they could be forced to surrender their arms. This was on Wounded Knee creek, northeast of Pine Ridge, and here the Indians were surrounded by the soldiers, who had Hotchkiss machine guns along with them. There were about four thousand Indians in this big camp, and the soldiers had the machine guns pointed at them from all around the village as the soldiers formed a ring about the tepees so that Indians could not escape.

The Indians were hungry and weak and they suffered from lack of clothing and furs because the whites had driven away all the game. When the soldiers had them all surrounded and they had their tepees set up, the officers sent troopers to each of them to search for guns and take them from the owners. If the Indians in the tepees did not at once hand over a gun, the soldier tore open their trunks and bundles and bags of robes or clothes,—looking for pistols and knives and ammunition. It was an ugly business, and brutal; they treated the Indians like they would torment a wolf with one foot in a strong trap; they could do this because the Indians were now in the white man's trap,—and they were helpless.

Then a shot was heard from among the Indian tepees. An Indian was blamed; the excitement began; soldiers ran to their stations; officers gave orders to open fire with the machine guns into the crowds of innocent men, women and children, and in a few minutes more than two hundred and twenty of them lay in the snow dead and dying. A terrible blizzard raged for two days covering the bodies with Nature's great white blanket; some lay in piles of four or five; others in twos or threes or singly, where they fell until the storm subsided. When a trench had been dug of sufficient length and depth to contain the frozen corpses, they were collected and piled, like cord-wood, in one vast icy tomb. While separating several stiffened forms which had fallen in a heap, two of them proved to be women, and hugged closely to their breasts were infant babes still alive after lying in the storm for two days in 20-below-zero weather.

I was there and saw the trouble,—but after the shooting was over; it was all bad.

DOCUMENT ANALYSIS

1. According to Black Elk, what atrocities took place at Wounded Knee? How did President Harrison describe these atrocities?

_____

_____

_____

2. Whom did Black Elk blame for the Wounded Knee Massacre? Whom did Harrison blame?

_____

_____

_____

3. According to President Harrison, what was the future of Native Americans? How did Black Elk's vision of the future compare with Harrison's vision?

_____

_____

_____

DOCUMENT 18.1
Samuel Gompers, *The American Labor Movement: Its Makeup, Achievements and Aspirations* (1914)

Samuel Gompers co-founded the American Federation of Labor (AFL or A.F. of L. below) in 1886, and he served as its president for most of the period until 1924. He composed this document at a time when the AFL was prospering, claiming almost 2 million members.

The Federation covers practically the whole field of industry. There are no limitations as to membership. The only requirement, so far as the A. F. of L. is concerned, is that the organization desiring affiliation shall be composed of wage-earners. . . .

The affiliated organizations are held together by moral obligation, a spirit of camaraderie, a spirit of group patriotism, a spirit of mutual assistance.

There are no coercive methods used by the A. F. of L. to prevent the withdrawal or secession of any affiliated organization. . . .

Similarly, no coercion is used in regard to national organizations which are not affiliated to the A. F. of L. We feel that it is the duty of every wage-worker to belong to the union of his trade or calling; that it is the duty of the local union of a trade or calling to belong to the national or international union of that trade or calling; and that it is equally the moral duty of every national or international organization of bona-fide workingmen to belong to the A. F. of L. But coercive methods are never employed. . . .

Recognizing the fact that associated effort is of greater influence and power to secure a given object than is individual effort the first purpose toward which the A. F. of L. directs its efforts is the encouragement of trade and labor unions and the closer federation of such unions. . . . They aim at the protection of the rights and the interests of the members and of all working people, the promotion and the advancement of their economic, political, and social rights. They aim to make life better worth living in our day. . . . In a word, the organizations leave no effort untried by which the working people may find betterment in any field of human activity. . . .

The A. F. of L. is in favor of a shorter workday, and a progressive decrease of working hours in keeping with the development of machinery and the use of productive forces. The Federation has recognized the need for greater opportunities and more time for rest, leisure and cultivation among the workers. . . . We insist upon one entire day of rest in each week. . . .

The Federation favors securing more effective inspection of workshops, factories, and mines, and has worked for the accomplishment of that purpose.

The Federation does not favor the employment of children under 16 years of age and has endeavored to forbid such employment.

It favors forbidding interstate transportation of the products of convict labor and the products of all non-inspected factories and mines. . . .

There is now a current movement to increase wages by a proposal to determine a minimum wage by political authorities. It is a maxim in law that once a court is given jurisdiction over an individual it has the power, the field, and authority to exercise that jurisdiction. . . . An attempt to entrap the American workmen into a species of slavery, under guise of an offer of this character is resented by the men and women of the American trade union movement.

When the question of fixing, by legal enactment, minimum wages for women was before the Executive Council of the A. F. of L. for investigation and discussion, and subsequently before the convention of the A. F. of L., there was a great diversion of views. . . . In my judgment the proposal to establish by law a minimum wage for women, though well meant, is a curb upon the rights, the natural development, and the opportunity for development of the women employed in the industries of our country. . . .

The A. F. of L. encourages the practice of its various affiliated organizations in endeavoring to secure a shorter workday by means of collective agreements with employers in the various industries, but it opposes reaching the same result by means of a law binding upon all employers in a given state, or throughout the union. If there were a movement and a possibility of establishing an eight-hour workday and a minimum wage by legal enactment throughout the land, the Federation would oppose such policies, because it has in a large measure accomplished the same purposes and will accomplish them by the initiative of the associations or the organizations and by the grit and courage of the manhood and womanhood of the men and women of the A. F. of L. That these results have been accomplished through the initiative and voluntary association of the workers precludes the question of having legal enactment for the same purpose. In addition, the giving of jurisdiction to government and to governmental agencies is always dangerous when it comes to governing the working people. . . .

The A. F. of L. encourages and stimulates the workmen in their efforts to secure a constantly increasing share in the products of labor, an increasing share in the consumption and use of things produced, thereby giving employment to the unemployed, the only effective way by which that can be done. . . .

In improving conditions from day to day the organized labor movement has no "fixed program" for human progress. If you start out with a program everything must conform to it. With theorists, if facts do not conform to their theories, then so much the worse for the facts. Their declarations of theories and actions refuse to be hampered by facts. We do not set any particular standard, but work for the best possible conditions immediately obtainable for the workers. When they are obtained then we strive for better.

It does not require any elaborate social philosophy or great discernment to know that a wage of $3 a day and a workday of eight hours in sanitary workshops are better than $2.50 a day and a workday of twelve hours under perilous conditions. The working people will not stop when any particular point is reached; they will never stop in their efforts to obtain a better life for themselves, for their wives, for their children, and for all humanity. The object is to attain complete social justice.

The Socialist party has for its purpose the abolition of the present system of wages. Many employers agree with that purpose—the abolition of wages. But the A. F. of L. goes beyond the system which those dreamers have conceived.

The movement of the working people, whether under the A. F. of L. or not, will simply follow the human impulse for improvement in conditions wherever that may lead, and wherever that may lead they will go without aiming at any theoretical goal. Human impulse for self-betterment will lead constantly to the material, physical, social, and moral betterment of the people. We decline to commit our labor movement to any species of speculative philosophy. . . .

DOCUMENT ANALYSIS

1. Though Gompers listed the positive achievements and aspirations of the AFL, he also described what the Federation would not do. Who might he be criticizing in these oblique references?

_____

_____

_____

2. What was the position of the AFL on the minimum wage?

_____

_____

_____

3. What goals did Gompers specifically list? From this short document, can you find enough information to outline the general AFL program? If so, what would you include?

_____

_____

_____

DOCUMENT 19.1
Richard K. Fox, from *Coney Island Frolics* (1883)

Coney Island, a beach off the coast of Brooklyn in New York City, featured an amusement park and beach resort built with the working-class and middle-class communities of the city in mind. It was a place where social conventions were loosened and patrons could revel in immediate satisfaction and fun. This selection is from an instruction manual or travel guide to Coney Island titled Coney Island Frolics: How New York's Gay Girls and Jolly Boys Enjoy Themselves by the Sea.

There are various ways of bathing at Coney Island. You can go in at the West End, where they give you a tumbledown closet like a sentry box stuck up in the sand, or at the great hotels where more or less approach to genuine comfort is afforded. The pier, too, is fitted up with extensive bathing houses, and altogether no one who wants a dip in the briny and has a quarter to pay for it need to go without it.

If a man is troubled with illusions concerning the female form divine and wishes to be rid of those illusions he should go to Coney Island and closely watch the thousands of women who bathe there every Sunday.

A woman, or at least most women, in bathing undergoes a transformation that is really wonderful. They waltz into the bathing-rooms clad in all the paraphernalia that most gladdens the feminine heart. The hair is gracefully dressed, and appears most abundant; the face is decorated with all that elaborate detail which defies description by one uninitiated in the mysteries of the boudoir; the form is molded by the milliner to distracting elegance of proportion, and the feet appear aristocratically slender and are arched in French boots.

Thus they appear as they sail past the gaping crowds of men, who make Coney Island a loafing place on Sundays. They seek out their individual dressing rooms and disappear. Somewhere inside of an hour, they make their appearance ready for the briny surf. If it were not for the men who accompany them it would be impossible to recognize them as the same persons who but a little while ago entered those diminutive rooms. . . .

The broad amphitheater at Manhattan Beach built at the water's edge is often filled with spectators. Many pay admission fees to witness the feats of swimmers, the clumsiness of beginners and the ludicrous mishaps of the never-absent stout persons. Under the bathing-house is a sixty horsepower engine. It rinses and washes the suits for the bathers, and its steady puffing is an odd accompaniment to the merry shouts of the bathers and the noise of the shifting crowd ashore. . . .

A person who intends to bathe at Manhattan or Brighton Beach first buys a ticket and deposits it in a box such as is placed in every elevated railroad station. If he carries valuables he may have them deposited without extra charge in a safe that weighs seven tons and has one thousand compartments. He encloses them in an envelope and seals it. Then he writes his name partly on the flap of the envelope and partly on the envelope itself. For this envelope he receives a metal check attached to an elastic string, in order that he may wear it about his neck while bathing. This check has been taken from one of the compartments of the safe which bears the same number as the check. Into the same compartment the sealed envelope is put. When the bather returns from the surf he must return the check and must write his name on piece of paper. This signature is compared with the one on the envelope. Should the bather report that his check has been lost or stolen his signature is deemed a sufficient warrant for return of the valuables. The safe has double doors in front and behind. Each drawer may be drawn out from either side. When the throng presses six men may be employed at this safe.

DOCUMENT ANALYSIS

1. How did Fox describe the women who come to Coney Island? Did he approve or disapprove of their behavior and appearance?

_____

_____

_____

2. Why would Coney Island appeal primarily to middle-class and working-class people?

_____

_____

_____

DOCUMENT 19.2
Adna Weber, "The Growth of Cities in the Nineteenth Century" (1899)

Adna Ferrin Weber was an urban demographer who wrote at the turn of the twentieth century. His work on population and cities offered a Darwinian approach to understanding how great cities were born. In this excerpt, he explains how human populations progressed from rural isolation to bustling urban centers such as New York and Chicago.

In a new country the rapid growth of cities is both natural and necessary, for no efficient industrial organization of a new settlement is possible without industrial centers to carry on the necessary work of assembling and distributing goods. A Mississippi Valley empire rising suddenly into being without its Chicago and its smaller centers of distribution is almost inconceivable to the nineteenth century economist. That America is the "land of mushroom cities" is therefore not at all surprising. But, on the other hand, it is astonishing that the development of the cities in a new country should outstrip that of the rural districts which they serve. The natural presumption would be that so long as land remains open to settlement, the superfluous population of the older States or of Europe would seek the fundamental, or food-producing, industry of agriculture, and build up cities only in a corresponding degree. Yet in the great cereal regions of the West, the cities have grown entirely out of proportion to the rural parts, resulting there, as in the East and in Europe, in an increasing concentration of the population. . . .

It is now clear that the growth of cities must be studied as a part of the question of distribution of population, which is always dependent upon the economic organization of society upon the constant striving to maintain as many people as possible upon a given area. The ever-present problem is so to distribute and organize the masses of men that they can render such services as favor the maintenance of the nation and thereby accomplish their own preservation. Population follows the line of least resistance in its distribution, and will consequently be affected by changes in the methods of production. When the industrial organization demands the presence of laborers in particular localities in order to increase its efficiency, laborers will be found there; the means of attraction will have been "better living"—in other words, an appeal to the motive of self-

interest. Economic forces are therefore the principal cause of concentration of population in cities. . . .

Now, without stretching the analogy, we may liken industrial society of today—embracing all countries within the circle of exchange of products—to a great organism composed of heterogeneous parts. This organism, however, is the product of ages of slow growth. Originally, in place of the one all-embracing social organism, there were myriads of small social units, each complete in itself and independent of the others, if not positively hostile to them. The history of civilization is simply the narrative description of the breaking down of the barriers that separated the primitive social units—the original family group, clan, patriarchal family, the enlarged village community or the manorial group. And the most conspicuous and influential role in the process was played by the trader, working upon men's desires for what they did not possess or produce. Neither war (conquest) nor religion has been of so vital and far-reaching influence in the integration and amalgamation of isolated social groups as trade and commerce. When, therefore, it is pointed out that towns owe their origin to trade, that the commercial metropolis of today is the successor of the primitive market-place established beside the boundary stone between hostile but avaricious tribal groups, that the extension of the market means the enlargement of the market-center—then one will readily perceive the connection of the growth of industrial society to its present world-wide dimensions with our problem of the concentration of population. . . .

If men were like other animals and had no further wants than bodily appetites and passions, there would be no large aggregations of people; for in order to produce food, men must live either in scattered habitations like American farmers, or in hamlets like the ancient family or tribal group, the village community, the Russian *mir,* and the modern agricultural village of Continental Europe. Even with a comparatively high grade of wants, men may live in these small groups, each of which is economically autonomous and self-sufficing, producing for itself and buying and selling little if anything. It is the period of the *Naturalwirthschaft,* in which all payments are in kind. The principle of division of labor finally led to the disruption of the village community, but its triumph was long delayed. The principle was of course grasped only imperfectly by primitive man. At first the only division was that based on sex, age, muscular power, or relation to the governing head of the group; in other respects there was no assignment of special tasks to particular individuals. Very

gradually men discovered among themselves differences of natural aptitude. The members of a community at length realized that it was more economical to have their flour made in a village mill by one member who should give all his time to that particular work, than to have it made by bits in a score of individual mills. One by one other industries have followed the mill—have departed from the separate households and taken up their abode in central establishment. Clothing ceased to be made at home; there arose a village weaver and a village shoemaker. To this process of development there is almost no conceivable end. Only a few years ago the American farmer not only raised his own food, but furnished his own fuel and sometimes made his own clothing. Now, however, he is a specialist, and thinks nothing of going to the market even for table supplies. Formerly, the farmer made his own tools; now he buys implements made in factories. But yesterday, and the men who reaped the fields of ripe grain were bound to the soil and compelled to dwell in isolated homes or small communities; today these men live in cities and make machinery to reap the grain. Thus, it appears that agriculture, the industry that disperses men, has ever narrowed its scope. Formerly, when men's wants were few and simple, agriculture was the all-embracing occupation. The agriculturist produced the necessary sustenance, and in his idle moments made whatever else he needed. But human wants have greatly multiplied and can no longer be satiated with food-products alone. Moreover, the business of providing for the new wants has been separated from agriculture. The total result is that the proportion of people who must devote themselves to the satisfaction of the elementary wants of society has vastly diminished and is still diminishing. And this result is attained not only by the diminishing importance of bread and butter in the realm of human wants, but also by the increased per capita product which a specialized body of workers can win from the soil. By the use of fertilizers, by highly scientific methods of cultivation, by labor-saving machinery, and by the construction of transportation systems to open up distant and virgin fields, the present century has immensely reduced the relative number of workers who must remain attached to the soil to provide society's food-supply. These facts are of fundamental importance in seeking the causes of urban growth. For cities are made up of persons who do not cultivate the soil; their existence presupposes a surplus food-supply, which in turn premises either great fertility of the soil or an advanced stage of the agricultural arts, and in either case convenient means of transportation.

DOCUMENT ANALYSIS

1. According to Weber, what forces spurred the growth of the first cities, or the "amalgamation" of isolated groups? What did they do that war could not?

_____

_____

_____

2. How important were the improved methods of food production to the growth of cities?

_____

_____

_____

3. What are the stages of development Weber described?

_____

_____

_____

DOCUMENT 20.1
Charlotte Perkins Gilman, "If I Were a Man" (1914)

Largely self-educated, Charlotte Perkins Gilman was a prolific writer who lectured on topics ranging from ethics to labor to the artificiality of gender roles. She wrote about issues, such as depression and mental illness that were often taboo, and she satirized the societal restrictions and hypocrisy women faced in their daily lives.

Mollie was "true to type." She was a beautiful instance of what is reverentially called "a true woman." Little, of course—no true woman may be big. Pretty, of course—no true woman could possibly be plain. Whimsical, capricious, charming, changeable, devoted to pretty clothes and always "wearing them well," as the esoteric phrase has it. (This does not refer to the clothes—they do not wear well in the least—but to some special grace of putting them on and carrying them about, granted to but few, it appears.)

She was also a loving wife and a devoted mother possessed of "the social gift" and the love of "society" that goes with it, and with all these was fond and proud of her home and managed it as capably as well, as most women do.

If ever there was a true woman it was Mollie Mathewson, yet she was wishing heart and soul she was a man.

And all of a sudden she was!

She was Gerald, walking down the path so erect and square-shouldered, in a hurry for his morning train, as usual, and, it must be confessed, in something of a temper. . . .

A man! Really a man—with only enough subconscious memory of herself remaining to make her recognize the differences.

At first there was a funny sense of size and weight and extra thickness, the feet and hands seemed strangely large, and her long, straight, free legs swung forward at a gait that made her feel as if on stilts.

This presently passed, and in its place, growing all day, wherever she went, came a new and delightful feeling of being the right size.

Everything fitted now. Her back snugly against the seat-back, her feet comfortably on the floor. Her feet? . . . His feet! She studied them carefully. Never before, since her early school days, had she felt such freedom and comfort as to feet—they were firm and solid on the ground when she walked; quick, springy, safe—as when, moved by an unrecognizable impulse, she had run after, caught, and swung aboard the car.

Another impulse fished in a convenient pocket for change—instantly, automatically, bringing forth a nickel for the conductor and a penny for the newsboy.

These pockets came as a revelation. Of course she had known they were there, had counted them, made fun of them, mended them, even envied them; but she never had dreamed of how it felt to have pockets.

Behind her newspaper she let her consciousness, that odd mingled consciousness, rove from pocket to pocket, realizing the armored assurance of having all those things at hand, instantly get-at-able, ready to meet emergencies. The cigar case gave her a warm feeling of comfort—it was full; the firmly held fountain pen, safe unless she stood on her head; the keys, pencils, letters, documents, notebook, checkbook, bill folder—all at once, with a deep rushing sense of power and pride, she felt what she had never felt before in all her life—the possession of money, of her own earned money—hers to give or to withhold, not to beg for, tease for, wheedle for—hers. . . .

When he took his train, his seat in the smoking car, she had a new surprise. All about him were the other men, commuters too, and many of them friends of his.

To her, they would have been distinguished as "Mary Wade's husband," "the man Belle Grant is engaged to," "that rich Mr. Shopworth," or "that pleasant Mr. Beale." And they would all have lifted their hats to her, bowed, made polite conversation if near enough—especially Mr. Beale.

Now came the feeling of open-eyed acquaintance, of knowing men—as they were. The mere amount of this knowledge was a surprise to her—the whole background of talk from boyhood up, the gossip of barber-shop and club, the conversation of morning and evening hours on trains, the knowledge of political affiliation, of business standing and prospects, of character—in a light she had never known before.

They came and talked to Gerald, one and another. He seemed quite popular. And as they talked, with this new memory and new understanding, an understanding which seemed to include all these men's minds, there poured in on the submerged consciousness beneath a new, a startling knowledge—what men really think of women.

Good, average, American men were there; married men for the most part, and happy—as happiness goes in general. In the minds of each and all there seemed to be a two-story department, quite apart from the rest of their ideas, a separate place where they kept their thoughts and feelings about women.

In the upper half were the most tender emotions, the most exquisite ideals, the sweetest memories, all lovely sentiments as to "home" and "mother," all delicate admiring adjectives, a sort of sanctuary, where a veiled statue, blindly adored, shared place with beloved yet commonplace experiences.

In the lower half—here that buried consciousness woke to keen distress—they kept quite another assortment of ideas. Here, even in this clean-minded husband of hers, was the memory of stories told at men's dinners, of worse ones overheard in street or car, of base traditions, coarse epithets, gross experiences—known, though not shared.

And all these in the department "woman," while in the rest of the mind—here was new knowledge indeed.

The world opened before her. Not the world she had been reared in—where Home had covered all the map, almost, and the rest had been "foreign," or "unexplored country," but the world as it was—man's world, as made, lived in, and seen, by men.

It was dizzying. To see the houses that fled so fast across the car window, in terms of builders' bills, or of some technical insight into materials and methods; to see a passing village with lamentable knowledge of who "owned it" and of how its Boss was rapidly aspiring in state power, or of how that kind of paving was a failure; to see shops, not as mere exhibitions of desirable objects, but as business ventures, many were sinking ships, some promising a profitable voyage—this new world bewildered her.

She—as Gerald—had already forgotten about that bill, over which she—as Mollie—was still crying at home. Gerald was "talking business" with this man, "talking politics" with that, and now sympathizing with the carefully withheld troubles of a neighbor.

Mollie had always sympathized with the neighbor's wife before.

She began to struggle violently with this large dominant masculine consciousness. She remembered with sudden clearness things she had read, lectures she had heard, and resented with increasing intensity this serene masculine preoccupation with the male point of view.

Mr. Miles, the little fussy man who lived on the other side of the street, was talking now. He had a large complacent wife; Mollie had never liked her much, but had always thought him rather nice—he was so punctilious in small courtesies.

And here he was talking to Gerald—such talk!

"Had to come in here," he said. "Gave my seat to a dame who was bound to have it. There's nothing they won't get when they make up their minds to it—eh?"

"No fear!" said the big man in the next seat. "They haven't much mind to make up, you know—and if they do, they'll change it."

"The real danger," began the Rev. Alfred Smythe, the new Episcopal clergyman, a thin, nervous, tall man with a face several centuries behind the times, "is that they will overstep the limits of their God-appointed sphere."

"Their natural limits ought to hold 'em, I think," said cheerful Dr. Jones. "You can't get around physiology, I tell you."

"I've never seen any limits, myself, not to what they want, anyhow," said Mr. Miles. "Merely a rich husband and a fine house and no end of bonnets and dresses, and the latest thing in motors, and a few diamonds—and so on. Keeps us pretty busy."

There was a tired gray man across the aisle. He had a very nice wife, always beautifully dressed, and three unmarried daughters, also beautifully dressed—Mollie knew them. She knew he worked hard, too, and she looked at him now a little anxiously.

But she smiled cheerfully.

"Do you good, Miles," he said. "What else would a man work for? A good woman is about the best thing on earth."

"And a bad one's the worse, that's sure," responded Miles.

"She's a pretty weak sister, viewed professionally," Dr. Jones averred with solemnity, and the Rev. Alfred Smythe added, "She brought evil into the world."

Gerald Mathewson sat up straight. Something was stirring in him which he did not recognize—yet could not resist.

"Seems to me we all talk like Noah," he suggested drily, "or the ancient Hindu scriptures. Women have their limitations, but so do we, God knows. Haven't we known girls in school and college just as smart as we were?"

"They cannot play our games," coldly replied the clergyman.

Gerald measured his meager proportions with a practiced eye.

"I never was particularly good at football myself," he modestly admitted, "but I've known women who could outlast a man in all-round endurance. Besides—life isn't spent in athletics!"

This was sadly true. They all looked down the aisle where a heavy ill-dressed man with a bad complexion sat alone. He had held the top of the columns once, with headlines and photographs. Now he earned less than any of them. . . .

"Yes, we blame them for grafting on us, but are we willing to let our wives work? We are not. It hurts our pride, that's all. We are always criticizing them for making mercenary marriages, but what do we call a girl who marries a chump with no money? Just a poor fool, that's all. And they know it.

"As for Mother Eve—I wasn't there and can't deny the story, but I will say this. If she brought evil into the world, we men have had the lion's share of keeping it going ever since—how about that?"

They drew into the city, and all day long in his business, Gerald was vaguely conscious of new views, strange feelings, and the submerged Mollie learned and learned.

DOCUMENT ANALYSIS

1. What things most surprised Mollie-as-Gerald?

_____

_____

_____

2. What point was Gilman making in this story? What did she identify as the gender inequalities of the day?

_____

_____

_____

3. Do the stereotypes concerning women that Gilman illustrates in this piece exist today?

_____

_____

_____

DOCUMENT 21.1
Pendleton Civil Service Act (1883)

In 1881, President James A. Garfield died from gunshot wounds inflicted by Charles J. Guiteau, who had failed to receive an appointment to a federal job. Garfield's assassination elevated public outrage to such a level that Congress could no longer ignore the growing demand to institute a new system of federal hiring. By 1881, the old system was out of control. Traditionally, a person who wanted a federal job had to rely on the party in office to appoint him or her. As the federal system grew, federal appointees increasingly had to pay to secure their jobs, and sometimes to continue to pay in order to keep them. Moreover, each change of administration in Washington resulted in a massive turnover in government workers. Not only was this system inefficient, but it encouraged corruption and ineptitude. Consequently, in 1883 Congress passed the Pendleton Act, which represented the first step in instituting a civil service system that relied on qualifications rather than patronage. Today, almost all federal jobs are filled through the civil service system.

Be it enacted by the Senate and House of Representatives of the United States of America in Congress assembled, That the President is authorized to appoint, by and with the advice and consent of the Senate, three persons, not more than two of whom shall be adherents of the same party, as Civil Service Commissioners, and said three commissioners shall constitute the United States Civil Service Commission. . . .

Sec. 2. That it shall be the duty of said commissioners:

First. To aid the President, as he may request, in preparing suitable rules for carrying this act into effect, and when said rules shall have been promulgated it shall be the duty of all officers of the United States in the departments and offices to which any such rules may relate to aid, in all proper ways, in carrying said rules, and any modifications thereof, into effect.

Second. And, among other things, said rules shall provide and declare, as nearly as the conditions of good administration will warrant, as follows:

First, for open, competitive examinations for testing the fitness of applicants for the public service now classified or to be classified hereunder. Such examinations shall be practical in their character, and so far as may be shall relate to those matters which will fairly test the relative capacity and fitness of the persons examined to discharge the duties of the service into which they seek to be appointed.

Second, that all the offices, places, and employments so arranged or to be arranged in classes shall be filled by selections according to grade from among those graded highest as the results of such competitive examinations.

Third, appointments to the public service aforesaid in the departments at Washington shall be apportioned among the several States and Territories and the District of Columbia upon the basis of population as ascertained at the last preceding census. . . .

Fifth, that no person in the public service is for that reason under any obligations to contribute to any political fund, or to render any political service, and that he will not be removed or otherwise prejudiced for refusing to do so.

Sixth, that no person in said service has any right to use his official authority or influence to coerce the political action of any person or body. . . .

Sec. 11. That no Senator, or Representative, or Territorial Delegate of the Congress, or Senator, Representative, or Delegate elect, or any officer or employee of either of said houses, and no executive, judicial, military, or naval officer of the United States, and no clerk or employee of any department, branch or bureau of the executive, judicial, or military or naval service of the United States, shall, directly, or indirectly, solicit or receive, or be in any manner concerned in soliciting or receiving, any assessment, subscription, or contribution for any political purpose whatever, from any officer, clerk, or employee of the United States, or any department, branch, or bureau thereof, or from any person receiving any salary or compensation from moneys derived from the Treasury of the United States . . .

DOCUMENT ANALYSIS

1. Examine the "Fifth" and "Sixth" paragraphs. What are these stipulations meant to deter? How do they differ from the stipulations in Section 11?

_____

_____

_____

2. Under this new system, how would a job candidate obtain a public service position?

_____

_____

_____

3. Do you know anyone who works for the federal government? If so, how did this person obtain her or his job?

_____

_____

_____

DOCUMENT 21.2
Mary Elizabeth Lease, from *Populist Crusader* (1892)

Mary Lease, an activist for the Populist movement, expresses her views regarding the Farmers' Alliance in the following selection. Lease was a very popular lecturer and agitator for farmers' rights. She is credited with telling farmers to "raise less corn and more hell," a good example of her particularly fiery style.

Yet, after all our years of toil and privation, dangers and hardships upon the Western frontier, monopoly is taking our homes from us by an infamous system of mortgage foreclosure, the most infamous that has ever disgraced the statures of a civilized nation. It takes from us at the rate of five hundred a month the homes that represent the best years of our life, our toil, our hopes, our happiness. How did it happen? The government, at the bid of Wall Street, repudiated its contracts with the people, the circulating medium was contracted in the interest of Shylock from $54 per capita to less than $8 per capita; or, as Senator Plumb tells us, "Our debts were increased, while the means to pay them was decreased;" or as grand Senator Steward puts it, "for twenty years the market value of the dollar has gone up and the market value of labor has gone down, till today the American laborer, in bitterness and wrath, asks which is the worst—the black slavery that has gone or the white slavery that has come?"

Do you wonder the women are joining the Alliance? I wonder if there is a woman in this broad land who can afford to stay out of the Alliance. Our loyal, white-ribbon women should be heart and hand in this Farmers' Alliance movement, for the men whom we have sent to represent us are the only men in the councils of this nation who have not been elected on a liquor platform; and I want to say here, with exultant pride, that the five farmer Congressmen and the United States Senator we have sent up from Kansas—the liquor traffic, Wall Street, "nor the gates of hell shall not prevail against them."

It would sound boastful were I to detail to you the active, earnest part the Kansas women took in the recent campaign. A Republican majority of 82,000 was reduced to less than 8,000, when we elected 97 representatives, 5 out of 7 Congressmen, and a United States Senator, for to the women of Kansas belongs the credit of defeating John J. Ingalls. He is feeling badly about it yet, too, for he said today that "women and Indians were the only class that would scalp a dead man." I rejoice that he realizes that he is politically dead.

I might weary you to tell you in detail how the Alliance women found time from cares of home and children to prepare the tempting, generous viands for the Alliance picnic dinners; where hungry thousands and tens of thousands gathered in the forests and groves to listen to the words of impassioned oratory, oftentimes from woman's lips, that nerved the men of Kansas to forget their party prejudice and vote for "Mollie and the babies." And not only did they find their way to the voters' hearts, through their stomachs, but they sang their way as well. I hold here a book of Alliance songs, composed and set to music by an Alliance woman, Mrs. Florence Olmstead of Butler County, Kan., that did much toward molding public sentiment. Alliance Glee Clubs composed of women gave us such stirring melodies as the nation has not heard since the Tippecanoe and Tyler campaign of 1840. And while I am individualizing, let me call your attention to a book written also by an Alliance woman. I wish a copy of it could be placed in the hands of every woman in this land. "The Fate of a Fool" is written by Mrs. Emma G. Curtis of Colorado. This book in the hands of women would teach them to be just and generous toward women, and help them to forgive and condemn in each other the sins so sweetly forgiven when committed by men.

Let no one for a moment believe that this uprising and federation of the people is but a passing episode in politics. It is a religious as well as a political movement, for we seek to put into practical operation the teachings and precepts of Jesus of Nazareth. We seek to enact justice and equity between man and man. We seek to bring the nation back to the constitutional liberties guaranteed us by our forefathers. The voice that is coming up today from the mystic chords of the American heart is the same voice that Lincoln heard blending with the guns of Fort Sumter and the Wilderness, and it is breaking into a clarion cry today that will be heard around the world.

Crowns will fall, thrones will tremble, kingdoms will disappear, the divine right of kings and the divine right of capital will fade away like the mists of the morning, when the Angel of Liberty shall kindle the fires of justice in the hearts of men. "Exact justice to all, special privileges to none." No more millionaires, and no more paupers; no more gold kings, silver kings and oil kings, and no more little waifs of humanity starving for a crust of bread. No more gaunt-faced, hollow-eyed girls in the factories, and no more little boys reared in poverty and crime for the penitentiaries and the gallows. But we shall have the golden age of which Isaiah sang and the prophets have so long foretold; when the farmers shall be prosperous and happy, dwelling under their own vine and fig tree; when the laborer shall gave that for which he toils; when occupancy and use shall be the only title to land, and everyone shall obey the divine injunction, "In the sweat of thy face shalt thou eat bread." When men shall be just and generous, little less than angels; when we shall have not a government of the people by capitalists, but a government of the people, by the people.

DOCUMENT ANALYSIS

1. What examples did Lease use to support her argument that women could make a difference in political struggles?

_____

_____

_____

2. How did Lease view the future of the United States? What role would women play?

_____

_____

_____

3. Which particular issue does Lease highlight in the opening paragraph as being especially oppressive for farmers?

_____

_____

_____

DOCUMENT 22.1
Mother Jones, "The March of the Mill Children" (1903)

Mary Harris Jones, a prominent labor organizer known as "Mother Jones," was especially active in the miners' strikes of the 1890s. One of her concerns was the exploitation of children. In this public-relations marvel, Jones marched mill children—many of whom had missing fingers and other work-related deformities—from Pennsylvania to President Theodore Roosevelt's home in Long Island, New York. Her work contributed to the passage of protective legislation for children in Pennsylvania. This selection comes from her autobiography.

In the spring of 1903 I went to Kensington, Pennsylvania, where seventy-five thousand textile workers were on strike. Of this number at least ten thousand were little children. The workers were striking for more pay and shorter hours. Every day little children came into Union Headquarters, some with their hands off, some with the thumb missing, some with their fingers off at the knuckle. They were stooped little things, round-shouldered and skinny. Many of them were not over ten years of age, although the state law prohibited their working before they were twelve years of age.

The law was poorly enforced and the mothers of these children often swore falsely as to their children's age. In a single block in Kensington, fourteen women, mothers of twenty-two children all under twelve, explained it was a question of starvation or perjury. That the fathers had been killed or maimed at the mines.

I asked the newspapermen why they didn't publish the facts about child labor in Pennsylvania. They said they couldn't because the mill owners had stock in the papers.

"Well, I've got stock in these little children," said I, "and I'll arrange a little publicity."

We assembled a number of boys and girls one morning in Independence Park, and from there were arranged to parade with banners to the courthouse where we would hold a meeting.

A great crowd gathered in the public square in front of the city hall. I put the little boys with their fingers off and hands crushed and maimed on a platform. I held up their mutilated hands and showed them to the crowd, and made the statement that Philadelphia's mansions were built on the broken bones, the quivering hearts and drooping heads of these children. That their little lives went out to make wealth for others. That neither state nor city officials paid any attention to these wrongs. That they did not care that these children were to be the future citizens of the nation. . . .

I called upon the millionaire manufacturers to cease their moral murders, and I cried to the officials in the open windows opposite, "Someday the workers will take possession of your city hall, and when we do, no child will be sacrificed on the altar of profit."

The reporters quoted my statement that Philadelphia mansions were built on the broken bones and quivering hearts of children. The Philadelphia papers and the New York papers got into squabble with each other over the question. The universities discussed it. Preachers began talking. That was what I wanted. Public attention on the subject of child labor.

The matter quieted down for a while and I concluded the people needed stirring up again. . . . I asked some of them if they would let me have their little boys and girls for a week or ten days, promising to bring them back safe and sound. They consented. A man named Sweeny was Marshall for our "army." A few men and women went with me to help with the children. They were on strike and I thought they might as well have a little recreation.

The children carried knapsacks on their backs in which was a knife and fork, a tin cup and a plate. We took along a wash boiler in which to cook the food on the road. One little fellow had a drum and another had a fife. That was our band. We carried banners that said, "We want more schools and less hospitals." "We want time to play." "Prosperity is here. Where is ours!"

We started from Philadelphia where we held a great mass meeting. I decided to go with the children to see President Roosevelt to ask him to have Congress pass a law prohibiting the exploitation of childhood. I thought that President Roosevelt might see these mill children and compare them with his own little ones who were spending the summer on the seashore at Oyster Bay. . . .

The children were very happy, having plenty to eat, taking baths in the brooks and rivers every day. I thought when the strike is over and they go back to the mills, they will never have another holiday like this. All along the line of the march the farmers drove out to meet us with wagonloads of fruit and vegetables. Their wives brought the children clothes and money. The interurban trainmen would stop their trains and give us free rides.

We were on the outskirts of New Trenton, New Jersey, cooking our lunch in the wash boiler, when the conductor on the interurban car stopped and told us the police were coming to notify us that we could not enter the town. There were mills in the town and the mill owners didn't like our coming.

I said, "All right, the police will be just in time for lunch."

Sure enough, the police came and we invited them to dine with us. They looked at the little gathering of children with their tin plates and cups around the wash boiler. They just smiled and spoke kindly to the children, and said nothing at all about not going into the city.

We went in, held our meeting, and it was the wives of the police who took the little children and cared for them that night sending them back in the morning with a nice lunch rolled up in paper napkins.

Everywhere we had meetings, showing up with living children, the horrors of child labor. . . .

I called on the mayor of Princeton and asked for permission to speak opposite the campus of the University. I said I wanted to speak on higher education. The mayor gave me permission. A great crowd gathered, professors and students and the people; and I told them that the rich robbed these little children of any education of the lowest order, that they might send their sons and daughters to places of higher education. . . . And I showed those professors children in our army who could scarcely read or write because they were working ten hours a day in the silk mills of Pennsylvania.

"Here's a text book on economics," I said, pointing to a little chap, James Ashworth, who was ten years old and who was stooped over like an old man from carrying bundles of yarn that weighed seventy-five pounds. "He gets three dollars a week.". . .

I sent a committee over to the New York Chief of Police, Ebstein, asking for permission to march up Fourth Avenue to Madison Square, where I wanted to hold a meeting. The chief refused and forbade our entrance to the city.

I went over myself to New York and saw Mayor Seth Low. The mayor was most courteous but he said he would have to support the commissioner. I asked him what the reason was for refusing us entrance to the city, and he said that we were not citizens of New York.

"Oh, I think we will clear that up, Mr. Mayor," I said. "Permit me to call your attention to an incident which took place in this nation just a year ago. A piece of rotten royalty came over here from Germany, called Prince Henry. The Congress of the United States voted $45,000 to dill that fellow's stomach for three weeks and to entertain him. His brother was getting $4,000,000 in dividends out of the blood of the workers in this country. Was he a citizen of this land?"

"And it was reported, Mr. Mayor, that you and all the officials of New York and the University Club entertained that chap." And I repeated, "Was he a citizen of New York?"

"No. Mother," said the mayor, "he was not.". . .

"Well, Mr. Mayor, these are the little citizens of the nation and they also produce its wealth. Aren't we entitled to enter your city?"

We marched to Twentieth Street. I told an immense crowd of the horrors of child labor in the mills around the anthracite region, and I showed them some of the children. I showed them Edie Dunphy, a little fellow of twelve, whose job it was to sit all day on a high stool, handing in

the right thread to another worker. Eleven hours a day he sat on the high stool with dangerous machinery all about him. All day long, winter and summer, spring and fall, for three dollars a week.

And then I showed them Gussie Rangnew, a little girl from whom all the childhood had gone. Her face was like an old woman's. Gussie packed stockings in a factory, eleven hours a day for a few cents a day.

We raised a lot of money for the strikers, and hundreds of friends offered their homes to the little ones while we were in the city.

The next day we went to Coney Island at the invitation of Mr. Bostick, who owned the wild animal show. The children had a wonderful time such as they never had in all their lives. After the exhibition of the trained animals, Mr. Bostick let me speak to the audience. . . . Right in front were the empty iron cages of the animals. I put my little children in the cages and they clung to the iron bars while I talked. . . .

"Fifty years ago there was a cry against slavery, and men gave up their lives to stop the selling of black children on the bloc. Today the white child is sold for two dollars a week to the manufacturers. Fifty years ago the black babies were sold C.O.D. Today the white baby is sold on the installment plan. . . .

"The trouble is that no one in Washington cares. I saw our legislators in one hour pass three bills for the relief of the railways, but when labor cries for aid for the children they will not listen.

"I asked a man in prison once how he happened to be there, and he said he had stolen a pair of shoes. I told him if he had stolen a railroad he would be a United States Senator.

"We are told that every American boy has the chance of being president. I tell you that these little boys in the iron cages would sell their chance any day for good square meals and a chance to play."

The next day we left Coney Island for Manhattan Beach to visit Senator Platt, who had made an appointment to me at nine o'clock in the morning. The children got stuck in the sandbanks and I had a time cleaning the sand off the littlest ones. So we started to walk on the railroad track. I was told it was private property and we had to get off. Finally a saloonkeeper showed us a shortcut in the sacred grounds of the hotel, and suddenly the army appeared in the lobby. The little fellows played "Hail, hail, the gang's all here" on their fifes and drums, and Senator Platt, when he saw the little army, ran away through the back door to New York.

I asked the manager if he would give the children breakfast, and charge it up to the Senator, as we had an invitation to breakfast that morning with him. He gave us a private room and he gave those children a breakfast, as they had never had in their lives. I had breakfast too, and a reporter from one of the Hearst papers and I charged it all up to Senator Platt.

We marched down to Oyster Bay, but the President refused to see us and he would not answer my letters. But our march had done its work. We had drawn the attention of the nation to the crime of child labor. And while the strike of the textile workers in Kensington was lost and the children driven back to work, not long afterward the Pennsylvania legislature passed a child labor law, sent thousands of children home from the mills, and kept thousands of others from entering the factory until they were fourteen years of age.

DOCUMENT ANALYSIS

1. According to this document, what type of horrors did children encounter in the factories?

_____

_____

_____

2. How did the various government officials treat Mother Jones and her mill children?

_____

_____

_____

3. What types of public relations schemes did Mother Jones use to gain publicity?

_____

_____

_____

DOCUMENT 23.1
Ernest Howard Crosby, "The Real 'White Man's Burden'" (1899)

From Ernest Howard Crosby, *Swords and Plowshares* (New York: Funk and Wagnall's, 1902), pp. 33–34.
Poem originally appeared in the *New York Times* (February 15, 1899).

Poet Ernest Crosby was an active anti-imperialist, poet, and social reformer who had experienced British imperialism firsthand in Egypt. After reading the Russian novelist Leo Tolstoy, he resigned from his position in Egypt as judge of the International Tribunal and devoted his life to promoting nonviolence. Crosby served as the president of the Anti-Imperialist League of New York and as vice president of the national Anti-Imperialist League. In 1899 he penned the parody poem below to answer Rudyard Kipling's "White Man's Burden."

THE REAL "WHITE MAN'S BURDEN"

Take up the White Man's burden.
  Send forth your sturdy kin,
And load them down with Bibles
  And cannon-balls and gin.
Throw in a few diseases
  To spread the tropic climes
For there the healthy niggers
  Are quite behind the times.
And don't forget the factories
  On those benighted shores
They have no cheerful iron mills
  Nor eke department stores.

They never work twelve hours a day,
  And live in strange content
Altho' they never have to pay
  A single sou of rent.
Take up the White Man's burden,
  And teach the Philippines
What interest and taxes are
  And what a mortgage means.
Give them electrocution chairs,
  And prisons, too, galore,
And if they seem inclined to kick
  Then spill their heathen gore.
They need our labor question, too,
  And politics and fraud—
We've made a pretty mess at home,
  Let's make a mess abroad.
And let us ever humbly pray
  The Lord of Hosts may deign
To stir our feeble memories
  Lest we forget—the Maine.

DOCUMENT ANALYSIS

1. What does Crosby define as the worst aspects of U.S. imperialism?

_____

_____

_____

2. Although Crosby's poem is a parody, it raised important issues of the day. Does the disagreement between Crosby and Kipling (and imperialists and anti-imperialists generally) sound familiar in the twenty-first century?

_____

_____

_____

3. Why did Crosby mention the Maine at the end of the poem? What message was he attempting to convey?

_____

_____

_____

DOCUMENT 23.2
William McKinley, "Decision on the Philippines" (1900)

In this speech to a group of ministers, U.S. President William McKinley outlined his rationale for annexing the Philippines in a treaty of 1898, paying the Spanish (under duress) $20 million for the privilege. It was a difficult decision, and it foreshadowed the path of U.S. foreign policy for much of the next century.

When next I realized that the Philippines had dropped into our laps, I confess I did not know what to do with them. I sought counsel from all sides—Democrats as well as Republican—but got little help. I thought first we would take only Manila; then Luzon; then other islands, perhaps, also.

I walked the floor of the White House night after night until midnight; and I am not ashamed to tell you, gentlemen, that I went down on my knees and prayed to Almighty God for light and guidance more than one night. And one night late it came to me this way—I don't know how it was, but it came:

(1) That we could not give them back to Spain—that would be cowardly and dishonorable;

(2) That we could not turn them over to France or Germany, our commercial rivals in the Orient—that would be bad business and discreditable;

(3) That we could not leave them to themselves—they were unfit for self-government, and they would soon have anarchy and misrule worse than Spain's was; and

(4) That there was nothing left for us to do but to take them all, and to educate the Filipinos, and uplift and civilize and Christianize them and by God's grace do the very best we could by them, as our fellow men for whom Christ also died.

And then I went to bed and went to sleep, and slept soundly, and the next morning I sent for the chief engineer of the War Department (our map-maker), and I told him to put the Philippines on the map of the United States [pointing to a large map on the wall of his office], and there they are and there they will stay while I am President!

DOCUMENT ANALYSIS

1. According to McKinley's speech, why couldn't the Filipinos rule themselves?

_____

_____

_____

2. Why and how did McKinley believe that U.S. rule would benefit the Filipinos?

_____

_____

_____

DOCUMENT 24.1
Eugene Kennedy, "A 'Doughboy' Describes the Fighting Front" (1918)

When the United States entered World War I in the spring of 1917, its soldiers were largely untrained and unprepared. However, the Allies desperately needed U.S. reinforcements, especially after the November 1917 Bolshevik Revolution led to a separate peace between Russia and Germany, which freed German soldiers on the Eastern Front to fight in the West. By May 1918, German forces were within 50 miles of Paris. Though Americans took part in various campaigns through the summer of 1918, it was not until September that large numbers saw action. Near St. Mihiel, France, more than 500,000 U.S. troops participated in a massive assault against the Germans. More than 1 million U.S. troops later took part in the final Meuse-Argonne offensive, which led to the signing of the armistice on November 11, 1918. U.S. soldiers were often hastily—and some people would argue poorly—trained, but their contribution to an Allied victory cannot be disputed. The selection below is from the diary of a U.S. soldier who saw action near St. Mihiel.

Thursday, September 12, 1918

Hiked through dark woods. No light allowed, guided by holding on the pack of the man ahead. Stumbled through underbrush for about half mile into an open field where we waited in soaking rain until about 10:00 P.M. We then started on our hike to the St. Mihiel front, arriving on the crest of a hill at 1:00 A.M. I saw a sight which I shall never forget. It was the zero hour and in one instant the entire front as far as the eye could reach in either direction was a sheet of flame while the heavy artillery made the earth quake. The barrage was so intense that for a time we could not make out whether the Americans or Germans were putting it over. After timing the interval between flash and report we knew that the heaviest artillery was less than a mile away and consequently it was ours. We waded through pools and mud across open lots into a woods on a hill and had to pitch tents in mud. Blankets all wet and we are soaked to the skin. Have carried full pack from 10:00 P.M. to 2:00 A.M., without a rest. . . . Despite the cannonading I slept until 8:00 A.M. and awoke to find every discharge of 14-inch artillery shaking our tent like a leaf. Remarkable how we could sleep. No breakfast. . . . The doughboys had gone over the top at 5:00 A.M. and the French were shelling the back areas toward Metz. . . . Firing is incessant, so is rain. See an air battle just before turning in.

Friday, September 13, 1918

Called at 3:00 A.M. Struck tents and started to hike at 5:00 A.M. with full packs and a pick. Put on gas mask at alert position and hiked about five miles to St. Jean, where we unslung full packs and went on about four miles further with short packs and picks. Passed several batteries and saw many dead horses who gave out at start of push. Our doughboys are still shoving and "Jerry" is dropping so many shells on road into no man's land that we stayed back in field and made no effort to repair shell-torn road. Plenty of German prisoners being brought back. . . . Guns booming all the time. . . .

Thursday, October 17, 1918

Struck tents at 8:00 A.M. and moved about four miles to Chatel. Pitched tents on a side hill so steep that we had to cut steps to ascend. Worked like hell to shovel out a spot to pitch tent on. Just across the val-ley in front of us about two hundred yards distant, there had occurred an explosion due to a mine planted by the "Bosche" [Germans] and set with a time fuse. It had blown two men (French), two horses, and the wagon into fragments. . . . Arriving on the scene we found Quinn ransacking the wagon. It was full of grub. We each loaded a burlap bag with cans of condensed milk, peas, lobster, salmon, and bread. I started back . . . when suddenly another mine exploded, the biggest I ever saw. Rocks and dirt flew sky high. Quinn was hit in the knee and had to go to hospital. . . . At 6:00 P.M. each of our four platoons left camp in units to go up front and throw three foot and one artillery bridge across the Aire River. On way to river we were heavily shelled and gassed. . . . We put a bridge across 75-foot span. . . . Third platoon men had to get into water and swim or stand in water to their necks. The toughest job we had so far. . . .

Monday, October 21, 1918

Fragment from shell struck mess-kit on my back. . . . Equipment, both American and German, thrown everywhere, especially Hun helmets and belts of machine gunners. . . . Went scouting . . . for narrow-gauge rails to replace the ones "Jerry" spoiled before evacuating. Negro engineers working on railroad same as at St. Mihiel, that's all they are good for. . . .

Friday, November 1, 1918

Started out at 4:00 A.M. The drive is on. Fritz is coming back at us. Machine guns cracking, flares and Verry lights, artillery from both sides. A real war and we are walking right into the zone, ducking shells all the way. The artillery is nerve racking and we don't know from which angle "Jerry" will fire next. Halted behind shelter of railroad track just outside of Grand Pre after being forced back off main road by shell fire. Trees splintered like toothpicks. Machine gunners on top of railroad bank. . . . "Jerry" drove Ewell and me into a two-by-four shell hole, snipers' bullets close.

Sunday, November 3, 1918

Many dead Germans along the road. One heap on a manure pile. . . . Devastation everywhere. Our barrage has rooted up the entire territory like a ploughed field. Dead horses galore, many of them have a hind quarter cut off—the Huns need food. Dead men here and there. The sight I enjoy better than a dead German is to see heaps of them. Rain again. Couldn't keep rain out of our faces and it was pouring hard. Got up at midnight and drove stakes to secure shelter—half over us, pulled our wet blankets out of mud and made the bed all over again. Slept like a log with all my equipment in the open. One hundred forty-two planes sighted in evening.

Sunday, November 10, 1918

First day off in over two months. . . . Took a bath and we were issued new underwear but the cooties [lice] got there first. . . . The papers show a picture of the Kaiser entitled "William the Lost," and stating that he had abdicated. Had a good dinner. Rumor at night that armistice was signed. Some fellows discharged their arms in the courtyard, but most of us were too well pleased with dry bunk to get up.

DOCUMENT ANALYSIS

1. What is the overall tone of Kennedy's diary? Is it emotional or merely a daily account? Did you find the tone surprising? Why or why not?

_____

_____

_____

2. Describe the physical conditions that Kennedy experienced daily.

_____

_____

_____

3. Notice the dates of each entry. What span of time does this excerpt cover? What themes recur throughout the selections?

_____

_____

_____

DOCUMENT 24.2
Henry Cabot Lodge's Objections to Article 10 of the Treaty of Versailles (1919)

The Treaty of Versailles consists of 440 Articles. Articles 1–26 form the Covenant of the League of Nations. Article 10 became the most contentious issue during the ratification debates within the U.S. Senate. Henry Cabot Lodge (R-Massachusetts) objected to many details of the Treaty of Versailles, particularly the League of Nations. He believed that membership in the League of Nations would entangle the United States in foreign affairs and prevent the country from acting independently in such matters. The following are selected portions of a speech that he delivered in the Senate on August 12, 1919.

Peace Treaty of Versailles—Article 10

The Members of the League undertake to respect and preserve as against external aggression the territorial integrity and existing political independence of all Members of the League. In case of any such aggression or in case of any threat or danger of such aggression the Council shall advise upon the means by which this obligation shall be fulfilled.

Lodge's Objections

I object in the strongest possible way to having the United States agree, directly or indirectly, to be controlled by a league which may at any time, and perfectly lawfully and in accordance with the terms of the covenant, be drawn in to deal with internal conflicts in other countries, no matter what those conflicts may be . . . There can be no genuine dispute whatever about the meaning of the first clause of article 10. . . . In article 10 the United States is bound on the appeal of any member of the league not only to respect but to preserve its independence and its boundaries, and that pledge if we give it, must be fulfilled.

. . . The broad fact remains that if any member of the league suffering from external aggression should appeal directly to the United States for support the United States would be bound to give that support in its own capacity and without reference to the action of other powers, because the United States itself is bound, and I hope the day will never come when the United States will not carry out its promises.

. . . There are, of course, many others, but these points, in the interest not only of the safety of the United States, but of the maintenance of the treaty and the peace of the world, should be dealt with here before it is too late. Once in the league the chance of amendment is so slight that it is not worth considering. Any analysis of the provisions of this league covenant, however, brings out in startling relief one great fact. Whatever may be said, it is not a league of peace; it is an alliance, dominated at the present moment by five great powers, really by three, and it has all the marks of an alliance. The development of international law is neglected. The court which is to decide disputes brought before it fills but a small place. The conditions for which this league really provides with the utmost care are political conditions, not judicial questions. . . . This league to enforce peace does a great deal for enforcement and very little for peace. It makes more essential provisions looking to war than to peace for the settlement of disputes.

. . . I am as anxious as any human being can be to have the United States render every possible service to the civilization and peace of mankind, but I am certain we can do it best by not putting ourselves in leading strings or subjecting our policies and our sovereignty to other nations. The independence of the United States is not only more precious to ourselves but to the world than any single possession. . . . The United States is the world's best hope, but if you fetter her in the interests and quarrels of other nations, if you tangle her in the intrigues of Europe, you will destroy her power for good and endanger her very existence . . .

DOCUMENT ANALYSIS

1. What were Lodge's primary objections to U.S. membership in the League of Nations?

_____

_____

_____

2. Do Lodge's arguments sound familiar? Are they relevant today, especially in discussions pertaining to the United Nations?

_____

_____

_____

3. Why do you think the Senate was more receptive to these arguments in 1919 than in 1945, when the United States joined the United Nations?

_____

_____

_____

DOCUMENT 25.1
John F. Carter, "'These Wild Young People' by One of Them" (1920)

*As the United States entered the "Roaring Twenties," it was recovering
from World War I. Some members of this Lost Generation who had lived
through, and sometimes participated in, the war reacted by questioning
traditional values and living their lives in ways that their parents and
grandparents often found bewildering. Artists and writers such as F. Scott
Fitzgerald, Ernest Hemingway, and Gertrude Stein were exploring new
ideas, and it became more popular to live for the moment and explore
life's possibilities. This excerpt describes the generation gap of this era.*

For some months past the pages of our more conservative magazines have been crowded with pessimistic descriptions of the younger
generation, as seen by their elders and, no doubt, their betters. Hardly a
week goes by that I do not read some indignant treatise depicting our extravagance, the corruption of our manners, the futility of our existence,
poured out in stiff, scared, shocked sentences before a sympathetic and
horrified audience of fathers, mothers, and maiden aunts—but particularly maiden aunts.

In the May issue of the *Atlantic Monthly* appeared an article entitled
"Polite Society," by a certain Mr. Grundy, the husband of a very old
friend of my family. In kindly manner he

Mentioned our virtues, it is true,
But dwelt upon our vices, too.

"Chivalry and Modesty are dead. Modesty died first," quoteth he,
but expressed the pious hope that all might yet be well if the oldsters
would but be content to "wait and see." His article is one of the best-
tempered and most gentlemanly of this long series of Jeremiads against
'these wild young people.' It is significant that it should be anonymous. In
reading it, I could not help but be drawn to Mr. Grundy personally, but
was forced to the conclusion that he, like everyone else who is writing
about my generation, has very little idea of what he is talking about. . . .

. . . Mrs. Katharine Fullerton Gerould has come forward as the latest
volunteer prosecuting attorney, in her powerful 'Reflections of a Grundy
Cousin' in the August *Atlantic*. She has little or no patience with us. She
disposes of all previous explanations of our degeneration in a series of
short paragraphs, then launches into her own explanation: the decay of
religion. She treats it as a primary cause, and with considerable effect. But
I think she errs in not attempting to analyze the causes for such decay,
which would bring her nearer to the ultimate truth.

A friend of mine has an uncle who, in his youth, was a wild, fast, extravagant young blood. His clothes were the amazement of even his
fastest friends. He drank, he swore, he gambled, bringing his misdeeds to
a climax by eloping with an heiress, a beautiful Philadelphian seraph, fascinated by this glittering Lucifer. Her family disowned her, and they fled
to a distant and wild country. He was, in effect, a brilliant, worthless, attractive, and romantic person. Now he is the sedate deacon of a Boston
Presbyterian church, very strong on morality in every shape, a terror to
the young, with an impeccable business career, and a very dull family circle. Mrs. Gerould must know of similar cases; so why multiply instances?
Just think how moral and unentertaining our generation will be when we
have emerged from the "roaring forties"!—and rejoice.

There is a story, illustrative of Californian civic pride, about a California funeral. The friends and relatives of the departed were gathered
mournfully around the bier, awaiting the arrival of the preacher who was
to deliver the funeral oration. They waited and waited and waited, but no
preacher appeared. Finally, a messenger-boy arrived with a telegram. It
was from the clergyman, and informed them that he had missed his train.
The chief mourner rose to the occasion and asked if anyone would like to
say a few kind words about the deceased. No one stirred. Finally a long,
lanky person got up, cleared his throat, and drawled, "Wa-a-al, if no one
else is goin' to speak, I'd like to say a few things about Los Angeles!"

I would like to say a few things about my generation.

In the first place, I would like to observe that the older generation
had certainly pretty well ruined this world before passing it on to us. They
give us this Thing, knocked to pieces, leaky, red-hot, threatening to blow
up; and then they are surprised that we don't accept it with the same attitude of pretty, decorous enthusiasm with which they received it, way back
in the eighteen-nineties, nicely painted, smoothly running, practically
fool-proof. "So simple that a child can run it!" But the child couldn't steer
it. He hit every possible telegraph-pole, some of them twice, and ended
with a head-on collision for which we shall have to pay the fines and damages. Now, with loving pride, they turn over their wreck to us; and, since
we are not properly overwhelmed with loving gratitude, shake their heads
and sigh, "Dear! dear! We were so much better-mannered than these wild
young people. But then we had the advantages of a good, strict, old-
fashioned bringing-up!" How intensely human these oldsters are, after
all, and how fallible! How they always blame us for not following precisely
in their eminently correct footsteps!

Then again there is the matter of outlook. When these sentimental
old world-wreckers were young, the world was such a different place. . . .
Life for them was bright and pleasant. Like all normal youngsters, they
had their little tin-pot ideals, their sweet little visions, their naive enthusi-
asms, their nice little sets of beliefs. Christianity had emerged from the
blow dealt by Darwin, emerged rather in the shape of social dogma. Man
was a noble and perfectible creature. Women were angels (whom they
smugly sweated in their industries and prostituted in their slums). Right
was downing might. The nobility and the divine mission of the race were
factors that led our fathers to work wholeheartedly for a millennium,
which they caught a glimpse of just around the turn of the century. Why,
there were Hague Tribunals! International peace was at last assured, and
according to current reports, never officially denied, the American delegates held out for the use of poison gas in warfare, just as the men of that
generation were later to ruin Wilson's great ideal of a league of nations,
on the ground that such a scheme was an invasion of American rights.
But still, everything, masked by ingrained hypocrisy and prudishness,
seemed simple, beautiful, inevitable.

Now my generation is disillusioned, and, I think, to a certain extent,
brutalized, by the cataclysm which their complacent folly engendered.
The acceleration of life for us has been so great that into the last few years
have been crowded the experiences and the ideas of a normal lifetime. We
have in our unregenerate youth learned the practicality and the cynicism
that is safe only in unregenerate old age. We have been forced to become
realists overnight, instead of idealists, as was our birthright. We have seen
man at his lowest, woman at her lightest, in the terrible moral chaos of
Europe. We have been forced to question, and in many cases to discard,
the religion of our fathers. We have seen hideous speculation, greed,
anger, hatred, malice, and all uncharitableness, unmasked and rampant
and unashamed. We have been forced to live in an atmosphere of "to-
morrow we die," and so, naturally, we drank and were merry. We have
seen the rottenness and shortcomings of all governments, even the best
and most stable. We have seen entire social systems overthrown, and our
own called in question. In short, we have seen the inherent beastliness of
the human race revealed in an infernal apocalypse.

It is the older generation who forced us to see all this, which has left
us with social and political institutions staggering blind in the fierce white
light that, for us, should beat only about the enthroned ideal. And now,
through the soft-headed folly of these painfully shocked Grundys, we
have that devastating wisdom which is safe only for the burned-out em-
bers of grizzled, cautious old men. We may be fire, but it was they who
made us play with gunpowder. And now they are surprised that a great
many of us, because they have taken away our apple-cheeked ideals, are
seriously considering whether or not their game be worth our candle.

But, in justice to my generation, I think that I must admit that most
of us have realized that, whether or no it be worth while, we must all play
the game, as long as we are in it. And I think that much of the hectic quality of our life is due to that fact and to that alone. We are faced with staggering problems and are forced to solve them, while the previous incum-
bents are permitted a graceful and untroubled death. All my friends are

working and working hard. Most of the girls I know are working. In one way or another, often unconsciously, the great burden put upon us is being borne, and borne gallantly, by that immodest, non-chivalrous set of ne'er-do-wells, so delightfully portrayed by Mr. Grundy and the amazing young Fitzgerald. A keen interest in political and social problems, and a determination to face the facts of life, ugly or beautiful, characterizes us, as it certainly did not characterize our fathers. We won't shut our eyes to the truths we have learned. We have faced so many unpleasant things already,—and faced them pretty well,—that it is natural that we should keep it up.

Now I think that this is the aspect of our generation that annoys the uncritical and deceives the unsuspecting oldsters who are now met in judgment upon us: our devastating and brutal frankness. And this is the quality in which we really differ from our predecessors. We are frank with each other, frank, or pretty nearly so, with our elders, frank in the way we feel toward life and this badly damaged world. It may be a disquieting and misleading habit, but is it a bad one? We find some few things in the world that we like, and a whole lot that we don't, and we are not afraid to say so or to give our reasons. In earlier generations this was not the case. The young men yearned to be glittering generalities, the young women to act like shy, sweet, innocent fawns toward one another. And now, when grown up, they have come to believe that they actually were figures of pristine excellence, knightly chivalry, adorable modesty, and impeccable propriety. But I really doubt if they were so. Statistics relating to, let us say, the immorality of college students in the eighteen-eighties would not compare favorably with those of the present. However, now, as they look back on it, they see their youth through a mist of muslin, flannels, tennis, bicycles, Tennyson, Browning, and the Blue Danube waltz. The other things, the ugly things that we know about and talk about, must also have been there. But our elders didn't care or didn't dare to consider them, and now they are forgotten. We talk about them unabashed, and not necessarily with Presbyterian disapproval, and so they jump to the conclusion that we are thoroughly bad, and keep pestering us to make us good.

The trouble with them is that they can't seem to realize that we are busy, that what pleasure we snatch must be incidental and feverishly hurried. We have to make the most of our time. We actually haven't got so much time for the noble procrastinations of modesty or for the elaborate rigmarole of chivalry, and little patience for the lovely formulas of an ineffective faith. Let them die for a while! They did not seem to serve the world too well in its black hour. If they are inherently good they will come back, vital and untarnished. But just now we have a lot of work, "old time is still a-flying," and we must gather rose-buds while we may.

Oh! I know that we are a pretty bad lot, but has not that been true of every preceding generation? At least we have the courage to act accordingly. Our music is distinctly barbaric, our girls are distinctly not a mixture of arbutus and barbed-wire. We drink when we can and what we can, we gamble, we are extravagant—but we work, and that's about all that we can be expected to do; for, after all, we have just discovered that we are all still very near to the Stone Age. The Grundys shake their heads. They'll make us be good. Prohibition is put through to stop our drinking, and hasn't stopped it. . . . A Draconian code is being hastily formulated at Washington and elsewhere, to prevent us from, by any chance, making any alteration in this present divinely constituted arrangement of things. The oldsters stand dramatically with fingers and toes and noses pressed against the bursting dykes. Let them! They won't do any good. They can shackle us down, and still expect us to repair their blunders, if they wish. But we shall not trouble ourselves very much about them any more. Why should we? What have they done? They have made us work as they never had to work in all their padded lives—but we'll have our cakes and ale for a' that.

For now we know our way about. We're not babes in the wood. . . . We're men and women, long before our time, in the flower of our full-blooded youth. We have brought back into civil life some of the recklessness and ability that we were taught by war. We are also quite fatalistic in our outlook on the tepid perils of tame living. All may yet crash to the ground for aught that we can do about it. Terrible mistakes will be made, but we shall at least make them intelligently and insist, if we are to receive the strictures of the future, on doing pretty much as we choose now.

Oh! I suppose that it's too bad that we aren't humble, starry-eyed, shy, respectful innocents, standing reverently at their side for instructions, playing pretty little games, in which they no longer believe, except for us. But we aren't, and the best thing the oldsters can do about it is to go into their respective backyards and dig for worms, great big pink ones—for the Grundy tribe are now just about as important as they are, and they will doubtless make company more congenial and docile than 'these wild young people,' the men and women of my generation.

DOCUMENT ANALYSIS

1. What role did World War I play in Carter's explanation of the differences between the older and younger generations?

_____

_____

_____

2. How would you describe the overall tone of Carter's article? Make a list of appropriate adjectives.

_____

_____

_____

3. How does this portrayal of the "generation gap" compare with today's differences between your generation and your parents'?

_____

_____

_____

DOCUMENT 26.1
Edward Earle Purinton, from "Big Ideas from Big Business" (1921)

In the 1920s business was booming in the United States, and its popularity was soaring as well. Nevertheless, many people expressed concerns about the coldness and callousness of businessmen. In the article reproduced below, Purinton addresses those concerns and argues that business, especially big business, is good for everyone, not just a select few.

Among the nations of the earth today America stands for one idea: Business. National opprobrium? National opportunity. For in this fact is, potentially, the salvation of the world.

Thru business, properly conceived, managed and conducted, the human race is finally to be redeemed. How and why a man works foretells what he will do, think, have, love and be. And real salvation is in doing, thinking, having, giving and being—not in sermonizing and theorizing. I shall base the facts of this article on the personal tours and minute examinations I have recently made of twelve of the world's largest business plants: U.S. Steel Corporation, International Harvester Company, Swift & Company, E. I. du Pont de Nemours & Company, National County Bank, National Cash Register Company, Western Electric Company, Sears, Roebuck & Company, H. J. Heinz Company, Peabody Coal Company, Statler Hotels, Wanamaker Stores.

These organizations are typical, foremost representatives of the commercial group of interests loosely termed "Big Business." A close view of these corporations would reveal to any trained, unprejudiced observer a new conception of modern business activities. Let me draw a few general conclusions regarding the best type of business house and business man.

What is the finest game? Business. The soundest science? Business. The truest art? Business. The fullest education? Business. The fairest opportunity? Business. The cleanest philanthropy? Business. The sanest religion? Business.

You may not agree. That is because you judge business by the crude, mean, stupid, false imitation of business that happens to be located near you.

The finest game is business. The rewards are for everybody, and all can win. There are no favorites—Providence always crowns the career of the man who is worthy. And in this game there is no "luck"—you have the fun of taking chances but the sobriety of guaranteeing certainties. The speed and size of your winnings are for you alone to determine; you needn't wait for the other fellow in the game—it is always your move. And your slogan is not "Down the Other Fellow!" but rather "Beat Your Own Record!" or "Do It Better Today!" or "Make Every Job a Masterpiece!" The great sportsmen of the world are the great business men.

The soundest science is business. All investigation is reduced to action, and by action proved or disproved. The idealistic motive animates the materialistic method. Hearts as well as minds are open to the truth. Capital is furnished for the researches of "pure science"; yet pure science is not regarded pure until practical. Competent scientists are suitably rewarded—as they are not in the scientific schools.

The truest art is business. The art is so fine, so exquisite, that you do not think of it as art. Language, color, form, line, music, drama, discovery, adventure—all the components of art must be used in business to make it of superior character.

The fullest education is business. A proper blend of study, work and life is essential to advancement. The whole man is educated. Human nature itself is the open book that all business men study; and the mastery of a page of this educates you more than the memorizing of a dusty tome from a library shelf. In the school of business, moreover, you teach yourself and learn most from your own mistakes. What you learn here you live out, the only real test.

The fairest opportunity is business. You can find more, better, quicker chances to get ahead in a large business house than anywhere else on earth. The biographies of champion business men show how they climbed, and how you can climb. Recognition of better work, of keener and quicker thought, of deeper and finer feeling, is gladly offered by the men higher up, with early promotion the rule for the man who justifies it. There is, and can be, no such thing as buried talent in a modern business organization.

The cleanest philanthropy is business. By "clean" philanthropy I mean that devoid of graft, inefficiency and professionalism, also of condolence, hysterics and paternalism. Nearly everything that goes by the name of Charity was born a triplet, the other two members of the trio being Frailty and Cruelty. Not so in the welfare departments of leading corporations. Savings and loan funds; pension and insurance provisions; health precautions, instructions and safeguards; medical attention and hospital care; libraries, lectures and classes; musical, athletic and social features of all kinds; recreational facilities and financial opportunities— these types of "charitable institutions" for employees add to the worker's self-respect, self-knowledge and self-improvement, by making him an active partner in the welfare program, a producer of benefits for his employer and associates quite as much as a recipient of bounty from the company. I wish every "charity" organization would send its officials to school to the heads of the welfare departments of the big corporations; the charity would mostly be transformed into capability, and the minimum of irreducible charity left would not be called by that name.

The sanest religion is business. Any relationship that forces a man to follow the Golden Rule rightfully belongs amid the ceremonials of the church. A great business enterprise includes and presupposes this relationship. I have seen more Christianity to the square inch as a regular part of the office equipment of famous corporation presidents than may ordinarily be found on Sunday in a verbalized but not vitalized church congregation. A man is not wholly religious until he is better on week-days than he is on Sunday. The only ripened fruits of creeds are deeds. You can fool your preacher with a sickly sprout or a wormy semblance of character, but you can't fool your employer. I would make every business house a consultation bureau for the guidance of the church whose members were employees of the house.

I am aware that some of the preceding statements will be challenged by many readers. I should not myself have made them, or believed them, twenty years ago, when I was a pitiful specimen of a callow youth and cocksure professional man combined. A thoro knowledge of business has implanted a deep respect for business and real business men.

The future work of the business man is to teach the teacher, preach to the preacher, admonish the parent, advise the doctor, justify the lawyer, superintend the statesman, fructify the farmer, stabilize the banker, harness the dreamer, and reform the reformer. Do all these needy persons wish to have these many kind things done to them by the business man? Alas, no. They rather look down upon him, or askance at him, regarding him as a mental and social inferior—unless he has money or fame enough to tilt their glance upward.

A large variety of everyday lessons of popular interest may be gleaned from a tour of the world's greatest business plants and a study of the lives of their founders. We suggest a few. . . .

Only common experiences will unite the laborer and the capitalist. Each must get the viewpoint of the other by sharing the work, duties and responsibilities of the other. The sons of the families of Swift, McCormick, Wanamaker, Heinz, du Pont, have learned the business from the ground up; they know the trials, difficulties and needs of workers because they are workers; and they don't have to settle agitations and strikes because there aren't any.

Further, by councils and committees of employees, management courses for department heads and foremen, plans of referendum and appeal, offers of stock and voting power to workers, employee representation on the board of directors, and other means of sharing authority and responsibility, owners of a business now give the manual workers a chance to think and feel in unison with themselves. All enmity is between strangers. Those who really know each other cannot fight.

DOCUMENT ANALYSIS

1. Though Purinton clearly supports big business, the way in which he formulates his arguments tells us a lot about its critics. Based on the issues that he addresses, what were critics saying?

_____

_____

_____

2. Notice which companies the author references. Are these businesses still "big" in the United States?

_____

_____

_____

3. How does this article sum up the spirit of 1920s America? What does the author say about labor relations?

_____

_____

_____

DOCUMENT 27.1
Franklin D. Roosevelt, First Inaugural Address (1932)

Franklin Roosevelt took office during the worst economic depression the nation had ever experienced. Unemployment was skyrocketing, almost half of the country's 24,000 banks had failed, inflation was climbing, and the nation's farmers were desperate to sell their goods. Roosevelt's first inaugural address is in many ways typical of his public approach to the problem. He used strong yet optimistic language and spoke of "attacking" the problem head-on. This speech is famous for his statement that Americans had "nothing to fear but fear itself."

I am certain that my fellow Americans expect that on my induction into the Presidency I will address them with a candor and a decision which the present situation of our Nation impels. This is preeminently the time to speak the truth, the whole truth, frankly and boldly. Nor need we shrink from honestly facing conditions in our country today. This great Nation will endure as it has endured, will revive and will prosper. So, first of all, let me assert my firm belief that the only thing we have to fear is fear itself—nameless, unreasoning, unjustified terror which paralyzes needed efforts to convert retreat into advance. In every dark hour of our national life a leadership of frankness and vigor has met with that understanding and support of the people themselves which is essential to victory. I am convinced that you will again give that support to leadership in these critical days.

In such a spirit on my part and on yours we face our common difficulties. They concern, thank God, only material things. Values have shrunken to fantastic levels; taxes have risen; our ability to pay has fallen; government of all kinds is faced by serious curtailment of income; the means of exchange are frozen in the currents of trade; the withered leaves of industrial enterprise lie on every side; farmers find no markets for their produce; the savings of many years in thousands of families are gone.

More important, a host of unemployed citizens face the grim problem of existence, and an equally great number toil with little return. Only a foolish optimist can deny the dark reality of the movement.

Yet our distress comes from no failure or substance. We are stricken by no plague of locusts. Compared with the perils which our forefathers conquered because they believed and were not afraid, we have still much to be thankful for. Nature still offers her bounty and human efforts have multiplied it. Plenty is at our doorstep, but a generous use of it languishes in the very sight of the supply. Primarily this is because rulers of the exchange of mankind's goods have failed through their own stubbornness and their own incompetence, have admitted their failure, and have abdicated. Practices of the unscrupulous money changers stand indicted in the court of public opinion, rejected by the hearts and minds of men.

True they have tried, but their efforts have been cast in the pattern of an outworn tradition. Faced by failure of credit they have proposed only the lending of more money. Stripped of the lure of profit by which to induce our people to follow their leadership, they have resorted to exhortations, pleading tearfully for restored confidence. They have known only the rules of a generation of self-seekers. They have no vision, and when there is no vision the people perish.

The money changers have fled from their high seats in the temple of our civilization. We may now restore that temple to the ancient truths. The measure of the restoration lies in the extent to which we apply social values more noble than mere monetary profit.

Happiness lies not in the mere possession of money; it lies in the joy of achievement, in the thrill of creative effort. The joy and moral stimulation of work no longer must be forgotten in the mad chase of evanescent profits. These dark days will be worth all they cost us if they teach us that our true destiny is not to be ministered unto but to minister to ourselves and to our fellow men.

Recognition of the falsity of material wealth as the standard of success goes hand in hand with the abandonment of the false belief that public office and high political position are to be valued only by the standards of pride of place and personal profit; and there must be an end to a conduct in banking and in business which too often has given to a sacred trust the likeness of callous and selfish wrongdoing. Small wonder that confidence languishes, for it thrives only on honesty, on honor, on the sacredness of obligations, on faithful protection, on unselfish performance; without them it cannot live.

Restoration calls, however, not for changes in ethics alone. This Nation asks for action, and action now.

Our greatest primary task is to put people to work. This is no unsolvable problem if we face it wisely and courageously. It can be accomplished in part by direct recruiting by the Government itself, treating the task as we would treat the emergency of a war, but at the same time, through this employment, accomplishing greatly needed projects to stimulate and reorganize the use of our natural resources.

Hand in hand with this we must frankly recognize the overbalance of population in our industrial centers and, by engaging on a national scale in a redistribution, endeavor to provide a better use of the land for those best fitted for the land. The task can be helped by definite efforts to raise the values of agricultural products and with this the power to purchase the output of our cities. It can be helped by preventing realistically the tragedy of the growing loss through foreclosure of our small homes and our farms. It can be helped by insistence that the Federal, State, and local governments act forthwith on the demand that their cost be drastically reduced. It can be helped by the unifying of relief activities which today are often scattered, uneconomical, and unequal. It can be helped by national planning for and supervision of all forms of transportation and of communications and other utilities which have a definitely public character. There are many ways in which it can be helped but it can never be helped merely by talking about it. We must act and act quickly.

Finally, in our progress toward a resumption of work we require two safeguards against a return of the evils of the old order: there must be a strict supervision of all banking and credits and investments, so that there will be an end to speculation with other people's money; and there must be provision for an adequate but sound currency.

These are the lines of attack. I shall presently urge upon a new Congress, in special session, detailed measures for their fulfillment, and I shall seek the immediate assistance of the several States.

Through this program of action we address ourselves to putting our own national house in order and making income balance outgo. Our international trade relations, though vastly important, are in point of time and necessity secondary to the establishment of a sound national economy. I favor as a practical policy the putting of first things first. I shall spare no effort to restore world trade by international economic readjustment, but the emergency at home cannot wait on that accomplishment.

The basic thought that guides these specific means of national recovery is not narrowly nationalistic. It is the insistence as a first consideration, upon the interdependence of the various elements in and parts of the United States—a recognition of the old and permanently important manifestation of the American spirit of the pioneer. It is the way to recovery. It is the immediate way. It is the strongest assurance that the recovery will endure.

In the field of world policy I would dedicate this Nation to the policy of the good neighbor—the neighbor who respects his obligations and respects the sanctity of his agreements in and with a world of neighbors.

If I read the temper of our people correctly, we now realize as we have never realized before our interdependence on each other; that we cannot merely take but we must give as well; that if we are to go forward, we must move as a trained and loyal army willing to sacrifice for the good of a common discipline, because without such discipline no progress is made, no leadership becomes effective. We are, I know, ready and willing to submit our lives and property to such discipline, because it makes possible a leadership which aims at a larger good. This I propose to offer, pledging that the larger purpose will bind upon us all as a sacred obligation with a unity of duty hitherto evoked only in time of armed strife.

With this pledge taken, I assume unhesitatingly the leadership of this great army of our people dedicated to a disciplined attack upon our common problems.

Action in this image and to this end is feasible under the form of government which we have inherited from our ancestors. Our Constitution is so simple and practical that it is possible always to meet extraordinary needs by changes in emphasis and arrangement without loss of essential form. That is why our constitutional system has proved itself the most superbly enduring political mechanism the modern world has produced. It has met every stress of vast expansion of territory, of foreign wars, of bitter internal strife, of world relations.

It is to be hoped that the normal balance of Executive and legislative authority may be wholly adequate to meet the unprecedented task before us. But it may be that an unprecedented demand and need for undelayed action may call for temporary departure from that normal balance of public procedure.

I am prepared under my constitutional duty to recommend the measures that a stricken Nation in the midst of a stricken world may require. These measures, or such other measures as the Congress may build out of its experience and wisdom, I shall seek, within my constitutional authority to bring to speedy adoption.

But in the event that the Congress shall fail to take one of these two courses and in the event that the national emergency is still critical, I shall not evade the clear course of duty that will then confront me. I shall ask the Congress for the one remaining instrument to meet the crisis—broad Executive power to wage a war against the emergency, as great as the power that would be given to me if we were in fact invaded by a foreign foe.

For the trust reposed in me I will return the courage and the devotion that befit the time. I can do no less.

We face the arduous days that lie before us in the warm courage of national unity; with the clear consciousness of seeking old and precious moral values; with the clear satisfaction that comes from the stern performance of duty by old and young alike. We aim at the assurance of a rounded and permanent national life.

We do not distrust the future of essential democracy. The people of the United States have not failed. In their need they have registered a mandate that they want direct, vigorous action. They have asked for discipline and direction under leadership. They have made me the present instrument of their wishes. In the spirit of the gift I take it.

In this dedication of a Nation we humbly ask the blessing of God. May He protect each and every one of us. May He guide me in the days to come.

DOCUMENT ANALYSIS

1. What is the general tone of Roosevelt's speech? How did he describe the existing situation?

_____

_____

_____

2. What, specifically, did Roosevelt indicate he was going to do?

_____

_____

_____

3. What makes this a particularly memorable political speech?

_____

_____

_____

DOCUMENT 28.1
Franklin D. Roosevelt, "The Four Freedoms" (1941)

In January 1941, the United States had not yet entered the war. Hitler had ravaged Western Europe, conducted a devastating bombing campaign against the United Kingdom, and seemed unstoppable. It was questionable how much longer Great Britain could hold out. Meanwhile the United States had begun to boldly assist the Allies, thereby increasing the chances of direct intervention. President Roosevelt's State of the Union message of January 6 was designed to remind Americans of the values we hold most dear and what our responsibility might be to preserve those ideals. The Four Freedoms gained even more popularity when famed artist Norman Rockwell used them as the basis of a series of paintings that graced the covers of issues of the Saturday Evening Post.

Armed defense of democratic existence is now being gallantly waged in four continents. If that defense fails, all the population and all the resources of Europe, Asia, Africa and Australia will be dominated by the conquerors. The total of those populations and their resources . . . greatly exceeds the sum total of the population and the resources of the whole of the Western Hemisphere—many times over.

In times like these it is immature—and incidentally untrue—for anybody to brag that an unprepared America, single-handed, and with one hand tied behind its back, can hold off the whole world.

No realistic American can expect from a dictator's peace international generosity, or return of true independence, or world disarmament, or freedom of expression, or freedom of religion—or even good business. . . .

The need of the moment is that our actions and our policy should be devoted primarily—almost exclusively—to meeting this foreign peril. For all our domestic problems are now a part of the great emergency.

Just as our national policy in internal affairs has been based upon a decent respect for the rights and the dignity of all our fellow men within our gates, so our national policy in foreign affairs has been based on a decent respect for the rights and dignity of all nations, large and small. And the justice of morality must and will win in the end.

Our national policy is this:

First, by an impressive expression of the public will and without regard to partisanship, we are committed to all-inclusive national defense.

Second, by an impressive expression of the public will and without regard to partisanship, we are committed to full support of all those resolute peoples, everywhere, who are resisting aggression and are thereby keeping war away from our hemisphere. By this support, we express our determination that the democratic cause shall prevail, and we strengthen the defense and security of our own nation.

Third, by an impressive expression of the public will and without regard to partisanship, we are committed to the proposition that principles of morality and considerations for our own security will never permit us to acquiesce in a peace dictated by aggressors and sponsored by appeasers. We know that enduring peace cannot be bought at the cost of other people's freedom. . . .

I also ask this Congress for authority and for funds sufficient to manufacture additional munitions and war supplies of many kinds, to be turned over to those nations which are now in actual war with aggressor nations.

Our most useful and immediate role is to act as an arsenal for them as well as for ourselves. They do not need man power. They do need billions of dollars' worth of the weapons of defense. . . .

Let us say to the democracies, "We Americans are vitally concerned in your defense of freedom. We are putting forth our energies, our resources, and our organizing powers to give you the strength to regain and maintain a free world. We shall send you, in ever-increasing numbers, ships, planes, tanks, guns. This is our purpose and our pledge.". . .

There is nothing mysterious about the foundations of a healthy and strong democracy. The basic things expected by our people of their political and economic systems are simple.

They are:

Equality of opportunity for youth and for others.

Jobs for those who can work.

Security for those who need it.

The ending of special privilege for the few.

The preservation of civil liberties for all.

The enjoyment of the fruits of scientific progress in a wider and constantly rising standard of living.

These are the simple and basic things that must never be lost sight of in the turmoil and unbelievable complexity of our modern world. The inner and abiding strength of our economic and political systems is dependent upon the degree to which they fulfill these expectations. . . .

In the future days, which we seek to make secure, we look forward to a world founded upon four essential human freedoms.

The first is freedom of speech and expression everywhere in the world.

The second is freedom of every person to worship God in his own way everywhere in the world.

The third is freedom from want, which, translated into world terms, means economic understandings which will secure to every nation a healthy peacetime life for its inhabitants everywhere in the world.

The fourth is freedom from fear—which, translated into world terms, means a world-wide reduction of armaments to such a point and in such a thorough fashion that no nation will be in a position to commit an act of physical aggression against any neighbor—anywhere in the world.

That is no vision of a distant millennium. It is a definite basis for a kind of world attainable in our own time and generation. That kind of world is the very antithesis of the so-called new order of tyranny which the dictators seek to create with the crash of a bomb.

To that new order we oppose the greater conception—the moral order. A good society is able to face schemes of world domination and foreign revolutions alike without fear.

Since the beginning of our American history we have been engaged in change—in a perpetual peaceful revolution—a revolution which goes on steadily, quietly adjusting itself to changing conditions—without the concentration camp or the quicklime in the ditch. The world order which we seek is the cooperation of free countries, working together in a friendly, civilized society.

DOCUMENT ANALYSIS

1. Roosevelt listed four essential human freedoms upon which a secure world should be founded. What are those four freedoms?

_____

_____

2. Early in the speech, Roosevelt maintained that "our national policy" is "an impressive expression of the public will and without regard to partisanship." Considering that Roosevelt delivered this speech early in 1941, what do you think he was trying to accomplish by making this assertion? How successful was he?

_____

_____

DOCUMENT 28.2
Albert Einstein, Letter to President Roosevelt (1939)

Even before the German invasion of Poland in September 1939, some U.S. scientists, many of them originally from Germany, were concerned about the implications of early experiments directed toward harnessing the process of nuclear fission to build weapons. Though the scientific community did not agree that weapons could actually be produced using this process, Leo Szilard, referenced below, did think it possible. He was concerned enough to want to inform President Roosevelt, but he did not have a way to do so personally. Therefore, he contacted his friend Albert Einstein, who agreed to write the letter that appears below. Its composition was a collaborative effort between Einstein and Szilard. The letter did not reach Roosevelt until October, and even then the administration was slow to act. Large-scale funding of nuclear research in the United States did not officially begin until the day before the Pearl Harbor attack, and it was not until August 1942 that the research became known as the Manhattan Project.

Albert Einstein
Old Grove Rd., Nassau Point
Peconic, Long Island
August 2nd, 1939

F. D. Roosevelt,
President of the United States,
White House
Washington, D.C.

Sir:

Some recent work by E. Fermi and L. Szilard, which has been communicated to me in manuscript, leads me to expect that the element uranium may be turned into a new and important source of energy in the immediate future. Certain aspects of the situation which has arisen seem to call for watchfulness and, if necessary, quick action on the part of the Administration. I believe therefore that it is my duty to bring to your attention the following facts and recommendations:

In the course of the last four months it has been made probable—through the work of Joliot in France as well as Fermi and Szilard in America—that it may become possible to set up a nuclear chain reaction in a large mass of uranium, by which vast amount of power and large quantities of new radium-like elements would be generated. Now it appears almost certain that this could be achieved in the immediate future.

This new phenomenon would also lead to the construction of bombs, and it is conceivable—though much less certain—that extremely powerful bombs of a new type may thus be constructed. A single bomb of this type, carried by boat and exploded in a port, might very well destroy the whole port together with some of the surrounding territory. However, such bombs might very well prove to be too heavy for transportation by air.

The United States has only very poor ores of uranium in moderate quantities. There is some good ore in Canada and the former Czechoslovakia, while the most important source of uranium is the Belgian Congo.

In view of this situation you may think it desirable to have some permanent contact maintained between the Administration and the group of physicists working on chain reactions in America. One possible way of achieving this might be for you to entrust with this task a person who has your confidence and who could perhaps serve in an inofficial capacity. His task might comprise the following:

a) to approach Government Departments, keep them informed of the further development, and put forward recommendations for Government action, giving particular attention to the problem of securing a supply of uranium ore for the United States:

b) to speed up the experimental work, which is at present being carried on within the limits of the budgets of University laboratories, by providing funds, if such funds be required, through his contacts with private persons who are willing to make contributions for this cause, and perhaps also by obtaining the co-operation of industrial laboratories which have the necessary equipment.

I understand that Germany has actually stopped the sale of uranium from the Czechoslovakian mines which she has taken over. That she should have taken such early action might perhaps be understood on the ground that the son of the German Under-Secretary of State, von Weizsacker, is attached to the Kaiser-Wilhelm-Institut in Berlin where some of the American work on uranium is now being repeated.

Yours very truly,

[signed] Albert Einstein

DOCUMENT ANALYSIS

1. If you had received this letter, would you have acted more quickly than Roosevelt did? What was Einstein actually encouraging Roosevelt to do?

_____

_____

_____

2. Einstein was a pacifist. Are you surprised he would write such a letter?

_____

_____

_____

3. Why do you think Einstein included the final paragraph on Germany?

_____

_____

_____

DOCUMENT 29.1
Ronald Reagan, Testimony Before the House Un-American Activities Committee (1947)

When the House Un-American Activities Committee (HUAC) began to investigate charges of communist influence in Hollywood, Ronald Reagan was president of the Screen Actors Guild. He was not yet a politician, but HUAC considered him a "friendly" witness because of his anticommunist stance. Significantly, Reagan was not the only future president present for that day's testimony. Richard Nixon was a member of the committee.

The Committes met at 10:30 A.M. [October 23, 1947], the Honorable J. Parnell Thomas (Chairman) presiding.

THE CHAIRMAN: The record will show that Mr. McDowell, Mr. Vail, Mr. Nixon, and Mr. Thomas are present. A Subcommittee is sitting.

Staff members present: Mr. Robert E. Stripling, Chief Investigator; Messrs. Louis J. Russell, H. A. Smith, and Robert B. Gatson, Investigators; and Mr. Benjamin Mandel, Director of Research.

MR. STRIPLING: When and where were you born, Mr. Reagan?

MR. REAGAN: Tampico, Illinois, February 6, 1911.

MR. STRIPLING: What is your present occupation?

MR. REAGAN: Motion-picture actor.

MR. STRIPLING: How long have you been engaged in that profession?

MR. REAGAN: Since June 1937, with a brief interlude of three and a half years, that at the time didn't seem very brief.

MR. STRIPLING: What period was that?

MR. REAGAN: That was during the late war.

MR. STRIPLING: What branch of the service were you in?

MR. REAGAN: Well, sir, I had been for several years in the Reserve as an officer in the United States Calvary, but I was assigned to the Air Corp.

MR. STRIPLING: Are you the president of the guild at the present time?

MR. REAGAN: Yes, sir. . . .

MR. STRIPLING: As a member of the board of directors, as president of the Screen Actors Guild, and as an active member, have you at any time observed or noted within the organization a clique of either Communists or Fascists who were attempting to exert influence or pressure on the guild?

MR. REAGAN: Well, sir, my testimony must be very similar to that of Mr. [George] Murphy and Mr. [Robert] Montgomery. There has been a small group within the Screen Actors Guild which has consistently opposed the policy of the guild board and officers of the guild, as evidenced by the vote on various issues. That small clique referred to has been suspected of more or less following the tactics that we associated with the Communist Party.

MR. STRIPLING: Would you refer to them as a disruptive influence within the guild?

MR. REAGAN: I would say that at times they have attempted to be a disruptive influence.

MR. STRIPLING: You have no knowledge yourself as to whether or not any of them are members of the Communist Party?

MR. REAGAN: No, sir, I have no investigative force, or anything, and I do not know.

MR. STRIPLING: Has it ever been reported to you that certain members of the guild were Communists?

MR. REAGAN: Yes, sir, I have heard different discussions and some of them tagged as Communists.

MR. STRIPLING: Would you say that this clique has attempted to dominate the guild?

MR. REAGAN: Well, sir, by attempting to put over their own particular views on various issues. . . .

MR. STRIPLING: Mr. Reagan, there has been testimony to the effect here that numerous Communist-front organizations have been set up in Hollywood. Have you ever been solicited to join any of those organizations or any organization which you consider to be a Communist-front organization?

MR. REAGAN: Well, sir, I have received literature from an organization called the Committee for a Far-Eastern Democratic Policy. I don't know whether it is Communist or not. I only know that I didn't like their views and as a result I didn't want to have anything to do with them. . . .

MR. STRIPLING: Would you say from your observation that this is typical of the tactics or strategy of the Communists, to solicit and use the names of prominent people to either raise money or gain support?

MR. REAGAN: I think it is in keeping with their tactics, yes, sir.

MR. STRIPLING: Do you think there is anything democratic about those tactics?

MR. REAGAN: I do not, sir.

MR. STRIPLING: Mr. Reagan, what is your feeling about what steps should be taken to rid the motion-picture industry of any Communist influences?

MR. REAGAN: Well, sir, ninety-nine percent of us are pretty well aware of what is going on, and I think, within the bounds of our democratic rights and never once stepping over the rights given us by democracy, we have done a pretty good job in our business of keeping those people's activities curtailed. After all, we must recognize them at present as a political party. On that basis we have exposed their lies when we came across them, we have opposed their propaganda, and I can certainly testify that in the case of the Screen Actors Guild we have been eminently successful in preventing them from, with their usual tactics, trying to run a majority of an organization with a well-organized minority. In opposing those people, the best thing to do is make democracy work. . . .

Sir, I detest, I abhor their philosophy, but I detest more than that their tactics, which are those of the fifth column, and are dishonest, but at the same time I never as a citizen want to see our country become urged, by either fear or resentment of this group that we ever compromise with any of our democratic principles through that fear or resentment. I still think that democracy can do it.

DOCUMENT ANALYSIS

1. Which aspects of Reagan's testimony would make the committee consider him a friendly witness?

_____

_____

_____

2. What did Reagan have to say about communists in Hollywood? Did he seem to fear their influence?

_____

_____

_____

DOCUMENT 29.2
Executive Order 9981 (1948)

In 1941, President Franklin D. Roosevelt had issued Executive Order 8802, which prohibited government contractors from discriminating on the basis of race, color, or national origin. After World War II, in July 1948, President Harry S Truman issued Executive Order 9981, excerpted below, which desegregated the U.S. armed forces. This order constituted a great milestone in the fight for civil rights. However, there was immense opposition to the order, and actual desegregation of the military took years to accomplish. For example, it was not until October 1953 that the army announced that 95 percent of its African American soldiers were actually part of integrated units.

WHEREAS it is essential that there be maintained in the armed services of the United States the highest standards of democracy, with equality of treatment and opportunity for all those who serve in our country's defense:

NOW, THEREFORE, by virtue of the authority vested in me as President of the United States, by the Constitution and the statutes of the United States, and as Commander-in-Chief of the armed services, it is hereby ordered as follows:

It is hereby declared to be the policy of the President that there shall be equality of treatment and opportunity for all persons in the armed services without regard to race, color, religion or national origin. This policy shall be put into effect as rapidly as possible, having due regard to the time required to effectuate any necessary changes without impairing efficiency or morale.

There shall be created in the National Military Establishment an advisory committee to be known as the President's Committee on Equality of Treatment and Opportunity in the Armed Services, which shall be composed of seven members to be designated by the President.

The Committee is authorized on behalf of the President to examine into the rules, procedures and practices of the armed services in order to determine in what respect such rules, procedures and practices may be altered or improved with a view to carrying out the policy of this order. The Committee shall confer and advise with the Secretary of Defense, the Secretary of the Army, the Secretary of the Navy, and the Secretary of the Air Force, and shall make such recommendations to the President and to said Secretaries as in the judgment of the Committee will effectuate the policy hereof.

All executive departments and agencies of the Federal Government are authorized and directed to cooperate with the Committee in its work, and to furnish the Committee such information or the services of such persons as the Committee may require in the performance of its duties.

DOCUMENT ANALYSIS

1. How long did the military have to comply with this order?

_____

_____

_____

2. What was the purpose of the President's Committee on Equality of Treatment and Opportunity in the Armed Forces?

_____

_____

_____

3. The first paragraph of the order states that its purpose is to maintain the "highest standards of democracy." How might those who opposed integration have argued against that goal?

_____

_____

_____

DOCUMENT 30.1
The Southern Manifesto (1956)

The landmark 1954 U.S. Supreme Court decision in Brown v. Board of Education *mandated an end to public school segregation in the United States. Popular reaction throughout the South, especially, was predictable. One very public response to the decision was the Southern Manifesto, read before Congress, preserved in the* Congressional Record, *and published in newspapers throughout the country. One hundred southern senators and representatives signed the Manifesto, which detailed their objection to the Brown decision.*

Declaration of Constitutional Principles

The unwarranted decision of the Supreme Court in the public school cases is now bearing the fruit always produced when men substitute naked power for established law.

The Founding Fathers gave us a Constitution of checks and balances because they realized the inescapable lesson of history that no man or group of men can be safely entrusted with unlimited power. They framed this Constitution with its provisions for change by amendment in order to secure the fundamentals of government against the dangers of temporary popular passion or the personal predilections of public officeholders.

We regard the decision of the Supreme Court in the school cases as a clear abuse of judicial power. It climaxes a trend in the Federal judiciary undertaking to legislate, in derogation of the authority of Congress, and to encroach upon the reserved rights of the States and the people.

The original Constitution does not mention education. Neither does the 14th Amendment nor any other amendment. The debates preceding the submission of the 14th Amendment clearly show that there was no intent that it should affect the systems of education maintained by the States.

The very Congress which proposed the amendment subsequently provided for segregated schools in the District of Columbia.

When the amendment was adopted, in 1868, there were 37 States of the Union. Every one of the 26 States that had any substantial racial differences among its people either approved the operation of segregated schools already in existence or subsequently established such schools by action of the same lawmaking body which considered the 14th Amendment.

As admitted by the Supreme Court in the public school case (*Brown v. Board of Education*), the doctrine of separate but equal schools "apparently originated in *Roberts v. City of Boston . . .* (1849), upholding school segregation against attack as being violative of a State constitutional guarantee of equality." This constitutional doctrine began in the North—not in the South, and it was followed not only in Massachusetts, but in Connecticut, New York, Illinois, Indiana, Michigan, Minnesota, New Jersey, Ohio, Pennsylvania, and other northern States until they, exercising their rights as States through the constitutional processes of local self-government, changed their school systems.

In the case of *Plessy v. Ferguson,* in 1896, the Supreme Court expressly declared that under the 14th Amendment no person was denied any of his rights if the States provided separate but equal public facilities. This decision has been followed in many other cases. It is notable that the Supreme Court, speaking through Chief Justice Taft, a former President of the United States, unanimously declared, in 1927, in *Lum v. Rice,* that the "separate but equal" principle is "within the discretion of the State in regulating its public schools and does not conflict with the 14th amendment."

This interpretation, restated time and again, became a part of the life of the people of many of the States and confirmed their habits, customs, traditions, and way of life. It is founded on elemental humanity and commonsense, for parents should not be deprived by Government of the right to direct the lives and education of their own children.

Though there has been no constitutional amendment or act of Congress changing this established legal principle almost a century old, the Supreme Court of the United States, with no legal basis for such action, undertook to exercise their naked judicial power and substituted their personal political and social ideas for the established law of the land.

This unwarranted exercise of power by the Court, contrary to the Constitution, is creating chaos and confusion in the States principally affected. It is destroying the amicable relations between the white and Negro races that have been created through 90 years of patient effort by the good people of both races. It has planted hatred and suspicion where there has been heretofore friendship and understanding.

Without regard to the consent of the governed, outside agitators are threatening immediate and revolutionary changes in our public-school systems. If done, this is certain to destroy the system of public education in some of the States.

With the gravest concern for the explosive and dangerous condition created by this decision and inflamed by outside meddlers:

We reaffirm our reliance on the Constitution as the fundamental law of the land.

We decry the Supreme Court's encroachments on rights reserved to the States and to the people, contrary to established law and to the Constitution.

We commend the motives of those States which have declared the intention to resist forced integration by any lawful means.

We appeal to the States and people who are not directly affected by these decisions to consider the constitutional principles involved against the time when they, too, on issues vital to them, may be the victims of judicial encroachment.

Even though we constitute a minority in the present Congress, we have full faith that a majority of the American people believe in the dual system of Government which has enabled us to achieve our greatness and will in time demand that the reserved rights of the State and of the people be made secure against judicial usurpation.

We pledge ourselves to use all lawful means to bring about a reversal of this decision which is contrary to the Constitution and to prevent the use of force in its implementation.

In this trying period, as we all seek to right this wrong, we appeal to our people not to be provoked by the agitators and troublemakers invading our States and to scrupulously refrain from disorders and lawless acts.

Signed by:

[Nineteen] Members of the United States Senate

[Eighty-one] Members of the United States House of Representatives

DOCUMENT ANALYSIS

1. What is the basis of the opposition to the Brown decision as expressed in this document?

_____

_____

_____

2. According to the Manifesto, whose power would the federal government usurp by implementing Brown?

_____

_____

_____

3. What role did "habits," "customs," and "traditions" play in the arguments presented in the document?

_____

_____

_____

DOCUMENT 30.2
John Lewis, Address at the March on Washington (1963)

The 1963 March on Washington had its roots in the planned, but postponed, march organized by labor and civil rights leader A. Philip Randolph in 1942. The 1963 march took place as Congress was debating a landmark civil rights bill. Martin Luther King, Jr., delivered his famous "I Have a Dream" speech. White and black leaders, politicians, activists, and actors turned out to support the march. Finally, John Lewis, a representative of the Student Nonviolent Coordinating Committee (SNCC) and the youngest speaker at the march, made a speech that made many of the more traditional leadership nervous. He focused on the shortcomings of the proposed bill and called for more action. This speech is actually a watered-down version of his original draft, which he changed after a personal appeal from Randolph and King.

It is interesting to note that Lewis used the term "black" rather than "negro," more commonly used at the time, in this speech.

We march today for jobs and freedom, but we have nothing to be proud of, for hundreds and thousands of our brothers are not here—they have no money for their transportation, for they are receiving starvation wages . . . or no wages, at all.

In good conscience, we cannot support the Administration's civil rights bill, for it is too little, and too late. There's not one thing in the bill that will protect our people from police brutality.

The voting section of the bill will not help the thousands of citizens who want to vote. . . .

What is in the bill that will protect the homeless and starving people of this nation? What is there in this bill to ensure the equality of a maid who earns $5.00 a week in the home of a family whose income is $100,000 a year?

The bill will not protect young children and old women from police dogs and fire hoses for engaging in peaceful demonstrations. . . .

For the first time in 100 years this nation is being awakened to the fact that segregation is evil and it must be destroyed in all forms. Our presence today proves that we have been aroused to the point of action.

We are now involved in a serious revolution. This nation is still a place of cheap political leaders who build their careers on immoral compromise and ally themselves with open forms of political, economic, and social exploitation. . . . The party of Kennedy is also the party of Eastland. The party of Javits is also the party of Goldwater. Where is our party?

I want to know—which side is the federal government on?

The revolution is at hand, and we must free ourselves of the chains of political and economic slavery. The non-violent revolution is saying, "We will not wait for the courts to act, for we have been waiting hundreds of years. We will not wait for the President, nor the Justice Department, nor Congress, but we will take matters into our own hands, and create a great source of power, outside of any national structure that could and would assure us victory." . . . We cannot be patient, we do not want to be free gradually, we want our freedom, and we want it now. We can not depend on any political party, for both the Democrats and Republicans have betrayed the basic principles of the Declaration of Independence. . . .

The revolution is a serious one. Mr. Kennedy is trying to take the revolution out of the streets and put it in the courts. Listen, Mr. Kennedy, listen. Mr. Congressman, listen, fellow citizens—the black masses are on the march for jobs and freedom, and we must say to the politicians that there won't be a "cooling-off period."

We won't stop now. All of the forces of Eastland, Barnett, and Wallace won't stop this revolution. The next time we march, we won't march on Washington, but will march through the South, through the Heart of Dixie, the way Sherman did—nonviolently. We will make the action of the past few months look petty. And I say to you, WAKE UP AMERICA!

DOCUMENT ANALYSIS

1. Why would this speech have angered, or at least concerned, some other civil rights leaders?

_____

_____

_____

2. What charges did Lewis level at politicians, both Democrats and Republicans?

_____

_____

_____

3. What is the overall tone of Lewis's speech? Is it surprising that this sort of rhetoric came from a man committed to nonviolence?

_____

_____

_____

DOCUMENT 31.1
National Defense Education Act (1958)

The Cold War and, specifically, the "space race" set in motion by the successful 1957 launch of the Soviet satellite Sputnik *led many Americans to fear that their country had fallen behind the Soviets in science and technology. As a result, Congress passed the National Defense Education Act (NDEA), which provided $575 million to enhance math, science, and foreign language education in primary and secondary schools, graduate fellowships, foreign language and area studies, and vocational-technical training. Perhaps the act's most important provision for U.S. college students, both in 1958 and today, was the funding of low-interest loans for students.*

Title I: General Provisions

Sec. 101. The Congress hereby finds and declares that the security of the Nation requires the fullest development of the mental resources and technical skills of its young men and women. The present emergency demands that additional and more adequate education opportunities be made available. The defense of this Nation depends upon the mastery of modern techniques developed from complex scientific principles. It depends as well upon the discovery and development of new principles, new techniques, and new knowledge.

We must increase our efforts to identify and educate more of the talent of our Nation. This requires programs that will give assurance that no student of ability will be denied an opportunity for higher education because of financial need; will correct as rapidly as possible the existing imbalances in our education programs which have led to an insufficient pro-

portion of our population educated in science, mathematics, and modern foreign languages and trained in technology.

The Congress reaffirms the principle and declares that the states and local communities have and must retain control over and primary responsibility for public education. The national interest requires, however, that the Federal Government give assistance to education for programs which are important to our defense. To meet the present educational emergency requires additional effort at all levels of government. It is therefore the purpose of this act to provide substantial assistance in various forms to individuals, and to States and their subdivisions, in order to insure trained manpower of sufficient quality and quantity to meet the national defense needs of the United States.

Sec. 102. Nothing contained in this act shall be construed to authorize any department, agency, officer, or employee of the United States to exercise any direction, supervision, or control over the curriculum, program of instruction, administration, or personnel of any educational institution or school system. . .

Title III: Financial Assistance for Strengthening Science, Mathematics, and Modern Foreign Language Instruction . . .

Sec. 301. There are hereby authorized to be appropriated $70,000,000 for the fiscal year ending June 30, 1959, and for each of the three succeeding fiscal years, for (1) making payments to State educational agencies under this title for the acquisition of equipment (suitable for use in providing education in science, mathematics, or modern foreign language) . . .

DOCUMENT ANALYSIS

1. Is the connection between education and national defense still a topic of interest in the United States? For example, do Americans make similar connections today between education and the "war on terror"?

_____

_____

_____

2. Why is Section 102 important? Who might have been threatened by this unprecedented venture by the federal government into education?

_____

_____

_____

3. What is the meaning of the phrase "the existing imbalances in our education programs" in Section 101? In your opinion, do such "imbalances" exist today?

_____

_____

_____

DOCUMENT 31.2
Shirley Chisholm, "Equal Rights for Women" (May 21, 1969)

Shirley Chisholm was the first African American woman to be elected to the U.S. House of Representatives. She represented her New York City district in Congress from 1969 until her retirement in 1982. She gained national fame in 1972 as the first African American to run for president when she campaigned for the Democratic nomination. In the speech reproduced below Chisholm calls for a constitutional amendment to guarantee equal rights for women.

HON. SHIRLEY CHISHOLM of New York

In the House of Representatives, May 21, 1969

Mr. Speaker, when a young woman graduates from college and starts looking for a job, she is likely to have a frustrating and even demeaning experience ahead of her. If she walks into an office for an interview, the first question she will be asked is, "Do you type?"

There is a calculated system of prejudice that lies unspoken behind that question. Why is it acceptable for women to be secretaries, librarians, and teachers, but totally unacceptable for them to be managers, administrators, doctors, lawyers, and Members of Congress?

The unspoken assumption is that women are different. They do not have executive ability, orderly minds, stability, leadership skills, and they are too emotional.

It has been observed before, that society for a long time discriminated against another minority, the blacks, on the same basis—that they were different and inferior. The happy little homemaker and the contented "old darkey" on the plantation were both produced by prejudice.

As a black person, I am no stranger to race prejudice. But the truth is that in the political world I have been far oftener discriminated against because I am a woman than because I am black.

Prejudice against blacks is becoming unacceptable although it will take years to eliminate it. But it is doomed because, slowly, white America is beginning to admit that it exists. Prejudice against women is still acceptable. There is very little understanding yet of the immorality involved in double pay scales and the classification of most of the better jobs as "for men only."

More than half of the population of the United States is female. But women occupy only 2 percent of the managerial positions. They have not even reached the level of tokenism yet. No women sit on the AFL-CIO council or Supreme Court. There have been only two women who have held Cabinet rank, and at present there are none. Only two women now hold ambassadorial rank in the diplomatic corps. In Congress, we are down to one Senator and 10 Representatives.

Considering that there are about 3 1/2 million more women in the United States than men, this situation is outrageous.

It is true that part of the problem has been that women have not been aggressive in demanding their rights. This was also true of the black population for many years. They submitted to oppression and even cooperated with it. Women have done the same thing. But now there is an awareness of this situation particularly among the younger segment of the population.

As in the field of equal rights for blacks, Spanish-Americans, the Indians, and other groups, laws will not change such deep-seated problems overnight. But they can be used to provide protection for those who are most abused, and to begin the process of evolutionary change by compelling the insensitive majority to reexamine its unconscious attitudes.

It is for this reason that I wish to introduce today a proposal that has been before every Congress for the last 40 years and that sooner or later must become part of the basic law of the land— the equal rights amendment.

Let me note and try to refute two of the commonest arguments that are offered against this amendment. One is that women are already protected under the law and do not need legislation. Existing laws are not adequate to secure equal rights for women. Sufficient proof of this is the concentration of women in lower paying, menial, unrewarding jobs and their incredible scarcity in the upper level jobs. If women are already equal, why is it such an event whenever one happens to be elected to Congress?

It is obvious that discrimination exists. Women do not have the opportunities that men do. And women that do not conform to the system, who try to break with the accepted patterns, are stigmatized as "odd" and "unfeminine." The fact is that a woman who aspires to be chairman of the board, or a Member of the House, does so for exactly the same reasons as any man. Basically, these are that she thinks she can do the job and she wants to try.

A second argument often heard against the equal rights amendment is that it would eliminate legislation that many States and the Federal Government have enacted giving special protection to women and that it would throw the marriage and divorce laws into chaos.

As for the marriage laws, they are due for a sweeping reform, and an excellent beginning would be to wipe the existing ones off the books. Regarding special protection for working women, I cannot understand why it should be needed. Women need no protection that men do not need. What we need are laws to protect working people, to guarantee them fair pay, safe working conditions, protection against sickness and layoffs, and provision for dignified, comfortable retirement. Men and women need these things equally. That one sex needs protection more than the other is a male supremacist myth as ridiculous and unworthy of respect as the white supremacist myths that society is trying to cure itself of at this time.

DOCUMENT ANALYSIS

1. What persuasive tools did Representative Chisholm use to convey her message? Is the message effective to you as a reader? Why or why not?

_____

_____

_____

2. Given the racial and gender situations in America in 1969, can Chisholm be considered a trailblazer for African Americans and women? Why or why not?

_____

_____

_____

3. How did Chisholm compare the situation of women in the United States with that of other minority groups?

_____

_____

_____

DOCUMENT 32.1
Ronald Reagan, Address to the National Association of Evangelicals (1983)

President Reagan firmly believed that the Cold War would end with a winner and a loser, not in a draw, and that the Western world, led by the United States, would be the winner. In his speeches, Reagan liked to throw out challenges, and this speech did just that. It affirmed the moral superiority of the West, and it identified this superiority as the West's strongest weapon. At the time, many commentators accused the president of dangerous brinksmanship. The debate over Reagan's role in the end of the Cold War and the collapse of the Soviet Union continues. Conservatives generally credit Reagan's policies while liberals also highlight internal weaknesses of the USSR and the activities of Soviet reformers, particularly Soviet leader Mikhail Gorbachev.

During my first press conference as President, in answer to a direct question, I pointed out that, as good Marxist-Leninists, the Soviet leaders have openly and publicly declared that the only morality they recognize is that which will further their cause, which is world revolution. I think I should point out I was only quoting Lenin, their guiding spirit, who said in 1920 that they repudiate all morality that proceeds from supernatural ideas—that's their name for religion—or ideas that are outside class conceptions. Morality is entirely subordinate to the interests of class war. And everything is moral that is necessary for the annihilation of the old, exploiting social order and for uniting the proletariat.

Well, I think the refusal of many influential people to accept this elementary fact of Soviet doctrine illustrates an historical reluctance to see totalitarian powers for what they are. We saw this phenomenon in the 1930s. We see it too often today.

This doesn't mean we should isolate ourselves and refuse to seek an understanding with them. I intend to do everything I can to persuade them of our peaceful intent, to remind them that it was the West that refused to use its nuclear monopoly in the forties and fifties for territorial gain and which now proposes a 50-percent cut in strategic ballistic missiles and the elimination of an entire class of land-based, intermediate-range nuclear missiles.

At the same time, however, they must be made to understand that we will never compromise our principles and standards. We will never give away our freedom. We will never abandon our belief in God. And we will never stop searching for a genuine peace. But we can assure none of these things America stands for through the so-called nuclear freeze solutions proposed by some.

The truth is that a freeze now would be a very dangerous fraud, for that is merely the illusion of peace. The reality is that we must find peace through strength.

I would agree to a freeze if only we could freeze the Soviets' global desires. A freeze at current levels of weapons would remove any incentive for the Soviets to negotiate seriously in Geneva and virtually end our chances to achieve the major arms reductions which we have proposed. Instead, they would achieve their objectives through the freeze.

A freeze would reward the Soviet Union for its enormous and unparalleled military buildup. It would prevent the essential and long-overdue modernization of United States and allied defenses and would leave our aging forces increasingly vulnerable. And an honest freeze would require extensive prior negotiations on the systems and numbers to be limited and on the measures to ensure effective verification and compliance. And the kind of freeze that has been suggested would be virtually impossible to verify. Such a major effort would divert us completely from our current negotiations on achieving substantial reductions.

A number of years ago, I heard a young father, a very prominent young man in the entertainment world, addressing a tremendous gathering in California. It was during the time of the cold war, and communism and our own way of life were very much on people's minds. And he was speaking to that subject. And suddenly, though, I heard him saying, "I love my little girls more than anything—" And I said to myself, "Oh, no, don't. You can't—don't say that." But I had underestimated him. He went on: "I would rather see my little girls die now, still believing in God, than have them grow up under communism and one day die no longer believing in God."

There were thousands of young people in that audience. They came to their feet with shouts of joy. They had instantly recognized the profound truth in what he had said, with regard to the physical and the soul and what was truly important.

Yes, let us pray for the salvation of all of those who live in that totalitarian darkness—pray they will discover the joy of knowing God. But until they do, let us be aware that while they preach the supremacy of the state, declare its omnipotence over individual man, and predict its eventual domination of all peoples on the Earth, they are the focus of evil in the modern world.

It was C. S. Lewis who, in his unforgettable "Screwtape Letters," wrote: "The greatest evil is not done now in those sordid 'dens of crime' that Dickens loved to paint. It is not even done in concentration camps and labor camps. In those we see its final result. But it is conceived and ordered (moved, seconded, carried and minuted) in clear, carpeted, warmed, and well-lighted offices, by quiet men with white collars and cut fingernails and smooth-shaven cheeks who do not need to raise their voice."

Well, because these "quiet men" do not "raise their voices," because they sometimes speak in soothing tones of brotherhood and peace, because, like other dictators before them, they're always making "their final territorial demand," some would have us accept them at their word and accommodate ourselves to their aggressive impulses. But if history teaches anything, it teaches that simple-minded appeasement or wishful thinking about our adversaries is folly. It means the betrayal of our past, the squandering of our freedom.

So, I urge you to speak out against those who would place the United States in a position of military and moral inferiority. You know, I've always believed that old Screwtape reserved his best efforts for those of you in the church. So, in your discussions of the nuclear freeze proposals, I urge you to beware the temptation of pride—the temptation of blithely declaring yourselves above it all and label both sides equally at fault, to ignore the facts of history and the aggressive impulses of an evil empire, to simply call the arms race a giant misunderstanding and thereby remove yourself from the struggle between right and wrong and good and evil.

I ask you to resist the attempts of those who would have you withhold your support for our efforts, this administration's efforts, to keep America strong and free, while we negotiate real and verifiable reductions in the world's nuclear arsenals and one day, with God's help, their total elimination.

While America's military strength is important, let me add here that I've always maintained that the struggle now going on for the world will never be decided by bombs or rockets, by armies or military might. The real crisis we face today is a spiritual one; at root, it is a test of moral will and faith.

Whittaker Chambers, the man whose own religious conversion made him a witness to one of the terrible traumas of our time, the Hiss-Chambers case, wrote that the crisis of the Western World exists to the degree in which the West is indifferent to God, the degree to which it collaborates in communism's attempt to make man stand alone without God. And then he said, for Marxism-Leninism is actually the second oldest faith, first proclaimed in the Garden of Eden with the words of temptation, "Ye shall be as gods."

The Western World can answer this challenge, he wrote, "but only provided that its faith in God and the freedom He enjoins is as great as communism's faith in Man."

I believe we shall rise to the challenge. I believe that communism is another sad, bizarre chapter in human history whose last pages even now are being written. I believe this because the source of our strength in the quest for human freedom is not material, but spiritual. And because it knows no limitation, it must terrify and ultimately triumph over those who would enslave their fellow man. For in the words of Isaiah: "He

giveth power to the faint; and to them that have no might He increased strength. . . . But they that wait upon the Lord shall renew their strength; they shall mount up with wings as eagles; they shall run, and not be weary. . . ."

Yes, change your world. One of our Founding Fathers, Thomas Paine, said, "We have it within our power to begin the world over again." We can do it, doing together what no one church could do by itself. God bless you, and thank you very much.

DOCUMENT ANALYSIS

1. Reagan considered morality to be a determining force in politics, both national and international. Many people, however, believe that politics is amoral, if not immoral. Does morality have a place in politics? Why or why not?

_____

_____

_____

2. Speculate as to the effect this speech had on its intended audience, on the American public at large, and on the world community.

_____

_____

_____

3. What role did God play in Reagan's version of the Cold War? Which historical figures or events did Reagan cite to prove his points?

_____

_____

_____

DOCUMENT 33.1
George W. Bush, Address to Congress (September 20, 2001)

In the week that followed the 9/11 terrorist attack on the World Trade Center and the Pentagon, President Bush gave several speeches and made several appearances. He had hoped to rally the American people, but his language was often imprecise and bellicose. He failed to instill confidence in the American people that the government was doing the right thing or was even in the right hands. Like many people, he was angry that the United States had been attacked and that so many civilians had been killed. The still-new president let his emotions show and did not choose his words carefully. Then, on September 20, 2001, Bush, his speechwriters, and his administrative team silenced the critics with a carefully prepared speech that calmed the American public and convinced many people of the administration's resolve and ability.

. . . My fellow citizens, for the last nine days, the entire world has seen for itself the state of our Union—and it is strong. (*Applause.*)

Tonight we are a country awakened to danger and called to defend freedom. Our grief has turned to anger, and anger to resolution. Whether we bring our enemies to justice, or bring justice to our enemies, justice will be done. (*Applause.*) . . .

On September the 11th, enemies of freedom committed an act of war against our country. Americans have known wars—but for the past 136 years, they have been wars on foreign soil, except for one Sunday in 1941. Americans have known the casualties of war—but not at the center of a great city on a peaceful morning. Americans have known surprise attacks—but never before on thousands of civilians. All of this was brought upon us in a single day—and night fell on a different world, a world where freedom itself is under attack.

Americans have many questions tonight. Americans are asking: Who attacked our country? The evidence we have gathered all points to a collection of loosely affiliated terrorist organizations known as al Qaeda. They are the same murderers indicted for bombing American embassies in Tanzania and Kenya, and responsible for bombing the USS *Cole.*

Al Qaeda is to terror what the mafia is to crime. But its goal is not making money; its goal is remaking the world—and imposing its radical beliefs on people everywhere.

The terrorists practice a fringe form of Islamic extremism that has been rejected by Muslim scholars and the vast majority of Muslim clerics—a fringe movement that perverts the peaceful teachings of Islam. The terrorists' directive commands them to kill Christians and Jews, to kill all Americans, and make no distinction among military and civilians, including women and children.

This group and its leader—a person named Osama bin Laden—are linked to many other organizations in different countries, including the Egyptian Islamic Jihad and the Islamic Movement of Uzbekistan. There are thousands of these terrorists in more than 60 countries. They are recruited from their own nations and neighborhoods and brought to camps in places like Afghanistan, where they are trained in the tactics of terror. They are sent back to their homes or sent to hide in countries around the world to plot evil and destruction.

The leadership of al Qaeda has great influence in Afghanistan and supports the Taliban regime in controlling most of that country. In Afghanistan, we see al Qaeda's vision for the world.

Afghanistan's people have been brutalized—many are starving and many have fled. Women are not allowed to attend school. You can be jailed for owning a television. Religion can be practiced only as their leaders dictate. A man can be jailed in Afghanistan if his beard is not long enough.

The United States respects the people of Afghanistan—after all, we are currently its largest source of humanitarian aid—but we condemn the Taliban regime. (*Applause.*) It is not only repressing its own people, it is threatening people everywhere by sponsoring and sheltering and supplying terrorists. By aiding and abetting murder, the Taliban regime is committing murder.

And tonight, the United States of America makes the following demands on the Taliban: Deliver to United States authorities all the leaders of al Qaeda who hide in your land. (*Applause.*) Release all foreign nationals, including American citizens, you have unjustly imprisoned. Protect foreign journalists, diplomats and aid workers in your country. Close immediately and permanently every terrorist training camp in Afghanistan, and hand over every terrorist, and every person in their support structure, to appropriate authorities. (*Applause.*) Give the United States full access to terrorist training camps, so we can make sure they are no longer operating.

These demands are not open to negotiation or discussion. (*Applause.*) The Taliban must act, and act immediately. They will hand over the terrorists, or they will share in their fate.

I also want to speak tonight directly to Muslims throughout the world. We respect your faith. It's practiced freely by many millions of Americans, and by millions more in countries that America counts as friends. Its teachings are good and peaceful, and those who commit evil in the name of Allah blaspheme the name of Allah. (*Applause.*) The terrorists are traitors to their own faith, trying, in effect, to hijack Islam itself. The enemy of America is not our many Muslim friends; it is not our many Arab friends. Our enemy is a radical network of terrorists, and every government that supports them. (*Applause.*)

Our war on terror begins with al Qaeda, but it does not end there. It will not end until every terrorist group of global reach has been found, stopped and defeated. (*Applause.*)

Americans are asking, why do they hate us? They hate what we see right here in this chamber—a democratically elected government. Their leaders are self-appointed. They hate our freedoms—our freedom of religion, our freedom of speech, our freedom to vote and assemble and disagree with each other.

They want to overthrow existing governments in many Muslim countries, such as Egypt, Saudi Arabia, and Jordan. They want to drive Israel out of the Middle East. They want to drive Christians and Jews out of vast regions of Asia and Africa.

These terrorists kill not merely to end lives, but to disrupt and end a way of life. With every atrocity, they hope that America grows fearful, retreating from the world and forsaking our friends. They stand against us, because we stand in their way.

We are not deceived by their pretenses to piety. We have seen their kind before. They are the heirs of all the murderous ideologies of the 20th century. By sacrificing human life to serve their radical visions—by abandoning every value except the will to power—they follow in the path of fascism, and Nazism, and totalitarianism. And they will follow that path all the way, to where it ends: in history's unmarked grave of discarded lies. (*Applause.*) . . .

This is not, however, just America's fight. And what is at stake is not just America's freedom. This is the world's fight. This is civilization's fight. This is the fight of all who believe in progress and pluralism, tolerance and freedom. . . .

I ask you to live your lives, and hug your children. I know many citizens have fears tonight, and I ask you to be calm and resolute, even in the face of continuing threat.

I ask you to uphold the values of America, and remember why so many have come here. We are in a fight for our principles, and our first responsibility is to live by them. No one should be singled out for unfair treatment or unkind words because of their ethnic background or religious faith. (*Applause.*) . . .

I will not forget this wound to our country or those who inflicted it. I will not yield; I will not rest; I will not relent in waging the struggle for freedom and security for the American people. . .

DOCUMENT ANALYSIS

1. Presidential speeches are usually aimed at a number of audiences. Read through the document and identify different passages that were designed to give information to a specific audience. How many audiences could you identify? What was the president's primary message to the American people in general?

_____

_____

_____

2. What is the overall tone of this address? Is it appropriate? Is it reassuring?

_____

_____

_____

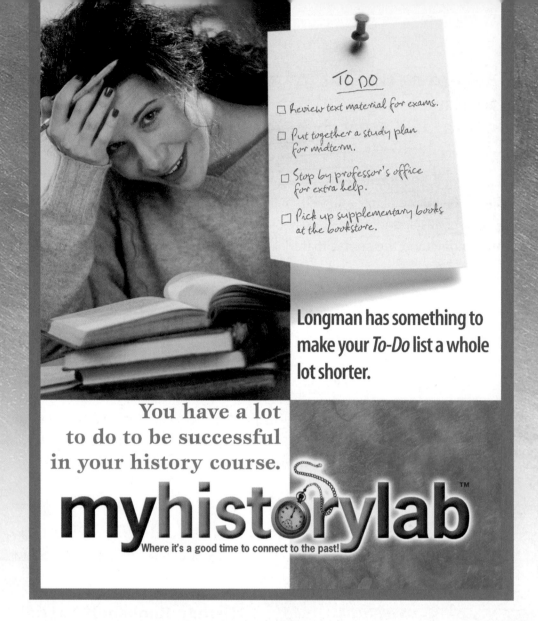
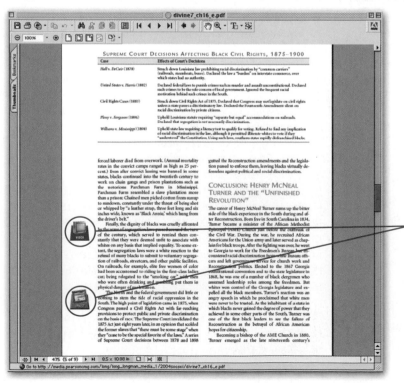

Are you overwhelmed by the time it takes to find primary source documents, images, and maps for your research papers?

MyHistoryLab contains over **1,100 documents, images, maps, and video clips**— all in one place —to help make writing your research paper easier and more effective, and to help you better understand the course material.

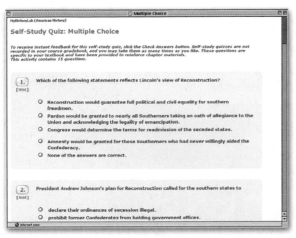

Are you sometimes overwhelmed when you study for exams?

MyHistoryLab gives you a **quizzing and testing program** that shows what you've mastered, as well as where you need more work. Look for these icons on MyHistoryLab—

 PRE-TEST POST TEST EXAM

Did your professor assign other books to read?

50 FREE BOOKS!

MyHistoryLab allows you to read, download, or print fifty of the most commonly assigned works for this course —all at no additional cost!

History Bookshelf Partial Listing.

1. *Common Sense,* Thomas Paine (1776)
2. *The Federalist Papers;* Alexander Hamilton, John Jay, and James Madison (1787-1788)
3. *The Autobiography of Benjamin Franklin* (1788)
4. *The Last of the Mohicans,* James Fennimore Cooper (1826)
5. *Democracy in America* (Two Volumes), Alexis De Tocqueville (1835)
6. *The Narrative of the Life of Frederick Douglass, An American Slave* (1845)
7. *Civil Disobedience,* Henry David Thoreau (1849)
8. *Uncle Tom's Cabin,* Harriet Beecher Stowe (1852)
9. *Walden,* Henry David Thoreau (1854)
10. *Incidents in the Life of a Slave Girl,* Harriet Jacobs (1861)
11. *The Adventures of Huckleberry Finn,* Mark Twain (1885)
12. *Looking Backward, 2000-1887,* Edward Bellamy (1888)
13. *The Yellow Wallpaper,* Charlotte Perkins Gilman (1892)
14. *The Red Badge of Courage,* Stephen Crane (1895)
15. *The Awakening and Selected Short Stories,* Kate Chopin (1899)
16. *Up From Slavery,* Booker T. Washington (1901)
17. *The Jungle,* Upton Sinclair (1906)
18. *Rise of the New West,* Frederick Jackson Turner (1906)
19. *Anarchism and Other Essays,* Emma Goldman (1917)
20. *Babbitt,* Sinclair Lewis (1922)

Now, flip through this text. You will find the icons shown on the next page. Each icon will direct you to a place in MyHistoryLab to help you better understand the material. For example, when reading about the 1700's, you will find an icon that links you to a letter by an indentured servant; when reading about the 20th century, you will find an icon that links you to a video clip about the Cold War.

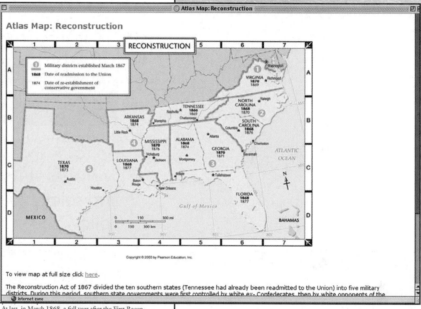

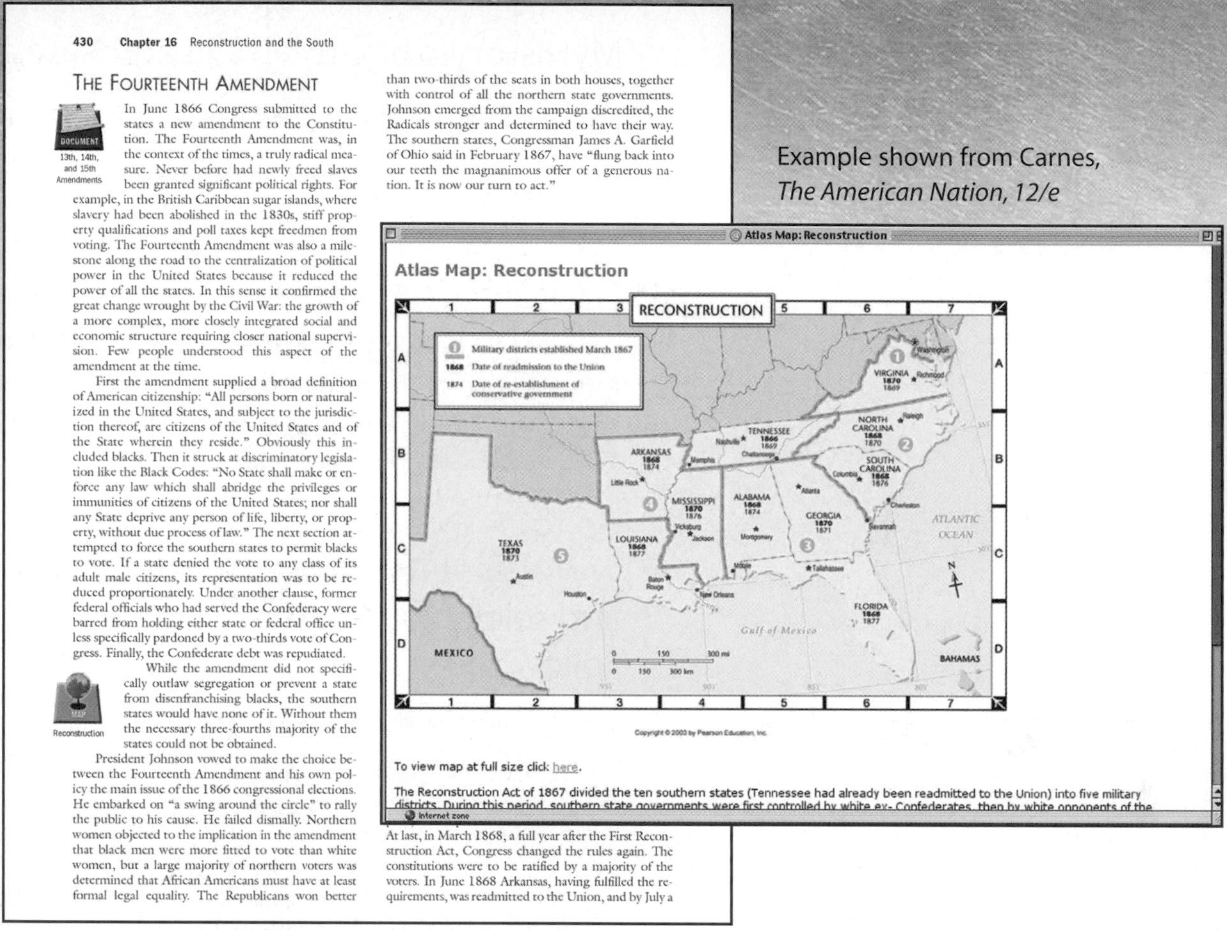

Example shown from Carnes,
The American Nation, 12/e

Within the shown textbook page:

430 Chapter 16 Reconstruction and the South

THE FOURTEENTH AMENDMENT

13th, 14th, and 15th Amendments

In June 1866 Congress submitted to the states a new amendment to the Constitution. The Fourteenth Amendment was, in the context of the times, a truly radical measure. Never before had newly freed slaves been granted significant political rights. For example, in the British Caribbean sugar islands, where slavery had been abolished in the 1830s, stiff property qualifications and poll taxes kept freedmen from voting. The Fourteenth Amendment was also a milestone along the road to the centralization of political power in the United States because it reduced the power of all the states. In this sense it confirmed the great change wrought by the Civil War: the growth of a more complex, more closely integrated social and economic structure requiring closer national supervision. Few people understood this aspect of the amendment at the time.

First the amendment supplied a broad definition of American citizenship: "All persons born or naturalized in the United States, and subject to the jurisdiction thereof, are citizens of the United States and of the State wherein they reside." Obviously this included blacks. Then it struck at discriminatory legislation like the Black Codes: "No State shall make or enforce any law which shall abridge the privileges or immunities of citizens of the United States; nor shall any State deprive any person of life, liberty, or property, without due process of law." The next section attempted to force the southern states to permit blacks to vote. If a state denied the vote to any class of its adult male citizens, its representation was to be reduced proportionately. Under another clause, former federal officials who had served the Confederacy were barred from holding either state or federal office unless specifically pardoned by a two-thirds vote of Congress. Finally, the Confederate debt was repudiated.

Reconstruction

While the amendment did not specifically outlaw segregation or prevent a state from disenfranchising blacks, the southern states would have none of it. Without them the necessary three-fourths majority of the states could not be obtained.

President Johnson vowed to make the choice between the Fourteenth Amendment and his own policy the main issue of the 1866 congressional elections. He embarked on "a swing around the circle" to rally the public to his cause. He failed dismally. Northern women objected to the implication in the amendment that black men were more fitted to vote than white women, but a large majority of northern voters was determined that African Americans must have at least formal legal equality. The Republicans won better

than two-thirds of the seats in both houses, together with control of all the northern state governments. Johnson emerged from the campaign discredited, the Radicals stronger and determined to have their way. The southern states, Congressman James A. Garfield of Ohio said in February 1867, have "flung back into our teeth the magnanimous offer of a generous nation. It is now our turn to act."

At last, in March 1868, a full year after the First Reconstruction Act, Congress changed the rules again. The constitutions were to be ratified by a majority of the voters. In June 1868 Arkansas, having fulfilled the requirements, was readmitted to the Union, and by July a

Atlas Map: Reconstruction

To view map at full size click here.

The Reconstruction Act of 1867 divided the ten southern states (Tennessee had already been readmitted to the Union) into five military districts. During this period, southern state governments were first controlled by white ex- Confederates, then by white opponents of the

---

DOCUMENT

DOCUMENT.
This icon will lead you to primary source documents, so you can see the original documents that pertain to the people and events you're studying.

IMAGE

IMAGE.
You'll find photos, cartoons, and art work that relate to the topic you're reading.

MAP

MAP.
Interactive maps will help you visualize the geography you are exploring in this course. You will also find printable map activities from one of Longman's workbooks, along with atlas maps.

AUDIO

AUDIO CLIP.
Hear the sounds of the past by listening to historical music in original recordings, or more contemporary performances of original works.

VIDEO

VIDEO CLIP.
Historical and political video clips from the last century bring history to life.

The American Nation,
Twelfth Edition, Primary Source Edition
It has everything students need to master the course!

A rich text with a clear, relevant, and balanced presentation of the social, economic, and cultural issues in the United States. A wealth of original primary source documents (at the end of this text) help make the material come alive by supporting the chapter content. Accompanying *Document Analysis* questions encourage students to delve deeper into the documents and explore how they relate to the events of the time. Documents are organized to correlate with chapter material.

How to Analyze Primary Source Documents

Would you like even more primary source documents?

myhistorylab™

Where it's a good time to connect to the past!

FREE when bundled with this book!

All of the primary source documents in this text plus hundreds more at no additional cost can be found on Longman's exclusive Web site— www.ablongman.com/myhistorylab

MyHistoryLab also contains a wealth of other resources including:

- **Images** (photos, cartoons, and artwork), **maps** (including interactive maps), and **audio and video clips** (with historical music and historical and political video clips from the last century).

- **The electronic textbook** (eBook) with multimedia icons that link to exciting resources, expanding upon the key topics students encounter as they read through the text.

- **An integrated quizzing and testing program**—including pre-tests, post-tests, and chapter exams—to help students identify areas of strength and weakness.

- **"The History Bookshelf"** where fifty of the most commonly assigned works like Thomas Paine's *Common Sense*, Upton Sinclair's *The Jungle*, or Booker T. Washington's *Up from Slavery* can be read, downloaded, or printed.

Professors get a wealth of instructor resources including a course management system, test bank, instructor's manual, PowerPoint® presentations, and more.

Go to www.myhistorylab.com, or read more about this exciting new Web site on the insert included in this textbook.

CENTRAL TEXAS COLLEGE EDITION

THE AMERICAN NATION
A HISTORY OF THE UNITED STATES

MARK C. CARNES • JOHN A. GARRATY

Taken from:

The American Nation: A History of the United States
by Mark C. Carnes and John A. Garraty

CENTRAL TEXAS COLLEGE

Excerpts taken from:

The American Nation: A History of the United States, Twelfth Edition
by Mark C. Carnes and John A. Garraty

Copyright © 2006 by John A. Garraty. Maps, graphs, and all illustration captions and related text copyright © by
Pearson Education, Inc.
Published by Pearson Longman

Copyright © 2006 by Pearson Custom Publishing
All rights reserved.

Printed in the United States of America

10   9   8   7   6   5   4   3

ISBN 0-536-21408-5

2006300063

AO

Please visit our web site at *www.pearsoncustom.com*

PEARSON CUSTOM PUBLISHING
75 Arlington Street, Suite 300, Boston, MA 02116
A Pearson Education Company

Brief Contents

Detailed Contents

Additional maps, arranged by topic, appear in the "Mapping the Past" features.

Maps for every presidential election, 1889 to 2004, appear in the Appendix, pp. A19–A31.

GRAPHS

Maps and Graphs

MAPS

DEBATING THE PAST

Features

Features

Debating the Past

Preface

From the Prologue ("Beginnings") tens of thousands of years ago to the war in Iraq and the 2004 election (Chapter 33), this edition of *The American Nation* includes many enhancements and new features. Yet the backbone remains the same. We focus on how the voices and actions of its many people have produced a particular political structure—the United States, a single nation—and how that nation has in turn influenced the lives of everyone.

FEATURES

New! Debating the Past

"Debating the Past" is a new feature in this edition of *The American Nation*. Historians argue about nearly every aspect of the nation's complex past, and each chapter now includes an essay on an important historiographical debate. Because such issues are hard to fix in memory, we have provided a photograph or picture to "trigger" the historiographical essay. For example, the question for Chapter 2—"Were puritan communities peaceful?"—is prefaced by a contemporary painting of a seventeenth-century puritan village, the question for Chapter 12—"Did the frontier change women's roles?"—commences with a photograph of a farm woman hauling buffalo chips in a wheelbarrow. Each essay concludes with a list of the major works cited. Our final debate—"Do historians ever get it right?" (Chapter 33)—poses a question that we hope will stimulate discussion.

In addition to "Debating the Past," each chapter of *The American Nation* contains one of three special features: an essay on a Hollywood movie's version of history ("Re-Viewing the Past"); a grouping of maps on a central topic in the chapter ("Mapping the Past"); or a biographical account of a major or representative person ("American Lives").

Re-Viewing the Past

The "Re-Viewing the Past" feature shows how particular movies shape our understanding of history. Directors often spend scores of millions of dollars to show what the past looked like. For example, *The Crucible* (discussed in Chapter 2), provides a vivid evocation of puritan Salem, and *Saving Private Ryan* (Chapter 28) of the Normandy invasion in World War II. Yet moviemakers often alter people and events for dramatic purposes; "reel history" should never be confused with "real history." These essays help our readers make sense of the bewildering array of historical facts and fictions presented in many historical movies. By offering guidance on which of Hollywood's reconstructions contain some measure of truthfulness, which do not, and how viewers can tell the difference, the "Re-Viewing the Past" essays help readers examine Hollywood's version of the past more critically. This edition of *The American Nation* includes two new "Re-Viewing the Past" essays: *Cold Mountain* (Chapter 15) and *Chicago* (Chapter 25).

Mapping the Past

Maps provide another visual way of representing the past. In addition to the standard maps depicting the routes of explorers, battles, or territorial acquisitions, more than half the chapters in *The American Nation* include separate map portfolios on social, economic, cultural, and political history. Topics examined in the "Mapping the Past" features range from "A Water Route to the Pacific?" (Chapter 6), which discusses the search for a water passage to the Pacific during the early 1800s; "Fertility and the Frontier," (Chapter 12), which considers whether frontier women had more children than women elsewhere; to "Planning Nuclear War" (Chapter 29), which describes the various strategies for winning a world war fought with thermonuclear weapons. *The American Nation*, even by its title, implies that we are one; yet

this truism overlooks the persistence and significance of regional bonds and local variations. Many of the maps in the "Mapping the Past" features spotlight particular states, counties, cities, and towns. Such maps show how local factors influence national trends and vice versa. Because students often need help in determining how to read and understand a map, the "Mapping the Past" essay in Chapter 5, "Depicting History with Maps" includes a discussion of the various elements of a map and the information that each element conveys. Eight of the "Mapping the Past" essays are new to the twelfth edition of *The American Nation:*

- Depicting History with Maps (Chapter 5)
- Nature as a Civilizing Force (Chapter 11)
- Cholera: A New Disease Strikes the Nation (Chapter 19)
- Isolationism of the 1930s (Chapter 27)
- Planning Nuclear War (Chapter 29)
- School Segregation After the *Brown* Decision (Chapter 30)
- *Roe* v. *Wade* (1978) and the Abortion Controversy (Chapter 31)
- Twenty Years of Terrorism (Chapter 33)

American Lives

Biographies underscore the human dimension of historical complexity. The "American Lives" essays in the twelfth edition of *The American Nation* range from Tisquantum, the Indian who famously assisted the Pilgrims (Chapter 1), to Bill Gates, founder of Microsoft and the richest man in the world (Chapter 32). Two new "American Lives" essays have been added: Nat Love, a black cowboy who claimed to have been source of the "Deadeye Dick" legend (Chapter 17), and Emma Goldman, a radical leftist (Chapter 22).

MORE MAPS

In addition to the "Mapping the Past" feature, we have reconceptualized and redrawn many of the maps in the text and have added dozens more. Many of the latter offer visual representations and interpretations of uniquely specialized information: Loss of Indian Lands, 1850–2000 (Chapter 17), The Forging of U.S. Steel (Chapter 18), Prostitution in Nineteenth-Century New York (Chapter 19), The Advance of Woman Suffrage (Chapter 22), Japanese Expansion, 1920–1941, and German Expansion, 1938–1939 (both in Chapter 27), and Air Relief to Berlin (Chapter 29). The section on Presidential Elections

in the Appendix for the twelfth edition includes a color map of the election results for every presidential election from 1789 to 2004.

PICTURES

In addition to its many maps, its evocation of Hollywood history, and its use of pictures to introduce the "Debating the Past" essays, *The American Nation* includes hundreds of pictures and artwork to accompany the text and enhance the narrative. Much as readers should examine Hollywood history critically and engage with historiographical debates, they should apply similar skills to paintings, photographs, and other visual representations of the past. Our captions are meant to stimulate thought, to provoke debate, and on occasion, to amuse. Each chapter opens with a work of art, ranging from an Aztec artist's depiction of a Spanish sailing ship (Chapter 1) to a famous photograph of the collapse of the World Trade Center (Chapter 33). We think that the pictures and photographs in themselves constitute a history of the nation's visual and material culture.

The text is as concise as we could make it. Yet the history of our nation is comprised of the words and actions of hundreds of millions of people over many decades. The story must be told in all its depth and complexity. It is not enough to know what happened; we also need to understand why.

INSTRUCTOR SUPPLEMENTS

For Qualified College Adopters

MyHistoryLab provides students with an online package complete with the entire textbook, numerous study aids, and course management. With over 1000 primary sources, images, audio clips, video clips, and over 150 map activities with gradable quizzes, geographic case studies, map workbook activities, and atlas maps, the site offers students a unique, interactive experience that brings history to life. The comprehensive site also includes a history bookshelf with twenty of the most commonly assigned books in history classes and a history toolkit with tutorials and helpful links.

LongmanAmericanHistory.com provides the same resources as MyHistoryLab, but without an e-book or course management.

History Digital Media Archive CD-ROM. The Digital Media Archive CD-ROM contains electronic

images and interactive and static maps, along with media elements such as video. These media assets are fully customizable and ready for classroom presentation or easy downloading into your PowerPoint™ presentations or any other presentation software. ISBN: 0-321-14976-9.

Visual Archives of American History, **Updated Second Edition.** Now on two CD-ROMs and with added content, this encyclopedic collection contains dozens of narrated vignettes and videos as well as hundreds of photos and illustrations ready for use in your own PowerPoint™ presentations, course websites, or online courses. Free to qualified college adopters.

The American Nation Companion Website (www.ablongman.com/carnes). This Website, designed specifically for this book, is an invaluable tool for both students and instructors. It contains student resources such as self-testing, chapter outlines, and links to outside sources; instructor resources such as the instructor's manual, PowerPoint presentations, maps, graphs, and tables from the text, blank maps for quizzes, and helpful web links; and our unique syllabus manager that gives instructors and students access to the up-to-date syllabus at any time from any computer.

Instructor's Resource Manual. Written by Michael Mayer of the University of Montana, this tool is designed to aid both the novice and experienced instructor in teaching American history. Each chapter included a concise chapter overview, a list of points for student mastery, lecture supplements, and questions for class discussion. A special feature of each chapter is a set of excerpted documents with accompanying questions for student analysis.

Test Bank. Written by Larry Peterson of North Dakota State University, the test bank contains over 2000 test items, including multiple choice, true/false, and essay. The questions are keyed to topic, difficulty level, cognitive type, and relevant text page.

Computerized TestGen-EQ Computerized Testing System. This flexible, easy-to-use computerized test bank includes all the test items in the printed test bank. Available on a dual platform CD-ROM, the software allows you to edit existing questions and add your own items. Tests can be printed in several different formats and can include graphs and tables.

Text-specific Transparencies. A set of map transparencies from the text is available.

Comprehensive American History Transparency Set. This vast collection of American history transparencies is a necessary teaching aid. It includes over 200 maps covering social trends, wars, elections, immigration, and demographics. Included is a set of reproducible map exercises.

Discovering American History Through Maps and Views Transparency Set. Created by Gerald Danzer of the University of Illinois at Chicago, the recipient of the AHA's 1990 James Harvey Robinson Prize for his work in the development of map transparencies, this set of 140 four-color acetates is a unique instructional tool. It contains an introduction on teaching history through maps and a detailed commentary on each transparency. The collection includes cartographic and pictorial maps, views, and photos, urban plans, building diagrams, and works of art.

STUDENT SUPPLEMENTS

MyHistoryLab provides students with an online package complete with the entire textbook, numerous study aids, and course management. With over 1000 primary sources, images, audio clips, video clips, as well as 150+ map activities with gradable quizzes, geographic case studies, map workbook activities, and atlas maps, the site offers students a unique, interactive experience that brings history to life. The comprehensive site also includes a history bookshelf with twenty of the most commonly assigned books in history classes and a history toolkit with tutorials and helpful links.

LongmanAmericanHistory.com provides the same resources as MyHistoryLab, but without an e-book or course management.

SafariX Textbooks Online is an exciting new choice for students looking to save money. As an alternative to purchasing the print textbook, students can subscribe to the same content online and save up to 50 percent off the suggested list price of the print text. With a SafariX WebBook, students can search the text, make notes online, print out reading assignments that incorporate lecture notes, and bookmark important passages for later review. For more information, or to subscribe to the SafariX WebBook, visit www.safarix.com.

Study Cards for American History. Colorful, affordable, and packed with useful information, Allyn & Bacon/Longman's Study Cards make studying easier, more efficient, and more enjoyable. Course information is distilled down to the basics, helping you quickly master the fundamentals, review a subject for understanding, or prepare for an exam. Because they're laminated for durability, you can keep these

Study Cards for years to come and pull them out whenever you need a quick review.

The American Nation Companion Website (www .ablongman.com/carnes). This Website, designed specifically for this book, is an invaluable tool for both students and instructors. It contains student resources such as self-testing, chapter outlines, and links to outside sources; instructor resources such as the instructor's manual; PowerPoint presentations, maps, graphs, and tables from the text, blank maps for quizzes, and helpful web links; and our unique syllabus manager that gives instructors and students access to the up-to-date syllabus at any time from any computer.

Study Guides. Written by Ken Weatherbie of Del Mar College are designed to provide students with a comprehensive review of the text material and to encourage applications and critical analysis of the material. Each chapter contains a chapter overview, learning objectives, important glossary terms, identification, map and critical thinking exercises, and multiple choice and essay questions.

Research Navigator Guide. This guidebook includes exercises and tips on how to use the Internet. It also includes an access code for Research Navigator™— the easiest way for students to start a research assignment or research paper. Research Navigator™ is composed of three exclusive databases of credible and reliable source material, including EBSCO's ContentSelect™ Academic Journal Database, New York Times Search by Subject Archive, and "Best of the Web" Link Library. This comprehensive site also includes a detailed help section by qualified college adopters.

Longman American History Atlas. A four-color reference tool and visual guide to American history that includes almost 100 maps and covers the full scope of history. Atlas overhead transparencies available to adopters. $3.00 when bundled by qualified college adopters.

Mapping American History: Student Activities. Written by Gerald Danzer of the University of Illinois at Chicago, this free map workbook for students features exercises designed to teach how to interpret and analyze cartographic materials as historical documents. Available free when bundled in advance with the textbook.

Mapping America: A Guide to Historical Geography, **Second Edition.** Written by Ken Weatherbie of Del Mar College, this two-volume workbook contains 35 exercises correlated to the text that review basic American historical geography and ask students to interpret the role geography has played in American

history. *Mapping America* is available free to qualified college adopters when bundled with the text in advance.

American History in a Box. Created by editors Julie Roy Jeffrey and Peter Frederick, this unique "reader in a box" is designed to give students an up-close and personal view of history. The collection includes loose facsimilies of written documents, visual materials and artifacts, songs and sheet music, portraits, cartoons, film posters, and more, so that students can learn first-hand what history is and what historians do. "Placing the Sources in Context" and "Questions to Consider" accompanying each set of materials in the collection help guide students through the practice of historical analysis.

America Through the Eyes of Its People, **Second Edition.** This single-volume collection of primary documents reflects the rich and varied tapestry of American life. The revised edition includes more social history and enhanced pedagogy. It is available shrinkwrapped with *The American Nation* at no charge to qualified college adopters when requested by the instructor in advance.

Sources of the African American Past, **Second Edition.** Edited by Roy Finkenbine of the University of Detroit at Mercy, this collection of primary sources covers key themes in the African American experience from the West African background to the present. Balanced between political and social history, it offers a vivid snapshot of the lives of African Americans in different historical periods, and includes documents representing women and different regions of the United States. Available at a minimum cost to qualified college adopters when bundled with the text.

Women and the National Experience, **Second Edition.** Edited by Ellen Skinner of Pace University, this primary source readers contains both classic and unusual documents describing the history of women in the United States. The documents provide dramatic evidence that outspoken women attained a public voice and participated in the development of national events and policies long before they could vote. Chronologically organized and balanced between social and political history, this reader offers a striking picture of the lives of women across American history. Available at a minimum cost to qualified college adopters when bundled in advance with the text.

Reading the American West. Edited by Mitchel Roth of Sam Houston State University, this primary source reader uses letters, diary excerpts, speeches, interviews, and newspaper articles to let students experience how historians research and how history is written. Every document is accompanied by a contextual

headnote and study questions. The book is divided into chapters with extensive introductions. Available at a minimum cost to qualified college adopters when bundled with the text.

A Short Guide to Writing About History, **Fourth Edition.** Written by Richard Marius (late) and Melvin E. Page, this practical text teaches students how to incorporate their own ideas into their papers and to tell a story about history that interests them and their peers. Focusing on more than just the conventions of good writing, this text shows students how first to think about history, and then how to organize their thoughts into coherent essays. The *Short Guide* covers both brief essays and the document resource paper as it explores the writing and researching processes, examines different modes of historical writing including argument, and concludes with guidelines for improving style.

Library of American Biography Series. Each of these interpretive biographies focuses on a figure whose actions and ideas significantly influenced the course of American history and national life. At the same time, each biography relates the life of its subjects to the broader theme and developments of the times. Brief and inexpensive, they are ideal for any U.S. history course. Editions include Edmund S. Morgan, *The Puritan Dilemma: The Story of John Winthrop;* Charles W. Akers, *Abigail Adams: An American Woman;* Harold C. Livesay, *Andrew Carnegie and the Rise of Big Business;* Randolph B. Campbell, *Sam Houston and the American Southwest;* Walter L. Hixson, *Charles Lindbergh: Lone Eagle;* Jack N. Rakove, *James Madison and the Creation of the American Republic;* Sam W. Haynes, *James K. Polk and the Expansionist Impulse;* and J. William T. Youngs, *Eleanor Roosevelt: A Personal and Public Life.*

Penguin Books. The partnership between Penguin-Putnam USA and Longman Publishers offers your students a discount on many titles when bundled with any Longman survey. Available titles include *Narrative of the Life of Frederick Douglass* by Frederick Douglass; *Why We Can't Wait* by Martin Luther King, Jr.; *Beloved* by Toni Morrison; and *Uncle Tom's Cabin* by Harriet Beecher Stowe.

ACKNOWLEDGMENTS

We wish to thank the many friends, colleagues, and students who, over the years, have given us the benefit of their advice and encouragement in keeping this book up to date. We are particularly grateful to Mary Elin Korchinsky for invaluable assistance, especially with the illustration program for this edition. We also thank the following reviewers for their comments and suggestions regarding this revision.

Larry Engelmann, San Jose State University

Howard Jablon, Purdue University, North Central

Juli Jones, St. Charles Community College

Timothy W. Kneeland, Nazareth College of Rochester

Suzanne Marshall, Jacksonville State University

David B. Parket, Kennesaw State University

Anne Paulet, Humboldt State University

Horacio Salinas Jr., Laredo Community College

John E. Sarles, University of the Incarnate Word

Robert M. Spector, Worcester State College

Amos St. Germain, Wentworth Institute of Technology

Ruth L. Suyanna, Los Angeles Mission College

Ken L. Weatherbie, Del Mar College

MARK C. CARNES
Ann Whitney Olin Professor of History
Barnard College, Columbia University

JOHN A. GARRATY
Gouverneur Morris Professor of History, Emeritus
Columbia University

About the Authors

Mark C. Carnes received his undergraduate degree from Harvard and his Ph.D. in history from Columbia University, where he studied and trained with Professor John A. Garraty. The Ann Whitney Olin Professor History at Barnard College, Columbia University, Professor Carnes has chaired both the departments of History and American Studies at Barnard. In addition to this textbook, Carnes and Garraty have co-authored *Mapping America's Past: A Historical Atlas* and are co-general editors of the 24-volume *American National Biography,* for which they were awarded the Waldo Leland Prize of the American Historical Association, the Darmouth Prize of the American Library Association, and the Hawkins Prize of the American Association of Publishers. In addition, Carnes has published numerous books in American social and cultural history, including *Past Imperfect: History According to the Movies* (1995), *Novel History: Historians and Novelists Confront America's Past (and Each Other)* (2001), and *Invisible Giants: 50 Americans That Shaped the Nation but Missed the History Books* (2002). Carnes also created "Reacting to the Past," which won the Theodore Hesburgh Award, sponsored by TIAA-CREF, as the outstanding pedagogical innovation of 2004.

"Garraty preaches a particular doctrine on historical writing, expounding on the details of a complex process whereby the murky abstractions of the past are distilled into clean, clear narrative. He insists that the writer's sole duty is to readers. This literary alchemy is all the more wondrous for being so devoid of artifice," Carnes observes.

▶ John A. Garraty *(left)* and
Mark C. Carnes *(right)*

©1999 Joel Gordon

John A. Garraty. Holding a Ph.D. from Columbia University and an L.H.D. from Michigan State University, Professor Garraty is Gouverneur Morris Professor Emeritus of History at Columbia. He is the author, co-author, and editor of scores of books and articles, among them biographies of Silas Wright, Henry Cabot Lodge, Woodrow Wilson, George W. Perkins, and Theodore Roosevelt. Along with Mark Carnes, he is co-editor of the *American National Biography.* Garraty has also contributed a volume—*The New Commonwealth* —to the New American Nation series and edited *Quarrels That Shaped the Constitution.* He was a member of the Board of Directors of *American Heritage* magazine and served as both vice president and head of the teaching division of the American Historical Association. His areas of research interest include the Gilded Age, unemployment (in a historical sense), and the Great Depression of the 1930s. Of his collaboration with Carnes on *The American Nation,* Garraty says, "Although this volume is the work of two authors, it is as nearly the product of a single historical sensibility as is possible. Mark's scholarly specialization in cultural and social issues, especially gender, complements mine in politics and the economy. The book has benefited, too, from his special interest in postwar America. Over the many years of our collaborations, one of our favorite topics of discussion has been the craft of historical writing. We share a commitment to clarity and conciseness. We strive to avoid jargon and verbiage. We believe that while the political history of the nation provides a useful narrative framework, its people are what give the story meaning."

The
American Nation

Beginnings

▼ Abstract geometric shapes such as rectangles and squares were common to the art of the early peoples of the Americas. The thousand-year-old ruins of the Anasazi cliff community at Mesa Verde, Colorado, reveal this tendency, with rectangular residential towers rising above circular pits, called *kivas,* used for ceremonial purposes.

CHAPTER CONTENTS

DEBATING THE PAST **Who—or what—killed the big mammals?**

Although human beings emerged in Africa more than two million years ago, it was only about 50,000 years ago that the peoples who most resemble us in their aptitude for tools and facility with language appeared. Paleontologists—scientists who study fossils and prehistoric life—identify them as Cro-Magnon after a cave in France where their bones and tools were first found. At the same time humans were also making similar stone tools in east Africa and western Asia. These peoples developed stone-tipped spears and harpoons, bone fishhooks and needles, and other implements that made them adept at hunting, fighting, and protecting themselves from the elements. They also devised complex languages. Their ability to communicate strengthened emotional bonds and promoted cooperation. They spread through much of Africa and Europe, displacing those humans that had preceded them, and forcing others to adopt their innovations.

PASSAGE TO ALASKA

For tens of thousands of years the frozen wasteland of Siberia remained impenetrable to these tool-making humans. But as the supply of big mammals grew increasingly scarce elsewhere in Asia, hunters ventured farther north. What drew them especially were woolly mammoths. Weighing 16,000 pounds, about as much as a large elephant, a single mammoth provided enough meat to feed two dozen hunters nearly all winter. Its fur could be worn as clothing and its fat could be burned for heat. Its bones, when stretched with fur, functioned as simple tents. A woolly mammoth was a kind of movable mall, and hunters regarded it with the avidity of shoppers at a clearance sale. As mammoths moved deeper into the arctic tundra, so did their human predators.

About 12,000 years ago, perhaps far earlier, some of these hunters crossed what is now the Bering Strait to Alaska. This was during the last Ice Age, when so much ocean water had been captured as glacial ice

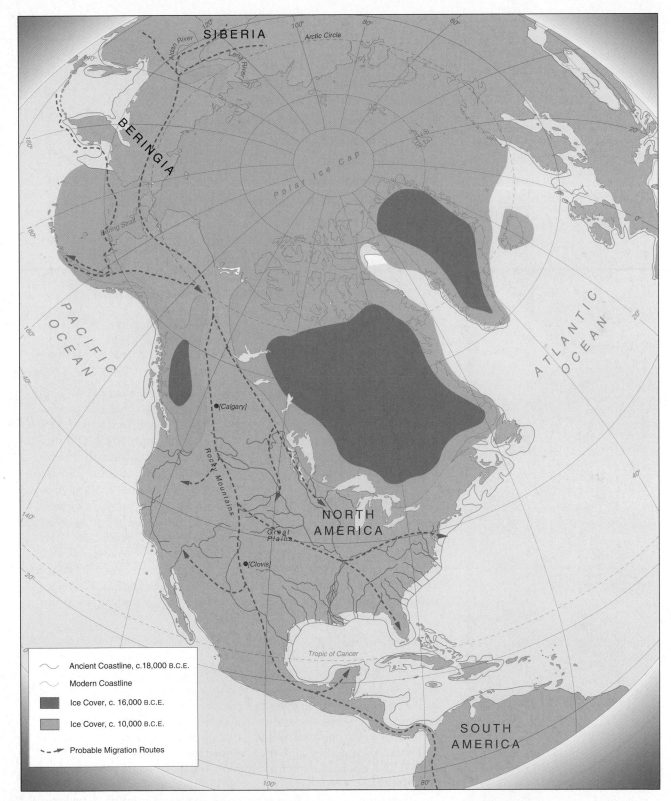

▲ **Ancient Asian Migrations to North America**

that ocean levels were 300–400 feet lower than nowadays. These hunters did not know that they had entered a new continent. Some trekked east, skirting the northern reaches of the Rocky Mountains. Beyond the foothills of the Rockies they encountered a shimmering plateau of ice that extended to the eastern horizon. Eventually they reached an ice-free corridor that funneled the mammoths and hunters southward.

In the vicinity of what is now Calgary, Canada, the hunters happened upon the Great Plains. The sight must have astonished them. On a limitless expanse of high, lush grass roamed vast herds of large animals. There were plenty of mammoths, but also equally enormous mastodons, with massive legs and stout feet; giant beavers the size of bears; 20-foot-long ground sloths weighing over 6000 pounds; strange monsters such as glyptodonts, which resembled armadillos but weighed over a ton, and also countless camels, horses, cheetahs, caribou, and deer.

THE DEMISE OF THE BIG MAMMALS

These animals had evolved over millions of years in the absence of human beings. If the big animals were unprepared to encounter humans, the hunters were ready for the big beasts. They had learned to divide spears into two 3-foot-long sections and connect them with a strip of leather. By swinging the lower shaft in a circular motion, the upper shaft, tipped with a sharp stone projectile, would whip forward with great force. The hunters also painstakingly chiseled long stone blades, which could more readily penetrate thick hides. Archaeologists have named these hunters after their ingenious blades, first found at Clovis, New Mexico.

Loosed upon herds of unwary animals, Clovis hunters seemingly slaughtered them almost at will, or stampeded them over cliffs. Archaeologists have found the blades of Clovis peoples in nearly every present-day American state and even at the southern tip of South America.

But the climate was warming; the Ice Age ended. Glacial ice melted and ocean levels rose, flooding the "land bridge" between Alaska and Asia. In the western region of what is now the United States, grasslands that had sustained the big mammals shrank.

And then the big mammals were gone. By about 9000 B.C.E.[1] most of the large mammals of North America had become extinct, including the mammoths, mastodons, saber-toothed cats, giant beavers, bears, horses, and camels. Whether the Clovis peoples killed off all the big mammals or the warming climate caused the blubbery, heavily furred animals to become extinct is a source of debate. (See Debating the Past, "Who—or what—killed the big mammals?" p. 6.) What is beyond dispute, however, is that the absence of large mammals had a profound effect on the subsequent course of human events.

THE ARCHAIC PERIOD: A WORLD WITHOUT BIG MAMMALS, 9000 B.C.E.–1000 B.C.E.

The loss of the big mammals marked the end of the Clovis culture. Descendants of the Clovis peoples had no choice but to find new sources of food, clothing, and shelter. For the next several thousand years, their lives were characterized by scarcity. A prolonged drought, or an especially severe winter, could lead to starvation. This period—known as the early Archaic—encompassed perhaps a hundred human generations.

The Archaic peoples learned to adapt to particular habitats. In woodland areas east of the Mississippi River, they hunted small animals, like rabbits and beaver, that had previously not been worth the bother; or they learned to find stealthy animals like bear and caribou or to sneak up on skittish ones like elk and deer. On the Great Plains, hunters for a time thrived on bison, which could be stampeded over cliffs. (The larger species of bison were among those that had disappeared around 10,000 B.C.E., but another species of bison still exists in North America.)

Most Archaic bands searched for game continuously. They migrated from one place to another according to a seasonal schedule, often returning to

---

[1] B.C.E. stands for "before the common era," and C.E. for "common era." These abbreviations are synonyms for B.C. and A.D., respectively. In this book dates not followed by B.C.E. refer to C.E.

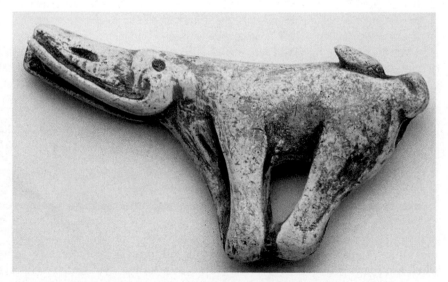

▲ Ice Age art—or artifact: Carved into this shoulder bone of a large animal is a figure of a woolly mammoth, as suggested by the long curved tusk. This affirms the centrality of the animals to Ice Age peoples.

DEBATING THE PAST

Who—or what—killed the big mammals? Paul S. Martin (1984) estimated that Clovis peoples, numbering several hundred thousand at their peak, hunted to extinction some 93 billion pounds of animals throughout the western hemisphere. Critics of what has been dubbed the "overkill" hypothesis insisted that Martin's rendering of a swarm of human predators devouring entire species was far-fetched. Clovis "hunters" were mostly scavengers who rarely succeeded in killing woolly mammoths (see museum reconstruction above) and other huge beasts. The big mammals died off because the climate of North America grew far warmer and drier after 11,000 B.C.E.: this damaged the ecosystem on which the big, furry mammals depended. Proponents of the "overkill" hypothesis responded that the big mammals had previously endured millions of years of climate fluctuations, some far more severe than the waning of the last Ice Age. That all these species would vanish during a climate shift that coincided with the arrival of human predators seems an improbable coincidence. And if the climate change was so extreme, why did it not result in the demise of species of birds and fish? Alfred Crosby (1986) also showed that the disappearance of many species of large mammals in Australia coincided with the arrival of human beings to that continent. This debate has nevertheless raged for nearly a half century. It reminds us that history is not fixed; facts change, as does our way of looking at them.

Paul S. Martin and Richard G. Klein, eds., *Quaternary Extinctions* (1984), which includes Martin's essay and also those of supporters and critics; also Alfred Crosby, *Ecological Imperialism* (1986).

the same campsites year after year. In the spring, when fish spawn, Archaic peoples moved to rivers and streams. In the summer, they hunted small animals. In the fall, they shifted to upland woods to gather protein-rich nuts, some of which they hid in caves for

emergencies. In winter, they often migrated to forests in search of deer, bear, and caribou.

As Archaic peoples became more knowledgeable about local food sources, they traveled less frequently. They provided for special needs through a

remarkably far-ranging trading system, as goods were passed from one band to another. Copper, used for tools and decorative objects, was acquired from the Lake Superior region; it was traded for chert, a crystalline stone that fractured into sharp, smooth surfaces, ideal for tool making.

Often perilously hungry, they discovered that sunflower seeds and sumpweed (a type of spinach) were edible. Around 2500 B.C.E., peoples in the Midwest planted some of the best seeds. They were the first inhabitants of what is now the United States to domesticate plants; plant cultivation gradually spread, though Archaic peoples remained primarily hunters and foragers.

THE FIRST SEDENTARY COMMUNITIES, 1000 B.C.E.

Some Archaic peoples happened on unusually rich habitats that could sustain them throughout the year. Peoples living along the coast and rivers of the Pacific Northwest and Alaska found fish so plentiful they could sometimes be scooped up in baskets. These people also learned to make nets and fishhooks and, in time, boats from bark and animal skins. Those living along the New England coast discovered a seemingly inexhaustible supply of shellfish. But for even these people, survival was a full-time job.

As tribes remained longer in one area, they began to regard it as their own. They built more substantial habitations, developed pottery to carry water and cook food, and buried the dead with distinctive rituals in special places, often marked with mounds.

One of the earliest sedentary communities was located at what is now Poverty Point, on the Mississippi River floodplains north of Delhi, Louisiana. It was founded around 1000 B.C.E. Poverty Point peoples, like those of the Pacific Northwest, became adept at fishing with nets. They also supplemented their diet with bottle gourd seeds and squash.

Poverty Point peoples filled countless grass baskets with earth and dumped them onto enormous mounds. One mound, shaped like an octagon, had six terraced levels on which were built some 400 to 600 houses. Another was more than 700 feet long and 70 feet high. Viewed from above, it resembled a hawk. In all, the mounds consisted of over a million cubic yards of dirt.

The enormity of their construction projects reveals much about the culture of Poverty Point peoples. They could not have diverted so much time and energy to construction if they were not proficient at acquiring food. Moreover, while most Archaic bands were egalitarian, with little differentiation in

▲ An infrared aerial photograph of Poverty Point, Louisiana. During the Archaic period, workers dumped a million cubic yards of earth in six layers—like a wedding cake—each layer nine feet high. These layers were in the shape of concentric circles (or, perhaps, octagons) and are still visible nearly three thousand years later.

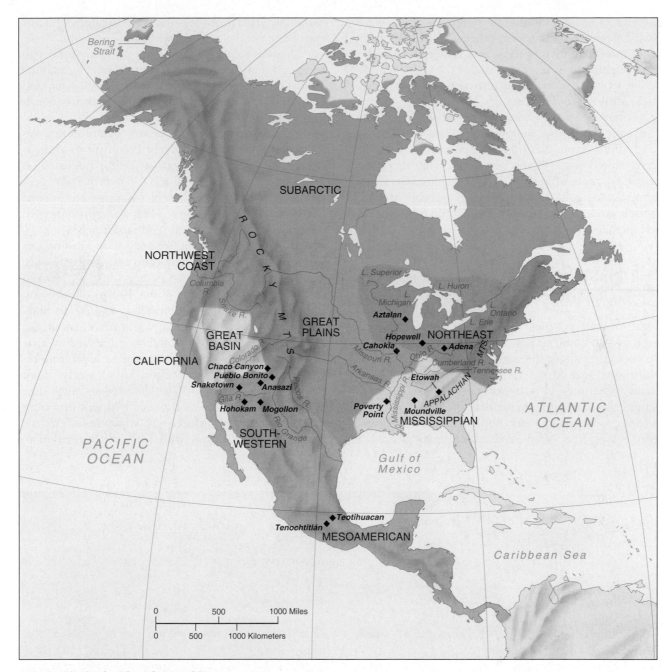

▲ **Ancient Native American Communities**

status, the social structure of Poverty Point was hierarchical. Leaders conceived the plans and directed the labor to build the earthworks.

After about five hundred years, Poverty Point was abandoned. No one knows why. Several hundred years later, scores of smaller mound communities, known as Adena, sprouted in the Ohio and Mississippi River valleys. The inhabitants of these communities were also hunters and foragers who cultivated plants in their spare time. Analysis of burial artifacts indicates that they engaged in long-distance trade and were dominated by elites, distinguished by the exotic

goods found in their graves. The Adena communities lasted several hundred years.

From about 200 B.C.E. to 500 C.E., another cluster of mound builders, known as Hopewell, flourished in Ohio and Illinois. Hopewell mounds were often shaped into squares, circles, and cones; but some, viewed from above, resembled birds or serpents. One Ohio burial mound contained 300 pounds of obsidian, found in Yellowstone, Wyoming; others included seashells from the Atlantic, silver from Canada, and bear teeth from the Rocky Mountains. Around 500 C.E. the Hopewell sites were abandoned.

▲ An aerial view of the Great Serpent Mound, in Locust Grove Ohio, built by Mississippian peoples around 1100 C.E. Some Mississippian mounds were in the shape of squares, circles, or cones, but others resembled hawks or panthers, and still others, like this one, depicted a mythical creature or perhaps a snake devouring an egg. Scholars speculate that the shapes reflected religious beliefs or functioned as territorial markers for different clans.

The impermanence of these communities suggests the fragility of sedentary life and serves as a reminder that the transition from a hunting and gathering way of life to one based on settled agriculture was slow and uneven.

CORN TRANSFORMS THE SOUTHWEST

About two thousand years ago, when most of the peoples of North America lived in hunting bands, an urban civilization flourished in the central Mexican highlands; Teotihuacán, about forty miles north of what is now Mexico City, had a population approaching 100,000 and featured miles of paved streets and a pyramid as large as those of the Egyptians. Another civilization with impressive small cities and pyramids was emerging in the

Andes Mountains in Peru. The difference between the simpler peoples in what is now the United States and Canada and the classic civilizations of Mesoamerica and South America can be explained in a single word: corn. The people of the valley of Mexico and the high Andes of Peru had it; the peoples farther north did not.

Originally, corn was unimpressive. Its cobs were only an inch long. Mesoamericans domesticated corn by planting the seeds of the largest and hardiest plants. The improved corn made possible a Neolithic revolution, the transition from hunting and gathering to a predominantly farming way of life. By 2000 B.C.E. nearly every valley in central Mexico and mountainside above the central and South American rainforests bristled with cornstalks.

Eventually corn came to the attention of the people of the Southwest: the Hohokam and Mogollon of Arizona and New Mexico; and the Anasazi of the Colorado

▲ Anasazi earthenware jars, from about 1200 C.E. The development of pottery was part of the ascent of a farming life. Corn could be stored in such jars, warding off starvation in lean winter months. Note the juxtaposition of straight lines and circles, an artistic pattern common among early American peoples. (Compare these pottery designs with the photograph of Anasazi architecture, pp. 2–3.)

Plateau. Corn transformed the lives of these people. Communities abandoned hunting grounds and settled near rivers, built trenches and canals to channel water to the crops, dammed gullies to capture runoff from flash floods, and constructed homes near the cornfields.

Their culture revolved around corn. Sun and water became the focus of their religious beliefs, symbols of life and rebirth. Priest-astronomers carefully measured changes of the seasons. If corn was planted too early, it might shrivel before the late summer rains; if planted

too late, it might be destroyed by frost. The centrality of corn to religious beliefs was underscored by the proximity of corn storage to sacred ceremonial pits, known as kivas. Corn Mother symbolism, suggesting a relationship between the fertility of the earth and of women, dominated religious practices. Moreover, control of the corn surplus was a key to political power.

Despite the aridity and blistering heat of the Southwest, the corn-cultivating peoples increased in number after 800 C.E. The Chaco Canyon, a 22-mile-long gorge in western New Mexico, witnessed the development of a most improbable human habitat. The Anasazi, who grew corn there, carved entire villages into the sandstone and shale cliffs. As population increased, the Anasazi built dozens of towns and villages linked by an elaborate system of roads. The largest of these cliff towns, Pueblo Bonito, had buildings more than five stories tall. The Hohokam constructed an irrigation canal system over hundreds of miles containing an intricate network of dams, sluices, and headgates. Snaketown, a Hohokam village 250 miles west of modern Phoenix, had a population of several thousand.

These communities were far smaller than those of their mightier neighbors to the south. But the triumph of the corn-growing Anasazi, Hohokam, and Mogollon is measured not by wealth and numbers but by the magnitude of the environmental challenges they overcame.

THE DIFFUSION OF CORN

Corn cultivation spread from the Southwestern deserts eastward. By about 200, cornfields dotted the southern Mississippi River valley. Thereafter, the advance of corn slowed. Farther north, early cold snaps killed existing varieties of the plant. Moreover, corn cultivation required unremitting labor, and few were eager to subject themselves to its incessant demands. Fields had to be cleared, usually by burning away the undergrowth. Then the soil was hoed using flat stones, clamshells, or the shoulder blades of large animals. After planting, the fields required constant weeding. When ripe, the corn had to be shucked and dried. In addition, hunters and foragers were accustomed to the thrill of the hunt, the taste of game, and the varied and often interesting tasks of foraging. They regarded farming as a subsidiary activity, a task best relegated to women.

But over time many hunting and gathering peoples learned that the alternative to agricultural work was starvation. Fields farther north and east were cleared and planted with corn, beans, and squash. Old skeletons provide a precise means of tracking corn's advance. When corn is chewed, enzymes in the mouth convert its carbohydrates to sugar, a major cause of dental cavities. Radiocarbon dating of skeletons from the vicinity

of what is now St. Louis first shows cavities around 700 and those from southern Wisconsin, around 900. By 1000 cavities can be found in skeletons throughout the Midwest and the East. Corn had become king.

POPULATION GROWTH AFTER 800

Corn stimulated population growth. An acre of woodlands fed two or three hunters or foragers; that same acre, planted in corn, provided for as many as two hundred people. Most hunting and foraging peoples found enough to eat in summer and fall, but in winter, the threat of starvation was acute, but dried corn, stored in glazed pots or sealed in underground pits, sustained large numbers of farming peoples over long periods. Corn cultivators may not have had a particularly nutritious diet, but they were less likely to starve.

Pre-Columbian Societies of the Americas

Corn cultivators also had more children than hunting and gathering peoples. The high caloric corn diet caused women to menstruate at an earlier age, making it possible for them to have more children. Corn also promoted fertility by shortening the duration of breastfeeding. Even toothless infants could be fed a soft mush of boiled corn, they could be weaned earlier; and once mothers ceased breastfeeding, they were far more likely to become pregnant. Thus while hunter-gathering women would likely conceive no more frequently than once every four years, women in corn-consuming societies were likely to have children twice as often.

A sedentary lifestyle promoted population growth in other ways. Infants and toddlers were a nuisance on the trail; some hunting and foraging peoples practiced abortion or even infanticide to ensure mobility and reduce the number of mouths to feed. But farming peoples nearly always could make use of additional hands, even young ones, to help with plowing, hoeing, weeding, and harvesting. Because farmers rarely moved, they built more permanent homes and more successfully sheltered infants from inclement weather and physical dangers.

As in the Southwest, the corn-cultivating peoples of the Mississippi Valley responded to increasing population by clearing more woodland and planting more corn. At first, corn cultivators and hunting-foraging peoples successfully cohabited within the same ecosystem: hunters traded for corn, essential for survival during winter, and corn cultivators traded for game, a source of complex protein. A mutually advantageous trade system evolved. But over time the two groups often came into conflict, and when they did, the much more numerous corn cultivators prevailed.

The corn-cultivating societies expanded west into Dakota, east through the Carolinas, south into

Florida, and north into Wisconsin. Their villages consisted of clusters of homes, surrounded by cornfields. They shared a constellation of beliefs and ritual practices. Like the Hopewell, they built burial mounds, but those of the corn cultivators were much larger. Some villages became towns and even small cities. Large temples and granaries and the homes of the governing elite were located on top of the mounds.

The most important and populous of these communities was located in the vicinity of St. Louis. Archaeologists call it Cahokia.

CAHOKIA: THE HUB OF MISSISSIPPIAN CULTURE

By 1000, Cahokia was a major center of trade, shops and crafts, and religious and political activities. It was the first true urban center in what is now the United States. By 1150, at the height of its development, it covered 6 square miles and had about 15,000 inhabitants.

The earthworks at Cahokia included some 20 huge mounds around a downtown plaza, with another 100 large mounds in the outlying areas. The largest mound was 110 feet high, covered 14 acres, and contained 20 million cubic yards of earth. It was probably the largest earthen structure in the Americas. Atop the mound was a 50-foot-high wood-framed temple.

Cahokian society was characterized by sharp class divisions. The elite lived in larger homes and consumed a better and more varied diet (their garbage pits included bones from the best cuts of meat). The corpse of one chieftain was buried upon a bed of 20,000 beaded shells; nearby was a long piece of shaped copper from Lake Superior, several bushels of bird and animal sculptures made of mica, and over 1000 arrows, many with beautiful quartz or obsidian points. Near the chieftain's bones were the skeletons of 50 women ranging from 18 to 23 years old, likely sacrifices to the gods. Their bones were genetically different from the Cahokian skeletons, suggesting that the young women were captives in war or tribute sent by vassal states.

▲ An artist's rendering of downtown Cahokia, around 1150 C.E. The palisade, composed of enormous tree trunks, is the large oval surrounding the main mounds. The largest of these, in the center, was 100 feet high. Here the elite of Cahokia lived and performed some of the fundamental ceremonial tasks of Mississippian culture. The open space in the center was probably filled with the stalls of craftspeople.

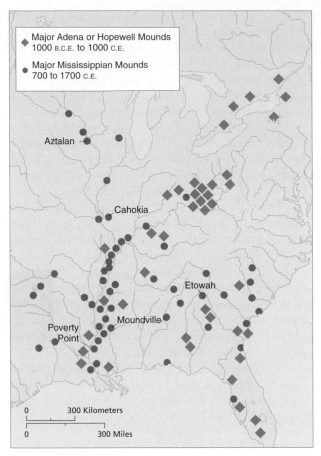

▲ Adena, Hopewell, and Mississippian Mounds

In a pit near these skeletons were those of four men whose heads and hands had been cut off; their necks and vertebrae bore multiple cuts indicating torture or mutilation. Another nearby burial pit included a mass grave. Some skeletons had been decapitated or their skulls smashed; a few of the fingers were in a vertical position, suggesting that the people were not dead at the time of burial and attempted to scratch their way out.

That the Cahokia had enemies is suggested by the existence of a 3-mile-long wooden palisade surrounding the central core of the city. It consisted of 20,000 enormous tree trunks, pounded deep into the ground, interspersed with several dozen watchtowers from which defenders could unloose arrows upon besiegers.

Despite its daunting fortifications, or perhaps because of them, the elite did not command a large army. Its power derived chiefly from its ability to create a compelling religious worldview and express it in tangible symbols. Cahokia was a cultural and religious center rather than a fortress. In the central plaza, skilled workers carved religious figurines from quartz, mica, and galena. Others painted similar symbols on pottery or etched them in copper goods. Lesser chieftains brought corn and other foodstuffs into Cahokia, perhaps as tribute, while the Cahokia rulers reciprocated with gifts of

figurines and copper or, in times of famine, grants of surplus corn. In Cahokia, too, priest-astronomers scrutinized the movements of the sun, moon, and stars.

Cahokia dominated a region of several hundred miles. Smaller mound-building communities emerged throughout the eastern woodlands and the Southeast. Two of the largest were Moundville, Alabama, and Etowah, Mississippi. Cahokia also established (or perhaps inspired) the creation of distant satellite communities. Around 800, Mississippian peoples moved into southern Wisconsin and built Aztalan (in what is now Jefferson County), with similar corn storage depots and large ceremonial mounds surrounding a central plaza.

Like Cahokia, Aztalan erected a massive tree-trunk palisade with watchtowers. Archaeologists have found burned and butchered body parts throughout the ruins, evidence of warfare. Some speculate that the corn-growing Mississippians encroached on the Oneota, a hunting and gathering people, and that the communities long remained hostile.

The Mississippian elites did more than supervise construction of their own massive earthen tombs. They also solved complicated problems of political and social organization.

THE COLLAPSE OF URBAN CENTERS

Cahokia and Aztalan soon declined. By 1200 Cahokia's population had been reduced to several thousand people; by 1350, it was deserted. Etowah and Moundville went into decline somewhat later.

The major towns and villages of the Southwest civilizations faded as well. By 1200, the inhabitants of Chaco Canyon had vanished and nearly all of the pueblos of the Anasazi had been abandoned. Snaketown and dozens of towns of the Hohokam had become empty ruins, their canals choked with weeds.

What caused the collapse of these communities has long been a source of debate. Some scholars cite protracted droughts during the 1200s and 1300s. Others note that population growth harmed the environment. Slash-and-burn wood clearance thinned the eastern forests, and corn cultivation exhausted the soil. Archaeologists have determined that each Cahokian house required 80 large wooden posts—a half million for the entire city. The palisade at Cahokia consisted of thousands of the trunks of fully grown trees, and it was repeatedly rebuilt. Denuded of big trees, the watershed around Cahokia became susceptible to erosion and flooding, further depleting exhausted topsoils.

The people of the Southwest also stripped their lands of trees for house and kiva construction, and for fuel. The wooden buildings at Chaco Canyon alone required nearly a quarter of a million trees. The irrigation system of the Hohokam harmed the environment in a different way. The canal networks distributed water

from the Gila and (aptly named) Salt rivers, and in so doing deposited thousands of tons of mineral salts on cornfields. With little rainfall to leach the soils, the salt residues eventually reached toxic levels.

Crop yields declined as the demand for food in towns and villages was increasing. Studies of human skeletons in Mississippian burial mounds show higher incidences of disease and malnutrition after 1250. What happened next is unclear. Some archaeologists believe that many people left the cities and villages and quietly reverted to the hunting and foraging life of their Archaic forebears. Others argue that the end was calamitous. Late Mississippian skeletons were smaller and more likely to show signs of disease; they also had more broken bones; often arms, feet, and hands were dismembered. Recurrent famines and disease may have undermined the credibility of elites and the cultural system they supervised, weakening their control of poor urban people as well as chieftains in the hinterlands. The towering log palisades of the Mississippians and the impenetrable cliff dwellings of the Anasazi were manifestations of this collective insecurity.

Warfare became endemic among the corn-growing tribes of the Northeast. By 1300, the Iroquoian peoples of New York and Pennsylvania were building forts with defensive earthworks and palisades. Some tribes joined together to form military alliances. Soil exhaustion, perhaps aggravated by the droughts that had parched the cornfields of the Southwest, may have forced tribes to compete for land and resources.

▼ Anasazi paintings dating from 1350 C.E. on the walls of kivas, subterranean rooms used for religious ceremonies. Are the birds, as spiritual couriers, bringing gifts of corn seed? The human figure, with an animal mask and feathered headdress, represents a spirit. It stares directly at the viewer who, seven centuries ago, was likely a young man about to learn the religious mysteries of the tribe.

Some scholars propose that gender tensions may have exacerbated these conflicts. Men performed most of the hunting and foraging tasks, while women did most of the work in the cornfields. As corn supplanted game and fish as staples of the diet, women acquired more status and power. To reassert male dominance, men embarked on raids and warfare.

By 1500 nearly all of the large towns had been abandoned. Survivors puzzled over who had inhabited the ruins, or who had erected the massive earthen mounds. The Navajo Indians referred to their predecessors as the "Anasazi," the "Ancient Ones."

The collapse of the cities disrupted trade networks. Some goods continued to move many, many miles, being passed from one tribe to another; but the flow of trade goods slowed to a trickle. Tribes were becoming more self-sufficient. Moreover, if the rise of powerful urban communities had forced earlier groups to band together, the demise of the urban communities encouraged the breakup of large groups and tribes. Hundreds, perhaps thousands of small bands lived in relative isolation.

To them, the great Aztec city of Tenochtitlán, beyond the Mexican desert, was only a rumor. Of Europe, Africa, and Asia, they knew nothing. That was about to change.

AMERICAN BEGINNINGS IN EURASIA AND AFRICA

If the Neolithic revolution had made but fitful progress in North America by 1500, its advance through Africa and Eurasia was nearly complete. Wheat, first domesticated in Southwest Asia after 9000 B.C.E., spread through the Nile Valley and the Mediterranean and eastward to India and China. Rice, domesticated in China around the same time, diffused throughout Eurasia. These lead crops were followed by others—oats, peas, olives, grapes, almonds, barley, oranges, lentils, and millet. Several thousand years later, farmers in Africa domesticated sorghum, palm oil, and yams.

Location of Major Indian Groups and Culture Areas in the 1600s

The flow of people and crops between Eurasia and Africa was hindered after about 6000 B.C.E., when the climate of Africa shifted and the Sahara broadened into a nearly impenetrable desert the size of the United States. The animals of Eurasia were as diverse as its crops. In the Americas, few large mammals survived the era of the Clovis hunters. But the ancient peoples of Eurasia learned how to domesticate horses, pigs, cows, goats, sheep, and oxen. In addition to protein-rich meat, cows and goats provided milk and dairy products such as cheese that could be stored for

winter; horses and oxen dragged trees and boulders from fields, pulled ploughs through tough sod, and contributed manure for fertilizer. Eurasians greatly increased the power of oxen and horses by harnessing them to wheeled vehicles. Because of the diversity and nutritional value of its food sources, the Eurasian population increased rapidly.

To accommodate the growing demand for food, Eurasian farmers cut down forests, filled in marshlands, and terraced hillsides. Monarchs joined with merchants and bankers to build port facilities, canals, and fleets of ships.

If cereal crops and animals dispersed throughout the vast Eurasian landmass, so did new diseases. The close physical proximity of people to their cows, pigs, goats, and sheep made them vulnerable to diseases borne by these animals. New strains of viruses and bacteria appeared in animal herds and spread to the humans that kept them. Diseases also spread readily, especially in large cities whose sanitation facilities were inadequate. Recurrent plagues swept across Eurasia. But those who survived acquired biological resistance.

West Africa evolved differently. The grassy savannah just south of the Sahara became the home for mostly herding peoples. Cities emerged in response to the growth of a trans-Sahara trade in gold, salt, kola—a caffeine rich nut—and slaves. Warlords leading horse-mounted cavalry vied for control of the trade routes across the Sahara. Conflict led to the great kingdoms of West Africa: Ghana, Mali, Songhay. Seldom did the kings of these empires penetrate far south into the tropical coastal region of west Africa. There the tsetse fly, carrier of sleeping sickness, decimated horse and cattle herds. Malaria, too, discouraged invaders. Relatively insulated from the imperial struggles farther north, peoples of the west African coast mostly kept to themselves, growing crops and harvesting the lush vegetation of the forest. By 1500, their lives, too, were about to change.

EUROPE IN FERMENT

During the 1400s Europe's population increased by nearly a third; by 1500, population pressure was acute. When harvests were poor or grain shipments failed to

▲ Like most world-changing innovations, the printing press of fifteenth-century Europe took advantage of technological innovations, chiefly improvements in metallurgy (to cast letters and to carve the ridges of the pressing screw), and new concepts, such as increasingly standardized rules for writing. By facilitating the spread of ideas, the printing press generated further technological advances.

arrive, hunger riots destabilized the political order. From 1413 to 1453, for example, Genoa, in Italy, was convulsed by 14 revolutions. Overpopulation was one reason why Jews, a vulnerable minority, were expelled from Spain and Portugal in 1492, and from Sicily in 1493.

Scarcity shook many peasants from the land and drove the urban poor from one city to another. Christoforo Colombo—or Columbus, as we call him—was among the restless youths who left home and took to the sea in search of a better life.

New ideas further unsettled European society. Movable type, which made the printing of books profitable, was perfected during the 1440s. By 1500, over 100 cities in Europe had at least one printing press and as many as 20 million volumes had been published. Books advanced new ideas and weakened the hold of traditional ones. Within a few decades, the treatises of Martin Luther and John Calvin initiated the Protestant Reformation. Books also excited the imagination and gave tangible expression to all manner of dreams and longings. (Columbus's restless curiosity had been stimulated by books on geography and navigation.)

Incessant squabbles over land resulted in nearly constant warfare. The military arts advanced accordingly. Improvements in metallurgy made it possible to cast bronze and iron cannon capable of containing

larger charges of gunpowder. By the early 1500s weapons weighing a ton or more were mounted in sailing ships or upon carriages pulled by teams of horses. Warfare of this nature was expensive; the cost of constructing fleets, equipping armies, and building massive fortifications required the collective resources of many thousands. No longer an activity of rival cities or contending noblemen, warfare demanded the resources of entire nations.

A restless hunger for land, a population made resistant to biological pathogens through recurrent exposure to them, an explosion in communication and knowledge, an avid acceptance of the new technology and organization of warfare, and the emergence of powerful and contentious monarchs all imparted a fateful dynamism to late fifteenth-century European society. Plainly, fifteenth-century Europeans had not solved their problems: population growth exceeded available food sources; poverty undermined political order; and war loomed larger and more ominous. Equally plainly, the people of North America had failed to solve basic social problems: those who practiced a hunting-gathering lifestyle were vulnerable to

starvation as well as to encroachments by the more numerous peoples of the corn-farming tribes. Farming peoples, on the other hand, despite new modes of social organization and cultural expression, found it difficult to sustain even small urban communities over a long period. In the absence of writing systems and larger "national" political organizations, few could join in broad enterprises; none possessed military technologies comparable to the Europeans. And the peoples of the Americas lacked the immunity from infectious diseases that so many Europeans had acquired.

Separating these two worlds was the impenetrable void of the Atlantic Ocean. Five hundred years earlier a Norseman, Leif Ericson, had sailed along the coast of Greenland to the shores of Labrador, but little came of his expeditions. But toward the close of the fifteenth century, European sailors of a different type, adept at navigating through the open sea and willing to sail far from land, were about to venture across the expanses of the Atlantic. In so doing they would transform it into a bridge that would join these worlds, and the west African coast as well, bringing all three into fateful collision.

MILESTONES

c. 12,000 B.C.E. (perhaps earlier)	Humans from Asia cross Beringia to Alaska	**c. 500 B.C.E.**	Corn cultivation begins in the Southwest
c. 12,000– 9000 B.C.E.	Humans diffuse throughout Americas	**c. 200 C.E.**	Corn cultivation begins in the lower Mississippi Valley
	Many species of large mammals become extinct in western hemisphere	**c. 700 C.E.**	Cahokia is founded near today's St. Louis, Missouri
	Clovis era ends	**c. 900 C.E.**	Corn cultivation begins in Wisconsin
	Eurasians domesticate wheat and rice	**c. 1200s– 1300s**	Protracted droughts in North America disrupt food supply; urban areas are abandoned
c. 3500 B.C.E.	Mesoamerican peoples cultivate corn and initiate Neolithic revolution		
c. 2500 B.C.E.	Peoples of midwestern North America domesticate sunflowers and sumpweed		
c. 1000 B.C.E.	First sedentary North American community is founded at today's Poverty Point, Louisiana		

SUPPLEMENTARY READING

During the 1990s the prehistoric era in North America has witnessed an explosion of interest, especially among archaeologists. A global perspective, focusing on geography as a causal force, is outlined in Jared Diamond, *Guns, Germs, and Steel* (1997). David Hurst Thomas, *Exploring Native North America* (2000), provides detailed analyses of representative archaeological sites.

A good survey of the first peoples of North America is David J. Meltzer, *Search for the First Americans* (1993). The "overkill hypothesis" is developed in Paul Martin and Richard Klein, eds., *Quaternary Extinctions* (1984). The best survey on the southwestern peoples is Linda S. Cordell, *Prehistory of the Southwest* (1997). See also J. J. Brody, *The Anasazi* (1990), David Roberts, *In Search of the Old Ones:*

Exploring the Anasazi World of the Southwest (1995), R. Gwinn Vivian, *The Chacoan Prehistory of the San Juan Basin* (1990), John P. Andrews and Todd W. Bostwick, *Desert Farmers at the River's Edge: The Hohokam and Pueblo Grande* (1997), and, on early agriculture, R. G. Matson, *The Origins of Southwestern Agriculture* (1991). For a study of Hopewell peoples, see Bruce D. Smith, *Rivers of Change* (1992).

On the Mississippian societies, see Thomas E. Emerson, *Cahokia and the Archaeology of Power* (1997), Thomas E. Emerson and R. Barry Lewis, eds., *Cahokia and the Hinterlands: Middle Mississippian Cultures of the Midwest* (1991), Biloine W. Young and Robert Fowler, *Cahokia, The Great Native American Metropolis* (2000), Timothy Pauketat, *The Ascent of Chiefs: Cahokia and Mississippian Politics in Native North America* (1994), and Robert A. Birmingham and Leslie Eisenberg, *Indian Mounds of Wisconsin* (2000). For early peoples elsewhere, see Vance T. Holliday, *Paleoindian Geoarchaeology of the Southern High Plains* (1997) and Ruth Kirk and Richard D. Daugherty, *Hunters of the Whale* (1974), for the Makah of the Northwest.

For an overview of political structures, see Robert D. Drennan, *Chiefdoms in the Americas* (1987). That warfare was a product of gender tensions is explored in Bruce G. Trigger, *Natives and Newcomers* (1985). The contention that the early peoples of North America lived in perfect harmony with nature is rebutted in Shepard Krech, *The Ecological Indian* (1999). Another common assumption, based on Native American folklore, of the essentially peaceful character of Southwestern peoples has been challenged by recent studies such as Glen E. Rice and Steven A. Leblanc, eds., *Deadly Landscapes: Case Studies in Prehistoric Southwestern Warfare* (2001), and Tim D. White, *Prehistoric Cannibalism at Mancos* (1992). In *Eve's Seed: Biology, the Sexes and the Course of History* (2001), Robert S. McElvaine argues that men enshrined raids and warfare in response to women's increasingly important economic role in farming activities.

SUGGESTED WEBSITES

Pre-Contact and Colonial Maps
http://www.lib.utexas.edu/maps/americas/
This University of Texas site contains numerous maps from the pre-contact and colonial periods.

Ancient Mesoamerican Civilization
http://www.angelfire.com/ca/humanorigins/index.html
Kevin L. Callahan of the University of Minnesota Department of Anthropology maintains this page that supplies information regarding Mesoamerican civilizations with well-organized essays and photos.

National Museum of the American Indian
http://www.si.edu/nmai
The Smithsonian Institution museum is dedicated to the Native American experience.

Cahokia Mounds
http://medicine.wustel/edu/~mckinney/cahokia/cahokia.html
The Cahokia Mounds State Historical site gives information about this fascinating pre-Columbian North American culture.

Alien Encounters: Europe in the Americas

An Aztec artist's depiction of the arrival of the Spaniards, whose blank faces scarcely appear human. Compare them to the detailed, grim expression of the Aztec scout, hidden at the top of the palm tree *(upper right)*. Historical interpretation always depends on one's point of view.

CHAPTER CONTENTS

At about two o'clock on the morning of October 12, 1492, a sailor named Roderigo de Triana, clinging in a gale to the mast of the *Pinta,* saw a gleam of white on the moonlit horizon and shouted: *"Tierra! Tierra!"* The land he had spied was an island in the West Indies called Guanahani by its inhabitants, a place distinguished neither for beauty nor size. Nevertheless, when Triana's master, Christopher Columbus, went ashore bearing the flag of Spain, he named it San Salvador, or Holy Savior. Columbus selected this imposing name for the island out of gratitude and wonder at having found it—he had sailed with three frail vessels more than 3000 miles for 33 days without sighting land.

San Salvador was the gateway to two continents. Columbus did not know it, and he refused to accept the truth, but his voyage threw open to exploitation by the peoples of western Europe more than a quarter of all the land in the world, a region of more than 16 million square miles, an area lushly endowed with every imaginable resource. He made possible a mass movement into the New World from Europe—and later from Africa and other regions. By 1600, about 240,000 Spaniards had made their way to the Americas. Gathering force rapidly, this movement brought over 100 million persons from throughout the world to the western hemisphere.

COLUMBUS

Columbus was an intelligent as well as a dedicated and skillful mariner. He failed to grasp the significance of his accomplishment because he had no idea that he was on the edge of two huge continents previously unknown to Europeans. He was seeking a way to China and Japan and the Indies, the amazing countries described by the Venetian Marco Polo in the late thirteenth century.

Having read carefully Marco Polo's account of his adventures in the service of Kublai Khan, Columbus had decided that these rich lands could be reached by sailing directly west from Europe. The idea was not original, but while others merely talked about it, Columbus pursued it with brilliant persistence.

If one could sail to Asia directly, the trading possibilities and the resulting profits would be limitless. Asian products were highly valued all over Europe. Spices such as pepper, cinnamon, ginger, nutmeg, and cloves were of primary importance, their role being not so much to titillate the palate as to disguise the taste of spoiled meats in regions that had little ice. Europeans also prized such tropical foods as rice, figs, and oranges, as well as perfumes (often used as a substitute for soap), silk and cotton, rugs, textiles such as muslin and damask, dyestuffs, fine steel products, precious stones, and various drugs.

But the cost of Asian products remained high. To transport spices from the Indies, silk from China, or rugs, cloth, and steel from the Middle East was extremely costly. The combined routes through central Asia were long and complicated—across strange seas, through deserts, over high mountain passes—with pirates or highwaymen a constant threat. Every petty tyrant through whose domain the caravans passed levied taxes, a quasi-legal form of robbery. Few merchants operated on a continental scale; typically, goods passed from hand to hand and were loaded and unloaded many times between Eastern producer and Western consumer, with each middleman exacting as large a profit as he could. In the end the western European consumer had to pay for all this.

If the produce of eastern Asia could be carried to Europe by sea, the trip would be both cheaper and more comfortable. The goods would have to be loaded and unloaded only once. A small number of sailors could provide all the necessary labor, and the free wind would supply the power to move the cargo to its destination. By the fifteenth century, this idea was beginning to be transformed into action.

The great figure in the transformation was Prince Henry the Navigator, third son of John I, king of Portugal. After distinguishing himself in 1415 in the capture of Ceuta, on the African side of the Strait of Gibraltar, he became interested in navigation and exploration. Sailing a vessel out of sight of land was still, in Henry's day, more an art than a science and was extremely hazardous. Ships were small and clumsy. Primitive compasses and instruments for reckoning latitude existed, but under shipboard conditions they were very inaccurate. Navigators could determine longitude only by keeping track of direction and estimating speed; even the most skilled could place little faith in their estimates.

Henry attempted to improve and codify navigational knowledge. At his court at Sagres, hard by Cape St. Vincent, the extreme southwestern point of Europe, he built an observatory and supervised the preparation of tables measuring the declination of the sun and other navigational data. But most improvements in navigation were the result of practical experience. Searching for a new route to Asia, Henry's captains sailed westward to the Madeiras and the Canaries and south along the coast of Africa, seeking a way around that continent. In 1445 Dinis Dias reached Cape Verde, site of present-day Dakar.

For 20 years after Henry's death in 1460, the Portuguese concentrated on exploiting his discoveries. In the 1480s King John II undertook systematic new explorations focused on reaching India. Gradually his caravels probed southward along the sweltering coast—to the equator, to the region of Angola, and beyond.

Into this bustling, prosperous, expectant little country in the corner of Europe came Christopher Columbus in 1476. Columbus was a weaver's son from Genoa, born in 1451. He had taken to the sea early, ranging widely in the Mediterranean. His arrival in Portugal was unplanned, since it resulted from the loss of his ship in a battle off the coast. For a time he worked as a chartmaker in Lisbon. He married a local woman. Then he was again at sea. He cruised northward, perhaps as far as Iceland, south to the equator, westward in the Atlantic to the Azores. Had his interest lain in that direction, he might well have been the first person to reach Asia by way of Africa, for in 1488 in Lisbon he met and talked with Bartholomeu Dias, just returned from his voyage around the southern tip of Africa, which had demonstrated that the way lay clear for a voyage eastward to the Indies.

But by this time Columbus had committed himself to the westward route. When King John II refused to finance him, he turned to the Spanish court, where, after many disappointments, he persuaded Queen Isabella to equip his expedition. In August 1492 he set out from the port of Palos with his tiny fleet, the *Santa Maria*, the *Pinta*, and the *Niña*. A little more than two months later, after a stopover in the Canary Islands to repair the *Pinta*'s rudder, his lookout sighted land.

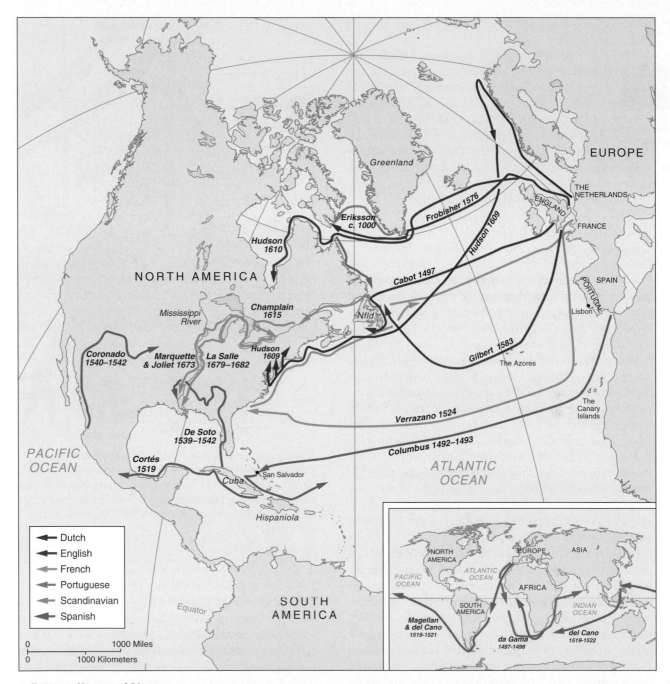

▲ **European Voyages of Discovery**

Columbus's success was due in large part to his single-minded conviction that the Indies could be reached by sailing westward for a relatively short distance and that a profitable trade would develop over this route. He had persuaded Isabella to grant him, in addition to the title Admiral of the Ocean Sea, political control over all the lands he might discover and 10 percent of the profits of the trade that would follow in the wake of his expedition. Now the combination of zeal and tenacity that had gotten him across the Atlantic cost him dearly. He refused to accept the plain evidence, which everywhere confronted him, that this was an entirely new world. All about were strange plants, known neither to Europe nor to Asia. The copper-colored people who paddled out to inspect his fleet could no more follow the Arabic widely understood in the East than they could Spanish. Yet Columbus, consulting his charts, convinced himself that he had reached the Indies. That is why he called the natives Indians, a misnomer that became nearly

universal, and was increasingly used even by the native peoples themselves.

Searching for treasure, Columbus pushed on to Cuba. When he heard the native word *Cubanocan*, meaning "middle of Cuba," he mistook it for *El Gran Can* (Marco Polo's "Grand Khan") and sent emissaries on a fruitless search through the tropical jungle for the khan's palace. He finally returned to Spain relatively empty-handed but certain that he had explored the edge of Asia. Three later voyages failed to shake his conviction.

SPAIN'S AMERICAN EMPIRE

Columbus died in 1506. By that time other captains had taken up the work, most of them more willing than he to accept what Europeans called the New World on its own terms. As early as 1493, Pope Alexander VI had divided the non-Christian world between Spain and Portugal. The next year, in the Treaty of Tordesillas, these powers negotiated an agreement about exploiting the new discoveries. In effect, Portugal continued to concentrate on Africa, leaving the New World, except for what eventually became Brazil, to the Spanish. Thereafter, from their base on Hispaniola (Santo Domingo), founded by Columbus, the Spaniards quickly fanned out through the Caribbean and then over large parts of the two continents that bordered it.

In 1513 Vasco Nuñez de Balboa crossed the Isthmus of Panama and discovered the Pacific Ocean. In 1519 Hernán Cortés landed an army in Mexico and overran the empire of the Aztecs, rich in gold and silver. That same year Ferdinand Magellan set out on his epic three-year voyage around the world. By discovering the strait at the southern tip of South America that bears his name, he gave the Spanish a clear idea of the size of the continent. In the 1530s Francisco Pizarro subdued the Inca empire in Peru, providing the Spaniards with still more treasure, drawn chiefly from the silver mines of Potosí.

Meanwhile other Spanish explorers had surveyed vast regions of what is now the United States. Juan Ponce de Léon, a shipmate of Columbus on the Admiral's second voyage, made the first Spanish landing on the mainland of North America, exploring the east coast of Florida in 1513. In the 1520s Pánfilo de Narváez explored the Gulf Coast of North America westward from Florida, and after his death his lieutenant, Alvar Núñez Cabeza de Vaca, wandered for years in the region north of the Gulf. Finally, along with three

▲ Horses (blindfolded) being loaded onto Spanish warships for shipment to the Americas. Native peoples had never seen horses (which had been extinct in the Americas for over ten thousand years). Nor had they seen enormous wooden warships, powered by sails and carrying heavy cannons, nor warriors, seated on horses and encased in armor.

companions, one a black slave named Esteban, Cabeza de Vaca made his way across what is now New Mexico and Arizona and then south to Mexico City. Between 1539 and 1543 Hernando de Soto traveled north from Florida to the Carolinas, then westward to the Mississippi River. During the same period Francisco Vásquez de Coronado ventured as far north as Kansas and west to the Grand Canyon. Fifty years after Columbus's first landfall, Spain was master of a huge American empire covering all of South America except Brazil, and also the southern fringe of North America, extending from California east to Florida. By the early 1600s Spanish explorers had reached Virginia, and there were small Spanish settlements at Saint Augustine in Florida and at Santa Fe in New Mexico.

The Spanish developed a distinct civilization in this enormous region. By the 1570s they had founded about 200 cities and towns, set up printing presses and published pamphlets and books, and

established universities in Mexico City and Lima. With the help of Indian artisans, they had constructed and decorated lavishly a large number of impressive cathedrals.

What explains this mighty surge of exploration, conquest, and development? Greed for gold and power certainly, but also a sense of adventure, the wish of ordinary Spaniards to make better lives for themselves, and the desire to Christianize the Indians—mixed motives propelled the *conquistadores* and their followers onward. Some saw the New World as a reincarnation of the Garden of Eden, a land of infinite promise. Ponce de Léon and many others actually expected to find the Fountain of Youth in America. Their visions, at once so selfish and so exalted, reveal the central paradox of New World history. This immense land brought out both the best and the worst in human beings. The "New" World, "Virgin" America inspired conflicting feelings in their hearts. They worshiped it for its purity and promise, yet they could not resist the opportunity to take advantage of its seeming innocence.

INDIANS AND EUROPEANS

The *conquistadores* were brave and imaginative men. It must not, however, be forgotten that they wrenched their empire from innocent hands; in an important sense, the settlement of the New World ranks among the most flagrant examples of unprovoked aggression in human history. When Columbus landed on San Salvador he planted a cross, "as a sign," he explained to Ferdinand and Isabella, "that your Highnesses held this land as your own." Of the Lucayans, the native inhabitants of San Salvador, Columbus wrote: "The people of this island . . . are artless and generous with what they have, to such a degree as no one would believe. . . . If it be asked for, they never say no, but rather invite the person to accept it, and show as much lovingness as though they would give their hearts."

The Indians of San Salvador behaved this way because to them the Spaniards seemed the very gods. "All believe that power and goodness dwell in the sky," Columbus reported, "and they are firmly convinced that I have come from the sky."

The products of Europe fascinated the Indians. The early observer Thomas Harriot noticed that such everyday things as compasses, magnets, and clocks seemed to them "rather the works of gods than of men."

Columbus also remarked of the Lucayans: "These people are very unskilled in arms . . . with fifty men they could all be subjected and made to do all that one wished." He and his compatriots tricked and cheated the Indians at every turn. Before entering a new area, Spanish generals customarily read a *Requerimiento* (requirement) to the inhabitants. This long-winded document recited a Spanish version of the history of the human race from the Creation to the division of the non-Christian world by Pope Alexander VI and then called on the Indians to recognize the sovereignty of the reigning Spanish monarch. ("If you do so . . . we shall receive you in all love and charity.") If this demand was rejected, the Spanish promised: "We shall powerfully enter into your country, and . . . shall take you, your wives, and your children, and shall make slaves of them. . . . The death and losses which shall accrue from this are your fault." This arrogant harangue was read in Spanish and often out of earshot of the Indians. When they responded by fighting, the Spaniards decimated them, drove them from their lands, and held the broken survivors in contempt.

Wherever they went, Europeans mistreated and sometimes slaughtered the people they encountered. The French philosopher Montaigne wrote that in the East Indies (now Indonesia), cities were ransacked and "the best part of the world topsi-turvied" by Spain merely to profit from "the

Conquistadores Torturing Native Amerindians

traffic of Pearls and pepper." When the Portuguese reached Africa, they carried off thousands into slavery. The Dutch behaved shamefully in the East Indies, as did the French in their colonial possessions.

English settlers described the Indians as being "of a tractable, free, and loving nature, without guile or treachery," yet in most instances they exploited and all but exterminated them. "Why should you take by force from us that which you can obtain by love?" one puzzled chief asked an early Virginia colonist, according to the latter's own account.

The first settlers of New England dealt fairly with the local inhabitants. They made honest, if somewhat misguided, efforts to Christianize and educate them and to respect their rights. But within a few years their relations with the Indians deteriorated. The settelers seized more land and their livestock ruined Indian crops and hunting grounds. In King Philip's War (1675–1676), a protracted slaughter on both sides, culminated in the massacre of perhaps 4000 Indians at the Great Swamp in Rhode Island.

RELATIVITY OF CULTURAL VALUES

If some of the natives were naive in thinking that the invaders, with their potent fire sticks and huge ships, which seemed to be "moving islands," were

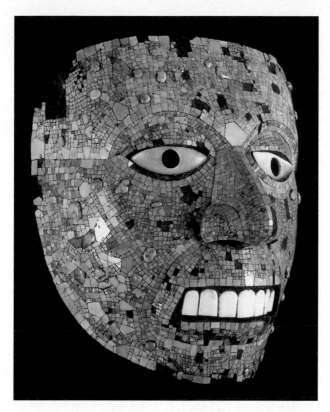

▲ A turquoise Aztec burial mask from about the time of Spanish contact. Such masks conveyed the Aztec sense of social hierarchy—only the most prominent were adorned with masks like this one—and its notion of an afterlife. The beautiful turquoise "face" would resist, as mortal flesh did not, the ravages of time.

gods, these "gods" were equally naive in their thinking. Since the Indians did not worship the Christian God and indeed worshiped a large number of other gods, the Europeans dismissed them as contemptible heathens. Some insisted that the Indians were servants of Satan. "Probably the devil decoyed these miserable savages hither," one English colonist explained.

In fact, many Indians were deeply religious people. But their religious values were so different from those of the Europeans that many of the latter believed that even if the Indians were not minions of Satan, they were unworthy of becoming Christians. Others, such as the Spanish friars, did try to convert the Indians, and with considerable success; but as late as 1569, when Spain introduced the Inquisition into its colonies, the natives were exempted from its control on the ground that they were incapable of rational judgment and thus not responsible for their "heretical" religious beliefs.

That the Indians allowed their environment to remain pristine is a myth. Long before contact with the Europeans, they had cleared fields, burned the underbrush of forests, diverted rivers and streams, built roads and settlements, and deposited immense quantities of earth upon mounds. The Europeans, nevertheless, left a deeper imprint on the American landscape. Their iron-tipped ploughs dug into the earth and made more of it accessible to cultivation, and their iron axes and saws enabled them to clear vast forests and use the lumber for construction.

Indians who depended on hunting and fishing had small use for personal property that was not easily portable. They had little interest in amassing wealth, as individuals or as tribes. Even the Aztecs, with their treasures of gold and silver, valued the metals for their durability and the beautiful things that could be made with them rather than as objects of commerce. The Narragansett Indians had a ritual in which they collected "almost all the riches they have to their gods"—kettles, hatchets, beads, knives—and burned them in a great fire.

This lack of concern for material things led Europeans to conclude that the native people of America were childlike creatures, not to be treated as equals. "[Indians] do but run over the grass, as do also foxes and wild beasts," an Englishman wrote in 1622, "so it is lawful now to take a land, which none useth, and make use of it." In the sense that the Indians lived in close harmony with nature, the first part of this statement contained a grain of truth, although of course the second did not follow from it logically.

Other troubles grew out of similar misunderstandings. English colonists assumed that Indian chiefs ruled with the same authority as their own kings. For example, the Wampanoag called their leader Metacom; the English referred to him as "King Philip," likely a term of derision. When Indians, whose loyalties were shaped by complex kinship relations more than by identification with any one leader, sometimes failed to honor commitments made by their chiefs, the English accused them of treachery.

For their part, Indians found many aspects of European society incomprehensible. When a group of Indians were presented to the 12-year-old king of Spain, Charles IX, they could not understand why his Swiss guards, "so many grown men, bearded, strong, and armed . . . should submit to obey a child" instead of putting one of their members in command.

The Europeans' inability to grasp the communal nature of land tenure among Indians also led to innumerable quarrels. Traditional tribal boundaries were neither spelled out in deeds or treaties nor

▲ European soldiers, clad in armor and wielding iron weapons, were nearly invincible in close fighting—all the more so when their foes were unarmed, as in this drawing. Here Cortés and his men slash through Montezuma's Aztec court.

marked by fences or any other sign of occupation. Often corn grown by a number of families was stored in a common bin and drawn on by all as needed. Such practices were utterly alien to the European mind. Indians resented, too, the intensity of English cultivation. Algonquians taunted English captives while burying them alive: "You English have grown exceedingly above the Ground. Let us now see how you will grow when planted into the ground." Nowhere was the cultural chasm between Indians and Europeans more evident than in warfare. Indians did not seek to possess land, so they sought not so much to destroy the enemy as to display their valor, to avenge an insult or perceived wrong, or to acquire captives who could take the place of missing family members. The Indians preferred to ambush an opponent and seize the stragglers; when confronted by a superior force, they usually melted into the woods. The Europeans preferred to fight in heavily armed masses in order to obliterate the enemy. Colonists denounced Indian perfidy for burning houses and towns; but they saw no inconsistency in burning Indian "nests," "wigwams," and "camps." Conversely, the Indians thought it within their rights to slaughter the cattle that devoured their crops and spoiled their hunting

grounds. But when the Indians tortured the beasts in fury, the colonists regarded them as savages.

DISEASE AND POPULATION LOSSES

Native American Population Loss, 1500–1700

Scholars agree on only one fact concerning the population history of the North American Indians following the arrival of Columbus: the number of Indians declined. (See the feature essay Debating the Past: "How many Indians perished with European settlement?" on p. 26.) Historian David Stannard's book on the subject, *American Holocaust,* was pointedly published in 1992, the five hundredth anniversary of Columbus's famous excursion. He contended that Columbus's actions constituted "genocide" against the native peoples of the Americas.

The terms *holocaust* and *genocide* usually refer to the systematic destruction of entire peoples, such as the Nazi attempt to exterminate the European Jews. But the objectives of the Europeans who came to the Americas were as different as the people themselves: soldiers, farmers, missionaries, women as well as men, Protestants, Catholics, and Jews. Many colonists depended on the Indians: The Spanish needed them to work the mines, till the soil, and build roads and buildings; French traders needed them to provide furs and other items for export; English settlers depended on them for additional food and knowledge. For most Europeans, a live Indian was better than a dead one.

Yet millions did die; and from the outset of the Europeans' invasion of the New World, sensitive observers had been appalled by their barbarity. The first to come under sharp scrutiny were the Spaniards. Bartolomé de Las Casas, a Dominican missionary who arrived in Hispaniola nearly a decade after Columbus, compiled a passionate and grisly indictment:

> It was the general rule among Spaniards to be cruel; not just cruel, but extraordinarily cruel so that harsh and bitter treatment would prevent Indians from daring to think of themselves as human beings or having a minute to think at all. So they would cut an Indian's hands and leave them dangling by a shred of skin and they would send him on saying "Go now, spread the news to your chiefs." They would test their swords and their manly strength on captured Indians and place bets on the slicing off of heads or the cutting of bodies in half with one blow.

These and countless similar stories gave rise to the "Black Legend" of Spanish tyranny and oppression, a standard so low that English and French

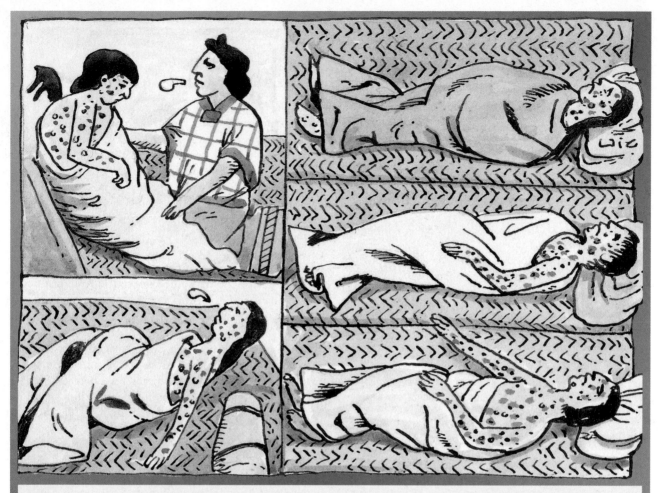

Debating the Past

How many Indians perished with European settlement? In 1518 smallpox, long a scourge in Europe, ravaged the native peoples of the New World. This picture shows Aztec victims being attended by a medicine man. "Those who did survive," reported Cortes's secretary, "having scratched themselves, were left in such a condition that they frightened the others with the many deep pits on their faces, hands, and bodies."

To calculate the magnitude of Indian losses, scholars had to determine the population at first contact with Europeans, a difficult task in the absence of Indian records. Early in the twentieth century, scholars gathered fragmentary population statistics as compiled by Catholic priests, Spanish officials, travelers, and soldiers. By aggregating this information for all tribes, including guesses where no data was available, the scholars estimated an Indian population in the United States and Canada in the early sixteenth century of a little more than 1 million.

By the 1960s and 1970s, some thought this estimate far too low. They complained that it minimized both the achievements of Indian civilizations as well as the extent of the destruction wrought by European diseases and guns. Anthropologist Henry Dobyns (1983) found that when smallpox, measles, or tuberculosis struck an Indian village, 19 out of 20 Indians would die. He thought this ratio characteristic of populations that lacked immunity to such diseases. He therefore multiplied the earlier population figures by twenty. After a few adjustments, he calculated the Indian population of the United States and Canada at 10 to 12 million, and of the entire western hemisphere, at over 100 million.

Dobyns's methodology came under fire, but Thornton (1987) and others devised pre-contact estimates ranging from 4 to 8 million. Since then, mathematicians have concluded that the data are so riddled with guesswork that no numerical estimates are reliable. But it is probably safe to conclude that Indian losses north of the Rio Grande numbered in the millions, and in the remainder of the western hemisphere, tens of millions.

Henry Dobyns, *Their Number Became Thinned: Native American Population Dynamics in Eastern North America* (1983), Russell Thornton, *American Indian Holocaust and Survival: A Population History Since 1492* (1987).

colonists believed they could not sink beneath it. In fact, English barbarities rivaled those of the Spaniards.

In Virginia in 1610, for example, George Percy, an English officer, when ordered to punish a Powhatan chief for insolence, proudly described how his men marched into an Indian town, seized some of the natives, "putt some fiftene or sixtene to the Sworde" and cut off their heads. Then he ordered his men to burn the houses and crops. When the expedition returned to its boats, his men complained that Percy had spared an Indian "quene and her Children." Percy relented, and threw the children overboard "shoteinge owtt their Braynes in the water." His men insisted that he burn the queen alive, but Percy, less cruel, stabbed her to death.

Of all the weapons the Europeans brought to the New World, the most potent was one they could not see and of which they were unaware: microorganisms that carried diseases such as smallpox, measles, bubonic plague, diphtheria, influenza, malaria, yellow fever, and typhoid. Most Europeans had been exposed to these diseases and thus carried antibodies for them in their blood; but the Indians initially lacked these antibodies. When these diseases first struck, many Indian villages were nearly wiped out.

In 1585, for example, Sir Francis Drake, preparing for a raid against the Spanish, stopped at the Cape Verde Islands. There some of his men contracted a fever—probably typhus—but sailed for Florida undaunted by their discomfort. When they landed at St. Augustine, the disease spread to the Indians who, according to Drake, "died verie fast and said amongst themselves, it was the Englisshe God that made them die so faste." Some 30 years later an outbreak of smallpox almost wiped out the Indians of Plymouth Bay, prompting the puritan divine, Cotton Mather, to offer thanks to God for having cleared the lands "of those pernicious creatures, to make room for better growth." Over the next three centuries, the Indian losses from such diseases were incalculable, though the lowest estimates begin in the millions.

SPAIN'S EUROPEAN RIVALS

DOCUMENT
Letters of Patent Granted to John Cabot

While Spain waxed fat on the wealth of the Americas, the other nations of western Europe did little. In 1497 and 1498 King Henry VII of England sent Captain John Cabot to explore the New World. Cabot visited Newfoundland and the northeastern coast of the continent. His explorations formed the basis for later British claims in North America, but they were not followed up for many decades. In 1524

Giovanni da Verrazano made a similar voyage for France, coasting the continent from Carolina to Nova Scotia. Some ten years later the Frenchman Jacques Cartier explored the St. Lawrence River as far inland as present-day Montréal. During the sixteenth century, fishermen from France, Spain, Portugal, and England began exploiting the limitless supplies of cod and other fish they found in the cold waters off Newfoundland. They landed at many points along the mainland coast from Nova Scotia to Labrador to collect water and wood and to dry their catches, but they made no permanent settlements until the next century.

There were many reasons for this delay, the most important probably being the fact that Spain had achieved a large measure of internal tranquility by the sixteenth century, while France and England were still torn by serious religious and political conflicts. The Spanish also profited from having seized on those areas in America best suited to producing quick returns. Furthermore, in the first half of the sixteenth century, Spain, under Charles V, dominated Europe as well as America. Charles controlled the Low Countries, most of central Europe, and part of Italy. Reinforced by the treasure of the Aztecs and the Incas, Spain seemed too mighty to be challenged in either the New World or the Old World.

Under Philip II, who succeeded Charles in 1556, Spanish strength seemed at its peak, especially after Philip added Portugal to his domain in 1580. But beneath the pomp and splendor (so well captured by such painters as Velázquez and El Greco) the great empire was in trouble. The corruption of the Spanish court had much to do with this. So did the ever-increasing dependence of Spain on the gold and silver of its colonies, which tended to undermine the local Spanish economy. Even more important was the disruption of the Catholic Church throughout Europe by the Protestant Reformation.

THE PROTESTANT REFORMATION

The spiritual lethargy and bureaucratic corruption besetting the Roman Catholic Church in the early sixteenth century made it a fit target for reform. The thriving business in the sale of indulgences, payments that were supposed to win for departed loved ones forgiveness for their earthly sins and thus release from purgatory, was a public scandal. The luxurious lifestyle of the popes and the papal court in Rome was another. Yet there had been countless earlier religious reform movements that had led to little or no change. The fact that the movement launched by Martin Luther in 1517 and carried

▲ St. Peter's Basilica in the Vatican was built between 1506 and 1626. Catholic popes defended the magnificent church as a suitable expression of man's love for a God who had redeemed mankind. Protestant critics denounced St. Peter's as a form of idolatry that celebrated man's attainments rather than those of God. Puritans insisted that their houses of worship be simple and their altars plain.

forward by men like John Calvin addressed genuine shortcomings in the Roman Catholic Church does not entirely explain why it led so directly to the rupture of Christendom.

The charismatic leadership of Luther and the compelling brilliance of Calvin made their protests more effective than earlier efforts at reform. Probably more important, so did the political possibilities let loose by their challenge to Rome's spiritual authority. German princes seized on Luther's campaign against the sale of indulgences to stop all payments to Rome and to confiscate church property within their domains. Swiss cities like Geneva, where Calvin took up

residence in 1536, and Zurich joined the Protestant revolt for spiritual reasons, but also to establish their political independence from Catholic kings. Francis I of France remained a Catholic, but he took advantage of Rome's troubles to secure control over the clergy of his kingdom. The efforts of Spain to suppress Protestantism in the Low Countries only further stimulated nationalist movements there, especially among the Dutch.

The decision of Henry VIII of England in 1534 to break with Rome was at bottom a political one. The refusal of Pope Clement VII to agree to an annulment of Henry's marriage of 20 years to Catherine of Aragon, the daughter of Ferdinand and Isabella, provided the occasion. Catherine had given birth to six children, but only a daughter, Mary, survived childhood; Henry was without a male heir. By repudiating the pope's spiritual authority and declaring himself head of the English (Anglican) church, Henry freed himself to divorce Catherine and to marry whomever—and however often—he saw fit. By the time of his death five wives and 13 years later, England had become a Protestant nation. More important for our story, the dominant character of the future English colonies in America had also been determined.

The growing political and religious conflict had economic overtones. Modern students have exploded the theory that the merchant classes were attracted to Protestantism because the Catholic Church, preaching outdated concepts like "just price" and frowning on the accumulation of wealth as an end in itself, stifled their acquisitiveness. Few merchants were more devoted to the quests for riches than the Italians, yet they remained loyal Catholics. So did the wool merchants of Flanders, among the most important in all Europe. Nonetheless, in some lands the business classes tended to support Protestant leaders, in part because the new sects, stressing simplicity, made fewer financial demands on the faithful than the Catholics did.

As the commercial classes rose to positions of influence, England, France, and the United Provinces of the Netherlands experienced a flowering of trade and industry. The Dutch built the largest merchant fleet in the world. Dutch traders captured most of the Far Eastern business once monopolized by the Portuguese, and they infiltrated Spain's Caribbean stronghold. A number of English merchant companies, soon to play a vital role as colonizers, sprang up in the last half of the sixteenth century. These joint-stock companies, ancestors of the modern corporation, enabled groups of investors to pool their capital and limit their individual

responsibilities to the sums actually invested—a very important protection in such risky enterprises. The Muscovy Company, the Levant Company, and the East India Company were the most important of these ventures.

ENGLISH BEGINNINGS IN AMERICA

English merchants took part in many kinds of international activity. The Muscovy Company spent large sums searching for a passage to China around Scandinavia and dispatched six overland expeditions in an effort to reach East Asia by way of Russia and Persia. In the 1570s Martin Frobisher made three voyages across the Atlantic, hoping to discover a northwest passage to East Asia or new gold-bearing lands.

Such projects, particularly in the area of North America, received strong but concealed support from the Crown. Queen Elizabeth I (1558–1603) invested heavily in Frobisher's expeditions. England was still too weak to challenge Spain openly, but Elizabeth hoped to break the Spanish overseas monopoly just the same. She encouraged her boldest sea dogs to plunder Spanish merchant ships on the high seas. When Captain Francis Drake was about to set sail on his fabulous round-the-world voyage in 1577, the queen said to him: "Drake . . . I would gladly be revenged on the King of Spain for divers injuries that I have received." Drake took her at her word. He sailed through the Strait of Magellan and terrorized the west coast of South America, capturing the Spanish treasure ship *Cacafuego,* heavily laden with Peruvian silver. After exploring the coast of California, which he claimed for England, Drake crossed the Pacific and went on to circumnavigate the globe, returning home in triumph in 1580. Although Elizabeth took pains to deny it to the Spanish ambassador, Drake's voyage was officially sponsored. Elizabeth being the principal shareholder in the venture, most of the ill-gotten Spanish bullion went into the Royal Treasury rather than Drake's pocket.

When schemes to place settlers in the New World began to mature at about this time, the queen again became involved. The first English effort was led by Sir Humphrey Gilbert, an Oxford educated soldier and courtier. The queen authorized him to explore and colonize "heathen lands not actually possessed by any Christian prince."

We know almost nothing about Gilbert's first attempt except that it occurred in 1578 and 1579; in 1583 he set sail again with five ships and over 200 settlers. He landed them on Newfoundland, then evidently decided to seek a more congenial site farther south. However, no colony was established, and on his way back to England his ship went down in a storm off the Azores.

Gilbert's half-brother, Sir Walter Raleigh, took up the work. Handsome, ambitious, and impulsive, Raleigh was a great favorite of Elizabeth. He sent a number of expeditions to explore the east coast of North America, a land he named Virginia in honor of his unmarried sovereign. In 1585 he settled about a hundred men on Roanoke Island, off the North Carolina coast, but these settlers returned home the next year. In 1587 Raleigh sent another group to Roanoke, including a number of women and children. Unfortunately, the supply ships sent to the colony in 1588 failed to arrive; when help did get there in 1590, not a soul could be found. The fate of the settlers has never been determined.

▲ Elizabeth I, standing upon a map of England. This contemporary miniature (1592) might have struck viewers as ludicrous were it not for the fact that Queen Elizabeth was a consummate political strategist and formidable military foe. She built the fleet that destroyed the Spanish Armada in 1588.

One reason for the delay in getting aid to the Roanoke colonists was the attack of the Spanish Armada on England in 1588. Angered by English raids on his shipping and by the assistance Elizabeth was giving to the rebels in the Netherlands, King Philip II decided to invade England. His motives were religious as well as political and economic, for England now seemed committed to Protestantism. His great fleet of some 130 ships bore huge crosses on the sails as if on another crusade. The Armada carried 30,000 men and 2400 guns, the largest naval force ever assembled up to that time. However, the English fleet of 197 ships shattered this armada, and a series of storms completed its destruction. Thereafter, although the war continued and Spanish sea power remained formidable, Spain could no longer block English penetration of the New World.

Experience had shown that the cost of planting settlements in a wilderness 3000 miles from England was more than any individual purse could bear. (Raleigh lost about £40,000 in his overseas ventures; early in the game he began to advocate government support of colonization.) As early as 1584 Richard Hakluyt, England's foremost authority on the Americas and a talented propagandist for colonization, made a convincing case for royal aid. In his *Discourse on Western Planting,* Hakluyt stressed the military advantages of building "two or three strong fortes" along the Atlantic coast of North America. Ships operating from such bases would make life uncomfortable for "King Phillipe" by intercepting his treasure fleets—a matter, Hakluyt added coolly, "that toucheth him indeede to the quicke." Colonies in America would also spread the Protestant religion and enrich the parent country by expanding the market for English woolens, bringing in valuable tax revenues, and providing employment for the swarms of "lustie youthes that be turned to no provitable use" at home. From the great American forests would come the timber and naval stores needed to build a bigger navy and merchant marine.

Queen Elizabeth read Hakluyt's essay, but she was too cautious and too devious to act boldly on his suggestions. Only after her death in 1603 did full-scale efforts to found English colonies in America begin, and even then the organizing force came from merchant capitalists, not from the Crown.

The Settlement of Virginia

In September 1605 two groups of English merchants petitioned the new king, James I, for a license to colonize Virginia, as the whole area claimed by England was then named. This was granted the following April, and two joint-stock companies were organized, one controlled by London merchants, the other by a group from the area around Plymouth and Bristol.[1] Both were under the control of a Royal Council for Virginia, but James appointed prominent stockholders to the council, which meant that the companies had considerable independence.

This first charter revealed the commercial motivation of both king and company in the plainest terms. Although it spoke of spreading Christianity and bringing "the Infidels and Savages, living in those Parts, to human Civility," it stressed the right "to dig, mine, and search for all Manner of Mines of Gold, Silver, and Copper." On December 20, 1606, the London Company dispatched about a hundred settlers aboard the *Susan Constant, Discovery,* and *Godspeed.* This little band reached the Chesapeake Bay area in May 1607 and founded Jamestown, the first permanent English colony in the New World.

From the start everything seemed to go wrong. The immigrants established themselves in what was a mosquito-infested swamp simply because it appeared easily defensible against Indian attack. They failed to get a crop in the ground because of the lateness of the season and were soon almost without food. Their leaders, mere deputies of the London merchants, did not respond to the challenges of the wilderness. The settlers lacked the skills pioneers need. More than a third of them were "gentlemen" unused to manual labor, and many of the rest were the gentlemen's servants, almost equally unequipped for the task of colony building. During the first winter more than half of the settlers died.

All the land belonged to the company, and aside from the gentlemen and their retainers, most of the settlers were only hired laborers who had contracted to work for it for seven years. This was unfortunate. The situation demanded people skilled in agriculture, and such a labor force was available. In England times were bad. The growth of the textile industry had led to an increased demand for wool, and great landowners were dismissing laborers and tenant farmers and shifting from labor-intensive agriculture to sheep-raising. Inflation, caused by a shortage of goods to supply the needs of a growing population and by the influx of large amounts of American silver into Europe, worsened the plight of the dispossessed. Many landless farmers were eager to migrate if offered a decent opportunity to obtain land and make new lives for themselves.

---

[1]The London Company was to colonize southern Virginia, while the Plymouth Company, the Plymouth-Bristol group of merchants, was granted northern Virginia.

The merchant directors of the London Company, knowing little or nothing about Virginia, failed to provide the colony with effective guidance. They set up a council of settlers, but they kept all real power in their own hands. Instead of stressing farming and public improvements, they directed the energies of the colonists into such futile labors as searching for gold (the first supply ship devoted precious space to two goldsmiths and two "refiners"), glassblowing, silk raising, winemaking, and exploring the local rivers in hopes of finding a water route to the Pacific and the riches of China.

One colonist, Captain John Smith, tried to stop some of this foolishness. Smith had come to Virginia after a fantastic career as a soldier of fortune in eastern Europe, where he had fought many battles, been enslaved by a Turkish pasha, and triumphed in a variety of adventures, military and amorous. He quickly realized that building houses and raising food were essential to survival, and he soon became an expert forager and Indian trader. Smith was as eager as any seventeenth-century European to take advantage of the Indians and he had few compunctions about the methods employed in doing so. But he recognized both the limits of the colonists' power and the vast differences between Indian customs and values and his own. It was necessary, he insisted, to dominate the "proud Savages" yet to avoid bloodshed.

Smith pleaded with company officials in London to send over more people accustomed to working with their hands, such as farmers, fishermen, carpenters, masons, "diggers up of trees," and fewer gentlemen and "Tuftaffety humorists."[2] "A plaine soldier who can use a pickaxe and a spade is better than five knights," he said.

Whether Smith was actually rescued from death at the hands of the Indians by the princess Pocahontas is not certain, but there is little doubt that without his direction, the colony would have perished in the early days. However, he stayed in Virginia only two years.

Lacking intelligent leaders and faced with appalling hardships, the Jamestown colonists failed to develop a sufficient sense of common purpose. Each year they died in wholesale lots from disease, starvation (there was even a case of cannibalism among the desperate survivors), Indian attack, and, above all, ignorance and folly. Between 1606 and 1622 the London Company invested more than £160,000 in Virginia and sent over about 6000 settlers. Yet no dividends were ever earned, and of the 6000, fewer

---

[2]Smith was referring to the gold tassels worn by titled students at Oxford and Cambridge at that time.

▲ This 1616 portrait depicts Pocahontas, daughter of Powhatan, the foremost chief of coastal Virginia. The colonists, in a dispute with Powhatan, took her hostage in 1613 and kept her in Jamestown. The next year she converted to Anglicanism, took the name "Lady Rebecca," and married John Rolfe, an alliance that helped defuse tensions between colonists and Indians. In 1616 the couple came to England with their infant son, where "Lady Rebecca" was received by King James I. She became celebrated as the "belle sauvage." She was the most prominent exemplar of those "intermediaries" who readily crossed the porous boundaries between colonist and Indian cultures.

than 2000 were still alive in 1622. In 1625 the population was down to about 1300. The only profits were those taken by certain shrewd investors who had organized a joint-stock company to transport women to Virginia "to be made wives" by the colonists.

One major problem, the mishandling of the local Indians, was largely the colonists' doing. It is quite likely that the settlement would not have survived if the Powhatan Indians had not given the colonists food in the first hard winters, taught them the ways of the forest, introduced them to valuable new crops such as corn and yams, and showed them how to clear dense timber by girdling the trees and burning them down after they were dead. The settlers accepted Indian aid, then took whatever else they wanted by force.

The Indians did not submit meekly to such treatment. They proved brave, skillful, and ferocious fighters once they understood that their very existence was at stake. The burden of Indian fighting might easily have been more than the frail settlement could bear.

What saved the white Virginians was not the brushing aside of the Indians but the gradual realization that they must produce their own food—cattle raising was especially important—and the cultivation of tobacco, which flourished there and could be sold profitably in England. Once the settlers discovered tobacco, no amount of company pressure could keep them at wasteful tasks like looking for gold. The "restraint of plantinge Tobacco," one company official commented, "is a thinge so distastefull to them that they will with no patience indure to heare of it."

John Rolfe, who is also famous for marrying Pocahontas, introduced West Indian tobacco—much milder than the local "weed" and thus more valuable—in 1612. With money earned from the sale of tobacco, the colonists could buy the manufactured articles they could not produce in a raw new country; this freed them from dependence on outside subsidies. It did not mean profit for the London Company, however, for by the time tobacco caught on, the surviving original colonists had served their seven years and were no longer hired hands. To attract more settlers, the company had permitted first tenancy and then outright ownership of farms. Thus the profits of tobacco went largely to the planters, not to the "adventurers" who had organized the colony.

Important administrative reforms helped Virginia to forge ahead. A revised charter in 1612 extended the London Company's control over its own affairs in Virginia. Despite serious intracompany rivalry between groups headed by Sir Thomas Smythe and Sir Edwin Sandys, a somewhat more intelligent direction of Virginia's affairs resulted. First, the merchants appointed a single resident governor and gave him sufficient authority to control the settlers. Then they made it much easier for settlers to obtain land of their own. In 1619 a rudimentary form of self-government was instituted: A House of Burgesses, consisting of delegates chosen in each district, met at Jamestown to advise the governor on local problems. The company was not bound by the actions of the burgesses, but from this seed sprang the system of representative government that became the American pattern.

These reforms, however, came too late to save the fortunes of the London Company. In 1619 the Sandys faction won control and started an extensive development program, but in 1622 a bloody Indian attack took the lives of 347 colonists. Morale sank, and James I, who disliked Sandys, decided that the colony was being badly managed. In 1624 the charter was revoked and Virginia became a royal colony, subject to direct control by the royal bureaucracy in London. As a financial proposition the company was a fiasco; the shareholders lost every penny they had invested. Nonetheless, by 1624 Virginia was firmly established and beginning to prosper.

"PURIFYING" THE CHURCH OF ENGLAND

Through all the social and political reshuffling that occurred in Virginia in its opening decades, the people, by and large, kept their eyes fixed on the main change. But although the prospect of a better material life brought most English settlers to America, for some, economic opportunity was not the only reason they abandoned what their contemporary William Shakespeare called "dear mother England." A profound unease with England's spiritual state—and therefore with their own while they remained there—explains why many colonists embarked on their "errand into the wilderness."

Despite the attempt of Henry VIII's older daughter, Queen Mary, to reinstate Catholicism during her brief reign (1553–1558), the Anglican Church became once and for all the official Church of England during the long reign of Elizabeth I (1558–1603). Like her father, Elizabeth took more interest in politics than in religion. So long as England had its own church, with her at its head, and with English rather than Latin as its official language, she was content. Aside from these changes, the Anglican Church under Elizabeth closely resembled the Catholic Church it had replaced.

This middle way satisfied most, but not all, of Elizabeth's subjects. Steadfast Catholics could not accept it. Some left England; the rest practiced their faith in private. At the other extreme, more radical Protestants, including a large percentage of England's university-trained clergy, insisted that Elizabeth had not gone far enough. The Anglican Church was still too much like the Church of Rome, they claimed. They objected to the richly decorated vestments worn by the clergy and to the use of candles, incense, and music in church services. They insisted that emphasis should be put on reading the Bible and analyzing the meaning of the Scriptures in order to encourage ordinary worshipers to truly understand their faith. Since they wanted to "purify" Anglicanism, these critics were called puritans. At first the name was a pejorative assigned to them by their opponents, but later it became a badge of honor.

Puritans objected to the way Elizabeth's bishops interpreted the Protestant doctrine of predestination. Their reading of the Book of Genesis convinced them

that all human beings were properly damned by Adam's original sin and that what one did on earth had no effect on a person's fate after death. To believe otherwise was to limit God's power, which was precisely what the Catholic Church did in stressing its ability to forgive sins by granting indulgences. The Anglicans implied that while God had already decided whether or not a person was saved, an individual's efforts to lead a good life could somehow cause God to change His mind. The Anglican clergy did not come right out and say that good works could win a person admission to Heaven—that heresy was called Arminianism. But they encouraged people to hope that good works were something more than ends in themselves. Puritans differed as to whether or not the ideal church should have any structure beyond the local congregation. Some—later called Congregationalists—favored a completely decentralized arrangement, with the members of each church and their chosen minister beholden only to one another. Others, called Presbyterians, favored some organization above the local level, but one controlled by elected laymen, not by the clergy.

Puritans were also of two minds as to whether reform could be accomplished within the Anglican Church. During Elizabeth's reign most hoped that it could. Whatever they did in their local churches, the puritans remained professed Anglicans. After James I succeeded Elizabeth I in 1603, however, their fears that the royal court might be backsliding into its old "popish" ways mounted. James was married to a Catholic, and the fact that he favored toleration for Catholics gave further substance to the rumor that he was himself a secret member of that church. This rumor proved to be false, but in his 22-year reign (1603–1625) James did little to advance the Protestant cause. His one contribution—which had a significance far beyond what he or anyone else anticipated—was to authorize a new translation of the Bible. The King James Version (1611) was both a monumental scholarly achievement and a literary masterpiece of the first order.

BRADFORD AND PLYMOUTH COLONY

Plymouth Colony

In 1606, worried about the future of their faith, members of the church in Scrooby, Nottinghamshire, "separated" from the Anglican Church, declaring it corrupt beyond salvage. In seventeenth-century England, Separatists had to go either underground or into exile. Since only the latter would permit them to practice

▲ The story of the first 30 years of pilgrim life in Plymouth, Massachusetts, is preserved in Governor William Bradford's *Of Plymouth Plantation*. A glimpse of the first colony is shown in this reconstruction.

their religious faith openly, exile it was. In 1608 some 125 of the group departed England for the Low Countries. They were led by their pastor, John Robinson; church elder William Brewster; and a 16-year-old youth, William Bradford. After a brief stay in Amsterdam, the group settled in the town of Leyden. In 1619, however, disheartened by the difficulties they had encountered in making a living, disappointed by the failure of others in England to join them, and distressed because their children were being "subjected to the great licentiousness of the youth" in Holland, these "Pilgrims" decided to move again—to seek "a place where they might have liberty and live comfortably."

Negotiations between the Pilgrims in Leyden and Sir Edwin Sandys of the Virginia Company raised the possibility of America. Although unsympathetic to their religious views, Sandys appreciated the Pilgrims' inherent worth and supported their request to establish a settlement near the mouth of the Hudson River, on the northern boundary of the Virginia Company's grant. Since the Pilgrims were short of money, they formed a joint-stock company with other prospective emigrants and some optimistic investors who agreed to pay the expenses of the group in return for half the profits of the venture. In September 1620, about 100 strong—only 35 of them Pilgrims from Leyden—they set out from Plymouth, England, on the *Mayflower*.

▶ *text continues on page 36*

American Lives

Tisquantum

In March 1621 Samoset, an Algonquian Indian who spoke broken English, introduced the Pilgrims to a friend named Tisquantum, a member of the Patuxet tribe, which inhabited the area around Plymouth. He explained that Tisquantum "had been in England and could speak better English than himself." For this reason, the Pilgrims were delighted to make his acquaintance.

Tisquantum, whose name the Pilgrims soon shortened to Squanto, had up to this point lived a life that had been unusual to say the least. In 1605 George Waymouth, an English captain in the employ of Sir Ferdinando Gorges, an official of the Plymouth Company, brought Tisquantum and four other Indians from a region now part of Maine to Bristol, England, where he "delivered" Tisquantum and two of the others to Gorges. Gorges, who was eager to learn all he could about the New World, took Tisquantum "into his own house." In time all three of the Indians "acquired a sufficient command of the English tongue to communicate to him a knowledge of their country."

How long Tisquantum remained in Sir Ferdinando's household is unclear, but in 1614 when Gorges sent two ships commanded by Captain John Smith to New England to prepare to found a colony, Tisquantum went along as interpreter. However, after Smith returned to England, his second in command, Captain Thomas Hunt, kidnapped Tisquantum and a number of other Indians, took them to Malaga, Spain, and sold them as slaves.

Nothing is known of Tisquantum's life in Malaga except that after several years he escaped aboard a vessel sailing, perhaps by way of Newfoundland, for England. (It seems likely that because he could speak English, Tisquantum attracted the sympathy of one or more English sailors, who agreed to take him aboard when they left

▲ Tisquantum

Malaga.) In London he was befriended by John Slany, the treasurer of the Newfoundland Company. Thereafter he made two trips to New England as a pilot, one in 1618 to an English settlement in Newfoundland, the other in 1619 to New England as a pilot on a vessel commanded by Captain Thomas Dermer. He left Dermer's ship somewhere on Cape Cod and made his way to Patuxet, only to discover that the Patuxet had been wiped out by a plague.

Tisquantum's first service to the Pilgrims was to act as interpreter at a dramatic meeting of the Pilgrim leaders with the most powerful chief of the region, the Wampanoag sachem, Massasoit. At this conference, after an elaborate exchange of gifts and speeches, a treaty of peace and mutual defense was negotiated. Tisquantum's services as interpreter were of inestimable value in reaching this agreement.

Thereafter, as Governor William Bradford explained in a famous passage in his history *Of Plymouth Plantation,* his value to the Pilgrims increased enormously. "Squanto," Bradford wrote, "was a special instrument sent of God for their good beyond their expectation. He directed them how to set their corn [and] where to take fish" to be used to fertilize the crop, a practice he almost certainly learned from English settlers in Newfoundland, since the Wampanoag were unfamiliar with the practice. "Squanto," Bradford added, "was also their pilot to bring them to unknown places for their profit, and never left them till he died."

That event occurred in November 1622, when Tisquantum contracted a fever while on a trading expedition with the Pilgrims on Cape Cod. According to Governor Bradford, his dying words were a request that Bradford "pray for him that he might go to the Englishmen's God in Heaven."

▲ The "deer" on the left side of the stream carry bows and arrows: the English engraver was impressed by the Indians' ability to disguise themselves as their prey. The acquisition of such skills helped the English survive in an unfamiliar environment. Europeans and colonists learned about the "new world" by reading pamphlets and books—such as the one in which this engraving appeared. Indians learned about the newcomers only from what they saw or heard by word of mouth. This left the Indians at a disadvantage.

Tisquantum's life in the brief months between his meeting the Pilgrims and his death was not, however, the idyll this passage suggests. Rather it illustrates an ambivalence common when the two cultures, European and Indian, coexist in the same person. As the historian James Phinney Baxter put it, Tisquantum's "mind has been enlarged beyond his fellows by contact with European civilization and a knowledge of the great world." This, in effect, made him an alien in both camps. At times he exaggerated his influence on the Pilgrims in an effort to "aggrandize himself in the estimation of the Indians." Bradford admitted that "Squanto . . . played his own game by putting the Indians in fear and drawing gifts from them to enrich himself."

Such behavior naturally caused the Indians to resent him. At one point Massasoit, citing terms of the treaty, demanded that the Pilgrims turn Tisquantum over to him for "punishment," clearly a euphemism for execution. Bradford

was able to avoid doing so, but the incident compelled Tisquantum "to stick close to the English," and goes a long way to explain why, in Bradford's above-quoted words, he "never left them till he died."

For their part the Pilgrims were sincerely thankful for the many services their "Squanto" provided. When the powerful Narragansett chief Corbitant was reported to have killed him, the Pilgrims sent 15 armed men to "cut off Corbitant's head," if the rumor proved true. (Fortunately it did not.) But the Pilgrims treated neither Tisquantum nor any other Indian as an equal. Despite their generally harmonious relations with the Wampanoag, they routinely referred to them as "savages." After his moving description of Squanto's death in his history, Bradford continued his account of the trading expedition with a routine summary of the goods collected—"about 26 or 28 hogs-heads of corn and beans. . . ."

Had the *Mayflower* reached the passengers' intended destination, the Pilgrims might have been soon forgotten. Instead their ship touched America slightly to the north, on Cape Cod Bay. Unwilling to remain longer at the mercy of storm-tossed December seas, they decided to settle where they were. Since they were outside the jurisdiction of the London Company, some members of the group claimed to be free of all governmental control. Therefore, before going ashore, the Pilgrims drew up the Mayflower Compact. "We whose names are underwritten," the Compact ran, "do by these Presents, solemnly and mutually in the presence of God and one another covenant and combine ourselves under into a civil Body Politick . . . and by Virtue hereof do enact . . . such just and equal laws . . . as shall be thought most meet and convenient for the general Good of the Colony."

Thus early in American history the idea was advanced that a society should be based on a set of rules chosen by its members, an idea carried further in the Declaration of Independence. The Pilgrims chose William Bradford as their first governor. In this simple manner, ordinary people created a government that they hoped would enable them to cope with the unknown wilderness confronting them.

DOCUMENT

Bradford, from *History of Plymouth Plantation*

The story of the first 30 years of the Pilgrims' colony has been preserved in *Of Plymouth Plantation,* written by Bradford. Having landed on the bleak Massachusetts shore in December 1620 at a place they called Plymouth, the Pilgrims had to endure a winter of desperate hunger. About half of them died. But by great good luck there was an Indian in the area, named Squanto, who spoke English! In addition to serving as an interpreter, he showed them the best places to fish and what to plant and how to cultivate it. They, in turn, worked hard, got their crops in the ground in good time, and after a bountiful harvest the following November, they treated themselves and their Indian neighbors to the first Thanksgiving feast.

But if the Pilgrims had quickly secured themselves a safe place in the wilderness, what followed was hardly all cranberries and drumsticks. Bradford's flock grew neither rich nor numerous on the thin New England soil. In 1650 there were still fewer than a thousand settlers, most of them living beyond the reach of the original church. Among these were a few who tried to take advantage of the freedom from social control afforded by the wilderness. In 1628 a group led by one Thomas Morton, "Lord of Misrule" of the outlying community of Mount Wollaston, which he renamed Merrymount, declared their liberation from all restraints by setting up a maypole. They then invited neighboring

Indian women to join them, provided drinks all round, and began (as the disapproving Bradford described the doings) "dancing and frisking together like so many fairies." Troops were dispatched to break up the carousing and take Morton into custody, after which he was packed off to England.

Morton was not a Pilgrim, and his antics do not jeopardize the Pilgrims' place in American history. That place is one of honor. Theirs were victories won not with sword and gunpowder like those of Cortés or with bulldozer and dynamite like those of modern pioneers, but with simple courage and practical piety.

WINTHROP AND MASSACHUSETTS BAY COLONY

The Pilgrims were not the first English colonists to inhabit the northern regions. The Plymouth Company had settled a group on the Kennebec River in 1607. These colonists gave up after a few months, but fishermen and traders continued to visit the area, which was christened New England by Captain John Smith after an expedition there in 1614.

In 1620 the Plymouth Company was reorganized as the Council for New England, which had among its principal stockholders Sir Ferdinando Gorges and his friend John Mason, former governor of an English settlement on Newfoundland. Their particular domain included a considerable part of what is now Maine and New Hampshire. More interested in real estate deals than in colonizing, the council disposed of a number of tracts in the area north of Cape Cod. The most significant of these grants was a small one made to a group of puritans from Dorchester, who established a settlement at Salem in 1629.

Later that year these Dorchester puritans organized the Massachusetts Bay Company and obtained a royal grant to the area between the Charles and Merrimack rivers. The Massachusetts Bay Company was organized like any other commercial venture, but the puritans, acting with single-minded determination, made it a way of obtaining religious refuge in America.

Unlike the Separatists in Plymouth, most puritans had managed to satisfy both Crown and conscience while James I was king. The England of his son Charles I, who succeeded to the throne in 1625, posed a more serious challenge. Whereas James had been content to keep puritans at bay, Charles and his favorite Anglican cleric, William Laud, intended to bring them to heel. With the king's support, Laud proceeded to embellish the already elaborate Anglican ritual and to tighten the central control that the

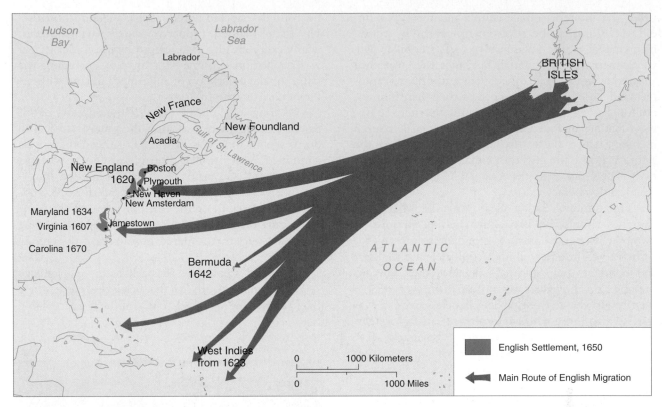

▲ **The Great English Migration**

puritans found so distasteful. He removed ministers with puritan leanings from their pulpits and threatened church elders who harbored such ministers with imprisonment.

No longer able to remain within the Anglican fold in good conscience and now facing prison if they tried to worship in the way they believed right, many puritans decided to migrate to America. In the summer of 1630 nearly a thousand of them set out from England, carrying the charter of the Massachusetts Bay Company with them. By fall, they had founded Boston and several other towns. The puritan commonwealth was under way.

Massachusetts settlers suffered fewer hardships in the early years than had the early Jamestown and Plymouth colonists. Luck played a part in this, but so did the careful planning that went into the transplantation. They also benefited from a constant influx of new recruits, who came with families and worldly possessions in tow. Continuing bad times and the persecution of puritans at home led to the Great Migration of the 1630s. Only a minority came to Massachusetts (many thousands more poured into new English colonies in the West Indies), but by 1640 well over 10,000 had arrived. This concentrated group of industrious, well-educated, and fairly prosperous colonists swiftly created a complex and distinct culture on the edge of what one of the pessimists among them called "a hideous and desolate wilderness, full of wild beasts and wild men."

The directors of the Massachusetts Bay Company believed their enterprise to be divinely inspired. Before leaving England, they elected John Winthrop, a 29-year-old Oxford-trained attorney, as governor of the colony. Throughout his 20 years of almost continuous service as governor, Winthrop spoke for the solid and sensible core of the puritans and their high-minded experiment. His lay sermon, "A Modelle of Christian Charity," delivered in mid-Atlantic on the deck of the *Arbella* in 1630, made clear his sense of the momentousness of that experiment:

DOCUMENT

Winthrop, "A Model of Christian Charity"

> Wee must Consider that wee shall be as a Citty upon a Hill, the eies of all people are upon us; soe that if wee shall deale falsely with our god in this worke wee have undertaken and soe cause him to withdrawe his present help from us, wee shall be made a story and a by-word through the world, wee shall open the mouthes of enemies to speake evill of the wayes of god and all professours for Gods sake.

The colonists created an elected legislature, the General Court. Their system was not democratic in the modern sense because the right to vote and hold

office was limited to male church members, but this did not mean that the government was run by clergymen or that it was not sensitive to the popular will. Clergymen were influential, but since they were not allowed to hold public office, their authority was indirect and based on the respect of their parishioners, not on law or force. At least until the mid-1640s, most families included at least one adult male church member. Since these "freemen" soon secured the right to choose the governor and elect the representatives ("deputies") to the General Court, a kind of practical democracy existed.

The puritans had a clear sense of what their churches should be like. After getting permission from the General Court, a group of colonists who wished to form a new church could select a minister and conduct their spiritual affairs as they saw fit. Membership, however, was not open to everyone or even to all who led outwardly blameless lives. It was restricted to those who could present satisfactory evidence of their having experienced "saving grace," such as by a compelling recounting of some extraordinary emotional experience, some mystical sign of intimate contact with God. This meant that full membership in the churches of early Massachusetts was reserved for "visible saints." During the 1630s, however, few applicants were denied membership. Having removed oneself from England was considered in most cases sufficient proof of spiritual purity.

TROUBLEMAKERS: ROGER WILLIAMS AND ANNE HUTCHINSON

As Winthrop had on more than one occasion to lament, most of the colony's early troublemakers came not from those of doubtful spiritual condition but from its certified saints. The "godly and zealous" Roger Williams was a prime example. The Pilgrim leader William Bradford described Williams as possessed of "many precious parts, but very unsettled in judgment." Even by Plymouth's standards Williams was an extreme separatist. He was ready to bring down the wrath of Charles I on New England rather than accept the charters signed by him or his father, even if these documents provided the only legal basis for the governments of Plymouth and Massachusetts Bay.

Williams had arrived in Massachusetts in 1631. Following a short stay in Plymouth, he joined the church in Salem, which elected him minister in 1635. Well before then, however, his opposition to the alliance of church and civil government turned both ministers and magistrates against him. Part of his contrariness stemmed from his religious libertarianism. Magistrates should have no voice in spiritual matters,

he insisted—"forced religion stinks in God's nostrils." He also offended property owners (which meant nearly everyone) by advancing the radical idea that it was "a Nationale sinne" for anyone, including the king, to take possession of any American land without buying it from the Indians.

As long as Williams enjoyed the support of his Salem church, there was little the magistrates could do to silence him. But his refusal to heed those who counseled moderation—"all truths are not seasonable at all times," Governor Winthrop reminded him—swiftly eroded that support. In the fall of 1635, economic pressure put on the town of Salem by the General Court turned his congregation against him. The General Court then ordered him to leave the colony within six weeks.

Williams departed Massachusetts in January 1636, traveling south to the head of Narragansett Bay. There he worked out mutually acceptable

▲ On this headstone in a puritan graveyard in Salem, Massachusetts, two images preach a sermon. On top is an hourglass lying on its side: for the deceased, the "clock" of mortal existence has stopped. Below is a "death's head" atop wings to carry the soul to heaven. But every puritan who walked past this gravestone doubtless wondered whether God had indeed selected the deceased to be among His Saints.

arrangements with the local Indians and founded the town of Providence. In 1644, after obtaining a charter in England from Parliament, he established the colony of Rhode Island and Providence Plantations. The government was relatively democratic, all religions were tolerated, and church and state were rigidly separated. Whatever Williams's temperamental excesses, he was more than ready to practice what he preached when given the opportunity.

Anne Hutchinson, who arrived in Boston in 1631, was another "visible saint" who, in the judgment of the puritan establishment, went too far. Hutchinson was not to be taken lightly. According to Governor Winthrop, her husband William was "a man of mild temper and weak parts, wholly guided by his wife." (He was not so weak as to be unable to father Anne's 15 children.) Duties as a midwife brought her into the homes of other Boston women, with whom she discussed and more than occasionally criticized the sermons of their minister, John Wilson.

The issue in dispute was whether God's saints could be confident of having truly received His gift of eternal life. Wilson and most of the ministers of the colony thought not. God's saints should ceaselessly monitor their thoughts and behavior. But Hutchinson thought this emphasis on behavior was similar to the Catholic belief that an individual's good deeds and penitence could bring God's salvation. Ministers should not demean God, Hutchinson declared, by suggesting that He would be impressed by human actions. She insisted that God's saints knew who they were; those presumed "saints" who had doubts on the matter were likely destined for eternal hell instead.

Hutchinson suggested that those possessed of God's grace were exempt from the rules of good behavior and even from the laws of the commonwealth. As her detractors pointed out, this was the conclusion some of the earliest German Protestants had reached, for which they were judged guilty of the heresy of antinomianism ("against the law") and burned at the stake.

In 1636 the General Court charged Hutchinson with defaming the clergy and brought her to trial. When her accusers quoted the Bible ("Honor thy father and thy mother") to make their case, she coolly announced that even the Ten Commandments must yield to one's own insights if these were directly inspired by God. When pressed for details, she acknowledged that she was a regular recipient of divine insights, communicated, as they were to Abraham, "by the voice of His own spirit in my soul." The General Court, on hearing this claim, banished her.

Hutchinson, together with her large family and a group of supporters, left Massachusetts in the spring of 1637 for Rhode Island, thereby adding to the reputation of that colony as the "sink" of New England.

After her husband died in 1642, she and six of her children moved to the Dutch colony of New Netherland, where, the following year, she and all but her youngest daughter were killed by Indians.

The banishment of dissenters like Roger Williams and Anne Hutchinson did not endear the Massachusetts puritans to posterity. In both cases outspoken individualists seem to have been done in by frightened politicians and self-serving ministers. Yet Williams and Hutchinson posed genuine threats to the puritan community. Massachusetts was truly a social experiment. Could it accommodate such uncooperative spirits and remain intact? When forced to choose between the peace of the commonwealth and sending dissenters packing, Winthrop, the magistrates, and the ministers did not hesitate.

OTHER NEW ENGLAND COLONIES

From the successful Massachusetts Bay Colony, settlement radiated outward to other areas of New England, propelled by an expanding population and puritan intolerance. In 1629 Sir Ferdinando Gorges and John Mason divided their holdings, Gorges taking the Maine section (enlarged in 1639) and Mason, New Hampshire, but neither succeeded in making much of his claim. Massachusetts gradually took over these areas. The heirs of Gorges and Mason managed to regain legal possession briefly in the 1670s, but Massachusetts bought title to Maine for a pittance (£1250) in 1677. New Hampshire became a royal colony in 1680.

Meanwhile, beginning in 1635, a number of Massachusetts congregations had pushed southwestward into the fertile valley of the Connecticut River. A group headed by the Reverend Thomas Hooker founded Hartford in 1636. Hooker was influential in the drafting of the Fundamental Orders, a sort of constitution creating a government for the valley towns, in 1639. The Fundamental Orders resembled the Massachusetts system, except that they did not limit voting to church members. Other groups of puritans came directly from England to settle towns in and around New Haven in the 1630s. These were incorporated into Connecticut shortly after the Hooker colony obtained a royal charter in 1662.

FRENCH AND DUTCH SETTLEMENTS

While the English were settling Virginia and New England, other Europeans were challenging Spain's monopoly in the New World. French explorers had pushed up the St. Lawrence as far as the site of Montréal in the 1530s, and beginning in 1603, Samuel de

Champlain made several voyages to the region. In 1608 he founded Québec, and he had penetrated as far inland as Lake Huron before the Pilgrims left Leyden. The French also planted colonies in St. Christopher, Guadeloupe, Martinique, and other islands in the West Indies after 1625.

Through their West India Company, the Dutch also established themselves in the West Indies. On the mainland they founded New Netherland in the Hudson Valley, basing their claim to the region on the explorations of Henry Hudson in 1609. As early as 1624 they established an outpost, Fort Orange, on the site of present-day Albany. Two years later they founded New Amsterdam at the mouth of the Hudson River, and Peter Minuit, the director general of the West India Company, purchased Manhattan Island from the Indians for trading goods worth about 60 guilders.

The Dutch traded with the Indians for furs and plundered Spanish colonial commerce enthusiastically. Through the Charter of Privileges of Patroons, which authorized large grants of land to individuals who would bring over 50 settlers, they tried to encourage large-scale agriculture. Only one such estate—Rensselaerswyck, on the Hudson south of Fort Orange, owned by the rich Amsterdam merchant Kiliaen Van Rensselaer—was successful. Peter Minuit was removed from his post in New Amsterdam in 1631, but he organized a group of Swedish settlers several years later and founded the colony of New Sweden on the lower reaches of the Delaware River. New Sweden was in constant conflict with the Dutch, who finally overran it in 1655.

MARYLAND AND THE CAROLINAS

The Virginia and New England colonies were essentially corporate ventures. Most of the other English colonies in America were founded by individuals or by a handful of partners who obtained charters from the ruling sovereign. It was becoming easier to establish settlements in America, for experience had taught the English a great deal about the colonization process. Settlers knew better what to bring with them and what to do after they arrived. Moreover, the psychological barrier was much less formidable. Like a modern athlete seeking to run a mile in less than four minutes, colonizers knew after about 1630 that what they were attempting could be accomplished. And conditions in Europe in the mid-seventeenth century encouraged thousands to migrate. Both in England and on the Continent the economic future seemed unpromising, while political and religious persecution erupted in one country after another, each time supplying America with new waves of refugees.

▲ In this 1670 illustration by the court painter for King Charles II, young Cecilius Calvert receives a map of Maryland from his grandfather, the second Lord Baltimore. The king's charter for Maryland provided that Cecilius's father and his heirs (first, Cecilius) were to hold the province as "true and absolute lords." The notion was as preposterous as Cecilius's aristocratic clothing. Cecilius died in 1682, before he could even attempt to rule Maryland like a feudal lord.

Numbers of influential Englishmen were eager to try their luck as colonizers. The grants they received made them "proprietors" of great estates, which were, at least in theory, their personal property. By granting land to settlers in return for a small annual rent, they hoped to obtain a steadily increasing income while holding a valuable speculative interest in all undeveloped land. At the same time, their political power, guaranteed by charter, would become increasingly important as their colonies expanded. In practice, however, the realities of life in America limited their freedom of action and their profits.

One of the first proprietary colonies was Maryland, granted by Charles I to George Calvert, Lord Baltimore. Calvert had a deep interest in America, being a member both of the London Company and of the Council for New England. He hoped to profit

financially from Maryland, but, since he was a Catholic, he also intended the colony to be a haven for his co-religionists.

Calvert died shortly before Charles approved his charter, so the grant went to his son Cecilius. The first settlers arrived in 1634, founding St. Mary's, just north of the Potomac. The presence of the now well-established Virginia colony nearby greatly aided the Marylanders; they had little difficulty in getting started and in developing an economy based, like Virginia's, on tobacco. According to the Maryland charter, Lord Baltimore had the right to establish feudal manors, hold people in serfdom, make laws, and set up his own courts. He soon discovered, however, that to attract settlers he had to allow them to own their farms and that to maintain any political influence at all he had to give the settlers considerable say in local affairs. Other wise concessions marked his handling of the religious question. He would have preferred an exclusively Catholic colony, but while Catholics did go to Maryland, there existed from the beginning a large Protestant majority. Baltimore dealt with this problem by agreeing to a Toleration Act (1649) that guaranteed freedom of religion to anyone "professing to believe in Jesus Christ." Though religious disputes persisted, the Calvert's compromise enabled them to make a fortune and maintain an influence in Maryland until the Revolution.

The Carolina charter, like that of Maryland, accorded the proprietors wide authority. With the help of the political philosopher John Locke, they drafted a grandiose plan of government called the Fundamental Constitutions, which created a hereditary nobility and provided for huge paper land grants to a hierarchy headed by the proprietors and lesser "landgraves" and "caciques." The human effort to support the feudal society was to be supplied by peasants (what the Fundamental Constitutions called "leet-men").

This complicated system proved unworkable. The landgraves and caciques got grants, but they could not find leet-men willing to toil on their domains. Probably the purpose of all this elaborate feudal nonsense was promotional; the proprietor hoped to convince investors that they could make fortunes in Carolina rivaling those of English lords. Life followed a more mundane pattern similar to what was going on in Virginia and Maryland, with property relatively easy to obtain.

The first settlers arrived in 1670, most of them from the sugar plantations of Barbados, where slave labor was driving out small independent farmers. Charles Town (now Charleston) was founded in 1680. Another center of population sprang up in the Albemarle district, just south of Virginia, settled largely by individuals from that colony. Two quite different societies grew up in these areas. The Charleston

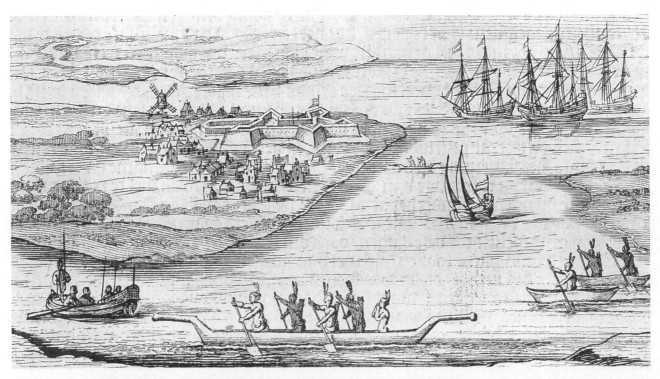

▲ This 1651 engraving, the first known view of Manhattan Island, shows the fort of New Amsterdam in the 1620s. Indians bring beaver pelts in their canoes to trade with the Dutch.

▲ Historian James Merrell notes several errors in Benjamin West's famous 1771 painting, *William Penn's Treaty with the Indians.* In 1682, when the treaty was negotiated, Penn was not yet so fat; the colonists' clothing and brick buildings resemble a scene in Philadelphia in the 1750s, not the 1680s; and the Indians are implausibly posed like Greek and Roman statues. Most important, the painting includes no translator, the one indispensable figure in the proceedings. All Indian and settler exchanges required "go-betweens" or "negotiators" to help each group explain itself to the other.

colony, with an economy based on a thriving trade in furs and on the export of foodstuffs to the West Indies, was prosperous and cosmopolitan. The Albemarle settlement, where the soil was less fertile, was poorer and more primitive. Eventually, in 1712, the two were formally separated, becoming North and South Carolina.

THE MIDDLE COLONIES

Gradually it became clear that the English would dominate the entire coast between the St. Lawrence Valley and Florida. After 1660 only the Dutch challenged their monopoly. The two nations, once allies against Spain, had fallen out because of the fierce competition of their textile manufacturers and merchants.

England's efforts to bar Dutch merchant vessels from its colonial trade also brought the two countries into conflict in America. Charles II precipitated a showdown by granting his brother James, Duke of York, the entire area between Connecticut and Maryland. This was tantamount to declaring war. In 1664 English forces captured New Amsterdam without a fight—there were only 1500 people in the town—and soon the rest of the Dutch settlements capitulated. New Amsterdam became New York. The duke did not interfere much with the way of life of the Dutch settlers, and they were quickly reconciled to English rule. New York had no local assembly until the 1680s, but there had been no such body under the Dutch either.

In 1664, even before the capture of New Amsterdam, the Duke of York gave New Jersey, the region between the Hudson and the Delaware, to John,

Lord Berkeley, and Sir George Carteret. To attract settlers, these proprietors offered land on easy terms and established freedom of religion and a democratic system of local government. A considerable number of puritans from New England and Long Island moved to the new province.

In 1674 Berkeley sold his interest in New Jersey to two Quakers. Quakers believed that they could communicate directly with their Maker; their religion required neither ritual nor ministers. Originally a sect emotional to the point of fanaticism, by the 1670s the Quakers had come to stress the doctrine of the Inner Light—the direct, mystical experience of religious truth—which they believed possible for all persons. They were at once humble and fiercely proud, pacifistic yet unwilling to bow before any person or to surrender their right to worship as they pleased. They distrusted the intellect in religious matters and, while ardent proselytizers of their own beliefs, they tolerated those of others cheerfully. When faced with opposition, they resorted to passive resistance, a tactic that embroiled them in grave difficulties in England and in most of the American colonies. In Massachusetts Bay, for example, four Quakers were executed when they refused either to conform to puritan ideas or to leave the colony.

The acquisition of New Jersey gave the Quakers a place where they could practice their religion in peace. The proprietors, in keeping with their principles, drafted an extremely liberal constitution for the colony, the Concessions and Agreements of 1677, which created an autonomous legislature and guaranteed settlers freedom of conscience, the right of trial by jury, and other civil rights.

The main Quaker effort at colonization came in the region immediately west of New Jersey, a fertile area belonging to William Penn, the son of a wealthy English admiral. Penn had early rejected a life of ease and had become a Quaker missionary. As a result, he was twice jailed. Yet he possessed qualities that enabled him to hold the respect and friendship of people who found his religious ideas abhorrent. From his father, Penn had inherited a claim to £16,000 that the admiral had lent Charles II. The king, reluctant to part with that much cash, paid off the debt in 1681 by giving Penn the region north of Maryland and west of the Delaware River, insisting only that it be named Pennsylvania, in honor of the admiral. In 1682 Penn founded Philadelphia. The Duke of York then added Delaware, the region between Maryland and the Delaware Bay, to Penn's holdings.

William Penn considered his colony a "Holy Experiment." He treated the Indians fairly, buying title to their lands and trying to protect them in their dealings with settlers and traders. Anyone who believed in "one Almighty and Eternal God" was entitled to freedom of worship. Penn's political ideas were paternalistic rather than democratic; the assembly he established could only approve or reject laws proposed by the governor and council. But individual rights were as well protected in Pennsylvania as in New Jersey.

Penn's altruism, however, did not prevent him from taking excellent care of his own interests. He sold both large and small tracts of land to settlers on easy terms but reserved huge tracts for himself. He promoted Pennsylvania tirelessly, writing glowing, although perfectly honest, descriptions of the colony, which were circulated widely in England and, in translation, in Europe. These attracted many settlers, including large numbers of Germans—the Pennsylvania "Dutch" (a corruption of *Deutsch,* meaning "German").

William Penn was neither a doctrinaire nor an ivory tower philosopher. He came to Pennsylvania himself when trouble developed between settlers and his representatives and agreed to adjustments in his first Frame of Government when he realized that local conditions demonstrated the need for change. His combination of toughness, liberality, and good salesmanship helped the colony to prosper and grow rapidly. Of course the presence of well-settled colonies on all sides and the richness of the soil had much to do with this happy state of affairs. By 1685 there were almost 9000 settlers in Pennsylvania, and by 1700 twice that number, a heartening contrast to the early history of Virginia and Plymouth. Pennsylvania produced wheat, corn, rye, and other crops in abundance and found a ready market for its surpluses on the sugar plantations of the West Indies.

INDIANS AND EUROPEANS AS "AMERICANIZERS"

Increase Mather, a puritan leader, worried that "Christians in this Land have become too like unto the Indians." Little wonder, he observed, that God had "afflicted us by them" through disease and other trials. Yet Mather's comments suggested that interaction between European settlers and the native peoples was characteristic of life in all the colonies. *Interaction* is the key word in this sentence. The so-called Columbian Exchange between Indian and European was a two-way street. The colonists learned a great deal about how to live in the American forest from the Indians: the names of plants and animals (hickory, pecan, raccoon, skunk, moose); what to eat in their new home and how to catch or grow it; what to wear (leather leggings and especially moccasins);

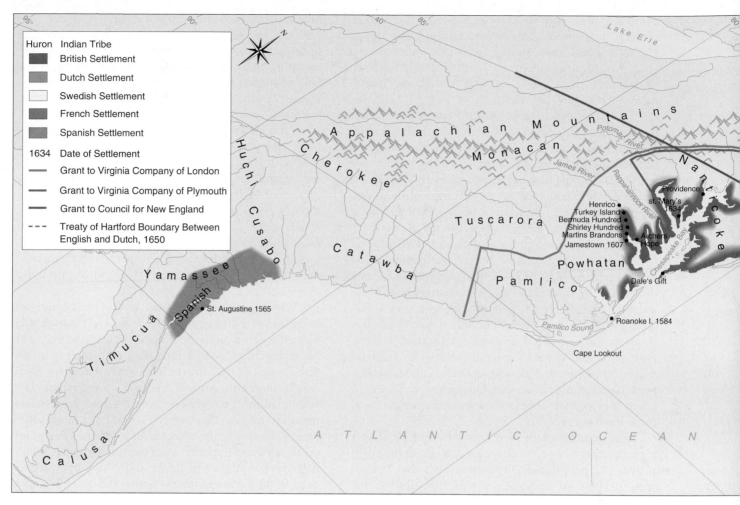

▲ European Footholds Along the Atlantic, 1584–1650

how best to get from one place to another; how to fight; and in some respects how to think.

The colonists learned from the Indians how best to use many plants and animals for food and clothing, but they would probably have discovered most of these if the continent had been devoid of human life when they arrived. Corn, however, the staple of the diet of agricultural tribes, was something the Indians had domesticated. Its contribution to the success of English colonization was enormous.

The colonists also took advantage of that marvel of Indian technology, the birchbark canoe. An early explorer, Martin Pring, brought one back to England in 1603; it was 17 feet long and 4 feet wide and capable, according to Pring, of carrying nine full-grown men. Yet it weighed "not at the most above sixtie pounds," a thing, Pring added, "almost incredible in regard to the largenesse and capacitie thereof."

For their part, the Indians adopted European technology eagerly. All metal objects were indeed of great usefulness to them, although the products and

tools that metals replaced were neither crude nor inefficient in most cases. (A bowman could get off six times as many shots in a given time as a seventeenth-century soldier armed with a firelock, and would probably hit the target more frequently.)

Indians took on many of the Europeans' attitudes along with their tools, clothing, weapons, alcohol, and ornaments. Some tribes used the products of European technology to tyrannize tribes in more remote areas. During wars, Indians fought almost as often with European settlers against other Indians as with other Indians against settlers.

The fur trade illustrates the pervasiveness of Indian-European interaction. It was in some ways a perfect business arrangement. Both groups profited greatly. The colonists got "valuable" furs for "cheap" European products, while the Indians got "priceless" tools, knives, and other trade goods in exchange for "cheap" beaver pelts and deerskins. The demand for furs caused the Indians to become more efficient hunters and trappers and even to

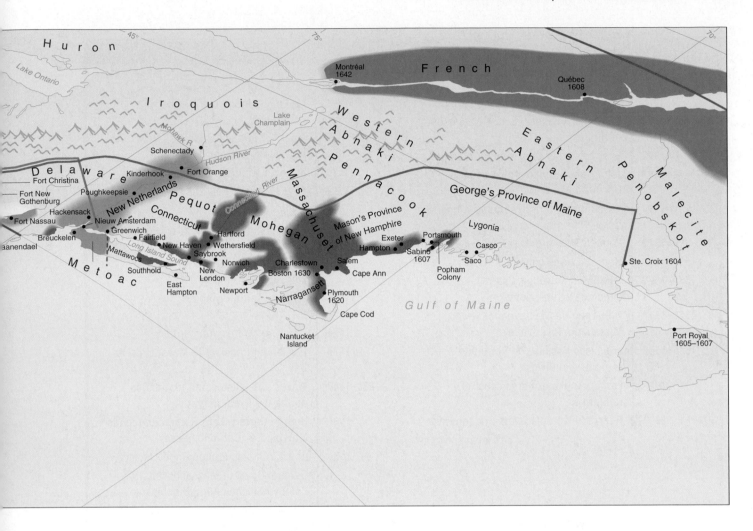

absorb some of the settlers' ideas about private property and capitalist accumulation. Hunting parties became larger. Farming tribes shifted their villages in order to be nearer trade routes and waterways. In some cases tribal organization was altered: small groups combined into confederations in order to control more territory when their hunting reduced the supplies of furs nearer home. Early in the seventeenth century, Huron Indians in the Great Lakes region, who had probably never seen a Frenchman, owned French products obtained from eastern tribes in exchange for Huron corn.

Although the colonists learned much from the Indians and adopted certain elements of Indian culture and technology eagerly, their objective was not to be like the Indians, whom they considered the epitome of savagery and barbarism. That they feared they might become "Indianized" is clear from the adage "It is very easy to make an Indian out of a white man, but you cannot make a white man out of an Indian." Yet this repudiation of the Indians was part of the

collective identity of the settlers, part of what made them Americans rather than transplanted Europeans. The constant conflicts with Indians forced the colonists to band together and in time gave them a sense of having shared a common history. And later, when they broke away from Great Britain, they used the image of the Indian to symbolize the freedom and independence they sought for themselves.

In sum, during the first 200-odd years that followed Columbus's first landfall in the Caribbean, a complex development had taken place in the Americas. Sometimes these alien encounters were amiable, as Indians and colonists exchanged ideas, skills, and goods; sometimes the encounters were hostile and bloody, with unimaginable cruelties inflicted by and on both sides. But mostly the coming together of Indians and European settlers was characterized by ambiguity and confusion, as markedly different peoples drew from their own traditions to make sense of a new world that little resembled what they knew. In time, their world would become our own.

MILESTONES

EXPLORATION	
c. 1000	Leif Eriksson reaches Newfoundland
1445–1488	Portuguese sailors explore west coast of Africa
1492	First voyage of Christopher Columbus
1497	John Cabot explores east coast of North America
1498	Vasco da Gama sails around Africa to India
1513	Ponce de Leon explores Florida
1519–1521	Hernán Cortes conquers Mexico
1519–1522	Ferdinand Magellan's crew circumnavigates globe
1539–1542	Hernando de Soto explores lower Mississippi River Valley
1540–1542	Francisco Vasquez de Coronado explores Southwest
1579	Francis Drake explores coast of California
1609	Henry Hudson discovers Hudson River

SETTLEMENT	
1493	Columbus founds La Navidad, Hispaniola
1494	Treaty of Tordesillas divides New World between Spain and Portugal
1576	Spanish settle St. Augustine
1587	English found "Lost Colony" of Roanoke Island
1607	English settle Jamestown
1608	French found Québec
1612	John Rolfe introduces tobacco cultivation in Virginia
1620	Pilgrims settle Plymouth, sign Mayflower Compact
1624	Dutch settle New Amsterdam
1630	English puritans settle Massachusetts Bay
1630–1640	Waves of English come to America during the Great Migration
1634	George Calvert, Lord Baltimore, founds Maryland as Catholic haven
1636	Roger Williams founds Rhode Island
	General Court of Massachusetts Bay Colony banishes Anne Hutchinson
1639	Thomas Hooker founds Connecticut
1642	French found Montréal
1664	English conquer Dutch New Amsterdam
1670	First settlers arrive in Carolina
1680	Charles Town (now Charleston) is settled
1682	William Penn founds Philadelphia

SUPPLEMENTARY READING

On the explorers and the world they opened up, see Samuel E. Morison, *The European Discovery of America* (1971–1974). Morison's biography of Columbus, *Admiral of the Ocean Sea* (1942), is a classic; for a recent study see Miles Davidson, *Columbus Then and Now* (1997). David Stannard, *American Holocaust* (1992), and Kirkpatrick Sale, *The Conquest of Paradise* (1990), are highly critical of Columbus. The history of Spanish colonization in the Southwest is treated in David J. Weber, *The Spanish Frontier in North America* (1992) and, in the Southeast, in Paul E. Hoffman, *A New Andalucia and a Way to the Orient* (1991) and *Florida's Frontiers* (2002). The classic study is Charles Gibson, *Spain in America* (1966). For an imaginative attempt to reconstruct the Native American response,

see Ramon Guitierrez, *When Jesus Came, The Corn Mothers Went Away* (1991).

Accounts of the English background of colonization can be found in Nicholas Canny, ed., *The Oxford History of the British Empire: The Origins of Empire* (1998). On French colonization, see William J. Eccles, *The French in North America, 1500–1765* (1998), Carl J. Ekberg, *French Roots in the Illinois Country* (1998), and Carole Blackburn, *Harvest of Souls* (2000), which focuses on the Jesuit Missionaries.

Contemporary scholarship on Indian-colonist relations focuses on their interactions. Important studies in that vein include Richard White, *Indians, Empires and Republics in the Great Lakes Region, 1650–1815* (1991), James Merrell, *Into the American Woods: Negotiators on the Pennsylvania*

Frontier (1999), Jill Lepore, *Name of War: King Philip's War and the Origins of American Identity* (1999), and Karen Kupperman, *Indians and English: Facing Off in Early America* (2000).

The impact of the Europeans is discussed in the Debating the Past (p. 26). See also Alfred W. Crosby, *Ecological Imperialism: The Biological Expansion of Europe, 900–1900* (1993) and, though it deals with a later period, Robert Boyd, *The Coming of the Spirit of Pestilence: Introduced Infectious Diseases and Population Decline among Northwest Coast Indians* (1999). Joyce E. Chaplin, *Subject Matter: Technology, the Body, and Science on the Anglo-American Frontier, 1500–1676* (2001) argues that Europeans did not assume that they were racially superior until they saw how readily native peoples died of diseases.

For a general study of American slave trade, see David Eltis, *The Rise of African Slavery in the Americas* (2000). General surveys of slavery include Ira Berlin, *Many Thousands Gone* (1998), and Peter Kolchin, *American Slavery, 1619–1877* (1993).

On Virginia, see David H. Fischer and James C. Kelly, *Bound Away: Virginia and the Westward Movement* (2000), and Edmund S. Morgan, *American Slavery, American Freedom* (1975). Jack P. Greene, *Pursuits of Happiness* (1988), argues for the centrality of the Chesapeake in the formation of American identity. On Roanoke, see Ivor

Noel Hume, *The Virginia Adventure* (1994). See also Everett Emerson, *Captain John Smith* (1993). For Maryland, consult Gloria T. Main, *Tobacco Colony* (1982), and A. C. Land, *Colonial Maryland* (1981); for Carolina, see Roger Ekirch, *Poor Carolina* (1981).

For the middle colonies, see Michael Kammen, *Colonial New York* (1975) and Donna Merwick, *Possessing Albany, 1630–1710: The Dutch and English Experiences* (1990). In addition to Merrell, see Mary Geiter, *William Penn* (2000);

On New England, Edmund Morgan's *The Puritan Dilemma: The Story of John Winthrop* (1958), long a classic, has been superseded by Francis J. Bremer, *John Winthrop: America's Forgotten Founding Father* (2003). The dispute over Anne Hutchinson has been enlivened by Michael P. Winship, *Making Heretics: Militant Protestantism and Free Grace in Massachusetts, 1636–1641* (2002), who notes that few at the time accused Hutchinson of antinomianism; see also his *Anne Hutchinson* (2005). Louise A. Breen, *Transgressing the Bounds: Subversive Enterprises among the Puritan Elite in Massachusetts, 1630–1692* (2001) draws a connection between religious dissenters such as Hutchinson and economic entrepreneurship. For Rhode Island, see Edwin S. Gaustad, *Liberty of Conscience: Roger Williams in America* (1991). William Bradford's classic, *Of Plymouth Plantation*, is also well worth sampling.

SUGGESTED WEBSITES

Vikings in the New World
http://www.anthro.mankato.msus.edu/prehistory/vikings/vikhome.html
This site explores the history of some of the earliest European visitors to the Americas.

The Columbus Doors
http://xroads.virginia.edu/~cap/columbus/col1.html
On this University of Virginia Website, historians discuss the Columbus myth and how it has changed over time.

1492: An Ongoing Voyage
http://www.ibiblio.org/expo/1492.exhibit/Intro.html
An exhibit of the Library of Congress, Washington, D.C., that includes brief essays and images about early civilizations and contact in the Americas.

The Computerized Information Retrieval System on Columbus and the Age of Discovery
http://www.millersv.edu/~columbus/
The History Department and Academic Computing Services of Millersville University, Pennsylvania, provide this text retrieval system containing more than 1000 articles from various magazines, journals, newspapers, speeches, official calendars, and other sources relating to various encounter themes.

Interacting with Native Americans in New Hampshire
http://seacoastnh.com/history/contact/index.html
This brief history of contact era New Hampshire has interesting links and gives a good picture of the earliest contacts.

The Discoverers' Web
http://www.win.tue.nl/cs/fm/engels/discovery/
Andre Engels offers information on the various exploration efforts.

The Plymouth Colony Archives Project at the University of Virginia
http://www.people.virginia.edu/~jfd3a/
This site contains extensive information about late seventeenth-century Plymouth colony.

Jamestown Rediscovery
http://www.apva.org/
This site, mounted by the Association for the Preservation of Virginia Antiquity, has excellent material on archaeological excavations at Jamestown.

Jamestown
http://www.nps.gov/colo/
This National Park Service site has information on Jamestown and other important colonial historical sites.

Williamsburg
http://www.history.org/
This commercial site explores colonial Williamsburg, Virginia.

William Penn, Visionary Proprietor
http://xroads.virginia.edu/~CAP/PENN/pnhome.html
William Penn had an interesting life, and this University site is a good introduction to the man and some of his achievements.

American Society in the Making

CHAPTER CONTENTS

▼ *The Fishing Lady,* a needlepoint depicting the "genteel culture" of the colonial elite. Gentility entailed good posture, delicate detail, and refined conversation. Nature was tamed, as evidenced by the ordered landscape, the frolicking animals, and the accommodating fish.

The colonies were settled chiefly by English people at first, with a leavening of Germans, Scots, Scots-Irish, Dutch, French, Swedes, Finns, a scattering of other nationalities, a handful of Sephardic Jews, and a gradually increasing number of black African slaves. The cultures these people brought with them varied according to the nationality, social status, and taste of the individual. The newcomers never lost this heritage entirely, but they—and certainly their descendants—became something quite different from their relatives who remained in the Old World. They became what we call Americans.

But not right away.

WHAT IS AN AMERICAN?

Why did America become something different from Europe? Why was New England not merely a new England, the struggling Spanish outpost at Santa Fe not a miniature Cadíz or Córdoba? If not just another "poor European immigrant" away from home, a French settler, Hector St. John de Crèvecoeur, wondered in 1762, "what then is the American, this new man?" And how did he—and she—come to be?

The fact of physical separation provides an important part of the answer. America was isolated from Europe by 3000 miles of ocean, or, as a poet put it, by "nine hundred leagues of roaring seas." The crossing took anywhere from a few weeks to several months, depending on wind and weather. No one undertook an ocean voyage lightly, and few who made the westward crossing ever thought seriously of returning. The modern mind can scarcely grasp the awful isolation that enveloped all the settlers. Each had to construct a new life or perish—if not of hunger, then of loneliness.

More than physical separation went into the process by which the colonists fashioned for themselves a new national identity and the outlines of a distinctive civilization. Varying conditions affected some settlers differently than others. Factors as material as the landscape encountered, as quantifiable as population patterns, as elusive as chance and calculation all shaped colonial social arrangements. Their cumulative impact did not at first produce anything like a uniform society. The "Americans" who evolved in what is now the United States were in many ways as different from each other as all were from their foreign cousins. The process by which these identities merged into an American nation remained incomplete. It was—and is—ongoing.

▲ In building mission churches, Spanish Franciscan friars exploited Indian materials to achieve precise symmetry, like the cross at the apex of their faith. The towers resembled those of the great churches of Spain.

SPANISH SETTLEMENT

Life in Spanish North America was shaped principally by Franciscan friars who, backed by soldiers and the financial support of kings Philip IV and Charles II, established strings of mission settlements among the Pueblo Indians of the upper reaches of the Rio Grande and among the tribes of northern Florida and the coastal regions of present-day Georgia and South Carolina. The actual construction of the missions was the work of local Indians, whom the friars intended to convert to Christianity in order to free them, as one priest put it, "from the obscure darkness of their idolatry."

The friars were for the most part dedicated men. Thousands of mission Indians were baptized and instructed in the rudiments of the Catholic faith. They were also taught to use European tools, to grow wheat and other European crops, and to raise chickens and pigs and other barnyard animals. But being

dedicated to their holy task, the friars paid little heed to how their activities undermined the Indians' traditional way of life.

The friars also exacted a heavy price in labor from the people they presumed to enlighten and civilize. The Indians built and maintained the missions, tilled the surrounding fields, and served the every need of the friars and other Spanish colonists. For this they were paid and fed little or nothing.

During the seventeenth century this kind of treatment led to rebellions in many of the missions in New Mexico and Florida, rebellions that, being isolated during most of the period, were easily repressed. In 1680, however, the Pueblo Indians came together under a religious leader named Popé. They caught the Spaniards entirely by surprise, killing some 400 of them. They then razed the town of Santa Fe and drove the surviving mission Spaniards all the way back to El Paso.

DOCUMENT

Legal statement by Pedro Hidalgo, soldier, Santa Fe 1680

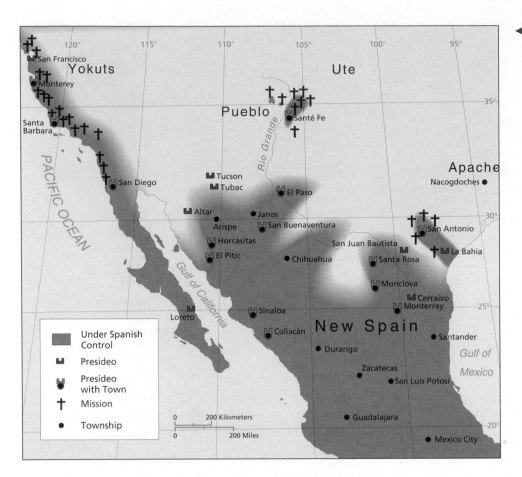

In the mid-1690s the Spaniards regained control of most of the upper Rio Grande and thereafter maintained control without difficulty. There were no more rebellions, partly because the Spaniards had learned to deal less harshly with the Pueblo people and partly because of their common need to repel attacks by the Ute, the Apache, and other Indian tribes.

The mission settlements in Florida were also badly battered in the last decades of the century, partly by mistreated Indians, partly by English colonists from Carolina. Many of the mission converts were enslaved by the Carolinians and shipped off to Barbados and other English colonies.

THE CHESAPEAKE COLONIES

The southern parts of English North America comprised three regions: the Chesapeake Bay, consisting of "tidewater" Virginia and Maryland; the "low country" of the Carolinas (and eventually Georgia); and the "back country," a vast territory that extended from the "fall line" in the foothills of the Appalachians, where falls and rapids put an end to navigation on the tidal rivers, to the farthest point of western settlement. Not until well into the eighteenth century

would the emergence of common features—export-oriented agricultural economies, a labor force in which black slaves figured prominently, the absence of towns of any size—prompt people to think of the "South" as a single region. When the English philosopher Thomas Hobbes wrote in 1651 that human life tended to be "nasty, brutish, and short," he might well have had in mind the royal colony of Virginia. Although the colony grew from about 1300 to nearly 5000 in the decade after the Crown took it over in 1624, the death rate remained appalling. Since more than 9000 immigrants had entered the colony, nearly half the population died during that decade.

The climate helped make the Chesapeake area a death trap. "Hot and moist" is how Robert Beverly described the weather in *The History and Present State of Virginia* (1705), the dampness "occasioned by the abundance of low grounds, marshes, creeks, and rivers." Almost without exception newcomers underwent "seasoning," a period of illness that in its mildest form consisted of "two or three fits of a feaver and ague." Actually the relatively dry summers were the chief cause of the high death rate. During the summer the slower flow of the James River allowed relatively dense salt water to penetrate inland. This blocked the flow of polluted river water, which the colonists drank.

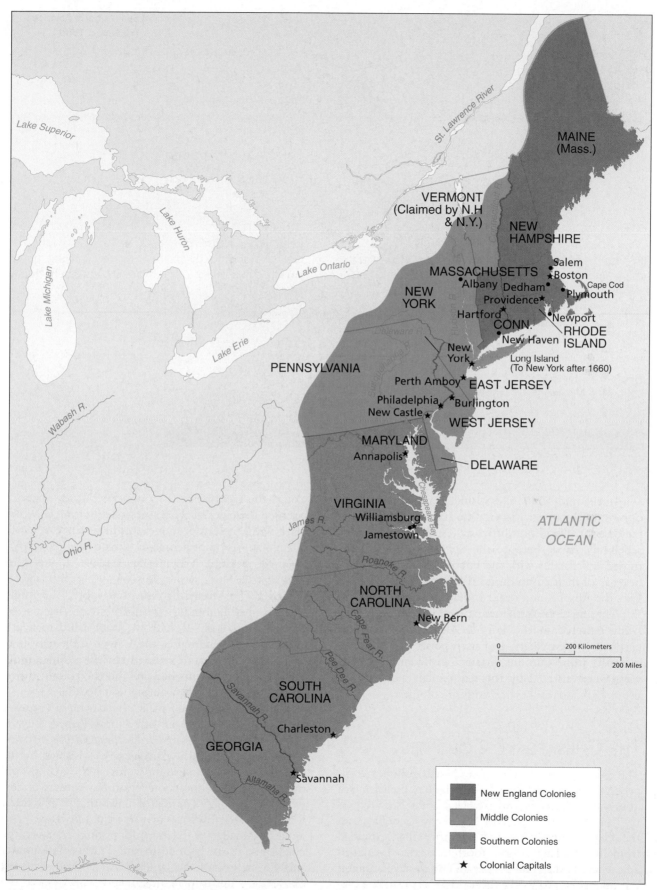

Lake Superior

Lake Michigan

Lake Huron

Lake Ontario

Lake Erie

St. Lawrence River

MAINE
(Mass.)

VERMONT
(Claimed by N.H
& N.Y.)

NEW
HAMPSHIRE

Salem
Boston
Cape Cod
Plymouth
Newport

MASSACHUSETTS
Albany   Dedham
Providence
Hartford
CONN.
New Haven

RHODE
ISLAND

NEW
YORK

New
York

Long Island
(To New York after 1660)

PENNSYLVANIA

Perth Amboy   EAST JERSEY

Philadelphia   Burlington
New Castle
WEST JERSEY

MARYLAND
Annapolis

DELAWARE

VIRGINIA
Williamsburg
Jamestown

James R.

Chesapeake Bay

ATLANTIC
OCEAN

Ohio R.

Wabash R.

Roanoke R.

NORTH
CAROLINA

New Bern

Cape Fear R.

Pee Dee R.

Savannah R.

SOUTH
CAROLINA

Charleston

GEORGIA

Altamaha R.

Savannah

Delaware R.
Susquehanna R.
Hudson R.

0   200 Kilometers
0   200 Miles

	New England Colonies
	Middle Colonies
	Southern Colonies
★	Colonial Capitals

▲ **English Colonies on the Atlantic Seaboard**

The result was dysentery, the "bloody flux." If they survived the flux, and a great many did not, settlers still ran the seasonal risk of contracting a particularly virulent strain of malaria, which, though seldom fatal in itself, could so debilitate its victims that they often died of typhoid fever and other ailments.

Long after food shortages and Indian warfare had ceased to be serious problems, life in the Chesapeake remained precarious. Well into the 1700s a white male of 20 in Middlesex County, Virginia, could look forward only to about 25 more years of life. Across Chesapeake Bay, in Charles County, Maryland, life expectancy was even lower. The high death rate had important effects on family structure. Because relatively few people lived beyond their forties, more often than not children lost at least one of their parents before they reached maturity and in many instances both. Remarriage was a way of life. Apparently this situation did not cause drastic emotional problems for most people of the region. Men provided generously for their families in their wills, despite knowing that their wives would probably remarry quickly. The effects on children of the deaths of their parents are hard to gauge but apparently were not often psychologically damaging, no doubt because they were so common and because, with the acute shortage of labor, someone could always be found to take in and care for an orphan. Being brought up entirely by step-parents was so common that children tended to accept it almost as a matter of course.

Because of the persistent shortage of women in the Chesapeake region (men outnumbered women by three to two even in the early 1700s), widows easily found new husbands. Many men spent their entire lives alone or in the company of other men. Others married Indian women and became part of Indian society.

All Chesapeake settlers felt the psychological effects of their precarious and frustrating existence. Random mayhem and calculated violence posed a continuous threat to life and limb. Life was coarse at best and often as "brutish" as Hobbes had claimed, even allowing for the difficulties involved in carving out a community in the wilderness.

THE LURE OF LAND

Agriculture was the bulwark of life for the Chesapeake settlers and the rest of the colonial South; the tragic experiences of the Jamestown settlement revealed this quickly enough. Jamestown also suggested that a colony could not succeed unless its inhabitants were allowed to own their own land. The first colonists, it will be recalled, had agreed to work for seven years in return for a share of the profits. When their contracts expired there were few profits. To satisfy these settlers and to attract new capital, the London Company declared a

"dividend" of land, its only asset. The surviving colonists each received 100 acres. Thereafter, as prospects continued poor, the company relied more and more on grants of land to attract both capital and labor. A number of wealthy Englishmen were given immense tracts, some running to several hundred thousand acres. Lesser persons willing to settle in Virginia received more modest grants. Whether dangled before a great tycoon, a country squire, or a poor farmer, the offer of land had the effect of encouraging immigration to the colony. This was a much-desired end, for without the labor to develop it the land was worthless.

Soon what was known as the headright system became entrenched in both Virginia and Maryland. Behind the system lay the eminently sound principle that land should be parceled out according to the availability of labor to cultivate it. For each "head" entering the colony authorities issued a "right" to take any 50 acres of unoccupied land. To "seat" a claim and receive title to the property, the holder of the headright had to mark out its boundaries, plant a crop, and construct some sort of habitation. This system was adopted in all the southern colonies and in Pennsylvania and New Jersey.

The first headrights were issued with no strings attached, but generally the grantor demanded a small annual payment called a quitrent. A quitrent was actually a tax, perhaps a shilling for 50 acres, which provided a way for the proprietors to derive incomes from their colonies. Quitrents were usually resented and difficult to collect.

The headright system encouraged landless Europeans to migrate to America. More often than not, however, those most eager to come could not afford passage across the Atlantic. To bring such people to America, the indentured servant system was developed. Indenture resembled apprenticeship. In return for transportation indentured servants agreed to work for a stated period, usually about five years. During that time they were subject to strict control by the master and received no compensation beyond their keep. Indentured women were forbidden to marry and if they became pregnant (as many did in a land where men outnumbered women by seven to one) the time lost from work that resulted was added to their terms of service.

DOCUMENT

Wessell Webling, His Indenture, 1622

Servants lacked any incentive to work hard, whereas masters tended to "abuse their servantes . . . with intollerable oppression." In this clash of wills the advantage lay with the master; servants lacked full political and civil rights, and masters could administer physical punishment and otherwise abuse them. An indenture, however, was a contract; servants could and did sue when planters failed to fulfill their parts of the bargain, and surviving court records suggest that they fared reasonably well when they did so.

Servants who completed their years of labor became free. Usually the former servant was entitled to an "outfit" (a suit of clothes, some farm tools, seed, and perhaps a gun). Custom varied from colony to colony. In the Carolinas and in Pennsylvania, for example, servants also received small grants of land from the colony when their service was completed.

The headrights issued when indentured servants entered the colonies went to whoever paid their passage, not to the servants. Thus the system gave a double reward to capital—land and labor for the price of the labor alone. Since well over half of the white settlers of the southern colonies came as indentured servants, the effect on the structure of southern society was enormous.

Most servants eventually became landowners, but with the passage of time their lot became harder. The best land belonged to the large planters, and low tobacco prices and high local taxes combined to keep many former servants in dire poverty. Some were forced to become "squatters" on land along the fringes of settlement that no one had yet claimed. Squatting often led to trouble; eventually, when someone turned up with a legal title to the land, the squatters demanded "squatters' rights," the privilege of buying the land from the legal owner without paying for the improvements they had made upon it. This led to lawsuits and sometimes to violence.

In the 1670s conflicts between Virginians who owned choice land and former servants on the outer edge of settlement brought the colony to the brink of class warfare. The costs of meeting the region's ever-growing need for labor with indentured servants were becoming prohibitive. Some other solution was needed.

"Solving" the Labor Shortage: Slavery

Probably the first African blacks brought to English North America arrived on a Dutch ship and were sold at Jamestown in 1619. Early records are vague and incomplete, so it is not possible to say whether these Africans were treated as slaves or freed after a period of years like indentured servants. What is certain is that by about 1640 *some* blacks were slaves (a few, with equal certainty, were free) and that by the 1660s local statutes had firmly established the institution in Virginia and Maryland.

▲ The Cape Coast Castle, on the slave coast of West Africa, looking out on the Atlantic Ocean. One of a dozen such forts operated by Britain, Spain, or the Netherlands, this castle held hundreds of African captives. Captains of slaving ships paid about 6 ounces of gold or 200 gallons of rum for each slave. The price was lower if the captains wanted to deal directly with African chieftains, but this required long, dangerous trips inland.

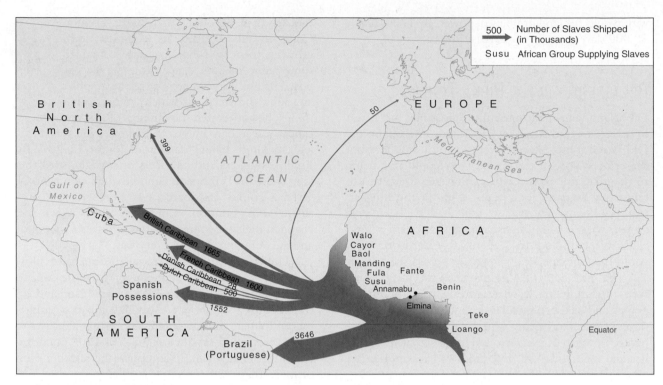

▲ **African Slave Trade, 1451–1870**

Whether slavery produced race prejudice in America or prejudice led to slavery is a hotly debated, important, and difficult-to-answer question. Most seventeenth-century Europeans were prejudiced against Africans; the usual reasons that led them to look down on "heathens" with customs other than their own were in the case of Africans greatly reinforced by the latter's blackness, which the English equated with dirt, the Devil, danger, and death. "Black is the Colour of Night, Frightful, Dark and Horrid," a popular disquisition of 1704 proclaimed. Yet the English knew that the Portuguese and Spaniards had enslaved blacks—*negro* is Spanish for black. Since the English adopted the word as a name for Africans, their treatment of Africans in the New World may also have derived from the Spanish, which suggests that they treated the first blacks in their colonies as slaves from the start. Prejudice and existing enslavement interacted with each other as both cause and effect. Slavery soon spread throughout the colonies. As early as 1626 there were 11 slaves in New Netherland, and when the English conquered that colony in 1664 there were 700 slaves in a population of about 8000. The Massachusetts Body of Liberties of 1641—strange title—provided that "there shall never be any bond-slavery . . . amongst us; unless it be lawful captives taken in just warrs [*i.e.*, Indians] and such strangers as willingly sell themselves, or *are solde* to us." However, relatively few blacks were imported until late in the seventeenth century, even in the southern colonies. In 1650 there were only 300 blacks in Virginia and as late as 1670 no more than 2000.

White servants were much more highly prized. The African, after all, was almost entirely alien to both the European and the American ways of life. In a country starved for capital, the cost of slaves—roughly five times that of indentured servants—was another disadvantage. In 1664 the governor of Maryland informed Lord Baltimore that local planters would use more "neigros" "if our purses would endure it." For these reasons, so long as white servants could be had in sufficient numbers, there were few slaves in the Chesapeake, and those that were generally worked alongside white servants and shared roughly the same food, clothing, and quarters.

In the 1670s the flow of indentured servants slackened, the result of improving economic conditions in England and the competition of other colonies for servants. At the same time, the formation of the Royal African Company (1672) made slaves more readily available. Then in 1689 a war in Europe cut off a principal market for tobacco, causing the price to fall and thus making migration to the colonies less attractive. The indenture system began to give way to slavery as the "permanent" solution to the southern colonies' chronic need for labor. An additional inducement causing planters and politicians to switch was the recognition that, unlike white servants, black slaves (and their offspring) would be forever barred from competing

with whites for land or political power. By 1700, nearly 30,000 slaves lived in the English colonies.

PROSPERITY IN A PIPE: TOBACCO

Labor and land made agriculture possible, but it was necessary to find a market for American crops in the Old World if the colonists were to enjoy anything but the crudest sort of existence. They could not begin to manufacture all the articles they required; to obtain from England such items as plows and muskets and books and chinaware, they had to have cash crops, what their English creditors called "merchantable commodities." Here, at least, fortune favored the Chesapeake.

The founders of Virginia tried to produce all sorts of things that were needed in the old country: grapes and silk in particular, indigo, cotton, oranges, olives, sugar, and many other plants. But it was tobacco, unwanted, even strongly opposed at first, that became for farmers on both sides of Chesapeake Bay "their darling."

Tobacco was unknown in Europe until Spanish explorers brought it back from the West Indies. It was not common in England until the time of Sir Walter Raleigh. Then it quickly proved irresistible to

DOCUMENT

James I, "A Counterblaste to Tobacco"

thousands of devotees. At first the London Company discouraged its colonists from growing tobacco. Since it clearly contained some habit-forming drug, many people opposed its use. King James I wrote a pamphlet attacking the weed, in which, among other things, he anticipated the findings of modern cancer researchers by saying that smoking was a "vile and stinking" habit "dangerous to the Lungs." But English smokers and partakers of snuff ignored their king, and the Virginians ignored their company. By 1617 a pound of tobacco was worth more than 5 shillings in London. Company and Crown then changed their tune, granting the colonists a monopoly and encouraging them in every way.

Unlike wheat, which required expensive plows and oxen to clear the land and prepare the soil, tobacco plants could be set on semicleared land and cultivated with a simple hoe. Although tobacco required lots of human labor, a single laborer working two or three acres could produce as much as 1200 pounds of cured tobacco, which, in a good year, yielded a profit of more than 200 percent. This being the case, production in America leaped from 2500 pounds in 1616 to nearly 30 million pounds in the late seventeenth century, or roughly 400 pounds of tobacco for every man, woman, and child in the Chesapeake colonies.

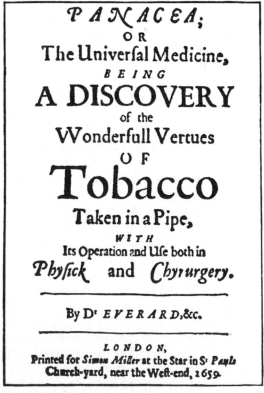

▲ Tobacco companies advertised their product as far back as the seventeenth century. This 1659 advertisement lauds tobacco as a medical "panacea."

The tidewater region was blessed with many navigable rivers and the planters spread along their banks, giving the Chesapeake a shabby, helter-skelter character of rough habitations and growing tobacco, mostly planted in stump-littered fields, surrounded by fallow land and thickets interspersed with dense forest. There were no towns and almost no roads. English ships made their way up the rivers from farm to farm, gathering the tobacco at each planter's wharf. The vessels also served as general stores of a sort where planters could exchange tobacco for everything from cloth, shoes, tools, salt, and nails to such exotic items as tea, coffee, chocolate, and spices.

However, the tremendous increase in the production of tobacco caused the price to plummet in the late seventeenth century. This did not stop the expansion of the colonies, but it did alter the structure of their society. Small farmers found it more difficult to make a decent living. At the same time men with capital and individuals with political influence were amassing large tracts of land. If well managed, a big plantation gave its owner important competitive advantages over the small farmer. Tobacco was notorious for the speed with which it exhausted the fertility of the soil. Growers with a lot of land could shift frequently to new fields within their holdings, allowing the old fields to lie fallow and thus maintain high yields, but the only option that small farmers had when their land gave out was to move to unsettled land on the frontier. To do that in the 1670s was to risk trouble with properly indignant Indians. It might also violate colonial laws designed to slow westward migration and limit tobacco production. Neither was about to stop settlement.

BACON'S REBELLION

Chesapeake settlers showed little respect for constituted authority, partly because most people lived on isolated plantations and partly because the London authorities were usually ignorant of their needs. The first Virginians often ignored directives of the London Company, while early Marylanders regularly disputed the right of the Calverts' agents to direct the affairs of the proprietorship. The most serious challenge took place in Virginia in 1676. Planters in the outlying counties heartily disliked the officials in Jamestown who ran the colony. The royal governor, Sir William Berkeley, and his "Green Spring" faction (the organization took its name from the governor's plantation) had ruled Virginia for more than 30 years. Outsiders resented the way Berkeley and his henchmen used their offices to line their pockets. They also resented their social pretensions, for Green Springers made no effort to conceal their opinion, which had considerable basis in fact, that western planters were a crude and vulgar lot.

▲ Sir William Berkeley looks every inch the autocrat in this portrait, a copy of one painted by Sir Peter Lely. After Bacon's death, Berkeley took his revenge and had 23 rebels hanged. Said King Charles II: "The old fool has killed more people in that naked country than I have done for the murder of my father."

Early in 1676 planters on the western edge of settlement, always looking for excuses to grab land by doing away with the Indians who owned it, asked Berkeley to authorize an expedition against Indians who had been attacking nearby plantations. Berkeley refused. The planters then took matters into their own hands. Their leader, Nathaniel Bacon, was (and remains today) a controversial figure. His foes described him as extremely ambitious and possessed "of a most imperious and dangerous hidden Pride of heart." But even his sharpest critics conceded that he was "of an inviting aspect and powerful elocution" and well qualified "to lead a giddy and unthinking multitude."

When Berkeley refused to authorize him to attack the Indians, Bacon promptly showed himself only too willing to lead that multitude not only against Indians but against the governor. Without permission he raised an army of 500 men, described by the Berkeley faction as "rabble of the basest sort." Berkeley then declared him a traitor.

Several months of confusion followed. Bacon murdered some peaceful Indians, marched on Jamestown and forced Berkeley to legitimize his authority, then headed west again to kill more Indians. In September he returned to Jamestown and burned it to the ground. Berkeley fled across Chesapeake Bay to the Eastern Shore. The Baconites plundered the estates of some of

the Green Spring faction. But a few weeks later, Bacon came down with a "violent flux"—probably it was a bad case of dysentery—and he died. Soon thereafter an English naval squadron arrived with enough soldiers to restore order. Bacon's Rebellion came to an end.

On the surface, the uprising changed nothing. No sudden shift in political power occurred. Indeed, Bacon had not sought to change either the political system or the social and economic structure of the colony. But if the *rebellion* did not change anything, nothing was ever again quite the same after it ended. With seeming impartiality, the Baconites had warred against Indians and against other planters. But which was the real enemy? Surely the Baconite and Green Springer factions had no differences that could not be compromised. And their common interest extended beyond the question of how to deal with Indians. Both wanted cheap labor.

In the quarter-century following Bacon's Rebellion the Chesapeake region thus became committed to black slavery. And slave ownership resulted in large differences in the wealth and lifestyles of growers of tobacco. The few who succeeded in accumulating 20 or more slaves and enough land to keep them occupied grew richer. The majority either grew poorer or at best had to struggle to hold their own.

More important, however, Bacon's Rebellion sealed an implicit contract between the inhabitants of the "great houses" and those who lived in more modest lodgings: Southern whites might differ greatly in wealth and influence, but they stood as one and forever behind the principle that Africans must have neither. This was the basis—the price—of the harmony and prosperity achieved by those who survived "seasoning" in the Chesapeake colonies.

The Carolinas

The English and, after 1700, the Scots-Irish settlers of the tidewater parts of the Carolinas turned to agriculture as enthusiastically as had their Chesapeake neighbors. In substantial sections of what became North Carolina, tobacco flourished. In South Carolina, after two decades in which furs and cereals were the chief products, Madagascar rice was introduced in the low-lying coastal areas in 1696. It quickly proved its worth as a cash crop. By 1700 almost 100,000 pounds were being exported annually; by the eve of the Revolution rice exports from South Carolina and Georgia exceeded 65 million pounds a year.

Rice culture required water for flooding the fields. At first freshwater swamps were adapted to the crop, but by the middle of the eighteenth century the chief rice fields lay along the tidal rivers and inlets. Dikes and floodgates allowed fresh water to flow across the fields with the rising tide; when the tide fell, the gates closed automatically to keep the water in. The process was reversed when it was necessary to drain the land. Then the water ran out as the tide ebbed, and the pressure of the next flood pushed the gates shut.

In the 1740s another cash crop, indigo, was introduced in South Carolina by Eliza Lucas. Indigo did not compete with rice either for land or labor. It prospered on high ground and needed care in seasons when the slaves were not busy in the rice paddies. The British were delighted to have a new source of indigo because the blue dye was important in their woolens industry. Parliament quickly placed a bounty—a bonus—on it to stimulate production.

Their tobacco, rice, and indigo, along with furs and forest products such as lumber, tar, and resin, meant that the southern colonies had no difficulty in obtaining manufactured articles from abroad. Planters dealt with agents in England and Scotland, called factors, who managed the sale of their crops, filled their orders for manufactures, and supplied them with credit. This was a great convenience but not necessarily an advantage, for it prevented the development of a diversified economy. Throughout the colonial era, while small-scale manufacturing developed rapidly in the North, it was stillborn in the South.

Reliance on European middlemen also retarded the development of urban life. Until the rise of Baltimore in the 1750s, Charleston was the only city of importance in the entire South. But despite its rich export trade, its fine harbor, and the easy availability of excellent lumber, Charleston's shipbuilding industry never remotely rivaled that of Boston, New York, or Philadelphia.

On the South Carolina rice plantations, slave labor predominated from the beginning, for free workers would not submit to its backbreaking and unhealthy regimen. The first quarter of the eighteenth century saw an enormous influx of Africans into all the southern colonies. By 1730 roughly three out of every ten people south of Pennsylvania were black, and in South Carolina the blacks outnumbered the whites by two to one. "Carolina," remarked a newcomer in 1737, "looks more like a negro country than like a country settled by white people."

Given the existing race prejudice and the degrading impact of slavery, this demographic change had an enormous impact on life wherever African Americans were concentrated. In each colony regulations governing the behavior of blacks, both free and slave, increased in severity as the density of the black population increased. The South Carolina Negro Act of 1740 denied slaves "freedom of movement, freedom of assembly, freedom to raise [their own] food, to earn money, to learn to read English." The blacks had no civil rights under any of these codes, and punishments

▲ Slaves on a South Carolina plantation, around 1790. Likely of Yoruba descent, they play west African instruments, such as the banjo, and also wear elaborate headgear, another Yoruba trait. But unlike their Yoruban contemporaries, who adorned faces and limbs with elaborate tattoos or scars, these slaves bear no evident body decorations. These people are African, indisputably, but also American.

were sickeningly severe. For minor offenses, whipping was common, for serious crimes, death by hanging or by being burned alive. Slaves were sometimes castrated for sexual offenses—even for lewd talk about white women—or for repeated attempts to escape.

The "master" race sought to acculturate the slaves in order to make them more efficient workers. A slave who could understand English was easier to order about; one who could handle farm tools or wait on tables was more useful than one who could not; a carpenter or a mason was more valuable still. But acculturation increased the slave's independence and mobility, and this posed problems. Most field hands seldom tried to escape; they expressed their dissatisfactions by pilferage and petty sabotage, by laziness, or by feigning stupidity. Most runaways were artisans who hoped to "pass" as free in a nearby town. It was one of the many paradoxes of slavery that the more valuable a slave became, the harder that slave was to control.

Few runaway slaves became rebels, however. Indeed, organized slave rebellions were rare, and while individual assaults by blacks on whites were common enough, personal violence was also common among whites, then and throughout American history. But

the masters had sound reasons for fearing their slaves; the particular viciousness of the system lay in the fact that oppression bred resentment, which in turn produced still greater oppression.

What is superficially astonishing is that the whites grossly exaggerated the danger of slave revolts. They pictured the black as a kind of malevolent ogre, powerful, bestial, and lascivious, a caldron of animal emotions that had to be restrained at any cost. Probably the characteristics they attributed to the blacks were really projections of their own passions. The most striking illustration was white fear that if blacks were free, they would breed with whites. Yet in practice, the interbreeding, which indeed took place, was almost exclusively the result of white men using their power as masters to have sexual relations with female slaves.

Thus the "peculiar institution" was fastened on America with economic, social, and psychic barbs. Ignorance and self-interest, lust for gold and for the flesh, primitive prejudices and complex social and legal ties, all combined to convince the whites that black slavery was not so much good as a fact of life. A few Quakers attacked the institution on the religious ground that all human beings are equal before God:

"Christ dyed for all, both *Turks, Barbarians, Tartarians,* and *Ethyopians.*" Yet some Quakers owned slaves, and even the majority who did not usually succumbed to color prejudice. Blackness was a defect, but it was no justification for enslavement, they argued. But the Quaker view attracted little attention anywhere—none in areas where slavery was important.

HOME AND FAMILY IN THE SOUTH

Life for all but the most affluent planters was by modern standards uncomfortable. Houses were mostly one- and two-room affairs, small, dark, and crowded. Furniture and utensils were sparse and crudely made. Chairs were rare; if a family possessed one it was reserved for the head of the house. People sat, slept, and ate on benches and planks. The typical dining table (the term itself was not in use) was made of two boards covered, if by anything, with a "board cloth." Toilets and plumbing of any kind were unknown; even chamber pots, which eliminated the nighttime trek to the privy, were beyond the reach of poorer families.

Clothes were equally crude and, since soap was expensive, rarely washed and therefore foul-smelling and often infested with vermin. Food was plentiful. Corn, served as bread, hominy, pancakes, and in various other forms, was the chief staple. But there was plenty of beef, pork, and game, usually boiled with various vegetables over an open fire.

White women (even indentured ones) rarely worked in the fields. Household maintenance, including tending to farm animals, making butter and cheese, pickling and preserving, spinning and sewing, and, of course, caring for children, which often involved orphans and stepchildren because of the fragility of life in the region, was their responsibility. For exceptional women, the labor shortage created opportunities. Some managed large plantations; Eliza Lucas ran three in South Carolina for her absent father while still in her teens, and after the death of her husband, Charles Pinckney, she managed his extensive property holdings.

Southern children were not usually subjected to as strict discipline as children in New England were, but the difference was relative. Formal schooling for all but the rich was nonexistent; the rural character of society made the maintenance of schools prohibitively expensive. Whatever most children learned, they got from their parents or other relatives. A large percentage of Southerners were illiterate. As in other regions, children were put to some kind of useful work at an early age.

More well-to-do, "middling" planters had more comfortable lifestyles, but they still lived in relatively crowded quarters, having perhaps three rooms to house a family of four or five and a couple of servants.

To sleep between sheets in a soft bed under blankets and quilts was luxury indeed in that world. Food in greater variety and abundance was another indication of a higher standard of living.

Until the early eighteenth century only a handful achieved real affluence. (The richest by far was Robert "King" Carter of Lancaster County, Virginia, who at the time of his death in 1732 owned 1000 slaves and 300,000 acres.) Those fortunate few, masters of several plantations and many slaves, lived in solid, two-story houses of six or more rooms, furnished with English and other imported carpets, chairs, tables, wardrobes, chests, china, and silver. When the occasion warranted, the men wore fine broadcloth, the women the latest (or more likely the next-to-latest) fashions. Some even sent their children abroad for schooling. The founding of the College of William and Mary in Williamsburg, Virginia, in 1693 was an effort to provide the region with its own institution of higher learning, mainly in order to train clergymen. For decades, however, the College of William and Mary was not much more than a grammar school. Lawyers were relatively numerous, though rarely learned in the law. Doctors were so scarce that one sick planter wrote a letter to his brother in England describing his symptoms and asking him to consult a physician and let him know the diagnosis.

These large planters also held the commissions in the militia, the county judgeships, and the seats in the colonial legislatures. The control that these "leading families" exercised over their neighbors was not entirely unearned. They were, in general, responsible leaders. And they recognized the necessity of throwing open their houses and serving copious amounts of punch and rum to ordinary voters when election time rolled around. Such gatherings served to acknowledge the representative character of the system.

No matter what their station, southern families led relatively isolated lives. Churches, which might be expected to serve as centers of community life, were few and far between. By the middle of the eighteenth century the Anglican Church was the "established" religion, its ministers supported by public funds. The Virginia assembly had made attendance at Anglican services compulsory in 1619. In Maryland, Lord Baltimore's Toleration Act did not survive the settlement in the colony of large numbers of militant puritans. It was repealed in 1654, reenacted in 1657, then repealed again in 1692 when the Anglican Church was established.

For all its legal standing, the Anglican Church was not a powerful force in the South. Most of the ministers the Bishop of London sent to America were second-rate men who had been unable to obtain decent livings at home. If they had intellectual or spiritual ambitions when they arrived, their rural circumstances

▲ The harbor of Charleston, South Carolina, as depicted in the 1730s. Nearly a half dozen church steeples can be seen behind the commercial buildings along the bustling waterfront. Americans usually think of the 1600s as the great age of religion, but most colonial churches were founded after the 1740s.

provided little opportunity to develop them. Most people had few opportunities to attend formal services. One result was that marriages tended to become civil rather than religious ceremonies.

Social events of any kind were great occasions. Births, marriages, and especially funerals called for much feasting; if there were neither heirs nor debts to satisfy, it was possible to "consume" the entire contents of a modest estate in celebrating the deceased's passing. (At one Maryland funeral the guests were provided with 55 gallons of an alcoholic concoction composed of brandy, cider, and sugar.)

Other forms of entertainment and relaxation included hunting and fishing, cockfighting, and horse racing. Horses were widely owned, but used for getting from place to place rather than as draft animals, since tobacco was transported by water and cultivated with hoes, not plows.

Even the most successful planters were conserving types, not idle grandees chiefly concerned with conspicuous display. The vast, undeveloped country encouraged them to produce and then invest their savings in more production. William Byrd II (1674–1744), one of the richest men in Virginia, habitually rose before dawn. Besides his tobacco fields, he operated a sawmill and a grist mill, prospected for iron and coal, and engaged in the Indian trade.

GEORGIA AND THE BACK COUNTRY

West of the fall line of the many rivers that irrigated tidewater Chesapeake and Carolina lay the back country. This region included the Great Valley of Virginia, the Piedmont, and what became the final English colony, Georgia, founded by a group of London philanthropists in 1733. These men were concerned over the plight of honest persons imprisoned for debt, whom they intended to settle in the New World. (Many Europeans were still beguiled by the prospect of regenerating their society in the colonies. All told, about 50,000 British convicts were "transported" to America in the colonial period, partly to get rid of "undesirables," but partly for humane reasons.) The government, eager to create a buffer between South Carolina and the hostile Spanish in Florida, readily granted a charter (1732) to the group, whose members agreed to manage the colony without profit to themselves for a period of 21 years.

In 1733 their leader, James Oglethorpe, founded Savannah. Oglethorpe was a complicated person, vain, high-handed, and straitlaced, yet idealistic. He hoped to people the colony with sober and industrious yeoman farmers. Land grants were limited to 50 acres and made nontransferable. To ensure sobriety, rum and other "Spirits and Strong Waters" were banned. To guarantee that the colonists would have to work hard, the entry of "any Black . . . Negroe" was prohibited. The Indian trade was to be strictly regulated in the interest of fair dealing.

Oglethorpe intended that silk, wine, and olive oil would be the main products—none of which, unfortunately, could be profitably produced in Georgia. His noble intentions came to naught. The settlers swiftly found ways to circumvent all restrictions. Rum flowed, slaves were imported, large land holdings amassed. Georgia developed an economy much like South Carolina's. In 1752 the founders, disillusioned, abandoned their responsibilities. Georgia then became a royal colony.

Now settlers penetrated the rest of the southern back country. So long as cheap land remained available

closer to the coast and Indians along the frontier remained a threat, only the most daring and footloose hunters or fur traders lived far inland. But once settlement began, it came with a rush. Chief among those making the trek were Scots-Irish and German immigrants. By 1770 the back country contained about 250,000 settlers, 10 percent of the population of the colonies.

This internal migration did not proceed altogether peacefully. In 1771 frontiersmen in North Carolina calling themselves Regulators fought a pitched battle with 1200 troops dispatched by the Carolina assembly, which was dominated by low-country interests. The Regulators were protesting their lack of representation in the assembly. They were crushed and their leaders executed. This was neither the last nor the bloodiest sectional conflict in American history.

PURITAN NEW ENGLAND

If survival in the Chesapeake required junking many European notions about social arrangements and submitting to the dictates of the wilderness, was this also true in Massachusetts and Connecticut? Ultimately it probably was, but at first puritan ideas certainly fought the New England reality to a draw.

Boston is located slightly more than 5° latitude north of Jamestown and almost 10° north of Charleston. Like other early New England towns and unlike these southern ones, Boston had a dependable water supply. The surrounding patchwork of forest, pond, dunes, and tide marsh was much more open than the malaria-infected terrain of the tidewater and low-country South. As a consequence New Englanders escaped "the agues and fevers" that beset settlers to the south, leaving them free to attend to their spiritual, economic, and social well-being. These differences alone made New England a much healthier habitat for settlers.

THE PURITAN FAMILY

New England's puritans were set apart from other English settlers by how much—and how long—they lived out of their baggage. The supplies the first arrivals brought with them eased their adjustment, as did the wherewithal of later, equally heavily laden arrivals. The puritans' baggage, however, included besides pots and pans, and saws and shovels, a plan for the proper ordering of society.

At the center of the plan was a covenant, or agreement, to ensure the upright behavior of all who took up residence. They sought to provide what John Winthrop described to the passengers on the *Arbella*

as the imperative of human existence: "that every man might have need of other, and from hence they might be all knitt more nearly together in the Bond of brotherly affection."

The first and most important covenant governing puritan behavior was that binding family members. The family's authority was backed by the Fifth Commandment: "Honor thy father and thy mother, that thy days may be long upon the land." In a properly ordered puritan family, as elsewhere in the colonies, authority flowed downward. Sociologists describe such a family as nuclear and patriarchal; each household contained one family, and in it, the father was boss. His principal responsibilities consisted of providing for the physical welfare of the household, including any servants, and making sure they behaved properly. All economic dealings between the family and other parties were also transacted by him, even when the property involved had been owned by his wife prior to their marriage.

The Reverend John Cotton's outline of a woman's responsibilities clearly establishes her subordinate position: she should keep house, educate the children, and improve "what is got by the industry of the man." The poet Anne Bradstreet reduced the functions of a puritan woman to two: "loving Mother and obedient Wife." Colonial New England, and the southern colonies as well, did have their female blacksmiths, silversmiths, shipwrights, gunsmiths, and butchers as well as shopkeepers and teachers. Such early examples of domestic "liberation," however, were mostly widows and the wives of incapacitated husbands. Even so, most widows, especially young ones, quickly remarried.

PURITAN WOMEN AND CHILDREN

Dealings with neighbors and relatives and involvement in church activities marked the outer limits of the social range of most puritan women. Care of the children was a full-time occupation when broods of 12 or 14 were more common than those of 1 or 2. Fewer children died in New England than in the Chesapeake or in Europe, though few families escaped a miscarriage or a child's death along the way. Childbearing and motherhood, therefore, commonly extended over three decades of a woman's life. Meanwhile, she also functioned as the chief operating officer of the household. Cooking, baking, sewing, and supervising servants, as well as mastering such arcane knowledge as the chemistry needed to make cheese from milk, bacon from pork, bread from grain, and beer from malt, all fell to her. These jobs were physically demanding, though not so debilitating as to prevent large numbers of New England wives from seeing one or more husbands off to the hereafter.

TO THE MOST HIGH AND MIGHTIE Prince, IAMES by the grace of God King of Great Britaine, France and Ireland, Defender of the Faith, &c.

THE TRANSLATORS OF *THE BIBLE*, *wiſh Grace, Mercie, and Peace, through* IESVS CHRIST *our* LORD.

Reat and manifold were the bleſſings (moſt dread Soueraigne) which Almighty GOD, the Father of all Mercies, beſtowed vpon vs the people of ENGLAND, when firſt he ſent your Maieſties Royall perſon to rule and raigne ouer vs. For whereas it was the expectation of many, who wiſhed not well vnto our SION, that vpon the ſetting of that bright *Occidentall Starre* Queene ELIZABETH of moſt happy memory, ſome thicke and palpable cloudes of darkeneſſe would ſo haue ouerſhadowed this land, that men ſhould haue bene in doubt which way they were to walke, and that it ſhould hardly be knowen, who was to direct the vnſetled State: the appearance of your MAIESTIE, as of the *Sunne* in his ſtrength, inſtantly diſpelled thoſe ſuppoſed and ſurmiſed miſts, and gaue vnto all that were well affected, exceeding cauſe of comfort; eſpecially when we beheld the gouernment eſtabliſhed in your HIGHNESSE, and your hopefull Seed, by an vndoubted Title, and this alſo accompanied with Peace and tranquillitie, at home and abroad.

But amongſt all our Ioyes, there was no one that more filled our hearts, then the bleſſed continuance of the Preaching of GODS ſacred word amongſt vs, which is that ineſtimable treaſure, which excelleth all the riches of the earth, becauſe the fruit thereof extendeth it ſelfe, not onely to the time ſpent in this tranſitory world, but directeth and diſpoſeth men vr to that Eternall happineſſe which is aboue in Heauen.

Then, not to ſuffer this to fall to the ground, but rather to take it vp, and to continue it in that ſtate, wherein the famous predeceſſour of your HIGHNESSE did leaue it; Nay, to goe forward with the confidence and reſo-
A 2   lution

▲ This 1611 Bible is dedicated "To the most high and mightie Prince, James." King James maintained that kings were "God's lieutenant's on earth," a martial analogy well-suited to the bloody religious disputes of the age. It took 47 ministers and 7 years to prepare the King James Bible.

As puritan social standards required husbands to rule over wives, so parents ruled over children. The virtue most insistently impressed on New England children was obedience; refusal to submit to parental direction was disturbing in itself and for what it implied about the child's eternal condition. Cotton Mather's advice, "better whipt, than damned," graced many a New England rod taken up by a parent in anger, from there to be rapidly transferred to the afterparts of misbehaving offspring. But household chores kept children out of mischief. By age six or seven girls did sewing and helped with housework and boys were put to work outdoors. Older children might be sent to live with another family to work as servants or apprentices.

Such practices, particularly when set beside portraits of early New England families that depict toddlers as somber-faced miniature adults wearing clothes indistinguishable from those of their parents, may convey the impression that puritans hustled their young through childhood with as little love as possible. New Englanders harbored no illusions. "Innocent vipers" is how one minister described children, having 14 of his own to submit as evidence. Anne Bradstreet, mother of eight, characterized one as harboring "a perverse will, a love of what's forbid / a serpent's sting in pleasing face lay hid." Yet for all their acceptance of the doctrine of infant damnation, puritan parents were not indifferent to the fate of their children. "I do hope," Cotton Mather confessed at the burial of one of the eight children he lost before the age of two, "that when my children are gone they are not lost; but carried unto the Heavenly Feast with Abraham." Another minister assigned children who died in infancy "the easiest room in hell."

Population growth reinforced puritan ideas about the family. When the outbreak of the English Civil War put an end to the Great Migration in the early 1640s, immigration declined sharply. Thereafter growth was chiefly due to the region's extraordinarily high birthrate (50 births for every 1000 population, which is more than three times the rate today) and strikingly low mortality rate (about 20 per 1000). This resulted in a population much more evenly distributed by age and sex than that in the South. The fact that most New England women married in their early twenties rather than their late teens suggests that the demand for women matched the supply. Demographic realities joined with puritan expectations to create a society of nuclear families distinct to the region.

VISIBLE PURITAN SAINTS AND OTHERS

When it came to religion, puritans believed that church membership ought to be the joint decision of a would-be member and those already in the church. Those seeking admission would tell the congregation why they believed that they had received God's grace. Obvious sinners and those ignorant of Christian doctrine were rejected out of hand. But what of pious and God-fearing applicants who lacked compelling evidence of salvation? In the late 1630s, with the Great Migration in full swing and new arrivals clamoring for admission to the churches, such "merit-mongers"

▲ New England children like David, Joanna, and Abigail Mason (painted by an unknown artist around 1670) were expected to emulate adults in their chores and their appearance. Nevertheless, diaries and letters indicate that children were cherished by their parents in a way closer to modern family love than what their European contemporaries experienced.

were excluded, thereby limiting church membership to the community's "visible saints." A decade later, the Great Migration over and applications down, some of the saints began to have second thoughts.

By the early 1650s fewer than half of all New England adults were church members, and so exacting had the examination for membership become, particularly in churches where the minister and elders outdid each other in the ferocity of their questioning, that most young people refused to submit themselves to it. How these growing numbers of nonmembers could be compelled to attend church services was a problem ministers could not long defer. Meanwhile, the magistrates found it harder to defend the policy of not letting taxpayers vote because they were not church members. But what really forced reconsideration of the membership policy were the concerns of nonmember parents about the souls of their children, who could not be baptized.

At first the churches permitted baptism of the children of church members. Later, some biblical purists came out against infant baptism altogether, but most puritans approved this practice, which allowed them the hope that a child who died after receiving baptism might at least be spared Hell's hottest precincts. Since most of the first generation were church members, nearly all the second-generation New Englanders were baptized, whether they became church members or not. The problem began with the third generation, the

offspring of parents who had been baptized but who did not become church members. By the mid-1650s it was clear that if nothing were done, soon a majority of the people would be living in a state of original sin. If that happened, how could the churches remain the dominant force in New England life?

Fortunately, a way out was at hand. In 1657 an assembly of Massachusetts and Connecticut ministers recommended a form of intermediate church membership that would permit the baptism of people who were not visible saints. Five years later, some 80 ministers and laymen met at Boston's First Church to hammer out what came to be called the Half-Way Covenant. It provided limited (halfway) membership for any applicant not known to be a sinner who was willing to accept the provisions of the church covenant. They and their children could be baptized, but the sacrament of communion and a voice in church decision making were reserved for full members.

The General Court of Massachusetts endorsed the recommendations of the Half-Way Synod and urged all the churches of the Commonwealth to adopt them. Two years later it quietly extended the right to vote to halfway church members.

Opponents of the Half-Way Covenant argued that it reflected a slackening of religious fervor. Michael Wigglesworth gave poetic voice to these views in "God's Controversy with New England" and "The Day of Doom," both written in 1662. Perry Miller, an authority on puritan New England, argued that the early 1660s marked the beginning of the decline, or "declension," of the puritan experiment. Some loss of religious intensity there may have been, but the rise in church memberships, the continuing prestige accorded ministers, and the lessening of the intrachurch squabbling after the 1660s suggest that the secularization of New England society had a long way to go.

DEMOCRACIES WITHOUT DEMOCRATS

Like the southern colonies, the New England colonies derived their authority from charters granted by the Crown or Parliament. Except for rare fits of meddling by London bureaucrats, they were largely left to their own devices where matters of purely local interest were concerned. This typically involved maintaining order by regulating how people behaved.

According to puritan theory, government was both a civil covenant, entered into by all who came within its jurisdiction, and the principal mechanism for policing the institutions on which the maintenance of the social order depended. When Massachusetts and Connecticut passed laws requiring church attendance, levying taxes

for the support of the clergy, and banning Quakers from practicing their faith, they were acting as "shield of the churches." When they provided the death penalty both for adultery and for blaspheming a parent, they were defending the integrity of families. When they set the price a laborer might charge for his services or even the amount of gold braid that servants might wear on their jackets, they believed they were enforcing the puritan principle that people must accept their assigned stations in life. Puritan communities were, for a time, close-knit: murder, assault, and theft were rare. Disputes were adjudicated through an active court system.

But puritan civil authorities and ministers of the puritan (Congregational) church came under sharp attack from English Anglicans, Presbyterians, and Quakers. When the Massachusetts General Court hanged four stubborn Quakers who returned after being expelled from the colony, a royal order of 1662 forbade further executions.

Laws like these have prompted historians and Americans generally to characterize New England colonial legislation as socially repressive and personally invasive. Yet many of the laws remained in force through the colonial period without rousing much local opposition. Others, particularly those upholding religious discrimination or restricting economic activity, were repealed at the insistence of Parliament.

A healthy respect for the backsliding ways of humanity obliged New Englanders not to depend too much on provincial governments, whose jurisdiction extended over several thousand square miles. Almost of necessity, the primary responsibility for maintaining "Good Order and Peace" fell to the more than 500 towns of the region. These differed greatly in size and development. By the early eighteenth century the largest, Boston, Newport, and Portsmouth, were on their way toward becoming urban centers. This was before "frontier" towns like Amherst, Kent, and Hanover had even been founded. Nonetheless, town life gave New England the distinctiveness it has still not wholly lost.

THE DOMINION OF NEW ENGLAND

The most serious threat to these arrangements occurred in the 1680s. Following the execution of Charles I in 1649, England was ruled by one man, the Lord Protector, Oliver Cromwell, a puritan. Cromwell's death in 1658 led to the restoration of the Stuart monarchy in the person of Charles II (1660–1685). During his reign and the abbreviated one of his brother, James II (1685–1688), the government sought to bring the colonies under effective royal control.

Massachusetts seemed in particular need of supervision. Accordingly, in 1684 its charter was annulled and the colony, along with all those north of Pennsylvania, became part of the Dominion of New England, governed by Edmund Andros.

Andros arrived in Boston in late 1686 with orders to make the northern colonies behave like colonies, not like sovereign powers. He set out to abolish popular assemblies, to change the land-grant system so as to provide the king with quitrents, and to enforce religious toleration, particularly of Anglicans. Andros, being a professional soldier and administrator, scoffed at those who resisted his authority. "Knoweing no other government than their owne," he said, they "think it best, and are wedded to . . . it."

Fortunately for New Englanders so wedded, the Dominion fell victim two years later to yet another political turnabout in England, the Glorious Revolution. In 1688 Parliament decided it had had enough of the Catholic-leaning Stuarts and sent James II packing. In his place it installed James's daughter Mary and her resolutely Protestant Dutch husband, William of Orange. When news of these events reached Boston in the spring of 1689, a force of more than a thousand colonists led by a contingent of ministers seized Andros and lodged him in jail. Two years later Massachusetts was made a royal colony that also included Plymouth and Maine. As in all such colonies the governor was appointed by the king. The new General Court was elected by property owners; church membership was no longer a requirement for voting.

SALEM BEWITCHED

In 1666, families living in the rural outback of the thriving town of Salem petitioned the General Court for the right to establish their own church. For political and economic reasons this was a questionable move, but in 1672 the General Court authorized the establishment of a separate parish. In so doing the Court put the 600-odd inhabitants of the village on their own politically as well.

Over the next 15 years three preachers came and went before, in 1689, one Samuel Parris became minister. Parris had spent 20 years in the Caribbean as a merchant and had taken up preaching only three years before coming to Salem. Accompanying him were his wife; a daughter, Betty; a niece, Abigail; and the family's West Indian slave, Tituba, who told fortunes and practiced magic on the side.

Parris proved as incapable of bringing peace to the feuding factions of Salem Village as had his predecessors. In January 1692 the church voted to dismiss him. At this point Betty and Abigail, now 9 and 11,

DOCUMENT

Ann Putnam's Deposition (1692)

along with Ann Putnam, a 12-year-old, started "uttering foolish, ridiculous speeches which neither they themselves nor any others could make sense of." A doctor diagnosed the girls' ravings as the work of the "Evil Hand" and declared them bewitched.

But who had done the bewitching? The first persons accused were three women whose unsavory reputations and frightening appearances made them likely candidates. Sarah Good, a pauper with a nasty tongue; Sarah Osborne, a bedridden widow; and the slave Tituba, who had brought suspicion on herself by volunteering to bake a "witch cake," made of rye meal and the girls' urine. The cake should be fed to a dog, Tituba said. If the girls were truly afflicted, the dog would show signs of bewitchment!

AUDIO
"Lookie There!"

The three women were brought before the local deputies to the General Court. As each was questioned, the girls went into contortions: "their arms, necks and backs turned this way and that way . . . their mouths stopped, their throats choked, their limbs wracked and tormented." Tituba, likely impressed by the powers ascribed to her, promptly confessed to being a witch. Sarah Good and Sarah Osborne each claimed to be innocent, although Sarah Good expressed doubts about Sarah Osborne. All three were sent to jail on suspicion of practicing witchcraft.

These proceedings triggered new accusations. By the end of April 1692, 24 more people had been charged with practicing witchcraft. Officials in neighboring Andover, lacking their own "bewitched," called in the girls to help with their investigations. By May the hunt had extended to Maine and Boston and up the social ladder to some of the colony's most prominent citizens, including Lady Mary Phips, whose husband, William, had just been appointed governor.

By June, when Governor Phips convened a special court consisting of members of his council, more than 150 persons (Lady Phips no longer among them) stood formally charged with practicing witchcraft. In the next four months the court convicted 28 of them, most of them women. Five "confessed" and were spared; the rest were condemned to death. Several others escaped. But 19 persons were hanged. The husband of a convicted witch refused to enter a plea when charged with being a "wizard." He was executed by having stones piled on him until he suffocated.

Anyone who spoke in defense of the accused was in danger of being charged with witchcraft, but some brave souls challenged both the procedures and the findings of the court. Finally, at the urging of the leading ministers of the Commonwealth, Governor Phips adjourned the court and forbade any further executions.

No one involved in these gruesome proceedings escaped with reputation intact, but those whose reputations suffered most were the ministers. Among the clergy only Increase Mather deserves any credit. He persuaded Phips to halt the executions, arguing that "it were better that ten witches should escape, than that one innocent person should be condemned." The behavior of his son Cotton defies apology. It was not that Cotton Mather accepted the existence of witches—at the time everyone did, which incidentally suggests that Tituba was not the only person in Salem who practiced witchcraft—or even that Mather took such pride in being the resident expert on demonology. It was rather his vindictiveness. He even stood at the foot of the gallows bullying hesitant hangmen into doing "their duty."

The episode also highlights the anxieties puritan men felt toward women. Many puritans believed that Satan worked his will especially through the allure of female sexuality. Moreover, many of the accused witches were widows of high status or older women who owned property; some of the women, like Tituba, had mastered herbal medicine and other suspiciously potent healing arts. Such women, especially those who lived apart from the daily guidance of men, potentially subverted the patriarchal authorities of church and state. (For more on this topic, see the feature essay, Re Viewing the Past "*The Crucible*," pp. 68–69.)

HIGHER EDUCATION IN NEW ENGLAND

Along with the farmers and artisans who settled in New England with their families during the Great Migration came nearly 150 university-trained colonists. Nearly all had studied divinity. These men became the first ministers in Massachusetts and Connecticut, and a brisk "seller's market" existed for them. Larger churches began stockpiling candidates by hiring newly arrived Cambridge and Oxford graduates as assistants or teachers in anticipation of the retirement of their senior ministers. But New England puritans could not forever remain dependent on the graduates of English universities.

In 1636 the Massachusetts General Court appropriated £400 to found "a schoole or colledge." Two years later, just as the first freshmen gathered in Cambridge, John Harvard, a recent arrival who had died of tuberculosis, left the college £800 and his library. After a shaky start, during which students conducted a hunger strike against a sadistic and larcenous headmaster, Harvard settled into an annual pattern of admitting a dozen or so 14-year-old boys, stuffing their heads with four years of theology, logic, and mathematics, and then sending them out into

▲ *Examination of a Witch.* A stern puritan patriarch adjusts his glasses to better examine a beautiful—and partially disrobed—young woman. Ostensibly, he's looking for the "witch's teats" with which she suckled "black dogs" and other creatures of the Devil. Completed in 1853 by T. H. Matteson, this painting subtly indicts puritan men as lecherous hypocrites. In fact, most accused witches were in their forties or fifties. The painting thus reveals more about the nineteenth-century reaction against puritanism than about the puritans themselves.

the wider world of New England. In 1650 Harvard received from the General Court the charter under which it is still governed.

Immediately below Harvard on the educational ladder came the grammar schools, where boys spent seven years learning Latin and Greek "so far as they may be fitted for the Universitie." Boston founded the first—the Boston Latin School—in 1636. Massachusetts and Connecticut soon passed education acts, which required all towns of any size to establish such schools. New Englanders hoped, as the preamble to the Massachusetts law of 1647 stated, to thwart "that old deluder, Satan," whose "chief object was to keep men from the knowledge of the Scriptures," by ensuring "that Learning may not be buried in the graves of our forefathers." Not every New England town required to maintain a school actually did so. Those that did often paid their teachers poorly. Only the most dedicated Harvard graduates took up teaching as a career. Some parents kept their children at their chores rather than at school.

Yet the cumulative effect of the puritan community's educational institutions, the family and the church as well as the school, was impressive. A majority of men in mid-seventeenth-century New England could read and a somewhat smaller percentage could also write. By the middle of the eighteenth century, male literacy was almost universal. In Europe only Scotland and Sweden had achieved this happy state so early. Literacy among women also improved steadily, despite the almost total neglect of formal education for girls.

Spreading literacy created a thriving market for the printed word. Many of the first settlers brought impressive libraries with them, and large numbers of English books were imported throughout the colonial period. The first printing press in the English colonies was founded in Cambridge in 1638, and by 1700 Boston was producing an avalanche of printed matter. Most of these publications were reprints of sermons; ministers required only the smallest encouragement

▶ *text continues on page 70*

Re-Viewing the Past

The Crucible

Winona Ryder stars in the 1996 movie based on Arthur Miller's 1953 play, *The Crucible,* an interpretation of the Salem witch trials of 1692. Ryder plays Abigail Williams, consumed with desire for John Proctor (Daniel Day-Lewis), a married man. Proctor has broken off their affair and reconciled with his wife, Elizabeth (Joan Allen). As the movie begins, Abigail and some other girls have sneaked into the woods with Tituba, a slave who practices black magic. They ask about their future husbands, and some beg her to cast a spell on their favorites. Abigail whispers something to Tituba, who recoils in horror. Abigail's dark eyes, glowing with fury, inform the movie audience of her message: she wants Elizabeth Proctor dead. Tituba slips into a trance and begins conjuring. Exhilarated by their illicit flouting of puritan convention, and quivering with sexual energy, the girls dance wildly around a fire, some throwing off all their clothes.

Then the minister happens onto the scene. The girls flee in terror. Some become hysterical. When confronted by church elders Abigail, glancing furtively at the other girls, blurts out that Tituba was a witch who was trying to steal their souls. Tituba initially denies the charges, but after being whipped she confesses. Pressed further, she names two other women as accomplices. At the mention of their names, Abigail's face contorts with pain and she moans; taking the cue, the other girls scream and writhe upon the floor. They supply the names of more witches. Alarmed by the enormity of Satan's plot, Massachusetts authorities initiate a thorough investigation.

After one court session, Abigail saunters over to John, standing by the side of the church. When he asks what "mischief" she has been up to, Abigail averts her eyes demurely and then gives him a wicked grin. John smiles at this prodigy in the seductive arts. She responds with a kiss, her hand groping for his groin. He hesitates, but then roughly pushes her away. Her eyes blaze with hatred.

The girls' hysterics intensify. Eventually over 100 suspected witches, most of them women, are arrested. The Proctors themselves come under suspicion. Asked to recite the Ten Commandments, John omits the injunction against adultery; the magistrate looks at him searchingly. When Abigail accuses Elizabeth of being a witch, John lashes out at the girl.

"She is a whore," he declares in court. "I have known her, sir."

"He is lying," she hisses. Suddenly her eyes widen, horror-stricken, and she screams that he, too, is in league with Satan. Her flawless histrionics again prevail: he is arrested.

During the trials, the magistrates look for physical evidence of satanic possession: unnatural flaps of skin or unusual warts—witch's teats—with which Satan's minions sap human souls. Family and neighbors, too, furnish evidence. Some cite occasions when the accused lost their tempers or stole livestock. But the main evidence is the behavior of the girls themselves, who squirm and howl, claiming that the spirits of the accused torment them. This "spectral" evidence unsettles the magistrates. Seeking stronger proof, they urge prisoners to confess. Those who do will be spared, for the act of confession signifies their break with Satan. Those who refuse must be hanged.

▼ Few portraits of single puritan women exist; their invisibility may help explain why some sought attention, perhaps by making witchcraft accusations. The young woman in this portrait became "visible" by becoming a mother.

The Proctors are among those convicted and sentenced to death. (Because Elizabeth is pregnant, her execution is postponed.) When given the opportunity to save himself, John signs a confession. But inspired by his wife's quiet courage, he repudiates it, choosing to die with honor rather than live in shame. His noble death at the scaffold, and the deaths of others like him, cause the people of Massachusetts to end the witch hunt.

The movie warrants consideration apart from Ryder's remarkable performance. For one, the movie vividly recreates a puritan world inhabited by palpable spirits. Contemporary viewers may snicker at scenes of adults scanning the night sky for flying witches and evil birds, but the puritans believed in such things. They regarded comets, meteors, and lightning as signals from God. When Cotton Mather lost the pages of some lectures, he concluded that "Spectres, or Agents in the invisible World, were the Robbers."

Episodes and language taken directly from trial records, though sometimes altered, infuse the movie with verisimilitude. For example, the Proctors were in fact interrogated on their biblical knowledge. Whereas in the movie John falters by omitting the commandment against adultery, in history, the fatal mistake was Elizabeth's. Asked to recite the Lord's Prayer, she substituted "hollowed be thy name" for "hallowed be thy name." The magistrates declared this to be a "depraving" act, for she had transformed the prayer into a curse—proof of satanic possession.

The movie's rendering of the girls' hysteria mostly corresponds with what we know from the historical record. A bewildered John Hale, a minister from Beverly, recorded that Abigail and her cousin were

> bitten and pinched by invisible agents. Their arms, necks and backs turned this way and that way, and returned back again, so as it was impossible for them to do of themselves. . . . Sometimes they were taken dumb, their mouths stopped, their throats choked, their limbs wracked and tormented so as might move an heart of stone . . . with bowels of compassion for them.

Historians still puzzle over the girls' behavior. Probably they were seeking attention, or venting anxiety over their fate as women in a patriarchal society; certainly their choice of victims suggests that they were voicing parental enmity toward neighbors. The movie alludes to such issues, but mostly attributes the girls' hysteria to sexual frustration, a consequence of puritan repression.

Ryder's Abigail symbolizes adolescent sexuality: her lust for John (and corresponding hatred of Elizabeth) precipitates the witch hunt. In point of fact, the real Abigail did accuse Elizabeth of witchcraft. The trial record reports that when Elizabeth denied the charge, Abigail raised her hand as if to strike her, but instead touched Elizabeth's hood "very lightly" and cried out, "My fingers! My fingers—burned!" Then Abigail swooned to the floor. But if these few details provide some basis for Abigail's conjectured affair with Elizabeth's husband, others call it into question, the most awkward being the gap in their ages: The real Abigail was 11 and Proctor, 60.

▶ Winona Ryder as a young puritan who accuses others of witchcraft.

Whatever the merits of playwright Arthur Miller's speculation about Abigail and John, his larger questions have long intrigued historians: Were the puritans sexually repressive? If so, did young people assent to puritan strictures or rebel against them?

Such questions cannot be answered with certainty. Few puritans left written accounts of their illicit thoughts and sexual behavior. Social historians have approached the matter from a different angle. Nearly all marriages and births in colonial New England (and most other places) were recorded. Scholars have scoured such records to determine how many brides gave 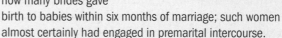 birth to babies within six months of marriage; such women almost certainly had engaged in premarital intercourse.

This data for about a dozen communities in puritan New England indicate an extraordinarily low rate of premarital intercourse, far below England's at the same time or New England's a century later. This confirms that young puritan couples were watched closely. Governor William Bradford of Plymouth Colony, commenting on the relative absence of premarital pregnancy, concluded that sinners there were "more discovered and seen and made public by due search, inquisition and due punishment; for the churches look narrowly to their members, and the magistrates over all, more strictly than in other places." On the other hand, the low rate of premarital pregnancy might not signify puritan repression so much as young people's acceptance of puritan values.

When critics confronted Arthur Miller on his deviations from the historical record, and especially when they expressed skepticism over whether young Abigail Williams and the elderly John Proctor had an affair, Miller was unrepentant. "What's real?" he retorted. "We don't know what these people were like." Perhaps so, but one suspects that Winona Ryder's Abigail would have had a hard time of it in Salem in 1692. Could a bloom of such pungent and venomous precocity have emerged through the stony soil of New England Puritanism, and if so, could it have survived the assiduous weeding of the puritans themselves?

from their congregations to send off last Sunday's remarks to the local printer. But if ministers exercised a near monopoly of the printed word, they did not limit their output to religious topics. They also produced modest amounts of history, poetry, reports of scientific investigations, and treatises on political theory.

Colonial Families: Adult and Child Reading

By the early eighteenth century the intellectual life of New England had taken on a character potentially at odds with the ideas of the first puritans. In the 1690s Harvard acquired a reputation for encouraging religious toleration. According to orthodox puritans, its graduates were unfit for the ministry and its professors were no longer interested in training young men for the clergy. In 1701 several Connecticut ministers, most of them Harvard graduates, founded a new "Collegiate School" designed to uphold the puritan values that Harvard seemed ready to abandon. The new college was named after its first English benefactor, Elihu Yale. It fulfilled its founders' hopes by sending more than half of its early graduates into the ministry. Nonetheless, as became all too clear at commencement ceremonies in 1722 when its president and six tutors announced themselves Anglicans, Yale quickly acquired purposes well beyond those assigned it by its creators.

The assumption that the clergy had the last word on learned matters, still operative at the time of the witchcraft episode, came under direct challenge in 1721. When a smallpox epidemic swept through Boston that summer, Cotton Mather, at the time the most prestigious clergyman in New England, recommended that the citizenry be inoculated. Instead of accepting Mather's authority, his heretofore silent critics seized on his support of the then-radical idea of inoculation to challenge both his motives and his professional credentials. They filled the unsigned contributor columns of New England's first newspaper, the *Boston Gazette*, and the *New England Courant,* which started in the midst of the inoculation controversy, with their views.

The *Courant* was published by James Franklin and his 16-year-old brother, Benjamin. The younger Franklin's "Silence Dogood" essays were particularly infuriating to members of the Boston intellectual establishment. Franklin described Harvard as an institution where rich and lazy "blockheads . . . learn little more than how to carry themselves handsomely . . . and from whence they return, after Abundance of Trouble, as Blockheads as ever, only more proud and conceited."

James Franklin was jailed in 1722 for criticizing the General Court, and shortly thereafter the *New England Courant* went out of business. Meanwhile, Ben had departed Boston for Philadelphia, where fame and fortune awaited him.

PROSPERITY UNDERMINES PURITANISM

Prior experience (and the need to eat) turned the first New Englanders to farming. They grew barley (used to make beer), rye, oats, green vegetables, and also native crops such as potatoes, pumpkins, and, most important, Indian corn, or maize. Corn was easily cultivated, and its yield per acre under rough frontier conditions exceeded that of other grains. It proved versatile and tasty when prepared in a variety of ways and also made excellent fodder for livestock. In the form of corn liquor, it was easy to store, to transport, and, in a pinch, to imbibe.

The colonists also had plenty of meat. They grazed cattle, sheep, and hogs on the common pastures or in the surrounding woodlands. Deer, along with turkey and other game birds, abounded. The Atlantic provided fish, especially cod, which was easily preserved by salting. In short, New Englanders ate an extremely nutritious diet. Abundant surpluses of firewood kept the winter cold from their doors. The combination contributed significantly to their good health and longevity.

The trouble was that virtually everything that New England farmers grew could be grown in Europe. The shortness of the growing season, the rocky and often hilly terrain, and careless methods of cultivation, which exhausted the soil, meant that farmers did not produce large surpluses. Thus, while New Englanders could feed themselves without difficulty, they had relatively little to spare and no place to sell it.

The earliest puritans accepted this economic marginality. The more pious positively welcomed it as insurance against "the serpent prosperity," which might otherwise deflect their spiritual mission into commercial opportunism. No prominent English merchants joined the Great Migration, though many were devoted puritans and some had invested in the Massachusetts Bay Company. Settlers who turned to business on arrival attracted suspicion, if not open hostility. Laws against usury (lending money at excessive rates) and profiteering in scarce commodities were in effect from the first days of settlement. Robert Keayne, a prosperous Boston merchant, was twice fined £200 by the General Court and admonished by his church for "taking above six-pence in the shilling profit; in some above eight-pence; and in some small things, above two for one." Keayne paid the fines and made "penitential acknowledgment" to his church, all the while convinced that "my goods and prices were cheap pennyworths."

Early puritan leaders resisted the argument of people like Keayne that business was a calling no less socially useful than the ministry or public office.

DEBATING THE PAST

Were puritan communities peaceable? A smooth, quiet river flows past this eighteenth-century puritan town. A church spire rises, treelike, from its center. The painting is a composition in harmony. In *The Scarlet Letter* (1850), however, Nathaniel Hawthorne shattered this placid image: Puritan towns were plagued with envy, intolerance, and hypocrisy. Hawthorne's harsh assessment, which many historians shared, persisted into the twentieth century. This view changed with Perry Miller (1933), whose elegant analysis of puritan sermons and writings amply demonstrated "the majesty and coherence of Puritan thinking." The rise of atheistic communism in the Soviet Union after World War II further contributed to an appreciation of the nation's puritan roots. Daniel Boorstin (1958) wrote approvingly of the strong families, religious faith, and democratic governance of puritan towns. During the 1960s a new generation of historians examined the issue. They had been influenced by Fernand Braudel, a French scholar. Braudel encouraged historians to reconstruct the "total history" of particular communities, rather like anthropologists. The publication of four such studies in 1970 reinvigorated colonial social history. John Demos discovered that families in Plymouth, Massachusetts, were beset with psychological conflicts; Philip Greven and Kenneth Lockridge found that Dedham and Andover, Massachusetts lost cohesion rapidly; Paul Zuckerman, on the other hand, concluded that his puritan towns most nearly resembled "peaceable kingdoms." Other studies complicated the picture further: Paul Boyer and Stephen Nissenbaum (1974) contended that Salem was wracked with class and religious tensions, while other scholars found communities that became increasingly cohesive. Which towns reflected the characteristic puritan pattern? The focus in recent decades has shifted from individual towns. David Hackett Fischer (1989) and Alan Taylor (2001) insisted that the puritans should be examined not in towns such as this one, but in relation to a much larger, even trans-Atlantic, context.

Perry Miller, *Orthodoxy in Massachusetts* (1933) and *The New England Mind* (1939), Daniel Boorstin, *The Colonial Experience* (1958), John Demos, *A Little Commonwealth* (1970), Philip J. Greven, *Four Generations* (1970), Kenneth Lockridge, *A New England Town* (1970), Michael Zuckerman, *Peaceable Kingdoms* (1970), Paul Boyer and Stephen Nissenbaum, *Salem Possessed* (1974), David Hackett Fischer, *Albion's Seed* (1989), Alan Taylor, *American Colonies* (2001).

Differences in wealth should be modest and should favor those to whom the community looked for leadership. In the puritan scheme of things, since Governor Winthrop was a far more valuable member of the community than Robert Keayne, he should stand higher than Keayne in all rankings, wealth included.

But Winthrop died in 1649 broke and in debt, whereas Keayne died three years later in sufficient prosperity (despite those stiff fines) to leave the town of Boston and Harvard College impressive benefactions. The gap between the puritan ideal and the emerging reality was becoming embarrassingly clear.

A MERCHANT'S WORLD

Winthrop's generation had tried to minimize dependence on European-manufactured goods such as iron tools, glass, and cloth by producing their own. When their efforts failed, they next pinned their hopes on establishing direct trade links with European suppliers by offering the skins of beaver and such other fur-bearing animals as otter, muskrat, and mink. Unfortunately, the beavers soon caught wind of what was going on and took off for points west and north. By the end of the late 1650s the New Englanders were back where they started. As one English merchant wrote, as trading partners New Englanders "have noe returns."

The colonists then turned to indirect trading schemes, in which merchants like Robert Keayne played a central role and from which they ultimately derived stature as well as wealth. The anticommercial bias of the early puritans did not, however, vanish as quickly as the elusive beaver had. At the beginning of the eighteenth century a Boston minister could still tell his congregation this story with every confidence that they shared his belief that his colleague got the better of the Maine fisherman: Once, some years after Keayne's death, a minister in Maine was reminding his flock that "the main end of planting this wilderness" was religion. A prominent member of the congregation could not contain his disagreement. "Sir," he cried out, "you are mistaken. You think you are preaching to the people of the Bay; our main end was to catch fish."

Colonial Products

Fish, caught offshore on grounds that extended from Cape Cod to Newfoundland, provided merchants with their opening into the world of transatlantic commerce. In 1643 five New England vessels set out with their holds packed with fish that they sold in Spain and the Canary Islands; they took payment in sherry and madeira, for which a market existed in England. One of these ships also had the dubious distinction of initiating New England into the business of trafficking in human beings when its captain took payment in African slaves, whom he subsequently sold in the West Indies. This was the start of the famous "triangular trade." Only occasionally was the pattern truly triangular; more often, intermediate legs gave it a polygonal character. So long as their ships ended up with something that could be exchanged for English goods needed at home, it did not matter what they started out with or how many things they bought and sold along the way.

So maritime trade and those who engaged in it became the driving force of the New England economy, important all out of proportion to the number of persons directly involved. Because those engaged

congregated in Portsmouth, Salem, Boston, Newport, and New Haven, these towns soon differed greatly from towns in the interior. They were larger and faster growing, and a smaller percentage of their inhabitants was engaged in farming.

The largest and most thriving town was Boston, which by 1720 had become the commercial hub of the region. It had a population of more than 10,000; in the entire British Empire, only London and Bristol were larger. More than one-quarter of Boston's male adults had either invested in shipbuilding or were directly employed in maritime commerce. Ship captains and merchants held most of the public offices.

Beneath this emergent mercantile elite lived a stratum of artisans and small shopkeepers, and beneath these a substantial population of mariners, laborers, and "unattached" people with little or no property and still less political voice. In the 1670s, at least a dozen prostitutes plied their trade in Boston. By 1720 crime and poverty had become serious problems; public relief rolls frequently exceeded 200 souls, and dozens of criminals languished in the town jail. Boston bore little resemblance to what the first puritans had in mind when they planted their "Citty upon a Hill." But neither was it like any eighteenth-century European city. It stood there on Massachusetts Bay, midway between its Puritan origins and its American future.

THE MIDDLE COLONIES: ECONOMIC BASIS

New York, New Jersey, Pennsylvania, and Delaware owe their collective name, the Middle Colonies, to geography. Sandwiched between New England and the Chesapeake region, they often receive only passing notice in accounts of colonial America. The lack of a distinctive institution, such as slavery or the town meeting, explains part of this neglect.

The Colonies to 1740

Actually, both institutions existed there. Black slaves made up about 10 percent of the population; indeed, one New York county in the 1740s had proportionally more blacks than large sections of Virginia. And eastern Long Island was settled by people from Connecticut who brought the town meeting system with them.

This quality of "in-betweenness" extended to other economic and social arrangements. Like colonists elsewhere, most Middle Colonists became farmers. But where northern farmers concentrated on producing crops for local consumption and southerners for export, Middle Colony farmers did both. In

addition to raising foodstuffs and keeping livestock, they grew wheat, which the thin soil and shorter growing season of New England did not permit but for which there existed an expanding market in the densely settled Caribbean sugar islands.

Social arrangements differed more in degree than in kind from those in other colonies. Unlike New England settlers, who clustered together in agricultural villages, families in the Hudson Valley of New York and in southeastern Pennsylvania lived on the land they cultivated, often as spatially dispersed as the tobacco planters of the Chesapeake. In contrast with Virginia and Maryland, however, substantial numbers congregated in the seaport centers of New York City and Philadelphia. They also settled interior towns like Albany, an important center of the fur trade on the upper Hudson, and Germantown, an "urban village" northwest of Philadelphia where many people were engaged in trades like weaving and tailoring and flour milling.

THE MIDDLE COLONIES: AN INTERMINGLING OF PEOPLES

The Middle Colonists also possessed traits that later would be seen as distinctly "American." Their ethnic and religious heterogeneity is a case in point. In the 1640s, when New Amsterdam was only a village, one visitor claimed to have heard 18 languages spoken there. Traveling through Pennsylvania a century later, the Swedish botanist Peter Kalm encountered "a very mixed company of different nations and religions." In addition to "Scots, English, Dutch, Germans, and Irish," he reported, "there were Roman Catholics, Presbyterians, Quakers, Methodists, Seventh day men, Moravians, Anabaptists, and one Jew." In New York City one embattled English resident complained: "Our chiefest unhappiness here is too great a mixture of nations, & English the least part."

Scandinavian and Dutch settlers outnumbered the English in New Jersey and Delaware even after the English took over these colonies. William Penn's first success in attracting colonists was with German Quakers and other persecuted religious sects, among them Mennonites and Moravians from the Rhine Valley. The first substantial influx of immigrants into New York after it became a royal colony consisted of French Huguenots.

Early in the eighteenth century, hordes of Scots-Irish settlers from northern Ireland and Scotland descended on Pennsylvania. These colonists spoke English but felt little loyalty to the English government,

▲ This painting is presumably of Lord Cornbury, the royal governor of New York and New Jersey in the early 1700s, in a dress. Why it was painted and by whom is unknown. Some regard the painting as proof that the eighteenth century tolerated a wide range of sexual behaviors. In *The Lord Cornbury Scandal* (1998), however, Patricia Bonomi views the painting as part of a plot to unseat a brusque and high-handed governor. Some of his enemies in the colonies dispatched letters to officials in London complaining of Cornbury's penchant for wearing women's clothing in public. Bonomi doubts that the charges were true.

which had treated them badly back home, and less to the Anglican Church, since most of them were Presbyterians. Large numbers of them followed the valleys of the Appalachians south into the back country of Virginia and the Carolinas.

Why so few English in the Middle Colonies? Here, again, timing provides the best answer. The English economy was booming. There seemed to be work for all. Migration to North America, while never drying up, slowed to a trickle. The result was colonies in which English settlers were a minority.

The intermingling of ethnic groups gave rise to many prejudices. Benjamin Franklin, though generally complimentary toward Pennsylvania's hardworking Germans, thought them clannish to a fault.

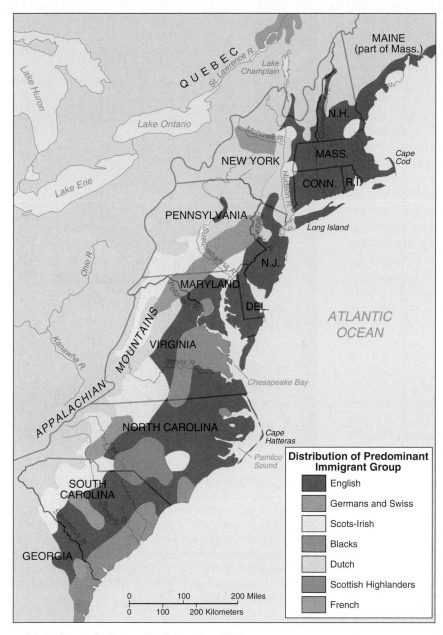

▲ **Ethnic Groups in Eastern North America, 1750**

"THE BEST POOR MAN'S COUNTRY"

Ethnic differences seldom caused conflict in the Middle Colonies because they seldom limited opportunity. The promise of prosperity (promotional pamphlets proclaimed Pennsylvania "the best poor man's country in the world") had attracted all in the first place, and achieving prosperity was relatively easy, even for those who came with only a willingness to work. From its founding, Pennsylvania granted upward of 500 acres of land to families on arrival, provided they would pay the proprietor an annual quitrent. Similar arrangements existed in New Jersey and Delaware. Soon travelers in the Middle Colonies were being struck by "a pleasing uniformity of decent competence."

New York was something of an exception to this favorable economic situation. When the English took over New York, they extended the Dutch patroon system by creating 30 manorial estates covering about 2 million acres. But ordinary New Yorkers never lacked ways of becoming landowners. A hundred acres along the Hudson River could be bought in 1730 for what an unskilled laborer could earn in three months. Even tenants on the manorial estates could obtain long-term leases that had most of the advantages of ownership but did not require the investment of any capital. "One may think oneself to be a great lord," one frustrated "lord" of a New York manor wrote a colleague, "but it does not amount to much, as you well know."

Mixed farming offered the most commonly trod path to prosperity in the Middle Colonies, but not the only one. Inland communities offered comfortable livelihoods for artisans. Farmers always needed barrels, candles, rope, horseshoes and nails, and dozens of other articles in everyday use. Countless opportunities awaited the ambitious settler in the shops, yards, and offices of New York and Philadelphia. Unlike Boston, New York and Philadelphia profited from navigable rivers that penetrated deep

The already cited French traveler Hector St. John de Crèvecoeur, while marveling at the adaptive qualities of "this promiscuous breed," complained that "the Irish . . . love to drink and to quarrel; they are litigious, and soon take to the gun, which is the ruin of everything." Yet by and large the various types managed to get along with each other successfully enough. Crèvecoeur attended a wedding in Pennsylvania where the groom's grandparents were English and Dutch and one of his uncles had married a Frenchwoman. The groom and his three brothers, Crèvecoeur added with some amazement, "now have four wives of different nations."

into the back country. Although founded half a century after New York and Boston, Philadelphia grew more rapidly than either. In the 1750s, when its population reached 15,000, it passed Boston to become the largest city in English America.

Most Philadelphians who stuck to their business, particularly if it happened to be maritime commerce, did well for themselves. John Bringhurst, a merchant, began his career as a clerk. At his death in 1751 he left an estate of several thousand pounds. The city's "leather-apron" artisans often accumulated estates of more than £400, a substantial sum at the time. By way of contrast, in Boston after 1710, economic stagnation made it much more difficult for a skilled artisan to rise in the world.

THE POLITICS OF DIVERSITY

"Cannot more friendly and private courses be taken to set matters right in an infant province?" an exasperated William Penn asked the people of Pennsylvania in 1704. "For the love of God, me, and the poor country, be not so governmentish." However well-intentioned Penn's advice, however justified his annoyance, the Pennsylvanians ignored him. Instead, they and their fellows throughout the region constructed a political culture that diverged sharply from the patterns of New England and the South both in contentiousness and in the sophistication required of local politicians.

Superficially the governments of the Middle Colonies closely resembled those of earlier settlements. All had popularly elected representative assemblies, and most white male adults could vote. In Pennsylvania, where Penn had insisted that there be no religious test and where 50 acres constituted a freehold, something close to white universal manhood suffrage existed. In New York even non-property-holding white male residents voted in local elections, and rural tenants with lifetime leases enjoyed full voting rights.

In Pennsylvania and most of New York, representatives were elected by counties. In this they resembled Virginia and Maryland. But unlike the Southerners, voters did not tend to defer in politics to the landed gentry. In New York, in 1689, during the political vacuum following the abdication of King James II, Jacob Leisler, a disgruntled merchant and militia captain, seized control of the government. "Leisler's Rebellion" did not amount to much. He held power for less than two years before he was overthrown and sent to the gallows. Yet for two decades New York politics continued to be a struggle between the Leislerians, and other self-conscious "outs" who shared Leisler's dislike of English rule, and anti-Leislerians, who had in common only that they had opposed his takeover. Each group sought the support of a succession of ineffective governors,

and the one that failed to get it invariably proceeded to make that poor man's tenure as miserable as possible.

New York lapsed into political tranquility during the governorship of Robert Hunter (1710–1719), but in the early 1730s conflict broke out over a claim for back salary by Governor William Cosby. When Lewis Morris, the chief justice of the supreme court, opposed Cosby's claim, the governor replaced him. Morris and his assembly allies responded by establishing the *New York Weekly Journal*. To edit the paper they hired an itinerant German printer, John Peter Zenger.

Governor Cosby might have tolerated the *Weekly Journal*'s front-page lectures on the right of the people to criticize their rulers had the back pages not contained advertisements referring to his supporters as spaniels and to him as a monkey. After submitting to two months of "open and implacable malice against me," he shut down the paper, arrested Zenger, and charged him with seditious libel.

What began as a squalid salary dispute became one of the most celebrated tests of freedom of the press in the history of journalism. At the trial Zenger's attorney, James Hamilton, argued that the truth of his client's criticisms of Cosby constituted a proper defense against seditious libel. This reasoning (though contrary to English law at the time) persuaded the jury to acquit Zenger.

Politics in Pennsylvania turned on conflict between two interest groups, one clustered around the proprietor, the other around the assembly, which was controlled by a coalition of Quaker representatives from Philadelphia and the German-speaking Pennsylvania Dutch.

Neither the proprietary party nor the Quaker party qualifies as a political party in the modern sense of being organized and maintained for the purpose of winning elections. Nor can they be categorized as standing for "democratic" or "aristocratic" interests. But their existence guaranteed that the political leaders had to take popular opinion into account. Moreover, having once appealed to public opinion, they had to be prepared to defer to it. Success turned as much on knowing how to follow as on knowing how to lead.

The 1763 uprising of the "Paxton Boys" of western Pennsylvania put this policy to a full test. The uprising was triggered by eastern indifference to Indian attacks on the frontier—an indifference made possible by the fact that the east outnumbered the west in the assembly, 26 to 10. Fuming because they could obtain no help from Philadelphia against the Indians, a group of Scots-Irish from Lancaster county fell on a village of peaceful Conestoga Indians and murdered them in cold blood. Then these Paxton Boys marched on Philadelphia, several hundred strong.

Fortunately a delegation of burghers, headed by Benjamin Franklin, talked the Paxton Boys out of

attacking the town by acknowledging the legitimacy of their grievances about representation and by promising to vote a bounty on Indian scalps! It was just such fancy footwork that established Franklin, the leader of the assembly party, as Pennsylvania's consummate politician. "Tell me, Mr. Franklin," a testy member of the proprietary party asked, "how is it that you are always with the majority?" Soon thereafter, the assembly sent Franklin to London to defend local interests against the British authorities, a situation in which he would definitely not be "with the majority."

REBELLIOUS WOMEN

Overlaying the political disputes and contentions of the era was a general anxiety over the role of women. Anne Hutchinson had drawn the wrath of Massachusetts puritan authorities by criticizing their teachings and humiliating them in public debate; puritan anxieties toward unattached or independent women surfaced later in the Salem witch trials. This concern was not confined to New England. In 1661 Governor Berkeley of Virginia issued a proclamation threatening Quaker women, but not men, with imprisonment if they persisted in disseminating "schismaticall and hereticall doctrines." These and other attempts to suppress women's activity in church and political meetings backfired. Many women endorsed Bacon's Rebellion; some were imprisoned when it was crushed. The governor's inability to control refractory women was symptomatic of widespread uneasiness toward women among the seemingly omnipotent planter elite. If men could not control their wives, how could they claim to be gentlemen at all?

The authority of husbands, and indeed of male political leaders and elites, differed over time and place. But the general trend was away from a model of social and political power derived from the hierarchical example of a family, where the authority of the husband was analogous to that of the monarch. Although this shift was toward political egalitarianism, it did not empower women. Before the eighteenth century, women who headed a family could assume authority in public matters. But by the mid-eighteenth century, white women were expected to confine themselves to private matters within the home.

MILESTONES

1619	First Africans are sold in Virginia	1692	Salem village holds witchcraft trials
1636	Puritans found Boston Latin School and Harvard College	1696	Virginia colonists found College of William and Mary
1657	Half-Way Covenant leads to rise in puritan church memberships		Rice cultivation is introduced in South Carolina
1676	Western planters launch Bacon's Rebellion in Virginia	1701	Connecticut ministers found Yale College
1684–1688	Edmund Andros rules Dominion of New England	1733	George Oglethorpe leads settlement of Georgia
1689	Leisler's Rebellion in New York seizes control of government		

SUPPLEMENTARY READING

Among general interpretations, D. J. Boorstin's *The Americans: The Colonial Experience* (1958), emphasizes the modern aspects of colonial society; Jon Butler's *Becoming America: The Revolution before 1776* (2000) similarly and more broadly emphasizes the rapid evolution of colonial society. Alan Kulikoff, *From British Peasants to Colonial American Farmers* (2000) underscores the importance of land in defining American life. Alan Taylor, *American Colonies* (2001) emphasizes the links between European and American societies.

On economic conditions, see John J. McCusker and Russell R. Menard, eds., *The Economy of British America, 1607–1789* (1991). For the economic growth of colonial New England, see Margaret Ellen Newell, *From Dependency to Independence* (1998). On the chronologically and geographically uneven development of slavery in America, consult Ira Berlin, *Generations of Captivity: A History of African-American Slaves* (2003) and *Many Thousands Gone* (1998). See also Philip D. Morgan, *Slave Counterpoint* (1998) and P. D. Curtin, *The Rise and Fall of the Plantation Complex* (1990). Alan Gallay, *The Indian Slave Trade* (2002) uncovers an issue that has long been overlooked.

On life in the colonial South, see T. W. Tate and David Ammerman, eds., *The Chesapeake in the Seventeenth Century* (1979), Allan Kulikoff, *Tobacco and Slaves* (1986),

D. B. and A. H. Rutman, *A Place in Time* (1984), and Timothy H. Breen and Stephen Innes, *"Myne Owne Ground": Race and Freedom on Virginia's Eastern Shore* (1980).

Family and community life are surveyed in D. F. Hawke, *Everyday Life in Early America* (1988), and Edmund S. Morgan, *The Puritan Family* (1966). The places of women and children are effectively presented in Laurel T. Ulrich, *Good Wives: Image and Reality in the Lives of Women in Northern New England* (1982), and Philip Greven, *The Protestant Temperament: Patterns of Child-Rearing, Religious Experience, and the Self in Early America* (1980). Richard Godbeer, *Sexual Revolution in Early America* (2002) corrects the stereotype of the puritans as sexually repressive.

The works of Perry Miller remain the starting point for any serious study of the cultural life of colonial New England. Among them, *Errand into the Wilderness* (1956) provides a good introduction. More recent studies, most of which modify Miller's judgments, include D. D. Hall, *Worlds of Wonder, Days of Judgment* (1989), and Patricia U. Bonomi, *Under the Cope of Heaven* (1986). Some recent scholarship contends that Puritan practices complemented economic development: for example, John Frederick Martin, *Profits in the Wilderness* (1991), Stephen Innes, *Creating the Commonwealth* (1995), and Mark A. Peterson, *The Price of Redemption* (1997).

Larry D. Gragg, *The Salem Witch Crisis* (1992) provides a narrative account. Paul Boyer and Stephen Nissenbaum, *Salem Possessed* (1974), argue that the episode grew out of tensions between different factions within the community. Mary Beth Norton, *In the Devil's Snare: The Salem Witchcraft*

Crisis of 1692 (2002), views the crisis as a response to fear of Indians. The subject is considered more generally in John Demos, *Entertaining Satan: Witchcraft and the Culture of Early New England* (1982). On women and witchcraft, see Elizabeth Reis, *Damned Women* (1997), Elaine G. Breslaw, *Tituba, Reluctant Witch of Salem* (1996), and Carol F. Karlsen, *The Devil in the Shape of a Woman* (1987).

For an engaging overview of the ideology of gender authority in the seventeenth century, see Mary Beth Norton, *Founding Mothers and Fathers* (1996). On women and religion in New England, see also Susan Juster, *Disorderly Women* (1994). Karin Wolf, *Not All Wives* (2000), describes the range of women's activities in Philadelphia. For the role of women in Virginia, see Kathleen M. Brown, *Good Wives, Nasty Wenches and Anxious Patriarchs* (1996).

Educational and intellectual developments are treated in Bernard Bailyn, *Education in the Forming of American Society* (1960), and L. A. Cremin, *American Education: The Colonial Experience* (1970).

In the past decade there has been a profusion of studies on the interrelationship between settlers and Indians: Jane T. Merritt, *At the Crossroads: Indians and Empire on a Mid-Atlantic Frontier* (2003), Richard White, *The Middle Ground* (1991), Daniel K. Richter, *Ordeal of the Longhouse* (1992), Daniel H. Usner, *Indians, Settlers, and Slaves in a Frontier Exchange Economy* (1992), Colin G. Calloway, *New Worlds for All: Indians, Europeans, and the Remaking of Early America* (1997), Karen O. Kupperman, *Indians and English* (2001), and James F. Brooks, *Captives and Cousins* (2002).

SUGGESTED WEBSITES

LVA Colonial Records Project—Index of Digital Facsimiles of Documents on Early Virginia
http://ajax.lva.lib.va.us/F/?func=file&file_name=find-b-clas27&local_base=CLAS27
This site contains reproductions of numerous documents.

DSL Archives: Slave Movement During the Eighteenth and Ninteenth Centuries (Wisconsin)
http://dpls.dacc.wisc.edu/slavedata/index.html
This site explores the slave ships and the slave trade that carried thousands of Africans to the New World.

Witchcraft in Salem Village
http://etext.virginia.edu/salem/witchcraft/
This University of Virginia site offers an extensive archive of the 1692 trials as well as life in late seventeenth-century Massachusetts.

Salem Witchcraft Trials (1692)
http://www.law.umkc.edu/faculty/projects/ftrials/salem/salem.htm
Images, chronology, court and officials documents by Dr. Doug Linder of the University of Missouri–Kansas City Law School.

Benjamin Franklin
http://sln.fi.edu/franklin/rotten.html
This Benjamin Franklin Institute site contains information and sources treating one of early-America's most well-known figures.

Religion and the Founding of the American Republic
http://lcweb.loc.gov/exhibits/religion/religion.html
This Library of Congress site is an online exhibit about religion and the formation of the United States.

DoHistory, Harvard University Film Center
http://www.dohistory.org/
Focusing on the life of Martha Ballard, a late eighteenth-century New England woman, this site employs selections from her diary, excerpts from a book and film about her life, and other primary documents that enable students to conduct their own historical investigation.

Anglicans, Puritans, and Quakers in Colonial America
http://www.mun.ca/rels/ang/texts/
This site provides information on the major religious movements in colonial America.

▼ British warships at anchor off New York harbor. The British Empire offered protection to its colonies, and the colonies provided advantageous terms of trade to the mother country. The fleet doubtless reassured the people of New York, yet it also reminded them of their subordination.

CHAPTER CONTENTS

Since the colonies were founded piecemeal by persons with varying motives and backgrounds, common traditions and loyalties developed slowly. For the same reason, the British government was slow to think of its American possessions as a unit or to deal with them in any centralized way. They were the king's possessions. As a good sovereign he was obligated to use them in a manner consonant with the public interest, but it was left to him and his advisers to decide what that interest was. No authority challenged the monarch's right to dispose of one section of the American domain to this group of merchants under such-and-such terms and another to that personal friend or creditor under a different arrangement. The specific form of each colony's government and the degree of local independence similarly depended on the nature of those particular arrangements.

THE BRITISH COLONIAL SYSTEM

There was a pattern basic to all colonial governments and a general framework of imperial control for all the king's overseas plantations. English political and legal institutions took hold everywhere in British America. While the colonists and the home authorities often had different motives in establishing new settlements, their motives seldom conflicted. Ruler and ruled alike sought prosperity, political and economic expansion, and the reproduction of Old World civilization.

In the earliest days of any settlement, the need to rely on home authorities was so obvious that few questioned England's sovereignty. Thereafter, as the fledglings grew strong enough to think of using their own wings, distance and British political inefficiency combined to allow them a great deal of freedom. External affairs were controlled entirely by London, and royal representatives in America tried to direct colonial policy. But in practice the Crown generally yielded the initiative in local matters to the colonies while reserving the right to veto actions it deemed to be against the national interest.

▲ Lewis Morris, a wealthy landowner, had extensive holdings in the Middle Colonies. He was named New Jersey's first governor when the colony became politically independent from New York in 1738. Honest but overbearing, Morris quarreled constantly with the state assembly over taxation, the militia, and land titles.

Each colony had a governor. By the eighteenth century he was an appointed official, except in Rhode Island and Connecticut. Governors were chosen by the king in the case of the royal colonies and by the proprietors of Maryland, Delaware, and Pennsylvania. The governors' powers were much like those of the king in Great Britain. They executed the local laws, appointed many minor officials, summoned and dismissed the colonial assemblies, and proposed legislation to them. They possessed the right to veto colonial laws, but in most colonies, again like the king, they were financially dependent on their "subjects."

Each colony also had a legislature. Except in Pennsylvania, these assemblies consisted of two houses. The lower house, chosen by qualified voters, had general legislative powers, including control of the purse. In all the royal colonies members of the upper house, or council, were appointed by the king, except in Massachusetts, where they were elected by the General Court. The councils served primarily as advisors to the governors, but they also had some judicial and legislative powers. Judges were appointed by the king and served at his pleasure. Yet both councilors and judges were normally selected from among the leaders of the local communities; London had neither the time nor the will to investigate their political beliefs. The system therefore tended to strengthen the influence of the entrenched colonials.

Although the power of the lower houses was severely restricted in theory, they dominated the government in nearly every colony. Financial power (including the right to set the governor's salary) gave them some importance, and as did the fact that they usually had the backing of public opinion.

Most colonial legislators were practical men. Knowing their own interests, they pursued them steadily, without much regard for political theories or the desires of the royal authorities. They extended their influence by slow accretion. They saw themselves as miniature Houses of Commons, steadily "nibbling" at the authority of the Crown. The king appointed their governors, but governors came and went. The lawmakers remained, accumulating experience, building on precedent, widening decade by decade their control over colonial affairs.

The official representatives of the Crown, whatever their powers, whatever their intentions, were prisoners of their surroundings. A royal governor lived thousands of miles from London, alone in a colonial world. Governors had no security of tenure; they served at the whim of the government in London. In their dealings with the assemblies they were often bound by rigid and impractical royal instructions. They had few jobs and favors to offer in their efforts to influence the legislators. Judges might

interpret the law according to English precedents, but in local matters colonial juries had the final say. And juries were seldom awed by precedents that clashed with their own conceptions of justice.

Within the British government the king's Privy Council had the responsibility for formulating colonial policy. It could and did disallow (annul) specific colonial laws, but it did not proclaim constitutional principles to which all colonial legislatures must conform. It acted as a court of last appeal in colonial disputes and handled each case individually. One day the council might issue a set of instructions to the governor of Virginia, the next a different set to the governor of South Carolina. No one person or committee thought broadly about the administration of the overseas empire.

At times British authorities, uneasy about their lack of control over the colonies, attempted to create a more effective system. Whenever possible the original, broadly worded charters were revoked. In the 1680s James II brought New York, New Jersey, and all of New England under one administration, the Dominion of New England; he apparently planned to unify the southern colonies in a similar manner. But James's actions were deeply resented by the colonists, and after the Glorious Revolution and the collapse of the Dominion of New England, no further important efforts at unification were attempted. Instead, the tendency was in the other direction. Delaware partially separated from Pennsylvania in 1704, and the two Carolinas formally split in 1712.

In 1696 colonial policy was effectively determined by a new Board of Trade, which nominated colonial governors and other high officials. It reviewed all the laws passed by the colonial legislatures, recommending the disallowance of those that seemed to conflict with imperial policy. The efficiency, assiduousness, and wisdom of the Board of Trade fluctuated over the years, but the Privy Council and the Crown nearly always accepted its recommendations.

Colonists naturally disliked having their laws disallowed, but London exercised this power with considerable restraint; only about 5 percent of the laws reviewed were rejected. Furthermore, the board served as an important intermediary for colonists seeking to influence king and Parliament. All the colonies in the eighteenth century maintained agents in London to present the colonial point of view before board members. The most famous colonial agent was Benjamin Franklin, who represented Pennsylvania, Georgia, New Jersey, and Massachusetts at various times during his long career. In general, however, colonial agents were seldom able to exert much influence on British policy.

The British never developed an effective, centralized government for the American colonies. By and large, their American "subjects" ran their own affairs. This fact more than any other explains our present federal system and the wide areas in which the state governments are sovereign and independent.

MERCANTILISM

The Board of Trade was concerned with commerce as well as colonial administration. According to prevailing European opinion, colonies were important for economic reasons, chiefly as a source of raw materials. To obtain these, British officials developed a number of loosely related policies that later economists called mercantilism. The most important raw materials in the eyes of mercantilists were gold and silver, since these metals, being universally valued and relatively rare, could be exchanged at any time for anything the owner desired or, being durable and compact, stored indefinitely for future use. For these reasons, how much gold and silver ("treasure" according to mercantilists) a nation possessed was considered the best barometer of its prosperity and power.

Since gold and silver could not be mined in significant amounts in western Europe, every early colonist dreamed of finding "El Dorado." The Spanish were the winners in this search; from the mines of Mexico and South America a treasure in gold and silver poured into the Iberian peninsula. Failing to control the precious metals at the source, the other powers tried to obtain them by guile and warfare (witness the exploits of Francis Drake).

In the mid-seventeenth century another method, less hazardous and in the long run far more profitable, called itself to the attention of the statesmen of western Europe. If a country could make itself as self-sufficient as possible and also keep its citizens busy producing items sought in other lands, it could sell more goods abroad than it imported. This was known as having "a favorable balance of trade." A country with an unfavorable balance was obliged to make up the difference by "exporting" gold and silver. Mercantilists regarded colonies as a means of acquiring precious metals by helping the mother country generate a favorable trade balance. Colonists thus were to supply raw materials that would otherwise have to be purchased from foreign sources or colonists were to buy substantial amounts of manufactured goods produced in the mother country.

Of the English colonies in the New World, those in tropical and subtropical climes were valued for their raw materials. The more northerly ones were important as markets, but because they were small in the seventeenth century, in English eyes they took second place. In

DOCUMENT
Mun, "England's Treasure by Foreign Trade"

▲ *Sea Captains Carousing in Surinam* by John Greenwood, a late eighteenth-century oil painting that describes the effects of alcohol—one man guzzles his rum punch straight from the bowl, another vomits onto the floor, while a third pours his punch onto an insensate colleague. Greenwood implicitly denounces as well the trade in sugar (rum) and slaves in which these captains were engaged.

1680 the sugar imported from the single West Indian island of Barbados was worth more than the goods sent to England by all the mainland colonies.

If the possession of gold and silver signified wealth, trade was the route that led to riches, and merchants were the captains who would pilot the ship of state to prosperity. "Trade is the Wealth of the World," Daniel Defoe wrote in 1728. One must, of course, have something to sell, so internal production must be stimulated. Parliament encouraged the British people to concentrate on manufacturing by placing tariffs on foreign manufactured goods and subsidizing British-made textiles, iron, and other products.

THE NAVIGATION ACTS

The nurture of commerce was fundamental. Toward this end Parliament enacted the Navigation Acts. These laws, put into effect over a period of half a century and more, were designed to bring gold and silver into the Royal Treasury, to develop the imperial merchant fleet, to channel the flow of colonial raw materials into England, and to keep foreign goods and vessels out of colonial ports.

The system originated in the 1650s in response to stiff commercial competition by the Dutch, whose sailors roamed the world's oceans in search of business. Before 1650 a large share of the produce of the English colonies in America reached Europe in Dutch vessels; the first slaves in Virginia, it will be recalled, arrived on a Dutch ship and were doubtless paid for in tobacco that was later burned in the clay pipes of the burghers of Amsterdam and Rotterdam.

The Navigation Act of 1660 reserved the entire trade of the colonies to English ships and required that the captain and three-quarters of his crew be English. (Colonists, of course, were English, and their ships were treated on the same terms as those sailing out of London or Liverpool.) The act also provided that certain colonial "enumerated articles"—sugar, tobacco, cotton, ginger, and dyes like indigo (purple) and fustic (yellow)—could not be "shipped, carried, conveyed or transported" outside the empire. Three years later Parliament required that with trifling exceptions all European products destined for the colonies be brought to England before being shipped across the Atlantic. Since trade between England and the colonies was reserved to English vessels, this meant that the goods would have to be unloaded and reloaded in England.

Early in the eighteenth century the list of enumerated articles was expanded to include rice, molasses, naval stores, furs, and copper.

The English looked on the empire broadly; they envisioned the colonies as part of an economic unit, not as servile dependencies to be exploited for England's selfish benefit. The growing of tobacco in England was prohibited, and valuable bounties were paid to colonial producers of indigo and naval stores. A planned economy, England specializing in manufacturing and the colonies in the production of raw materials, was the grand design. By and large the system suited the realities of life in an underdeveloped country rich in raw materials and suffering from a chronic labor shortage.

Much has been made by some historians of the restrictions that the British placed on colonial manufacturing. The Wool Act of 1699 prohibited the export (but not the manufacture for local sale) of colonial woolen cloth. A similar law regarding hats was passed in 1732, and in 1750 an Iron Act outlawed the construction of new rolling and slitting mills in America. No other restrictions on manufacturing were imposed.

At most the Wool Act stifled a potential American industry; the law was directed chiefly at Irish woolens rather than American ones. The hat industry cannot be considered a major one. Iron, however, was important; by 1775 the industry was thriving in Virginia, Maryland, New Jersey, and Pennsylvania, and America was turning out one-seventh of the world supply. Yet the Iron Act was designed to steer the American iron industry in a certain direction, not to destroy it. Eager for iron to feed English mills, Parliament eliminated all duties on colonial pig and bar iron entering England, a great stimulus to the basic industry.

THE EFFECTS OF MERCANTILISM

AUDIO

"The Connecticut Peddler"

Colonists increasingly complained about mercantilism, but did it harm them? The chronic colonial shortage of hard money was superficially caused by the flow of specie—gold and silver—to England to meet the "unfavorable" balance of trade. The rapidly growing colonial economy consumed far more manufactured products than it could pay for out of current production. To be "in debt" to England really meant that the English were investing capital in America, a state of affairs that benefited lender and borrower alike.

Important colonial products for which no market existed in England (such as fish, wheat, and corn) were never enumerated and moved freely and directly to foreign ports. Most colonial manufacturing was untouched by English law. Shipbuilding benefited from the Navigation Acts, since many English merchants bought vessels built in the colonies. Between 1769 and 1771, Massachusetts, New Hampshire, and Rhode Island yards constructed perhaps 250 ships of 100 to 400 tons for transatlantic commerce and twice that many sloops and schooners for fishermen and coastal traders.

Two forces that worked in opposite directions must be considered before arriving at any judgment about English mercantilism. While the theory presupposed a general imperial interest above that of both colony and mother country, when conflicts of interest arose the latter nearly always predominated. Whenever Parliament or the Board of Trade resolved an Anglo-American disagreement, the colonists tended to lose.

Complementary interests conspired to keep conflicts at a minimum, but in the long run, as the American economy became more complex, the colonies would have been seriously hampered and much more trouble would have occurred had the system continued to operate.

On the other hand, the restrictions of English mercantilism were greatly lessened by inefficiency. The king and his ministers handed out government posts to win political favor or to repay political debts, regardless of the recipient's ability to perform the duties of the office.

Transported to remote America, this bumbling and cynical system scarcely functioned at all when local opinion resisted it. Smuggling became a respected profession, bribery of English officials standard practice. Despite a supposedly prohibitive duty of sixpence a gallon imposed by the Molasses Act of 1733, molasses from the French West Indies continued to be imported. The duty was seldom collected. A customs officer in Salem offered to pass French molasses for 10 percent of the legal tax, and in New Jersey the collectors "entered into a composition with the Merchants and took a Dollar a Hogshead or some such small matter."

Mercantilist policies hurt some colonists such as the tobacco planters, who grew far more tobacco than British consumers could smoke. Tobacco planters wanted to ship directly to Dutch or French ports. But the policies helped others, and most people proved adept at getting around those aspects of the system that threatened them. In any case, the colonies enjoyed almost continuous prosperity, as even so dedicated a foe of mercantilist restrictions as Adam Smith admitted.

By the same token, England profited greatly from its overseas possessions. With all its inefficiencies, mercantilism worked. Prime Minister Sir Robert Walpole's famous policy of "salutary neglect," which involved looking the other way when Americans violated the Navigation Acts, was partly a bowing to the inevitable, partly the result of complacency. English manufactures were better and cheaper than those of other nations. This fact, together with ties of language and a common heritage, predisposed Americans toward doing business in England. All else followed naturally; the mercantilist laws merely steered the American economy in a direction it had already taken.

▶ **Colonial Trade with England, 1700–1774**

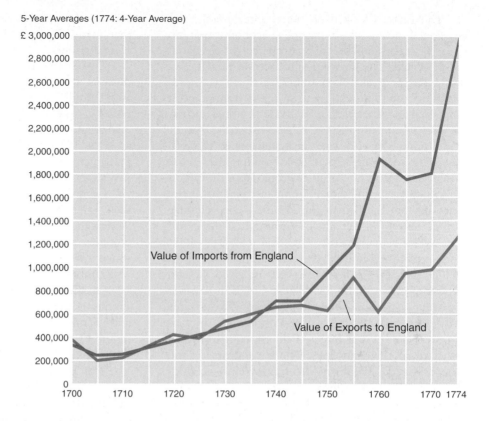

5-Year Averages (1774: 4-Year Average)

Value of Imports from England

Value of Exports to England

THE GREAT AWAKENING

Although a majority of the settlers were of English, Scotch, or Scotch-Irish descent, and their interests generally coincided with those of their cousins in the mother country, people in the colonies were beginning to recognize their common interests and character. Their loyalties were still predominantly local, but by 1750 the word American, used to describe something characteristic of all the British possessions in North America, had entered the language. Events in one part of America were beginning to have direct effects on other regions. One of the first of these developments was the so-called Great Awakening.

By the early eighteenth century, religious fervor had slackened in all the colonies. Prosperity turned many colonists away from their forebears' preoccupation with the rewards of the next world to the more tangible ones of this one. John Winthrop invested his faith in God and his own efforts in the task of creating a spiritual community; his grandsons invested in Connecticut real estate.

The proliferation of religious denominations made it impracticable to enforce laws requiring regular religious observances. Even in South Carolina, the colony that came closest to having an "Anglican Establishment," only a minority were churchgoers. Settlers in frontier districts lived beyond the reach of church or clergy. The result was a large and growing number of "persons careless of all religion."

This state of affairs came to an abrupt end with the Great Awakening of the 1740s. The Awakening began in the Middle Colonies as the result of religious developments that originated in Europe. In the late 1720s two newly arrived ministers, Theodore Frelinghuysen, a Calvinist from Westphalia, and William Tennent, an Irish-born Presbyterian, sought to instill in their sleepy Pennsylvania and New Jersey congregations the evangelical zeal and spiritual enthusiasm they had witnessed among the Pietists in Germany and the Methodist followers of John Wesley in England. Their example inspired other clergymen, including Tennent's two sons.

A more significant surge of religious enthusiasm followed the arrival in 1738 in Georgia of the Reverend George Whitefield, a young Oxford-trained Anglican minister. Whitefield was a marvelous pulpit orator and no mean actor. He played on the feelings of his audience the way a conductor directs a symphony. Whitefield undertook a series of fund-raising tours throughout the colonies. The most successful began in Philadelphia in 1739. Benjamin Franklin, not a very religious person and not easily moved by emotional appeals, heard one of these sermons. "I silently resolved he should get nothing from me," he later recalled.

DOCUMENT

Franklin on George Whitefield (1771)

I had in my Pocket a Handful of Copper Money, three or four silver Dollars, and five Pistoles in Gold. As he proceeded I began to soften and concluded to give the Coppers. Another Stroke of his Oratory . . . determin'd me to give the Silver; and he finish'd so admirably that I empty'd my Pocket wholly into the Collector's Dish.

Whitefield's visit changed the "manners of our inhabitants," Franklin added.

Wherever Whitefield went he filled the churches. If no local clergyman offered his pulpit, he attracted thousands to meetings out of doors. During a three-day visit to Boston, 19,000 people (more than the population of the town) thronged to hear him. His oratorical brilliance aside, Whitefield succeeded in releasing an epidemic of religious emotionalism because his message was so well suited to American ears. By preaching a theology that one critic said was "scaled down to the comprehension of twelve-year-olds," he spared his audiences the rigors of hard thought. Though he usually began by chastising his listeners as sinners, "half animals and half devils," he invariably took care to leave them with the hope that eternal salvation could be theirs. While not denying the doctrine of predestination, he preached a God responsive to good intentions. He disregarded sectarian differences and encouraged his listeners to do the same. "God help us to forget party names and become Christians in deed and truth," he prayed.

Whitefield attracted some supporters among ministers with established congregations, but many more from among younger "itinerants," as preachers who lacked permanent pulpits were called. A visit from him or one of his followers inevitably prompted comparisons between this new, emotionally charged style and the more restrained "plaine style" favored by the typical settled minister. Parishioners who had heard a revivalist preacher listened the next Sunday to the droning of their regular minister with what one of Whitefield's imitators claimed was the fear that their souls were at risk because they had been "living under the ministry of dead men."

Of course not everyone found the Whitefield style edifying. When those who did not spoke up, churches sometimes split into factions. Those who supported the incumbent minister were called, among Congregationalists, "Old Lights," and among Presbyterians, "Old Sides," while those who favored revivalism were known as "New Lights" and "New Sides." These splits often ran along class lines. The richer, better-educated, and more influential members of the church tended to stay with the traditional arrangements.

But many were deeply moved by the new ideas. Persons chafing under the restraints of puritan authoritarianism, or feeling guilty over their preoccupation with material goods, now found release in religious ferment. For some the release was more than spiritual; Timothy Cutler, a conservative Anglican clergyman, complained that as a result of the Awakening "our presses are forever teeming with books and our women with bastards." Whether or not Cutler was correct, the Great Awakening helped some people to rid themselves of the idea that disobedience to authority entailed damnation. Anything that God justified, human law could not condemn.

Other institutions besides the churches were affected by the Great Awakening. In 1741 the president of Yale College criticized the theology of itinerant ministers. One of these promptly retorted that a Yale faculty member had no more divine grace than a chair! Other revivalists called on the New Light churches of Connecticut to withdraw their support from Yale and endow a college of their own. The result was the

▲ In this painting evangelist George Whitefield appears to be cross-eyed. This is no fault of John Wollaston, the painter. Whitefield had eye problems; his detractors called him "Dr. Squintum." The woman's rapturous gaze is unaffected by Whitefield's own curious visage.

College of New Jersey (now Princeton), founded in 1746 by New Side Presbyterians. Three other educational by-products of the Great Awakening followed: the College of Rhode Island (Brown), founded by Baptists in 1765; Queen's College (Rutgers), founded by Dutch Reformers in 1766; and Dartmouth, founded by New Light Congregationalists in 1769.

These institutions promptly set about to refute the charge that the evangelical temperament was hostile to learning.

THE RISE AND FALL OF JONATHAN EDWARDS

Jonathan Edwards, the most famous native-born revivalist of the Great Awakening, was living proof that the evangelical temperament need not be hostile to learning. Edwards, though deeply pious, was passionately devoted to intellectual pursuits. But in 1725, four years after graduating from Yale, he was offered the position of assistant at his grandfather Solomon Stoddard's church in Northampton, Massachusetts. He accepted, and when Stoddard died two years later, Edwards became pastor.

During his six decades in Northampton, Stoddard had so dominated the ministers of the Connecticut Valley that some referred to him as "pope." His prominence came in part from the "open enrollment" admission policy he adopted for his own church. Evidence of saving grace was neither required nor expected of members: mere good behavior sufficed. As a result, the grandson inherited a congregation whose members were possessed of an "inordinate engagedness after this world." How ready they were to meet their Maker in the next was another question.

DOCUMENT

Edwards, "Sinners in the Hands of an Angry God"

For all his learning and intellectual brilliance, Edwards did not stick at dramatizing what unconverted listeners had to look forward to. The heat of Hell's consuming fires and the stench of brimstone became palpable at his rendering. In his most famous sermon, "Sinners in the Hands of an Angry God," delivered at Enfield, Connecticut, in 1741, he pulled out all the stops, depicting a "dreadfully provoked" God holding the unconverted over the pit of Hell, "much as one holds a spider, or some loathsome insect." Later, on the off-chance that his listeners did not recognize themselves among the "insects" in God's hand, he declared that "this is the dismal case of every soul in this congregation that has not been born again, however moral and strict, sober and religious, they may otherwise be." A great moaning reverberated through the church. People cried out, "What must I do to be saved?"

Unfortunately for some church members, Edwards's warnings about the state of their souls caused much anxiety. One disconsolate member, Joseph Hawley, slit his throat. Edwards took the suicide calmly. "Satan seems to be in a great rage," he declared. But for some of Edwards's most prominent parishioners, Hawley's death roused doubts. They began to miss the forgiving God of Solomon Stoddard.

Rather than soften his message, Edwards persisted, and in 1749 his parishioners voted unanimously to dismiss him. He became a missionary to some Indians in Stockbridge, Massachusetts. In 1759 he was appointed president of Princeton, but he died of smallpox before he could take office.

By the early 1750s a reaction had set in against religious "enthusiasm" in all its forms. Except in the religion-starved South, where traveling New Side Presbyterians and Baptists continued their evangelizing efforts, the Great Awakening had run its course. Whitefield's tour of the colonies in 1754 attracted little notice.

Although it caused divisions, the Great Awakening also fostered religious toleration. If one group claimed the right to worship in its own way, how could it deny to other Protestant churches equal freedom? The Awakening was also the first truly national event in American history. It marks the time when the previously distinct histories of New England, the Middle Colonies, and the South began to intersect. Powerful links were being forged. As early as 1691 there was a rudimentary intercolonial postal system. In 1754, not long after the Awakening, the farsighted Benjamin Franklin advanced his Albany Plan for a colonial union to deal with common problems, such as defense against Indian attacks on the frontier. Thirteen once-isolated colonies, expanding to the north and south as well as westward, were merging.

THE ENLIGHTENMENT IN AMERICA

The Great Awakening pointed ahead to an America marked by religious pluralism; by the 1740s many colonists were rejecting not only the stern Calvinism of Edwards but even the easy Arminianism of Solomon Stoddard in favor of a far less forbidding theology, one more in keeping with the ideas of the European Enlightenment.

The Enlightenment had an enormous impact in America. The founders of the colonies were contemporaries of the astronomer Galileo Galilei (1564–1642), the philosopher-mathematician René Descartes (1596–1650), and Sir Isaac Newton (1642–1727), the genius who revealed to the world the workings of gravity and other laws of motion. American society developed amid the excitement generated by these

DEBATING THE PAST

Was economic gain the colonists' main motivation? This bustling New York farm scene was painted in 1732 on a wood plank. Were those who first placed it above their mantelpiece enshrining their prosperity or their family? Perhaps the first important account of the eighteenth century was by James Truslow Adams (1927), a Wall Street broker who amassed a fortune, retired at age 34, and turned to history. The colonists, he believed, were likewise consumed with acquiring better and more abundant food, clothing, furnishings, housing, and the status such goods signified. He doubted that they cared much about anything else. In the 1950s many scholars, flush with post–World War II patriotism, insisted that the colonists cared deeply about religious, political, and family values. Edmund Morgan (1958) best exemplified this viewpoint. But Adams's position resurfaced several decades later. James Lemon (1972) claimed that Pennsylvania attracted middle-class immigrants who quickly became profit-maximizing farmers. Jack Greene (1988) and Alan Kulikoff (1992) showed that farmers in the Chesapeake and the South had almost from the start been preoccupied with money and land. The studies of colonial towns during the 1970s transformed the debate. Philip Greven (1970) and others discovered that while nearly everyone craved land, they did so chiefly for their families. Parents sought enough land to give or bequeath to their many children, who otherwise, on attaining adulthood, would be forced to scatter. This focus on parents and family life also spotlighted the central role of women in colonial society, a theme that was developed by Linda Kerber (1980), Mary Beth Norton (1980), and many others.

James Truslow Adams, *Provincial Society* (1927), Edmund Morgan, *A Puritan Dilemma* (1958), James Lemon, *Best Poor Man's Country* (1972), Jack Greene, *Pursuits of Happiness* (1988), Alan Kulikoff, *Agrarian Origins of American Capitalism* (1992), Philip Greven, *Four Generations* (1970), Linda Kerber, *Women of the Republic* (1980), Mary Beth Norton, *Liberty's Daughters* (1980).

great discoverers, who provided both a new understanding of the natural world and a mode of thought that implied that impersonal, scientific laws governed the behavior of all matter, animate and inanimate. Earth and the heavens, human beings and the lower animals—all seemed parts of an immense, intricate machine. God had set it all in motion and remained the master technician (the divine watchmaker) overseeing it, but He took fewer and fewer occasions to interfere with its immutable operation. If human reasoning powers and direct observation of natural phenomena rather than God's revelations provided the key to knowledge, it followed that knowledge of the laws of nature, by enabling people to understand the workings of the universe, would enable them to control their earthly destinies and to have at least a voice in their eternal destinies.

Most creative thinkers of the European Enlightenment realized that human beings were not entirely rational and that a complete understanding of the physical world was beyond their grasp. They did, however, believe that human beings were becoming more rational and would be able, by using their rational powers, to discover the laws governing the physical world. Their faith in these ideas produced the so-called Age of Reason. And while their confidence in human rationality now seems naive and the "laws" they formulated no longer appear so mechanically perfect (the universe is far less orderly than they imagined) they added immensely to knowledge.

Many churchgoing colonists, especially better educated ones, accepted the assumptions of the Age of Reason wholeheartedly. Some repudiated the doctrine of original sin and asserted the benevolence of God. Others came to doubt the divinity of Christ and eventually declared themselves Unitarians. Still others, among them Benjamin Franklin, embraced Deism, a faith that revered God for the marvels of His universe rather than for His power over humankind.

The impact of Enlightenment ideas went far beyond religion. The writings of John Locke and other political theorists found a receptive audience. So did the work of the Scottish philosophers Francis Hutcheson and David Hume and the French *philosophes*, particularly Montesquieu and Voltaire. Ideas generated in Europe often reached America with startling speed.

No colonial political controversy really heated up in America until all involved had published pamphlets citing half a dozen European authorities. Radical ideas that in Europe were discussed only by an intellectual elite became almost commonplace in the colonies.

As the topics of learned discourse expanded, ministers lost their monopoly on intellectual life. By the 1750s, only a minority of Harvard and Yale graduates were becoming ministers. The College of Philadelphia (later the University of Pennsylvania), founded in 1751, and King's College (later Columbia), founded in New York in 1754, added two institutions to the growing ranks of American colleges, which were never primarily training grounds for clergymen.

Lawyers, who first appeared in any number in colonial towns in the 1740s, swiftly asserted their intellectual authority in public affairs. Physicians and the handful of professors of natural history declared themselves better able to make sense of the new scientific discoveries than clergymen. Yet because fields of knowledge were far less specialized than in modern times, self-educated amateurs could also make useful contributions.

The most famous instances of popular participation occurred in Philadelphia. It was there, in 1727, that 21-year-old Benjamin Franklin founded the Junto, a club at which he and other young artisans gathered on Friday evenings to discuss "any point of morals, politics, or natural philosophy." In 1743 Franklin established an expanded version of the Junto, the American Philosophical Society, which he hoped would "cultivate the finer arts and improve the common stock of knowledge."

▲ Benjamin Franklin is most often depicted as he looked in later life, with his own thinning hair rather than the wig that was de rigueur for an eighteenth-century man of good family. In this 1767 portrait, a younger Franklin follows the fashion.

COLONIAL SCIENTIFIC ACHIEVEMENTS

America produced no Galileo or Newton, but colonists contributed significantly to the collection of scientific knowledge. The unexplored continent provided a laboratory for the study of natural phenomena. The Philadelphia Quaker John Bartram, a "down right plain Country Man," ranged from Florida to the Great Lakes during the middle years of the eighteenth century, gathering and classifying hundreds of plants. Bartram also studied Indians closely, speculating about their origins and collecting information about their culture.

Benjamin Franklin's far-ranging curiosity extended to science. "No one of the present age has made more important discoveries," Thomas Jefferson declared. One of Franklin's biographers has similarly called him a "harmonious human multitude." His studies of electricity, which he capped in 1752 with his famous kite experiment, established him as a scientist of international stature. He also invented the lightning rod, the iron Franklin stove (a far more efficient way to heat a room than an open fireplace), bifocal spectacles, and several other ingenious devices. In addition he served 14 years (1751–1764) in the Pennsylvania assembly. He founded a circulating library and helped to get the first hospital in Philadelphia built. He came up with the idea of a lottery to raise money for public purposes. In his spare time he taught himself Latin, French, Spanish, and Italian.

Franklin wrote so much about the virtues of hard work and thrift that some historians have described him as stuffy and straitlaced. Nothing could be further from the truth. He recognized the social value of conventional behavior, but he was no slave to convention. He wrote satirical essays on such subjects as the advantage of having affairs with older and plain-looking women (who were, he claimed, more likely to appreciate the attention). And he had the perfect temperament, being open-minded and imaginative as well as shrewd and judicious—an unbeatable combination.

Franklin's international fame notwithstanding, the theoretical contributions of American thinkers and scientists were modest. No colony produced a Voltaire, or Gibbon, or Rousseau. Most were practical rather than speculative types, tinkerers rather than constructors of grand designs. As one observer noted, they were easily diverted "by Business or Inclination

from profound Study, and prying into the Depth of Things." Thomas Jefferson, for example, made no theoretical discovery of importance, but his range was almost without limit: linguist, bibliophile, political scientist, architect, inventor, scientific farmer, and—above all—apostle of reason. "Fix reason firmly in her seat," he wrote, "and call to her tribunal every fact, every opinion."

Involvement at even the most marginal level in the intellectual affairs of Europe gave influential New Englanders, Middle Colonists, and Southerners a chance to get to know one another. Although their role in what Jefferson called "the Republic of Letters" was still minor, by mid-century their influence on the intellectual climate of the colonies was growing. That climate was one of eager curiosity, flexibility of outlook, and confidence.

REPERCUSSIONS OF DISTANT WARS

The British colonies were part of a great empire that was part of a still larger world. Seemingly isolated in their remote communities, scattered like a broken string of beads between the wide Atlantic and the trackless Appalachian forests, Americans were constantly affected by outside events both in the Old World and in the New. Under the spell of mercantilist logic, the western European nations competed fiercely for markets and colonial raw materials. War—hot and cold, declared and undeclared—was almost a permanent condition of seventeenth- and eighteenth-century life, and when the powers clashed they fought wherever they could get at one another, in America, in Europe, and elsewhere.

Although the American colonies were minor pieces in the game and were sometimes casually exchanged or sacrificed by the masterminds in London, Paris, and Madrid in pursuit of some supposedly more important objective, the colonists quickly generated their own international animosities. Frenchmen and Spaniards clashed savagely in Florida as early as the sixteenth century. Before the landing of the Pilgrims, Samuel Argall of Virginia was sacking French settlements in Maine and carrying off Jesuit priests into captivity at Jamestown. Instead of fostering tranquility and generosity, the abundance of America seemed to make the settlers belligerent and greedy.

The North Atlantic fisheries quickly became a source of trouble between Canadian and New England colonists, despite the fact that the waters of the Grand Banks teemed with cod and other fish. To dry and salt their catch the fishermen needed land bases, and French and English Americans struggled constantly over the harbors of Maine, Nova Scotia, and Newfoundland.

Even more troublesome was the fur trade. The yield of the forest was easily exhausted by indiscriminate slaughter, and traders contended bitterly to control valuable hunting grounds. The French in Canada conducted their fur trading through tribes such as the Algonquin and the Huron. This brought them into conflict with the Five Nations, the powerful Iroquois confederation of central New York. As early as 1609 the Five Nations were at war with the French and their Indian allies. For decades this struggle flared sporadically, the Iroquois more than holding their own both as fighters and as traders. The Iroquois brought quantities of beaver pelts to the Dutch at Albany, some obtained by their own trappers, others taken by ambushing the fur-laden canoes of their enemies. They preyed on and ultimately destroyed the Huron in the land north of Lake Ontario and dickered with Indian trappers in far-off Michigan. When the English took over the New Amsterdam colony they eagerly adopted the Iroquois as allies, buying their furs and supplying them with trading goods and guns.

By the last decade of the seventeenth century it had become clear that the Dutch lacked the strength to maintain a big empire and that Spain was fast declining. The future, especially in North America, belonged to England and France. In the wars of the next 125 years European alliances shifted dramatically, yet the English and what the Boston lawyer John Adams called "the turbulent Gallicks" were always on opposite sides.

In the first three of these conflicts colonists played only minor parts. The fighting in America consisted chiefly of sneak attacks on isolated outposts. In King William's War (1689–1697), the American phase of the War of the League of Augsburg, French forces raided Schenectady in New York and frontier settlements in New England. English colonists retaliated by capturing Port Royal, Nova Scotia, only to lose that outpost in a counterattack in 1691. The Peace of Ryswick in 1697 restored all captured territory in America to the original owners.

The next struggle was the War of the Spanish Succession (1702–1713), fought to prevent the union of Spain and France under the Bourbons. The Americans named this conflict Queen Anne's War. French-inspired Indians razed Deerfield, Massachusetts (see the feature essay, American Lives, "Eunice Williams/Gannenstenhawi," pp. 90–91). A party of Carolinians burned St. Augustine in Spanish Florida. The New Englanders retook Port Royal. In the Treaty of Utrecht in 1713, France yielded Nova Scotia, Newfoundland, and the Hudson Bay region to Great Britain.

► *text continues on page 92*

American Lives

Eunice Williams/Gannenstenhawi

The sound of glass shattering and wood splintering woke seven-year-old Eunice Williams. Indians were ransacking the house. Her father shouted for help. Then footsteps pounded up the stairs and strangers rushed into her room. Strong hands yanked her out of bed and pushed her toward the stairs and down. John, only six, clung to her. The barn was ablaze. Her father, arms tied, was in his nightshirt. Indians taunted him with strange words and waved their hatchets before his face. After a time several grabbed John and the baby and took them outside; another Indian followed with a club. Eunice's mother screamed but they held her back. After a few moments the Indians came back in and seized Parthena, a slave. They dragged her outside and her screams stopped.

Soon, morning light filtered through the broken window. The Indians untied one of Eunice's father's arms, gave him his pants and gestured for him to dress. They also thrust clothes toward her, and she put them on. Then she and her family were herded outside, where Parthena and Little John lay dead in the snow, and the baby in a heap near a boulder. The Indians rushed them into the meeting house. Inside, many of Eunice's neighbors were huddled against a wall. The Indians gave them all moccasins, and forced them to run toward the woods. Gunshots clattered at the far edge of the village, and the Indians made them run faster, deep into the forest. Those who lingered were dispatched with clubs or hatchets.

Throughout the day the captives scrambled onward. When Eunice stumbled and fell, exhausted, an Indian carried her on his shoulders, mile after mile. At night he covered her with a blanket. Sunrise brought the same frantic rush to the north. Eunice's mother, weakened from the new baby, fell behind. Her father tried to help her but could not. He paused with her to pray, but the Indians pushed him forward. Eunice never saw her mother again.

The Indians broke into smaller groups, and Eunice was separated from her father and brothers. The same Indian as before carried her. When they rested, he gave her the best pieces of meat. He smiled, saying something she didn't understand.

During the weeks that followed she was taken several hundred miles to a large Mohawk settlement near Montréal. There, the captive men were stripped naked and forced to run past the villagers, who beat and poked them with clubs and burning sticks. The women and children were treated more leniently. Their hair was cut; some had their ears pierced. Amidst great ceremony, they were immersed in water and their bodies were painted. Then they were given Mohawk clothing. Women wore loose sleeveless tunics, skirts that hung to their knees, leggings ornamented with moosehair, and leather moccasins. Their hair was greased and pulled back, fastened with a ribbon of eelskin.

Eunice was settled among a Mohawk family, and she came to understand that she had been adopted by them. But the family was unlike the one she had known. Mohawk husbands and wives lived apart from each other, with their own parents; children stayed with their mother and her large group of relatives.

In 1706, two years after Eunice had been taken from Deerfield, her father, a puritan minister, was ransomed and returned home. Her brothers were similarly "redeemed" soon afterward. But the Mohawk made no offer to redeem Eunice. In response to written pleas from her father, the Mohawk stated that they "would as soon part with their hearts" as with Eunice; besides, they added, the girl was "unwilling to return" to Massachusetts. In 1713 her father received word that his daughter had married a Mohawk.

Shortly afterward, English and French officials prevailed on the Mohawk to allow Eunice to speak with a trader sent by her father. By then, she had forgotten English, so the trader was obliged to speak to her through an interpreter. He pleaded for her to return home. She sat in stony silence. Finally, she uttered two Mohawk words: "Jaghte Oghte"— "maybe not." She would remain with her people: the Mohawk.

Decades later, she agreed to visit her English brothers. The women of Deerfield gave her a dress and invited her to stay in their homes, but she wrapped herself in an Indian blanket and slept in an orchard with her husband. She returned to Canada and died there in 1785, where she was known by the name, Gannenstenhawi, "she who brings in corn."

▲ In *The Death of Jane McCrae* (1803–1804), the young painter John Vanderlyn, who had been studying in Europe, poses the Indians and their victim in the manner of ancient Greek sculpture. Although little is known about the real McCrae, she was captured and killed, at age 25, while sneaking off to marry a British soldier. She became one of the American nation's first heroines. Such scenes, though, were unusual. Indians such as the Mohawks fought "mourning wars" specifically to acquire captives to replace population losses from disease and war. Abenaki Indians, who also participated in the raid on Deerfield, preferred to sell their captives or hold them for ransom.

If the colonies were mere pawns in these wars, battle casualties were proportionately high and the civilian population of New England (and of Canada) paid heavily because of the fighting. Many frontier settlers were killed in the raids. Hundreds of townspeople died during the campaigns in Nova Scotia. Massachusetts taxes went up sharply and the colony issued large amounts of paper currency to pay its bills, causing an inflation that ate into the living standards of wage earners.

The American phase of the third Anglo-French conflict, the War of the Austrian Succession (1740–1748), was called King George's War. The usual Indian raids were launched in both directions across the lonely forests that separated the St. Lawrence settlements from the New York and New England frontier. A New England force captured the strategic fortress of Louisbourg on Cape Breton Island, guarding the entrance to the Gulf of St. Lawrence. The Treaty of Aix-la-Chapelle in 1748, however, required the return of Louisbourg, much to the chagrin of the New Englanders.

As this incident suggests, the colonial wars generated a certain amount of trouble between England and the colonies; matters that seemed unimportant in London might loom large in American eyes, and vice versa. But the conflicts were seldom serious. The wars did, however, increase the bad feelings between settlers north and south of the St. Lawrence. Every Indian raid was attributed to French provocateurs, although more often than not the English colonists themselves were responsible for the Indian troubles. Conflicting land claims further aggravated the situation. Massachusetts, Connecticut, and Virginia possessed overlapping claims to the Ohio Valley, and Pennsylvania and New York also had pretensions in the region. Yet the French, ranging broadly across the mid-continent, insisted that the Ohio country was exclusively theirs.

THE GREAT WAR FOR THE EMPIRE

In this beautiful, almost untouched land, a handful of individuals determined the future of the continent. Over the years the French had established a chain of forts and trading posts running from Mackinac Island in northern Michigan to Kaskaskia on the Mississippi and Vincennes on the Wabash, and from Niagara in the east to the Bourbon River, near Lake Winnipeg, in the west. By the 1740s, however, Pennsylvania fur traders, led by George Croghan, a rugged Irishman, were setting up posts north of the Ohio River and bargaining with Miami and Huron Indians, who ordinarily sold their furs to the French. In 1748 Croghan

built a fort at Pickawillany, deep in the Miami country, in what is now western Ohio. That same year agents of a group of Virginia land speculators who had recently organized what they called the Ohio Company reached this area.

With trifling exceptions, an insulating band of wilderness had always separated the French and English in America. Now the two powers came into contact. The immediate result was a showdown battle for control of North America, the "great war for the empire." Thoroughly alarmed by the presence of the English on land they had long considered their own, the French struck hard. Attacking suddenly in 1752, they wiped out Croghan's post at Pickawillany and drove his traders back into Pennsylvania. Then they built a string of barrier forts south from Lake Erie along the Pennsylvania line: Fort Presque Isle, Fort Le Boeuf, Fort Venango.

The Pennsylvania authorities chose to ignore this action, but Lieutenant Governor Robert Dinwiddie of Virginia (who was an investor in the Ohio Company) dispatched a 21-year-old surveyor named George Washington to warn the French that they were trespassing on Virginia territory.

Washington, a gangling, inarticulate, and intensely ambitious young planter, made his way northwest in the fall of 1753 and delivered Dinwiddie's message to the commandant at Fort Le Boeuf. It made no impression. "[The French] told me," Washington reported, "that it was their absolute Design to take Possession of the Ohio, and by G— they would do it." Governor Dinwiddie thereupon promoted Washington to lieutenant colonel and sent him back in the spring of 1754 with 150 men to seize a strategic junction south of the new French forts, where the Allegheny and Monongahela rivers join to form the Ohio.

Eager but inexperienced in battle, young Washington botched his assignment. As his force labored painfully through the tangled mountain country southeast of the fork of the Ohio, he received word that the French had already occupied the position and were constructing a powerful post, Fort Duquesne. Outnumbered by perhaps four to one, Washington foolishly pushed on. He surprised and routed a French reconnaissance party, but this brought on him the main body of enemy troops.

Hastily he threw up a defensive position, aptly named Fort Necessity, but the ground was ill chosen; the French easily surrounded the fort and Washington had to surrender. After tricking the young officer, who could not read French, into signing an admission that he had "assassinated" the leader of the reconnaissance party, his captors, with the gateway to the Ohio country firmly in their hands, permitted

him and his men to march off. Nevertheless, Washington returned to Virginia a hero, for although still undeclared, this was war, and he had struck the first blow against the hated French.

In the resulting conflict, which historians call the French and Indian War (to the colonists it was simply "the French War"), the English outnumbered the French by about 1.5 million to 90,000. But the English were divided and disorganized, the French disciplined and united. The French controlled the disputed territory, and most of the Indians took their side. As a colonial official wrote, together they made formidable forest fighters, "sometimes in our Front, sometimes in our Rear, and often on all sides of us, Hussar Fashion, taking the Advantage of every Tree and Bush." With an ignorance and arrogance typical of eighteenth-century colonial administration, the British mismanaged the war and failed to make effective use of local resources. For several years they stumbled from one defeat to another.

General Edward Braddock, a competent but uninspired soldier, was dispatched to Virginia to take command. In June 1755 he marched against Fort Duquesne with 1400 Redcoats and a smaller number of colonials, only to be decisively defeated by a much smaller force of French and Indians. Braddock died bravely in battle, and only 500 of his men, led by Colonel Washington, who was serving as his aide-de-camp, made their way back to Virginia.

Elsewhere Anglo-American arms fared little better in the early years of the war. Expeditions against Fort Niagara, key to all French defenses in the west, and Crown Point, gateway to Montréal, bogged down. Meanwhile Indians, armed by the French, bathed the frontier in blood. Venting the frustration caused by 150 years of white advance, they attacked defenseless outposts with unrestrained brutality.

The most feared of the "French" Indians were the Delaware, a once-peaceful Pennsylvania tribe that had been harried from their homelands by English and Iroquois. General Braddock paid his Indian allies only £5 each for French scalps but offered £200 for the hair of Shinngass, the Delaware chieftain.

The Seven Years' War

In 1756 the conflict spread to Europe to become the Seven Years' War. Prussia sided with Great Britain, Austria with the French. On the world stage, too, things went badly for the British. Finally, in 1758, as defeat succeeded defeat, King George II was forced to allow William Pitt, whom he detested, to take over leadership of the war effort. Pitt, grandson of "Diamond" Pitt, a nouveau riche East India merchant, was an unstable man who spent much of his life on the verge of madness, but he was a brilliant strategist and capable of inspiring the nation in its hour of trial.

▲ This, the first portrait of George Washington, was done by Charles Willson Peale in 1772. Washington's right hand is inside his vest, a convention later associated with Napoleon; his left hand is behind his back. Perhaps this was to spare the painter of the trouble of rendering hands and fingers, always a challenge.

Pitt recognized, as few contemporaries did, the potential value of North America. Instead of relying on the tightfisted and shortsighted colonial assemblies for men and money, he poured regiment after regiment of British regulars and the full resources of the British treasury into the contest, mortgaging the future recklessly to secure the prize. Grasping the importance of sea power in fighting a war on the other side of the Atlantic, he used the British navy to bottle up the enemy fleet and hamper French communications with Canada. He possessed a keen eye for military genius, and when he discovered it, he ignored seniority and the outraged feelings of mediocre generals and promoted talented young officers to top commands. (His greatest find was James Wolfe, whom he made a brigadier at age 31.)

In the winter of 1758, as Pitt's grand strategy matured, Fort Duquesne fell. It was appropriately

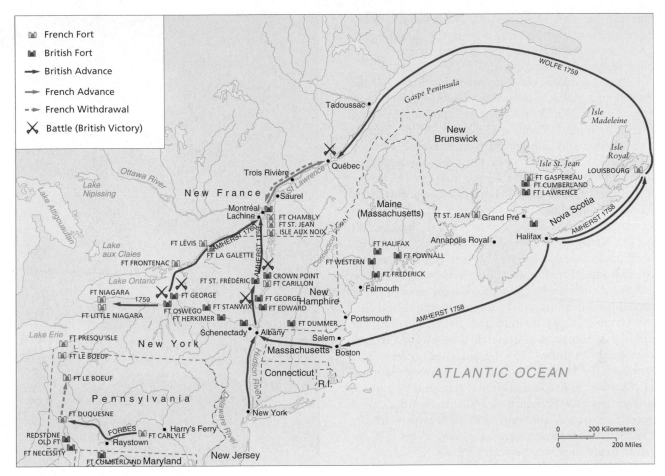

Legend:
- 🏰 French Fort
- 🏰 British Fort
- → British Advance
- → French Advance
- -→ French Withdrawal
- ✕ Battle (British Victory)

▲ **British Successes, 1758–1763**

renamed Fort Pitt, the present Pittsburgh. The following summer Fort Niagara was overrun. General Jeffrey Amherst took Crown Point, and Wolfe sailed up the St. Lawrence to Québec. There General Louis Joseph de Montcalm had prepared formidable defenses, but after months of probing and planning, Wolfe found and exploited a chink in the city's armor and captured it. Both he and Montcalm died in the battle. In 1760 Montréal fell and the French abandoned all Canada to the British. The British also won major victories against Spanish forces in Cuba and Manila, and against the French in the West Indies and India.

THE PEACE OF PARIS

Peace was restored in 1763 by the Treaty of Paris. Its terms were moderate considering the extent of the British triumph. France abandoned all claim to North America except for two small islands near Newfoundland; Great Britain took over Canada and the eastern half of the Mississippi Valley. Spain got back both the Philippine Islands and Cuba, but in exchange ceded East and West Florida to Great Britain. In a separate treaty, Spain also got New Orleans and the huge area of North America west of the Mississippi River.

"Half the continent," the historian Francis Parkman wrote, "had changed hands at the scratch of a pen." From the point of view of the English colonists in America, the victory was overwhelming. All threat to their frontiers seemed to have been swept away. Surely, they believed in the first happy moments of victory, their peaceful and prosperous expansion was ensured for countless generations.

No honest American could deny that the victory had been won chiefly by British troops and with British gold. Colonial militiamen fought well in defense of their homes or when some highly prized objective seemed ripe for the plucking; they lacked discipline and determination when required to fight far from home and under commanders they did not know. As one American official admitted, it was difficult to get New Englanders to enlist "unless assurances can be given that they shall not march to the southward of certain limits."

Colonials were delighted that scarlet-clad British regulars had borne the brunt of the fighting and hap-

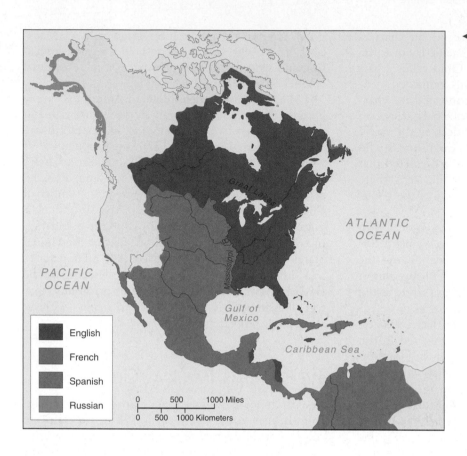

pier still that the Crown had shouldered most of the financial burden of the long struggle. The local assemblies contributed to the cost, but except for Massachusetts and Virginia their outlays were trivial compared with the £82 million poured into the worldwide conflict by the British.

Little wonder that the great victory produced a burst of praise for king and mother country throughout America. Parades, cannonading, fireworks, banquets, the pealing of church bells—these were the order of the day in every colonial town. "Nothing," said Thomas Pownall, wartime governor of Massachusetts and a student of colonial administration, "can eradicate from [the colonists'] hearts their natural, almost mechanical affection to Great Britain." A young South Carolinian who had been educated in England claimed that the colonists were "more wrapped up in a king" than any people he had ever heard of.

PUTTING THE EMPIRE RIGHT

In London peace proved a time for reassessment; that the empire of 1763 was not the same as the empire of 1754 was obvious. The new, far larger dominion would be much more expensive to maintain. Pitt had spent a huge sum winning and securing it,

much of it borrowed money. Great Britain's national debt had doubled between 1754 and 1763. Now this debt must be serviced and repaid, and the strain that this would place on the economy was clear to all. Furthermore, the day-to-day cost of administering an empire that extended from the Hudson Bay to India was far larger than that which the already burdened British taxpayer could be expected to bear. Before the great war for the empire, Britain's North American possessions were administered for about £70,000 a year; after 1763 the cost was five times as much.

The American empire had also become far more complex. A system of administration that treated it as a string of separate plantations struggling to exist on the edge of the forest would no longer suffice. The war had been fought for control of the Ohio Valley. Now that the prize had been secured, ten thousand hands were eager to make off with it. The urge to expand was, despite the continent's enormous empty spaces, an old American drive. As early as the 1670s eastern stay-at-homes were lamenting the "insatiable desire after Land" that made people willing to "live like Heathen, only that so they might have Elbow-room enough in the world." Frontier warfare had frustrated this urge for seven long years. How best could it be satisfied now that peace had come?

Conflicting colonial claims, based on charters drafted by men who thought the Pacific lay over the next hill, threatened to make the Ohio valley a battleground once more. The Indians remained "unpacified." Rival land companies contested for charters, while fur traders strove to hold back the wave of settlement that must inevitably destroy the world of the beaver and the deer. One Englishman who traveled through America at this time predicted that if the colonists were left to their own devices, "there would soon be civil war from one end of the continent to the other."

Apparently only Great Britain could deal with these problems and rivalries, for when Franklin had proposed a rudimentary form of colonial union—the Albany Plan of 1754—it was rejected by almost everyone. Unfortunately, the British government did not rise to the challenge. Perhaps this was to be expected. A handful of aristocrats (fewer than 150 peers were active in government affairs) dominated British politics, and they were more concerned with local offices and personal advantage than with large questions of policy. An American who spent some time in London in 1764 trying to obtain approval for a plan for the development of the West reported: "The people hear Spend thire time in Nothing but abuseing one Another and Strieving who shall be in power with a view to Serve themselves and Thire friends." King George III was not a tyrant, as once was commonly believed, but he was an inept politician and the victim of frequent bouts of illness.

Serene in their ignorance, most English leaders insisted that colonials were uncouth and generally inferior beings. During the French and Indian War, British commanders repeatedly expressed contempt for colonial militiamen, whom they considered fit only for "fatigue" duties such as digging trenches, chopping wood, and other noncombat tasks. General Wolfe characterized colonial troops as the "most contemptible cowardly dogs you can conceive," and another English officer, annoyed by their unsanitary habits, complained that they "infect the air with a disagreeable stink." The British officers failed to understand that colonial soldiers were volunteers who had formally contracted to serve under specific conditions. Lord Loudoun, the British commander-in-chief during the French and Indian War, was flabbergasted to discover that New England troops refused to obey one of his direct orders on the ground that it violated their contracts. Little wonder that any officer with a royal commission outranked all officers of the colonial militia, regardless of title. Young Colonel Washington, for example, had to travel all the way from Virginia to the headquarters of the commander-in-chief in Boston to establish his precedence over one Captain John Dagworthy, a Maryland officer who had formerly held a royal commission and who did not propose to let a mere colonial colonel outrank him.

Many English people resented Americans simply because the colonies were rapidly becoming rich and powerful. They were growing at an extraordinary rate. Between 1750 and 1770 the population of British America increased from 1 million to more than 2 million. As early as 1751, Benjamin Franklin predicted that in a century "the greatest number of Englishmen will be on this Side of the Water." (His guess was nearly on the mark: in 1850 the population of Great Britain was 20.8 million, that of the United States 23.1 million, including some 4 million slaves and others who were not of British descent.) If the English did not say much about this possibility, they too considered it from time to time—without Franklin's complacency.

TIGHTENING IMPERIAL CONTROLS

The attempt of the inefficient, ignorant, and indignant British government to deal with the intricate colonial problems that resulted from the great war for the empire led to the American Revolution. Trouble began when the British decided after the French and Indian War to intervene more actively in American affairs. Theoretically the colonies were entirely subordinate to Crown and Parliament, yet except for the disastrous attempt to centralize control of the colonies in the 1680s, they had been allowed a remarkable degree of freedom to manage their own affairs. Of course they had come to expect this as their right.

Parliament had never attempted to tax American colonists. "Compelling the colonies to pay money without their consent would be rather like raising contributions in an enemy's country than taxing Englishmen for their own benefit," Benjamin Franklin wrote. Sir Robert Walpole, initiator of the policy of salutary neglect, recognized the colonial viewpoint. He responded to a suggestion that Parliament tax the colonies by saying: "I will leave that for some of my successors, who may have more courage than I have." Nevertheless, the *legality* of parliamentary taxation, or of other parliamentary intervention in colonial affairs, had not been seriously contested. During King George's War and again during the French and Indian War many British officials in America suggested that Parliament tax the colonies.

Despite the peace treaty of 1763, the American colonies continued to be a drain on the British treasury. Mostly this was due to the cost of fighting Indians. Freed of the restraint posed by French competition,

▲ This engraving depicts Pontiac confronting Colonel Henry Bouquet. Pontiac had good reason to be angry. In a letter dated July 16, 1763 Sir Jeffrey Amherst, commander of British forces in North America, advised Bouquet to infect Pontiac's Indians with smallpox: "You will do well to try to Innoculate the Indians by means of Blacketts, as well as to try Every other method that can serve to Extirpate this Execrable Race." Bouquet responded a week later: "all your directions will be observed."

This Proclamation of 1763 excited much indignation in America. The frustration of dozens of schemes for land development in the Ohio Valley angered many influential colonists. Colonel Washington referred to the proclamation contemptuously as "a temporary expedient to quiet the minds of Indians," and he continued to stake out claims to western lands.

Originally the British had intended the proclamation to be temporary. With the passage of time, however, checking westward expansion seemed a good way to save money, prevent trouble with the Indians, and keep the colonies tied closely to the mother country. The proclamation line, the Board of Trade declared, was "necessary for the preservation of the colonies in due subordination."[1] Naturally this attitude caused resentment in America. To close off the West temporarily in order to pacify the Indians made some sense; to keep it closed was like trying to contain a tidal wave.

Englishmen and colonists increased their pressure on the Indians. Fur traders cheated them outrageously, while callous military men hoped to exterminate them like vermin. One British officer expressed the wish that they could be hunted down with dogs.

Led by an Ottawa chief named Pontiac, the tribes made one last effort to drive the whites back across the mountains. What the whites called Pontiac's "Rebellion" caused much havoc, but it failed. By 1764 most of the western tribes had accepted the peace terms offered by a royal commissioner, Sir William Johnson, one of the few whites who understood and sympathized with them. The British government then placed 15 regiments, some 6000 soldiers, in posts along the entire arc of the frontier, as much to protect the Indians from the settlers as the settlers from the Indians. It proclaimed a new western policy: no settlers were to cross the Appalachian divide. Only licensed traders might do business with the Indians beyond that line. The purchase of Indian land was forbidden. In compensation, three new colonies—Québec, East Florida, and West Florida—were created, but they were not permitted to set up local assemblies.

THE SUGAR ACT

Americans disliked the new western policy but realized that the problems were knotty and that no simple solution existed. Their protests were somewhat muted. Great Britain's effort to raise money in America to help support the increased cost of colonial administration caused far more vehement complaints. George Grenville, who became prime minister in 1763, was a fairly able man, although long-winded and rather narrow in outlook. His reputation as a financial expert was based chiefly on his eagerness to reduce government spending. Under his leadership Parliament passed, in April 1764, the so-called Sugar Act. This law placed tariffs on sugar, coffee, wines, and other things imported into America in substantial amounts. At the same time, measures aimed at en-

---

[1]The British were particularly concerned about preserving the colonies as markets for their manufactures. They feared that the spread of population beyond the mountains would stimulate local manufacturing because the high cost of land transportation would make British goods prohibitively expensive.

▶ **Proclamation of 1763**

George III's Proclamation of 1763 in effect reserved for the Indians the vast area across the Appalachians (except for the new royal colonies of Québec, East Florida, and West Florida) as far west as Spanish Louisiana and as far north as the Hudson Bay Company preserve.

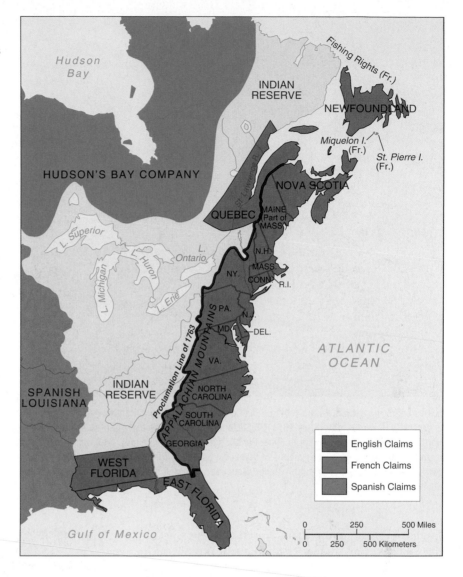

forcing all the trade laws were put into effect. Those accused of violating the Sugar Act were to be tried before British naval officers in vice admiralty courts. Grenville was determined to end smuggling, corruption, and inefficiency. Soon the customs service was collecting each year 15 times as much in duties as it had before the war.

DOCUMENT

Otis, The Rights of the British Colonies Asserted and Proved

More alarming was the nature of the Sugar Act and the manner of its passage. The Navigation Act duties had been intended to regulate commerce, and the sums collected had not cut deeply into profits. Indeed, the Navigation Acts might well be considered an instrument of imperial foreign policy, an area of government that everyone willingly conceded to London. Yet few Americans were willing to concede that Parliament

had the right to tax them. As *Englishmen* they believed that no one should be deprived arbitrarily of property and that, as James Otis put it in his stirring pamphlet *The Rights of the British Colonies Asserted and Proved* (1764), written during the controversy over writs of assistance, everyone should be "free from all taxes but what he consents to in person, or by his representative." John Locke had made clear in his *Second Treatise on Government* (1690) that property ought never be taken from people without their consent, not because material values transcend all others but because human liberty can never be secure when arbitrary power of any kind exists. "If our Trade may be taxed why not our Lands?" the Boston town meeting asked when news of the Sugar Act reached America. "Why not the produce of our Lands and every Thing we possess or make use of?"

AMERICAN COLONISTS DEMAND RIGHTS

To most people in Great Britain the colonial protest against taxation without representation seemed a hypocritical quibble, and it is probably true that in 1764 many of the protesters had not thought the argument through. The distinction between tax laws and other types of legislation was artificial, the British reasoned. Either Parliament was sovereign in America or it was not, and only a fool or a traitor would argue that it was not. If the colonists were loyal subjects of George III, as they claimed, they should bear cheerfully their fair share of the cost of governing his widespread dominions. As to representation, the colonies *were* represented in Parliament; every member of that body stood for the interests of the entire empire. If Americans had no say in the election of members of Commons, neither did most English subjects.

This concept of "virtual" representation accurately described the British system. But it made no sense in America, where from the time of the first settlements members of the colonial assemblies had represented the people of the districts in which they stood for office. The confusion between virtual and actual (geographically based) representation revealed the extent to which colonial and British political practices had diverged over the years.

The British were correct in concluding that selfish motives influenced colonial objections to the Sugar Act. The colonists denounced taxation without representation, but an offer of a reasonable number of seats in Parliament would not have satisfied them. They would probably have complained about paying taxes to support imperial administration even if imposed by their own assemblies. American abundance and the simplicity of colonial life had enabled them to prosper without assuming any considerable tax burden. Now their maturing society was beginning to require communal rather than individual solutions to the problems of existence. Not many of them were prepared to face up to this hard truth.

Over the course of colonial history Americans had taken a narrow view of imperial concerns. They had avoided complying with the Navigation Acts whenever they could profit by doing so. Colonial militiamen had compiled a sorry record when asked to fight for Britain or even for the inhabitants of colonies other than their own. True, most Americans professed loyalty to the Crown, but not many would voluntarily open their purses except to benefit themselves. In short they were provincials, in attitude and in fact.

Although the colonists were opposed in principle to taxation without representation, they failed to agree on a common plan of resistance. Many of the assemblies drafted protests, but these varied in force as well as in form. Merchant groups that tried to organize boycotts of products subject to the new taxes met with indifferent success. Then in 1765 Parliament provided the flux necessary for welding colonial opinion by passing the Stamp Act.

THE STAMP ACT: THE POT SET TO BOILING

The Stamp Act placed stiff excise taxes on all kinds of printed matter. No one could sell newspapers or pamphlets, or convey licenses, diplomas, or legal papers without first buying special stamps and affixing them to the printed matter. Stamp duties were intended to be relatively painless to pay and cheap to

Stamp Act Stamps

▲ Outraged at the Stamp Act of 1765, which implemented a direct tax on printed matter, an angry mob burned the stamps in protest. Note the enthusiastic participation of women and a young black; that they are not wearing shoes indicates that they were of working-class background.

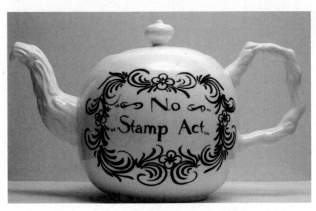

▲ By the mid-eighteenth century, tea had become a staple of the colonists' diet. (In 1766, for example, the residents of the Philadelphia poor house demanded that they be served Bohea tea rather than cheaper substitutes.) But colonial ceramics could not withstand boiling water. Thus tea cups and tea pots were manufactured in Staffordshire, England, which had perfected high-temperature ceramics. This "No Stamp Tax" teapot—ironically—was manufactured in England.

collect; in England similar taxes brought in about £100,000 annually. Grenville hoped the Stamp Act would produce £60,000 a year in America, and the law provided that all revenue should be applied to "defraying the necessary expenses of defending, protecting, and securing, the . . . colonies."

Hardly a farthing was collected. As the Boston clergyman Jonathan Mayhew explained, "Almost every British American . . . considered it as an infraction of their rights, or their dearly purchased privileges." The Sugar Act had been related to Parliament's uncontested power to control colonial trade, but the Stamp Act was a direct tax. When Parliament ignored the politely phrased petitions of the colonial assemblies, more vigorous protests quickly followed.

Virginia took the lead. In late May 1765 Patrick Henry introduced resolutions asserting redundantly that the Burgesses possessed "the only and sole and exclusive right and power to lay taxes" on Virginians and suggesting that Parliament had no legal authority to tax the colonies at all. Henry spoke for what the royal governor called the "Young, hot and Giddy Members" of the legislature (most of whom, incidentally, had absented themselves from the meeting). The more extreme of Henry's resolutions were defeated, but the debate they occasioned attracted wide and favorable attention. On June 6 the Massachusetts assembly proposed an intercolonial Stamp Act Congress, which, when it met in New York City in October, passed another series of resolutions of protest. The Stamp Act and other recent acts of Parliament were "burthensome and grievous," the delegates declared.

"It is unquestionably essential to the freedom of a people . . . that no taxes be imposed on them but with their own consent."

During the summer irregular organizations known as Sons of Liberty began to agitate against the act. Far more than anyone realized, this marked the start of the revolution. For the first time extralegal organized resistance was taking place, distinct from protest and argument conducted by constituted organs of government like the House of Burgesses and the Massachusetts General Court.

Although led by men of character and position, the "Liberty Boys" frequently resorted to violence to achieve their aims. In Boston they staged vicious riots, looting and vandalizing the houses of the stamp master and his brother-in-law, Lieutenant Governor Thomas Hutchinson. In Connecticut stamp master Jared Ingersoll, a man of great courage and dignity, faced an angry mob demanding his resignation. When threatened with death if he refused, he coolly replied that he was prepared to die "perhaps as well now as another Time." Probably his life was not really in danger, but the size and determination of the crowd convinced him that resistance was useless, and he capitulated.

The stamps were printed in England and shipped to stamp masters (all Americans) in the colonies well in advance of November 1, 1765, the date the law was to go into effect. The New York stamp master had resigned, but the stamps were stored in the city under military guard. Radicals distributed placards reading: "The first Man that either distributes or makes use of Stampt Paper let him take care of his House, Person, and Effects. We dare." When Major Thomas James, the British officer who had charge of the stamps, promised that "the stamps would be crammed down New Yorkers' throats," a mob responded by breaking into his house, drinking all his wine, and smashing his furniture and china.

In some colonies the stamps were snatched by mobs and put to the torch amid rejoicing. Elsewhere they were locked up in secret by British officials or held on shipboard. For a time no business requiring stamped paper was transacted; then, gradually, people began to defy the law by issuing and accepting unstamped documents. Threatened by mob action should they resist, British officials stood by helplessly. The law was a dead letter.

The looting associated with this crisis alarmed many colonists, including some prominent opponents of the Stamp Act. "When the pot is set to boil," the lawyer John Adams remarked sadly, "the scum rises to the top." Another Bostonian called the vandalizing of Thomas Hutchinson's house a "flagrant instance of to what a pitch of infatuation an

DOCUMENT

Franklin, Testimony Against the Stamp Act

incensed populace can rise." Such people worried that the protests might be aimed at the wealthy and powerful in America as well as at British tyranny. This does not mean that they disapproved of crowd protests, or even the destruction of property during such protests, as distinct from stealing. Many such people took part in the rioting. "State-quakes," John Adams also said, this time complacently, were comparable to "earthquakes" and other kinds of natural violence.

RIOTERS OR REBELS?

That many of the poor resented the colonial elite goes without saying, as does the fact that in many instances the rioting got out of hand and took on a social as well as a political character. Times were hard, and the colonial elite, including most of the leading critics of British policy, had little compassion for the poor, whom they feared could be corrupted by anyone who offered them a square meal or a glass of rum. Once roused, laborers and artisans may well have directed their energies toward righting what they considered local wrongs.

Yet the mass of the people, being owners of property and capable of influencing political decisions, were not social revolutionaries. They might envy and resent the wealth and power of the great landowners and merchants, but there is little evidence that they wished to overthrow the established order.

The British were not surprised that Americans disliked the Stamp Act. They had not anticipated, however, that Americans would react so violently and so unanimously. Americans did so for many reasons. Business continued to be poor in 1765, and at a time when 3 shillings was a day's wage for an urban laborer, the stamp tax was 2 shillings for an advertisement in a newspaper, 5 shillings for a will, and 20 shillings for a license to sell liquor. The taxes would hurt the business of lawyers, merchants, newspaper editors, and tavernkeepers. Even clergymen dealt with papers requiring stamps. The protests of such influential and articulate people had a powerful impact on public opinion.

The greatest cause of concern to the colonists was Great Britain's flat rejection of the principle of no taxation without representation. This alarmed them for two closely related reasons. First of all, *as Americans* they objected to being taxed by a legislative body they had not been involved in choosing. To buy a stamp was to surrender all claim to self-government. Secondly, as *British subjects* they valued what they called "the rights of Englishmen." They saw the Stamp Act as only the worst in a series of arbitrary invasions of these rights.

Already Parliament had passed still another measure, the Quartering Act, requiring local legislatures to house and feed new British troops sent to the colonies. Besides being a form of indirect taxation, a standing army was universally deemed to be a threat to liberty. Why were Redcoats necessary in Boston and New York where there was no foreign enemy for thousands of miles in any direction? In hard times, soldiers were particularly unwelcome because, being miserably underpaid, they took any odd jobs they could get in their off hours, thus competing with unemployed colonists.

Reluctantly, many Americans were beginning to fear that the London authorities had organized a conspiracy to subvert the liberties of all British subjects.

TAXATION OR TYRANNY?

In the eighteenth century the English were universally recognized to be the freest people in the world. In Mozart's opera, *The Abduction from the Seraglio* (1782), when the Turk Osmin tells the kidnapped Blonda that she is his slave, a "gift" from his master, she replies contemptuously: "A slave! I am an Englishwoman, born to freedom." Americans, like their English cousins, attributed their freedom to what they called their balanced government. In Britain power appeared to be shared by the Crown, the House of Lords (representing the aristocracy), and the House of Commons (representing the rest of the realm). The governors, councils, and assemblies seemed to play analogous roles in the colonies.

In reality this balance of separate forces never existed, either in Britain or in America. The apparent harmony of society was in both instances the product of a lack of seriously divisive issues, not of dynamic tension between rival forces. But the new laws seemed to Americans to threaten the balance, and this idea was reinforced by their observations of the corruption of English elections. Benjamin Franklin, being a colonial agent in London, knew British politics well. He complained that the entire country was "at market" and "might be bought . . . by the Devil himself" for about £12 million. A clique seeking unlimited power was trying to destroy balanced government in Britain and in America, or so many colonists thought.

There was no such conspiracy, yet no certain answer can be made to the question, Were American rights actually in danger? Grenville and his successors were English politicians, not tyrants. They looked down on bumptious colonials but surely had no wish to destroy them or their prosperity. The British attitude was like that of a parent making a recalcitrant youngster swallow a bitter medicine: protests were

understandable, but in the patient's own interest they must be ignored. Franklin reported one high official in London as saying: "His Majesty's Instructions . . . are the LAW OF THE LAND; *they are*, the Law of the Land, and as such *ought to be* OBEYED."

At the same time, British leaders believed that the time had come to assert royal authority and centralize imperial power at the expense of colonial autonomy. The need to maintain a substantial British army in America to control the western Indians tempted the government to use some of the troops to "control" white Americans as well. This attitude probably had as much to do with the coming of the revolution as any specific act of Parliament because it flew in the face of the reality that the colonies had progressed beyond the "childhood" stage. They were no longer entirely dependent on "the mother country." Indeed, an increasing number of important colonists believed that America would soon become what Franklin called "a great country, populous and mighty . . . able to shake off any shackles that may be imposed on her."

This view of America's future place in the world did not necessarily mean breaking away from the British Empire. However, it surely meant dealing with Great Britain on terms approaching equality. But psychologically British leaders were not ready to deal with Americans as equals or to consider American interests on a par with their own. In the long run, American liberty would be destroyed if this attitude was not changed.

Besides refusing to use stamps, Americans responded to the Stamp Act by boycotting British goods. Nearly a thousand merchants signed nonimportation agreements. These struck British merchants hard in their pocketbooks, and they began to pressure Parliament for repeal. After a hot debate—Grenville, whose ministry had fallen over another issue, advocated using the army to enforce the act—the hated law was repealed in March 1766. In America there was jubilation at the news. The ban on British goods was lifted and the colonists congratulated themselves on having stood fast in defense of principle.

THE DECLARATORY ACT

The great controversy over the constitutional relationship of colony to mother country was only beginning. The same day that it repealed the Stamp Act, Parliament passed a Declaratory Act stating that the colonies were "subordinate" and that Parliament could enact any law it wished "to bind the colonies and people of America."

To most Americans this bald statement of parliamentary authority seemed unconstitutional—a flagrant violation of their understanding of how the

British imperial system was supposed to work. Actually the Declaratory Act highlighted the degree to which British and American views of the system had drifted apart. The English and the colonials were using the same words but giving them different meanings. Their conflicting definitions of the word *representation* was a case in point. Another involved the word *constitution,* the term that James Otis had used in his attack on writs of assistance. To the British the Constitution meant the totality of laws, customs, and institutions that had developed over time and under which the nation functioned. In America, partly because governments were based on specific charters, the word meant a written document or contract spelling out, and thus limiting, the powers of government. If in England Parliament passed an "unconstitutional" law, the result might be rebellion, but that the law existed none would deny. "If the parliament will positively enact a thing to be done which is unreasonable," the great eighteenth-century English legal authority Sir William Blackstone wrote, "I know of no power that can control it." In America people were beginning to think that an unconstitutional law simply had no force.

Even more basic were the differing meanings that English and Americans were giving to the word *sovereignty.* Eighteenth-century English political thinkers believed that sovereignty (ultimate political power) could not be divided. Government and law being based ultimately on force, some "final, unqualified, indivisible" authority had to exist if social order was to be preserved. The Glorious Revolution in England had settled the question of where sovereignty resided—in Parliament. The Declaratory Act, so obnoxious to Americans, seemed to the English the mere explication of the obvious. That colonial governments had passed local laws the English did not deny, but they had done so at the sufferance of the sovereign legislative power, Parliament.

Given these ideas and the long tradition out of which they had sprung, one can sympathize with the British failure to follow the colonists' reasoning (which had not yet evolved into a specific proposal for constitutional reform). But most responsible British officials refused even to listen to the American argument.

THE TOWNSHEND DUTIES

Despite the repeal of the Stamp Act, the British did not abandon the policy of taxing the colonies. If direct taxes were inexpedient, indirect ones like the Sugar Act certainly were not. To persuade Parliament to repeal the Stamp Act, some Americans (most notably Benjamin Franklin) had claimed that the

colonists objected only to direct taxes. To draw such a distinction as a matter of principle was absurd, and in fact few colonists had done so. British leaders saw the absurdity but easily convinced themselves that Americans were making the distinction.

Therefore, in June 1767, the chancellor of the exchequer, Charles Townshend, introduced a series of levies on glass, lead, paints, paper, and tea imported into the colonies. Townshend was a charming man experienced in colonial administration, but he was something of a playboy (his nickname was Champagne Charlie), and he lacked both integrity and common sense. He liked to think of Americans as ungrateful children; he once said he would rather see the colonies turned into "Primitive Desarts" than treat them as equals. Townshend thought it "perfect nonsense" to draw a distinction between direct and indirect taxation, yet in his arrogance he believed the colonists were stupid enough to do so.

By this time the colonists were thoroughly on guard, and they responded quickly to the Townshend levies with a new boycott of British goods. In addition they made elaborate efforts to stimulate colonial manufacturing. By the end of 1769 imports from the mother country had been almost halved. Meanwhile, administrative measures enacted along with the Townshend duties were creating more ill will. A Board of Customs Commissioners, with headquarters in Boston, took charge of enforcing the trade laws, and new vice admiralty courts were set up at Halifax, Boston, Philadelphia, and Charleston to handle violations. These courts operated without juries, and many colonists considered the new commissioners rapacious racketeers who systematically attempted to obtain judgments against honest merchants in order to collect the huge forfeitures—one-third of the value of ship and cargo—that were their share of all seizures.

The struggle forced Americans to do some deep thinking about both American and imperial political affairs. The colonies' common interests and growing economic and social interrelationships probably made some kind of union inevitable. Trouble with England speeded the process. In 1765 the Stamp Act Congress (another extralegal organization and thus a further step in the direction of revolution) had brought the delegates of nine colonies to New York. Now, in 1768, the Massachusetts General Court took the next step. It sent the legislatures of the other colonies a "Circular Letter" expressing the "humble opinion" that the Townshend Acts were "Infringements of their natural & constitutional Rights."

The question of the limits of British power in America was much debated, and this too was no doubt inevitable, again because of change and growth. Even in the late seventeenth century the assumptions that led Parliament to pass the Declaratory Act would have been unrealistic. By 1766 they were absurd.

After the passage of the Townshend Acts, John Dickinson, a Philadelphia lawyer, published "Letters from a Farmer in Pennsylvania to the Inhabitants of the British Colonies." Dickinson considered himself a loyal British subject trying to find a solution to colonial troubles. "Let us behave like dutiful children, who have received unmerited blows from a beloved parent," he wrote. Nevertheless, he stated plainly that Parliament had no right to tax the colonies. Another moderate Philadelphian, John Raynell, put it this way: "If the Americans are to be taxed by a Parliament where they are not . . . Represented, they are no longer Englishmen but Slaves."

Some Americans were much more radical than Dickinson. Samuel Adams of Boston, a genuine revolutionary agitator, believed by 1768 that Parliament had no right at all to legislate for the colonies. If few were ready to go that far, fewer still accepted the reasoning behind the Declaratory Act.

The British ignored American thinking. The Massachusetts Circular Letter had been framed in moderate language and clearly reflected the convictions of most of the people in the Bay Colony, yet when news of it reached England, the secretary of state for the colonies, Lord Hillsborough, ordered the governor to dissolve the legislature. Two regiments of British troops were transferred from the frontier to Boston, part of the aforementioned policy of bringing the army closer to the centers of colonial unrest.

THE BOSTON MASSACRE

These acts convinced more Americans that the British were conspiring to destroy their liberties. Resentment was particularly strong in Boston, where the postwar depression had come on top of two decades of economic stagnation. Crowding 4000 tough British soldiers into a town of 16,000 people, many of them as capable of taking care of themselves when challenged as any Redcoat, was a formula for disorder.

How many brawls and minor riots took place in the waterfront taverns and darkened alleys of the colonial ports that winter is lost to history. In January 1770 scuffles between Liberty Boys and Redcoats in the Golden Hill section of New York City resulted in a number of injuries. Then, in Boston on March 5, 1770, real trouble erupted. Late that afternoon a crowd of idlers began tossing snowballs at a company of Redcoats guarding the Custom House. Some of these missiles had been carefully wrapped around suitably sized rocks. Gradually the crowd increased in size and its mood grew meaner. The

▲ This portrait is from 1772, when Samuel Adams was furious over the Boston massacre. The painter was John Singleton Copley. Although his parents were impoverished Irish immigrants, Copley had recently married the daughter of a rich Tory merchant. Did Copley side with his father-in-law, who detested Adams as a tribune of the "mob," or with Adams?

soldiers panicked and began firing their muskets. When the smoke cleared, five Bostonians lay dead and dying on the bloody ground.

This so-called Boston Massacre infuriated the populace. The violence played into the hands of radicals like Samuel Adams. But just as at the time of the Stamp Act riots, cooler heads prevailed. Announcing that he was "defending the rights of man and unconquerable truth," John Adams volunteered his services to make sure the soldiers got a fair trial. Most were acquitted; the rest were treated leniently by the standards of the day. In Great Britain, confrontation also gave way to adjustment. In April 1770 all the Townshend duties except a threepenny tax on tea were repealed. The tea tax was maintained as a matter of principle. "A peppercorn in acknowledgment of the right was of more value than millions without it," one British peer declared smugly—a glib fallacy.

At this point the nonimportation movement collapsed; although the boycott on tea was continued, many merchants imported British tea and paid the tax too. "Drank green tea," one patriot wrote in describing an afternoon at the merchant John Hancock's. "From Holland, I hope, but don't know."

A kind of postmassacre truce settled over Boston and the rest of British America. During the next two years no serious crisis erupted. Imports of British goods were nearly 50 percent higher than before the nonimportation agreement. So long as the British continued to be conciliatory, the colonists seemed satisfied with their place in the empire.

THE POT SPILLS OVER

In 1772 this informal truce ended and new troubles broke out. The first was plainly the fault of the colonists involved. Early in June the British patrol boat *Gaspee* ran aground in Narragansett Bay, south of Providence, while pursuing a suspected smuggler. The *Gaspee*'s commander, Lieutenant Dudingston, had antagonized everyone in the area by his officiousness and zeal; that night a gang of local people boarded the helpless *Gaspee* and put it to the torch. This action was clearly criminal, but when the British attempted to bring the culprits to justice no one would testify against them. The British, frustrated and angry, were strengthened in their conviction that the colonists were utterly lawless.

Then Thomas Hutchinson, now governor of Massachusetts, announced that henceforth the Crown rather than the local legislature would pay his salary. Since control over the salaries of royal officials gave the legislature a powerful hold on them, this development was disturbing. Groups of radicals formed "committees of correspondence" and stepped up communications with one another, planning joint action in case of trouble. This was another monumental step along the road to revolution; an organized colony-wide resistance movement, lacking in any "legitimate" authority but ready to consult and act in the name of the public interest, was taking shape.

THE TEA ACT CRISIS

In the spring of 1773 an entirely unrelated event precipitated the final crisis. The British East India Company held a monopoly of all trade between India and the rest of the empire. This monopoly had yielded fabulous returns, but decades of corruption and inefficiency together with heavy military expenses in recent years had weakened the company until it was almost bankrupt.

Unhappy Boston! see thy Sons deplore,
Thy hallow'd Walks besmear'd with guiltless Gore
While faithless P——n and his savage Bands,
With murd'rous Rancour stretch their bloody Hands,
Like fierce Barbarians grinning o'er their Prey,
Approve the Carnage and enjoy the Day.

If scalding drops from Rage from Anguish Wrung
If speechless Sorrows lab'ring for a Tongue
Or if a weeping World can ought appease
The plaintive Ghosts of Victims such as these;
The Patriot's copious Tears for each are shed,
A glorious Tribute which embalms the Dead.

But know Fate summons to that awful Goal,
Where Justice strips the Murd'rer of his Soul:
Should venal C——ts the scandal of the Land,
Snatch the relentless Villain from her Hand,
Keen Execrations on this Plate inscrib'd,
Shall reach a Judge who never can be brib'd.

The unhappy Sufferers were Messrs Saml Gray Saml Maverick, Jams Caldwell, Crispus Attucks & Patk Carr Killed. Six wounded, two of them (Christr Monk & John Clark) Mortally

▲ This engraving of the Boston Massacre (1770) became the most reprinted depiction of the event, and probably the most inaccurate. It was done by Paul Revere, engraver, silversmith, and eventual patriot. The British soldiers did not form ranks and fire on command at the crowd. The judge at the subsequent trial of the British soldiers warned jurors not to be influenced by "the prints exhibited in our houses" that added "wings to fancy"—prints, specifically, such as this one. The jury of colonists acquitted all the British soldiers but two, who received mild punishments.

however, to preserve (as Lord North said when the East India Company directors suggested its repeal) the principle of Parliament's right to tax the colonies.

The company then shipped 1700 chests of tea to colonial ports. Though the idea of high-quality tea offered at bargain prices was tempting, after a little thought nearly everyone in America appreciated the dangers involved in buying it. If Parliament could grant the East India Company a monopoly of the tea trade, it could parcel out all or any part of American commerce to whomever it pleased. More important, the act appeared utterly diabolical, a dastardly trick to trap them into paying the tea tax. The plot seemed obvious: the real price of Lord North's tea was American submission to parliamentary taxation.

Public indignation was so great in New York and Philadelphia that when the tea ships arrived, the authorities ordered them back to England without attempting to unload. The tea could be landed only "under the Protection of the Point of the Bayonet and Muzzle of the Cannon," the governor of New York reported. "Even then," he added, "I do not see how the Sales or Consumption could be effected."

The situation in Boston was different. The tea ship *Dartmouth* arrived on November 27. The radicals, marshaled by Sam Adams, were determined to prevent it from landing its cargo; Governor Hutchinson (who had managed to have two of his sons appointed to receive and sell the tea) was equally determined to collect the tax and enforce the law. For days the town seethed. Crowds milled in the streets, harangued by Adams and his friends, while the *Dartmouth* and two later arrivals swung with the tides on their moorings. Then, on the night of December 16, as Hutchinson was preparing to seize the tea for nonpayment of the duty, a band of colonists disguised as Indians rowed out to the ships and dumped the hated tea chests into the harbor.

The destruction of the tea was a serious crime and it was obvious that a solid majority of the people of Boston approved of it. The painted "Patriots" who

Among the assets of this venerable institution were some 17 million pounds of tea stored in English warehouses. The decline of the American market, a result first of the boycott and then of the smuggling of cheaper Dutch tea, partly accounted for the glut. Normally, East India Company tea was sold to English wholesalers. They in turn sold it to American wholesalers, who distributed it to local merchants for sale to the consumer. A substantial British tax was levied on the tea as well as the threepenny Townshend duty. Now Lord North, the new prime minister, decided to remit the British tax and to allow the company to sell directly in America through its own agents. The savings would permit a sharp reduction of the retail price and at the same time yield a nice profit to the company. The Townshend tax was retained,

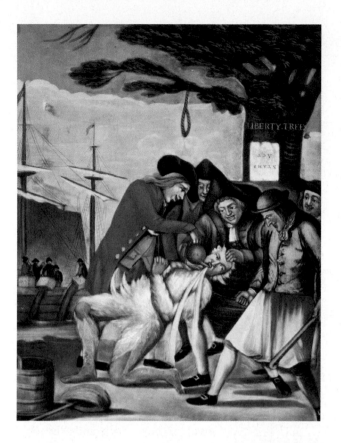

◄ A noose hanging from a "Liberty Tree" reveals this artist's bias: the "tar-and-feathering" of a British official would doubtless culminate in greater violence. As historian Gordon Wood points out, however, the mob actions of the colonists often "grew out of folk festivals and traditional popular rites." A "tar-and-feathering," though painful and occasionally dangerous, was mostly a humiliation. By the early 1770s, though, the mockery was becoming tinged with violence.

jettisoned the chests were a veritable cross-section of society, and a huge crowd gathered at wharfside and cheered them on. The British burned with indignation when news of the "Tea Party" reached London. People talked (fortunately it was only talk) of flattening Boston with heavy artillery. Nearly everyone, even such a self-described British friend of the colonists as Edmund Burke, agreed that the colonists must be taught a lesson. George III himself said, "We must master them or totally leave them to themselves."

What particularly infuriated the British was the certain knowledge that no American jury would render a judgment against the criminals. The memory of the *Gaspee* affair was fresh in everyone's mind in England, as undoubtedly it was in the minds of those Bostonians who, wearing the thinnest of disguises, brazenly destroyed the tea.

FROM RESISTANCE TO REVOLUTION

Parliament responded in the spring of 1774 by passing the Coercive Acts. The Boston Port Act closed the harbor of Boston to all commerce until its citizens paid for the tea. The Administration of Justice Act provided for the transfer of cases to courts outside Massachusetts when the governor felt that an impartial trial could not be had within the colony. The Massachusetts Government Act revised the colony's charter drastically, strengthening the power of the governor, weakening that of the local town meetings, making the council appointive rather than elective, and changing the method by which juries were selected. These were unwise laws—they cost Great Britain an empire. All of them, and especially the Port Act, were unjust laws as well. Parliament was punishing the entire community for the crimes of individuals. Even more significant, they marked a drastic change in British policy—from legislation and strict administration to treating colonial protesters as criminals, from attempts to persuade and conciliate to coercion and punishment.

The Americans named the Coercive Acts the Intolerable Acts. That the British answer to the crisis was coercion the Americans found unendurable. Although neither the British nor the colonists yet realized it, the American Revolution had begun.

▲ This British caricature of 1775 mocks the protest of the "Patriotic Ladies at Edenton in North Carolina." While women in the background empty their tea canisters, others (amidst some distractions) sign a pledge "not to Conform to the Pernicious Custom of Drinking Tea."

▲ A Philadelphia street scene such as might have been viewed by delegates to the First Continental Congress in 1774. Public space in the colonial city often brought together many different peoples—artisans and gentlemen, black servants (or slaves), and fashionable ladies.

Step by step, in the course of a single decade, a group of separate political bodies, inhabited by people who (if we put aside the slaves who were outside the political system) were loyal subjects of Great Britain, had been forced by the logic of events—by new British policies and by a growing awareness of their common interests—to take political power into their own hands and to unite with one another to exercise that power effectively. Ordinary working people, not just merchants, lawyers, and other well-to-do people, played increasingly more prominent roles in public life as crisis after crisis roused their indignation. This did not yet mean that most Americans wanted to be free from British rule. Nearly every colonist was willing to see Great Britain continue to control, or at least regulate, such things as foreign relations, commercial policy, and other matters of general American interest. Parliament, however—and in the last analysis George III and most Britishers—insisted that their authority over the colonies was unlimited. Behind their stubbornness lay the arrogant psychology of the European: "*Colonists are inferior. . . . We own you.*"

Lord North directed the Coercive Acts at Massachusetts alone because he assumed that the other colonies, profiting from the discomfiture of Massachusetts, would not intervene, and because of the British tendency to think of the colonies as separate units connected only through London. His strategy failed because his assumption was incorrect: the colonies began at once to act in concert.

Extralegal political acts now became a matter of course. In June 1774 Massachusetts called for a meeting of delegates from all the colonies to consider common action. This First Continental Congress met at Philadelphia in September; only Georgia failed to send delegates. Many points of view were represented, but even the so-called conservative proposal, introduced by Joseph Galloway of Pennsylvania,

called for a thorough overhaul of the empire. Galloway suggested an *American* government, consisting of a president general appointed by the king and a grand council chosen by the colonial assemblies, that would manage intercolonial affairs and possess a veto over parliamentary acts affecting the colonies.

This was not what the majority wanted. If taxation without representation was tyranny, so was all legislation. Therefore Parliament had no right to legislate in any way for the colonies. John Adams, while prepared to *allow* Parliament to regulate colonial trade, now believed that Parliament had no inherent right to control it. "The foundation . . . of all free government," he declared, "is a right in the people to participate in their legislative council." Americans "are entitled to a free and exclusive power of legislation in their several provincial legislatures."

Propelled by the reasoning of Adams and others, the Congress passed a declaration of grievances and resolves that amounted to a complete condemnation of Britain's actions since 1763. A Massachusetts proposal

that the people take up arms to defend their rights was endorsed. The delegates also organized a "Continental Association" to boycott British goods and to stop all exports to the empire. To enforce this boycott, committees were appointed locally "to observe the conduct of all persons touching this association" and to expose violators to public scorn.

If the Continental Congress reflected the views of the majority—there is no reason to suspect that it did not—it is clear that the Americans had decided that drastic changes must be made. It was not merely a question of mutual defense against the threat of British power, not only (in Franklin's aphorism) a matter of hanging together lest they hang separately. A nation was being born.

Looking back many years later, one of the delegates to the First Continental Congress made just these points. He was John Adams of Massachusetts, and he said: "The revolution was complete, in the minds of the people, and the Union of the colonies, before the war commenced."

MILESTONES

1650–1696	Parliament enacts Navigation Acts
1689–1697	King William's War (War of the League of Augsburg)
1699–1750	Parliament enacts laws regulating colonial manufacturing
1702–1713	Queen Anne's War (War of the Spanish Succession): France loses Nova Scotia, Newfoundland, and Hudson Bay to Britain
1733	Molasses Act's duty leads to smuggling
1738–1742	Religious enthusiasm surges during Great Awakening
1740–1748	King George's War (War of the Austrian Succession)
1743	Benjamin Franklin founds American Philosophical Society
1752	Franklin discovers nature of lightning
1754	Albany Congress paves way for Stamp Act Congress and Continental Congress
1754–1763	British and American Colonists fight French and Indians in French and Indian War (Seven Years' War)

1760	George III becomes king of England
1763	George III's Proclamation forbids settlement beyond Appalachians
1764	Sugar Act places tariffs on sugar, coffee, wines, and other imports
1765	Stamp Act places excise taxes on all printed matter, leads to Stamp Tax Congress
1766	Stamp Act is repealed; Declaratory Act asserts parliamentary authority over colonies
1767	Townshend Duties lead to Massachusetts Circular Letter
1770	Five American colonists die in Boston Massacre
1772	Colonists burn *Gaspee*
1773	Tea Act leads to Boston Tea Party
1774	Coercive Acts lead to First Continental Congress

SUPPLEMENTARY READING

A full analysis of the British imperial system can be found in the early volumes of L. H. Gipson's *British Empire Before the American Revolution* (1936–1968). See also James A. Henretta, *The Evolution of American Society* (1973), and Michael Kammen, *Empire and Interest* (1974). Jack P. Greene, *Peripheries and Center* (1989), describes how the colonists extended their control of political affairs. On colonial trade and the mercantilist system, see J. J. McCusker and R. R. Menard, *The Economy of British America* (1985), and P. J. Marshall, ed., *The Oxford History of the British Empire: The Eighteenth Century* (1998).

On the Great Awakening, Richard Bushman, *From Puritan to Yankee* (1967) emphasizes psycho-social factors while Frank Lambert, *Inventing the "Great Awakening"* (1999) focuses on the intersection of religion and economics. Catherine A. Brekus, *Strangers and Pilgrims: Female Preaching in America* (1998) addresses a long-neglected subject. See also P. U. Bonami, *Under the Cope of Heaven: Religion, Society, and Politics in Colonial America* (1986). For the Enlightenment, see H. F. May, *The Enlightenment in America* (1976). Fred Anderson, *The Crucible of War* (2000) is a readable and thorough narrative of the Great War for the Empire; see also his *A People's Army: Massachusetts Soldiers and Society in the Seven Years' War* (1984).

On the causes of the Revolution, see Pauline Maier, *From Resistance to Revolution* (1972), Edmund S. Morgan, *The Birth of the Republic* (1977), and Edward Countryman, *The American Revolution* (1985). Valuable local studies include T. H. Breen, *Tobacco Culture* (1985), on Virginia; Countryman's *A People in Revolution* (1989), on New York; and T. M. Doerflinger, *A Vigorous Spirit of Enterprise* (1986), on Philadelphia. Specific issues during the period are treated in E. S. and H. M. Morgan, *The Stamp Act Crisis* (1953), John Shy, *Toward Lexington* (1965), and Alfred F. Young, *The Shoemaker and the Tea Party* (1999).

Bernard Bailyn's *The Ideological Origins of the American Revolution* (1967) and *The Origins of American Politics* (1968) are brilliant analyses of the political thinking and political structure of eighteenth-century America. Other seminal works include Gordon S. Wood, *The Radicalism of the American Revolution* (1992), and Edmund S. Morgan, *Inventing the People: The Rise of Popular Sovereignty in England and America* (1988). See also Pauline Maier, *The Old Revolutionaries* (1980). On Benjamin Franklin, see two good recent biographies, by Edmund Morgan (2002) and Walter Isaacson (2003).

The full story of Eunice Williams/Gannenstenhawi is brilliantly told in John Demos, *The Unredeemed Captive* (1994); for the Indian perspective of the same event, see *Evan Haefeli* and *Kevin Sweeney, Captors and Captives: The 1704 French and Indian Raid on Deerfield* (2003).

SUGGESTED WEBSITES

Colonial Era Timeline
www.historyplace.com/unitedstates/revolution/
rev-col.htm
This site provides information about colonial-era issues.

Colonial Documents
http://www.yale.edu/lawweb/avalon/18th.htm
The key documents are reproduced on this Yale University site, as are some important documents from other periods of U.S. history.

Jonathan Edwards
http://www.jonathanedwards.com/
This site includes the text of speeches delivered by Preacher Jonathan Edwards.

The French and Indian War
http://web.syr.edu/~laroux/
This site, treating the French and Indian War, includes chronologies and documents, as well as materials dealing with the French soldiers who fought in the conflict.

The Early America Review
http://earlyamerica.com/
This site explores the colonies through the colonial media.

White Oak Fur Post
http://www.whiteoak.org/
This site documents an eighteenth-century fur trading post among the Indians in the region that would become Minnesota.

BOSTON

CHARLES TOWN

▼ On June 17, 1775, the British tried to dislodge Continentals from fortified (and concealed) positions atop Breed's Hill. The misnamed Battle of Bunker Hill resulted in the loss of 1000 Redcoats, and only 400 colonists.

CHAPTER CONTENTS

The actions of the First Continental Congress led the British authorities to force a showdown with their bumptious colonial offspring. "The New England governments are in a state of rebellion," George III announced. "Blows must decide whether they are to be subject to this country or independent." General Thomas Gage, veteran of Braddock's ill-fated expedition against Fort Duquesne and now commander-in-chief of all British forces in North America, had already been appointed governor of Massachusetts. Some 4000 Redcoats were concentrated in Boston, camped on the town common once peacefully reserved for the citizens' cows.

Parliament echoed with demands for a show of strength in America. After the Tea Party the general impression was that resistance to British rule was concentrated in Massachusetts. Based on the behavior of colonial militia in the French and Indian War, most Britishers did not think people in the other colonies would be inclined to fight outside their own region. General James Grant announced that with 1000 men he "would undertake to go from one end of America to the other, and geld all the males, partly by force and partly by a little coaxing."

Some opposed the idea of crushing the colonists, and others believed that it could not be easily managed, but they were a small minority. The House of Commons listened to Edmund Burke's magnificent speech on conciliating the colonies and then voted 270 to 78 against him.

"THE SHOT HEARD ROUND THE WORLD"

The London government decided to use troops against Massachusetts in January 1775, but the order did not reach General Gage until April. In the interim both sides were active. Parliament voted new troop levies and declared Massachusetts to be in a state of rebellion. The Massachusetts Patriots, as they were now calling themselves, formed an extralegal provincial assembly, reorganized the militia, and began training "Minute Men" and other fighters. Soon companies armed with anything that would shoot were drilling on town commons throughout Massachusetts and in other colonies too.

When Gage received his orders on April 14, he acted swiftly. The Patriots had been accumulating

arms at Concord, some 20 miles west of Boston. On the night of April 18, Gage dispatched 700 crack troops to seize these supplies. The Patriots were prepared. Paul Revere and other horsemen rode off to alert the countryside and warn John Hancock and Sam Adams, leaders of the provincial assembly, whose arrests had been ordered.

Warren, "Account of the Battle of Lexington"

When the Redcoats reached Lexington early the next morning, they found the common occupied by about 70 Minute Men. After an argument, the Americans began to withdraw. Then someone fired a shot. There was a flurry of gunfire and the Minute Men fled, leaving eight of their number dead. The British then marched on to Concord, where they destroyed whatever supplies the Patriots had been unable to carry off.

But militiamen were pouring into the area from all sides. A hot skirmish at Concord's North Bridge forced the Redcoats to yield that position. Becoming alarmed, they began to march back to Boston. Soon they were being subjected to a withering fire from American irregulars along their line of march. A strange battle developed on a "field" 16 miles long and only a few hundred yards wide. Gage was obliged to send out an additional 1500 soldiers, and total disaster was avoided only by deploying skirmishers to root out snipers hiding in barns and farmhouses along the road to Boston. When the first day of the Revolutionary War ended, the British had sustained 273 casualties, the Americans fewer than 100. "The Rebels are not the despicable rabble too many have supposed them to be," General Gage admitted.

For a brief moment of history tiny Massachusetts stood alone at arms against an empire that had humbled France and Spain. Yet Massachusetts assumed the offensive! The provincial government organized an expedition that captured Fort Ticonderoga and Crown Point, on Lake Champlain. The other colonies rallied quickly to the cause, sending reinforcements to Cambridge. When news of the battle reached Virginia, George Washington wrote sadly, "A brother's sword has been sheathed in a brother's breast and the once happy and peaceful plains of America are either to be drenched in blood or inhabited by a race of slaves." And then he added: "Can a virtuous man hesitate in his choice?"

▲ Two weeks after the battle of Lexington and Concord, Ralph Earl, a colonial militiaman from Connecticut, was ordered to make sketches and paintings of what had transpired. Earl revisited the battlefield and interviewed those who had fought. He was an accurate painter, but not a very good one. Note that each of the British formations, facing officers, contains exactly 25 men.

THE SECOND CONTINENTAL CONGRESS

On May 10, 1775, the day Ticonderoga fell, the Second Continental Congress met in Philadelphia. It was a distinguished group, more radical than the First

Congress. Besides John and Sam Adams, Patrick Henry and Richard Henry Lee of Virginia, and Christopher Gadsden of South Carolina, all holdovers from the First Congress, there was Thomas Jefferson, a lanky, sandy-haired young planter from Virginia. Jefferson had recently published "A Summary View of the Rights of British America," an essay criticizing the institution of monarchy and warning George III that "kings are the servants, not the proprietors of the people." The Virginia convention had also sent George Washington, who knew more than any other colonist about commanding men and who wore his buff-and-blue colonel's uniform, a not-too-subtle indication of his willingness to place this knowledge at the disposal of the Congress. The renowned Benjamin Franklin was a delegate, moving rapidly to the radical position.

The Boston merchant John Hancock was chosen president of the Congress, which, like the first, had no legal authority. Yet the delegates had to make agonizing decisions under the pressure of rapidly unfolding military events, with the future of every American depending on their actions. Delicate negotiations and honeyed words might yet persuade king and Parliament to change their ways, but precipitate, bold effort was essential to save Massachusetts.

In this predicament the Congress naturally dealt first with the military crisis. It organized the forces gathering around Boston into the so-called Continental Army and appointed George Washington commander-in-chief. After Washington and his staff left for Massachusetts on June 23, the Congress turned to the task of requisitioning men and supplies.

THE BATTLE OF BUNKER HILL

Meanwhile, in Massachusetts, the first major battle of the war had been fought. The British position on the peninsula of Boston was impregnable to direct assault, but high ground north and south, at Charlestown and Dorchester Heights, could be used to pound the city with artillery. When the Continentals seized Bunker Hill and Breed's Hill at Charlestown and set up defenses on the latter, Gage determined at once to drive them off. This was accomplished on June 17. Twice the Redcoats marched in close ranks, bayonets fixed, up Breed's Hill, each time being driven back after suffering heavy losses. Stubbornly they came again, and this time they carried the redoubt, for the defenders had run out of ammunition.

The British then cleared the Charlestown peninsula, but the victory was really the Americans', for they had proved themselves against professional soldiers and had exacted a terrible toll. More than 1000 Redcoats had fallen in a couple of hours, out of a

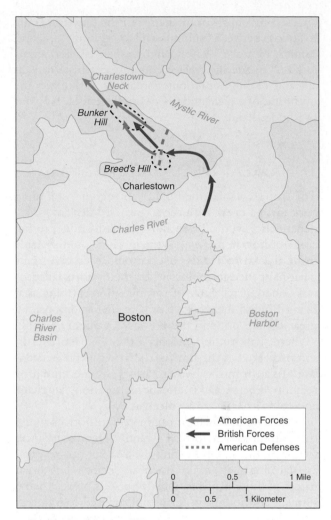

▲ **The Battle of Bunker Hill**
Most of the so-called Battle of Bunker Hill actually took place on Breed's Hill nearby. This area today is all part of the city of Boston.

force of some 2500, while the Continentals lost only 400 men, most of them cut down by British bayonets after the hill was taken. "The day ended in glory," a British officer wrote, "but the loss was uncommon in officers for the number engaged."

The Battle of Bunker Hill, as it was called for no good reason, greatly reduced whatever hope remained for a negotiated settlement. The spilling of so much blood left each side determined to force the other's submission. The British recalled General Gage, replacing him with General William Howe, a respected veteran of the French and Indian War, and George III formally proclaimed the colonies to be "in open rebellion." The Continental Congress dispatched one last plea to the king (the Olive Branch Petition), but this was a sop to the moderates. Immediately thereafter it adopted the Declaration of the Causes and Necessity of Taking Up Arms, which condemned everything the British had done since 1763. Americans were "a people

attacked by unprovoked enemies"; the time had come to choose between "submission" to "tyranny" and "resistance by force." The Congress then ordered an attack on Canada and created committees to seek foreign aid and to buy munitions abroad. It authorized the outfitting of a navy under Commodore Esek Hopkins of Rhode Island.

THE GREAT DECLARATION

The Congress (and the bulk of the people) still hung back from a break with the Crown. To declare for independence would be to burn the last bridge, to become traitors in the eyes of the mother country. Aside from the word's ugly associations, everyone knew what happened to traitors when their efforts failed. It was sobering to think of casting off everything that being English meant: love of king, the traditions of a great nation, pride in the power of a mighty empire. "Where shall we find another Britain?" John Dickinson had asked at the time of the Townshend Acts crisis. "Torn from the body to which we are united by religion, liberty, laws, affections, relation, language and commerce, we must bleed at every vein."

Then, too, rebellion might end in horrors worse than submission to British tyranny. The disturbances following the Stamp Act and the Tea Act had revealed an alarming fact about American society. The organizers of those protests, mostly persons of wealth and status, had thought in terms of "ordered resistance." They countenanced violence only as a means of forcing the British authorities to pay attention to their complaints. But protest meetings and mob actions had brought thousands of ordinary citizens into the struggle for local self-government. Some of the upper-class leaders among the Patriots, while eager to have their support, were concerned about what they would make of actual independence. In addition, not all the property that had been destroyed belonged to Loyalists and British officials. Too much exalted talk about "rights" and "liberties" might well give the poor (to say nothing of the slaves) an exaggerated impression of their importance.

Finally, in a world where every country had some kind of monarch, could common people *really* govern themselves? The most ardent defender of American rights might well hesitate after considering all the implications of independence.

Yet independence was probably inevitable by the end of 1775. The belief that George III had been misled by evil or stupid advisers on both sides of the Atlantic became progressively more difficult to sustain. Mistrust of Parliament—indeed, of the whole of British society—grew apace.

Two events in January 1776 pushed the colonies a long step toward a final break. First came the news that the British were sending hired Hessian soldiers to fight against them. Colonists associated mercenaries with looting and rape and feared that the German-speaking Hessians would run amok among them. Such callousness on the part of Britain made reconciliation seem out of the question.

The second decisive event was the publication of *Common Sense*. This tract was written by Thomas Paine, a one-time English corsetmaker and civil servant turned pamphleteer, a man who had been in America scarcely a year. *Common Sense* called boldly for complete independence. It attacked not only George III but the idea of monarchy itself. Paine applied the uncomplicated logic of the zealot to the recent history of America. Where the colonists had been humbly petitioning George III and swallowing their resentment when he ignored them, Paine called George a "Royal Brute" and "the hardened sullen-tempered Pharaoh of England." Many Americans had wanted to control their own affairs but feared the instability of untried republican government. To them Paine said: "We have it in our power to begin the world again." "A government of our own is our natural right," he insisted. "O! ye that love mankind! Ye that dare oppose not only tyranny but the tyrant, stand forth!"

Virtually everyone in the colonies must have read *Common Sense* or heard it explained and discussed. About 150,000 copies were sold in the critical period between January and July. Not every Patriot was impressed by Paine's arguments. John Adams dismissed *Common Sense* as "a tolerable summary of arguments which I had been repeating again and again in Congress for nine months." But no one disputed the impact of Paine's pamphlet on public opinion.

The tone of the debate changed sharply as Paine's slashing attack took effect. In March 1776 the Congress unleashed privateers against British commerce; in April it opened American ports to foreign shipping; in May it urged the Patriots who had set up extralegal provincial conventions to frame constitutions and establish state governments.

On June 7 Richard Henry Lee of Virginia introduced a resolution of the Virginia Convention:

> RESOLVED: That these United Colonies are, and of right ought to be, free and independent States, that they are absolved from all allegiance to the British Crown, and that all political connection between them and the State of Great Britain is, and ought to be, totally dissolved.

This momentous resolution was not passed until July 2; the Congress first appointed a committee

▲ This 1857 painting depicts the destruction of a statue of King George III during the Revolution. This rendering purges the "mob" action of its menacing violence: the arm gestures are celebratory rather than threatening, and the women and children are well-to-do. This is a middle-class view of the American Revolution, bloodless, public-spirited, and consensual.

consisting of Thomas Jefferson, Benjamin Franklin, John Adams, Roger Sherman, and Robert Livingston to frame a suitable justification of independence. Livingston, a member of one of the great New York landowning families, was put on the committee in an effort to push New York toward independence. Sherman, a self-educated Connecticut lawyer and merchant, was a conservative who opposed parliamentary control over colonial affairs. Franklin, the best known of all Americans and an experienced writer, was a natural choice; so was John Adams, whose devotion to the cause of independence combined with his solid conservative qualities made him perhaps the typical man of the Revolution.

Thomas Jefferson was probably placed on the committee because politics required that a Virginian be included and because of his literary skill and general intelligence. Aside from writing *A Summary View of the Rights of British America,* he had done little to attract notice. At age 33 he was the youngest member of the Continental Congress and was only marginally interested in its deliberations. He had been slow to take his seat in the fall of 1775, and he had gone home to Virginia before Christmas. He put off returning several times and arrived in Philadelphia only on May 14. Had he delayed another month, someone else would have written the Declaration of Independence.

The committee asked Jefferson to prepare a draft. The result, with a few amendments made by Franklin and Adams and somewhat toned down by the whole Congress, was officially adopted by the delegates on July 4, 1776, two days after the delegates had voted for the decisive break with Great Britain.

Jefferson's Declaration of Independence (see the text of the document in the Appendix, pp. A3–A4) consisted of two parts. The first, introductory part justified the abstract

DOCUMENT

Jefferson, "Rough Draft" of the Declaration of Independence

right of any people to revolt and described the theory on which the Americans based their creation of a new, republican government. The second, much longer section was a list of the "injuries and usurpations" of George III, a bill of indictment explaining why the colonists felt driven to exercise the rights outlined in the first part of the document. Here Jefferson stressed the monarch's interference with the functioning of representative government in America, his harsh administration of colonial affairs, his restrictions on civil rights, and his maintenance of troops in the colonies without their consent.

Jefferson sought to marshal every possible evidence of British perfidy, and he made George III, rather than Parliament, the villain because the king was the personification of the nation against which America was rebelling. He held the monarch responsible for Parliament's efforts to tax the colonies and restrict their trade, for many actions by subordinates that George III had never deliberately authorized, and for some things that never happened. He even blamed the king for the existence of slavery in the colonies, a charge the Congress cut from the document not entirely because of its concern for accuracy. The long bill of particulars reads more like a lawyer's brief than a careful analysis, but it was intended to convince the world that the Americans had good reasons for exercising their right to form a government of their own.

Jefferson's general statement of the right of revolution has inspired oppressed peoples all over the world for more than 200 years:

> We hold these truths to be self-evident, that all men are created equal, that they are endowed by their Creator with certain unalienable Rights, that among these are Life, Liberty and the pursuit of Happiness. That to secure these rights, Governments are instituted among Men, deriving their just powers from the consent of the governed, That whenever any Form of Government becomes destructive of these ends, it is the Right of the People to alter or to abolish it, and to institute new Government. . . .

The Declaration was intended to influence foreign opinion, but its proclamation had little immediate effect outside Great Britain, and there it only made people angry and determined to subdue the rebels. A substantial number of European military men offered their services to the new nation, and a few of these might be called idealists, but most were adventurers and soldiers of fortune, thinking mostly of their own advantage. Why, then, has the Declaration had so much influence on modern history? Not because the thought was original with Jefferson. As John Adams later pointed out—Adams viewed his great contemporary with a mixture of affection, respect, and jealousy—the basic idea was

commonplace among eighteenth-century liberals. "I did not consider it any part of my charge to invent new ideas," Jefferson explained, "but to place before mankind the common sense of the subject, in terms so plain and firm as to command their assent. . . . It was intended to be an expression of the American mind."

Revolution was not new, but the spectacle of a people solemnly explaining and justifying their right, in an orderly manner, to throw off their oppressors and establish a new system on their own authority was almost without precedent. Soon the French would be drawing on this example in their revolution, and rebels everywhere have since done likewise. And if Jefferson did not create the concept, he gave it a nearly perfect form.

1776: THE BALANCE OF FORCES

A formal declaration of independence merely cleared the way for tackling the problems of founding a new nation. Lacking both traditions and authority based in law, the Congress had to create political institutions and a new national spirit, all in the midst of war.

Always the military situation took precedence, for a single disastrous setback might make everything else meaningless. At the start the Americans already possessed their lands (except for the few square miles occupied by British troops). Although thousands of colonists fought for George III, the British soon learned that to put down the American rebellion they would have to bring in men and supplies from bases on the other side of the Atlantic. This was a most formidable task.

Certain long-run factors operated in America's favor. Although His Majesty's soldiers were brave and well disciplined, the army was as inefficient and ill directed as the rest of the British government. Whereas nearly everyone in Great Britain wanted to crack down on Boston after the Tea Party, many boggled at engaging in a full-scale war against all the colonies. Aside from a reluctance to spill so much blood, there was the question of expense. Finally, the idea of dispatching the cream of the British army to America while powerful enemies on the Continent still smarted from past defeats seemed risky. For all these reasons the British approached gingerly the task of subduing the rebellion. When Washington fortified Dorchester Heights overlooking Boston, General Howe withdrew his troops to Halifax rather than risk another Bunker Hill.

For a time, the initiative remained with the Americans. An expedition under General Richard Montgomery captured Montréal in November 1775,

The American Revolution

▲ Forts were crucial in eighteenth-century warfare. They provided a repository for gunpowder and munitions, and a platform for heavy cannon. Fort Stanwix *(above)* was located at a crucial site on the Mohawk River. In 1777, a British army under Barry St. Leger surrounded the fort and nearly forced it to surrender when an audacious Patriot general arrived and forced St. Leger to retreat. His name was Benedict Arnold.

and another small force under Benedict Arnold advanced to the gates of Québec after a grueling march across the wilderness from Maine. Montgomery and Arnold attempted to storm the Québec defenses on December 31, 1775, but were repulsed with heavy losses. Even so, the British troops in Canada could not drive the remnants of the American army—perhaps 500 men in all—out of the province until reinforcements arrived in the spring.

Awareness of Britain's problems undoubtedly spurred the Continental Congress to the bold actions of the spring of 1776. However, on July 2, 1776, the same day that Congress voted for independence, General Howe was back on American soil, landing in force on Staten Island in New York harbor in preparation for an assault on the city. Soon Howe had at hand 32,000 well-equipped troops and a powerful fleet commanded by his brother, Richard, Lord Howe. If the British controlled New York City and the Hudson River, they could, as Washington realized, "stop intercourse between the northern and southern Colonies, upon which depends the Safety of America."

Suddenly the full strength of the empire seemed to have descended on the Americans. Superior British resources (a population of 9 million to the colonies' 2.5 million, large stocks of war materials and the industrial capacity to boost them further, mastery of the seas, a well-trained and experienced army, a highly centralized and, when necessary, ruthless government) were now all too evident.

The demonstration of British might in New York harbor accentuated American military and economic weaknesses: Both money and the tools of war were continually in short supply in a predominantly agricultural country. Many of Washington's soldiers were armed with weapons no more lethal than spears and tomahawks. Few had proper uniforms. Even the most patriotic resisted conforming to the conventions of military discipline; the men hated drilling and all parade-ground formality. And all these problems were complicated by the fact that Washington had to create an army organization out of whole cloth at the same time that he was fighting a war.

Supply problems were handled inefficiently and often corruptly. Few officers knew much about such mundane but vital matters as how to construct and maintain proper sanitary facilities when large numbers of soldiers were camped at one place for extended periods of time. What was inelegantly known as "the itch" afflicted soldiers throughout the war.

Loyalists

Behind the lines, the country was far from united. Whereas nearly all colonists had objected to British policies, many still hesitated to take up arms against the mother country. Even Massachusetts harbored many Loyalists, or Tories, as they were called; about a thousand Americans left Boston with General Howe, abandoning their homes rather than submit to the rebel army.

No one knows exactly how the colonists divided on the question of independence. John Adams's off-the-cuff estimate was that a third of the people were ardent Patriots, another third loyal to Great Britain, and the rest neutral or tending to favor whichever side seemed to be winning. This guess is probably as useful as any, although in keeping with Adams's character he may have understated the number who agreed with him and overstated those opposed to his position. Most historians think that about a fifth of the people were Loyalists and about two-fifths Patriots, but there are few hard figures to go by. What is certain is that large elements, perhaps a majority of the people, were more or less indifferent to the conflict or, in Tom Paine's famous phrase, were summer soldiers and sunshine patriots—they supported the Revolution when all was going well and lost their enthusiasm in difficult hours.

The divisions cut across geographical, social, and economic lines. A high proportion of those holding royal appointments and many Anglican clergymen remained loyal to King George, as did numbers of merchants with close connections in Britain. There were important pockets of Tory strength in rural sections of New York, in the North Carolina backcountry, and among persons of non-English origin and other minority groups who tended to count on London for protection against the local majority.

Many became Tories simply out of distaste for change or because they were pessimistic about the condition of society and the possibility of improving it. "What is the whole history of human life," wrote the Tory clergyman and schoolmaster Jonathan Boucher of Virginia, "but a series of disappointments?" Still others believed that the actions of the British, however unfair and misguided, did not justify rebellion. Knowing that they possessed a remarkably free and equitable system of government, they could not stomach shedding blood merely to avoid paying more taxes or to escape from what they considered minor restrictions on their activities. "The Annals of no Country can produce an Instance of so virulent a Rebellion . . . originating from such trivial Causes," one Loyalist complained.

The Tories lacked organization. While Patriot leaders worked closely together, many of the Tory "leaders" did not even know one another. They had no central committee to lay plans or coordinate their efforts. When the revolutionaries took over a colony, some Tories fled; others sought the protection of the British army; others took up arms; and still others accommodated themselves silently to the new regime.

If the differences separating Patriot from Loyalist are unclear, feelings were nonetheless bitter. Individual Loyalists were often set upon by mobs, tarred and feathered, and otherwise abused. Some were thrown into jail for no legitimate reason; others were exiled and their property confiscated. Battles between Tory units and the Continental Army were often exceptionally bloody. "Neighbor was against neighbor, father against son and son against father," one Connecticut Tory reported. "He that would not thrust his own blade through his brother's heart was called an infamous villain."

Early British Victories

General Howe's campaign against New York brought to light another American weakness—the lack of military experience. Washington, expecting Howe to attack New York, had moved south to meet the threat immediately after Howe had abandoned Boston. But both he and his men failed badly in this first major test. Late in August Howe crossed from Staten Island to Brooklyn. In the Battle of Long Island he easily outflanked and defeated Washington's army. Had he acted decisively, he could probably have ended the war on the spot, but Howe could not make up his mind whether to be a peacemaker or a conqueror. This hesitation in consolidating his gains permitted Washington to withdraw his troops to Manhattan Island.

Howe could still have trapped Washington simply by using his fleet to land troops on the northern end of Manhattan; instead he attacked New York City directly, leaving the Americans an escape route to the north. Again Patriot troops proved no match for British regulars. Although Washington threw his hat to the ground in a rage and threatened to shoot cowardly Connecticut soldiers as they fled the battlefield, he could not stop the rout and had to fall back on Harlem Heights in upper Manhattan. Yet once more Howe failed to pursue his advantage promptly.

Still, Washington refused to see the peril in remaining on an island while the enemy commanded the surrounding waters. Only when Howe shifted a powerful force to Westchester, directly threatening his rear, did Washington move north to the mainland. Finally, after several narrow escapes, he crossed the Hudson River and marched south to New Jersey, where the British could not use their naval superiority against him.

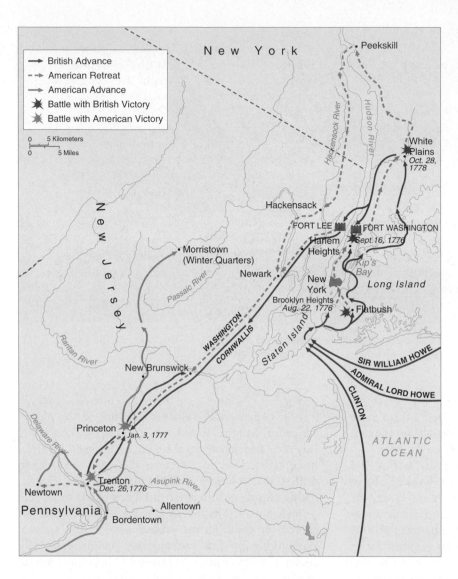

◀ **New York and New Jersey Campaigns, 1776–1777**

The battles in and around New York City seemed to presage an easy British triumph. Yet somehow Washington salvaged a moral victory from these ignominious defeats. He learned rapidly; seldom thereafter did he place his troops in such vulnerable positions. And his men, in spite of repeated failure, had become an army. In November and December 1776 they retreated across New Jersey and into Pennsylvania. General Howe then abandoned the campaign, going into winter quarters in New York but posting garrisons at Trenton, Princeton, and other strategic points.

The troops at Trenton were hated Hessian mercenaries, and Washington decided to attack them. He crossed the ice-clogged Delaware River with 2400 men on Christmas night during a wild storm. The little army then marched nine miles to Trenton, arriving at daybreak in the midst of a sleet storm. The Hessians were taken completely by surprise. Those who could fled in disorder; the rest—900 of them—surrendered.

The Hessians were first-class professional soldiers, probably the most competent troops in Europe at that time. The victory gave a boost to American morale. A few days later Washington outmaneuvered General Cornwallis, who had rushed to Trenton with reinforcements, and won another battle at Princeton. These engagements had little strategic importance, since both armies then went into winter quarters. Without them, however, there might not have been an army to resume the war in the spring.

SARATOGA AND THE FRENCH ALLIANCE

When spring reached New Jersey in April 1777, Washington had fewer than 5000 men under arms. Great plans—far too many and too complicated, as it turned out—were afoot in the British camp. The strategy called for General John Burgoyne to lead a large army from Canada down Lake Champlain toward Albany while a smaller force under Lieutenant Colonel Barry St. Leger pushed eastward toward Albany from Fort Oswego on

▲ The British generals were criticized at home for their losses during the Revolutionary War. This 1779 cartoon shows a British commander in America relaxing in his command tent while his defeated colleagues surrender at Saratoga.

Lake Ontario. General Howe was to lead a third force north up the Hudson. The Patriots would be trapped and the New England states isolated from the rest.

As a venture in coordinated military tactics, the British campaign of 1777 was a fiasco. General Howe had spent the winter in New York wining and dining his officers and prominent local Loyalists and having a torrid affair with the wife of the officer in charge of prisoners of war. He was less attentive to his responsibilities for the British army advancing south from Canada.

General "Gentleman Johnny" Burgoyne, a charming if somewhat bombastic character, part politician, part poet, part gambler, part ladies' man, yet also a brave soldier, had begun his march from Canada in mid June. By early July his army, which consisted of 500 Indians, 650 Loyalists, and 6000 regulars, had captured Fort Ticonderoga at the southern end of Lake Champlain. He quickly pushed beyond Lake George but then bogged down. Burdened by a huge baggage train that included 138 pieces of generally useless artillery, more than 30 carts laden with his personal wardrobe and supply of champagne, and his mistress, he could advance at but a snail's pace through the dense woods north of Saratoga.[1] Patriot militia impeded his way by felling trees across the forest trails.

---

[1]Many soldiers, enlisted men as well as officers, were accompanied by their wives or other women on campaigns. More than 2000 accompanied the Burgoyne expedition. At one point Washington complained of "the multitude of women . . . especially those who are pregnant, or have children [that] clog upon every movement." Actually, women in eighteenth-century armies worked hard, doing most of the cooking, washing, and other "housekeeping" tasks.

St. Leger was also slow in carrying out his part of the grand design. He did not leave Fort Oswego until July 26, and when he stopped to besiege a Patriot force at Fort Stanwix, General Benedict Arnold had time to march west with 1000 men from the army resisting Burgoyne and drive him back to Oswego.

Meanwhile, with magnificent disregard for the agreed-on plan, Howe wasted time trying to trap Washington into exposing his army in New Jersey. This enabled Washington to send some of his best troops to buttress the militia units opposing Burgoyne. Then, just when St. Leger was setting out for Albany, Howe took the bulk of his army off by sea to attack Philadelphia, leaving only a small force commanded by General Sir Henry Clinton to aid Burgoyne.

When Washington moved south to oppose Howe, the Britisher taught him a series of lessons in tactics, defeating him at the Battle of Brandywine, then feinting him out of position and moving unopposed into Philadelphia. But by that time it was late September, and disaster was about to befall General Burgoyne.

The American forces under Philip Schuyler and later under Horatio Gates and Benedict Arnold had erected formidable defenses immediately south of Saratoga near the town of Stillwater. Burgoyne struck at this position twice and was thrown back both times with heavy losses. Each day more local militia swelled the American forces. Soon Burgoyne was under siege, his troops pinned down by withering fire from every direction, unable even to bury their dead. The only hope was General Clinton, who had finally started up the Hudson from New York. Clinton got as far as

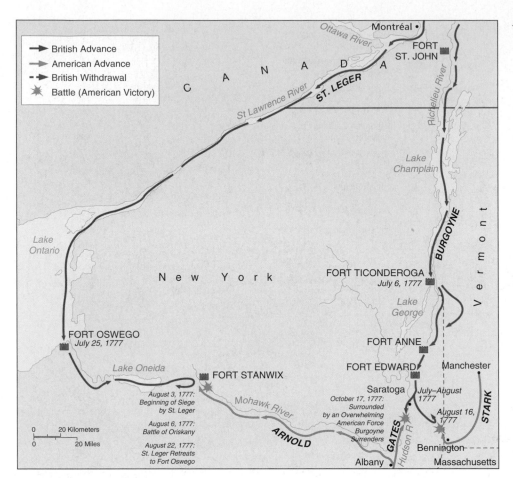

Kingston, about 80 miles below Saratoga, but on October 16 he decided to return to New York for reinforcements. The next day, at Saratoga, Burgoyne surrendered. Some 5700 British prisoners were marched off to Virginia.

This overwhelming triumph changed the course and character of the war. France would probably have entered the war in any case; the country had never reconciled itself to its losses in the Seven Years' War and for years had been building a navy capable of taking on the British. Helping the Americans was simply another way of weakening their British enemy. As early as May 1776 the Comte de Vergennes, France's foreign minister, had persuaded Louis XVI to authorize the expenditure of 1 million livres for munitions for America, and more was added the next year. Spain also contributed, not out of sympathy for the Revolution but because of its desire to injure Great Britain. Soon vital supplies were being funneled secretly to the rebels through a dummy company, Roderigue Hortalez et Cie. When news of the victory at Saratoga reached Paris, the time seemed ripe and Louis XVI recognized the United States. Then Vergennes and three American commissioners in Paris,

Benjamin Franklin, Arthur Lee, and Silas Deane, drafted a commercial treaty and a formal treaty of alliance. The two nations agreed to make "common cause and aid each other mutually" should war "break out" between France and Great Britain. Meanwhile, France guaranteed "the sovereignty and independence absolute and unlimited" of the United States. The help of Spain and France, Washington declared, "will not fail of establishing the Independence of America in a short time."

When the news of Saratoga reached England, Lord North realized that a Franco-American alliance was almost inevitable. To forestall it, he was ready to give in on all the issues that had agitated the colonies before 1775. Both the Coercive Acts and the Tea Act would be repealed; Parliament would pledge never to tax the colonies.

Instead of implementing this proposal promptly, Parliament delayed until March 1778. Royal peace commissioners did not reach Philadelphia until June, a month after Congress had ratified the French treaty. The British proposals were icily rejected, and while the peace commissioners were still in Philadelphia, war broke out between France and Great Britain.

► Campaign in the South, 1779–1781

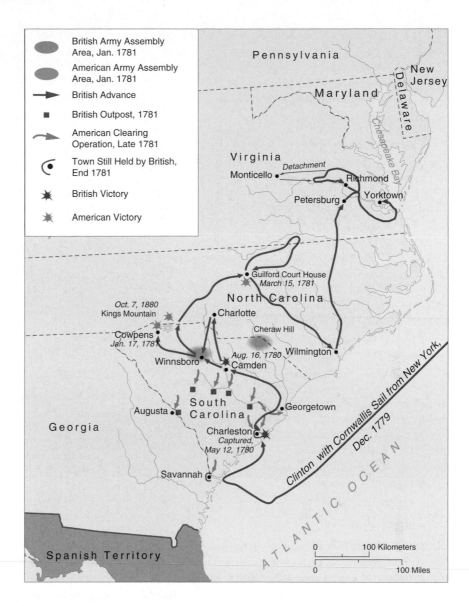

The American Revolution, however, had yet to be won. After the loss of Philadelphia, Washington had settled his army for the winter at Valley Forge, 20 miles to the northwest. The army's supply system collapsed. Often the men had nothing to eat but "fire cake," a mixture of ground grain and water molded on a stick or in a pan and baked in a campfire. According to the Marquis de Lafayette, one of many Europeans who volunteered to fight on the American side, "the unfortunate soldiers . . . had neither coats, nor hats, nor shirts, nor shoes; their feet and legs froze till they grew black, and it was often necessary to amputate them."

To make matters worse, there was grumbling in Congress over Washington's failure to win victories and talk of replacing him as commander-in-chief with Horatio Gates, the "hero" of Saratoga. (In fact, Gates was an indifferent soldier, lacking in decisiveness and unable to instill confidence in his subordinates.)

As the winter dragged on, the Continental Army melted away. So many officers resigned that Washington was heard to say that he was afraid of "being left Alone with the Soldiers only." Since enlisted men could not legally resign, they deserted by the hundreds. Yet the army survived. Gradually the soldiers who remained became a tough, professional fighting force.

THE WAR MOVES SOUTH

Spring brought a revival of American hopes in the form of more supplies, new recruits, and, above all, word of the French alliance. In May 1778 the British replaced General Howe as commander with General Clinton, who decided to transfer his base back to New York. While Clinton was moving across New Jersey, Washington attacked him at Monmouth Court

House. The fight was inconclusive, but the Americans held the field when the day ended and were able to claim a victory.

Thereafter British strategy changed. Fighting in the northern states degenerated into skirmishes and other small-unit clashes. Instead, relying on sea power, the supposed presence of many Tories in the South, and the possibility of obtaining the help of slaves, the British concentrated their efforts in South Carolina and Georgia. Savannah fell to them late in 1778, and most of the settled parts of Georgia were overrun during 1779. In 1780 Clinton led a massive expedition against Charleston. When the city surrendered in May, more than 3000 soldiers were captured, the most overwhelming American defeat of the war. Leaving General Cornwallis and some 8000 men to carry on the campaign, Clinton then sailed back to New York.

The Tories in South Carolina and Georgia came closer to meeting British expectations than in any other region, but the callous behavior of the British troops persuaded large numbers of hesitating citizens to join the Patriot cause. Guerrilla bands led by Francis Marion, the "Swamp Fox," Thomas Sumter, after whom Fort Sumter, famous in the Civil War, was named, and others like them provided a nucleus of resistance in areas that had supposedly been subdued.

But the tide soon turned. In 1779 the Spanish governor of Louisiana, José de Gálvez, administered a stinging defeat to British troops in Florida, and in 1780 and 1781 he captured the British-held Gulf ports of Pensacola and Mobile. More important, in June 1780 Congress placed Horatio Gates in charge of a southern army consisting of the irregular militia units and a hard core of Continentals transferred from Washington's command. Gates encountered Cornwallis at Camden, South Carolina. Foolishly, he entrusted a key sector of his line to untrained militiamen, who panicked when the British charged with fixed bayonets. Gates suffered heavy losses and had to fall back. Congress then recalled him, sensibly permitting Washington to replace him with General Nathanael Greene, a first-rate officer.

A band of militiamen had trapped a contingent of Tories at King's Mountain and forced its surrender. Greene, avoiding a major engagement with Cornwallis's superior numbers, divided his troops and staged a series of raids on scattered points. In January 1781, at the Battle of Cowpens in northwestern South Carolina, General Daniel Morgan inflicted a costly defeat on Colonel Banastre Tarleton, one of Cornwallis's most effective officers. Cornwallis pursued Morgan hotly, but the American rejoined Greene, and at Guilford Court House they again

inflicted heavy losses on the British. Then Cornwallis withdrew to Wilmington, North Carolina, where he could rely on the fleet for support and reinforcements. Greene's Patriots quickly regained control of the Carolina backcountry.

VICTORY AT YORKTOWN

Seeing no future in the Carolinas and unwilling to vegetate at Wilmington, Cornwallis marched north into Virginia, where he joined forces with troops under Benedict Arnold. (Disaffected by what he considered unjust criticism of his generalship, Arnold had sold out to the British in 1780. He intended to betray the bastion of West Point on the Hudson River. The scheme was foiled when incriminating papers were found on the person of a British spy, Major John André. Arnold fled to the British and André was hanged.) As in the Carolina campaign, the British had numerical superiority at first but lost it rapidly when local militia and Continental forces concentrated against them. Cornwallis soon discovered that Virginia Tories were of little help in such a situation. "When a Storm threatens, our friends disappear," he grumbled.

General Clinton ordered Cornwallis to establish a base at Yorktown, where he could be supplied by sea. It was a terrible mistake. The British navy in American waters far outnumbered American and French vessels, but the Atlantic is wide, and in those days communication was slow. The French had a fleet in the West Indies under Admiral François de Grasse and another squadron at Newport, Rhode Island, where a French army was stationed. In the summer of 1781 Washington, de Grasse, and the Comte de Rochambeau, commander of French land forces, designed and carried out with an efficiency unparalleled in eighteenth-century warfare a complex plan to bottle up Cornwallis.

The British navy in the West Indies and at New York might have forestalled this scheme had it moved promptly and in force. But Admiral Sir George Rodney sent only part of his Indies fleet. As a result, de Grasse, after a battle with a British fleet commanded by Admiral Thomas Graves, won control of the Chesapeake and cut Cornwallis off from the sea.

The next move was up to Washington, and this was his finest hour as a commander. He desperately wanted to attack the British base at New York, but at the urging of Rochambeau he agreed instead to strike

▶ *text continues on page 126*

Re-Viewing the Past

The Patriot

As the opening credits roll, Benjamin Martin (played by Mel Gibson) pries open a wooden box. It contains yellowing papers, a few medals and a tomahawk. He lifts the tomahawk, fingers its handle gingerly, and stares at the blade. "I had long feared that my sins would revisit me," a voice intones, "and the cost is more than I can bear." The viewer suspects—rightly, it turns out—that Martin's sins were violent, and that they had something to do with hacking people apart. But at the outset of *The Patriot,* Hollywood's $100-million blockbuster on the American Revolution, Martin is more pacifist than patriot. When the South Carolina legislature votes to go to war with Great Britain, he publicly declares that his chief obligation is to his family: "I will not fight." He soon changes his mind.

The British capture of Charleston (1780) brings onto the scene a villainous British cavalry officer, Colonel Tavington. Ordered by General Cornwallis to subdue the insurrection in the countryside, Tavington ransacks plantations, forces slaves into the King's service, and hounds the rebel militia. He also arrests Gabriel (Heath Ledger), Martin's oldest son, and orders the boy's execution as a spy. When Gabriel's younger brother tries to intervene, Tavington shoots the boy dead. Overcome with rage, Martin races to his room, grabs the hatchet, and proceeds to bury it—repeatedly—in the chests and skulls of countless British soldiers. He takes command of the militia, recruits more Patriots, and harries the British at every turn.

Tavington responds by intensifying his campaign against the rebels. His culminating barbarity is to round up the villagers of Wakefield (including Gabriel's fiancé), corral them in a church, and set it ablaze. All perish in unimaginable (and mercifully unfilmed) agony. Martin checks his rage long enough to plot the defeat of Cornwallis's army. This occurs at the Battle of Cowpens, where the militia holds its position despite being blasted by British artillery and decimated by repeated fusillades. When Tavington leads a cavalry charge, Martin's eyes widen and he reaches for the tomahawk. Tavington dies at Martin's hands, and Cornwallis is routed, too; the latter's subsequent surrender at Yorktown is now a foregone conclusion.

Historians have found much to criticize in the movie's retelling of the war in the South. There was no such person as Benjamin Martin, though elements of his story can be

▲ Francis Marion, a Patriot whose guerrilla warfare helped drive the British from South Carolina.

found in the exploits of guerrilla leaders such as Francis Marion ("the Swamp Fox"), Thomas Sumter, Andrew Pickens, and General Daniel Morgan, who commanded the Continentals at Cowpens. Although the British cavalry wear red uniforms in the movie, they were known as the Green Dragoons for a reason that seemingly eluded the filmmakers. The movie's version of the Battle of Cowpens featured a glorious display of fireworks, though neither army's artillery in South Carolina was capable of firing explosive shells. Cornwallis was not humiliated at Cowpens because he was not there. In the movie the British are caricatured as either evil geniuses or bungling twits; and the Patriots, as largehearted rogues or pious patriarchs. The real combatants doubtless adhered less predictably to type. The most serious deviation from the historical record was the incineration of the occupied church: there is no record of any such event. "*The Patriot* is to history what Godzilla was to biology," declared historian David Hackett Fischer.

However, *The Patriot* raises and thoughtfully addresses an important historical issue: How can any society reconcile peaceable virtues—love for family, neighborliness, cooperation—with the violence of war? In *The Patriot,* the dilemma is symbolized by Martin's tomahawk. This weapon helps free his captured son and vanquish the evil Tavington; and yet it is also a manifestation of Martin's savage, even pathological, rage. Martin's secret shame, alluded to in the opening scene, was his dismembering corpses after a particularly brutal battle during the French and Indian War.

Eighteenth-century Europeans were in fact preoccupied with reconciling the violence of war with the need for social order. Their particular refinement in the military arts was the ordered massing of musket fire. Because muskets were highly inaccurate, a troop of soldiers, dispersed and firing on their own, were unlikely to drive an enemy from the field. But when the soldiers were brought together in concentrated formations and ordered to fire at the same moment, the enemy would be decimated. The technology of warfare required intense military discipline; and the new penchant for military order imposed seeming coherence upon the chaos of the battlefield.

The Patriot provides a vivid rendering of this juxtaposition. Soldiers in beautifully colored uniforms march in straight, regular columns to the steady cadence of drums while officers bark precise commands: "Circle right. Face forward. Lift weapons . . . " These stately preliminaries, depicted on ripening fields beneath a summer sun, provide an unsettling backdrop for the ensuing violence: volleys of musket fire shatter the formations; low-velocity cannon balls decapitate individual soldiers; soldiers thrust bayonets into the chests of enemies.

Martin, once he has again taken up his tomahawk, concludes that the British cannot be defeated in this type of battle. And, in fact, they seldom were. Martin advocates guerrilla warfare, as did many southern Patriot militiamen. The British had good reason to doubt the legitimacy of this type of warfare. When men went wild on the battlefield, or fired shots and then hid among civilians, they were criminals, not soldiers. If such behavior were condoned, warfare would become barbarity.

▼ Mel Gibson as Patriot leader with Jason Isaacs as Colonel Tavington, a barbarous British officer.

▶ Colonel Banastre Tarleton, on whom Tavington was based.

The movie develops this point at considerable length. During a truce, Martin confers with Cornwallis, who complains that the Patriot militia aimed at officers at the beginning of battles. Such behavior was inconsistent with "civilized warfare." Officers, as gentlemen, were bound by codes of honor. If they were killed, who would "restrain" the regular soldiers—keep them from reverting, as did Martin, to a frenzy of terror and rage?

The movie's debate over the nature of "civilized" warfare parallels an ongoing debate at the time. At the outset of the conflict, British officers took an oath affirming the British Articles of War, which protected citizens and soldiers who had surrendered. The American Congress also adopted the British Articles of War as the basis for discipline and military justice. But with the outbreak of guerrilla warfare in the South, both sides frequently ignored these rules.

"Colonel Tavington" was obviously based on Banastre Tarleton, the actual commander of the Green Dragoons. Tarleton became notorious after his soldiers raped three plantation women and killed several militiamen who had surrendered. This behavior worried Cornwallis, who sent a dispatch commending his subordinate's courage and zeal but also warning: "Use your utmost endeavors to prevent the troops under your command from committing irregularities." In a subsequent engagement at Waxhaws, however, Tarleton again lost control of his men, who stabbed and slashed vanquished foes. An American officer discovered that the American corpses at Waxhaws had each received, on the average, 16 wounds.

British and American officers sought to affirm that the war could be civilized. But such high-minded notions were repeatedly subverted during tomahawk-wielding guerrilla warfare and by excessively zealous commanders. The question then remained, as it does today, whether unchecked aggression is, among soldiers, a virtue or a vice. *The Patriot* raises these issues but does not resolve them. Martin, surely, should have kept his tomahawk in its locked box; but if he had, would the Patriots have won?

▶ **The Yorktown Campaign,
April–September 1781**

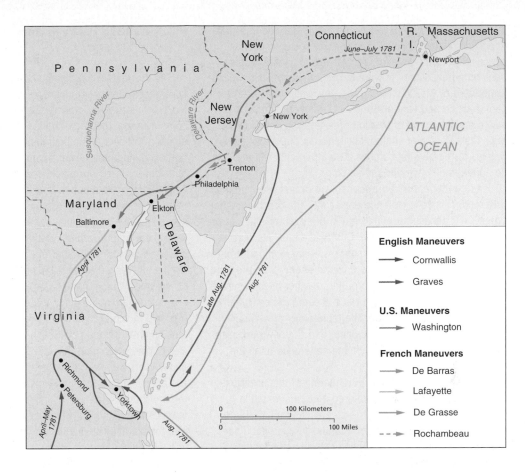

at Yorktown. After tricking Clinton into thinking he was heading for New York, he pushed boldly south. In early September he reached Yorktown and joined up with an army commanded by Lafayette and troops from de Grasse's fleet. He soon had nearly 17,000 French and American veterans in position.

"The Liberty Song"

Cornwallis was helpless. He held out until October 17 and then asked for terms. Two days later more than 7000 British soldiers marched out of their lines and laid down their arms. Then the jubilant Lafayette ordered his military band to play "Yankee Doodle."

THE PEACE OF PARIS

The British gave up trying to suppress the rebellion after Yorktown, but the event that confirmed the existence of the United States as an independent nation was the signing of a peace treaty with Great Britain. Yorktown had been only one of a string of defeats suffered by British arms in the Mediterranean, the West Indies, Africa, and Asia. The national debt had doubled again since 1775. In March 1782 Lord North resigned after Parliament renounced all further efforts to coerce the colonies. At once the new ministry of

Lord Rockingham prepared to negotiate a peace settlement with America.

The problem of peacemaking was complicated. The United States and France had pledged not to make a separate peace. Spain, at war with Great Britain since 1779, was allied with France but not with America. Although eager to profit at British expense, the Spanish hoped to limit American expansion beyond the Appalachians, for they had ambitions of their own in the eastern half of the Mississippi Valley. France, while ready enough to see America independent, did not want the new country to become *too* powerful; in a conflict of interest between America and Spain, France tended to support Spain.

The Continental Congress appointed John Adams, Benjamin Franklin, John Jay, Thomas Jefferson, and Henry Laurens as a commission to conduct peace talks. Franklin and Jay did most of the actual negotiating. Congress, grateful for French aid during the Revolution, had instructed the commissioners to rely on the advice of the Comte de Vergennes. In Paris, however, the commissioners soon discovered that Vergennes was not the perfect friend of America that Congress believed him to be. He was, after all, a French official, and France had other interests far more important than concern for its American ally. Vergennes "means to keep his hand under our chin to

▲ The surrender of Cornwallis at Yorktown on October 19, 1781, by John Trumbull in 1820. In 1789 Trumbull, who had served as an aide to Washington, wrote to Thomas Jefferson that he wanted to make paintings "to preserve and diffuse the memory of the noblest series of actions which have e'er presented themselves to the history of man"—the American revolution. The next year he went to London to study painting with Benjamin West; he was promptly arrested as an American spy. Fortunately, West had made connections with King George III and managed to spare Trumbull from the gallows.

prevent us from drowning," Adams complained, "but not to lift our head out of the water."

Franklin, whose fame as a scientist and sage had spread to Europe, was wined and dined by the cream of Paris and petted and fussed over by some of the city's most beautiful women. He did not press the American point of view as forcefully as he might have. But this was because he took the long view, which was to achieve a true reconciliation with the British, not simply to drive the hardest bargain possible. John Jay was somewhat more tough-minded. But on basic issues all the Americans were in agreement. They hinted to the British representative, Richard Oswald, that they would consider a separate peace if it were a generous one and suggested that Great Britain would be far better off with America, a nation that favored free trade, in control of the trans-Appalachian region than with a mercantilist power like Spain.

The British government reacted favorably, authorizing Oswald "to treat with the Commissioners appointed by the Colonys, under the title of Thirteen United States." Soon the Americans were deep in negotiations with Oswald. They told Vergennes what they were doing but did not discuss details.

Oswald was cooperative, and the Americans drove a hard bargain. One scrap of conversation reveals the tenor of the talks.

OSWALD: We can never be such damned sots as to disturb you.

ADAMS: Thank you. . . . But nations don't feel as you and I do, and your nation, when it gets a little refreshed from the fatigues of the war, and when men and money become plentiful, and allies at hand, will not feel as it does now.

OSWALD: We can never be such damned sots as to think of differing again with you.

ADAMS: Why, in truth I have never been able to comprehend the reason why you ever thought of differing with us.

By the end of November 1782 a preliminary treaty had been signed. "His Britannic Majesty," Article 1

DEBATING THE PAST

Was the American Revolution rooted in class struggle? This 1795 engraving of a Stamp Act protest delineates a class division. The three British Tories—one suspended, two sprawled below—are wealthy. The Patriots surrounding them are not. The progressive historian Carl Becker declared that the Revolution was fought "not only about home rule but also about who should rule at home." The leaders of the Revolution sought not only to defeat the Crown in England but also the rabble in Boston and New York—the Patriots as depicted here. Another progressive historian, Arthur Schlesinger, Sr. (1918) wrote that commercial elites "instigated" popular opposition to British policies, grew alarmed at the "engulfing tide of radicalism" that led to war, and then turned against the farmers and workers who did most of the fighting. Edmund Morgan rejected the notion that the Revolution grew out of class divisions. It did not constitute a victory of the rich over the poor, but "a union of three million cantankerous colonists into a new nation." Historians during the tumultuous 1960s underscored the divisions in American society. Gary B. Nash showed how declining opportunities had radicalized urban workers. Other social historians found yet other cleavages: Mary Beth Norton between men and women; Sylvia R. Frey between masters and slaves; Colin Calloway between colonists and Indians.

Carl Becker, *History of Political Parties in New York* (1909), Arthur M. Schlesinger, Sr., *The Colonial Merchants and the American Revolution* (1918), Edmund Morgan, *The Birth of the Republic* (1956), Gary B. Nash, *The Urban Crucible* (1989), Mary Beth Norton, *Founding Mothers and Fathers* (1996), Sylvia R. Frey, *Water from the Rock* (1991), Colin Calloway, *American Revolution in Indian Country* (1995).

began, "acknowledges the said United States . . . to be free, sovereign and independent States." Other terms were equally in line with American hopes and objectives. The boundaries of the nation were set at the Great Lakes, the Mississippi River, and 31° north latitude (roughly the northern boundary of Florida, which the British turned over to Spain).[2] Britain recognized the right of Americans to take fish on the Grand Banks off Newfoundland and, far more important, to dry and cure their catch on unsettled beaches in Labrador and Nova Scotia. The British agreed to withdraw their troops from American soil "with all convenient speed." Where the touchy problem of Tory property seized during the Revolution was concerned, the Americans agreed only that Congress would "earnestly recommend" that the states "provide for the restitution of all estates, rights and properties which have been confiscated." They promised to prevent further property confiscation and prosecutions of Tories—certainly a wise as well as a humane policy—and they agreed not to impede the collection of debts owed British subjects. Vergennes was flabbergasted by the success of the Americans. "The English buy the peace more than they make it," he wrote. "Their concessions . . . exceed all that I should have thought possible."

The American commissioners obtained these favorable terms because they were shrewd diplomats and because of the rivalries that existed among the great European powers. In the last analysis, Britain preferred to have a weak nation of English-speaking people in command of the Mississippi Valley rather than France or Spain.

From their experience at the peace talks, the American leaders learned the importance of playing one power against another without committing themselves completely to any. This policy demanded constant contact with European affairs and skill at adjusting policies to changes in the European balance of power. It enabled the United States, a young and relatively feeble country, to grow and prosper.

FORMING A NATIONAL GOVERNMENT

Independence was won on the battlefield and at the Paris Peace Conference, but it could not have been achieved without the work of the Continental Congress and the new state governments. The delegates recognized that the Congress was essentially a legislative body rather than a complete government and

DOCUMENT

The Articles of Confederation

---

[2]Much of this vast region, of course, was controlled not by the British but by various Indian tribes.

from the start they struggled to create a workable central authority. But their effort was handicapped by much confusion and bickering, and early military defeats sapped their energy and morale. In July 1776 John Dickinson prepared a draft national constitution, but it could not command much support. The larger states objected to equal representation of all the states, and the states with large western land claims refused to cede them to the central government. It was not until November 1777 that the Articles of Confederation were submitted to the states for ratification.

It was necessary to obtain the approval of all the states before the Articles could go into effect. All acted fairly promptly but Maryland, which did not ratify the document until 1781. Maryland held out in order to force a change that would authorize Congress to determine the western limits of states with land claims beyond the Appalachians. There were many good reasons why this should be done. The state claims to the West were overlapping, vaguely defined, and in some instances preposterous. To have permitted a few states to monopolize the West would have unbalanced the Union from the start.

Many people in the "landed" states recognized the justice of Maryland's suggestion, yet Maryland had a more selfish motive. Land speculators in the state had obtained from the Indians rights to large tracts in the Ohio Valley claimed by Virginia. Under Virginia, the Maryland titles would be worthless, but under a national administration they might be made to stand up.

Virginia resented its neighbor's efforts to grasp these valuable lands by indirection, but with the British about to advance into the state, Virginia agreed to surrender its claim to all land west and north of the Ohio River. It thwarted the Maryland speculators by insisting that all titles based on Indian purchases be declared void. Maryland then had no recourse but to ratify the Articles.

The Articles merely provided a legal basis for authority that the Continental Congress had already been exercising. Each state, regardless of size, was to have but one vote; the union it created was only a "league of friendship." Article 2 defined the limit of national power: "Each state retains its sovereignty, freedom, and independence, and every Power, jurisdiction, and right, which is not by this confederation expressly delegated to the United States, in Congress assembled."

Time proved this an inadequate arrangement, chiefly because the central government lacked the authority to impose taxes and had no way of enforcing the powers it did have.

FINANCING THE WAR

In practice, Congress and the states carried on the war cooperatively. General officers were appointed by Congress, lesser ones locally. The Continental Army, the backbone of Washington's force, was supported by Congress. The states raised militia chiefly for short-term service. Militiamen fought well at times but often proved unreliable, especially when asked to fight at any great distance from their homes. Washington continually fretted about their "dirty mercenary spirit" and their "intractable" nature, yet he could not have won the war without them.

The fact that Congress's requisitions of money often went unhonored by the states does not mean that the states failed to contribute heavily to the war effort. Altogether they spent about $5.8 million in hard money, and they met Congress's demands for beef, corn, rum, fodder, and other military supplies. In addition, Congress raised large sums by borrowing. Americans bought bonds worth between $7 and $8 million during the war. Foreign governments lent another $8 million, most of this furnished by France. Congress also issued more than $240 million in paper money, the states over $200 million more. This currency fell rapidly in value, resulting in an inflation that caused hardship and grumbling. The people, in

▲ The Continental Army brought together men from all over the colonies and from a wide range of backgrounds. Their variety is suggested in this watercolor by a French officer who served in America during the Revolution. From left to right are a black infantryman with a light rifle, a musketman, a soldier carrying a heavy rifle, and an artilleryman.

effect, paid much of the cost of the war through the depreciation of their savings, but it is hard to see how else the war could have been financed, given the prejudice of the populace against paying taxes to fight a war against British taxation.

At about the time the Articles of Confederation were ratified, Congress established Departments of Foreign Affairs, War, and Finance, with individual heads responsible to it. The most important of the new department heads was the superintendent of finance, Robert Morris, a Philadelphia merchant. When Morris took office, the Continental dollar was worthless, the system of supplying the army chaotic, the credit of the government exhausted. He set up an efficient method of obtaining food and uniforms for the army, persuaded Congress to charter a national Bank of North America, and aided by the slackening of military activity after Yorktown, got the country back on a hard money basis. New foreign loans were obtained, partly because Morris's efficiency and industry inspired confidence.

STATE REPUBLICAN GOVERNMENTS

However crucial the role of Congress, in an important sense the real revolution occurred when the individual colonies broke their ties with Great Britain. Using their colonial charters as a basis, the states began framing new constitutions even before the Declaration of Independence. By early 1777 all but Connecticut and Rhode Island, which continued under their colonial charters well into the nineteenth century, had taken this decisive step.

On the surface the new governments were not drastically different from those they replaced. The most significant change was the removal of outside control, which had the effect of making the governments more responsive to public opinion. Gone were the times when a governor could be appointed and maintained in office by orders from London. The new constitutions varied in detail, but all provided for an elected legislature, an executive, and a system of courts. In general the powers of the governor and of judges were limited, the theory being that elected rulers no less than those appointed by kings were subject to the temptations of authority, that, as one Patriot put it, all men are "tyrants enough at heart." The typical governor had no voice in legislation and little in appointments. Pennsylvania went so far as to eliminate the office of governor, replacing it with an elected council of 12.

Power was concentrated in the legislature, which the people had come to count on to defend their interests. In addition to the lawmaking authority exercised by the colonial assemblies, the state constitutions gave the legislatures the power to declare war, conduct foreign relations, control the courts, and perform many other essentially executive functions. While continuing to require that voters be property owners or taxpayers, the constitution makers remained suspicious even of the legislature.

They rejected the British concept of virtual representation. They saw legislators as representatives, that is, agents reflecting the interests of the voters of a particular district rather than superior persons chosen to decide public issues according to their own best judgment. Where political power was involved, the common American principle was every man for himself, but also everyone for the nation, the republic. People were no longer subjects, but citizens, *parts* of government, obedient to its laws, but not blindly subordinate to governmental authority epitomized in the monarch.

A majority of the constitutions contained bills of rights (such as the one George Mason wrote for Virginia) protecting the people's civil liberties against all branches of the government. In Britain such guarantees checked only the Crown; the Americans invoked them against their elected representatives as well.

The state governments combined the best of the British system, including its respect for status, fairness, and due process, with the uniquely American stress on individualism and a healthy dislike of too much authority. The idea of drafting written frames of government—contracts between the people and their representatives that carefully spelled out the powers and duties of the latter—grew out of the experience of the colonists after 1763, when the vagueness of the unwritten British constitution had caused so much controversy, and from the compact principle, the heart of republican government as described so eloquently in the Declaration of Independence. This constitutionalism represented one of the most important innovations of the Revolutionary era: a peaceful method for altering the political system. In the midst of violence, the states changed their frames of government in an orderly, legal manner—a truly remarkable achievement that became a beacon of hope to reformers all over the world. The states' example, the Reverend Simeon Howard of Massachusetts predicted, "will encourage the friends and rouse a spirit of liberty through other nations."

SOCIAL REFORM

Many states seized the occasion of constitution making to introduce important political and social reforms. In Pennsylvania, Virginia, North Carolina, and

other states the seats in the legislature were reapportioned in order to give the western districts their fair share. Primogeniture, entail (the right of an owner of property to prevent heirs from ever disposing of it), and quitrents were abolished wherever they had existed. Steps toward greater freedom of religion were taken, especially in states where the Anglican Church had enjoyed a privileged position. In Virginia the movement to separate church and state was given the force of law by Jefferson's Statute of Religious Liberty, enacted in 1786. "Our civil rights have no dependence on our religious opinions, any more than our opinions in physics or geometry," the statute declared. "Truth is great and will prevail if left to herself." Therefore, "no man shall be compelled to frequent or support any religious worship, place, or ministry . . . nor shall otherwise suffer on account of his religious opinions or belief."

Many states continued to support religion; Massachusetts did not end public support of Congregational churches until the 1830s. But after the Revolution the states usually distributed the money roughly in accordance with the numerical strength of the various Protestant denominations.

A number of states moved tentatively against slavery. In attacking British policy after 1763, colonists had frequently claimed that Parliament was trying to make slaves of them. No less a personage than George Washington wrote in 1774: "We must assert our rights, or submit to every imposition, that can be heaped upon us, till custom and use shall make us tame and abject slaves." However exaggerated the language, such reasoning led to denunciations of slavery, often vague but significant in their effects on public opinion. The fact that practically every important thinker of the European Enlightenment (Montesquieu, Voltaire, Diderot, and Rousseau in France, David Hume, Samuel Johnson, and Adam Smith in England, to name the most important) had criticized slavery on moral and economic grounds also had an impact on educated opinion. Then, too, the forthright statements in the Declaration of Independence about liberty and equality seemed impossible to reconcile with slaveholding. "How is it," asked Dr. Johnson, who opposed independence vehemently, "that we hear the loudest yelps for liberty among the drivers of negroes?"

The war opened direct paths to freedom for some slaves. In November 1775 Lord Dunmore, the royal governor of Virginia, proclaimed that all slaves "able and willing to bear arms" for the British would be liberated. In fact, the British treated slaves as captured property, seizing them by the thousands in their campaigns in the south. The fate of these blacks is obscure. Some ended up in the West Indies, still slaves. Others were evacuated to Canada and liberated, and

some of them settled the British colony of Sierra Leone in West Africa, founded in 1787. Probably many more escaped from bondage by running away during the confusion accompanying the British campaigns in the South.

About 5000 blacks served in the Patriot army and navy. Most black soldiers were assigned noncombat duties, but there were some black soldiers in every major battle from Lexington to Yorktown.

Beginning with Pennsylvania in 1780, the northern states all did away with slavery. In most cases slaves born after a certain date were to become free on reaching maturity. Since New York did not pass a gradual emancipation law until 1799 and New Jersey not until 1804, there were numbers of slaves in the so-called free states well into the nineteenth century—more than 3500 as late as 1830. But the institution was on its way toward extinction. All the states prohibited the importation of slaves from abroad, and except for Georgia and South Carolina, the southern states passed laws removing restrictions on the right of individual owners to free their slaves. The greatest success of voluntary emancipation came in Virginia, where, between 1782 and 1790, as many as 10,000 blacks were freed.

These advances encouraged foes of slavery to hope that the institution would soon disappear. But slavery died only where it was not economically important. Except for owners whose slaves were "carried off" by the British, only in Massachusetts, where the state supreme court ruled slavery unconstitutional in 1783, were owners deprived of existing slaves against their will.

Despite the continuing subordination of blacks, there is no question that the Revolution permanently changed the tone of American society. In the way they dressed, in their manner of speech, and in the way they dealt with one another in public places, Americans paid at least lip service to the idea of equality.

After the publication of *Common Sense* and the Declaration of Independence, with their excoriations of that "Royal Brute," King George III, it became fashionable to denounce the granting of titles of nobility, all "aristocrats," and any privilege based on birth. In 1783 a group of army officers founded a fraternal organization, the Society of Cincinnati. Although the revered George Washington was its president, many citizens found the mere existence of a club restricted to officers alarming; the fact that membership was to be hereditary, passing on the death of a member to his oldest son, caused a furor.

Nevertheless, little of the social and economic upheaval usually associated with revolutions occurred, before, during, or after 1776. At least part of the urban violence of the period (just how large a part is difficult to determine at this distance) had no

social objective. America had its share of criminals, mischievous youths eager to flex their muscles, and other people unable to resist the temptation to break the law when it could be done without much risk of punishment. Certainly there was no wholesale proscription of any class, faith, or profession.

The property of Tories was frequently seized by the state governments, but almost never with the idea of redistributing wealth or providing the poor with land. While some large Tory estates were broken up and sold to small farmers, others passed intact to wealthy individuals or to groups of speculators. The war disrupted many traditional business relationships. Some merchants were unable to cope with the changes; others adapted well and grew rich. But the changes occurred without regard for the political beliefs or social values of either those who profited or those who lost.

During the war, conflicts erupted over economic issues involving land and taxation, yet no single class or interest triumphed in all the states or in the national government. In Pennsylvania, where the western radical element was strong, the constitution was extremely democratic; in Maryland and South Carolina the conservatives maintained control handily. Throughout the country, many great landowners were ardent Patriots, but others became Tories—and so did many small farmers.

In some instances the state legislatures wrote the new constitutions. In others the legislatures ordered special elections to choose delegates to conventions empowered to draft the charters. The convention method was a further important product of the Revolutionary era, an additional illustration of the idea that constitutions are contracts between the people and their leaders. Massachusetts even required that its new constitution be ratified by the people after it was drafted.

Finally, the new governments became more responsive to public opinion, no matter what the particular shape of their political institutions. This was true principally because *Common Sense,* the Declaration of Independence, and the experience of participating in a revolution had made people conscious of their rights in a republic and of their power to enforce those rights. Conservatives swiftly discovered that state constitutions designed to insulate legislators and officials from popular pressures were ineffective when the populace felt strongly about any issue.

EFFECTS OF THE REVOLUTION ON WOMEN

In the late eighteenth century there was a trend in the Western world, barely perceptible at the time, toward increasing the legal rights of women. This movement

was strengthened in America by the events leading up to the break with Great Britain and still more by the Declaration of Independence. When Americans began to think and talk about the rights of the individual and the evils of arbitrary rule, subtle effects on relations between the sexes followed. For example, it became somewhat easier for women to obtain divorces. In colonial times divorces were relatively rare, but easier for men to obtain than for women. After the Revolution the difference did not disappear, but it became considerably smaller. In Massachusetts, before the 1770s no woman is known to have obtained a divorce on the ground of her husband's adultery. Thereafter, successful suits by wives against errant husbands were not unusual. In 1791 a South Carolina judge went so far as to say that the law protecting "the absolute dominion" of husbands was "the

▲ A 1797 engraving of Deborah Sampson, the first woman to serve as a soldier in the Revolution. Born in 1760, Sampson in 1782 put on men's clothes and enlisted in the Massachusetts Militia under the name of Timothy Thayer. Her imposture was discovered and she was expelled. She then enlisted as Robert Shurtlieff in the Continental army. At a battle against Loyalists at Tarrytown, New York she was wounded in the thigh. Rather than let a doctor treat her—and discover her gender—she extracted the musket ball herself. After the war, she continued to wear men's clothing until she married and had children.

However, the war effort increased the influence of women in several ways. With so many men in uniform, women took over the management of countless farms, shops, and businesses, and they became involved in the handling of other day-to-day matters that men had normally conducted. Their experiences made both them and in many cases their fathers and husbands more aware of their ability to take on all sorts of chores previously considered exclusively masculine in character. At the same time, women wanted to contribute to the winning of independence, and their efforts to do so made them conscious of their importance. Furthermore, the rhetoric of the Revolution, with its stress on liberty and equality, affected women in the same way that it caused many whites of both sexes to question the morality of slavery.

Attitudes toward the education of women also changed because of the Revolution. According to the best estimates, at least half the white women in America could not read or write as late as the 1780s. In a land of opportunity like the United States, women seemed particularly important, not only because they themselves were citizens, but because of their role in training the next generation. "You distribute 'mental nourishment' along with physical," one orator told the women of America in 1795. "The reformation of the world is in your power. . . . The solidity and stability of your country rest with you." The idea of female education began to catch on. Schools for girls were founded, and the level of female literacy gradually rose.

▲ Abigail Adams, in asking her husband John to "remember the ladies" when reforming society, was not advocating political rights for women. Rather, she wanted fairer treatment for women within the family. "Do not put such unlimited power into the hands of the husbands," she wrote him. "Remember all men would be tyrants if they could."

GROWTH OF A NATIONAL SPIRIT

American independence and control of a wide and rich domain were the most obvious results of the Revolution. Changes in the structure of society, as we have seen, were relatively minor. Economic developments, such as the growth of new trade connections and the expansion of manufacturing in an effort to replace British goods, were of only modest significance. By far the most important social and economic changes involved the Tories and were thus by-products of the political revolution rather than a determined reorganization of a people's way of life.

There was another important result of the Revolution: the growth of American nationalism. Most modern revolutions have been *caused* by nationalism and have *resulted* in independence. In the case of the American Revolution, the desire to be free antedated any intense national feeling. The colonies entered into a political union not because they felt an overwhelming desire to bring all Americans under one rule but because unity offered the only hope of winning a war against Great Britain. That

offspring of a rude and barbarous age." The "progress of civilization," he continued, "has tended to ameliorate the condition of women, and to allow even to wives, something like personal identity."

As the tone of this "liberal" opinion indicates, the change in male attitudes that took place in America because of the Revolution was small. Courts in New York and Massachusetts refused to take action against Tory women whose husbands were Tories on the ground that it was the duty of women to obey their husbands, and when John Adams's wife Abigail warned him in 1776 that if he and his fellow rebels did not "remember the ladies" when reforming society, the women would "foment a Rebellion" of their own, he treated her remarks as a joke. Adams believed that voting (and as he wrote on another occasion, writing history) was "not the Province of the Ladies."[3]

---

[3]Adams's distaste for women historians may have been based on the fact that in his friend Mercy Otis Warren's *History of the Rise, Progress, and Termination of the American Revolution* (1805) Warren claimed that Adams sometimes allowed his "prejudices" to distort his judgment.

they remained united after throwing off British rule reflects the degree to which nationalism had developed during the conflict.

By the middle of the eighteenth century the colonists had begun to think of themselves as a separate society distinct from Europe and even from Britain. Benjamin Franklin described himself not as a British subject but as "an American subject of the King," and in 1750 a Boston newspaper could urge its readers to drink "American" beer in order to free themselves from being "beholden to Foreigners" for their alcoholic beverages. Little political nationalism existed before the Revolution, however, in part because most people knew little about life outside their own colony. When a delegate to the first Continental Congress mentioned "Colonel Washington" to John Adams soon after the Congress met, Adams had to ask him who this "Colonel Washington" was. He had never heard the name before.

Local ties remained predominant. A few might say, with Patrick Henry in 1774, "The distinctions between Virginians, Pennsylvanians, New Yorkers, and New Englanders are no more. I am not a Virginian, but an American." But Henry was being carried away by his own oratory; he was actually of two minds on the subject of national versus local loyalty. People who really put America first were rare indeed before the final break with Great Britain.

The new nationalism arose from a number of sources and expressed itself in different ways. Common sacrifices in war certainly played a part; the soldiers of the Continental Army fought in the summer heat of the Carolinas for the same cause that had led them to brave the ice floes of the Delaware in order to surprise the Hessians. Such men lost interest in state boundary lines; they became Americans.

John Marshall of Fauquier County, Virginia, for example, was a 20-year-old militiaman in 1775. The next year he joined the Continental Army. He served in Pennsylvania, New Jersey, and New York and endured the winter of 1777–1778 at Valley Forge. "I found myself associated with brave men from different states who were risking life and everything valuable in a common cause," he later wrote. "I was confirmed in the habit of considering America as my country and Congress as my government."

Andrew Jackson, child of the Carolina frontier, was only nine years old when the Revolution broke out. One brother was killed in battle; another died as a result of untreated wounds. Young Andrew took up arms and was captured by the Redcoats. A British officer ordered Jackson to black his boots and, when the boy refused, struck him across the face with the flat of his sword. Jackson bore the scar to his grave— and became an ardent nationalist on the spot. He and

Marshall had very different ideas and came to be bitter enemies in later life. Nevertheless, they were both American nationalists—and for the same reason.

Civilians as well as soldiers reacted in this way. A Carolina farmer whose home and barn were protected against British looters by men who spoke with the harsh nasal twang of New England adopted a broader outlook toward politics. When the news came that thousands of Redcoats had stacked their arms in defeat after Yorktown, few people cared what state or section had made the victory possible—it was an American triumph.

The war caused many people to move from place to place. Soldiers traveled as the tide of war fluctuated; so too—far more than in earlier times— did prominent leaders. Members of Congress from every state had to travel to Philadelphia; in the process they saw much of the country and the people who inhabited it. Listening to their fellows and serving with them on committees almost inevitably broadened these men, most of them highly influential in their local communities.

With its 13 stars and 13 stripes representing the states, the American flag symbolized national unity and reflected the common feeling that such a symbol was necessary. Yet the flag had separate stars and stripes; local interests and local loyalties remained extremely strong, and these could be divisive when conflicts of interest arose.

Certain practical problems that demanded common solutions also drew the states together. No one seriously considered having 13 postal systems or 13 sets of diplomatic representatives abroad. Every new diplomatic appointment, every treaty of friendship or commerce signed, committed all to a common policy and thus bound them more closely together. And economic developments had a unifying effect. Cutting off English goods encouraged manufacturing, making America more self-sufficient and stimulating both interstate trade and national pride.

THE GREAT LAND ORDINANCES

The western lands, which had divided the states in the beginning, became a force for unity once they had been ceded to the national government. Everyone realized what a priceless national asset they were, and all now understood that no one state could determine the future of the West.

Western Land Claims Ceded by the States

The politicians argued hotly about how these lands should be developed. Some advocated selling the land in township units in the traditional New England manner to groups or companies; others favored

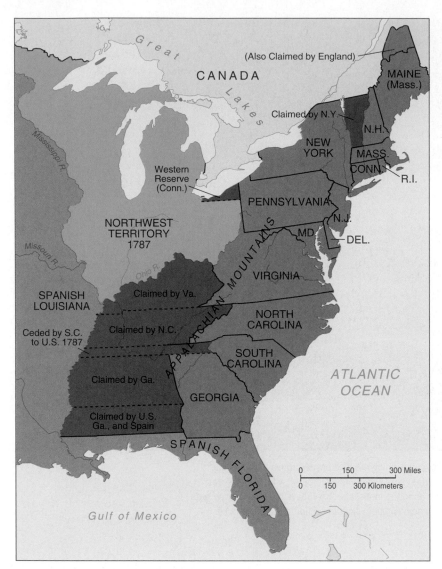

New York and Virginia gave up their claims to the vast area that became the Northwest Territory and thus set a precedent for trans-Appalachian land policy. By 1802 the various state claims had been ceded to the national government. The original Northwest Territory (the Old Northwest) was bounded by the Ohio River, the Mississippi, and the Great Lakes.

letting individual pioneers stake out farms in the hel-ter-skelter manner common in the colonial South. The decision was a compromise. The Land Ordinance of 1785 provided for surveying western territories into 6-mile-square townships before sale. Every other township was to be further subdivided into 36 sections of 640 acres (1 square mile) each. The land was sold at auction at a minimum price of $1 an acre. The law favored speculative land-development companies, for even the 640-acre units were far too large and expensive for the typical frontier family. But the fact that the land was to be surveyed and sold by the central government was a nationalizing force. It ensured orderly development of the West and simplified the task of defending the frontier in the event of Indian attack. Congress set aside the sixteenth section of every township for the maintenance of schools, another farsighted decision.

Still more significant was the Northwest Ordinance of 1787, which established governments for the West. As early as 1775 settlers in frontier districts were petitioning Congress to allow them to enter the Union as independent states, and in 1780 Congress had resolved that all lands ceded to the nation by the existing states should be "formed into distinct republican States" with "the same rights of sovereignty, freedom and independence" as the original 13. In 1784 a committee headed by Thomas Jefferson worked out a plan for doing this, and in 1787 it was enacted into law. The area bounded by the Ohio, the Mississippi, and the Great Lakes was to be carved into not fewer than three or more than five territories. Until the adult male population of the entire area reached 5000, it was to be ruled by a governor and three judges, all

DOCUMENT

Northwest Ordinance, 1787

▲ The Land Ordinance of 1785 called for surveying and dividing the Western Territories into one-mile square mile subdivisions—640 acres. These were further subdivided and sold as 40 acre tracts. Few pieces of legislation have left a more visible imprint upon the landscape. Nowadays the Midwest, as seen from an airplane, resembles a patchwork quilt of 40-acre squares, like the section of Kansas above.

appointed by Congress. When 5000 men of voting age had settled in the territory, the Ordinance authorized them to elect a legislature, which could send a nonvoting delegate to Congress. Finally, when 60,000 persons had settled in any one of the political subdivisions, it was to become a state. It could draft a constitution and operate in any way it wished, save that the government had to be "republican" and that slavery was prohibited.

Seldom has a legislative body acted more wisely. That the western districts must become states everyone conceded from the start. The people had had their fill of colonialism under British rule, and the rebellious temper of frontier settlers made it impossible even to consider maintaining the West in a dependent status. (When North Carolina ceded its trans-Appalachian lands to the United States in 1784, the settlers there, uncertain how they would fare under federal rule, hastily organized an extralegal state of Franklin, and it was not until 1789 that

the national government obtained control.) But it would have been unfair to turn the territories over to the firstcomers, who would have been unable to manage such large domains and would surely have taken advantage of their priority to dictate to later arrivals. A period of tutelage was necessary, a period when the "mother country" must guide and nourish its growing offspring.

Thus the intermediate territorial governments corresponded almost exactly to the governments of British royal colonies. The appointed governors could veto acts of the assemblies and could "convene, prorogue, and dissolve" them at their discretion. The territorial delegates to Congress were not unlike colonial agents. Yet it was vital that this intermediate stage end and that its end be determined in advance so that no argument could develop over when the territory was ready for statehood.

The system worked well and was applied to nearly all the regions absorbed by the nation as it

advanced westward. Together with the Ordinance of 1785, which branded its checkerboard pattern on the physical shape of the West, this law gave the growing country a unity essential to the growth of a national spirit.

NATIONAL HEROES

Benjamin Franklin, c. 1794–1802

The Revolution further fostered nationalism by giving the people their first commonly revered heroes. Benjamin Franklin was widely known before the break with Great Britain through his experiments with electricity, his immensely successful *Poor Richard's Almanack,* and his invention of the Franklin stove. His staunch support of the Patriot cause, his work in the Continental Congress, and his diplomatic successes in France, where he was extravagantly admired, added to his fame. Franklin demonstrated, to Europeans and to Americans themselves, that not all Americans need be ignorant rustics.

Washington, however, was "the chief human symbol of a common Americanism." Stern, cold, a man of few words, the great Virginian did not seem a likely candidate for hero worship. "My countenance never yet revealed my feelings," he himself admitted. Yet he had qualities that made people name babies after him and call him "the Father of His Country" long before the war was won: his personal sacrifices in the cause of independence, his integrity, and above all, perhaps, his obvious desire to retire to his Mount Vernon estate (for many Americans feared any powerful leader and worried lest Washington seek to become a dictator).

As a general, Washington was not a brilliant strategist like Napoleon. Neither was he a tactician of the quality of Caesar or Robert E. Lee. But he was a remarkable organizer and administrator—patient, thoughtful, conciliatory. In a way, his lack of genius made his achievements all the more impressive. He held his forces together in adversity, avoiding both useless slaughter and catastrophic defeat. People of all sections, from every walk of life, looked on Washington as the embodiment of American virtues: a man of deeds rather than words; a man of substance accustomed to luxury yet capable of enduring great hardships stoically and as much at home in the wilderness as an Indian; a bold Patriot, quick to take arms against British tyranny, yet eminently respectable. The Revolution might have been won without Washington, but it is unlikely that the free United States would have become so easily a true nation had he not been at its call.

A NATIONAL CULTURE

Breaking away from Great Britain accentuated certain trends toward social and intellectual independence and strengthened the national desire to create an American culture. The Anglican Church in America had to form a new organization once the connection with the Crown was severed. It painfully weaned itself from government support, and in 1786 it became the Protestant Episcopal Church. The Dutch and German Reformed churches also became independent of their European connections. Roman Catholics in America had been under the administration of the vicar apostolic of England; after the Revolution, Father John Carroll of Baltimore assumed these duties, and in 1789 he became the first American Roman Catholic bishop.

The impact of post-Revolutionary nationalism on American education was best reflected in the immense success of the textbooks of Noah Webster, later famous for his American dictionary. Webster was an ardent patriot. "We ought not to consider ourselves as inhabitants of a particular state only," he wrote in 1785, "but as *Americans.*" Webster's famous *Spelling Book* appeared in 1783 when he was a young schoolteacher in Goshen, New York. It emphasized American forms and usage and contained a patriotic preface urging Americans to pay proper respect to their own literature. Webster's *Reader,* published shortly thereafter, included selections from the speeches of Revolutionary leaders, who, according to the compiler, were the equals of Cicero and Demosthenes as orators. Some 15 million copies of the *Speller* were sold in the next five decades, several times that number by 1900. The *Reader* was also a continuing best-seller.

Webster's work was not the only sign of nationalism in education. In 1787 John M'Culloch published the first American history textbook. The colleges saw a great outburst of patriotic spirit. King's College (founded in 1754) received a new name, Columbia, in 1784. Everywhere it was recognized that the republic required educated and cultivated leaders.

Nationalism affected the arts and sciences in the years after the Revolution. Jedidiah Morse's popular *American Geography* (1789) was a paean in praise of the "astonishing" progress of the country, all the result of the "natural genius of Americans." The American Academy of Arts and Sciences, founded at Boston during the Revolution, was created "to advance the interest, honor, dignity and happiness of a free, independent and virtuous people."

American painters and writers of the period usually chose extremely patriotic themes. Mercy Otis Warren, a sister of James Otis, published an impressive *History of the Rise, Progress and Termination of the American Revolution* in 1805. The artist John Trumbull helped capture Dorchester Heights and force the evacuation of Boston, took part in the defense of northern New York against Burgoyne, and fought in Pennsylvania and Rhode Island. When he took up painting, he went to London to study, but he produced such pictures as *The Battle of Bunker's Hill, The Surrender of Lord Cornwallis at Yorktown,* and *The Declaration of Independence.* Trumbull referred to these and similar efforts as his "national work." Joel Barlow intended his *Vision of Columbus,* written between 1779 and 1787, to prove that America was "the noblest and most elevated part of the earth." Royall Tyler's play *The Contrast,* which was produced in New York in 1787, compared American virtue (the hero was called Colonel Manly) with British vice and contained such chauvinistic lines as these:

*Why should our thoughts to distant countries roam
When each refinement may be found at home?*

In a more subtle way, American nationalism revealed itself in the fondness of the Revolutionary generation for ancient Greek and Roman architecture, which it saw as expressing democratic and republican values. Jefferson, for example, built his home at Monticello in a classical style and modeled the Virginia Capitol on the Roman *Maison Carré* in Nimes, France.

The United States in the 1780s was far from the powerful centralized nation it has since become. Probably most citizens still gave their first loyalty to their own states. In certain important respects the confederation was pitifully ineffectual. However, people were increasingly aware of their common interests and increasingly proud of their common heritage. The motto of the new nation, *E pluribus unum*—"from many, one"—describes a process that was gradually gathering force in the years after Yorktown.

MILESTONES

Year	Event
1774	Thomas Jefferson writes *A Summary View of the Rights of British America*
	General Thomas Gage, commander-in-chief of British army in North America, is named governor of Massachusetts
1775	Colonists fight British in Battles of Lexington and Concord
	Second Continental Congress names George Washington commander-in-chief (of Continental Army)
	Gage is replaced as British commander by General Sir William Howe after Battle of Bunker Hill
1776	Thomas Paine publishes *Common Sense*
	Washington's troops occupy Boston
	Second Continental Congress issues Declaration of Independence
	Washington's troops are defeated in Battle of Long Island
	Washington evacuates New York City
	Washington's victory at Battle of Trenton boosts morale
1777	Washington's troops win Battle of Princeton
	American victory at Saratoga turns the tide and leads to alliance with France
	British occupy Philadelphia after Battle of Germantown
1777–1778	Continental Army winters at Valley Forge
1778	British capture Savannah
1780	British capture Charleston
1781	States ratify Articles of Confederation
	General Cornwallis surrenders at Yorktown
1783	Great Britain recognizes independence of United States by signing Peace of Paris
1785	Congress passes Land Ordinance of 1785
1787	Northwest Ordinance establishes governments for the West

SUPPLEMENTARY READING

Good brief surveys of the Revolutionary years are Edward Countryman, *The American Revolution* (1985) and E. S. Morgan, *The Birth of the Republic* (1977). The best one-volume account of the war is Piers Mackesey, *The War for America, 1775–1783* (1964). See also Jack Greene, *Understanding the American Revolution* (1995). David Hackett Fischer's account of the battle of Lexington and Concord in *Paul Revere's Ride* (1994) shows why the colonists won the war; his *Washington's Crossing* (2004) outlines the importance of the New Jersey campaign. See also John W. Shy, *A People Numerous and Armed* (1990).

For a short biography of Washington, see James MacGregor Burns and Susan Dunn, *George Washington* (2004). Longer biographies include Richard Norton Smith, *Patriarch: George Washington and the New American Nation* (1993), and Henry Wiencek, *Imperfect God: George Washington, His Slaves, and the Creator of America* (2003). John E. Ferling, *Setting the World Ablaze* (2000) and his *A Leap in the Dark* (2003) provide a good overview of how Washington, Jefferson, and John Adams interacted. See also Joseph Ellis, *Founding Brothers: The Revolutionary Generation* (2000), and David McCullough *John Adams* (2001).

On the broader context of the Revolution, see Lester Langley, *The Americas in the Age of Revolution, 1750–1850* (1996); Eliga Gould emphasizes the continuity in America of British political culture, *The Persistence of Empire* (2000).

On the Continental Congress and the Articles of Confederation, see Jackson T. Main, *The Sovereign States* (1973) and Jack N. Rakove, *The Beginnings of National Politics* (1979). P. S. Onuf, *Statehood and Union* (1987), deals with the Northwest Ordinance. Eric Foner, *Tom Paine and Revolutionary America* (1976), is an excellent brief biography. James K. Martin makes a case for his subject in *Benedict Arnold, Revolutionary Hero* (1997).

The classic study of the Declaration of Independence is C. L. Becker, *The Declaration of Independence* (1922); for contemporary analysis see Pauline Maier, *American Scripture* (1997), and Jay Fliegelman, *Declaring Independence* (1993).

The early history of the state governments is covered in W. P. Adams, *The First American Constitutions* (1980). Edward Countryman, *A People in Revolution* (1982), deals with conditions in New York; for Maryland, see Jean B. Lee, *The Price of Nationhood* (1994). The development of political and social ideas, before, during, and after the Revolution, is admirably described and analyzed in G. S. Wood, *The Creation of the American Republic* (1969) and *The Radicalism of the American Revolution* (1992).

The effects of the Revolution on slavery are treated in W. D. Jordan, *White over Black* (1968), and on the Indians, in Colin G. Calloway, *The American Revolution in Indian Country* (1995). For an account of Indians, debtors, and slaves in Virginia, see Woody Holton, *Forced Founders* (1999). L. K. Kerber, *Women of the Republic* (1980), M. B. Norton, *Liberty's Daughters* (1980), and Joy Day Buel and Richard Buel, *The Way of Duty* (1984) discuss the effects of the Revolution on women and the family.

SUGGESTED WEBSITES

Revolutionary War Songs

http://www.mcneilmusic.com/rev.html

This site contains colonial and revolutionary era songs.

Maryland Loyalists and the American Revolution

http://users.erols.com/candidus/index.htm

This examination of Maryland's Loyalists promotes the author's book on that subject. Nonetheless, the site has good information about an underappreciated phenomenon, including Loyalist songs and poems.

The American Revolution

http://revolution.h-net.msu.edu/

This site accompanies the PBS series *Revolution* with essays and resource links.

Georgia's Rare Map Collection

http://scarlett.libs.uga.edu/darchive/hargrett/maps/colamer.html

http://scarlett.libs.uga.edu/darchive/hargrett/maps/revamer.html

These two University of Georgia sites contain maps of colonial and revolutionary America.

Canada History

http://www.civilization.ca

Canada and the United States shared a colonial past, but developed along different lines. This site is part of the virtual museum of the Canadian Museum of Civilization Corporation.

The Federalist Era: Nationalism Triumphant

▼ George Washington, "father of the nation," also designed his home, Mount Vernon: a broad, solid edifice which, though it evolved over decades, retained a rigid symmetry. "Everything," he instructed the builders, was to be "exactly answerable and uniform." He held a similar view about the structure of government.

CHAPTER CONTENTS

At first, only a relative handful of Americans resented the constraints imposed by the confederation on the power of the central government. Once the war was over, the need for unity seemed less pressing and interstate conflicts reasserted themselves. Modern research has modified but not contradicted the thesis, advanced by John Fiske in *The Critical Period of American History* (1888), that the national government was demoralized and inadequate. If, as Washington said, it moved "on crutches . . . tottering at every step," it did move. The negotiation of a successful peace treaty ending the Revolutionary War, the humane and farsighted federal land policies, and even the establishment of a rudimentary federal bureaucracy to manage routine affairs were remarkable achievements, all carried out under the Articles. Yet the country's evolution placed demands on the national government that its creators had not anticipated.

Border Problems

The government had to struggle to win actual control over the territory granted the United States in the treaty ending the Revolution. Both Great Britain and Spain stood in the way of this objective. The British had promised to withdraw all their troops from American soil promptly, and so they did—within the settled portions of the 13 states. Beyond the frontier, however, they had established a string of seven military posts, running from the northern end of Lake Champlain through Niagara and Detroit to the tip of the Michigan peninsula. These, despite the Treaty of Paris, they refused to surrender. Pressing against America's exposed frontier like hot coals, the posts seared national pride. They threatened to set off another Indian war, for the British intrigued constantly to stir up the tribes. The great prize was the rich fur trade of the region, which the British still controlled.

The British justified holding on to these positions by citing the failure of the Americans to live up to some terms of the peace treaty. The United States had agreed not to impede British creditors seeking to collect prewar debts and to "earnestly recommend" that the states restore confiscated Tory property. The national government complied with both requirements (which called only for words on Congress's part), but the states did not cooperate. Many passed laws making it impossible for British creditors to collect debts, and the property of Tory émigrés was not returned.

Yet those violations of the peace terms had little to do with the continued presence of the British. They would probably not have evacuated the posts at this time even if every farthing of the debt had been paid and every acre of confiscated land restored. Americans found the presence of British troops galling. When the French had pushed a line of forts into the Ohio country in the 1750s, it had seemed to most colonists a matter of local concern, to be dealt with by Virginia or Pennsylvania. Three decades later the inability to eject the British seemed a national disgrace.

Then there was the question of the Spanish in the Southwest. Spain had been a co-belligerent, not an ally, in the war with Great Britain. In the peace negotiations it had won back Florida and the Gulf Coast region east of New Orleans. Spanish troops had captured Natchez during the war, and although the post lay far north of the boundary, Spain refused to turn it over to the United States. Far more serious, in 1784 the Spaniards had closed the lower Mississippi River to American commerce. Because of the prohibitive cost of moving bulky farm produce over the mountains, settlers beyond the Appalachians depended on the Mississippi and its network of tributaries to get their corn, tobacco, and other products to eastern and European markets. The Spanish governor of Louisiana, Esteban Miró, soon opened the river to American produce, subject only to a modest tariff, but if Spain ever denied them the right to "deposit" goods at New Orleans while awaiting oceangoing transportation, Westerners could not sell their surpluses. A stronger central government might have dealt with these foreign problems more effectively, but it could not have eliminated them. United or decentralized, until the country grew more powerful, or until the Europeans began to fight among themselves, the United States was bound to suffer at their hands.

▲ New Orleans, by linking flatboats on the Mississippi River with seagoing vessels, became a major commercial port. Like most ports, it sustained a profitable business in prostitution. These tidy white cottages with shuttered windows were likely homes of the city's mulatto mistresses and prostitutes. Neighborhood children, crouching behind a wall, keenly watch the proceedings.

FOREIGN TRADE

The fact that the Revolution freed American trade from the restrictions of British mercantilism proved a mixed blessing in the short run. The commercial benefits that Tom Paine had described in *Common Sense* did not materialize. Americans could now trade directly with Europe, and commercial treaties were negotiated with a number of European nations. Beginning in 1784, when the 360-ton *Empress of China* reached Canton with a cargo of furs and cotton to be exchanged for silks, tea, and spices, a valuable East Asian trade sprang up where none had existed before. But exclusion from Britain's imperial trade union brought losses of a much larger magnitude.

Immediately after the Revolution a controversy broke out in Great Britain over fitting the former colonies into the mercantilist system. Some people, influenced by Adam Smith's *The Wealth of Nations*, published in 1776, argued that any restriction on the buying and selling of goods was wasteful; if people could trade freely, all parties would benefit. Others, while remaining mercantilists, realized how important the American trade was for British prosperity and argued that special treatment should be afforded the former colonists. Unfortunately, a proud empire recently humbled in war could hardly be expected to exercise such forbearance. Persuaded in part by the reasoning of Lord Sheffield's pamphlet *Observations on the Commerce of the American States* that Britain could get all the American commerce it wished without making concessions, Parliament voted to try building up exports to America while holding imports to a minimum, all according to the best tenets of mercantilism.

At the same time British merchants, eager to regain markets closed to them during the Revolution, poured low-priced manufactured goods of all kinds into the United States. Americans, long deprived of British products, rushed to take advantage of the bargains. Soon imports of British goods were approaching the levels of the early 1770s, while exports to the empire reached no more than half their earlier volume.

The influx of British goods aggravated the situation just when the economy was suffering a certain dislocation as a result of the ending of the war. From 1784 to 1786 the country went through a period of bad times. The inability of Congress to find money to pay the nation's debts undermined public confidence. Veterans who had still not been paid, and private individuals and foreign governments that had lent the government money during the Revolution, were clamoring for their due. In some regions crop failures compounded the difficulties.

The depression made the states stingier than ever about supplying the requisitions of Congress; at the same time many of them levied heavy property taxes in order to pay off their own war debts. Everywhere people were hard-pressed for cash. "As Money has ever been considered the root of all evils," one Massachusetts man commented sourly, "may we not presage happy times, as this source is almost done away?"

An obvious way of dealing with these problems would have been to place tariffs on British goods in order to limit imports or force the British to open the West Indies to all American goods, but the Confederation lacked the authority to do this. When individual states erected tariff barriers, British merchants easily got around them by bringing their goods in through states that did not. That the central government lacked the power to control commerce disturbed merchants, other businessmen, and the ever-increasing number of national-minded citizens in every walk of life.

Thus a movement developed to give the Confederation the power to tax imports, and in 1781 Congress sought authority to levy a 5 percent tariff duty. This would enable Congress to pay off some of its obligations and also put pressure on the British to relax their restrictions on American trade with the West Indies. Every state but Rhode Island agreed, but the measure required the unanimous consent of the states and therefore failed.

Defeat of the tariff pointed up the need for revising the Articles of Confederation, for here was a case where a large percentage of the states were ready to increase the power of the national government yet were unable to do so. Although many individuals in every region were worried about creating a centralized monster that might gobble up the sovereignty of the states, the practical needs of the times convinced many others that this risk must be taken.

THE SPECTER OF INFLATION

The depression and the unfavorable balance of trade led to increased pressures in the states for the printing of paper money and the passage of laws designed to make life easier for debtors. Before the Revolution the colonists had grappled with the chronic shortage of hard money resulting from their unfavorable balance of trade in many ways—declaring various staple products such as furs, tobacco, and even Indian wampum to be legal tender; deliberately overvaluing foreign coins to discourage their export; making it illegal to ship coins abroad; and printing paper currency. In response to wartime needs, both the Continental Congress and the states issued large amounts of paper

money during the Revolution, with inflationary results (the Continental dollar became utterly worthless by 1781, and Virginia's paper money nearly so).

After the war some states set out to restore their credit by imposing heavy taxes and severely restricting new issues of money. Combined with the postwar depression and the increase in imports, this sharply lowered prices and wages. Soon debtors, especially farmers, were crying for relief, both in the form of laws that would make it difficult to collect debts and through the printing of more paper money. If more money were put in circulation, wages and prices would rise and debts would be easier to pay.

More than half the states yielded to this pressure in 1785 and 1786. Issues in South Carolina, New York, and Pennsylvania were conservatively handled and succeeded, but some states printed up so much money it depreciated rapidly. The most disastrous experience was that of Rhode Island, where the government attempted to legislate public confidence in £100,000 of paper. Any landowner could borrow a share of this money from the state for 14 years, using real estate as security. Creditors feared that the loans would never be repaid, but the legislature passed a law fining persons who refused to accept it £100. When creditors fled the state to avoid being confronted, the legislature authorized debtors to discharge their obligations by turning the necessary currency over to a judge. A conservative poet described Rhode Island as a "realm of rogues, renown'd for fraud and guile" where "Bankrupts their creditors with rage pursue."

Daniel Shays's "Little Rebellion"

Although the Rhode Island case was atypical, it alarmed conservatives. Then, close on its heels, came a disturbing outbreak of violence in Massachusetts. The Massachusetts legislature was determined to pay off the state debt and maintain a sound currency. Taxes amounting to almost £1.9 million were levied between 1780 and 1786, the burden falling most heavily on those of moderate income. The average Massachusetts farmer paid about a third of every year's income in taxes. Bad times and deflation led to many foreclosures, and the prisons were crowded with honest debtors. "Our Property is torn from us," one town complained, "our Gaols filled & still our Debts are not discharged."

In the summer of 1786 mobs in the western communities began to stop foreclosures by forcibly preventing the courts from holding their sessions. Under the leadership of Daniel Shays, a veteran of Bunker Hill, Ticonderoga, and Saratoga, the "rebels" marched on Springfield and prevented the state

▲ This broadside lauds Daniel Shays *(left),* who headed the armed rebellion against Massachusetts, which was cracking down on debtors. Shays is pictured in his Continental uniform. For his efforts at the battle of Saratoga in 1777, Marquis de Lafayette had presented Shays with a ceremonial sword, pictured here. Shays sold the sword to pay off his debts.

supreme court from meeting. When the state government sent troops against them, the rebels attacked the Springfield arsenal. They were routed, and the uprising then collapsed. Shays fled to Vermont.

As Thomas Jefferson observed at safe remove from the trouble in Paris, where he was serving as minister to France, Shays's uprising was only "a *little* rebellion" and as such "a medicine necessary for the sound health of government." But Shays and his followers were genuinely exasperated by the refusal of the government even to try to provide relief for their troubles. By taking up arms they forced the authorities to heed them: At its next session the legislature made some concessions to their demands.

But unlike Jefferson, most well-to-do Americans considered the uprising "Liberty run mad." "What, gracious God, is man! that there should be such inconsistency and perfidiousness in his conduct?" the usually unexcitable George Washington asked when news of the riots reached Virginia. "We are fast verging to anarchy and confusion!" During the crisis private persons had had to subscribe funds to put the rebels down, and when Massachusetts had appealed to Congress for help there was little Congress could legally do. The lessons seemed plain: Liberty must not become an excuse for license; greater authority must be vested in the central government.

DOCUMENT

Military Reports on Shays's Rebellion

The Rhode Island excesses and the uprising in Massachusetts illustrated the clash between local and national interests. Newspapers in all the states followed the bizarre spectacle of debtors in Rhode Island pursuing their creditors with fistfuls of worthless paper money. The revolt of Daniel Shays worried planters in far-off Virginia and the Carolinas almost as much as it did the merchants of Boston. Bacon's Rebellion, a far more serious affair, had evoked no such reaction in the seventeenth century, nor had the Regulator War in North Carolina as late as 1771.

To Philadelphia, and the Constitution

If most people wanted to increase the power of Congress, they were also afraid to shift the balance too far lest they destroy the sovereignty of the states and the rights of individuals. The machinery for change established in the Articles of Confederation, which required the unanimous consent of the states for all amendments, posed a particularly delicate problem. Experience had shown it unworkable, yet to bypass it would be revolutionary and therefore dangerous.

The first fumbling step toward reform was taken in March 1785 when representatives of Virginia and Maryland, meeting at the home of George Washington to settle a dispute over the improvement of navigation on the Potomac River, suggested a conference of all the states to discuss common problems of commerce. In January 1786 the Virginia legislature sent out a formal call for such a gathering to be held in September at Annapolis. However, the Annapolis Convention disappointed advocates of reform; delegates from only five states appeared; even Maryland, supposedly the host state, did not send a representative. Being so few the group did not feel it worthwhile to propose changes.

Alexander Hamilton—Portrait

Among the delegates was a young New York lawyer named Alexander Hamilton, a brilliant, imaginative, and daring man who was convinced that only drastic centralization would save the nation from disintegration. Hamilton described himself as a "nationalist." While the war still raged he contrasted the virtues of "a great Federal Republic" with the existing system of "petty states with the appearance only of union, jarring, jealous, and perverse." Instead of giving up, he proposed calling another convention to meet at Philadelphia to deal generally with constitutional reform. Delegates should be empowered to work out a broad plan for correcting "such defects as may be discovered to exist" in the Articles of Confederation.

The Annapolis group approved Hamilton's suggestion, and Congress reluctantly endorsed it. This time all the states but Rhode Island sent delegates. On May 25, 1787, the convention opened its proceedings at the State House in Philadelphia and unanimously elected George Washington its president. When it adjourned four months later, it had drafted the Constitution.

The Great Convention

As the decades have passed and the Constitution has grown more and more tradition-encrusted without losing any of its flexibility, each generation has tried to explain how a people so young and inexperienced, so free-swinging and unruly, could have produced it. At the time of the hundredth anniversary of its signing, the British statesman William E. Gladstone called it "the most wonderful work ever struck off at a given time by the brain of man." One reason for its durability was the ability of those who drafted it. The Founders were remarkable men. Although he later had reason to quarrel with certain aspects of their handiwork, Jefferson, who was on a foreign assignment and did not attend the convention, called them "demigods." A presumably more impartial French diplomat said that "even in Europe," he had never seen "an assembly more respectable for the talents, knowledge, disinterestedness, and patriotism."

Collectively the delegates possessed a rare combination of talents. Most of them had had considerable experience in politics, and the many lawyers among them were skilled in logic and debate. Furthermore, the times made them acutely aware of their opportunities. It was "a time when the greatest lawgivers of antiquity would have wished to live," an opportunity to "establish the wisest and happiest government that human wisdom can contrive," John Adams wrote. "We . . . decide for ever the fate of republican government," James Madison said during the deliberations.

If these remarks overstated the importance of their deliberations, they nonetheless represented the opinion of most of those present. They were boldly optimistic about their country. "We are laying the foundation of a great empire," Madison predicted. At the same time the delegates recognized the difficulties they faced. The ancient Roman republic was one model, and all knew that it had been overthrown by tyrants and eventually overrun by barbarians. The framers were also familiar with Enlightenment thinkers such as John Locke, Thomas Hobbes, and Montesquieu, and also with the ideas that swirled around the great disputes between Parliament and the Stuart monarchs during the seventeenth century.

▲ James Madison was a key figure at the Great Convention of 1787. He not only influenced the shaping of the Constitution but also kept the most complete record of the proceedings. "Every person," wrote one delegate, "seems to acknowledge his greatness."

Fortunately, they were nearly all of one mind on basic questions. That there should be a federal system, with both independent state governments and a national government with limited powers to handle matters of common interest, was accepted by all but one or two of them. Republican government, drawing its authority from the people and remaining responsible to them, was a universal assumption. A measure of democracy followed inevitably from this principle, for even the most aristocratic delegates agreed that ordinary citizens should share in the process of selecting those who were to make and execute the laws.

All agreed that no group within society, no matter how numerous, should have unrestricted authority. They looked on political power much as we today view nuclear energy: a force with tremendous potential value for humankind, but one easily misused and therefore dangerous to unleash. People meant well and had limitless possibilities, the constitution makers believed, but they were selfish by nature and could not be counted on to respect the interests of others. The ordinary people—small farmers, artisans, any taxpayer—should have a say in government in order to be able to protect themselves against those who would exploit their weakness, and the majority must

somehow be prevented from plundering the rich, for property must be secure or no government could be stable. No single state or section must be allowed to predominate, nor should the legislature be supreme over the executive or the courts. Power, in short, must be divided, and the segments must be balanced one against the other.

At the outset the delegates decided to keep the proceedings secret. That way no one was tempted to play to the gallery or seek some personal political advantage at the expense of the common good. Next they agreed to go beyond their instructions to revise the Articles of Confederation and draft an entirely new form of government. This was a bold, perhaps illegal act, but it was in no way irresponsible because nothing the convention might recommend was binding on anyone, and it was absolutely essential because under the Articles a single state could have prevented the adoption of any change. Alexander Hamilton captured the mood of the gathering when he said: "We can only propose and recommend—the power of ratifying or rejecting is still in the States. . . . We ought not to sacrifice the public Good to narrow Scruples."

THE COMPROMISES THAT PRODUCED THE CONSTITUTION

The delegates voted on May 30, 1787 that "a national Government ought to be established." They then set to work hammering out a specific plan. Furthermore, the delegates believed that the national government should have separate executive and judicial branches as well as a legislature. But two big questions had to be answered. The first—*What powers should this national government be granted?*—occasioned relatively little discussion. The right to levy taxes and to regulate interstate and foreign commerce was assigned to the central government almost without debate. So was the power to raise and maintain an army and navy and to summon the militia of the states to enforce national laws and suppress insurrections. With equal absence of argument, the states were deprived of their rights to issue money, to make treaties, and to tax either imports or exports without the permission of Congress. Thus, in summary fashion, was brought about a massive shift of power, a shift made necessary by the problems that had brought the delegates to Philadelphia and made practicable by the new nationalism of the 1780s.

The second major question—*Who shall control the national government?*—proved more difficult to answer in a manner satisfactory to all. Led by Virginia, the larger states pushed for representation in

the national legislature based on population. The smaller states wished to maintain the existing system of equal representation for each state regardless of population. The large states rallied behind the Virginia Plan, drafted by James Madison and presented to the convention by Edmund Randolph, governor of the state. The small states supported the New Jersey Plan, prepared by William Paterson, a former attorney general of that state. The question was important; equal state representation would have been undemocratic, whereas a proportional system would have effectively destroyed the influence of all the states as states. But the delegates saw it in terms of combinations of large or small states, and this old-fashioned view was unrealistic: When the states combined, they did so on geographic, economic, or social grounds that seldom had anything to do with size. Nevertheless, the debate was long and heated, and for a time it threatened to disrupt the convention.

Day after day in the stifling heat of high summer, the weary delegates struggled to find a suitable compromise. Madison and a few others had to use every weapon in their arsenal of argument to hold the group together. (All told, during the 88 sessions of the convention, a total of 569 votes were taken.) July 2 was perhaps the most fateful day of the whole proceedings. "We are at full stop," said Roger Sherman of Connecticut, who had been one of the drafters of the Declaration of Independence. "If we do not concede on both sides," a North Carolina delegate warned, "our business must soon be at an end."

But the delegates did "concede on both sides," and the debates went on. Again on July 17 collapse threatened as the representatives of the larger states caucused to consider walking out of the convention. Fortunately they did not walk out, and finally the delegates adopted what is known as the Great Compromise. In the lower branch of the new legislature—the House of Representatives—places were to be assigned according to population and filled by popular vote. In the upper house—the Senate—each state was to have two members, elected by its legislature.

Then a complicated struggle took place between northern and southern delegates, occasioned by the institution of slavery and the differing economic interests of the regions. About one American in seven in the 1780s was a slave. Northerners contended that slaves should be counted in deciding each state's share of direct federal taxes. Southerners, of course, wanted to exclude slaves from the count. Yet Southerners wished to include slaves in determining each district's representation in the House of Representatives, although they had no intention of permitting the slaves to vote. In the Three-fifths Compromise it was agreed that "three-fifths of all other Persons"

should be counted for both purposes. (As it turned out, the compromise was a victory for the Southerners, for direct taxes were only rarely levied by Congress before the Civil War.) Settlement of the knotty issue of the African slave trade was postponed by a clause making it illegal for Congress to outlaw the trade before 1808.

Questions involving the regulation of less controversial commerce also caused sectional disagreement. Southerners disliked export taxes because their staple products were largely sold abroad. In return for a clause prohibiting such taxes, they dropped their demand that all laws regulating foreign commerce be approved by two-thirds of both houses of Congress. Many other differences of opinion were resolved by the give-and-take of practical compromise.

The final document (see the text of the Constitution in the Appendix, pp. A9–A18), signed on September 17, established a legislature of two houses; an executive branch, consisting of a president with wide powers and a vice president whose only function was to preside over the Senate; and a national judiciary consisting of a Supreme Court and such "inferior courts" as Congress might decide to create. The lower, popularly elected branch of the Congress was supposed to represent especially the mass of ordinary citizens. It was given the sole right to introduce bills for raising revenue. The 26-member Senate was looked on by many as a sort of advisory council similar to the upper houses of the colonial legislatures. Its consent was required before any treaty could go into effect and for major presidential appointments. The Founders also intended the Senate to represent in Congress the interests not only of the separate states but of what Hamilton called "the rich and the well-born" as contrasted with "the great mass of the people."

The creation of a powerful president was the most drastic departure from past experience, and it is doubtful that the Founders would have gone so far had everyone not counted on Washington, a man universally esteemed for character, wisdom, and impartiality, to be the first to occupy the office. Besides giving him general responsibility for executing the laws, the Constitution made the president commander-in-chief of the armed forces of the nation and general supervisor of its foreign relations. He was to appoint federal judges and other officials, and he might veto any law of Congress, although his veto could be overridden by a two-thirds majority of both houses. While not specifically ordered to submit a program of legislation to Congress, he was to deliver periodic reports on the "State of the Union" and recommend "such Measures as he shall judge necessary and expedient." Most modern presidents have interpreted this requirement as authorizing

Debating the Past

What ideas shaped the Constitution? In this 1788 cartoon, the angel "Concord" presents the Constitution to "Columbia"—an embodiment of the United States; a Greek temple sits in the background, upheld by thirteen pillars representing the colonies. Were the authors of the Constitution inspired by classical antiquity? No, declared Charles A. Beard. Their chief concerns were to protect their property and business interests.

Few historians found much confirmation of Beard's thesis; but what, then, *were* they thinking? Daniel Boorstin regarded the Founders as practical men who "found a refuge from the diversity of ideas in the satisfying concreteness of experience." Bernard Bailyn rejected this argument. His research revealed that the revolutionary leaders learned to cherish republican virtue and citizenship from ancient Roman philosophers such as Plutarch and Tacitus, from thinkers of the European Enlightenment, and from critics of eighteenth-century British monarchs. Joyce Appleby countered that if ideas were at the heart of the Constitution, they came from John Locke, a seventeenth-century philosopher who enshrined property rights. The Constitution was a blueprint for capitalist development. Jack Rakove searched in vain to find the "original intent" of the Founders. They favored a government strong enough to protect people and promote their interests; they also favored individual rights and freedom. Which mattered more, they could not agree.

Charles A. Beard, *An Economic Interpretation of the Constitution of the United States* (1913), Daniel Boorstin, *The Lost World of Thomas Jefferson* (1948), Bernard Bailyn, *The Ideological Origins of the American Revolution* (1967), Joyce Appleby, *Capitalism and a New Social Order* (1984), Jack Rakove, *Original Meanings* (1996).

them to submit detailed legislative proposals and to use the full power and prestige of the office to get Congress to enact them.

Looking beyond Washington, whose choice was sure to come about under any system, the Constitution established a cumbersome method of electing presidents. Each state was to choose "electors" equal in number to its representation in Congress. The electors, meeting separately in their own states, were to vote for two persons for president. Supposedly the procedure would prevent anyone less universally admired than Washington from getting a majority in the "electoral college," in which case the House of Representatives would choose the president from among the leading candidates, each state having but one vote. However, the swift rise of national political parties prevented the expected fragmentation of the electors' votes, and only two elections have ever gone to the House for settlement.

The national court system was set up to adjudicate disputes under the laws and treaties of the United States. No such system had existed under the Articles, a major weakness. Although the Constitution did not specifically authorize the courts to declare laws void when they conflicted with the Constitution, the courts soon exercised this right of "judicial review" in cases involving both state and federal laws.

That the Constitution reflected the commonly held beliefs of its framers is everywhere evident in the document. It greatly expanded the powers of the central government yet did not seriously threaten the independence of the states. Foes of centralization, at the time and ever since, have predicted the imminent disappearance of the states as sovereign bodies. But despite a steady trend toward centralization, probably inevitable as American society has grown ever more complex, the states remain powerful political organizations that are sovereign in many areas of government.

The Founders believed that since the new powers of government might easily be misused, each should be held within safe limits by some countervailing force. The Constitution is full of ingenious devices ("checks and balances") whereby one power controls and limits another without reducing it to impotence. "Let Congress Legislate, let others execute, let others judge," John Jay suggested. This separation of legislative, executive, and judicial functions is the fundamental example of the principle. Other examples are the president's veto; Congress's power of impeachment, cleverly divided between House and Senate; the Senate's power over treaties and appointments; and the balance between Congress's right to declare war and the president's control of the armed forces.

RATIFYING THE CONSTITUTION

Influenced by the widespread approval of the decision of Massachusetts to submit its state constitution of 1780 to the voters for ratification, the framers of the Constitution provided (Article VII) that their handiwork be ratified by special state conventions. This procedure gave the Constitution what Madison called "the highest source of authority"—the endorsement of the people, expressed through representatives chosen specifically to vote on it. The framers may also have been motivated by a desire to bypass the state legislatures, where many members might resent the reductions being made in state authority. This was not of central importance because the legislatures could have blocked ratification by refusing to call conventions. Only Rhode Island did so, and since the Constitution was to go into operation when nine states had approved it, Rhode Island's stubbornness did no vital harm.

Such a complex and controversial document as the Constitution naturally excited argument throughout the country. Those who favored it called themselves Federalists, thereby avoiding the more accurate but politically unattractive label of Centralizers. Their opponents thus became the Anti-Federalists.

It is difficult to generalize about the members of these groups. The Federalists tended to be substantial individuals, members of the professions, well-to-do, active in commercial affairs, and somewhat alarmed by the changes wrought by the Revolution. They were more interested, perhaps, in orderly and efficient government than in safeguarding the maximum freedom of individual choice.

The Anti-Federalists were more often small farmers, debtors, and persons to whom free choice was more important than power and who resented those who sought and held power. "Lawyers and men of learning and money men . . . expect to be the managers of the Const[itution], and get all the power and all the money into their own hands," a Massachusetts Anti-Federalist complained. "Then they will swallow up all us little folks . . . just as the whale swallowed up *Jonah*." But many rich and worldly citizens opposed the Constitution, and many poor and obscure persons were for it. It seems likely that most did not support or oppose the new system for narrowly selfish reasons. The historian David Ramsay, who lived at the time when these groups were forming, was probably correct when he wrote that "the great body of independent men who saw the necessity of an energetic government" swung the balance in favor of the Constitution.

Whether the Anti-Federalists were more democratic than the Federalists is an interesting question. Those who are loud for local autonomy do not necessarily believe in equal rights for all the locals. Many Anti-Federalist leaders, including Richard Henry Lee, the man who had introduced the resolution that resulted in the Declaration of Independence, had reservations about democracy. On the other hand, even Hamilton, no admirer of democracy, believed that ordinary citizens should have some say about their government. In general, practice still stood well ahead of theory when it came to popular participation in politics.

It is important to keep in mind that the country was large and sparsely settled, that communication was primitive, and that the central government did not influence the lives of most people to any great degree. Many persons, including some who had been in the forefront of the struggle for independence, believed that a centralized republican system would not work in a country so large and with so many varied interests as the United States. Patrick Henry considered the Constitution "horribly frightful." It "squints toward monarchy," he added. That Congress could pass all laws "necessary and proper" to carry out the functions assigned it and legislate for the "general welfare" of the country

DOCUMENT

Henry Against Ratification of the Constitution

▲ Patrick Henry, an ardent revolutionary, was perhaps the main opponent to ratification of the Constitution. Such a "consolidated government," he declared in 1788, would be "extremely pernicious, impolitic, and dangerous." This painting by Thomas Sully dates from the mid-nineteenth century.

▲ New Yorkers honor Hamilton during a parade marking ratification of the Constitution. That Hamilton stood on a ship was fitting, not only because he sought to strengthen the federal "ship of state" but also because New York merchants were among his staunchest backers.

seemed alarmingly all-inclusive. The first sentence of the Constitution, beginning "We the people of the United States" rather than "We the states," convinced many that the document represented centralization run wild. Another old revolutionary who expressed doubts was Samuel Adams, who remarked: "As I enter the Building I stumble at the Threshold."

Very little of the opposition to the Constitution grew out of economic issues. Most people wanted the national debt paid off; nearly everyone opposed an unstable currency; most favored uniform trade policies; most were ready to give the new government a chance if they could be convinced that it would not destroy the states. When backers agreed to add amendments guaranteeing the civil liberties of the people against challenge by the national government and reserving all unmentioned power to the states, much of the opposition disappeared. Sam Adams ended up voting for the Constitution in the Massachusetts convention after the additions had been promised.

No one knows exactly how public opinion divided on the question of ratification. The Federalists were usually able to create an impression of strength far beyond their numbers and to overwhelm doubters with the mass of their arguments. They excelled in political organization and in persuasiveness. James Madison, for example, demolished the thesis that a centralized republican government could not function efficiently in a large country. In rule by the majority lay protection against the "cabals" of special interest groups. "Extend the sphere," Madison argued, "and you take in a greater variety of parties and interests; you make it less probable that a majority of the whole will have a common motive to invade the rights of other citizens." Moreover, the management of national affairs would surely attract leaders of greater ability and sounder character to public service than the handling of petty local concerns ever could in a decentralized system.

DOCUMENT

Madison Defends
the Constitution

The Constitution met with remarkably little opposition in most of the state ratifying conventions, considering the importance of the changes it instituted. Delaware acted first, ratifying unanimously on December 7, 1787. Pennsylvania followed a few days later, voting for the document by a 2 to 1 majority. New Jersey approved unanimously on December 18; so did Georgia on January 2, 1788. A week later Connecticut fell in line, 128 to 40.

The Massachusetts convention provided the first close contest. Early in February, after an extensive debate, the delegates ratified by a vote of 187 to 168. In April, Maryland accepted the Constitution by nearly 6 to 1, and in May, South Carolina approved, 149 to 73. New Hampshire came along on June 21, voting 57 to 47 for the Constitution. This was the ninth state, making the Constitution legally operative.

Before the news from New Hampshire had spread throughout the country, the Virginia convention debated the issue. Virginia, the largest state and the home of so many prestigious figures, was absolutely essential if the Constitution was to succeed. With unquestioned patriots like Richard Henry Lee and Patrick Henry opposed, the result was not easy to predict. But when the vote came on June 25, Virginia ratified, 89 to 79. Aside from Rhode Island, this left only New York and North Carolina outside the Union.

New York politics presented a complex and baffling picture. Resistance to independence had been strong there in 1776 and remained a problem all through the war. Although New York was the third largest state, with a population rapidly approaching 340,000, it sided with the small states at Philadelphia, and two of its three delegates (Hamilton was the exception) walked out of the convention and took the lead in opposing ratification. A handful of great landowning and mercantile families dominated politics, but they were divided into shifting factions. In general, New York City, including most ordinary working people as well as the merchants, favored ratification and the rural areas were against it.

The Anti-Federalists, well organized and competently led in New York by Governor George Clinton, won 46 of the 65 seats at the ratifying convention. The New York Federalists had one great asset in the fact that so many states had already ratified and another in the person of Alexander Hamilton. Although contemptuous of the *weakness* of the Constitution, Hamilton supported it with all his energies as being incomparably stronger than the old government. Working with Madison and John Jay, he produced the *Federalist Papers,* a series of brilliant essays explaining and defending the new system. In his articles, Hamilton stressed the need for a strong federal executive, while Madison sought to allay fears that the new national government would have too much power by emphasizing the many checks and balances in the Constitution. The essays were published in the local press and later in book form. Although generations of judges and lawyers have treated them almost as parts of the Constitution, their impact on contemporary public opinion was probably slight. Open-minded members of the convention were undoubtedly influenced, but few delegates were open-minded.

Hamilton became a kind of one-man army in defense of the Constitution, plying hesitating delegates with dinners and drinks, facing obstinate ones with the threat that New York City would secede from the state if the Constitution were rejected. Once New Hampshire and Virginia had ratified, opposition in New York became a good deal less intransigent. In the end, by promising to support a call for a second national convention to consider amendments, the Federalists carried the day, 30 to 27. With New York in the fold, the new government was free to get under way. North Carolina finally ratified in November 1789, Rhode Island the following year, in May 1790.

WASHINGTON AS PRESIDENT

Elections took place in the states during January and February 1789, and by early April enough congressmen had gathered in New York, the temporary national capital, to commence operation. The ballots of the presidential electors were officially counted in the Senate on April 6, Washington being the unanimous choice. John Adams, with 34 electoral votes, won the vice-presidency.

When he left Mount Vernon for the eight-day trip to New York for his inauguration, Washington's progress was a series of celebrations. In every town he was met by bands, honor guards, local dignitaries, and crowds of cheering citizens. The people were informally ratifying the decision to create a new and more powerful United States. On April 30 Washington took the oath of office at New York's Federal Hall.

IMAGE

Washington's Arrival in New York City, 1789

Washington made a firm, dignified, conscientious, but cautious president. His acute sense of responsibility led him to face the task "with feelings not unlike those of a culprit who is going to the place of his execution." Each presidential action must of necessity establish a precedent. "The eyes of Argus are upon me," he complained, "and no slip will pass unnoticed." Hoping to make the presidency appear respectable in the eyes of the world, he saw to it that his

▶ *text continues on page 154*

Mapping the Past

Depicting History with Maps

History consists of the stories people tell about the past. Because historians work mostly with written sources, they use words to describe the past. Pictures help too, which is why this book has so many of them. But maps effectively show movement over time and through space.

An Indian Map

Maps come in many different forms. Consider the map below by Lean Wolf, a Hidatsa warrior. It depicts his raid on a Sioux village to steal horses. In the map, Lean Wolf represents himself as a wolf—four legs, with dark black snout. The lodges of the Hidatsa village are shown as circles, with the dots representing support poles: a lodge with five poles contains a large extended family, a lodge with two, a small one. His route to the Sioux village is indicated by a dashed line. Crosses identify Sioux lodges; squares mark whites' houses. A cross with a square denotes a Hidatsa–Sioux intermarriage; a cross within a square indicates where a white man lives with a Sioux woman. Lean Wolf used forward-facing hoofprints to show the route back home. Thus, the map indicates that his venture succeeded; he did manage to steal horses from the Sioux.

Lean Wolf's map displays complicated information that doubtless was informative to him and other Hidatsa warriors. The rest of us may not find it so easy to decipher.

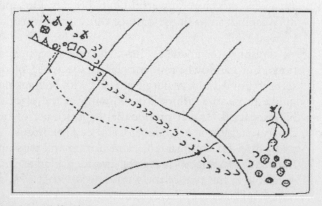

▲ Lean Wolf's Map

For one thing, the map lacks a title to convey the main idea. What was the relationship between the horse raid and the information on Sioux dwellings and marriage patterns? Did he refrain from taking horses from Sioux habitations occupied by mixed Hidatsa-Sioux couples? We don't know.

Second, the map lacks a key—a list of the various pictographic symbols and an explanation of what they represent. Third, it lacks geographical reference points and distance markers. How far did Lean Wolf travel and in what direction? From the map, we do not know that the villages were located near Fort Buford, North Dakota. Fourth, the base map lacks labels. Did the nearly straight line between the villages represent a stream, a trail, or something else?

Examples of Modern Maps: Ratification of the Constitution

All the maps in this book tell stories about the past, but they include titles, keys, geographical and chronological references, and other labels. Consider the map on the right that represents one of the key events discussed in this chapter.

The map's title—Ratification of the Federal Constitution, 1787–1790—explains its theme. The key provides information necessary to understand the map: teal green represents areas where a majority voted for the Constitution, and red where a majority voted against the Constitution, and so on. Latitude and longitude lines on the map show precisely where the votes occurred. The compass point indicates north. (In maps of North America, north is customarily toward the top of the page; but sometimes it makes more sense to reorient the page. For example, the map of the long Atlantic seaboard in the seventeenth century stretches across two pages in Chapter 1 of this book (see pp. 44–45); the compass therefore points not to the top of the page, but to the upper right-hand corner.

Beneath the compass is a scale of miles and kilometers. Labels on the map indicate the relevant dates and identify relevant geographic and political features. (Many historical maps, but not this one, convey movement; Lean Wolf used hoofprints to indicate movement; most mapmakers use an Indian implement—an arrow—for this purpose.)

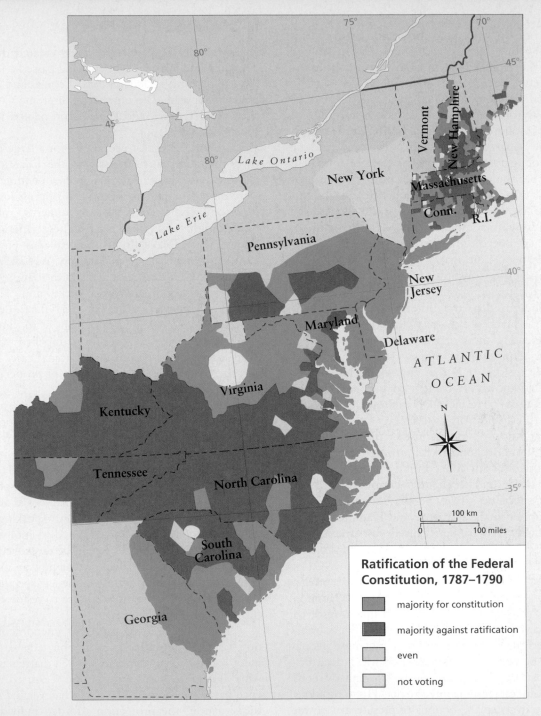

Ratification of the Federal Constitution, 1787–1790

majority for constitution

majority against ratification

even

not voting

Historians use maps to formulate and illustrate interpretations. Jackson Turner Main regarded this map on ratification as visual confirmation of his thesis: those favoring the Constitution (the green areas) generally lived in the more settled and economically prosperous regions along the coast; those opposed (red areas) were concentrated in "backwoods" New England and the western frontiers of Pennsylvania, Virginia, and the Carolinas.

But why, if Main's thesis is true, were there some red areas (opposing the Constitution) in coastal North Carolina and Maryland, and a few townships in coastal New England? And why

were there some green areas (favoring the Constitution) in backcountry New England, Pennsylvania, and the South?

Maps alone cannot answer these questions. It is also necessary to learn what people thought, said, and did. The search for answers leads historians to written sources—diaries, letters, newspaper accounts—and also to paintings, cartoons, and other visual sources. From information gleaned from all these sources, a more complete picture gradually emerges, although readers must decide for themselves the persuasiveness of any historical argument.

carriage was drawn by six cream-colored horses, and when he rode (he was a magnificent horseman), it was on a great white charger, with the saddle of leopard skin and the cloth edged in gold. Twenty-one servants (seven of them slaves) attended his needs at the presidential mansion on Broadway.

Washington meticulously avoided treading on the toes of Congress, for he took seriously the principle of the separation of powers. Never would he speak for or against a candidate for Congress, nor did he think that the president should push or even propose legislation. When he knew a controversial question was to be discussed in Congress, he avoided the subject in his annual message. The veto, he believed, should be employed only when the president considered a bill unconstitutional.

Although the Constitution said nothing about a presidential Cabinet, Washington established the system of calling his department heads together for general advice, a practice that was followed by his successors. In selecting these department heads and other important administrators, he favored no particular faction. He insisted only that appointees be competent and "of known attachment to the Government we have chosen." He picked Hamilton for secretary of the treasury, Jefferson for secretary of state, General Henry Knox of Massachusetts for secretary of war, and Edmund Randolph for attorney general. He called on them for advice according to the logic of his particular needs and frequently without regard for their own specialties. Thus he sometimes consulted Jefferson about financial matters and Hamilton about foreign affairs. This system caused resentment and confusion, especially when rival factions began to coalesce around Hamilton and Jefferson.

Despite his respect for the opinions of others, Washington was a strong chief executive. As Hamilton put it, he "consulted much, pondered much, resolved slowly, resolved surely." His stress on the dignity of his office suited the needs of a new country whose people tended to be perhaps too informal. It was indeed important that the first president be particularly concerned about establishing precedents. His scrupulous care lest he overstep the bounds of presidential power helped erase the prejudices of those who feared that republican government must inevitably succumb to dictatorship and tyranny. When each step is an experiment, when foreign dangers loom at the end of every errant path, it is surely wise to go slowly. And no one should forget that Washington's devotion to duty did not always come easily. Occasionally he exploded. Thomas Jefferson has left us a graphic description of the president at a Cabinet meeting, in a rage because of some unfair criticism, swearing that "by god he had rather be on his farm than to be made emperor of the world."

CONGRESS UNDER WAY

By September 1789 Congress had created the State, Treasury, and War departments and passed a Judiciary Act establishing 13 federal district courts and 3 circuit courts of appeal. The number of Supreme Court justices was set at six, and Washington named John Jay the chief justice.

True to Federalist promises—for a large majority of both houses were friendly to the Constitution—Congress prepared a list of a dozen amendments (ten were ratified) guaranteeing what Congressman James Madison, who drafted the amendments, called the "great rights of mankind." These amendments, known as the Bill of Rights (See Amendments to the Constitution in the Appendix, pp. A14–A18), provided that Congress should make no law infringing freedom of speech, the press, or religion. The right of trial by jury was reaffirmed, the right to bear arms guaranteed. No one was to be subject to "unreasonable" searches or seizures or compelled to testify against himself or herself in a criminal case. No one was to "be deprived of life, liberty, or property, without due process of law."

Despite Washington's reluctance to interfere with the activities of Congress, he urged acceptance of these amendments so that the "rights of freemen" would be "impregnably fortified." The Bill of Rights was unique; the English Bill of Rights of 1689 was much less broad-gauged and, being an act of Parliament, was subject to repeal by Parliament at any time. The Tenth Amendment—not, strictly speaking, a part of the Bill of Rights—was designed to mollify those who feared that the states would be destroyed by the new government. It provided that powers not delegated to the United States or denied specifically to the states by the Constitution were to reside either in the states or in the people.

As experts pointed out, the amendments were not logically necessary because the federal government had no authority to act in such matters to begin with. But many had wanted to be reassured. Experience has proved repeatedly that whatever the logic of the situation, the protection afforded individuals by the Bill of Rights has been anything but unnecessary.

The Bill of Rights did much to convince doubters that the new government would not become too powerful. More complex was the task of proving that it was powerful enough to deal with those national problems that the Confederation had not been able to solve: the threat to the West posed by the British, Spaniards, and Indians; the disruption of the pattern of American foreign commerce resulting from independence; and the collapse of the financial structure of the country.

HAMILTON AND FINANCIAL REFORM

One of the first acts of Congress in 1789 was to employ its new power to tax. The simplest means of raising money seemed to be that first attempted by the British after 1763, a tariff on foreign imports. Congress levied a 5 percent duty on all foreign products entering the United States, applying higher rates to certain products, such as hemp, glass, and nails, as a measure of protection for American producers. The Tariff Act of 1789 also placed heavy tonnage duties on all foreign shipping, a mercantilist measure designed to stimulate the American merchant marine.

Raising money for current expenses was a small and relatively simple aspect of the financial problem faced by Washington's administration. The nation's debt was large, its credit shaky, its economic future uncertain. In October 1789 Congress deposited on the slender shoulders of Secretary of the Treasury Hamilton the task of straightening out the fiscal mess and stimulating the country's economic development.

Hamilton at age 34 had already proved himself a remarkable man. Born in the British West Indies, the illegitimate son of a shiftless Scot who was little better than a beachcomber, and raised by his mother's family, he came to New York in 1773 to attend King's College. When the Revolution broke out, he joined the Continentals. At 22 he was a staff colonel, aide-de-camp to Washington. Later, at Yorktown, he led a line regiment, displaying a bravery approaching foolhardiness. He married the daughter of Philip Schuyler, a wealthy and influential New Yorker, and after the Revolution he practiced law in that state.

Hamilton was a bundle of contradictions. Witty, charming, possessed of a mind like a sharp knife, he was sometimes the soul of practicality, sometimes an incurable romantic. No more hard-headed realist ever lived, yet he was quick to resent any slight to his honor, even—tragically—ready to fight a duel though he abhorred the custom of dueling. A self-made man, he admired aristocracy and disparaged the abilities of the common run of mankind who, he said, "seldom judge or determine right." Although granting that Americans must be allowed to govern themselves, he was as apprehensive of the "turbulence" of the masses as a small boy passing a graveyard in the dark. "No popular government was ever without its Catilines and its Caesars," he warned—a typical example of that generation's concern about the fate of the Roman republic.

The country, Hamilton insisted, needed a strong national government. "I acknowledge," he wrote in one of the *Federalist Papers*, "my aversion to every project that is calculated to disarm the government of a single weapon, which in any possible contingency

▲ "To confess my weakness," Hamilton wrote when he was only 14, "my ambition is prevalent." This pastel drawing by James Sharples was made about 1796.

might be usefully employed for the general defense and security." He avowed that government should be "a great Federal Republic," not "a number of petty states, with the appearance only of union, jarring, jealous, perverse, without any determined direction." He wished to reduce the states to mere administrative units, like English counties.

As secretary of the treasury, Hamilton proved to be a farsighted economic planner. The United States, a "Hercules in the cradle," needed capital to develop its untapped material and human resources. To persuade investors to commit their funds in America, the country would have to convince them that it would meet every obligation in full. His *Report on the Public Credit* outlined a plan for the federal government to borrow money to pay all of its debts as well as those of the states.

While most members of Congress agreed, albeit somewhat grudgingly, that the debt should be paid in full, they had misgivings as to who should get those payments. Many of the soldiers, farmers, and merchants who had been forced to accept government securities in lieu of cash for goods and services, had sold their securities for a fraction of their face value to speculators; under Hamilton's proposal, the speculators—now paid for the full value of the securities— would make a killing. To the argument for divided

payment, Hamilton answered coldly: "[The specula-tor] paid what the commodity was worth in the mar-ket, and took the risks. . . . He . . . ought to reap the benefit of his hazard."

Hamilton was essentially correct, and in the end Congress had to go along. After all, the speculators had not caused the securities to fall in value; indeed, as a group they had favored sound money and a strong government. The best way to restore the na-tion's credit was to convince investors that the gov-ernment would honor all obligations in full. What in-furiated his contemporaries and still attracts the scorn of many historians was Hamilton's motive. He delib-erately intended his plan to give a special advantage to the rich. The government would be strong, he thought, only if well-to-do Americans enthusiastically supported it. What better way to win them over than to make it worth their while financially to do so?

In part, opposition to the funding plan was sec-tional, for citizens of the northern states held more than four-fifths of the national debt. The scheme for assuming the state debts aggravated the controversy, since most of the southern states had already paid off much of their Revolutionary War obligations. For months Congress was deadlocked. Finally, in July 1790, Hamilton worked out a compromise with Rep-resentative James Madison and Secretary of State Jef-ferson. The two Virginians swung a few southern votes, and Hamilton induced some of his followers to support the southern plan for locating the permanent capital of the Union on the Potomac River.

Jefferson later claimed that Hamilton had hood-winked him. Having only recently returned from Eu-rope, he said, "I was really a stranger to the whole subject." Hamilton had persuaded him to "rally around" by the false tale that "our Union" was threatened with dissolution. This was nonsense; Jef-ferson agreed to the compromise because he expected that Virginia and the rest of the South would profit from having the capital so near at hand.

The assumption bill passed, and the entire funding plan was a great success. Soon the United States had the highest possible credit rating in the world's finan-cial centers. Foreign capital poured into the country.

DOCUMENT

Alexander Hamilton, "Bank"

Hamilton next proposed that Congress charter a national bank. Such an institution would provide safe storage for government funds and serve as an agent for the govern-ment in the collection, movement, and ex-penditure of tax money. Most important, because of its substantial resources a bank could fi-nance new and expanding business enterprises, greatly speeding the economic growth of the nation. It would also be able to issue bank notes, thereby

providing a vitally needed medium of exchange for the specie-starved economy. This Bank of the United States was to be partly owned by the government, but 80 percent of the $10 million stock issue was to be sold to private individuals.

The country had much to gain from such a bank, but again—Hamilton's cleverness was never more in evidence—the well-to-do commercial classes would gain still more. Government balances in the bank be-longing to all the people would earn dividends for a handful of rich investors. Manufacturers and other capitalists would profit from the bank's credit facilities. Public funds would be invested in the bank, but con-trol would remain in private hands, since the govern-ment would appoint only 5 of the 25 directors. Never-theless, the bill creating the bank passed both houses of Congress with relative ease in February 1791.

President Washington, however, hesitated to sign it, for the bill's constitutionality had been questioned during the debate in Congress. Nowhere did the Constitution specifically authorize Congress to char-ter corporations or engage in the banking business. As was his wont when in doubt, Washington called on Jefferson and Hamilton for advice.

Hamilton defended the legality of the bank by enunciating the doctrine of "implied powers." If a logical connection existed between the purpose of the bill and powers clearly stated in the Constitution, he wrote, the bill was constitutional.

> If the *end* be clearly comprehended within any of the specified powers, and if the measure have an obvious relation to that *end* . . . it may safely be deemed to come within the compass of the national authority.
> . . . A bank has a natural relation to the power of col-lecting taxes—to that of regulating trade—to that of providing for the common defence.

Jefferson disagreed. Congress could only do what the Constitution specifically authorized, he said. The "elastic clause" granting it the right to pass "all Laws which shall be necessary and proper" to carry out the specified powers must be interpreted literally or Congress would "take possession of a boundless field of power, no longer susceptible to any definition." Because a bank was obviously not necessary, it was not authorized.

Although not entirely convinced, Washington ac-cepted Hamilton's reasoning and signed the bill. He could just as easily have followed Jefferson, for the Constitution is not clear. If one stresses *proper* in the "necessary and proper" clause in Article I, Section 8 of the Constitution, one ends up a Hamiltonian; if one stresses *necessary*, then Jefferson's view is correct. His-torically (and this is the important point) politicians

have nearly always adopted the "loose" Hamiltonian "implied powers" interpretation when they favored a measure and the "strict" Jeffersonian one when they do not. Jefferson disliked the bank; therefore, he claimed it was unconstitutional. Had he approved, he doubtless would have taken a different tack.

In 1819 the Supreme Court officially sanctioned Hamilton's construction of the "necessary and proper" clause, and in general that interpretation has prevailed. Because the majority tends naturally toward an argument that increases its freedom of action, the pressure for this view has been continual and formidable. The Bank of the United States succeeded from the start. When its stock went on sale, investors snapped up every share in a matter of hours. People eagerly accepted its bank notes at face value. Business ventures of all kinds found it easier to raise new capital. Soon state-chartered banks entered the field. There were only 3 state banks in 1791; by 1801, there were 32.

Hamilton had not finished. In December 1791 he submitted his *Report on Manufactures,* a bold call for economic planning. The pre-Revolutionary non-importation agreements and wartime shortages had stimulated interest in manufacturing. Already a number of joint-stock companies had been founded to manufacture textiles, and an elaborate argument for economic diversification had been worked out by American economists such as Tench Coxe and Mathew Carey. Hamilton was familiar with these developments. In his *Report* he called for government tariffs, subsidies, and awards to encourage American manufacturing. He hoped to change an essentially agricultural nation into one with a complex, self-sufficient economy. Once again business and commercial interests in particular would benefit. They would be protected against foreign competition and otherwise subsidized, whereas the general taxpayer, particularly the farmer, would pay the bill in the form of higher taxes and higher prices on manufactured goods. Hamilton argued that in the long run every interest would profit, and he was undoubtedly sincere, being too much the nationalist to favor one section at the expense of another. A majority of the Congress, however, balked at so broad-gauged a scheme. Hamilton's *Report* was set aside, although many of the specific tariffs he recommended were enacted into law in 1792.

Nevertheless, the secretary of the treasury had managed to transform the financial structure of the country and to prepare the ground for an economic revolution. The constitutional reforms of 1787 had made this possible, and Hamilton turned possibility into reality.

THE OHIO COUNTRY: A DARK AND BLOODY GROUND

The western issues and those related to international trade proved more difficult because other nations were involved. The British showed no disposition to evacuate their posts on American soil simply because the American people had decided to strengthen their central government, nor did the western Indians suddenly agree to abandon their hunting grounds to the white invaders.

Trouble came swiftly when white settlers moved onto the land north of the Ohio River in large numbers. The Indians, determined to hold this country at all costs, struck hard at the invaders. In 1790 the Miami chief Little Turtle, a gifted strategist, inflicted a double defeat on militia units commanded by General Josiah Harmar. The next year Little Turtle and his men defeated the forces of General Arthur St. Clair still more convincingly. Both Harmar and St. Clair resigned from the army, their careers ruined, but the defeats led Congress to authorize raising a regular army of 5000 men.

By early 1792 the Indians had driven the whites into "beachheads" at Marietta and Cincinnati on the Ohio. Resentment of the federal government in the western counties of every state from New York to the Carolinas mounted, the people feeling that it was ignoring their interests. They were convinced that the British were inciting the Indians to attack them, yet the supposedly powerful national government seemed unable to force Great Britain to surrender its forts in the West.

Still worse, the Westerners believed, was the way the government was taxing them. In 1791, as part of his plan to take over the debts of the states, Hamilton had persuaded Congress to adopt an excise tax of 8 cents a gallon on American-made whiskey. Excise taxes were particularly disliked by most Americans. A duty on imported products was collected from merchants and passed on to consumers as part of the price, and it was by its nature imposed only on foreign-made products. People who did not want to pay it usually could find a domestic alternative. But the collection of excise taxes on American goods required hordes of tax collectors, armed with the power to snoop into one's affairs. Westerners, who were heavy drinkers and who turned much of their grain into whiskey in order to cope with the high cost of transportation, were especially angered by the tax on whiskey.

Knowing that the tax would be unpopular, Hamilton promised that the distillers would "be secured from every species of injury by the misconduct of the officers to be employed" in collecting it. But

he was determined to enforce the law. To western complaints, he coolly suggested that farmers drank too much to begin with. If they found the tax oppressive, they should cut down on their consumption. Of course this did nothing to reduce western opposition to the tax. Resistance was especially intense in western Pennsylvania. When treasury agents tried to collect it there, they were forcibly prevented from doing so.

REVOLUTION IN FRANCE

Momentous events in Europe were also affecting the situation. In 1789 the French Revolution erupted, and four years later war broke out between France and Great Britain and most of the rest of Europe. With France fighting Great Britain and Spain, there arose the question of America's obligations under the Alliance of 1778. That treaty required the United States to defend the French West Indies "forever against all other powers." Suppose the British attacked Martinique; must America then go to war? Morally the United States was so obligated, but no

▲ King Louis XVI of France, beheaded in Paris, January 21, 1793. Alexander Hamilton recommended termination of the nation's alliance with France. Thomas Jefferson argued that the treaty should be preserved because it had been made with the French people and not the monarch. As the French Revolution became still bloodier, American enthusiasm for the French radicals, and for radicalism in general, began to wane.

responsible American statesman urged such a policy. With the British in Canada and Spanish forces to the west and south, the nation would be in serious danger if it entered the war. Instead, in April 1793, Washington issued a proclamation of neutrality committing the United States to be "friendly and impartial" toward both sides in the war.

Meanwhile the French had sent a special representative, Edmond Charles Genet, to the United States to seek support. During its early stages, especially when France declared itself a republic in 1792, the revolution had excited much enthusiasm in the United States, for it seemed to indicate that American democratic ideas were already engulfing the world. The increasing radicalism in France tended to dampen some of the enthusiasm, yet when "Citizen" Genet landed at Charleston, South Carolina, in April 1793, the majority of Americans probably wished the revolutionaries well. As Genet, a charming, ebullient young man, made his way northward to present his credentials, cheering crowds welcomed him in every town. Quickly concluding that the proclamation of neutrality was "a harmless little pleasantry designed to throw dust in the eyes of the British," he began, in plain violation of American law, to license American vessels to operate as privateers against British shipping and to grant French military commissions to a number of Americans in order to mount expeditions against Spanish and British possessions in North America.

Washington received Genet coolly, and soon thereafter demanded that he stop his illegal activities. Genet, whose capacity for self-deception was monumental, appealed to public opinion over the president's head and continued to commission privateers. Even Jefferson was soon exasperated by Genet, whom he described as "hot headed, all imagination, no judgment and even indecent toward the P[resident]." Washington then requested his recall. The incident ended on a ludicrous note. When Genet left France, he had been in the forefront of the Revolution. But events there had marched swiftly leftward, and the new leaders in Paris considered him a dangerous reactionary. His replacement arrived in America with an order for his arrest. To return might well mean the guillotine, so Genet asked the government that was expelling him for political asylum! Washington agreed, for he was not a vindictive man. A few months later the bold revolutionary married the daughter of the governor of New York and settled down as a farmer on Long Island, where he raised a large family and "moved agreeably in society."

The Genet affair was incidental to a far graver problem. Although the European war increased the

foreign demand for American products, it also led to attacks on American shipping by both France and Great Britain. Each power captured American vessels headed for the other's ports whenever it could. In 1793 and 1794 about 600 United States ships were seized.

The British attacks caused far more damage, both physically and psychologically, because the British fleet was much larger than France's, and France at least professed to be America's friend and to favor freedom of trade for neutrals. In addition the British issued secret orders late in 1793 turning their navy loose on neutral ships headed for the French West Indies. Pouncing without warning, British warships captured about 250 American vessels and sent them off as prizes to British ports. The merchant marine, one American diplomat declared angrily, was being "kicked, cuffed, and plundered all over the Ocean."

The attacks roused a storm in America, reviving hatreds that had been smoldering since the Revolution. The continuing presence of British troops in the Northwest (in 1794 the British began to build a new fort in the Ohio country) and the restrictions imposed on American trade with the British West Indies raised tempers still further. To try to avoid a war, for he wisely believed that the United States should not become embroiled in the Anglo-French conflict, Washington sent Chief Justice John Jay to London to seek a settlement with the British.

FEDERALISTS AND REPUBLICANS: THE RISE OF POLITICAL PARTIES

The furor over the violations of neutral rights focused attention on a new development, the formation of political parties. Why national political parties emerged after the ratification of a Constitution that made no provision for such organizations is a question that has long intrigued historians. Probably the main reason was the obvious one: By creating a strong central government the Constitution produced national issues and a focus for national discussion and settlement of these issues. Furthermore, by failing to create machinery for nominating candidates for federal offices, the Constitution left a vacuum, which informal party organizations filled. That the universally admired Washington headed the government was a force limiting partisanship, but his principal advisers, Hamilton and Jefferson, were in sharp disagreement, and they soon became the leaders around which parties coalesced.

In the spring of 1791 Jefferson and James Madison began to sound out other politicians about forming an informal political organization. Jefferson also appointed the poet Philip Freneau to a minor state department post and Freneau then began publishing a newspaper, the *National Gazette,* to disseminate the views of what became known as the Republican party. The *Gazette* was soon describing Jefferson as a "Colossus of Liberty" and flailing away editorially at Hamilton's policies. Hamilton hit back promptly, organizing his own followers in the Federalist party, the organ of which was John Fenno's *Gazette of the United States.*

The personal nature of early American political controversies goes far toward explaining why the party battles of the era were so bitter. So does the continuing anxiety that plagued partisans of both persuasions about the supposed frailty of a republican government. The United States was still very much an experiment; leaders who sincerely proclaimed their own devotion to its welfare suspected that their opponents wanted to undermine its institutions. Federalists feared that the Jeffersonians sought a dictatorship based on "mob rule," Republicans that the Hamiltonians hid "under the mask of Federalism hearts devoted to monarchy."

At the start Hamilton had the ear of the president, and his allies controlled a majority in Congress. Jefferson, who disliked controversy, avoided a direct confrontation as long as he could. He went along with Hamilton's funding plan and traded the assumption of state debts for a capital on the Potomac. However, when Hamilton proposed the Bank of the United States, he dug in his heels. It seemed designed to benefit the northeastern commercial classes at the expense of southern and western farmers. He sensed a dastardly plot to milk the producing masses for the benefit of a few capitalists.

The growing controversy over the French Revolution and the resulting war between France and Great Britain widened the split between the parties. After the radicals in France executed Louis XVI and instituted the Reign of Terror, American conservatives were horrified. The Jeffersonians were also deeply shocked. However, they continued to defend the Revolution. Great southern landlords whose French counterparts were losing their estates—some their heads—extolled "the glorious successes of our Gallic brethren." In the same way the Federalists began to idealize the British, whom they considered the embodiment of the forces that were resisting French radicalism.

This created an explosive situation. Enthusiasm for a foreign country might tempt Americans, all unwittingly, to betray their own. Hamilton came to believe that Jefferson was so prejudiced in favor of

France as to be unable to conduct foreign affairs rationally, and Jefferson could say contemptuously: "Hamilton is panick struck, if we refuse our breech to every kick which Great Britain may choose to give it." This, of course, was an exaggeration, but Hamilton was certainly predisposed toward England. As he put it to an English official, "*we think in English.*"

In fact, Jefferson never lost his sense of perspective. When the Anglo-French war erupted, he recommended neutrality. In the Genet affair, although originally sympathetic to the young envoy, Jefferson cordially approved Washington's decision to send Genet packing. Hamilton perhaps went a little too far in his friendliness to Great Britain, but the real danger was that some of Hamilton's and Jefferson's excitable followers might become so committed as to forget the true interests of the United States.

1794: CRISIS AND RESOLUTION

During the summer of 1794 several superficially unrelated events brought the partisan conflicts of the period to a peak. For the better part of two years the government had been unable to collect Hamilton's whiskey tax in the West. In Pennsylvania, mobs had burned the homes of revenue agents, and several men had been killed. Late in July, 7000 "rebels" converged on Pittsburgh, threatening to set fire to the town. They were turned away by the sight of federal

▲ In 1792 farmers in western Pennsylvania, outraged over Hamilton's tax on liquor, rose up in rebellion against tax collectors. Their banners included the slogan of the French revolutionaries: "Liberty, Equality, and Fraternity!" Washington crushed the rebellion.

artillery and the liberal dispensation of whiskey by the frightened inhabitants.

Early in August President Washington determined "to go to every length that the Constitution and laws would permit" to enforce the law. He mustered an enormous army of nearly 13,000 militiamen. This had the desired effect; when the troops arrived in western Pennsylvania, rebels were nowhere to be seen. The expected Whiskey Rebellion simply did not happen. Good sense had triumphed. Moderates in the region (not everyone, after all, was a distiller) agreed that even unpopular laws should be obeyed.

More important, perhaps, than the militia in pacifying the Pennsylvania frontier was another event that occurred while that army was being mobilized. This was the Battle of Fallen Timbers in Ohio near present-day Toledo, where the regular army troops of Major General "Mad Anthony" Wayne won a decisive victory over the Indians. Wayne's victory opened the way for the settlement of the region. Some 2000 of the whiskey tax rebels simply pulled up stakes and headed for Ohio after the effort to avoid the excise collapsed.

JAY'S TREATY

Still more significant was the outcome of President Washington's decision to send John Jay to England to seek a treaty settling the conflicts that vexed the relations of the two nations. The British genuinely wanted to reach an accommodation with the United States—as one minister quipped, the Americans "are so much in debt to this country that we scarcely dare to quarrel with them." Jay was received by both the King and Queen and wined and dined by the foreign secretary, the prime minister, and other officials. The British also feared that the two new republics, France and the United States, would draw together in a battle against Europe's monarchies. On the other hand, the British were riding the crest of a wave of important victories in the war in Europe and were not disposed to make concessions to the Americans simply to avoid trouble.

The treaty that Jay brought home did contain a number of concessions. The British agreed to evacuate the posts in the West. They also promised to compensate American

shipowners for seizures in the West Indies and to open up their colonies in Asia to American ships. They conceded nothing, however, to American demands that the rights of neutrals on the high seas be respected; no one really expected them to do so in wartime. A provision opening the British West Indies to American commerce was so hedged with qualifications limiting the size of American vessels and the type of goods allowed that the United States refused to accept it.

Jay also committed the United States to paying pre-Revolutionary debts still owed British merchants, a slap in the face to many states whose courts had been impeding their collection. Yet nothing was said about the British paying for the slaves they had "abducted" during the fighting in the South.

Although Jay might have driven a harder bargain, this was a valuable treaty for the United States. But it was also a humiliating one. Most of what the United States gained already legally belonged to it, and the treaty sacrificed principles of importance to a nation dependent on foreign trade. When the terms became known, they raised a storm of popular protest. It seemed possible that President Washington would repudiate the treaty or that if he did not, the Senate would refuse to ratify it.

1795: ALL'S WELL THAT ENDS WELL

Washington did not repudiate the Jay Treaty and after long debate the Senate ratified it in June 1795. After a bitter debate, with most Republicans opposing the

◀ **The United States, 1787–1802**
The United States on the eve of the Louisiana Purchase. In 1804 Georgia's cession became part of the Mississippi Territory. The seven British western forts were evacuated as a result of Jay's Treaty (1795).

measure, the House passed the requisite funding resolution. The treaty marked an important step toward the regularization of Anglo-American relations, which in the long run was essential for both the economic and political security of the nation. And the evacuation of the British forts in the Northwest was of enormous immediate benefit.

Still another benefit was totally unplanned. Unexpectedly, the Jay Treaty enabled the United States to solve its problems on its southeastern frontier. During the early 1790s Spain had entered into alliances with the Cherokee, Creek, and other Indian tribes hostile to the Americans and built forts on territory ceded to the United States by Great Britain in the Treaty of Paris. In 1795, however, Spain intended to withdraw from the European war against France. Fearing a joint Anglo-American attack on Louisiana and its other American possessions, it decided to improve relations with the United States. Therefore the king's chief minister, Manuel de Godoy, known as "the Prince of Peace," offered the American envoy Thomas Pinckney a treaty that granted the United States the free navigation of the Mississippi River and the right of deposit at New Orleans that western Americans so urgently needed. This Treaty of San Lorenzo, popularly known as Pinckney's Treaty, also accepted the American version of the boundary between Spanish Florida and the United States.

The Senate ratified the Jay Treaty in June. Pinckney signed the Treaty of San Lorenzo in October that same year. These agreements put an end, at least temporarily, to European pressures in the trans-Appalachian region. Between the signings, in August 1795, as an aftermath of the Battle of Fallen Timbers, 12 tribes signed the Treaty of Greenville. The Indians surrendered huge sections of their lands, thus ending a struggle that had consumed a major portion of the government's revenues for years.

After the events of 1794 and 1795, settlers poured into the West as water bursts through a broken dike. "I believe scarcely anything short of a Chinese Wall or a line of Troops will restrain . . . the Incroachment of Settlers, upon the Indian Territory," President Washington explained in 1796. Kentucky had become a state in 1792; now, in 1796, Tennessee was admitted. Two years later the Mississippi Territory was organized, and at the end of the century, the Indiana Territory. The great westward flood reached full tide.

WASHINGTON'S FAREWELL

Settlement of western problems did not, however, put an end to partisan strife. Even the sainted Washington was neither immune to attack nor entirely

George Washington, Farewell Address

above the battle. On questions of finance and foreign policy he usually sided with Hamilton and thus increasingly incurred the anger of the Jeffersonians. But he was, after all, a Virginian. Only the most rabid partisan could think him a tool of northern commercial interests. He remained as he intended himself to be, a symbol of national unity. But he was determined to put away the cares of office at the end of his second term. In September 1796 he announced his retirement in a "Farewell Address" to the nation.

Washington found the acrimonious rivalry between Federalists and Republicans most disturbing. Hamilton advocated national unity, yet he seemed prepared to smash any individual or faction that disagreed with his vision of the country's future. Jefferson had risked his neck for independence, but he opposed the economic development needed to make America strong enough to defend that independence. Washington was less brilliant than either Hamilton or Jefferson but wiser. He appreciated how important it was that the new nation should remain at peace—with the rest of the world and with itself. In his farewell he deplored the "baneful effects of the spirit of party" that led honest people to use unscrupulous means to win a mean advantage over fellow Americans. He tried to show how the North benefited from the prosperity of the South, the South from that of the North, and the East and West also, in reciprocal fashion.

Washington urged the people to avoid both "inveterate antipathies" and "passionate attachments" to any foreign nation. Nothing had alarmed him more than the sight of Americans dividing into "French" and "English" factions. Furthermore, France had repeatedly interfered in American domestic affairs. "Against the insidious wiles of foreign influence," Washington now warned, "the jealousy of a free people ought to be constantly awake." America should develop its foreign trade but steer clear of foreign political connections as far as possible. "Permanent alliances" should be avoided, although "temporary alliances for extraordinary emergencies" might sometimes be useful.

THE ELECTION OF 1796

Washington's Farewell Address was destined to have a long and important influence on American thinking, but its immediate impact was small. He had intended it to cool political passions. Instead, in the words of Federalist congressman Fisher Ames, people took it as

"a signal, like dropping a hat, for the party racers to start." By the time the 1796 presidential campaign had ended, many Federalists and Republicans were refusing to speak to one another.

Jefferson was the only Republican candidate seriously considered in 1796. The logical Federalist was Hamilton, but, as was to happen so often in American history with powerful leaders, he was not considered "available" because his controversial policies had made him many enemies. Gathering in caucus, the Federalists in Congress nominated Vice President John Adams for the top office and Thomas Pinckney of South Carolina, negotiator of the popular Spanish treaty, for vice president. In the election the Federalists were victorious.

Hamilton, hoping to run the new administration from the wings, preferred Pinckney to Adams. He arranged for some of the Federalist electors from South Carolina to vote only for Pinckney. (Pinckney, who was on the high seas at the time, did not even know he was running for vice president!) Catching wind of this, a number of New England electors retaliated by cutting Pinckney. As a result, Adams won in the electoral college, 71 to 68, over *Jefferson*, who thus became vice president. Pinckney got only 59 electoral votes.

That Adams would now be obliged to work with a vice president who led the opposition seemed to presage a decline in partisanship. Adams actually preferred the Virginian to Pinckney for the vice presidency, while Jefferson said that if Adams would "relinquish his bias to an English constitution," he might make a fine chief executive. The two had in common a distaste for Hamilton—a powerful bond.

However, the closeness of the election indicated a trend toward the Republicans, who were making constant and effective use of the charge that the Federalists were "monocrats" (monarchists) determined to destroy American liberty. Without Washington to lead them, the Federalist politicians were already quarreling among themselves; honest, able, hardworking John Adams was too caustic and too scathingly frank to unite them. Everything seemed to indicate a Republican victory at the next election.

THE XYZ AFFAIR

At this point occurred one of the most remarkable reversals of public feeling in American history. French attacks on American shipping, begun out of irritation at the Jay Treaty and in order to influence

▲ This flattering portrait of John Adams by John Trumbull was done in 1793. Jeffersonian newspapers referred to Adams derisively as "His Rotundity." Benjamin Bache, editor of the Philadelphia *Aurora*, described him as "blind, bald, toothless, querulous," which was three-quarters true but irrelevant.

the election, continued after Adams took office. Hoping to stop them, Adams appointed three commissioners (Charles Pinckney, United States minister to France, and elder brother of Thomas[1]; John Marshall, a Virginia Federalist lawyer; and Elbridge Gerry of Massachusetts, who was not closely identified with either party) to try to negotiate a settlement. They were instructed to seek a moderate settlement, to "terminate our differences . . . without referring to the merits."

Their mission was a fiasco. Talleyrand, the French foreign minister, sent an agent later spoken of as X to demand "something for the pocket," a "gratification,"—read a bribe—as the price of making a deal. Later two other Tallyrand agents, Y and Z, made the same demand. The Americans refused, more because they suspected Talleyrand's good faith than because of any particular distaste for bribery. "No, no, not a sixpence," Pinckney later told X. The talks broke up, and in April 1798 President Adams released the commissioners' reports.

---

[1]The Pinckney brothers were children of Eliza Pinckney, the woman responsible for the introduction of indigo cultivation to America.

▲ The 1797 cartoon refers to the infamous XYZ affair. Here the five-headed monster (France) demands "Money, Money, Money!!" while the three American representatives answer, "We will not give you six pence."

They caused a sensation. Americans' sense of national honor, perhaps overly tender because the country was so young and insecure, was outraged. Pinckney's laconic refusal to pay a bribe was translated into the grandiose phrase "Millions for defense, but not one cent for tribute!" and broadcast throughout the land. John Adams, never a man with mass appeal, suddenly found himself a national hero. Federalist hotheads burned for a fight. Congress unilaterally abrogated the French Alliance, created a Navy Department, and appropriated enough money to build 40-odd warships and triple the size of the army. Washington came out of retirement to lead the forces, with Hamilton, now a general, as second in command. On the seas American privateers began to attack French shipping.

Adams did not much like the French and he could be extremely stubborn. A declaration of war would have been immensely popular. But perhaps—it is not an entirely illogical surmise about John Adams, who later in life described himself with some relish as "obnoxious, suspected, and unpopular"—

the president did not want to be popular. Instead of calling for war, he contented himself with approving the buildup of the armed forces.

The Republicans, however, committed to friendship with France, did not appreciate Adams's moderation. Although angered by the XYZ Affair, they tried, one Federalist complained, "to clog the wheels of government" by opposing the military appropriations. John Daly Burk of the New York *Time Piece* called Adams a "mock Monarch" surrounded by a "court composed of tories and speculators," which of course was a flat lie.

Many Federalists expected the Republicans to side with France if war broke out. Hysterical and near panic, they easily persuaded themselves that the danger of subversion was acute. The French Revolution and the resulting war were churning European society to the depths, stirring the hopes of liberals and striking fear in the hearts of conservatives. Refugees of both persuasions were flocking to the United States. Suddenly the presence of these foreigners seemed threatening to "native" Americans.

THE ALIEN AND SEDITION ACTS

Conservative Federalists saw in this situation a chance to smash the opposition. In June and July 1798 they pushed through Congress a series of repressive measures known as the Alien and Sedition Acts. The least offensive of these laws, the Naturalization Act, increased the period a foreigner had to reside in the United States before being eligible for citizenship from 5 to 14 years. The Alien Enemies Act gave the president the power to arrest or expel aliens in time of "declared war," but since the quasi-war with France was never declared, this measure had no practical importance. The Alien Act authorized the president to expel all aliens whom he thought "dangerous to the peace and safety of the United States." (Adams never invoked this law, but a number of aliens left the country out of fear that he might.)

DOCUMENT
The Alien and
Sedition Acts

Finally, there was the Sedition Act. Its first section, making it a crime "to impede the operation of any law" or to attempt to instigate a riot or insurrection, was reasonable enough; but the act also made it illegal to publish, or even to utter, any "false, scandalous and malicious" criticism of high government officials. Although milder than British sedition laws, this proviso rested, as James Madison said, on "the exploded doctrine" that government officials "are the masters and not the servants of the people."

As the election of 1800 approached, the Federalists made a systematic attempt to silence the leading Republican newspapers. Twenty-five persons were prosecuted and ten convicted, all in patently unfair trials. In typical cases, the editor Thomas Cooper, an English-born radical, later president of the University of South Carolina, was sentenced to six months in jail and fined $400; the editor Charles Holt got three months and a $200 fine; and the editor James Callender got nine months and a $200 fine.

THE KENTUCKY AND VIRGINIA RESOLVES

While Thomas Jefferson did not object to state sedition laws, he believed that the Alien and Sedition Acts violated the First Amendment's guarantees of freedom of speech and the press and were an invasion of the rights of the states. In 1798 he and Madison decided to draw up resolutions arguing that the laws were unconstitutional. Madison's draft was presented to the Virginia legislature and Jefferson's to the legislature of Kentucky.

Jefferson argued that since the Constitution was a compact made by sovereign states, each state had "an equal right to judge for itself" when the compact had been violated. Thus a state could declare a law of Congress unconstitutional. Madison's Virginia Resolves took an only slightly less forthright position.

DOCUMENT
The Virginia and
Kentucky
Resolutions

Neither Kentucky nor Virginia tried to implement these resolves or to prevent the enforcement of the Alien and Sedition Acts. Jefferson and Madison were protesting Federalist high-handedness and firing the opening salvo of Jefferson's campaign for the presidency, not advancing a new constitutional theory of extreme states' rights. "Keep away all show of force," Jefferson advised his supporters.

This was sound advice, for events were again playing into the hands of the Republicans. Talleyrand had never wanted war with the United States. When he discovered how vehemently the Americans had reacted to his little attempt to replenish his personal fortune, he let Adams know that new negotiators would be properly received.

President Adams quickly grasped the importance of the French change of heart. Other leading Federalists, however, had lost their heads. By shouting about the French danger, they had roused the country against radicalism, and they did not intend to surrender this advantage tamely. Hamilton in particular wanted war at almost any price—if not against France, then against Spain. He saw himself at the head of the new American army sweeping first across Louisiana and the Floridas, then on to the South. "We ought to squint at South America," he suggested. "Tempting objects will be without our grasp."

But the Puritan John Adams was a specialist at resisting temptation. At this critical point his intelligence, his moderate political philosophy, and his stubborn integrity stood him in good stead. He would neither go to war merely to destroy the political opposition in America nor follow "the fools who were intriguing to plunge us into an alliance with England . . . and wild expeditions to South America." Instead he submitted to the Senate the name of a new minister plenipotentiary to France, and when the Federalists tried to block the appointment, he threatened to resign. That would have made Jefferson president! So the furious Federalists had to give in, although they forced Adams to send three men instead of one.

Napoleon had taken over France by the time the Americans arrived, and he drove a harder bargain than Talleyrand would have. But in the end he signed an agreement (the Convention of 1800) abrogating the Franco-American treaties of 1778. Nothing was said about the damage done to American shipping by the French, but the war scare was over.

MILESTONES

1781	States fail to approve Congress's tariff
1786	Rhode Island Supreme Court upholds state legal tender act (*Trevett* v. *Weeden*)
	Shays's Rebellion collapses in Springfield, Massachusetts
	Only five states send delegates to Annapolis Convention
1787	Delegates meet at Philadelphia Constitutional Convention
1787–1788	All states but North Carolina and Rhode Island ratify Constitution
1789	President Washington is inaugurated
	Storming of Paris Bastille begins French Revolution
1790	Hamilton issues his *Report on Public Credit*
1791	Hamilton issues his *Report on Manufactures*
	First Ten Amendments (Bill of Rights) to the Constitution are ratified
	Republican and Federalist political parties are organized
	Philip Freneau's *National Gazette* and John Fenno's *Gazette of the United States* are founded

1793	French revolutionaries execute King Louis XVI
	Washington issues Declaration of Neutrality
1794	"Mad Anthony" Wayne's troops defeat Indians at Battle of Fallen Timbers
	Washington's militiamen thwart Whiskey Rebellion in Pennsylvania
1795	Senate ratifies humiliating Jay Treaty
1796	Washington announces his retirement in Farewell Address
	John Adams is elected president
1798	French demand bribe during XYZ Affair
	Congress passes Alien and Sedition Acts
1798–1799	Jefferson presents Kentucky Resolutions
	Madison presents Virginia Resolutions

SUPPLEMENTARY READING

On the Constitution, in addition to the works cited in the Debating the Past (p. 148), see Reginald Horsman, *The New Republic* (2000), a good brief survey. Bernard Bailyn, To Begin the World Anew (2003) shows how the founders embraced ambiguity. For Madison's role, see Lance Banning, *The Sacred Fire of Liberty* (1995), Drew R. McCoy, *The Last of the Fathers* (1989), and Gary Rosen, *American Compact* (1999). On Hamilton, Ronald Chernow, *Alexander Hamilton* (2004) offers a balanced account while Richard Brookhiser's brief *Alexander Hamilton, American* (1999) is more partisan. See also Karl-Friedrich Walling, *Republican Empire: Alexander Hamilton on War and Free Government* (1999). The *Federalist Papers* of Hamilton, Madison, and Jay, available in many editions, are essential for the arguments of the supporters of the new government. For the Bill of Rights, consult Bernard Schwartz, *The Great Rights of Mankind* (1977).

For Washington, in addition to the works cited in the previous chapter, see Alexander De Conde, *Entangling Alliance: Politics and Diplomacy Under George Washington* (1958), Harry Ammon, *The Genet Mission* (1973), two volumes by S. F. Bemis, *Jay's Treaty* (1923) and *Pinckney's Treaty* (1926), Alexander De Conde, *The Quasi-War* (1966), and William Stinchcombe, *The XYZ Affair* (1980). On economic development, see E. J. Ferguson, *The Power of the Purse* (1968), and C. P. Nettels, *The Emergence of a National Economy* (1962), which puts this subject in the broader perspective of the period 1775–1815. On the radical western movements, see D. P. Szatmary, *Shays' Rebellion* (1980) and Thomas P. Slaughter, *The Whiskey Rebellion* (1986).

John Patrick Diggins, *John Adams* (2003) is a useful brief biography. Excellent full-length biographies include Joseph J. Ellis, *Passionate Sage* (1993), and David McCullough, *John*

Adams (2001). Stanley Elkins and Eric McKitrick, *The Age of Federalism* (1993), and James Roger Sharp, *American Politics in the Early Republic* (1993), provide detailed accounts of the politics of this period. For the Alien and Sedition Acts, see J. M. Smith, *Freedom's Fetters* (1956), and L. W. Levy, *Freedom of Speech and Press in Early American History* (1963). Paul Nagel's collective biography, *The Adams Women* (1987), provides a superb account of a remarkable family.

On the role of maps generally, see Susan Schulten, *The Geographical Imagination in America, 1880–1950 (2001).*

SUGGESTED WEBSITES

George Washington at Home
http://www.mountvernon.org/
Pictures and documents from Mount Vernon, the home of the first president, George Washington.

George Washington
http://memory.loc.gov/ammem/gwhtml/gwhome.html
This Library of Congress site contains information on Washington and his papers.

Biographies of the Founders
http://www.colonialhall.com/
This site provides interesting information about the men who signed the Declaration of Independence and includes a trivia section.

The *Federalist Papers*
http://www.law.emory.edu/FEDERAL/federalist/
This Emory University site is a collection of the most important *Federalist Papers,* a series of documents designed to convince people to support the new Constitution and the Federalist Party.

The Continental Congress and the Constitutional Convention, 1774–1798
http://memory.loc.gov/ammem/bdsds/bdsdhome.html
The Continental Congress Broadside Collection (253 titles) and the Constitutional Convention Broadside Collection (21 titles) contain 274 documents relating to the work of Congress and the drafting and ratification of the Constitution.

The Constitution and the Amendments
http://www.law.emory.edu/FEDERAL/usconst.html
A searchable Constitution site, especially useful for its information on the Bill of Rights and other constitutional amendments.

The George Washington Papers
http://www.virginia.edu/gwpapers/
This site provides information on the University of Virginia publishing project, with selected documents, essays, and an index to the published volumes.

Archiving Early America
http://earlyamerica.com
Old newspapers provide a window into issues of the past. This site includes the Keigwin and Matthews collection of historic newspapers.

Alexander Hamilton
http://odur.let.rug.nl/~usa/B/hamilton/hamilxx.htm
This site from *A Hypertext of American History* examines Hamilton's life and influence in the United States during the early national period.

The XYZ Affair
http://ap.grolier.com/article?assetid=0425920-00&templatename=/article/article.html
This site examines the XYZ affair, the first major crisis of U.S. foreign policy.

Jeffersonian Democracy

▼ Jefferson envisioned an American democracy consisting of sturdy, yeoman farmers such as these, painted by 22-year-old Francis Alexander (1822). Notwithstanding this charming rendering of farm life, Alexander took up painting to escape farm chores.

CHAPTER CONTENTS

Once the furor over war and subversion subsided, public attention focused on the presidential contest between Adams and Jefferson. Because of his stand for peace, Adams personally escaped the brunt of popular indignation against the Federalist party. His solid qualities had a strong appeal to conservatives, and fear that the Republicans would introduce radical "French" social reforms did not disappear when the danger of war with France ended. Many nationalist-minded voters worried that the Republicans, waving the banner of states' rights, would weaken the strong government established by the Federalists. The economic progress stimulated by Hamilton's financial reforms also seemed threatened. But when the electors' votes were counted in February 1801, the Republicans were discovered to have won narrowly, 73 to 65.

But which Republican was to be president? The Constitution did not distinguish between presidential and vice presidential candidates; it provided only that each elector vote for two candidates, the one with the most votes becoming president and the runner-up vice president. The development of national political parties made this system impractical. The vice presidential candidate of the Republicans was Aaron Burr of New York, a former senator and a rival of Hamilton in law and politics. But Republican party solidarity had been perfect; Jefferson and Burr received 73 votes each. Because of the tie, the Constitution required that the House of Representatives (voting by states) choose between them.

In the House the Republicans could control only 8 of the 16 state delegations. On the first ballot Jefferson got these 8 votes, 1 short of election, while 6 states voted for Burr. Two state delegations, being evenly split, lost their votes. Through 35 ballots the deadlock

persisted; the Federalist congressmen, fearful of Jefferson's supposed radicalism, voted solidly for Burr.

Pressures were exerted on both candidates to make deals to win additional support. Officially at least, both refused. Burr put on a great show of remaining above the battle. (Had he been an honorable man, he would have withdrawn, since the voters had clearly intended him for the second spot.) Whether Jefferson made any promises is uncertain; there is some evidence that to break the deadlock he assured the Federalists that he would preserve Hamilton's financial system and continue the Washington-Adams foreign policy.

In the end, Alexander Hamilton decided who would be the next president. Although he considered Jefferson "too much in earnest in his democracy" and "not very mindful of truth," he detested Burr. He exerted his considerable influence on Federalist congressmen on Jefferson's behalf. Finally, on February 17, 1801, Jefferson was elected. Burr became vice president.

To make sure that this deadlock would never be repeated, the Twelfth Amendment was drafted, providing for separate balloting in the Electoral College for president and vice president. This change was ratified in 1804, shortly before the next election.

THE FEDERALIST CONTRIBUTION

On March 4, 1801, in the raw new national capital on the Potomac River named in honor of George Washington, the Father of his Country, Thomas Jefferson took the presidential oath and delivered his inaugural address. His goal was to recapture the simplicity and austerity—the "pure republicanism"—that had characterized "the spirit of '76." The new president believed that a revolution as important as that heralded by his immortal Declaration of Independence had occurred, and for once most of his political enemies agreed with him.

Certainly an era had ended. In the years between the Peace of Paris and Jay's Treaty, the Federalists had practically monopolized the political good sense of the nation. In the perspective of history they were "right" in strengthening the federal government, in establishing a sound fiscal system, in trying to diversify the economy, in seeking an accommodation with Great Britain, and in refusing to be carried away with enthusiasm for France despite the bright dreams inspired by the French Revolution.

The Federalists had displayed remarkable self-control and moderation at least until 1798. They were nationalists who did not try to destroy local patriotism, aristocrats willing to live with the spirit of democracy. The Constitution—with its wise compromises, its

balance of forces, its restraints, and its practical concessions to local prejudices—is their monument.

But the Federalists were unable to face up to defeat. When they saw the Republicans gathering strength by developing clever new techniques of party organization and propaganda, mouthing slogans about liberty, attacking "monocrats," glorifying both the past with its satisfying simplicity and the future with its promise of a glorious day when all men would be free, equal, and brothers, they panicked. Abandoning the sober wisdom of their great period, they fought to save themselves at any cost. The effort turned defeat into rout. The Republican victory, close in the Electoral College, approached landslide proportions in the congressional elections, where popular feeling expressed itself directly.

Jefferson erred, however, in calling this triumph a revolution. The real upheaval had been attempted in 1798; it was Federalist-inspired, and it failed. In 1800 the voters expressed a preference for the old over the new; that is, for individual freedom and limited national power. And Jefferson, despite Federalist fears that he would destroy the Constitution and establish a radical social order, presided instead over a regime that confirmed the great achievements of the Federalist era.

What was most significant about the election of 1800 was that it was *not* a revolution. After a bitter contest, the Jeffersonians took power and proceeded to change the policy of the government. They did so peacefully. Thus American republican government passed a crucial test: Control of its machinery had changed hands in a democratic and orderly way. And only slightly less significant, the informal party system had demonstrated its usefulness. The Jeffersonians had organized popular dissatisfaction with Federalist policies, formulated a platform of reform, chosen leaders to put their plans into effect, and elected those leaders to office.

THOMAS JEFFERSON: POLITICAL THEORIST

Jefferson hardly seemed cut out for politics. Although in some ways a typical, pleasure-loving southern planter, he had in him something of the Spartan. He grew tobacco but did not smoke, and he partook only sparingly of meat and alcohol. Unlike most planters he never hunted or gambled, though he was a fine horseman and enjoyed dancing, music, and other social diversions. His practical interests ranged enormously—from architecture and geology to natural history and scientific farming—yet he displayed little interest in managing men. Controversy dismayed him, and he tended to avoid it by assigning to some

DEBATING THE PAST

Did Thomas Jefferson father a child by his slave? The photo *(left)* shows Thomas Jefferson's bedroom at Monticello. He designed the alcove to ensure privacy. A page from his farm accounts *(right)* in his own writing lists as slaves Sally Hemings and several of her children, including Madison, born in 1805, and Eston, born in 1808. In 1787, Sally Hemings, a young slave from the Jefferson plantation, was sent to Paris to serve Thomas Jefferson, U.S. minister to France, and his two daughters. Jefferson's wife had died five years earlier. When Jefferson was elected president in 1800, a newspaper published several articles claiming that he had fathered all of Hemings's children. Jefferson ignored the charges and his political allies denounced them as lies. In 1873 Madison Hemings told an Ohio reporter that his mother, Sally Hemings, had said that his father was Thomas Jefferson. Few took the story seriously. Jefferson scholar Merrill Peterson (1960) was the first to mention Madison Hemings's story, which he attributed to Federalists seeking to embarrass Jefferson and abolitionists seeking to discredit slavery. Dumas Malone (1948–1981), the preeminent Jefferson biographer, flatly rejected the possibility of a Jefferson-Hemings liaison. Among scholars, Malone's views went mostly unchallenged for decades. But Gordon-Reed (1997), a lawyer, accumulated considerable evidence in support of Madison Hemings's story, though she did not think it proven. The next year a forensic pathologist compared a DNA sample of a descendant of Field Jefferson, Thomas Jefferson's uncle, to that of a descendant of Eston Hemings. A genetic sequence matched. Eston had been fathered by a Jefferson. Some pointed to Jefferson's younger brother, Randolph, as the father, but most Jefferson scholars concluded that Thomas Jefferson was the more likely father. No such revelations could diminish Jefferson's significance as statesman, but they further complicate our understanding of one of the nation's foremost apostles of freedom.

Merrill Peterson, *The Jefferson Image in the American Mind* (1960), Dumas Malone, *Jefferson and His Time*, 6 volumes (1948–1981), Anette Gordon-Reed, *Thomas Jefferson and Sally Hemings* (1997). See also Joseph Ellis, *American Sphynx* (1998).

thicker-skinned associate the task of attacking his enemies. Nevertheless, he wanted to have a say in shaping the future of the country, and once engaged, he fought stubbornly and at times deviously to get and hold power.

Like Hamilton, Jefferson thought human beings basically selfish. "Lions and tigers are mere lambs compared with men," he once said. Although he claimed to have some doubts about the subject, he suspected that blacks were "inferior to whites in the endowments both of body and mind." (Hamilton, who also owned slaves, stated flatly of blacks: "Their natural faculties are as good as ours.") Jefferson's pronouncements on race are yet more troubling in light of recent research, including DNA studies, that point to the likelihood that he fathered one or more children by Sally Hemings, one of his slaves.

Yet like a good child of the Enlightenment, Jefferson believed that "no definite limits can be assigned to the improvability of the human race" and that unless people were free to follow the dictates of reason, the

DOCUMENT

"Memoirs of a Monticello Slave"

march of civilization would grind quickly to a halt. "To preserve the freedom of the human mind," he wrote, "every spirit should be ready to devote itself to martyrdom." Democracy seemed to him not so much an ideal as a practical necessity. If people could not govern themselves, how could they be expected to govern their fellows? He had no patience with Hamilton's fondness for magnifying the virtues of the rich and the well-born. He believed that "genius" was a rare quality but one "which nature has shown as liberally among poor as rich." When a very old man he wrote: "The mass of mankind has not been born with saddles on their backs, nor a favored few booted and spurred, ready to ride them legitimately, by the grace of God."

Jefferson believed *all* government a necessary evil at best, for by its nature it restricted the freedom of the individual. For this reason, he wanted the United States to remain a society of small independent farmers. Such a nation did not need much political organization.

Jefferson's main objection to Hamilton was that Hamilton wanted to commercialize and centralize the country. This Jefferson feared, for it would mean the growth of cities, which would complicate society and hence require more regulation. "The mobs of great cities add just as much to the support of pure government," he said, "as sores do to the strength of the human body." Later in life he warned a nephew to avoid "populous cities" because, he said, in such places young men acquire "habits and partialities which do not contribute to the happiness of their afterlife." Like Hamilton, he believed that city workers were easy prey for demagogues. "I consider the class of artificers as the panders of vice, and the instruments by which the liberties of a country are usually overturned," he said. "Those who labor in the earth," he also said, "are the chosen people of God, if ever He had a chosen people."

Jefferson objected to what he considered Hamilton's pro-British orientation. Despite his support of the Revolution, Hamilton admired English society and the orderliness of the British government, and he modeled much of his financial program on the British example. To the author of the Declaration of Independence, these attitudes passed all understanding. Jefferson thought English society immoral and decadent, the British system of government fundamentally corrupt. Toward France, the two took opposite positions. Jefferson was in Paris when the French Revolution broke out; he was delighted to see another blow struck at tyranny. Leading French liberals consulted him at every turn. Later, as secretary of state, he excused the excesses of the French upheaval far more than most Americans. To Hamilton, the violence and social disruption caused by the French Revolution were anathema.

JEFFERSON AS PRESIDENT

The novelty of the new administration lay in its style and its moderation. Both were apparent in Jefferson's inaugural address. The new president's opening remarks showed that he was neither a demagogue nor a firebrand. "The task is above my talents," he said modestly, "and . . . I approach it with . . . anxious and awful presentiments." The people had spoken, and their voice must be heeded, but the rights of dissenters must be respected. "All . . . will bear in mind this sacred principle," he said, "that though the will of the majority is in all cases to prevail, that will to be rightful must be reasonable; that the minority possess their equal rights, which equal law must protect, and to violate would be oppression."

Thomas Jefferson, First Inaugural Address

Jefferson spoke at some length about specific policies. He declared himself against "entangling alliances" and for economy in government, and he promised to pay off the national debt, preserve the government's credit, and stimulate both agriculture and its "handmaid," commerce. His main stress was on the cooling of partisan passions. "Every difference of opinion is not a difference of principle. We have called by different names brethren of the same principle. We are all Republicans—we are all Federalists." And he promised the country "a wise and frugal Government, which shall restrain men from injuring one another" and "leave them otherwise free to regulate their own pursuits."

Jefferson quickly demonstrated the sincerity of his remarks. He saw to it that the whiskey tax and other Federalist excises were repealed, and he made sharp cuts in military and naval expenditures to keep the budget in balance. The national debt was reduced from $83 million to $57 million during his eight years in office. The Naturalization Act of 1798 was repealed, and the old five-year residence requirement for citizenship restored. The Sedition Act and the Alien Act expired of their own accord in 1801 and 1802.

The changes were not drastic. Jefferson made no effort to tear down the fiscal structure that Hamilton had erected. "We can pay off his debt," the new president confessed, "but we cannot get rid of his financial system." Nor did the author of the Kentucky Resolves try to alter the balance of federal-state power.

Yet there was a different tone to the new regime. Jefferson had no desire to surround himself with pomp and ceremony; the excessive formality of the Washington and Adams administrations had been distasteful to him. From the moment of his election, he played down the ceremonial aspects of the presidency. He asked that he be notified of his election by mail rather than by a committee, and he would have preferred to have taken

the oath at Charlottesville, near Monticello, his home, rather than at Washington. After the inauguration, he returned to his boardinghouse on foot and took dinner in his usual seat at the common table.

In the White House he often wore a frayed coat and carpet slippers, even to receive the representatives of foreign powers when they arrived, resplendent with silk ribbons and a sense of their own importance, to present their credentials. At social affairs he paid little heed to the status and seniority of his guests. When dinner was announced, he offered his arm to whichever lady he was talking to at the moment and placed her at his right; other guests were free to sit wherever they found an empty chair. During business hours congressmen, friends, foreign officials, and plain citizens coming to call took their turn in the order of their arrival. "The principle of society with us," Jefferson explained, "is the equal rights of all. . . . Nobody shall be above you, nor you above anybody, *pell-mell* is our law."

"Pell-mell" was also good politics, and Jefferson turned out to be a superb politician. He gave dozens of small stag dinner parties for congressmen, serving the food personally from a dumbwaiter connected with the White House kitchen. The guests, carefully chosen to make congenial groups, were seated at a round table to encourage general conversation, and the food and wine were first-class. These were ostensibly social occasions—shoptalk was avoided—yet they paid large political dividends. Jefferson learned to know every congressman personally, Democratic Republican and Federalist alike, and not only their political views but their strengths, their quirks, and their flaws as well. And he worked his personal magic on them, displaying the breadth of his knowledge, his charm and wit, his lack of pomposity. "You see, we are alone, and *our walls have no ears*," he would say, and while the wine flowed and the guests sampled delicacies prepared by Jefferson's French chef, the president manufactured political capital. "You drink as you please and converse at your ease," one guest reported.

Jefferson made effective use of his close supporters in Congress and of Cabinet members as well, in persuading Congress to go along with his proposals. His state papers were models of reason, minimizing conflicts, stressing areas where all honest people must agree. After all, as he indicated in his inaugural address, nearly all Americans believed in having both a federal government and a republican system. No great principle divided them into irreconcilable camps. Jefferson set out to bring them all into *his* camp, and he succeeded so well in four years that when he ran for reelection against Charles Pinckney, he got 162 of the 176 electoral votes cast. Eventually

▲ This 1800 painting of Thomas Jefferson was by Rembrandt Peale (1800). Rembrandt's father—the painter Charles Willson Peale—named his other sons after painters, too: Rubens, Titian, and Raphaelle, and Titian II. Rembrandt Peale did this painting, adjudged to be extremely accurate, when he was twenty.

even John Quincy Adams, son of the second president, became a Jeffersonian.

At the same time, Jefferson was anything but nonpartisan in the sense that Washington had been. His Cabinet consisted exclusively of men of his own party. He exerted almost continuous pressure on Congress to make sure that his legislative program was enacted into law. He did not remove many Federalist officeholders, and at one point he remarked ruefully that government officials seldom died and never resigned. But when he could, he used his power of appointment to reward his friends and punish his enemies.

JEFFERSON'S ATTACK ON THE JUDICIARY

Although notably open-minded and tolerant, Jefferson had a few stubborn prejudices. One was against kings, another against the British system of government. A third was against judges, or rather, against

entrenched judicial power. While recognizing that judges must have a degree of independence, he feared what he called their "habit of going out of the question before them, to throw an anchor ahead, and grapple further hold for future advances of power." The biased behavior of Federalist judges during the trials under the Sedition Act had enormously increased this distrust, and it burst all bounds when the Federalist majority of the dying Congress rammed through the Judiciary Act of 1801.

The Judiciary Act created six new circuit courts, presided over by 16 new federal judges and a small army of attorneys, marshals, and clerks. The expanding country needed the judges, but with the enthusiastic cooperation of President Adams, the Federalists made shameless use of the opportunity to fill all the new positions with conservative members of their own party. The new appointees were dubbed "midnight justices" because Adams had stayed up until midnight on March 3, his last day as president, feverishly signing their commissions.

The Republicans retaliated as soon as the new Congress met by repealing the Judiciary Act of 1801, but on taking office Jefferson had discovered that in the confusion of Adams's last hours, the commissions of a number of justices of the peace for the new District of Columbia had not been distributed. While these were small fry indeed, Jefferson was so angry that he ordered the commissions held up even though they had been signed by Adams.

One of the appointees, William Marbury, then petitioned the Supreme Court for a writ of mandamus (Latin for "we order") directing the new secretary of state, James Madison, to give him his commission.

DOCUMENT

Opinion of the Supreme Court for *Marbury* v. *Madison*

The case of *Marbury* v. *Madison* (1803) placed Chief Justice John Marshall, one of Adams's "midnight" appointments, in an embarrassing position. Marbury had a strong claim; if Marshall refused to issue a mandamus, everyone would say he dared not stand up to Jefferson, and the prestige of the Court would suffer. If he issued the writ, however, he would place the Court in direct conflict with the executive. Jefferson particularly disliked Marshall. He would probably tell Madison to ignore the order, and in the prevailing state of public opinion nothing could be done about it. This would be a still more staggering blow to the judiciary. What should the chief justice do?

Marshall had studied law only briefly and had no previous judicial experience, but in this crisis he first displayed the genius that was to mark him as a great judge. By right Marbury should have his commission, he announced. However, the Court could not require Madison to give it to him. Marbury's request for a mandamus had been based on an ambiguous clause in the Judiciary Act of 1789. That clause was unconstitu-

tional, Marshall declared, and therefore void. Congress could not legally give the Supreme Court the right to issue writs of mandamus in such circumstances.

With the skill and foresight of a chess grand master, Marshall turned what had looked like a trap into a triumph. By sacrificing the pawn, Marbury, he established the power of the Supreme Court to invalidate federal laws that conflicted with the Constitution. Jefferson could not check him because Marshall had *refused* power instead of throwing an anchor ahead, as Jefferson had feared. Yet he had certainly grappled a "further hold for future advances of power," and the president could do nothing to stop him.

The Marbury case made Jefferson more determined to strike at the Federalist-dominated courts. He decided to press for the impeachment of some of the more partisan judges. First he had the House of Representatives bring charges against District Judge John Pickering. Pickering was clearly deranged—he had frequently delivered profane and drunken harangues from the bench—and the Senate quickly voted to remove him. Then Jefferson went after a much larger fish, Samuel Chase, associate justice of the Supreme Court.

Chase had been prominent for decades, an early leader of the Sons of Liberty, a signer of the Declaration of Independence, active in the affairs of the Continental Congress. Washington had named him to the Supreme Court in 1796, and he had delivered a number of important opinions. But his handling of cases under the Sedition Act had been outrageously high-handed. Defense lawyers had become so exasperated as to throw down their briefs in disgust at some of his prejudiced rulings. However, the trial demonstrated that Chase's actions had not constituted the "high crimes and misdemeanors" required by the Constitution to remove a judge. Even Jefferson became disenchanted with the efforts of some of his more extreme followers and accepted Chase's acquittal with equanimity.

THE BARBARY PIRATES

Aside from these perhaps salutary setbacks, Jefferson's first term was a parade of triumphs. Although he cut back the army and navy sharply in order to save money, he temporarily escaped the consequences of leaving the country undefended because of the lull in the European war signalized by the Treaty of Amiens between Great Britain and France in March 1802. Despite the fact that he had only seven frigates, he even managed to fight a small naval war with the Barbary pirates without damage to American interests or prestige.

The North African Arab states of Morocco, Algiers, Tunis, and Tripoli had for decades made a

business of piracy, seizing vessels all over the Mediterranean and holding crews and passengers for ransom. The European powers found it simpler to pay them annual protection money than to crush them. Under Washington and Adams, the United States joined in the payment of this tribute; while large, the sums were less than the increased costs of insurance for shippers when the protection was not purchased.

Such spinelessness ran against Jefferson's grain. "When this idea comes across my mind, my faculties are absolutely suspended between indignation and impatience," he said. When the pasha of Tripoli tried to raise the charges, he balked. Tripoli then declared war in May 1801, and Jefferson dispatched a squadron to the Mediterranean.

In the words of one historian, the action was "halfhearted and ill-starred." The pirates were not overwhelmed, and a major American warship, the frigate *Philadelphia,* had to be destroyed after running aground off the Tripolitan coast. The payment of tribute continued until 1815. Just the same, America, though far removed from the pirate bases, was the only maritime nation that tried to resist the blackmail. Although the war failed to achieve Jefferson's purpose of ending the payments, the pasha agreed to a new treaty more favorable to the United States, and American sailors, led by Commodore Edward Preble, won valuable experience and a large portion of fame. The greatest hero was Lieutenant Stephen Decatur, who captured two pirate ships, led ten men in a daring raid on another in which he took on a gigantic sailor in a wild battle of cutlass against boarding pike,[1] and snatched the stricken *Philadelphia* from the pirates by sneaking aboard and setting it afire.

THE LOUISIANA PURCHASE

The Louisiana Purchase

The major achievements of Jefferson's first term had to do with the American West, and the greatest by far was the acquisition of the huge area between the Mississippi River and the Rocky Mountains. In a sense the purchase of this region, called Louisiana, was fortuitous, an accidental by-product of European political adjustments and the whim of Napoleon Bonaparte. Certainly Jefferson had not planned it, for in his inaugural address he had expressed the opinion that the country already had all the land it would need "for a thousand generations." It was nonetheless the perfectly logical—one might almost say inevitable—result of a long series of events in the history of the Mississippi Valley.

Along with every other American who had even a superficial interest in the West, Jefferson understood that the United States must have access to the mouth of the Mississippi and the city of New Orleans or eventually lose everything beyond the Appalachians. "There is on the globe one single spot, the possessor of which is our natural and habitual enemy," he was soon to write. "It is New Orleans." Thus when he learned shortly after his inauguration that Spain had given Louisiana back to France, he was immediately on his guard. Control of Louisiana by Spain, a "feeble" country with "pacific dispositions," could be tolerated; control by a resurgent France dominated by Napoleon, the greatest military genius of the age, was entirely different. Did Napoleon have designs on Canada? Did he perhaps mean to resume the old Spanish and British game of encouraging the Indians to harry the American frontier? And what now would be the status of Pinckney's precious treaty?

Deeply worried, the president instructed his minister to France, Robert R. Livingston, to seek assurances that American rights in New Orleans would be respected and to negotiate the purchase of West Florida in case that region had also been turned over to France.

Jefferson's concern was well founded; France was indeed planning new imperial ventures in North America. Immediately after settling its difficulties with the United States through the Convention of 1800, France signed the secret Treaty of San Ildefonso with Spain, which returned Louisiana to France. Napoleon hoped to use this region as a breadbasket for the French West Indian sugar plantations, just as colonies like Pennsylvania and Massachusetts had fed the British sugar islands before the Revolution.

However, the most important French island, Saint Domingue (Hispaniola), at the time occupied entirely by the nation of Haiti, had slipped from French control. During the French Revolution, the slaves of the island had revolted. In 1793 they were granted personal freedom, but they fought on under the leadership of the "Black Napoleon," a self-taught genius named Toussaint Louverture, and by 1801 the island was entirely in their hands. The original Napoleon, taking advantage of the slackening of war in Europe, dispatched an army of 20,000 men under General Charles Leclerc to reconquer it.

When Jefferson learned of the Leclerc expedition, he had no trouble divining its relationship to Louisiana. His uneasiness became outright alarm. In April 1802 he again urged Minister Livingston to attempt the purchase of New Orleans and Florida or, as an alternative, to buy a tract of land near the mouth of the Mississippi where a new port could be constructed. Of necessity, the mild-mannered, idealistic president now became an aggressive realist. If the

---

[1]Decatur killed the pirate by drawing a small pistol from his pocket as his opponent was about to skewer him.

▲ New Orleans in 1803, when the city was acquired—along with much of the modern United States—in the Louisiana Purchase. It was known as the Crescent City because of the way it hugged a curved section of the Mississippi River. In 1803, its population was about 8000, including 4000 whites, 2700 slaves, and about 1300 free "persons of color."

right of deposit could not be preserved through negotiation, it must be purchased with gunpowder, even if that meant acting in conjunction with the despised British. "The day that France takes possession of New Orleans," he warned, "we must marry ourselves to the British fleet and nation."

In October 1802 the Spanish, who had not yet actually turned Louisiana over to France, heightened the tension by suddenly revoking the right of deposit at New Orleans. We now know that the French had no hand in this action, but it was beyond reason to expect Jefferson or the American people to believe it at the time. With the West clamoring for relief, Jefferson appointed his friend and disciple James Monroe minister plenipotentiary and sent him to Paris with instructions to offer up to $10 million for New Orleans and Florida. If France refused, he and Livingston should open negotiations for a "closer connection" with the British.

The tension broke before Monroe even reached France. General Leclerc's Saint Domingue expedition ended in disaster. Although Toussaint surrendered, Haitian resistance continued. Yellow fever raged

through the French army; Leclerc himself fell to the fever, which wiped out practically his entire force.

When news of this calamity reached Napoleon early in 1803, he began to have second thoughts about reviving French imperialism in the New World. Without Saint Domingue, the wilderness of Louisiana seemed of little value. Napoleon was preparing a new campaign in Europe. He could no longer spare troops to recapture a rebellious West Indian island or to hold Louisiana against a possible British attack, and he needed money.

For some weeks the commander of the most powerful army in the world mulled the question without consulting anyone. Then, with characteristic suddenness, he made up his mind. On April 10 he ordered Foreign Minister Talleyrand to offer not merely New Orleans but all of Louisiana to the Americans. The next day Talleyrand summoned Livingston to his office on the rue du Bac and dropped this bombshell. Livingston was almost struck speechless but quickly recovered his composure. When Talleyrand asked what the United States would give for the province, he suggested the French equivalent of about $5 million. Tal-

leyrand pronounced the sum "too low" and urged Livingston to think about the subject for a day or two.

DOCUMENT

The Louisiana Purchase

Livingston faced a situation that no modern diplomat would ever have to confront. His instructions said nothing about buying an area almost as large as the entire United States, and there was no time to write home for new instructions. The offer staggered the imagination. Luckily, Monroe arrived the next day to share the responsibility. The two Americans consulted, dickered with the French, and finally agreed—they could scarcely have done otherwise—to accept the proposal. Early in May they signed a treaty. For 60 million francs—about $15 million—the United States was to have all of Louisiana.

No one knew exactly how large the region was or what it contained. When Livingston asked Talleyrand about the boundaries of the purchase, he replied: "I can give you no direction. You have made a noble bargain for yourselves, and I suppose you will make the most of it." Never, as the historian Henry Adams wrote, "did the United States government get so much for so little."

Napoleon's unexpected concession caused consternation in America, though there was never real doubt that the treaty would be ratified. Jefferson did not believe that the government had the power under the Constitution to add new territory or to grant American citizenship to the 50,000 residents of Louisiana by executive act, as the treaty required. He even drafted a constitutional amendment: "The province of Louisiana is incorporated with the United States and made part thereof," but his advisers convinced him that it would be dangerous to delay approval of the treaty until an amendment could be acted on by three-fourths of the states. Jefferson then suggested that the Senate ratify the treaty and submit an amendment afterward "confirming an act which the nation had not previously authorized." This idea was so obviously illogical that he quickly dropped it. Finally, he came to believe "that the less we say about constitutional difficulties the better." Since what he called "the good sense of our country" clearly wanted Louisiana, he decided to "acquiesce with satisfaction" while Congress overlooked the "metaphysical subtleties" of the problem and ratified the treaty.

DOCUMENT

Fisher Ames on the Louisiana Purchase

Some of the more partisan Federalists, who had been eager to fight Spain for New Orleans, attacked Jefferson for undermining the Constitution. One such critic described Louisiana contemptuously as a "Gallo-Hispano-Indian" collection of "savages and adventurers." Even Hamilton expressed hesitation about absorbing "this new, immense, unbounded world," though he had dreamed of seizing still larger domains himself. In the end Hamilton's nationalism reasserted itself, and he urged ratification of the treaty, as did such other important Federalists as John Adams and John Marshall. And in a way the Louisiana Purchase was as much Hamilton's doing as Jefferson's. Napoleon accepted payment in United States bonds, which he promptly sold to European investors. If Hamilton had not established the nation's credit so soundly, such a large issue could never have been so easily disposed of.

It was ironic—and a man as perceptive as Hamilton must surely have recognized the irony—that the acquisition of Louisiana ensured Jefferson's reelection and further contributed to the downfall of the Federalists. The purchase was popular even in the New England bastions of that party. While the negotiations were progressing in Paris, Jefferson had written of partisan political affairs: "If we can settle happily the difficulties of the Mississippi, I think we may promise ourselves smooth seas during our time." These words turned out to be no more accurate than most political predictions, but the Louisiana Purchase drove another spike into the Federalists' coffin.

THE FEDERALISTS DISCREDITED

The West and South were solidly for Jefferson, and the North was rapidly succumbing to his charm. The addition of new western states would soon further

▲ The 1790 slave rebellion in Haiti, led by Toussaint Louverture, caused thousands of French to flee the island; many settled in South Carolina. Their stories fueled fears of a slave uprising in the South.

reduce New England's power in national affairs. So complete did the Republican triumph seem that a handful of diehard Federalists in New England began to think of secession. Led by former secretary of state Timothy Pickering, a sour, implacable conservative, a group known as the Essex Junto organized in 1804 a scheme to break away from the Union and establish a "northern confederacy."

Even within the dwindling Federalist ranks the junto had little support. Nevertheless, Pickering and his friends pushed ahead, drafting a plan whereby, having captured political control of New York, they would take the entire Northeast out of the Union. Since they could not begin to win New York for anyone in their own ranks, they hit on the idea of supporting Vice President Aaron Burr, who was running against the "regular" Republican candidate for governor of New York. Although Burr did not promise to bring New York into their confederacy if elected, he encouraged them enough to win their backing. The foolishness of the plot was revealed in the April elections: Burr was overwhelmed by the regular Republican. The junto's scheme collapsed.

▲ Pistols used in the duel between Aaron Burr and Alexander Hamilton. Before the duel Hamilton's lawyer drew up a contract specifying the terms: the duelists were to shoot from 10 paces, and the barrels of the guns were to be no longer than eleven inches. Hamilton seems never to have discharged his pistol, but Burr took deadly aim, firing a .54-calibre ball that hit Hamilton in the chest. It ricocheted off his rib, punctured his liver, and lodged in his backbone. He died the next day.

The incident, however, had a tragic aftermath. Hamilton had campaigned against Burr, whom he considered "an embryo Caesar." When he continued after the election to cast aspersions on Burr's character (not a very difficult assignment, since Burr, despite being a grandson of the preacher Jonathan Edwards, frequently violated both the political and sexual mores of the day), Burr challenged him to a duel. It was well known that Hamilton opposed dueling in principle, his own son having been slain in such an encounter, and he certainly had no need to prove his courage. But he believed that his honor was at stake. The two met with pistols on July 11, 1804, at Weehawken, New Jersey, across the Hudson from New York City. Hamilton made no effort to hit the challenger, but Burr took careful aim. Hamilton fell, wounded; he died the next day. Thus a great, if enigmatic, man was cut off in his prime. His work, in a sense, had been completed, and his philosophy of government was being everywhere rejected, yet the nation's loss was large.

LEWIS AND CLARK

While the disgruntled Federalists dreamed of secession, Jefferson was planning the exploration of Louisiana and the region beyond. He especially hoped to find a water route to connect the upper Mississippi or its tributaries with the Pacific Ocean. Early in 1803 he got $2500 from Congress and obtained the permission of the French to send his exploring party across Louisiana. To command the expedition he appointed his private secretary, Meriwether Lewis, a young Virginian who had seen considerable service with the army in the West and who possessed, according to Jefferson, "a great mass of accurate information on all the subjects of nature." Lewis chose as his companion officer William Clark, another soldier (he had served with General Anthony Wayne at the Battle of Fallen Timbers) who had much experience in negotiating with Indians.

Jefferson, whose interest in the West was scientific as well as political, issued precise instructions to Lewis:

DOCUMENT

Thomas Jefferson to Meriwether Lewis

> Other objects worthy of notice will be, the soil and face of the country . . . the remains and accounts of any animals which may be deemed, or are extinct; the mineral productions of every kind . . . climate, as characterized by the thermometer, by the proportion of rainy, cloudy, and clear days, by lightning, hail, snow, ice, by the access and recess of frost, by the winds prevailing at different seasons, the dates at which particular plants put forth or lose their

flower or leaf, times of appearance of particular birds, reptiles or insects . . .

Scientific matters were inextricably intertwined with practical ones, such as the fur trade, for in his nature studies Jefferson concentrated on "useful" plants and animals. He was haunted by imperialistic visions of an expanding America that were not unlike those of Hamilton. After the consummation of the Louisiana Purchase, he instructed Lewis to try to establish official relations with the Indians in the Spanish territories beyond. Lewis should assure the tribes that "they will find in us faithful friends and protectors," Jefferson said. That the expedition would be moving across Spanish territory need not concern the travelers because of "the expiring state of Spain's interests there."

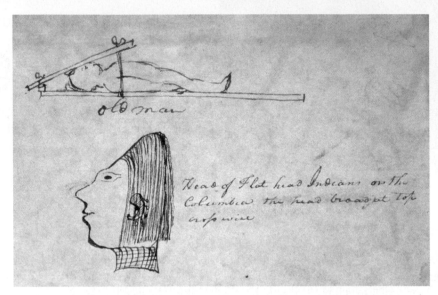

▲ The "Flat Head" (Chinook Indians) acquired their name through shaping in infancy, as shown in a diagram from the Lewis and Clark journals. More remarkable to the explorers than the shape of the Indian heads was the tribeswomen's open sexuality. "The young females are fond of the attention of our men and appear to meet the sincere approbation of their friends and connections for thus obtaining their favors," Captain Clark confided in his diary.

Lewis and Clark gathered a group of 48 experienced men near St. Louis during the winter of 1803–1804. In the spring they made their way slowly up the Missouri River in a 55-foot keelboat and two dugout canoes, called pirogues. By late fall they had reached what is now North Dakota, where they built a small station, Fort Mandan, and spent the winter there. In April 1805, having shipped back to the president more than 30 boxes of plants, minerals, animal skins and bones, and Indian artifacts, they struck out again toward the mountains, accompanied by a Shoshone woman, Sacajawea, and her French-Canadian husband, Toussaint Charbonneau, who acted as interpreters and guides. They passed the Great Falls of the Missouri and then clambered over the Continental Divide at Lemhi Pass in southwestern Montana. Soon thereafter the going became easier, and they descended to the Pacific by way of the Clearwater and Columbia Rivers, reaching their destination in November. They had hoped to return by ship, but during the long, damp winter not a single vessel appeared. In the spring of 1806 they headed back by land, reaching St. Louis on September 23.

DOCUMENT

Lewis and Clark Meet the Shoshone

The country greeted the news of their return with delight. Besides locating several passes across the Rockies, Lewis and Clark had established friendly relations with a great many Indian tribes to whom they presented gifts, medals, American flags, and a sales talk designed to promote peace and the fur trade. They brought back a wealth of data about the country and its resources. The journals kept by members of the group were published and, along with their accurate maps, became major sources for scientists, students, and future explorers. To Jefferson's great personal satisfaction, Lewis provided him with many specimens of the local wildlife, including two grizzly bear cubs, which he kept for a time in a stone pit in the White House lawn.

The success of Lewis and Clark did not open the gates of Louisiana very wide. Other explorers sent out by Jefferson accomplished far less. Thomas Freeman, an Irish-born surveyor, led a small party up the Red River but ran into a powerful Spanish force near the present junction of Arkansas, Oklahoma, and Texas and was forced to retreat. Between 1805 and 1807 Lieutenant Zebulon Pike explored the upper Mississippi Valley and the Colorado region. (He discovered but failed to scale the peak south of Denver that bears his name.) Pike eventually made his way to Santa Fe and the upper reaches of the Rio Grande, but he was not nearly so careful and acute an observer as Lewis and Clark were and consequently brought back much less information. By 1808 fur traders based at St. Louis were beginning to invade the Rockies, and by 1812 there were 75,000 people in the southern section of the new territory, which was admitted to the Union that year as the state of Louisiana. The northern region lay almost untouched until much later.

▶ *text continues on page 182*

Mapping the Past

A Water Route to the Pacific?

Jefferson's Dream

In the fall of 1802, President Thomas Jefferson asked the Spanish minister whether his government would take offense if a small group of Americans explored the sources of the Missouri River. The expedition, Jefferson assured the Spaniard, would have no purpose other than "the advancement of geography." The minister coolly replied that such an adventure "could not fail to give umbrage to our government." After the meeting, the diplomat promptly alerted his superiors in Madrid that Jefferson was "a lover of glory." The American president's goal, he wrote, was to find a water route to the Pacific, thus facilitating American settlement of the region.

The Spaniard was exactly right. Several months after his meeting with the Spanish minister, Jefferson sent a secret message to Congress. In it he requested an appropriation of $2500 for an expedition to determine whether the Missouri River connected, "possibly with a single portage," to the Western (Pacific) Ocean. Congress approved the resolution. Jefferson chose Meriwether Lewis, his private secretary, and William Clark, an army officer, to head the expedition.

Jefferson's belief in a water route to the Pacific via the Missouri was based on several sources. The first was a book published in 1763 by Simon le Page du Pratz, a French traveler. Du Pratz wrote that an Indian, Moncacht-Apé, followed the Missouri to its source, dragged a canoe over a short portage, and then paddled upon a "Beautiful River" (Belle Rivière) that emptied into a western ocean. A rendering of du Pratz's map appears below, left.

In 1784 Peter Pond, an employee of the North West Company, prepared a map based on similar reports by the company's fur traders (see map far right). They told him that the Missouri River originated within the

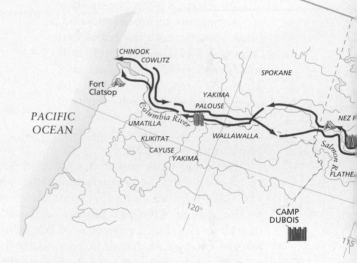

Le Page du Pratz, 1758

"Stony (Rocky) Mountains." Beyond them lay the Naberkistagen River, which emptied into the South Sea (presumably the Pacific Ocean). Inspired by such reports, Alexander Mackenzie, a Scotsman in the fur trade, crossed the Continental Divide further north and, after an easy portage, came to the Fraser River, which flowed into the Pacific. Although the raging Fraser was unsuited for commercial navigation, Mackenzie believed that a satisfactory route to the Pacific could be found. In 1801 he published a book advancing this hypothesis and urged Great Britain to develop the route that would ultimately join the Atlantic and the Pacific.

Jefferson, alarmed by British interest in the Northwest, immediately ordered a copy of Mackenzie's book. It arrived at Monticello in the summer

of 1802. Jefferson and Lewis poured over the maps. They compared Mackenzie's account with du Pratz's map, and also with a map compiled by Jedidiah Morse. Morse's map, too, suggested that the source of the Missouri nearly connected with the River of the West (see map right). Lewis's mission was to find the easiest route to the Pacific.

Lewis And Clark's Expedition

In the spring of 1804 Lewis and Clark started out with a group of 48 men up the Missouri. By late fall they had reached what is now North Dakota, where they built a small station, Fort Mandan, and spent the winter. In April 1805, they continued their westward journey on small boats and canoes. Among their party was Sacajawea, a 16-year-old Shoshone, then six months pregnant. In June they arrived at the Great Falls of the Missouri. It took them a month to make the portage—hardly the easy trip Moncacht-Apé had related. Nor did

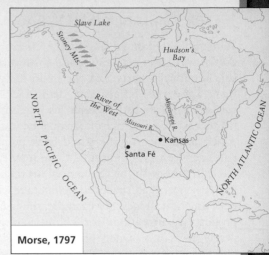

Morse, 1797

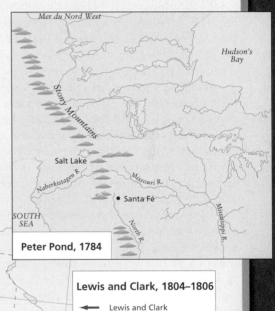

Peter Pond, 1784

the jagged mountains in the distance bear much resemblance to the Appalachians.

Yet Lewis, seemingly oblivious to the boulder-strewn streams and deep ravines that impeded his portage, remained optimistic. On August 10 he wrote that if the Columbia River beyond the mountains was like what he had so far encountered, "a communication across the continent by water will be practicable and safe." A week later, they came to the Shoshone settlement, where Sacajawea was reunited with some of her family. Then Lewis's party began the long climb into the Bitterroot Mountains, eventually coming to the Continental Divide near the Lemhi Pass. Beyond the summit, Lewis saw an endless range of "unknown formidable snow clad Mountains." A navigable water route through the Rockies did not exist.

Lewis and Clark, 1804–1806

←	Lewis and Clark
←	Lewis
←	Clark
←	Ordway and Gass
⛺	support camps
👥	encounter with Indians
✕	battle

JEFFERSONIAN DEMOCRACY

With the purchase of Louisiana, Jefferson completed the construction of the political institution known as the Republican party and the philosophy of government known as Jeffersonian democracy. From what sort of materials had he built his juggernaut? In part his success was a matter of personality; in the march of American democracy he stood halfway, temperamentally, between Washington and Andrew Jackson, perfectly in tune with the thinking of his times. The colonial American had practiced democracy without really believing in it; hence, for example, the maintenance of property qualifications for voting in regions where nearly everyone owned property. Stimulated by the libertarian ideas of the Revolution, Americans were rapidly adjusting their beliefs to conform with their practices. However, it took Jefferson, a man of large estates, possessed of the general prejudice in favor of the old-fashioned citizen rooted in the soil, yet deeply committed to majority rule, to oversee the transition.

Jefferson's marvelous talents as a writer help explain his success. He expounded his ideas in language that few people could resist. He had a remarkable facility for discovering practical arguments to justify his beliefs—as when he suggested that by letting everyone vote, elections would be made more honest because with large numbers going to the polls, bribery would become prohibitively expensive.

Jefferson prepared the country for democracy by proving that a democrat could establish and maintain a stable regime. The Federalist tyranny of 1798 was compounded of selfishness and stupidity, but it was also based in part on honest fears that an egalitarian regime would not protect the fabric of society from hotheads and crackpots. The impact of the French Revolution on conservative thinking in the mid-1790s cannot be overestimated. America had fought a seven-year revolution without executing a single Tory, yet during the few months that the Reign of Terror ravaged France, nearly 17,000 persons were officially put to death for political "crimes" and many thousands more were killed in civil disturbances. Worse, in the opinion of many, the French extremists had attempted to destroy Christianity, substituting for it a "cult of reason." They confiscated property, imposed price controls, and abolished slavery in the French colonies. Little wonder that many Americans feared that the Jeffersonians, lovers of France and of *liberté, égalité, fraternité* would try to remodel American society in a similar way.

Jefferson calmed these fears. "Pell-mell" might scandalize the British and Spanish ministers and a few locals, but it was scarcely revolutionary. The most partisan Federalist was hard put to see a Robespierre, leader during the Reign of Terror in France, in the amiable president scratching out state papers at his desk or chatting with a Kentucky congressman at a "republican" dinner party. Furthermore, Jefferson accepted Federalist ideas on public finance, even learning to live with Hamilton's bank. As a good democrat, he drew a nice distinction between his own opinions and the wishes of the majority, which he felt must always take priority. Even in his first inaugural he admitted that manufacturing and commerce were, along with agriculture, the "pillars of our prosperity," and while believing that these activities would thrive best when "left most free to individual enterprise," he accepted the principle that the government should protect them when necessary from "casual embarrassments." Eventually he gave his backing to modest proposals for spending federal money on roads, canals, and other projects that, according to his political philosophy, ought to have been left to the states and private individuals.

During his term the country grew and prospered, the commercial classes sharing in the bounty along with the farmers so close to Jefferson's heart. Blithely he set out to win the support of all who could vote. "It is material to the safety of Republicanism," he wrote in 1803, "to detach the mercantile interests from its enemies and incorporate them into the body of its friends."

Thus Jefferson undermined the Federalists all along the line. They had said that the country must pay a stiff price for prosperity and orderly government, and they demanded prompt payment in full, both in cash (taxes) and in the form of limitations on human liberty. Under Jefferson these much-desired goals had been achieved cheaply and without sacrificing freedom. A land whose riches could only be guessed at had been obtained without firing a shot and without burdening the people with new taxes. "What farmer, what mechanic, what laborer, ever sees a taxgatherer of the United States?" the president could ask in 1805, without a single Federalist rising to challenge him. Order without discipline, security without a large military establishment, prosperity without regulatory legislation, freedom without license—truly the Sage of Monticello appeared to have led his fellow Americans into a golden age.

THE BURR CONSPIRACY

Republican virtue seemed to have triumphed, both at home and abroad. But Jefferson soon found himself in trouble at home and abroad.

In part his difficulties arose from the extent of the Republican victory. In 1805 his Federalist opponents had no useful ideas, no intelligent leadership, no effective numbers. They held only a quarter of the seats

▲ This engraving by J. Stoner, *American Stage Wagon,* depicts the common mode of transportation along federal roads during the Jefferson administration.

in Congress. As often happens in such situations, lack of opposition weakened party discipline and encouraged factionalism among the Republicans.

The Republican who caused Jefferson the most trouble was Aaron Burr, and the president was partly to blame for the difficulty. After their contest for the presidency in 1801, Jefferson pursued Burr vindictively, depriving him of federal patronage in New York and replacing him as the 1804 Republican vice presidential candidate with Governor George Clinton, Burr's chief rival in the state.

While still vice president, Burr began to flirt with treason. He approached Anthony Merry, the British minister in Washington, and offered to "effect a separation of the Western part of the United States." His price was £110,000 and the support of a British fleet off the mouth of the Mississippi. The British did not fall in with his scheme, but Burr went ahead nonetheless. Exactly what he had in mind has long been in dispute. Certainly he dreamed of acquiring a western empire for himself; whether he intended to wrest it from the United States or from Spanish territories beyond Louisiana is unclear. He joined forces with General James Wilkinson, whom Jefferson had appointed governor of the Louisiana Territory, who was secretly in the pay of Spain.

The opening of the Ohio and Mississippi valleys had not totally satisfied land-hungry Westerners. In 1806 Burr and Wilkinson had no difficulty raising a small force at a place called Blennerhassett Island, in the Ohio River. Some six dozen men began to move downriver toward New Orleans under Burr's command. Whether the objective was New Orleans or some part of Mexico, the scheme was clearly illegal. For some reason, however—possibly because he was incapable of loyalty to anyone[2]—Wilkinson betrayed Burr to Jefferson at the last moment. Burr tried to escape to Spanish Florida but was captured in February 1807, brought to Richmond, Virginia, under guard, and charged with high treason.

Any president will deal summarily with traitors, but Jefferson's attitude during Burr's trial reveals the depth of his hatred. He "made himself a party to the prosecution," personally sending evidence to the United States attorney who was handling the case and offering blanket pardons to associates of Burr who would agree to turn state's evidence. In stark contrast, Chief Justice Marshall, presiding at the trial in his capacity as judge of the circuit court, repeatedly showed favoritism to the prisoner.

In this contest between two great men at their worst, Jefferson as a vindictive executive and Marshall

---

[2]John Randolph said of him: "Wilkinson is the only man that I ever saw who was from the bark to the very core a villain."

▲ John Randolph, a Congressman from Roanoke, Virginia, was the most prominent of the Republican critics of Jefferson. He made a fetish of preserving states' rights against invasion by the central government. "Asking one of the States to surrender part of her sovereignty is like asking a lady to surrender part of her chastity," he remarked in one of his typical epigrams.

as a prejudiced judge, the victory went to the judge. Organizing "a military assemblage," Marshall declared on his charge to the jury, "was not a levying of war." To "advise or procure treason" was not in itself treason. Unless two independent witnesses testified to an overt act of treason as thus defined, the accused should be declared innocent. The jury, deliberating only 25 minutes, found Burr not guilty.

Throughout the trial, Burr never lost his self-possession. He seemed to view the proceedings with amiable cynicism. Then, since he was wanted either for murder or for treason in six states, he went into exile in Europe. Some years later he returned to New York, where he spent an unregenerate old age, fathering two illegitimate children in his seventies and being divorced by his second wife on grounds of adultery at 80.

The Burr affair was a blow to Jefferson's prestige; it left him more embittered against Marshall and the federal judiciary, and it added nothing to his reputation as a statesman.

NAPOLEON AND THE BRITISH

Jefferson's difficulties with Burr may be traced at least in part to the purchase of Louisiana, which, empty and unknown, excited the greed of men like Burr and Wilkinson. But problems infinitely more serious were also related to Louisiana.

Napoleon had jettisoned Louisiana to clear the decks before resuming the battle for control of Europe. This war had the effect of stimulating the American economy, for the warring powers needed American goods and American vessels. Shipbuilding boomed; foreign trade, which had quintupled since 1793, nearly doubled again between 1803 and 1805. By the summer of 1807, however, the situation had changed: a most unusual stalemate had developed in the war.

In October 1805 Britain's Horatio Nelson demolished the combined Spanish and French fleets in the Battle of Trafalgar, off the coast of Spain. Napoleon, now at the summit of his powers, quickly redressed the balance, smashing army after army thrown against him by Great Britain's continental allies. By 1807 he was master of Europe, while the British controlled the seas around the Continent. Neither nation could strike directly at the other.

They therefore resorted to commercial warfare, striving to disrupt each other's economy. Napoleon struck first with his Berlin Decree (November 1806), which made "all commerce and correspondence" with Great Britain illegal. The British retaliated with a series of edicts called Orders in Council, blockading most continental ports and barring from them all foreign vessels unless they first stopped at a British port and paid customs duties. Napoleon then issued his Milan Decree (December 1807), declaring any vessel that submitted to the British rules "to have become English property" and thus subject to seizure.

The blockades and counterblockades seemed designed to stop commerce completely, yet this was not the case. Napoleon's "Continental System" was supposed to make Europe self-sufficient and isolate Great Britain, yet he was willing to sell European products to the British (if the price was right); his chief objective was to deprive them of their continental markets. The British were ready to sell anything on the Continent, and to allow others to do so too, provided they first paid a toll. The Continental System was, in John Quincy Adams's pithy phrase, "little more than extortion wearing the mask of prohibition," and British policy was equally immoral—a kind of piracy practiced with impunity because the Royal Navy controlled the seas.

When war first broke out between Britain and France in 1792, the colonial trade of both sides had fallen largely into American hands because the danger of capture drove many belligerent merchant vessels

from the seas. This commerce had engaged Americans in some devious practices. Under the Rule of War of 1756, the British denied neutrals the right in time of war to engage in trade from which they were barred by mercantilist regulations in time of peace. If an American ship carried sugar from the French colony of Martinique to France, for example, the British claimed the right to capture it because such traffic was normally confined to French ships by French law.

To avoid this risk, American merchants brought the sugar first to the United States, a legal peacetime voyage under French mercantilism. Then they reshipped it to France as American sugar. Since the United States was a neutral nation and sugar was not contraband of war, the Americans expected the British to let their ships pass with impunity. Continental products likewise reached the French West Indies by way of United States ports, and the American government encouraged the traffic in both directions by refunding customs duties on foreign products reshipped within a year. Between 1803 and 1806 the annual value of foreign products reexported from the United States jumped from $13 million to $60 million! In 1806 the United States exported 47 million pounds of coffee—none, of course, of local origin. An example of this type of trade is offered by Samuel Eliot Morison in his *Maritime History of Massachusetts*:

The brig *Eliza Hardy* of Plymouth enters her home port from Bordeaux, on May 20, 1806, with a cargo of claret wine. Part of it is immediately reexported to Martinique in the schooner *Pilgrim* which also carries a consignment of brandy that came from Alicante in the brig *Commerce* and another of gin that came from Rotterdam in the barque *Hannah* of Plymouth. The rest of the *Eliza Hardy*'s claret is taken to Philadelphia by coasters, and thence reexported in seven different vessels to Havana, Santiago de Cuba, St. Thomas, and Batavia.

This underhanded commerce irritated the British. In the cases of the *Essex* and the *William* (1805–1806), a British judge, Sir William Grant, decreed that American ships could no longer rely on "mere voluntary *ceremonies*" to circumvent the Rule of 1756. Thus just when Britain and France were cracking down on direct trade by neutrals, Britain determined to halt the American reexport trade, thereby gravely threatening American prosperity.

THE IMPRESSMENT CONTROVERSY

More dismaying were the cruel indignities being visited on American seamen by the British practice of impressment. Under British law any able-bodied subject could be drafted for service in the Royal Navy in an emergency. Normally, when the commander of a warship found himself shorthanded, he put into a British port and sent a "press gang" ashore to round up the necessary men in harborside pubs. When far from home waters, he might hail any passing British merchant ship and commandeer the necessary men, though this practice was understandably unpopular in British maritime circles. He might also stop a *neutral* merchant vessel on the high seas and remove any British subject. Since the United States owned by far the largest merchant fleet among the neutrals, its vessels bore the brunt of this practice.

Impressment had been a cause of Anglo-American conflict for many years; American pride suffered every time a vessel carrying the flag was forced to back topsails and heave to at the command of a British man-of-war. Still more galling was the contemptuous behavior of British officers when they boarded American ships. In 1796 an American captain named Figsby was stopped twice by British warships while carrying a cargo of poultry and other livestock to Guadeloupe. First a privateer, the *Sea Nymph*, impressed two of his crew, confiscated most of his chickens, "abused" him, and stole his ship's flag. Two days later HMS *Unicorn* took another of Figsby's men, the rest of his poultry, four sheep, and three hogs.

Many British captains made little effort to be sure they were impressing British subjects; any likely looking lad might be taken when the need was great. Furthermore, there were legal questions in dispute. When did an English immigrant become an American? When he was naturalized, the United States claimed. Never, the British retorted; "once an Englishman, always an Englishman."

America's lax immigration laws compounded the problem. A foreigner could become a citizen with ridiculous ease; those too impatient to wait the required five years could purchase false naturalization papers for as little as a dollar. Because working conditions in the American merchant marine were superior to those of the British, at least 10,000 British-born sailors were serving on American ships. Some became American citizens legally; others obtained false papers; some admitted to being British subjects; some were deserters from the Royal Navy. From the British point of view, all were liable to impressment.

The Jefferson administration conceded the right of the British to impress their own subjects from American merchant ships. When naturalized Americans were impressed, however, the administration was irritated, and when native-born Americans were taken, it became incensed. Impressment, Secretary of State Madison said in 1807, was "anomalous in principle . . . grievous in practice, and . . . abominable in

▲ Completed in 1797, the 44-gun *Constitution*, one of the largest ships in the U.S. Navy, was no match for the largest British warships, which had twice as many cannon. The *Constitution*'s subsequent success (and the reason that it was preserved) was largely due to the skill of American captains and sailors.

abuse." Between 1803 and 1812 at least 5000 sailors were snatched from the decks of United States vessels and forced to serve in the Royal Navy. Most of them—estimates run as high as three out of every four—were Americans.

The British did not claim the right to impress native-born Americans, and when it could be proved that boarding officers had done so, the men in question were released by higher authority. During the course of the controversy, the British authorities freed 3800 impressed Americans, which suggests that many more were seized. However, the British refused to abandon impressment. "The Pretension advanced by Mr. Madison that the American Flag should protect every Individual sailing under it," one British foreign secretary explained, "is too extravagant to require any serious Refutation."

The combination of impressment, British interference with the reexport trade, and the general harassment of neutral commerce instituted by both Great Britain and France would have perplexed the most informed and hardheaded of leaders, and in dealing with these problems Jefferson was neither informed nor hardheaded. He believed it much wiser to stand up for one's rights than to compromise, yet he hated the very thought of war. Perhaps, being a Southerner, he was less sensitive than he might have been to the needs of New England commercial interests. While the American merchant fleet passed 600,000 tons and continued to grow at an annual rate of over 10 percent, Jefferson kept only a skeleton navy on active service, despite the fact that the great powers were fighting a worldwide, no-holds-barred

war. Instead of building a navy that other nations would have to respect, he relied on a tiny fleet of frigates and a swarm of gunboats that were useless against the Royal Navy—" a macabre monument," in the words of one historian, "to his hasty, ill-digested ideas" about defense.[3]

THE EMBARGO ACT

The frailty of Jefferson's policy became obvious once the warring powers began to attack neutral shipping in earnest. Between 1803 and 1807 the British seized more than 500 American ships, Napoleon more than 200 more. The United States could do nothing.

The ultimate in frustration came on June 22, 1807, off Norfolk, Virginia. The American 46-gun frigate *Chesapeake* had just left port for patrol duty in the Mediterranean. Among its crew were a British sailor who had deserted from HMS *Halifax* and three Americans who had been illegally impressed by the captain of HMS *Melampus* and had later escaped. The *Chesapeake* was barely out of sight of land when HMS *Leopard* (56 guns) approached and signaled it to heave to. Thinking that *Leopard* wanted to make some routine communication, Captain James Barron did so. A British officer came aboard and demanded that the four "deserters" be handed over to him. Barron refused, whereupon as soon as the officer was back on board, *Leopard* opened fire on the unsuspecting American ship, killing three sailors. Barron had to surrender. The "deserters" were seized, and then the crippled *Chesapeake* was allowed to limp back to port.

The attack was in violation of international law, for no nation claimed the right to impress sailors from warships. The British government admitted this, though it delayed making restitution for years. The American press clamored for war, but the country had nothing to fight with. Jefferson contented himself with ordering British warships out of American territorial waters. However, he was determined to put a stop to the indignities being heaped on the flag by Great Britain and France. The result was the Embargo Act.

---

[3]The gunboats had performed effectively against the Barbary pirates, but Jefferson was enamored of them mainly because they were cheap. A gunboat cost about $10,000 to build, a frigate well over $300,000.

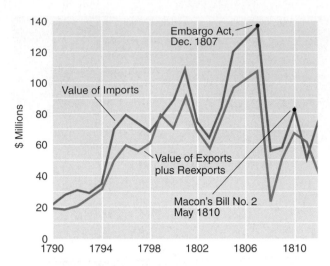

▲ **American Foreign Trade, 1790–1812**
The embargo's effects are shown graphically here. The space between the upper (import) and the lower (export) line indicates a persistent foreign-trade deficit.

The Embargo Act prohibited all exports. American vessels could not clear for any foreign port, and foreign vessels could do so only if empty. Importing was not forbidden, but few foreign ships would come to the United States if they had to return without a cargo. Although the law was sure to injure the American economy, Jefferson hoped that it would work in two ways to benefit the nation. By keeping U.S. merchant ships off the seas, it would end all chance of injury to them and to the national honor. By cutting off American goods and markets, it would put great economic pressure on Britain and France to moderate policies toward American shipping. The fact that boycotts had repeatedly wrested concessions from the British during the crises preceding the Revolution was certainly in Jefferson's mind when he devised the embargo.

Seldom has a law been so bitterly resented and resisted by a large segment of the public. It demanded of the maritime interests far greater sacrifices than they could reasonably be expected to make. Massachusetts-owned ships alone were earning over $15 million a year in freight charges by 1807, and Bay State merchants w0ere making far larger gains from the buying and selling of goods. Foreign commerce was the most expansive force in the economy,

the chief reason for the nation's prosperity. As John Randolph remarked in a typical sally, the administration was trying "to cure the corns by cutting off the toes."

The Embargo Act had catastrophic effects. Exports fell from $108 million in 1807 to $22 million in 1808, imports from $138 million to less than $57 million. Prices of farm products and manufactured goods reacted violently; seamen were thrown out of work; merchants found their businesses disrupted.

How many Americans violated the law is difficult to determine, but they were ingenious at discovering ways to do so. The most obvious way was to smuggle goods back and forth between Canada and the northeastern states. As James Madison recalled in later years, the political boundary lost all significance. People on both sides made the region "a world of itself," treating the Embargo Act as though the laws of Congress did not apply to them.

As for ocean commerce, American ships made hastily for blue water before the machinery of enforcement could be put into operation, not to return until the law was repealed. Shipping between American ports had not been outlawed, and coasting vessels were allowed to put into foreign ports when in distress. Suddenly, mysterious storms began to drive experienced skippers leagues off their courses, some as far as Europe. The brig *Commerce* en route from Massachusetts to New Orleans, was "forced" by a shortage of water to make for Havana. Having replenished its casks, the brig exchanged its cargo for sugar.

▲ The Ograbme ("embargo" spelled backward), a unique snapping turtle created by cartoonist Alexander Anderson, effectively frustrates an American tobacco smuggler.

▲ The East India Wharf in Salem, Massachusetts in 1806. One of the richest cities in the nation, Salem had a fleet of 200 ships and thirty wharves. Its wealth was chiefly derived from a trade in tea and textiles with India.

The law permitted merchants with property abroad to send ships to fetch it. About 800 ships went off on such errands. Lawbreakers were difficult to punish. In the seaport towns juries were no more willing to convict anyone of violating the Embargo Act than their fathers had been to convict those charged with violating the Townshend Acts. A mob at Gloucester, Massachusetts, destroyed a revenue cutter in the same spirit that Rhode Islanders exhibited in 1772 when they burned the *Gaspee*.

Surely the embargo was a mistake. The United States ought either to have suffered the indignities heaped on its vessels for the sake of profits or, by constructing a powerful navy, made it dangerous for the belligerents to treat its merchant ships so roughly. Jefferson was too proud to choose the former alternative, too parsimonious to choose the latter. Instead he applied harsher and harsher regulations in a futile effort to accomplish his purpose. Militiamen patrolled the Canadian border; revenuers searched out smuggled goods without proper warrants. The illegal trade continued, and in his last months as president Jefferson simply gave up. Even then he would not admit that the embargo was a fiasco and urge its repeal. Only in Jefferson's last week in office did a leaderless Congress finally abolish it, substituting the Non-Intercourse Act, which forbade trade only with Great Britain and France and authorized the president to end the boycott against either power by proclamation when and if it stopped violating the rights of Americans.

Thus Jefferson's political career ended on a sour note. Several weeks after he had left office and returned to Monticello, he privately advised his successor, James Madison, to trust his own judgment to govern because the people readily succumbed to "the floating lies of the day."

MILESTONES

1800	Jefferson is elected president (Revolution of 1800)	1804–1806	Lewis and Clark explore West
1801	Judiciary Act of 1801 allows Adams to appoint many Federalist judges	1806	Aaron Burr schemes to take land in West during Burr Conspiracy
1801–1805	U.S. wages war against Barbary pirates in North Africa	1806–1807	Napoleon issues Berlin and Milan decrees in order to disrupt British shipping and economy
1803	Supreme Court declares part of Judiciary Act of 1789 unconstitutional (*Marbury* v. *Madison*)	1807	HMS *Leopard* attacks USS *Chesapeake*
	Jefferson negotiates Louisiana Purchase with France		Embargo Act prohibits all exports
1804	Aaron Burr kills Alexander Hamilton in duel	1809	Non-Intercourse Act forbids trade with Great Britain and France
	Jefferson is reelected		

SUPPLEMENTARY READING

No student interested in Jefferson's political and social philosophy should miss sampling his writings. A useful compilation is Merrill D. Peterson, ed., *Thomas Jefferson* (1984). Lance Banning, *The Jeffersonian Persuasion* (1978), is valuable, as are the books on Jefferson mentioned in Debating the Past (p. 171).

For the election of 1800, see Bernard A. Weisberger, *America Afire* (2000). Arnold Rogow, *Fatal Friendship* (1998), describes the relationship of Hamilton and Burr; see also Joanne B. Freeman, *Affairs of Honor* (2001) on politics and dueling more generally.

For a general treatment of the Jeffersonian era, consult Marshall Smelser, *The Democratic Republic* (1968). On the parties of the era, see James Roger Sharp, *American Politics in the Early Republic* (1993) and N. E. Cunningham, Jr., *The Jeffersonian Republicans in Power* (1963); a useful monograph is Anthony F. C. Wallace, *Jefferson and the Indians* (1999).

Jefferson's battle with the judges can be followed in R. E. Ellis, *The Jeffersonian Crisis* (1971). For *Marbury* v. *Madison*, see J. A. Garraty, ed., *Quarrels That Have Shaped the Constitution* (1964), and D. O. Dewey's more detailed *Marshall Versus Jefferson* (1970) as well as R. Kent Newmeyer, *John Marshall and the Heroic Age of the Supreme Court* (2001).

Thomas Fleming, *The Louisiana Purchase* (2003) is a brief, clear account; Jon Kukla, *A Wilderness So Immense: The Louisiana Purchase and the Destiny of America* (2003) argues that the region was acquired chiefly as a place for resettling Indians.

An excellent general treatment of western exploration is contained in R. A. Billington, *Westward Expansion* (1967). On Lewis and Clark, see Stephen E. Ambrose, *Undaunted Courage* (1996). Thomas P. Slaughter, *Exploring Lewis and Clark* (2003) is a scholarly examination of the explorers' writings.

The best account of the neutral rights question is Bradford Perkins, *Prologue to War* (1961).

SUGGESTED WEBSITES

Thomas Jefferson
http://www.pbs.org/jefferson/
This site, the companion to the PBS series on Jefferson, includes material on how people understand Jefferson today.

Lewis and Clark—The PBS Website
http://www.pbs.org/lewisandclark
This is a companion site to Ken Burns's film, containing a timeline of the expedition, a collection of related links, a bibliography, and more than 800 minutes of unedited, full-length Real Player interviews with seven experts featured in the film.

Thomas Jefferson Resources Online
http://etext.virginia.edu/jefferson/
"Mr. Jefferson's University," The University of Virginia, provides resources about Jefferson and his times.

The Jefferson Home
http://www.monticello.org/
This site explores Jefferson's gifted mind through an examination of Monticello, Jefferson's unique home.

▼ "Hail, Bright Aurora" (c.1815), by an unknown artist. Aurora, the goddess of dawn, represents the ascent of the American nation. The metaphor may have come from the poem, "An Hymn to the Morning," by Phyllis Wheatley, a black slave: "Aurora hail, and all the thousand dies/ Which deck thy progress through the vaulted skies."

CHAPTER CONTENTS

MADISON IN POWER

It is a measure of Jefferson's popularity and of the political ineptitude of the Federalists that the Republicans won the election of 1808 handily despite the embargo. James Madison got 122 of the 173 electoral votes for the presidency, and the party carried both houses of Congress, although by reduced majorities.

In his inaugural address, Madison observed that the "present situation" of the United States was "full of difficulties" and that war continued to rage among European powers. Yet he assumed the presidency, he said, "with no other discouragement than what springs from my own inadequacy." The content of the speech was as modest as its delivery; virtually no one could hear it.

Madison was a small, neat, rather precise person, narrower in his interests than Jefferson but in many ways a deeper thinker. He was more conscientious in the performance of his duties and more consistent in adhering to his principles. Ideologically, however, they were as close as two active and intelligent people could be. Madison had no better solution to offer for the problem of the hour than had Jefferson. The Non-Intercourse Act proved difficult to enforce—once an American ship left port, there was no way to prevent the skipper from steering for England or France—and it exerted little economic pressure on the British, who continued to seize American vessels.

Late in 1809, at the urging of Secretary of the Treasury Gallatin, who was concerned because the government was operating at a deficit, Representative Nathaniel Macon of North Carolina introduced a bill permitting American ships to go anywhere but closing United States ports to the ships of Britain and France. After protracted bickering in Congress, this measure was replaced by another, known as Macon's Bill No. 2, which removed all restrictions on commerce with France and Britain, although French and British warships were still barred from American waters. The bill authorized the president to reapply the principle of nonintercourse to either of the major powers if the other should "cease to violate the neutral commerce of the United States." This bill became law in May 1810.

The volume of United States commerce with the British Isles swiftly zoomed to pre-embargo levels. Trade with France remained much more limited because of the British fleet. Napoleon therefore announced that the Berlin and Milan decrees would be revoked in November with the understanding that Great Britain would abandon its own restrictive policies. Treating this ambiguous proposal as a statement of French policy (which it decidedly was not), and hoping to win concessions from the British, Madison reapplied the nonintercourse policy to Great Britain. Napoleon, having thus tricked Madison into closing American ports to British ships and goods, continued to seize American ships and cargoes whenever it suited him to do so.

The British grimly refused to modify the Orders in Council unless it could be shown that the French had actually repealed the Berlin and Milan decrees—and this despite mounting complaints from their own businessmen that the new American nonimportation policy was cutting off a major market for their manufactures. Madison, on the other hand, could not afford either to admit that Napoleon had deceived him or to reverse American policy still another time. Reluctantly he came to the conclusion that unless Britain repealed the Orders, the United States must declare war.

TECUMSEH AND INDIAN RESISTANCE

There were other reasons for fighting besides British violations of neutral rights. The Indians were again restive, and western farmers believed that the British in Canada were egging them on. This had been true in the past but was no longer the case in 1811 and 1812. American domination of the southern Great Lakes region was no longer in question. Canadian officials had no desire to force a showdown between the Indians and the Americans, for that could have but one result. Aware of their own vulnerability, the Canadians wanted to preserve Indian strength in case war should break out between Great Britain and the United States.

American political leaders tended to believe that Indians should be encouraged to become farmers and to copy the "civilized" ways of whites. However, no government had been able to control the frontiersmen, who by bribery, trickery, and force were driving the tribes back year after year from the rich lands of the Ohio Valley. General William Henry Harrison, governor of the Indiana Territory, a tough, relentless soldier, kept constant pressure on them. He wrested land from one tribe by promising it aid against a traditional enemy, from another as a penalty for having murdered a white man, from others by corrupting a few chiefs. Harrison justified his sordid behavior by citing the end in view—that "one of the fairest portions of the globe" be secured as "the seat of civilization, of science, and of true religion." The "wretched savages" should not be allowed to stand in the path of this worthy objective. As early as 1805 it was clear that unless something drastic was done, Harrison's aggressiveness, together with the corroding effects of white civilization, would soon obliterate the tribes.

At this point the Shawnee chief, Tecumseh, made a bold and imaginative effort to reverse the trend by binding all the tribes east of the Mississippi into a great confederation. Traveling from the Wisconsin country to the Floridas, he persuaded tribe after tribe to join him. "Let the white race perish," Tecumseh declared. "They seize your land; they corrupt your women. . . . Back whence they came, upon a trail of blood, they must be driven!"

To Tecumseh's political movement his brother Tenskwatawa, known as "The Prophet," added the force of a moral crusade. Instead of aping white customs, the Prophet said, Indians must give up white ways, white clothes, and white liquor and reinvigorate their own culture. Ceding lands to the whites must stop because the Great Spirit intended that the land be used in common by all.

▲ As a young man Tecumseh *(left)* was a superb hunter and warrior; his younger brother, Tenskwatawa *(right)* was awkward and inept with weapons; he accidentally gouged out his right eye with an arrow. In 1805 he had a religious vision, became known as "The Prophet," and inspired Tecumseh's warriors.

The Prophet was a fanatic who saw visions and claimed to be able to control the movement of heavenly bodies. Tecumseh, however, possessed true genius. A powerful orator and a great organizer, he had deep insight into the needs of his people. Harrison himself said of Tecumseh: "He is one of those uncommon geniuses which spring up occasionally to produce revolutions and overturn the established order of things." The two brothers made a formidable team. By 1811 thousands of Indians were organizing to drive the whites off their lands. Alarms swept through the West.

With about a thousand soldiers, General Harrison marched boldly against the brothers' camp at Prophetstown, where Tippecanoe Creek joins the Wabash, in Indiana. Tecumseh was away recruiting men, and the Prophet recklessly ordered an assault on Harrison's camp outside the village on November 7, 1811. When the white soldiers held their ground despite the Prophet's magic, the Indians lost confidence and fell back. Harrison then destroyed Prophetstown.

While the Battle of Tippecanoe was pretty much a draw, it disillusioned the Indians and shattered their confederation. Frontier warfare continued, but in the disorganized manner of former times. Like all such fighting it was brutal and bloody.

Unwilling as usual to admit that their own excesses were the chief cause of the trouble, the settlers directed their resentment at the British in Canada. "This combination headed by the Shawanese prophet is a British scheme," a resolution adopted by the citizens of Vincennes, Indiana, proclaimed. As a result, the cry for war with Great Britain rang along the frontier.

DEPRESSION AND LAND HUNGER

Some Westerners pressed for war because they were suffering an agricultural depression. The prices they received for their wheat, tobacco, and other products in the markets of New Orleans were falling, and they attributed the decline to the loss of foreign markets and the depredations of the British. American commercial restrictions had more to do with the western depression than the British, and in any case the slow and cumbersome transportation and distribution system that western farmers were saddled with was the major cause of their difficulties. But the farmers were no more inclined to accept these explanations than they were to absolve the British from responsibility for the Indian difficulties. If only the seas were free,

DEBATING THE PAST

How did Indians and settlers interact? Two Indians *(above)* gaze at a frontier settlement. In 1893 historian Frederick Jackson Turner, the most important historian of his era, credited frontier conditions for creating the stalwart individualists that made the United States distinctive. In his view, the frontier had not been a particular zone or region, but "the outer edge of the wave—the meeting point between savagery and civilization." The nature of the interaction between Indians and settlers was one-sided: the Indians fell back. But in recent decades, historians have challenged this concept not only because it disparaged Indian societies and cultures, but also because it ignored the many ways in which Indians and settlers interacted. Abandoning the concept of an Indian-settler frontier, Richard White (1991) described a "middle ground" and James Merrell (1999) the "edge of the woods," a region where Indians and settlers resolved disputes, traded goods, and exchanged ideas. The concept of a "middle ground" put Indians and settlers on equal footing. But that also may be its chief difficulty. Daniel K. Richter (2001) and Jane T. Merritt (2003) showed that while Indians preferred to co-exist with the settlers rather than fight them, by the eighteenth century raw power prevailed—as did, usually, the settlers.

Frederick Jackson Turner, "The Significance of the Frontier in American History" (1893), Patricka Nelson Limerick, *The Legacy of Conquest* (1987), Richard White, *The Middle Ground* (1991), James Merrell, *Into the Woods* (1999), Daniel K. Richter, *Facing East from Indian Country* (2001), Gregory H. Nobles, *American Frontiers* (1997), Jane T. Merritt, *At the Crossroads* (2003).

they reasoned, costs would go down, prices would rise, and prosperity would return.

To some extent western expansionism also heightened the war fever. The West contained immense tracts of virgin land, but Westerners wanted more. Canada would surely fall to American arms in the event of war, the frontiersmen believed. So, apparently, would Florida, for Spain was now Britain's ally. Florida in itself provided no cause for a war, for it was sure to fall into American hands before long. In 1810

Madison had snapped up the extreme western section without eliciting any effective response from Spain.

So it was primarily because of Canada, nearby and presumably vulnerable, that Westerners wanted war. President Madison probably regarded an attack on Canada as a way to force the British to respect neutral rights. Still more important in Madison's mind, if the United States conquered Canada, Britain's hope of obtaining food in Canada for its West Indian sugar islands would be shattered. Then it would have to end

its hateful assaults and restrictions on American merchant ships or the islands' economy would collapse.

But Westerners, and many Easterners too, were more patriots than imperialists or merchants in 1811 and 1812. When the "War Hawks" (their young leaders in Congress) called for war against Great Britain, they did so because they saw no other way to defend the national honor and force repeal of the Orders in Council. The choice seemed to lie between war and surrender of true independence. As Madison put it, to bow to British policy would be to "recolonize" American foreign commerce.

OPPONENTS OF WAR

Large numbers of people, however, thought that a war against Great Britain would be a national calamity. Some Federalists would have resisted anything the administration proposed; Congressman Josiah Quincy of Massachusetts declared that he "could not be kicked" into the war, which he considered a cowardly, futile, and unconstitutional business designed primarily to ensure the reelection of Madison. (Quincy saw no inconsistency between this opinion and his conviction that Madison was a pacifist.) According to Quincy the War Hawks were "backwoodsmen" willing to wage a "cruel, wanton, senseless and wicked" war in order to swallow up Canada.

But other people based their objections on economics and a healthy realism. No shipowner could view with equanimity the idea of taking on the largest navy in the world. Such persons complained sincerely enough about impressment and the Orders in Council, but war seemed worse to them by far. Self-interest led them to urge patience.

Such a policy would have been wise, for Great Britain did not represent a real threat to the United States. British naval officers were high-handed, officials in London complacent, British diplomats in Washington second-rate and obtuse. Yet language, culture, and strong economic ties bound the two countries. Napoleon, on the other hand, represented a tremendous potential danger. He had offhandedly turned over Louisiana, but even Jefferson, the chief beneficiary of his largess, hated everything he stood for. Jefferson called Napoleon "an unprincipled tyrant who is deluging the continent of Europe with blood."

No one understood the Napoleonic danger to America more clearly than the British; part of the stubbornness and arrogance of their maritime policy grew out of their conviction that Napoleon was a threat to all free nations. The *Times* of London declared: "The Alps and the Apennines of America are the British Navy. If ever that should be removed, a short time will

suffice to establish the headquarters of a [French] Duke-Marshal at Washington." Yet by going to war with Britain, the United States was aiding Napoleon.

What made the situation even more unfortunate was the fact that by 1812 conditions had changed in England in a way that made a softening of British maritime policy likely. A depression caused chiefly by the increasing effectiveness of Napoleon's Continental System was plaguing the country. Manufacturers, blaming the slump on the loss of American markets, were urging repeal of the Orders in Council. Gradually, though with exasperating slowness, the government prepared to yield. On June 23, after a change of ministries, the new foreign secretary, Lord Castlereagh, suspended the Orders. Five days earlier, alas, the United States had declared war.

THE WAR OF 1812

The illogic of the War Hawks in pressing for a fight was exceeded only by their ineffectiveness in planning and managing the struggle. By what possible strategy could the ostensible objective of the war be achieved? To construct a navy capable of challenging the British fleet would have been the work of many years and a more expensive proposition than the War Hawks were willing to consider. So hopeless was that prospect that Congress failed to undertake any new construction in the first year of the conflict. Several hundred merchant ships lashed a few cannon to their decks and sailed off as privateers to attack British commerce. The navy's seven modern frigates, built during the war scare after the XYZ affair, put to sea. But these forces could make no pretense of disputing Britain's mastery of the Atlantic.

For a brief moment the American frigates held center stage, for they were faster, tougher, larger, and more powerfully armed than their British counterparts. Barely two months after the declaration of war, Captain Isaac Hull in USS *Constitution* chanced upon HMS *Guerrière* in mid-Atlantic, outmaneuvered *Guerrière* brilliantly, brought down its mizzenmast with his first volley, and then gunned it into submission, a hopeless wreck. In October USS *United States,* captained by Stephen Decatur, hero of the war against the Barbary pirates, caught HMS *Macedonian* off the Madeiras, pounded it unmercifully at long range, and forced the British ship to surrender. *Macedonian* was taken into New London as a prize; over a third of the 300-man crew were casualties, while American losses were but a dozen. Then, in December, *Constitution*, now under Captain William Bainbridge, took on the British frigate *Java* off Brazil. "Old Ironsides" shot away *Java's* mainmast and reduced it to a hulk too battered for salvage.

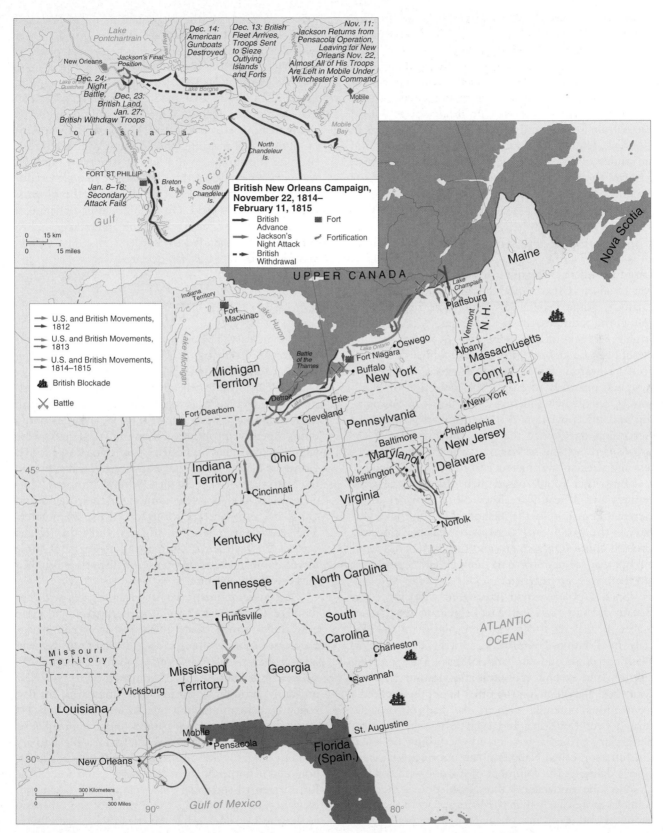

Dec. 14: American Gunboats Destroyed

Dec. 13: British Fleet Arrives, Troops Sent to Sieze Outlying Islands and Forts

Nov. 11: Jackson Returns from Pensacola Operation, Leaving for New Orleans Nov. 22, Almost All of His Troops Are Left in Mobile Under Winchester's Command

Dec. 24: Night Battle

Dec. 23: British Land, **Jan. 27:** British Withdraw Troops

Jan. 8–18: Secondary Attack Fails

FORT ST PHILLIP

British New Orleans Campaign, November 22, 1814– February 11, 1815

→ British Advance
→ Jackson's Night Attack
--→ British Withdrawal

■ Fort
⚓ Fortification

U.S. and British Movements, 1812
U.S. and British Movements, 1813
U.S. and British Movements, 1814–1815
British Blockade
✕ Battle

▲ **The War of 1812**

These victories had little influence on the outcome of the war. The Royal Navy had 34 frigates, 7 more powerful ships of the line, and dozens of smaller vessels. As soon as these forces could concentrate against them, the American frigates were immobilized, forced to spend the war gathering barnacles at their moorings while powerful British squadrons ranged offshore. The privateering merchantmen were more effective because they were so numerous; they captured more than 1300 British vessels during the war. The best of them—vessels like *America* and *True-Blooded Yankee*—were redesigned, given more sail to increase their speed, and formidably armed. *America* captured 26 prizes valued at more than a million dollars. *True-Blooded Yankee* took 27 vessels and destroyed 7 more in a Scottish harbor.

Great Britain's one weak spot seemed to be Canada. The colony had but half a million inhabitants to oppose 7.5 million Americans. Only 2257 British regulars guarded the long border from Montréal to Detroit. The Canadian militia was feeble, and many of its members, being American-born, sympathized with the "invaders." According to the War Hawk congressman Henry Clay of Kentucky, the West was one solid horde of ferocious frontiersmen, armed to the teeth and thirsting for Canadian blood. Yet such talk was mostly brag and bluster; when Congress authorized increasing the army by 25,000 men, Kentucky produced 400 enlistments.

American military leadership proved extremely disappointing. Madison showed poor judgment by relying on officers who had served with distinction in the Revolution. In most cases, as one biographer suggested, their abilities "appeared to have evaporated with age and long disuse." Instead of a concentrated strike against Canada's St. Lawrence River lifeline, which would have isolated Upper Canada, the generals planned a complicated three-pronged attack. It failed dismally. In July 1812 General William Hull, veteran of the battles of Trenton, Saratoga, and Monmouth and now governor of the Michigan Territory, marched forth with 2200 men against the Canadian positions facing Detroit. Hoping that the Canadian militia would desert, he delayed his assault, only to find his communications threatened by hostile Indians led by Tecumseh. Hastily he retreated to Detroit, and when the Canadians, under General Isaac Brock, pursued him, he surrendered the fort without firing a shot! In October another force attempted to invade Canada from Fort Niagara. After an initial success it was crushed by superior numbers, while a large contingent of New York militiamen watched from the east bank of the Niagara River, unwilling to fight outside their own state.

▲ With a few exceptions, American forces in the War of 1812 were ill-trained and ill-led, and poor strategy resulted in several disgraceful defeats. Here, a resplendently dressed militia officer consults a map.

The third arm of the American "attack" was equally unsuccessful. Major General Henry Dearborn, who had fought honorably in the Revolution from Bunker Hill to Yorktown, but who had now grown so fat that he needed a specially designed cart to get from place to place, set out from Plattsburgh, New York, at the head of an army of militiamen. Their objective was Montréal, but when they reached the border, the troops refused to cross. Dearborn meekly marched them back to Plattsburgh.

Meanwhile, the British had captured Fort Michilimackinac in northern Michigan, and the Indians had taken Fort Dearborn (now Chicago), massacring 85 captives. Instead of sweeping triumphantly through Canada, the Americans found themselves trying desperately to keep the Canadians out of Ohio.

Stirred by these disasters, Westerners rallied somewhat in 1813. General Harrison, the victor of

▲ In the heat of the Battle of Lake Erie, Perry had to abandon his flagship, the *Lawrence,* which had been shot to pieces by enemy fire. (Over three-fourths of the ship's crew were killed or wounded.) He was rowed to the *Niagara,* from which he directed the rest of the engagement.

Tippecanoe, headed an army of Kentuckians in a series of inconclusive battles against British troops and Indians led by Tecumseh. He found it impossible to recapture Detroit because a British squadron controlling Lake Erie threatened his communications. President Madison therefore assigned Captain Oliver Hazard Perry to the task of building a fleet to challenge this force. In September 1813, at Put-in-Bay near the western end of the lake, Perry destroyed the British vessels in a bloody battle in which 85 of the 103 men on Perry's flagship were casualties. "We have met the enemy and they are ours," he reported. About a quarter of Perry's 400 men were blacks, which led him to remark that "the color of a man's skin" was no more an indication of his worth than "the cut and trimmings" of his coat. With the Americans in control of Lake Erie, Detroit became untenable for the British, and when they fell back, Harrison gave chase and defeated them at the Thames River, some 60 miles northeast of Detroit. Although little more than a skirmish, this battle had large repercussions. Tecumseh

was among the dead (an eccentric American colonel, Richard Mentor Johnson, was to base a long and successful political career, culminating in his election as vice president of the United States in 1836, on his claim of having personally done in the great chief), and without him the Indians lost heart. But American attempts to win control of Lake Ontario and to invade Canada in the Niagara region were again thrown back. Late in 1813 the British captured Fort Niagara and burned the town of Buffalo. The conquest of Canada was as far from realization as ever.

The British fleet had intensified its blockade of American ports, extending its operations to New England waters previously spared to encourage the antiwar sentiments of local maritime interests. All along the coast, patrolling cruisers, contemptuous of Jefferson's puny gunboats, captured small craft, raided shore points to commandeer provisions, and collected ransom from port towns by threatening to bombard them. One captain even sent a detail ashore to dig potatoes for his ship's mess.

BRITAIN ASSUMES THE OFFENSIVE

Until 1814 the British put relatively little effort into the American war, being concerned primarily with the struggle against Napoleon. However, in 1812 Napoleon had invaded Russia and been thrown back; thereafter, one by one, his European satellites rose against him. Gradually he relinquished his conquests; the Allies—his enemies—marched into France, Paris fell, and in April 1814 the emperor abdicated. Then the British, free to strike hard at the United States, dispatched some 14,000 veterans to Canada.

By the spring of 1814 British strategists had devised a master plan for crushing the United States. One army, 11,000 strong, was to march from Montréal, tracing the route that General Burgoyne had followed to disaster in the Revolution. A smaller amphibious force was to make a feint at the Chesapeake Bay area, destroying coastal towns and threatening Washington and Baltimore. A third army was to assemble at Jamaica and sail to attack New Orleans and bottle up the West.

It is necessary, in considering the War of 1812, to remind oneself repeatedly that in the course of the conflict many brave young men lost their lives. Without this sobering reflection it would be easy to dismiss the conflict as a great farce compounded of stupidity, incompetence, and brag. The British, despite their years of experience against Napoleon, were scarcely more effective than the Americans when they assumed the offensive. They achieved significant success only in the diversionary attack in the Chesapeake Bay area.

While the main British army was assembling in Canada, some 4000 veterans under General Robert Ross sailed from Bermuda for the Chesapeake. After making a rendezvous with a fleet commanded by Vice Admiral Sir Alexander Cochrane and Rear Admiral Sir George Cockburn, which had been terrorizing the coast, they landed in Maryland at the mouth of the Patuxent River, southeast of Washington. A squadron of gunboats "protecting" the capital promptly withdrew upstream; when the British pursued, their commander ordered them blown up to keep them from being captured.

DOCUMENT

Dolley Payne Madison to Lucy Payne Todd

The British troops marched rapidly toward Washington. At Bladensburg, on the outskirts of the city, they came upon an army twice their number, commanded by General William H. Winder, a Baltimore lawyer who had already been captured and released by the British in the Canadian fighting. While President Madison and other officials watched, the British charged—and Winder's army turned tail almost without firing a shot. The British swarmed into the capital and put most public buildings to the torch. Before personally setting fire to the White House, Admiral Cockburn took one of the president's hats and a cushion from Dolley Madison's chair as souvenirs, and, finding the table set for dinner, derisively drank a toast to "Jemmy's health," adding, an observer coyly recalled, "pleasantries too vulgar for me to repeat."

This was the sum of the British success. When they attempted to take Baltimore, they were stopped by a formidable line of defenses devised by General Samuel Smith, a militia officer. General Ross fell in the attack. The fleet then moved up the Patapsco River and pounded Fort McHenry with its cannon, raining 1800 shells upon it in a 25-hour bombardment on September 13 and 14.

"THE STAR SPANGLED BANNER"

While this attack was in progress, an American civilian, Francis Scott Key, who had been temporarily detained on one of the British ships, watched anxiously through the night. Key had boarded the vessel before the attack in an effort to obtain the release of an American doctor who had been taken into custody in Washington. As twilight faded, Key had seen the Stars and Stripes flying proudly over the battered fort. During the night the glare of rockets and bursting of bombs gave proof that the defenders were holding out. Then, by the first light of the new day, Key saw again the flag, still waving over Fort McHenry. Drawing an old letter from his pocket, he dashed off the words to "The Star Spangled Banner," which, when set to music, was to become the national anthem of the United States.

To Key that dawn seemed a turning point in the war. He was roughly correct, for in those last weeks of the summer of 1814 the struggle began to move toward resolution. Unable to crack the defenses of Baltimore, the British withdrew to their ships; shortly after, they sailed to Jamaica to join the forces preparing to attack New Orleans.

The destruction of Washington had been a profound shock. Thousands came forward to enlist in the army. The new determination and spirit were strengthened by news from the northern front, where General Sir George Prevost had been leading the main British invasion force south from Montréal. At Plattsburgh, on the western shore of Lake Champlain, his 1000 Redcoats came up against a well-designed defense line manned by 3300 Americans under General Alexander Macomb. Prevost called up his supporting fleet of four ships and a dozen gunboats. An American fleet of roughly similar strength under Captain Thomas Macdonough, a youthful officer who had served with Decatur against the Barbary pirates, came forward to oppose the British. On September 11, in a

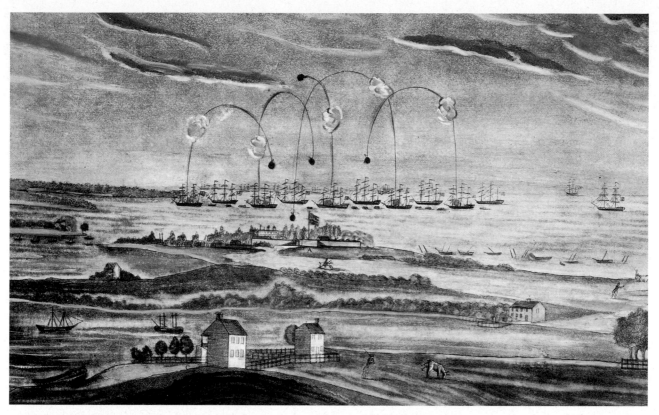

▲ *The Bombardment of Fort McHenry* by John Bower, with the Stars and Stripes flying over the fort *(center)*. The British fleet fired 1800 bombs and red-glaring incendiary rockets. The fort did not return fire because the British ships were beyond the range of its cannon. Although "The Star Spangled Banner" celebrates the "home of the brave," the defenders of Fort McHenry sensibly fled the ramparts and took cover below during the bombardment; they sustained only 30 casualties.

brutal battle at point-blank range, Macdonough destroyed the British ships and drove off the gunboats. With the Americans now threatening his flank, Prevost lost heart and retreated to Canada.

THE TREATY OF GHENT

The war might as well have ended with the battles of Plattsburgh, Washington, and Baltimore, for later military developments had no effect on the outcome. Earlier in 1814 both sides had agreed to discuss peace terms. Commissioners were appointed and negotiations begun during the summer at Ghent, in Belgium. The American delegation consisted of former secretary of the treasury Albert Gallatin; Speaker Henry Clay of the House of Representatives; James A. Bayard, a former senator; and two veteran diplomats, Jonathan Russell, minister to Sweden, and John Quincy Adams, minister to Russia. Adams was chairman. The British commissioners were lesser men by far, partly because they could refer important questions to the Foreign Office in nearby London

for decision and partly because Britain's topflight diplomats were engaged in settling the future of Europe at the Congress of Vienna.

The talks at Ghent were drawn out and frustrating. The British were in no hurry to sign a treaty, believing that their three-pronged offensive in 1814 would swing the balance in their favor. They demanded at first that the United States abandon practically all the Northwest Territory to the Indians and cede other points along the northern border to Canada. On the issues of impressment and neutral rights, they would make no concessions at all. The Americans would yield no territory, for public opinion at home would have been outraged if they had. Old John Adams, for example, told President Madison at this time, "I would continue this war forever rather than surrender an acre. . . ."

Fortunately, the British came to realize that by pressing this point they would only spur the Americans to fight on. News of the defeat at Plattsburgh modified their ambitions, and when the Duke of Wellington advised that from a military point of view they had no

DOCUMENT

The Treaty of Ghent

case for territorial concessions so long as the United States controlled the Great Lakes, they agreed to settle for *status quo ante bellum,* to leave things as they were before the war. The other issues, everyone suddenly realized, had simply evaporated. The mighty war triggered by the French Revolution seemed finally over. The seas were free to all ships, and the Royal Navy no longer had need to snatch sailors from the vessels of the United States or of any other power. On Christmas Eve 1814 the treaty, which merely ended the state of hostilities, was signed. Although, like other members of his family, he was not noted for tact, John Quincy Adams rose to the spirit of the occasion. "I hope," he said, "it will be the last treaty of peace between Great Britain and the United States." And so it was.

THE HARTFORD CONVENTION

Before news of the treaty could cross the Atlantic, two events took place that had important effects but that would not have occurred had the news reached America more rapidly. The first was the Hartford Convention, a meeting of New England Federalists held in December 1814 and January 1815 to protest the war and to plan for a convention of the states to revise the Constitution.

Sentiment in New England had opposed the war from the beginning. The governor of Massachusetts titled his annual address in 1813 "On the Present Unhappy War," and the General Court went on record calling the conflict "impolitic, improper, and unjust." The Federalist party had been quick to employ the discontent to revive its fortunes. Federalist-controlled state administrations refused to provide militia to aid in the fight and discouraged individuals and banks from lending money to the hard-pressed national government. Trade with the enemy flourished as long as the British fleet did not crack down on New England ports, and goods flowed across the Canadian line in as great or greater volume as during Jefferson's embargo.

Their attitude toward the war made the Federalists even more unpopular with the rest of the country, and this in turn encouraged extremists to talk of seceding from the Union. After Massachusetts summoned the meeting of the Hartford Convention, the fear was widespread that the delegates would propose a New England Confederacy, thereby striking at the Union in a moment of great trial.

Luckily for the country, moderate Federalists controlled the convention. They approved a statement that in case of "deliberate, dangerous and palpable infractions of the Constitution" a state has the right "to interpose its authority" to protect itself. This concept, similar to that expressed in the Kentucky and Virginia resolutions by the Republicans when they were in the minority, was accompanied by a list of proposed constitutional amendments designed to make the national government conform more closely to the New England ideal. These would have (1) repealed the Three-fifths Compromise on representation and direct taxes, which favored the slaveholding states; (2) required a two-thirds vote of Congress for the admission of new states and for declaring war; (3) reduced Congress's power to restrict trade by measures such as an embargo; (4) limited presidents to a single term; and (5) made it illegal for naturalized citizens to hold national office.

Nothing formally proposed at Hartford was treasonable, but the proceedings were kept secret, and rumors of impending secession were rife. In this atmosphere came the news from Ghent of an honorable peace. The Federalists had been denouncing the war and predicting a British triumph; now they were discredited.

THE BATTLE OF NEW ORLEANS

Still more discrediting to Federalists was the second event that would not have happened had communications been more rapid: the Battle of New Orleans. During the fall of 1814 the British had gathered an army at Negril Bay in Jamaica, commanded by Major General Sir Edward Pakenham, brother-in-law of the Duke of Wellington. Late in November an armada of 60 ships set out for New Orleans with 11,000 soldiers. Instead of sailing directly up from the mouth of the Mississippi as the Americans expected, Pakenham approached the city by way of Lake Borgne, to the east. Proceeding through a maze of swamps and bayous, he advanced close to the city's gates before being detected. Early on the afternoon of December 23, three mud-spattered local planters burst into the headquarters of General Andrew Jackson, commanding the defenses of New Orleans, with the news.

For once in this war of error and incompetence the United States had the right man in the right place at the right time. After his Revolutionary War experiences, Jackson had studied law, then moved West, settling in Nashville, Tennessee. He served briefly in both houses of Congress and was active in Tennessee affairs. Jackson was a hard man and fierce-tempered, frequently involved in brawls and duels, but honest and, by western standards, a good public servant. When the war broke out, he was named major general of volunteers. Almost alone among nonprofessional troops during the conflict, his men won impressive

victories, savagely crushing the Creek Indians in a series of battles in Alabama.

Jackson's success was due to his toughness and determination. Discipline based on fear, respect, and their awareness of his genuine concern for their well-being made his individualistic frontier militiamen into an army. His men called Jackson Old Hickory; the Indians called him Sharp Knife.

Following these victories, Jackson was assigned the job of defending the Gulf Coast against the expected British strike. Although he had misjudged Pakenham's destination, he was ready when the news of the British arrival reached him. "By the Eternal," he vowed, "they shall not sleep on our soil." "Gentlemen," he told his staff officers, "the British are below, we must fight them tonight."

While the British rested and awaited reinforcements, planning to take the city the next morning, Jackson rushed up men and guns. At 7:30 P.M. on December 23 he struck hard, taking the British by surprise. But Pakenham's veterans rallied quickly, and the battle was inconclusive. With Redcoats pouring in from the fleet, Jackson fell back to a point 5 miles below New Orleans and dug in.

He chose his position wisely. On his right was the Mississippi, on his left an impenetrable swamp, to the front an open field. On the day before Christmas (while the commissioners in Ghent were signing the peace treaty), Jackson's army, which included a segregated unit of free black militiamen, erected an earthen parapet about 10 yards behind a dry canal bed. Here the Americans would make their stand.

For two weeks Pakenham probed the American line. Jackson strengthened his defenses daily. At night, patrols of silent Tennesseans slipped out with knife and tomahawk to stalk British sentries. They called this grim business "going hunting." On January 8, 1815, Pakenham ordered an all-out frontal assault. The American position was formidable, but these were men who had defeated Napoleon. At dawn, through the lowland mists, the Redcoats moved forward with fixed bayonets. Pakenham assumed that the undisciplined Americans—about 4500 strong—would run at the sight of bare steel.

The Americans did not run. Perhaps they feared the wrath of their commander more than enemy bayonets. Artillery raked the advancing British, and when the range closed to about 150 yards, the riflemen opened up. Jackson had formed his men in three ranks behind the parapet. One rank fired, then stepped down as another took its place. By the time the third had loosed its volley, the first had reloaded and was ready to fire again. Nothing could stand against this rain of lead. General Pakenham was wounded twice, then killed by a shell fragment while calling up his last reserves. During the battle a single brave British officer reached the top of the parapet. When retreat was finally sounded, the British had suffered almost 2100 casualties, including nearly 300 killed. Thirteen Americans lost their lives, and 58 more were wounded or missing.

VICTORY WEAKENS THE FEDERALISTS

Word of Jackson's magnificent triumph reached Washington almost simultaneously with the good news from Ghent. People found it easy to confuse the chronology and consider the war a victory won on the battlefield below New Orleans instead of the standoff it had been. Jackson became the "Hero of New Orleans"; his proud fellow citizens rated his military abilities superior to those of the Duke of Wellington. The nation rejoiced. One sour Republican complained that the Federalists of Massachusetts had fired off more powder and wounded more men celebrating the victory than they had during the whole course of the conflict. The Senate ratified the peace treaty unanimously, and the frustrations and failures of the past few years were forgotten. Moreover, American success in holding off Great Britain despite internal frictions went a long way toward convincing European nations that both the United States and its republican form of government were here to stay. The powers might accept these truths with less pleasure than the Americans, but accept them they did.

The nation had suffered relatively few casualties and little economic loss, except to the shipping interests. The Indians were the main losers in the contest. When Jackson defeated the Creeks, for example, he forced them to surrender 23 million acres, constituting three-fifths of what is now Alabama and one-fifth of Georgia.

The war completed the destruction of the Federalist party. The success of the Jeffersonians' political techniques had inspired younger Federalists in many parts of the country to adopt the rhetoric of democracy and (more important) to perfect local organizations. In 1812 the party made significant gains in the Northeast, electing numbers of congressmen and winning many state and local offices. They did not run a candidate for president, but their support enabled the dissident New York Republican DeWitt Clinton to obtain 89 electoral votes to Madison's 128.

Their private correspondence reveals that these Federalists were no more enchanted by the virtues of mass democracy than were their elders, but by mouthing democratic slogans they revived the party

▲ In warfare, Indians adopted some of the weapons and strategy of white soldiers. Here Indians congregate in a massed formation, armed with guns and tomahawks, to defend their village; one downed Indian is holding a gun and wearing boots. The federal officers are mounted on horses.

in many districts. Now the results of the war undermined their efforts. They had not supported the war effort; they had argued that the British could not be defeated; they had dealt clandestinely with the enemy; they had even threatened to break up the Union. So long as the issue remained in doubt, these policies won considerable support, but New Orleans made the party an object of ridicule and scorn. It soon disappeared even in New England, swamped beneath a wave of patriotism that flooded the land.

The chief reason for the happy results of the war had little to do with American events. After 1815 Europe settled down to what was to be a century of relative peace. With peace came an end to serious foreign threats to America and a revival of commerce. European emigration to the United States, long held back by the troubled times, spurted ahead, providing the expanding country with its most valuable asset— strong, willing hands to do the work of developing the land. The mood of Jefferson's first term, when democracy had reigned amid peace and plenty, returned with a rush. And the nation, having had its fill of international complications, turned in on itself as Jefferson had wished. The politicians, ever sensitive to public attitudes, had learned what seemed at the time

a valuable lesson. Foreign affairs were a potent cause of domestic conflict. The volatile character of sectional politics was thus another reason why America should escape from involvement in European affairs.

ANGLO-AMERICAN RAPPROCHEMENT

There remained a few matters to straighten out with Great Britain, Spain, and Europe generally. Since no territory had changed hands at Ghent, neither signatory had reason to harbor a grudge. There was no sudden flowering of Anglo-American friendship. Yet for years no serious trouble marred Anglo-American relations. The war had taught the British to respect Americans, if not to love them.

In this atmosphere the two countries worked out peaceful solutions to a number of old problems. American trade was becoming ever more important to the British, that of the sugar islands less so. In July 1815 they therefore signed a commercial convention ending discriminatory duties and making other adjustments favorable to trade. Boundary difficulties also moved toward resolution. At Ghent the diplomats had created several joint commissions to settle

the disputed boundary between the United States and Canada. Many years were to pass before the line was finally drawn, but establishing the principle of defining the border by negotiation was important. In time, a line extending over 3000 miles was agreed to without the firing of a single shot.

Immediately after the war the British reinforced their garrisons in Canada and began to rebuild their shattered Great Lakes fleet. The United States took similar steps. But both nations found the cost of rearming more than they cared to bear. When the United States suggested demilitarizing the lakes, the British agreed. The Rush-Bagot Agreement of 1817 limited each country to one 100-ton vessel armed with a single 18-pounder on Lake Champlain and another on Lake Ontario. They were to have two each for all the other Great Lakes.

Gradually, as an outgrowth of this decision, the entire border was demilitarized, a remarkable achievement. In the Convention of 1818 the two countries agreed to the 49th parallel as the northern boundary of the Louisiana Territory between the Lake of the Woods and the Rockies, and to the joint control of the Oregon country for ten years. The question of the rights of Americans in the Labrador and Newfoundland fisheries, which had been much disputed during the Ghent negotiations, was settled amicably.

THE TRANSCONTINENTAL TREATY

The acquisition of Spanish Florida and the settlement of the western boundary of Louisiana were also accomplished as an aftermath of the War of 1812, but in a far different spirit. Spain's control of the Floridas was feeble. West Florida had passed into American hands by 1813, and frontiersmen in Georgia were eyeing East Florida greedily. Indians struck frequently into American territory from Florida, then fled to sanctuary across the line. American slaves who escaped across the border could not be recovered. In 1818 James Monroe, who had been elected president in 1816, ordered General Andrew Jackson to clear raiding Seminole Indians from American soil and to pursue them into Florida if necessary. Seizing on these instructions, Jackson marched into Florida and easily captured two Spanish forts.

Although Jackson eventually withdrew from Florida, the impotence of the Spanish government made it obvious even in Madrid that if nothing were done, the United States would soon fill the power vacuum by seizing the territory. The Spanish also feared for the future of their tottering Latin American empire, especially the northern provinces of Mexico, which stood in the path of American westward expansion.

Spain and the United States had never determined where the Louisiana Territory ended and Spanish Mexico began. In return for American acceptance of a boundary as far east of the Rio Grande as possible, Spain was ready to surrender Florida.

For these reasons the Spanish minister in Washington, Luis de Onís, undertook in December 1817 to negotiate a treaty with John Quincy Adams, Monroe's secretary of state. Adams pressed the minister mercilessly on the question of the western boundary, driving a bargain that would have done credit to the most tightfisted of his Yankee ancestors. Onís opened their talks by proposing a line in the middle of what is now Louisiana, and when Adams countered by demanding a boundary running through present-day Texas, Onís professed to be shocked. Abstract right, not power, should determine the settlement, he said. "Truth is of all times, and reason and justice are founded upon immutable principles." To this Adams replied: "That truth is of all times and that reason and justice are founded upon immutable principles has never been contested by the United States, but neither truth, reason, nor justice consists in stubbornness of assertion, nor in the multiplied repetition of error."

In the end Onís could only yield. He saved Texas for his monarch but accepted a boundary to the Louisiana Territory that followed the Sabine, Red, and Arkansas Rivers to the Continental Divide and the 42nd parallel to the Pacific, thus abandoning Spain's claim to a huge area beyond the Rockies that had no connection at all with the Louisiana Purchase. Adams even compelled him to agree that when the boundary followed rivers, United States territory was to extend to the farthest bank, not merely to midstream. The United States obtained Florida in return for a mere $5 million, and that paid not to Spain but to Americans who held claims against the Spanish government.

This "Transcontinental Treaty" was signed in 1819, although ratification was delayed until 1821. Most Americans at the time thought the acquisition of Florida the most important part of the treaty, but Adams, whose vision of America's future was truly continental, knew better. "The acquisition of a definite line of boundary to the [Pacific] forms a great epoch in our history," he recorded in his diary.

THE MONROE DOCTRINE

Concern with defining the boundaries of the United States did not reflect a desire to limit expansion; rather, the feeling was that there should be no more quibbling and quarreling with foreign powers that might distract the people from the great task of national development. The classic enunciation of this

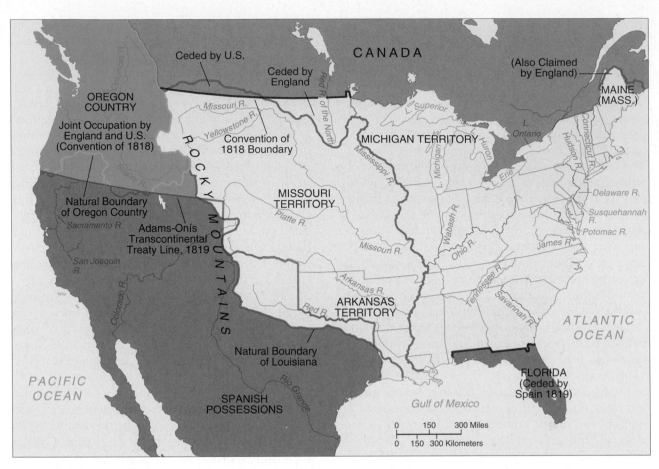

▲ The United States, 1819

point of view, the completion of America's withdrawal from Europe, was the Monroe Doctrine.

Two separate strands met in this pronouncement. The first led from Moscow to Alaska and down the Pacific Coast to the Oregon country. Beginning with the explorations of Vitus Bering in 1741, the Russians had maintained an interest in fishing and fur trading along the northwest coast of North America. In 1821 the czar extended his claim south to the 51st parallel and forbade the ships of other powers to enter coastal waters north of that point. This announcement was disturbing.

The second strand ran from the courts of the European monarchs to Latin America. Between 1817 and 1822 practically all of the region from the Rio Grande to the Strait of Magellan had won its independence. Spain, former master of all the area except Brazil, was too weak to win it back by force, but Austria, Prussia, France, and Russia decided at the Congress of Verona in 1822 to try to regain the area for Spain in the interests of "legitimacy." There was talk of sending a large French army to South America. This possibility also caused grave concern in Washington.

To the Russian threat, Monroe and Secretary of State Adams responded with a terse warning: "The American continents are no longer subjects for any new European colonial establishments." This statement did not impress the Russians, but they had no intention of colonizing the region. In 1824 they signed a treaty with the United States abandoning all claims below the present southern limit of Alaska (54° 40′ north latitude) and removing their restrictions on foreign shipping.

The Latin American problem was more complex. The United States was not alone in its alarm at the prospect of a revival of French or Spanish power in that region. Great Britain, having profited greatly from the breakup of the mercantilist Spanish empire by developing a thriving commerce with the new republics, had no intention of permitting a restoration of the old order. But the British monarchy preferred not to recognize the new revolutionary South American republics, for England itself was only beginning to recover from a period of social upheaval as violent as any in its history. Bad times and high food prices had combined to cause riots, conspiracies, and angry demands for parliamentary reform.

In 1823 the British foreign minister, George Canning, suggested to the American minister in London that the United States and Britain issue a joint statement opposing any French interference in South America, pledging that they themselves would never annex any part of Spain's old empire, and saying nothing about recognition of the new republics. This proposal of joint action with the British was flattering to the United States but scarcely in its best interests. The United States had already recognized the new republics, and it had no desire to help Great Britain retain its South American trade. As Secretary Adams pointed out, to agree to the proposal would be to abandon the possibility of someday adding Cuba or any other part of Latin America to the United States. America should act independently, Adams urged. "It would be more candid, as well as more dignified, to avow our principles explicitly . . . than to come in as a cockboat in the wake of the British man-of-war."

Monroe heartily endorsed Adams's argument and decided to include a statement of American policy in his annual message to Congress in December 1823. "The American continents," he wrote, "by the free and independent condition which they have assumed and maintain, are henceforth not to be considered as subjects for future colonization by any European powers." Europe's political system was "essentially different" from that developing in the New World, and the two should not be mixed. The United States would not interfere with existing European colonies in North or South America and would avoid involvement in strictly European affairs, but any attempt to extend European control to countries in the hemisphere that had already won their independence would be considered, Monroe warned, "the manifestation of an unfriendly disposition toward the United States" and consequently a threat to the nation's "peace and safety."

DOCUMENT

Monroe Doctrine

This policy statement—it was not dignified with the title Monroe Doctrine until decades later—attracted little notice in Europe or Latin America and not much more at home. Obviously the United States, whose own capital had been overrun by a mere raiding party less than ten years before, could not police the entire Western Hemisphere. European statesmen dismissed Monroe's message as "arrogant" and "blustering," worthy only of "the most profound contempt." Latin Americans, while appreciating the intent behind it, knew better than to count on American aid in case of attack.

Nevertheless, the principles laid down by President Monroe so perfectly expressed the wishes of the people of the United States that when the country grew powerful enough to enforce them, there was little need to alter or embellish his pronouncement. However understood at the time, the doctrine may be seen as the final stage in the evolution of American independence.

From this perspective, the famous Declaration of 1776 merely began a process of separation and self-determination. The peace treaty ending the Revolutionary War was a further step, and Washington's Declaration of Neutrality in 1793 was another, demonstrating as it did the capacity of the United States to determine its own best interests despite the treaty of alliance with France. The removal of British troops from the northwest forts, achieved by the otherwise ignominious Jay Treaty, marked the next stage. Then the Louisiana Purchase made a further advance toward true independence by ensuring that the Mississippi River could not be closed to the commerce so vital to the development of the western territories.

The standoff War of 1812 ended any lingering British hope of regaining control of America, the Latin American revolutions further weakened colonialism in the Western Hemisphere, and the Transcontinental Treaty pushed the last European power from the path of westward expansion. Monroe's "doctrine" was a kind of public announcement that the sovereign United States had completed its independence and wanted nothing better than to be left alone to concentrate on its own development. Better yet if Europe could be made to allow the entire hemisphere to follow its own path.

THE ERA OF GOOD FEELINGS

The person who gave his name to the so-called doctrine was an unusually lucky man. James Monroe lived a long life in good health and saw close up most of the great events in the history of the young republic. At the age of 18 he shed his blood for liberty at the Battle of Trenton. He was twice governor of Virginia, a United States senator, and a Cabinet member. He was at various times the nation's representative in Paris, Madrid, and London. Elected president in 1816, his good fortune continued. The world was finally at peace, the country united and prosperous. A person of good feeling who would keep a steady hand on the helm and hold to the present course seemed called for, and Monroe possessed exactly the qualities that the times required. "He is a man whose soul might be turned wrongside outwards, without discovering a blemish," Jefferson said, and John Quincy Adams, a harsh critic of public figures, praised Monroe's courtesy, sincerity, and sound judgment.

Courtesy and purity of soul do not always suffice to make a good president. In more troubled times Monroe might well have brought disaster, for he was

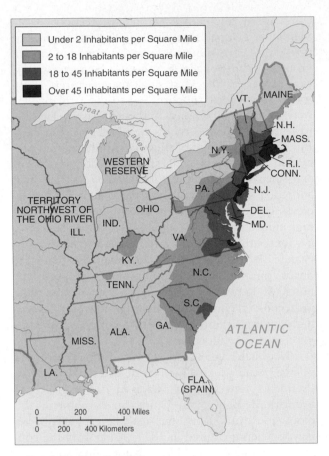

▲ **Population Density, 1790**

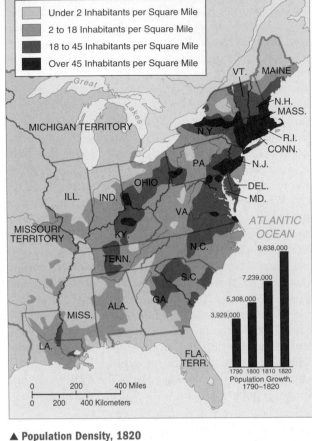

▲ **Population Density, 1820**
The 30 years from 1790 to 1820 saw a sizable increase in population. The growth was especially great in the decade from 1810 to 1820, with a 33.1 percent increase.

neither a person of outstanding intellect nor a forceful leader. He blazed few paths, organized no personal machine. The Monroe Doctrine, by far the most significant achievement of his administration, was as much the work of Secretary of State Adams as his own. No one ever claimed that Monroe was much better than second-rate, yet when his first term ended, he was reelected without organized opposition.

By 1817 the divisive issues of earlier days had vanished. Monroe dramatized their disappearance by beginning his first term with a goodwill tour of New England, heartland of the opposition. The tour was a triumph. Everywhere the president was greeted with tremendous enthusiasm. After he visited Boston, once the headquarters and now the graveyard of Federalism, a Federalist newspaper, the *Columbian Centinel*, gave the age its name. Pointing out that the celebrations attending Monroe's visit had brought together in friendly intercourse many persons "whom party politics had long severed," it dubbed the times the "Era of Good Feelings."

It has often been said that the harmony of Monroe's administrations was superficial, that beneath the calm lay potentially disruptive issues that had not yet begun to influence national politics. The dramatic change from the unanimity of Monroe's second election to the fragmentation of four years later, when four candidates divided the vote and the House of Representatives had to choose the president, supports the point.

Nevertheless, the people of the period had good reasons for thinking it extraordinarily harmonious. Peace, prosperity, liberty, and progress all flourished in 1817 in the United States. The heirs of Jefferson had accepted, with a mixture of resignation and enthusiasm, most of the economic policies advocated by the Hamiltonians.

The Jeffersonian balance between individual liberty and responsible government, having survived both bad management and war, had justified itself to the opposition. The new unity was symbolized by the restored friendship of Jefferson and John Adams. In

1801 Adams had slipped sulkily out of Washington without waiting to attend his successor's inauguration, but after ten years of icy silence, the two old collaborators, abetted by Dr. Benjamin Rush, effected a reconciliation. Although they continued to disagree vigorously about matters of philosophy and government, the bitterness between them disappeared entirely. By Monroe's day, Jefferson was writing long letters to "my dear friend," ranging over such subjects as theology, the proper reading of the classics, and agricultural improvements, and receiving equally warm and voluminous replies. "Whether you or I were right," Adams wrote amiably to Jefferson, "Posterity must judge."

When political divisions appeared again, as they soon did, it was not because the old balance had been shaky. Few of the new controversies challenged Republican principles or revived old issues. Instead, these controversies were children of the present and the future, products of the continuing growth of the country. From 1790 to 1820, the area of the United States doubled, but very little of the Louisiana Purchase had been settled. More significant, the population of the nation had more than doubled, from 4 million to 9.6 million. The pace of the westward movement had also quickened; by 1820 the moving edge of the frontier ran in a long, irregular curve from Michigan to Arkansas.

New Sectional Issues

Sectional tensions led to many disputes over banking, the tariff, federal land policy, and internal improvements. Overshadowing all of these was the debate over slavery.

The War of 1812 and the depression that struck the country in 1819 had shaped many of the controversies. The tariff question was affected by both. Before the War of 1812 the level of duties averaged about 12.5 percent of the value of dutiable products, but to meet the added expenses occasioned by the conflict, Congress doubled all tariffs. In 1816, when the revenue was no longer needed, a new act kept duties close to wartime levels. Infant industries that had grown up during the years of embargo, nonintercourse, and war were able to exert considerable pressure. The act especially favored textiles because the British were dumping cloth in America at bargain prices in their attempt to regain lost markets. Unemployed workers and many farmers became convinced that prosperity would return only if American industry were shielded against foreign competition.

There was backing for high duties in every section. Except for New England, where the shipping interests favored free trade and where the booming textile mills were not seriously injured by foreign competition, the North favored protection. A few Southerners hoped that textile mills would spring up in their region; more supported protection on the ground that national self-sufficiency was necessary in case of war. In the West small manufacturers in the towns added their support, and so did farmers, who were counting on workers in the new eastern factories to consume much of their wheat and corn and hogs. But with the passage of time the South rejected protection almost completely. Industry failed to develop, and since Southerners exported most of their cotton and tobacco, they soon concluded that besides increasing the cost of nearly everything they bought, high duties on imports would limit the foreign market for southern staples by inhibiting international exchange. As this fact became clear, the West tended to divide on the tariff question: the Northwest and much of Kentucky, which had a special interest in protecting its considerable hemp production, favored high duties; the Southwest, where cotton was the major crop, favored low duties.

National banking policy was another important political issue affected by the war and the depression. Presidents Jefferson and Madison had managed to live with the Bank of the United States despite its dubious constitutionality, but its charter was not renewed when it expired in 1811. Aside from the constitutional question, the major opposition to recharter came from state banks eager to take over the business of the Bank for themselves. The fact that English investors owned most of the Bank's stock was also used as an argument against recharter.

Many more state banks were created after 1811, and most extended credit recklessly. When the British raid on Washington and Baltimore in 1814 sent panicky depositors scurrying to convert their deposits into gold or silver, the overextended financiers could not oblige them. All banks outside New England suspended specie payments; that is, they stopped exchanging their bank notes for hard money on demand. Paper money immediately fell in value; a paper dollar was soon worth only 85 cents in coin in Philadelphia, less in Baltimore. Government business also suffered from the absence of a national bank. In October 1814 Secretary of the Treasury Alexander J. Dallas submitted a plan for a second Bank of the United States, and after considerable wrangling over its precise form, the institution was authorized in April 1816.

The new Bank was much larger than its predecessor, being capitalized at $35 million. However, unlike Hamilton's creation, it was badly managed at the start. Its first president, William Jones, a former secretary of the treasury, allowed his institution to join in the irresponsible creation of credit. By the summer of

▲ The Bank of Philadelphia (1801), designed by Benjamin Latrobe, combined the Ionic columns of an ancient Athenian temple and the circular dome of ancient Rome. By appropriating the grandeur of antiquity, Americans were seeking to liberate themselves from modern Europe.

1818 the Bank's 18 branches had issued notes in excess of ten times their specie reserves, far more than was prudent, considering the Bank's responsibilities. When depression struck the country in 1819, the Bank of the United States was as hard pressed as many of the state banks. Jones resigned.

The new president, Langdon Cheves of South Carolina, was as rigid as Jones had been permissive. During the bad times, when easy credit was needed, he pursued a policy of stern curtailment. The Bank thus regained a sound position at the expense of hardship to borrowers. "The Bank was saved," the contemporary economist William Gouge wrote somewhat hyperbolically, "and the people were ruined." Indeed, the bank reached a low point in public favor. Irresponsible state banks resented it, as did the advocates of hard money.

Regional lines were less sharply drawn on the Bank issue than on the tariff. Northern congressmen voted against the Bank 53 to 44 in 1816—many of them because they objected to the particular proposal, not because they were against any national bank. Those from other sections favored it, 58 to 30. The collapse occasioned by the Panic of 1819 produced further opposition to the institution in the West.

Land policy in the West also caused sectional controversy. No one wished to eliminate the system of survey and sale, but there was continuous pressure to reduce the price of public land and the minimum unit offered for sale. The Land Act of 1800 set $2 an acre

as the minimum price and 320 acres (a half section) as the smallest unit. In 1804 the minimum was cut to 160 acres, which could be had for about $80 down, roughly a quarter of what the average artisan could earn in a year.

Since banks were pursuing an easy-credit policy, land sales boomed. In 1818 the government sold nearly 3.5 million acres. Thereafter, continuing expansion and the rapid shrinkage of the foreign market as European farmers resumed production after the Napoleonic Wars led to disaster. Prices fell, the panic struck, and western debtors were forced to the wall by the hundreds.

Sectional attitudes toward the public lands were fairly straightforward. The West wanted cheap land; the North and South tended to look on the national domain as an asset that should be converted into as much cash as possible. Northern manufacturers feared that cheap land in the West would drain off surplus labor and force wages up, while Southern planters were concerned about the competition that would develop when the virgin lands of the Southwest were put to the plow to make cotton. The West, however, was ready to fight to the last line of defense over land policy, while the other regions would usually compromise on the issue to gain support for their own vital interests.

Sectional alignments on the question of internal improvements were similar to those on land policy, but this issue, soon to become very important, had

▲ A slave family is broken up in this mordant painting titled, *After the Sale: Slaves Going Home from Richmond (1853)*, by Eyre Crowe (British). The man at the lower right, holding a whip, is taking money; an American flag flies from the auctioneer's carriage. The moral was obvious.

not greatly agitated national affairs before 1820. As we have seen, the only significant federal internal improvement project undertaken before that date was the National Road.

The most divisive sectional issue was slavery. After the compromises affecting the "peculiar institution" made at the Constitutional Convention, it caused remarkably little conflict in national politics before 1819. Although the importation of blacks rose in the 1790s, Congress abolished the African slave trade in 1808 without major incident. As the nation expanded, free and slave states were added to the Union in equal numbers, Ohio, Indiana, and Illinois being balanced by Louisiana, Mississippi, and Alabama. In 1819 there were 22 states, 11 slave and 11 free. The expansion of slavery occasioned by the cotton boom led Southerners to support it more aggressively, which tended to irritate many Northerners, but most persons considered slavery mainly a local issue.

To the extent that it was a national question, the North opposed it and the South defended it ardently. The West leaned toward the southern point of view, for in addition to the southwestern slave states, the Northwest was sympathetic, partly because much of its produce was sold on southern plantations and partly because at least half of its early settlers came from Virginia, Kentucky, and other slave states.

Northern Leaders

By 1824 the giants of the Revolutionary generation had completed their work. Washington, Hamilton, Franklin, Samuel Adams, Patrick Henry, and most of their peers were dead. John Adams (88), Thomas Jefferson (81), and James Madison (73) were passing their declining years quietly on their ancestral acres, full of memories and sage advice, but no longer active

in national affairs. In every section new leaders had come forward, men shaped by the past but chiefly concerned with the present. Quite suddenly, between the war and the panic, they had inherited power. They would shape the future of the United States.

John Quincy Adams was the best-known political leader of the North in the early 1820s. Just completing his brilliant work as secretary of state under Monroe, highlighted by his negotiation of the Transcontinental Treaty and his design of the Monroe Doctrine, he had behind him a record of public service dating to the Confederation period. At age 11 he was giving English lessons to the French minister to the Continental Congress and his secretary. ("He shows us no mercy and makes us no compliments," the minister remarked.) While in his teens he served as secretary of legation in Russia and Great Britain. Later he was American minister to the Netherlands and to Prussia, and a Federalist United States senator from Massachusetts. Then he gradually switched to the Republican point of view, supporting the Louisiana Purchase and even the Embargo Act.

Adams was farsighted, imaginative, hardworking, and extremely intelligent, but he was inept in personal relations. He had all the virtues and most of the defects of the puritan, being suspicious both of others and of himself. He suffered in two ways from being his father's child: As the son of a president he was under severe pressure to live up to the Adams name, and his father expected a great deal of him. When the boy was only 7, John Adams wrote his wife: "Train [the children] to virtue. Habituate them to industry, activity, and spirit. Make them consider vice as shameful and unmanly. Fire them with ambition to be useful."

Such training made John Quincy an indefatigable worker. Even in winter he normally rose at 5 A.M., and he could never convince himself that most of his associates were not lazy dolts. He set a standard no one could meet and consequently was continually dissatisfied with himself. As one of his grandsons remarked, "He was disappointed because he was not supernatural."

Like his father, John Quincy Adams was a strong nationalist. While New England was still antiprotectionist, he was at least open-minded on the subject of high tariffs. Unlike most Easterners, he believed that the federal government should spend freely on roads and canals in the West. To slavery he was, like most New Englanders, personally opposed. As Monroe's second term drew toward its close, Adams seemed one of the most likely candidates to succeed him, and at this period his ambition to be president was his great failing. It led him to make certain compromises with his principles, which in turn plagued his oversensitive conscience and had a corrosive effect on his peace of mind.

Daniel Webster was recognized as one of the coming leaders of New England. Born in New Hampshire in 1782, he graduated from Dartmouth College in 1801, and by the time of the War of 1812 he had made a local reputation as a lawyer and orator. After serving two terms in Congress during the conflict, he moved to Boston to concentrate on his legal practice. He soon became one of the leading constitutional lawyers of the country. In 1823 he was again elected to Congress.

Webster owed much of his reputation to his formidable presence and his oratorical skill. Dark, broadchested, large-headed, craggy of brow, with deep-set, brooding eyes and a firm mouth, he projected a remarkable appearance of heroic power and moral strength. His thunderous voice, his resourceful vocabulary, his manner—all backed by the mastery of every oratorical trick—made him unique.

Webster had a first-rate mind, powerful and logical. His faults were largely those of temperament. He was too fond of money, good food, and fine broadcloth, of alcohol and adulation. Generally he bestirred himself only with great effort and then usually to advance his

▲ Eyes like "anthracite furnaces," the English historian Thomas Carlyle remarked of Daniel Webster; this is the "Black Dan" portrait by Francis Alexander (1835).

own cause. He borrowed large sums from his well-to-do admirers but rarely paid them back. Webster could have been a lighthouse in the night, guiding his fellow citizens to safe harbor. More often he was a weather vane, shifting to accommodate the strongest breeze.

Unlike the independent-minded Adams, Webster nearly always reflected the beliefs of the dominant business interests of New England. His opposition to the embargo and the War of 1812 got him into Congress, where he faithfully supported the views of New England merchants. He opposed the high tariff of 1816 because the merchants favored free trade, and he voted against establishing the Bank chiefly on partisan grounds. (His view changed when the Bank hired him as its lawyer.) He was against cheap land and federal construction of internal improvements, but basically he was a nationalist, as was seen in his arguments before the Supreme Court. Ahead of him lay fame, considerable constructive service, but also bitter frustration.

New York's man of the future was a sandy-haired politico named Martin Van Buren. The Red Fox, as he was called, was one of the most talented politicians ever to play a part in American affairs. He was clever and hardworking, but his mind and his energy were always devoted to some political purpose. From 1812 to 1820 he served in the state legislature; in 1820 he was elected United States senator.

Van Buren had great charm and immense tact. By nature affable, he never allowed partisanship to mar his personal relationships with other leaders. The members of his political machine, known as the Albany Regency, were almost fanatically loyal to him, but even his enemies could seldom dislike him as a person.

Somehow Van Buren could reconcile deviousness with honesty. He "rowed to his objective with muffled oars," said Randolph of Roanoke, yet Van Buren was neither crooked nor venal. Politics for him was like a game or a complex puzzle: The object was victory, but one must play by the rules or lose all sense of achievement. Only a fool will cheat at solitaire, and despite his gregariousness Van Buren was at heart a solitary operator.

His positions on the issues of the 1820s are hard to determine because he never took a position if he could avoid doing so. In part this was his politician's desire to straddle every fence; it also reflected his quixotic belief that issues were means rather than ends in the world of politics. No one could say with assurance what he thought about the tariff, and since slavery did not arouse much interest in New York, it is safe to suppose that at this time he had no opinion at all about the institution. Any intelligent observer in the 1820s would have predicted that "the Little Magician" would go far. How far, and in what direction, no one could have guessed.

SOUTHERN LEADERS

The most prominent southern leader was William H. Crawford, Monroe's secretary of the treasury. Following service in the Georgia legislature, where he spoke for the large planters against the interests of yeomen farmers, in 1807 he was elected to the United States Senate. Crawford was direct and friendly, a marvelous storyteller, and one of the few persons in Washington who could teach the fledgling senator Martin Van Buren anything about politics. Crawford was one of the first politicians to try to build a national machine. "Crawford's Act" of 1820, limiting the term of minor federal appointees to four years, was passed, as the name suggests, largely through his efforts, for he realized before nearly anyone else that a handful of petty offices, properly distributed, could win the allegiance of thousands of voters.

Crawford was controversial. Many of his contemporaries considered him no more than a cynical spoilsman, although his administration of the Treasury department was first-rate. Yet he had many friends. His ambition was vast, his power great. Fate, however, was about to strike Crawford a crippling blow.

▲ This striking portrait of John C. Calhoun was painted sometime between 1818 and 1825, probably by Charles Bird King. Calhoun was in his thirties.

John C. Calhoun, the other outstanding southern leader, was born in South Carolina in 1782 and graduated from Yale in 1804. After serving in the South Carolina legislature, he was elected to Congress in 1811. In Congress he took a strong nationalist position on all the issues of the day. In 1817 Monroe made him secretary of war.

Calhoun, a well-to-do planter, was devoted to the South and its institutions, but he took the broadest possible view of political affairs. "Our true system is to look to the country," he said in 1820, "and to support such measures and such men, without regard to sections, as are best calculated to advance the general interest." John Quincy Adams, seldom charitable in his private opinions of colleagues (he called Crawford "a worm" and Henry Clay a "gamester" with an "undigested system of ethics"), praised Calhoun's "enlarged philosophic views" and considered him "above all sectional and factional prejudices."

Calhoun was intelligent, bookish, and given to the study of abstractions. Legend has it that he once tried to write a poem but after putting down the word "Whereas" gave it up as beyond his powers. Some obscure failing made it impossible for him to grasp the essence of the human condition. An English observer once said that Calhoun had "an imperfect acquaintance with human nature." Few contemporaries could maintain themselves in debate against his powerful intelligence, yet that mind—so sharp, so penetrating—was the blind bondsman of his ambition.

Western Leaders

The outstanding western leader of the 1820s was Henry Clay of Kentucky, one of the most charming and colorful of American statesmen. Clay was the kind of person who made men cheer and women swoon. On the platform he ranked with Webster; behind the political scenes he was the peer of Van Buren. In every environment he was warm and open—what a modern political scientist might call a charismatic personality. Clay loved to drink, swear, tell tales, and play poker. At one sitting he won $40,000 from a friend and then cheerfully told him that a note for $500 would wipe out the obligation. He was a reasonable man, skilled at arranging political compromises, but he possessed a reckless streak: Twice in his career he challenged men to duels for having insulted him. Fortunately, all concerned were poor shots.

Clay was elected to Congress in 1810. He led the War Hawks in 1811 and 1812 and was Speaker of the House from 1811 to 1820 and from 1823 to 1825.

Intellectually the inferior of Adams, Calhoun, and Webster, Clay nevertheless had a perfect temperament

▲ Henry Clay of Kentucky. "Life itself is but a compromise between death and life." He applied this principle to politics.

for politics. He loved power and understood that in the United States it had to be shared to be exercised. His great gift was in seeing national needs from a broad perspective and fashioning a program that could inspire ordinary citizens with something of his vision.

In the early 1820s he was just developing his "American System." In return for eastern support of a policy of federal aid in the construction of roads and canals, the West would back the protective tariff. He justified this deal on the widest national grounds. America has a "great diversity of interests," ranging from agriculture and fishing to manufacturing, shipbuilding, and commerce. "The good of each . . . and of the whole should be carefully consulted. This is the only mode by which we can preserve, in full vigor, the harmony of the whole Union." Stimulating manufacturing, for example, would increase the demand for western raw materials, while western prosperity would lead to greater consumption of eastern manufactured goods.

Although himself a slaveowner, Clay called slavery the "greatest of human evils." He favored freeing the slaves and "colonizing" them in Africa, which could, he said, be accomplished gradually and at relatively minor cost.

The West had other spokesmen in the 1820s. Thomas Hart Benton, elected to the Senate by the new state of Missouri, was an expansionist and a hard-money man of the uncompromising sort, suspicious of paper currency and therefore of all banks. His friends called him "Old Bullion"; his detractors, "Big Bully Bottom." Benton championed the small western farmer, favoring free homesteads for pioneers and an extensive federal internal improvements program. Another western leader was General William Henry Harrison. Although he sat in the Ohio legislature and in both houses of Congress between 1816 and 1828, Harrison was primarily a soldier. He did not identify himself closely with any policy other than the extermination of Indians. He had little to do with the newly developing political alignments of the 1820s.

Much like Harrison was Andrew Jackson, the "Hero of New Orleans," whose popularity greatly exceeded Harrison's. He had many friends, shrewd in the ways of politics, who were working devotedly, if not entirely unselfishly, to make him president. No one knew his views on most questions, but few cared. His chief assets as a presidential candidate were his military reputation and his forceful personality, but both, and especially the latter, were likely to get him into political hot water.

THE MISSOURI COMPROMISE

The sectional concerns of the 1820s repeatedly influenced politics. The depression of 1819 to 1822 increased tensions by making people feel more strongly about the issues of the day. For example, manufacturers who wanted high tariffs in 1816 were more vehemently in favor of protection in 1820 when their business fell off. Even when economic conditions improved, geographic alignments on key issues tended to solidify.

One of the first and most critical of the sectional questions concerned the admission of Missouri as a slave state. When Louisiana entered the Union in 1812, the rest of the Louisiana Purchase was organized as the Missouri Territory. Building on a nucleus of Spanish and French inhabitants, the region west and north of St. Louis grew rapidly, and in 1817 the Missourians petitioned for statehood. A large percentage of the settlers—the population exceeded 60,000 by 1818—were Southerners who had moved into the valleys of the Arkansas and Missouri rivers. Since many of them owned slaves, Missouri would become a slave state.

DOCUMENT

Missouri
Enabling Act

The admission of new states had always been a routine matter, in keeping with the admirable pattern established by the Northwest Ordinance. But during the debate on the Missouri Enabling Act in February 1819, Congressman James Tallmadge of New York introduced an amendment prohibiting "the further introduction of slavery" and providing that all slaves born in Missouri after the territory became a state should be freed at age 25.

While Tallmadge was merely seeking to apply in the territory the pattern of race relations that had developed in the states immediately east of Missouri, his amendment represented, at least in spirit, something of a revolution. The Northwest Ordinance had prohibited slavery in the land between the Mississippi and the Ohio, but that area had only a handful of slaveowners in 1787 and little prospect of attracting more. Elsewhere no effort to restrict the movement of slaves into new territory had been attempted. If one assumed (as whites always had) that the slaves themselves should have no say in the matter, it appeared democratic to let the settlers of Missouri decide the slavery question for themselves. Nevertheless, the Tallmadge amendment passed the House, the vote following sectional lines closely. The Senate, however, resoundingly rejected it. The less populous southern part of Missouri was then organized separately as the Arkansas Territory, and an attempt to bar slavery there was stifled. The Missouri Enabling Act failed to pass before Congress adjourned.

When the next Congress met in December 1819, the Missouri issue came up at once. The vote on Tallmadge's amendment had shown that the rapidly growing North controlled the House of Representatives. It was vital, Southerners felt, to preserve a balance in the Senate. Yet Northerners objected to the fact that Missouri extended hundreds of miles north of the Ohio River, which they considered slavery's natural boundary. Angry debate raged in Congress for months.

The debate did not turn on the morality of slavery or the rights of blacks. Northerners objected to adding new slave states because under the Three-fifths Compromise these states would be overrepresented in Congress (60 percent of their slaves would be counted in determining the size of the states' delegations in the House of Representatives) and because they did not relish competing with slave labor. Since the question was political influence rather than the rights and wrongs of slavery, a compromise was worked out in 1820. Missouri entered the Union as a slave state and Maine, having been separated from Massachusetts, was admitted as a free state to preserve the balance in the Senate.

To prevent further conflict, Congress adopted the proposal of Senator Jesse B. Thomas of Illinois, which "forever prohibited" slavery in all other parts of the Louisiana Purchase north of 36° 30′ latitude, the westward extension of Missouri's southern boundary. Although this division would keep slavery out of most of the territory, Southerners accepted it cheerfully. The land south of the line, the present states of Arkansas and Oklahoma, seemed ideally suited for the expanded plantation economy, and most persons considered the treeless northern regions little better than

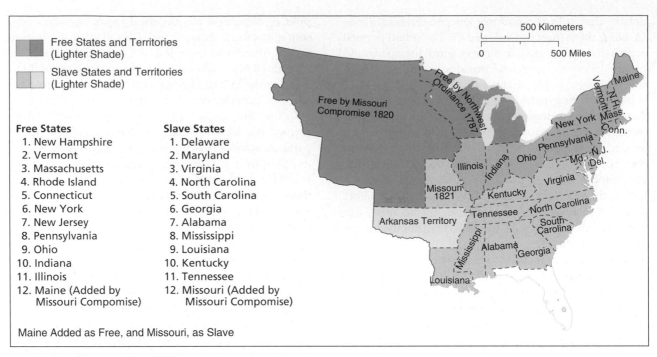

Free States and Territories
(Lighter Shade)

Slave States and Territories
(Lighter Shade)

Free States
1. New Hampshire
2. Vermont
3. Massachusetts
4. Rhode Island
5. Connecticut
6. New York
7. New Jersey
8. Pennsylvania
9. Ohio
10. Indiana
11. Illinois
12. Maine (Added by
    Missouri Compromise)

Slave States
1. Delaware
2. Maryland
3. Virginia
4. North Carolina
5. South Carolina
6. Georgia
7. Alabama
8. Mississippi
9. Louisiana
10. Kentucky
11. Tennessee
12. Missouri (Added by
    Missouri Compromise)

Maine Added as Free, and Missouri, as Slave

▲ **The Missouri Compromise, 1820**
The Missouri Compromise temporarily put aside the congressional debate over slavery, with the slave states (12) and free states (12) being in perfect balance. This meant, of course, that the Senate was evenly divided as well. But what would happen when other parts of the Missouri Territory sought admission to the Union as states?

a desert. One northern senator, decrying the division, contemptuously described the land north and west of Missouri, today one of the world's richest agricultural regions, as "a prairie without food or water."

The Missouri Compromise did not end the crisis. When Missouri submitted its constitution for approval by Congress (the final step in the admission process), the document, besides authorizing slavery and prohibiting the emancipation of any slave without the consent of the owner, required the state legislature to pass a law barring free blacks and mulattos from entering the state "under any pretext whatever." This provision plainly violated Article IV, Section 2, of the United States Constitution: "The Citizens of each State shall be entitled to all Privileges and Immunities of Citizens in the several States." It did not, however, represent any more of a break with established racial patterns, North or South, than the Tallmadge amendment; many states east of Missouri barred free blacks without regard for the Constitution.

Nevertheless, northern congressmen hypocritically refused to accept the Missouri constitution. Once more the debate raged. Again, since few Northerners cared to defend the rights of blacks, the issue was compromised. In March 1821 Henry Clay found a face-saving formula: Out of respect for the "supreme law of the land," Congress accepted the Missouri constitution with the demurrer that no law

passed in conformity to it should be construed as contravening Article IV, Section 2.

Every thinking person recognized the political dynamite inherent in the Missouri controversy. The sectional lineup had been terrifyingly compact. What meant the Union if so trivial a matter as one new state could so divide the people? Moreover, despite the timidity and hypocrisy of the North, everyone realized that the rights and wrongs of slavery lay at the heart of the conflict. "We have the wolf by the ears, and we can neither safely hold him, nor safely let him go," Jefferson wrote a month after Missouri became a state. The dispute, he said, "like a fire bell in the night, awakened and filled me with terror." Jefferson knew that the compromise had not quenched the flames ignited by the Missouri debates. "This is a reprieve only," he said. John Quincy Adams called it the "title page to a great tragic volume." Yet one could still hope that the fire bell was only a false alarm, that Adams's tragic volume would remain unread.

THE ELECTION OF 1824

Other controversies that aroused strong feelings did not seem to divide the country so deeply. The question of federal internal improvements caused endless

debate that split the country on geographical lines. In 1816 the nationalist-minded Calhoun had pressed a plan to set up a $1.5 million fund for roads and canals. Congress approved this despite strong opposition in New England and a divided South. In 1822 a bill providing money for the upkeep of the National Road caused another sectional split. Both measures were vetoed, but in 1824 Monroe approved a differently worded internal improvement act. Such proposals excited intense reactions. John Randolph, opposing the 1824 bill with his usual ferocity, threatened to employ "every . . . means short of actual insurrection" to defeat it. Yet no one—not even Randolph, it will be noted—threatened the Union on this issue.

The tariff continued to divide the country. When a new, still higher tariff was enacted in 1824, the slave states voted almost unanimously against it, the North and Northwest in favor, and New England remained of two minds. Webster (after conducting a poll of business leaders before deciding how to vote) made a powerful speech against the act, but the measure passed without creating a major storm.

These divisions were not severely disruptive, in part because the major politicians, competing for the presidency, did not dare risk alienating any section by taking too extreme a position. Calhoun, for example, had changed his mind about protective tariffs by 1824, but he avoided declaring himself because of his presidential ambitions. Another reason was that the old party system had broken down; the Federalists had disappeared as a national party and the Jeffersonians, lacking an organized opposition, had become less aggressive and more troubled by factional disputes.

The presidential fight was therefore waged on personal grounds, although the heat generated by the contest began the process of reenergizing party politics. Besides Calhoun the candidates were Jackson, Crawford, Adams, and Clay. The maneuvering among them was complex, the infighting savage. In March 1824, Calhoun, who was young enough to wait for the White House, withdrew and declared for the vice presidency, which he won easily. Crawford, who had the support of many congressional leaders, seemed the likely winner, but he suffered a series of paralytic strokes that gravely injured his chances.

Despite the bitterness of the contest, it attracted relatively little public interest; barely a quarter of those eligible took the trouble to vote. In the Electoral College Jackson led with 99, Adams had 84, Crawford 41, and Clay 37. Since no one had a majority, the contest was thrown into the House of Representatives, which, under the Constitution, had to choose from among the three leaders, each state delegation having one vote. By employing his great influence in the House, Clay swung the balance. Not wishing to advance the fortunes of a rival Westerner like Jackson and feeling, with reason, that Crawford's health made him unavailable, Clay gave his support to Adams, who was thereupon elected.

JOHN QUINCY ADAMS AS PRESIDENT

Adams, who took a Hamiltonian view of the future of the country, hoped to use the national authority to foster all sorts of useful projects. He asked Congress for a federal program of internal improvements so vast that even Clay boggled when he realized its scope. He came out for aid to manufacturing and agriculture, for a national university,

DOCUMENT

John Quincy Adams, Inaugural Address

▲ This cartoon for the 1824 election shows Adams's "low pressure" ship sailing toward the victory dock, while Jackson's "high pressure" ship explodes before reaching the dock and the victory prize of the White House. Although Jackson won a plurality of both the popular and electoral votes in the election, he failed to win the necessary majority, and the House of Representatives had to choose the winner from among the top three candidates. When Henry Clay's supporters in the House gave their votes—and the victory—to John Quincy Adams, the Jacksonians complained of having been cheated by a "corrupt bargain."

and even for a government astronomical observatory. For a nationalist of unchallengeable Jeffersonian origins like Clay or Calhoun to have pressed for so extensive a program would have been politically risky. For the son of John Adams to do so was disastrous; every doubter remembered his Federalist background and decided that he was trying to overturn the glorious "Revolution of 1800."

Adams proved to be his own worst enemy, for he was as inept a politician as ever lived. Although capable on occasion of turning a phrase—in his first annual message to Congress he described astronomical observatories as "light-houses of the skies"—his general style of public utterance was bumbling and cumbersome. Knowing that many citizens considered things like observatories impractical extravagances, he urged Congress not to be "palsied by the will of our constituents." To persuade Americans, who were almost pathological on the subject of monarchy, to support his road building program, he cited with approval the work being done abroad by "the nations of Europe and . . . their rulers," which revived fears that all Adamses were royalists at heart. He was insensitive to the ebb and flow of public feeling; even when he wanted to move with the tide, he seldom managed to dramatize and publicize his stand effectively. There was wide support in the country for a federal bankruptcy law, but instead of describing himself in plain language as a friend of poor debtors, Adams called for the "amelioration" of the "often oppressive codes relating to insolvency" and buried the recommendation at the tail end of a dull state paper.

One of Adams's worst political failings was his refusal to use his power of appointment to win support. "I will not dismiss . . . able and faithful political opponents to provide for my own partisans," he said. The attitude was traditional at the time, but Adams carried it to extremes—in four years he removed only 12 men from office. Nevertheless, by appointing Henry Clay secretary of state, he laid himself open to the charge that he had won the presidency by a "corrupt bargain." Thus, despite his politically suicidal attitude toward federal jobs, he was subject to the annoyance of a congressional investigation of his appointments, out of which came no less than six bills designed "to reduce the patronage of the executive."

CALHOUN'S EXPOSITION AND PROTEST

The tariff question added to the president's troubles. High duties, increasingly more repulsive to the export-conscious South, attracted more and more favor in the North and West. Besides manufacturers, lead

miners in Missouri, hemp raisers in Kentucky, wool growers in New York, and many other interests demanded protection against foreign competition. The absence of party discipline provided an ideal climate for "logrolling" in Congress. Legislators found themselves under pressure from their constituents to raise the duties on products of local importance; to satisfy these demands, they traded votes with other congressmen similarly situated. In this way massive "support" for protection was generated.

In 1828 a new tariff was hammered into shape by the House Committee on Manufactures. Northern and western agricultural interests were in command; they wrote into the bill extremely high duties on raw wool, hemp, flax, fur, and liquor. New England manufacturers protested vociferously, for although their products were protected, the proposed law would increase the cost of their raw materials. This gave Southerners, now hopelessly in the minority on the tariff question, a chance to block the bill. When the New Englanders proposed amendments lowering the duties on raw materials, the Southerners voted nay, hoping to force them to reject the measure on the final vote. This desperate strategy failed. New England had by this time committed its future to manufacturing, a change signaled by the somersault of Webster, who, ever responsive to local pressures, now voted for protection. After winning some minor concessions in the Senate, largely through the intervention of Van Buren, enough New Englanders accepted the so-called Tariff of Abominations to ensure its passage.

Vice President Calhoun, who had watched the debate from the vantage point of his post as president of the Senate, now came to a great turning point in his career. He had thrown in his lot with Jackson, whose running mate he was to be in the coming election, and had been assured that the Jacksonians would oppose the bill. Yet northern Jacksonians had been responsible for drafting and passing it. The new tariff would impoverish the South, he believed. He warned Jackson that relief must soon be provided or the Union would be shaken to its foundations. Then he returned to his South Carolina plantation and wrote an essay, *The South Carolina Exposition and Protest,* repudiating the nationalist philosophy he had previously championed.

The South Carolina legislature released this document to the country in December 1828, along with eight resolutions denouncing the protective tariff as unfair and unconstitutional. The theorist Calhoun, however, was not content with outlining the case against the tariff. His *Exposition* provided an ingenious defense of the right of the people of a state to reject a

▶ *text continues on page 220*

Mapping the Past

North–South Sectionalism Intensifies

Origins of the "Tariff of Abominations"

After the Napoleonic wars, the "infant industries" of the United States sought and received "protection" against foreign competition in the form of high tariffs on imports. By raising the prices of imported goods, American producers would enjoy a competitive advantage.

A protective tariff was enacted in 1816 without serious controversy. But manufacturers in Massachusetts, New York, and Pennsylvania wanted still higher tariffs. In 1827

Daniel Webster of Massachusetts proposed a law to add an 83-cent tax to every dollar's worth of imported woolen cloth. This would ensure that American woolen manufacturers, many of them located in Massachusetts, would dominate the market; it would also raise the price of woolen cloth to American consumers. The measure was tied in the Senate; Vice President Calhoun cast the deciding vote against the woolen tariff.

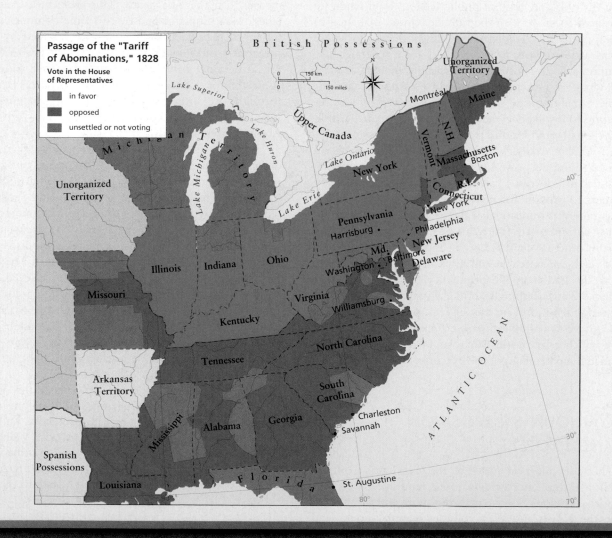

Passage of the "Tariff of Abominations," 1828

Vote in the House of Representatives

- in favor
- opposed
- unsettled or not voting

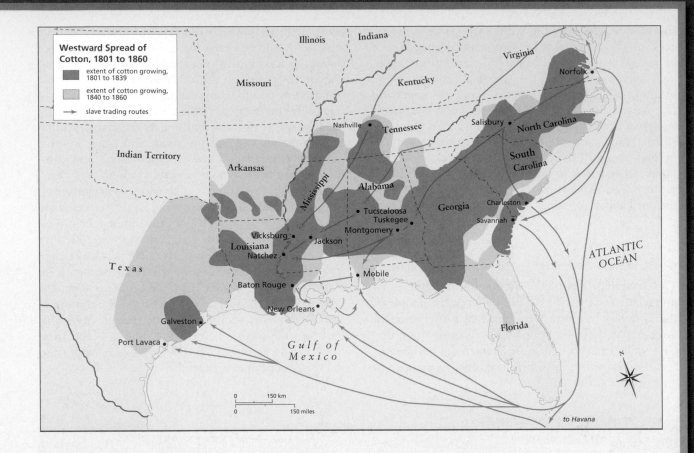

Westward Spread of Cotton, 1801 to 1860

extent of cotton growing, 1801 to 1839
extent of cotton growing, 1840 to 1860
slave trading routes

Redoubling their efforts, the manufacturers convened at Harrisburg, Pennsylvania. They called for far higher duties on woolens and many other products. Their duties would double the price of most woolen goods. Should that happen, a Southerner declared, South Carolina would within a year become "an independent State and her ports will be free ports." But once Congress got hold of the bill, it was transformed. Southerners, to ensure its defeat, attempted to drive a wedge between western farmers and northeastern manufacturers. The Southerners added high taxes on imports of raw materials, such as wool, hemp, and molasses; such measures pleased the sheep farmers and hemp growers of the Mid-Atlantic states and the Midwest, but harmed woolen manufacturers in New England as well as those engaged in shipping. When the final vote came, congressmen in eastern Massachusetts, Rhode Island, and the New York City region voted against the "Tariff of Abominations"; nearly all other northeastern congressmen voted for it, as did nearly every congressman in the West. The vote reflected a profound shift in the nation's political geography. Early in the national period, the most prominent division was often between the more prosperous peoples along the east coast—tidewater planters and urban merchants—and the rough frontiersmen in the western hinterlands. But the vote on the "Tariff of Abominations" of 1828 was an early indication of the emerging political geography reflecting the South's isolation.

Cotton Belt, 1801–1860

Most of the opposition to the "Tariff of Abominations" came from cotton-growing regions—and thus, those dependent on slavery. Slavery had long existed in North America, but by the time of the Revolution the growth of the "peculiar institution" appeared to have been checked. But in 1793 Eli Whitney, a young graduate of Yale College, invented the cotton gin, a simple, hand-operated machine that revitalized cotton cultivation—and slavery. In 1793 only 3000 bales of cotton were produced in the United States. In 1800 output reached 100,000 bales, roughly 500 million pounds; then, there were fewer than a million slaves in the United States, and by the 1820s annual production was averaging more than 400,000 bales. This was only the beginning. Output exceeded 1 million bales in the mid-1830s and nearly 4 million by 1860.

This growth required a huge expansion of the area where cotton was grown. First, cotton took over the fertile Appalachian Piedmont in a band running from southern Virginia into Georgia. Then it spread westward across central Alabama and Mississippi and into the rich alluvial soil of the banks of the Mississippi River, in a broad band from Tennessee and Arkansas to southern Louisiana. Finally, in the 1840s and 1850s, the crop spread into the eastern sections of Texas.

The westward expansion of cotton cultivation served to exacerbate an inherently bad institution. Planters in the Upper South increasingly sold their "surplus" slaves to the more fertile lands in the Mississippi delta, Alabama, and East Texas.

law of Congress. Starting with John Locke's revered concept of government as a contractual relationship, he argued that since the states had created the Union, logic dictated that they be the final arbiters of the meaning of the Constitution, which was its framework. If a special state convention, representing the sovereignty of the people, decided that an act of Congress violated the Constitution, it could interpose its authority and "nullify" the law within its boundaries. Calhoun did not seek to implement this theory in 1828, for he hoped that the next administration would lower the tariff and make nullification unnecessary.

THE MEANING OF SECTIONALISM

The sectional issues that occupied the energies of politicians and strained the ties between the people of the different regions were produced by powerful forces that actually bound the sections together. Growth caused differences that sometimes led to conflict, but growth itself was the product of prosperity.

People were drawn to the West by the expectation that life would be better there, as more often than not it was, at least in the long run. Henry Clay based his American System on the idea that sectional economic differences could be mutually beneficial. He argued plausibly that western farmers would profit by selling their crops to eastern city dwellers and that spending public money on building roads and other internal improvements would make transportation and communication less expensive and thus benefit everyone.

Another force unifying the nation was patriotism; the increasing size and prosperity of the nation made people proud to be part of a growing, dynamic society. Still another was the uniqueness of the American system of government and the people's knowledge that their immediate ancestors had created it. John Adams and Thomas Jefferson died on the same day, July 4, 1826, the fiftieth anniversary of the signing of the Declaration of Independence. People took this not as a remarkable coincidence, but as a sign from the heavens, an indication that God looked with favor on the American experiment.

MILESTONES

Year	Event
1808	James Madison is elected president
1810	Macon's Bill No. 2 removes all restrictions on commerce with Britain and France
1811	Battle of Tippecanoe shatters Indian confederation
1812	James Madison is reelected president
	Congress declares war on Great Britain
	USS *Constitution* and *United States* win naval victories
1813	Captain Oliver Hazard Perry destroys British fleet in Battle of Lake Erie
	General William Henry Harrison defeats British in Battle of the Thames
	Tecumseh dies at Battle of the Thames
1814	British burn Washington, D.C.
	Francis Scott Key writes "The Star Spangled Banner" during bombardment of Fort McHenry
	New England Federalists meet at Hartford Convention
	Treaty of Ghent officially ends war of 1812
1815	General Andrew Jackson defeats British at Battle of New Orleans
1816	James Monroe is elected president
1817	Rush-Bagot Agreement limits American and British forces on Lake Champlain and Great Lakes
1819	United States signs Transcontinental Treaty with Spain
1819–1822	United States experiences economic depression
1820	James Monroe is reelected president
1820–1821	Missouri Compromise closes Missouri Territory to slavery, but opens Arkansas Territory to slavery
1820–1850	Cities and manufacturing grow rapidly
1823	Monroe Doctrine says U.S. will consider future European colonization in western hemisphere a threat to American peace and safety
1824–1825	House of Representatives decides election of 1824 in favor of John Quincy Adams, leading to claims of "corrupt bargain" with Henry Clay
1828	Congress passes Tariff of Abominations, leading to nullification debate

SUPPLEMENTARY READING

On Madison, see Lance Banning, *Sacred Fire of Liberty* (1995), and Jack N. Rakove, *James Madison and the Creation of the American Republic* (1999). The best modern account of the causes and course of the War of 1812 is J. C. A. Stagg, *Mr. Madison's War* (1983). Irving Brant, *James Madison: Commander-in-Chief* (1961), vigorously defends Madison's handling of the war. Jackson's part in the conflict is described in R. V. Remini, *Andrew Jackson and the Course of American Empire* (1977). Richard Barbuto, *Niagara 1814: America Invades Canada* (2000), and David Curtis Skaggs and Larry L. Nelson, *The Sixty Years' War for the Great Lakes* (2001), provide accounts of the war in the North.

On the Treaty of Ghent, see F. L. Engelman, *The Peace of Christmas Eve* (1962), and Bradford Perkins, *Castlereagh and Adams* (1964). For the decline of the Federalist party and the Hartford Convention, consult D. H. Fischer, *The Revolution of American Conservatism* (1965), and J. M. Banner, *To the Hartford Convention* (1981).

For the postwar diplomatic settlements and the Era of Good Feelings, see James Lewis, *The American Union and the Problem of Neighborhood: The United States and the Collapse of the Spanish Empire, 1783–1829* (1998), George Dangerfield, *The Era of Good Feelings* (1952), and Harry Ammon, *James Monroe: The Quest for National Identity* (1971), and on his famous doctrine, Ernest May, *The Making of the Monroe Doctrine* (1976).

Merrill D. Peterson, *The Great Triumvirate* (1987), is an interesting study of Clay, Calhoun, and Webster. Other biographies of statesmen of the period include Paul C. Nagel, *John Quincy Adams* (1997), Robert Remini, *Daniel Webster* (1997), Irving Bartlett, *John C. Calhoun* (1993), Maurice Baxter, *Henry Clay and the American System* (1995), and C. C. Mooney, *William H. Crawford* (1974). On the Missouri Compromise, see Glover Moore, *The Missouri Controversy* (1953). See also P. C. Nagel, *One Nation Indivisible* (1965).

On Indians, in addition to the works cited in Debating the Past (p. 194) see John Sugden, *Tecumseh* (1998), R. David Edmonds, *The Potawatomis* (1978), and Michael N. McConnell, *A Country Between: The Upper Ohio Valley and Its Peoples* (1992).

SUGGESTED WEBSITES

Documents from the War of 1812

http://www.yale.edu/lawweb/avalon/diplomacy/britian/brtreaty.htm

This site includes the important documents from the War of 1812.

The War of 1812

http://members.tripod.com/~war1812/index.html

This site provides in-depth information about the War of 1812.

The Monroe Doctrine

http://www.yale.edu/lawweb/avalon/monroe.htm

Read the Monroe Doctrine, an important early articulation of U.S. foreign policy, online.

The Seminole Indians of Florida

http://www.seminoletribe.com/

Before becoming president, Andrew Jackson began a war against the Seminole Indians.

Toward a National Economy

▼ St. Louis during the 1830s, by George Catlin, a lawyer turned painter. Twenty-five years earlier, Catlin's wife had complained of "this wild Country." But by 1830s St. Louis had over 5000 people and regular steamboat service.

Politicians might attribute the growth of the country and the preservation of the Union to their own patriotism and ingenuity, but without the economic and technological developments of the period, neither of these much-to-be-desired objectives could have been attained. The country was still overwhelmingly agricultural in 1820, but the nation was on the brink of a major economic readjustment. Certain obscure seeds planted in the early years of the republic had taken root. Almost unnoticed, new attitudes toward material goods, along with new ways of producing them, were beginning to take hold. The industrial revolution was coming to America with a rush.

GENTILITY AND THE CONSUMER REVOLUTION

The democratic revolution was accompanied by widespread emulation of aristocratic behavior. Sometimes the most ardent American democrats proved the most susceptible to the blandishments of European gentility. Thus young John Adams, while lampooning "the late Refinements in modern manners," nevertheless advised his future wife, Abigail, to be more attentive to posture: "You very often hang your Head like a Bulrush, and you sit with your legs crossed to the ruin of the figure." On his trip to Paris in 1778 on behalf of the Continental Congress, he denounced the splendor of the houses, furniture, and clothing. "I cannot help suspecting that the more

▲ Americans enshrined the simple life and a homespun equality; yet they coveted the cultural markers of aristocracy, such as imported porcelain tea services. This one, made in France, was given to Alexander Hamilton. Gentility spread, historian Richard Bushman writes, "because people longed to be associated with the 'best society.'"

Elegance, the less Virtue," he concluded. Yet despite the exigencies of war, Adams purchased a lavish carriage. On returning to America, he bought a three-story mansion and furnished it with Louis XV chairs and, among other extravagances, an ornate wine cooler from Vincennes.

Among aristocratic circles in Europe, gentility was the product of ancestry and cultivated style; but in America it was largely defined by possession of material goods. Houses with parlors, dining rooms, and hallways bulged with countless articles of consumption: porcelain plates, silver tea services, woolen carpets, walnut tables. By the mid-eighteenth century the "refinement of America" had touched the homes of some Southern planters and urban merchants; but a half century later porcelain plates made by English craftsman Josiah Wedgwood and mahogany washstands by Thomas Chippendale were appearing even in frontier communities. Americans were demanding more goods than such craftsmen could turn out. Everywhere producers sought to expand their workshops, hire and train more artisans, and acquire large stocks of materials and labor-saving machines.

But first they had to locate the requisite capital, find ways to supervise large numbers of workers, and discover how to get raw materials to factories and products to customers. The solutions to these problems, taken together, constituted the "market revolution" of the early nineteenth century. The "industrial revolution" came on its heels.

BIRTH OF THE FACTORY

By the 1770s British manufacturers, especially those in textiles, had made astonishing progress in mechanizing their operations, bringing workers together in buildings called factories where waterpower, and later steam, supplied the force to run new spinning and weaving devices that increased productivity and reduced labor costs.

Because machine-spun cotton was cheaper and of better quality than that spun by hand, producers in other countries were eager to adopt British methods. Americans had depended on Great Britain for such products until the Revolution cut off supplies; then the new spirit of nationalism gave impetus to the development of local industry. A number of state legislatures offered bounties to anyone who would introduce the new machinery. The British, however, guarded their secrets vigilantly. It was illegal to export any of the new machines or to send their plans abroad. Workers skilled in their construction and use were forbidden to leave the country. These restrictions were effective for a time; the principles on which the new machines were based were simple enough, but to construct workable models without plans was another matter. Although a number of persons tried to do so, it was not until Samuel Slater installed his machines in Pawtucket, Rhode Island, that a successful factory was constructed.

Slater, born in England, was more than a skilled mechanic. Attracted by stories of the rewards offered in the United States, he slipped out of England in 1789. Not daring to carry any plans, he depended on his memory and his mechanical sense for the complicated specifications of the necessary machines. Moses Brown brought Slater to Rhode Island to help run his textile-manufacturing operation. Slater insisted on scrapping the crude machinery Brown's company had assembled. Then, working in secrecy with a carpenter who was "under bond not to steal the patterns nor disclose the nature of the work," Slater built and installed his machinery. In December 1790 the first American factory began production.

It was a humble beginning indeed. Slater's machines made only cotton thread, which Brown's company sold in its Providence store and "put out"

This physical separation of masters and journeymen is reflected in the maps on page 226. In 1827, for example, most journeymen lived near their masters' shops. But by 1834 journeymen were scattered throughout Rochester. A similar separation of journeymen and masters was found among skilled workers in the building trades. In Johnson's words, the journeymen and apprentices "worked for men they seldom saw." Often such men were becoming estranged from those who paid their wages.

Johnson found the same shift, from apprentice and journeyman to wage earner, and from master to merchant capitalist, in many other trades.

The Journey to Work, Philadelphia, 1850

During the next two decades, the expanding scale of manufacturing operations made the craft-dominated workshop nearly an anachronism. Larger operations required more work space, and the need to locate near suppliers, customers, or a source of waterpower meant that the owner's home could no longer serve as a workplace. By about 1850, Boston, New York, Philadelphia, and other cities had sorted themselves into commercial and residential districts; the residential districts further separated into working-class and employer-class neighborhoods.

Nowadays the term *inner city* often connotes poverty, and *suburbs*, prosperity. But the relationship was reversed in the mid-nineteenth-century city, as historian Sam Bass Warner has shown in his study of Philadelphia. In 1850 affluent Philadelphians resided in the core of the city while factory workers lived in shanties and boardinghouses along its outskirts. The map *(left)*, based on census data for 1850, shows that fewer factory workers lived in downtown Philadelphia than were employed by the factories there. Each day, thousands of factory workers from Penn Township and the eastern section of Passyunk Township walked into town to work in downtown factories.

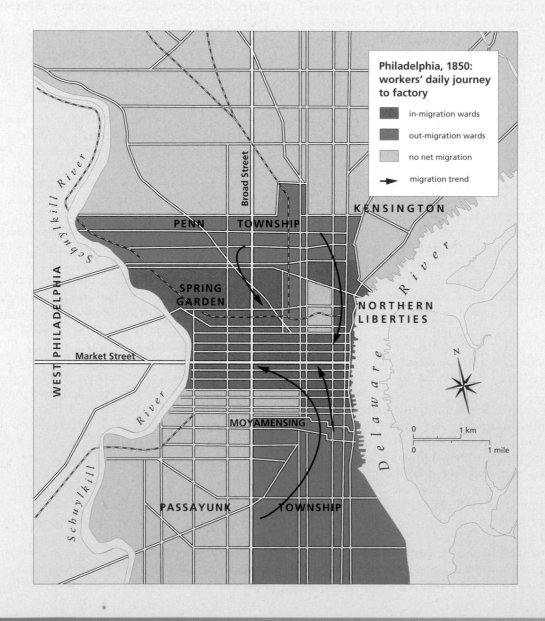

AN INDUSTRIAL PROLETARIAT?

As machines displaced skilled labor, the ability of laborers to influence working conditions declined. If skilled, they either became employers and developed entrepreneurial and managerial skills, or they descended into the mass of wage earners. Simultaneously, the changing structure of production widened the gap between owners and workers and blurred the distinction between skilled and unskilled labor.

These trends might have been expected to generate hostility between workers and employers. To some extent they did. There were strikes for higher wages and to protest work speedups throughout the 1830s and again in the 1850s. Efforts to found unions and to create political organizations dedicated to advancing the interests of workers were also undertaken. But well into the 1850s Americans displayed few signs of the class solidarity common among European workers.

Why America did not produce a self-conscious working class is a question that has long intrigued historians. As with most such large questions, no single answer has been forthcoming. Some historians argue that the existence of the frontier siphoned off displaced and dissatisfied workers. The number of urban laborers who went West could not have been large, but the fact that the expanding economy created many opportunities for laborers to rise out of the working class was surely another reason why so few of them developed strong class feelings.

Other historians believe that ethnic and racial differences kept workers from seeing themselves as a distinct class with common needs and common enemies. The influx of needy immigrants willing to accept almost any wage was certainly resented by native-born workers. The growing number of free blacks in northern cities—between 1800 and 1830 the number tripled in Philadelphia and quadrupled in New York—also inhibited the development of a self-identified working class.

These answers help explain the relative absence of class conflict during the early stages of the industrial revolution in America, but so does the fact that conditions in the early shops and factories represented an improvement for the people who worked in them. This was the case with nearly all European immigrants, though less so for urban free blacks, since in the South many found work in the skilled trades.

Most workers in the early textile factories were drawn from outside the regular labor market. Relatively few artisan spinners and weavers became factory workers; indeed, some of them continued to work as they had, for it was many years before the factories could even begin to satisfy the ever-increasing demand for cloth. Nor did immigrants attend the new machines. Instead, the mill owners relied chiefly on women and children. They did so because machines lessened the need for skill and strength and because the labor shortage made it necessary to tap unexploited sources. By the early 1820s about half the cotton textile workers in the factories were under 16 years of age.

Most people of that generation considered this a good thing. They reasoned that the work was easy and that it kept youngsters busy at useful tasks while providing their families with extra income. Roxanna Foote, whose daughter, Harriet Beecher Stowe, wrote *Uncle Tom's Cabin*, came from a solid middle-class family in Guilford, Connecticut. Nevertheless, she worked full-time before her marriage in her grandfather's small spinning mill. "This spinning-mill was a favorite spot," a relative recalled many years later. "Here the girls often received visitors, or read or chatted while they spun." Roxanna explained her daily regimen as a mill girl matter-of-factly: "I generally rise with the sun, and, after breakfast, take my wheel, which is my daily companion, and the evening is generally devoted to reading, writing, and knitting."

This seems a somewhat idealized picture, or perhaps working for one's grandfather made a difference. Another young girl, Emily Chubbock, later a well-known writer, had a less pleasant recollection of her experience as an 11-year-old factory hand earning $1.25 a week. "My principal recollections . . . are of noise and filth, bleeding hands and aching feet, and a very sad heart." In any case, a society accustomed to seeing the children of fairly well-to-do farmers working full-time in the fields was not shocked by the sight of children working all day in mills. In factories where laborers were hired in family units, no member earned very much, but with a couple of adolescent daughters and perhaps a son of 9 or 10 helping out, a family could take home enough to live decently. For most working Americans, then as now, that was success enough.

LOWELL'S WALTHAM SYSTEM: WOMEN AS FACTORY WORKERS

Instead of hiring children, the Boston Associates developed the "Waltham System" of employing young, unmarried women in their new textile mills. For a

▲ The first mill operations performed only the task of spinning wool, cotton, and other fibers into thread; soon weaving was also mechanized, so that fabric ready to be cut and sewn was manufactured. Note that the workers are all women, supervised by a male foreman.

DOCUMENT

The Harbinger,
"Female Workers
at Lowell"

generation after the opening of the Merrimack Manufacturing Company in 1823, the thriving factory towns of Lowell, Chicopee, and Manchester provided the background for a remarkable industrial idyll. Young women came from farms all over New England to work for a year or two in the mills. They were lodged in company boardinghouses, which, like college dormitories, became centers of social life and not merely places to eat and sleep. Unlike modern college dormitories, the boardinghouses were strictly supervised; straitlaced New Englanders did not hesitate to permit their daughters to live in them. The regulations laid down by one company, for example, required that all employees "show that they are penetrated by a laudable love of temperance and virtue." "Ardent spirits" were banished from company property, "games of hazard and cards" prohibited. A 10 P.M. curfew was strictly enforced.

The women earned between $2.50 and $3.25 a week, about half of which went for room and board. Some of the remainder they sent home, the rest (what there was of it) they could spend as they wished.

Most of these young women did not have to support themselves. They worked to save for a trousseau, to help educate a younger brother, or simply for the experience and excitement of meeting new people and escaping the confining environment of the farm. "The feeling that at this new

work, the few hours they had of every-day leisure was entirely their own was a satisfaction to them," one Lowell worker recalled. Anything but an industrial proletariat, they filled the windows of the factories with flowering plants, organized sewing circles, edited their own literary periodicals, and attended lectures on edifying subjects. That such activity was possible on top of a 70-hour work week is a commentary on both the resiliency of youth and the leisurely pace of these early factories. The English novelist Charles Dickens, though scarcely enchanted by other American ways, was impressed by his visit to Lowell, which he compared most favorably to "those great haunts of misery," the English manufacturing towns. "They were all well dressed," he wrote of the workers. "They were healthy in appearance, many of them remarkably so, and had the manners and deportment of young women. . . . The rooms in which they worked were as well ordered as themselves."

Life in the mills was not all it might have been. Although they made up 85 percent of the workforce, women were kept out of supervisory positions. In 1834 workers in several mills "turned out" to protest cuts in their wages and a hike in what they paid for board. This work stoppage did not force a reversal of management policy. Another strike two years later in response to a work speedup was somewhat more successful. But when a drop in prices in

DOCUMENT

Regarding Life
in the Mills

the 1840s led the owners to introduce new rules designed to increase production, workers lacked the organizational strength to block them. By then young women of the kind that had flocked to the mills in the 1820s and 1830s were beginning to find work as schoolteachers and clerks. Mill owners turned increasingly to Irish immigrants to operate their machines.

IRISH AND GERMAN IMMIGRANTS

Between 1790 and 1820 the population of the United States had more than doubled to 9.6 million. The most remarkable feature of this growth was that it resulted almost entirely from natural increase. The birthrate in the early nineteenth century exceeded 50 per 1000 population, a rate as high as that of any country in the world today. Fewer than 250,000 immigrants entered the United States between 1790 and 1820. European wars, the ending of the slave trade, and doubts about the viability of the new republic slowed the flow of humanity across the Atlantic to a trickle.

But soon after the final defeat of Napoleon in 1815, immigration began to pick up. In the 1820s, some 150,000 European immigrants arrived; in the 1830s, 600,000; in the 1840s, 1.7 million. The 1850 census, the first to make the distinction, estimated that of the nation's population of 23 million, more than 10 percent were foreign-born. In the Northeast the proportion exceeded 15 percent.

Most of this human tide came from Germany and Ireland, but substantial numbers also came from Great Britain and the Scandinavian countries. As with earlier immigrants, most were drawn to America by what are called "pull" factors: the prospect of abundant land, good wages, and economic opportunity generally, or by the promise of political and religious freedom. But many came because of "push" factors: to stay where they were meant to face starvation. This was particularly true of those from Ireland, where a potato blight triggered the flight of tens of thousands. This Irish exodus continued; by the end of the century there were more people of Irish origin in America than in Ireland.

Once ashore in New York, Boston, or Philadelphia, most relatively prosperous immigrants pushed directly westward. Others found work in the new factory towns along the route of the Erie Canal, in the lower Delaware Valley southeast of Philadelphia, or along the Merrimack River north of Boston. But most of the Irish immigrants, "the poorest and most wretched population that can be found in the world," one of their priests called them, lacked the means to go West. Aside from the cost of transportation, starting a farm required far more capital than they could raise. Like it or not, they had to settle in the eastern cities.

Viewed in historical perspective, this massive wave of immigration stimulated the American economy. In the short run, the influx of the 1830s and 1840s depressed living standards and strained the social fabric. For the first time the nation had acquired a culturally distinctive, citybound, and propertyless class. The poor Irish immigrants had to accept whatever wages employers offered them. By doing so they caused resentment among native workers, resentment exacerbated by the unfamiliarity of the Irish with city ways and by their Roman Catholic faith, which the Protestant majority associated with European authoritarianism and corruption.

THE PERSISTENCE OF THE HOUSEHOLD SYSTEM

Since technology affected American industry unevenly, contemporaries found the changes difficult to evaluate. Interchangeable firing pins for rifles did not lead at once even to matching pairs of shoes. More than 15 years passed after John Fitch built and launched the world's first regularly scheduled steamboat in 1790 before it was widely accepted. Few people in the 1820s appreciated how profound the impact of the factory system would be. The city of Lowell seemed remarkable and important but not necessarily a herald of future trends.

Yet in nearly every field apparently minor changes were being made. Beginning around 1815, small improvements in the design of waterwheels, such as the use of leather transmission belts and metal gears, made possible larger and more efficient machinery in mills and factories. The woolen industry gradually became as mechanized as the cotton. Iron production advanced beyond the stage of the blacksmith's forge and the small foundry only slowly; nevertheless, by 1810 machines were stamping out nails at a third of the cost of the hand-forged type, and a few years later sheet iron, formerly hammered out laboriously by hand, was being produced in efficient rolling mills. At about this time the puddling process for refining pig iron made it possible to use coal for fuel instead of expensive charcoal.

Key improvements were made soon after the War of 1812 in the manufacture of paper, glass, and pottery. The commercial canning of sterilized foods

▲ The West Point Foundry in Cold Spring, New York, by Robert Weir Ferguson. This painting conveys how the machines of the industrial revolution are dominating workers' lives.

in airtight containers began about 1820. The invention in that year of a machine for cutting ice, which reduced the cost by over 50 percent, had equally important effects on urban eating habits.

RISE OF CORPORATIONS

Mechanization required substantial capital investment, and capital was chronically in short supply. The modern method of organizing large enterprises, the corporation, was slow to develop. Between 1781 and 1801 only 326 corporations were chartered by the states, and only a few of them were engaged in manufacturing.

The general opinion was that only quasi-public projects, such as roads and waterworks, were entitled to the privilege of incorporation. Anyone interested in organizing a corporation had to obtain a special act

of a state legislature. And even among businessmen there was a tendency to associate corporations with monopoly, with corruption, and with the undermining of individual enterprise. In 1820 the economist Daniel Raymond wrote: "The very object . . . of the act of incorporation is to produce inequality, either in rights, or in the division of property. Prima facie, therefore all money corporations are detrimental to national wealth. They are always created for the benefit of the rich. . . ." Such feelings help explain why as late as the 1860s most manufacturing was being done by unincorporated companies.

While the growth of industry did not suddenly revolutionize American life, it reshaped society in various ways. For a time it lessened the importance of foreign commerce. Some relative decline from the lush years immediately preceding Jefferson's embargo was no doubt inevitable, especially in the fabulously profitable reexport trade. But American

industrial growth reduced the need for foreign products and thus the business of merchants. Only in the 1850s, when the wealth and population of the United States were more than three times what they had been in the first years of the century, did the value of American exports climb back to the levels of 1807. As the country moved closer to self-sufficiency (a point it never reached), nationalistic and isolationist sentiments were subtly augmented. During the embargo and the War of 1812 a great deal of capital had been transferred from commerce to industry; afterward new capital continued to prefer industry, attracted by the high profits and growing prestige of manufacturing. The rise of manufacturing affected farmers too, for as cities grew in size and number, the need to feed the populace caused commercial agriculture to flourish. Dairy farming, truck gardening, and fruit growing began to thrive around every manufacturing center.

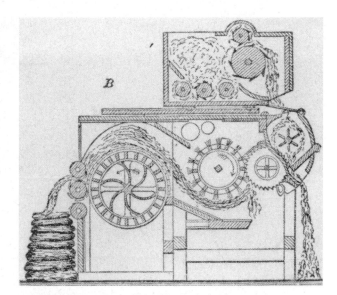

▲ Eli Whitney's cotton gin was based on a simple concept: the cotton, embedded with seeds, moved through interlocking combs, moving in opposite directions. In the above rendering, the cotton is fed from above; the combed cotton came out lower left, and the seeds, lower right.

COTTON REVOLUTIONIZES THE SOUTH

By far the most important indirect effect of industrialization occurred in the South, which soon began to produce cotton to supply the new textile factories of Great Britain and New England. The possibility of growing large amounts of this crop in America had not been seriously considered in colonial times, but by the 1780s the demand for raw cotton to feed the voracious British mills was causing many American farmers to experiment with the crop. Most of the world's cotton at this time came from Egypt, India, and the East Indies. The plant was considered tropical, most varieties being unable to survive the slightest frost. Hamilton, who missed nothing that related to the economic growth of the country, reported: "It has been observed . . . that the nearer the place of growth to the equator, the better the quality of the cotton."

Beginning in 1786, "sea-island" cotton was grown successfully in the mild, humid lowlands and offshore islands along the coasts of Georgia and South Carolina. This was a high-quality cotton, silky and long-fibered like the Egyptian. But its susceptibility to frost severely limited the area of its cultivation. Elsewhere in the South, "green-seed," or upland, cotton flourished, but this plant had little commercial value because the seeds could not be easily separated from the lint. When sea-island cotton was passed between two rollers, its shiny black seeds simply popped out; with upland cotton the seeds were pulled

through with the lint and crushed, the oils and broken bits destroying the value of the fiber. To remove the seeds by hand was laborious; a slave working all day could clean scarcely a pound of the white fluff. This made it an uneconomical crop. In 1791 the usually sanguine Hamilton admitted in his *Report on Manufactures* that "the extensive cultivation of cotton can, perhaps, hardly be expected."

Early American cotton manufacturers used the sea-island variety or imported the foreign fiber, in the latter case paying a duty of 3 cents a pound. However, the planters of South Carolina and Georgia, suffering from hard times after the Revolution, needed a new cash crop. Rice production was not expanding, and indigo, the other staple of the area, had ceased to be profitable when it was no longer possible to claim the British bounty. Cotton seemed an obvious answer. Farmers were experimenting hopefully with varieties of the plant and mulling the problem of how upland cotton could be more easily deseeded.

This was the situation in the spring of 1793, when Eli Whitney was a guest at Mulberry Grove, the plantation of Catherine Greene, widow of General Nathanael Greene, some dozen miles from Savannah.[2] Whitney had accepted a position as private

---

[2]The property, formerly owned by a prominent Georgia Tory, had been given to Greene by the state in gratitude for his having driven out the British during the Revolution.

tutor at 100 guineas a year with a nearby family and had stopped to visit a friend, Phineas Miller, who was overseer of the Greene plantation. While at Mulberry Grove, Whitney, who had never seen a cotton plant before, met a number of the local landowners.

> I heard [he wrote his father] much of the extreme difficulty of ginning Cotton, that is, separating it from its seed. There were a number of very respectable Gentlemen at Mrs. Greene's who all agreed that if a machine could be invented that would clean the Cotton with expedition, it would be a great thing both to the Country and to the inventor.

Whitney thought about the problem for a few days and then "struck out a plan of a machine." He described it to Miller, who enthusiastically offered to finance the invention. Since Whitney had just learned that his job as tutor would pay only 50 guineas, he accepted Miller's proposal.

Within ten days he had solved the problem that had baffled the planters. His gin (engine) consisted of a cylinder covered with rows of wire teeth rotating in a box filled with cotton. As the cylinder turned, the teeth passed through narrow slits in a metal grating. Cotton fibers were caught by the teeth and pulled through the slits. The seeds, too thick to pass through the openings, were left behind. A second cylinder, with brushes rotating in the opposite direction to sweep the cotton from the wires, prevented matting and clogging.

This "absurdly simple contrivance" almost instantly transformed southern agriculture. With a gin a slave could clean 50 times as much cotton as by hand; soon larger models driven by mules and horses were available. The machines were so easy to construct (once the basic idea was understood) that Whitney and Miller were never able to enforce their patent rights effectively. Rival manufacturers shamelessly pirated their work, and countless farmers built gins of their own. Cotton production increased from 3000 bales in 1790 to well over 400,000 bales a year in the early 1820s.

Despite this avalanche, the price of cotton remained high. During the 1790s it ranged between 26 and 44 cents a pound, a veritable bonanza. In the next decade the price was lower (15 to 19 cents), but it still provided high profits even for inefficient planters. The price rose again after 1815, and only once before 1826 did the price fall below 14 cents. With prices at these levels, profits of $50 an acre were not unusual, and the South boomed.

Upland cotton would grow wherever there were 200 consecutive days without frost and 24 inches of rain. The crop engulfed Georgia and South Carolina and spread north into parts of Virginia. After Andrew Jackson smashed the southwestern Indians during the War of 1812, the rich "Black Belt" area of central Alabama and northern

▲ **Cotton Production and Slave Population, 1800–1860**

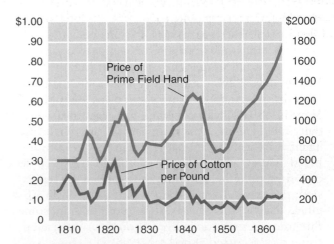

▲ **Prices for Cotton and for Slaves, 1802–1860**
The vertical axis on the left shows cents, and the curve for the price of cotton should be read against it; the right vertical axis shows dollars, and the price of slaves should be read against it. These prices are from New Orleans records. The rising trend of slave prices (and a growing slave population) shows the continuing profitability and viability of slavery up to 1860.

Mississippi and the delta region along the lower Mississippi River were rapidly taken over by the fluffy white staple. In 1821 Alabama alone raised 40,000 bales. Central Tennessee also became important cotton country.

Cotton stimulated the economy of the rest of the nation as well. Most of it was exported, the sale paying for much-needed European products. The transportation, insurance, and final disposition of the crop fell largely into the hands of northern merchants, who profited accordingly. And the surplus corn and hogs of western farmers helped feed the slaves of the new cotton plantations. Cotton was the major force in the economy for a generation, beginning about 1815.

REVIVAL OF SLAVERY

Amid the national rejoicing over this prosperity, one aspect both sad and ominous was easily overlooked. Slavery, a declining or at worst stagnant institution in the decade of the Revolution, was revitalized in the following years.

Libertarian beliefs inspired by the Revolution ran into the roadblock of race prejudice as soon as some of the practical aspects of freedom for blacks became apparent. As disciples of John Locke, the Revolutionary generation had a deep respect for property rights; in the last analysis most white Americans placed these rights ahead of the personal liberty of black Americans in their constellation of values. Forced abolition of slavery therefore attracted few recruits. Moreover, the rhetoric of the Revolution had raised the aspirations of blacks. Increasing signs of rebelliousness appeared among them, especially after the slave uprising in Saint Domingue, which culminated, after a great bloodbath, in the establishment of the black Republic of Haiti in 1804. This example of a successful slave revolt filled white Americans with apprehension. Their fears were irrational (Haitian blacks outnumbered whites and mulattos combined by seven to one) but nonetheless real. And fear led to repression; the exposure in 1801 of a plot to revolt in Virginia, led by the slave Gabriel, resulted in some three dozen executions even though no actual uprising had occurred.

The mood of the Revolutionary decade had led a substantial number of masters to free their slaves. Unfortunately this led many other whites to have second thoughts about ending slavery. "If the blacks see all of their color slaves, it will seem to them a disposition of Providence, and they will be content," a

Virginia legislator, apparently something of an amateur psychologist, claimed. "But if they see others like themselves free . . . they will repine." As the number of free blacks rose, restrictions on them were everywhere tightened.

In the 1780s many opponents of slavery began to think of solving the "Negro problem" by colonizing freed slaves in some distant region—in the western districts or perhaps in Africa. The colonization movement had two aspects. One, a manifestation of an embryonic black nationalism, reflected the disgust of black Americans with local racial attitudes and their interest in African civilization. Paul Cuffe, a Massachusetts Quaker, managed to finance the emigration of 38 of his fellow blacks to British Sierra Leone in 1815, but few others followed. Most influential northern blacks, the most conspicuous among them the Reverend Richard Allen, bishop of the African Methodist Church, opposed the idea vigorously.

The other colonization movement, led by whites, was paternalistic. Some white colonizationists genuinely abhorred slavery. Others could not stomach living with free blacks; to them colonization was merely a polite word for deportation. Most white colonizationists were conservatives who considered themselves realists. Whether they thought African Americans degenerate by nature or the victims of their surroundings, they were sure that American conditions gave them no chance to better their lot and that both races would profit from separation.

The colonization idea became popular in Virginia in the 1790s, but nothing was achieved until after the founding of the American Colonization Society in 1817. The society purchased African land and established the Republic of Liberia. However, despite the cooperation of a handful of black nationalists and the patronage of many important white Southerners, including Presidents Madison and Monroe and Chief Justice Marshall, it accomplished little. Although some white colonizationists expected exslaves to go to Africa as enthusiastic Christian missionaries who would convert and "civilize" the natives, few blacks in fact wished to migrate to a land as alien to their own experience as to their masters'. Only about 12,000 went to Liberia, and the toll taken among them by tropical diseases was large. As late as 1850 the black American population of Liberia was only 6000.

The cotton boom of the early nineteenth century acted as a brake on the colonization movement. As cotton production expanded, the need for labor in the South grew apace. The price of slaves doubled between 1795 and 1804. As it rose, the inclination of

even the most kindhearted masters to free their slaves began to falter. Although the importation of slaves from abroad had been outlawed by all the states, perhaps 25,000 were smuggled into the country in the 1790s. In 1804 South Carolina reopened the trade, and between that date and 1808, when the constitutional prohibition of importation became effective, some 40,000 were brought in. Thereafter the miserable traffic in human beings continued clandestinely, though on a small scale.

The cotton boom triggered an internal trade in slaves that frequently wreaked havoc among them. While it had always been legal for owners to transport their own slaves to a new state if they were settling there, many states forbade, or at least severely restricted, interstate commercial transactions in human flesh. A Virginia law of 1778, for example, prohibited the importation of slaves for purposes of sale, and persons entering the state with slaves had to swear that they did not intend to sell them. Once cotton became important, these laws were either repealed or systematically evaded. There was a surplus of slaves in one part of the United States and an acute shortage in another. A migration from the upper South to the cotton lands quickly sprang up. Slaves from "free" New York and New Jersey and even from New England began to appear on the auction blocks of Savannah and Charleston. Early in the Era of Good Feelings, newspapers in New Orleans were carrying reports such as: "Jersey negroes appear to be particularly adapted to this market. . . . We have the right to calculate on large importations in the future, from the success which hitherto attended the sale."

By about 1820 the letter of the law began to be changed. Soon the slave trade became an organized business, cruel and shameful, frowned on by the "best" people of the South, managed by the depraved and the greedy, yet patronized by nearly anyone who needed labor. "The native land of Washington, Jefferson, and Madison," one disgusted Virginian told a French visitor, "[has] become the Guinea of the United States."

The lot of African Americans in the northern states was almost as bad as that of southern free blacks. Except in New England, where there were few blacks to begin with, most were denied the vote, either directly or by extralegal pressures. They could not testify in court, intermarry with whites, obtain decent jobs or housing, or get even a rudimentary education. Most states segregated blacks in theaters, hospitals, and churches and on public transportation facilities. They were barred from hotels and restaurants patronized by whites.

Northern blacks could at least protest and try to convince the white majority of the injustice of their treatment. These rights were denied their southern brethren. They could and did publish newspapers and pamphlets, organize for political action, petition legislatures and the Congress for redress of grievance—in short, they applied methods of peaceful persuasion in an effort to improve their position in society.

ROADS TO MARKET

Inventions and technological improvements were extremely important in the settlement of the West. On superficial examination, this may not seem to have been the case, for the hordes of settlers who struggled across the mountains immediately after the War of 1812 were no better equipped than their ancestors who had pushed up the eastern slopes in previous generations. Many plodded on foot over hundreds of miles, dragging crude carts laden with their meager possessions. More fortunate pioneers traveled on horseback or in heavy, cumbersome wagons, the best known being the hearselike, canvas-topped Conestoga "covered wagons," pulled by horses or oxen.

Expanding America and Internal Improvements

In many cases the pioneers followed trails and roads no better than those of colonial days—quagmires in wet weather, rutted and pitted with potholes a good part of the year. When they settled down, their way of life was no more advanced than that of the Pilgrims. At first they were creatures of the forest, feeding on its abundance, building their homes and simple furniture with its wood, clothing themselves in the furs of forest animals. They usually planted the first crop in a natural glade; thereafter, year by year, they pushed back the trees with ax and saw and fire until the land was cleared. Any source of power more complicated than an ox was beyond their ken. Until the population of the territory had grown large enough to support town life, settlers were as dependent on crude household manufacturers as any earlier pioneer.

The spread of settlement into the Mississippi Valley created challenges that required technological advances if they were to be met. In the social climate of that age in the United States, these advances were not slow in coming. Most were related to transportation, the major problem for Westerners. Without economical means of getting their produce to market, they were condemned to lives of crude self-sufficiency. Everyone recognized that an efficient

▲ This stage, having just passed over a solid road of made of tree trunks, must now make its way across an all-dirt road. Already its wheels have sunk several inches into the mud.

transportation network would increase land values, stimulate domestic and foreign trade, and strengthen the entire economy.

The Mississippi River and its tributaries provided a natural highway for western commerce and communication, but it was one that had grave disadvantages. Farm products could be floated down to New Orleans on rafts and flatboats, but the descent along the Ohio River from Pittsburgh to the Mississippi took at least a month. Transportation upstream was out of the question for anything but the lightest and most valuable products, and even for them it was extremely expensive. In any case, the natural flow of trade was between East and West. That is why, from early in the westward movement, much attention was given to building roads linking the Mississippi Valley to the eastern seaboard.

Constructing decent roads over the rugged Appalachians was a formidable task. The steepest grades had to be reduced by cutting through hills

and filling in low places, all without modern blasting and earth-moving equipment. Streams had to be bridged. Drainage ditches were essential if the roads were not to be washed out by the first rains, and a firm foundation of stones, topped with a well-crowned gravel dressing, had to be provided if they were to stand up under the pounding of heavy wagons. The skills required for building roads of this quality had been developed in Great Britain and France, and the earliest American examples, constructed in the 1790s, were similar to good European highways. The first such road, connecting Philadelphia and Lancaster, Pennsylvania, opened to traffic in 1794.

In heavily populated sections the volume of traffic made good roads worth their cost, which ran to as much as $13,000 a mile where the terrain was difficult, though the average was perhaps half that figure. In some cases good roads ran into fairly remote areas. In New York, always a leading state in the movement

for improved transportation, an excellent road had been built all the way from Albany to Lake Erie by the time of the War of 1812, and by 1821 the state had some 4000 miles of good roads.

TRANSPORTATION AND THE GOVERNMENT

Most of the improved highways and many bridges were built as business ventures by private interests. Promoters charged tolls, the rates being set by the states. Tolls were collected at gates along the way; hinged poles suspended across the road were turned back by a guard after receipt of the toll. Hence these thoroughfares were known as turnpikes, or simply pikes.

The profits earned by a few early turnpikes, such as the one between Philadelphia and Lancaster, caused the boom in private road building, but even the most fortunate of the turnpike companies did not make much money. Maintenance was expensive, traffic spotty. (Ordinary public roads paralleling turnpikes were sometimes called "shunpikes" because penny-pinching travelers used them to avoid the tolls.) Some states bought stock to bolster weak companies, and others built and operated turnpikes as public enterprises. Local governments everywhere provided considerable support, for every town was eager to develop efficient communication with its neighbors.

Despite much talk about individual self-reliance and free enterprise, local, state, and national governments contributed heavily to the development of what in the jargon of the day were called "internal improvements." They served as "primary entrepreneurs," supplying capital for risky but socially desirable enterprises, with the result that a fascinating mixture of private and public energy went into the building of these institutions. At the federal level even the parsimonious Jeffersonians became deeply involved. In 1808 Secretary of the Treasury Albert Gallatin drafted a comprehensive plan for constructing much-needed roads at a cost of $16 million. This proposal was not adopted, but the government poured money in an erratic and unending stream into turnpike companies and other organizations created to improve transportation.

Logically, the major highways, especially those over the mountains, should have been built by the national government. Strategic military requirements alone would have justified such a program. One major artery, the Old National Road, running from Cumberland, Maryland, to Wheeling, in western Virginia, was constructed by the United States between 1811 and 1818. In time it was extended as far west as Vandalia, Illinois. However, further federal road building was hampered by political squabbles in Congress, usually phrased in constitutional terms but in fact based on sectional rivalries and other economic conflicts. Thus no comprehensive highway program was undertaken in the nineteenth century.

While the National Road, the New York Pike, and other, rougher trails such as the Wilderness Road into the Kentucky country were adequate for the movement of settlers, they did not begin to answer the West's need for cheap and efficient transportation. Wagon freight rates averaged at least 30 cents a ton-mile around 1815. At such rates, to transport a ton of oats from Buffalo to New York would have cost 12 times the value of the oats! To put the problem another way, four horses could haul a ton and a half of oats about 18 or 20 miles a day over a good road. If they could obtain half their feed by grazing, the horses would still consume about 50 pounds of oats a day. It requires little mathematics to figure out how much oats would be left in the wagon when it reached New York City, almost 400 miles away.

Turnpikes made it possible to transport such goods as clothing, hardware, coffee and books across the Appalachians, but the expense was considerable. It cost more to ship a ton of freight 300 miles over the mountains from Philadelphia to Pittsburgh than from Pittsburgh to Philadelphia by way of New Orleans, more than ten times as far. Until the coming of the railroad, which was just being introduced in England in 1825, the cost of shipping bulky goods by land over the great distances common in America was prohibitive. Businessmen and inventors concentrated instead on improving water transport, first by designing better boats and then by developing artificial waterways.

DEVELOPMENT OF STEAMBOATS

Rafts and flatboats were adequate for downstream travel, but the only practical solution to upstream travel was the steamboat. After John Fitch's work around 1790, a number of others made important contributions to the development of steam navigation. One early enthusiast was John Stevens, a wealthy New Jerseyite, who designed an improved steam boiler for which he received one of the first patents issued by the United States. Stevens got his brother-in-law, Robert R. Livingston, interested in

DEBATING THE PAST

Was early nineteenth-century America transformed by a "market revolution"? In this 1847 painting by George Caleb Bingham, a steamboat in the distance has run aground; the men in the flatboat are considering, perhaps, whether to help lighten its load. Their faces brim with satisfaction. *They* are not soot-begrimed wage slaves who shovel coal into smoke-belching machines. *They* work when and where they wish, moved only by the pull of the current and the sweat of their muscles. And yet the viewer senses that their satisfaction will be fleeting. The steamboat will get going again. George Rogers Taylor (1951) proposed that the key factor in the transformation of the economy during the early nineteenth century was a "transportation revolution," the development of a system of canals, steamboats, and railroads. But in the 1990s some suggested that the "transportation revolution" was merely a component of a larger and more powerful process: a "market revolution." The thesis was proposed by Charles Sellers (1991), Harry Watson (1990), and others. They argued that early in the nineteenth century some well-connected entrepreneurs used public funds to establish banks and corporations and to construct the nation's transportation infrastructure. This transformed craftsmen into factory workers and subsistence farmers into petty capitalists. In the frenzy to make money, such people turned their backs on family and community. The "market revolution" thesis has provoked many debates, not the least of which is whether it was a good thing. Sellers had no doubts. "Capitalism commodifies and exploits all life," he declared. But the only judgment that matters was that of the people such as those depicted above. If the steamboat captain were to offer them higher wages and steady work, would they accept?

George Rogers Taylor, *The Transportation Revolution* (1951), Charles Sellers, *The Market Revolution* (1991), Harry Watson, *Liberty and Power* (1990).

▲ On August 17, 1807 thousands of New Yorkers gathered along the Hudson River. Many had come to ridicule the noisy, spark-spuming contraption built by Robert Fulton—a steam-powered boat. But as the paddle wheels began to churn and the boat moved, the jeers turned to cheers. The boat made the 150-mile trip to Albany in eight hours.

the problem, and the latter used his political influence to obtain an exclusive charter to operate steamboats on New York waters. In 1802, while in France trying to buy New Orleans from Napoleon, Livingston got to know Robert Fulton, a young American artist and engineer who was experimenting with steam navigation, and agreed to finance his work. In 1807, after returning to New York, Fulton constructed the *North River Steam Boat,* famous to history as the *Clermont.*

The *Clermont* was 142 feet long, 18 feet abeam, and drew 7 feet of water. With its towering stack belching black smoke, its side wheels could push it along at a steady 5 miles an hour. Nothing about it was radically new, but Fulton brought the essentials—engine, boiler, paddle wheels, and hull—into proper balance and thereby produced an efficient vessel.

No one could patent a steamboat; soon the new vessels were plying the waters of every navigable river from the Mississippi east. After 1815 steamers were making the run from New Orleans as far as Ohio. By 1820 at least 60 vessels were operating between New Orleans and Louisville, and by the end of

the decade there were more than 200 steamers on the Mississippi.

The day of the steamboat had dawned, and although the following generation would experience its high noon, even in the 1820s its major effects were clear. The great Mississippi Valley, in the full tide of its development, was immensely enriched. Produce poured down to New Orleans, which soon ranked with New York and Liverpool among the world's great ports. Only 80,000 tons of freight reached New Orleans from the interior in 1816 and 1817, more than 542,000 tons in 1840 and 1841. Upriver traffic was affected even more spectacularly. Freight charges plummeted, in some cases to a tenth of what they had been after the War of 1812. Around 1818 coffee cost 16 cents a pound more in Cincinnati than in New Orleans, a decade later less than 3 cents more. The Northwest emerged from self-sufficiency with a rush and became part of the national market.

Steamboats were far more comfortable than any contemporary form of land transportation, and competition soon led builders to make them positively luxurious. The *General Pike*, launched in 1819, set the fashion. Marble columns, thick carpets, mirrors, and crimson curtains adorned its cabins and public rooms. Soon the finest steamers were floating palaces where passengers could dine, drink, dance, and gamble in luxury as they sped smoothly to their destinations. Yet raft and flatboat traffic increased. Farmers, lumbermen, and others with goods from upriver floated down in the slack winter season and returned in comfort by steamer after selling their produce—and their rafts as well, for lumber was in great demand in New Orleans. Every January and February New Orleans teemed with Westerners and Yankee sailors, their pockets jingling, bent on a fling before going back to work. The shops displayed everything from the latest Paris fashions to teething rings made of alligator teeth mounted in silver. During the carnival season the city became one great festival, where every human pleasure could be tasted, every vice indulged.

THE CANAL BOOM

While the steamboat was conquering western rivers, canals were being constructed that further improved the transportation network. Since the midwestern rivers all emptied into the Gulf of Mexico, they did not provide a direct link with the eastern seaboard. If an artificial waterway could be cut between the great central valley and some navigable

stream flowing into the Atlantic, all sections would profit immensely.

Canals were more expensive than roads, but so long as the motive power used in overland transportation was the humble horse, they offered enormous economic advantages to shippers. Because there is less friction to overcome, a team plodding along a towpath could pull a canal barge with a 100-ton load and make better time over long distances than it could pulling a single ton in a wagon on the finest road.

Although canals were as old as Egypt, only about 100 miles of them existed in the United States as late as 1816. Construction costs aside, in a rough and mountainous country canals presented formidable engineering problems. To link the Mississippi Valley and the Atlantic meant somehow circumventing the Appalachian Mountains. Most people thought this impossible.

Mayor DeWitt Clinton of New York believed that such a project was feasible in New York State. In 1810, while serving as state canal commissioner, he traveled across central New York and convinced himself that it would be practicable to dig a canal from Buffalo, on Lake Erie, to the Hudson River. The Mohawk Valley cuts through the Appalachian chain just north of Albany, and at no point along the route to Buffalo does the land rise more than 570 feet above the level of the Hudson. Marshaling a mass of technical, financial, and commercial information and using his political influence cannily, Clinton placed his proposal before the New York legislature. In its defense he was eloquent and farsighted:

> As an organ of communication between the Hudson, the Mississippi, the St. Lawrence, the great lakes of the north and west, and their tributary rivers, [the canal] will create the greatest inland trade ever witnessed. The most fertile and extensive regions of America will avail themselves of its facilities for a market. All their surplus . . . will concentrate in the city of New York. . . . That city will, in the course of time, become the granary of the world, the emporium of commerce, the seat of manufactures, the focus of great moneyed operations. . . . And before the revolution of a century, the whole island of Manhattan, covered with habitations and replenished with a dense population, will constitute one vast city.

The legislators were convinced, and in 1817 the state began construction along a route 363 miles long, most of it across densely forested wilderness. At the time the longest canal in the United States ran less than 28 miles!

AUDIO
The Erie Canal

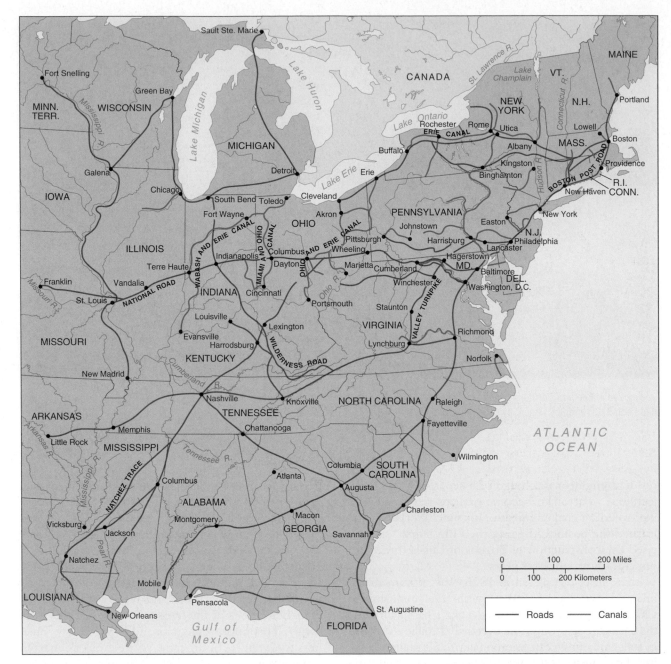

▲ **Canals and Roads, 1820–1850**

DOCUMENT
Erie Canal 1819

The construction of the Erie Canal, as it was called, was a remarkable accomplishment. The chief engineer, Benjamin Wright, a surveyor-politician from Rome, New York, had had almost no experience with canal building. One of his chief associates, James Geddes, possessed only an elementary school education and knew virtually nothing about surveying. Both learned rapidly by trial and error. Fortunately, Wright proved to be a good organizer and a fine judge of engineering talent. He quickly spotted young men of ability among the workers and pushed them forward. One of his finds, Canvass White, was sent to study British canals. White became an expert on the design of locks; he also discovered an American limestone that could be made into waterproof cement, a vital product in canal construction that had previously been imported at a substantial price from England. Another of Wright's protégés, John B. Jervis, began as an axman, rose in two years to

▲ *Junction of Erie and Northern Canals* by John Hill, c. 1835. Freight rates from Buffalo to New York City had been $100 a ton by wagon; by canal, the cost was only $10.

resident engineer in charge of a section of the project, and went on to become perhaps the outstanding American civil engineer of his time. Workers who learned the business digging the "Big Ditch" supervised the construction of dozens of canals throughout the country in later years.

The Erie, completed in 1825, was an immediate financial success. Together with the companion Champlain Canal, which linked Lake Champlain and the Hudson, it brought in over half a million dollars in tolls in its first year. Soon its entire $7 million cost had been recovered, and it was earning profits of about $3 million a year. The effect of this prosperity on New York State was enormous. Buffalo, Rochester, Syracuse, and half a dozen lesser towns along the canal flourished.

NEW YORK CITY: EMPORIUM OF THE WESTERN WORLD

New York City had already become the largest city in the nation, thanks chiefly to its merchants, who had established a reputation for their rapid and or-derly way of doing business. In 1818 the Black Ball Line opened the first regularly scheduled freight and passenger service between New York and England. Previously shipments might languish in port for weeks while a skipper waited for additional cargo. Now merchants on both sides of the Atlantic could count on the Black Ball packets to move their goods between Liverpool and New York on schedule whether or not the transporting vessel had a full cargo. This improvement brought much new business to the port. In the same year New York enacted an auction law requiring that imported goods placed on the block could not be withdrawn if a bid satisfactory to the seller was not forthcoming. This, too, was a boon to businessmen, who could be assured that if they outbid the competition, the goods would be theirs.

Now the canal cemented New York's position as the national metropolis. Most European-manufactured goods destined for the Mississippi Valley entered the country at New York and passed on to the West over the canal. The success of the Erie also sparked a nationwide canal-building boom. Most canals were constructed either by the states, as in the case of the Erie, or as "mixed enterprises" that combined public and private energics.

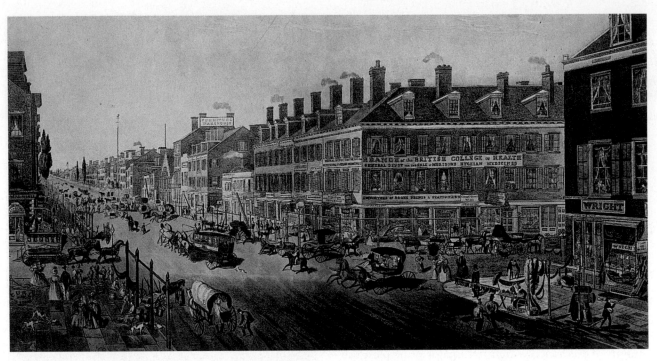

▲ A view of New York's Broadway in 1835. The broad avenue was home to many of the large, modern stores that helped make New York City the commercial center of the nation.

No state profited as much from this construction as New York, for none possessed New York's geographic advantages. The rocky hills of New England discouraged all but fanatics. Canals were built connecting Worcester and Northampton, Massachusetts, with the coast, but they were financial failures. The Delaware and Hudson Canal, running from northeastern Pennsylvania across northern New Jersey and lower New York to the Hudson, was completed by private interests in 1828. It managed to earn respectable dividends by barging coal to the eastern seaboard, but it made no attempt to compete with the Erie for the western trade. Pennsylvania, desperate to keep up with New York, engaged in an orgy of construction. In 1834 it completed a complicated system, part canal and part railroad, over the mountains to Pittsburgh. This Mainline Canal cost a staggering sum for that day. With its 177 locks and cumbersome "inclined-plane railroad" it was slow and expensive to operate and never competed effectively with the Erie. Efforts of Maryland to link Baltimore with the West by water failed utterly.

Beyond the mountains there was even greater zeal for canal construction in the 1820s and still more in the 1830s. Once the Erie opened the way across New York, farmers in the Ohio country demanded that links be built between the Ohio River and the Great Lakes so that they could ship their produce by water directly to the East. Local feeder canals seemed equally necessary; with corn worth 20 cents a bushel at Columbus selling for 50 cents at Marietta, on the Ohio, the value of cheap transportation became obvious to Ohio farmers.

Even before the completion of the Erie, Ohio had begun construction of the Ohio and Erie Canal running from the Ohio River to Cleveland. Another, from Toledo to Cincinnati, was begun in 1832. Meanwhile, Indiana had undertaken the 450-mile Wabash and Erie Canal. These canals were well conceived, but the western states overextended themselves building dozens of feeder lines, trying, it sometimes seemed, to supply all farmers west of the Appalachians with water connections from their barns to the New York docks. Politics made such programs almost inevitable, for in order to win support for their pet projects, legislators had to back the schemes of their fellows. The result was frequently financial disaster. There was not enough traffic to pay for all the waterways that were dug. By 1844, $60 million in state "improvement" bonds were in default. Nevertheless, the canals benefited both western farmers and the national economy.

THE MARSHALL COURT

The most important legal advantages bestowed on business in the period were the gift of Chief Justice John Marshall. Historians have tended to forget that Chief Justice John Marshall had six colleagues on the Supreme Court, and that is easy to understand. Marshall's particular combination of charm, logic, and forcefulness made the Court during his long reign, if not a rubber stamp, remarkably submissive to his view of the Constitution. Marshall's belief in a powerful central government explains his tendency to hand down decisions favorable to manufacturing and business interests. He also thought that "the business community was the agent of order and progress" and tended to interpret the Constitution in a way that would advance its interests.

Many important cases came before the Court between 1819 and 1824, and in each one Marshall's decision was applauded by most of the business community. The cases involved two major principles: the "sanctity" of contracts and the supremacy of federal legislation over the laws of the states. Marshall shared the conviction of the Revolutionary generation that property had to be protected against arbitrary seizure if liberty was to be preserved. Contracts between private individuals and between individuals and the government must be strictly enforced, he believed, or chaos would result. He therefore gave the widest possible application to the constitutional provision that no state could pass any law "impairing the Obligation of Contracts."

In *Dartmouth College* v. *Woodward* (1819), which involved an attempt by New Hampshire to alter the charter granted to Dartmouth by King George III in 1769, Marshall held that such a charter was a contract and might not be canceled or altered without the consent of both parties. The state had sought not to destroy the college but to change it from a private to a public institution, yet Marshall held that to do so would violate the contract clause.

Marshall's decisions concerning the division of power between the federal government and the states were even more important. The question of the constitutionality of a national bank, first debated by Hamilton and Jefferson, had not been submitted to the courts during the life of the first Bank of the United States. By the time of the second Bank there were many state banks, and some of them felt that their interests were threatened by the national institution. Responding to pressure from local banks, the Maryland legislature placed an annual tax of

▲ The artist Chester Harding painted John Marshall in 1828, during the Chief Justice's twenty-seventh year on the Supreme Court. "The unpretentious dignity [and] the sober factualism" of Harding's style (as art historian Oliver Larkin describes it) was well suited to Marshall's character.

$15,000 on "foreign" banks, including the Bank of the United States! The Maryland branch of the Bank of the United States refused to pay, whereupon the state brought suit against its cashier, John W. McCulloch. *McCulloch* v. *Maryland* was crucial to the Bank, for five other states had levied taxes on its branches, and others would surely follow suit if the Maryland law were upheld.

Marshall extinguished the threat. The Bank of the United States was constitutional, he announced in phrases taken almost verbatim from Hamilton's 1791 memorandum to Washington on the subject; its legality was implied in many of the powers specifically

granted to Congress. Full "discretion" must be allowed Congress in deciding exactly how its powers "are to be carried into execution." Since the Bank was legal, the Maryland tax was unconstitutional. Marshall found a "plain repugnance" in the thought of "conferring on one government a power to control the constitutional measures of another." He put this idea in the simplest possible language: "The power to tax involves the power to destroy . . . the power to destroy may defeat and render useless the power to create." The long-range significance of the decision lay in its strengthening of the implied powers of Congress and its confirmation of the Hamiltonian or "loose" interpretation of the Constitution. By establishing the legality of the Bank, it also aided the growth of the economy.

In 1824 Marshall handed down an important decision involving the regulation of interstate commerce. This was the "steamboat case," *Gibbons* v. *Ogden*. In 1815 Aaron Ogden, former United States senator and governor of New Jersey, had purchased the right to operate a ferry between Elizabeth Point, New Jersey, and New York City from Robert Fulton's backer, Robert R. Livingston, who held a New York monopoly of steamboat navigation on the Hudson. When Thomas Gibbons, who held a federal coasting license, set up a competing line, Ogden sued him. Ogden argued in effect that Gibbons could operate his boat (whose captain was Cornelius Vanderbilt, later a famous railroad magnate) on the New Jersey side of the Hudson but had no right to cross into New York waters. After complicated litigation in the lower courts, the case reached the Supreme Court on appeal. Marshall decided in favor of Gibbons, effectively destroying the New York monopoly. A state can regulate commerce which begins and ends in its own territory but not when the transaction involves crossing a state line; then the national authority takes precedence. "The act of Congress," he said, "is supreme; and the law of the state . . . must yield to it."

This decision threw open the interstate steamboat business to all comers, and since an adequate 100-ton vessel could be built for as little as $7000, dozens of small operators were soon engaged in it. Their competition tended to keep rates low and service efficient, to the great advantage of the country. More important in the long run was the fact that in order to include the ferry business within the federal government's power to regulate interstate commerce, Marshall had given the word the widest possible meaning. "Commerce, undoubtedly, is traffic, but it is something more,—it is intercourse." By construing the "commerce" clause so broadly, he

made it easy for future generations of judges to extend its coverage to include the control of interstate electric power lines and even radio and television transmission.

Many of Marshall's decisions aided the economic development of the country in specific ways, but his chief contribution lay in his broadly national view of economic affairs. When he tried consciously to favor business by making contracts inviolable, his influence was important but limited—and, as it worked out, impermanent. In the steamboat case and in *McCulloch* v. *Maryland,* where he was really deciding between rival property interests, his work was more truly judicial in spirit and far more lasting. In such matters his nationalism enabled him to add form and substance to Hamilton's vision of the economic future of the United States.

Marshall and his colleagues firmly established the principle of judicial limitation on the power of legislatures and made the Supreme Court a vital part of the American system of government. In an age plagued by narrow sectional jealousies, Marshall's contribution was of immense influence and significance, and on it rests his claim to greatness.

John Marshall died in 1835. Two years later, in the *Charles River Bridge* case, the court handed down another decision that aided economic development. The state of Massachusetts had built a bridge across the Charles River between Boston and Cambridge that drew traffic from an older, privately owned toll bridge nearby. Since no tolls were collected from users of the state bridge after construction costs were recovered, owners of the older bridge sued for damages on the ground that the free bridge made the stock in their company worthless. They argued that in building the bridge, Massachusetts had violated the contract clause of the Constitution.

The Court, however, now speaking through the new Chief Justice, Roger B. Taney, decided otherwise. The state had a right to place "the comfort and convenience" of the whole community over that of a particular company, Taney declared. "Improvements" that add to public "wealth and property" take precedence. How John Marshall would have voted in this case, in which he would have had to choose between his Dartmouth College and steamboat case arguments, will never be known. But like most of the decisions of the Court that were made while Marshall was Chief Justice, the Charles River Bridge case advanced the interests of those who favored economic development. Whether they were pursuing political advantage or economic, the Americans of the early nineteenth century seemed committed to a policy of compromise and accommodation.

MILESTONES

1790	Samuel Slater sets up first American factory
1793	Eli Whitney invents cotton gin
1794	Philadelphia–Lancaster turnpike is built
1807	Robert Fulton constructs *North River Steam Boat (Clermont)*
1808	Constitutional prohibition of importation of slaves goes into effect
1813	Boston Manufacturing Company opens in Waltham, Massachusetts
1816	Second Bank of the United States is created
1817	American Colonization Society is founded in order to establish republic of Liberia for freed slaves
1819	Chief Justice John Marshall asserts "sanctity" of contracts in *Dartmouth College* v. *Woodward*
	Chief Justice Marshall strengthens implied powers of Congress in *McCulloch* v. *Maryland* (Bank of United States)
1824	Chief Justice Marshall defends supremacy of federal government over states in *Gibbons* v. *Ogden* (steamboat case)
1825	Erie Canal is completed
1837	Chief Justice Roger B. Taney rules in favor of the whole community over a particular company in *Charles River Bridge* v. *Warren Bridge*

SUPPLEMENTARY READING

On the consumer revolution, see especially Richard Bushman, *The Refinement of America* (1992). In addition to the works cited in Debating the Past (p. 238) on the market revolution, see Melvyn Stokes and Stephen Conway, eds., *The Market Revolution in America* (1996), and Christopher Clark, *The Roots of Rural Capitalism: Western Massachusetts, 1780–1860* (1991). See also Laurel Thatcher Ulrich, *The Age of Homespun* (2001).

On the industrial revolution in America, see A. D. Chandler, Jr., *The Visible Hand: The Managerial Revolution in American Business* (1977). On the role of inventors, see Carroll Pursell, *The Machine in America* (1995), and B. M. Tucker, *Samuel Slater and the Origins of the American Textile Industry* (1984).

The growth of cities in the Jacksonian era can be traced in Richard C. Wade, *The Urban Frontier* (1957), and Howard Chudacoff, *The Evolution of American Urban Society* (1981). Allen F. Davis and Mark Halle, eds., *The Peoples of Philadelphia* (1973), Oscar Handlin, *Boston's Immigrants* (1968 ed.), and P. R. Knights, *The Plain People of Boston* (1971), deal with individual cities.

On immigration and ethnicity, see P. T. Knoble, *Paddy and the Republic* (1986), J. P. Dolan, *Immigrant Church: New York's Irish and German Catholics* (1982), and, generally, Philip Taylor, *The Distant Mirror: European Migration to the United States* (1971), and Stephan Thernstrom, ed., *Harvard Encyclopedia of American Ethnic Groups* (1980).

On changes in the nature of work, consult Paul Johnson, *A Shopkeeper's Millennium* (1978), Sean Wilentz, *Chants Democratic* (1984), Bruce Laurie, *Artisans into Workers* (1989), Norman Ware, *The Industrial Worker* (1990), and Anthony F. C. Wallace, *Rockdale* (1978); on women in the early factories, see Mary Blewett, *Men, Women, and Work* (1988), and Thomas Dublin, *Women at Work* (1979). On the lengthening commute to work, see Sam Bass Warner, *The Private City: Philadelphia in Three Periods of Its Growth* (1968).

Evan Cornog describes the origins and impact of the Erie Canal in *The Birth of Empire* (1998). On canal building, consult R. E. Shaw, *Canals for a Nation* (1990). Two works by Carter Goodrich, *Government Promotion of American Canals and Railroads* (1960) and *Canals and American Economic Development* (1961), describe the role of government aid in canal construction authoritatively. John Lauritz Larson, *Internal Improvement: National Public Works and the Promise of Popular Government in the Early United States* (2001), blames Andrew Jackson for the abandonment of public support for transportation infrastructure.

R. Kent Newmyer, *John Marshall and the Heroic Age of the Supreme Court* (2001) is strongly supportive of Marshall's actions; see also G. Edward White, *The Marshall Court and Cultural Change* (1991), as well as the sources cited in previous chapters.

SUGGESTED WEBSITES

The Marshall Cases
http://odur.let.rug.nl/~usa/D/1801-1825/marshallcases/marxx.htm
John Marshall, and the cases he heard, shaped the form and function of the judicial system in the United States.

Whole Cloth: Discovering Science and Technology Through American Textile History
http://www.si.edu/lemelson/centerpieces/whole_cloth/
The Jerome and Dorothy Lemelson Center for the Study of Invention and Innovation/Society for the History of Technology put together this site, which includes activities and sources about early-American manufacturing and industry.

Erie Canal Online
http://www.syracuse.com/features/eriecanal
This site, built around the diary of a 14-year-old girl who traveled from Amsterdam to Syracuse, New York, in the early nineteenth century, explores the construction and importance of the Erie Canal.

The Era of the Mountain Men
http://www.xmission.com/~drudy/amm.html
Private letters help students learn about the concerns and environment of the writers and recipients. This site has correspondence from early settlers west of the Mississippi River.

CHAPTER 9 Jacksonian Democracy

▼ Critics lampooned the raucous behavior of "King Mob" at the White House following the inauguration of Andrew Jackson; but public gatherings taught Americans to think of themselves as partisans in a national political system.

CHAPTER CONTENTS

At 11 A.M. on March 4, 1829, a bright sunny day, Andrew Jackson, hatless and dressed severely in black, left his quarters at Gadsby's Hotel. Accompanied by a few close associates, he walked up Pennsylvania Avenue to the Capitol. At a few minutes after noon he emerged on the East Portico with the justices of the Supreme Court and other dignitaries. Before a throng of more than 15,000 people he delivered an almost inaudible and thoroughly commonplace inaugural address and then took the presidential oath. The first man to congratulate him was Chief Justice Marshall, who had administered the oath. The second was "Honest George" Kremer, a Pennsylvania congressman best known for the leopardskin coat that he affected, who led the cheering crowd that brushed past the barricade and scrambled up the Capitol steps to wring the new president's hand.

Jackson shouldered his way through the crush, mounted a splendid white horse, and rode off to the White House. A reception had been announced, to which "the officially and socially eligible as defined by precedent" had been invited. The day was unseasonably warm after a hard winter, and the streets of Washington were muddy. As Jackson rode down Pennsylvania Avenue, the crowds that had turned out to see the Hero of New Orleans followed—on horseback, in rickety wagons, and on foot. Nothing could keep them out of the executive mansion, and the result was chaos. Long tables laden with cakes, ice cream, and orange punch had been set up in the East Room, but

these scarcely deflected the well-wishers. Jackson was pressed back helplessly as men tracked mud across valuable rugs and clambered up on delicate chairs to catch a glimpse of him. The White House shook with their shouts. Glassware splintered, furniture was overturned, women fainted.

Jackson was a thin old man despite his toughness, and soon he was in danger. Fortunately, friends formed a cordon and managed to extricate him through a rear door. The new president spent his first night in office at Gadsby's hotel.

Only a generation earlier Jefferson had felt obliged to introduce pell-mell to encourage informality in the White House (see p. 173). Now a man whom John Quincy Adams called "a barbarian" held Jefferson's office, and, as one Supreme Court justice complained, "The reign of King 'Mob' seemed triumphant."

"DEMOCRATIZING" POLITICS

Jackson's inauguration, and especially this celebration in the White House, symbolized the triumph of "democracy," the achievement of place and station by "the common man." Having been taught by Jefferson that all men are created equal, the Americans of Jackson's day (conveniently ignoring males with black skins, to say nothing of women, regardless of color) found it easy to believe that every person was as competent and as politically important as his neighbor.

The difference between Jeffersonian democracy and the Jackson variety was more one of attitude than of practice. Jefferson had believed that ordinary citizens could be educated to determine what was right. Jackson insisted that they knew what was right by instinct. Jefferson's pell-mell encouraged the average citizen to hold up his head; by the time of Jackson, the "common man" gloried in ordinariness and made mediocrity a virtue. The slightest hint of distinctiveness or servility became suspect. That President Washington required his footmen to wear uniforms was taken as a matter of course in the 1790s, but the British minister in Jackson's day found it next to impossible to find Americans willing to don his splendid livery. While most middle-class families could still hire people to do their cooking and housework, the word *servant* itself fell out of fashion, replaced by the egalitarian *help*.

The Founders had not foreseen all the implications of political democracy for a society like the one that existed in the United States. They believed that the ordinary man should have political power in order to protect himself against the superior man, but they assumed that the latter would always lead. The people would naturally choose the best men to manage public affairs. In Washington's day and even in Jefferson's this was generally the case, but the inexorable logic of democracy gradually produced a change. The new western states, unfettered by systems created in a less democratic age, drew up constitutions that eliminated property qualifications for voting and holding office. Many more public offices were made elective rather than appointive. The eastern states revised their own frames of government to accomplish the same purposes.

Even the presidency, designed to be removed from direct public control by the Electoral College, felt the impact of the new thinking. By Jackson's time only two states, Delaware and South Carolina, still provided for the choice of presidential electors by the legislature; in all others they were selected by popular vote. The system of permitting the congressional caucus to name the candidates for the presidency came to an end before 1828. Jackson and Adams were put forward by state legislatures, and soon thereafter the still more democratic system of nomination by national party conventions was adopted.

Certain social changes reflected a new way of looking at political affairs. The final disestablishment of churches further reveals the dislike of special privilege. The beginnings of the free-school movement, the earliest glimmerings of interest in adult education, and the slow spread of secondary education all bespeak a concern for improving the knowledge and judgment of the ordinary citizen. The rapid increase in the number of newspapers, their declining prices, and their ever-greater concentration on political affairs indicate an effort to bring political news to the common man's attention.

All these changes emphasized the idea that every citizen was equally important and the conviction that all should participate in government. Officeholders began to stress the fact that they were *representatives* as well as leaders and to appeal more openly and much more intensively for votes. The public responded. At each succeeding presidential election, more people went to the polls. Roughly 300,000 ballots were cast in 1824, 1.1 million four years later, and 2.4 million in 1840.

As voting became more important, so did competition among candidates, and this led to changes in the role and structure of political parties. Running campaigns and getting out the vote required money, people, and organized effort. Party managers, often holders of relatively minor offices, held rallies, staged parades, dreamed up catchy slogans, and printed broadsides, party newspapers, and ballots containing the names of the party's nominees for distribution to their supporters. Parties became powerful institutions that instilled loyalty among adherents.

The parties first formed at the state level. The 1828 election stimulated party formation because

instead of several sectional candidates, each dominant in his own region, competing for the presidency, it pitted two nationally known men against each other. This compelled local leaders to make a choice and then to organize their forces in order to convince local voters to accept their judgment. This was especially true in states where neither Adams nor Jackson had a preponderance of backers. Thus the new system established itself much faster in New York and Pennsylvania than in New England, where Adams was strong, or Tennessee, where the native son Jackson had overwhelming support.

Like most institutions, the new parties created bureaucracies to keep them running smoothly. Devoted party workers were rewarded with political office when their efforts were successful. "To the victors belong the spoils," said the New York politician William L. Marcy, and the image, drawn from war and piracy, was appropriate. Although the vigorous wooing of voters constituted recognition of their importance and commitment to keeping them informed, campaigning—another military term—frequently degenerated into demagoguery. The most effective way to attract the average voter, politicians soon decided, was by flattery.

1828: The New Party System in Embryo

The new system could scarcely have been imagined in 1825 while John Quincy Adams ruled over the White House; Adams was not well equipped either to lead King Mob or to hold it in check. Indeed, it was the battle to succeed Adams that caused the system to develop. The campaign began almost on the day of his selection by the House of Representatives. Jackson felt that he, the man who had received the largest number of votes, had been cheated of the presidency in 1824 by "the corrupt bargain" that he believed Adams had made with Henry Clay, and he sought vindication.

Relying heavily on his military reputation and on Adams's talent for making enemies, Jackson avoided taking a stand on issues and on questions where his views might displease one or another faction. The political situation thus became chaotic, one side unable to marshal support for its policies, the other unwilling to adopt policies for fear of losing support.

The campaign was disgraced by character assassination and lies of the worst sort. Administration supporters denounced Jackson as a bloodthirsty military tyrant, a drunkard, and a gambler. His wife Rachel, ailing and shy, was dragged into the campaign, her

▲ Rachel Jackson, wife of Andrew Jackson. At 17 she had married Lewis Robards, but theirs was a tempestuous marriage. After two years she returned to her family in Natchez, Mississippi. Robards sued for divorce in Virginia on grounds of desertion. Several months later she married Jackson in Mississippi. But, unbeknownst to Jackson, Robards would not finalize the divorce until a year after Rachel's marriage to Jackson. In defending Rachel's honor from a charge of bigamy, Jackson killed a man in a duel. During the 1824 and 1828 presidential campaigns, critics denounced their marriage as immoral.

good name heartlessly besmirched. Previously married to a cruel, unbalanced man named Lewis Robards, she had begun living with Jackson before her divorce from Robards had been legally completed. When this fact came to light, she and Jackson had to remarry. Seizing on this incident, an Adams pamphleteer wrote: "Ought a convicted adulteress and her paramour husband be placed in the highest offices of this free and christian land?"

Furious, the Jacksonians (now calling themselves Democrats) replied in kind. They charged that while American minister to Russia, Adams had supplied a beautiful American virgin for the delectation of the czar. Discovering that while president Adams had purchased a chess set and a billiard table for the White House, they accused him of squandering public money on gambling devices. They translated his long

and distinguished public service into the statistic that he had received over the years a sum equal to $16 for every day of his life in government pay. The great questions of the day were largely ignored.

All this was inexcusable, and both sides must share the blame. But as the politicians noticed when the votes were counted, their efforts had certainly brought out the electorate. *Each* candidate received far more votes than all four candidates had received in the preceding presidential election.

When inauguration day arrived, Adams refused to attend the ceremonies because Jackson had failed to pay the traditional preinaugural courtesy call on him at the White House, but the Old Puritan may have been equally, if unconsciously, motivated by shame at tactics he had countenanced during the campaign. Jackson felt vindication, not shame, but in any case, deep personal feelings were uppermost in everyone's mind at the formal changing of the guard. The real issues, however, remained. Andrew Jackson would now have to deal with them.

The Jacksonian Appeal

Although Jackson's supporters liked to cast him as the political heir of Jefferson, he was in many ways like the conservative Washington: a soldier first, an inveterate speculator in western lands, the owner of a fine plantation and of many slaves, a man with few intellectual interests and only sketchily educated.

Nor was Jackson quite the rough-hewn frontier character he sometimes seemed. True, he could not spell (again, like Washington), he possessed the unsavory habits of the tobacco chewer, and he had a violent temper. But his manners and lifestyle were those of a southern planter. "I have always felt that he was a perfect savage," Grace Fletcher Webster, wife of Senator Daniel Webster, explained. "But," she added, "his manners are very mild and gentlemanly." Jackson's judgment was intuitive yet usually sound; his frequent rages were often feigned, designed to accomplish some carefully thought-out purpose. Once, after scattering a delegation of protesters with an exhibition of wrath, he turned to an observer and said impishly: "They thought I was mad."

Whatever his personal convictions, Jackson stood as the symbol for a movement supported by a new, democratically oriented generation. That he was both a great hero and in many ways a most extraordinary person helps explain his mass appeal. He had defeated a mighty British army and killed hosts of Indians, but he acted on hunches and not always consistently, shouted and pounded his fist when angry, put loyalty to old comrades above efficiency when making appointments,

▲ This painting of Jackson is by Ralph E. W. Earl (1833), whose father, a soldier, had been assigned to do accurate paintings of the battles of Lexington and Concord. The son married a niece of Andrew Jackson and completed this imposing portrait.

distrusted "aristocrats" and all special privilege. Perhaps he was rich, perhaps conservative, but he was a man of the people, born in a frontier cabin, familiar with the problems of the average citizen.

Jackson epitomized many American ideals. He was intensely patriotic, generous to a fault, natural and democratic in manner (at home alike in the forest and in the ballroom of a fine mansion). He admired good horseflesh and beautiful women, yet no sterner moralist ever lived; he was a fighter, a relentless foe, but a gentleman in the best American sense. That some special providence watched over him (as over the United States) appeared beyond argument to those who had followed his career. He seemed, in short, both an average and an ideal American, one the people could identify with and still revere.

For these reasons Jackson drew support from every section and every social class: western farmers and southern planters, urban workers and bankers and merchants. In this sense he was profoundly democratic—and in the sense, too, that whatever his

position on public issues, he believed in equality of opportunity, distrusted entrenched status of every sort, and rejected no free American because of humble origins or inadequate education.

THE SPOILS SYSTEM

DOCUMENT

Jackson, First Annual Message to Congress

Jackson took office with the firm intention of punishing the "vile wretches" who had attacked him so viciously during the campaign. (Rachel Jackson died shortly after the election, and her devoted husband was convinced that the indignities heaped on her by Adams partisans had hastened her decline.) The new concept of political office as a reward for victory seemed to justify a housecleaning in Washington. Henry Clay captured the fears of anti-Jackson government workers. "Among the official corps here there is the greatest solicitude and apprehension," he said. "The members of it feel something like the inhabitants of Cairo when the plague breaks out; no one knows who is next to encounter the stroke of death."

Eager for the "spoils," an army of politicians invaded Washington. There was nothing especially innovative about this invasion, for the principle of filling offices with one's partisans was almost as old as the republic. However, the long lapse of time since the last real political shift, and the recent untypical example of John Quincy Adams, who rarely removed or appointed anyone for political reasons, made Jackson's policy appear revolutionary. His removals were not entirely unjustified, for many government workers had grown senile and others corrupt. A number of officials were found to be short in their accounts; a few were hopeless drunks. Jackson was determined to root out the thieves. Even Adams admitted that some of those Jackson dismissed deserved their fate.

Aside from going along with the spoils system and eliminating crooks and incompetents, Jackson advanced another reason for turning experienced government employees out of their jobs: the principle of rotation. "No man has any more intrinsic right to official station than another," he said. Those who hold government jobs for a long time "are apt to acquire a habit of looking with indifference upon the public interests and of tolerating conduct from which an unpracticed man would revolt." By "rotating" jobholders periodically, more citizens could participate in the tasks of government, and the danger of creating an entrenched bureaucracy would be eliminated. The problem was that the constant replacing of trained workers by novices was not likely to increase the efficiency of the government. Jackson's response to this argument was typical: "The duties of all public officers are . . . so plain and simple that men of intelligence may readily qualify themselves for their performance."

Contempt for expert knowledge and the belief that ordinary Americans can do anything they set their minds to became fundamental tenets of Jacksonian democracy. To apply them to present-day government would be to court disaster, but in the early nineteenth century it was not so preposterous, because the role that government played in American life was simple and nontechnical.

Furthermore, Jackson did not practice what he preached. By and large his top appointees were anything but common men. A majority came from the same social and intellectual elite as those they replaced. He did not try to rotate civil servants in the War and Navy departments, where to do so might have been harmful. In general, he left pretty much alone what a modern administrator would call middle management, the backbone of every organization.

Nevertheless, the spoilsmen roamed the capital in force during the spring of 1829, seeking, as the forthright Jackson said, "a tit to suck the treasury pap." Their philosophy was well summarized by a New Yorker: "No d——d rascal who made use of his office . . . for the purpose of keeping Mr. Adams in, and Genl. Jackson out of power is entitled to the least lenity or mercy. . . . Whether or not I shall get anything in the general scramble for plunder, remains to be proven, but I rather guess I shall."

PRESIDENT OF ALL THE PEOPLE

President Jackson was not cynical about the spoils system. As a strong man who intuitively sought to increase his authority, the idea of making government workers dependent on him made excellent sense. His opponents had pictured him as a simple soldier fronting for a rapacious band of politicians, but he soon proved he would exercise his authority directly. Except for Martin Van Buren, the secretary of state, his Cabinet was not distinguished, and he did not rely on it for advice. He turned instead to an informal "Kitchen Cabinet," which consisted of the influential Van Buren and a few close friends. But these men were advisers, not directors; Jackson was clearly master of his own administration.

More than any earlier president, he conceived of himself as the direct representative of all the people and therefore the embodiment of national power. From Washington to John Quincy Adams, his predecessors together had vetoed only nine bills, all on the ground that they believed the measures unconstitutional. Jackson vetoed a dozen, some simply because he thought the legislation inexpedient. Yet he had no

ambition to expand the scope of federal authority at the expense of the states. Basically he was a Jeffersonian; he favored a "frugal," constitutionally limited national government. Furthermore, he was a poor administrator, given to penny-pinching and lacking in imagination. His strong prejudices and his contempt for expert advice, even in fields such as banking where his ignorance was almost total, did him no credit and the country considerable harm.

Jackson's great success (not merely his popularity) was primarily the result of his personality. A shrewd French observer, Michel Chevalier, after commenting on "his chivalric character, his lofty integrity, and his ardent patriotism," pointed out what was probably the central element in Jackson's appeal. "His tactic in politics, as well as in war," Chevalier wrote in 1824, "is to throw himself forward with the cry of *Comrades, follow me!*" Sometimes he might be wrong, but always he was a leader.

SECTIONAL TENSIONS REVIVED

In office Jackson had to say something about western lands, the tariff, and other issues. He tried to steer a moderate course, urging a slight reduction of the tariff and "constitutional" internal improvements. He suggested that once the rapidly disappearing federal debt had been paid off, the surplus revenues of the government might be "distributed" among the states.

Even these cautious proposals caused conflict, so complex were the interrelations of sectional disputes. If the federal government turned its expected surplus over to the states, it could not afford to reduce the price of public land without going into the red. This disturbed Westerners, notably Senator Thomas Hart Benton of Missouri, and western concern suggested to southern opponents of the protective tariff an alliance of South and West. The Southerners argued that a tariff levied only to raise revenue would increase the cost of foreign imports, bring more money into the treasury, and thus make it possible to reduce the price of public land.

The question came up in the Senate in December 1829, when Senator Samuel A. Foot of Connecticut suggested restricting the sale of government land. Benton promptly denounced the proposal. On January 19, 1830, Senator Robert Y. Hayne of South Carolina, a spokesman for Vice President Calhoun, supported Benton vigorously, suggesting an alliance of South and West based on cheap land and low tariffs. Daniel Webster then rose to the defense of northeastern interests, cleverly goading Hayne by accusing South Carolina of advocating disunionist policies. Responding to this attack, the South Carolinian, a glib speaker but a rather imprecise thinker,

launched into an impassioned exposition of the states' rights doctrine.

Webster then took the floor again and for two days, before galleries packed with the elite of Washington society, cut Hayne's argument to shreds. The Constitution was a compact of the American people, not merely of the states, he insisted, the Union perpetual and indissoluble. Webster made the states' rights position appear close to treason; his "second reply to Hayne" effectively prevented the formation of a West-South alliance and made Webster a presidential candidate.

JACKSON: "THE BANK . . . I WILL KILL IT!"

In the fall of 1832 Jackson was reelected president, handily defeating Henry Clay. The main issue in this election, aside from Jackson's personal popularity, was the president's determination to destroy the second Bank of the United States. In this "Bank war," Jackson won a complete victory, yet the effects of his triumph were anything but beneficial to the country.

After *McCulloch* v. *Maryland* had presumably established its legality and the conservative Langdon Cheves had gotten it on a sound footing, the Bank of the United States had flourished. In 1823 Cheves was replaced as president by Nicholas Biddle, who managed it brilliantly. A talented Philadelphian, only 37 when he took over the Bank, Biddle was experienced in literature, the law, and diplomacy as well as in finance. Almost alone in the United States, Biddle realized that his institution could act as a rudimentary central bank, regulating the availability of credit throughout the nation by controlling the lending policies of the state banks. Small banks, possessing limited amounts of gold and silver, sometimes overextended themselves in making large amounts of bank notes available to borrowers in order to earn interest. All this paper money was legally convertible into hard cash on demand, but in the ordinary run of business people seldom bothered to convert their notes so long as they thought the issuing bank was sound.

Bank notes passed freely from hand to hand and from bank to bank in every section of the country. Eventually much of the paper money of the local banks came across the counter of one or another of the 22 branches of the Bank of the United States. By collecting these notes and presenting them for conversion into coin, Biddle could compel the local banks to maintain adequate reserves of gold and silver—in other words, make them hold their lending policies within bounds. "The Bank of the United States," he explained, "has succeeded in keeping in

▲ Although the American dollar was the unit of currency in the young nation, the paper currency itself mostly consisted of bank notes, such as this $10 note. The bearer of this note could redeem it in Philadelphia for $10 in gold or silver, unless the bank had issued too many such notes and lacked sufficient specie.

check many institutions which might otherwise have been tempted into extravagant and ruinous excesses."

Biddle's policies in the 1820s were good for the Bank of the United States, which earned substantial profits, for the state banks, and probably for the country. Pressures on local bankers to make loans were enormous. The nation had an insatiable need for capital, and the general mood of the people was optimistic. Everyone wanted to borrow, and everyone expected values to rise, as in general they did. But by making liberal loans to produce merchants, for example, rural bankers indirectly stimulated farmers to expand their output beyond current demand, which eventually led to a decline in prices and an agricultural depression. In every field of economic activity, reckless lending caused inflation and greatly exaggerated the ups and downs of the business cycle. It can be argued, however, that by restricting the lending of state banks, Biddle was slowing the rate of economic growth and that in a predominantly agricultural society an occasional slump was not a large price to pay for rapid economic development.

Biddle's policies acted to stabilize the economy, and many interests, including a substantial percentage of state bankers, supported them. They also provoked a great deal of opposition. In part the opposition originated in pure ignorance: Distrust of paper money did not disappear, and people who disliked all paper saw the Bank as merely the largest (and thus the worst) of many bad institutions. At the other extreme, some bankers chafed under Biddle's restraints because by discouraging them from lending freely, he was limiting their profits. Few financiers realized what

Biddle was trying to accomplish. The historian Bray Hammond estimated that in this period no more than one banker in four understood what was happening when he made a loan. What was "sound" banking practice? Honest people disagreed, and many turned against the ideas of Nicholas Biddle.

Bankers who did understand what Biddle was doing also resisted him. New York bankers resented the fact that a Philadelphia institution could wield so much power over their affairs. New York was the nation's largest importing center; huge amounts of tariff revenue were collected there. Yet since this money was deposited to the credit of the Bank of the United States, Biddle controlled it from Philadelphia.

Finally, some people objected to the Bank because it was a monopoly. Distrust of chartered corporations as agents of special privilege tended to focus on the Bank, which had a monopoly of public funds but was managed by a private citizen and controlled by a handful of rich men. Biddle's wealth and social position intensified this feeling. Like many brilliant people, he sometimes appeared arrogant. He was unused to criticism and disdainful of ignorant and stupid attacks, failing to see that they were sometimes the most dangerous.

JACKSON'S BANK VETO

This formidable opposition to the Bank was diffuse and unorganized until Andrew Jackson brought it together. When he did, the Bank was quickly destroyed. Jackson can be included among the ignorant enemies

of the institution, a hard-money man suspicious of all commercial banking. "I think it right to be perfectly frank with you," he told Biddle in 1829. "I do not dislike your Bank any more than all banks. But ever since I read the history of the South Sea Bubble I have been afraid of banks."

Jackson's attitude dismayed Biddle. It also mystified him, since the Bank was the country's best defense against a speculative mania like the eighteenth-century South Sea Bubble, in which hundreds of naive British investors had been fleeced. Almost against his will, Biddle found himself gravitating toward Clay and the new National Republican party, offering advantageous loans and retainers to politicians and newspaper editors in order to build up a following. Thereafter, events moved inevitably toward a showdown, for the president's combative instincts were easily aroused. "The Bank," he told Van Buren, "is trying to kill me, *but I will kill it!*"

Henry Clay, Daniel Webster, and other prominent National Republicans hoped to use the Bank controversy against Jackson. They reasoned that the institution was so important to the country that Jackson's opposition to it would undermine his popularity. They therefore urged Biddle to ask Congress to renew the Bank's charter. The charter would not expire until 1836, but by pressing the issue before the 1832 presidential election, they could force Jackson either to approve the recharter bill or to veto it (which would give candidate Clay a lively issue in the campaign). The banker yielded to this strategy and a recharter bill passed Congress early in July 1832. Jackson promptly vetoed it.

DOCUMENT

Jackson, Veto of the Bank Bill

Jackson's message explaining why he had rejected the bill was immensely popular, but it adds nothing to his reputation as a statesman. Being a good Jeffersonian—and no friend of John Marshall—he insisted that the Bank was unconstitutional. (*McCulloch* v. *Maryland* he brushed aside, saying that as president he had sworn to uphold the Constitution as *he* understood it.) The Bank was inexpedient, he argued. A dangerous private monopoly that allowed a handful of rich men to accumulate "many millions" of dollars, the Bank was making "the rich richer and the potent more powerful." Furthermore, many of its stockholders were foreigners: "If we must have a bank . . . it should be *purely American*." Little that he said made any more sense than this absurdity.[1]

The most unfortunate aspect of Jackson's veto was that he could have reformed the Bank instead of

▲ "King Andrew the First," standing atop the United States Constitution—a scepter in one hand, and a veto in another. Compare this drawing to the one of Queen Elizabeth on page 29.

destroying it. The central banking function was too important to be left in private hands. Biddle once boasted that he could put nearly any bank in the United States out of business simply by forcing it to exchange specie for its bank notes. He thought he was demonstrating his forbearance, but in fact he was revealing a dangerous flaw in the system. When the Jacksonians called him Czar Nicholas, they were not far from the mark. Moreover, private bankers were making profits that in justice belonged to the people, for the government received no interest from the large sums it kept on deposit in the Bank. Jackson would not consider reforms. He set out to smash the Bank of the United States without any real idea of what might be put in its place—a foolhardy act.

Biddle considered Jackson's veto "a manifesto of anarchy," its tone like "the fury of a chained panther biting the bars of his cage." A large majority of the voters, however, approved of Jackson's hard-hitting attack.

---

[1]The country needed all the foreign capital it could attract. Foreigners owned only $8 million of the $35 million stock, and in any case they could not vote their shares.

Buttressed by his election triumph, Jackson acted swiftly. "Until I can strangle this hydra of corruption, the Bank, I will not shrink from my duty," he said. Shortly after the start of his second term, he decided to withdraw the government funds deposited in its vaults. Under the law only the secretary of the treasury could remove the deposits. When Secretary Louis McLane refused to do so, believing that the alternative depositories, the state banks, were less safe, Jackson promptly "promoted" him to secretary of state and appointed William J. Duane, a Pennsylvania lawyer, to the treasury post. Foolishly, he failed to ask Duane his views on the issue before appointing him. Too late he discovered that the new secretary agreed with McLane! It would not be "prudent" to entrust the government's money to "local and irresponsible" banks, Duane said.

Believing that Cabinet officers should obey the president as automatically as a colonel obeys a general, Jackson dismissed Duane, replacing him with Attorney General Roger B. Taney, who had been advising him closely on Bank affairs. Taney carried out the order by depositing new federal receipts in seven state banks in eastern cities while continuing to meet government expenses with drafts on the Bank of the United States.

The situation was confused and slightly unethical. Set on winning the Bank war, Jackson lost sight of his fear of unsound paper money. Taney, however, knew exactly what he was doing. One of the state banks receiving federal funds was the Union Bank of Baltimore. Taney owned stock in this institution, and its president was his close friend. Little wonder that Jackson's enemies were soon calling the favored state banks "pet" banks. This charge was not entirely fair because Taney took pains to see that the deposits were placed in financially sound institutions. Furthermore, by 1836 the government's funds had been spread out reasonably equitably in about 90 banks. But neither was the charge entirely unfair; the administration certainly favored institutions whose directors were politically sympathetic to it.

When Taney began to remove the deposits, the government had $9,868,000 to its credit in the Bank of the United States; within three months the figure fell to about $4 million. Faced with the withdrawal of so much cash, Biddle had to contract his operations. He decided to exaggerate the contraction, pressing the state banks hard by presenting all their notes and checks that came across his counter for conversion into specie and drastically limiting his own bank's business loans. He hoped that the resulting shortage of credit would be blamed on Jackson and that it would force the president to return the deposits. "Nothing but the evidence of suffering . . . will produce any effect," he reasoned.

For a time the strategy appeared to be working. Paper money became scarce, specie almost unobtainable. A serious panic threatened. New York banks were soon refusing to make any loans at all. "Nobody buys; nobody can sell," a French visitor to the city observed. Memorials and petitions poured in on Congress. Worried and indignant delegations of businessmen began trooping to Washington seeking "relief." Clay, Webster, and John C. Calhoun thundered against Jackson in the Senate.

The president would not budge. "I am fixed in my course as firm as the Rockey Mountain," he wrote Vice President Van Buren. No "frail mortals" who worshiped "the golden calf" could change his mind. To others he swore he would sooner cut off his right arm and "undergo the torture of ten Spanish inquisitions" than restore the deposits. When delegations came to him, he roared: "Go to Nicholas Biddle. . . . Biddle has all the money!" And in the end—because he was right—business leaders began to take the old general's advice. Pressure on Biddle mounted swiftly, and in July 1834 he suddenly reversed his policy and began to lend money freely. The artificial crisis ended.

JACKSON VERSUS CALHOUN

The Webster-Hayne debate had revived discussion of Calhoun's argument about nullification. Although southern-born, Jackson had devoted too much of his life to fighting for the entire United States to countenance disunion. Therefore, in April 1830, when the states' rights faction invited him to a dinner to celebrate the anniversary of Jefferson's birth, he came prepared. The evening reverberated with speeches and toasts of a states' rights tenor, but when the president was called on to volunteer a toast, he raised his glass, fixed his eyes on John C. Calhoun, and said: "Our *Federal* Union: It must be preserved!" Calhoun took up the challenge at once. "The Union," he retorted, "next to our liberty, most dear!"

It is difficult to measure the importance of the animosity between Jackson and Calhoun in the crisis to which this clash was a prelude. Calhoun wanted very much to be president. He had failed to inherit the office from John Quincy Adams and had accepted the vice presidency again under Jackson in the hope of succeeding him at the end of one term, if not sooner, for Jackson's health was known to be frail. Yet Old Hickory showed no sign of passing on or retiring. Jackson also seemed to place special confidence in the shrewd Van Buren, who, as secretary of state, also had claim to the succession.

A silly social fracas in which Calhoun's wife appeared to take the lead in the systematic snubbing of

Peggy Eaton, wife of the secretary of war, had estranged Jackson and Calhoun. (Peggy was supposed to have had an affair with Eaton while she was still married to another man, and Jackson, undoubtedly sympathetic because of the attacks he and Rachel had endured, stoutly defended her good name.) Then, shortly after the Jefferson Day dinner, Jackson discovered that in 1818, when he had invaded Florida, Calhoun, then secretary of war, had recommended to President Monroe that Jackson be summoned before a court of inquiry and charged with disobeying orders. Since Calhoun had repeatedly led Jackson to believe that he had supported him at the time, the revelation convinced the president that Calhoun was not a man of honor.

The personal difficulties are worth stressing because Jackson and Calhoun were not far apart ideologically except on the ultimate issue of the right of a state to overrule federal authority. Jackson was a strong president, but he did not believe that the area of national power was large or that it should be expanded. His interests in government economy, in the distribution of federal surpluses to the states, and in interpreting the powers of Congress narrowly were all similar to Calhoun's. Like most Westerners, he favored internal improvements, but he preferred that local projects be left to the states. In 1830 he vetoed a bill providing aid for the construction of the Maysville Road because the route was wholly within Kentucky. There were political reasons for this veto, which was a slap at Kentucky's hero, Henry Clay, but it could not fail to please Calhoun.

INDIAN REMOVALS

The president also took a states' rights position in the controversy that arose between the Cherokee Indians and Georgia. Jackson subscribed to the theory, advanced by Jefferson, that Indians were "savage" because they roamed wild in a trackless wilderness. The "original inhabitants of our forests" were "incapable of self-government," Jackson claimed, ignoring the fact that the Cherokee lived settled lives and had governed themselves without trouble before the whites arrived.

The Cherokee inhabited a region coveted by whites because it was suitable for growing cotton. Since most Indians preferred to maintain their tribal ways, Jackson pursued a policy of removing them from the path of white settlement. This policy seems heartless to modern critics, but since few Indians were willing to adopt the white way of life, most contemporary whites considered removal the only humane solution if the nation was to continue to expand. Jackson insisted that the Indians receive fair prices for their lands and that the government bear

▲ When a Sac chief signed a treaty abandoning lands east of the Mississippi River and moved the tribe to Iowa, Black Hawk decided to go to war. In 1832, the year of this painting, he led several hundred warriors back across the Mississippi. Although they repeatedly drew U.S. soldiers into ambushes, Black Hawk and his warriors were driven back. He was captured in 1833 and imprisoned in St. Louis. Later, he was introduced to President Andrew Jackson and was returned to a reservation in Iowa, where he died.

the expense of resettling them. He believed that moving them beyond the Mississippi would protect them from the "degradation and destruction to which they were rapidly hastening . . . in the States."

Many tribes resigned themselves to removal without argument. Between 1831 and 1833, some 15,000 Choctaw migrated from their lands in Mississippi to the region west of the Arkansas Territory.

MAP

Native American
Removal

In *Democracy in America*, the Frenchman Alexis de Tocqueville described "the frightful sufferings that attend these forced migrations," and he added sadly that the migrants "have no longer a country, and

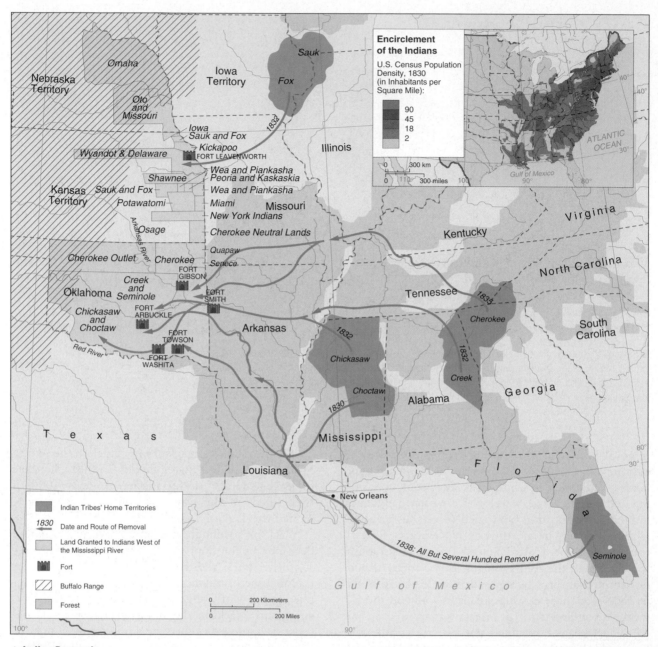

▲ **Indian Removals**

soon will not be a people." He vividly described a group of Choctaw crossing the Mississippi River at Memphis in the dead of winter:

> The cold was unusually severe; the snow had frozen hard upon the ground, and the river was drifting huge masses of ice. The Indians had their families with them, and they brought in their train the wounded and the sick, with children newly born and old men upon the verge of death. They possessed neither tents nor wagons, but only their arms and some provisions. I saw them embark to pass the mighty river, and never will that solemn spectacle fade from my remembrance. No cry, no sob, was heard among the assembled crowd; all were silent.

Tocqueville was particularly moved by the sight of an old woman whom he described in a letter to his mother. She was "naked save for a covering which left visible, at a thousand places, the most emaciated figure imaginable. . . . To leave one's country at that age to seek one's fortune in a foreign land, what misery!"

A few tribes, such as Black Hawk's Sac and Fox in Illinois and Osceola's Seminole in Florida, resisted

▲ Several hundred Seminole Indians in Florida refused to abandon their tribal lands and move west. Although their leader, Osceola, was treacherously captured in 1837 and soon died in prison, other Seminole fought on until forced to surrender in 1842; the warriors in this picture are attacking a federal fort. Some Seminole hid in the swamps and never surrendered.

removal and were subdued by troops. One Indian nation, the Cherokee, sought to hold on to their lands by adjusting to white ways. They took up farming and cattle raising, developed a written language, drafted a constitution, and tried to establish a state within a state in northwestern Georgia. Several treaties with the United States seemed to establish the legality of their government. But Georgia would not recognize the Cherokee Nation. It passed a law in 1828 declaring all Cherokee laws void and the region part of Georgia.

The Indians challenged this law in the Supreme Court. In *Cherokee Nation* v. *Georgia* (1831), Chief Justice John Marshall had ruled that the Cherokee were "not a foreign state, in the sense of the Constitution" and therefore could not sue in a United States court. However, in *Worcester* v. *Georgia* (1832), a case involving two missionaries to the Cherokee who had not procured licenses required by Georgia law, he ruled that the state could not control the Cherokee or their territory. Later, when a Cherokee named Corn Tassel, convicted in a Georgia court of the murder of another Indian, appealed on the ground that the crime had taken place in Cherokee territory, Marshall agreed and declared the Georgia action unconstitutional.

Jackson backed Georgia's position. No independent nation could exist within the United States, he insisted. Georgia thereupon hanged Corn Tassel. In 1838, after Jackson had left the White House, the United States forced 15,000 Cherokee to leave Georgia for Oklahoma. At least 4000 of them died on the way; the route has been aptly named the Trail of Tears.

Jackson's willingness to allow Georgia to ignore decisions of the Supreme Court persuaded extreme southern states' righters that he would not oppose the doctrine of nullification should it be formally applied to a law of Congress. They deceived themselves egregiously. Jackson did not challenge Georgia because he approved of the state's position. He spoke of "the poor deluded . . . Cherokees" and called William Wirt, the distinguished lawyer who defended their cause, a "truly wicked" man. Jackson was not one to worry about being inconsistent. When South Carolina revived the talk of nullification in 1832, he acted in quite a different manner.

THE NULLIFICATION CRISIS

The proposed alliance of South and West to reduce the tariff and the price of land had not materialized, partly because Webster had discredited the South in the eyes of western patriots and partly because the planters of South Carolina and Georgia, fearing the competition of fertile new cotton lands in Alabama

and Mississippi, opposed the rapid exploitation of the West almost as vociferously as northern manufacturers did. When a new tariff law was passed in 1832, it lowered duties much less than the Southerners desired. At once talk of nullifying it began to be heard in South Carolina.

In addition to the economic woes of the up-country cotton planters, the great planter-aristocrats of the rice-growing Tidewater, though relatively prosperous, were troubled by northern criticisms of slavery. In the rice region, blacks outnumbered whites two to one; it was the densest concentration of blacks in the United States. Thousands of these slaves were African-born, brought in during the burst of importations before Congress outlawed the trade in 1808. Controlled usually by overseers of the worst sort, the slaves seemed to their masters like savage beasts straining to rise up against their oppressors. In 1822 the exposure in Charleston of a planned revolt organized by Denmark Vesey, who had bought his freedom with money won in a lottery, had alarmed many whites. News of a far more serious uprising in Virginia led by the slave Nat Turner in 1831, just as the tariff controversy was coming to a head, added to popular concern. Radical South Carolinians saw protective tariffs and agitation against slavery as the two sides of one coin; against both aspects of what appeared to them the tyranny of the majority, nullification seemed the logical defense. Yield on the tariff, editor Henry L. Pinckney of the influential *Charleston Mercury* warned, and "abolition will become the order of the day."

Endless discussions of Calhoun's doctrine after the publication of his *Exposition and Protest* in 1828 had produced much interesting theorizing without clarifying the issue. Admirers of Calhoun praised his "power of analysis & profound philosophical reasonings," but his idea was ingenious rather than profound. Plausible at first glance, it was based on false assumptions: that the Constitution was subject to definitive interpretation; that one party could be permitted to interpret a compact unilaterally without destroying it; that a minority of the nation could reassume its sovereign independence but that a minority of a state could not.

President Jackson was in this respect Calhoun's exact opposite. The South Carolinian's mental gymnastics he brushed aside; intuitively he realized the central reality: If a state could nullify a law of Congress, the Union could not exist. "Tell . . . the Nullifiers from me that they can talk and write resolutions and print threats to their hearts' content," he warned a South Carolina representative when Congress adjourned in July 1832. "But if one drop of blood be shed there in defiance of the laws of the United States, I will hang the first man of them I can get my hands on to the first tree I can find."

The warning was not taken seriously in South Carolina. In October the state legislature provided for the election of a special convention, which, when it met, contained a solid majority of nullifiers. On November 24, 1832, the convention passed an ordinance of nullification prohibiting the collection of tariff duties in the state after February 1, 1833. The legislature then authorized the raising of an army and appropriated money to supply it with weapons.

Jackson quickly began military preparations of his own, telling friends that he would have 50,000 men ready to move in a little over a month. He also made a statesmanlike effort to end the crisis peaceably. First he suggested to Congress that it lower the tariff further. On December 10 he delivered a "Proclamation to the People of South Carolina." Nullification could only lead to the destruction of the Union, he said. "The laws of the United States must be executed. I have no discretionary power on the subject. . . . Those who told you that you might peaceably prevent their execution deceived you." Old Hickory added sternly: "Disunion by armed force is *treason*. Are you really ready to incur its guilt?" Jackson's reasoning profoundly shocked even opponents of nullification. If South Carolina did not back down, the president's threat to use force would mean civil war and possibly the destruction of the Union he claimed to be defending.

Calhoun sought desperately to control the crisis. By prearrangement with Senator Hayne, he resigned as vice president and was appointed to replace Hayne in the Senate, where he led the search for a peaceful solution. Having been defeated in his campaign for the presidency, Clay was a willing ally. In addition, many who admired Jackson nonetheless, as Van Buren later wrote, "distrusted his prudence," fearing that he would "commit some rash act." They believed in dealing with the controversy by discussion and compromise.

DOCUMENT

South Carolina's Ordinance of Nullification

As a result, administration leaders introduced both a new tariff bill and a Force Bill granting the president additional authority to execute the revenue laws. Jackson was perfectly willing to see the tariff reduced but insisted that he was determined to enforce the law. As the February 1 deadline approached, he claimed that he could raise 200,000 men if needed to suppress resistance. "Union men, fear not," he said. "*The Union will be preserved.*"

Jackson's determination sobered the South Carolina radicals. Their appeal for the support of other southern states fell on deaf ears: All rejected the idea of nullification. The unionist minority in South

▲ A South Carolina belle sewing—albeit languorously—a palmetto (a stylized palm leaf) onto a "nullification hat."

Carolina added to the radicals' difficulties by threatening civil war if federal authority were defied. Calhoun, though a brave man, was alarmed for his own safety, for Jackson had threatened to "hang him as high as Haman" if nullification were attempted. Observers described him as "excessively uneasy." He was suddenly eager to avoid a showdown.

Ten days before the deadline, South Carolina postponed nullification pending the outcome of the tariff debate. Then, in March 1833, Calhoun and Clay pushed a compromise tariff through Congress. As part of the agreement Congress also passed the Force Bill, mostly as a face-saving device for the president.

The compromise reflected the willingness of the North and West to make concessions in the interest of national harmony. Senator Silas Wright of New York, closely affiliated with Van Buren, explained the situation: "People will neither cut throats nor dismember the Union for protection. There is more patriotism and love of country than that left yet. The People will never balance this happy government against ten cents a pound upon a pound of wool."

And so the Union weathered the storm. Having stepped to the brink of civil war, the nation had drawn hastily back. The South Carolina legislature professed to be satisfied with the new tariff (in fact it made few immediate reductions, providing for a gradual lowering of rates over a ten-year period) and repealed the Nullification Ordinance, saving face by nullifying the Force Act, which was now a dead letter. But the radical South Carolina planters were becoming convinced that only secession would protect slavery. The nullification fiasco had proved that they could not succeed without the support of other slave states. Thereafter they devoted themselves ceaselessly to obtaining it.

BOOM AND BUST

During 1833 and 1834 Secretary of the Treasury Taney insisted that the pet banks maintain large reserves. But other state banks began to offer credit on easy terms, aided by a large increase in their reserves of gold and silver resulting from causes unconnected with the policies of either the government or Biddle's Bank. A decline in the Chinese demand for Mexican silver led to increased exports of the metal to the United States, and the rise of American interest rates attracted English capital into the country. Heavy English purchases of American cotton at high prices also increased the flow of specie into American banks. These developments caused bank notes in circulation to jump from $82 million in January 1835 to $120 million in December 1836. Bank deposits rose even more rapidly.

Much of the new money flowed into speculation in land; a mania to invest in property swept the country. The increased volume of currency caused prices to soar 15 percent in six months, buoying investors' spirits and making them ever more optimistic about the future. By the summer of 1835 one observer estimated that in New York City, which had about 250,000 residents, enough house lots had been laid out and sold to support a population of 2 million. Chicago at this time had only 2000 to 3000 inhabitants, yet most of the land for 25 miles around had been sold and resold in small lots by speculators anticipating the growth of the area. Throughout the West farmers borrowed money from local banks by mortgaging their land, used the money to buy more land from the government, and then borrowed still more money from the banks on the strength of their new deeds.

So long as prices rose, the process could be repeated endlessly. In 1832, while the Bank of the United States still regulated the money supply, federal

income from the sale of land was $2.6 million. In 1834 it was $4.9 million; in 1835, $14.8 million. In 1836 it rose to $24.9 million, and the government found itself totally free of debt and with a surplus of $20 million!

Finally Jackson became alarmed by the speculative mania. In the summer of 1836 he issued the Specie Circular, which provided that purchasers must henceforth pay for public land in gold or silver. At once the rush to buy land came to a halt. As demand slackened, prices sagged. Speculators, unable to dispose of lands mortgaged to the banks, had to abandon them to the banks, but the banks could not realize enough on the foreclosed property to recover their loans. Suddenly the public mood changed. Commodity prices tumbled 30 percent between February and May. Hordes of depositors sought to withdraw their money in the form of specie, and soon the banks exhausted their supplies. Panic swept the country in the spring of 1837 as every bank in the nation was forced to suspend specie payments. The boom was over.

Major swings in the business cycle can never be attributed to the actions of a single person, however powerful, but there is no doubt that Jackson's war against the Bank exaggerated the swings of the economic pendulum, not so much by its direct effects as by the impact of the president's ill-considered policies on popular thinking. His Specie Circular did not prevent speculators from buying land—at most it caused purchasers to pay a premium for gold or silver. But it convinced potential buyers that the boom was going to end and led them to make decisions that in fact ended it. Old Hickory's combination of impetuousness, combativeness, arrogance, and ignorance rendered the nation he loved so dearly a serious disservice.

JACKSONIANISM ABROAD

Jackson's emotional and dogmatic side also influenced his handling of foreign affairs. His patriotism was often so extravagant as to be ludicrous; in less peaceful times he might well have embroiled the country in far bloodier battles than his war with Nicholas Biddle produced. By pushing relentlessly for the solution of minor problems, he won a number of diplomatic successes. Several advantageous reciprocal trade agreements were negotiated, including one with Great Britain that finally opened British West Indian ports to American ships. American claims dating from the Napoleonic Wars were pressed vigorously. The most important result of this policy came in 1831, when France agreed to pay about $5 million to compensate for damages to American property during that long conflict.

This settlement, however, led to trouble because the French Chamber of Deputies refused to appropriate the necessary funds. When the United States submitted a bill for the first installment in 1833, it was unable to collect. Jackson at once adopted a belligerent stance, his ire further aroused by a bill for $170,041.18 submitted by Nicholas Biddle for the services of the Bank of the United States in attempting to collect the money. When France ignored the second installment, Jackson sent a blistering message to Congress, full of such phrases as "not to be tolerated" and "take redress into our own hands." He asked for a law "authorizing reprisals upon French property" if the money was not paid.

Jackson's case was ironclad, yet it did not merit such vigorous prosecution. Congress wisely took no action. Jackson suspended diplomatic relations with France and ordered the navy readied. The French—in part, no doubt, because they were clearly in the wrong—were insulted by Jackson's manner. Irresponsible talk of war was heard in both countries. Fortunately the French Chamber finally appropriated the money, Jackson moderated his public pronouncements, and the issue subsided.

Similarly, when a snag delayed the negotiation of the West Indian treaty, Jackson had suggested forcing Great Britain to make concessions by imposing a boycott on trade with Canada. In both cases he showed poor judgment, being ready to take monumental risks to win petty victories. His behavior reinforced the impression held by foreigners that the United States was a rash young country with a chip on its shoulder, pathologically mistrustful of the good faith of European powers.

THE JACKSONIANS

Jackson's personality had a large impact on the shape and tone of American politics and thus with the development of the second party system. When he came to office, nearly everyone professed to be a follower of Jefferson. By 1836 being a Jeffersonian no longer meant much; what mattered was how one felt about Andrew Jackson. He had ridden to power at the head of a diverse political army, but he left behind him an organization with a fairly cohesive, if not necessarily consistent, body of ideas. This Democratic party contained rich citizens and poor, Easterners and Westerners, abolitionists as well as slaveholders. It was not yet a close-knit national organization, but—always allowing for individual exceptions—the Jacksonians agreed on certain underlying principles. These included suspicion of special privilege and large business corporations, both typified by the Bank of the United States; freedom of economic opportunity, unfettered by private or governmental

DEBATING THE PAST

For whom did Jackson fight? In 1837, his last year as president, Jackson here distributes hunks of a 1400-pound cheese, a gift from New York farmers. They thought it the best present the "farming class" could give to someone who so forcefully had represented "their interest." In 1855 historian George Bancroft maintained that Jackson *was all* America, for he "shared and possessed all the creative ideas of his country and his time." (This is the sort of twaddle that gives nineteenth-century historians a bad name.) In 1945 Arthur M. Schlesinger, Jr.—son of the progressive historian—praised Jackson for battling on behalf of farmers and workers against big business. Jackson approached politics in terms of class rather than geography, and in that sense anticipated Franklin Delano Roosevelt. In both eras, Schlesinger observed, "the business community" had brought "national affairs to a state of crisis." Richard Hofstadter (1948) conceded that Jackson's fight against business had "many superficial points in common" with Roosevelt's. But Jackson had been no friend of the "common man," for he had consistently promoted the interests of well-to-do farmers and local entrepreneurs. This point received some confirmation from Edward Pessen's (1969) study of wealth accumulation during the Jacksonian era: the rich grew richer and the poor, poorer. Robert Remini (1984), on the other hand, argued that Jackson adhered to republican ideals: he did what was good for the nation as a whole. Whatever the reality, many different people *believed* that Jackson represented them. Note that at the public reception above, some wore formal attire and others, work clothes. But all got cheese.

George Bancroft, *Literary and Historical Miscellanies* (1855), Arthur M. Schlesinger, Jr., *Age of Jackson* (1945), Richard Hofstadter, *The American Political Tradition*, Edward Pessen, *Jacksonian America* (1969), Lee Benson, *The Concept of Jacksonian Democracy* (1961), Robert Remini, *Andrew Jackson and the Course of American Democracy* (1984).

restrictions; absolute political freedom, at least for white males; and the conviction that any ordinary man is capable of performing the duties of most public offices.

Jackson's ability to reconcile his belief in the supremacy of the Union with his conviction that national authority should be held within narrow limits tended to make the Democrats the party of those who believed that the powers of the states should not be diminished. Tocqueville caught this aspect of Jackson's philosophy perfectly: "Far from wishing to extend Federal power," he wrote, "the president belongs to the party that wishes to limit that power."

Although the radical Locofoco[2] wing of the party championed the idea, nearly all Jacksonians, like their leader, favored giving the small man his chance—by supporting public education, for example, and by refusing to place much weight on a person's origin, dress, or manners. "One individual is as good as another" (for accuracy we must insert the adjective *white*) was their axiom. This attitude helps explain why immigrants, Catholics, and other minority groups usually voted Democratic. However, the Jacksonians showed no tendency either to penalize the wealthy or to intervene in economic affairs to aid the underprivileged. The motto "That government is best which governs least" graced the masthead of the chief Jacksonian newspaper, the *Washington Globe,* throughout the era.

Rise of the Whigs

The opposition to Jackson was far less cohesive. Henry Clay's National Republican party provided a nucleus, but Clay never dominated that party as Jackson dominated the Democrats. Its orientation was basically anti-Jackson. It was as though the American people were a great block of granite from which some sculptor had just fashioned a statue of Jackson, the chips scattered about the floor of the studio representing the opposition.

While Jackson was president, the impact of his personality delayed the formation of a true two-party system, but as soon as he surrendered power, the opposition, taking heart, began to coalesce. Many Democrats could not accept the odd logic of Jacksonian finance. As early as 1834 they, together with the Clay element, the extreme states' righters who followed Calhoun, and other dissident groups, were calling

themselves Whigs. The name harkened back to the Revolution. It implied patriotic distaste for too-powerful executives, expressed specifically as resistance to the tyranny of "King Andrew."

This coalition possessed great resources of wealth and talent. Anyone who understood banking was almost obliged to become a Whig unless he was connected with one of Jackson's "pets." Those spiritual descendants of Hamilton who rejected the administration's refusal to approach economic problems from a broadly national perspective also joined in large numbers. Those who found the coarseness and "pushiness" of the Jacksonians offensive were another element in the new party. The anti-intellectual and antiscientific bias of the administration (Jackson rejected proposals for a national university, an observatory, and a scientific and literary institute) drove many ministers, lawyers, doctors, and other well-educated people into the Whig fold.

The philosopher Ralph Waldo Emerson was no doubt thinking of these types when he described the Whigs as "the enterprizing, intelligent, well-meaning & wealthy part of the people," but Whig arguments also appealed to ordinary voters who were predisposed to favor strong governments that would check the "excesses" of unrestricted individualism.

The Whigs were slow to develop effective party organization. They had too many generals and not enough troops. It was hard for them to agree on any issue more complicated than opposition to Jackson. Furthermore, they stood in conflict with the major trend of the age: the glorification of the common man.

Lacking a dominant leader in 1836, the Whigs relied on "favorite sons," hoping to throw the presidential election into the House of Representatives. Daniel Webster ran in New England. For the West and South, Hugh Lawson White of Tennessee, a former friend who had broken with Jackson, was counted on to carry the fight. General William Henry Harrison was supposed to win in the Northwest and to draw support everywhere from those who liked to vote for military heroes. This sorry strategy failed; Jackson's handpicked candidate, Martin Van Buren, won a majority of both the popular and the electoral votes.

Martin Van Buren: Jacksonianism Without Jackson

Van Buren's brilliance as a political manipulator—the Red Fox, the Little Magician—has tended to obscure his statesmanlike qualities and his engaging

---

[2]A locofoco was a type of friction match. The name was first applied in politics when a group of New York Jacksonians used these matches to light candles when a conservative faction tried to break up their meeting by turning off the gaslights.

personality. He made a powerful argument, for example, that political parties were a force for unity, not for partisan bickering. In addition, high office sobered him, and improved his judgment. He fought the Bank of the United States as a monopoly, but he also opposed irresponsible state banks. New York's Safety Fund System, requiring all banks to contribute to a fund, supervised by the state, to be used to redeem the notes of any member bank that failed, was established largely through his efforts. Van Buren believed in public construction of internal improvements, but he favored state rather than national programs, and he urged a rational approach: Each project must stand on its own as a useful and profitable public utility.

He continued to equivocate spectacularly on the tariff—in his *Autobiography* he described two of his supporters walking home after listening to him talk on the tariff, each convinced that it had been a brilliant speech, but neither having obtained the slightest idea as to where Van Buren stood on the subject—but he was never in the pocket of any special interest group or tariff lobbyist. He accounted himself a good Jeffersonian, tending to prefer state action to federal, but he was by no means doctrinaire. Basically he approached most questions rationally and pragmatically.

Van Buren

Van Buren had outmaneuvered Calhoun easily in the struggle to succeed Jackson, winning the old hero's confidence and serving him well. In 1832 he was elected vice president and thereafter was conceded to be the "heir apparent." In 1835 the Democratic National Convention unanimously nominated him for president.

Van Buren took office just as the Panic of 1837 struck the country. Its effects were frightening but short-lived. When the banks stopped converting paper money into gold and silver, they outraged conservatives but in effect eased the pressure on the money market: Interest rates declined and business loans again became relatively easy to obtain. In 1836, at the height of the boom in land sales, Congress had voted to "distribute" the new treasury surplus to the states, and this flow of money, which the states promptly spent, also stimulated the revival. Late in 1838 the banks resumed specie payments.

But in 1839 a bumper crop caused a sharp decline in the price of cotton. Then a number of state governments that had overextended themselves in road- and canal-building projects were forced to default on their debts. This discouraged investors, particularly foreigners. A general economic depression ensued that lasted until 1843.

Van Buren was not responsible for the panic or the depression, but his manner of dealing with economic issues was scarcely helpful. He saw his role as being concerned only with problems plaguing the government, ignoring the economy as a whole. "The less government interferes with private pursuits the better for the general prosperity," he pontificated. As Daniel Webster scornfully pointed out, Van Buren was following a policy of "leaving the people to shift for themselves," one that many Whigs rejected.

Such a hands-off approach to the depression seems foolish by modern standards. Van Buren's refusal to assume any responsibility for the general welfare appears to explode the theory that the Jacksonians were deeply concerned with the fate of ordinary citizens. In *The Concept of Jacksonian Democracy*, Lee Benson argues that the Whigs, rather than the Democrats, were the "positive liberals" of the era. Benson cites many statements by Whigs about applying "the means of the state boldly and liberally to aid . . . public works."

This approach helps correct past oversimplifications, but it judges the period by the standards of a later age. The country in the 1830s was still mainly agricultural, and for most farmers the depression, though serious, did not spell disaster. Moreover, many Jacksonians were perfectly willing to see the states act to stimulate economic growth in bad times—as indeed most states did.

Van Buren's chief goal was finding a substitute for the state banks as a place to keep federal funds. The depression and the suspension of specie payments embarrassed the government along with private depositors. He soon settled on the idea of "divorcing" the government from all banking activities. His independent treasury bill called for the construction of government owned vaults where federal revenues could be stored until needed. To ensure absolute safety, all payments to the government were to be made in hard cash. After a battle that lasted until the summer of 1840, the Independent Treasury Act passed both the House and the Senate.

Opposition to the Independent Treasury Act had been bitter, and not all of it was partisan. Bankers and businessmen objected to the government's withholding so much specie from the banks, which needed all the hard money they could get to support loans that were the lifeblood of economic growth. It seemed irresponsible for the federal government to turn its back on the banks, which so obviously performed a semipublic function. These criticisms made good sense, but through a lucky

combination of circumstances, the system worked reasonably well for many years.

By creating suspicion in the public mind, officially stated distrust of banks acted as a damper on their tendency to overexpand. No acute shortage of specie developed because heavy agricultural exports and the investment of much European capital in American railroads beginning in the mid-1840s brought in large amounts of new gold and silver. After 1849 the discovery of gold in California added another important source of specie. The supply of money and bank credit kept pace roughly with the growth of the economy, but through no fault of the government. "Wildcat" banks proliferated. Fraud and counterfeiting were common, and the operation of everyday business affairs was inconvenienced in countless ways. The disordered state of the currency remained a grave problem until corrected by Civil War banking legislation.

THE LOG CABIN CAMPAIGN

It was not his financial policy that led to Van Buren's defeat in 1840. The depression naturally hurt the Democrats, and the Whigs were far better organized than in 1836. The Whigs also adopted a different strategy. The Jacksonians had come to power on the coattails of a popular general whose views on public questions they concealed or ignored. They had maintained themselves by shouting the praises of the common man. Now the Whigs seized on these techniques and carried them to their logical—or illogical—conclusion. Not even bothering to draft a program, and passing over Clay and Webster, whose views were known and therefore controversial, they nominated General William Henry Harrison for president. The "Hero of Tippecanoe" was counted on to conquer the party created in the image of the Hero of New Orleans. To "balance" the ticket, the Whigs chose a former Democrat, John Tyler of Virginia, an ardent supporter of states' rights, as their vice presidential candidate.

The Whig argument was specious but effective: General Harrison is a plain man of the people who lives in a log cabin (where the latchstring is always out). Contrast him with the suave Van Buren, luxuriating amid "the Regal Splendor of the President's Palace." Harrison drinks ordinary hard cider and eats hog meat and grits, while Van Buren drinks expensive foreign wines and fattens on fancy concoctions prepared by a French chef. The general's furniture is plain and sturdy; the president dines off gold plates and treads on Royal Wilton carpets that cost the people $5

▲ The 1840 presidential campaign was the first to use circus hoopla and the techniques of mass appeal that came to characterize political contests in the United States. This photograph is of a log cabin with a "hard cider" keg that was carried on a pole at rallies for William Henry Harrison.

a yard. In a country where all are equal, the people will reject an aristocrat like "Martin Van Ruin" and put their trust in General Harrison, a simple, brave, honest, public-spirited common man.

Harrison came from a distinguished family, being the son of Benjamin Harrison, a signer of the Declaration of Independence and a former governor of Virginia. He was well educated and in at least comfortable financial circumstances, and he certainly did not live in a log cabin. The Whigs ignored these facts. The log cabin and the cider barrel became their symbols, which every political meeting saw reproduced in a dozen forms. The leading Whig campaign newspaper, edited by a vigorous New Englander named Horace Greeley, was called the *Log Cabin*. Cartoons, doggerel, slogans, and souvenirs were everywhere substituted for argument.

The Democrats used the same methods as the Whigs and were equally well organized, but they had little heart for the fight. The best they could come up with was the fact that their vice presidential candidate,

▶ *text continues on page 270*

Horace Greeley

Zaccheus ("Zack") Greeley, a farmer in Amherst, New Hampshire, was the son and grandson of men who bore that name, but for some unexplained reason when his first son was born in 1811 he named him Horace. Zack Greeley owned 40 acres of stony land on which he grew corn, oats, and rye, along with hops, a key ingredient in the making of beer. The local soil tended to become hard packed. Every few years it had to be "broken up" by plowing it with four pairs of oxen, led by a horse. To "ride horse to plough" was one of Horace's tasks by the time he was 5. "I was early made acquainted with labor," Horace recalled many years later. His other jobs included keeping the oxen out of the corn on frosty autumn mornings while the harvesters had their breakfast, and digging out worms and grubs around the corn hills.

The hard times following the Panic of 1819, combined with ill health and a poor head for business, caused Zack Greeley to lose his farm in 1820. Indeed, to avoid debtors' prison, he had to leave his family and hurry across the state line into Vermont. But after working as a day laborer for a few months he was able to rent a house in Westhaven, Vermont, and send for his family. There the Greeleys experienced what Horace called "genuine poverty,—not beggary, nor dependence, but the manly American sort." During the winter Zack chopped wood for 50 cents a day. In the spring he contracted to clear 50 acres of wild land. For the next two years Zack and his two sons, aged 10 and 8 in 1821, cleared the 50 acres at a rate of $7 an acre, plus half the usable wood they had cut. They chopped down trees, sawed the wood into manageable lengths, and uprooted and burned rotting stumps and brush. Horace described the work as "rugged and grimy, but healthy." The next year the Greeleys moved to a nearby small farm called Flea Knoll. That spring was too wet, the summer too dry, the fields thick with thistles. Farming, Horace had by this time decided, was "a mindless, monotonous drudgery." He was determined to seek a different vocation.

Fortunately he was a bright boy and his parents apparently noticed his talent early. Before he was 3 they sent him to school in the winter months in a one-room schoolhouse near his grandfather's farm. He proved particularly adept at mastering Webster's *Spelling-Book* and soon outdistanced much

older pupils in the school's weekly spelling bees. Reading proved equally easy for him, and by the time he was 5, with a little help from his mother, he had made his way through the entire Bible. Word of his talent spread throughout the community, and when he was 9 a group of "leading men" offered to send him to Phillips Academy in Exeter, New Hampshire. His parents, however, politely declined the offer, saying "they would give their children the best education they could afford, and then stop."

After the family moved to Vermont, young Greeley continued to go to school in the winter months when his labor was not needed on the farm. But he was not exposed to any of the sciences or to any math as far advanced as algebra. Despite his lack of much formal education, however, he hoped to become a newspaper man. In 1826 he learned of an opening for an apprentice on the *Northern Spectator* in the town of East Poultney, Vermont. He was 15.

He was offered the post and with his father's approval he signed on to work until the age of 20 for room and board and $40 a year for clothing. East Poultney, he recalled many years later, was an excellent place to learn a trade—there were, he explained, perhaps with tongue in cheek, "few villages wherein the incitements to dissipation and vice are fewer." The paper was loosely run, editors and printers came and went frequently. Thus "every one had perfect liberty to learn whatever he could." Greeley worked at his job very hard but also found time to scour the shelves of the East Poultney Public Library.

When his apprenticeship ended, Greeley paid a brief visit to his family, which had settled in Erie County, Pennsylvania. Then he found a couple of jobs on papers in Chautauqua County, New York, before accepting a post as a journeyman on the Erie [Pennsylvania] *Gazette* for $15 a month. After five months, however, he was let go. Finding that "the West seemed to be laboring under a surfeit of printers," he paid a final visit to his parents and, as he later explained, "with $25 in my pocket, and very little extra clothing in my bundle, I set my face toward New York." He arrived in the city by Hudson River steamer on August 17, 1831. He was five months short of 21 years old.

▲ Greeley reading his newspaper, the *New York Tribune*.

After buying a new suit for $5, Greeley had only $10 to his name. For a year and a half he lived hand-to-mouth, working for a series of printers as a journeyman. Then he managed to set himself up on his own and in 1834 began publishing the *New-Yorker,* a literary magazine. He became heavily involved in Whig politics and on April 10, 1841, launched the newspaper that became his life work, the *New York Tribune.*

Greeley is best known for the line "Go West, young man, go West," advice many mid-nineteenth-century young people of both sexes eagerly accepted. Greeley used, though he did not invent, that expression, but his own career was typical of a far different pattern, the movement of ambitious men and women from farm to city.

Richard Mentor Johnson, had killed Tecumseh, not merely defeated him. Van Buren tried to focus public attention on issues, but his voice could not be heard above the huzzahs of the Whigs. When the Whigs chanted "Tippecanoe and Tyler too!" and "Van, Van, is a used-up man" and rolled out another barrel of hard cider, the best the Democrats could come up with was:

Rumpsey, Dumpsey,
Colonel Johnson
Killed Tecumseh.

A huge turnout (four-fifths of the eligible voters) carried Harrison to victory by a margin of almost 150,000. The electoral vote was 234 to 60.

The Democrats had been blown up by their own bomb. In 1828 they had portrayed John Quincy Adams as a bloated aristocrat and Jackson as a simple farmer. The lurid talk of Van Buren dining off golden plates was no different from the stories that made Adams out to be a passionate gambler. If Van Buren

was a lesser man than Adams, Harrison was a pale imitation indeed of Andrew Jackson.

The Whigs continued to repeat history by rushing to gather the spoils of victory. Washington was again flooded by office seekers, the political confusion was monumental. Harrison had no ambition to be an aggressive leader. He believed that Jackson had misused the veto and professed to put as much emphasis as had Washington on the principle of the separation of legislative and executive powers. This delighted the Whig leaders in Congress, who had had their fill of the "executive usurpation" of Jackson. Either Clay or Webster seemed destined to be the real ruler of the new administration, and soon the two were squabbling over their old general like sparrows over a crust.

At the height of their squabble, less than a month after his inauguration, Harrison fell gravely ill. Pneumonia developed, and on April 4 he died. John Tyler of Virginia, honest and conscientious but doctrinaire, became president of the United States. The political climate of the country was changed dramatically. Events began to march in a new direction.

MILESTONES

1828	Andrew Jackson is elected president	1833	Treasury Secretary Roger B. Taney orders Treasury funds removed from Bank of the United States
1829	Crowds cause chaos at Jackson's White House inaugural reception		Calhoun and Clay push through Compromise Tariff
	Jackson relies on his "Kitchen Cabinet"	1836	Jackson issues Specie Circular to control speculation
1830	Daniel Webster, in his "Second Reply to Hayne," calls Union perpetual and indissoluble		Martin Van Buren is elected president
	Jackson vetoes the Maysville Road Bill	1837–1838	Panic sweeps nation, ending boom
1831	Nat Turner leads slave rebellion in Virginia	1838	4000 Cherokee die on Trail of Tears to Oklahoma
	Chief Justice Marshall denies Cherokee rights in *Cherokee Nation* v. *Georgia*	1840	Independent Treasury Act divorces federal government from all banking activities
1831–1838	Southern Indians are removed to Oklahoma		"Log Cabin" Campaign is first to use "hoopla"
1832	South Carolina defends states' rights in Ordinance of Nullification		William Henry Harrison is elected president
	Force Bill grants president authority to execute revenue laws	1841	Harrison dies one month after inauguration; John Tyler becomes president
	Jackson vetoes Bank Recharter Bill		
	Chief Justice Marshall rules in Cherokees' favor in *Worcester* v. *Georgia*		
	Jackson is reelected president		

SUPPLEMENTARY READING

The nature of Jacksonian democracy was analyzed brilliantly by Alexis de Tocqueville, *Democracy in America* (1835–1840). Other commentaries by foreigners throw much light on Jacksonian democracy. See especially, in addition to Tocqueville, Frances Trollope, *Domestic Manners of the Americans* (1832), Michel Chevalier, *Society, Manners and Politics in the United States* (1961), Harriet Martineau, *Retrospect of Western Travel* (1838) and *Society in America* (1837), and F. J. Grund, *Aristocracy in America* (1859).

In addition to the works on Jackson cited in Debating the Past (p. 264), see Bray Hammond, *Banks and Politics in America from the Revolution to the Civil War* (1957), and J. M. McFaul, *The Politics of Jacksonian Finance* (1972). Peter Temin, *The Jacksonian Economy* (1969), minimizes the effects of Jackson's policies on economic conditions. Jill Norgren, *The Cherokee Cases* (1996) is critical of Jackson's policies toward Indians; Robert Remini is more supportive in *Andrew Jackson and His Indian Wars* (2001).

On the transformation of political parties, see Richard P. McCormick, *The Second American Party System* (1966), and Michael Holt, *The Rise and Fall of the American Whig Party* (1999), which focuses on variations at the state level. Gerald Leonard, *The Invention of Party Politics* (2002) provides a detailed study of Illinois.

On the nullification controversy, see R. E. Ellis, *The Union at Risk* (1987), and William W. Freehling, *The Road to Disunion* (1990), which stresses the close relationship between the nullifiers and the slavery issue.

For the Van Buren administration, see John Niven, *Martin Van Buren* (1983), and M. L. Wilson, *The Presidency of Martin Van Buren* (1984). The election of 1840 is treated in R. G. Gunderson, *The Log-Cabin Campaign* (1957).

Louis Masur's *1831, Year of Eclipse* (2001), provides an interesting perspective on that pivotal year.

SUGGESTED WEBSITES

Indian Affairs: Laws and Treaties, Compiled and Edited by Charles J. Kappler (1904)
http://digital.library.okstate.edu/kappler/
This digitized text at Oklahoma State University includes preremoval treaties with the Five Civilized Tribes and other tribes.

Andrew Jackson and Indian Removal
http://www.iwchildren.org/genocide/murderer1.htm
This site offers a critical appraisal of Jackson's Indian removal policy.

The Second Bank of the United States, 1816–1836
http://odur.let.rug.nl/~usa/E/usbank/bank04.htm
The political fighting surrounding the Second Bank of the United States occupied the United States during the Jackson era, and led to the rise of the Whig party.

Daniel Webster
http://www.dartmouth.edu/~dwebster
Background information and selected writings from one of the nineteenth century's most noted orators.

The American Whig Party, 1834–1856
http://odur.let.rug.nl/~usa/E/uswhig/whigsxx.htm
This site treats the rise and fall of an important nineteenth-century political movement.

National Museum of the American Indian
http://www.si.edu/nmai
The Smithsonian Institution maintains this site, providing information about the museum that is dedicated to everything about Native Americans.

The Making of Middle-Class America

▲ A view of Samuel Slater's cotton textile mill at Pawtucket Falls; the fast-running water turned the wheels that powered the machinery.

to individual artisans, who, working for wages, wove it into cloth in their homes. The machines were tended by a labor force of nine children, for the work was simple and the pace slow. The young operatives' pay ranged from 33 to 67 cents a week, about what a youngster could earn in other occupations.[1]

The factory was profitable from the start. Slater soon branched out on his own, and others trained by him opened their own establishments. By 1800 seven mills possessing 2000 spindles were in operation; by 1815, after production had been stimulated by the War of 1812, there were 130,000 spindles turning in 213 factories. Many of the new factories were inefficient, but the well-managed ones earned large profits. Slater began with almost nothing. When he died in 1835 he owned mill properties in Rhode Island, Massachusetts, Connecticut, and New Hampshire in addition to other interests. By the standards of the day he was a rich man.

Before long the Boston Associates, a group of merchants headed by Francis Cabot Lowell, added a new dimension to factory production. Beginning

at Waltham, Massachusetts, where the Charles River provided the necessary waterpower, between 1813 and 1850 they revolutionized textile production. Some early factory owners had set up hand looms in their plants, but the weavers could not keep pace with the whirring spinning jennies. Lowell, after an extensive study of British mills, smuggled the plans for an efficient power loom into America. His Boston Manufacturing Company at Waltham, capitalized at $300,000, combined machine production, large-scale operation, efficient management, and centralized marketing procedures. It concentrated on the mass production of a standardized product.

Lowell's cloth, though plain and rather coarse, was durable and cheap. His profits averaged almost 20 percent a year during the Era of Good Feelings. In 1823 the Boston Associates began to harness the power of the Merrimack River, setting up a new $600,000 corporation at the sleepy village of East Chelmsford, Massachusetts (population 300), where there was a fall of 32 feet in the river. Within three years the town, appropriately renamed Lowell, had 2000 inhabitants.

---

[1] This labor pattern persisted for several decades. In 1813 a cotton manufacturer placed the following advertisement in the *Utica* (N.Y.) *Patriot:* "A few sober and industrious families of at least five children each, over the age of eight years are wanted at the Cotton Factory. Widows with large families would do well to attend this notice."

► *text continues on page 228*

Mapping
the Past

The Making of the Working Class

Increasing Physical Separation of Masters and Workers

During the 1700s boys in their teens learned a skill by serving as apprentices to master workmen. After five to seven years of training, apprentices usually became wage-earning journeymen. The master's workshop commonly functioned as both a tiny factory and small store. One journeyman shoemaker in Rochester, New York explained

> It was customary for the boss, with the younger apprentices, to occupy the room in front where, with bared arms and leather aprons, they performed their work and met their customers. A shop in the rear or above would be occupied by the tramping journeyman and the older apprentice. . . . The shops were low rooms in which from fifteen to twenty men worked . . .

Because they lived and worked under the same roof, masters commonly treated apprentices almost as their children. Journeymen usually lived in boardinghouses near the masters'

workshops; if they proved industrious, talented, and frugal, they became master workers, opened a shop of their own, and hired apprentices.

But economic growth during the 1820s and 1830s eroded the ties between masters and workers. Historian Paul Johnson described how this process worked in Rochester, New York. In 1823, the Erie Canal had been completed as far as that city, enabling grain from the Genesee Valley to be loaded onto canal boats and taken to markets in New York City. During the next ten years Rochester became the fastest growing city in the nation. Master workers in Rochester enlarged their shops, hired more workers, and focused more keenly on profits rather than their traditional obligations to workers. They increasingly moved manufacturing processes out of their shops, which now became shoe stores. Journeymen, with paid assistants, performed the work of shoemaking in separate locations.

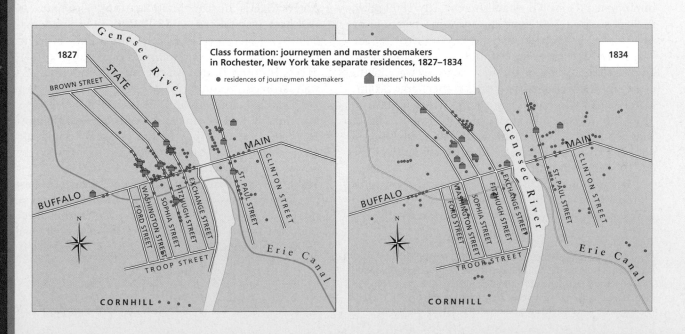

Class formation: journeymen and master shoemakers in Rochester, New York take separate residences, 1827–1834

● residences of journeymen shoemakers   🏠 masters' households

CHAPTER CONTENTS

▼ *Joseph Moore and His Family* (1839), by Erastus Salisbury Field, reflects the emerging middle-class family. Although the painting is named after the father, the mother is carefully placed in a precisely equivalent position; each child has a space of his or her own.

O n May 12, 1831, two French aristocrats, Alexis de Tocqueville and Gustave de Beaumont, arrived in New York City from Le Havre on the packet *President*. Their official purpose was to make a study of American prisons for the French government. But they really came, as Tocqueville explained, "to see what a great republic is like."

Tocqueville and Beaumont were only the most insightful of dozens of Europeans who visited the United States during the first half of the nineteenth century in order to study the "natives." Their visit, for example, overlapped with that of Frances Trollope, whose *Domestic Manners of Americans* (1834) advised English readers that Americans were just as uncouth as they had imagined. A decade later, Charles Dickens made what by then had become for foreigners an almost obligatory pass through this crude outpost of civilization, before publishing his report on his "sharp dealing" cousins in *American Notes* (1842). A little later, in a novel, Dickens described the United States as a "Republic . . . full of sores and ulcers."

TOCQUEVILLE AND BEAUMONT IN AMERICA

Unlike Trollope, Dickens, and other uncharitable foreign visitors, Tocqueville and Beaumont believed that Europe was passing from its aristocratic past into a democratic future. How better to prepare for the change, they believed, than by studying the United States, where democracy was already the "enduring and normal state" of the land. In the nine months they spent in America, they traveled from New York to Boston, then back through New York in order to inspect the state prison at Auburn, then on to Ohio. ("No one has been born

there; no one wants to stay there," Tocqueville later said.) They examined conditions on the frontier in the Michigan Territory, then sailed down the Mississippi River to New Orleans, where they heard an opera good enough to make them imagine they were back in France, and attended a "Quadroon ball," where, according to Tocqueville, "all the men [were] white, all the women coloured."

From New Orleans they went on to "semi-barbarous" Alabama before turning north to Washington, a city that Beaumont declared to be "very ugly." Finally back to New York, whence they sailed for France on February 20, 1832. All told, they had met and interviewed some 250 individuals, ranking from President Jackson—Beaumont insisted on referring to Old Hickory as "Monsieur"—to a number of Chippewa Indians.

▲ *The Dinner Party* (c. 1825) was perhaps Henry Sargent's most successful painting. It was taken on tour to New York, Boston, Philadelphia, and Salem, with viewers paying 25 cents apiece to see it. It helped establish a genteel standard in interior decoration: ornamented moldings, sideboards, thick carpeting, and tasteful paintings.

It had indeed been a "useful" trip for the two Frenchmen. It resulted in their prison report and in *Marie, ou l'Esclavage aux Etats Unis* (1835), Beaumont's account of American race problems, cast in the form of a novel. But above all else, the visit provided the material for Tocqueville's classic *De la Démocratie en Amérique,* published in France in 1835 and a year later in an English translation. *Democracy in America* has been the starting point for virtually all subsequent writers who have tried to describe what Tocqueville called "the creative elements" of American institutions.

TOCQUEVILLE IN JUDGMENT

The gist of *Democracy in America* is contained in the book's first sentence: "No novelty in the United States struck me more vividly during my stay there than the equality of conditions." Tocqueville meant not that Americans lived in a state of total equality, but that the inequalities that did exist among white Americans were not enforced by institutions or supported by public opinion. Moreover, the inequalities paled when compared with those of Europe. "In America," he concluded, "men are nearer equality than in any other country in the world." The circumstances of one's birth meant little, one's education less, and one's intelligence scarcely anything. Economic differences, while real and certainly "paraded" by those who enjoyed "a pre-eminence of wealth," were transitory. "Such wealth," Tocqueville assured his readers, "is within reach of all."

These sweeping generalizations, however comforting to Americans then and since, are simplifications. Few modern students of Jacksonian America would accept them without qualification. In the 1830s and 1840s a wide and growing gap existed between the rich and poor in the eastern cities. According to one study, the wealthiest 4 percent of the population of New York controlled about half the city's wealth in 1828, about two-thirds in 1845. The number of New Yorkers worth $100,000 or more tripled in that period. A similar concentration of wealth was occurring in Philadelphia and Boston.

Moreover, Tocqueville failed to observe the many poor people in Jacksonian America. Particularly in the cities, bad times forced many unskilled laborers and their families into dire poverty. Tocqueville took little notice of such inequalities, in part because he was so captivated by the theme of American equality. He also had little interest in how industrialization and urbanization were affecting society. When he did take notice of working conditions, he

remarked that wages were higher in America than in Europe and the cost of living was lower, facts obvious to the most obtuse European visitor. Furthermore, as with most foreign visitors, nearly all his contacts were with members of the upper crust. "We hardly see anyone," he acknowledged, "except people of distinction."

Despite his blind spots, Tocqueville realized that America was undergoing some fundamental social changes. These changes, he wrote, were being made by "an innumerable crowd who are . . . not exactly rich nor yet quite poor [and who] have enough property to want order and not enough to excite envy." In his notes he put it even more succinctly: "The whole society seems to have turned into one middle class."

A RESTLESS PEOPLE

"In America, men never stay still," Tocqueville noted. "Something is almost always provisional about their lives." Other European observers came away equally struck by the restlessness of Americans, without necessarily agreeing that democratic institutions made them so. Frances Trollope thought their "incessant bustling" similar to their eating too fast and spitting too often. It stemmed from their "universal pursuit of money," she claimed.

One reason Americans seemed continually on the move was that every year there were more of them. The first federal census in 1790 recorded that there were 3.9 million people in the country. In the early 1850s there were six times as many. The population was doubling every 22 years—just about what Franklin had predicted in 1751! The growth can be measured geographically by the admission of new states in the 1830s and 1840s: Arkansas in 1836, Michigan in 1837, Florida in 1845, Texas in 1846, and Wisconsin in 1848.

Yet by contemporary European standards, even the settled parts of the United States were sparsely populated in the 1830s and 1840s. But for people accustomed to the wide open spaces, the presence of more than a handful of neighbors was reason enough for moving on. Abraham Lincoln's father Thomas (1778–1851) was typical: He grew up in Kentucky, pioneered in Indiana, and died in Illinois.

The urge to move had an urban dimension as well. For every "young man" who took the advice of the New York newspaperman Horace Greeley to "go west," several young men and women went instead to town. By the tens of thousands they exchanged the rigors of farming for the uncertain risks and

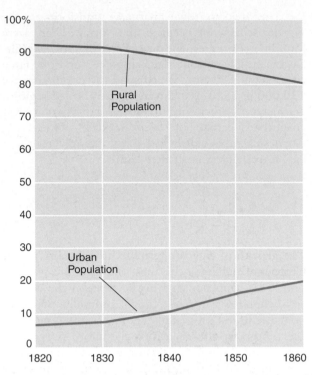

▲ **Rural Versus Urban Population, 1820–1860**
As the balance of rural and urban population began to shift during the years from 1820 to 1860, the number of cities with populations over 100,000 grew from one in 1820—New York—to nine in 1870, including southern and western cities like New Orleans and San Francisco.

rewards of city life. Boston, New York, and Philadelphia had a combined population of 50,000 at the time of the Revolution. Each expanded rapidly during the first half of the next century. Boston had 40,000 residents in 1820, nearly 140,000 in 1850. Philadelphia grew even more rapidly, from just under 100,000 in 1820 to almost 400,000 in 1850. New York, which had forged ahead of Philadelphia around 1810, grew from 125,000 in 1820 to more than 500,000 in 1850.

However spectacular the growth of the largest cities, the emergence of new towns was more significant. In 1820 the Northeast contained 5 cities with populations above 25,000 and 13 with populations above 10,000. Thirty years later, 26 cities had more than 25,000 residents and 62 had more than 10,000.

Even though the Old Northwest remained primarily agricultural, its towns grew as fast as its farms. Pittsburgh, St. Louis, Cincinnati, Louisville, and Lexington attracted settlers in such numbers that by 1850 all but Lexington had populations of over 35,000. Cincinnati, "the Emporium of the West," with a population of 100,000, ranked seventh in the country.

The trek to town that was transforming the Northeast did not occur in the South. There were four cities of respectable size in the region—Mobile, Savannah, Charleston, and Baltimore—and one large city, New Orleans, which had a population of 120,000 in 1850. Yet all were located on the region's perimeter. Neither Virginia nor North Carolina had an urban center of even modest dimensions. Charleston, the oldest and most typically southern city, scarcely grew at all after 1830.

THE FAMILY RECAST

The growth of cities undermined the importance of home and family as the unit of economic production. This happened first in the cities of the Northeast, then in the West, and eventually wherever nonagricultural jobs occupied a substantial percentage of the workforce. More and more people did their work in shops, in offices, or on factory floors. Whether a job was skilled or unskilled, white-collar or blue-collar, or strictly professional, it took the family breadwinner out of the house during working hours six days a week. This did not mean that the family necessarily ceased to be an economic unit. But the labor of the father and any children with jobs came home in the form of cash, thus at least initially in the custody of the individual earners. The social consequences of this change were enormous for the traditional "head of the family" and for his wife and children.

DOCUMENT

Carey, *Rules for Husbands and Wives*

Because he was away so much the husband had to surrender to his wife some of the power in the family that he had formerly exercised, if for no other reason than that she was always there. The situation bore a superficial resemblance to the relationship of the king of England to the colonies in the seventeenth century: Whatever the king's power under the law, his authority was limited by his lack of close contact with his colonial "offspring." Perhaps this is what Noah Webster had in mind when he used a similar comparison in describing the ideal father's authority as "like the mild dominion of a limited monarch, and not the iron rule of an austere tyrant." It certainly explains why Tocqueville concluded that "a sort of equality reigns around the domestic hearth" in America. It also explains why American men began to place women on a pedestal, presuming them to be by nature almost saintly, pure of mind and body, selflessly devoted to the care of others.

The new power and prestige that wives and mothers enjoyed were not obtained without cost. Since they were exercising day-to-day control over household affairs, they were expected to tend only to those affairs. Expanding their interest to other fields of human endeavor was frowned on. Where the typical wife had formerly been a partner in a family enterprise, she now left earning a living entirely to her husband. She was certainly not encouraged to have an independent career as, say, a lawyer or doctor. Time spent away from home or devoted to matters unrelated to the care of husband and family was, according to the new doctrine of "separate spheres," time misappropriated.

This trend widened the gap between the middle and lower classes. For a middle-class wife and mother to take a job or, still worse, to devote herself to any "frivolous" activity outside the home was considered a dereliction of duty. Such an attitude could not possibly develop in lower-class families where everyone had to work simply to keep food on the table.

Some women objected to making a cult out of "womanhood": by placing an ideal on so high a pedestal, all real women would fall short. Others escaped its more suffocating aspects by forming close friendships with other women. But most women, including such forceful proponents of women's rights as the educator Catharine Beecher and Sarah Hale, the editor of *Godey's Ladies Book*, subscribed to the view that a woman's place was in the home. "The formation of the moral and intellectual character of the young is committed mainly to the female hand," Beecher wrote in *A Treatise on Domestic Economy for the Use of Young Ladies* (1841). "The mother forms the character of the future man."

DOCUMENT

Beecher, from *A Treatise on Domestic Economy*

Another reason for the switch in power and influence from husbands to wives was that women began to have fewer children. Here again, the change happened earliest and was most pronounced among families in the rapidly urbanizing Northeast. But the birthrate gradually declined all over the country. People married later than in earlier periods. Long courtships and broken engagements were common, probably because prospective marriage partners were becoming more selective. On average, women began having their children two or three years later than their mothers had, and they stopped two or three years sooner. Apparently many middle-class couples made a conscious effort to limit family size, even when doing so required sexual abstinence.

Having fewer children led parents to value children more highly, or so it would seem from the

▲ Middle-class parents practiced sexual abstinence and even simple forms of contraception to limit family size. By having fewer children, they could lavish more attention and economic resources on each one. Middle-class fathers occupied themselves with business; mothers, with child rearing. Such people often sought to persuade others to similarly control their desires.

additional time and affection they lavished on them. Here again, the mother provided most of both. Child rearing fell within her "sphere" and occupied the time that earlier generations of mothers had devoted to such tasks as weaving, sewing, and farm chores. Not least of these new responsibilities was overseeing the children's education, both secular and religious.

DOCUMENT

Mother's Magazine

As families became smaller, relations within them became more caring. Parents ceased to think of their children mostly as future workers. The earlier tendency even among loving parents to keep their children at arm's length, yet within reach of the strap, gave way to more intimate relationships. Gone was the puritan notion that children possessed "a perverse will, a love of what's forbid," and with it the belief that parents were responsible for crushing all juvenile resistance to their authority. In its place arose the view described by Lydia Maria Child in *The Mother's Book* (1831) that children "come to us from heaven, with their little souls full of innocence and peace." Mothers "should not

interfere with the influence of angels," Child advised her readers.

Bronson Alcott, another proponent of gentle child-rearing practices, went still further. Children, he insisted, were the moral superiors of their parents. Alcott banished "the rod and all its appendages" from his own household, wherein four daughters (one, Louisa May, later the author of *Little Women* and other novels) were raised, and urged other parents to follow his example. "Childhood hath saved me!" he wrote. The English poet William Wordsworth's "Ode on Intimations of Immortality," in which babies entered the world "trailing clouds of glory," served some American parents as a child-rearing manual.

THE SECOND GREAT AWAKENING

Belief in the innate goodness of children was of course in direct conflict with the Calvinist doctrine of infant damnation, to which most American Protes-

▲ Religious revivals stirred passions, as this rendering of an 1839 camp meeting suggests: people are gesticulating, swooning, and writhing on the ground. Finney endorsed such "excitements" as essential for conversion. But some doubted the wisdom of eliciting passions so as to persuade people to exercise more restraint and sin less often.

tant churches formally subscribed. "Of all the impious doctrines which the dark imagination of man ever conceived," Bronson Alcott wrote in his journal, "the worst [is] the belief in original and certain depravity of infant nature." Alcott was far from alone in thinking infant damnation a "debased doctrine," despite its standing as one of the central tenets of orthodox Calvinism.

The inclination to set aside other Calvinist tenets, such as predestination, became more pronounced as a new wave of revivalism took shape in the 1790s. This Second Great Awakening began as a counteroffensive to the deistic thinking and other forms of "infidelity" that New England Congregationalists and southern Methodists alike identified with the French Revolution. Prominent New England ministers, who considered themselves traditionalists but also revivalists,

men such as Yale's president, Timothy Dwight, and Dwight's student, the Reverend Lyman Beecher, placed less stress in their sermons on God's arbitrary power over mortals, more on the promise of the salvation of sinners because of God's mercy and "disinterested benevolence." When another of Dwight's students, Horace Bushnell, declared in a sermon on "Christian nurture" in 1844 that Christian parents should prepare their children "for the skies," he meant that parents could contribute to their children's salvation.

Calvinism came under more direct assault from Charles Grandison Finney, probably the most effective of a number of charismatic evangelists who brought the Second Great Awakening to its crest. In 1821 Finney abandoned a promising career as a

DOCUMENT

Finney, "What a Revival of Religion Is"

lawyer and became an itinerant preacher. His most spectacular successes occurred during a series of revivals conducted in towns along the Erie Canal, a region Finney called "the burned-over district" because it had been the site of so many revivals before his own. From Utica, where his revival began in 1826, to Rochester, where it climaxed in 1831, he exhorted his listeners to take their salvation into their own hands. He insisted that people could control their own fate. He dismissed Calvinism as a "theological fiction." Salvation was available to anyone. But the day of judgment was just around the corner; there was little time to waste.

During and after Finney's efforts in Utica, declared conversions increased sharply. In Rochester, church membership doubled in six months. Elsewhere in the country, churches capitalized on the efforts of other evangelists to fill their pews. In 1831 alone, church membership grew by 100,000, an increase, according to a New England minister, "unparalleled in the history of the church." The success of the evangelists of the Second Great Awakening stemmed from the timeliness of their assault on Calvinist doctrine and even more from their methods. Finney, for example, consciously set out to be entertaining as well as edifying. The singing of hymns and the solicitation of personal testimonies provided his meetings with emotional release and human interest. Prominent among his innovations was the "anxious bench," where leading members of the community awaited the final prompting from within before coming forward to declare themselves saved.

But the economic changes of the times and the impact of these changes on family life had as important effects on the Second Awakening as even the most accomplished of the evangelists. The growth of industry and commerce that followed the completion of the Erie Canal in 1825, along with the disappearance of undeveloped farmland, led hundreds of young men to leave family farms to seek their fortunes in Utica and other towns along the canal. There, uprooted, uncertain, buffeted between ambition, hope, and anxiety, they found it hard to resist the comfort promised by the revivalists to those who were saved.

Women, and especially the wives of the business leaders of the community, felt particularly responsible for the Christian education of their children, which fell within their separate sphere. Many women had servants and thus had time and energy to devote to their own and their offsprings' salvation.

Paradoxically, this caused many of them to venture out of that sphere and in doing so they moved further out of the shadow of their husbands. They founded the Oneida County Female Missionary Society, an association that did most of the organizing and a good deal of the financing of the climactic years of the Second Awakening. The Female Missionary Society raised more than $1000 a year (no small sum at that time) to support the revival in Utica, in its environs, and throughout the burned-over district. Apparently without consciously intending to do so, women challenged the authority of the paternalistic, authoritarian churches they so fervently embraced. Then, by mixtures of exhortation, example, and affection, they set out to save the souls of their loved ones, first their children and ultimately their husbands too.

THE ERA OF ASSOCIATIONS

Alongside the recast family and the "almost revolutionized" church, a third pillar of the emerging American middle class was the voluntary association. Unlike the other two, it had neither colonial precedents nor contemporary European equivalents. The voluntary association of early nineteenth-century America was unique. "In France," Tocqueville wrote of this phenomenon, "if you want to proclaim a truth or propagate some feeling . . . you would find the government or in England some territorial magnate." In America, however, "you are sure to find an association."

The leaders of these associations tended to be ministers, lawyers, or merchants, but the rank and file consisted of tradesmen, foremen, clerks, and their wives. Some of these associations were formed around a local cause that some townspeople wished to advance, such as the provision of religious instruction for orphaned children; others were affiliated with associations elsewhere for the purposes of combating some national evil, such as drunkenness. Some, such as the American Board of Commissioners of Foreign Missions, founded in Boston in 1810, quickly became large and complex enterprises. (By 1860 the board had sent 1250 missionaries into the "heathen world" and raised $8 million to support them.) Others lasted only as long as it took to accomplish a specific good work, such as the construction of a school or a library.

In a sense the associations were assuming functions previously performed in the family, such as caring for old people and providing moral guidance to the young, but without the paternalistic discipline of the old way. They constituted a "benevolent empire," eager to make society over into their members' idea of how God wanted it to be.

BACKWOODS UTOPIAS

Americans frequently belonged to several associations at the same time and more than a few made reform their life's work. The most adventuresome tested their reform theories by withdrawing from workaday American society and establishing experimental communities. The communitarian point of view aimed at "commencing a wholesale social reorganization by first establishing and demonstrating its principles completely on a small scale." The first communitarians were religious reformers. In a sense the Pilgrims fall into this category, along with a number of other groups in colonial times, but only in the nineteenth century did the idea flourish.

One of the most influential of the earlier communities were the Shakers, founded by an Englishwoman, Ann Lee, who came to America in 1774. Mother Ann, as she was called, saw visions that convinced her that Christ would come to earth again as a woman and that she was that woman. With a handful of followers she founded a community near Albany,

New York. The group grew rapidly, and after Ann Lee's death in 1784 her movement continued to expand. By the 1830s her followers had established about 20 successful communities.

The Shakers practiced celibacy; believing that the millennium was imminent, they saw no reason for perpetuating the human race. Each group lived in a large Family House, the sexes strictly segregated. Property was held in common but controlled by a ruling hierarchy. So much stress was placed on equality of labor and reward and on voluntary acceptance of the rules, however, that the system does not seem to have been oppressive.

The Shaker religion, joyful and fervent, was marked by much group singing and dancing, which provided the members with emotional release from their tightly controlled regimen. An industrious, skillful people, they made a special virtue of simplicity; some of their designs for buildings and, especially, furniture achieved a classic beauty seldom equaled among untutored artisans. Despite their odd customs, the Shakers were universally tolerated and even admired.

▲ The Shakers segregated the sexes and enforced celibacy. Pent-up sexual tensions were released in religious ecstasy expressed through church dances, as the lines of men and women approached each other—but never touched.

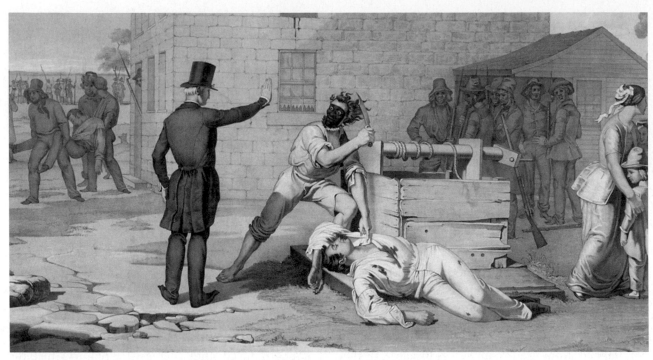

▲ Persecution forced the Mormons to move from New York to Ohio to Missouri, before settling for a time in Nauvoo, Illinois. There, in 1844 Joseph Smith, the Mormon leader, announced his candidacy for presidency of the United States. Smith and his brother Hyrum were arrested by local authorities and murdered in their jail cell by a hostile mob.

Utopian Communities before the Civil War

There were many other religious colonies, such as the Amana Community, which flourished in New York and Iowa in the 1840s and 1850s, and John Humphrey Noyes's Oneida Community, where the members practiced "complex" marriage—a form of promiscuity based on the principle that every man in the group was married to every woman. They prospered by developing a number of manufacturing skills.

The most important of the religious communitarians were the Mormons. A remarkable Vermont farm boy, Joseph Smith, founded the religion in western New York in the 1820s. Smith saw visions; he claimed to have discovered and translated an ancient text, the Book of Mormon, written in hieroglyphics on plates of gold, which described the adventures of a tribe of Israelites that had populated America from biblical times until their destruction in a great war in 400 C.E. With a small band of followers, Smith established a community in Ohio in 1831. The Mormons' dedication and economic efficiency attracted large numbers of converts, but their unorthodox religious views and their exclusivism, a product of their sense of being a chosen people, caused resentment among unbelievers. The Mormons were forced to move first to Missouri and then back to Illinois, where in 1839 they founded the town of Nauvoo.

Nauvoo flourished—by 1844 it was the largest city in the state, with a population of 15,000—but once again the Mormons ran into local trouble. They quarreled among themselves, especially after Smith secretly authorized polygamy (he called it "celestial marriage") and a number of other unusual rites for members of the "Holy Order," the top leaders of the church.[1] They created a paramilitary organization, the Nauvoo Legion, headed by Smith, envisaging themselves as a semi-independent state within the Union. Smith announced that he was a candidate for president of the United States. Rumors circulated that the Mormons intended to take over the entire Northwest for their "empire." Once again local "gentiles" rose against them. Smith was arrested, then murdered by a mob.

Under a new leader, Brigham Young, the Mormons sought a haven beyond the frontier. In 1847

---

[1]One justification of polygamy, paradoxically, was that marriage was a sacred, eternal state. If a man remarried after his wife's death, eventually he would have two wives in Heaven. Therefore why not on earth?

they marched westward, pressing through the mountains until they reached the desolate wilderness on the shores of the Great Salt Lake. There, at last, they established their Zion and began to make their truly significant impact on American history. Irrigation made the desert flourish, precious water wisely being treated as a community asset. Hard, cooperative, intelligently directed effort spelled growth and prosperity; more than 11,000 people were living in the area when it became part of the Utah Territory in 1850. In time the communal Mormon settlement broke down, but the religion has remained—known as the Church of Latter-Day Saints, a major force in the shaping of the West. The Mormon Church is still by far the most powerful single influence in Utah and is a thriving organization in many other parts of the United States and in Europe.

Despite their many common characteristics, the religious communities varied enormously; subordination of the individual to the group did not destroy group individualism. Their sexual practices, for example, ranged from the "complex marriage" of the Oneidans through Mormon polygamy and ordinary monogamy to the reluctant acceptance of sexual intercourse by the Amana Community and the celibacy of the Shakers. The communities are more significant as reflections of the urgent reform spirit of the age than they are for their accomplishments.

The communities had some influence on reformers who wished to experiment with social organization. When Robert Owen, a British utopian socialist who believed in economic as well as political equality and who considered competition debasing, decided to create an ideal community in America, he purchased the Rappite settlement at New Harmony, Indiana. Owen's advocacy of free love and "enlightened atheism" did not add to the stability of his group or to its popularity among outsiders. The colony was a costly failure.

The American followers of Charles Fourier, a French utopian socialist who proposed that society should be organized in cooperative units called phalanxes, fared better. Fourierism did not seek to tamper with sexual and religious mores. Its advocates included important journalists, such as Horace Greeley of the *New York Tribune* and Parke Godwin of the *New York Evening Post*. In the 1840s several dozen Fourierist colonies were established in the northern and western states. Members worked at whatever tasks they wished and only as much as they wished. Wages were paid according to the "repulsiveness" of the tasks performed; the person who "chose" to clean out a cesspool would receive more than someone hoeing corn or mending a fence or

engaging in some task requiring complex skills. As might be expected, none of the communities lasted very long.

THE AGE OF REFORM

The communitarians were the most colorful of the reformers, their proposals the most spectacular. More effective, however, were the many individuals who took on themselves responsibility for caring for the physically and mentally disabled and for the rehabilitation of criminals. The work of Thomas Gallaudet in developing methods for educating deaf people reflects the spirit of the times. Gallaudet's school in Hartford, Connecticut, opened its doors in 1817; by 1851 similar schools for the deaf had been established in 14 states.

Dr. Samuel Gridley Howe did similar work with the blind, devising means for making books with raised letters (Louis Braille's system of raised dots was not introduced until later in the century) that the blind could "read" with their fingers. Howe headed a school for the blind in Boston, the pioneering Perkins Institution, which opened in 1832. Of all that Charles Dickens observed in America, nothing so favorably impressed him as Howe's success in educating 12-year-old Laura Bridgman, who was deaf, mute, and blind. Howe was also interested in trying to educate the mentally defective and in other causes, including antislavery. "Every creature in human shape should command our respect," he insisted. "The strong should help the weak, so that the whole should advance as a band of brethren."

One of the most striking aspects of the reform movement was the emphasis reformers placed on establishing special institutions for dealing with social problems. In the colonial period, orphans, indigent persons, the insane, and the feebleminded were usually cared for by members of their own families or boarded in a neighboring household. They remained part of the community. Even criminals were seldom "locked away" for extended jail terms; punishment commonly consisted of whipping, being placed in stocks in the town square, or (for serious crimes) execution. But once persuaded that people were primarily shaped by their surroundings, reformers demanded that deviant and dependent members of the community be taken from their present corrupting circumstances and placed in specialized institutions where they could be trained or rehabilitated. Almshouses, orphanages, reformatories, prisons, and lunatic asylums sprang up throughout the United States like mushrooms in a forest after a summer rain.

DEBATING THE PAST

Did the antebellum reform movement improve society? The Eastern State Penitentiary in Philadelphia was built in the 1820s. The picture at left was done by Samuel Cowperthwaite, Convict # 2954. Eastern State consisted of seven rows of cells radiating out from the central tower. The design ensured continuous supervision and isolation. The reformers who conceived of the prison thought it would teach an inmate to "listen to the reproaches of his conscience." The dessert plate *(right)* commemorating the jail is proof that some people believed in its mission. After visiting the prison, however, Charles Dickens described its system of confinement as "rigid, strict and hopeless." In *Madness and Civilization* (1961) and *Discipline and Punish* (1975), the French philosopher Michel Foucault similarly regarded such institutions as part of the process whereby modern societies squelched individuality. Those who refused to accept the discipline of teachers, employers, and government officials were labeled "deviants" and sent to institutions that would "reform" them through the imposition of order, a thesis that David J. Rothman (1971) applied to antebellum penitentiaries and asylums. Before Foucault, most scholars had endorsed antebellum reforms. Now these reforms were reassessed more critically. Michael B. Katz (1968) and Stanley K. Schultz (1973) argued that the public schools were means for preparing the young for industrial labor by instilling discipline and regimentation. Movements to promote temperance and suppress prostitution, similarly, were increasingly viewed as unwarranted intrusions on private matters. But in the 1980s women's historians altered this debate. Mary Ryan (1981) and others showed that women dominated nearly all antebellum reform movements, and for good reason. The child who could not attend a school was often subjected to the ceaseless drudgery of farm or factory. The exuberant individualist who tarried at the tavern sometimes beat his wife on returning home. The Eastern State Penitentiary and the antebellum insane asylums were fearsome places, but would their inmates have been better off on the streets? Excessive discipline erodes individuality; excessive individuality erodes social cohesion.

Michel Foucault, *Madness and Civilization* (1961), Michael B. Katz, *The Irony of Early School Reform* (1968), Stanley K. Schultz, *The Culture Factory* (1973), David J. Rothman, *The Discovery of the Asylum* (1971), Carl F. Kaestle, *Pillars of the Republic* (1983), Mary Ryan, *Cradle of the Middle Class* (1981).

The rationale for this movement was scientific; elaborate statistical reports attested to the benefits that such institutions would bring to both inmates and society as a whole. The motivating spirit of the founders of these asylums was humane, although many of the institutions seem anything but humane to the modern eye. The highly regarded Philadelphia prison system was based on strict solitary confinement, which was supposed to lead culprits to reflect on their sins and then reform their ways. The prison was literally a penitentiary, a place to repent. In fact, the system drove some inmates mad, and soon a rival Auburn system was introduced in New York State, which allowed for some social contact among prisoners and for work in shops and stone quarries. Absolute silence was required at all times. The prisoners were herded about in lock step and punished by flogging for the slightest infraction of the rules. Regular "moral and religious instruction" was provided, which the authorities believed would lead inmates to reform their lives. Tocqueville and Beaumont, in their report on American prisons, concluded that the

Philadelphia system produced "the deepest impression on the soul of the convict," while the Auburn system made the convict "more conformable to the habits of man in society."

The hospitals for mental patients were intended to cure inmates, not merely to confine them. The emphasis was on isolating them from the pressures of society; on order, quiet, routine; on control but not on punishment. The unfortunates were seen as *de*ranged; the task was to *ar*range their lives in a rational manner. In practice, shortages of trained personnel, niggardly legislative appropriations, and the inherent difficulty of managing violent and irrational patients often produced deplorable conditions in the asylums.

This situation led Dorothea Dix, a woman of almost saintlike selflessness, to devote 30 years of her life to a campaign to improve the care of the insane. She traveled to every state in the Union, and as far afield as Turkey and Japan, inspecting asylums and poorhouses. Insane persons in Massachusetts, she wrote in a memorial intended to shock state legislators into action, were being kept in cages and closets, "*chained, naked, beaten with rods, and lashed into obedience!*" Her reports led to some improvement in conditions in Massachusetts and other states, but in the long run the bright hopes of the reformers were never realized. Institutions founded to uplift the deviant and dependent all too soon became places where society's "misfits" might safely be kept out of sight.

"DEMON RUM"

Beecher, "Six Sermons on Intemperance"

Reformers must of necessity interfere with the affairs of others; thus there is often something of the busybody and arrogant meddler about them. How they are regarded usually turns on the observer's own attitude toward their objectives. What is to some an unjustified infringement on a person's private affairs is to others a necessary intervention for that person's own good and for the good of society. Consider the temperance movement, the most widely supported and successful reform of the Age of Reform.

Americans in the 1820s consumed prodigious amounts of alcohol, more than ever before or since. Not that the colonists had been teetotalers. Liquor, mostly in the form of rum or hard apple cider, was cheap and everywhere available; taverns were an integral part of colonial society. There were alcoholics in colonial America, but because neither political nor religious leaders considered drinking dangerous, there was no alcohol "problem." Most doctors recommended the regular consumption of alcohol as healthy. John Adams, certainly the soul of propriety, drank a tankard of hard cider every day for breakfast. Dr. Benjamin Rush's *Inquiry into the Effects of Ardent Spirits* (1784), which questioned the medicinal benefits of alcohol, fell on deaf ears.

However, alcohol consumption increased markedly in the early years of the new republic, thanks primarily to the availability of cheap corn and rye whiskey distilled in the new states of Kentucky and Tennessee. In the 1820s the per capita consumption of hard liquor reached 5 gallons, well over twice what it is today. Since small children and many grown people did not drink that much, others obviously drank a great deal more. Many women drank, if mostly at home; and reports of carousing among 14-year-old college freshmen show that youngsters did too. But the bulk of the heavy drinking occurred when men got together, at taverns or grogshops and at work. Many prominent politicians, including Clay and Webster, were heavy consumers. Webster is said to have kept several thousand bottles of wine, whiskey, and other alcoholic beverages in his cellar.

Artisans and common laborers regarded their twice-daily "dram" of whiskey as part of their wages. In workshops, masters were expected to halt production periodically to drink with their apprentices and journeymen. Trips to the neighborhood grogshop also figured into the workaday routine. In 1829 Secretary of War John Eaton estimated that three-quarters of the nation's laborers drank at least 4 ounces of distilled spirits a day.

The foundation of the American Temperance Union in 1826 signaled the start of a national crusade against drunkenness. Employing lectures, pamphlets, rallies, essay contests, and other techniques, the union set out to persuade people to "sign the pledge" not to drink liquor. Primitive sociological studies of the effects of drunkenness (reformers were able to show a high statistical correlation between alcohol consumption and crime) added to the effectiveness of the campaign.

In 1840 an organization of reformed drunkards, the Washingtonians, set out to reclaim alcoholics. One of the most effective Washingtonians was John B. Gough, rescued by the organization after seven years in the gutter. "Crawl from the slimy ooze, ye drowned drunkards," Gough would shout, "and with suffocation's blue and livid lips speak out against the drink!"

Revivalist ministers like Charles Grandison Finney argued that alcohol was one of the great barriers to conversion, which helps explain why Utica, a town of fewer than 13,000 residents in 1840, supported four separate temperance societies in that year. Employers all over the country also signed on, declaring their businesses henceforward to be "cold-water" enterprises. Soon the temperance movement claimed a million members. Although women did much of the work at the local level in all antebellum reforms, they were especially active in the temperance movement.

The temperance people aroused bitter opposition, particularly after they moved beyond calls for restraint to demands for prohibition of all alcohol. German and Irish immigrants, for the most part Catholics, and also members of Protestant sects that used wine in their religious services, objected to being told by reformers that their drinking would have to stop. But by the early 1840s the reformers had secured legislation in many states that imposed strict licensing systems and heavy liquor taxes. Local option laws permitted towns and counties to ban the sale of alcohol altogether.

In 1851 Maine passed the first effective law prohibiting the manufacture and sale of alcoholic beverages. The leader of the campaign was Mayor Neal Dow of Portland, a businessman who became a prohibitionist after seeing the damage done by drunkenness among workers in his tannery. By 1855 a dozen other states had passed laws based on the Maine statute, and the nation's per capita consumption of alcohol had plummeted to 2 gallons a year.

THE ABOLITIONIST CRUSADE

No reform movement of this era was more significant, more ambiguous, or more provocative of later historical investigation than the drive to abolish slavery. That slavery should have been a cause of indignation to reform-minded Americans was inevitable. Humanitarians were outraged by the master's whip and by the practice of disrupting families. Democrats protested the denial of political and civil rights to slaves. Perfectionists of all stripes deplored the fact that slaves had no chance to improve themselves. However, well into the 1820s, the abolitionist cause attracted few followers because there seemed to be no way of getting rid of slavery short of revolution. While a few theorists argued that the Fifth Amendment, which provides that no one may be "deprived of life, liberty, or property, without due process of law," could be interpreted to mean

▲ William Lloyd Garrison founded *The Liberator* and edited it for 35 years; the newspaper was one of the nation's leading antislavery publications.

that the Constitution outlawed slavery, the great majority believed that the institution was not subject to federal control.

Particularly in the wake of the Missouri Compromise, antislavery Northerners neatly compartmentalized their thinking. Slavery was wrong; they would not tolerate it in their own communities. But since the Constitution obliged them to tolerate it in states where it existed, they felt no responsibility to fight it. The issue was explosive enough even when limited to the question of the expansion of slavery into the territories. People who advocated any kind of forced abolition in states where it was legal were judged irresponsible in the extreme. In 1820 presidential hopeful John Quincy Adams called slavery "the great and foul stain upon the North American Union." "If the Union must be dissolved," he added, "slavery is precisely the question upon which it ought to break." But Adams expressed these opinions in the privacy of his diary, not in a public speech. Most critics of slavery therefore confined themselves to urging

▶ *text continues on page 288*

American
Lives

Sojourner Truth

Isabella was the youngest of ten, or perhaps twelve, children; she was born in 1797, or perhaps 1799. Most details of her early life are unknown. No one bothered to record them because she was a slave. We do know that she was born in Ulster County, New York, and that her owner was Colonel Ardinburgh, a Dutch farmer. He grew tobacco, corn, and flax. Because the rocky hills west of the Hudson River could not sustain large farms, he could make use of only a handful of slaves. He therefore sold most of the slave children, including Isabella's siblings, when they were young.

Isabella's mother used to tell her of the time when Ardinburgh had gathered up her five-year-old brother and three-year-old sister to take them for a sleigh ride. They were initially delighted, but when he tried to lock them into a box, the boy broke free, ran into the house and hid under a bed. He was found and both children were dragged away, never to be seen by their parents again. Isabella lived in terror of being similarly torn from her parents.

In 1807 Ardinburgh died. His heirs sold his "slaves, horses, and other cattle" at auction. A local farmer bought Isabella for $100. Her parents, too old and decrepit to be of value, were given their freedom. Destitute and virtually homeless, they died shortly afterward.

Isabella, who spoke only Dutch, found herself at odds with her new master and his family. Sometimes she did not understand what they wanted her to do. "If they sent me for a frying pan, not knowing what they meant, perhaps I carried them the pot hooks," she recalled. "Then, oh! How angry mistress would be with me." Once, for an order that she did not understand, the master whipped her with a bundle of rods. The lacerations permanently scarred her back.

In 1810 she was sold to John Dumont, a farmer. She remained with him for nearly eighteen years. Though she came to regard him "as a God," she claimed that his wife subjected her to cruel and "unnatural" treatment. What exactly transpired, she refused "from motives of delicacy" to say. Historian Nell I. Painter contends that the mistress likely abused her sexually.

In 1815 Dumont arranged for Isabella to marry another of his slaves. (Slave marriages were recognized by law in most northern states, but not in the South.) Isabella had no say in the choice of a husband, who had previously been mated to at least two other slaves. She had five children by him.

Isabella labored in the fields, sowing and harvesting crops. She also cooked and cleaned the house. In recognition of her diligence, Dumont promised to set her free on July 4, 1826, exactly one year prior to the date set by the New York State legislature to end slavery. But during that final year Isabella injured her hand and could not work as effectively as before. On the proposed date of liberation, Dumont reneged on his promise to release her. Isabella chafed at his decision but said nothing. She dutifully spun 100 pounds of wool—the amount of labor she thought she owed him—and then, as winter was setting in, she heard the voice of God tell her to leave. She picked up her baby and walked to a neighbor's house. When Dumont came to collect her, the neighbor Isaac Van Wagenen paid him $25 for Isabella and the baby and set them free. In gratitude, Isabella took the surname Van Wagenen.

But Isabella learned that her five-year-old son, Peter, had been sold to a planter in Alabama, where no date had been set for the ending of slavery. She angrily confronted the Dumonts, who scoffed at her concern for "a paltry nigger." "I'll have my child again," Isabella retorted. She consulted with a Quaker lawyer, who assured her that New York law forbade such sales. He filed suit in her behalf and in 1828 the boy was returned.

Now on her own, Isabella went to New York City. During these years New York City, like much of the nation, was awash in religious ferment. Isabella, whose views on religion were a complex amalgam of African folkways, spiritualism, temperance, and dietary asceticism, was attracted to various unorthodox religious leaders. The most curious of these was Robert Matthews, a bearded, thundering tyrant who claimed to be the Old Testament prophet Matthias. He proposed to restore the practices of the ancient patriarchs,

especially an insistence that men dominate women. Matthews converted Elijah Pierson, a wealthy New York merchant, and persuaded him to finance a religious commune. Matthews acquired a house in the town of Sing Sing, named it Mount Zion, housed nearly a dozen converts, and ruled it with an iron hand. Isabella was among those who joined the commune.

In 1834, Pierson died. Local authorities, who had heard stories of sexual and other irregularities at Mount Zion, arrested Matthews on charges of poisoning Pierson. This sensational story boosted sales of the city's penny press, then in its infancy. When one published story accused Isabella of the murder, she sued the author for libel and collected a judgment of $125.

Isabella then gravitated to William Miller, a zealot who claimed that the world would end in 1843. When it did not, his movement did.

Although she had nearly always been subject to the authority of powerful men, Isabella had by this time become a preacher. Tall and severe in manner, she jabbed at the air with bony fingers and demanded the obedience she had formerly given to others. Now she changed her name to Sojourner Truth, a journeyer conveying God's true spirit, and embarked on a career of antislavery feminism.

▲ Sojourner Truth

"colonization" or persuading slaveowners to treat their property humanely.

One of the few Americans in the 1820s to go further was the Quaker Benjamin Lundy, editor of the Baltimore-based newspaper *The Genius of Universal Emancipation*. Lundy was no fanatic; he urged the use of persuasion in the South rather than interference by the federal government. He also explored the possibility of colonizing free blacks and slaves in Haiti and Canada. But he refused to mince words, and consequently he was subject to frequent harassment.

DOCUMENT

Garrison, First issue of *The Liberator*

Even more provocative and less accommodating to local sensibilities was Lundy's youthful assistant, William Lloyd Garrison of Massachusetts. Garrison pronounced himself for "immediate" abolition. When his extreme position made continued residence in Baltimore impossible, he returned to Boston, where in 1831 he established his own newspaper, *The Liberator*. "I am in earnest," he announced in the first issue. "I will not equivocate—I will not excuse—I will not retreat a single inch—and I will be heard."

Garrison's position, and that espoused by the New England Anti-Slavery Society, which he organized in 1831, was absolutely unyielding: Slaves must be freed immediately and treated as equals; compensated emancipation was unacceptable, colonization unthinkable. Because the United States government countenanced slavery, Garrison refused to engage in political activity to achieve his ends. Burning a copy of the Constitution—that "agreement with hell"—became a regular feature at Society-sponsored public lectures.

Few white Americans found Garrison's line of argument convincing, and many were outraged by his confrontational tactics. Whenever he spoke in public, he risked being mobbed by what newspaper accounts approvingly described as "gentlemen of property and standing." In 1833 a Garrison meeting in New York City was broken up by colonizationists. Two years later a mob dragged Garrison through the streets of his own Boston. That same day a mob broke up the convention of the New York Anti-Slavery Society in Utica. In 1837 Elijah Lovejoy, a Garrisonian newspaper editor in Alton, Illinois, first saw his press destroyed by fire and then was himself murdered by a mob. When the proprietors of Philadelphia's Pennsylvania Hall booked an abolitionist meeting in 1838, a mob burned the hall to the ground to prevent the meeting from taking place.

In the wake of this violence some of Garrison's backers had second thoughts about his call for an immediate end to slavery. The wealthy New York businessmen Arthur and Lewis Tappan, who had subsidized *The Liberator*, turned instead to Theodore Dwight Weld, a young minister who was part of Charles Grandison Finney's "holy band" of revivalists. Weld and his followers spoke of "immediate" emancipation "gradually" achieved, and they were willing to engage in political activity to achieve that goal.

In 1840 the Tappans and Weld broke with Garrison over the issue of involvement in politics and the participation of female abolitionists as public lecturers. Garrison, ever the radical, supported the women; Weld thought they would needlessly antagonize would-be supporters. The Tappans then organized the Liberty Party, which nominated as its presidential candidate James G. Birney, a Kentucky slaveholder who had been converted to evangelical Christianity and abolitionism by Weld. Running on a platform of universal emancipation to be gradually brought about through legislation, Birney received only 7000 votes.

▲ Frederick Douglass in 1847, having escaped from slavery nine years earlier. He attracted large audiences as an antislavery lecturer, though his white supporters worried that he neither looked nor sounded like a former slave. Lest audiences think him an imposter, William Lloyd Garrison counseled him to not sound too "learned." Another thought it would be better if he had "a little of the plantation in his speech." Douglass rejected such suggestions.

Many blacks were abolitionists long before the white movement began to attract attention. In 1830 some 50 black antislavery societies existed, and thereafter these groups grew in size and importance, being generally associated with the Garrisonian wing. White abolitionists eagerly sought out black speakers, especially runaway slaves, whose heart-rending accounts of their experiences aroused sympathies and who, merely by speaking clearly and with conviction, stood as living proof that blacks were neither animals nor fools.

The first prominent black abolitionist was David Walker, whose powerful *Appeal to the Coloured Citizens of the World* (1829) is now considered one of the roots of the modern black nationalist movement. Walker was born free and had experienced American racism extensively in both the South and the North. He denounced white talk of democracy and freedom as pure hypocrisy and predicted that when God finally brought justice to America white "tyrants will wish they were never born!"

Frederick Douglass, a former slave who had escaped from Maryland, was one of the most remarkable Americans of his generation. While a bondsman he had received a full portion of beatings and other indignities, but he had been allowed to learn to read and write and to master a trade, opportunities denied the vast majority of slaves. Settling in Boston, he became an agent of the Massachusetts Anti-Slavery Society and a featured speaker at its public meetings.

DOCUMENT

Passages from
*The Autobiography
of Frederick
Douglass*

Douglass was a tall, majestically handsome man who radiated determination and indignation. Slavery, he told white audiences, "brands your republicanism as a sham, your humanity as a base pretense, your Christianity as a lie." In 1845 he published his *Narrative of the Life of Frederick Douglass,* one of the most gripping autobiographical accounts of a slave's life ever written. Douglass insisted that freedom for blacks required not merely emancipation but full equality, social and economic as well as political. Not many white Northerners accepted his reasoning, but few who heard him or read his works could afterward maintain the illusion that all blacks were dull-witted or resigned to inferior status.

At first Douglass was, in his own words, "a faithful disciple" of Garrison, prepared to tear up the Constitution and destroy the Union to gain his ends. In the late 1840s, however, he changed his mind, deciding that the Constitution, created to "establish Justice, insure domestic Tranquility . . . and secure the Blessings of Liberty," as its preamble states, "could not well have been designed at the same time to maintain and perpetuate a system of rapine and murder like slavery." Thereafter he fought slavery and race prejudice from within the system, something Garrison was never willing to do.

Garrison's importance cannot be measured by the number of his followers, which was never large. Unlike more moderately inclined enemies of slavery, he recognized that abolitionism was a revolutionary movement, not merely one more middle-class reform. He also understood that achieving racial equality, not merely "freeing" the slaves, was the only way to reach the abolitionists' professed objective: full justice for blacks. And he saw clearly that few whites, even among abolitionists, believed that blacks were their equals.

At the same time, Garrison seemed utterly indifferent to what effect the "immediate" freeing of the slaves would have on the South. He and his followers came close to claiming that all southern whites were villains, all blacks saints. Garrison said he would rather be governed by "the inmates of our penitentiaries" than by southern congressmen, whom he characterized as "desperadoes." The life of the slave-owner, he wrote, is "one of unbridled lust, of filthy amalgamation, of swaggering braggadocio, of haughty domination, of cowardly ruffianism, of boundless dissipation, of matchless insolence, of infinite self-conceit, of unequaled oppression, of more than savage cruelty." His followers were no less fanatical in their judgments. "Slavery and cruelty cannot be disjoined," one wrote. "Consequently every slaveholder must be inhuman."

Both Garrison's insights into the limits of northern racial egalitarianism and his blind contempt for southern whites led him to the conclusion that American society was rotten to the core. Hence his refusal to make any concession to the existing establishment, religious or secular. He was hated in the North as much for his explicit denial of the idea that a constitution that supported slavery merited respect as for his implicit denial of the idea that a professed Christian who tolerated slavery for even an instant could hope for salvation. He was, in short, a perfectionist, a trafficker in moral absolutes who wanted his Kingdom of Heaven in the here and now. By contrast, most other American reformers were willing to settle for perfection on the installment plan.

WOMEN'S RIGHTS

The question of slavery was related to another major reform movement of the era, the crusade for women's rights. The relationship was personal and

▲ Anna Elizabeth Klumpke's portrait of Elizabeth Cady Stanton (1887). In 1848 Stanton helped draft the Declaration of Sentiments, spelling out the injustices of man to woman. The conclusion: "He has endeavored, in every way he could, to destroy her confidence in her own powers, to lessen her self-respect, and to make her willing to lead a dependent and abject life."

ideological, direct and indirect, simple and profound. Superficially, the connection can be explained in this way: Women were as likely as men to find slavery offensive and to protest against it. When they did so, they ran into even more adamant resistance, the prejudices of those who objected to abolitionists being reinforced by their feelings that women should not speak in public or participate in political affairs. Thus female abolitionists, driven by the urgencies of conscience, were almost forced to become advocates of women's rights. "We have good cause to be grateful to the slave," the feminist Abby Kelley wrote. "In striving to strike his irons off, we found most surely, that we were manacled ourselves."

At a more profound level, the reference that abolitionists made to the Declaration of Independence to justify their attack on slavery radicalized women with regard to their own place in society. Were only all men created equal and endowed by God with unalienable rights? For many women the question was a consciousness-raising experience; they began to believe that, like blacks, they were imprisoned from birth in a caste system, legally subordinated and assigned menial social and economic roles that prevented them from developing their full potentialities. Such women considered themselves in a sense worse off than blacks, who had at least the psychological advantage of confronting an openly hostile and repressive society rather than one concealed behind the cloying rhetoric of romantic love.

With the major exception of Margaret Fuller, whose book *Women in the Nineteenth Century* (1844) made a frontal assault on all forms of sexual discrimination, the leading advocates of equal rights for women began their public careers in the abolitionist movement. Among the first were Sarah and Angelina Grimké, South Carolinians who abandoned their native state and the domestic sphere to devote themselves to speaking out against slavery. (In 1841 Angelina married Theodore Dwight Weld.) Male objections to the Grimkés' activities soon made them advocates of women's rights. Similarly, the refusal of delegates to the World Anti-Slavery Convention held in London in 1840 to let women participate in their debates precipitated the decision of two American abolitionists, Lucretia Mott and Elizabeth Cady Stanton, to turn their attention to the women's rights movement.

Slavery aside, there were other aspects of feminist consciousness-raising. Some women rejected the idea that they should confine themselves to a sphere of activity consisting mostly of child rearing and housekeeping. The very effort to enforce this kind of specialization made women aware of their second-class citizenship and thus more likely to be dissatisfied. They lacked not merely the right to vote, of which they did not make a major issue, but if married, the right to own property or to make a will. Lydia Maria Child, a popular novelist, found this last restriction particularly offensive. It excited her "towering indignation" that her husband had to sign her will. David Child was not what today would be called a chauvinist, but, as she explained, "I was indignant for womankind made chattels personal from the beginning of time."

As Lydia Child noted, the subordination of women was as old as civilization. The attack on it came not because of any new discrimination but for the same reasons that motivated reformers against other forms of injustice: belief in progress, a sense of personal responsibility, the conviction that institutions could be changed and that the time for changing them was limited.

When women sought to involve themselves in reform, they became aware of perhaps the most serious handicap that society imposed on them—the conflict

between their roles as wives and mothers and their urge to participate in the affairs of the larger world. Elizabeth Cady Stanton has left a striking description of this dilemma. She lived in the 1840s in Seneca Falls, a small town in central New York. Her husband was frequently away on business; she had a brood of growing children and little domestic help. When, stimulated by her interest in abolition and women's rights, she sought to become active in the movements, her family responsibilities made it almost impossible even to read about them.

"I now fully understood the practical difficulties most women had to contend with," she recalled in her autobiography, *Eighty Years and More* (1898):

> The general discontent I felt with woman's portion as wife, mother, housekeeper, physician, and spiritual guide, the chaotic condition into which everything fell without her constant supervision, and the wearied, anxious look of the majority of women, impressed me with the strong feeling that some active measures should be taken.

DOCUMENT

Stanton, Declaration of Sentiments

Active measures she took. Together with Lucretia Mott and a few others of like mind, she organized a meeting, the Seneca Falls Convention (July 1848), and drafted a Declaration of Sentiments patterned on the Declaration of Independence. "We hold these truths to be self-evident: that all men and women are created equal," it stated, and it went on to list the "injuries and usurpations" of men, just as Jefferson had outlined those of George III.

From this seed the movement grew. During the 1850s a series of national conventions was held, and more and more reformers, including William Lloyd Garrison, joined the cause. Of the recruits, Susan B. Anthony was the most influential, for she was the first to see the need for thorough organization if effective pressure was to be brought to bear on male-dominated society. Her first campaign, mounted in 1854 and 1855 in behalf of a petition to the New York legislature calling for reform of the property and divorce laws, accumulated 6000 signatures. But the petition did not persuade the legislature to act. Indeed, the feminists achieved very few practical results during the Age of Reform. Their leaders, however, were persevering types, most of them extraordinarily long-lived. Their major efforts lay in the future.

Despite the aggressiveness of many reformers and the extremity of some of their proposals, little social conflict blighted these years. Most citizens readily accepted the need for improving society and showed a healthy tolerance for even the most harebrained

schemes for doing so. When Sylvester Graham, inventor of the graham cracker, traveled up and down the land praising the virtues of hard mattresses, cold showers, and homemade bread, he was mobbed by professional bakers, but otherwise, as his biographer says, "he was the subject of jokes, lampoons, and caustic editorials" rather than violence. Americans argued about everything from prison reform to vegetarianism, from women's rights to phrenology (a pseudoscience much occupied with developing the diagnostic possibilities of measuring the bumps on people's heads). But they seldom came to blows. Even the abolitionist movement might not have caused serious social strife if the territorial expansion of the late 1840s had not dragged the slavery issue back into politics. When that happened, politics again assumed center stage, public discourse grew embittered, and the first great Age of Reform came to an end.

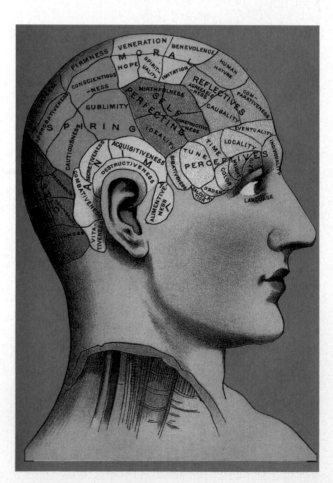

▲ Phrenology sought to determine aptitude and character from the size and shape of a person's head. In the nineteenth century, many regarded it as a science. Bumps in certain parts of the skull suggested an innate penchant for love, while protuberances elsewhere for destructiveness or acquisitiveness.

MILESTONES

1774	Mother Ann Lee founds first Shaker community
1784	Dr. Benjamin Rush's *Inquiry into the Effects of Ardent Spirits* questions alcohol's benefits
1826	American Temperance Union begins campaign against drunkenness
1829	Black abolitionist David Walker publishes *Appeal to the Coloured Citizens of the World*
1830s	Second Great Awakening stresses promise of salvation
	Prison reformers debate Auburn versus Philadelphia system
1830–1850	Utopian communities flourish
1830	Joseph Smith shares his "vision" in *Book of Mormon*
1831	Abolitionist William Lloyd Garrison founds *The Liberator* and New England Anti-Slavery Society
1831–1832	Alexis de Tocqueville and Gustave de Beaumont tour America
1832	Perkins Institution for the Blind opens in Boston
1837	Illinois abolitionist Elijah Lovejoy is murdered
1843	Dorothea Dix exposes treatment of the insane in *Memorial to the Legislature of Massachusetts*
1844	Margaret Fuller condemns sexual discrimination in *Women in the Nineteenth Century*
	Nauvoo mob murders Joseph Smith
1845	Frederick Douglass describes slave life in *Narrative of the Life of Frederick Douglass*
1847	Brigham Young leads Mormon migration to Great Salt Lake
1848	Elizabeth Cady Stanton and Lucretia Mott organize Seneca Falls Convention and draft Declaration of Sentiments
1851	Maine bans alcoholic beverages
1854–1855	Susan B. Anthony leads petition campaign against New York property and divorce laws

SUPPLEMENTARY READING

On Tocqueville and his views of America, see Alexis de Tocqueville, *Democracy in America*, J. P. Mayer, ed. (1966 edition); also Andre Jardin, *Alexis de Tocqueville* (1988). For an analysis of the middle class, see Stuart M. Blumin, *The Emergence of the Middle Class* (1989).

On the changing place of the family and the changes within it, see Mary P. Ryan, *Cradle of the Middle Class: The Family in Oneida, New York* (1981), Catherine E. Kelly, *In the New England Fashion: Reshaping Women's Lives in the Nineteenth Century* (1999), Nancy Cott, *The Bonds of Womanhood* (1977), and Carl Degler, *At Odds: Women and Family in America from the Revolution to the Present* (1980).

The Second Great Awakening has been examined both as a religious and as a social phenomenon. Still useful is Whitney Cross, *The Burned-Over District* (1950), but see also Paul E. Johnson, *A Shopkeeper's Millennium* (1978). Mark A. Noll, *America's God: From Jonathan Edwards to Abraham Lincoln* (2002) provides a broader study of the religious dimension of reform movements. For the Shakers, see Stephen J. Stein, *The Shaker Experience in America* (1992). Richard Bushman, *Joseph Smith and the Beginnings*

of Mormonism (1984), provides a good introduction to the subject. For a broader study see Leonard J. Arrington, *The Mormon Experience* (1992).

For the origins of feminism, see Nancy Cott, *The Grounding of Modern Feminism* (1987), Ellen C. DuBois, *Feminism and Suffrage: The Emergence of an Independent Women's Movement in America, 1848–1869* (1978), and Linda K. Kerber, *No Constitutional Right to Be Ladies* (1998). Bruce Dorsey, *Reforming Men and Women* (2002) shows how men often initiated reforms but women took control of them.

On utopianism generally, see Ronald G. Walters, *American Reformers, 1815–1860* (1978). Accounts of the temperance movement include Barbara L. Epstein, *The Politics of Domesticity* (1981), and W. J. Rorabaugh, *The Alcoholic Republic* (1979).

For a general study of the context of abolitionism, see Richard S. Newman, *The Transformation of American Abolitionism* (2002). For sharply contrasting views of the abolitionist movement, see Stanley Elkins, *Slavery* (1975), and Lewis Perry and Michael Fellman, eds., *Anti-Slavery*

Reconsidered (1979). Women's role in the movement is discussed in Julie Roy Jeffrey, *The Great Silent Army of Abolitionism* (1998). The persistence of slavery in the North, a topic that is often overlooked, is examined in Joanne P. Melish, *Disowning Slavery* (1998). Biographical accounts include John L. Thomas, *The Liberator: William Lloyd Garrison* (1963), Gerda Lerner, *The Grimké Sisters from South Carolina* (1967), and Nathan Huggins, *Slave and Citizen: The Life of Frederick Douglass* (1980).

Carolyn L. Karcher, *The First Woman in the Republic: A Cultural Biography of Lydia Maria Child* (1994), Charles Capper, *Margaret Fuller* (1992), Elizabeth Griffith, *In Her Own Rights: The Life of Elizabeth Cady Stanton* (1984), and Kathryn K. Sklar, *Catharine Beecher* (1973), are solid biographies of important women in the era.

On Sojourner Truth, see Nell Irvin Painter, *Sojourner Truth* (1996) and, for her time with Mathias, Paul F. Johnson and Sean Wilentz, *Kingdom of Mathias* (1994).

SUGGESTED WEBSITES

The Alexis de Tocqueville Tour: Exploring Democracy in America

http://www.tocqueville.org/

Text, images, and teaching suggestions are all part of this companion site to C-SPAN's recent programming on de Tocqueville.

Votes for Women: Selections from the National Women Suffrage Association Collection, 1848–1921

http://memory.loc.gov/ammem/naw/nawshome.html

This Library of Congress site contains books, pamphlets, and other artifacts that document the suffrage campaign.

By Popular Demand: "Votes for Women" Suffrage Pictures, 1850–1922

http://memory.loc.gov/ammem/vfwhtml/vfwhome.html

Portraits, suffrage parades, picketing suffragists, an anti-suffrage display, and cartoons commenting on the movement are all part of this Library of Congress site.

Important Black Abolitionists

http://www.loc.gov/exhibits/african/afam006.html

An exhibit from the Library of Congress, with pictures and text, that discuss some of the key African American abolitionists and their efforts to end slavery.

Pioneering the Upper Midwest: Books from Michigan, Minnesota, and Wisconsin, ca. 1820–1910

http://memory.loc.gov/ammem/umhtml/umhome.html

This Library of Congress site looks at first-person accounts, biographies, promotional literature, ethnographic and antiquarian texts, colonial archival documents, and other works from the seventeenth to early twentieth century. It covers many topics and issues that affected Americans in the settlement and development of the upper Midwest.

History of the Suffrage Movement

http://www.rochester.edu/SBA

This site includes a chronology, important texts relating to women's suffrage, and bibliographical information about Susan B. Anthony and Elizabeth Cady Stanton.

An American Culture

▼ Frederic Edwin Church conveyed the romantic sensibility in *Twilight in the Wilderness* (1860). The clouds glow with religious portent, and their reflected light pervades Nature.

As the United States grew larger, richer, and more centralized, it began to evolve a more distinctive culture. Still the child of Europe, by mid-century it was clearly the offspring rather than an imitation of the parent society. Jefferson had drawn most of his ideas from classical authors and seventeenth-century English thinkers. He gave an American cast to these doctrines, as when he stressed the separation of church and state or the pursuit of happiness instead of property in describing the "unalienable rights" of men. But Ralph Waldo Emerson, whose views were roughly similar to Jefferson's and who was also influenced by European thinkers, was an American philosopher. He and his generation of writers, painters, and architects drew quite self-consciously on native sources and inspirations. Some worshiped the pristine beauty of Nature while others celebrated the ebullient energies of a democratic people. Collectively they described convincingly the emergence of a distinctly American culture.

IN SEARCH OF NATIVE GROUNDS

Early nineteenth-century literary groups such as Boston's Anthology Club and the Friendly Club in New York consciously set out to "foster American genius" and to encourage the production of a distinctively American literature. But of the novelists before 1830, only James Fenimore Cooper made successful use of the national heritage. Beginning with *The Spy* (1821), *The Pioneers* (1823), and *The Last of the Mohicans* (1826), he wrote a long series of tales of Indians and settlers that

▲ Part of the mid-nineteenth-century literary renaissance, James Fenimore Cooper was the first American novelist to explore native themes, settings, and characters.

presented a vivid, if romanticized, picture of frontier life. (Cooper's Indians, Mark Twain quipped, belonged to "an extinct tribe that never existed.") Cooper's work marked a shift from the classicism of the eighteenth century, which emphasized reason and orderliness in writing, to the romanticism of the early nineteenth century, with its stress on highly subjective emotional values and its concern for the beauties of nature and the freedom of the individual.

The novel developed along with its readership, which was composed, increasingly, of middle-class women. In novels such as *A New England Tale* (1822) and *Redwood* (1824), Catharine M. Sedgwick painstakingly chronicled the simple virtues of the home and family.

Most of the early novelists slavishly imitated British writers. Some looked to the sentimental novels of Samuel Richardson and Susanna Rowson (Rowson's *Charlotte Temple* went through 150 American editions). Others copied the style of satirical writers like Daniel Defoe and Tobias Smollett. Most popular were historical romances done in the manner of the Waverley novels of Sir Walter Scott. None approached the level of the best British writers, and as a result American novelists were badly outdistanced in their

own country by the British, both in prestige and popularity. Since foreign copyrights were not recognized in the United States, British books were shamelessly pirated and sold cheaply. Half a million volumes of Scott were sold in America before 1823. American readers benefited but not American writers.

New York City was the literary capital of the country. Its leading light was Washington Irving, whose comical *Diedrich Knickerbocker's History of New York* (1809) made its young author famous on both sides of the Atlantic. Yet Irving soon abandoned the United States for Europe. *The Sketch Book* (1819), which included "Rip Van Winkle" and other well-known tales and legends of the Dutch in the Hudson Valley, was written while the author was residing in Birmingham and London. Outside New York there was much less literary activity. New England was only on the verge of its great literary flowering.

American painting in this period reached a level comparable to that of contemporary European work, but the best artists received most of their training in Europe. Benjamin West, the first and in his day the most highly regarded, went to Europe before the Revolution and never returned; he can scarcely be considered an American. John Singleton Copley, whose stern, straight-forward portraits display a more distinctly American character than the work of any of his contemporaries, was a Bostonian. No one so well captured the vigor and integrity of the Revolutionary generation. Charles Willson Peale, after studying under West in London, settled in Philadelphia, where he established a museum containing fossils, stuffed animals, and various natural curiosities as well as paintings. Peale helped found the Pennsylvania Academy of the Fine Arts, and he did much to encourage American painting. Not the least of his achievements was the production of a large brood of artistic children to whom he gave such names as Rembrandt, Titian, and Rubens. The most talented of Peale's children was (appropriately) Rembrandt, whose portrait of Jefferson, executed in 1800, is one of the finest likenesses of the Sage of Monticello.

Another outstanding artist of this generation was Gilbert Stuart, who is best known for his many studies of George Washington. Stuart studied in England with Benjamin West, and his brush was much in demand in London. He was probably the most technically accomplished of the early American portrait painters. He was fond of painting his subjects with ruddy complexions (produced by means of a judicious mixture of vermilion, purple, and white pigment), which made many of his elderly sitters appear positively cherubic. He once remarked that the pallid flesh tones used by a rival looked "like putrid veal a little blown with green flies."

▲ In *The Course of Empire, Destruction* (1836), painter Thomas Cole shows an ancient civilization, evocative of Rome, in apocalyptic decline. Man should not overestimate the permanence or the value of "civilization," Cole suggested, a sentiment that fit with a new American sensibility that enshrined nature and feelings.

In general, the painting of the period was less obviously imitative of European models than the national literature. Wealthy merchants, manufacturers, and planters wished their likenesses preserved, and the demand for portraits of the nation's Revolutionary heroes seemed insatiable. Since paintings could not be reproduced as books could be, American artists did a flourishing business. Yet they remained unmistakably in the European tradition.

THE ROMANTIC VIEW OF LIFE

In the Western world the romantic movement was a revolt against the bloodless logic of the Age of Reason. It was a noticeable if unnamed point of view in Germany, France, and England as early as the 1780s and in America a generation later; by the second quarter of the nineteenth century, few intellectuals were unmarked by it. "Romantics" believed that change and growth were the essence of life, for individuals and for institutions. They valued feeling and intuition over pure thought, and they stressed the dif-

ferences between individuals and societies rather than the similarities. Ardent love of country characterized the movement; individualism, optimism, ingenuousness, and emotion were its bywords. Whereas the puritans, believing that nearly everyone was destined to endure the tortures of Hell for all eternity, contemplated death with dread, romantics, assuming that good people would go to Heaven, professed to look forward to death.

Romanticism perfectly fitted the mood of nineteenth-century America. Interest in raw nature and in primitive peoples, worship of the individual, praise of folk culture, the subordination of intellect to feeling—were these primarily romantic ideas or American ideas? Jacksonian democracy with its self-confidence, careless prodigality, contempt for learning, glorification of the ordinary—was it a product of the American experience or a reflection of a wider world view?

The romantic way of thinking found its greatest American expression in the transcendentalist movement. Transcendentalism, a New England creation, is difficult to describe because it emphasized the inde-

finable and the unknowable. It was a mystical, intuitive way of looking at life that subordinated facts to feelings. Its literal meaning was "to go beyond the world of the senses," by which the transcendentalists meant the material and observable world. To the transcendentalists, human beings were truly divine because they were part of nature, itself the essence of divinity. Their intellectual capacities did not define their capabilities, for they could "transcend" reason by having faith in themselves and in the fundamental benevolence of the universe. Transcendentalists were complete individualists, seeing the social whole as no more than the sum of its parts. Organized religion, indeed all institutions were unimportant if not counterproductive; what mattered was the single person and that people aspire, stretch *beyond* their known capabilities. Failure resulted only from lack of effort. The expression "Hitch your wagon to a star" is of transcendentalist origin.

EMERSON AND THOREAU

The leading transcendentalist thinker was Ralph Waldo Emerson. Born in 1803 and educated at Harvard, Emerson became a minister, but in 1832 he gave up his pulpit, deciding that "the profession is antiquated." After traveling in Europe, where he met many romantic writers, including Samuel Taylor Coleridge, William Wordsworth, and (especially important) the historian Thomas Carlyle, he settled in Concord, Massachusetts, where he had a long career as an essayist, lecturer, and sage.

DOCUMENT

Emerson, *The Concord Hymn*

Emerson managed to restore to what he called "corpse-cold" Unitarianism the fervor and purposefulness characteristic of seventeenth-century puritanism. His philosophy was at once buoyantly optimistic and rigorously intellectual, self-confident, and conscientious. In "The American Scholar," a notable address he delivered at Harvard in 1837, he urged Americans to put aside their devotion to things European and seek inspiration in their immediate surroundings. Emerson saw himself as pitting "spiritual powers" against "the mechanical powers and the mechanical philosophy of this time." The new industrial society of New England disturbed him profoundly.

Emerson favored change and believed in progress. It was America's destiny to fulfill "the postponed expectations of the world." Temperamentally, however, he was too serene and too much his own man to fight for the causes other reformers espoused, and he was too idealistic to accept the compromises

that most reformers make to achieve their ends. To abolitionist friends who sought his aid he said: "God must govern his own world. . . . I have quite other slaves to face than those Negroes, to wit, imprisoned thoughts . . . which have no watchman or lover or defender but me."

Because he put so much emphasis on self-reliance, Emerson disliked powerful governments. "The less government we have the better," he said. In a sense he was the prototype of some modern alienated intellectuals, so repelled by the world as it was that he would not actively try to change it. Nevertheless he thought strong leadership essential, perhaps being influenced in this direction by his friend Carlyle's glorification of the role of great men in history. Emerson also had a strong practical streak. He made his living by lecturing, tracking tirelessly across the country, talking before every type of audience for fees ranging from $50 to several hundreds.

Closely identified with Emerson was his Concord neighbor Henry David Thoreau. After graduating

▲ In 1838 Ralph Waldo Emerson told a bookish audience in Boston that man was "almost smothered under his own institutions." Amongst the stifling encumbrances he enumerated were law, property, church, customs—and books.

▲ Walden Pond, as seen today, where Henry David Thoreau lived from 1845 to 1847: "I went to the woods because I wished to live deliberately, to front only the essential facts of life, and see if I could not learn what it had to teach, and not, when I came to die, to discover that I had not lived."

from Harvard in 1837, Thoreau taught school for a time and helped out in a small pencil-making business run by his family. He was a strange man, gentle, a dreamer, content to absorb the beauties of nature almost intuitively, yet stubborn and individualistic to the point of selfishness. "He is the most unmalleable fellow alive," one acquaintance wrote. The hectic scramble for wealth that Thoreau saw all about him he found disgusting—and alarming, for he believed it was destroying both the natural and the human resources of the country.

Like Emerson, Thoreau objected to many of society's restrictions on the individual. "That government is best which governs not at all," he said, going both Emerson and the Jeffersonians one better. He was perfectly prepared to see himself as a majority of one. Emerson reduced him to a phrase when he called him "a born protestant." "When were the good and the brave ever in a majority?" Thoreau asked. "If a man does not keep pace with his companions," he wrote on another occasion, "perhaps it is because he hears a different drummer."

In 1845 Thoreau decided to put to the test his theory that a person need not depend on society for a satisfying existence. He built a cabin at Walden Pond on some property owned by Emerson and lived there alone for two years. He did not try to be entirely self-sufficient: He was not above returning to his family or to Emerson's for a square meal on occasion, and he generally purchased the building materials and other manufactured articles that he needed. Instead he set out, by experimenting, to prove that *if necessary,* an individual could get along without the products of

civilization. He used manufactured plaster in building his Walden cabin, but he also gathered a bushel of clamshells and made a small quantity of lime himself, to prove that it could be done.

At Walden, Thoreau wrote *A Week on the Concord and Merrimack Rivers* (1849), which used an account of a trip he had taken with his brother as a vehicle for a discussion of his ideas about life and literature. He spent much time observing the quiet world around the pond, thinking, and writing in his journal. The best fruit of this period was that extraordinary book *Walden* (1854). Superficially, *Walden* is the story of Thoreau's experiment, movingly and beautifully written. It is also an acid indictment of the social behavior of the average American, an attack on unthinking conformity, on subordinating one's own judgment to that of the herd.

The most graphic illustration of Thoreau's confidence in his own values occurred while he was living at Walden. At that time the Mexican War was raging. Thoreau considered the war immoral because it advanced the cause of slavery. To protest, he refused to pay his Massachusetts poll tax. For this he was arrested and lodged in jail, although only for one night because an aunt promptly paid the tax for him. His essay "Civil Disobedience," explaining his view of the proper relation between the individual and the state, resulted from this experience. Like Emerson, however, Thoreau refused to participate in practical reform movements. "I love Henry," one of his friends said, "but I cannot like him; and as for taking his arm, I should as soon think of taking the arm of an elm tree."

EDGAR ALLAN POE

The work of all the imaginative writers of the period reveals romantic influences, and it is possibly an indication of the affinity of the romantic approach to American conditions that a number of excellent writers of poetry and fiction first appeared in the 1830s and 1840s. Edgar Allan Poe, one of the most remarkable, seems almost a caricature of the romantic image of the tortured genius. Poe was born in Boston in 1809, the son of poor actors who died before he was three years old. He was raised by a wealthy Virginian, John Allan.

Few persons as neurotic as Poe have been able to produce first-rate work. In college he ran up debts of $2500 in less than a year and had to withdraw. He won an appointment to West Point but was discharged after a few months for disobedience and "gross neglect of duty." He was a lifelong alcoholic and an occasional taker of drugs. He married a child of 13.

▲ In 1845 Edgar Allan Poe, impoverished and an alcoholic, was living in the "greatest wretchedness." His young wife was dying of tuberculosis. That same year he wrote "The Raven," a poem about an ill-omened bird that intrudes on a young man's grief over the death of his beloved. "Take thy beak from out of my heart" the man screams. Quoth the raven—famously—"Nevermore."

Poe was obsessed with death. Once he attempted to poison himself; repeatedly he was down and out, even to the verge of starvation. He was haunted by melancholia and hallucinations. Yet he was an excellent magazine editor, a penetrating critic, a poet of unique if somewhat narrow talents, and a fine short story writer. Although he died at age 40, he turned out a large volume of serious, highly original work.

Poe responded strongly to the lure of romanticism. His works abound with examples of wild imagination and fascination with mystery, fright, and the occult. If he did not invent the detective story, he perfected it; his tales "The Murders in the Rue Morgue" and "The Purloined Letter" stressed the thought processes of a clever detective in solving a mystery by reasoning from evidence. Poe was also one of the earliest writers to deal with what are today called science fiction themes, and "The Pit and the Pendulum" and "The Cask of Amontillado" show that he was a master of the horror tale.

Although dissolute in his personal life, when Poe touched pen to paper, he became a disciplined craftsman. The most fantastic passages in his works are the result of careful, reasoned selection; not a word, he believed, could be removed without damage to the whole. And despite his rejection of most of the values prized by middle-class America, Poe was widely read in his own day. His poem "The Raven" won instantaneous popularity when it was published in 1845. Had he been a little more stable, he might have made a good living with his pen—but in that case he might not have written as he did.

NATHANIEL HAWTHORNE

Another product of the prevailing romanticism was Nathaniel Hawthorne of Salem, Massachusetts. Hawthorne was born in 1804. When he was a small child, his father died and his grief-stricken mother became a recluse. Left largely to his own devices, he grew to be a lonely, introspective person. Wandering about New England by himself in summertime, he soaked up local lore, which he drew on in writing short stories. For a time he lived in Concord, where he came to know most of the leading transcendentalists. However, he disliked the egoism of the transcendental point of view and rejected its bland optimism outright. He called Emerson an "everlasting rejector of all that is," a "seeker for he knows not what."

Hawthorne was fascinated by the past, particularly by the puritan heritage of New England and its

▲ "The House of the Seven Gables" in Salem, Massachusetts, on which Nathaniel Hawthorne's novel was based. The house symbolized the past's stranglehold on the present. "If each generation were allowed and expected to build its own houses, that single change . . . would imply almost every reform which society is now suffering for." Love, Hawthorne suggested, was a means to break free of the fetters of the past.

continuing influence on his own generation. He scorned "minute fidelity" to the real world in his fiction, seeking "a severer truth . . . the truth of the human heart." But he was active in politics and an admirer of Andrew Jackson. Three Democratic presidents—Martin Van Buren, James K. Polk, and Franklin Pierce—appointed him to minor political offices.

Hawthorne's early stories, originally published in magazines, were brought together in *Twice-Told Tales* (1837). They made excellent use of New England culture and history for background but were concerned chiefly with the struggles of individuals with sin, guilt, and especially the pride and isolation that often afflict those who place too much reliance on their own judgment. His greatest works were two novels written after the Whigs turned him out of his government job in 1849. *The Scarlet Letter* (1850), a grim yet sympathetic analysis of adultery, condemned not the woman, Hester Prynne, but the people who presumed to judge her. *The House of the Seven Gables* (1851) was a gripping account of the decay of an old New England family brought on by the guilt feelings of the current owners of the

house, caused by the way their ancestors had cheated the original owners of the property.

Like Poe, Hawthorne was appreciated in his own day and widely read; unlike Poe, he made a modest amount of money from his work. Yet he was never very comfortable in the society he inhabited. He had no patience with the second-rate. And despite his success in creating word pictures of a somber, mysterious world, he considered America too prosaic a country to inspire good literature. "There is no shadow, no antiquity, no mystery, no picturesque and gloomy wrong, nor anything but a commonplace prosperity," he complained.

HERMAN MELVILLE

In 1850, while writing *The House of the Seven Gables,* Hawthorne's publisher introduced him to another writer who was in the midst of a novel. The writer was Herman Melville; the book, *Moby Dick.* Hawthorne and Melville became good friends at once, for despite their dissimilar backgrounds, they

had a great deal in common. Melville was a New Yorker, born in 1819, one of eight children of a merchant of distinguished lineage. His father, however, lost all his money and died when the boy was 12. Herman left school at 15, worked briefly as a bank clerk, and in 1837 went to sea. For 18 months, in 1841 and 1842, he was crewman on the whaler *Acushnet.* Then he jumped ship in the South Seas. For a time he lived among a tribe of cannibals in the Marquesas; later he made his way to Tahiti, where he idled away nearly a year. After another year at sea he returned to America in the fall of 1844.

Although he had never before attempted serious writing, in 1846 he published *Typee,* an account of his life in the Marquesas. The book was a great success, for Melville had visited a part of the world almost unknown to Americans, and his descriptions of his bizarre experiences suited the taste of a romantic age. Success inspired him to write a sequel, *Omoo* (1847); other books followed quickly.

As he wrote Melville became conscious of deeper powers. In 1849 he began a systematic study of Shakespeare, pondering the bard's intuitive grasp of human nature. Like Hawthorne, Melville could not accept the prevailing optimism of his generation. Unlike his friend, he admired Emerson, seconding the Emersonian demand that Americans reject European ties and develop their own literature. "Believe me," he wrote, "men not very much inferior to Shakespeare are this day being born on the banks of the Ohio." Yet he considered Emerson's vague talk about striving and the inherent goodness of mankind complacent nonsense.

Experience made Melville too aware of the evil in the world to be a transcendentalist. His novel *Redburn* (1849), based on his adventures on a Liverpool packet, was, as the critic F. O. Matthiessen put it, "a study in disillusion, of innocence confronted with the world, of ideals shattered by facts." Yet Melville was no cynic; he expressed deep sympathy for the Indians and for immigrants, crowded like animals into the holds of transatlantic vessels. He denounced the brutality of discipline in the United States Navy in *White-Jacket* (1850). His essay "The Tartarus of Maids," a moving if somewhat overdrawn description of young women working in a paper factory, protested the subordination of human beings to machines.

Hawthorne, whose dark view of human nature coincided with Melville's, encouraged him to press ahead with *Moby Dick* (1851). This book, Melville said, was "broiled in hellfire." Against the background of a whaling voyage (no better account of whaling has ever been written), he dealt subtly and symbolically with the problems of good and evil, of courage and cowardice, of faith, stubbornness, pride. In Captain Ahab, driven relentlessly to hunt down the huge white whale Moby Dick, which had destroyed his leg, Melville created one of the great figures of literature; in the book as a whole, he produced one of the finest novels written by an American, comparable to the best in any language.

As Melville's work became more profound, it lost its appeal to the average reader, and its originality and symbolic meaning escaped most of the critics. *Moby Dick,* his masterpiece, received little attention and most of that unfavorable. He kept on writing until his death in 1891 but was virtually ignored. Only in the 1920s did the critics rediscover him and give him his merited place in the history of American literature. His "Billy Budd, Foretopman," now considered one of his best stories, was not published until 1924.

WALT WHITMAN

Walt Whitman, whose *Leaves of Grass* (1855) was the last of the great literary works of this brief outpouring of genius, was the most romantic and by far the most

▲ Some scholars regard Walt Whitman as the poet of nature, and others, of the body—a reference to erotic lines such as: "Without shame the man I like knows and avows the deliciousness of his sex, /Without shame the woman I like knows and avows hers." Whitman's *Leaves of Grass* had every leaf in nature, complained critic E. P. Whipple, except the fig leaf.

distinctly American writer of his age. He was born on Long Island, outside New York City, in 1819. At 13 he left school and worked for a printer; thereafter he held a succession of newspaper jobs in the metropolitan area. He was an ardent Jacksonian and later a Free Soiler, which got him into hot water with a number of the publishers for whom he worked.

Although genuinely a "common man," thoroughly at home among tradesmen and laborers, he was surely not an ordinary man. Deeply introspective, he read omnivorously, if in a rather disorganized fashion, while working out a new, intensely personal mode of expression. During the early 1850s, while employed as a carpenter and composing the poems that made up *Leaves of Grass*, he regularly carried a book of Emerson in his lunch box. "I was simmering, simmering, simmering," he later recalled. "Emerson brought me to a boil." The transcendental idea that inspiration and aspiration are at the heart of all achievement captivated him. A poet could best express himself, he believed, by relying uncritically on his natural inclinations without regard for rigid metrical forms.

Leaves of Grass consisted of a preface, in which Whitman made the extraordinary statement that Americans had "probably the fullest poetical nature" of any people in history, and 12 poems in free verse: rambling, uneven, appearing to most readers shocking both in the commonplace nature of the subject matter and the coarseness of the language. Emerson, Thoreau, and a few others saw a fresh talent in these poems, but most

DOCUMENT

Whitman,
*Preface to
Leaves of Grass*

DEBATING THE PAST

Was there an "American Renaissance"? With the exception of Hawthorne's *The Scarlet Letter* (1850), the extraordinary literary achievements at mid-century went mostly unnoticed. Melville's *Moby Dick* and Thoreau's *Walden* (1854) each sold only a few thousand copies, and Walt Whitman's *Leaves of Grass* (1955) far fewer. A half century later critic Van Wyck Brooks identified these works as distinctly American, but he was unimpressed with what he called *America's Coming of Age* (1915). Transcendentalism he dismissed as "one shining deluge

of righteousness, purity, and practical mysticism." Ever since publication of Emerson's "American Scholar," he added, "the whole of American literature has had the semblance of one vast, all embracing baccalaureate address." Critic F. O. Matthiessen (1941) took a sharply different view. He identified the mid-nineteenth century as an "American Renaissance," a period when American writers ceased to be overshadowed by Europeans. Emerson, Thoreau, and Whitman drew from the energy and optimism of the people of the American nation, and Hawthorne and Melville from its soul. The relationship between American nationalism and letters was overdrawn, Leo Marx (1964) suggested. The great writers of the nineteenth century were reacting against urbanization and industrialization, moving symbolically "away from sophistication toward simplicity, away from the city toward the country." The social upheavals of the 1960s precipitated a backlash against the "elitist" focus on high-brow writers. Ann Douglas (1977) claimed that the "split between elite and mass culture" had occurred precisely during the mid-nineteenth century, when most readers ignored Melville and Whitman and devoured sentimental novels by Harriet Beecher Stowe, Susan Warner, and others, many of which were serialized in *Godey's Ladys' Book*, edited by Sarah Hale. Douglas, however, sided with the elitists, denouncing such novels for their "debased religiosity, their sentimental peddling of Christian belief for its nostalgic value." Nevertheless, one suspects that the girl pictured here in *Godey's Ladys' Book* (1855) was not reading *Moby Dick*.

Van Wyck Brooks, *America's Coming of Age* (1915), F. O. Matthiessen, *The American Renaissance* (1941), Leo Marx, *The Machine in the Garden* (1964), Ann Douglas, *The Feminization of American Culture* (1977), David S. Reynolds, *Beneath the American Renaissance* (1988).

readers and reviewers found them offensive. Indeed, the work was so undisciplined and so much of it had no obvious meaning that it was easy to miss the many passages of great beauty and originality.

Part of Whitman's difficulty arose because there was much of the charlatan in his makeup; often his writing did not ring true. He loved to use foreign words and phrases, and since he had no more than a smattering of any foreign language, he sounded pretentious and sometimes downright foolish when he did so. In reality a sensitive, gentle person, he tried to pose as a great, rough character. (Later in his career he bragged of fathering no less than six illegitimate children, which was assuredly untrue.) He never married, and his work suggests that his strongest emotional ties were with men. Thomas Carlyle once remarked shrewdly that Whitman thought he was a big man because he lived in a big country.

Whitman's work was more authentically American than that of any contemporary. His egoism—he titled one of his finest poems "Song of Myself"—was tempered by his belief that he was typical of all humanity:

> I celebrate myself and sing myself
> And what I assume you shall assume,
> For every atom belonging to me as good belongs to you.

He had a remarkable ear for rendering common speech poetically, for employing slang, for catching the breezy informality of Americans and their faith in themselves:

> Earth! you seem to look for something at my hands,
> Say, old top-knot, what do you want?
> I bequeath myself to the dirt to grow from the grass I
>   love,
> If you want me again look for me under your boot-soles.

Because of these qualities and because in his later work, especially during the Civil War, he occasionally struck a popular chord, Whitman was never as neglected as Melville. When he died in 1892, he was, if not entirely understood, at least widely appreciated.

THE WIDER LITERARY RENAISSANCE

Emerson, Thoreau, Poe, Hawthorne, Melville, and Whitman were the great figures of American literature before the Civil War. A number of others, if they lacked genius, were leading literary lights in their own day and are still worth reading. One was Henry Wadsworth Longfellow. In 1835, while still in his twenties, Longfellow became professor of modern languages at Harvard. Although he published a fine translation of Dante's *Divine Comedy* and was expert

in many languages, his fame came from his poems: "The Village Blacksmith"; "Paul Revere's Ride"; *The Courtship of Miles Standish*, a sentimental tale of Pilgrim days; and *The Song of Hiawatha*, the romantic retelling of an Indian legend. These brought him excellent critical notices and considerable fortune; his work was widely translated and reprinted.

Although musical, polished, and full of vivid images, Longfellow's poetry, like the man, lacked profundity, originality, and force. But it was neither cheap nor trivial. When Longfellow wrote "Life is real! life is earnest! / And the grave is not its goal," he expressed the heartfelt belief of most of his generation. In this sense he captured the spirit of his times better than any of his great contemporaries, better even than Whitman.

Longfellow was the most talented of a group of minor New England writers who collectively gave that region great intellectual vitality. John Greenleaf Whittier, a poet nearly as popular as Longfellow, believed ardently in the abolition of slavery. A few of his poems can still be read with pleasure, among them "The Barefoot Boy," dealing with his rural childhood. Somewhat more weighty was the achievement of James Russell Lowell, the first editor of the *Atlantic Monthly*, founded in Boston in 1857. Lowell's humorous stories written in the New England dialect made an original and influential contribution to the national literature. Dr. Oliver Wendell Holmes, professor of medicine at Harvard, was widely known as a poet and essayist. A few of his poems, such as "The Chambered Nautilus" and "Old Ironsides," are interesting examples of American romantic verse.

Collectively these minor writers had a beneficial effect on American culture, for if rather smug and narrow, they were serious and industrious. They fixed their gaze upward and encouraged their readers to do likewise.

So did the important historians of the period, all of them New Englanders. George Bancroft, one of the first Americans to study in Germany, began in 1834 to publish a ten-volume *History of the United States*, based on thorough research. William Hickling Prescott, though nearly blind, wrote extensively on the history of Spain and Spain's American empire, his *Conquest of Mexico* (1843) and *Conquest of Peru* (1847) being his most important works. John Lothrop Motley, another German-trained historian, published his *Rise of the Dutch Republic* in 1856, and Francis Parkman began his great account of the struggle between France and Great Britain for the control of North America with *Conspiracy of Pontiac* in 1851.

Southern literature was even more markedly romantic than that of New England. John Pendleton

Kennedy of Baltimore wrote several novels with regional historical themes, much in the manner of Sir Walter Scott. Kennedy was also a Whig politician of some importance who served several terms in Congress; in 1852 he became secretary of the navy in the Fillmore Cabinet. The more versatile and influential William Gilmore Simms of South Carolina wrote nearly two dozen novels, several volumes of poetry, and a number of biographies. At his peak in the 1830s he earned as much as $6000 a year with his pen. *The Partisan* (1835), one of a series of novels dealing with the Revolution, and *The Yemassee* (1835), the story of an early eighteenth-century Indian war, seem too melodramatic for modern tastes. His portraits of the planter class are too bloodless and reverential to be convincing. His female characters are nearly all pallid and fragile. Only when Simms wrote of frontier life and its people did his work possess much power.

DOMESTIC TASTES

Architecture flourished in the northern cities chiefly as a result of the work of Charles Bulfinch and some of his disciples. Bulfinch was influenced by British architects, but he developed a manner all his own. His

▲ How, in a democracy, could women assent to the authority of husbands? Catharine Beecher, a popular writer, responded that women could promote "intellectual and moral elevation" by transforming their home into a "glorious temple." Women, as homemakers, were to spearhead the nation's religious and moral regeneration.

"Federal" style gave parts of Boston a dignity and charm equal to the finest sections of London. The State House, numerous other public buildings, and, best of all, many of Bulfinch's private houses—austere yet elegant, solid yet airy and graceful—gave the town a distinction it had lacked before the Revolution.

In the 1830s and 1840s new techniques made it possible to weave colored patterns into cloth by machine, to manufacture wallpaper printed with complicated designs, and to produce rugs and hangings that looked like tapestries. Combined with the use of machine methods in the furniture business, these inventions had a powerful impact on public taste. That impact, at least in the short run, was aesthetically unfortunate. In these years the parlor evolved as a room whose chief purpose was to display a piano, stuffed chairs and sofas with flowered prints, wallpaper with vertical stripes, heavy drapes with frilled edges, and all manner of bibelots. "Though your parlor may be crowded," one decorator advised, "it is crowded only with love."

Wood-turning machinery added to the popularity of the elaborately decorated "Gothic" style of architecture. The irregularity and uniqueness of Gothic buildings suited the prevailing romanticism, their aspiring towers, steeples, and arches and their flexibility (a new wing or extension could always be added without spoiling the effect) made them especially attractive to a people enamored of progress. The huge pile of pink masonry of the Smithsonian Institution Building in Washington, with its nine distinct types of towers, represents American Gothic at its most giddy and lugubrious stage. The building, which was designed in 1846 by James Renwick, confounded generations of architects, but with the passage of time it came to seem the perfect setting for the vast collection of mementos that fill "the nation's attic." "Greek" and "Italian" styles also flourished in this period, the former particularly in the South; elsewhere the Gothic was by all odds the most popular.

Increasingly, Americans of the period were purchasing native art. George Catlin, who painted hundreds of pictures of Indians and their surroundings, all rich in authentic detail, displayed his work before admiring crowds in many cities. Genre painters (artists whose canvases told stories, usually drawn from everyday life) were wildly popular. The best were William Sidney Mount of New York and George Caleb Bingham of Missouri. Rumor had it that Mount received $1000 for his first important canvas; Bingham's paintings commanded excellent prices; and the public bought engravings of the work of both men in enormous numbers.

The more academic artists of the period were popular as well. The "luminists" and members of the

▲ The Smithsonian Institution Building, made of red sandstone, is popularly known as "The Castle" because of its crenellated towers. Its architect, James Renwick, Jr., also designed New York's Grace Church and St. Patrick's Cathedral in the popular Gothic Revival style.

petent American works of art into middle-class homes.

Beginning in the late 1850s, the prints of the firm of Currier and Ives brought a crude but charming kind of art to a still wider audience. Currier and Ives lithographs portrayed horse racing, trains, rural landscapes, and "every tender domestic moment, every sign of national progress, every regional oddity, every private or public disaster from a cut finger to a forest fire." They were issued in very large editions and sold for as little as 15 cents.

romantic Hudson River School specialized in grandiose pictures of wild landscapes. In the 1840s Thomas Doughty regularly collected $500 each for his paintings. The works of Asher B. Durand, John Kensett, and Thomas Cole were in demand. The collector Luman Reed commissioned five large Cole canvases for an allegorical series, *The Course of Empire*, and crowds flocked to see another of Cole's series, *The Voyage of Life*, when it was exhibited in New York.

In 1839 the American Art-Union was formed in New York to encourage native art. The Art-Union hit on the ingenious device of selling what were in effect lottery tickets and using the proceeds to purchase paintings, which became the prizes in the lottery. Annual "memberships" sold for $5; 814 people subscribed in 1839, nearly 19,000 ten years later. Soon the Art-Union was giving every member an engraving of one of its principal prizes. The organization had to disband after a New York court outlawed the lottery in 1851, but in 1854 a new Cosmopolitan Art-Union was established in Ohio. In the years before the Civil War it boomed, reaching a peak of 38,000 members and paying as much as $6000 for an individual work—the sculptor Hiram Powers's boneless female nude, *The Greek Slave*. It also distributed an art magazine and each year gave a young artist a gold medal and $2000 for foreign study.

The art unions made little effort to encourage innovators, but they were a boon to many artists. The American Art-Union paid out as much as $40,000 for its prizes in a single year. By distributing thousands of engravings and colored prints, they introduced com-

EDUCATION FOR DEMOCRACY

Except on the edge of the frontier and in the South, most youngsters between the ages of five and ten attended a school for at least a couple of months of the year. These schools, however, were privately run and charged fees. Attendance was not required and fell off sharply once children learned to read and do their sums well enough to get along in day-to-day life. The teachers were usually young men waiting for something better to turn up.

All this changed with the rise of the common school movement. At the heart of the movement was the belief, widely expressed in the first days of the republic, that a government based on democratic rule must provide the means, as Jefferson put it, to "diffuse knowledge throughout the mass of the people." This meant free tax-supported schools, which all children were expected to attend. It also came to mean that such an educational system should be administered on a statewide basis and that teaching should become a profession that required formal training.

DOCUMENT

Mann, Report of the Massachusetts Board of Ed.

The two most effective leaders of the common school movement were Henry Barnard and Horace Mann. Both were New Englanders, Whigs, trained in the law, and in other ways conservative types. They shared an unquenchable faith in the improvability of the human race through education. Barnard served in educational posts in Connecticut, Rhode Island, and New York in the 1840s and 1850s and as editor of the *American Journal of Education* from 1855 until 1882. Mann drafted the 1837 Massachusetts law creating a state school board and then became its first secretary. Over the next decade Mann's annual reports carried the case for common schools to every

▲ James J. Audubon was perhaps the nation's foremost chronicler of nature in antebellum America. The "Roseate Spoonbill" is from his *The Birds of America* (1827–1838). "I am not a scholar," Audubon wrote in 1830. "But no man living knows better than I do the habits of our birds."

corner of the land. Seldom given to understatement, Mann called common schools "the greatest discovery ever made by man." In his reports he criticized wealthy parents who sent their children to private academies rather than bring them into contact with their poorer neighbors in the local school. He encouraged young women to become teachers while commending them to school boards by claiming that they could get along on lower salaries than men.

By the 1850s every state outside the South provided free elementary schools and supported institutions for training teachers. Many extended public education to include high schools, and Michigan and Iowa even established publicly supported colleges.

Historians differ in explaining the success of the common school movement. Some stress the arguments Mann used to win support from employers by appealing to their need for trained and well-disciplined workers. Others see the schools as designed to "Americanize" the increasing numbers of non-English and non-Protestant immigrants who were flooding into the country. (Supporting this argument is the fact that Catholic bishops in New York and elsewhere opposed laws requiring Catholic children to attend these "Protestant" schools and set up their own private, parochial schools.)

Still other scholars argue that middle-class reformers favored public elementary schools on the theory that they would instill the values of hard work, punctuality, and submissiveness to authority in children of the laboring classes. (See Debating the Past, "Did the antebellum reform movement improve society?" in Chapter 10 [p. 283]).

All these reasons played a part in advancing the cause of the common schools. Yet it remains the case that the most compelling argument for common schools was cultural; more effectively than any other institution, they brought Americans of different economic circumstances and ethnic backgrounds into early and mutually beneficial contact with one another. They served the two roles that Mann assigned to them: "the balance wheel of the social machinery" and "the great equalizer."

READING AND THE DISSEMINATION OF CULTURE

As the population grew and became more concentrated, and as society, especially in the North, was permeated by a middle-class point of view, popular concern for "culture" in the formal sense increased. A

▲ Artist Henry Inman's *Dismissal of School on an October Afternoon* celebrated the one-room schoolhouse, but suggested that life's greater lessons could be learned out-of-doors, amidst the beauty of nature.

largely literate people, committed to the idea of education but not generally well educated, set their hearts on being "refined" and "cultivated." Industrialization made it easier to satisfy this new demand for culture, though the new machines also tended to make the artifacts of culture more stereotyped.

Improved printing techniques reduced the cost of books, magazines, and newspapers. In the 1850s one publisher sold a 50-volume set of Sir Walter Scott for $37.50. The first penny newspaper was the *New York Sun* (1833), but James Gordon Bennett's *New York Herald,* founded in 1835, brought the cheap new journalism to perfection. The *Boston Daily Times* and the *Philadelphia Public Ledger* soon followed. The penny newspapers depended on sensation, crime stories, and society gossip to attract readers, but they covered important national and international news too.

In the 1850s the moralistic and sentimental "domestic" novel entered its prime. The most successful writers in this genre were women, which prompted Hawthorne to complain bitterly that "a

d——d mob of scribbling women" was taking over American literature. Typical were Susan Warner, whose *The Wide, Wide World* (1850) was the sad tale of a pious, submissive girl who cried "more readily and more steadily" than any other tormented child in a novel at the time, and Maria Cummins, author of *The Lamplighter* (1854), the story of little Gerty, an orphan rescued by a kindly lamplighter, appropriately named Trumena Flint. *The Lamplighter* sold 70,000 copies within a year of publication. During these years arboreal pseudonyms were in vogue, among them Fanny Fern and Grace Greenwood. Although some scholars scorn the novels of such writers as sentimental drivel, the nineteenth-century equivalent of television soaps, others regard their books (and perhaps the soaps) as a means of creating imaginative "feminine" communities.

Besides reading countless volumes of sentimental romances (the books of another novelist, Mary Jane Holmes, sold over a million copies in these years), Americans consumed reams of religious literature. In 1840 the American Tract Society distrib-

uted 3 million copies of its publications; in 1855, more than 12 million. The society had hundreds of missionary-salesmen, called colporteurs, who fanned out across the country preaching the gospel and selling or giving away religious pamphlets and books. These publications played down denominational differences in favor of a generalized brand of evangelical Christianity. They bore titles such as *Quench Not the Spirit* (over 900,000 copies distributed by 1850) and *The Way to Heaven*. The American Bible Society issued hundreds of thousands of copies of the Old and New Testaments each year. Americans also devoured books on self-improvement, some aimed at uplifting the reader's character; others, which would today be called "how-to" books, at teaching everything from raising chickens to carving tombstones.

Philanthropists contributed large sums to charity and other good causes: Stephen Girard left $6 million for "educating poor white orphan boys" in his adopted Philadelphia; John Jacob Astor of New York and George Peabody of Massachusetts endowed libraries; John Lowell, son of the pioneer cotton manufacturer, left $500,000 to establish the Lowell Institute in Boston to sponsor free public lectures. In the late 1850s the industrialist Peter Cooper founded the Cooper Institute in New York City, where workers could take free courses in practical subjects. Mechanics' libraries sprang up in every industrial center and attracted so many readers that pressure was soon applied to grant them state funds. In 1848 Massachusetts led the way by authorizing the use of public money to back the Boston Public Library, and soon several states were encouraging local communities to found tax-supported libraries.

The desire for knowledge and culture in America is well illustrated by the success of the mutual improvement societies known as lyceums. The movement began in Great Britain; in the United States its prime mover was Josiah Holbrook, an itinerant lecturer and sometime schoolmaster from Connecticut. Holbrook founded the first lyceum in 1826 at Millbury, Massachusetts; within five years there were over a thousand scattered across the country. The lyceums conducted discussions, established libraries, and lobbied for better schools. Soon they began to sponsor lecture series on topics of every sort. Many of the nation's political and intellectual leaders, such as Webster, Emerson, Melville, and Lowell, regularly graced their platforms. So did other less famous lecturers who in the name of culture pronounced on subjects ranging from "Chemistry Applied to the Mechanic Arts" to a description of the tombs of the Egyptian pharaohs.

THE STATE OF THE COLLEGES

Unlike common schools, with their democratic overtones, private colleges had at best a precarious place in Jacksonian America. For one thing, there were too many of them. Any town with pretensions of becoming a regional center felt it had to have a college. Ohio had 25 in the 1850s, Tennessee 16. Many of these institutions were short-lived. Of the 14 colleges founded in Kentucky between 1800 and 1850, only half were still operating in 1860.

The problem of supply was compounded by a demand problem—too few students. Enrollment at the largest, Yale, never topped 400 until the mid-1840s. On the eve of the Civil War the largest state university, North Carolina, had fewer than 500. Higher education was beyond the means of the average family. Although most colleges charged less than half the $55 tuition required by Harvard, that was still too much for most families, wages being what they were. So desperate was the shortage that colleges accepted applicants as young as 11 and 12 and as old as 30.

Once enrolled, students had little worry about making the grade, not least because grades were not given. Since students were hard to come by and classwork was considered relatively unimportant, discipline was lax. Official authority was frequently challenged, and rioting was known to break out over such weighty matters as the quality of meals. A father who visited his son's college dormitory in 1818 found it inhabited by "half a dozen loungers in a state of oriental lethargy, each stretched out upon two or three chairs, with scarce any indication of life in them [other] than the feeble effort to keep up the fire of their cigars."

The typical college curriculum, dominated by the study of Latin and Greek, had almost no practical relevance except for future clergymen. The Yale faculty, most of them ministers, defended the classics as admirably providing for both "the discipline and the furniture of the mind," but these subjects commended themselves to college officials chiefly because they did not require costly equipment or a faculty that knew anything else. Professors spent most of their time in and out of the classroom trying to maintain a semblance of order, "to the exclusion of any great literary undertakings to which their choice might lead them," one explained. "Our country is yet too young for old professors," a Bostonian informed a foreign visitor in the 1830s, "and, besides, they are too poorly paid to induce first rate men to

▶ *text continues on page 312*

Mapping
the Past

Nature as a Civilizing Force

Thoreau had gone off to Walden Pond to escape the constraints of civilization. "We need the tonic of wildness," he declared. (His wildness, to be sure, was subdued: he was referring to a pasture.) A few years later landscape architect Andrew Jackson Downing similarly conceived of nature as a balm "to soften and humanize" those whose nerves had been rubbed raw by city life. Rather than flee into the woods, Downing proposed to bring nature to every home. Partly this could be accomplished through proper design: houses themselves should blend with nature, and open up to it with broad porches and large windows. Moreover, homes should be *surrounded* by nature. This could be accomplished even in cities by providing for well-landscaped lawns.

Suburban Arcadia

Another solution was to build homes in the suburbs. The first effort in this direction was Llewellyn Park, built in 1856 in West Orange, New Jersey, by Llewellyn S. Haskell, a wealthy New York merchant. Jackson hired Alexander Jackson Davis, author of *Rural Residences* (1837) and a friend of Downing's, to plan the community. Davis conceived of the community as a place for New York City businessmen seeking "accessible, retired, and healthful homes in the country." He cleared expansive vistas and framed the clearing with rocks and trees, constructed seven miles of winding roads with names such as Tulip, Mountain, and Passive, and built a 50-acre pedestrian "Ramble" through adjacent woods (*top right*).

Creation of Central Park

Llewellyn Park was a bucolic idyll for rich business-men. But those who most needed the "softening" and "humanizing" tonic of nature were urban workers. Surrounded by machinery or immured in office buildings and counting rooms, they returned "home" to brick and concrete tenements or apartment buildings. "Nature" could be brought into the city in the form of urban parks. Spirited citizens—or as historian Charles Beard contended in 1926—real estate speculators—initiated plans for a park in New York City in the early 1850s.

Frederick Law Olmsted, a landscape architect, travel writer, and editor, and Calvert Vaux, an English landscape architect who was an associate of Downing, submitted the "Greensward" plan for the design of Central Park. Olmsted and Vaux rejected as models the broad boulevards and symmetrical designs of European parks. They did not want the park to serve as an adornment to the city. Central Park was instead to be a place of refuge from urban life. The roads that would transverse the park would be dropped below eye level. Paths would meander around hills and ponds. Clusters of trees would block out the encroaching city. Pastoral vistas would reveal gentle hills and rock outcroppings.

Manmade structures, too, would harmonize with nature; bridges would reiterate the natural curves of nature, as illustrated in the recent picture (left). This idyllic conception of

Central Park was at variance with the wishes of workers who flocked there to play baseball or to listen to band concerts. "Greensward" became "The People's Playground."

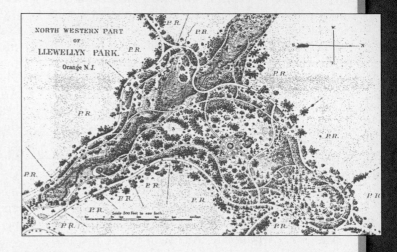

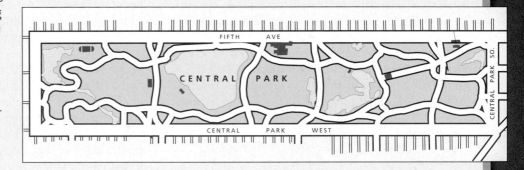

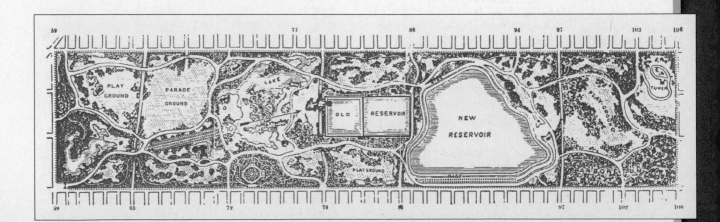

devote themselves to the business of lecturing. . . . We consider professors as secondary men."

Fortunately for the future of higher education, some college officials recognized the need for a drastic overhaul of their institutions. President Francis Wayland of Brown University used his 1842 address, "On the Present Collegiate System," to call for a thorough revamping of the curriculum to make it responsive to the economic realities of American society. This meant more courses in science, economics (where Wayland's own *Elements of Political Economy* might be used), modern history, and applied mathematics; fewer in Hebrew, biblical studies, Greek, and ancient history.

Yale established a separate school of science in 1847, which it hoped would attract serious-minded students and research-minded professors. At Harvard, which also opened a scientific school, students were allowed to choose some of their courses and were compelled to earn grades as a stimulus to study. Colleges in the West and the South began to offer mechanical and agricultural subjects relevant to their regional economies. Oberlin enrolled four female students in 1837, and the first women's college, the Georgia Female College, opened its doors in 1839.

These reforms slowed the downward spiral of colleges; they did not restore them to the honored place they had enjoyed in the Revolutionary era. Of the first six presidents of the United States, only Washington did not graduate from college. Beginning in 1829, seven of the next eleven did not. In this Presidents Jackson, Van Buren, Harrison, Taylor, Fillmore, Lincoln, and Johnson were like 98 of every 100 white males, all blacks and Indians, and all but a handful of white women in mid-nineteenth-century America. Going to college had yet, in Wayland's words, to "commend itself to the good sense and patriotism of the American people."

CIVIC CULTURES

Unlike the capitals of Europe, which were centers of art and culture, Washington was a cultural backwater, and the politicians seemed content to keep it that way. Whether the United States had *any* cultural center, and if so, where it was, is another matter. Boston, Philadelphia, and New York vied for primacy, but many smaller cities, such as Lexington, Kentucky, the self-proclaimed "Athens of the West," set the tone for the surrounding hinterland.

In the cities members of the "learned professions," especially lawyers, were generally accepted as the arbiters of taste in literature and art. "At the bar or the bench the American aristocracy is found," and there too resides "the most intellectual section of society,"

the ever-insightful Tocqueville reported. Lawyers came mostly from the upper reaches of the city's economic order, usually from families long in residence.

Emerson only half mockingly called Boston "the hub of the universe," but this was a case when local pride triumphed over his usual good judgment. Boston was indeed the home of the country's leading literary magazine, the *North American Review*, founded in 1815, but Philadelphia had *Graham's*, the country's first illustrated magazine, and *Godey's Ladies Book*, which reached 150,000 subscribers in the 1850s, an enormous number for that date. By 1825 New York's House of Harper, organized in 1817, was the largest book publisher in the nation. Boston was the home of the nation's leading historians, and Philadelphia, with the Pennsylvania Academy of Fine Arts (1815) and the Philadelphia Academy of Music (1857), was conceded by all but blind Bostonians and tin-eared New Yorkers to predominate in artistic and musical matters.

In the West, Cincinnati could point to its seven weekly and two daily newspapers, a literary monthly, a medical journal, and a magazine for teenagers. The first Beethoven symphony ever heard in America was performed in Cincinnati in 1817. By the 1830s such coups had enabled the "Queen City" to replace the "Athens of the West" as the center of trans-Allegheny culture. Having quickly accomplished so much, its boosters reasoned, Cincinnati would soon assume national leadership in cultural matters, as it already had in the processing of pork bellies.

Even smaller cities like Portland, Providence, Hartford, Albany, and Pittsburgh had literary and natural history societies and were regular stops on the lyceum circuit. All in all, American cities had a vitality and diversity that foreign visitors both celebrated and decried. Life in the towns was by some standards crude; many of the people were pushy, crass, and dedicated to the accumulation of wealth. But on this last count, the English novelist Charles Dickens offered some international perspective. "The golden calf they worship," he wrote of Americans in 1841, "is a pigmy compared with the giant effigies set up in other parts of that vast counting-house which lies beyond the Atlantic; and the almighty dollar sinks into something comparatively insignificant amidst a whole Pantheon of better gods."

AMERICAN HUMOR

The clash between the desire of a few for a "high" culture and the simpler tastes of the majority led James Fenimore Cooper to conclude that Americans would be forever "wanting in most of the high tastes,

Vol. 2.]   "GO AHEAD!!"   [No. 3.

THE CROCKETT ALMANAC 1841.

Tussel with a Bear. See page 9.

Containing Adventures, Exploits, Sprees & Scrapes in the West, & Life and Manners in the Backwoods.

Nashville, Tennessee. Published by Ben Harding.

▲ *The Crockett Almanacs* were the precursors to modern comic books. These illustrated books included tall-tales of hard-drinking, hard-fighting, and loose-loving heroes. In *Beneath the American Renaissance* (1988), David S. Reynolds argues that the major literary figures of the day derived themes and ideas from such raucous and subversive elements of antebellum culture.

DOCUMENT

James Fenimore Cooper *Notions of America*

pretensions of colonial sophisticates and the ways of common folk to good comic effect. But the possibilities of this kind of humor were greatly enlarged in the Jacksonian era. Where else was there a country theoretically based on equality whose inhabitants were so strikingly varied?

One of the first to exploit the comic aspects of Jackson was Seba Smith, a newspaperman from Portland, Maine. Smith's fictional creation, Major Jack Downing, was a Jackson man from a part of the country suspicious of both the general's politics and intelligence. Smith had Downing accompany the president on his tour of New England, which included, among other adventures, an appearance at Harvard to receive an honorary degree. In the presence of so many learned gentlemen with political views contrary to his own, Downing advised the president "jest to say nothing, but look as knowing as any of them." Which was what Jackson did, even when faced by snickering "sassy students." "The General stood it out like a hero," the major assured readers, "and got through very well."

Life in the Old Southwest provided chroniclers with more than enough violence to capture the attention of their "gentle readers." Violence figures prominently in Augustus Baldwin Longstreet's story "The Fight," in which one Ransy Sniffle, "who, in his earlier days, had fed copiously upon red clay and blackberries," promoted a wrestling match between two toughs, Bill and Bob. After provoking both to do battle, Ransy sat back to enjoy the slaughter. And slaughter it was. Bob, the victor, "entirely lost his left ear and a large piece of his left cheek." As for Bill, he

> presented a hideous spectacle. About a third of his nose, at the lower extremity, was bit off, and his face so swelled and bruised that it was difficult to discover anything of the human visage, much more the fine features which he carried into the fight.

and consequently in the high enjoyments." But other writers were not so sure, and some, rather than despair over the cultural incongruities, found in them a rich source of humor.

They were hardly the first to do so. The comic potential in juxtaposing high ideals and low reality had been exploited by the Greek playwright Aristophanes; by Rabelais, the creator of *Gargantua;* and by Cervantes in *The Adventures of Don Quixote*—all, incidentally, works available in mid-century America. William Byrd and Benjamin Franklin had both used the differences between the

During the 1830s and 1840s, the Davy Crockett Almanacs provided outrageous and ribald tales about frontier life; because they also included humorous pictures, they were akin to modern comic books. An 1837 Crockett story told about a sixteen-year-old girl who on her wedding night "sucked forty rattlesnake eggs, just to give her a sweet breath." Once when she was fighting wildcats, they "scratched her backside so tarnaciously its never itched since." In a new country, it made sense not to take oneself too seriously. While the outcome of the nation's experiment in combining democracy and cultural aspiration remained in doubt, most Americans took their laughs where they could find them.

MILESTONES

1830s–1850s	Hudson River School is first coherent American school of art	1845	Edgar Allan Poe publishes "The Raven"
1830s–1860s	Machine-made decorations adorn American Gothic architecture	1845–1846	Henry David Thoreau lives alone at Walden Pond
1834	George Bancroft publishes 10-volume *History of the United States*	1846	Smithsonian Institution opens for research
1834–1836	Thomas Cole paints allegorical *The Course of Empire*	1850	Nathaniel Hawthorne publishes *The Scarlet Letter*
1835	James Gordon Bennett founds *New York Herald*	1851	Herman Melville publishes *Moby Dick*
1836	John Lowell endows Lowell Institute, free public lectures		Francis Parkman publishes *The Conspiracy of Pontiac*
1837	Ralph Waldo Emerson delivers "The American Scholar" at Harvard	1854	Henry David Thoreau attacks conformity in *Walden*
	Oberlin enrolls 4 female students	1855–1892	Walt Whitman publishes *Leaves of Grass* (various editions)
	Horace Mann and Henry Barnard call for common schools	1857	*Atlantic Monthly* is founded
1839	American Art-Union is formed to encourage native art	1858	Frederick Law Olmsted and Calvert Vaux win New York Central Park competition
1842–1843	Herman Melville lives in Tahiti and other South Pacific islands	1859	Cooper Institute offers free courses to workers
1843	Hiram Powers sculpts *The Greek Slave*	1850s–1907	Currier & Ives prints reach wide audience

SUPPLEMENTARY READING

Useful surveys of cultural and intellectual currents in this period are Daniel Boorstin, *The Americans: The National Experience* (1967), and Rush Welter, *The Mind of America, 1820–1860* (1975). See also Richard Hofstadter, *Anti-intellectualism in American Life* (1963), and Stow Persons, *The Decline of American Gentility* (1975), for a more critical assessment.

For Emerson and Thoreau, see the biographies by Robert D. Richardson, *Emerson: The Mind on Fire* (1995), and *Henry Thoreau: The Life of the Mind* (1986). For Poe, the biography by Kenneth Silverman (1991) is excellent. David S. Reynold's *Walt Whitman's America* (1995) examines the poet's relation to other trends in American life. See also Hershel Parker, *Herman Melville: 1819–1851* (1996) and *Herman Melville: 1851–1891* (2002).

On the cultural life of the South, see Bertram Wyatt-Brown, *Hearts of Darkness* (2003), and Drew Faust, *A Sacred Circle* (1977).

On education, in addition to works cited in the previous chapter, see Lawrence A. Cremin, *American Education: The National Experience* (1980), and C. F. Kaestle, *Pillars of the Republic* (1983). Jill Lepore, *A Is For American* (2002) is also useful.

Neil Harris, *The Artist in American Society* (1966), puts art in its social setting. See also Barbara Novak, *Nature and Culture: American Landscape Painting* (1980).

Scholars have recently been interested in the proliferation of unconventional popular ideas during these years. See David S. Reynolds, *Beneath the American Renaissance* (1988), and John M. Brooke, *The Refiner's Fire* (1994). In *Carnival on the Page: Popular Print Media in Antebellum America* (2000), Isabelle Lehuu argues that a rowdy and "subversive" popular press was another manifestation of this subversive culture.

SUGGESTED WEBSITES

America's First Look into the Camera: Daguerreotype Portraits and Views, 1839–1862
http://memory.loc.gov/ammem/daghtml/daghome.html
The Library of Congress's daguerreotype collection consists of more than 650 photographs from the 1839–1864 period. Portraits, architectural views, and some street scenes make up most of the collection.

The Era of the Mountain Men
http://www.xmission.com/~drudy/amm.html
Private letters help students of the past learn about the concerns and environment of the writers and recipients. This site has correspondence from early settlers in the area west of the Mississippi River.

Edgar Allan Poe
http://www.eapoe.org/index.html
The Edgar Allan Poe Society of Baltimore provides the original works, history, criticism, images, and more about the writer.

Eastern State Penitentiary Official Homepage
http://www.easternstate.com/index.html
This is the official Website for America's most historic prison; the model for 300 prisons worldwide. Eastern State Penitentiary is now open to the public as an historic site.

CHAPTER 12

Westward Expansion

▼ In *American Progress* (1872), John Gast depicts a feminized (and eroticized!) America moving westward, a school book in one hand and telegraph wire in the other. Confronted with the onslaught of "civilization," the buffalo flee and the Indians cringe.

John Tyler, who became president after the death of William Henry Harrison, was a thin, rather delicate-appearing man with pale blue eyes and a long nose. Courteous, tactful, soft-spoken, he gave the impression of being weak, an impression reinforced by his professed belief that the president should defer to Congress in the formulation of policy. This was a false impression; John Tyler was stubborn and proud, and these characteristics combined with an almost total lack of imagination to make him worship consistency, as so many second-raters do. He had turned away from Jackson because of the aggressive way the president had used his powers of appointment and the veto, but he also disagreed with Henry Clay and the northern Whigs about the Bank, protection, and federal internal improvements. Being a states' rights Southerner, he considered such measures unconstitutional. Nevertheless, he was prepared to cooperate with Clay as the leader of what he called the "more immediate representatives" of the people, the members of Congress. But he was not prepared to be Clay's puppet. He asked all of Harrison's Cabinet to remain in office.

TYLER'S TROUBLES

Tyler and Clay did not get along, and for this Clay was chiefly to blame. He behaved in an overbearing manner that was out of keeping with his nature, probably because he resented having been passed over by the

▲ John Tyler posed for a daguerreotypist about 1850, after he had retired from public life. Never fully committed to the cause of the party that put him in power, he proved to be an ineffective president.

Whigs in 1840. (When news of Harrison's nomination reached him in Washington, he was half drunk. His face darkened. "I am the most unfortunate man in the history of parties," he said, "always run . . . when sure to be defeated, and now betrayed for a nomination when I, or anyone, would be sure of an election.") He considered himself the real head of the Whig party and intended to exercise his leadership.

In Congress, Clay announced a comprehensive program that ignored Tyler's states' rights view of the Constitution. Most important was his plan to set up a new Bank of the United States. A bill to repeal the Independent Treasury Act caused no difficulty, but when Congress passed a new Bank bill, Tyler vetoed it. The entire Cabinet except Secretary of State Daniel Webster thereupon resigned in protest.

Abandoned by the Whigs, Tyler attempted to build a party of his own. He failed to do so, and for the remainder of his term the political squabbling in Washington was continuous. Clay wanted to distribute the proceeds from land sales to the states, presumably to bolster their sagging finances but actually to reduce federal revenues in order to justify raising the tariff. To win western votes for distribution, he

agreed to support the Preemption Act of 1841 legalizing the right of squatters to occupy unsurveyed land and to buy it later at $1.25 an acre without bidding for it at auction. However, the Southerners insisted on an amendment pledging that distribution would be stopped if the tariff were raised above the 20 percent level, and when the Whigs blithely tried to push a high tariff through Congress without repealing the Distribution Act, Tyler vetoed the bill. Finally, the Distribution Act was repealed and Tyler signed the new Tariff Act of 1842, raising duties to about the levels of 1832.

THE WEBSTER-ASHBURTON TREATY

Webster's decision to remain in the Cabinet was motivated in part by his desire to settle the boundary between Maine and New Brunswick. The intent of the peace treaty of 1783 had been to award the United States all land in the area drained by rivers flowing into the Atlantic rather than into the St. Lawrence, but the wording was obscure and the old maps conflicting. In 1842 the British sent a new minister, Lord Ashburton, to the United States to try to settle all outstanding disputes. Ashburton and Webster easily worked out a compromise boundary. The British needed only a small part of the territory to build a military road connecting Halifax and Quebec. Webster, who thought any settlement desirable simply to eliminate a possible cause of war, willingly agreed.

The problem of placating Maine and Massachusetts, which wanted every acre of the land in dispute, Webster solved in an extraordinary manner. It was known that during the peace negotiations ending the Revolution, Franklin had marked the boundary between Maine and Canada on a map with a heavy red line, but no one could find the Franklin map. Webster obtained an old map of the area and had someone mark off in red a line that followed the British version of the boundary. He showed this document to representatives of Maine and Massachusetts, convincing them that they had better agree to his compromise before the British got wind of it and demanded the whole region! It later came out that the British had a true copy of the Franklin map, which showed that the entire area rightfully belonged to the United States.

Nevertheless, Webster's generosity made excellent sense. Lord Ashburton, gratified by having obtained the strategic territory, made concessions elsewhere along the Canadian and American border. British dependence on foreign foodstuffs was increasing; America's need for British capital was rising. War, or even unsettled affairs, would have injured vital business relations and produced no compensating gains.

THE TEXAS QUESTION

The settlement with Great Britain won support in every section of the United States, but the same could not be said for Tyler's attempt to annex the Republic of Texas, for this involved the question of slavery. In the Transcontinental Treaty of 1819 with Spain, the boundary of the United States had been drawn in such a way as to exclude Texas. This seemed unimportant at the time, yet within months of the treaty's ratification in February 1821, Americans led by Stephen F. Austin had begun to settle in the area. Almost simultaneously Mexico threw off the last vestiges of Spanish rule.

Cotton flourished on the fertile Texas plains, and for a time, the new Mexican authorities offered free land and something approaching local autonomy to groups of settlers from the United States. By 1830 there were some 20,000 white Americans in Texas, about 2000 slaves, and only a few thousand Mexicans.

President John Quincy Adams had offered Mexico $1 million for Texas, and Jackson was willing to pay $5 million, but Mexico would not sell. Nevertheless, by the late 1820s, the flood of American settlers was giving the Mexican authorities second thoughts. The immigrants apparently felt no loyalty to Mexico. Most were Protestants, though Mexican law required that all immigrants be Catholics; few attempted to learn more than a few words of Spanish. When Mexico outlawed slavery in 1829, American settlers evaded the law by "freeing" their slaves and then signing them to lifetime contracts as indentured servants. In 1830 Mexico prohibited further immigration of Americans into Texas, though again the law proved impossible to enforce.

As soon as the Mexican government began to restrict them, the Texans began to seek independence. In 1835 a series of skirmishes escalated into a full-scale rebellion. The Mexican president, Antonio López de Santa Anna, marched north with

▲ *The Fall of the Alamo*, by Robert Onderdonk, commemorating one of the legends of Texan—and American—history. Though valuable for propaganda purposes, the heroic defense of the Alamo was a military debacle. On learning that the entire force had been wiped out, Sam Houston, commander of the Texans, railed against his commanders at the Alamo for allowing their men to be "forted up" and destroyed.

6000 soldiers to subdue the rebels. Late in February 1836 he reached San Antonio.

DOCUMENT

Travis, *Letter from the Alamo*

A force of 187 men under Colonel William B. Travis held the city. They took refuge behind the stout walls of a former mission called the Alamo. For ten days they beat off Santa Anna's assaults, inflicting terrible casualties on the attackers. Finally, on March 6, the Mexicans breached and scaled the walls. Once inside they killed everyone, even the wounded. Among the dead were the legendary Davy Crockett and Jim Bowie, inventor of the Bowie knife.

After the Alamo and a similar slaughter at another garrison at Goliad, southeast of San Antonio, peaceful settlement of the dispute between Texas and Mexico was impossible. Meanwhile, on March 2, 1836, Texas had declared its independence. Sam Houston, a former congressman and governor of Tennessee and an experienced Indian fighter, was placed in charge of the rebel army. For a time Houston retreated before Santa Anna's troops, who greatly outnumbered his own. At the San Jacinto

▲ This portrait, Davy Crockett's favorite of himself, emphasizes his refinement. It is at odds with the rough-hewn, bawdy frontiersman of Crockett lore, spread especially through dime novels read mostly by middle-class boys.

River he took a stand. On April 21, 1836, shouting "Forward! Charge! Remember the Alamo! Remember Goliad!" his troops routed the Mexican army, which soon retreated across the Rio Grande. In October, Houston was elected president of the Republic of Texas, and a month later a plebiscite revealed that an overwhelming majority favored annexation by the United States.

President Jackson hesitated. To take Texas might lead to war with Mexico. Assuredly it would stir up the slavery controversy. On his last day in office he recognized the republic, but he made no move to accept it into the Union, nor did his successor, Van Buren. Texas thereupon went its own way, which involved developing friendly ties with Great Britain. An independent Texas suited British tastes perfectly, for it could provide an alternative supply of raw cotton and a market for manufactures unfettered by tariffs.

These events caused alarm in the United States, especially among Southerners, who dreaded the possibility that a Texas dominated by Great Britain might abolish slavery. As a Southerner, Tyler shared these feelings; as a beleaguered politician, spurned by the Whigs and held in contempt by most Democrats, he saw in annexation a chance to revive his fortunes. When Webster resigned as secretary of state in 1843, Tyler replaced him with a fellow Virginian, Abel P. Upshur, whom he ordered to seek a treaty of annexation. The South was eager to take Texas, and in the West and even the Northeast the patriotic urge to add such a magnificent new territory to the national domain was great. Counting noses, Upshur convinced himself that the Senate would approve annexation by the necessary two-thirds majority. He negotiated a treaty in February 1844, but before he could sign it he was killed by the accidental explosion of a cannon on USS *Princeton* during a weapons demonstration.

To ensure the winning of Texas, Tyler appointed John C. Calhoun secretary of state. This was a blunder; by then Calhoun was so closely associated with the South and with slavery that his appointment alienated thousands of Northerners who might otherwise have welcomed annexation. Suddenly Texas became a hot political issue. Clay and Van Buren, who seemed assured of the 1844 Whig and Democratic presidential nominations, promptly announced that they opposed annexation, chiefly on the ground that it would probably lead to war with Mexico. With a national election in the offing, northern and western senators refused to vote for annexation, and in June the Senate rejected the treaty, 35 to 16. The Texans were angry and embarrassed, the British eager again to take advantage of the situation.

MANIFEST DESTINY

The Senate, Clay, and Van Buren had all misinterpreted public opinion. John C. Calhoun, whose world was so far removed from that of the average citizen, in this case came much closer to comprehending the mood of the country than any of its other leaders.

For two centuries Americans had been gradually conquering a continent. The first colonists had envisaged a domain extending from the Atlantic to the Pacific, although they had not realized the immensity of the New World. By the time their descendants came to appreciate its size, they had been chastened by the experience of battling the Indians for possession of the land and then laboriously developing it. The Revolution and its aftermath of nationalism greatly stimulated expansion, and then, before the riches of trans-Appalachia had even been inventoried, Jefferson had stunned the country with the purchase of Louisiana, an area so large that the mere thought of it left Americans giddy.

The westward march from the seventeenth century to the 1840s had seemed fraught with peril, the prize golden but attainable only through patient labor and fearful hardships. Wild animals and wild men, mighty forests and mighty foreign powers beset the path. John Adams wrote of "conquering" the West "from the trees and rocks and wild beasts." He was "enflamed" by the possibilities of "that vast scene which is opening in the West," but to win it the United States would have to "march *intrepidly* on."

Quite rapidly (as historians measure time) the atmosphere changed. Each year of national growth increased the power and confidence of the people, and every forward step revealed a wider horizon. Now the West seemed a ripe apple, to be picked almost casually. Where pioneers had once stood in awe before the majesty of the Blue Ridge, then hesitated to venture from the protective shadows of the forest into the open prairies of Illinois, they now shrugged their shoulders at great deserts and began to talk of the Rocky Mountains as "mere molehills" along the road to the Pacific. After 200 years of westward expansion had brought them as far as Missouri and Iowa, Americans perceived their destined goal. *The whole continent was to be theirs!* Theirs to exploit, and theirs to make into one mighty nation, a land of opportunity, a showcase to display the virtues of democratic institutions, living proof that Americans were indeed God's chosen people. A New York journalist, John L. O'Sullivan, captured the new mood in a sentence. Nothing must interfere, he wrote in 1845, with "the fulfillment of our *manifest destiny* to overspread the continent allotted by Providence for the free development of our yearly multiplying millions."

The expansion, stimulated by the natural growth of the population and by a revived flood of immigration, was going on in every section and with little regard for political boundaries. New settlers rolled westward in hordes. Between 1830 and 1835, some 10,000 entered "foreign" Texas, and this was a trickle compared to what the early 1840s were to bring. The politicians did not sense the new mood in 1844; even Calhoun, who saw the acquisition of Texas as part of a broader program, was thinking of balancing sectional interests rather than of national expansion.

LIFE ON THE TRAIL

The romantic myths attached by later generations to this mighty human tide have obscured the adjustments forced on the pioneers and focused attention on the least significant of the dangers they faced and the hardships they endured. For example, Indians could of course be deadly enemies, but pioneers were more likely to complain that the Indians they encountered were dirty, lazy, and pitiably poor than to worry about the danger of Indian attack. Women tended to fear their strangeness, not their actual behavior. One reported that Indian men were commonly "guiltless of clothing."

The greater dangers were accidents on the trail, particularly to children, and also unsanitary conditions and exposure to the elements. "Going west" had always been laborious, but in the 1840s the distances covered were longer by far and the comforts and conveniences of "civilization" that had to be left behind, being more extensive than those available to earlier generations, tended to be more painful to surrender.

Travel on the plains west of the Mississippi was especially taxing for women. Some assumed tasks traditionally performed by men. "I keep close to my gun and dog," a woman from Illinois wrote in her diary. But most found the experience disillusioning. Guidebooks promised them that "regular exercise, in the open air . . . gives additional vigor and strength." But the books did not prepare women for having to collect dried buffalo dung for fuel, for the heat and choking dust of summer, for enduring a week of steady rain, for the monotony, the dirt, the cramped quarters. Caring for an infant or a two-year-old in a wagon could be torture week after week on the trail.

In their letters and journals pioneer women mostly complained of being bone weary. "It is impossible to keep anything clean," one recorded, and it is not hard to envisage the difficulty of doing so while

DOCUMENT

Geer, Oregon Trail Journal

▶ *text continues on page 324*

Mapping
the Past

Fertility and the Frontier

In 1798 English philosopher Thomas Malthus remarked that the sudden population increase in the United States was "probably without parallel in history." This he attributed to the "extreme cheapness of good land." He reasoned that while the cost of farmland in Europe obliged couples in Europe to marry late and curb sexual desires, frontier couples in the United States, who needed more hands to farm its vast open spaces, married earlier and had many children.

The census of 1800 provided some statistical foundation for Malthus's assertions. It showed that the average white

▲ John Kleeb and his wife are posed with their seven children in Custer County, Nebraska (1880s); all of the children are young; more siblings likely followed. On the frontier, where labor was scarce, even young children could soon earn their keep.

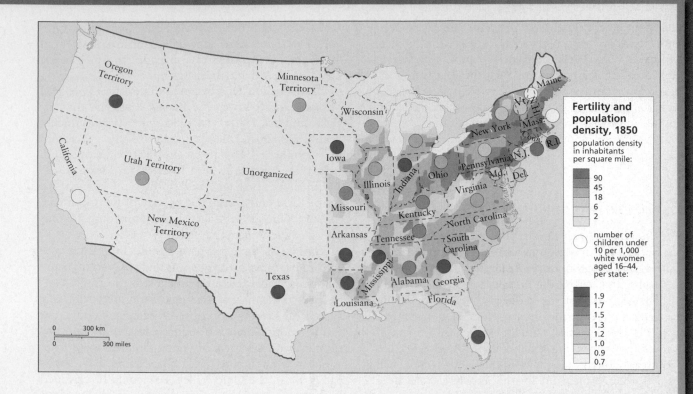

Fertility and population density, 1850

population density in inhabitants per square mile:

- 90
- 45
- 18
- 6
- 2

number of children under 10 per 1,000 white women aged 16–44, per state:

- 1.9
- 1.7
- 1.5
- 1.3
- 1.2
- 1.0
- 0.9
- 0.7

woman had many children—on the average, seven. Moreover, census data confirmed that in the frontier regions, where cheap land was most plentiful, women had more children than their counterparts in the more congested East. This geographic gradient—high fertility in the western states, low in New England and the Northeast—persisted during the nineteenth century.

The map "Fertility and Population Density, 1850" *(above)* shows that white women in the most densely populated states, especially New England, had the lowest fertility levels while those in the western states had the highest fertility levels. For example, women between the ages of 16 and 44 in New England had, on the average, fewer than one child under the age of 10; conversely, women in the Oregon Territory, as well as Texas, Louisiana, Arkansas, Iowa, Indiana, Mississippi, Georgia, and Florida had twice as many (2.15) young children as their New England counterparts. (Comparable data are unavailable for African American mothers.)

While this map seems to confirm a direct relationship between frontier life and fertility, a closer examination of the census data suggests the salience of other factors, too. For example, Missouri and Wisconsin were sparsely settled, and yet their fertility rates were lower than Indiana, which was relatively well developed.

Historians have observed that in the late eighteenth and early nineteenth centuries an ideology of domesticity confined women to the home even as it enshrined their role as custodians of the young. Mothers intent on guiding each child's moral development, and fathers intent on saving enough money to establish a foothold in the emerging middle class,

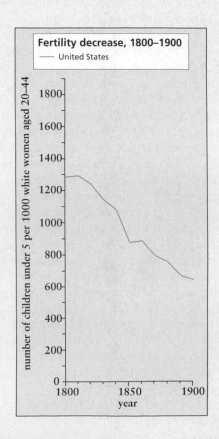

Fertility decrease, 1800–1900
— United States

y-axis: number of children under 5 per 1000 white women aged 20–44

x-axis: year

together decided to limit their families by marrying later, by abstaining from sexual relations for long periods, and perhaps by practicing contraception.

living for weeks on end on the trail. "Felt very tired indeed—went to bed early," was the typical woman's diary entry. "Oh dear," another wrote in her journal, "I do so want to get there, it is now almost four months since we have slept in a house." What sort of a house a pioneer family would actually sleep in when they reached their destination is a question this woman did not record, which was probably fortunate for her peace of mind.

CALIFORNIA AND OREGON

By 1840 many Americans had settled far to the west in California, which was unmistakably Mexican territory, and in the Oregon country, jointly claimed by the United States and Great Britain; and it was to these distant regions that the pioneers were going in increasing numbers as the decade progressed. California was a sparsely settled land of some 7000 Spanish-speaking ranchers and a handful of "Anglo" settlers from the United States. Until the 1830s, when their estates were broken up by the anticlerical Mexican government, 21 Catholic missions, stretching north from San Diego to San Francisco, controlled more than 30,000 Indian converts, who were little better off than slaves. Richard Henry Dana, a Harvard College student, sailed around South America to California as an ordinary seaman on the brig *Pilgrim* in 1834. His account of that voyage in *Two Years Before the Mast* (1840) contains a fine description of what life was like in the region: "There is no working class (the Indians being practically serfs and doing all the hard work) and every rich man looks like a grandee, and every poor scamp like a broken-down gentleman."

Oregon, a vaguely defined area between California and Russian Alaska, proved still more alluring to Americans. Captain Robert Gray had sailed up the Columbia River in 1792, and Lewis and Clark had visited the region on their great expedition. In 1811 John Jacob Astor's Pacific Fur Company had established trading posts on the Columbia. Two decades later Methodist, Presbyterian, and Catholic missionaries began to find their way into the Willamette Valley, a green land of rich soil, mild climate, and tall forests teeming with game. Gradually a small number of settlers followed, until by 1840 there were about 500 Americans in the Willamette area.

In the early 1840s, fired by the spirit of manifest destiny, the country suddenly burned with "Oregon fever." In dozens upon dozens of towns, societies were founded to collect information and organize groups to make the march to the Pacific. Land hunger (stimulated by glowing reports from the scene) drew the new migrants most powerfully, but the patriotic concept of manifest destiny gave the trek

across the 2000 miles of wilderness separating Oregon from the western edge of American settlement in Missouri the character of a crusade. In 1843 nearly 1000 pioneers made the long trip.

The Oregon Trail began at the western border of Missouri and followed the Kansas River and the perverse, muddy Platte ("a mile wide and six inches deep") past Fort Laramie to the Rockies. It crossed the Continental Divide by the relatively easy South Pass, veered south to Fort Bridger, on Mexican soil, and then ran north and west through the valley of the Snake River and eventually, by way of the Columbia, to Fort Vancouver, a British post guarding the entrance to the Willamette Valley.

Over this tortuous path wound the canvas-covered caravans with their scouts and their accompanying herds. Each group became a self-governing community on the march, with regulations democratically agreed on "for the purpose of keeping good order and promoting civil and military discipline." Most of the travelers consisted of young families, some from as far away as the east coast cities, more from towns and farms in the Ohio Valley. Few could be classified as poor because the cost of the trip for a family of four was about $600, no small sum at that time. (The faster and less fatiguing trip by ship around South America cost about $600 per person.)

For large groups Indians posed no great threat (though constant vigilance was necessary), but the five-month trip was full of labor, discomfort, and uncertainty. "It became so monotonous after a while that I would have welcomed an Indian fight if awake," one man wrote. And at the end lay the regular tasks of pioneering. The spirit of the trailblazers is caught in an entry from the diary of James Nesmith:

Friday, October 27.—Arrived at Oregon City at the falls of the Willamette.
Saturday, October 28.—Went to work.

Although many women had doubts about their austere new world—"Nothing can atone for the loss of society of friends," one wrote—others took satisfaction. Another homesteader wrote that "any woman who can stand her own company, can see the beauty of the sunset, loves growing things, and is willing to put in as much time at careful labor as she does over the washtub, will certainly succeed, will have independence, plenty to eat all the time, and a home of her own in the end."

Behind the dreams of the Far West as an American Eden lay the commercial importance of the three major west coast harbors: San Diego, San Francisco, and the Strait of Juan de Fuca leading into Puget Sound. Eastern merchants considered these harbors the keys to the trade of the Orient. That San Diego

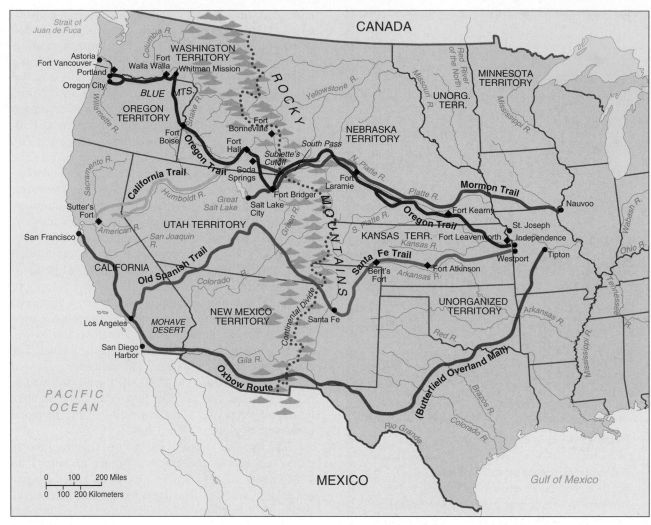

▲ **Trails West**
The Old Spanish Trail was the earliest of the trails west. Part of it was mapped in 1776 by a Franciscan missionary. The Santa Fe Trail came into use after 1823. The Oregon Trail was pioneered by trappers and missionaries. The Mormon Trail was first traversed in 1847, while the Oxbow Route, developed under a federal mail contract, was used from 1858 to 1861.

and San Francisco were Mexican and the Puget Sound district was claimed by Great Britain only heightened their desire to possess them. As early as 1835, Jackson tried to buy the San Francisco region. Even Calhoun called San Francisco the future New York of the Pacific and proposed buying all of California from Mexico.

THE ELECTION OF 1844

In the spring of 1844 expansion did not seem likely to affect the presidential election. The Whigs nominated Clay unanimously and ignored Texas in their party platform. When the Democrats gathered in convention at Baltimore in May, Van Buren appeared to have the nomination in his pocket. He too wanted to keep

Texas out of the campaign. John C. Calhoun, however, was determined to make Texas a campaign issue.

That a politician of Van Buren's caliber, controlling the party machinery, could be upset at a national convention seemed unthinkable. But upset he was, for the southern delegates rallied round the Calhoun policy of taking Texas to save it for slavery. "I can beat Clay and Van Buren put together on this issue," Calhoun boasted. "They are behind the age." With the aid of a few northern expansionists the Southerners forced through a rule requiring that a candidate must be approved by a two-thirds majority. Van Buren could not muster that much support. After a brief deadlock, a "dark horse," James K. Polk of Tennessee, swept the convention.

Polk was a good Jacksonian; his supporters called him "Young Hickory." He opposed high tariffs and

DEBATING THE PAST

Did the frontier change women's roles? Ada McColl here gathers buffalo chips to be burned for fuel. Women were missing from Frederick Jackson Turner's famous argument (1893) on the centrality of the frontier to American history. Subsequent scholars provided some anecdotal accounts of women on the frontier, but it was not until the 1970s that scholars flocked to the subject. John Mack Faragher (1979) concluded that women on the overland trail had not experienced feminist liberation but had instead been exploited. Women worked ceaselessly—preparing meals, caring for children, cleaning clothes—in nearly impossible conditions. That same year Julie Roy Jeffrey added that husbands still made the "major decisions." Equally important, frontier women themselves endorsed the "cult of true womanhood": They sought to civilize the frontier. Sandra L. Myres (1982), on the other hand, argued that while frontier women accepted traditional women's roles, they also sought to "enlarge the scope of women's place" and in so doing undermined traditions.

Frederick Jackson Turner, "The Significance of the Frontier in American History" (1893), John Mack Faragher, *Women and Men on the Overland Trail* (1979), Julie Roy Jeffrey, *Frontier Women* (1979), Sandra L. Myres, *Westering Women and the Frontier Experience* (1982).

was dead set against establishing another national bank. But he believed in taking Texas, and he favored expansion generally. To mollify Van Buren's supporters, the convention nominated Senator Silas Wright of New York for vice president, but Wright was Van Buren's friend and equally opposed to annexation. When the word was flashed to him in Washington over the new "magnetic telegraph" that Samuel F. B. Morse had just installed between the convention hall in Baltimore and the Capitol, he refused to run. The delegates then picked George M. Dallas of Pennsylvania, who favored annexation of Texas. The Democratic platform demanded that Texas be "reannexed" (implying that it had been part of the Louisiana Purchase) and that all of Oregon be "reoccupied" (suggesting that the joint occupation of the region with Great Britain, which had been agreed to in the Convention of 1818, be abrogated).

Texas was now in the campaign. When Clay sensed the new expansionist sentiment of the voters, he tried to hedge on his opposition to annexation, but by doing so he probably lost as many votes as he gained. The election was extremely close. The campaign followed the pattern established in 1840, with stress on parades, mass meetings, and slogans. Polk carried the country by only 38,000 of 2.7 million votes. In the Electoral College the vote was 170 to 105.

The decisive factor in the contest was the Liberty party, an antislavery splinter group organized in 1840. Only 62,000 voters supported Liberty party candidate James G. Birney, a "reformed" Kentucky slaveholder, but nearly 16,000 of them lived in New York, most in the western part of the state, a Whig stronghold. Since Polk carried New York by barely 5000 votes, the votes cast for Birney probably cost Clay the state. Had Clay won New York's 36 electoral votes, he would have been elected with 141 electoral votes to Polk's 134.

Polk's victory was nevertheless taken as a mandate for expansion. Tyler promptly called on Congress to take Texas by joint resolution, which would avoid the necessity of obtaining a two-thirds majority in the Senate. This was done a few days before Tyler left the White House. Under the resolution, if the new state agreed, as many as four new states might be carved from its territory. Polk accepted this arrangement, and in December 1845 Texas became a state.

POLK AS PRESIDENT

President Polk, a slightly built, erect man with grave, steel-gray eyes, was approaching 50 years of age. His mind was not of the first order, for he was too tense and calculating to allow his intellect free rein, but he

was an efficient, hard worker with a strong will and a tough skin, qualities that stood him in good stead in the White House, and he made politics his whole life. It was typical of the man that he developed a special technique of handshaking in order better to cope with the interminable reception lines that every leader has to endure. "When I observed a strong man approaching," he once explained, "I generally took advantage of him by . . . seizing him by the tip of his fingers, giving him a hearty shake, and thus preventing him from getting a full grip upon me." In four years in office he was away from his desk in Washington for a total of only six weeks.

Polk was uncommonly successful in doing what he set out to do as president. He persuaded Congress to lower the tariff of 1842 and to restore the independent treasury. He opposed federal internal improvements and managed to have his way. He made himself the spokesman of American expansion by committing himself to obtaining, in addition to Texas, both Oregon and the great Southwest. Here again, he succeeded.

DOCUMENT

John O'Sullivan, "Annexation"

Oregon was the first order of business. In his inaugural address Polk stated the American claim to the entire region in the plainest terms, but he informed the British minister in Washington, Richard Pakenham, that he would accept a boundary following the 49th parallel to the Pacific. Pakenham rejected this proposal without submitting it to London, and Polk thereupon decided to insist again on the whole area. When Congress met in December 1845, he asked for authority to give the necessary one year's notice for abrogating the 1818 treaty of joint occupation. "The only way to treat John Bull," he told one congressman, "was to look him straight in the eye." Following considerable discussion, Congress complied and in May 1846 Polk notified Great Britain that he intended to terminate the joint occupation.

The British then decided to compromise. Officials of the Hudson's Bay Company had become alarmed by the rapid growth of the American settlement in the Willamette Valley. By 1845 there were some 5000 people there, whereas the country north of the Columbia contained no more than 750 British subjects. A clash between the groups could have but one result. The company decided to shift its base from the Columbia to Vancouver Island. And British experts outside the company reported that the Oregon country could not possibly be defended in case of war. Thus, when Polk accompanied the one-year notice with a hint that he would again consider a compromise, the British foreign secretary, Lord Aberdeen, hastily suggested Polk's earlier proposal, dividing the Oregon territory along the 49th parallel. Polk, abandoning his belligerent attitude, agreed.

▲ "This Is the House That Polk Built" is the title of this 1846 cartoon directed against the president. Polk hatches his eggs and schemes for territorial expansion, reduction of the tariff, and fame—aims the cartoonist saw as flimsy as a house of cards. Contrary to the cartoonist's view, Polk succeeded in his expansion goals.

The treaty followed that line from the Rockies to Puget Sound, but Vancouver Island, which extends below the line, was left entirely to the British, so that both nations retained free use of the Strait of Juan de Fuca. Although some northern Democrats accused Polk of treachery because he had failed to fight for all of Oregon, the treaty so obviously accorded with the national interest that the Senate approved it by a large majority in June 1846. Polk was then free to take up the Texas question in earnest.

WAR WITH MEXICO

One reason for the popularity of the Oregon compromise was that the country was already at war with Mexico and wanted no trouble with Great Britain. The war had broken out in large measure because of the expansionist spirit, and the confidence born of its overwhelming advantages of size and wealth certainly encouraged the United States to bully Mexico. In addition, Mexico had defaulted on debts owed the United States, which caused some people to suggest using force to obtain the money. But Mexican pride was also involved. Texas had been independent for the better part of a decade, and Mexico had made no

▶ The War with
Mexico,
1846–1848

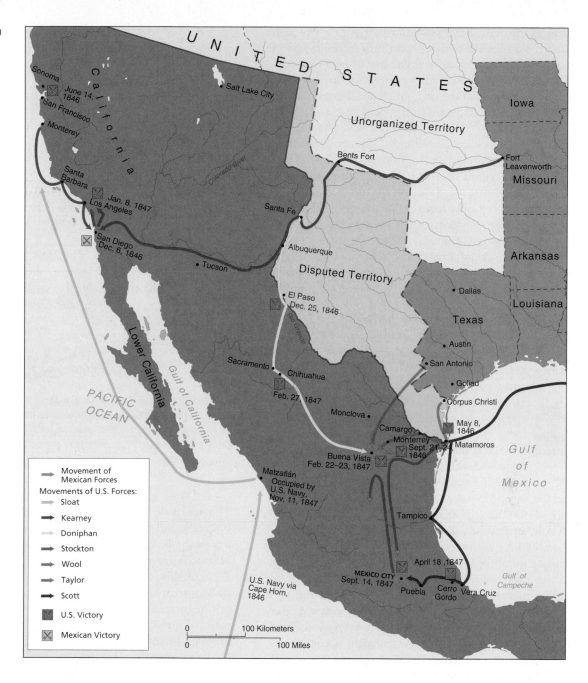

serious effort to reconquer it; nevertheless, Mexico never recognized its independence and promptly broke off diplomatic relations when the United States annexed the republic.

Polk then ordered General Zachary Taylor into Texas to defend the border. However, the location of that border was in dispute. Texas claimed the Rio Grande; Mexico insisted that the boundary was the Nueces River, which emptied into the Gulf of Mexico about 150 miles to the north. Taylor reached the Nueces in July 1845 with about 1500 troops and crossed into the disputed territory. He stopped on the southern bank at Corpus Christi, not wishing

to provoke the Mexicans by marching to the Rio Grande.

In November, Polk sent an envoy, John Slidell, on a secret mission to Mexico to try to obtain the disputed territory by negotiation. He authorized Slidell to cancel the Mexican debt in return for recognition of the annexation of Texas and acceptance of the Rio Grande boundary. The president also empowered Slidell to offer as much as $30 million if Mexico would sell the United States all or part of New Mexico and California.

It would probably have been to Mexico's advantage, at least in the short run, to have made a deal

with Slidell. The area Polk wanted, lying in the path of American expansion, was likely to be engulfed as Texas had been, without regard for the actions of the American or Mexican governments. But the Mexican government refused to receive Slidell. Amid a wave of anti-American feeling, a military coup occurred and General Mariano Paredes, the new head of state, promptly reaffirmed his country's claim to all of Texas. Slidell returned to Washington convinced that the Mexicans would not give an inch until they had been "chastised."

Polk had already ordered Taylor to advance to the Rio Grande. By late March 1846 the army, swelled to about 4000, had taken up positions near the Mexican town of Matamoros. The Mexicans crossed the river on April 25 and attacked an American mounted patrol. They were driven back easily, but when news of the fighting reached Washington, Polk asked Congress to declare war. He treated the matter as a *fait accompli:* "War exists," he stated flatly. Congress accepted this reasoning and without actually declaring war voted to raise and supply an additional 50,000 troops.

From the first battle, the outcome of the Mexican War was never in doubt. At Palo Alto, north of the Rio Grande, 2300 Americans scattered a Mexican force more than twice their number. Then, hotly pursuing, 1700 Americans routed 7500 Mexicans at Resaca de la Palma. Fewer than 50 United States soldiers lost their lives in these engagements, while Mexican losses in killed, wounded, and captured exceeded 1000. Within a week of the outbreak of hostilities, the Mexicans had been driven across the Rio Grande and General Taylor had his troops firmly established on the southern bank.

The Mexican army was poorly equipped and, despite a surfeit of high-ranking officers, poorly led. The well-supplied American forces had a hard core of youthful West Pointers eager to make their reputations and regulars trained in Indian warfare to provide the leadership needed to turn volunteer soldiers into first-rate fighting men. Yet Mexico was a large, rugged country with few decent roads; conquering it proved to be a formidable task.

TO THE HALLS OF MONTEZUMA

President Polk insisted not only on directing grand strategy (he displayed real ability as a military planner) but on supervising hundreds of petty details, down to the purchase of mules and the promotion of enlisted men. But he allowed party considerations to control his choice of generals. This partisanship caused unnecessary turmoil in army ranks. He wanted, as

Thomas Hart Benton said, "a small war, just large enough to require a treaty of peace, and not large enough to make military reputations dangerous for the presidency."

Unfortunately for Polk, both Taylor and Winfield Scott, the commanding general in Washington, were Whigs. Polk, who tended to suspect the motives of anyone who disagreed with him, feared that one or the other would make political capital of his popularity as a military leader. The examples of his hero, Jackson, and of General Harrison loomed large in Polk's thinking.

Polk's attitude was narrow, almost unpatriotic, but not unrealistic. Zachary Taylor was not a brilliant soldier. He had joined the army in 1808 and made it his whole life. He cared so little for politics that he had never bothered to cast a ballot in an election. Polk believed that he lacked the "grasp of mind" necessary for high command, and General Scott complained of his "comfortable, laborsaving contempt for learning of every kind." But Taylor commanded the love and respect of his men (they called him "Old Rough and Ready" and even "Zack"), and he knew how to deploy them in the field. He had won another victory against a Mexican force three times larger than his own at Buena Vista in February 1847.

The dust had barely settled on the field of Buena Vista when Whig politicians began to pay Taylor court. "Great expectations and great consequences rest upon you," a Kentucky politician explained to him. "People everywhere begin to talk of converting you into a political leader, when the War is done."

Polk's concern was heightened because domestic opposition to the war was growing. Many Northerners feared that the war would lead to the expansion of slavery. Others—among them an obscure Illinois congressman named Abraham Lincoln—felt that Polk

▲ This 1846 daguerreotype is the earliest known American war photograph. U.S. General John E. Wood poses with his staff in Saltillo, Mexico.

▲ The landing of Scott's army near Veracruz on March 9, 1847. Veracruz surrendered within several weeks. Scott then advanced to the interior and encountered the Mexican army, under Santa Anna, dug in along the National Road. Scott seized two hills and outflanked the Mexicans. Mexico City fell to Scott in September.

DOCUMENT

Thomas Corwin, "Against the Mexican War"

had misled Congress about the original outbreak of fighting and that the United States was the aggressor. The farther from the Rio Grande one went in the United States, the less popular "Mr. Polk's war" became; in New England opposition was almost as widespread as it had been to "Mr. Madison's war" in 1812.

Polk's design for prosecuting the war consisted of three parts. First, he would clear the Mexicans from Texas and occupy the northern provinces of Mexico. Second, he would take possession of California and New Mexico. Finally, he would march on Mexico City. Proceeding west from the Rio Grande, Taylor swiftly overran Mexico's northern provinces. In June 1846, American settlers in the Sacramento Valley seized Sonoma and raised the Bear Flag of the Republic of California. Another group, headed by Captain John C. Frémont, leader of an American exploring party that happened to be in the area, clashed with the Mexican authorities around Monterey,

California, and then joined with the Sonoma rebels. A naval squadron under Commodore John D. Sloat captured Monterey and San Francisco in July 1846, and a squadron of cavalry joined the other American units in mopping-up operations around San Diego and Los Angeles. By February 1847 the United States had won control of nearly all of Mexico north of the capital city.

The campaign against Mexico City was the most difficult of the war. Fearful of Taylor's growing popularity and entertaining certain honest misgivings about his ability to oversee a complicated campaign, Polk put Winfield Scott in charge of the offensive. He tried to persuade Congress to make Thomas Hart Benton a lieutenant general so as to have a Democrat in nominal control, but the Senate had the good sense to vote down this absurd proposal.

About Scott's competence no one entertained a doubt. But he seemed even more of a threat to the Democrats than Taylor, because he had political ambitions as well as military ability. In 1840 the Whigs

had considered running him for president. Scion of an old Virginia family, Scott was nearly 6½ feet tall; in uniform his presence was commanding. He was intelligent, even-tempered, and cultivated, if somewhat pompous. After a sound but not spectacular record in the War of 1812, he had added to his reputation by helping modernize military administration and strengthen the professional training of officers. The vast difference between the army of 1812 and that of 1846 was chiefly his doing. On the record, and despite the politics of the situation, Polk had little choice but to give him this command.

Scott landed his army south of Veracruz, Mexico, on March 9, 1847, laid siege to the city, and obtained its surrender in less than three weeks with the loss of only a handful of his 10,000 men. Marching westward through hostile country, he maintained effective discipline, avoiding atrocities that might have inflamed the countryside against him. Finding his way blocked by well-placed artillery and a large army at Cerro Gordo, where the National Road rose steeply toward the central highlands, Scott outflanked the Mexican position and then carried it by storm, capturing more than 3000 prisoners and much equipment. By mid-May he had advanced to Puebla, only 80 miles southeast of Mexico City.

After delaying until August for the arrival of reinforcements, he pressed on, won two hard-fought victories at the outskirts of the capital, and on September 14 hammered his way into the city. In every engagement the American troops had been outnumbered, yet they always exacted a far heavier toll from the defenders than they themselves were forced to pay. In the fighting on the edge of Mexico City, for example, Scott's army sustained about 1000 casualties, for the Mexicans defended their capital bravely. But 4000 Mexicans were killed or wounded in the engagements, and 3000 (including eight generals, two of them former presidents of the republic) were taken prisoner. No less an authority than the Duke of Wellington, the conqueror of Napoleon, called Scott's campaign the most brilliant of modern times.

THE TREATY OF GUADALUPE HIDALGO

The Mexicans were thoroughly beaten, but they refused to accept the situation. As soon as the news of the capture of Veracruz reached Washington, Polk sent Nicholas P. Trist, chief clerk of the State Department, to accompany Scott's army and to act as peace commissioner after the fall of Mexico City. Trist possessed impeccable credentials as a Democrat, for he had married a granddaughter of Thomas Jefferson and had served for a time as secretary to Andrew Jackson. Long residence as United States consul at Havana had given him an excellent command of Spanish.

Trist joined Scott at Veracruz in May. The two men took an instant dislike to each other. Scott considered it a "personal dishonor" to be asked to defer to what he considered a State Department flunky, and his feelings were not salved when Trist sent him an officious 30-page letter discoursing on the nature of his assignment. However, Scott was eager to end the war and realized that a petty quarrel with the president's emissary would not advance that objective. Trist fell ill, and Scott sent him a jar of guava marmalade; after that they became good friends.

Because of the confused state of affairs following the fall of Mexico City, Trist was unable to open negotiations with Mexican peace commissioners until January 1848. Polk, unable to understand the delay, became impatient. Originally he had authorized Trist to pay $30 million for New Mexico, Upper and Lower California, and the right of transit across Mexico's narrow isthmus of Tehuantepec. Now, observing the disorganized state of Mexican affairs, he began to consider demanding more territory and paying less for it. He summoned Trist home.

▲ Winfield Scott, hero of the Mexican War, glares at the observer. Timothy Dwight Johnson, a biographer, wrote that Scott's "ambition fed his arrogance and, in turn, his arrogance fed his ambition." Indisputably, Scott was well fed.

Trist, with Scott's backing, ignored the order. He realized that unless a treaty was arranged soon, the Mexican government might disintegrate, leaving no one in authority to sign a treaty. He dashed off a 65-page letter to the president, in effect refusing to be recalled, and proceeded to negotiate. Early in February the Treaty of Guadalupe Hidalgo was completed. By its terms Mexico accepted the Rio Grande as the boundary of Texas and ceded New Mexico and Upper California to the United States. In return the United States agreed to pay Mexico $15 million and to take on the claims of American citizens against Mexico, which by that time amounted to another $3.25 million.

When he learned that Trist had ignored his orders, the president seethed. Trist was "contemptibly base," he thought, an "impudent and unqualified scoundrel." He ordered Trist placed under arrest and fired from his State Department job.[1] Yet Polk had no choice but to submit the treaty to the Senate, for to have insisted on more territory would have meant more fighting, and the war had become increasingly unpopular. The relatively easy military victory made some people ashamed that their country was crushing a weaker neighbor. Abolitionists, led by William Lloyd Garrison, called it an "invasion . . . waged solely for the detestable and horrible purpose of extending and perpetuating American slavery." The Senate, subject to the same pressures as the president, ratified the agreement by a vote of 38 to 14.

THE FRUITS OF VICTORY: FURTHER ENLARGEMENT OF THE UNITED STATES

The Mexican War, won quickly and at relatively small cost in lives and money, brought huge territorial gains. The Pacific coast from south of San Diego to the 49th parallel and all the land between the coast and the Continental Divide had become the property of the American people. Immense amounts of labor and capital would have to be invested before this new territory could be made to yield its bounty, but the country clearly had the capacity to accomplish the job.

United States Territorial Expansion in the 1850s

In this atmosphere came what seemed a sign from the heavens. In January 1848, while Scott's veterans rested on their victorious arms in Mexico City, a mechanic named James W. Marshall was building a sawmill on the American River in the Sacramento

Valley east of San Francisco. One day, while supervising the deepening of the millrace, he noticed a few flecks of yellow in the bed of the stream. These he gathered up and tested. They were pure gold.

Other strikes had been made in California and been treated skeptically or as matters of local curiosity; since the days of Jamestown, too many pioneers had run fruitlessly in search of El Dorado, and too much fool's gold had been passed off as the real thing. Yet this discovery produced an international sensation. The gold was real and plentiful—$200 million of it was extracted in four years—but equally important was the fact that everyone was ready to believe the news. The gold rush reflected the heady confidence inspired by Guadalupe Hidalgo; it seemed the ultimate justification of manifest destiny. Surely an era of continental prosperity and harmony had dawned.

SLAVERY: THE FIRE BELL IN THE NIGHT RINGS AGAIN

Prosperity came in full measure but harmony did not, for once again expansion brought the nation face to face with the divisive question of slavery. This giant chunk of North America, most of it vacant, its future soon to be determined—should it be slave or free? The question, in one sense, seems hardly worth the national crisis it provoked. Slavery appeared to have little future in New Mexico and California, none in Oregon. Why did the South fight so hard for the right to bring slaves into a region that seemed so poorly suited to their exploitation?

Narrow partisanship provides part of the explanation. In districts where slavery was entrenched, a congressman who zealously defended the institution against the most trivial slight usually found himself a popular hero. In the northern states, the representatives who were vigilant in what they might describe as "freedom's cause" seldom regretted it on election day. But slavery raised a moral question. Most Americans tried to avoid confronting this truth; as patriots they assumed that any sectional issue could be solved by compromise. However, while the majority of whites had little respect for blacks, slave or free, few persons, northern or southern, could look upon the ownership of one human being by another as simply an alternative form of economic organization and argue its merits as they would those of the protective tariff or a national bank. Twist the facts as they might, slavery was either right or it was wrong; being on the whole honest and moral, they could not, having faced that truth, stand by unconcerned while the question was debated.

The question could come up in Congress only indirectly, for the Constitution did not give the federal

---

[1]Trist was retired to private life without being paid for his time in Mexico. In 1870, when he was on his deathbed, Congress finally awarded him $14,299.20.

government any control over slavery in the states. But Congress had complete control in the territories. Therefore the fact that slavery had no future in the Mexican cession was unimportant—in fact, for the foes of slavery, it was an advantage. By attacking slavery where it did not and probably never could exist, they could conceal from the slaveholders—and perhaps even from themselves—their hope ultimately to extinguish the institution.

Slavery had complicated the Texas problem from the start, and it beclouded the future of the Southwest even before the Mexican flag had been stripped from the staffs at Santa Fe and Los Angeles. The northern, Van Burenite wing of the Democratic party had become increasingly uneasy about the proslavery cast of Polk's policies, which were unpopular in their part of the country. Once it became likely that the war would bring new territory into the Union, these Northerners felt compelled to try to check the president and to assure their constituents that they would resist the admission of further slave territory. On August 8, 1846, during the debate on a bill appropriating money for the conduct of the war, Democratic Congressman David Wilmot of Pennsylvania introduced an amendment that provided "as an express and fundamental condition to the acquisition of any territory from the Republic of Mexico" that "neither slavery nor involuntary servitude shall ever exist in any part of said territory, except for crime, whereof the party shall first be duly convicted."

Southerners found the Wilmot Proviso particularly insulting. Nevertheless, it passed the House, where northern congressmen outnumbered southern. But it was defeated in the Senate, where Southerners held the balance. To counter the Proviso, Calhoun, once again serving as senator from South Carolina, introduced resolutions in 1846 arguing that Congress had no right to bar slavery from any territory; because territories belonged to all the states, slave and free, all should have equal rights in them. From this position it was only a step (soon taken) to demanding that Congress guarantee the right of slave owners to bring slaves into the territories and establish federal slave codes in the territories. Most Northerners considered this proposal as repulsive as Southerners found the Wilmot Proviso.

Calhoun's resolutions could never pass the House of Representatives, and Wilmot's Proviso had no chance in the Senate. Yet their very existence threatened the Union; as Senator Benton remarked, they were like the blades of a pair of scissors, ineffective separately, an efficient cutting tool taken together.

To resolve the territorial problem, two compromises were offered. One, eventually backed by President Polk, would extend the Missouri Compromise line to the Pacific. The majority of Southerners were willing to go along with this scheme, but most Northerners would no longer agree to the reservation of *any* new territory for slavery. The other possibility, advocated by Senator Lewis Cass of Michigan, called for organizing new territories without mention of slavery, thus leaving it to local settlers, through their territorial legislatures, to determine their own institutions. Cass's "popular sovereignty," known more vulgarly as "squatter sovereignty," had the superficial merit of appearing to be democratic. Its virtue for the members of Congress, however, was that it allowed them to escape the responsibility of deciding the question themselves.

THE ELECTION OF 1848

One test of strength occurred in August, before the 1848 presidential election. After six months of acrimonious debate, Congress passed a bill barring slavery from Oregon. The test, however, proved little. If it required half a year to settle the question for Oregon, how could an answer ever be found for California and New Mexico? Plainly the time had come, in a democracy, to go to the people. The coming presidential election seemed to provide an ideal opportunity.

The opportunity was missed. The politicians of the parties hedged, fearful of losing votes in one section or another. With the issues blurred, voters had no real choice. That the Whigs should behave in such a manner was perhaps to be expected of the party of "Tippecanoe and Tyler Too," but in 1848 they outdid even their 1840 performance, nominating Zachary Taylor for president. They chose the general despite his lack of political sophistication and after he had flatly refused to state his opinion on any current subject. The party offered no platform. Taylor was a brave man and a fine general; the Democrats had mistreated him; he was a common, ordinary fellow, unpretentious and warmhearted. Such was the Whig "argument." Taylor's contribution to the campaign was so naive as to be pathetic. "I am a Whig, *but not an ultra Whig*. . . . If elected . . . I should feel bound to administer the government untrammeled by party schemes."

The Democratic party had little better to offer. All the drive and zeal characteristic of it in the Jackson period had gradually seeped away. Polk's espousal of Texas's annexation had driven many Northerners from its ranks. James Buchanan of Pennsylvania, Polk's secretary of state, and William L. Marcy of New York, his secretary of war, and others like them—cautious, cynical politicians interested chiefly in getting and holding office—now came to the fore in northern Democratic politics.

The Democratic nominee was Lewis Cass, the father of popular sovereignty, but the party did not endorse that or any other solution to the territorial question. Cass was at least an experienced politician,

having been governor of the Michigan Territory, secretary of war, minister to France, and senator. Nevertheless, his approach to life was exemplified by an annoying habit he displayed at Washington social functions: A teetotaler, he would circulate among the guests with a glass in hand, raising it to his lips repeatedly but never swallowing a drop.

The Van Buren wing of the Democratic party was known as the Barnburners to call attention to their radicalism—supposedly they would burn down the barn to get rid of the rats. The Barnburners could not stomach Cass, in part because he was willing to countenance the extension of slavery into new territories, in part because he had led the swing to Polk at the 1844 Democratic convention. Combining with the antislavery Liberty party, they formed the Free Soil party and nominated Van Buren.

Van Buren knew he could not be elected, but he believed the time had come to take a stand. "The minds of nearly all mankind have been penetrated by a conviction of the evils of slavery," the onetime "Fox" and "Magician" declared. The Free Soil party polled nearly 300,000 votes, about 10 percent of the total, in a very dull campaign. Offered a choice between the honest ignorance of Taylor and the cynical opportunism of Cass, the voters—by a narrow margin—chose the former, Taylor receiving 1.36 million votes to Cass's 1.22 million. Taylor carried 8 of the 15 slave states and 7 of the 15 free states, proof that the sectional issue had been avoided.

5000 South Americans, and numbers of Europeans joined the rush.

The rough limits of the gold country had been quickly marked out. For 150 miles and more along the western slope of the Sierra stretched the great mother lode. Along the expanse any stream or canyon, any ancient gravel bed might conceal a treasure in nuggets, flakes, or dust. Armed with pickaxes and shovels, with washing pans, even with knives and spoons, eager prospectors hacked and dug and sifted, each accumulating a hoard, some great, some small, of gleaming yellow metal.

The impact on the region was enormous. Between 1849 and 1860 about 200,000 people, nearly all of them males, crossed the Rockies to California and thousands more reached California by ship via Cape Horn. Almost overnight the Spanish American population was reduced to the status of a minority. Disregarding justice and reason alike, the newcomers from the East, as one observer noted, "regarded every man but a native [North] American as an interloper." They referred to people of Latin American origin as "greasers" and sought by law and by violence to keep them from mining for gold. Even the local Californians (now American citizens) were discriminated against. The few free blacks in California and the several thousand more who came in search of gold were treated no better. As for the far larger Indian population, it was almost wiped out. There were about 150,000 Indians in California in the mid-1840s but only 35,000 in 1860.

THE GOLD RUSH

It was now clear that the question of slavery in the territories had to be faced. The discovery of gold had brought an army of prospectors into California. By the summer of 1848 San Francisco had become almost a ghost town, and an estimated two-thirds of the adult males of Oregon had hastened south to the gold fields. After President Polk confirmed the "extraordinary character" of the strike in his annual message of December 1848, there was no containing the gold seekers. During 1849, some 25,000 Americans made their way to California from the East by ship; more than 55,000 others crossed the continent by overland routes. About 8000 Mexicans,

▲ Gold prospectors used a "long Tom" to wash gold from gravel in a stream. The California gold rush brought mostly men—along with a few women—west in search of their fortunes.

The ethnic conflict was only part of the problem. Rough, hard men, separated from women, lusting for gold in a strange wild country where fortunes could be made in a day, gambled away in an hour, or stolen in an instant—the situation demanded the establishment of a territorial government. President Taylor appreciated this, and in his gruff, simple-hearted way he suggested an uncomplicated answer: admit California directly as a state, letting the Californians decide for themselves about slavery. The rest of the Mexican cession could be formed into another state. No need for Congress, with its angry rivalries, to meddle at all, he believed. In this way the nation could avoid the divisive effects of sectional debate.

The Californians reacted favorably to Taylor's proposal. They were overwhelmingly opposed to slavery, though not for humanitarian reasons. On the contrary, they tended to look on blacks as they did Mexicans and feared that if slavery were permitted, white gold seekers would be disadvantaged. "They would be unable," one delegate to the California constitutional convention predicted, "to compete with the bands of negroes who would be set to work under the direction of capitalists. It would become a monopoly." By October 1849 they had drawn up a constitution that outlawed slavery, and by December the new state government was functioning.

Taylor was the owner of a large plantation and more than 100 slaves; Southerners had assumed (without bothering to ask) that he would fight to keep the territories open to slavery. But being a military man, he was above all a nationalist; he disliked the divisiveness that partisan discussion of the issue was producing. Southerners were horrified by the president's reasoning. To admit California would destroy the balance between free and slave states in the Senate; to allow all the new land to become free would doom the South to wither in a corner of the country, surrounded by hostile free states. Should that happen, how long could slavery sustain itself, even in South Carolina? Radicals were already saying that the South would have to choose between secession and surrender. Taylor's plan played into the hands of extremists.

THE COMPROMISE OF 1850

DOCUMENT

Clay, Speech to the U.S. Senate

This was no longer a squabble over territorial governments. With the Union itself at stake, Henry Clay rose to save the day. He had been as angry and frustrated when the Whigs nominated Taylor as he had been when they passed him over for Harrison. Now, well beyond age 70 and in ill health, he put away his ambition and his resentment and for the last time concentrated his remarkable vision on a great, multifaceted national problem. California must be free and soon admitted to the Union, but the South must have some compensation. For that matter, why not seize the opportunity to settle every outstanding sectional conflict related to slavery? Clay wondered long and hard, drew up a plan, then consulted his old Whig rival Webster and obtained his general approval. On January 29, 1850, he laid his proposal, "founded upon mutual forbearance," before the Senate. A few days later he defended it on the floor of the Senate in the last great speech of his life.

California should be brought directly into the Union as a free state, he argued. The rest of the Southwest should be organized as a territory without mention of slavery: The Southerners would retain the right to bring slaves there, while in fact none would do so. "You have got what is worth more than a thousand Wilmot Provisos," Clay pointed out to his northern colleagues. "You have nature on your side." Empty lands in dispute along the Texas border should be assigned to the New Mexico Territory, Clay continued, but in exchange the United States should take over Texas's preannexation debts. The slave trade should be abolished in the District of Columbia (but not slavery itself), and a more effective federal fugitive slave law should be enacted and strictly enforced in the North.

Clay's proposals occasioned one of the most magnificent debates in the history of the Senate. Every important member had his say. Calhoun, perhaps even more than Clay, realized that the future of the nation was at stake and that his own days were numbered (he died four weeks later). He was so feeble that he could not deliver his speech himself. He sat impassive, wrapped in a great cloak, gripping the arms of his chair, while Senator James M. Mason of Virginia read it to the crowded Senate. Calhoun thought his plan would save the Union, but his speech was an argument for secession; he demanded that the North yield completely on every point, ceasing even to discuss the question of slavery. Clay's compromise was unsatisfactory; he himself had no other to offer. If you will not yield, he said to the northern senators, "let the States . . . agree to separate and part in peace. If you are unwilling we should part in peace, tell us so, and we shall know what to do."

Three days later, on March 7, Daniel Webster took the floor. He too had begun to fail. Years of heavy drinking and other forms of self-indulgence had taken their toll. The brilliant volubility and the thunder were gone, and when he spoke his face was bathed in sweat and there were strange pauses in his delivery. But his argument was lucid. Clay's proposals should be adopted. Since the future of all the territories had already been fixed by geographic and economic factors, the Wilmot Proviso was unnecessary. The

DOCUMENT

Webster, Speech to the U.S. Senate

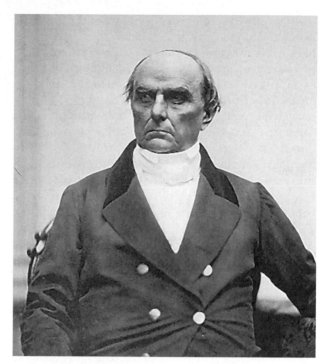

▲ Two leading lights of the day, Clay and Webster, as they looked at about the time they played major roles in the Compromise of 1850. The daguerreotype of Clay *(left)* dates from the late 1840s; that of Webster *(right)* from 1851, a year before his death. Both are by the noted Boston firm of Southworth and Hawes.

North's constitutional obligation to yield fugitive slaves, he said, braving the wrath of New England abolitionists, was "binding in honor and conscience." (A cynic might say that once again Webster was placing property rights above human rights.) The Union, he continued, could not be sundered without bloodshed. At the thought of that dread possibility, the old fire flared: "Peaceable secession!" Webster exclaimed, "Heaven forbid! Where is the flag of the republic to remain? Where is the eagle still to tower?" The debate did not end with the aging giants. Every possible viewpoint was presented, argued, rebutted, rehashed. Senator William H. Seward of New York, a new Whig leader, close to Taylor's ear, caused a stir while arguing against concessions to the slave interests by saying that despite the constitutional obligation to return fugitive slaves, a "higher law" than the Constitution, the law of God, forbade anything that countenanced the evil of slavery.

The majority clearly favored some compromise, but nothing could have been accomplished without the death of President Taylor on July 9, 1850. Obstinate, probably resentful because few people paid him half the heed they paid Clay and other prominent members of Congress, the president had insisted on his own plan to bring both California and New Mexico directly into the Union. When Vice President Millard Fillmore, who was a politician, not an ideologue, succeeded Taylor, the deadlock between the White House and Capitol Hill was broken. Even so, each part of the

compromise had to be voted on separately, for too many stubborn congressmen were willing to overturn the whole plan because they objected to specific parts of it. Senator Benton, for example, announced against Clay's omnibus bill because he objected to the fugitive slave provision and the Texas boundary settlement.

The final congressional maneuvering was managed by another relative newcomer, Senator Stephen A. Douglas of Illinois, who took over when Washington's summer heat prostrated the exhausted Clay. Partisanship and economic interests complicated Douglas's problem. According to rumor, Clay had persuaded an important Virginia newspaper editor to back the compromise by promising him a $100,000 government printing contract. This inflamed many Southerners. New York merchants, fearful of the disruption of their southern business, submitted a petition bearing 25,000 names in favor of compromise, a document that had a favorable effect in the South. The prospect of the federal government's paying the debt of Texas made ardent compromisers of a horde of speculators. Between February and September, Texas bonds rose erratically from 29 to over 60, while men like W. W. Corcoran, whose Washington bank held more than $400,000 of these securities, entertained legislators and supplied lobbyists with large amounts of cash.

In the Senate and then in the House, tangled combinations pushed through the separate measures, one by one. California became the thirty-first state. The rest

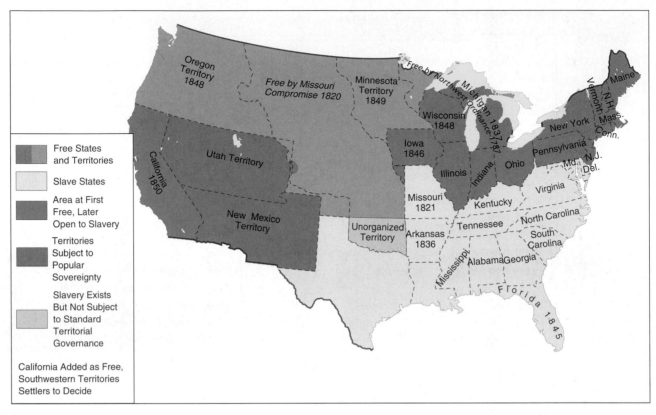

Free States and Territories

Slave States

Area at First Free, Later Open to Slavery

Territories Subject to Popular Sovereignty

Slavery Exists But Not Subject to Standard Territorial Governance

California Added as Free, Southwestern Territories Settlers to Decide

▲ **Compromise of 1850**

DOCUMENT

The Fugitive Slave Act (1850)

of the Mexican cession was divided into two territories, New Mexico and Utah, each to be admitted to the Union when qualified, "with or without slavery as [its] constitution may prescribe." Texas received $10 million to pay off its debt in return for accepting a narrower western boundary. The slave trade in the District of Columbia was abolished as of January 1, 1851. The Fugitive Slave Act of 1793 was amended to provide for the appointment of federal commissioners with authority to issue warrants, summon posses, and compel citizens under pain of fine or imprisonment to assist in the capture of fugitives. Commissioners who decided that an accused person was a runaway received a larger fee than if they declared the person legally free. The accused could not testify in their own defense. They were to be returned to the South without jury trial merely on the submission of an affidavit by their "owner."

Only 4 senators and 28 representatives voted for all these bills. The two sides did not meet somewhere in the middle as is the case with most compromises. Each bill passed because those who preferred it outnumbered those opposed. In general, the Democrats gave more support to the compromise than the Whigs, but party lines never held firmly. In the Senate, for example, 17 Democrats and 15 Whigs voted to admit California as a free state. A large number of congressmen absented themselves when parts of the

settlement unpopular in their home districts came to a vote; 21 senators and 36 representatives failed to commit themselves on the new fugitive slave bill. Senator Jefferson Davis of Mississippi voted for the fugitive slave measure and the bill creating Utah Territory, remained silent on the New Mexico bill, and opposed the other measures. Senator Salmon P. Chase of Ohio, an abolitionist, supported only the admission of California and the abolition of the slave trade.

In this piecemeal fashion the Union was preserved. The credit belongs mostly to Clay, whose original conceptualization of the compromise enabled lesser minds to understand what they must do.

Everywhere sober and conservative citizens sighed with relief. Mass meetings throughout the country "ratified" the result. Hundreds of newspapers gave the compromise editorial approval. In Washington patriotic harmony reigned. "You would suppose that nobody had ever thought of disunion," Webster wrote. "All say they always meant to stand by the Union to the last." When Congress met again in December it seemed that party discord had been buried forever. "I have determined never to make another speech on the slavery question," Senator Douglas told his colleagues. "Let us cease agitating, stop the debate, and drop the subject." If this were done, he predicted, the compromise would be accepted as a "final settlement." With this bit of wishful thinking the year 1850 passed into history.

MILESTONES

1835	Alamo falls to Santa Anna's Mexican army	1846	U.S. and Britain settle Oregon boundary dispute
1836	Sam Houston routs Santa Anna at Battle of San Jacinto	1846–1848	U.S. wages "Mr. Polk's War" with Mexico
1837	U.S. recognizes Republic of Texas	1846	House of Representatives adopts Wilmot Proviso prohibiting slavery in Mexican cession, but Senate defeats it
1840	Richard Henry Dana describes voyage to California in *Two Years Before the Mast*	1847	General Winfield Scott captures Mexico City
	William Henry Harrison is elected president	1848	James W. Marshall discovers gold at Sutter's Mill, California
1841	William Henry Harrison dies; Vice President John Tyler becomes president		Treaty of Guadalupe Hidalgo brings U.S. huge territorial gains
	Preemption Act grants "squatters' rights" in West		Zachary Taylor is elected president
1842	Webster-Ashburton Treaty determines Maine boundary	1850	Taylor dies; Vice President Millard Fillmore becomes president
1843	Oregon Trail opens		Henry Clay's Compromise of 1850 preserves Union
1844	James K. Polk is elected president		
1845	U.S. annexes Texas		
	John L. O'Sullivan coins the expression *manifest destiny*		

SUPPLEMENTARY READING

For John Tyler, perhaps the least examined of the presidents, see Dan Monroe, *The Republican Vision of John Tyler* (2003); on the Whigs more generally, see Michael F. Holt, *The Rise and Fall of the American Whig Party* (1999), and Daniel Walker Howe, *The Political Culture of the American Whigs* (1979).

On diplomatic affairs, see P. A. Varg, *United States Foreign Relations: 1820–1860* (1979), and D. M. Pletcher, *The Diplomacy of Annexation: Texas, Oregon, and the Mexican War* (1973).

The new expansionism is discussed in Frederick Merk, *Manifest Destiny and Mission in American History* (1963) and *The Monroe Doctrine and American Expansionism* (1966). H. N. Smith, *Virgin Land* (1950), is also important for an understanding of this subject. The course of western development is treated in R. A. Billington and Martin Ridge, *The Far Western Frontier* (1982). Important recent studies of the California gold rush include Malcolm J. Rohrbough, *Days of Gold* (1997), and Susan Lee Johnson, *Roaring Camp: The Social World of the California Gold Rush* (2000). On the effects of the settling of the Great Plains, see Elliott West, *The Contested Plains: Indians, Goldseekers and the Rush to Colorado* (1998) and J. D. Unruh, *The Plains Across* (1979). Francis Parkman's classic account, *The Oregon Trail* (1849) is absorbing.

For the election of 1844, see J. C. N. Paul, *Rift in the Democracy* (1961). Two recent, brief biographies of Polk

are John Seigenthaler, *James K. Polk* (2004), and Thomas M. Leonard, *James K. Polk: A Clear and Unquestionable Destiny* (2001). The standard biography of Polk is Charles G. Sellers's *James K. Polk* (1957–1966). William Dusinberre, *Slavemaster President: The Double Career of James Polk* (2003) is sharply critical.

On the Mexican War, see Richard Bruce Winders, *Mr. Polk's Army* (1997), R. W. Johannsen, *To the Halls of the Montezumas* (1987), and K. J. Bauer, *The Mexican War* (1974). J. H. Schroeder, *Mr. Polk's War* (1973), discusses American opposition to the conflict. See also Marshall De Bruhl, *Sword of San Jacinto* (1993), a biography of Sam Houston. Randy Roberts and James S. Olson, *A Line in the Sand: The Alamo in Blood and Memory* (2001) is an accessible account.

For the Compromise of 1850, see David M. Potter, *The Impending Crisis, 1848–1861* (1976), and Holman Hamilton, *Prologue to Conflict* (1964). See also Robert Remini, *Daniel Webster: The Man and His Time* (1997), and Irving H. Bartlett, *John C. Calhoun* (1993).

Fertility and the frontier is examined in Yasukichi Yasuba, *Birth Rates of the White Population in the U.S., 1800–1860* (1962), and John Modell, "Family and Fertility on the Indiana Frontier, 1820," in *American Quarterly* (1971). See also Mary Ryan, *The Cradle of the Middle Class* (1981).

SUGGESTED WEBSITES

From Slave to Master

http://moa.umdl.umich.edu/cgi/sgml/
moa-idx?notisid=ABT6752

This site contains an autobiography of a slave who became a master, with strong comments on the place of blacks in pre-Civil War America.

Sam Houston and the Texas Revolution, 1825–1836

http://www.lnstar.com/mall/texasinfo/shouston.htm

This site provides information on the revolution, including the dynamic Sam Houston.

On the Trail in Kansas

http://www.ukans.edu/heritage/owk/128/trails.htm/
#Oregon

This Kansas Collection site provides good primary sources and images relating to the Oregon Trial and America's early movement westward.

"Been Here So Long": Selections from the WPA American Slave Narratives

http://newdeal.feri.org/asn/index.htm

Slave narratives are some of the most interesting primary sources about slavery.

Slave Narratives

http://docsouth.unc.edu/neh/texts.html

This site presents narratives of several slaves housed at the Documents of the American South collection and the University of North Carolina.

The Settlement of African Americans in Liberia

http://www.loc.gov/exhibits/african/afam003.html

This site contains images and text relating to the colonization movement to return African Americans to Africa.

Images of African Americans from the Nineteenth Century

http://digital.nypl.org/schomburg/images_aa19/

The New York Public Library–Schomburg Center for Research in Black Culture site contains numerous visuals of nineteenth-century African Americans.

The Compromise of 1850 and the Fugitive Slave Act

http://www.pbs.org/wgbh/aia/part4

From the series on Africans in America, an analysis of the Compromise of 1850 and the effect of the Fugitive Slave Act on black Americans.

Words and Deeds in American History

http://lcweb2.loc.gov/ammem/mcchtml/
corhome.html

A Library of Congress site containing links to Frederick Douglas, the Compromise of 1850, as well as speeches by John C. Calhoun, Daniel Webster, and Henry Clay; and other topics from the Civil War era.

CHAPTER

13 The Sections Go Their Ways

▼ A railroad engine pierces the darkening wilderness. Man-made light supplants the setting sun, and nature flees before the encroaching machine. The painting is by Andrew W. Melrose.

CHAPTER CONTENTS

A nation growing as rapidly as the United States in the middle decades of the nineteenth century changed continually in hundreds of ways. It was developing a national economy marked by the dependence of each area on all the others, the production of goods in one region for sale in all, the increased specialization of agricultural and industrial producers, and the growth in size of units of production.

Cotton remained the most important southern crop and the major American export. However, manufacturing in the Northeast and the railroads, which revolutionized transportation and communication, became the mainsprings of economic growth. The continuing westward movement of agriculture had significant new effects. American foreign commerce changed radically, and the flood of European immigration had an impact on manufacturing, town life, and farming.

THE SOUTH

The South was less affected than other sections by urbanization, European immigration, the transportation revolution, and industrialization. The region remained predominantly agricultural; cotton was still king, slavery the most distinctive southern institution. But important changes were occurring. Cotton continued to march westward, until by 1859

fully 1.3 million of the 4.3 million bales grown in the United States came from beyond the Mississippi. In the upper South, Virginia held its place as the leading tobacco producer, but states beyond the Appalachians were raising more than half the crop. The introduction of Bright Yellow, a mild variety of tobacco that (miraculously) grew best in poor soil, gave a great stimulus to production. The older sections of Maryland, Virginia, and North Carolina shifted to the kind of diversified farming usually associated with the Northeast. By 1849 the wheat crop of Virginia was worth twice as much as the tobacco crop.

In the time of Washington and Jefferson, progressive Virginia planters had experimented with crop rotation and fertilizers. In the mid-nineteenth century, Edmund Ruffin introduced the use of marl, an earth rich in calcium, to counteract the acidity of worn-out tobacco fields. Ruffin discovered that dressings of marl, combined with the use of fertilizers and with proper drainage and plowing methods, doubled and even tripled the yield of corn and wheat. In the 1840s some Southerners began to import Peruvian guano, a high-nitrogen fertilizer of bird droppings, which increased yields. Others experimented with contour plowing to control erosion and with improved breeds of livestock, new types of plows, and agricultural machinery.

THE ECONOMICS OF SLAVERY

The increased importance of cotton in the South strengthened the hold of slavery on the region. The price of slaves rose until by the 1850s a prime field hand was worth as much as $1800, roughly three times the cost in the 1820s. While the prestige value of owning this kind of property affected prices, the rise chiefly reflected the increasing value of the South's agricultural output. "Crop value per slave" jumped from less than $15 early in the century to more than $125 in 1859.

In the cotton fields of the Deep South slaves brought several hundred dollars per head more than in the older regions; thus the tendency to sell them "down the river" continued. Mississippi took in some 10,000 slaves a year throughout the period; by 1830 the black population of the state exceeded the white. The westward shift of cotton cultivation was accompanied by the forcible transfer of more than a million African American slaves from the seaboard states to the dark, rich soil of regions watered by the Mississippi and Arkansas rivers and their tributaries. This "second great migration" of blacks greatly surpassed the original uprooting of blacks from Africa to the United States.

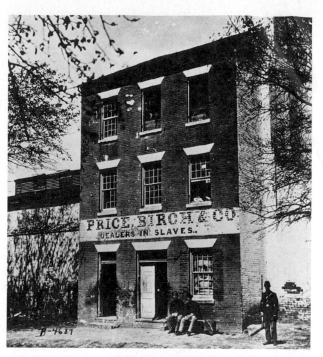

▲ Price, Birch & Company of Virginia, "dealers in Slaves." Such companies not only sold slaves but also arranged for them to work in nearby shops and factories.

Slave trading became a big business. In the 1850s there were about 50 dealers in Charleston and 200 in New Orleans. The largest traders were Isaac Franklin and John Armfield, who collected slaves from Virginia and Maryland at their "model jail" in Alexandria and shipped them by land and sea to a depot near Natchez. Each of the partners cleared half a million dollars before retiring, and some smaller operators did proportionately well.

The impact of the trade on the slaves was frequently disastrous. Husbands were often separated from wives, parents from children. This was somewhat less likely to happen on large, well-managed plantations than on small farms, but it was common enough everywhere. According to one study, one-third of all slave first "marriages" in the upper South were broken by forced separation and nearly half of all children were separated from at least one parent. Families were torn apart less frequently in the lower South, where far more slaves were bought than sold.

Because the business was so profitable, the prejudice against slave traders abated as the price of slaves rose. Men of high social status became traders, and persons of humble origin who had prospered in the trade had little difficulty in buying land and setting up as respectable planters.

As blacks became more expensive, the ownership of slaves became more concentrated. In 1860

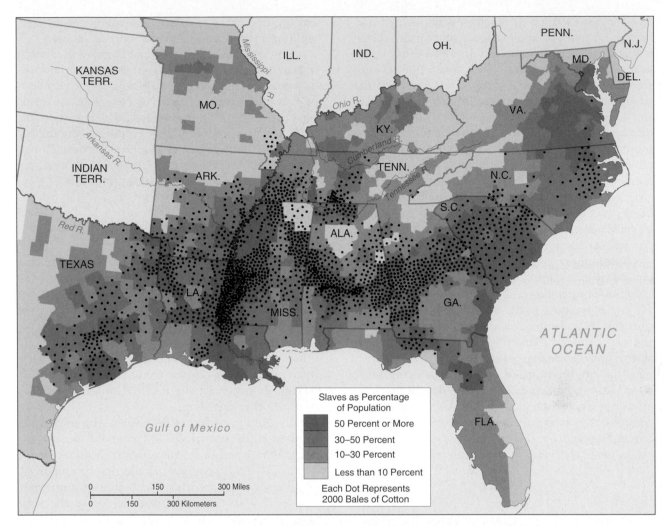

▲ **Cotton and Slaves in the South, 1860**
Not surprisingly, the areas of greatest cotton production were also the areas with the highest proportion of slaves in the population. Note the concentrations of both in the Piedmont, the Alabama Black Belt, and the lower Mississippi Valley, and the relative absence of both in the Appalachian Mountains.

Slavery in the South

only about 46,000 of the 8 million white residents of the slave states had as many as 20 slaves. When one calculates the cost of 20 slaves and the land to keep them profitably occupied, it is easy to understand why this figure is so small. The most efficient size of a plantation worked by gangs of slaves ranged between 1000 and 2000 acres. In every part of the South the majority of farmers cultivated no more than 200 acres, in many sections fewer than 100 acres. On the eve of the Civil War only one white family in four in the South owned any slaves at all. A few large plantations and many small farms— this was the pattern.

There were few genuine economies of scale in southern agriculture. Small farmers grew the staple crops; and many of them owned a few slaves, often working beside them in the fields. These yeomen farmers were hardworking, self-reliant, and moderately prosperous, quite unlike the "poor white trash" of the pine barrens and the remote valleys of the Appalachians who scratched a meager subsistence from substandard soils and lived in ignorance and squalor.

Well-managed plantations yielded annual profits of 10 percent and more, and, in general, money invested in southern agriculture earned at least a modest return. Considering the way the workforce was exploited, this is hardly surprising. Recent estimates indicate that after allowing for the cost of land and capital, the average plantation slave "earned" cotton worth $78.78 in 1859. It cost masters about $32 a year to feed, clothe, and house a slave. In other words, almost 60 percent of the product of slave labor was expropriated by the masters.

The South failed to develop locally owned marketing and transportation facilities, and for this slavery was at least partly responsible. In 1840 *Hunt's Merchant Magazine* estimated that it cost $2.85 to move a bale of cotton from the farm to a seaport and that additional charges for storage, insurance, port fees, and freight to a European port exceeded $15. Middlemen from outside the South commonly earned most of this money. New York capitalists gradually came to control much of the South's cotton from the moment it was picked, and a large percentage of the crop found its way into New York warehouses before being sold to manufacturers. The same middlemen supplied most of the foreign goods that the planters purchased with their cotton earnings.

Southerners complained about this state of affairs but did little to correct it. Capital tied up in the ownership of labor could not be invested in anything else, and social pressures in the South militated against investment in trade and commerce. Ownership of land and slaves yielded a kind of psychic income not available to any middleman. As one British visitor pointed out, the southern blacks were "a nonconsuming class." Still more depressing, under slavery the enormous reservoir of intelligence and skill that the blacks represented was almost entirely wasted. Many slave artisans worked on the plantations, and a few free blacks made their way in the South remarkably well, but the amount of talent unused, energy misdirected, and imagination smothered can only be guessed.

Foreign observers in New England frequently noted the alertness and industriousness of ordinary laborers and attributed this, justifiably, to the high level of literacy. Nearly everyone in New England could read and write. Correspondingly, the stagnation and inefficiency of southern labor could be attributed in part to the high degree of illiteracy, for over 20 percent of *white* Southerners could not read or write, another tragic squandering of human resources.

ANTEBELLUM PLANTATION LIFE

There was never any such thing as a "typical" plantation, but it is possible to describe, in a general way, what a medium-to-large operation employing 20 or more slaves was like in the two decades preceding the Civil War. Such a plantation was more like a small village than a northern-type agricultural unit, and in another way more like a self-sufficient colonial farm than a nineteenth-century commercial operation, although its major activity involved producing cotton or some other cash crop.

In addition to the master's house with its complement of barns and stables, there would usually be a kitchen, a smokehouse, a washhouse, a home for the overseer should one be employed, perhaps a schoolhouse, a gristmill, a forge, and of course the slave quarters, off at a distance (but not too far) from the center.

Slaveholding families were also quite different from northern families of similar status, in part because they were engaged in agriculture and in part because of their so-called peculiar institution. Husbands and wives did not function in separate spheres to nearly the same extent, although their individual functions were different and gender related.

Although planter families purchased their fine clothes, furniture, and china, as well as other manufactured products such as sewing machines, cooking utensils, books, and musical instruments, plantations were busy centers of household manufacture, turning out most of the clothing of slaves except for shoes and the everyday clothing of their own children, along with bedding and other textiles. Spinning,

▲ This painting of a slave auction highlights an awkward aspect of slavery. The slave woman has light skin, which suggests that her father was likely a slave owner. Those men bidding on her stare with an intensity portending that she will likely share her mother's fate.

weaving, and sewing were women's work, both for whites and blacks. Nearly all the food consumed was raised on the land; only tea and coffee and a few other food items were commonly purchased.

The master was in general charge and his word was law—the system was literally paternalistic. But his wife nearly always had immense responsibilities. Running the household meant supervising the servants (and punishing them when necessary, which often meant wielding a lash), nursing the sick, taking care of the vegetable and flower gardens, planning meals, and seeing to the education of her own children and the training of young slaves. It could also involve running the entire plantation on the frequent occasions when her husband was away on business. At the same time, her role entailed being a "southern lady," refined, graceful, supposedly untroubled by worldly affairs.

Most slaveholding women had to learn all these things by doing; in general, they married while still in their teens and had been given little or no training in the household arts. Unmarried "young ladies" had few responsibilities beyond caring for their own rooms and persons and perhaps such "ladylike" tasks as arranging flowers.

The majority of the slaves of both sexes were field hands who labored on the land from dawn to dusk. Household servants and artisans, indeed any slave other than small children and the aged and infirm, might be called on for such labor when needed. Slave women were expected to cook for their own families and do other chores after working in the fields.

DOCUMENT

Harper, "The Slave Mother"

Children, free and slave, were cared for by slaves, the former by household servants, the latter usually by an elderly woman, perhaps with the help of a girl only a little older than the children. Infants were brought to their mothers in the fields for nursing several times a day, for after a month or two at most, slave mothers were required to go back to work. Slave children were not put to work until they were six or seven years old, and until they were about ten they were given only small tasks such as feeding the chickens or minding a smaller child. Black and white youngsters played together and were often cared for by the same nursemaid.

Slave cabins were simple and crude; most consisted of a single room, dark, with a fireplace for cooking and heat. Usually the flooring was raised above ground level, though some were set on the bare earth. In 1827 Basil Hall, a British naval officer, reported that in a large South Carolina plantation, 140 slaves lived in 28 cottages or huts. These were "uncommonly neat and comfortable, and might have shamed those of many countries I have seen." Yet Hall dismissed the claims of white Southerners

that slaves were happier than the peasantry of England. Slavery was, above all, a "humiliation" imposed upon "the whole mass of the labouring population" of the South.

THE SOCIOLOGY OF SLAVERY

It is difficult to generalize about the peculiar institution because so much depended on the individual master's behavior. Although some ex-slaves told of masters who refused to whip them, Bennet Barrow of Louisiana, a harsh master, averaged one whipping a month. "The great secret of our success," another planter recalled years later, "was the great motive power contained in that little instrument." Overseers were commonly instructed to give 20 lashes for ordinary offences, such as shirking work or stealing, and 39 for more serious offenses, such as running away. Sometimes slaves were whipped to death though, by 1821, all southern states had passed laws allowing a master to be charged with murder if he caused a slave's death from excessive punishment. Conviction normally resulted in a fine. In 1840 a South Carolina woman convicted of killing a slave was fined $214.28.

Most owners provided adequate clothing, housing, and food for their slaves. Only a fool or a sadist would fail to take care of such valuable property. However, vital statistics indicate that infant mortality among slaves was twice the white rate, life expectancy at least five years less.

On balance, it is significant that the United States was the only nation in the Western Hemisphere where the slave population grew by natural increase. After the ending of the slave trade in 1808, the black population increased at nearly the same rate as the white. Put differently, during the entire period from the founding of Jamestown to the Civil War, only a little more than half a million slaves were imported into the country, about 5 percent of the number of Africans carried by slavers to the New World. Yet in 1860 there were about 4 million blacks in the United States.

Most owners felt responsibilities toward their slaves, and slaves were dependent on and in some ways imitative of white values. However, powerful fears and resentments, not always recognized, existed on both sides. The plantation environment forced the two races to live in close proximity. From this circumstance could arise every sort of human relationship. One planter, using the appropriate pseudonym Clod Thumper, could write: "Africans are nothing but brutes, and they will love you better for whipping, whether they deserve it or not." Another, describing a slave named Bug, could say: "No one

▲ A slave burial service, painted by John Antrobus in 1860. In an inversion of power relations, a slave preacher leads the mourners while the white overseer and the plantation owners watch uneasily, shunted (literally) to the sides.

knows but myself what feeling I have for him. Black as he is we were raised together." One southern white woman tended a dying servant with "the kindest and most unremitting attention." Another, discovered crying after the death of a slave she had repeatedly abused, is said to have explained her grief by complaining that she "didn't have nobody to whip no more."

Such diametrically conflicting sentiments often existed within the same person. And almost no white Southerners had any difficulty exploiting the labor of slaves for whom they felt genuine affection.

Slaves were without rights; they developed a distinctive way of life by attempting to resist oppression and injustice while accommodating themselves to the system. Their marriages had no legal status, but their partnerships seem to have been as loving and stable as those of their masters. Certainly they were acutely conscious of family relationships and responsibilities.

Slave religion, on the surface an untutored form of Christianity tinctured with some African survivals, seemed to most slave owners a useful instrument for teaching meekness and resignation and for providing

harmless emotional release, which it sometimes was and did. However, religious meetings, secret and open, provided slaves with the opportunity to organize, which led at times to rebellions and more often to less drastic ways of resisting white domination. Religion also sustained the slaves' sense of their own worth as beings made in the image of God, and it taught them, therefore, that while human beings can be enslaved in body, their spirits cannot be enslaved without their consent.

DOCUMENT

A Catechism for Slaves

Observing that slaves often seemed happy and were only rarely overtly rebellious, whites persuaded themselves that most blacks accepted the system without resentment and indeed preferred slavery to the uncertainties of freedom. There was much talk about "loyal and faithful servants." The Civil War, when slaves flocked to the Union lines once assured of freedom and fair treatment, would disabuse them of this illusion.

As the price of slaves rose and as northern opposition to the institution grew more vocal, the system hardened perceptibly. White Southerners made much

of the danger of insurrection. When a plot was uncovered or a revolt took place, instant and savage reprisals resulted. In 1822, after the conspiracy of Denmark Vesey was exposed by informers, 37 slaves were executed and another 30-odd deported, although no overt act of rebellion had occurred. After an uprising in Louisiana, 16 blacks were decapitated, their heads left to rot on poles along the Mississippi as a grim warning.

DOCUMENT

Turner, *The Confession of Nat Turner*

The Nat Turner revolt in Virginia in 1831 was the most sensational of the slave uprisings; 57 whites lost their lives before it was suppressed. White Southerners treated runaways almost as brutally as rebels, although they posed no real threat to whites. The authorities tracked down fugitives with bloodhounds and subjected captives to merciless lashings.

After the Nat Turner revolt, interest in doing away with slavery vanished in the white South. The southern states made it increasingly difficult for masters to free their slaves; during 1859 only about 3000 in a slave population of nearly 4 million were given their freedom.

Slavery did not flourish in urban settings, and cities did not flourish in societies where slavery was important. Most southern cities were small, and within them, slaves made up a small fraction of the labor force. The existence of slavery goes a long way toward explaining why the South was so rural and why it had so little industry. Blacks were much harder to supervise and control in urban settings. Individual slaves were successfully employed in southern manufacturing plants, but they made up only an insignificant fraction of the South's small industrial labor supply.

Southern whites considered the existence of free blacks undesirable, no matter where they lived. The mere fact that they could support themselves disproved the notion that blacks were by nature childlike and shiftless, unable to work efficiently without white guidance. From the whites' point of view, free blacks set a bad example for slaves. In a petition calling for the expulsion of free blacks from the state, a group of South Carolinians noted that slaves continualy have before their eyes, persons of the same color . . . freed from the control of masters, working where they please, going where they please, and expending their money how they please.

At a minimum, as another Southerner said, the sight of "a vile and lazy free negro lolling in the sunshine" might make slaves envious. Still worse, it might encourage them to try to escape, and worst of all, the free blacks might help them do so.

Many southern states passed laws aimed at forcing free blacks to emigrate, but these laws were not well enforced. There is ample evidence that the white people of, say, Maryland, would have liked to get rid of the state's large free-black population. Free blacks were barred from occupations in which they might cause trouble—no free black could be the captain of a ship, for example—and they were required by law to find a "respectable" white person who would testify as to their "good conduct and character." But whites, who needed slave labor, did not try very hard to expel them.

Some unscrupulous Southerners helped smuggle blacks from Africa. About 54,000 slaves were brought to America illegally after the trade was outlawed in 1808, not a very large number relative to the slave population. British, French, Portuguese, and American naval vessels patrolled the African coast continuously. The American navy alone seized more than 50 suspected slavers in the two decades before 1860. However, the fast, sharklike pirate cruisers were hard to catch, and the anti–slave trade laws were imperfectly worded and unevenly enforced. Many accounts tell of slaves in America long after 1808 with

▲ An 1844 advertisement from *The Western Citizen* for the "Liberty Line," a tongue-in-cheek reference to the volunteers who helped slaves escape from the South ("the Patriarchal Dominion") to get to Canada ("Libertyville"). Although the ad likened the effort to a railroad speeding hundreds of slaves northward, in fact relatively few slaves ever took this "northern tour."

filed teeth, tattoos, and other signs of African origin, yet no one owning such a person was ever charged with the possession of contraband goods.

Psychological Effects of Slavery

The injustice of slavery needs no proof; less obvious is the fact that it had a corrosive effect on the personalities of Southerners, slave and free alike. By "the making of a human being an animal without hope," the system bore heavily on all slaves' sense of their own worth. Some found the condition absolutely unbearable. They became the habitual runaways who collected whip scars like medals, the "loyal" servants who struck out in rage against a master knowing that the result would be certain death, and the leaders of slave revolts.

Denmark Vesey of South Carolina, even after buying his freedom, could not stomach the subservience demanded of slaves by the system. When he saw Charleston slaves step into the gutter to make way for whites, he taunted them: "You deserve to remain slaves!" For years he preached resistance to his fellows, drawing his texts from the Declaration of Independence and the Bible and promising help from black Haiti. So vehemently did he argue that some of his followers claimed they feared Vesey more than their masters, even more than God. He planned his uprising for five years, patiently working out the details, only to see it aborted at the last moment when a few of his recruits lost their nerve and betrayed him. For Denmark Vesey, death was probably preferable to living with such rage as his soul contained.

Yet Veseys were rare. Most slaves appeared, if not contented, at least resigned to their fate. Many seemed even to accept the whites' evaluation of their inherent abilities and place in society. Of course in most instances it is impossible to know whether this apparent subservience was feigned in order to avoid trouble.

Slaves had strong family and group attachments and a complex culture of their own, maintained, so to speak, under the noses of their masters. By a mixture of subterfuge, accommodation, and passive resistance, they erected subtle defenses against exploitation, achieving a sense of community that helped sustain the psychic integrity of individuals. But slavery discouraged, if it did not extinguish, independent judgment and self-reliance. These qualities are difficult enough to develop in human beings under the best of circumstances; when every element in white society encouraged slaves to let others do their thinking for them, to avoid questioning the status quo, to

lead a simple life, many did so willingly enough. Was this not slavery's greatest shame?

Whites, too, were harmed by the slave system. Associating working for others with servility discouraged many poor white Southerners from hiring out to earn a stake. Slavery provided the weak, the shiftless, and the unsuccessful with a scapegoat that made their own miserable state easier to bear but harder to escape.

More subtly, the patriarchal nature of the slave system reinforced the already existing tendency toward male dominance over wives and children typical of the larger society. For men of exceptional character, the responsibilities of ownership could be ennobling, but for hotheads, alcoholics, or others with psychological problems, the power could be brutalizing, with terrible effects on the whole plantation community, whites and blacks alike.

Aside from its fundamental immorality, slavery caused basically decent people to commit countless petty cruelties. "I feel badly, got very angry and whipped Lavinia," one Louisiana woman wrote in her diary. "O! for government over my temper." But for slavery, she would surely have had better self-control. The finest white Southerners were often warped by the institution. Even those who abhorred slavery sometimes let it corrupt their thinking: "I consider the labor of a breeding woman as no object, and that a child raised every 2 years is of more profit than the crop of the best laboring man." This cold calculation came from the pen of Thomas Jefferson, author of the Declaration of Independence, a man who, it now seems likely, fathered at least one child by a slave.

Manufacturing in the South

Although the temper of southern society discouraged business and commercial activities, considerable manufacturing developed. Small flour and lumber mills flourished. There were important rope-making plants in Kentucky and commercial cotton presses, used to compact cotton into 500-pound bales, in many southern cities. Iron and coal were mined in Virginia, Kentucky, and Tennessee. In the 1850s the Tredegar Iron Works in Richmond did an annual business of about $1 million.

The availability of the raw material and the abundance of waterpower along the Appalachian slopes made it possible to manufacture textiles profitably in the South. By 1825 a thriving factory was functioning at Fayetteville, North Carolina, and soon others sprang up elsewhere in North Carolina and in adjoining states. William Gregg's factory, at Graniteville, South Carolina, established in 1846, was employing about 300 people by 1850. It was a constant moneymaker. An able propagandist as well as a good businessman,

DEBATING THE PAST

Did slaves and masters form emotional bonds?
Slavery, Ulrich Bonnell Phillips (1918) declared, was a benign institution. "Severity was clearly the exception, and kindliness the rule," he remarked. Kenneth Stampp (1956), writing as the civil rights movement of the 1950s was gaining momentum, repudiated Phillips's thesis. Slavery ripped apart families, reduced human beings to chattel, and eroded the slave's sense of self. Stanley Elkins (1959) went further still, comparing southern slavery to the subjugation of inmates in Nazi concentration camps. Slavery was so absolute that the psyche of African Americans was crushed for generations. Two major works in the 1970s challenged this rendering but in different ways. Eugene D. Genovese (1974) argued that masters and slaves were locked in a system of mutual dependence. Slaves were bound to their owners "in an organic relationship so complex and ambivalent that neither could express the simplest human feelings without reference to each other." Their emotional ties, however complicated, were real. Herbert Gutman (1976) insisted that slaves did not bond with their masters. Slave parents, children, and other relatives formed lasting ties that endured. Because it is hard to know what people really felt, the issue resists historical analysis: Did the slave girl in this photograph know for sure how she felt about the child in her arms?

Ulrich Bonnell Phillips, *American Negro Slavery* (1918), Kenneth Stampp, *The Peculiar Institution* (1956), Stanley Elkins, *Slavery* (1959), Eugene D. Genovese, *Roll, Jordan, Roll* (1974), Herbert Gutman, *The Black Family in Slavery and Freedom* (1976).

Gregg saw the textile business not only as a source of profit but also as a device for improving the lot of the South's poor whites. He worked hard to weaken the southern prejudice against manufacturing and made his plant a model of benevolent paternalism similar to that of the early mills of Lowell, Massachusetts. As with every other industry, however, southern textile manufacturing amounted to very little when compared with that of the North. While Gregg was employing 300 textile workers in 1850, the whole state of South Carolina had fewer than 900. Lowell, Massachusetts, had more spindles turning in 1860 than the entire South.

Less than 15 percent of all the goods manufactured in the United States in 1860 came from the South; the region did not really develop an industrial society. Its textile manufacturers depended on the North for machinery, for skilled workers and technicians, for financing, and for insurance. When the English geologist Charles Lyell visited New Orleans in 1846, he was astounded to discover that the thriving city supported not a single book publisher. Even a local guidebook that he purchased bore a New York imprint.

THE NORTHERN INDUSTRIAL JUGGERNAUT

The most obvious change in the North in the decades before the Civil War was the rapid growth of industry. The best estimates suggest that immediately after the War of 1812 the United States was manufacturing less than $200 million worth of goods annually. In 1859 the northeastern states alone produced $1.27 billion of the national total of almost $2 billion.

Manufacturing expanded in so many directions that it is difficult to portray or to summarize its evolution. The factory system made great strides. The development of rich anthracite coal fields in Pennsylvania was particularly important in this connection. The coal could be floated cheaply on canals to convenient sites and used to produce both heat for smelting and metalworking and steam power to drive machinery. Steam permitted greater flexibility in locating factories and in organizing work within them, and since waterpower was already being used to capacity, steam was essential for the expansion of output.

American industry displayed a remarkable receptivity to technological change. The list of inventions and processes developed between 1825 and 1850, included—besides such obviously important items as the sewing machine, the vulcanization of rubber, and the cylinder press—the screw-making machine, the friction match, the lead pencil, and an apparatus for making soda water. A society in flux put a premium on resourcefulness; an environment that offered so

much freedom to the individual encouraged experimentation. The expanding market inspired businessmen to use new techniques. With skilled labor always in short supply, the pressure to substitute machines for trained hands was great.

In the 1820s a foreign visitor noted: "Everything new is quickly introduced here, and all the latest inventions. . . . The moment an American hears the word 'invention' he pricks up his ears." Twenty years later a Frenchman wrote: "If they continue to work with the same ardor, they will soon have nothing more to desire or to do. All the mountains will be flattened, the valleys filled, all matter rendered productive." By 1850 the United States led the world in the manufacture of goods that required the use of precision instruments, and in certain industries the country was well on the way toward modern mass production methods. American clocks, pistols, rifles, and locks were outstanding.

The American exhibits at the London Crystal Palace Exhibition of 1851 so impressed the British that they sent two special commissions to the United States to study manufacturing practices. After visiting the Springfield Arsenal, where a worker took apart ten muskets, each made in a different year, mixed up the parts, and then reassembled the guns, each in perfect working order, the British investigators placed a large order for gun-making machinery. They also hired a number of American technicians to help organize what became the Enfield rifle factory. They were amazed by the lock and clock factories of New England and by the plants where screws, files, and similar metal objects were turned out in volume by automatic machinery. Instead of resisting new laborsaving machines, the investigators noted, "the workingmen hail with satisfaction all mechanical improvements."

Invention alone does not account for the industrial advance. Every year new natural resources were discovered and made available by the westward march of settlement, and the expansion of agriculture produced an ever-larger supply of raw materials for the mills and factories. Of the ten leading industries in 1860, eight (flour milling, cotton textiles, lumber, shoes, men's clothing, leather, woolen goods, and liquor) relied on farm products for their raw materials.

In the 1850s the earlier prejudice against the corporation began to break down; by the end of the decade the northern and northwestern states had all passed general incorporation laws. Of course, the corporate device made possible larger accumulations of capital. While the federal government did not charter business corporations, two actions of Congress illustrate the shift in public attitudes. In 1840 a group of scientists sought a federal charter for a National Institution for the Promotion of Science. They were

turned down on constitutional grounds; if Congress "went on erecting corporations in this way," one legislator said, "they would come, at last, to have corporations for everything." In 1863, however, the bill creating the National Academy of Science passed both houses without debate.

Industrial growth led to a great increase in the demand for labor. The effects, however, were mixed. Skilled artisans, technicians, and toolmakers earned good wages and found it relatively easy to set themselves up first as independent craftsmen, later as small manufacturers. The expanding frontier drained off much agricultural labor that might otherwise have been attracted to industry, and the thriving new towns of the West absorbed large numbers of eastern artisans of every kind. At the same time, the pay of an unskilled worker was never enough to support a family decently, and the new machines weakened the bargaining power of artisans by making skill less important.

Many other forces acted to stimulate the growth of manufacturing. Immigration increased rapidly in the 1830s and 1840s. An avalanche of strong backs, willing hands, and keen minds descended on the country from Europe. European investors poured large sums into the booming American economy, and the savings of millions of Americans and the great hoard of new California gold added to the supply of capital. Improvements in transportation, population growth, the absence of internal tariff barriers, and the relatively high per capita wealth all meant an ever expanding market for manufactured goods.

DOCUMENT

Morse, "Foreign Immigration"

A NATION OF IMMIGRANTS

Rapid industrialization influenced American life in countless ways, none more significant than its effect on the character of the workforce and consequently on the structure of society. The jobs created by industrial expansion attracted European immigrants by the tens of thousands. It is a truism that America is a nation of immigrants—recall that even the ancestors of the Indians came to the New World from Asia. But only with the development of nationalism, that is, with the establishment of the independent United States, did the word *immigrant,* meaning a foreign-born resident, come into existence.

The "native" population (native in this case meaning those whose ancestors had come from Europe rather than native Americans, the Indians) tended to look down on immigrants, and many of the immigrants, in turn, developed prejudices of their own. The Irish, for example, disliked blacks, with whom they often competed for work. One Irish

leader in the old country, Daniel O'Connell, admitted that the American Irish were "among the worst enemies of the colored race." And of course blacks responded with equal bitterness. "Every hour sees us elbowed out of some employment to make room for some newly arrived emigrant from the Emerald Isle, whose hunger and color entitle him to special favor," one of them complained. Antiblack prejudice was less noticeable among other immigrant groups but by no means absent; most immigrants adopted the views of the local majority, which was often unfriendly to African Americans.

Social and racial rivalries aside, unskilled immigrants caused serious disruptions of economic patterns wherever they appeared. Their absorption into the factories of New England speeded the disintegration of the system of hiring young farm women. Already competition and technical advances in the textile industry were increasing the pace of the machines and reducing the number of skilled workers needed to run them. Fewer young farm women were willing to work under these conditions. Recent immigrants, who required less "coddling" and who seemed to provide the mills with a "permanent" working force, replaced the women in large numbers. By 1860 Irish immigrants alone made up more than 50 percent of the labor force in the New England mills.

HOW WAGE EARNERS LIVED

The influx of immigrants does not entirely explain the low standard of living of industrial workers during this period. Low wages and the crowding that resulted from the swift expansion of city populations produced slums that would make the most noisome modern ghetto seem a paradise. A Boston investigation in the late 1840s described one district as "a perfect hive of human beings . . . huddled together like brutes." In New York tens of thousands of the poor lived in dark, rank cellars, those in the waterfront districts often invaded by high tides. Tenement houses like great gloomy prisons rose back to back, each with many windowless rooms and often without heat or running water.

Out of doors, city life for the poor was almost equally squalid. Slum streets were littered with garbage and trash. Recreational facilities were almost nonexistent. Police and fire protection in the cities were pitifully inadequate. "Urban problems" were less critical than a century later only because they affected a smaller part of the population; for those who experienced them, they were, all too often, crushing. In the mid-1850s large numbers of children in New York scrounged a bare existence by begging and scavenging. They took shelter at night in coal bins and empty barrels.

In the early factory towns, most working families maintained small vegetable gardens and a few chickens; low wage rates did not necessarily reflect a low standard of living. But in the new industrial slums even a blade of grass was unusual. In 1851 the editor Horace Greeley's *New York Tribune* published a minimum weekly budget for a family of five. The budget, which allowed nothing for savings, medical bills, recreation, or other amenities (Greeley did include 12 cents a week for newspapers), came to $10.37. Since the weekly pay of a factory hand seldom reached $5, the wives and children of most male factory workers also had to labor in the factories merely to survive. And child labor in the 1850s differed fundamentally from child labor in the 1820s. The pace of the machines had become much faster by then, and the working environment more depressing.

Relatively few workers belonged to unions, but federations of craft unions sprang up in some cities, and during the boom that preceded the Panic of 1837, a National Trades Union representing a few northeastern cities managed to hold conventions. Early in the Jackson era, "workingmen's" political parties enjoyed a brief popularity, occasionally electing a few local officials. These organizations were made up mostly of skilled craftsmen, professional reformers, and even businessmen. They soon expired, destroyed by internal bickering over questions that had little or nothing to do with working conditions.

The depression of the late 1830s led to the demise of most trade unions. Nevertheless, skilled workers improved their lot somewhat in the 1840s and 1850s. The working day declined gradually from about $12\frac{1}{2}$ hours to 10 or 11 hours. Many states passed 10-hour laws and laws regulating child labor, but they were poorly enforced. Most states, however, enacted effective mechanic's lien laws, giving workers first call on the assets of bankrupt and defaulting employers, and the Massachusetts court's decision in the case of *Commonwealth* v. *Hunt* (1842), establishing the legality of labor unions, became a judicial landmark when other state courts followed the precedent.

The flush times of the early 1850s caused the union movement to revive. Many strikes occurred, and a few new national organizations appeared. However, most unions were local institutions, weak and with little control over their membership. The Panic of 1857 dealt the labor movement another body blow. Thus there was no trend toward the general unionization of labor between 1820 and the Civil War.

For this the workers themselves were partly responsible: Craftsmen took little interest in unskilled

▶ *text continues on page 354*

Mapping
the Past

Irish and German Immigration

From 1790 to 1820, about 8000 immigrants came into the United States each year. During the next four decades, immigrants flooded into the United States at the rate of about 120,000 annually. By 1860, one in eight of the nation's 32 million people was born in Europe.

The main source of immigrants was rural Ireland, which had been rocked by several economic blows. The first was caused by the end of the Napoleonic Wars in 1815. The return of millions of soldier-peasants to their farms on the European continent caused grain prices in Ireland to fall by nearly 50 percent. Landlords there plowed grain crops under, planted grass for animal fodder, and evicted tenants. Some dispossessed farmers sought work in Dublin, Belfast, or a few other Irish cities; others emigrated to Canada or the United States. But for a time most remained in rural Ireland, hoping to eke out enough food by growing potatoes on small, scrubby plots of land. Thus the population of Ireland, despite the diminishing acreage devoted to cropland, increased from 6.8 million in 1821 to more than 8 million in 1841.

In the fall of 1845, disaster struck when disease devastated the potato crop. Many Irish starved, others braved a winter voyage to the United States, willing to endure, as one said, any misery "save that of remaining in Ireland." The Great Famine persisted for six years. About a million Irish died; another million emigrated to the United States.

Sources of Irish Emigration

The demographic consequences of the Great Famine varied by region. The two maps (above, right) help explain who emigrated and why.

The first map shows that west coast counties of Ireland were the poorest. More than half the residents of Mayo, Galway, Kerry, Clare, and Limerick counties received extended public relief as paupers.

The second map, on population change during the 1840s, shows that tens of thousands of farmers flooded into Dublin, the largest city in Ireland. The prosperous east coast counties—Antrim, Down, Wexford—experienced little decline in population. And the highest population losses were in west and central Ireland. The desperately poor inhabitants of west Ireland—the counties of Mayo, Galway, Clare, and Cork—

lacked the wherewithal to book passage on sailing ships across the Atlantic. Here the population losses were likely a result of starvation. In central Ireland, in counties such as Cavan, Monaghan, Roscommon, and Queens, where poverty was less extreme and people could sell their farms, tools, and furnishings, the high rates of depopulation chiefly resulted from emigration to the United States.

▲ A fisherwoman from Kerry, one of the poorest counties in Ireland. Many were too poor to pay for passage to the United States. Tens of thousands starved.

German and Irish Settlement in the United States

The potato blight spread to the Continent and caused farmers there to emigrate, too. In Germany, the failed democratic revolution of 1848 contributed to the exodus to the United States. In 1854, the peak year of German emigration, some 215,000 made their way to the United States. The map at bottom shows that by 1870 many had settled in rural areas of the Midwest, especially Wisconsin, where they likely resumed farming. But many remained in eastern ports, especially New York, Philadelphia, and Baltimore. Others flocked to the emerging industrial cities of Cincinnati, Chicago, and Milwaukee.

Many Irish immigrants, having sold most of their assets for passage, often lacked the money to move west or buy farms there. Most settled in the port cities along the northeastern seaboard and along the Erie Canal. By 1870 more than a quarter of a million inhabitants of New York City (including Brooklyn) had been born in Ireland. Philadelphia, Jersey City, and Boston had the next largest Irish communities in the nation.

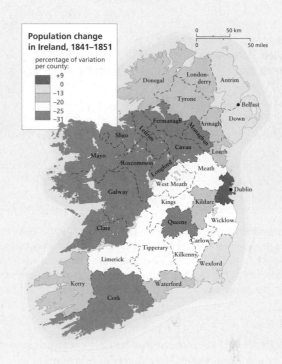

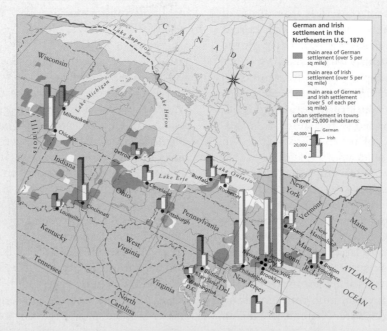

▲ A strike by 800 women shoemakers in Lynn, Massachusetts, 1860. In 1851 a Lynn shoemaker had adapted a Howe sewing machine so that it could pierce and sew leather, work normally performed by married women in their homes. Because these large machines required women to leave home and children and work at the shoe-stitching factories, few married women would do so; here they are protesting their displacement.

workers except to keep them down. Few common laborers considered themselves part of a permanent working class with different objectives from those of their employers. Although hired labor had existed throughout the colonial period, it was only with the growth of factories and other large enterprises that significant numbers of people worked for wages. To many, wage labor seemed almost un-American, a violation of the republican values of freedom and independence that had triumphed in the Revolution. Jefferson's professed dislike of urban life was based in part on his fear that people who worked for wages would be so beholden to their employers that they could not act independently.

This republican value system, along with the fluidity of society, the influx of job-hungry immigrants, and the widespread employment of women and children in unskilled jobs made labor organization difficult. The assumption was that nearly anyone who was willing to work could eventually escape from the wage-earning class. "If any continue through life in the condition of the hired laborer," Abraham Lincoln declared in 1859, "it is . . . because of either a dependent nature which prefers it, or improvidence, folly, or singular misfortune."

PROGRESS AND POVERTY

Any investigation of American society before the Civil War reveals a paradox that is obvious but difficult to resolve. The United States was a land of opportunity, a democratic society with a prosperous, expanding economy and few class distinctions. Its people had a high standard of living in comparison with the citizens of European countries. Yet within this rich, confident nation there existed a class of miserably underpaid and depressed unskilled workers, mostly immigrants, who were worse off materially than nearly any southern slave. The literature is full of descriptions of needleworkers earning 12 cents a day, of women driven to prostitution because they could not earn a living decently, of hunger marches and soup kitchens, of disease and crime and people sunk into apathy by hopeless

poverty. In 1848 more than 56,000 New Yorkers, about a quarter of the population, were receiving some form of public relief. A police drive in that city in 1860 brought in nearly 500 beggars.

The middle-class majority seemed indifferent to or at best unaware of these conditions. Reformers conducted investigations, published exposés, and labored to help the victims of urbanization and industrialization. They achieved little. Great fires burned in these decades to release the incredible energies of America. The poor were the ashes, sifting down silent and unnoticed beneath the dazzle and the smoke. Industrialization produced poverty and riches (in Marxian terminology, a proletarian class and an aristocracy of capitalists). Tenements sprang up cheek by jowl with the urban palaces of the new rich and the tree-lined streets of the prosperous middle class.

Economic opportunities were great, and taxation was minimal. Little wonder that as the generations passed, the rich got richer. Industrialization accelerated the process and, by stimulating the immigration of masses of poor workers, skewed the social balance still further. Society became more stratified, and differences in wealth and status among citizens grew greater. But the ideology of egalitarian democracy held its own. By the mid-nineteenth century Americans were convinced that all men were equal, and indeed all *white* men had equal political rights. Socially and economically, however, the distances between top and bottom were widening. This situation endured for the rest of the century, and in some respects it still endures.

FOREIGN COMMERCE

Changes in the pattern of foreign commerce were less noticeable than those in manufacturing but were nevertheless significant. After increasing erratically during the 1820s and 1830s, both imports and exports leapt forward in the next 20 years. The nation remained primarily an exporter of raw materials and an importer of manufactured goods, and in most years it imported more than it exported. Cotton continued to be the most valuable export, in 1860 accounting for a record $191 million of total exports of $333 million. Despite America's own thriving industry, textiles still held the lead among imports, with iron products second. As in earlier days, Great Britain was both the best customer of the United States and its leading supplier.

The success of sailing packets, those "square-riggers on schedule," greatly facilitated the movement of passengers and freight. Fifty-two packets were operating between New York and Europe by 1845, and many more plied between New York and other American ports. The packets accelerated the tendency for trade to concentrate in New York and to a lesser extent in Philadelphia, Baltimore, and New Orleans. The commerce of Boston and smaller New England towns like Providence and New Haven, which had flourished in earlier days, now languished.

New Bedford and a few other southern New England towns shrewdly saved their prosperity by concentrating on whaling, which boomed between 1830 and 1860. The supply of whales seemed unlimited—as indeed it was, given the primitive hunting techniques of the age of sail. By the mid-1850s, with sperm oil selling at more than $1.75 a gallon and the country exporting an average of $2.7 million worth of whale oil and whalebone a year, New Bedford boasted a whaling fleet of well over 300 vessels and a population approaching 25,000.

The whalers ranged the oceans of the world; they lived a hard, lonely life punctuated by moments of exhilaration when they sighted the great mammoths of the deep and drove the harpoon home. They also made magnificent profits. To clear 100 percent in a single voyage was merely routine.

The increase in the volume and value of trade and its concentration at larger ports had a marked effect on the construction of ships. By the 1850s the average vessel was three times the size of those built 30 years earlier. Startling improvements in design, culminating in the long, sleek, white-winged clipper ships, made possible speeds previously undreamed of. Appearing just in time to supply the need for fast transportation to the California gold fields, the clippers cut sailing time around Cape Horn to San Francisco from five or six months to three, the record of 89 days being held jointly by *Andrew Jackson* and Donald McKay's famous *Flying Cloud.* Another McKay-designed clipper, *Champion of the Seas,* once logged 465 nautical miles in 24 hours, far in excess of the best efforts of modern yachts. To achieve such speeds, cargo capacity had to be sacrificed, making clippers uneconomical for carrying the bulky produce that was the mainstay of commerce. But for specialty goods, in their brief heyday the clippers were unsurpassed. Hong Kong merchants, never known for extravagance, willingly paid 75 cents a cubic foot to ship tea by clipper to London even though slower vessels charged only 28 cents. In the early 1850s clippers sold for as much as $150,000; with decent luck a ship might earn its full cost in a voyage or two.

STEAM CONQUERS THE ATLANTIC

The reign of the clipper ship was short. Like so many other things, ocean commerce was being mechanized. Steamships conquered the high seas more slowly than the rivers because early models were unsafe in rough

▲ *Giant Steamboats on the Levee at New Orleans* (1853), a painting by Hippolyte Sebron, a Frenchman. A picture of stately elegance, these boats required unusually powerful engines to make way against the strong currents of the Mississippi. Improvements in engine design and iron casting helped boats meet the river's challenge.

waters and uneconomical. A riverboat could take on fuel along its route, whereas an Atlantic steamer had to carry tons of coal across the ocean, thereby reducing its capacity for cargo. However, by the late 1840s, steamships were capturing most of the passenger traffic, mail contracts, and first-class freight. These vessels could not keep up with the clippers in a heavy breeze, but their average speed was far greater, especially on the westward voyage against the prevailing winds. Steamers were soon crossing the Atlantic in less than ten days. Nevertheless, for very long voyages, such as the 15,000-mile haul around South America to California, fast sailing ships held their own for many years.

The steamship, and especially the iron ship, which had greater cargo-carrying capacity and was stronger and less costly to maintain, took away the advantages that American shipbuilders had held since colonial times. American lumber was cheap, but the British excelled in iron technology. Although the United States invested about $14.5 million in subsidies for the shipping industry, the funds were not employed intelligently and did little good. In 1858 government efforts to aid shipping were abandoned.

The combination of competition, government subsidy, and technological advance drove down shipping rates. Between the mid-1820s and the mid-1850s the cost of moving a pound of cotton from New York to Liverpool fell from 1 cent to about a third of a cent. Transatlantic passengers could obtain the best accommodations on the fastest ships for under $200, good accommodations on slower packets for as little as $75.

Rates were especially low for European emigrants willing to travel to America on cargo vessels. By the 1840s at least 4000 ships were engaged in carrying bulky American cotton and Canadian lumber to Europe. On their return trips with manufactured goods they had much unoccupied space, which they converted into rough quarters for passengers. Conditions on these ships were crowded, gloomy, and foul. Frequently epidemics took a fearful toll among steerage passengers. On one crossing of the ship *Lark,* 158 of 440 passengers died of typhus.

Yet without this cheap means of transportation, thousands of poor immigrants would simply have remained at home. Bargain freight rates also help

explain the clamor of American manufacturers for high tariffs, for transportation costs added relatively little to the price of European goods.

CANALS AND RAILROADS

Another dramatic change was the shift in the direction of the nation's internal commerce and its immense increase. From the time of the first settlers in the Mississippi Valley, the Great River had controlled the flow of goods from farm to market. The completion of the Erie Canal in 1825 heralded a shift, speeded by the feverish canal construction of the following decade. In 1830 there were 1277 miles of canal in the United States; by 1840 there were 3326 miles.

Each year saw more western produce moving to market through the canals. In 1845 the Erie Canal was still drawing over two-thirds of its west-east traffic from within New York, but by 1847, despite the fact that this local business held steady, more than half of its traffic came from west of Buffalo, and by 1851 more than two-thirds. The volume of western commerce over the Erie Canal in 1851 amounted to more than 20 times what it had been in 1836, while the value of western goods reaching New Orleans in this period increased only two and a half times.

The expanding traffic and New York's enormous share of it caused businessmen in other eastern cities whose canal projects had been unsuccessful to respond promptly when a new means of transport, the railroad, became available. The first railroads were built in England in the 1820s. In 1830 the first American line, the ambitiously named Baltimore and Ohio Railroad, carried 80,000 passengers over a 13-mile stretch of track.

By 1833 Charleston, South Carolina, had a line reaching 136 miles to Hamburg, on the Savannah River. Two years later the cars began rolling on the Boston and Worcester Railroad. The Panic of 1837 slowed construction, but by 1840 the United States had 3328 miles of track, equal to the canal mileage and nearly double the railroad mileage of all Europe.

The first railroads did not compete with the canals for intersectional traffic. The through connections needed to move goods economically over great distances materialized slowly. Of the 6000 miles of track operating in 1848, nearly all lay east of the Appalachians, and little of it had been coordinated into railroad systems. The intention of most early builders had been to monopolize the trade of surrounding districts, not to establish connections with competing centers. Frequently, railroads used tracks of different widths deliberately to prevent other lines from tying into their tracks.

Engineering problems held back growth. Steep grades and sharp curves—unavoidable in many parts of the country if the cost of the roads was not to be prohibitive—required more powerful and flexible engines than yet existed. Sparks from wood-burning locomotives caused fires. Wooden rails topped with strap iron wore out quickly and broke loose under the weight and vibration of heavy cars. In time the iron T rail and the use of crossties set in loose gravel to reduce vibration increased the durability of the tracks and made possible heavier, more efficient equipment. Modifications in the design of locomotives enabled the trains to negotiate sharp curves. Engines that could burn hard coal appeared, thereby eliminating the danger of starting fires along the right-of-way and reducing fuel costs.

▲ *First Railroad Train on the Mohawk and Hudson Road, 1835,* by Edward Lamson Henry (1892). Note how the shape and design of the railroad cars resembled the stagecoach they replaced.

Between 1848 and 1852 railroad mileage nearly doubled. Three years later it had doubled again, and by 1860 the nation had 30,636 miles of track. During this extraordinary burst of activity, four companies drove lines of gleaming iron from the Atlantic seaboard to the great interior valley. In 1851 the Erie Railroad, longest road in the world with 537 miles of track, linked the Hudson River north of New York City with Dunkirk on Lake Erie. Late the next year the Baltimore and Ohio reached the Ohio River at Wheeling, and in 1853 a banker named Erastus Corning consolidated eight short lines connecting Albany and Buffalo to form the New York Central Railroad. Finally, in 1858 the Pennsylvania Railroad completed a line across the mountains from Philadelphia to Pittsburgh.

In the states beyond the Appalachians, building went on at an even more feverish pace. By 1855 passengers could travel from Chicago or St. Louis to the east coast at a cost of $20 to $30, the trip taking, with luck, less than 48 hours. A generation earlier such a trip had required two to three weeks. Construction was slower in the South: Mississippi laid about 800 miles of track, Alabama 600.

FINANCING THE RAILROADS

Railroad building required immense amounts of labor and capital at a time when many other demands for these resources existed. Immigrants or (in the South) slaves did most of the heavy work. Raising the necessary money proved a more complex task.

Private investors supplied about three-quarters of the money invested in railroads before 1860, more than $800 million in the 1850s alone. Much of this capital came from local merchants and businessmen and from farmers along the proposed rights-of-way. Funds were easy to raise because subscribers seldom had to lay out the full price of their stock at one time; instead they were subject to periodic "calls" for a percentage of their commitment as construction progressed. If the road made money, much of the additional mileage could be paid for out of earnings from the first sections built. The Utica and Schenectady Railroad, one of the lines that became part of the New York Central, was capitalized in 1833 at $2 million (20,000 shares at $100). Only $75 per share was ever called; by 1844 the road had been completed, shares were selling at $129, and shareholders were receiving handsome cash dividends.

The Utica and Schenectady Railroad was a short road in a rich territory; for less favorably situated lines, stocks were hard to sell. Of the lines connecting the seaboard with the Middle West, the New York Central alone needed no public aid, chiefly because it ran through prosperous, well-populated country and across level terrain. The others were all "mixed enterprises," drawing about half their capital from state and local governments, the rest from bonds sold to American and foreign investors.

Public aid took many forms. Towns, counties, and the states themselves lent money to railroads and invested in their stock. Special privileges, such as exemption from taxation and the right to condemn property, were often granted, and in a few cases states built and operated roads as public corporations.

DOCUMENT

Senate Report on the Railroads

As with earlier internal improvement proposals, federal financial aid to railroads was usually blocked in Congress by a combination of eastern and southern votes. But in 1850 a scheme for granting federal lands to the states to build a line from Lake Michigan to the Gulf of Mexico passed both houses. The main beneficiary was the Illinois Central Railroad, which received a 200-foot right-of-way and alternate strips of land along the track 1 mile wide and 6 miles deep, a total of almost 2.6 million acres. By mortgaging this land and by selling portions of it to farmers, the Illinois Central raised nearly all the $23.4 million it spent on construction. The success of this operation led to additional grants of almost 20 million acres in the 1850s, benefiting more than 40 railroads. Far larger federal grants were made after the Civil War, when the transcontinental lines were built.

Frequently, the capitalists who promoted railroads were more concerned with making money out of the construction of the lines than with operating them. The banker Erastus Corning was a good railroad man; his lines were well maintained and efficiently run. Yet he was also mayor of Albany, an important figure in state and national politics, and a manufacturer of iron. He accepted no salary as president of the Utica and Schenectady, "asking only that he have the privilege of supplying all the rails, running gear, tools and other iron and steel articles used." When he could not himself produce rails of the proper quality, he purchased them in England, charging the railroad a commission for his services. Corning's actions led to stockholder complaints, and a committee was appointed to investigate. He managed to control this group easily enough, but it did report that "the practice of buying articles for the use of the Railroad Company from its own officers might in time come to lead to abuses of great magnitude." The prediction proved all too accurate in the generation following the Civil War.

Corning, it must be emphasized, was honest enough; his mistake, if mistake it was, lay in overestimating his own impartiality a little. Others in the

business were unashamedly crooked and avidly took advantage of the public passion for railroads. Some officials issued stock to themselves without paying for it and then sold the shares to gullible investors. Others manipulated the books of their corporations and set up special construction companies and paid them exorbitant returns out of railroad assets. These practices did not become widespread until after the Civil War, but all of them first sprang up in the decades preceding the war. At the same time that the country was first developing a truly national economy, it was also producing its first really big-time crooks.

RAILROADS AND THE ECONOMY

The effects of so much railroad construction were profound. Although the main reason that farmers put more land under the plow was an increase in the price of agricultural products, the railroad helped determine just what land was used and how profitably it could be farmed. Much of the fertile prairie through which the Illinois Central ran had been available for settlement for many years before 1850, but development had been slow because it was remote from navigable waters and had no timber. In 1840 the three counties immediately northeast of Springfield had a population of about 8500. They produced about 59,000 bushels of wheat and 690,000 bushels of corn. In the next decade the region grew slowly by the standards of that day: The three counties had about 14,000 people in 1850 and produced 71,000 bushels of wheat and 2.2 million bushels of corn. Then came the railroad and with it an agricultural revolution. By 1860 the population of the three counties had soared to over 38,000, wheat production had topped 550,000 bushels, and corn 5.7 million bushels. "Land-grant" railroads such as the Illinois Central stimulated agricultural expansion by advertising their lands widely and selling farm sites at low rates on liberal terms.

Access to world markets gave the farmers of the upper Mississippi Valley an incentive to increase output. Land was plentiful and cheap, but farm labor was scarce; consequently agricultural wages rose sharply, especially after 1850. New tools and machines appeared in time to ease the labor shortage. First came the steel plowshare, invented by John Deere, a Vermont-born blacksmith who had moved to Illinois in 1837. The prairie sod was tough and sticky, but Deere's smooth metal plows cut through it easily. In 1839 Deere turned out ten such plows in his little shop in Moline, Illinois. By 1857 he was selling 10,000 a year.

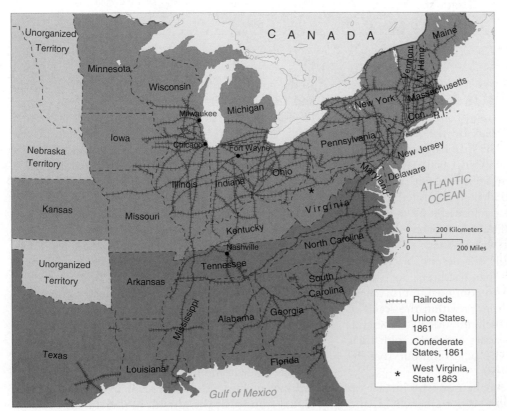

◀ **Railroads, 1860**
This map shows trunk lines (lines carrying through-traffic) in operation in 1860. Certain towns and cities owed their spectacularly rapid growth to the railroad, Chicago being an outstanding example. The map suggests the strong influence of the railroads on the expansion and economic prosperity of smaller cities such as Fort Wayne, Milwaukee, and Nashville. At the outbreak of the Civil War in 1861, the relative lack of railroads in the South was a major disadvantage for the Confederacy.

▶ **Agriculture, 1860**

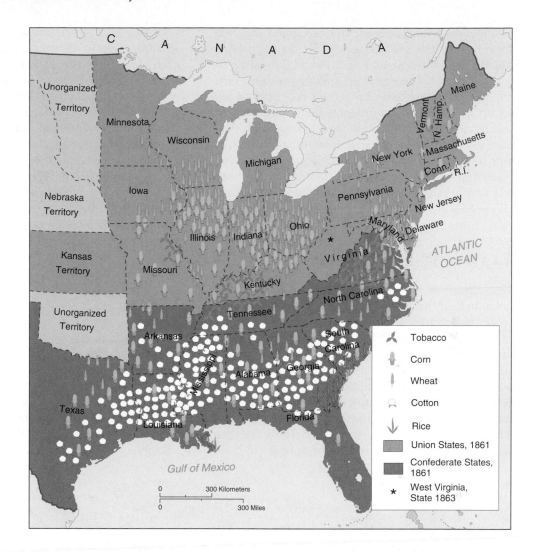

Still more important was the perfection of the mechanical reaper, for wheat production was limited more by the amount that farmers could handle during the brief harvest season than by the acreage they could plant and cultivate. The major figure in the development of the reaper was Cyrus Hall McCormick. McCormick's horse-drawn reaper bent the grain against the cutting knife and then deposited it neatly on a platform, whence it could easily be raked into windrows. With this machine, two workers could cut 14 times as much wheat as with scythes.

McCormick prospered, but despite his patents, he could not keep other manufacturers out of the business. Competition led to continual improvement of the machines and kept prices within the reach of most farmers. Installment selling added to demand. By 1860 nearly 80,000 reapers had been sold; their efficiency helps explain why wheat output rose by nearly 75 percent in the 1850s.

The railroad had an equally powerful impact on American cities. The eastern seaports benefited, and so did countless intermediate centers, such as Buffalo and Cincinnati. But no city was affected more profoundly by railroads than Chicago. In 1850 not a single line had reached there; five years later it was terminal for 2200 miles of track and controlled the commerce of an imperial domain. By extending half a dozen lines west to the Mississippi, it drained off nearly all the river traffic north of St. Louis. The Illinois Central sucked the expanding output of the prairies into Chicago as well. Most of this freight went eastward over the new railroads or on the Great Lakes and the Erie Canal. Nearly 350,000 tons of shipping plied the lakes by 1855.

The railroads, like the textile industry, stimulated other kinds of economic activity. They transformed agriculture, both real estate values and the buying and selling of land increased whenever the iron horse puffed into a new district. The railroads spurred regional concentration of industry and an increase in the size of business units. Their insatiable need for capital stimulated the growth of investment banking.

The complexity of their operations made them, as the historian Alfred D. Chandler, Jr., writes, "the first modern business enterprises," the first to employ large numbers of salaried managers and to develop "a large internal organizational structure with carefully defined lines of responsibility."

Although they apparently did not have much effect on general manufacturing before the Civil War, the railroads consumed nearly half the nation's output of bar and sheet iron in 1860. Probably more labor and more capital were occupied in economic activities resulting from the development of railroads than in the roads themselves—another way of saying that the railroads were immensely valuable internal improvements.

The proliferation of trunk lines and the competition of the canal system (for many products the slowness of canal transportation was not a serious handicap) led to a sharp decline in freight and passenger rates. Periodically, railroads engaged in "wars" to capture business. At times a person could travel from New York to Buffalo for as little as $4; anthracite was being shipped from the Pennsylvania mines to the coast for $1.50 a ton. The Erie Canal reduced its toll charges by more than two thirds in the face of railroad competition, and the roads in turn cut rates drastically until, on the eve of the Civil War, it cost less than 1 cent per ton-mile to send produce through the canal and only slightly more than 2 cents a mile on the railroads. By that time one could ship a bushel of wheat from Chicago to New York by railroad for less than 35 cents.

Cheap transportation had a revolutionary effect on western agriculture. Farmers in Iowa could now raise grain to feed the factory workers of Lowell and even of Manchester, England. Two-thirds of the meat consumed in New York City was soon arriving by rail from beyond the Appalachians. The center of American wheat production shifted westward to Illinois, Wisconsin, and Indiana. When the Crimean War (1853–1856) and European crop failures increased foreign demand, these regions boomed. Success bred success for farmers and for the railroads. Profits earned from carrying wheat enabled the roads to build feeder lines that opened up still wider areas to commercial agriculture and made it easy to bring in lumber, farm machinery, household furnishings, and the settlers themselves at low cost.

RAILROADS AND THE SECTIONAL CONFLICT

Increased production and cheap transportation boosted the western farmer's income and standard of living. The days of isolation and self-sufficiency, even for the family on the edge of the frontier, rapidly disappeared. Pioneers quickly became operators of businesses and, to a far greater extent than their forebears, consumers, buying all sorts of manufactured articles that their ancestors had made for themselves or done without. These changes had their costs. Like southern planters, they now became dependent on middlemen and lost some of their feeling of self-reliance. Overproduction became a problem. Buying a farm began to require more capital, for as profits increased, so did the price of land. Machinery was an additional expense. The proportion of farm laborers and tenants increased.

The linking of East and West had fateful effects on politics. The increased ease of movement from section to section and the ever more complex social and economic integration of East and West stimulated nationalism and thus became a force for the preservation of the Union. Without the railroads and canals, Illinois and Iowa would scarcely have dared to side against the South in 1861. When the Mississippi ceased to be essential to them, citizens of the upper valley could afford to be more hostile to slavery and especially to its westward extension. Economic ties with the Northeast reinforced cultural connections.

The South might have preserved its influence in the Northwest if it had pressed forward its own railroad-building program. It failed to do so. There were many southern lines but nothing like a southern system. As late as 1856 one could get from Memphis to Richmond or Charleston only by very indirect routes. As late as 1859 the land-grant road extending

▲ John Deere's steel-bladed plow was designed to cut through the tough prairie sod.

the Illinois Central to Mobile, Alabama, was not complete, nor did any economical connection exist between Chicago and New Orleans.

This state of affairs could be accounted for in part by the scattered population of the South, the paucity of passenger traffic, the seasonal nature of much of the freight business, and the absence of large cities. Southerners placed too much reliance on the Mississippi: The fact that traffic on the river continued to be heavy throughout the 1850s blinded them to the precipitous rate at which their relative share of the nation's trade was declining. But the fundamental cause of the South's backwardness in railroad construction was the attitude of its leaders. Southerners of means were no more interested in commerce than in industry; their capital found other outlets.

THE ECONOMY ON THE EVE OF CIVIL WAR

Between the mid-1840s and the mid-1850s the United States experienced one of the most remarkable periods of growth in the history of the world. Every economic indicator surged forward: manufacturing, grain and cotton production, population, railroad mileage, gold production, sales of public land. The building of the railroads stimulated business, and by making transportation cheaper, the completed lines energized the nation's economy. The American System that Henry Clay had dreamed of arrived with a rush just as Clay was passing from the scene.

Inevitably, this growth caused dislocations that were aggravated by the boom psychology that once again infected the popular mind. In 1857 there was a serious collapse. The return of Russian wheat to the world market after the Crimean War caused grain prices to fall. This checked agricultural expansion, which hurt the railroads and cut down on the demand for manufactures. Unemployment increased. Frightened depositors started runs on banks, most of which had to suspend specie payments.

People called this abrupt downturn the Panic of 1857. Yet the vigor of the economy was such that the bad times did not last long. The upper Mississippi Valley suffered most, for so much new land had been opened up that supplies of farm produce greatly exceeded demand. Elsewhere conditions improved rapidly.

The South, somewhat out of the hectic rush to begin with, was affected very little by the collapse of 1857, for cotton prices continued high. This gave planters the false impression that their economy was immune to such violent downturns. Some began to argue that the South would be better off out of the Union.

Before a new national upward swing could become well established, however, the sectional crisis between North and South shook people's confidence in the future. Then the war came, and a new set of forces shaped economic development.

MILESTONES

1808	Congress bans further importation of slaves		1840–1857	Economy surges during boom in manufacturing, railroad construction, and foreign commerce
1822	37 slaves are executed when Denmark Vesey's "conspiracy" is exposed		1842	Massachusetts declares unions legal in *Commonwealth v. Hunt*
1825	Erie Canal is completed, connecting East and Middle West		1846	Elias Howe invents sewing machine
1830	Baltimore and Ohio railroad begins operation		1850	Congress grants land to aid construction of Illinois Central Railroad
1831	Nat Turner's slave uprising kills 57 whites		1854	Clipper ship *Flying Cloud* sails from New York to San Francisco in 89 days
1837	Cyrus Hall McCormick invents reaper to harvest wheat		1857	Brief economic depression (Panic of 1857) collapses economy
1839	John Deere begins manufacturing steel plows			

SUPPLEMENTARY READING

Most of the volumes dealing with economic developments mentioned in earlier chapters continue to be useful for this period. On the Panic of 1857, see J. L. Huston, *The Panic of 1857 and the Coming of the Civil War* (1987). For a useful comparative study, see John Majewski, *A House Dividing: Economic Development in Pennsylvania and Virginia before the Civil War* (2000). On the economy of the South, see Gavin Wright, *The Political Economy of the Cotton South* (1978), and Michael Tadman, *Speculators and Slaves* (1989).

On slavery, in addition to the essential works listed in Debating the Past (p. 349), see Brenda Stevenson, *Life in Black and White* (1996), and Walter Johnson, *Soul by Soul: Life Inside the Antebellum Slave Market* (1999), which focuses on New Orleans. Recent evidence of slave resistance is documented in John Hope Franklin and Loren Schweninger, *Runaway Slaves* (1999), David Robertson, *Denmark Vesey* (1999), and Douglas R. Egerton, *Gabriel's Rebellion* (1993). An earlier study is Eugene D. Genovese, *From Rebellion to Revolution* (1979).

Excellent regional studies include Peter Coclanis, *The Shadow of a Dream* (1989), for South Carolina, as well as Charles E. Joyner, *Down by the Riverside: A South Carolina Slave Community* (1984), and Ann Patton Malone, *Sweet Chariot: Slave Family and Household Structure in Nineteenth-Century Louisiana* (1992).

Among specialized volumes, Bertram Wyatt-Brown, *Southern Honor* (1982), and Ira Berlin, *Slaves Without Masters* (1975), are important. Richard C. Wade, *Slavery in the Cities* (1964), contends that urban life eroded slavery, while Robert Starobin, *Industrial Slavery in the Old South* (1970), found that the institution could be adapted to industrial purposes. Most local studies take an intermediate position; see, for example, Midori Takagi, *"Rearing Wolves to Our Own Destruction": Slavery in Richmond, Virginia, 1782-1865* (1999).

Irish emigration is the subject of Tim Pat Coogan's expansive *Wherever Green Is Worn* (2000), and Edward Laxton, *The Famine Ships* (1997), as well as the scholarly collection edited by Arthur Gribben, *The Great Famine and the Irish Diaspora in America* (1999). J. Matthew Gallman, *Receiving Erin's Children* (2000) examines the arrival of Irish famine emigrants in Philadelphia. Although fewer sources on German emigration are available in English, see Marianne Wokeck, *Trade in Strangers* (1999).

On industrial developments, see H. J. Habbakuk, *American and British Technology in the Nineteenth Century* (1962), and Nathan Rosenberg, *Technology and American Economic Growth* (1972). John F. Stover, *American Railroads* (1997), is a good survey. Among the specialized studies of railroad development see Sarah Gordon, *Passage to Union* (1997), which considers the political implications of railroad development, as well as T. C. Cochran, *Railroad Leaders* (1953).

On labor history, many of the books cited in the three previous chapters apply to this one as well. On the New England shoe industry and labor organization, see Mary Blewett, *Men, Women and Work* (1988); for a more general study see her *Constant Turmoil: The Politics of Industrial Life in Nineteenth Century New England* (2000). For workingmen's political activities, Edward Pessen's *Most Uncommon Jacksonians* (1967) remains valuable.

SUGGESTED WEBSITES

"Been Here So Long": Selections from the WPA American Slave Narratives

http://newdeal.feri.org/asn/index.htm

Slave narratives are some of the most interesting primary sources about slavery.

The Settlement of African Americans in Liberia

http://www.loc.gov/exhibits/african/afam003.html

This site contains images and text relating to the colonization movement to return African Americans to Africa.

Images of African Americans from the Nineteenth Century

http://digital.nypl.org/schomburg/images_aa19/

The New York Public Library Schomburg Center for Research in Black Culture site contains numerous visuals of nineteenth-century African Americans.

The Coming of
the Civil War

SUPPLEMENTARY READING

Most of the volumes dealing with economic develop‑
ments mentioned in earlier chapters continue to be useful
for this period. On the Panic of 1857, see J. L. Huston,
The Panic of 1857 and the Coming of the Civil War (1987).
For a useful comparative study, see John Majewski, *A
House Dividing: Economic Development in Pennsylvania
and Virginia before the Civil War* (2000). On the economy
of the South, see Gavin Wright, *The Political Economy of
the Cotton South* (1978), and Michael Tadman, *Speculators
and Slaves* (1989).

On slavery, in addition to the essential works listed in
Debating the Past (p. 349), see Brenda Stevenson, *Life in
Black and White* (1996), and Walter Johnson, *Soul by Soul:
Life inside the Antebellum Slave Market* (1999), which fo‑
cuses on New Orleans. Recent evidence of slave resistance
is documented in John Hope Franklin and Loren
Schweninger, *Runaway Slaves* (1999), David Robertson,
Denmark Vesey (1999), and Douglas R. Egerton, *Gabriel's
Rebellion* (1993). An earlier study is Eugene D. Genovese,
From Rebellion to Revolution (1979).

Excellent regional studies include Peter Coclanis, *The
Shadow of a Dream* (1989), for South Carolina, as well as
Charles␣J. Joyner, *Down by the Riverside: A South Carolina
Slave Community* (1984), and Ann Patton Malone, *Sweet
Chariot: Slave Family and Household Structure in Nine‑
teenth Century Louisiana* (1992).

Among specialized volumes, Bertram Wyatt‑Brown,
Southern Honor (1982), and Ira Berlin, *Slaves Without Mas‑
ters* (1975), are important. Richard C. Wade, *Slavery in the
Cities* (1964), contends that urban life eroded slavery, while
Robert Starobin, *Industrial Slavery in the Old South*

(1970), found that the insti...
dustrial purposes. Most local...
position; see, for example, Ni...
*to Our Own Destruction": Sl...
1782–1865 (1990).

Irish emigration is the subj...
pansive *Wherever Green Is Wor...
ton, *The Famine Ships* (1997)...
lection edited by Arthur Gribb...
the Irish Diaspora in Ameri...
Raising Erin's Children (200...
Irish famine emigrants in Phil...
sources on German emigration a...
Marianne Wokeck, *Trade in Str...*

On industrial developments,
American and British Technology i...
(1962), and Nathan Rosenberg...
Economic Growth (1972), John F....
...(1997), is a good survey...
...ies of railroad development see Sar...
Union (1997), which considers the...
railroad development, as well as...
Landers (1953).

On labor history, many of the bo...
previous chapters apply to this one...
England shoe industry and labor org...
Blewett, *Men, Women and Work* (19...
study see her *Constant Turmoil: The...
Life in Nineteenth Century New England...*
ingmen's political activities, Edward Pe...
mon Jacksonians (1967) remains valuable...

SUGGESTED WEBSITES

"Been Here So Long": Selections from the WPA American Slave Narratives

http://newdeal.feri.org/asn/index.htm

Slave narratives are some of the most interesting primary
sources about slavery.

The Settlement of African Americans in Liberia

http://www.loc.gov/exhibits/african/afam003.html

This site contains images and text relating to the coloniza‑
tion movement to return African Americans to Africa.

Images of African Americans from the␣... Century

http://digital.nypl.org/schomburg/ima...

The New York Public Library Schomburg
Center for Black Culture site contains num...
nineteenth‑century African Americans.

▼ In *The Ride for Liberty—the Fugitive Slaves* (1863), painter Eastman Johnson foregrounds the slaves' own efforts to escape. In the background, though, the Union Army advances. Few slaves could effect their freedom on their own.

CHAPTER CONTENTS

The political settlement between North and South that Henry Clay designed in 1850 lasted only four years. One specific event wrecked it, but it was probably doomed in any case. Americans continued to migrate westward by the thousands, and as long as slaveholders could carry their human property into federally controlled territories, northern resentment would smolder. Slaves continued to seek freedom in the North, and the federal Fugitive Slave Act of 1850, which imposed fines for hiding or rescuing fugitive slaves, could not guarantee their capture and return. Abolitionists intensified their propaganda.

THE SLAVE POWER COMES NORTH

The new fugitive slave law encouraged more white Southerners to try to recover escaped slaves. Something approaching panic reigned in the black communities of northern cities when slave hunters arrived to seize former slaves. Thousands of blacks, not all of them fugitive slaves, fled to Canada, but many remained, and Northerners frequently refused to stand aside when such people were dragged off in chains.

Shortly after the passage of the act, James Hamlet was seized in New York City, convicted, and returned to slavery in Maryland without even being allowed to communicate with his wife and children. The New York black community was outraged, and with help from white neighbors it swiftly raised $800 to buy his freedom. In 1851 Eu-

▲ Anthony Burns, the subject of this Boston poster, was the third runaway slave to be seized and returned to the South under the hated Fugitive Slave Act of 1850. The Burns case galvanized public opinion just when Congress was debating the Kansas-Nebraska Act. The passage of that bill further outraged Northerners.

DOCUMENT

Drew, from *Narratives of Fugitive Slaves in Canada*

phemia Williams, who had lived for years as a free woman in Pennsylvania, was seized, her presumed owner claiming also her six children, all Pennsylvania-born. A federal judge released the Williamses, but the case caused alarm in the North.

Abolitionists often interfered with the enforcement of the law. When two Georgians came to Boston to reclaim William and Ellen Craft, admitted fugitives, a "vigilance committee" hounded them through the streets shouting "slave hunters, slave hunters," and forced them to return home empty-handed. The Crafts prudently—or perhaps in disgust—decided to leave the United States for England. Early in 1851 a Virginia agent captured Frederick "Shadrach" Jenkins, a waiter in a Boston coffeehouse. While Jenkins was being held for deportation, a mob of African Americans broke into the courthouse and hustled him off to Canada. That October a slave named Jerry, who had escaped from Missouri, was arrested in Syracuse, New York. Within minutes the whole town had the news. Crowds surged through the streets, and when night fell, a mob smashed into the building where Jerry was being held and spirited him away to safety in Canada.

Such incidents exacerbated sectional feelings. White Southerners accused the North of reneging on one of the main promises made in the Compromise of 1850, while the sight of harmless human beings being hustled off to a life of slavery disturbed many Northerners who were not abolitionists.

However, most white Northerners were not prepared to interfere with the enforcement of the Fugitive Slave Act themselves. Of the 332 blacks put on trial under the law, about 300 were returned to slavery, most without incident. In March 1854, Sherman M. Ableman, a Wisconsin newspaperman, was charged with having raised a mob to free a runaway. The Wisconsin Supreme Court freed him on the grounds that the Fugitive Slave Act was unconstitutional. However, in *Ableman* v. *Booth* (1859) the United States Supreme Court upheld the act's constitutionality and Booth was jailed. Nevertheless, enforcing the law in the northern states became steadily more difficult.

UNCLE TOM'S CABIN

Tremendously important in increasing sectional tensions and bringing home the evils of slavery to still more people in the North was Harriet Beecher Stowe's novel *Uncle Tom's Cabin* (1852). Stowe was neither a professional writer nor an abolitionist, and she had almost no firsthand knowledge of slavery. But her conscience had been roused by the Fugitive Slave Act. In gathering material for the book, she depended heavily on abolitionist writers, many of whom she knew. She dashed it off quickly; as she later recalled, it seemed to write itself. Nevertheless, *Uncle Tom's Cabin* was an enormous success: 10,000 copies were sold in a week; 300,000 in a year. It was translated into dozens of languages. Dramatized versions were staged in countries throughout the world .

DOCUMENT

Stowe, *Uncle Tom's Cabin*

Harriet Beecher Stowe was hardly a distinguished writer; it was her approach to the subject that explains the book's success. Her tale of the pious, patient slave Uncle Tom, the saintly white child Eva, and the callous slave driver Simon Legree appealed to an audience far wider than that reached by the abolitionists. She avoided the self-righteous, accusatory tone of most abolitionist tracts and did not seek to convert readers to belief in racial equality. Many of her southern white characters were fine, sensitive people, while the cruel Simon Legree was a transplanted Connecticut Yankee. There were many heart-rending scenes of pain, self-sacrifice, and heroism. The story proved especially effective on the stage: The slave Eliza crossing the frozen Ohio River to freedom, the death of Little Eva, Eva and Tom ascending to Heaven—these scenes left audiences in tears.

Southern critics pointed out, correctly enough, that Stowe's picture of plantation life was distorted, her slaves atypical. They called her a "coarse, ugly, long-tongued woman" and accused her of trying to

135,000 SETS, 270,000 VOLUMES SOLD.

UNCLE TOM'S CABIN

FOR SALE HERE.

AN EDITION FOR THE MILLION, COMPLETE IN 1 Vol., PRICE 37 1-2 CENTS.
" " IN GERMAN, IN 1 Vol., PRICE 50 CENTS.
" " IN 2 Vols., CLOTH, 6 PLATES, PRICE $1.50.
SUPERB ILLUSTRATED EDITION, IN 1 Vol., WITH 153 ENGRAVINGS,
PRICES FROM $2.50 TO $5.00.

The Greatest Book of the Age.

▲ A poster advertising *Uncle Tom's Cabin* in 1852, the year of its publication. The following year, Harriet Beecher Stowe published *A Key to Uncle Tom's Cabin,* intended to provide documentary evidence in support of disputed details of her indictment of slavery.

"awaken rancorous hatred and malignant jealousies" that would undermine national unity. Most Northerners, having little basis on which to judge the accuracy of the book, tended to discount southern criticism as biased. In any case, *Uncle Tom's Cabin* raised questions that transcended the issue of accuracy. Did it matter if every slave was not as kindly as Uncle Tom, as determined as George Harris? What if only one white master was as evil as Simon Legree? No earlier white American writer had looked at slaves as people.

Uncle Tom's Cabin touched the hearts of millions. Some became abolitionists; others, still hesitating to step forward, asked themselves as they put the book down: Is slavery just?

DIVERSIONS ABROAD: THE "YOUNG AMERICA" MOVEMENT

Clearly a distraction was needed to help keep the lid on sectional troubles. Some people hoped to find one in foreign affairs. The spirit of manifest destiny explains

this in large part; once the United States had reached the Pacific, expansionists began to think of transmitting the dynamic, democratic U.S. spirit to other countries by aiding local revolutionaries, opening new markets, perhaps even annexing foreign lands.

This "Young America" spirit was partly emotional, a mindless confidence that democracy would triumph everywhere, that public opinion was "stronger than the Bayonet." At the time of the European revolutions of 1848, Americans talked freely about helping the liberals in their struggles against autocratic governments. Horace Greeley's *New York Tribune* predicted that Europe would soon become "one great and splendid Republic . . . and we shall all be citizens of the world." When the Austrians crushed a rebellion in Hungary, Secretary of State Daniel Webster addressed an insulting note full of vague threats to the Austrian chargé d'affaires in Washington. Hungarian revolutionary hero Louis Kossuth visited the United States in search of aid in 1851 and 1852; President Fillmore put the USS *Mississippi* at his disposal, and great crowds turned out to cheer him.

The United States had no intention of going to war to win independence for the Hungarians, as Kossuth soon learned to his sorrow. However, the same democratic-expansionist sentiment led to dreams of conquests in the Caribbean area. In 1855 an adventurer named William Walker, backed by an American company engaged in transporting migrants to California across Central America, seized control of Nicaragua and elected himself president. He was ousted two years later but made repeated attempts to regain control until, in 1860, he died before a Honduran firing squad. Another would-be dictator, "General" George W. L. Bickley, claiming that he was disturbed by that "crookedest of all boundary lines, the Rio Grande," tried to organize an expedition to conquer Mexico.

Although many Northerners suspected them of engaging in plots to obtain more territory for slavery, Walker and Bickley were primarily adventurers trying to use the prevailing mood of buoyant expansionism for selfish ends. But there were reasons unrelated to slavery why Central America suddenly seemed important. The rapid development of California created a need for improved communication with the West Coast. A canal across Central America would cut weeks from the sailing time between New York and San Francisco. In 1850 Secretary of State John M. Clayton and the British minister to the United States, Henry Lytton Bulwer, negotiated a treaty providing for the demilitarization and joint Anglo-American control of any canal across the isthmus.

▶ *text continues on page 370*

Mapping the Past

Runaway Slaves: Hard Realities

The Myth of the Underground Railroad

The "Underground Railroad" is a commonplace of American history. The imagery is that of a subway moving masses of slaves out of the South. But the metaphor is deceptive. "The Underground Railroad" was neither as organized nor as extensive as legend suggests, nor did it exist in any slave state.

Each year tens of thousands of slaves fled, often from wrathful masters and overseers, by running into the swamps, hills, woods, or cities of the South. Few had any hope of making it to a free state, much less Canada. Few received help from abolitionists or anyone else. Of the nation's 4 million slaves, probably no more than several thousand a year escaped to a free state. Only a handful of slaves in the Cotton Belt of South Carolina, Georgia, Alabama, and Mississippi made it out of the South. Moreover, runaways in Texas and Louisiana did not go north to Canada, but west to Mexico, where nothing could be done to recover them.

The "Underground Railroad" endangered slavery not by enabling large numbers of slaves to escape, but by posing an explicit challenge to political leaders in the South. They insisted on passage of the Fugitive Slave Act to reaffirm their right to their "property" in slaves.

Actual Slave Escapes

The map "Escape Itineraries" *(right)* underscores the fact that few runaway slaves had much chance of making their way to freedom in the North. The map shows that the greatest concentrations of slaves were in South Carolina, Georgia, Alabama, Mississippi, and Louisiana. Most successful runaways lived near free states, and those who managed to escape possessed exceptional skills, cunning, or luck, and usually a combination of all three. The second map further suggests that escaped slaves generally originated from and fled to places with high proportions of free blacks.

The experience of William and Ellen Craft, slaves in Georgia, is illuminating. William, a cabinetmaker, worked evenings as a waiter and saved some money; his wife, Ellen, a seamstress, made a pair of men's trousers. Exemplary slaves, their master gave them a pass to visit relatives for Christmas and they used this occasion to escape. Ellen, who was light-skinned, put on men's clothing and green eyeglasses; to conceal her inability to write, she put her arm in a sling and, as further disguise, wrapped a bandage around one side of her face. She claimed to be a white gentleman traveling to Philadelphia to see an eye doctor, accompanied by her "servant"— William. With the money he had saved they bought

▲ A print of Ellen Craft, the slave, in the disguise "as a distinguished-looking gentleman" that effected her escape. The deceit was possible, she wrote, because she was "almost white" in appearance.

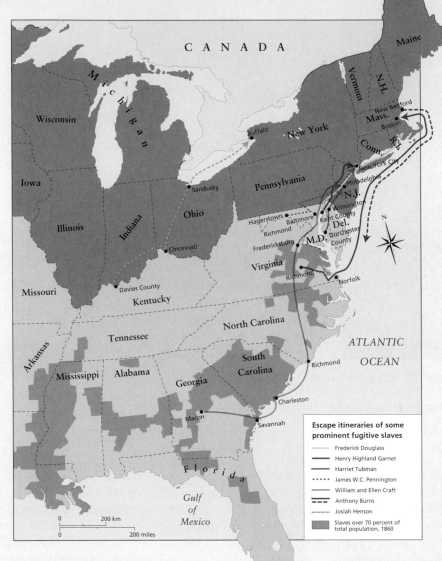

Escape itineraries of some prominent fugitive slaves

Frederick Douglass
Henry Highland Garnet
Harriet Tubman
James W.C. Pennington
William and Ellen Craft
Anthony Burns
Josiah Henson

Slaves over 70 percent of total population, 1860

0 ____ 200 km
0 ____ 200 miles

the Ohio River, headed into southern Indiana, and walked northeast to Cincinnati and then to Sandusky, Ohio. From there they sailed to Buffalo. Before the year was out, they passed over to Canada.

James W. C. Pennington escaped from a farm near Hagerstown, Maryland, in 1827. He walked toward Baltimore but was captured near Reisterstown. Then he escaped again, heading northwest into Pennsylvania, where he hid for several months. Then he journeyed northeast through Lancaster County to East Nautmeal in Chester County, Pennsylvania. He settled in New York.

Anthony Burns, who taught himself to read and write, became invaluable as a hired hand who worked at various crafts. While working as a stevedore on the docks in Richmond (see the poster on p. 366), he befriended a sailor who helped him stow away on a ship to Boston. There he was apprehended. Under the terms of the Fugitive Slave Law, he was returned to Richmond. The residents of Boston purchased his freedom in 1855.

train tickets in Macon and went to Savannah. Then they took several short boat trips: to Charleston and then to Wilmington, North Carolina, and again by train through Virginia and Maryland. They arrived at Philadelphia on Christmas Day, 1848.

Frederick Douglass escaped from Baltimore, Maryland, in 1838, disguised as a sailor, and with borrowed seaman's papers. He traveled by train to Wilmington, Delaware, by boat to Philadelphia, by train to New York City, and by boat to New Bedford, Massachusetts.

Josiah Henson was at a young age made superintendent of a plantation in Maryland. When his master went bankrupt, he was sent to a plantation in Davies County, Kentucky. Fearing he would be sold to the Deep South, in 1830 he escaped on foot with his wife and children. They crossed

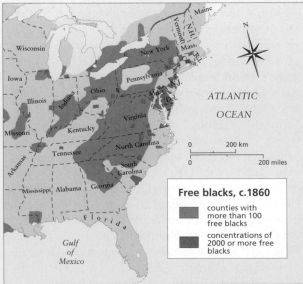

Free blacks, c.1860

counties with more than 100 free blacks

concentrations of 2000 or more free blacks

0 ____ 200 km
0 ____ 200 miles

▲ A photograph of Commodore Matthew Perry in 1855 *(left)* juxtaposed with a Japanese portrait of him. When Perry's squadron arrived in Edo Bay (Tokyo), the Japanese ordered him to leave. Japanese writers had long warned of the "barbarians of the west" who with "squinting eyes and limping feet" sought to override the "noble nations" of Asia.

As this area assumed strategic importance to the United States, the desire to obtain Cuba grew stronger. In 1854 President Franklin Pierce instructed his minister to Spain, Pierre Soulé of Louisiana, to offer $130 million for the island. Since Soulé was a hotheaded bungler, the administration arranged for him first to confer in Belgium with the American ministers to Great Britain and France, James Buchanan and John Y. Mason, to work out a plan for persuading Spain to sell. Out of this meeting came the Ostend Manifesto, a confidential dispatch to the State Department suggesting that if Spain refused to sell Cuba, "the great law of self-preservation" might justify "wresting" it from Spain by force.

News of the manifesto leaked out, and it had to be published. Northern opinion was outraged by this "slaveholders' plot." Europeans claimed to be shocked by such "dishonorable" and "clandestine" diplomacy. The government had to disavow the manifesto, and any hope of obtaining Cuba or any other territory in the Caribbean vanished.

The expansionist mood of the moment also explains President Fillmore's dispatching an expedition under Commodore Matthew C. Perry to try for commercial concessions in the isolated kingdom of Japan in 1854. Perry's expedition was a great success. The

Japanese, impressed by American naval power, agreed to establish diplomatic relations. In 1858 an American envoy, Townsend Harris, negotiated a commercial treaty that opened to American ships six Japanese ports heretofore closed to foreigners. President Pierce's negotiation of a Canadian reciprocity treaty with Great Britain in 1854 and an unsuccessful attempt, also made under Pierce, to annex the Hawaiian Islands are further demonstrations of the assertive foreign policy of the period.

STEPHEN DOUGLAS: "THE LITTLE GIANT"

The most prominent spokesman of the Young America movement was Stephen A. Douglas. The senator from Illinois was the Henry Clay of his generation. Like Clay at his best, Douglas was able to see the needs of the nation in the broadest perspective. He held a succession of state offices before being elected to Congress in 1842 at the age of 29. After only two terms in the House, he was chosen United States senator.

Douglas succeeded at almost everything he attempted. His law practice was large and prosperous.

He dabbled in Chicago real estate and made a fortune. Politics suited him to perfection. Rarely has a man seemed so closely attuned to his time and place in history. Although very short, he had powerful shoulders, a large head, strong features, and deep-set, piercing eyes. His high forehead was made to appear even bolder by the way he wore his hair, swept back in a pompadour and draped over his collar. His appearance was so imposing that friends called him "the Little Giant." "I live with my constituents," he once boasted, "drink with them, lodge with them, pray with them, laugh, hunt, dance, and work with them. I eat their corn dodgers and fried bacon and sleep two in a bed with them." Yet he was no mere backslapper. He read widely, wrote poetry, financed a number of young American artists, served as a regent of the Smithsonian Institution, and was interested in scientific farming.

The foundations of Douglas's politics were expansion and popular sovereignty. He had been willing to fight for all of Oregon in 1846, and he supported the Mexican War to the hilt, in sharp contrast to his one-term Illinois colleague in Congress, Abraham Lincoln. That local settlers should determine their own institutions was, to his way of thinking, axiomatic. Arguments over the future of slavery in the territories he believed a foolish waste of energy and time since he was convinced that natural conditions would keep the institution out of the West.

The main thing, he insisted, was to get on with the development of the United States. Let the nation build railroads, acquire new territory, expand its trade. He believed slavery "a curse beyond computation" for both blacks and whites, but he refused to admit that any moral issue was involved. He cared not, he boasted, whether slavery was voted up or voted down. This was not really true, but the question was interfering with the rapid exploitation of the continent. Douglas wanted it settled so that the country could concentrate on more important matters.

Douglas's success in steering the Compromise of 1850 through Congress added to his reputation. In 1851, he set out to win the Democratic presidential nomination, reasoning that since he was the brightest, most imaginative, and hardest-working Democrat around, he had every right to press his claim.

This brash aggressiveness proved his undoing. He expressed open contempt for James Buchanan and said of his other chief rival, Lewis Cass, who had won considerable fame while serving as minister to France, that his "reputation was beyond the C."

At the 1852 Democratic convention Douglas had no chance. Cass and Buchanan killed each other off, and the delegates finally chose a dark horse, Franklin Pierce of New Hampshire. The Whigs, rejecting the colorless Fillmore, nominated General Winfield Scott, who was known as "Old Fuss and Feathers" because of his "punctiliousness in dress and decorum." In the campaign both sides supported the Compromise of 1850. The Democrats won an easy victory, 254 electoral votes to 42.

So handsome a triumph seemed to ensure stability, but in fact it was a prelude to political chaos. The Whig party was crumbling fast. The shifting amalgam of ethnic and cultural issues that held the party together at the local level dissolved as the slavery debate became more heated. The "Cotton" Whigs of the South, alienated by the antislavery sentiments of their northern brethren, were flocking into the Democratic fold. In the North the Whigs, divided between an antislavery wing ("conscience Whigs") and another that was undisturbed by slavery, found themselves more and more at odds with each other. Congress fell overwhelmingly into the hands of proslavery southern Democrats, a development profoundly disturbing to northern Democrats as well as to Whigs.

THE KANSAS-NEBRASKA ACT

Franklin Pierce was a youthful-appearing 48 years old when he took office. He was generally well liked by politicians. His career had included service in both houses of Congress. Alcohol had become a problem for him in Washington, however, and in 1842 he had resigned from the Senate and returned home to try to best the bottle, a struggle in which he was successful. His law practice boomed, and he added to his reputation by serving as a brigadier general during the Mexican War. Although his nomination for president

▲ Stephen A. Douglas, dubbed the "Little Giant" for his height—he was five feet four inches tall—and his pugnacity. John Quincy Adams observed that during a debate Douglas worked himself into "such a heat that if his body had been made of combustible matter it would have burnt out."

▲ Franklin Pierce, a brigadier general during the Mexican War, was thrown from his horse and sustained pelvic and knee injuries. When he attempted to lead his men the next day, he fainted. Another officer, mistaking his unconsciousness, accused him of cowardice. For years, Whigs attacked Pierce's military record. Alluding to his fondness for liquor, they called him "hero of many a bottle."

came as a surprise, once made, it had appeared perfectly reasonable. Great things were expected of his administration, especially after he surrounded himself with men of all factions: To balance his appointment of a radical states' rights Mississippian, Jefferson Davis, as secretary of war, for example, he named a conservative Northerner, William L. Marcy of New York, as secretary of state.

Only a strong leader, however, can manage a ministry of all talents, and that President Pierce was not. The ship of state was soon drifting; Pierce seemed incapable of holding firm the helm.

This was the situation in January 1854 when Senator Douglas, chairman of the Committee on Territories, introduced what looked like a routine bill organizing the land west of Missouri and Iowa as the Nebraska Territory. Since settlers were beginning to trickle into the area, the time had arrived to set up a civil administration. But besides his expansionist motives, Douglas also acted because a territorial government was essential to railroad development. As a director of the Illinois Central line and as a land speculator, he hoped to make Chicago the terminus

of a transcontinental railroad, but construction could not begin until the route was cleared of Indians and brought under some kind of civil control.

Southerners, wishing to bring the transcontinental line to Memphis or New Orleans, pointed out that a right-of-way through organized territory already existed across Texas and the New Mexico Territory. In 1853 the United States minister to Mexico, James Gadsden, a prominent southern railroad executive, had engineered the purchase of more than 29,000 square miles of Mexican territory south of the Gila River, which provided an easy route through the mountains for such a railroad. Douglas, whose vision of the economic potentialities of the nation was Hamiltonian, would have been willing to support the construction of two or even three transcontinental railroads, but he knew that Congress would not go that far. In any case, he believed that the Nebraska region must be organized promptly.

The powerful southern faction in Congress would not go along with Douglas's proposal as it stood. The railroad question aside, Nebraska would presumably become a free state, for it lay north of latitude 36°30′ in a district from which slavery had been excluded by the Missouri Compromise. Under pressure from the Southerners, led by Senator David R. Atchison of Missouri, Douglas agreed first to divide the region into two territories, Kansas and Nebraska, and then—a fateful concession—to repeal the part of the Missouri Compromise that excluded slavery from land north of 36°30′. Whether the new territories should become slave or free, he argued, should be left to the decision of the settlers in accordance with the democratic principle of popular sovereignty. The fact that he might advance his presidential ambitions by making concessions to the South must have influenced Douglas too, as must the local political situation in Missouri, where slaveholders feared being "surrounded" on three sides by free states.

Douglas's miscalculation of northern sentiment was monumental. It was one thing to apply popular sovereignty to the new territories in the Southwest, quite another to apply it to a region that had been part of the United States for half a century and free soil for 34 years. Word that the area was to be opened to slavery caused an indignant outcry; many moderate opponents of slavery were radicalized. A group of abolitionist congressmen issued what they called their "Appeal of the Independent Democrats" (actually, all were Free Soilers and Whigs) denouncing the Kansas-Nebraska bill as "a gross violation of a sacred pledge" and calling for a campaign of letter writing, petitions, and public meetings to prevent its passage. The unanimity and force of the northern public's reaction was like nothing in America since the days of the Stamp Act and the Intolerable Acts.

The Compromise of 1850 and the Kansas-Nebraska Act

But protests could not defeat the bill. Southerners in both houses backed it regardless of party. Douglas, at his best when under attack, pushed it with all his power. The authors of the "Appeal," he charged, were "the pure unadulterated representatives of Abolitionism, Free Soilism, [and] Niggerism." President Pierce added whatever force the administration could muster. As a result, the northern Democrats split and the bill became law late in May 1854. In this manner the nation took the greatest single step in its march toward the abyss of secession and civil war.

The repeal of the Missouri Compromise struck the North like a slap in the face—at once shameful and challenging. Presumably the question of slavery in the territories had been settled forever; now, seemingly without justification, it had been reopened. On May 24, two days after the Kansas-Nebraska bill passed the House of Representatives, Anthony Burns, a slave who had escaped from Virginia by stowing away on a ship, was arrested in Boston. Massachusetts abolitionists brought suit against Burns's former master, charging false arrest. They also organized a protest meeting at which they inflamed the crowd into attacking the courthouse where Burns was being held. The mob broke into the building and a guard was killed, but federal marshals drove off the attackers.

President Pierce ordered the Boston district attorney to "incur any expense" to enforce the law. He also sent a revenue cutter to Boston to carry Burns back to Virginia. Thus Burns was returned to his master, but it required two companies of soldiers and 1000 police and marines to get him aboard ship. As the grim parade marched past buildings festooned with black crepe, the crowd screamed "Kidnappers! Kidnappers!" at the soldiers. Estimates of the cost of returning this single slave to his owner ran as high as $100,000. A few months later, northern sympathizers bought Burns his freedom—for a few hundred dollars.

In previous cases Boston's conservative leaders, Whig to a man, had tended to hold back; after the Burns incident, they were thoroughly radicalized. "We went to bed one night old fashioned . . . Whigs," one of them explained, "and waked up stark mad Abolitionists."

KNOW-NOTHINGS, REPUBLICANS, AND THE DEMISE OF THE TWO-PARTY SYSTEM

There were 91 free-state Democrats in the House of Representatives when the Kansas-Nebraska Act was passed, only 25 after the next election. With the Whig party already moribund, dissidents flocked to two new parties.

One was the American, or "Know-Nothing," party, so called because it grew out of a secret society whose members used the password "I don't know." The Know-Nothings were primarily nativists—immigration was soaring in the early 1850s, and the influx of poor foreigners was causing genuine social problems. Crime was on the rise in the cities along with drunkenness and other "diseases of poverty."

Several emotion-charged issues related to the fact that a large percentage of the immigrants were Irish and German Catholics also troubled the Know-Nothings. Questions such as public financing of parochial schools, lay control of church policies, the prohibition of alcoholic beverages, and increasing the time before an immigrant could apply for citizenship (the Know-Nothings favored 21 years) were matters of major importance to them. Since these were divisive issues, the established political parties tried to avoid them; hence the development of the new party.

The American party was important in the South as well as in the North, and while most Know-Nothings disliked blacks and considered them inherently inferior beings, they tended to adopt the dominant view of slavery in whichever section they were located. In the North most opposed the Kansas-Nebraska Act.

Operating often in tacit alliance with the antislavery forces (dislike of slavery did not prevent many abolitionists from being prejudiced against Catholics and immigrants), the northern Know-Nothings won a string of local victories in 1854 and elected more than 40 congressmen.

Far more significant in the long run was the formation of the Republican party, which was made up of former Free Soilers, Conscience Whigs, and "Anti-Nebraska" Democrats. The American party was a national organization, but the Republican party was purely sectional. It sprang up spontaneously throughout the Old Northwest and caught on with a rush in New England.

Republicans presented themselves as the party of freedom. They were not abolitionists (though most abolitionists were soon voting Republican), but they insisted that slavery be kept out of the territories. They believed that if America was to remain a land of opportunity, free white labor must have exclusive access to the West. Thus the party appealed not only to voters who disapproved of slavery, but also to those who wished to keep blacks—free or slave—out of their states. In 1854 the Republicans won more than a hundred seats in the House of Representatives and control of many state governments.

The Whig party had almost disappeared in the northern states and the Democratic party had been gravely weakened, but it was unclear how these two new parties would fare. The Know-Nothing party had the superficial advantage of being a nationwide organization, but where slavery was concerned, this was

DEBATING THE PAST

Was the Civil War avoidable? In 1855 Senator William H. Seward, New York's most prominent Whig, declared from the steps of the state capitol in Albany that his party was dead. He advised supporters to join the new Republican Party, which opposed slavery. Three years later Seward, a Republican, declared that conflict between the North and South was "irrepressible." Charles and Mary Beard used the term *irrepressible conflict* as a chapter title in their 1927 history text, arguing that

antithetical economic systems—one based on free labor and the other on slavery—could not coexist. The argument was fleshed out by Arthur Cole in *The Irrepressible Conflict* (1934), who added that slavery was both outmoded and immoral. War had been inevitable, as was the South's defeat. In *The Repressible Conflict* (1939), Avery Craven dismissed Cole's book as a "belated abolitionist tract." War arose, Craven insisted, when northern "fanatics" whipped up sentiment against the South and southern politicians responded with equal vituperation. The "molders of public opinion" divided the nation by creating "the fiction of two distinct peoples." James G. Randall (1942) similarly saw no differences between the North and South of sufficient magnitude to rip the nation apart. The leaders of both sides—he called them a "bungling generation"—should not have allowed overheated passions to ignite a civil war. In the 1970s and 1980s historians who embraced the "new political history," which focused on statistical analyses of voting behavior rather than the rhetoric of politicians, argued that war might have been avoided if the Whig party had not disintegrated. William Gienapp (1987) and Michael Holt (1999) credited the two-party system of the Whigs and Democrats with holding the nation together during difficult times; local coalitions on issues such as temperance and immigration had forestalled the divisive reckoning over slavery. It was the emergence of the Republican Party in these contexts, not the economic tension between the sections, that made war "irrepressible."

Charles and Mary Beard, *The Rise of American Civilization* (1927), Arthur Cole, *The Irrepressible Conflict* (1934), Avery Craven, *The Repressible Conflict* (1939), James G. Randall, *The Coming of the Civil War* (1942), William Gienapp, *The Origins of the Republican Party* (1987), and Michael Holt, *The Rise and Fall of the American Whig Party* (1999).

anything but advantageous. And many Northerners who disliked slavery were troubled by the harsh Know-Nothing policies toward immigrants and Catholics. If the Know-Nothings were in control, said former Whig congressman Abraham Lincoln in 1855, the Declaration of Independence would read "all men are created equal, except negroes, *and foreigners, and catholics.*"

"BLEEDING KANSAS"

The furor over slavery might have died down if settlement of the new territories had proceeded in an orderly manner. Almost none of the settlers who

flocked to Kansas owned slaves and relatively few of them were primarily interested in the slavery question. Most had a low opinion of blacks. ("I kem to Kansas to live in a free state," one Northerner explained. "I don't want niggers a-trampin' over my grave.") Like nearly all frontier settlers, they wanted land and local political office, lucrative government contracts, and other business opportunities.

When Congress opened the gates to settlement in May 1854, none of the land in the territory was available for sale. Treaties extinguishing Indian titles had yet to be ratified, and public lands had not been surveyed. In July Congress authorized squatters to occupy unsurveyed federal lands, but much of this

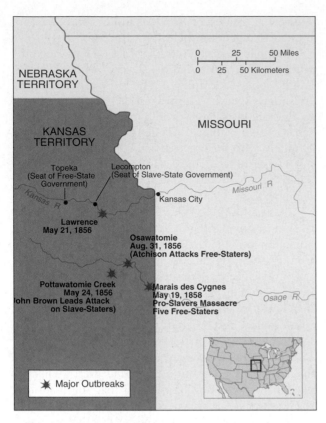

▲ **"Bleeding Kansas"**

property was far to the west of the frontier and practically inaccessible. The situation led to confusion over property boundaries, to graft and speculation, and to general uncertainty, thereby exacerbating the difficulty of establishing an orderly government.

The legal status of slavery in Kansas became the focus of all these conflicts. Both northern abolitionists and southern defenders of slavery were determined to have Kansas. They made of the territory first a testing ground and then a battlefield, thus exposing the fatal flaw in the Kansas-Nebraska Act and the idea of popular sovereignty. The law said that the people of Kansas were "perfectly free" to decide the slavery question. But the citizens of territories were not entirely free because territories were not sovereign political units. The Act had created a political vacuum, which its vague statement that the settlers must establish their domestic institutions "subject . . . to the Constitution" did not begin to fill. When should the institutions be established? Was it democratic to let a handful of first comers make decisions that would affect the lives of the thousands soon to follow? The virtues of the time-tested system of congressional control established by the Northwest Ordinance became fully apparent only when the system was discarded.

More serious was the fact that outsiders, North and South, refused to permit Kansans to work out

their own destiny. The contest for control began at once. The New England Emigrant Aid Society was formed, with grandiose plans for transporting antislavery settlers to the area. The society transported only a handful of New Englanders to Kansas. Yet the New Englanders were very conspicuous, and the society helped many Midwestern antislavery settlers to make the move.

Doing so stirred white Southerners to action. The proslavery forces enjoyed several advantages in this struggle. The first inhabitants in frontier regions nearly always came from lands immediately to the east. In this case they were proslavery Missourians. When word spread that "foreigners" from New England were seeking to "steal" Kansas, many Missourians rushed to protect their "rights." "If we win we carry slavery to the Pacific Ocean," Senator Atchison boasted.

In November 1854 an election was held in Kansas to pick a territorial delegate to Congress. A large band of Missourians crossed over specifically to vote for a proslavery candidate and elected him easily. In March 1855 some 5000 "border ruffians" again descended on Kansas and elected a territorial legislature. A census had recorded 2905 eligible voters, but 6307 votes were cast. The legislature promptly enacted a slave code and laws prohibiting abolitionist agitation. Antislavery settlers refused to recognize this regime and held elections of their own. By January 1856 two governments existed in Kansas, one based on fraud, the other extralegal.

By denouncing the free-state government located at Topeka, President Pierce encouraged the proslavery settlers to assume the offensive. In May, 800 of them sacked the antislavery town of Lawrence. An extremist named John Brown then took the law into his own hands in retaliation. By his reckoning, five Free Soilers had been killed by proslavery forces. In May 1856, together with six companions (four of them his sons), Brown stole into a settlement on Pottawatomie Creek in the dead of night. They dragged five unsuspecting men from their rude cabins and murdered them. This slaughter brought men on both sides to arms by the hundreds. Marauding bands came to blows and terrorized homesteads, first attempting to ascertain the inhabitants' position on slavery.

Brown and his followers escaped capture and were never indicted for the murders, but pressure from federal troops eventually forced him to go into hiding. He finally left Kansas in October 1856. By that time some 200 persons had lost their lives.

A certain amount of violence was normal in any frontier community, but it suited the political interests of the Republicans to make the situation in Kansas seem worse than it was. Exaggerated accounts of "bleeding Kansas" filled the pages of northern newspapers. The

Democrats were also partly to blame, for although residents of nearby states often tried to influence elections in new territories, the actions of the border ruffians made a mockery of the democratic process.

However, the main responsibility for the Kansas tragedy must be borne by the Pierce administration. Under popular sovereignty the national government was supposed to see that elections were orderly and honest. Instead, the president acted as a partisan. When the first governor of the territory objected to the manner in which the proslavery legislature had been elected, Pierce replaced him with a man who backed the southern group without question.

SENATOR SUMNER BECOMES A MARTYR FOR ABOLITIONISM

As counterpoint to the fighting in Kansas there arose an almost continuous clamor in the halls of Congress. Red-faced legislators traded insults and threats. Epithets like "liar" were freely tossed about. Prominent in these angry outbursts was a new senator, Charles Sumner of Massachusetts. Brilliant, learned, and articulate, Sumner had made a name for himself in New England as a reformer interested in the peace movement, prison reform, and the abolition of slavery. He possessed great magnetism and was, according to the tastes of the day, an accomplished orator, but he suffered inner torments of a complex nature that warped his personality. He was egotistical and humorless. His unyielding devotion to his principles was less praiseworthy than it seemed on casual examination, for it resulted from his complete lack of respect for the principles of others. Reform movements evidently provided him with a kind of emotional release; he became combative and totally lacking in objectivity when espousing a cause.

In the Kansas debates Sumner displayed an icy disdain for his foes. Colleagues threatened him with assassination, called him a "filthy reptile" and a "leper." He was impervious to such hostility. In the spring of 1856 he loosed a dreadful blast titled "The Crime Against Kansas." Characterizing administration policy as tyrannical, imbecilic, absurd, and infamous, he demanded that Kansas be admitted to the Union at once as a free state. Then he began a long and intemperate attack on both Douglas and the elderly Senator Andrew P. Butler of South Carolina, who was not present to defend himself.

Sumner described Butler as a "Don Quixote" who had taken "the harlot, slavery" as his mistress, and he spoke scornfully of "the loose expectoration" of Butler's speech. This was an inexcusable reference to the uncontrollable drooling to which the elderly senator was subject. While he was still talking, Douglas, who shrugged off most political name-calling as part of the game, was heard to mutter, "That damn fool will get himself killed by some other damn fool."

Such a "fool" quickly materialized in the person of Congressman Preston S. Brooks of South Carolina, a nephew of Senator Butler. Since Butler was absent from Washington, Brooks, who was probably as mentally unbalanced as Sumner, assumed the responsibility of defending his kinsman's honor. A southern romantic par excellence, he decided that caning Sumner would reflect his contempt more effectively than challenging him to a duel. Two days after the speech, Brooks entered the Senate as it adjourned. Sumner remained at his desk writing. Waiting until a talkative woman in the lobby had left so that she would be spared the sight of violence, Brooks then walked up to Sumner and rained blows on his head with a cane until Sumner fell, unconscious and bloody, to the floor. "I . . . gave him about 30 first-rate stripes," Brooks later boasted. "Towards the last he bellowed like a calf. I wore my cane out completely but saved the head which is gold." The physical damage suffered by Sumner was not life-threatening, but the incident so affected him psychologically that he was unable to return to his seat in Congress until 1859.

▲ Cartoon of Charles Sumner of Massachusetts being caned on the floor of the Senate by Preston Brooks of South Carolina.

Both sides made much of this disgraceful incident. When the House censured him, Brooks resigned, returned to his home district, and was triumphantly reelected. A number of well-wishers sent him souvenir canes. Northerners viewed the affair as illustrating the brutalizing effect of slavery on southern whites and made a hero of Sumner.

BUCHANAN TRIES HIS HAND

Such was the atmosphere surrounding the 1856 presidential election. The Republican party now dominated much of the North. It nominated John C. Frémont, "the Pathfinder," one of the heroes of the conquest of California during the war with Mexico. Frémont fit the Whig tradition of presidential candidates: a popular military man with almost no political experience. Unlike Taylor and Scott, however, he was sound and articulate on the issue of slavery in the territories. Although citizens of diverse interests had joined the party, Republicans expressed their objectives in one simple slogan: "Free soil, free speech, and Frémont."

The Democrats cast aside the ineffectual Pierce, but they did not dare nominate Douglas because he had raised such a storm in the North. They settled on James Buchanan, chiefly because he had been out of the country serving as minister to Great Britain during the long debate over Kansas! The American party nominated former president Millard Fillmore, a choice the remnants of the Whigs endorsed. Walt Whitman had been an ardent Democrat. But the party's stand on slavery in the territories disgusted him. In 1856 he wrote a poem, "The 18th Presidency," denouncing both Buchanan and Fillmore:

> *Two galvanized old men, close on*
> *the summons to depart this life*
> *. . . relics and proofs of the little*
> *political bargains . . .*

In the campaign, the Democrats concentrated on denouncing the Republicans as a sectional party that threatened to destroy the Union. On this issue they carried the day. Buchanan won only a minority of the popular vote, but he had strength in every section. He got 174 electoral votes to Frémont's 114 and Fillmore's 8. The significant contest took place in the populous states just north of slave territory—Pennsylvania, Ohio, Indiana, and Illinois. Of these, Buchanan carried all but Ohio, although by narrow margins.

No one could say that James Buchanan lacked political experience. Elected to the Pennsylvania legislature in 1815 when he was only 24 years old, he served for well over 20 years in Congress and had been minister to Russia, then Polk's secretary of state, then minister to Great Britain under Pierce.

Personally, Buchanan was a bundle of contradictions. Dignified in bearing and by nature cautious, he could consume enormous amounts of liquor without showing the slightest sign of inebriation. A big, heavy man, he was nonetheless remarkably graceful and light on his tiny feet, of which he was inordinately proud. He wore a very high collar to conceal a scarred neck, and because of an eye defect he habitually carried his head to one side and slightly forward, which gave him, as his biographer says, "a perpetual attitude of courteous deference and attentive interest" that sometimes led individuals to believe they had won a greater share of his attention and support than was actually the case. In fact he was extremely stubborn and sometimes vindictive.

Buchanan was said to be popular with women and attracted to them as well, and although he contemplated marriage on more than one occasion, he never took the final step. Over the years many strong men in politics had, like Walt Whitman, held him in contempt. Yet he was patriotic, conscientious, and anything but radical. While Republican extremists called him a "doughface"—they believed he lacked the force of character to stand up against southern extremists—many voters in 1856 thought he had the qualities necessary to steer the nation to calmer waters.

THE DRED SCOTT DECISION

Before Buchanan could fairly take the Kansas problem in hand, an event occurred that drove another deep wedge between North and South. Back in 1834 Dr. John Emerson of St. Louis joined the army as a surgeon and was assigned to duty at Rock Island, Illinois. Later he was transferred to Fort Snelling, in the Wisconsin Territory. In 1838 he returned to Missouri. Accompanying him on these travels was his body servant, Dred Scott, a slave. In 1846, after Emerson's death, Scott and his wife Harriet, whom he had married while in Wisconsin, with the help of a friendly lawyer brought suit in the Missouri courts for their liberty. They claimed that residence in Illinois, where slavery was barred under the Northwest Ordinance, and in the Wisconsin Territory, where the Missouri Compromise outlawed it, had made them free.

The future of Dred and Harriet Scott mattered not at all to the country or the courts; at issue was the question of whether Congress or the local legislatures had the power to outlaw slavery in the territories. After many years of litigation, the case reached the Supreme Court of the United States. On March 6, 1857, two days after Buchanan's inauguration, the high tribunal acted. Free or slave,

DOCUMENT

Opinion of the Supreme Court for *Dred Scott* v. *Sanford*

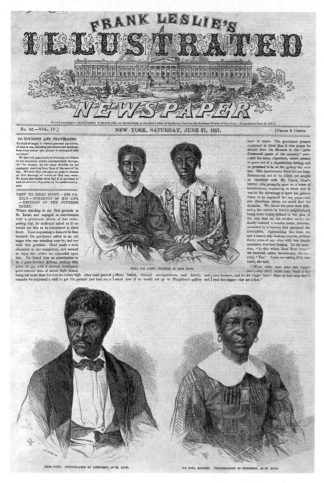

▲ Dred Scott and his wife, featured on the cover of *Frank Leslie's Illustrated Newspaper*. Historian Joshua Brown in *Beyond the Lines* (2002) argues that this publication was the precursor to today's popular news magazines. Its plentiful pictures were made possible by the new technology of mass-produced wood engraving.

the Court declared, blacks were not citizens; therefore, Scott could not sue in a federal court. This was dubious legal logic because many blacks were accepted as citizens in some states when the Constitution was drafted and ratified, and Article IV, Section 2, says that "the citizens of each state shall be entitled to all privileges and immunities of citizens in the several states." But the decision settled Scott's fate.

However, the Court went further. Since the plaintiff had returned to Missouri, the laws of Illinois no longer applied to him. His residence in the Wisconsin Territory—this was the most controversial part of the decision—did not make him free because the Missouri Compromise was unconstitutional. According to the Bill of Rights (the Fifth Amendment), the federal government cannot deprive any person of life, liberty, or property without due process of law.[1]

---

[1]Some state constitutions had similar provisions, but the slave states obviously did not.

Therefore, Chief Justice Roger B. Taney reasoned, "an Act of Congress which deprives a person . . . of his liberty or property merely because he came himself or brought his property into a particular Territory . . . could hardly be dignified with the name of due process of law."

The Dred Scott decision has been widely criticized on legal grounds. Each justice filed his own opinion, and on several important particulars there was no line of argument on which any five of the nine agreed. Some critics have reasoned that the justices should not have gone beyond the minimum of argument necessary to settle the case, and many have made much of the facts that a majority of the justices were Southerners and proslavery Northerners, and that President Buchanan had pressured them to decide the case against the Scotts. It would be going too far, however, to accuse them of plotting to extend slavery. They were trying to settle the vexing question of slavery in the territories once and for all. If this objective could only be accomplished by fuzzy reasoning, it would not be the first or the last time in the history of jurisprudence that an important result rested on shaky logic.

In addition to invalidating the already repealed Missouri Compromise, the decision threatened Douglas's principle of popular sovereignty, for if Congress could not exclude slaves from a territory, how could a mere territorial legislature do so? Until statehood was granted, slavery seemed as inviolate as freedom of religion or speech or any other civil liberty guaranteed by the Constitution. Where formerly freedom (as guaranteed in the Bill of Rights) was a national institution and slavery a local one, now, according to the Court, slavery was nationwide, excluded only where states had specifically abolished it.

The irony of employing the Bill of Rights to keep blacks in chains did not escape northern critics. Now slaves could be brought into the Minnesota Territory, even into Oregon. In his inaugural address Buchanan had sanctimoniously urged the people to accept the forthcoming ruling, "whatever this may be," as a final settlement. Many assumed (indeed, it was true) that he had put pressure on the Court to act as it did and that he knew in advance of his speech what the decision would be. If this "greatest crime in the judicial annals of the Republic" was allowed to stand, Northerners argued, the Republican party would have no reason to exist: Its program had been declared unconstitutional! The Dred Scott decision convinced thousands that the South was engaged in an aggressive attempt to extend the peculiar institution so far that it could no longer be considered peculiar.

THE LECOMPTON CONSTITUTION

Kansas soon provided a test for northern suspicions. Initially Buchanan handled the problem of Kansas well by appointing Robert J. Walker as governor. Although he was from Mississippi, Walker had no desire to foist slavery on the territory against the will of its inhabitants. He was a small man, only five feet tall, but he had more political stature by far than any previous governor of the territory. A former senator and Cabinet member, he was also courageous, patriotic, and tough-minded, much like Douglas in temperament and belief.

The proslavery leaders in Kansas had managed to convene a constitutional convention at Lecompton, but the Free Soil forces had refused to participate in the election of delegates. When this rump body drafted a proslavery constitution and then refused to submit it to a fair vote of all the settlers, Walker denounced its work and hurried back to Washington to explain the situation to Buchanan.

The president refused to face reality. His prosouthern advisers were clamoring for him to "save" Kansas. Instead of rejecting the Lecompton constitution, he asked Congress to admit Kansas to the Union with this document as its frame of government.

Buchanan's decision brought him head-on against Stephen A. Douglas, and the repercussions of their clash shattered the Democratic party. Principle and self-interest (an irresistible combination) forced Douglas to oppose the leader of his party. If he stood aside while Congress admitted Kansas, he not only would be abandoning popular sovereignty, but he would be committing political suicide as well. He was up for re-election to the Senate in 1858. All but one of the 56 newspapers in Illinois had declared editorially against the Lecompton constitution; if Douglas supported it, his defeat was certain. In a dramatic confrontation at the White House, he and Buchanan argued the question at length, tempers rising. Finally, the president tried to force him into line. "Mr. Douglas," he said, "I desire you to remember that no Democrat ever yet differed from an Administration of his own choice without being crushed." "Mr. President," Douglas replied contemptuously, "I wish you to remember that General Jackson is dead!" And he stalked out of the room.

Buchanan then compounded his error by putting tremendous political pressure on Douglas, cutting off his Illinois patronage on the eve of his reelection campaign. Of course Douglas persisted, openly joining the Republicans in the fight. Congress rejected the Lecompton bill.

Meanwhile, the extent of the fraud perpetrated at Lecompton became clear. In October 1857 a new legislature had been chosen in Kansas, antislavery voters participating in the balloting. It ordered a referendum on the Lecompton constitution in January 1858. The constitution was overwhelmingly rejected; this time the proslavery settlers boycotted the test. When Buchanan persisted in pressing Congress to admit Kansas under the Lecompton constitution, Congress ordered another referendum. To slant the case in favor of approval, the legislators stipulated that if the constitution was voted down, Kansas could not be admitted into the Union until it had a population of 90,000. Nevertheless, the Kansans rejected it by a ratio of six to one.

More than opposition to slavery influenced this vote, for by 1858 most Kansans were totally alienated from the Democratic administration in Washington because of its bungling and corrupt management of the public lands. After delaying sales unconscionably, Buchanan suddenly put 8 million acres up for auction in 1858. Squatters on this land were faced, in the midst of a depression, with finding $200 in cash to cover the minimum price of their quarter sections or losing their improvements. Local protests forced a delay of the sales, but Kansans by the thousands were convinced that Buchanan had thrown the land on the market out of pique at their rejection of the Lecompton constitution.

THE EMERGENCE OF LINCOLN

These were dark days. During the Panic of 1857 Northerners put the blame for the hard times on the southern-dominated Congress, which had just reduced tariff duties to the lowest levels in nearly half a century. As prices plummeted and unemployment rose, they attributed the collapse to foreign competition and accused the South of having sacrificed the prosperity of the rest of the nation for its selfish advantage. The South in turn read in its relative immunity from the depression proof of the superiority of the slave system, which further stimulated the running sectional debate about the relative merits of free and slave labor.

Dissolution threatened the Union. To many Americans, Stephen A. Douglas seemed to offer the best hope of preserving it. For this reason unusual attention was focused on his campaign for reelection to the Senate in 1858. The importance of the contest and Douglas's national prestige put great pressure on the Republicans of Illinois to nominate someone who would make a good showing against him. The man they chose was Abraham Lincoln.

After a towering figure has passed from the stage, it is always difficult to discover what he was like before his rise to prominence. This is especially true of Lincoln, who changed greatly when power, responsibility, and fame came to him. Lincoln was not unknown in 1858, but his public career had not been distinguished. He was born in Kentucky in 1809, and the story of his early life can be condensed, as he once

▲ How Lincoln aged during his term of office is evident in comparing Alexander Hesler's portrait, taken on June 3, 1860, with one by an unnamed photographer taken April 10, 1865.

said himself, into a single line from Gray's *Elegy:* "The short and simple annals of the poor." His illiterate father, Thomas Lincoln, was a typical frontier wanderer. When Abraham was seven years old, the family moved to Indiana. In 1830 they pushed west again into southern Illinois. The boy received almost no formal schooling.

However, Lincoln had a good mind, and he was extremely ambitious.[2] He cut loose from his family, made a trip to New Orleans, and for a time managed a general store in New Salem, Illinois. In 1834, when barely 25, he won a seat in the Illinois legislature as a Whig. Meanwhile, he studied law and was admitted to the bar in 1836.

Lincoln remained in the legislature until 1842, displaying a perfect willingness to adopt the Whig position on all issues. In 1846 he was elected to Congress. While not engaged in politics he worked at the law, maintaining an office in Springfield and following the circuit, taking a variety of cases, few of much importance. He earned a decent but by no means sumptuous living. After one term in Congress, marked by

_____
[2]His law partner, William Herndon, said that Lincoln's ambition was "a little engine that knows no rest."

his partisan opposition to Polk's Mexican policy, his political career petered out. He seemed fated to pass his remaining years as a small-town lawyer.

Even during this period Lincoln's personality was extraordinarily complex. His bawdy sense of humor and his endless fund of stories and tall tales made him a legend first in Illinois and then in Washington. He was admired in Illinois as an expert axman and a champion wrestler. He was thoroughly at home with toughs like the "Clary's Grove Boys" of New Salem and in the convivial atmosphere of a party caucus. But in a society where most men drank heavily, he never touched liquor. And he was subject to periods of melancholy so profound as to appear almost psychopathic. Friends spoke of him as having "cat fits," and he wrote of himself in the early 1840s: "I am now the most miserable man living. If what I felt were equally distributed to the whole human family, there would not be one cheerful face on earth."

In a region swept by repeated waves of religious revivalism, Lincoln managed to be at once a man of calm spirituality and a skeptic without appearing offensive to conventional believers. He was a party wheelhorse, a corporation lawyer, even a railroad lobbyist, yet his reputation for integrity was stainless.

The revival of the slavery controversy in 1854 stirred Lincoln deeply. No abolitionist, he had tried to take a "realistic" view of the problem. The Kansas-Nebraska bill led him to see the moral issue more clearly. "If slavery is not wrong, nothing is wrong," he stated with the directness and simplicity of expression for which he later became famous. Compromises made in the past for the sake of sectional harmony had always sought to preserve as much territory as possible for freedom. Yet unlike most Free Soilers, he did not blame the Southerners for slavery. "They are just what we would be in their situation," he confessed.

The moderation of his position combined with its moral force won Lincoln many admirers in the great body of citizens who were trying to reconcile their low opinion of blacks and their patriotic desire to avoid an issue that threatened the Union with their growing conviction that slavery was sinful. Anything that aided slavery was wrong, Lincoln argued. But before casting the first stone, Northerners should look into their own hearts: "If there be a man amongst us who is so impatient of [slavery] as a wrong as to disregard its actual presence among us and the difficulty of getting rid of it suddenly in a satisfactory way . . . that man is misplaced if he is on our platform." And Lincoln confessed:

> If all earthly power were given to me, I should not know what to do as to the existing institution. But . . . [this] furnishes no more excuse for permitting slavery to go into our free territory than it would for reviving the African slave trade.

Thus Lincoln was at once compassionate toward the slave owner and stern toward the institution. "A house divided against itself cannot stand," he warned. "I believe this government cannot endure permanently half slave and half free." Without minimizing the difficulties or urging a hasty or ill-considered solution, Lincoln demanded that the people look toward a day, however remote, when not only Kansas but the entire country would be free.

THE LINCOLN-DOUGLAS DEBATES

As Lincoln developed these ideas his reputation grew. In 1855 he almost won the Whig nomination for senator. He became a Republican shortly thereafter, and in June 1856, at the first Republican National Convention, he received 110 votes for the vice-presidential nomination. He seemed the logical man to pit against Douglas in 1858.

In July, Lincoln challenged Douglas to a series of seven debates. The senator accepted. The debates were well attended and widely reported, for the idea of a direct confrontation between candidates for an important office captured the popular imagination.

The choice of the next senator lay, of course, in the hands of the Illinois legislature. Technically, Douglas and Lincoln were campaigning for candidates for the legislature who were pledged to support them for the Senate seat. They presented a sharp physical contrast that must have helped voters sort out their differing points of view. Douglas was short and stocky, Lincoln long and lean. Douglas gave the impression of irrepressible energy. While speaking, he roamed the platform; he used broad gestures and bold, exaggerated arguments. He did not hesitate to call "Honest Abe" a liar. Lincoln, on his part, was slow and deliberate of speech, his voice curiously high-pitched. He seldom used gestures or oratorical tricks, trying rather to create an impression of utter sincerity to add force to his remarks.

The two employed different political styles, each calculated to project a particular image. Douglas epitomized efficiency and success. He dressed in the latest fashion, favoring flashy vests and the finest broadcloth. He was a glad-hander and a heavy drinker—he apparently died of cirrhosis of the liver. Ordinarily he arrived in town in a private railroad car, to be met by a brass band, then to ride at the head of a parade to the appointed place.

Lincoln appeared before the voters as a man of the people. He wore ill-fitting black suits and a stovepipe hat—repository for letters, bills, scribbled notes, and other scraps—that exaggerated his great height. He presented a worn and rumpled appearance, partly because he traveled from place to place on day coaches, accompanied by only a few advisers. When local supporters came to meet him at the station, he preferred to walk with them through the streets to the scene of the debate.

Lincoln and Douglas maintained a high intellectual level in their speeches, but these were political debates. They were seeking not to influence future historians (who have nonetheless pondered their words endlessly) but to win votes. Both tailored their arguments to appeal to local audiences—more antislavery in the northern counties, more proslavery in the southern. They also tended to exaggerate their differences, which were not in fact enormous. Neither wanted to see slavery in the territories or thought it economically efficient, and neither sought to abolish it by political action or by force. Both believed blacks congenitally inferior to whites, although Douglas took more pleasure in expounding on supposed racial differences than Lincoln did.

Douglas's strategy was to make Lincoln look like an abolitionist. He accused the Republicans of favoring racial equality and refusing to abide by the decision of the Supreme Court in the Dred Scott case. Himself he pictured as a heroic champion of democracy, attacked on one side by the "black" Republicans and on the other by Buchanan supporters, yet ready to fight to his last breath for popular sovereignty.

Lincoln tried to picture Douglas as proslavery and a defender of the Dred Scott decision. "Slavery is an unqualified evil to the negro, to the white man, to the soil, and to the State," he said. "Judge Douglas," he also said, "is blowing out the moral lights around us, when he contends that whoever wants slaves has a right to hold them."

However, Lincoln often weakened the impact of his arguments, being perhaps too eager to demonstrate his conservatism. "All men are created equal," he would say on the authority of the Declaration of Independence, only to add: "I am not, nor ever have been, in favor of bringing about in any way the social and political equality of the white and black races." He opposed allowing blacks to vote, to sit on juries, to marry whites, even to be citizens. He predicted the "ultimate extinction" of slavery, but when pressed he predicted that it would not occur "in less than a hundred years at the least." He took a fence-sitting position on the question of abolition in the District of Columbia and stated flatly that he did not favor repeal of the Fugitive Slave Act.

In the debate at Freeport, a town northwest of Chicago near the Wisconsin line, Lincoln asked Douglas if, considering the Dred Scott decision, the people of a territory could exclude slavery before the territory became a state. Unhesitatingly Douglas replied that they could, simply by not passing the local laws essential for holding blacks in bondage. "It matters not what way the Supreme Court may hereafter decide as to the abstract question," Douglas said. "The people have the lawful means to introduce or exclude it as they please, for the reason that slavery cannot exist . . . unless it is supported by local police regulations."

DOCUMENT

Douglas, Debate at Galesburg, Illinois

This argument saved Douglas in Illinois. The Democrats carried the legislature by a narrow margin, whereas it is almost certain that if Douglas had accepted the Dred Scott decision outright, the balance would have swung to the Republicans. But the so-called Freeport Doctrine cost him heavily two years later when he made his bid for the Democratic presidential nomination. "It matters not what way the Supreme Court may hereafter decide"—southern extremists would not accept a man who suggested that the Dred Scott decision could be circumvented, although in fact Douglas had only stated the obvious.

Probably Lincoln had not thought beyond the senatorial election when he asked the question; he was merely hoping to keep Douglas on the defensive and perhaps injure him in southern Illinois, where considerable proslavery sentiment existed. In any case, defeat did Lincoln no harm politically. He had more than held his own against one of the most formidable debaters in politics, and his distinctive personality and point of view had impressed themselves on thousands of minds. Indeed, the defeat revitalized his political career.

The campaign of 1858 marked Douglas's last triumph, Lincoln's last defeat. Elsewhere the elections in the North went heavily to the Republicans. When the old Congress reconvened in December, northern-sponsored economic measures (a higher tariff, the transcontinental railroad, river and harbor improvements, a free homestead bill) were all blocked by southern votes.

Whether the South could continue to prevent the passage of this legislation in the new Congress was

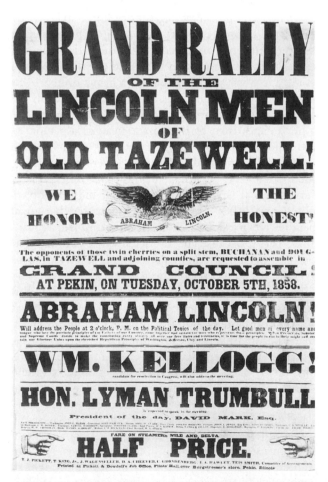

▲ The Lincoln-Douglas debates began in June 1858 with Lincoln's "House Divided" speech and lasted until October. At rallies such as the one announced in this poster, the tall awkward "Rail Splitter" challenged the "Little Giant" to examine thoroughly the slavery question.

problematical. In early 1859 even many moderate Southerners were uneasy about the future. The radicals, made panicky by Republican victories and their own failure to win in Kansas, spoke openly of secession if a Republican was elected president in 1860. Lincoln's "house divided" speech was quoted out of context, while Douglas's Freeport Doctrine added to southern woes. When Senator William H. Seward of New York spoke of an "irrepressible conflict" between freedom and slavery, white Southerners became still more alarmed.

Naturally they struck back. Led by such self-described "fire-eaters" as William L. Yancey of Alabama and Senators Jefferson Davis of Mississippi, John Slidell of Louisiana, and James H. Hammond of South Carolina, they demanded a federal slave code for the territories and talked of annexing Cuba and reviving the African slave trade.

John Brown's Raid

In October 1859, John Brown, the scourge of Kansas, made his second contribution to the unfolding sectional drama. Gathering a group of 18 followers, white and black, he staged an attack on Harpers Ferry, Virginia, a town on the Potomac River upstream from Washington. Having boned up on guerrilla tactics, he planned to seize the federal arsenal there; arm the slaves, whom he thought would flock to his side; and then establish a black republic in the mountains of Virginia.

Simply by overpowering a few night watchmen, Brown and his men occupied the arsenal and a nearby rifle factory. They captured several hostages, one of them Colonel Lewis Washington, a great-grand-nephew of George Washington. But no slaves came forward to join them. Federal troops commanded by Robert E. Lee soon trapped Brown's men in an engine house of the Baltimore and Ohio Railroad. After a two-day siege in which the attackers picked off ten of his men, Brown was captured.

No incident so well illustrates the role of emotion and irrationality in the sectional crisis as does John Brown's raid. Over the years before his Kansas escapade, Brown had been a drifter, horse thief, and swindler, several times a bankrupt, a failure in everything he attempted. His maternal grandmother, his mother, and five aunts and uncles were certifiably insane, as were 2 of his 20 children and many other relatives. After his ghastly Pottawatomie murders it should have been obvious to anyone that he was both a fanatic and mentally unstable: Some of the victims were hacked to bits with a broadsword. Yet numbers of high-minded Northerners, including Emerson and Thoreau, had supported Brown and his antislavery "work" after 1856. Some—among them Franklin B. Sanborn, a teacher; Thomas Wentworth Higginson, a clergyman; and the merchant George L. Stearns—contributed knowingly to his Harpers Ferry enterprise.

White Southerners reacted to Harpers Ferry with equal irrationality, some with a rage similar to Brown's. Dozens of hapless Northerners in the southern states were arrested, beaten, or driven off. One, falsely suspected of being an accomplice of Brown, was lynched.

Brown's fate lay in the hands of the Virginia authorities. Ignoring his obvious derangement, they charged him with treason, conspiracy, and murder. He was speedily convicted and sentenced to death by hanging.

Yet "Old Brown" had still one more contribution to make to the developing sectional tragedy. Despite the furor he had created, cool heads everywhere called for calm and denounced his attack. Most Republican politicians repudiated him. Even execution would probably not have made a martyr of Brown had he behaved like a madman after his capture. Instead, an enormous dignity descended on him as he lay in his Virginia jail awaiting death. Whatever his faults, he truly believed in racial equality. He addressed blacks who worked for him as "Mister" and arranged for them to eat at his table and sit with his family in church.

This conviction served him well in his last days. "If it is deemed necessary that I should forfeit my life for the furtherance of the ends of justice, and mingle my blood further with the blood of . . . millions in this slave country whose rights are disregarded by wicked, cruel, and unjust enactments," he said before the judge pronounced sentence, "I say, let it be done."

DOCUMENT
John Brown's
Address before
Sentencing

This John Brown, with his patriarchal beard and sad eyes, so apparently incompatible with the bloody terrorist of Pottawatomie and Harpers Ferry, led thousands in the North to ignore his past and treat him almost as a saint.

And so Brown, hanged on December 2, 1859, became to the North a hero and to the South a symbol of northern ruthlessness. Soon, as the popular song had it, Brown's body lay "a-mouldering in the grave," and the memory of his bloody act did indeed go "marching on."

The Election of 1860

By 1860 the nation was teetering on the brink of disunion. Radicals North and South were heedlessly provoking one another. When a disgruntled North Carolinian, Hinton Rowan Helper, published *The*

▲ After Brown's capture, Emerson called him "a martyr" who would "make the gallows as glorious as the cross." John Brown's principled radicalism found favor during the Depression decade of the 1930s. John Stewart Curry's mural, completed in 1943, depicted the demented John Brown in the pose of Christ on the cross. The image offended the Kansas legislature, which had commissioned Curry to portray Kansas history in a "sane and sensible manner."

Impending Crisis of the South (1857), an attempt to demonstrate statistically that slavery was ruining the South's economy and corrupting its social structure, the Republicans flooded the country with an abridged edition, although they knew that Southerners considered the book an appeal for social revolution. "I have always been a fervid Union man," one Southerner wrote in 1859, "but I confess the [northern] endorsement of the Harpers Ferry outrage and Helper's infernal doctrine has shaken my fidelity."

Extremism was more evident in the South, and to any casual observer that section must have seemed the aggressor in the crisis. Yet even in demanding the reopening of the African slave trade, southern radicals believed that they were defending themselves against attack. They felt surrounded by hostility. The North was growing at a much faster rate; if nothing was done, they feared, a flood of new free states would soon be able to amend the Constitution and emancipate the slaves. John Brown's raid, with its threat of an insurrection like Nat Turner's, reduced them to a state of panic.

When legislatures in state after state in the South cracked down on freedom of expression, made the manumission of slaves illegal, banished free blacks, and took other steps that Northerners considered blatantly provocative, the advocates of these policies believed that they were only defending the status quo. Perhaps, by seceding from the Union, the South

could raise a dike against the tide of abolitionism. Secession also provided an emotional release, a way of dissipating tension by striking back at criticism.

Stephen A. Douglas was probably the last hope of avoiding a rupture between North and South. But when the Democrats met at Charleston, South Carolina, in April 1860 to choose a presidential candidate, the southern delegates would not support him unless he promised not to disturb slavery in the territories. Indeed, they went further in their demands. The North, William L. Yancey of Alabama insisted, must accept the proposition that slavery was not merely tolerable but right. Of course the Northerners would not go so far. "Gentlemen of the South," said Senator George E. Pugh of Ohio in replying to Yancey, "you mistake us—you mistake us! We will not do it!" When southern proposals were voted down, most of the delegates from the deep South walked out and the convention adjourned without naming a candidate.

In June the Democrats reconvened at Baltimore. Again they failed to reach agreement. The two wings then met separately, the Northerners nominating Douglas, the Southerners John C. Breckenridge of Kentucky, Buchanan's vice-president. On the question of slavery in the territories, the Northerners promised to "abide by the decision of the Supreme Court," which meant, in effect, that they stood for Douglas's Freeport Doctrine. The Southerners

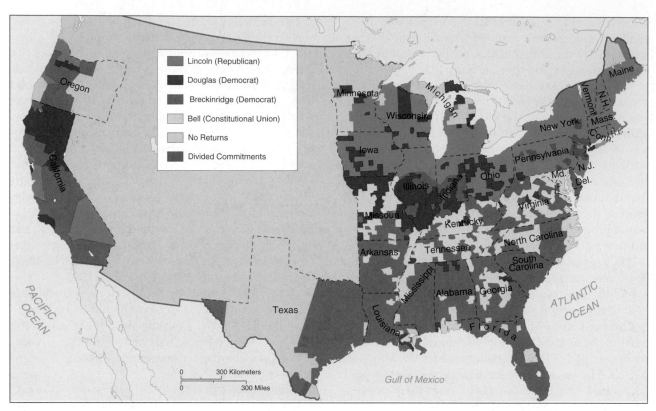

▲ **Presidential Election, 1860**

announced their belief that neither Congress nor any territorial government could prevent citizens from settling "with their property" in any territory.

Meanwhile, the Republicans, who met in Chicago in mid-May, had drafted a platform attractive to all classes and all sections of the northern and western states. For manufacturers they proposed a high tariff, for farmers a homestead law providing free land for settlers. Internal improvements "of a National character," notably a railroad to the Pacific, should receive federal aid. No restrictions should be placed on immigration. As to slavery in the territories, the Republicans did not equivocate: "The normal condition of all the territory of the United States is that of freedom." Neither Congress nor a local legislature could "give legal existence to Slavery in any Territory."

In choosing a presidential candidate the Republicans displayed equally shrewd political judgment. Senator Seward was the front-runner, but he had taken too extreme a stand and appeared unlikely to carry the crucial states of Pennsylvania, Indiana, and Illinois. He led on the first ballot but could not get a majority. Then the delegates began to look closely at Abraham Lincoln. His thoughtful and moderate views on the main issue of the times and his formidable debating skills attracted many, and so did his political personality. "Honest Abe," the "Railsplitter," a man of humble origins (born in a log cabin), self-educated, self-made, a common man but by no means an ordinary man—the combination seemed unbeatable.

It also helped that Lincoln was from a crucial state and had an excellent team of convention managers. Taking advantage of the fact that the convention was meeting in Lincoln's home state, they packed the gallery with leather-lunged Chicago ward heelers who were assigned the task of shouting for their man. They also made a series of deals with the leaders of other state delegations to win additional votes. "I authorize no bargains and will be bound by none," Lincoln telegraphed the convention. "Lincoln ain't here and don't know what we have to meet," one of his managers remarked—and proceeded to trade off two Cabinet posts for the votes of key states.

On the second ballot Lincoln drew shoulder to shoulder with Seward, on the third he was within two votes of victory. Before the roll could be called again, delegates began to switch their votes, and in a landslide, soon made unanimous, Lincoln was nominated.

A few days earlier the remnants of the American and Whig parties had formed the Constitutional Union party and nominated John Bell of Tennessee for president. "It is both the part of patriotism and of duty," they resolved, "to recognize no political principle other than the Constitution of the country, the union of the states, and the enforcement of the laws."

Ostrichlike, the Constitutional Unionists ignored the conflicts rending the nation. Only in the border states, where the consequences of disunion were sure to be most tragic, did they have any following.

With four candidates in the field, no one could win a popular majority, but it soon became clear that Lincoln was going to be elected. Breckenridge had most of the slave states in his pocket and Bell would run strong in the border regions, but the populous northern and western states had a majority of the electoral votes, and there the choice lay between the Republicans and the Douglas Democrats. In such a contest the Republicans, with their attractive economic program and their strong stand against slavery in the territories, were sure to come out on top.

Lincoln avoided campaigning and made no public statements. Douglas, recognizing the certainty of Lincoln's victory, accepted his fate and for the first time in his career rose above ambition. "We must try to save the Union," he said. "I will go South." In the heart of the Cotton Kingdom, he appealed to the voters to stand by the Union regardless of who was elected. He was the only candidate to do so; the others refused to remind the people that their election might result in secession and civil war.

When the votes were counted, Lincoln had 1.866 million, almost a million fewer than the combined total of his three opponents, but he swept the North and West, which gave him 180 electoral votes and the presidency. Douglas received 1.383 million votes, so distributed that he carried only Missouri and part of New Jersey. Breckenridge, with 848,000 popular votes, won most of the South; Bell, with 593,000, carried Virginia, Tennessee, and Kentucky. Lincoln was thus a minority president, but his title to the office was unquestionable. Even if his opponents could have combined their popular votes in each state, Lincoln would have won.

THE SECESSION CRISIS

DOCUMENT

South Carolina Declaration of the Causes of Secession

Only days after Lincoln's victory, the South Carolina legislature ordered an election of delegates to a convention to decide the state's future course. On December 20 the convention voted unanimously to secede, basing its action on the logic of Calhoun. "The State of South Carolina has resumed her position among the nations of the world," the delegates announced. By February 1, 1861, the six other states of the lower South had followed suit. A week later, at Montgomery, Alabama, a provisional government of the Confederate States of America was established. Virginia, Tennessee, North Carolina, and Arkansas did not leave the Union but announced that

if the federal government attempted to use force against the Confederacy, they too would secede.

Why were white Southerners willing to wreck the Union their forebears had put together with so much love and labor? No simple explanation is possible. The danger that the expanding North would overwhelm them was for neither today nor tomorrow. Lincoln had assured them that he would respect slavery where it existed. The Democrats had retained control of Congress in the election; the Supreme Court was firmly in their hands as well. If the North did try to destroy slavery, secession would perhaps be a logical tactic, but why not wait until the threat materialized? To leave the Union meant abandoning the very objectives for which the South had been contending for over a decade: a share of the federal territories and an enforceable fugitive slave law.

One reason why the South rejected this line of thinking was the tremendous economic energy generated in the North, which seemed to threaten the South's independence. As one Southerner complained at a commercial convention in 1855:

> From the rattle with which the nurse tickles the ear of the child born in the South to the shroud which covers the cold form of the dead, everything comes from the North. We rise from between sheets made in Northern looms, and pillows of Northern feathers, to wash in basins made in the North. . . . We eat from Northern plates and dishes; our rooms are swept with Northern brooms, our gardens dug with Northern spades . . . and the very wood which feeds our fires is cut with Northern axes, helved with hickory brought from Connecticut and New York.

Secession, white Southerners argued, would "liberate" the South and produce the kind of balanced economy that was proving so successful in the North. Moreover, the mere possibility of emancipation was a powerful force for secession. "We must either submit to degradation, and to the loss of property worth four billions," the Mississippi convention declared, "or we must secede."

The years of sectional conflict, the growing northern criticism of slavery, perhaps even an unconscious awareness that this criticism was well founded, had undermined and in many cases destroyed the patriotic feelings of white Southerners. Because of the constant clamor set up by New England antislavery groups, the South tended to identify all Northerners as "Yankee abolitionists" and to resent them with increasing passion. "I look upon the whole New England race as a troublesome unquiet set of meddlers," one Georgian wrote. In addition, a Republican president would not need the consent of Congress to flood the South with unfriendly federal officials—abolitionists and perhaps even blacks. Such a possibility

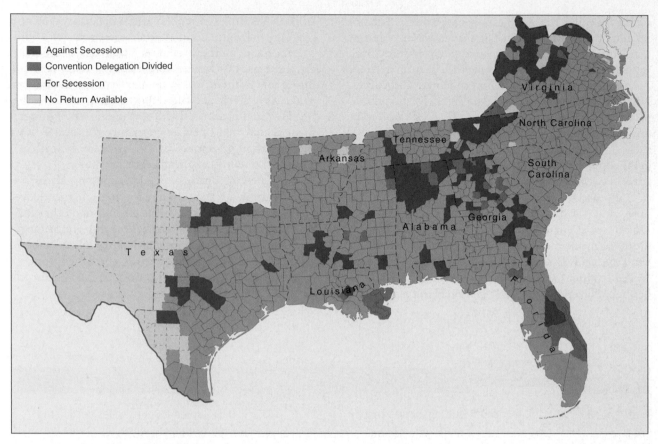

▲ **Secession of the South, 1860–1861**
A comparison of this map with the one on page 343 shows the minimal support for secession in the mainly nonslave mountain areas of the Appalachians. The strong antisecession sentiment in the mountainous areas of Virginia eventually led several counties there to break from Virginia in 1863 and form the new state of West Virginia.

most white Southerners found unsupportable. Fear approaching panic swept the region.

Although states' rights provided the rationale for leaving the Union, and Southerners expounded the strict constructionist interpretation of the Constitution with great ingenuity, the economic and emotional factors were far more basic. The lower South decided to go ahead with secession regardless of the cost. "Let the consequences be what they may," an Atlanta newspaper proclaimed. "Whether the Potomac is crimsoned in human gore, and Pennsylvania Avenue is paved ten fathoms in depth with mangled bodies . . . the South will never submit."

Not every slave owner could contemplate secession with such bloodthirsty equanimity. Some believed that the risks of war and slave insurrection were too great. Others retained a profound loyalty to the United States. Many accepted secession only after the deepest examination of conscience. Lieutenant Colonel Robert E. Lee of Virginia was typical of thousands. "I see only that a fearful calamity is upon us," he wrote during the secession crisis. "There is

no sacrifice I am not ready to make for the preservation of the Union save that of honour. If a disruption takes place, I shall go back in sorrow to my people & share the misery of my native state."

In the North there was a foolish but understandable reluctance to believe that the South really intended to break away. President-elect Lincoln was inclined to write off secession as a bluff designed to win concessions he was determined not to make. He also showed lamentable political caution in refusing to announce his plans or to cooperate with the outgoing Democratic administration before his inauguration.

In the South there was an equally unrealistic expectation that the North would not resist secession forcibly. The "Yankees" were timid materialists who would neither bear the cost nor risk their lives to prevent secession. It was commonly believed that "a lady's thimble will hold all the blood that will be shed." President Buchanan recognized the seriousness of the situation but professed himself powerless. Secession, he said, was illegal, but the federal government had no legal way to prevent it. (This was the same dilemma that had

surfaced during the nullification crisis, but as Senator Douglas had reminded him, Buchanan was no Andrew Jackson.) He urged making concessions to the South yet lacked the forcefulness to take the situation in hand.

Of course he faced unprecedented difficulties. His term was about to run out—Lincoln's inauguration day was March 4—and since he could not commit to his successor, his influence was minuscule. Yet a bolder president would have denounced secession in uncompromising terms. Instead Buchanan vacillated between compromise and aimless drift.

Appeasers, well-meaning believers in compromise, and those prepared to fight to preserve the Union were alike incapable of effective action. A group of moderates headed by Henry Clay's disciple, Senator John J. Crittenden of Kentucky, proposed a constitutional amendment in which slavery would be "recognized as existing" in all territories south of latitude 36°30′. Crittenden had a special reason for seeking to avoid a conflict. His oldest son was about to become a southern general, another son a northern general. His amendment also promised that no future amendment would tamper with the institution in the slave states and offered other guarantees to the South. But Lincoln refused to consider any arrangement that would open new territory to slavery. "On the territorial question," he wrote, "I am inflexible." The Crittenden Compromise got nowhere.

The new southern Confederacy set vigorously to work drafting a constitution, choosing Jefferson Davis as provisional president, seizing arsenals and other federal property within its boundaries, and preparing to dispatch diplomatic representatives to enlist the support of foreign powers. Buchanan bumbled helplessly in Washington. And out in Illinois, Abraham Lincoln juggled Cabinet posts and grew a beard.

MILESTONES

Year	Event	Year	Event
1850	Compromise of 1850 preserves Union	1857	U.S. Supreme Court issues decision in Dred Scott case, declaring slaves are not citizens
	U.S. and Great Britain sign Clayton-Bulwer Treaty on interoceanic canal		Panic of 1857 collapses economy
1851–1860	Northerners resist enforcement of Fugitive Slave Act	1858	Abraham Lincoln loses Senate race to Stephen Douglas after Lincoln-Douglas Debates, but wins national attention
1852	Harriet Beecher Stowe publishes *Uncle Tom's Cabin* depicting slavery	1859	John Brown raids Harpers Ferry, Virginia arsenal
	Franklin Pierce is elected president	1860	Abraham Lincoln is elected president
1854	U.S. disavows secret Ostend Manifesto on Cuba		South Carolina secedes from Union
	Kansas-Nebraska Act repeals Missouri Compromise	1861	Seven southern states establish Confederate States of America
	Commodore Matthew Perry forces Japan to open its ports to U.S. trade		Lincoln rejects Crittenden Compromise, last peaceful attempt to save Union
	Senate ratifies Gadsden Purchase of Mexican territory		
1855	William Walker seizes power in Nicaragua		
1856–1858	Proslavery forces oppose Free Soilers in "Bleeding Kansas" Territory		
1856	John Brown and followers murder five proslavery men in Pottawatomie Massacre		
	South Carolina's Preston Brooks canes Senator Charles Sumner of Massachusetts on Senate floor		
	James Buchanan is elected president		

SUPPLEMENTARY READING

On the origins of the Civil War, in addition to the Debating the Past (p. 374), see David M. Potter, *The Impending Crisis* (1976), Don E. Fehrenbacher, *Sectional Crisis and Southern Constitutionalism* (1995), and Marshall De Rosa, *The Politics of Dissolution* (1998). In *States' Rights and the Union* (2000), as in his other works, Forrest McDonald affirms the South's right to secede. William A. Link, *Roots of Secession: Slavery and Politics in Antebellum Virginia* (2003) is a useful state study.

On slave resistance, see especially John Hope Franklin and Loren Schweninger, *Runaway Slaves* (1999), William Dusinberre, *Them Dark Days: Slavery in the American Rice Swamps* (1996), and Steven Weisenburger, *Modern Medea: A Family Story of Slavery and Child-Murder from the Old South* (1998).

On the enforcement of the Fugitive Slave Act, see S. W. Campbell, *The Slave Catchers* (1970), and T. D. Morris, *Free Men All: The Personal Liberty Laws* (1974). Everyone should read Harriet Beecher Stowe's *Uncle Tom's Cabin*. Joan Hedrick's *Harriet Beecher Stowe* (1994) is excellent.

For the foreign policy of the 1850s, see C. H. Brown, *Agents of Manifest Destiny* (1980), and P. B. Wiley and Korogi Ichiro, *Yankees in the Land of the Gods* (1990).

On Stephen A. Douglas, see Robert W. Johannsen, *Stephen A. Douglas* (1973). Sumner's role in the deepening crisis is brilliantly discussed in David H. Donald, *Charles Sumner and the Coming of the Civil War* (1960) and *Charles Sumner and the Rights of Man* (1970); a more recent, brief study is Frederick J. Blue, *Charles Sumner and the Conscience of the North* (1994). Jean Baker, *James Buchanan* (2004) is solid and concise. On Dred Scott, see Paul Finkelman, *Dred Scott v. Sandford* (1997).

For Lincoln's own well-crafted words, see Abraham Lincoln, *Selections* (2 vols., 1989). The best modern biographies of Lincoln are David H. Donald, *Lincoln* (1995), and Mark Neely, *The Last Best Hope on Earth* (1993). Lincoln's early struggles are thoughtfully examined in Douglas L. Wilson, *Honor's Voice: The Transformation of Abraham Lincoln* (1998). W. E. Gienapp, *The Origins of the Republican Party* (1987), and Eric Foner, *Free Soil, Free Labor, Free Men* (1970), are excellent analyses of Republican ideas and policies. Allen Guelzo, *Lincoln's Emancipation Proclamation* (2004) is also useful.

John Stauffer, *Black Hearts of Men* (2001) examines John Brown and other radical abolitionists. See also Stephen B. Oates, *To Purge This Land with Blood* (1984).

SUGGESTED WEBSITES

Secession Era Editorial Project
http://history.furman.edu/~benson/docs/
Furman University is digitizing editorials about the secession crisis and already includes scores of them on this site.

John Brown Trial Links
http://www.law.umkc/edu/faculty/projects/ftrials/Brown.html
For information about the John Brown trial, this site provides a list of excellent links.

Harriett Beecher Stowe and *Uncle Tom's Cabin*
http://xroads.virginia.edu/~HYPER/STOWE/stowe.html
This site provides both text and description of Stowe's important books, as well as information about the author's life.

Abraham Lincoln
http://showcase.netins.net/web/creative/lincoln.html
This site both contains useful information about President Lincoln and links to other web destinations.

Abraham Lincoln Association
http://www.alincolnassoc.com/
This site allows the search of digital versions of Lincoln's papers.

The War to Save the Union

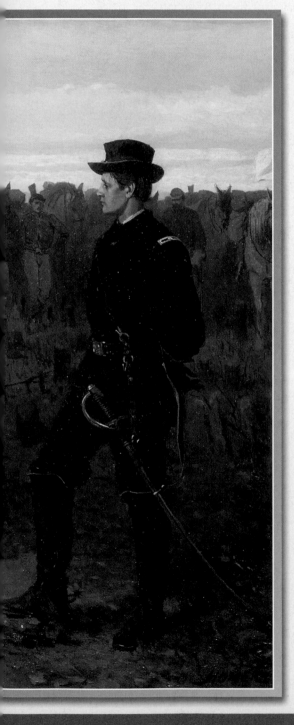

▼ *Prisoners from the Front* (1866) established Winslow Homer's reputation for spare truthfulness. But while the Union officer is depicted as intelligent and upright, the surrendering Confederate soldiers are mere caricatures—a dull-witted fellow, hands in pocket; a beaten patriarch; a defiant cavalier.

CHAPTER CONTENTS

The nomination of Lincoln had succeeded brilliantly for the Republicans, but was his election a good thing for the country? As the inauguration approached, many Americans had doubts. Honest Abe was a clever politician who had spoken well about the central issue of the times, but would he act decisively in this crisis? His behavior as president-elect was not reassuring. He spent much time closeted with politicians. Was he too obtuse to understand the grave threat to the Union posed by secession? People remembered uneasily that he had never held executive office, that his congressional career had been short and undistinguished. When he finally uprooted himself from Springfield in February 1861, his occasional speeches en route to Washington were vague, almost flippant. He kissed babies, shook hands, mouthed platitudes. Some people thought it downright cowardly that he let himself be spirited in the dead of night through Baltimore, where feeling against him ran high.

LINCOLN'S CABINET

Everyone waited tensely to see whether Lincoln would oppose secession with force, but Lincoln seemed concerned only with organizing his Cabinet. The final slate was not ready until the morning of inauguration day, March 4, and shrewd observers found it alarming, for the new president had chosen to construct a "balanced" Cabinet representing a wide range of opinion instead of putting together a group of harmonious advisers who could help him face the crisis.

William H. Seward, the secretary of state, was the ablest and best known of the appointees. Despite his reputation for radicalism, the hawk-nosed, chinless, tousle-haired Seward hoped to conciliate the South and was thus in bad odor with the radical wing of the Republican party. In time Seward proved himself Lincoln's strong right arm, but at the start he underestimated the president and expected to dominate him. Senator Salmon P. Chase, a bald, square-jawed, antislavery leader from Ohio, whom Lincoln named secretary of the treasury, represented the radicals. Chase was humorless and vain but able; he detested Seward. Many of the president's other selections worried thoughtful people.

DOCUMENT
Lincoln, First Inaugural Address

Lincoln's inaugural address was conciliatory but firm. Southern institutions were in no danger from his administration. Secession, however, was illegal, the Union "perpetual." "A husband and wife may be divorced," Lincoln said, employing one of his homely and unconsciously risqué metaphors, "but the different parts of our country cannot. . . . Intercourse, either amicable or hostile, must continue between them." His tone was calm and warm. His concluding words catch the spirit of the inaugural perfectly:

> I am loath to close. We are not enemies, but friends. We must not be enemies. Though passion may have strained, it must not break, our bonds of affection. The mystic chords of memory, stretching from every battlefield and patriot grave to every living heart . . . will yet swell the chorus of the Union when again touched, as surely they will be, by the better angels of our nature.

FORT SUMTER: THE FIRST SHOT

While denying the legality of secession, Lincoln had taken a temporizing position. The Confederates had seized most federal property in the Deep South.

Lincoln admitted frankly that he would not attempt to reclaim this property. However, two strongholds, Fort Sumter, on an island in Charleston harbor, and Fort Pickens, at Pensacola, Florida, were still in loyal Union hands. Most Republicans did not want to surrender them without a show of resistance. To do so, one wrote, would be to convert the American eagle into a "debilitated chicken."

Yet to reinforce the forts might mean bloodshed that would make reconciliation impossible. After weeks of indecision, Lincoln took the moderate step of sending a naval expedition to supply the beleaguered Sumter garrison with food. Unwilling to permit this, the Confederates opened fire on the fort on April 12 before the supply ships arrived. After holding out for 34 hours, Major Robert Anderson and his men surrendered.

The attack precipitated an outburst of patriotic indignation in the North. Lincoln issued a call for 75,000 volunteers; his request prompted Virginia, North Carolina, Arkansas, and Tennessee to secede. After years of crises and compromises, the nation chose to settle the great quarrel between the sections by force of arms.

Southerners considered Lincoln's call for troops an act of naked aggression. When the first Union regiment tried to pass through Baltimore in mid-April, it was attacked by a mob. The prosouthern chief of police telegraphed the Maryland state's attorney: "Streets red with blood. Send . . . for the riflemen to come, without delay. Fresh hordes will be down on us to-morrow." The chief and the mayor of Baltimore then ordered the railroad bridges connecting Baltimore with the northern states destroyed. Order was not restored until Union troops occupied key points in the city.

The Southerners were seeking to exercise what a later generation would call the right of self-determination. How, they asked, could the North square its professed belief in democracy with its refusal to permit the southern states to leave the Union when a majority of their citizens wished to do so?

Lincoln took the position that secession was a rejection of democracy. If the South could refuse to abide by the result of an election in which it had freely participated, then everything that monarchists and other conservatives had said about the instability of republican governments would be proved true. "The central idea of secession is the essence of anarchy," he said. The United States must "demonstrate to the world" that "when ballots have been fairly and constitutionally decided, there can be no successful appeal except to ballots themselves, at succeeding elections."

This was the proper ground to take, both morally and politically. A war against slavery would not have been supported by a majority of Northerners. Slavery was the root cause of secession but not of the North's determination to resist secession, which resulted from the people's commitment to the Union. Although abolition was to be one of the major results of the Civil War, the war was fought for nationalistic reasons, not to destroy slavery. Lincoln made this plain when he wrote in response to an editorial by Horace Greeley urging immediate emancipation: "I would save the Union. . . . If I could save the Union without freeing any slave, I would do it; and if I could save it by freeing all the slaves, I would do it; and if I could do it by freeing some and leaving others alone, I would also do that." He added, however, "I intend no modification of my oft-expressed personal wish that all men, everywhere, could be free."

THE BLUE AND THE GRAY

In any test between the United States and the Confederacy, the former possessed tremendous advantages. There were more than 20 million people in the northern states (excluding Kentucky and Missouri, where opinion was divided) but only 9 million in the South, including 3.5 million slaves whom the whites hesitated to trust with arms. The North's economic capacity to wage war was even more preponderant. It was manufacturing nine times as much as the Confederacy (including 97 percent of the nation's firearms) and had a far larger and more efficient railroad system than the South. Northern control of the merchant marine and the navy made possible a blockade of the Confederacy, a particularly potent threat to a region so dependent on foreign markets.

The Confederates discounted these advantages. Many doubted that public opinion in the North would sustain Lincoln if he attempted to meet secession with force. Northern manufacturers needed southern markets, and merchants depended heavily on southern business. Many western farmers still sent their produce down the Mississippi. War would threaten the prosperity of all these groups, Southerners maintained. Should the North try to cut Europe off from southern cotton, the European powers, particularly Great Britain, would descend on the land in their might, force open southern ports, and provide the Confederacy with the means of defending itself forever. Moreover, the South provided nearly three-fourths of the world's cotton,

essential for most textile mills. "You do not dare to make war on cotton," Senator Hammond of South Carolina had taunted his northern colleagues in 1858. "No power on earth dares to make war upon it. Cotton is king."

The Confederacy also counted on certain military advantages. The new nation need only hold what it had; it could fight a defensive war, less costly in men and material and of great importance in maintaining morale and winning outside sympathy. Southerners would be defending not only their social institutions but also their homes and families.

Luck played a part too; the Confederacy quickly found a great commander, while many of the northern generals in the early stages of the war proved either bungling or indecisive. In battle after battle Union armies were defeated by forces of equal or smaller size.

There was little to distinguish the enlisted men of the two sides. Both, conscious of their forefathers of 1776, fought for liberty, though they interpreted the concept in opposite ways.

Both sides faced massive difficulties in organizing for a war long feared but never properly anticipated. After southern defections, the regular Union army consisted of only 13,000 officers and enlisted men, far too few to absorb the 186,000 who had joined the colors by early summer, much less the additional 450,000 who had volunteered by the end of the year. Recruiting was left to the states, each being assigned a quota; there was little central organization. Natty companies of "Fire Zouaves" and "Garibaldi Guards" in gorgeous uniforms rubbed shoulders with slovenly units composed of toughs and criminals and with regiments of farm boys from

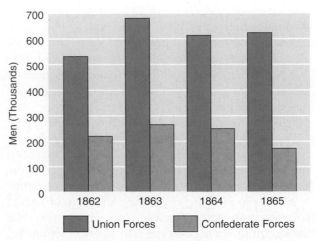

▲ **Men Present for Service in the Civil War**

▲ Young volunteers of the First Virginia Militia, in 1861. Why did they join the Confederate army? "It is better to spend our all in defending our country than to be subjugated and have it taken away from us," one explained, a sentiment that appeared often in the letters of Confederate soldiers. Soldiers on both sides believed that their cause was righteous.

character: He would willingly accept snubs and insults in order to advance the cause. He kept a close check on every aspect of the war effort, but found time for thought too. His young secretary John Nicolay reported seeing him sit sometimes for a whole hour like "a petrified image," lost in contemplation.

Gradually Lincoln's stock rose—first with men like Seward, who saw him close up and experienced both his steel and his gentleness, then with the people at large, who sensed his compassion, his humility, his wisdom. He was only 52 when he became president, and already people were calling him Old Abe. Before long they would call him Father Abraham.

The Confederacy faced far greater problems than the North, for it had to create an entire administration under pressure of war, with the additional handicap of the states' rights philosophy to which it was committed. The Confederate constitution explicitly recognized the sovereignty of the states and contained no broad authorization for laws designed to advance the general welfare. State governments repeatedly defied the central administration, located at Richmond after Virginia seceded, even with regard to military affairs.

Of course, the Confederacy made heavy use of the precedents and administrative machinery taken over from the United States. The government quickly decided that all federal laws would remain in force until specifically repealed, and many former federal officials continued to perform their duties under the new auspices.

The call to arms produced a turnout in the Confederacy perhaps even more impressive than that in the North; by July 1861 about 112,000 men were under arms. As in the North, men of every type enlisted, and morale was high. Some wealthy recruits brought slave servants with them to care for their needs in camp, cavalrymen supplied their own horses, and many men arrived with their own shotguns and hunting rifles. Ordinary militia companies sporting names like Tallapoosa Thrashers, Cherokee Lincoln Killers, and Chickasaw Desperadoes marched in step with troops of "character, blood, and social position"

Iowa, Illinois, and Michigan. Unlike later conflicts in which men from all parts of the country were mixed in each regiment, Civil War units were recruited locally. Men in each company tended to have known one another or had friends in common in civilian life. But few knew even the rudiments of soldiering. The hastily composed high command, headed by the elderly Winfield Scott, debated grand strategy endlessly while regimental commanders lacked decent maps of Virginia.

The Whig prejudice against powerful presidents was part of Lincoln's political heritage; consequently at the start he did not display the firmness of Jackson or Polk in his dealings with Congress and his Cabinet. But his strength lay in his ability to think problems through. When he did, he acted unflinchingly. Anything but a tyrant by nature, he boldly exceeded the conventional limits of presidential power in the emergency, expanding the army without congressional authorization, suspending the writ of habeas corpus, even emancipating the slaves when he thought military necessity demanded that action. Yet he also displayed remarkable patience and depth of

either a good politician or a popular leader. As president he devoted too much time to details, failed to delegate authority, and (unlike Lincoln) was impatient with garrulous and dull-witted people, types political leaders frequently have to deal with. Being a graduate of West Point, he fancied himself a military expert, but he was a mediocre military thinker. Unlike Lincoln, he quarreled frequently with his subordinates, held grudges, and allowed personal feelings to distort his judgment. "If anyone disagrees with Mr. Davis," his wife Varina Davis admitted, "he resents it and ascribes the difference to the perversity of his opponent."

DOCUMENT
Davis, Address to the Provisional Congress

▲ Jefferson Davis sat for this portrait in 1863 in his mansion in Richmond. It is the only wartime portrait from the life of the Confederate president.

bearing names like Richmond Howitzers and Louisiana Zouaves. ("Zouave" mania swept both North and South, prospective soldiers evidently considering broad sashes and baggy breeches the embodiment of military splendor.)

President Jefferson Davis represented the best type of southern planter, noted for his humane treatment of his slaves. In politics he had pursued a somewhat unusual course. While senator from Mississippi, he opposed the Compromise of 1850 and became a leader of the southern radicals. After Pierce made him secretary of war, however, he took a more nationalistic position, one close to that of Douglas. Davis supported the transcontinental railroad idea and spoke in favor of the annexation of Cuba and other Caribbean areas. He rejected Douglas's position during the Kansas controversy but tried to close the breach that Kansas had opened in Democratic ranks. After the 1860 election he supported secession only reluctantly, preferring to give Lincoln a chance to prove that he meant the South no harm.

Davis was courageous, industrious, and intelligent, but he was rather too reserved and opinionated to make

THE TEST OF BATTLE: BULL RUN

"Forward to Richmond!" "On to Washington!" Such shouts propelled the armies into battle long before either was properly trained. On July 21 at Manassas Junction, Virginia, some 20 miles below Washington, on a branch of the Potomac called Bull Run, 30,000 Union soldiers under General Irvin McDowell attacked a roughly equal force of Confederates commanded by the "Napoleon of the South," Pierre G. T. Beauregard. McDowell swept back the Confederate left flank. Victory seemed sure. Then a Virginia brigade under Thomas J. Jackson rushed to the field by rail from the Shenandoah Valley in the nick of time, held doggedly to a key hill, and checked the advance. (A South Carolina general, seeking to rally his own men, pointed to the hill and shouted: "Look, there is Jackson with his Virginians, standing like a stone wall against the enemy." Thus "Stonewall" Jackson received his nickname.)

The Southerners then counterattacked, driving the Union soldiers back. As often happens with green troops, retreat quickly turned to rout. McDowell's men fled toward the defenses of Washington, abandoning their weapons, stumbling through lines of supply wagons, trampling foolish sightseers who had come out to watch the battle. Panic engulfed Washington. Richmond exulted. Both sides expected the northern capital to fall within hours.

The inexperienced southern troops were too disorganized to follow up their victory. Casualties on both sides were light, and the battle had little direct effect on anything but morale. Southern confidence soared, while the North began to realize how immense the task of subduing the Confederacy would be.

After Bull Run, Lincoln devised a broader, more systematic strategy for winning the war. The

navy would clamp a tight blockade on all southern ports. In the West operations designed to gain control of the Mississippi would be undertaken. (This was part of General Scott's "Anaconda Plan," designed to starve the South into submission.) More important, a new army would be mustered at Washington to invade Virginia. Congress promptly authorized the enlistment of 500,000 three-year volunteers. To lead this army and—after General Scott's retirement in November—to command the Union forces, Lincoln appointed a 34-year-old major general, George B. McClellan.

McClellan was the North's first military hero. Units under his command had driven the Confederates from the pro-Union western counties of Virginia, clearing the way for the admission of West Virginia as a separate state in 1863. The fighting had been on a small scale, but McClellan, an incurable romantic and something of an egomaniac, managed to inflate its importance. "You have annihilated two armies," he proclaimed in a widely publicized message to his troops. Few Northerners noticed that they had "annihilated" only about 250 Confederates.

Despite his penchant for self-glorification, McClellan possessed solid qualifications for command. One was experience. After graduating from West Point second in his class in 1846, he had served in the Mexican War. During the Crimean War he spent a year in the field, talking with British officers and studying fortifications. McClellan had a fine military bearing, a flair for the dramatic, and the ability to inspire troops. He was a talented administrator and organizer. He liked to concoct bold plans and dreamed of striking swiftly at the heart of the Confederacy to capture Richmond, Nashville, even New Orleans. Yet he was sensible enough to insist on massive logistic support, thorough training for the troops, iron discipline, and meticulous staff work before making a move.

PAYING FOR THE WAR

After Bull Run, this policy was exactly right. By the fall of 1861 a real army was taking shape along the Potomac: disciplined, confident, adequately supplied. Northern shops and factories were producing guns, ammunition, wagons, uniforms, shoes, and the countless other supplies needed to fight a great war. Most manufacturers operated on a small scale, but with the armed forces soon wearing out 3 million pairs of shoes and 1.5 million uniforms a year and with men leaving their jobs by the hundreds of thousands to fight, the tendency of industry to mechanize and to increase the size of the average manufacturing unit became ever more pronounced.

At the beginning of the war Secretary of the Treasury Salmon P. Chase underestimated how much it would cost. He learned quickly. In August 1861 Congress passed an income tax law (3 percent on incomes over $800, which effectively exempted ordinary wage earners) and assessed a direct tax on the states. Loans amounting to $140 million were authorized. As the war dragged on and expenses mounted, new excise taxes on every imaginable product and service were passed, and still further borrowing was necessary. In 1863 the banking system was overhauled.

During the war the federal government borrowed a total of $2.2 billion and collected $667 million in taxes, slightly over 20 percent of its total expenditures.

▲ Eighteen-year-olds were the largest age group in the first year of the war in both armies. Soldiers were universally called "the boys"; and officers, even in their thirties, were called "old men." One of the most popular war songs was "Just Before the Battle, Mother."

▲ A family of a soldier in the 31st Philadelphia Infantry, camped near Washington, D.C. Although both armies discouraged women from following soldier-husbands, the practice was fairly common. Women proved indispensable as laundresses and cooks. Although women were initially excluded from army hospitals, the policy quickly changed and camp women often worked as nurses during battles.

These unprecedented large sums proved inadequate. Some obligations were met by printing paper money unredeemable in coin. About $431 million in "greenbacks"—the term distinguished this fiat money from the redeemable yellowback bills—were issued during the conflict. Public confidence in all paper money vacillated with each change in the fortunes of the Union armies, but by the end of the war the cost of living in the North had doubled.

On balance, the heavy emphasis on borrowing and currency inflation was expensive but not irresponsible. In a country still chiefly agricultural, people had relatively low cash incomes and therefore could not easily bear a heavy tax load. Many Americans considered it reasonable to expect future generations to pay part of the dollar cost of saving the Union when theirs was contributing so heavily in labor and blood.

POLITICS AS USUAL

Partisan politics was altered by the war but not suspended. The secession of the southern states left the Republicans with large majorities in both houses of Congress. Most Democrats supported measures necessary for the conduct of the war but objected to the way the Lincoln administration was conducting it. The sharpest conflicts came when slavery and race relations were under discussion. The Democrats adopted a conservative stance, as reflected in the slogan "The Constitution as it is; the Union as it was; the Negroes where they are." The Republicans divided into Moderate and Radical wings. Political divisions on economic issues such as tariffs and land policy tended to cut across party lines and, so far as the Republicans were concerned, to bear little relation to slavery and race. As the war progressed, the Radical faction became increasingly influential.

In 1861 the most prominent Radical senator was Charles Sumner, finally recovered from his caning by Preston Brooks and brimful of hatred for slaveholders. In the House, Thaddeus Stevens of Pennsylvania was the rising power. Sumner and Stevens were uncompromising on all questions relating to slaves; they insisted not merely on abolition but on granting full political and civil rights to blacks. Moderate Republicans objected vehemently to treating blacks as equals and opposed making abolition a war aim, and even many of the so-called Radicals disagreed with Sumner and Stevens on race relations. Senator Benjamin Wade of Ohio, for example, was a lifelong opponent of slavery, yet he had convinced himself that blacks (he habitually called them "niggers") had a distinctive and unpleasant smell. He considered the common white prejudice against blacks perfectly understandable. But prejudice, he maintained, gave no one the right "to do injustice to anybody"; he insisted that blacks were at least as intelligent as whites and were entitled not merely to freedom but to full political equality.

At the other end of the political spectrum stood the so-called Peace Democrats. These "Copperheads" (apparently the reference was not to the poisonous snake but to an earlier time when some hard-money Democrats wore copper pennies around their necks) opposed all measures in support of the war. They hoped to win control of Congress and force a negotiated peace. Few were actually disloyal, but their activities at a time when thousands of men were risking their lives in battle infuriated many Northerners.

Lincoln treated dissenters with a curious mixture of repression and tolerance. He suspended the writ of habeas corpus in critical areas and applied martial law

freely. Over 13,000 persons were arrested and held without trial, many, as it later turned out, unjustly. The president argued that the government dared not stand on ceremony in a national emergency. His object, he insisted, was not to punish but to prevent. Arbitrary arrests were rarely, if ever, made for purely political purposes, and free elections were held as scheduled throughout the war.

The federal courts compiled an admirable record in defending civil liberties, although when in conflict with the military, they could not enforce their decrees. In *Ex parte Merryman* (1861), Chief Justice Taney held General George Cadwalader in contempt for failing to produce a prisoner for trial when ordered to do so, but Cadwalader went unpunished and the prisoner continued to languish behind bars. After the war, in *Ex parte Milligan* (1866), the Supreme Court declared illegal the military trials of civilians in areas where the regular courts were functioning, but by that time the question was of only academic interest.

The most notorious domestic foe of the administration was the Peace Democrat Congressman Clement L. Vallandigham of Ohio, who was sent to prison by a military court. There were two rebellions in progress, Vallandigham claimed, "the Secessionist Rebellion" and "the Abolitionist Rebellion." "I am against both," he added. But Lincoln ordered him released and banished to the Confederacy. Once at liberty Vallandigham moved to Canada, from which refuge he ran unsuccessfully for governor of Ohio.

"Perish offices," he once said, "perish life itself, but do the thing that is right." In 1864 he returned to Ohio. Although he campaigned against Lincoln in the presidential election, he was not arrested. Lincoln was no dictator.

Behind Confederate Lines

The South also revised its strategy after Bull Run. Although it might have been wiser to risk everything on a bold invasion of the North, President Davis relied primarily on a strong defense to wear down the Union's will to fight. In 1862 the Confederate Congress passed a conscription act that permitted the hiring of substitutes and exempted many classes of people (including college professors, druggists, and mail carriers) whose work could hardly have been deemed essential. A provision deferring one slave owner or overseer for every plantation of 20 or more slaves led many to grumble about "a rich man's war and a poor man's fight."

Although the Confederacy did not develop a two-party system, there was plenty of internal political strife. Southern devotion to states' rights and individual liberty (for white men) caused endless trouble. Conflicts were continually erupting between Davis and southern governors jealous of their prerogatives as heads of "sovereign" states.

Finance was the Confederacy's most vexing problem. The blockade made it impossible to raise much money through tariffs. The Confederate Congress passed an income tax together with many excise taxes but all told they covered only 2 percent of its needs by taxation. The most effective levy was a tax in kind, amounting to one-tenth of each farmer's production. The South borrowed as much as it could ($712 million), even mortgaging cotton undeliverable because of the blockade, in order to gain European credits. But it relied mainly on printing paper currency; over $1.5 billion poured from the presses during the war. Considering the amount issued, this currency held its value well until late in the war, when the military fortunes of the Confederacy began to decline. Then the bottom fell out, and by early 1865 the Confederate dollar was worth less than 2 cents in gold.

Outfitting the army strained southern resources to the limit. Large supplies of small arms (some 600,000 weapons during the entire war) came from Europe through the blockade, along with other valuable matériel. As the blockade became more efficient, however, it became increasingly difficult to obtain European goods. The Confederates did manage to build a number of munitions plants, and they captured huge amounts of northern arms. No battle was lost because of a lack of guns or other military equipment, although shortages of shoes and uniforms handicapped the Confederate forces on some occasions.

Foreign policy loomed large in Confederate thinking, for the "cotton is king" theory presupposed that the great powers would break any northern blockade to get cotton for their textile mills. Southern expectations were not realized, however. The European nations would have been delighted to see the United States broken up, but none was prepared to support the Confederacy directly. The attitude of Great Britain was decisive. The cutting off of cotton did not hit the British as hard as the South had hoped. They had a large supply on hand when the war broke out, and when that was exhausted, alternative sources in India and Egypt took up part of the slack. Furthermore, British crop failures necessitated the importation of large amounts of northern wheat, providing a powerful reason for not antagonizing the United States. The fact that most ordinary people in Great Britain favored the North also influenced British policy.

Several times the two nations came to the brink of war. In November 1861 the USS *San Jacinto* stopped a British vessel, the *Trent,* on the high seas and forcibly arrested two Confederate envoys, James M. Mason and John Slidell, who were en route to London. This violation of international law would probably have led to war had not Lincoln decided to turn the Southerners loose. In 1862 two powerful cruisers, the *Florida* and the *Alabama,* were built for the Confederates in English shipyards under the most transparent of subterfuges. Despite American protests, they were permitted to put to sea and were soon wreaking havoc among northern merchant ships. When two ironclad "rams" were also built in Britain for the Confederates, the United States made it clear that it would declare war if the ships were delivered. The British government then confiscated the vessels, avoiding a showdown.

Charles Francis Adams, the American minister in London, ably handled the many vexing problems that arose. However, the military situation determined British policy; once the North obtained a clear superiority on the battlefield, the possibility of intervention vanished.

War in the West: Shiloh

After Bull Run no battles were fought until early 1862. Then, while McClellan continued his deliberate preparations to attack Richmond, important fighting occurred far to the west. Most of the Plains Indians sided with the Confederacy, principally because of their resentment of the federal government's policies toward them. White settlers from Colorado to California were mostly Unionists. In March 1862 a Texas army advancing beyond Santa Fe clashed with a Union force in the Battle of Glorieta Pass. The battle was indecisive, but a Union unit destroyed the Texans' supply train. The Texans felt compelled to retreat to the Rio Grande, thus ending the Confederate threat to the Far West.

Meanwhile, far larger Union forces, led by a shabby, cigar-smoking West Pointer named Ulysses S. Grant, had invaded Tennessee from a base at Cairo, Illinois. Making effective use of armored gunboats, Grant captured Fort Henry and Fort Donelson, strongholds on the Tennessee and Cumberland rivers, taking 14,000 prisoners. Next he marched toward Corinth, Mississippi, an important railroad junction.

To check Grant's advance, the Confederates massed 40,000 men under Albert Sidney Johnston. On April 6, while Grant slowly concentrated his forces,

Johnston struck suddenly at Shiloh, 20 miles north of Corinth. Some Union soldiers were caught half-dressed, others in the midst of brewing their morning coffee. A few died in their blankets. "We were more than surprised," one Illinois officer later admitted. "We were astonished." However, Grant's men stood their ground. At the end of a day of ghastly carnage the Confederates held the advantage, but fresh Union troops poured in during the night, and on the second day of battle the tide turned. The Confederates fell back toward Corinth, exhausted and demoralized.

Grant, shaken by the unexpected attack and appalled by his losses, allowed the enemy to escape. This cost him the fine reputation he had won in capturing Fort Henry and Fort Donelson. He was relieved of his command. Although Corinth eventually fell and New Orleans was captured by a naval force under the

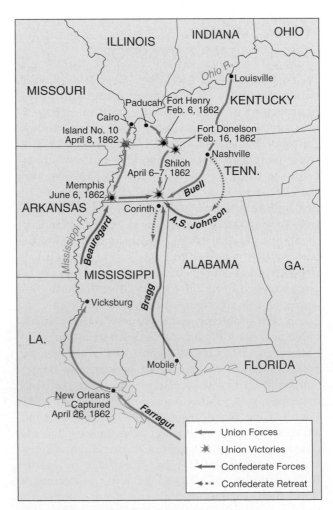

▲ **War in the West, 1862**
Although Union forces ultimately took Shiloh in April 1862, the city of Vicksburg, and thus control of the Mississippi, remained in southern hands.

command of Captain David Farragut, Vicksburg, key to control of the Mississippi, remained firmly in Confederate hands. A great opportunity had been lost.

Shiloh had other results. The staggering casualties shook the confidence of both belligerents. More Americans fell there in two days than in all the battles of the Revolution, the War of 1812, and the Mexican War combined. Union losses exceeded 13,000 out of 63,000 engaged; the Confederates lost 10,699, including General Johnston. Technology in the shape of more accurate guns that could be fired far more rapidly than the muskets of earlier times and more powerful artillery were responsible for the carnage. Gradually the generals began to reconsider their tactics and to experiment with field fortifications and other defensive measures. And the people, North and South, stopped thinking of the war as a romantic test of courage and military guile.

MCCLELLAN: THE RELUCTANT WARRIOR

In Virginia, General McClellan, after unaccountable delays, was finally moving against Richmond. Instead of trying to advance across the difficult terrain of northern Virginia, he transported his army by water to the tip of the peninsula formed by the York and James rivers in order to attack Richmond from the southeast. After the famous battle on March 9, 1862, between the USS *Monitor* and the Confederate *Merrimack*, the first fight in history between armored warships, control of these waters was securely in northern hands.

While McClellan's plan alarmed many congressmen because it seemed to leave Washington relatively unprotected, it simplified the problem of keeping the army supplied in hostile country. But McClellan now displayed the weaknesses that eventually ruined his career. His problems were both intellectual and psychological. Basically he approached tactical questions in the manner of a typical eighteenth-century general. He considered war a kind of gentlemanly contest (similar to chess with its castles and knights) in which maneuver, guile, and position determined victory. He saw the Civil War not as a mighty struggle over fundamental beliefs but as a sort of complex game that commanders played at a leisurely pace and for limited stakes. He believed it more important to capture Richmond than to destroy the army protecting it. With their capital in northern hands, surely the Southerners (outwitted and outmaneuvered by a brilliant general) would acknowledge defeat and agree to return to the Union. The idea of crushing the South seemed to him wrongheaded and uncivilized.

Beyond this, McClellan was temperamentally unsuited for a position of so much responsibility. Beneath the swagger he was profoundly insecure. He talked like Napoleon, but he did not like to fight. He called repeatedly for more men; when he got them, he demanded still more. He knew how to get ready, but he was never ready in his own mind. What was said of another Union general would have been better said of McClellan: He was "watching the enemy as fast as he can."

McClellan began the Peninsula campaign in mid-March. Proceeding deliberately, he floated an army of 112,000 men down the Potomac and by May 14 had established a base at White House Landing, less than 25 miles from Richmond. A swift thrust might have ended the war quickly, but McClellan delayed, despite the fact that he had 80,000 men in striking position and large reserves. As he pushed forward slowly, the Confederates caught part of his force separated from the main body by the rain-swollen Chickahominy River and attacked. The Battle of Seven Pines was indecisive yet resulted in more than 10,000 casualties.

At Seven Pines the Confederate commander, General Joseph E. Johnston, was severely wounded; leadership of the Army of Northern Virginia then passed to Robert E. Lee. Although a reluctant supporter of secession, Lee was a superb soldier. During the Mexican War his gallantry under fire inspired General Scott to call him the bravest man in the army; another officer rhapsodized over his "daring reconnaissances pushed up to the cannon's mouth." He also had displayed an almost instinctive mastery of tactics. Admiral Raphael Semmes, who accompanied Scott's army on the march to Mexico City, recalled in 1851 that Lee "seemed to receive impressions intuitively, which it cost other men much labor to acquire."

Lee was McClellan's antithesis. McClellan seemed almost deliberately to avoid understanding his foes, acting as though every southern general was a genius. Lee, a master psychologist on the battlefield, took the measure of each Union general and devised his tactics accordingly. Where McClellan was complex, egotistical, perhaps even unbalanced, Lee was courtly, tactful, and entirely without McClellan's vainglorious belief that he was a man of destiny. Yet on the battlefield Lee's boldness skirted the edge of foolhardiness.

To relieve the pressure on Richmond, Lee sent General "Stonewall" Jackson, soon to be his most trusted lieutenant, on a diversionary raid in the Shenandoah Valley, west of Richmond and Washington. Jackson struck hard and swiftly at scattered Union forces in the region, winning a number of battles and capturing vast stores of equipment. Lincoln dispatched 20,000 reserves to the Shenandoah to check him—to the dismay of McClellan, who wanted

▲ Lee in 1863, by Julian Vannerson. "So great is my confidence in General Lee," Stonewall Jackson remarked, "that I am willing to follow him blind-folded."

the troops to attack Richmond from the north. But after Seven Pines, Lee ordered Jackson back to Richmond. While Union armies streamed toward the valley, Jackson slipped stealthily between them. On June 25 he reached Ashland, directly north of the Confederate capital.

Before that date McClellan had possessed clear numerical superiority yet had only inched ahead; now the advantage lay with Lee, and the very next day he attacked. For seven days the battle raged. Lee's plan was brilliant but too complicated for an army yet untested: The full weight of his force never hit the northern army at any one time. Nevertheless, the shock was formidable. McClellan, who excelled in defense, fell back, his lines intact, exacting a fearful toll. Under difficult conditions he managed to transfer his troops to a new base on the James River at Harrison's Landing, where the guns of the navy could shield his position. Again the loss of life was terrible: Northern casualties totaled 15,800; those of the South nearly 20,000 in the Seven Days' Battle for Richmond.

LEE COUNTERATTACKS: ANTIETAM

McClellan was still within striking distance of Richmond, in an impregnable position with secure supply lines and 86,000 soldiers ready to resume battle. Lee had absorbed heavy losses without winning

any significant advantage. Yet Lincoln was exasperated with McClellan for having surrendered the initiative and, after much deliberation, reduced his authority by placing him under General Henry W. Halleck. Halleck called off the Peninsula campaign and ordered McClellan to move his army from the James to the Potomac, near Washington. He was to join General John Pope, who was gathering a new army between Washington and Richmond.

DOCUMENT

McClellan to Abraham Lincoln (July 7, 1862)

If McClellan had persisted and captured Richmond, the war might have ended and the Union been restored without the abolition of slavery, since at that point the North was still fighting for union, not for freedom for the slaves. By prolonging the war, Lee inadvertently enabled it to destroy slavery along with the Confederacy, though no one at the time looked at the matter this way.

For the president to have lost confidence in McClellan was understandable. Nevertheless, to allow Halleck to pull back the troops was a bad mistake. When they withdrew, Lee seized the initiative. With typical decisiveness and daring, he marched rapidly north. Late in August his Confederates drove General Pope's confused troops from the same ground, Bull Run, where the first major engagement of the war had been fought.

Thirteen months had passed since the first failure at Bull Run, and despite the expenditure of thousands of lives, the Union army stood as far from Richmond as ever. Dismayed by Pope's incompetence, Lincoln turned in desperation back to McClellan. When his secretary protested that McClellan had expressed contempt for the president, Lincoln replied gently: "We must use what tools we have."

While McClellan was regrouping the shaken Union Army, Lee once again took the offensive. He realized that no number of individual southern triumphs could destroy the enormous material advantages of the North. Unless some dramatic blow, delivered on northern soil, persuaded the people of the United States that military victory was impossible, the South would surely be crushed in the long run by the weight of superior resources. Lee therefore marched rapidly northwest around the defenses of Washington.

Acting with even more than his usual boldness, Lee divided his army of 60,000 into a number of units. One, under Stonewall Jackson, descended on weakly defended Harpers Ferry, capturing more than 11,000 prisoners. Another pressed as far north as Hagerstown, Maryland, nearly to the Pennsylvania line. McClellan pursued with his usual deliberation until a captured dispatch revealed to him Lee's dispositions. Then he moved a bit more swiftly, forcing Lee to stand and fight on September 17 at

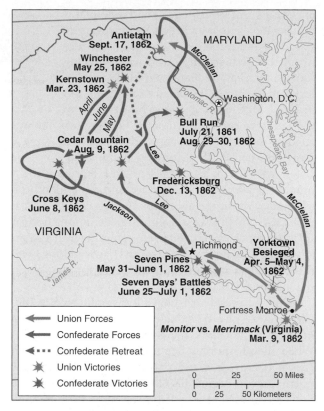

▲ War in the East, 1861–1862

After the first battle at Bull Run, in July of 1861, there was little action until the following spring, when McClellan launched his Peninsula campaign. The Battle of Antietam was the culmination of the fighting in the summer of 1862.

Sharpsburg, Maryland, between the Potomac and Antietam Creek.[1] On a field that offered Lee no room to maneuver, 70,000 Union soldiers clashed with 40,000 Confederates. When darkness fell, more than 22,000 lay dead or wounded on the bloody field.

Although casualties were evenly divided and the Confederate lines remained intact, Lee's position was perilous. His men were exhausted. McClellan had not yet thrown in his reserves, and new federal units were arriving hourly. A bold northern general would have continued the fight without respite through the night. One of ordinary aggressiveness would have waited for first light and then struck with every soldier who could hold a rifle, for with the Potomac at his back, Lee could not retreat under fire without inviting disaster. McClellan, however, did nothing. For an entire day, while Lee scanned the field in futile search of some weakness in the Union lines, he held his fire. That night the Confederates slipped back across the Potomac into Virginia.

---

[1]Southerners tended to identify battles by nearby towns, northerners by bodies of water. Thus Manassas and Bull Run, Sharpsburg and Antietam, Murfreesboro and Stone's River, and so on.

Lee's invasion had failed; his army had been badly mauled; the gravest threat to the Union in the war had been checked. But McClellan had let victory slip through his fingers. Soon Lee was back behind the defenses of Richmond, rebuilding his army.

Once again, this time finally, Lincoln dismissed McClellan from his command.

THE EMANCIPATION PROCLAMATION

Antietam, though hardly the victory he had hoped for, gave Lincoln the excuse he needed to take a step that changed the character of the war decisively. When the fighting started, fear of alienating the border states was reason enough for not making emancipation of the slaves a war aim. Lincoln even insisted on enforcing the Fugitive Slave Act for this reason. However, pressures to act against the South's "peculiar institution" mounted steadily. Slavery had divided the nation; now it was driving Northerners to war within themselves. Love of country led them to fight to save the Union, but fighting aroused hatreds and caused many to desire to smash the enemy. Sacrifice, pain, and grief made abolitionists of many who had no love for blacks—they sought to free the slave only to injure the master.

To make abolition an object of the war might encourage the slaves to revolt, but Lincoln disclaimed this objective. Nevertheless, the possibility existed. Already the slaves seemed to be looking to the North for freedom: Whenever Union troops invaded Confederate territory, slaves flocked into their lines.

As the war progressed, the Radical faction in Congress gradually chipped away at slavery. In April 1862 the Radicals pushed through a bill abolishing slavery in the District of Columbia; two months later another measure outlawed it in the territories; in July the Confiscation Act "freed" all slaves owned by persons in rebellion against the United States. In fighting for these measures and in urging general emancipation, some Radicals made statements harshly critical of Lincoln; but while he carefully avoided being identified with them or with any other faction, the president was never very far from their position. He resisted emancipation because he feared it would divide the country and injure the war effort, not because he personally disapproved. Indeed, he frequently cited Radical pressure as an excuse for doing what he wished to do on his own.

Lincoln would have preferred to see slavery done away with by state law, with compensation for slave owners and federal aid for former slaves willing to leave the United States. He tried repeatedly to persuade the loyal slave states to adopt this policy, but without success. By the summer of 1862

DOCUMENT

The Emancipation Proclamation

he was convinced that for military reasons and to win the support of liberal opinion in Europe, the government should make abolition a war aim. "We must free the slaves or be ourselves subdued," he explained to a member of his Cabinet. He delayed temporarily, fearing that a statement in the face of military reverses would be taken as a sign of weakness. The "victory" at Antietam Creek gave him his opportunity, and on September 22 he made public the Emancipation Proclamation. After January 1, 1863, it said, all slaves in areas in rebellion against the United States "shall be then, thenceforward, and forever free."

No single slave was freed directly by Lincoln's announcement, which did not apply to the border states or to those sections of the Confederacy, like New Orleans and Norfolk, Virginia, already controlled by federal troops. The proclamation differed in philosophy, however, from the Confiscation Act in striking at the institution, not at the property of rebels. Henceforth every Union victory would speed the destruction of slavery without regard for the attitudes of individual masters.

Some of the president's advisers thought the proclamation inexpedient, and others considered it illegal. Lincoln justified it as a way to weaken the enemy. The proclamation is full of phrases like "as a fit and necessary war measure" and "warranted by the Constitution upon military necessity."

Southerners considered the Emancipation Proclamation an incitement to slave rebellion—as one of them put it, an "infamous attempt to . . . convert the quiet, ignorant, and dependent black son of toil into a savage incendiary and brutal murderer." Most antislavery groups thought it did not go far enough. Lincoln "is only stopping on the edge of Niagara, to pick up a few chips," one abolitionist declared. "He and they will go over together." Foreign opinion was mixed: Liberals tended to applaud, conservatives to react with alarm or contempt.

As Lincoln anticipated, the proclamation had a subtle but continuing impact in the North. Its immediate effect was to aggravate racial prejudices. Millions of whites disapproved of slavery yet abhorred the idea of equality for blacks. David Wilmot, for example, insisted that his famous proviso was designed to preserve the territories for whites rather than to weaken slavery, and as late as 1857 the people of Iowa rejected black suffrage by a vote of 49,000 to 8000. To some, emancipation seemed to herald an invasion of the North by blacks who would compete for jobs, drive down wages, commit crimes, spread diseases, and eventually destroy the "purity" of the white race. The word *miscegenation* was coined in 1863 by David G. Croly, an editor of the *New York World*, directly as a result of the Emancipation Proclamation. Its original meaning was "the mingling of the white and black races on the continent *as a consequence of the freedom of the latter.*" Of course, the fact of miscegenation in its current, more general meaning of racial interbreeding long antedated the freeing of any slave.

The Democrats spared no effort to make political capital of these fears and prejudices even before Lincoln's Emancipation Proclamation, and they made large gains in the 1862 election, especially in the Northwest. So strong was antiblack feeling that most of the Republican politicians who defended emancipation did so with racist arguments. Far from encouraging southern blacks to move north, they claimed, the ending of slavery would lead to a mass migration of northern blacks to the South.

When the Emancipation Proclamation began actually to free slaves, the government pursued a policy of "containment," that is, of keeping the former slaves in the South. Panicky fears of an inundation of blacks subsided in the North. Nevertheless, emancipation remained a cause of social discontent. In March 1863, volunteering having fallen off, Congress passed a conscription act. The law applied to all men between ages 20 and 45, but it allowed draftees to hire substitutes and even to buy exemption for $300, provisions that were patently unfair to the poor. During the remainder of the war 46,000 men were actually drafted, whereas 118,000 hired substitutes, and another 161,000 "failed to report." Conscription represented an enormous expansion of national authority, since in effect it gave the government the power of life and death over individual citizens.

THE DRAFT RIOTS

After the passage of the Conscription Act, draft riots erupted in a number of cities. By far the most serious disturbance occurred in New York City in July 1863. Many workers resented conscription in principle and were embittered by the $300 exemption fee (which represented a year's wages). The idea of being forced to risk their lives to free slaves who would then, they believed, compete with them for jobs infuriated them. On July 13 a mob attacked the office where the names of conscripts were being drawn. Most of the rioters were poor Irish Catholic laborers who resented both the blacks and the middle-class Protestant whites who seemed to them responsible for the special attention blacks were suddenly receiving. For four days the city was an inferno. Public buildings, shops, and private residences were put to the torch. What began as a protest against the draft became an assault on blacks and the well-to-do. It took federal troops

and the temporary suspension of the draft in the city to put an end to the rioting. By the time order was restored more than a hundred people (most of them rioters) had lost their lives.

The Emancipation Proclamation does not entirely account for the draft riots. The new policy neither reflected nor triggered a revolution in white thinking about the race question. Its significance was subtle but real; both the naive view that Lincoln freed the slaves on January 1, 1863, and the cynical one that his action was a mere propaganda trick are incorrect. Northern hostility to emancipation arose from fear of change more than from hatred of blacks, while liberal disavowals of any intention to treat blacks as equals were in large measure designed to quiet this fear. To a degree the racial backlash that the proclamation inspired reflected the public's awareness that a change, frightening but irreversible, *had occurred*.

Most white Northerners did not surrender their comforting belief in black inferiority, and Lincoln was no exception. Yet Lincoln was evolving. He talked about deporting freed slaves to the tropics, but he did not send any there. And he began to receive black leaders in the White House and to allow black groups to hold meetings on the grounds.

Many other Americans were changing too. The brutality of the New York riots horrified many white citizens. Over $40,000 was swiftly raised to aid the victims, and some conservatives were so appalled by the Irish rioters that they began to talk of giving blacks the vote. The influential *Atlantic Monthly* commented: "It is impossible to name any standard . . . that will give a vote to the Celt [the Irish] and exclude the negro."

THE EMANCIPATED PEOPLE

To blacks, both slave and free, the Emancipation Proclamation served as a beacon. Even if it failed immediately to liberate one slave or to lift the burdens of prejudice from one black back, it stood as a promise of future improvement. "I took the proclamation for a little more than it purported," Frederick Douglass recalled in his autobiography, "and saw in its spirit a life and power far beyond its letter." Lincoln was by modern standards a racist, but

▲ Lithograph of the New York draft riots. Although the main targets of the rioters were blacks, the homes and businesses of prominent Republicans were also attacked. Brooks Brothers was burned. Horace Greeley's newspaper was besieged, as was the *Times*. (Winston Churchill's grandfather manned a Gatling gun on the second floor of the *Times* to drive away the rioters.)

his most militant black contemporaries respected him deeply. The *Anglo-African,* an uncompromising black newspaper (the position of which is revealed in an 1862 editorial that asked: "Poor, chicken-hearted, semi-barbarous Caucasians, when will you learn that 'the earth was made for MAN?'"), referred in 1864 to Lincoln's "many noble acts" and urged his reelection. Douglass said of him: "Lincoln was not . . . either our man or our model. In his interests, in his association, in his habits of thought and in his prejudices, he was a white man." Nevertheless, Douglass described Lincoln as "one whom I could love, honor, and trust without reserve or doubt."

As for the slaves of the South, after January 1, 1863, whenever the "Army of Freedom" approached, they laid down their plows and hoes and flocked to the Union lines in droves. "We-all knows about it," one black confided to a northern clergyman early in 1863. "Only we darsen't let on. We *pretends* not to know." Such behavior came as a shock to the owners. "[The slaves] who loved us best—as we thought—were the first to leave us," one planter mourned. Talk of slave "ingratitude" increased. Instead of referring to their workers as "servants" or "my black family," many owners began to describe them as "slaves" or "niggers."

AFRICAN AMERICAN SOLDIERS

A revolutionary shift occurred in white thinking about using black men as soldiers. Although they had fought in the Revolution and in the Battle of

▶ *text continues on page 408*

▲ The storming of Fort Wagner by the 54th Massachusetts on July 18, 1863. Composed of black volunteers but led by Robert Gould Shaw, a white abolitionist, the 54th Massachusetts breached the ramparts but was eventually thrown back, sustaining heavy losses. Although the focal point of this contemporary painting is the death of Shaw, the broader significance of the battle is shown in the foreground, where two black soldiers are bayoneting their Confederate foes. (See also Re-Viewing the Past: *"Glory,"* pp. 406–407.)

Re-Viewing the Past

Glory

Glory (1989) tells the story of the 54th Massachusetts Volunteer Infantry, a black regiment, from its establishment in the fall of 1862 through its attack on Fort Wagner, South Carolina, on July 18, 1863.

"Historical accuracy," director Edward Zwick declared, was "the goal of everyone involved in the production." Filmmakers of historical subjects commonly make such assertions, but Zwick proved that he had attended to the historical record. For example, he had the peak of Shaw's cap dyed the exact shade of medium green used by officers of the Massachusetts 54th; and when shoes were distributed to the recruits, there were no "lefts" or "rights": shoes were to shape themselves to either foot from wear. Few viewers could be expected to take note of such historical details, but Zwick included them nevertheless.

Zwick's evident commitment to history makes his deviations all the more interesting. Consider the opening scenes. The movie begins with a panoramic shot of rolling hills, dotted with tents. Fog blankets the valley and softens the morning light. The camera moves closer, focusing on Union soldiers around a campfire. Then the quiet is shattered: soldiers hasten to form ranks, trot toward a battlefield, and charge across it, a young officer in the van. (He is Captain Robert Gould Shaw, played by Matthew Broderick). The attackers are decimated. When Shaw turns to rally his troops, he sees that they are fleeing in terror. Then he is hit and loses consciousness.

Shaw is sent home to Boston to convalesce. At a reception, Governor Andrew offers the young officer command of the Massachusetts 54th, a black regiment being raised in Boston. Shaw hesitates for a moment. Then he confers privately with another officer, who is appalled.

"I knew how much you'd like to be a colonel, but a colored regiment?"

"I'm gonna do it," Shaw replies.

"You're not serious."

"Yeah."

These scenes contain truths without being entirely truthful. In fact, Governor Andrew did offer the commission and Shaw accepted it. But at the time Shaw was in Virginia. Andrew, in Boston, conveyed it through Shaw's father and young Shaw initially refused. Zwick has compressed the story chronologically, squeezing weeks into minutes; and he has rearranged it geographically to enable Andrew and young Shaw to meet. Such modifications are common in "reel history," and these do not impair historical understanding.

But *Glory* deviates from the historical record in more significant ways. It suggests, for example, that the Massachusetts 54th was composed mostly of former slaves whose hatred of slavery was based on personal experience. In truth, the Massachusetts 54th was recruited from blacks in northern states, most had been born free.

▼ Matthew Broderick, as Robert Gould Shaw, and Denzel Washington, as former slave recruit Trip, in the movie, *Glory*.

▲ Photographs of Robert Gould Shaw, Commander of the Massachusetts 54th, and private Charles Arnum, a free black volunteer from Springfield, Massachusetts.

The fiction that they had been slaves, however, made it possible for Zwick to examine a larger truth. Of the 178,000 blacks who served in the Union army, fewer than one-fifth were from the North; the great majority *were* former slaves. Nearly 100,000 were recruited from Louisiana, Mississippi, or Tennessee, among the first states occupied by the Union army. *Glory* thus merges the story of the free blacks of the Massachusetts 54th with that of former slaves who were recruited from the Deep South.

Zwick exploited the dramatic potential of the latter groups. How did slaves respond when, having just received their freedom, they were placed under the absolute power of white officers?

Glory develops the question chiefly through the character of Trip (Denzel Washington), a former slave who hates all whites, including Shaw. Shaw illuminates the other side of the question. An inveterate abolitionist, he reluctantly decides that former slaves must be whipped (literally) into shape. When Trip sneaks off one night and is captured for desertion, Shaw orders him flogged. When Trip's back is bared, Shaw sees that it is laced with scars from whippings by slave masters. During the flogging, Trip fixes Shaw with a hateful stare, a powerful scene that underscores the movie's central irony: To end slavery, Shaw has superseded the plantation master while Trip has again become a slave.

Whatever its dramatic merits, the scene is unhistorical. In 1861 Congress had outlawed flogging in the military. Disobedient soldiers were tied in a crouched position, or they were suspended by their thumbs, toes just touching the ground.

Physical punishment was, in fact, one of the chief sources of contention between ex-slave soldiers and white officers. "I am no slave to be driven," one black recruit informed a brutish commander. When an officer of the 38th Colored Infantry tied a black recruit up by the thumbs, his friends cut him down and forced the officers back with bayonets: "No white son of a bitch can tie a man up here," they declared. The blacks were charged with mutiny and several were executed, an incident that shows that former slaves did not willingly submit to army discipline tainted with racism. Though African Americans con-

stituted only 8 percent of the Union army, 80 percent of those executed for mutiny were black. Many white officers, as the movie suggests, did assert that former slaves must be treated like slaves. "I no longer wonder why slave drivers were cruel. I am," one white officer confided in a letter to his brother.

Could such soldiers—black recruits and white officers alike—have been good ones? The movie answers the question by recreating the actual attack on Fort Wagner, the first step in the offensive on Charleston. It shows the blacks of the Massachusetts 54th marching to the front of the line, and forming up along a narrow beach. On Shaw's command, they charge forward. Unlike the white troops in the opening scene, the blacks follow him to the ramparts; when he falls, they continue onward until they are wiped out.

Were the soldiers of the Massachusetts 54th as courageous as those in the movie? Shortly after the battle, Lieutenant Iredell Jones, a Confederate officer, reported: "The negroes fought gallantly, and were headed by as brave a colonel as ever lived." Of the 600 members of the 54th Massachusetts, 40 percent were casualties on that day, an extraordinarily high ratio. Did ex-slaves fight as courageously as the free blacks of the 54th? The answer to this question came not at Fort Wagner, but at other, less publicized battles. A few weeks earlier, for example, several companies of the Louisiana (Colored) Infantry, composed of former slaves who had been in the army only for several weeks, fought off a furious Confederate assault at Milliken's Bend near Vicksburg. The Confederate general was astonished when whites in the Union army fled but the blacks held their ground despite sustaining staggering casualties—45 percent—the highest of any single battle in the war.

Thus while *Glory* is a fictional composite—of free black and ex-slave recruits, and of the assault on Fort Wagner and Milliken's Bend—it conveys a broader truth about black soldiers. Howell Cobb, a Confederate senator from Georgia, declared: "If the black can make a good soldier, our whole system of government is wrong." *Glory* shows that although white officers and black recruits did not form a harmonious team, they together proved that slavery was doomed.

New Orleans during the War of 1812, a law of 1792 barred blacks from the army. During the early stages of the rebellion, despite the eagerness of thousands of free blacks to enlist, the prohibition remained in force. By 1862, however, the need for manpower was creating pressure for change. In August Secretary of War Edwin M. Stanton authorized the military government of the captured South Carolina sea islands to enlist slaves in the area. After the Emancipation Proclamation specifically authorized the enlistment of blacks, the governor of Massachusetts moved to organize a black regiment, the famous Massachusetts 54th. (See Re-Viewing the Past, "*Glory,*" pp. 406–407.) Swiftly thereafter, other states began to recruit black soldiers, and in May 1863 the federal government established a Bureau of Colored Troops to supervise their enlistment. By the end of the war one soldier in eight in the Union army was black.

DOCUMENT

Letter from a Free Black Volunteer to the *Christian Recorder* (1864)

Enlisting so many black soldiers changed the war from a struggle to save the Union to a kind of revolution. "Let the black man . . . get an eagle on his button and a musket on his shoulder," wrote Frederick Douglass, "and there is no power on earth which can deny that he has won the right to citizenship."

At first black soldiers received only $7 a month, about half what white soldiers were paid. But they soon proved themselves in battle; of the 178,000 who served in the Union army, 37,000 were killed, a rate of loss about 40 percent higher than that among white troops The Congressional Medal of Honor was awarded to 21 blacks.

The higher death rates among black soldiers were partly due to the fury of Confederate soldiers. Many black captives were killed on the spot. After overrunning the garrison of Fort Pillow on the Mississippi River, the Confederates massacred several dozen black soldiers, along with their white commander. Lincoln was tempted to order reprisals, but he and his advisers realized that to do so would have been both morally wrong (two wrongs never make a right) and likely to lead to still more atrocities. "Blood can not restore blood," Lincoln said in his usual direct way.

ANTIETAM TO GETTYSBURG

It was well that Lincoln seized on Antietam to release his proclamation; had he waited for a more impressive victory, he would have waited nearly a year. To

replace McClellan, he chose General Ambrose E. Burnside, best known to history for his magnificent side-whiskers (originally called burnsides, later, at first jokingly, sideburns). Burnside was a good corps commander, but he lacked the self-confidence essential to anyone who takes responsibility for major decisions. He knew his limitations and tried to avoid high command, but patriotism and his sense of duty compelled him, when pressed, to accept leadership of the Army of the Potomac. He prepared to march on Richmond.

MAP

The Civil War Part I: 1861–1862

Unlike McClellan, Burnside was aggressive—too aggressive. He planned to ford the Rappahannock River at Fredericksburg. Supply problems and bad weather delayed him until mid-December, giving Lee time to concentrate his army in impregnable positions behind the town. Although he had more than 120,000 men against Lee's 75,000, Burnside should have called off the attack when he saw Lee's advantage; instead he ordered the troops forward. Crossing the river over pontoon bridges, his divisions occupied Fredericksburg. Then, in wave after wave, they charged the Confederate defense line while Lee's artillery riddled them from nearby Marye's Heights. Watching the battle from his command post on the heights, General Lee was deeply moved. Turning to General James Longstreet, he said: "It is well that war is so terrible—we should grow too fond of it!"

On December 14, the day following this futile assault, General Burnside, tears streaming down his cheeks, ordered the evacuation of Fredericksburg. Shortly thereafter General Joseph Hooker replaced him.

Unlike Burnside, "Fighting Joe" Hooker was ill-tempered, vindictive, and devious. In naming him to command the Army of the Potomac, Lincoln sent him a letter that was a measure of his desperation but is now famous for what it reveals of the president's character:

> I think that during Gen. Burnside's command of the Army, you have taken counsel of your ambition, and thwarted him as much as you could, in which you did a great wrong to the country. . . . I have heard, in such a way as to believe it, of you, recently saying that both the Army and the Government need a Dictator. Of course it is not *for* this, but in spite of it, that I have given you the command. Only those generals who gain successes, can set up dictators. What I now ask of you is military success, and I will risk the dictatorship. . . . Beware of rashness, but with energy and sleepless vigilance, go forward, and give us victories.

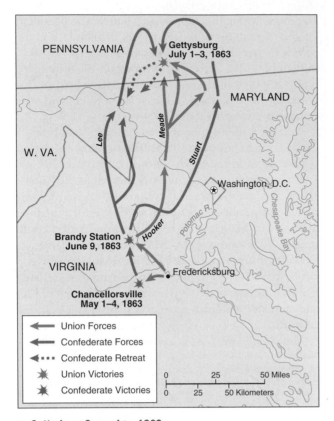

PENNSYLVANIA

Gettysburg
July 1–3, 1863

MARYLAND

W. VA.

Lee

Meade

Stuart

Washington, D.C.

Chesapeake Bay

Potomac R.

Brandy Station
June 9, 1863

Hooker

VIRGINIA

Fredericksburg

Chancellorsville
May 1–4, 1863

←	Union Forces
←	Confederate Forces
◄····	Confederate Retreat
✳	Union Victories
✳	Confederate Victories

0   25   50 Miles
0   25   50 Kilometers

▲ **Gettysburg Campaign, 1863**
Gettysburg, in July of 1863, marked the turning point of the war;
after it the South never again tried to invade the North.

abandoned the field and retreated in good order behind the Rappahannock.

Chancellorsville cost the Confederates dearly, for their losses, in excess of 12,000, were almost as heavy as the North's and harder to replace. They also lost Stonewall Jackson, struck down by the bullets of his own men while returning from a reconnaissance. Nevertheless, the Union army had suffered another fearful blow to its morale.

Lee knew that time was still on the side of the North; to defend Richmond was not enough. Already federal troops in the West were closing in on Vicksburg, threatening to cut Confederate communications with Arkansas and Texas. Now was the time to strike, while the morale of the North was at low ebb. With 75,000 soldiers he crossed the Potomac again, a larger Union force dogging his right flank. By late June his army had fanned out across southern Pennsylvania in a 50-mile arc from Chambersburg to the Susquehanna. Gray-clad soldiers ranged 50 miles *northwest* of Baltimore, within 10 miles of Harrisburg, Pennsylvania.

As Union soldiers had been doing in Virginia, Lee's men destroyed property and commandeered food, horses, and clothing wherever they could find them. They even seized a number of blacks and sent them south to be sold as slaves. On July 1 a Confederate division looking for shoes in the town of Gettysburg clashed with two brigades of Union cavalry northwest of the town. Both sides sent out calls for reinforcements. Like iron filings drawn to a magnet, the two armies converged. The Confederates won control of the town, but the Union army, now commanded by General George G. Meade, took a strong position on Cemetery Ridge, a hook-shaped stretch of high ground just to the south. Lee's men occupied Seminary Ridge, a parallel position.

On this field the fate of the Union was probably decided. For two days the Confederates attacked Cemetery Ridge, pounding it with the heaviest artillery barrage ever seen in America and sweeping bravely up its flanks in repeated assaults. During General George E. Pickett's famous charge, a handful of his men actually reached the Union lines, but reserves drove them back. By nightfall on July 3 the Confederate army was spent, the Union lines unbroken.

The following day was the Fourth of July. The two weary forces rested on their arms. Had the Union army attacked in force, the Confederates might have been crushed, but just as McClellan had hesitated after Antietam, Meade let opportunity pass. On July 5 Lee retreated to safety. For the first time he had been clearly bested on the field of battle.

Hooker proved no better than his predecessor, but his failings were more like McClellan's than Burnside's. By the spring of 1863 he had 125,000 men ready for action. Late in April he forded the Rappahannock and quickly concentrated at Chancellorsville, about 10 miles west of Fredericksburg. His army outnumbered the Confederates by more than two to one; he should have forced a battle at once. Instead he delayed, and while he did, Lee sent Stonewall Jackson's corps of 28,000 men across tangled countryside to a position directly athwart Hooker's unsuspecting flank. At 6 P.M. on May 2, Jackson attacked.

Completely surprised, the Union right crumbled, brigade after brigade overrun before it could wheel to meet Jackson's charge. At the first sound of firing, Lee had struck along the entire front to impede Union troop movements. If the battle had begun earlier in the day, the Confederates might have won a decisive victory; as it happened, nightfall brought a lull, and the next day the Union troops rallied and held their ground. Heavy fighting continued until May 5, when Hooker

Lincoln Finds His General: Grant at Vicksburg

On Independence Day, a day after Gettysburg, federal troops won another great victory far to the west. When General Halleck was called east in July 1862, Ulysses S. Grant resumed command of the Union troops. Grant was one of the most controversial officers in the army. At West Point he had compiled an indifferent record, ranking twenty-first in a class of 39. During the Mexican War he served well, but when he was later assigned to a lonely post in the West, he took to drink and was forced to resign his commission. Thereafter he was by turns a farmer, a real estate agent, and a clerk in a leather goods store. In 1861, approaching age 40, he seemed well into a life of frustration and mediocrity.

The war gave him a second chance. Back in service, however, his reputation as a ne'er-do-well and his unmilitary bearing worked against him, as did the heavy casualties suffered by his troops at Shiloh. Yet the fact that he knew how to manage a large army and win battles did not escape Lincoln. According to

tradition, when a gossip tried to poison the president against Grant by referring to his drinking, Lincoln retorted that if he knew what brand Grant favored, he would send a barrel of it to some of his other generals.[2] Grant never used alcohol as a substitute for courage. "Old Ulysses," one of his soldiers said, "he don't scare worth a damn."

Grant's major aim was to capture Vicksburg, a city of tremendous strategic importance. Together with Port Hudson, a bastion north of Baton Rouge, Louisiana, it guarded a 150-mile stretch of the Mississippi. The river between these points was inaccessible to federal gunboats. So long as Vicksburg remained in southern hands, the trans-Mississippi region could send men and supplies to the rest of the Confederacy.

Vicksburg sits on a bluff overlooking a sharp bend in the river. When it proved unapproachable from either the west or the north, Grant devised an audacious scheme for getting at it from the east. He

---

[2]Lincoln denied having said this, pointing out that it was a version of a remark about General James Wolfe attributed to King George II. When a critic remarked that Wolfe was a madman, the King is said to have replied: "I wish he would bite some of the others."

▲ Grant's bold initiative to seize Vicksburg depended on ferrying his army swiftly across the Mississippi. These Union steamboats brought reinforcements that saved Grant's army. The boats were converted into floating hospitals.

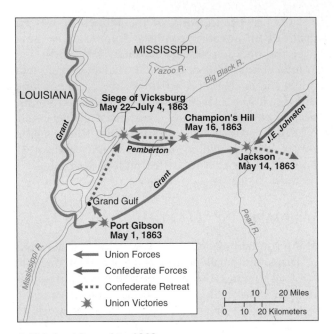

▲ Vicksburg Campaign, 1863
When Vicksburg fell to the Union troops on July 4, 1863, the Mississippi was reopened to the free passage of federal forces.

descended the Mississippi from Memphis to a point a few miles north of the city. Then, leaving part of his force behind to create the impression that he planned to attack from the north, he crossed the west bank and slipped quickly southward. Recrossing the river below Vicksburg, he abandoned his communications and supply lines and struck at Jackson, the capital of Mississippi. In a series of swift engagements his troops captured Jackson, cutting off the army of General John C. Pemberton, defending Vicksburg, from other Confederate units. Turning next on Pemberton, Grant defeated him in two decisive battles, Champion's Hill and Big Black River, and drove him inside the Vicksburg fortifications. By mid-May the city was under siege. Grant applied relentless pressure, and on July 4 Pemberton surrendered. With Vicksburg in Union hands, federal gunboats could range the entire length of the Mississippi.[3] Texas and Arkansas were for all practical purposes lost to the Confederacy.

Lincoln had disliked Grant's plan for capturing Vicksburg. Now he generously confessed his error and placed Grant in command of all federal troops west of the Appalachians. Grant promptly took charge of the fighting around Chattanooga, Tennessee, where Confederate advances, beginning with the Battle of Chickamauga (September 19–20), were

threatening to develop into a major disaster for the North. Shifting corps commanders and bringing up fresh units, he won another decisive victory at Chattanooga in a series of battles ending on November 25, 1863. This cleared the way for an invasion of Georgia. Suddenly this unkempt, stubby little man, who looked more like a tramp than a general, emerged as the military leader the North had been so desperately seeking. In March 1864 Lincoln summoned him to Washington, named him lieutenant general, and gave him supreme command of the armies of the United States.

ECONOMIC AND SOCIAL EFFECTS, NORTH AND SOUTH

Although much blood would yet be spilled, by the end of 1863 the Confederacy was on the road to defeat. Northern military pressure, gradually increasing, was eroding the South's most precious resource: manpower. An ever-tightening naval blockade was reducing its economic strength. Shortages developed that, combined with the flood of currency pouring from the presses, led to drastic inflation. By 1864 an officer's coat cost $2000 in Confederate money, cigars sold for $10 each, butter was $25 a pound, and flour went for $275 a barrel. Wages rose too, but not nearly as rapidly.

The southern railroad network was gradually wearing out, the major lines maintaining operations only by cannibalizing less vital roads. Imported products such as coffee disappeared; even salt became scarce. Efforts to increase manufacturing were only moderately successful because of the shortage of labor, capital, and technical knowledge. In general, southern prejudice against centralized authority prevented the Confederacy from making effective use of its scarce resources. Even blockade running was left in private hands until 1864. Precious cargo space that should have been reserved for medical supplies and arms was often devoted to high-priced luxuries.

In the North, after a brief depression in 1861 caused by the uncertainties of the situation and the loss of southern business, the economy flourished. Government purchases greatly stimulated certain lines of manufacturing, the railroads operated at close to capacity and with increasing efficiency, the farm machinery business boomed because so many farmers left their fields to serve in the army, and bad harvests in Europe boosted agricultural prices.

Congress passed a number of economic measures long desired but held up in the past by southern opposition. The Homestead Act (1862) gave 160 acres

---

[3]Port Hudson, isolated by Vicksburg's fall, surrendered on July 9.

to any settler who would farm the land for five years. The Morrill Land Grant Act of the same year provided the states with land at the rate of 30,000 acres for each member of Congress to support state agricultural colleges. Various tariff acts raised the duties on manufactured goods to an average rate of 47 percent in order to protect domestic manufacturers from foreign competition. The Pacific Railway Act (1862) authorized subsidies in land and money for the construction of a transcontinental railroad. And the National Banking Act of 1863 gave the country, at last, a uniform currency.

All these laws stimulated the economy. Whether the overall economic effect of the Civil War on the Union was beneficial is less clear. Since it was fought mostly with rifles, light cannon, horses, and wagons, it had much less effect on heavy industry than later wars would have. Although the economy grew, it did so more slowly during the 1860s than in the decades preceding and following. Prices soared beginning in 1862, averaging about 80 percent over the 1860 level by the end of the war. As in the South, wages did not keep pace. This did not make for a healthy economy; nor did the fact that there were chronic shortages of labor in many fields, shortages aggravated by a sharp drop in the number of immigrants.

As the war dragged on and the continuing inflation eroded purchasing power, resentment on the part of workers deepened. During the 1850s iron molders, cigar makers, and some other skilled workers had formed national unions. This trend continued through the war years. There were many strikes. Inflation and shortages encouraged speculation and fostered a selfish, materialistic attitude toward life. Many contractors took advantage of wartime confusion to sell the government shoddy goods. By 1864 cotton was worth $1.90 a pound in New England. It could be had for 20 cents a pound in the South. Although it was illegal to traffic in the staple across the lines, unscrupulous operators did so and made huge profits.

Yet the war undoubtedly hastened industrialization and laid the basis for many other aspects of modern civilization. It posed problems of organization and planning, both military and civilian, that challenged the talents of creative persons and thus led to a more complex and efficient economy. The mechanization of production, the growth of large corporations, the creation of a better banking system, and the emergence of business leaders attuned to these conditions would surely have occurred in any case, for industrialization was under way long before the South seceded. Nevertheless, the war greatly speeded all these changes.

Civilian participation in the war effort was far greater than in earlier conflicts. Some churches split over the question of emancipation, but North and South, church leaders took the lead in recruitment drives and in charitable activities aimed at supporting the armed forces. In the North a Christian Commission raised the money and coordinated the personnel needed to provide Union soldiers with half a million Bibles, several million religious tracts, and other books, along with fruit, coffee, and spare clothing.

WOMEN IN WARTIME

Many southern women took over the management of farms and small plantations when their menfolk went off to war. Others became volunteer nurses, and after an initial period of resistance, the Confederate

▲ Women workers filling cartridges at the U.S. arsenal at Watertown, Massachusetts (1861) from an engraving after Winslow Homer.

▲ Women in the South playing croquet during the war, preserving the amenities of plantation life. By 1864 southern leaders were complaining that many southern women had lost their zeal for the Cause. Poor women engaged in bread riots; and well-to-do women held "incessant parties and balls." Through such actions, women registered their discontent with the war—and with the paternalist ethos of southern chivalry, which had manifestly failed to protect and defend southern womanhood.

army began to enlist women in the medical corps. At least two female nurses, Captain Sally Tompkins and Kate Cumming, left records of their experiences that throw much light on how the wounded were treated during the war. Other southern women worked as clerks in newly organized government departments.

Southern "ladyhood" more generally was yet another casualty of the war. The absence or death of husbands or other male relations changed attitudes toward gender roles. When her husband obeyed a military order to abandon Atlanta to the advancing Union armies, Julia Davidson, about to give birth, denounced the "men of Atlanta" for having "run and left Atlanta" and their homes. Such women learned to fend for themselves. "Necessity," Davidson later wrote her husband, would "make a different woman of me."

Large numbers of women also contributed to the northern war effort. As in the South, farm women went out into fields to plant and harvest crops, aided in many instances by new farm machinery. Many others took jobs in textile factories; in establishments making shoes, uniforms, and other supplies for the army; and in government agencies. But as was usually the case, the low wages traditionally paid women acted as a brake on wage increases for their male colleagues.

Besides working in factories and shops and on farms, northern women, again like their southern counterparts, aided the war effort more directly. Elizabeth Blackwell, the first American woman doctor of medicine, had already founded the New York Infirmary for Women and Children. After war broke out she helped set up what became the United States Sanitary Commission, an organization of women similar to the Christian Commission dedicated to improving

sanitary conditions at army camps, supplying hospitals with volunteer nurses, and raising money for medical supplies. Many thousands of women volunteers took part in Sanitary Commission and related programs.

DOCUMENT

Barton, Memoirs about Medical Life at the Battlefield

An additional 3000-odd women served as regular army nurses during the conflict. At the start the high command of both armies resisted the efforts of women to help, but necessity and a grudging recognition of the competence of these women gradually brought the generals around. Clara Barton, a school teacher and government clerk, was among the first women to dress wounds at forward stations on the battlefield. After she ran out of bandages at Antietam, she dressed wounds with green corn leaves. The chief surgeon declared her to be "the angel of the battlefield." The "proper sphere" of American woman was expanding, another illustration of the modernizing effect of the war.

GRANT IN THE WILDERNESS

Grant's strategy as supreme commander was simple, logical, and ruthless. He would attack Lee and try to capture Richmond, Virginia. General William

Tecumseh Sherman would drive from Chattanooga toward Atlanta, Georgia. Like a lobster's claw, the two armies could then close to crush all resistance. Early in May 1864 Grant and Sherman commenced operations, each with more than 100,000 men.

Grant marched the Army of the Potomac directly into the tangled wilderness area south of the Rappahannock, where Hooker had been routed a year earlier. Lee, having only 60,000 men, forced the battle in the roughest possible country, where Grant found it difficult to make efficient use of his larger force. For two days (May 5–6) the Battle of the Wilderness raged. When it was over, the North had sustained another 18,000 casualties, far more than the Confederates. But unlike his predecessors, Grant did not fall back after being checked, nor did he expose his army to the kind of devastating counterattack at which Lee was so expert. Instead he shifted his troops to the southeast, attempting to outflank the Confederates. Divining his intent, Lee rushed his divisions southeastward and disposed them behind hastily erected earthworks in well-placed positions around Spotsylvania Court House. Grant attacked. After five more days, at a cost to the Union army of another 12,000 men, the Confederate lines were still intact.

Grant had grasped the fundamental truth that the war could be won only by grinding the South

▲ An 8.5-ton siege gun, mounted on a railroad flatcar, that hurled 200-pound bombs onto Confederate positions at Petersburg. Trench warfare ensued, a chilling harbinger of World War I in early twentieth-century Europe.

down beneath the weight of numbers. His own losses of men and equipment could be replaced; Lee's could not. When critics complained of the cost, he replied doggedly that he intended to fight on in the same manner if it took all summer. Once more he pressed southeastward in an effort to outflank the enemy. At Cold Harbor, 9 miles from Richmond, he found the Confederates once more in strong defenses. He attacked. It was a battle as foolish and nearly as one-sided as General Pakenham's assault on Jackson's line outside New Orleans in 1815. "At Cold Harbor," the forthright Grant confessed in his memoirs, "no advantage whatever was gained to compensate for the heavy losses we sustained."

Sixty thousand casualties in less than a month! The news sent a wave of dismay through the North. There were demands that "Butcher" Grant be removed from command. Lincoln, however, stood firm. Although the price was fearfully high, Grant was gaining his objective. At Cold Harbor, Lee had to fight without a single regiment in general reserve while Grant's army was larger than at the start of the offensive. When Grant next swung around his flank, striking south of the James River toward Petersburg, Lee had to rush his troops to that city to hold him.

As the Confederates dug in, Grant put Petersburg under siege. Soon both armies had constructed complicated lines of breastworks and trenches, running for miles in a great arc south of Petersburg, much like the fortifications that would be used in France in World War I. Methodically the Union forces extended their lines, seeking to weaken the Confederates and cut the rail connections supplying Lee's troops and the city of Richmond. Grant could not overwhelm him, but by late June, Lee was pinned to earth. Moving again would mean having to abandon Richmond—tantamount, in southern eyes, to surrender.

SHERMAN IN GEORGIA

The summer of 1864 saw the North submerged in pessimism. The Army of the Potomac held Lee at bay but appeared powerless to defeat him. In Georgia, General Sherman inched forward methodically against the wily Joseph E. Johnston, but when he tried a direct assault at Kennesaw Mountain on June 27, he was thrown back with heavy casualties. In July Confederate raiders under General Jubal Early dashed suddenly across the Potomac from the

▲ Although Sherman's 100,000 Union soldiers marched to Atlanta, his men were supplied by sixteen railway trains from Chattanooga, Tennessee, each day. After taking Atlanta late in the summer of 1864, Sherman pulled up the railway line and burned the depots. On his march to the sea, he destroyed several hundred miles of railroads.

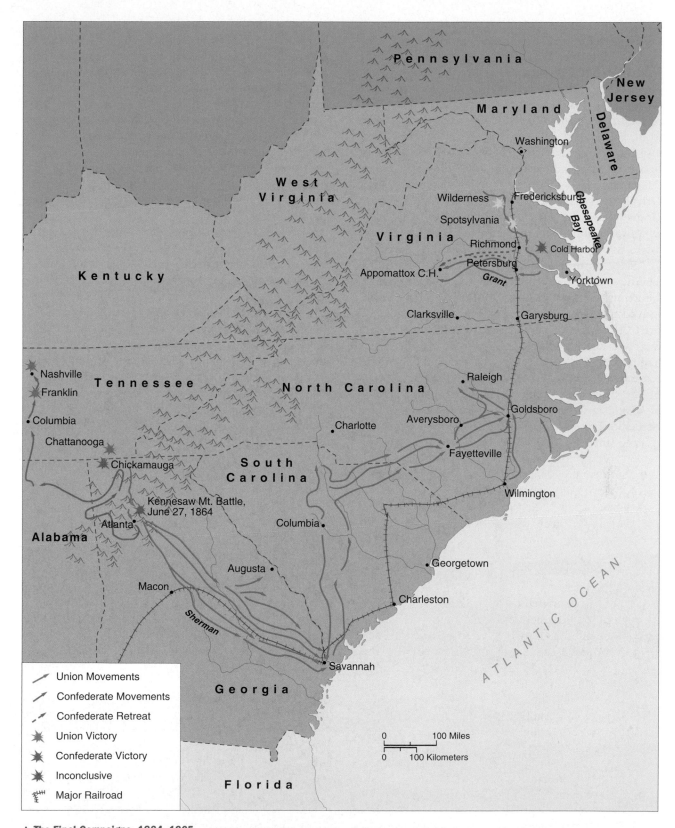

▲ **The Final Campaigns, 1864–1865**
Grant's repeated and costly (60,000 casualties the first month) attempts to outflank Lee are detailed
here. At Five Forks the long siege of Petersburg was broken; Richmond was evacuated. A week later,
Lee surrendered. Sherman's campaign in Georgia and the Carolinas is also depicted.

Shenandoah Valley to within five miles of Washington before being turned back. A draft call for 500,000 additional men did not improve the public temper. Huge losses and the absence of a decisive victory were taxing the northern will to continue the fight.

In June, Lincoln had been renominated on a National Union ticket, with the Tennessee Unionist Andrew Johnson, a former Democrat, as his running mate. He was under attack not only from the Democrats, who nominated General McClellan and came out for a policy that might almost be characterized as peace at any price, but also from the Radical Republicans, many of whom had wished to dump him in favor of Secretary of the Treasury Chase.

Then, almost overnight, the whole atmosphere changed. On September 2, General Sherman's army fought its way into Atlanta. When the Confederates countered with an offensive northward toward Tennessee,[4] Sherman did not follow. Instead he abandoned his communications with Chattanooga and marched unopposed through Georgia, "from Atlanta to the sea."

Sherman was in some ways quite like Grant. He was a West Pointer who resigned his commission only to fare poorly in civilian occupations. Back in the army in 1861, he suffered a brief nervous breakdown. After recovering he fought well under Grant at Shiloh and the two became close friends. "He stood by me when I was crazy," Sherman later recalled, "and I stood by him when he was drunk." Far more completely than most military men of his generation, Sherman believed in total war—in appropriating or destroying everything that might help the enemy continue the fight.

DOCUMENT

Sherman, "The March Through Georgia"

The march through Georgia had many objectives besides conquering territory. One obvious one was economic, the destruction of southern resources. "[We] must make old and young, rich and poor feel the hard hand of war," Sherman said. Before taking Atlanta he wrote his wife: "We have devoured the land. . . . All the people retire before us and desolation is behind. To realize what war is one should follow our tracks."

Another object of Sherman's march was psychological. "If the North can march an army right through the South," he told General Grant, Southerners will take it "as proof positive that the North

can prevail." This was certainly true of Georgia's blacks, who flocked to the invaders by the thousands, women and children as well as men, all cheering mightily when the soldiers put their former masters' homes to the torch. "They pray and shout and mix up my name with Moses," Sherman explained.

Sherman's victories staggered the Confederacy and the anti-Lincoln forces in the North. In November the president was easily reelected, 212 electoral votes to 21. The country was determined to carry on the struggle.

At last the South's will to resist began to crack. Sherman entered Savannah on December 22, having denuded a strip of Georgia 60 miles wide. Early in January 1865 he marched northward, leaving behind "a broad black streak of ruin and desolation—the fences all gone; lonesome smoke-stacks, surrounded by dark heaps of ashes and cinders, marking the spots where human habitations had stood." In February his troops captured Columbia, South Carolina. Soon they were in North Carolina, advancing relentlessly. In Virginia, Grant's vise grew tighter day by day while the Confederate lines became thinner and more ragged.

TO APPOMATTOX COURT HOUSE

On March 4 Lincoln took the presidential oath and delivered his second inaugural address. Photographs taken at about this time show how four years of war had marked him. Somehow he had become both gentle and steel-tough, both haggard and inwardly calm. With victory sure, he spoke for tolerance, mercy, and reconstruction. "Let us judge not," he said after stating again his personal dislike of slavery, "that we be not judged." He urged all Americans to turn without malice to the task of mending the damage and to make a just and lasting peace between the sections.

Now the Confederate troops around Petersburg could no longer withstand the federal pressure. Desperately Lee tried to pull his forces back to the Richmond and Danville Railroad at Lynchburg, but the swift wings of Grant's army enveloped them. Richmond fell on April 3. With fewer than

MAP

The Civil War Part II: 1863-1865

30,000 men to oppose Grant's 115,000, Lee recognized the futility of further resistance. On April 9 he and Grant met by prearrangement at Appomattox Court House.

It was a scene at once pathetic and inspiring. Lee was noble in defeat; Grant, despite his rough-

---

[4]This force was crushed before Nashville in December by a Union army under General George Thomas.

DEBATING THE PAST

Why did the South lose the Civil War? The answer to this question had long been answered with numbers: The South had too few people and factories. But many have rebutted this point by noting that the South nearly *did* win. Moreover, while southern commanders were plagued with shortages, they lost no battles because they ran out of bullets or shells. In a study of industrial output, Emory Thomas (1979) concluded that southern leadership "outdid its northern counterpart in mobilizing for total war." The South's chief deficiency was, surprisingly, in food production. Frank L. Owsley (1925) blamed the South's defeat on "state's rights jealousy and particularism." Confederate states failed to coordinate financing and production and thus made the South's defeat "inevitable." Jeffrey Hummel (1996), however, has advanced the opposite argument: Jefferson Davis's centralization of power strangled the South with bureaucratic inefficiency and deprived it of ideological coherence. Folklore holds that the genius of southern generals, especially Robert E. Lee, overcame all southern deficiencies. But in *Attack and Die* (1982), a book whose thesis is contained in its title, Grady McWhiney and Perry D. Jamieson insisted that Lee's audacity, and that of other southern generals, was ill-suited to the military technology of the day. Rifles were particularly effective at cutting down attacking armies. Detailed statistical analysis, however, has challenged this thesis: the North and South initiated attacks with nearly equal frequency and losses. Edward Channing (1925) proposed that the South was defeated because by 1865 Confederates "lost the will to fight." This is rather like saying that the South stopped fighting because it decided to stop fighting—an instance of circular reasoning. But many historians have found the argument, restated more subtly, to be persuasive. Herman Hattaway and Archer Jones (1986) proposed that while the Confederacy could field and equip an effective army for most of the war, "an insufficient nationalism" failed to "survive the strains imposed by lengthy hostilities." The scene above is of Richmond in April, 1865.

Emory Thomas, *The Confederate Nation* (1979), Frank L. Owsley, *State Rights in the Confederacy* (1925), Grady McWhiney and Perry D. Jamieson, *Attack and Die* (1982), Edward Channing, *History of the United States* (1925), Herman Hattaway and Archer Jones, *How the North Won* (1983), Jeffrey Hummel, *Emancipating Slaves, Enslaving Free Men* (1996).

hewn exterior, sensitive and magnanimous in victory. "I met you once before, General Lee, while we were serving in Mexico," Grant said after they had shaken hands. "I have always remembered your appearance, and I think I should have recognized you anywhere." They talked briefly of that earlier war, and then, acting on Lincoln's instructions, Grant outlined his terms. All that would be required was that the Confederate soldiers lay down their arms. They could return to their homes in peace. When Lee hinted (he was too proud to ask outright for the concession) that his men would profit greatly if allowed to retain possession of their horses, Grant agreed to let them do so.

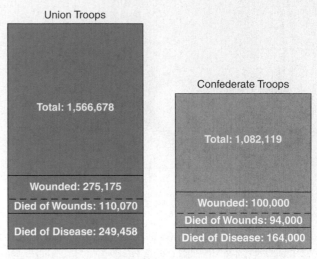

▲ **Casualties of the Civil War**
The Union death rate was 23 percent, the Confederate 24 percent. In general, twice as many soldiers were killed by disease as were killed by bullets.

WINNERS, LOSERS, AND THE FUTURE

And so the war ended. It had cost the nation more than 600,000 lives, nearly as many as in all other American wars combined. The story of one of the lost thousands must stand for all, Union and Confederate. Jones Budbury, a tall, 19-year-old redhead, was working in a Pennsylvania textile mill when the war broke out, and he enlisted at once. His regiment first saw action at Bull Run. He took part in McClellan's Peninsula campaign. He fought at Second Bull Run, at Chancellorsville, and at Gettysburg. A few months after Gettysburg he was wounded in the foot and spent some time in an army hospital. By the spring of 1864 he had risen through the ranks to first sergeant and his hair had turned gray. In June he was captured and sent to Andersonville military prison, near Macon, Georgia, but he fell ill and the Confederates released him. In March 1865 he was back with his regiment in the lines besieging Richmond. On April 6, three days before Lee's surrender, Jones Budbury was killed while pursuing Confederate units near Sailor's Creek, Virginia.

The war also caused enormous property losses, especially in the Confederacy. All the human and material destruction explains the eroding hatred and bitterness that the war implanted in millions of hearts. The corruption, the gross materialism, and the selfishness generated by wartime conditions were other disagreeable by-products of the conflict. Such sores fester in any society, but the Civil War bred conditions that inflamed and multiplied them. The war produced many examples of charity, self-sacrifice, and devotion to duty as well, yet if the general moral atmosphere of the postwar generation can be said to have resulted from the experiences of 1861 to 1865, the effect overall was bad.

What had been obtained at this price? Slavery was dead. Paradoxically, while the war had been fought to preserve the Union, after 1865 the people tended to see the United States not as a union of states but as a nation. After Appomattox, secession was almost literally inconceivable. In a strictly political sense, as Lincoln had predicted from the start, the northern victory heartened friends of republican government and democracy throughout the world. A better-integrated society and a more technically advanced and productive economic system also resulted from the war.

The Americans of 1865 estimated the balance between cost and profit according to their individual fortunes and prejudices. Only the wisest realized that no final accounting could be made until the people had decided what to do with the fruits of victory. That the physical damage would be repaired no one could reasonably doubt; that even the loss of human resources would be restored in short order was equally apparent. But would the nation make good use of the opportunities the war had made available? What would the former slaves do with freedom? How would whites, northern and southern, react to emancipation? To what end would the new technology and social efficiency be directed? Would the people be able to forget the recent past and fulfill the hopes for which so many brave soldiers had given their "last full measure of devotion"?

Re-Viewing the Past

Cold Mountain

Cold Mountain (2004), a movie based on Charles Frazier's novel, is a love story set during the Civil War. But this is an unusual love story. The lovers are seldom together; and the hero is a deserter.

Inman (Jude Law), a schoolteacher, and Ada (Nicole Kidman), the well-born daughter of the minister, meet in a town in western North Carolina in the shadows of Cold Mountain. They speak on several occasions, look searchingly at each other, and exchange a single resolute kiss. Then Inman enlists in the Confederate army. They send each other letters, many of which never arrive. They yearn for each other without knowing much about each other. In a world made ugly by war, they need something beautiful to love. They cherish their photographs of the other.

Inman is wounded in the neck during the siege of Petersburg. While convalescing in the hospital, he receives a letter from Ada: "If you are fighting, stop fighting . . . If you are marching, stop marching. Come back to me." He nods grimly and decides to desert. He sneaks out of the hospital and begins his long trek back to Cold Mountain.

The journey is an ordeal. He suffers from cold and hunger. Confederate soldiers chase, capture, and shoot him, leaving him for dead; rogues attack and rob him. If war is hell, leaving it is no picnic, either.

Ada suffers too. Her father dies and she sets the slaves free. A southern lady, she knows nothing about farming and goes hungry. Renée Zellweger, a plucky female farmhand, appears at the farm and sets it aright.

The movie reaches a climax when Inman staggers up Cold Mountain—and into the arms of

► Nicole Kidman, as Ada in *Cold Mountain*

Ada. He is closely pursued by ruffians in the Home Guard, a local militia, who shoot him dead.

Can any of this be regarded as history?

There was a man named Inman, the brother of author Frazier's great-great-grandfather. The real Inman had been wounded in the neck at Petersburg, deserted, and was killed in a gunfight with the Home Guard near Cold Mountain. But the known facts of Inman's story, Frazier explained, "could be scrawled on the back of the envelope." Frazier made up everything else, doubtless inspired by Homer's *Odyssey*, another story of a soldier's return home from war.

But if much of the story is the product of Frazier's imagination, it nevertheless illuminates several historically significant themes. *Cold Mountain* examines the psychological effects of the loss of morale in the South, which many historians now regard as the best explanation for its defeat. (See Debating the Past, p. 418.) Official statistics indicate that some 200,000 Union soldiers and 104,000 Confederates deserted. Many more simply walked unarmed into enemy camps and were arrested as "captured." When Robert E. Lee surrendered at Appomattox, his army had dwindled to 28,000 men; another 3800 were reported as deserted and another 14,000 as captured.

The problem of desertion was especially acute in the mountain region of North Carolina, where support for secession had never been strong. In late 1863 and early 1864 the legislature of North Carolina passed laws penalizing sheriffs who failed to assist in capturing deserters and draft dodgers; it also created the Home Guard, local militias composed of men exempt from conscription, and charged them with the task of rounding up deserters. By early 1865, Lee was complaining that

▲ Southern lady with Lookout Mountain, Tennessee, in the background.

entire units were deserting; he especially regretted that "the greatest number of desertions have occurred among the North Carolina troops."

If the movie accurately pinpoints the geography of desertion—North Carolina—was its psychological explanation equally valid? Did southern women, like Ada, encourage their menfolk to desert?

The historical evidence is ambivalent.

On the one hand, the Confederacy made a concerted effort to enlist the support of white women. The South's surprisingly strong economic performance suggests that plenty of women, like Ada, learned how to manage farms and plantations. There is evidence, too, that southern women encouraged their men to fight. In 1862 and again the next year, a letter appeared in many Confederate newspapers in which "The Women of the South" called on their men to enlist and fight. "Never turn your backs on the flag," it advised soldiers, for cowardly behavior would disgrace themselves and their "children's children." When Sergeant Edwin Fay of Louisiana wrote to his wife saying that he wanted to leave "this horrid war," she responded that while she missed him terribly she could not countenance his becoming a deserter.

The Confederacy's appeal to women reflected their increasing importance in public life. Historian Drew Gilpin Faust argues that women's role shifted further as the Confederacy and its menfolk failed to defend white southern "womanhood." "Of necessity," such women assumed a larger role in the management of farms and plantations and they became more assertive in public matters. Some took the lead—as did Ada—in encouraging their men to desert.

"Though the ladies may not be willing to concede the fact," a Confederate official in North Carolina declared, "they are nevertheless responsible for the desertion in the army." James Fowler, a private from North Carolina who had been sentenced to death for desertion, cited his wife's pleas in his appeal for clemency. "I received a letter from my wife stating there [sic] condition and my two children was both at the point of Death and I made evry [sic] effort to get permission to go home honorably."

Cold Mountain is not history. But the movie illuminates the anguish of those who cling to life and love rather than to a war effort that will likely fail.

MILESTONES

1861	Confederates attack Fort Sumter; Lincoln calls for 75,000 volunteers	**1863**	Congress passes Conscription and National Banking acts
	First Battle of Bull Run (Virginia) boosts Confederate morale		Federal troops subdue draft riots in New York City
	Lincoln appoints George B. McClellan Union commander		Union army defeats Confederates at turning point Battle of Gettysburg, Pennsylvania
	Supreme Court rules against Lincoln's suspension of habeas corpus in *Ex parte Merryman*		Union siege and capture of Vicksburg, Mississippi, gives Union control of entire Mississippi River
1862	Confederate Congress passes Conscription Act	**1864**	Grant pushes deep into Virginia in costly Battles of the Wilderness, Spotsylvania Court House, and Cold Harbor
	Battle of Glorieta Pass ends Confederate threat to Far West		Sherman captures Atlanta, Georgia; marches to sea; captures Savannah
	USS *Monitor* defeats Confederate *Merrimack* in first battle between ironclads	**1864**	Lincoln is reelected president
	Battle of Shiloh, Tennessee, leaves 23,000 dead, wounded, or missing	**1864–1865**	Grant takes Petersburg, Virginia, after 10-month siege
	Robert E. Lee assumes command of Confederate Army of Northern Virginia	**1865**	Sherman captures Columbia, South Carolina
	Lee and Stonewall Jackson defeat huge Union army at Seven Days' Battle for Richmond	**1865**	Lee surrenders to Grant at Appomattox Court House, Virginia
	Lee and Jackson defeat Union army at Second Battle of Bull Run		
	Lee's northern advance is stopped at Battle of Antietam; 22,000 die		
	Lincoln's Emancipation Proclamation frees slaves in "areas of rebellion"		
	Congress passes Homestead, Morrill Land Grant, and Pacific Railway acts		

SUPPLEMENTARY READING

The best survey of the Civil War period is James M. McPherson, *Battle Cry of Freedom* (1988), but see also Russell F. Weigley, *A Great Civil War* (2000).

On the precipitating events of the war, see Maury Klein, *Days of Defiance: Sumter, Secession and the Coming of the Civil War* (1997), and Wallace Hettle, *The Peculiar Democracy: Southern Democrats in Peace and Civil War* (2001).

For Lincoln, in addition to books mentioned in previous chapters, see Philip Paludan, *The Presidency of Abraham Lincoln* (1994). Lincoln's dealings with the Radicals have been extensively investigated. H. L. Trefousse, *The Radical Republicans: Lincoln's Vanguard for Racial Justice* (1969), which praises Lincoln's management of the Radicals and minimizes his differences with them, is a good summary, but see also Richard Franklin Bensel, *Yankee*

Leviathan: The Origins of Central State Authority in America (1990). Mark E. Neely, *The Fate of Liberty* (1991) examines Lincoln's position on civil liberties. Frank Klement, *The Limits of Dissent* (1998) focuses on Clement Vallandigham. For the movement to make abolition a war aim and the reaction to it, see Michael Vorenberg, *Final Freedom* (2001).

On economic issues, see Heather Cox Richardson, *The Greatest Nation on Earth: Republican Economy Policies during the Civil War* (1997), and Bray Hammond, *Sovereignty and an Empty Purse: Banks and Politics in the Civil War* (1970).

On African Americans in the Union army, see Joseph T. Glatthaar, *Forged in Battle: The Civil War Alliance of Black Soldiers and White Officers* (1990); Peter Burchard, *One*

Gallant Rush (1965), recounts the story of Robert Gould Shaw and the Massachusetts 54th. See also Martin H. Blatt, *Hope & Glory: Essays on the Legacy of the 54th Massachusetts Regiment* (2001).

For aspects of economic and social history, see Philip S. Paludan, *"A People's Contest": The Union at War* (1988). Edward L. Ayers, *In the Presence of Mine Enemies* (2003) examines the effect of the war on various communities. For women and the war, see Drew Gilpin Faust, *Mothers of Invention* (1997), Judith Ann Giesberg, *Civil War Sisterhood: The U.S. Sanitary Commission and Women's Politics in Transition* (2000), and Laura Edwards, *Scarlett Doesn't Live Here Anymore* (2000). Elizabeth Young considers the literary heritage of women and the war in *Disarming the Nation: Women's Writing and the American Civil War* (1999). See also Iver Bernstein, *The New York City Draft Riots* (1990).

For the Confederacy, see Gary W. Gallagher, *The Confederate War* (1997). See also his edited collection, *Lee the Soldier* (1996). On divisions within the Confederacy, see William W. Freehling, *The South vs. The South: How Anti-Confederate Southerners Shaped the Course of the Civil War* (2001). Important biographies include William Cooper, *Jefferson Davis, American* (2000). See also Mark Grimsley and Brooks D. Simpson, eds., *Collapse of the Confederacy* (2001), and Steven V. Ash, *When the Yankees Came: Conflict and Chaos in the Occupied South* (1995).

Gerald F. Linderman, *Embattled Courage* (1988) argues that the soldiers on both sides grew disillusioned with the fighting; the persistence of the initial ideals is a theme in James McPherson, *What They Fought For, 1861–1865*

(1994), and Reid Mitchell, *The Vacant Chair* (1993). Bertram Wyatt-Brown, *The Shaping of Southern Culture: Honor, Grace and War, 1760s–1880s* (2001) contends that while soldiers on both sides used the same rhetoric to defend their cause, they had different notions of what terms such as "honor" meant.

Among the biographies of Civil War generals, northern and southern, the following are especially noteworthy: Brooks D. Simpson, *Ulysses S. Grant: Triumph over Adversity, 1822–1865* (2000), Jean E. Smith, *Grant* (2001), William S. McFeely, *Grant* (1981), Michael Fellman, *The Making of Robert E. Lee* (2000), Douglass S. Freeman, *R. E. Lee* (1934–1935), James I. Robertson, *Stonewall Jackson* (1997), Stephen W. Sears, *George B. McClellan* (1988), Stanley P. Hirshson, *The White Tecumseh: A Biography of William T. Sherman* (1997), and Chester G. Hearn, *Admiral David Glasgow Farragut* (1998).

The diplomacy of the Civil War period is covered in two works by Howard Jones, *Union in Peril* (1992), on British intervention, and *Abraham Lincoln and a New Birth of Freedom* (1999), on issues of slavery. See also John Taylor, *William Henry Seward* (1991).

John C. Waugh, *Reelecting Lincoln* (1997) considers the election of 1864. The assassination of Lincoln and its aftermath is the subject of Jay Winik, *April 1865: The Month That Saved America* (2001).

The legacy of the Civil War is thoughtfully examined in David W. Blight, *Race and Reunion: The Civil War in American Memory* (2001), and Tony Horwitz, *Confederates in the Attic: Dispatches from the Unfinished Civil War* (1998).

SUGGESTED WEBSITES

The American Civil War Homepage

http://sunsite.utk.edu/civil-war/warweb.html

This site has a great collection of hypertext links to the most useful identified electronic files about the American Civil War.

Abraham Lincoln

http://showcase.netins.net/web/creative/lincoln.html

This site both contains useful information about President Lincoln and links to other web destinations.

Abraham Lincoln Association

http://www.alincolnassoc.com/

This site allows searches of Lincoln's papers.

Assassination of President Abraham Lincoln

http://memory.loc.gov/ammem/alhtml/alrintr.html

Part of the American memory series with introduction, timeline, and gallery.

National Civil War Association

http://www.ncwa.org/

This site documents one of the many Civil War reenactment organizations in the United States.

Selected Civil War Photographs

http://memory.loc.gov/ammem/cwphtml/cwphome.html

Library of Congress site has more than one thousand photographs, many from Matthew Brady.

A Timeline of the Civil War

http://www.historyplace.com/civilwar/index.html

This site offers a comprehensive Civil War timeline that includes photographs.

U.S. Civil War Center

http://www.cwc.lsu.edu/

The mission of this site is to "locate, index and/or make available all appropriate private and public data regarding the Civil War and to promote the study of the Civil War from the perspective of all professional, occupations, and academic disciplines."

Reconstruction and the South

▼ Robert B. Elliott of South Carolina, where blacks outnumbered whites, addressing Congress on civil rights issues in 1874. He had defeated white opponents in 1870 and 1872.

O n April 5, 1865, Abraham Lincoln visited Richmond. The fallen capital lay in ruins, sections blackened by fire, but the president was able to walk the streets unmolested and almost unattended. Everywhere black people crowded around him worshipfully; some fell to their knees as he passed, crying "Glory, Hallelujah," hailing him as a messiah. Even white townspeople seemed to have accepted defeat without resentment.

A few days later, in Washington, Lincoln delivered an important speech on Reconstruction, urging compassion and open-mindedness. On April 14 he held a Cabinet meeting at which postwar readjustment was considered at length. That evening, while Lincoln was watching a performance of the play *Our American Cousin* at Ford's Theater, a half-mad actor, John Wilkes Booth, slipped into his box and shot him in the back of the head with a small pistol. Early the next morning, without having regained consciousness, Lincoln died.

The murder was part of a complicated plot organized by die-hard pro-Southerners. Seldom have fanatics displayed so little understanding of their own interests, for with Lincoln perished the South's best hope for a mild peace. After his body had been taken home to Illinois, the national mood hardened; apparently the awesome drama was still unfolding—retribution and a final humbling of the South were inevitable.

PRESIDENTIAL RECONSTRUCTION

Despite its bloodiness, the Civil War had caused less intersectional hatred than might have been expected. Although civilian property was often seized or destroyed, the invading armies treated the southern

population with forbearance, both during the war and after Appomattox. While confederate President Davis was ensconced in Richmond behind Lee's army, Northerners boasted that they would "hang Jeff Davis to a sour apple tree," and when he was captured in Georgia in May 1865, he was at once clapped into irons preparatory to being tried for treason and murder. But feeling against Davis subsided quickly. In 1867 the military turned him over to the civil courts, which released him on bail. He was never brought to trial. A few other Confederate officials spent short periods behind bars, but the only Southerner executed for war crimes was Major Henry Wirz, the commandant of Andersonville military prison.

The legal questions related to bringing the defeated states back into the Union were extremely complex. Since Southerners believed that secession was legal, logic should have compelled them to argue that they were out of the Union and would thus have to be formally readmitted. Northerners should have taken the contrary position, for they had fought to prove that secession was illegal. Yet the people of both sections did just the opposite. Senator Charles Sumner and Congressman Thaddeus Stevens, in 1861 uncompromising expounders of the theory that the Union was indissoluble, now insisted that the Confederate states had "committed suicide" and should be treated like "conquered provinces." Lincoln believed the issue a "pernicious abstraction" and tried to ignore it.

The process of readmission began in 1862, when Lincoln reappointed provisional governors for those parts of the South that had been occupied by federal troops. On December 8, 1863, he issued a proclamation setting forth a general policy. With the exception of high Confederate officials and a few other special groups, all Southerners could reinstate themselves as United States citizens by taking a simple loyalty oath. When, in any state, a number equal to 10 percent of those voting in the 1860 election had taken this oath, they could set up state government. Such governments had to be republican in form, must recognize the "permanent freedom" of the slaves, and must provide for black education. The plan, however, did not require that blacks be given the right to vote.

The "Ten Percent Plan" reflected Lincoln's lack of vindictiveness and his political wisdom. He realized that any government based on such a small minority of the population would be, as he put it, merely "a tangible nucleus which the remainder . . . may rally around as fast as it can," a sort of puppet regime, like the paper government established in those sections of Virginia under federal control.[1] The regimes estab-

lished under this plan in Tennessee, Louisiana, and Arkansas bore, in the president's mind, the same relation to finally reconstructed states that an egg bears to a chicken. "We shall sooner have the fowl by hatching it than by smashing it," he remarked. He knew that eventually representatives of the southern states would again be sitting in Congress, and he wished to lay the groundwork for a strong Republican party in the section. Yet he realized that Congress had no intention of seating representatives from the "10 percent" states at once.

The Radicals in Congress disliked the 10 percent plan, partly because of its moderation and partly because it enabled Lincoln to determine Union policy toward the recaptured regions. In July 1864 they passed the Wade-Davis bill, which provided for constitutional conventions only after a majority of the others in a southern state had taken a loyalty oath. Confederate officials and anyone who had "voluntarily borne arms against the United States" were barred from voting in the election or serving at the convention. Besides prohibiting slavery, the new state constitutions would have to repudiate Confederate debts. Lincoln disposed of the Wade-Davis bill with a pocket veto and there matters stood when Andrew Johnson became president following the assassination.

Lincoln had picked Johnson for a running mate in 1864 because he was a border-state Unionist Democrat and something of a hero as a result of his courageous service as military governor of Tennessee. His political strength came from the poor whites and yeomen farmers of eastern Tennessee, and he was fond of extolling the common man and attacking "stuck-up aristocrats."

Thaddeus Stevens called Johnson a "rank demagogue" and a "damned scoundrel," and it is true that Johnson was a masterful rabble-rouser. But few men of his generation labored so consistently on behalf of small farmers. Free homesteads, public education, absolute social equality—such were his objectives. The father of communism, Karl Marx, a close observer of American affairs at this time, wrote approvingly of Johnson's "deadly hatred of the oligarchy."

Johnson was a Democrat, but because of his record and his reassuring penchant for excoriating southern aristocrats, the Republicans in Congress were ready to cooperate with him. "Johnson, we have faith in you," said Senator Ben Wade, author of the Wade-Davis bill, the day after Lincoln's death. "By the gods, there will be no trouble now in running the government!"

Johnson's reply, "Treason must be made infamous," delighted the Radicals, but the president proved temperamentally unable to work with them. Like Randolph of Roanoke, his antithesis intellectually and socially, opposition was his specialty; he soon alienated every powerful Republican in Washington.

---

[1]By approving the separation of the western counties that had refused to secede, this government provided a legal pretext for the creation of West Virginia.

▲ Andrew Johnson in 1855, from a painting by William Cooper. From origins even more lowly than Lincoln's, Johnson had risen to be congressman, governor of Tennessee, and United States senator. He was able and ambitious but fundamentally unsure of himself, as could be seen in his boastfulness and stubbornness.

Radical Republicans listened to Johnson's diatribes against secessionists and the great planters and assumed that he was anti-southern. Nothing could have been further from the truth. He had great respect for states' rights and he shared most of his poor white Tennessee constituents' contempt of blacks. "Damn the negroes, I am fighting these traitorous aristocrats, their masters," he told a friend during the war. "I wish to God," he said on another occasion, "every head of a family in the United States had one slave to take the drudgery and menial service off his family."

The new president did not want to injure or humiliate all white Southerners. He issued an amnesty proclamation only slightly more rigorous than Lincoln's. It assumed, correctly enough, that with the war over most southern voters would freely take the loyalty oath; thus it contained no 10 percent clause. More classes of Confederates, including those who owned taxable property in excess of $20,000, were excluded from the general pardon. By the time Congress convened in December 1865, all the southern states had organized governments, ratified the Thirteenth Amendment abolishing slavery, and elected senators and representatives. Johnson promptly recommended these new governments to the attention of Congress.

REPUBLICAN RADICALS

Peace found the Republicans in Congress no more united than they had been during the war. A small group of "ultra" Radicals were demanding immediate and absolute civil and political equality for blacks; they should be given, for example, the vote, a plot of land, and access to a decent education. Senator Sumner led this faction. A second group of Radicals, headed by Thaddeus Stevens in the House and Ben Wade in the Senate, agreed with the ultras' objectives but were prepared to accept half a loaf if necessary to win the support of less radical colleagues.

Nearly all Radicals distinguished between the "natural" God-given rights described in the Declaration of Independence, and social equality. "Equality," said Stevens, "does not mean that a negro shall sit in the same seat or eat at the same table with a white man. That is a matter of taste which every man must

▲ Mathew Brady's photograph of the stalwart radical Republican Thaddeus Stevens. Stevens insisted on being buried in a black cemetery. He wrote his own epitaph: "I repose in this quiet and secluded spot, not from any natural preference for solitude, but finding other cemeteries limited as to race, by charter rules, I have chosen this that I might illustrate in my death the principles which I advocated through a long life, equality of man before his Creator."

decide for himself." This did not reflect personal prejudice in Stevens's case. When he died, he was buried in a black cemetery.

The moderate Republicans wanted to protect the former slaves from exploitation and guarantee their basic rights but were unprepared to push for full political equality. A handful of Republicans sided with the Democrats in support of Johnson's approach, but all the rest insisted at least on the minimal demands of the moderates. Thus Johnsonian Reconstruction was doomed.

Johnson's proposal had no chance in Congress for reasons having little to do with black rights. The Thirteenth Amendment had the effect of increasing the representation of the southern states in Congress because it made the Three-fifths Compromise meaningless. Henceforth those who had been slaves would be counted as whole persons in apportioning seats in the House of Representatives. If Congress seated the Southerners, the balance of power might swing to the Democrats. To expect the Republicans to surrender power in such a fashion was unrealistic. Former Copperheads gushing with extravagant praise for Johnson put them instantly on guard.

In addition, the ex-Confederates were not overflowing with goodwill toward their conquerors. A minority would have nothing to do with amnesties and pardons:

> *Oh, I'm a good old rebel,*
> *Now that's just what I am;*
> *For the "fair land of freedom,"*
> *I do not care a dam.*
> *I'm glad I fit against it—*
> *I only wish we'd won*
> *And I don't want no pardon*
> *For anything I done.*

Southern voters had further provoked northern resentment by their choice of congressmen. Georgia elected Alexander H. Stephens, vice president of the Confederacy, to the Senate, although he was still in a federal prison awaiting trial for treason! Several dozen men who had served in the Confederate Congress had been elected to either the House or the Senate, together with four generals and many other high officials. The southern people understandably selected locally respected and experienced leaders, but it was equally reasonable that these choices would sit poorly with Northerners.

DOCUMENT

The Mississippi Black Code

Finally, the so-called Black Codes enacted by southern governments to control former slaves alarmed the North. These varied in severity from state to state, but all, as one planter admitted, set out to keep the blacks "as near to a state of bondage as possible."

When seen in historical perspective, even the strictest codes represented some improvement over slavery. Most permitted blacks to sue and to testify in court, at least in cases involving members of their own race. Blacks were allowed to own certain kinds of property; other rights were guaranteed. However, blacks could not bear arms, be employed in occupations other than farming and domestic service, or leave their jobs without forfeiting back pay. The Mississippi code required them to sign labor contracts for the year in January, and, in addition, drunkards, vagrants, beggars, "common night-walkers," and even "mischief makers" and persons who "misspend what they earn" and who could not pay the stiff fines assessed for such misbehavior were to be "hired out . . . at public outcry" to the white persons who would take them for the shortest period in return for paying the fines. Such laws, apparently designed to get around the Thirteenth Amendment, outraged Northerners.

CONGRESS REJECTS JOHNSONIAN RECONSTRUCTION

For all these reasons the Republicans in Congress rejected Johnsonian Reconstruction. Quickly they created a joint committee on Reconstruction, headed by Senator William P. Fessenden of Maine, a moderate, to study the question of readmitting the southern states.

The committee held public hearings that produced much evidence of the mistreatment of blacks. Colonel George A. Custer, stationed in Texas, testified: "It is of weekly, if not of daily occurrence that Freedmen are murdered." The nurse Clara Barton told a gruesome tale about a pregnant woman who had been brutally whipped. Others described the intimidation of blacks by poor whites. The hearings strengthened the Radicals, who had been claiming all along that the South was perpetuating slavery under another name.

President Johnson's attitude speeded the swing toward the Radical position. While the hearings were in progress, Congress passed a bill expanding and extending the Freedmen's Bureau, which had been established in March 1865 to care for refugees. The bureau, a branch of the War Department, was already exercising considerable coercive and supervisory power in the South. Now Congress sought to add to its authority in order to protect the black population. Although the bill had wide support, Johnson vetoed it, arguing that it was an unconstitutional extension of military authority in peacetime. Congress then passed a Civil Rights Act that, besides declaring specifically that blacks were citizens of the

DOCUMENT

Southern Skepticism of the Freedmen's Bureau

▲ Agents of the Freedmen's Bureau helped defend former slaves against white attacks and provided them with food, clothing, and medical care. They also set up schools. However, hostility toward the activities of the Freedmen's Bureau was widespread. In 1866, during a race riot in Memphis, mobs killed 46 blacks and burned this Freedmen's schoolhouse.

United States, denied the states the power to restrict their rights to testify in court, to make contracts for their labor, and to hold property. In other words, it put teeth in the Thirteenth Amendment.

Once again the president refused to go along, although his veto was sure to drive more moderates into the arms of the Radicals. On April 9, 1866, Congress repassed the Civil Rights Act by a two-thirds majority, the first time in American history that a major piece of legislation became law over the veto of a president. This event marked a revolution in the history of Reconstruction. Thereafter Congress, not President Johnson, had the upper hand.

In the clash between the president and Congress, Johnson was his own worst enemy. His language was often intemperate, his handling of opponents inept, his analysis of southern conditions incorrect. He had assumed that the small southern farmers who made up the majority in the Confederacy shared his prejudices against the planter class. They did not, as their choices in the postwar elections demonstrated. In fact, Johnson's hatred of the southern aristocracy may have been based more on jealousy than on principle. Under the Reconstruction plan, persons excluded from the blanket amnesty could apply individually for the restoration of their rights. When wealthy and socially prominent southerners flocked to Washington, hat in hand, he found their flattery and humility exhilarating. He issued pardons wholesale. "I did not expect to keep out all who were excluded from the amnesty," he explained. "I intended they should sue for pardon, and so realize the enormity of their crime."

The president misread northern opinion. He believed that Congress had no right to pass laws affecting the South before southern representatives had been readmitted to Congress. However, in the light of the refusal of most southern whites to grant any real power or responsibility to the freedmen (an attitude that Johnson did not condemn), the public would not accept this point of view. Johnson placed his own judgment over that of the overwhelming majority of northern voters, and this was a great error, morally and tactically. By encouraging white Southerners to resist efforts to improve the lot of blacks, Johnson played into the hands of the Radicals.

The Radicals encountered grave problems in fighting for their program. Northerners might object to the Black Codes and to seating "rebels" in Congress, but few believed in racial equality. Between 1865 and 1868, Wisconsin, Minnesota, Connecticut, Nebraska, New Jersey, Ohio, Michigan, and Pennsylvania all rejected bills granting blacks the vote.

The Radicals were in effect demanding not merely equal rights for freedmen but extra rights; not merely the vote but special protection of that right against the pressure that southern whites would surely apply to undermine it. This idea flew in the face of conventional American beliefs in equality before the law and individual self-reliance. Such protection would involve interference by the federal government in local affairs, a concept at variance with American practice. Events were to show that the Radicals were correct—that what amounted to a political revolution in state-federal relations was essential if blacks were to achieve real equality. But in the climate of that day their proposals encountered bitter resistance, and not only from white Southerners.

Thus, while the Radicals sought partisan advantage in their battle with Johnson and sometimes played on war-bred passions in achieving their ends, they were taking large political risks in defense of genuinely held principles. One historian has aptly called them the "moral trustees" of the Civil War.

THE FOURTEENTH AMENDMENT

DOCUMENT

13th, 14th, and 15th Amendments

In June 1866 Congress submitted to the states a new amendment to the Constitution. The Fourteenth Amendment was, in the context of the times, a truly radical measure. Never before had newly freed slaves been granted significant political rights. For example, in the British Caribbean sugar islands, where slavery had been abolished in the 1830s, stiff property qualifications and poll taxes kept freedmen from voting. The Fourteenth Amendment was also a milestone along the road to the centralization of political power in the United States because it reduced the power of all the states. In this sense it confirmed the great change wrought by the Civil War: the growth of a more complex, more closely integrated social and economic structure requiring closer national supervision. Few people understood this aspect of the amendment at the time.

First the amendment supplied a broad definition of American citizenship: "All persons born or naturalized in the United States, and subject to the jurisdiction thereof, are citizens of the United States and of the State wherein they reside." Obviously this included blacks. Then it struck at discriminatory legislation like the Black Codes: "No State shall make or enforce any law which shall abridge the privileges or immunities of citizens of the United States; nor shall any State deprive any person of life, liberty, or property, without due process of law." The next section attempted to force the southern states to permit blacks to vote. If a state denied the vote to any class of its adult male citizens, its representation was to be reduced proportionately. Under another clause, former federal officials who had served the Confederacy were barred from holding either state or federal office unless specifically pardoned by a two-thirds vote of Congress. Finally, the Confederate debt was repudiated.

MAP

Reconstruction

While the amendment did not specifically outlaw segregation or prevent a state from disenfranchising blacks, the southern states would have none of it. Without them the necessary three-fourths majority of the states could not be obtained.

President Johnson vowed to make the choice between the Fourteenth Amendment and his own policy the main issue of the 1866 congressional elections. He embarked on "a swing around the circle" to rally the public to his cause. He failed dismally. Northern women objected to the implication in the amendment that black men were more fitted to vote than white women, but a large majority of northern voters was determined that African Americans must have at least formal legal equality. The Republicans won better

than two-thirds of the seats in both houses, together with control of all the northern state governments. Johnson emerged from the campaign discredited, the Radicals stronger and determined to have their way. The southern states, Congressman James A. Garfield of Ohio said in February 1867, have "flung back into our teeth the magnanimous offer of a generous nation. It is now our turn to act."

THE RECONSTRUCTION ACTS

Had the southern states been willing to accept the Fourteenth Amendment, coercive measures might have been avoided. Their recalcitrance and continuing indications that local authorities were persecuting blacks finally led to the passage, on March 2, 1867, of the First Reconstruction Act. This law divided the former Confederacy—exclusive of Tennessee, which had ratified the Fourteenth Amendment—into five military districts, each controlled by a major general. It gave these officers almost dictatorial power to protect the civil rights of "all persons," maintain order, and supervise the administration of justice. To rid themselves of military rule, the former states were required to adopt new state constitutions guaranteeing blacks the right to vote and disenfranchising broad classes of ex-Confederates. If the new constitutions proved satisfactory to Congress, and if the new governments ratified the Fourteenth Amendment, their representatives would be admitted to Congress and military rule ended. Johnson's veto of the act was easily overridden.

Although drastic, the Reconstruction Act was so vague that it proved unworkable. Military control was easily established. But in deference to moderate Republican views, the law had not spelled out the process by which the new constitutions were to be drawn up. Southern whites preferred the status quo, even under army control, to enfranchising blacks and retiring their own respected leaders. They made no effort to follow the steps laid down in the law. Congress therefore passed a second act, requiring the military authorities to register voters and supervise the election of delegates to constitutional conventions. A third act further clarified procedures.

Still white Southerners resisted. The laws required that the constitutions be approved by a majority of the registered voters. Simply by staying away from the polls, whites prevented ratification in state after state. At last, in March 1868, a full year after the First Reconstruction Act, Congress changed the rules again. The constitutions were to be ratified by a majority of the voters. In June 1868 Arkansas, having fulfilled the requirements, was readmitted to the Union, and by July a

sufficient number of states had ratified the Fourteenth Amendment to make it part of the Constitution. But it was not until July 1870 that the last southern state, Georgia, qualified to the satisfaction of Congress.

CONGRESS SUPREME

To carry out this program in the face of determined southern resistance required a degree of single-mindedness over a long period seldom demonstrated by an American legislature. The persistence resulted in part from the suffering and frustrations of the war years. The refusal of the South to accept the spirit of even the mild reconstruction designed by Johnson goaded the North to ever more overbearing efforts to bring the ex-Confederates to heel. President Johnson's stubbornness also influenced the Republicans. They became obsessed with the need to defeat him. The unsettled times and the large Republican majorities, always threatened by the possibility of a Democratic resurgence if "unreconstructed" southern congressmen were readmitted, sustained their determination.

These considerations led Republicans to attempt a kind of grand revision of the federal government, one that almost destroyed the balance between judicial, executive, and legislative power established in 1789. A series of measures passed between 1866 and 1868 increased the authority of Congress over the army, over the process of amending the Constitution, and over Cabinet members and lesser appointive officers. Even the Supreme Court was affected. Its size was reduced and its jurisdiction over civil rights cases limited. Finally, in a showdown caused by emotion more than by practical considerations, the Republicans attempted to remove President Johnson from office.

Johnson was a poor president and out of touch with public opinion, but he had done nothing to merit ejection from office. While he had a low opinion of African Americans, his opinion was so widely shared by whites that it is unhistorical to condemn him as a reactionary on this ground. Johnson believed that he was fighting to preserve constitutional government. He was honest and devoted to duty, and his record easily withstood the most searching examination. When Congress passed laws taking away powers granted him by the Constitution, he refused to submit.

The chief issue was the Tenure of Office Act of 1867, which prohibited the president from removing officials who had been appointed with the consent of the Senate without first obtaining Senate approval. In February 1868 Johnson "violated" this act by dismissing Secretary of War Edwin M. Stanton, who had been openly in sympathy with the Radicals for some time. The House, acting under the procedure set up in the Constitution for removing the president, promptly impeached him before the bar of the Senate, Chief Justice Salmon P. Chase presiding.

In the trial, Johnson's lawyers easily established that he had removed Stanton only in an effort to prove the Tenure of Office Act unconstitutional. They demonstrated that the act did not protect Stanton to begin with, since it gave Cabinet members tenure "during the term of the President by whom they may have been appointed," and Stanton had been appointed in 1862, during Lincoln's first term!

Nevertheless the Radicals pressed the charges (11 separate articles) relentlessly. To the argument that Johnson had committed no crime, the learned Senator Sumner retorted that the proceedings were "political in character" rather than judicial. Thaddeus Stevens, directing the attack on behalf of the House, warned the senators that although "no corrupt or wicked motive" could be attributed to Johnson, they would "be tortured on the gibbet of everlasting obloquy" if they did not convict him. Tremendous pressure was applied to the handful of Republican senators who were unwilling to disregard the evidence.

Seven of them resisted to the end, and the Senate failed by a single vote to convict Johnson. This was probably fortunate. The trial weakened the presidency, but if Johnson had been forced from office on such flimsy grounds, the independence of the executive might have been permanently undermined. Then the legislative branch would have become supreme.

THE FIFTEENTH AMENDMENT

The failure of the impeachment did not affect the course of Reconstruction. The president was acquitted on May 16, 1868. A few days later, the Republican National Convention nominated General Ulysses S. Grant for the presidency. At the Democratic convention Johnson had considerable support, but the delegates nominated Horatio Seymour, a former governor of New York. In November Grant won an easy victory in the Electoral College, 214 to 80, but the popular vote was close: 3 million to 2.7 million. Although he would probably have carried the Electoral College in any case, Grant's margin in the popular vote was supplied by southern blacks enfranchised under the Reconstruction acts, about 450,000 of whom supported him. A majority of white voters probably preferred

► *text continues on page 434*

Mapping the Past

The Politics of Reconstruction

The map below, "Imposition of Union military control," summarizes the rise and fall of Reconstruction in the South. The Reconstruction Acts of 1867 divided the Confederacy into five military districts. In 1868 Arkansas was the first state to be readmitted to the Union; Georgia, in July 1870, was the last. The legislative enactments of Congress, led by the Radical Republicans, were enforced by the Union army. Republican electoral success in the South was similarly predicated on the presence of the Union army; but this map also shows that Democrats reestablished their political power in most states prior to the Compromise of 1877: Virginia (1869), Georgia (1872), Texas (1874), Arkansas (1874), and Mississippi (1876) are examples.

Triumph of the Republican Party in the South, 1870

In the late 1860s the rise of the Republican party was due both to the weakness of the southern Democrats and to the enfranchisement of black men. African Americans voted solidly Republican—the party of Lincoln—and they exercised their vote diligently. In many elections, the black voter turnout approached 90 percent. "It is the hardest thing in the world to keep a negro away from the polls," decried a white Alabama politician.

The power of the black vote in 1870 is demonstrated in the map at right, top. Of the 15 congressional districts that encompassed the interior counties from Louisiana through South Carolina, it was in the Cotton Belt, where blacks comprised the majority, that Republican candidates won 14 seats. Throughout the South, Republicans took 31 of the 57 seats in the House of Representatives. In the three states where blacks outnumbered whites—South Carolina, Mississippi, and Louisiana—the Republicans won every House seat.

Five blacks were among the Republican victors. With the exception of Josiah Walls, a former slave who had fought with the Union army and represented Florida, all of the blacks were from areas with a substantial black majority: three from South Carolina, the other from Alabama.

"Carpetbaggers," Republicans from the North, were also strong in the areas where blacks had a majority, especially Louisiana, Mississippi, and Virginia. Except for the two congressional districts in lower Louisiana, no "carpetbaggers" won House seats where blacks did not constitute a majority of the population.

"Scalawags," white Southerners who endorsed the Republican party, did take some seats in areas with white majorities. Usually these victories were in districts that had been Whig strongholds.

Collapse of the Republican Party in the South, 1878

With the Compromise of 1877 and subsequent withdrawal of Union troops, the Republican political power in the South collapsed. Tennessee, excluded from the Union military district, never experienced a period of Republican domination; in Virginia, the Democrats were firmly back in power by 1869.

The map at bottom right shows that by 1878, Democrats, all of them white, recaptured 77 of the 83 House seats in the South. All of the black House representatives had been defeated. No Republican was elected in Texas, Arkansas, Louisiana, Mississippi, Alabama, Georgia, South Carolina, or North Carolina. The South was not exactly "solid"—independent Democrats and Greenback representatives won a handful of seats. But the South would remain a Democratic bastion for over a century.

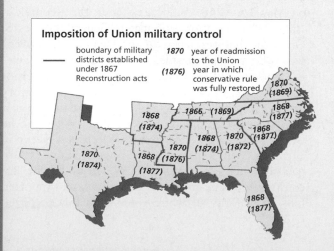

Imposition of Union military control

— boundary of military districts established under 1867 Reconstruction acts

1870 year of readmission to the Union

(1876) year in which conservative rule was fully restored

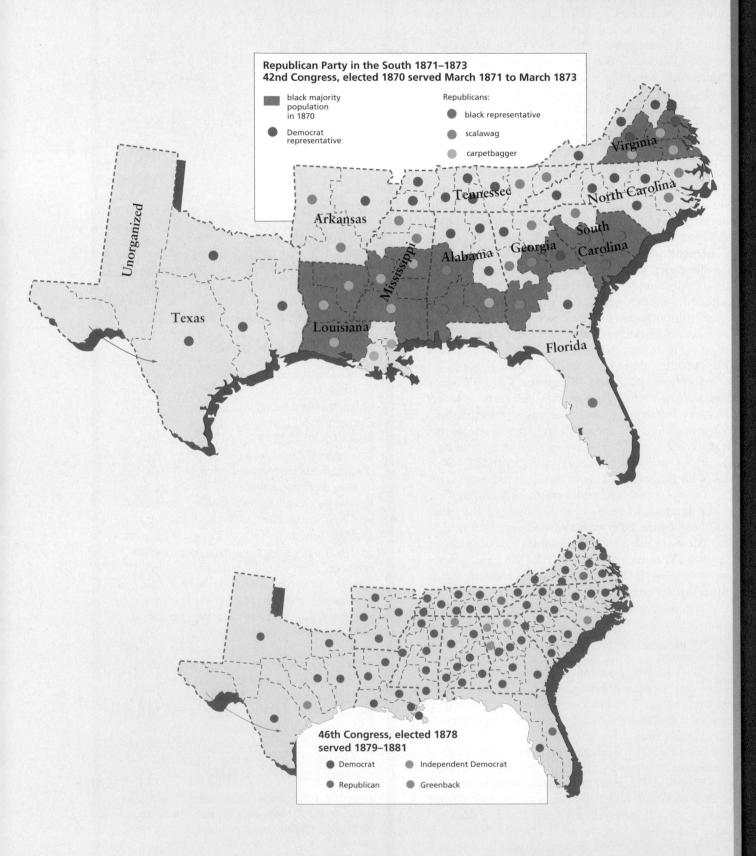

Republican Party in the South 1871–1873
42nd Congress, elected 1870 served March 1871 to March 1873

- black majority population in 1870
- Democrat representative

Republicans:
- black representative
- scalawag
- carpetbagger

Unorganized

Texas

Arkansas

Tennessee

Louisiana

Mississippi

Alabama

Georgia

South Carolina

North Carolina

Virginia

Florida

46th Congress, elected 1878 served 1879–1881

- Democrat
- Republican
- Independent Democrat
- Greenback

Seymour. Since many citizens undoubtedly voted Republican because of personal admiration for General Grant, the election statistics suggest that a substantial white majority opposed the policies of the Radicals.

The Reconstruction acts and the ratification of the Fourteenth Amendment achieved the purpose of enabling black Southerners to vote. The Radicals, however, were not satisfied; despite the unpopularity of the idea in the North, they wished to guarantee the right of blacks to vote in every state. Another amendment seemed the only way to accomplish this objective, but passage of such an amendment appeared impossible. The Republican platform in the 1868 election had smugly distinguished between blacks voting in the South ("demanded by every consideration of public safety, of gratitude, and of justice") and in the North (where the question "properly belongs to the people").

However, after the election had demonstrated how important the black vote could be, Republican strategy shifted. Grant had carried Indiana by fewer than 10,000 votes and lost New York by a similar number. If blacks in these and other closely divided states had voted, Republican strength would have been greatly enhanced.

Suddenly Congress blossomed with suffrage amendments. After considerable bickering over details, the Fifteenth Amendment was sent to the states for ratification in February 1869. It forbade all the states to deny the vote to anyone "on account of race, color, or previous condition of servitude." Once again nothing was said about denial of the vote on the basis of sex, which caused feminists, such as Elizabeth Cady Stanton, to be even more outraged than they had been by the Fourteenth Amendment.

Most southern states, still under federal pressure, ratified the amendment swiftly. The same was true in most of New England and in some western states. Bitter battles were waged in Connecticut, New York, Pennsylvania, and the states immediately north of the Ohio River, but by March 1870 most of them had ratified the amendment and it became part of the Constitution.

The debates occasioned by these conventions show that partisan advantage was not the only reason why voters approved black suffrage at last. The unfairness of a double standard of voting, North and South, the contribution of black soldiers during the war, and the hope that by passing the amendment the strife of Reconstruction could finally be ended all played a part.

When the Fifteenth Amendment went into effect, President Grant called it "the greatest civil change and . . . the most important event that has occurred since the nation came to life." The American Anti-Slavery Society formally dissolved itself, its work apparently completed. "The Fifteenth Amendment confers upon the African race the care of its own destiny,"

DEBATING THE PAST

Were Reconstruction governments corrupt? Racist depictions of Reconstruction were common. This one by Thomas Nast was entitled "Colored Rule in a Reconstructed (?) State" and appeared in *Harper's Weekly* (1874). In 1902 Columbia historian William A. Dunning similarly declared that free slaves were mere children, incapable of holding office. In 1910 W. E. B. Du Bois, an African American scholar, was the first to applaud Reconstruction for broadening educational opportunities and democratizing government, but few historians concurred. In the 1960s, as the civil rights movement was gaining momentum, more scholars came out in support of Reconstruction. In 1965 Kenneth Stampp emphasized the Reconstruction governments' attempts to protect freedmen; that same year, Joel Williamson turned Dunning's thesis on its head and endorsed nearly all aspects of Reconstruction. More recent scholars have generally taken a moderate position: Reconstruction may have failed, but its accomplishments under difficult circumstances of white opposition were substantial; see, for example, Eric Foner (1988). Certain facts are beyond argument. Black officeholders were neither numerous nor inordinately influential. None was ever elected governor of a state; fewer than a dozen and a half during the entire period served in Congress.

William A. Dunning, *Reconstruction and the Constitution* (1902), W. E. B. Du Bois, *Black Reconstruction in America* (1935), Kenneth Stampp, *The Peculiar Institution* (1965), Joel Williamson, *After Slavery* (1965), Eric Foner, *Reconstruction* (1988).

Radical Congressman James A. Garfield wrote proudly after the amendment was ratified. "It places their fortunes in their own hands."

Many of the celebrants lived to see the amendment subverted in the South. That it could be evaded by literacy tests and other restrictions was apparent at the time and may even have influenced some persons who voted for it. But a stronger amendment—one, for instance, that positively granted the right to vote to all men and put the supervision of elections under national control—could not have been ratified.

"Black Republican" Reconstruction: Scalawags and Carpetbaggers

The Radicals had at last succeeded in imposing their will on the South. Throughout the region former slaves had real political influence; they voted, held office, and exercised the "privileges" and enjoyed the "immunities" guaranteed them by the Fourteenth Amendment. Almost to a man they voted Republican.

The spectacle of blacks not five years removed from slavery in positions of power and responsibility attracted much attention at the time and has since been examined exhaustively by historians (see Debating the Past, p. 434). But the real rulers of the "black Republican" governments were white: the "scalawags"—Southerners willing to cooperate with the Republicans because they accepted the results of the war and wished to advance their own interests—and the "carpetbaggers"—Northerners who went to the South as idealists to help the freed slaves, as employees of the federal government, or more commonly as settlers hoping to improve themselves.

The scalawags were by far the more numerous. A few were prewar politicians or well-to-do planters, men such as the Mississippi planter John L. Alcorn and Joseph E. Brown, the Confederate governor of Georgia. General James Longstreet, one of Lee's most important lieutenants, was another prominent Southerner who cooperated with the Republicans. But most were people who had supported the Whig party before the secession crisis and who saw the Republicans as the logical successors of the Whigs.

The carpetbaggers were a particularly varied lot. Most had mixed motives for coming south and personal gain was certainly among them. But so were opposition to slavery and the belief that blacks deserved to be treated decently and given a chance to get ahead in the world.

Many northern blacks became carpetbaggers: former Union soldiers, missionaries from northern black churches, and also teachers, lawyers, and other members of the small northern black professional class. Many of these became officeholders, but like southern black politicians their influence was limited.

That blacks should fail to dominate southern governments is certainly understandable. They lacked experience in politics and were mostly poor and uneducated. They were nearly everywhere a minority. Those blacks who held office during Reconstruction tended to be better educated and more prosperous than most southern blacks. A disproportionate number had been free before the war. Of those freed by the Thirteenth Amendment, a large percentage had been house servants or artisans, not field hands. Mulatto politicians were also disproportionately numerous and (as a group) more conservative and economically better off than other black leaders.

In South Carolina and elsewhere, blacks proved in the main able and conscientious public servants: able because the best tended to rise to the top in such a fluid situation and conscientious because most of those who achieved importance sought eagerly to demonstrate the capacity of their race for self-government. Even at the local level, where the quality of officials was usually poor, there was little difference in the degree of competence displayed by white and black officeholders. In power, the blacks were not vindictive; by and large they did not seek to restrict the rights of ex-Confederates.

Not all black legislators and administrators were paragons of virtue. In South Carolina, despite their

▲ During Reconstruction, 14 blacks won election to the House of Representatives and two, Hiram Revels and Blanche K. Bruce, served in the Senate. Revels, at far left, won the Mississippi Senate seat that Jefferson Davis had once held. He later became president of Alcorn University. Congressman R. Brown Elliot, at far right, had been educated at Eton in England.

control of the legislature, they broke up into factions repeatedly and failed to press for laws that would improve the lot of poor black farm workers. In *The Prostrate South* (1874), James S. Pike, a northern newspaperman, wrote: "The rule of South Carolina should not be dignified with the name of government. It is the installation of a huge system of brigandage." Like many northern commentators, Pike exaggerated the immorality and incompetence of the blacks, but waste and corruption were common during Reconstruction governments. Half the budget of Louisiana in some years went for salaries and "mileage" for representatives and their staffs. One Arkansas black took $9000 from the state for repairing a bridge that had cost only $500 to build. A South Carolina legislator was voted an additional $1000 in salary after he lost that sum betting on a horse race.

However, the corruption must be seen in perspective. The big thieves were nearly always white; blacks got mostly crumbs. Furthermore, graft and callous disregard of the public interest characterized government in every section and at every level during the decade after Appomattox. Big-city bosses in the North embezzled sums that dwarfed the most brazen southern frauds. The New York City Tweed Ring probably made off with more money than all the southern thieves, black and white, combined. While the evidence does not justify the southern corruption, it suggests that the unique features of Reconstruction politics—black suffrage, military supervision, carpetbagger and scalawag influence—do not explain it.

The "black Republican" governments displayed qualities that grew directly from the ignorance and political inexperience of the former slaves. There was a tragicomic aspect to the South Carolina legislature during these years, its many black members—some dressed in old frock coats, others in rude farm clothes—rising to points of order and personal privilege without reason, discoursing ponderously on subjects they did not understand. But those who complained about the ignorance and irresponsibility of blacks conveniently forgot that the tendency of nineteenth-century American democracy was away from educational, financial, or any other restrictions on the franchise. Thousands of white Southerners were as illiterate and uncultured as the freedmen, yet no one suggested depriving them of the ballot.

In fact, the Radical southern governments accomplished a great deal. They spent money freely but not entirely wastefully. Tax rates zoomed, but the money financed the repair and expansion of the South's dilapidated railroad network, rebuilt crumbling levees, and expanded social services. Before the Civil War, southern planters possessed a disproportionate share of political as well as economic power, and they spent relatively little public money on education and public services of all kinds.

During Reconstruction an enormous gap had to be filled, and it took money to fill it. The Freedmen's Bureau made a major contribution. Northern religious and philanthropic organizations also did important work. Eventually, however, the state governments established and supported hospitals, asylums, and systems of free public education that, while segregated, greatly benefited everyone, whites as well as blacks. Much state money was also spent on economic development: land reclamation, repairing and expanding the war-ravaged railroads, maintaining levees.

The former slaves grasped eagerly at the opportunities to learn. Schools and other institutions were supported chiefly by property taxes, and these, of course, hit well-to-do planters hard. Hence much of the complaining about the "extravagance" of Reconstruction governments concealed traditional selfish objections to paying for public projects. Eventually the benefits of expanded government services to the entire population became clear, and when white supremacy was reestablished, most of the new services remained in force, and the corruption and inefficiency inherited from the carpetbagger governments continued.

THE RAVAGED LAND

The South's grave economic problems complicated the rebuilding of its political system. The section had never been as prosperous as the North, and wartime destruction left it desperately poor by any standard. In the long run the abolition of slavery released immeasurable quantities of human energy previously stifled, but the immediate effect was to create confusion. Freedom to move without a pass, to "see the world," was one of the former slaves' most cherished benefits of emancipation. Understandably, many at first equated legal freedom with freedom from having to earn a living, a tendency reinforced for a time by the willingness of the Freedmen's Bureau to provide rations and other forms of relief in war-devastated areas. Most, however, soon accepted the fact that they must earn a living; a small plot of land of their own ("40 acres and a mule") would complete their independence.

This objective was forcefully supported by the relentless Congressman Thaddeus Stevens, whose hatred of the planter class was pathological. "The property of the chief rebels should be seized," he stated. If the lands of the richest "70,000 proud, bloated and defiant rebels" were confiscated, the federal government would obtain 394 million acres. Every adult male ex-slave could easily be supplied with 40 acres.

▲ The Freedmen's Bureau built 4329 schools, attended by some 250,000 former slaves, in the postwar South. Many of the teachers in these schools were abolitionists or missionaries from New England. The schools drew African Americans of all ages, from children to grandparents, who were eager for the advantages offered by education.

The beauty of his scheme, Stevens insisted, was that "nine-tenths of the [southern] people would remain untouched." Dispossessing the great planters would make the South "a safe republic," its lands cultivated by "the free labor of intelligent citizens." If the plan drove the planters into exile, "all the better."

Although Stevens's figures were faulty, many Radicals agreed with him. "We must see that the freedmen are established on the soil," Senator Sumner declared. "The great plantations, which have been so many nurseries of the rebellion, must be broken up, and the freedmen must have the pieces." Stevens, Sumner, and others who wanted to give land to the freedmen weakened their case by associating it with the idea of punishing the former rebels; the average American had too much respect for property rights to support a policy of confiscation.

Aside from its vindictiveness, the extremists' view was simplistic. Land without tools, seed, and other necessities would have done the freedmen little good. Congress did throw open 46 million acres of poor-quality federal land in the South to blacks under the Homestead Act, but few settled on it. Establishing former slaves on small farms with adequate financial aid would have been of incalculable benefit to them. This would have been practicable, but extremely expensive. It was not done.

The former slaves therefore had either to agree to work for their former owners or strike out on their own. White planters, influenced by the precipitous decline of sugar production in Jamaica and other Caribbean islands that had followed the abolition of slavery there, expected freed blacks to be incapable of self-directed effort. If allowed to become independent farmers, they would either starve to death or descend into barbarism. Of course the blacks did neither. True, the output of cotton and other southern staples declined precipitously after slavery was abolished. Observers soon came to the conclusion that a free black produced much less than a slave had produced. "You can't get only about two-thirds as much out of 'em now as you could when they were slaves," an Arkansas planter complained.

However, the decline in productivity was not caused by the inability of free blacks to work independently. They simply chose no longer to work like slaves. They let their children play instead of forcing them into the fields. Mothers devoted more time to childcare and housework, less to farm labor. Elderly blacks worked less.

Noting these changes, white critics spoke scornfully of black laziness and shiftlessness. "You cannot make the negro work without physical compulsion," was the common view. Even General

Oliver O. Howard, head of the Freedmen's Bureau, used the phrase "wholesome compulsion" in describing the policy of forcing blacks to sign exploitive labor contracts. A leading southern magazine complained in 1866 that black women now expected their husbands "to support them in idleness." It would never have made such a comment about white housewives. Moreover, studies show that emancipated blacks earned almost 30 percent more than the value of the subsistence provided by their former masters.

The family life of ex-slaves was changed in other ways. Male authority increased when husbands became true heads of families. (Under slavery the ultimate responsibility for providing for women and children was the master's.) When blacks became citizens, the men acquired rights and powers denied to all women, such as the right to hold public office and serve on juries. Similarly, black women became more like white women, devoting themselves to separate "spheres" where their lives revolved around housekeeping and child rearing.

SHARECROPPING AND THE CROP-LIEN SYSTEM

Before the passage of the Reconstruction acts, plantation owners tried to farm their land with gang labor, the same system as before, only now paying wages to the former slaves. This method did not work well for two entirely different reasons. Money was scarce, and capital, never adequate even before the collapse of the Confederacy, accumulated slowly. Interest rates were extremely high. This situation made it difficult for landowners to pay their laborers in cash. More important, blacks did not like working for wages because it kept them under the direction of whites and thus reminded them of slavery. They wanted to be independent, to manage not merely their free time but their entire lives for themselves. "The colored people of this vicinity are so proud," a white Virginian noted, "that they think it is somewhat a second slavery to hire by the month or year." Since the voluntary withdrawal of so much black labor from the workforce had produced a shortage, the blacks had their way. "I had to yield," another white planter admitted, "or lose my labor."

Quite swiftly, a new agricultural system known as sharecropping emerged. Instead of cultivating the land by gang labor as in antebellum times, planters broke up their estates into small units and established on each a black family. The planter provided housing, agricultural implements, draft animals, seed, and

▲ After the Civil War, most blacks worked as sharecroppers on land owned by whites. In this photograph, black sharecroppers pick cotton, a major cash crop of the South with the owner of the land getting a share of the crop (crop-lien). The crop-lien system injured everyone. Diversified farming would have reduced the farmers' need for cash, preserved the fertility of the soil, and, by placing a premium on imagination and shrewdness, aided the best of them to rise in the world. Because the price for cotton remained low, sharecroppers often fell into debt and were tied to the land almost as tightly as under slavery.

other supplies, and the family provided labor. The crop was divided between them, usually on a fifty-fifty basis. If the landlord supplied only land and housing, the laborer got a larger share. This was called share tenancy.

Sharecropping gave blacks the day-to-day control of their lives that they craved and the hope of earning enough to buy a small farm. Consider the example of Daniel Trotter, a Louisiana black who worked for several years as a farm laborer. He then spent four years as a sharecropper on land owned by a man named Clurman, then two more on the farm of one J. H. C. Cosgrove, with whom he split the crop fifty-fifty. He was then able to rent land from Cosgrove and a series of other white farmers. While renting, his wife earned money by sewing and by raising chickens, whose eggs she sold "one or two dozen at a time." The Trotters also raised a few pigs for the market, and

DOCUMENT

A Sharecrop Contract

Daniel, evidently possessing mechanical skills, made some "cash money" repairing farm machinery, clocks, and guns. After 14 years the Trotters had saved $175 in greenbacks and $33 in silver, enough to buy what Trotter proudly described as a "plantation." But relatively few blacks possessed the Trotters' energy, determination, and good luck. As late as 1880 blacks owned less than 10 percent of the agricultural land in the South, although they made up more than half of the region's farm population. Mississippi actually prohibited the purchase of farmland by blacks.

Many white farmers in the South were also trapped by the sharecropping system and by white efforts to keep blacks in a subordinate position. New fencing laws kept them from grazing livestock on undeveloped land, a practice common before the Civil War. But the main cause of southern rural poverty for whites as well as for blacks was the lack of enough capital to finance the sharecropping system. Like their colonial ancestors, the landowners had to borrow against October's harvest to pay for April's seed. Thus the crop-lien system developed.

Under the crop-lien system, both landowner and sharecropper depended on credit supplied by local bankers, merchants, and storekeepers for everything from seed, tools, and fertilizer to overalls, coffee, and salt. Crossroads stores proliferated, and a new class of small merchants appeared. The prices of goods sold on credit were high, adding to the burden borne by the rural population. The small southern merchants were almost equally victimized by the system, for they also lacked capital, bought goods on credit, and had to pay high interest rates.

IMAGE
Five Generations of a Slave Family

Seen in broad perspective, the situation is not difficult to understand. The South, drained of every resource by the war, was competing for funds with the North and West, both vigorous and expanding and therefore voracious consumers of capital. Reconstruction, in the literal sense of the word, was accomplished chiefly at the expense of the standard of living of the producing classes. The crop-lien system and the small storekeeper were only agents of an economic process dictated by national, perhaps even worldwide, conditions.

Compared with the rest of the country, progress was slow. Just before the Civil War cotton harvests averaged about 4 million bales. During the conflict, output fell to about half a million, and the former Confederate states did not enjoy a 4-million-bale year again until 1870. In contrast, national wheat production in 1859 was 175 million bushels and in 1878, 449 million. About 7000 miles of railroad were built in the South between 1865 and 1879; in the rest of the nation nearly 45,000 miles of track were laid.

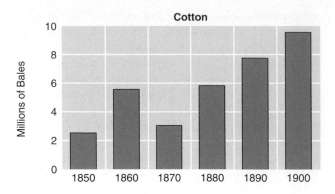

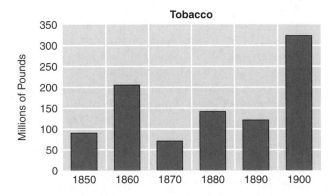

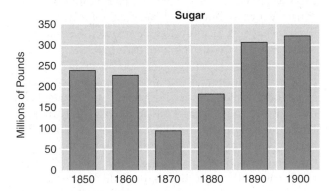

▲ **Southern Agriculture, 1850–1900**
Cotton production recovered to its prewar level by 1880, but tobacco and sugar production lagged. Not until 1900 did tobacco growers have a better year than they had in 1860. The years following 1870 saw a general downward trend in wholesale prices for farm commodities. (Statistics are for the 11 states of the Confederacy.)

But in the late 1870s, cotton production revived. It soon regained, and thereafter long retained, its title as "king" of the southern economy. This was true in large measure because of the crop-lien system.

The South made important gains in manufacturing after the war. The tobacco industry, stimulated by the sudden popularity of the cigarette, expanded rapidly. Virginia and North Carolina tobacco towns like Richmond, Lynchburg, and Durham flourished. The exploitation of the coal and iron deposits of

northeastern Alabama in the early 1870s made a boomtown of Birmingham. The manufacture of cotton cloth increased, productive capacity nearly doubling between 1865 and 1880. Yet the mills of Massachusetts alone had eight times the capacity of the entire South in 1880. Despite the increases, the South's share of the national output of manufactured goods declined sharply during the Reconstruction era.

THE WHITE BACKLASH

Radical southern governments could sustain themselves only as long as they had the support of a significant proportion of the white population, for except in South Carolina and Louisiana, the blacks were not numerous enough to win elections alone. The key to survival lay in the hands of the wealthy merchants and planters, mostly former Whigs. People of this sort had nothing to fear from black economic competition. Taking a broad view, they could see that improving the lot of the former slaves would benefit all classes.

Southern white Republicans used the Union League of America, a patriotic club founded during the war, to control the black vote. Employing secret rituals, exotic symbols, and other paraphernalia calculated to impress unsophisticated people, they enrolled the freedmen in droves and marched them to the polls en masse.

Powerless to check the League by open methods, dissident Southerners established a number of secret terrorist societies, bearing such names as the Ku Klux Klan, the Knights of the White Camelia, and the Pale Faces. The most notorious of these organizations was the Klan, which originated in Tennessee in 1866. At first it was purely a social club, but by 1868 it had been taken over by vigilante types dedicated to driving blacks out of politics, and it was spreading rapidly across the South. Sheet-clad nightriders roamed the countryside, frightening the impressionable and chastising the defiant. Klansmen, using a weird mumbo jumbo and claiming to be the ghosts of Confederate soldiers, spread horrendous rumors and published broadsides designed to persuade the freedmen that it was unhealthy for them to participate in politics:

> *Niggers and Leaguers, get out of the way,*
> *We're born of the night and we vanish by day.*
> *No rations have we, but the flesh of man—*
> *And love niggers best—the Ku Klux Klan;*
> *We catch 'em alive and roast 'em whole,*
> *Then hand 'em around with a sharpened pole.*
> *Whole Leagues have been eaten, not leaving a man,*
> *And went away hungry—the Ku Klux Klan....*

When intimidation failed, the Klansmen resorted to force. After being whipped by one group in Ten-

▲ A graphic warning by the Alabama Klan "of the fate in store for" scalawags and carpetbaggers, "those great pests of Southern society," from the *Tuscaloosa Independent Monitor,* September 1, 1868.

nessee, a recently elected justice of the peace reported: "They said they had nothing particular against me . . . but they did not intend any nigger to hold office." In hundreds of cases the KKK murdered their opponents, often in the most gruesome manner.

Accounts from Victims of the Ku Klux Klan

Congress struck at the Klan with three Force Acts (1870–1871), which placed elections under federal jurisdiction and imposed fines and prison sentences on persons convicted of interfering with any citizen's exercise of the franchise. Troops were dispatched to areas where the Klan was strong, and by 1872 the federal authorities had arrested enough Klansmen to break up the organization.

Nevertheless the Klan contributed substantially to the destruction of Radical regimes in the South. Its depredations weakened the will of white Republicans (few of whom really believed in racial equality), and it intimidated many blacks, who gave up trying to exercise their rights. The fact that the army had to be called in to suppress it was a glaring illustration of the weakness of the Reconstruction governments.

Gradually it became respectable to intimidate black voters. Beginning in Mississippi in 1874, terrorism spread through the South. Instead of hiding behind masks and operating in the dark, these terrorists donned red shirts, organized into military companies, and paraded openly. Mississippi redshirts seized militant blacks and whipped them publicly. Killings were frequent. When blacks dared to fight back, heavily armed whites put them to rout. In other states similar results followed.

Terrorism fed on fear, fear on terrorism. White violence led to fear of black retaliation and thus to even more brutal attacks. The slightest sign of resistance came to be seen as the beginning of race war, and when the blacks suffered indignities and persecutions

in silence, the awareness of how much they must resent the mistreatment made them appear more dangerous still. Thus self-hatred was displaced, guilt suppressed, aggression justified as self-defense, individual conscience submerged in the animality of the mob.

Before long the blacks learned to stay home on election day. One by one, "Conservative" parties—Democratic in national affairs—took over southern state governments. Intimidation was only a partial explanation of this development. The increasing solidarity of whites, northern and southern, was equally significant.

The North had subjected the South to control from Washington while preserving state sovereignty in the North itself. In the long run this discrimination proved unworkable. Many Northerners had supported the Radical policy only out of irritation with President Johnson. After his retirement their enthusiasm waned. The war was fading into the past and with it the worst of the anger it had generated.

Northern voters could still be stirred by references to the sacrifices Republicans had made to save the Union and by reminders that the Democratic party was the organization of rebels, Copperheads, and the Ku Klux Klan. "If the Devil himself were at the helm of the ship of state," wrote the novelist Lydia Maria Child in 1872, "my conscience would not allow me to aid in removing him to make room for the Democratic party." Yet emotional appeals could not convince Northerners that it was still necessary to maintain a large army in the South. In 1869 the occupying forces were down to 11,000 men. After Klan disruption and intimidation had made a farce of the 1874 elections in Mississippi, Governor Ames appealed to Washington for help. President Grant's attorney general, Edwards Pierrepont, refused to act. "The whole public are tired out with these autumnal outbreaks in the South," he told Ames. "Preserve the peace by the forces of your own state."

Nationalism was reasserting itself. Had not Washington and Jefferson been Virginians? Was not Andrew Jackson Carolina-born? Since most Northerners had little real love or respect for blacks, their interest in racial equality flagged once they felt reasonably certain that blacks would not be re-enslaved if left to their own devices in the South.

Another, much subtler force was also at work. The prewar Republican party had stressed the common interest of workers, manufacturers, and farmers in a free and mobile society, a land of equal opportunity where all could work in harmony. Southern whites had insisted that laborers must be disciplined if large enterprises were to be run efficiently. By the 1870s, as large industrial enterprises developed in the northern states, the thinking of business leaders changed—the southern argument began to make sense to them, and they became more sympathetic to the southern demand for more control over "their" labor force.

GRANT AS PRESIDENT

Other matters occupied the attention of northern voters. The expansion of industry and the rapid development of the West, stimulated by a new wave of railroad building, loomed more important to many than the fortunes of the former slaves. Beginning in 1873, when a stock market panic struck at public confidence, economic difficulties plagued the country for nearly a decade. Heated controversies arose over tariff policy, with western agricultural interests seeking to force reductions from the high levels established during the war, and over the handling of the wartime greenback paper money, with debtor groups and many manufacturers favoring further expansion of the supply of dollars and conservative merchants and bankers arguing for retiring the greenbacks in order to return to a "sound" currency.

More damaging to the Republicans was the failure of Ulysses S. Grant to live up to expectations as president. Qualities that had made Grant a fine military leader for a democracy—his dislike of political maneuvering and his simple belief that the popular will could best be observed in the actions of Congress—made him a poor chief executive. When Congress failed to act on his suggestion that the quality of the civil service needed improvement, he announced meekly that if Congress did nothing, he would assume the country did not want anything done. Grant was honest, but his honesty was of the naive type that made him the dupe of unscrupulous friends and schemers.

His most serious weakness as president was his failure to deal effectively with economic and social problems, but the one that injured him and the Republicans most was his inability to cope with government corruption. The worst of the scandals—such as the Whiskey Ring affair, which implicated Grant's private secretary, Orville E. Babcock, and cost the government millions in tax revenue, and the corruption of Secretary of War William W. Belknap in the management of Indian affairs—did not become public knowledge during Grant's first term. However, in 1872 Republican reformers, alarmed by rumors of corruption and disappointed by Grant's failure to press for civil service reform, organized the Liberal Republican party and nominated Horace Greeley, the able but eccentric editor of the *New York Tribune,* for president.

The Liberal Republicans were mostly well-educated, socially prominent types—editors, college presidents, economists, along with a sprinkling of businessmen and politicians. Their liberalism was of

▲ This cartoon—"A Strong Man at the Head of Government"—pokes fun at Grant, whose presidency was weighed down with scandal. Grant did not cause the corruption, nor did he participate in the remotest way in the rush to "fatten at the public trough," as the reformers of the day might have put it. But he did nothing to prevent the scandals that disgraced his administration. Out of a misplaced belief in the sanctity of friendship, he protected some of the worst culprits and allowed calculating tricksters to use his good name and the prestige of his office to advance their own interests at the country's expense. "Mistakes have been made, as all can see and I admit," Grant conceded in his final report to Congress.

The Democrats also nominated Greeley in 1872, although he had devoted his political life to flailing the Democratic party in the *Tribune*. That surrender to expediency, together with Greeley's temperamental unsuitability for the presidency, made the campaign a fiasco for the reformers. Grant triumphed easily, with a popular majority of nearly 800,000.

Nevertheless, the defection of the Liberal Republicans hurt the Republican party in Congress. In the 1874 elections, no longer hampered as in the presidential contest by Greeley's notoriety and Grant's fame, the Democrats carried the House of Representatives. It was clear that the days of military rule in the South were ending. By the end of 1875 only three southern states—South Carolina, Florida, and Louisiana—were still under Republican control.

The Republican party in the South was "dead as a doornail," a reporter noted. He reflected the opinion of thousands when he added: "We ought to have a sound sensible republican . . . for the next President as a measure of safety; but only on the condition of absolute noninterference in Southern local affairs, for which there is no further need or excuse."

THE DISPUTED ELECTION OF 1876

Against this background the presidential election of 1876 took place. Since corruption in government was the most widely discussed issue, the Republicans passed over their most attractive political personality, the dynamic James G. Blaine, Speaker of the House of Representatives, who had been connected with some chicanery involving railroad securities. Instead they nominated Governor Rutherford B. Hayes of Ohio, a former general with an untarnished reputation. The Democrats picked Governor Samuel J. Tilden of New York, a wealthy lawyer who had attracted national attention for his part in breaking up the Tweed Ring in New York City.

In November early returns indicated that Tilden had carried New York, New Jersey, Connecticut, Indiana, and all the southern states, including Louisiana, South Carolina, and Florida, where Republican regimes were still in control. This seemed to give him 203 electoral votes to Hayes's 165, and a popular plurality in the neighborhood of 250,000 out of more than 8 million votes cast. However, Republican leaders had anticipated the possible loss of Florida, South Carolina, and Louisiana and were prepared to use their control of the election machinery in those states to throw out sufficient Democratic ballots to alter the results if doing so would change the national outcome. Realizing that the electoral votes of those states were exactly enough to elect their man, they telegraphed their henchmen on the scene, ordering them to go into

the laissez-faire variety; they were for low tariffs and sound money, and against what they called "class legislation," meaning measures benefiting particular groups, whether labor unions or railroad companies or farm organizations. Nearly all had supported Reconstruction at the start, but by the early 1870s most were including southern blacks among the special interests that ought to be left to their own devices. Their observation of urban corruption and of unrestricted immigration led them to disparage universal suffrage, which, one of them said, "can only mean in plain English the government of ignorance and vice."

action. The local Republicans then invalidated Democratic ballots in wholesale lots and filed returns showing Hayes the winner. Naturally the local Democrats protested vigorously and filed their own returns.

The Constitution provides (Article II, Section 1) that presidential electors must meet in their respective states to vote and forward the results to "the Seat of the Government." There, it adds, "the President of the Senate shall, in the Presence of the Senate and House of Representatives, open all the Certificates, and the Votes shall then be counted." But who was to do the counting? The House was Democratic, the Senate Republican; neither would agree to allow the other to do the job. On January 29, 1877, scarcely a month before inauguration day, Congress created an electoral commission to decide the disputed cases. The commission consisted of five senators (three Republicans and two Democrats), five representatives (three Democrats and two Republicans), and five justices of the Supreme Court (two Democrats, two Republicans, and one "independent" judge, David Davis). Since it was a foregone conclusion that the others would vote for their party no matter what the evidence, Davis would presumably swing the balance in the interest of fairness.

But before the commission met, the Illinois legislature elected Davis senator! He had to resign from the Court and the commission. Since independents were rare even on the Supreme Court, no neutral was available to replace him. The vacancy went to Associate Justice Joseph P. Bradley of New Jersey, a Republican.

Evidence presented before the commission revealed a disgraceful picture of election shenanigans. On the one hand, in all three disputed states Democrats had clearly cast a majority of the votes; on the other, it was unquestionable that many blacks had been forcibly prevented from voting.

In truth, both sides were shamefully corrupt. The governor of Louisiana was reported willing to sell his state's electoral votes for $200,000. The Florida election board was supposed to have offered itself to Tilden for the same price. "That seems to be the standard figure," Tilden remarked ruefully.

Most modern authorities take the view that in a fair election the Republicans would have carried South Carolina and Louisiana but that Florida would have gone to Tilden, giving him the election, 188 electoral votes to 181. In the last analysis, this opinion has been arrived at simply by counting white and black noses: Blacks were in the majority in South Carolina and Louisiana. Amid the tension and confusion of early 1877, however, even a Solomon would have been hard-pressed to judge rightly amid the rumors, lies, and contradictory statements, and the electoral commission was not composed of Solomons. The Democrats had some hopes that Justice Bradley would be sympathetic to their case, for he was known to be opposed to harsh Reconstruction policies. On the eve of the commission's decision in the Florida controversy, he was apparently ready to vote in favor of Tilden. But the Republicans subjected him to tremendous political pressure. When he read his opinion on February 8, it was for Hayes. Thus, by a vote of 8 to 7, the commission awarded Florida's electoral votes to the Republicans.

The rest of the proceedings was routine. The commission assigned all the disputed electoral votes (including one in Oregon where the Democratic governor had seized on a technicality to replace a single Republican elector with a Democrat) to Hayes.

Democratic institutions, shaken by the South's refusal to go along with the majority in 1860 and by the suppression of civil rights during the rebellion, and further weakened by military intervention and the intimidation of blacks in the South during Reconstruction, seemed now a farce. According to Tilden's campaign manager, angry Democrats in 15 states, chiefly war veterans, were readying themselves to march on Washington to force the inauguration of Tilden. Tempers flared in Congress, where some spoke ominously of a filibuster that would prevent the recording of the electoral vote and leave the country, on March 4, with no president at all.

THE COMPROMISE OF 1877

Forces for compromise had been at work behind the scenes in Washington for some time. Although northern Democrats threatened to fight to the last

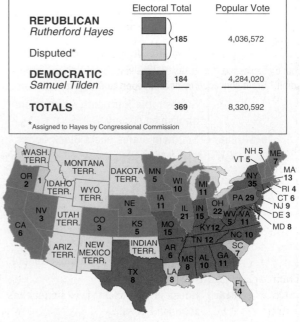

▲ The Compromise of 1877

ditch, many southern Democrats were willing to accept Hayes if he would promise to remove the troops and allow the southern states to manage their internal affairs by themselves. Ex-Whig planters and merchants who had reluctantly abandoned the carpetbag governments and who sympathized with Republican economic policies hoped that by supporting Hayes they might contribute to the restoration of the two-party system that had been destroyed in the South during the 1850s. Ohio Congressman James A. Garfield urged Hayes to find "some discreet way" of showing these Southerners that he favored "internal improvements." Hayes replied: "Your views are so nearly the same as mine that I need not say a word."

Tradition has it that a great compromise between the sections was worked out during a dramatic meeting at the Wormley Hotel[2] in Washington on February 26. Actually the negotiations were drawn out and informal, and the Wormley conference was but one of many. With the tacit support of many Democrats, the electoral vote was counted by the president of the Senate on March 2, and Hayes was declared elected, 185 votes to 184.

---

[2]Ironically, the hotel was owned by James Wormley, reputedly the wealthiest black in Washington.

Like all compromises, this agreement was not entirely satisfactory; like most, it was not honored in every detail. Hayes recalled the last troops from South Carolina and Louisiana in April. He appointed a former Confederate general, David M. Key of Tennessee, postmaster general and delegated to him the congenial task of finding Southerners willing to serve their country as officials of a Republican administration. But the alliance of ex-Whigs and northern Republicans did not flourish; the South remained solidly Democratic. The major significance of the compromise, one of the great intersectional political accommodations of American history, was that it ended Reconstruction and inaugurated a new political order in the South. More than the Constitutional amendments and federal statutes, this new regime would shape the destinies of the four million freedmen.

For most, this future was to be bleak. Forgotten in the North, manipulated and then callously rejected by the South, rebuffed by the Supreme Court, voiceless in national affairs, they and their descendants were condemned in the interests of sectional harmony to lives of poverty, indignity, and little hope. Meanwhile, the rest of the United States continued its golden march toward wealth and power.

MILESTONES

1863	Lincoln announces "Ten Percent Plan" for Reconstruction	**1868**	Fourth Reconstruction Act requires a majority of Southern voters to ratify state constitutions
1865	Federal government sets up Freedmen's Bureau to ease transition from slavery to freedom		Senate acquits Johnson
	General Lee surrenders at Appomattox Court House		States ratify Fourteenth Amendment extending rights to freed slaves
	Abraham Lincoln is assassinated; Andrew Johnson becomes president		Ulysses S. Grant is elected president
	Johnson issues amnesty proclamation		Ku Klux Klan uses intimidation and force throughout South
	States ratify Thirteenth Amendment abolishing slavery	**1870**	States ratify Fifteenth Amendment granting black suffrage
1865–1866	Southern states enact Black Codes	**1870–1871**	Force (Ku Klux Klan) Act destroys Klan
1866	Civil Rights Act passes over Johnson's veto	**1872**	Liberal Republican party nominates Horace Greeley for president
	Johnson campaigns for his Reconstruction policy		Grant is reelected president
1867	First Reconstruction Act puts former Confederacy under military rule	**1876**	Rutherford B. Hayes runs against Samuel Tilden in disputed presidential election
	Tenure of Office Act protects Senate appointees	**1877**	Electoral Commission awards disputed votes to Rutherford B. Hayes who becomes president
1868	House of Representatives impeaches Johnson		Hayes agrees to Compromise of 1877 ending Reconstruction

SUPPLEMENTARY READING

Lincoln's ideas about Reconstruction are analyzed in William C. Harris, *With Charity for All* (1997) and in many of the Lincoln volumes mentioned in earlier chapters. Hans Trefousse, *Andrew Johnson: A Biography* (1989) is a balanced account. See also Brooks D. Simpson, *The Reconstruction Presidents* (2001), Eric L. McKitrick, *Andrew Johnson and Reconstruction* (1960), and M. L. Benedict, *The Impeachment and Trial of Andrew Johnson* (1973).

A number of biographies provide information helpful in understanding the Radicals. The most important are Hans Trefousse, *Thaddeus Stevens* (1997), and David Donald, *Charles Sumner and the Rights of Man* (1970). J. M. McPherson, *The Struggle for Equality: Abolitionists and the Negro in the Civil War and Reconstruction* (1964) is also valuable. On the Fourteenth Amendment, see W. E. Nelson, *The Fourteenth Amendment* (1988); on the Fifteenth Amendment, see William Gillette, *The Right to Vote* (1965).

Conditions in the South during Reconstruction are discussed in Edward Ayers, *The Promise of the New South* (1992). The Freedmen's Bureau is examined in Paul Cimbala, *Under the Guardianship of the Nation* (1997). See also R. H. Abbott, *The Republican Party and the South* (1986), Michael Perman, *Reunion Without Compromise* (1973), H. N. Rabinowitz, *Race Relations in the Urban South* (1978), J. L. Roark, *Masters Without Slaves* (1977), and Leon Litwack, *Been in the Storm Too Long* (1979). For recent general studies, see Don E. Fehrenbacher, *The Slaveholding Republic* (2001), and Pamela Brandwein, *Reconstructing Reconstruction* (1999). Daniel Stowell's *Rebuilding Zion* (1998) explores the religious dimensions of Reconstruction.

Of state studies see, for Virginia, Jane E. Dailey, *Before Jim Crow* (2000); for South Carolina, Julie Saville, *The Work of Reconstruction* (1994), W. L. Rose, *Rehearsal for Reconstruction* (1964), Thomas Holt, *Black over White: Negro Political Leadership in South Carolina* (1977); for Texas, Randolph B. Campbell, *Grass-Roots Reconstruction in Texas* (1997). Much recent work on the Ku Klux Klan similarly focuses on particular states: see Lou F. Williams, *The Great South Carolina Ku Klux Klan Trials* (1996), Glenn Feldman, *Politics, Society and the Klan in Alabama* (1999), and Noel Fisher, *War at Every Door* (1997), which examines East Tennessee.

On the economic and social effects of Reconstruction, see G. D. Jaynes, *Branches Without Roots: Genesis of the Black Working Class* (1986), R. L. Ransom and Richard Sutch, *One Kind of Freedom: The Economic Consequences of Emancipation* (1977), Robert Higgs, *Competition and Coercion* (1977), and C. F. Oubre, *Forty Acres and a Mule* (1978). The ambiguities of dependence and independence as they relate to racial and gender issues are explored in Laura F. Edwards, *Gendered Strife and Confusion* (1997), and Amy Dru Stanley, *From Bondage to Contract* (1998).

On Grant's presidency, see Jean Edwards Smith, *Grant* (2001), Geoffrey Perret, *Ulysses S. Grant* (1997), and W. S. McFeely, *Grant* (1981). On the Republican reform movement, see J. G. Sproat, *"The Best Men": Liberal Reformers in the Gilded Age* (1968). For the disputed election of 1876 and the compromise following it, consult C. V. Woodward, *Reunion and Reaction* (1951), and William Gillette, *Retreat from Reconstruction* (1980).

David W. Blight, *Race and Reunion* (2001) considers the Civil War and Reconstruction in a deeper historical perspective.

SUGGESTED WEBSITES

The Impeachment of Andrew Johnson
http://www.impeach-andrewjohnson.com/
This HarpWeek site about the impeachment includes images and text from the Reconstruction period.

Diary and Letters of Rutherford B. Hayes
http://www.ohiohistory.org/onlinedoc/hayes/index.cfm
The Rutherford B. Hayes Presidential Center in Fremont, Ohio, maintains this searchable database of Hayes's writings.

Rutherford B. Hayes
http://www.ipl.org/ref/POTUS/rbhayes.html
This site contains information relating to Hayes and his presidency.

Images of African Americans from the Nineteenth Century
http://digital.nypl.org/schomburg/images_aa19/
The New York Public Library–Schomburg Center for Research in Black Culture site contains numerous visuals.

Freedman and Southern Society Project (University of Maryland, College Park)
http://www.inform.umd.edu/ARHU/Depts/History/Freedman/home.html
This site contains a chronology and sample documents from several collections or primary sources about emancipation and freedom in the 1860s.

In the Wake of War

▼ In Charles Russell's *Trail of the Iron Horse* (1910) the steel rails stretch nearly to the sun, while wispy brush strokes depict the Indians almost as ghosts.

After Appomattox the immense resources of the United States, combined with the high value most Americans assigned to work and achievement, made the people strongly materialistic. From colonial times they had assumed that prosperity was the natural state of things, and they had shown an inordinate respect for wealth. The Civil War further encouraged the glorification of money and the things it could buy. The North's capacity to produce the tools of war had helped preserve the Union; the role of businessmen and manufacturers in winning the struggle was clear to every soldier from General Grant to the lowliest private.

After the failures of Reconstruction, Americans seemed even more enamored of material values. They were tired of sacrifice, eager to act for themselves. Never especially noted for their sophistication, taste, or interest in preserving the resources of the country, the people now tolerated the grossest kind of waste and seemed to care little about corruption in high places, so long as no one interfered with their personal pursuit of profit. Mark Twain, raised in an earlier era, called this a Gilded Age, dazzling on the surface, base metal below. A later writer, Vernon Parrington, named the period the Great Barbecue, a time when everyone rushed to gobble up the national inheritance like hungry picnickers crowding around the savory roast at one of the big political outings common in those years.

CONGRESS ASCENDANT

Most students of the subject have concluded that the political history of the United States in the last quarter of the nineteenth century was

singularly divorced from the meaningful issues of that day. On the rare occasions that important, supposedly controversial measures were debated, they excited far less argument than they merited. A graduated income tax, the greatest instrument for orderly economic and social change that a democratic society has devised, was enacted during the Civil War, repealed after that conflict, reenacted in 1894 as part of the maneuvering over tariff reform, and then declared unconstitutional in 1895 without causing much more than a ripple in the world of partisan politics. This was typical; as the English observer James Bryce noted in *The American Commonwealth* (1888), a brilliant analysis of the American political system, politicians were "clinging too long to outworn issues" and "neglecting to discover and work out new principles capable of solving the problems which now perplex the country." Congress, another critic wrote, "does not solve the problems, the solution of which is demanded by the life of the nation."

A succession of weak presidents presided over the White House. Although the impeachment proceedings against Andrew Johnson had failed, Congress dominated the government. Within Congress, the Senate generally overshadowed the House of Representatives. In his novel *Democracy* (1880), the cynical Henry Adams wrote that the United States had a "government of the people, by the people, for the benefit of Senators." Critics called the Senate a "rich man's club," and it did contain many millionaires, among them Leland Stanford, founder of the Central Pacific Railroad; the mining tycoon James G. "Bonanza" Fair of Nevada; Philetus Sawyer, a self-made Wisconsin lumberman; and Nelson Aldrich of Rhode Island, whose wealth derived from banking and a host of corporate connections. However, the true sources of the Senate's influence lay in the long tenure of many of its members (which enabled them to master the craft of politics), in the fact that it was small enough to encourage real debate, and in its long-established reputation for wisdom, intelligence, and statesmanship.

The House of Representatives, on the other hand, was one of the most disorderly and inefficient legislative bodies in the world. "As I make my notes," a reporter wrote in 1882 while sitting in the House gallery,

> I see a dozen men reading newspapers with their feet on their desks. . . . "Pig Iron" Kelley of Pennsylvania has dropped his newspaper and is paring his fingernails. . . . The vile odor of . . . tobacco . . . rises from the two-for-five-cents cigars in the mouths of the so-called gentlemen below. . . . They chew, too! Every desk has a spittoon of pink and gold china beside it to catch the filth from the statesman's mouth.

An infernal din rose from the crowded chamber. Desks slammed; members held private conversations, hailed pages, shuffled from place to place, clamored for the attention of the Speaker—and all the while some poor orator tried to discuss the question of the moment. Speaking in the House, one writer said, was like trying to address the crowd on a passing Broadway bus from the curb in front of the Astor House in New York. On one occasion in 1878 the adjournment of the House was held up for more than 12 hours because most of the members of an important committee were too drunk to prepare a vital appropriations bill for final passage.

The great political parties professed undying enmity to each other, but they seldom took clearly opposing positions on the questions of the day. Democrats were separated from Republicans more by accidents of geography, religious affiliation, ethnic background, and emotion than by economic issues. Questions of state and local importance, unrelated to national politics, often determined the outcome of congressional elections and thus who controlled the federal government.

The fundamental division between Democrats and Republicans was sectional, a result of the Civil War. The South, after the political rights of blacks had been drastically circumscribed, became heavily Democratic. Most of New England was solidly Republican. Elsewhere the two parties stood in fair balance, although the Republicans tended to have the advantage. A preponderance of the well-to-do, cultured Northerners were Republicans. Perhaps in reaction to this concentration, immigrants, Catholics, and—except for blacks—other minority groups tended to vote Democratic. But there were so many exceptions that these generalizations are of little practical importance. German and Scandinavian immigrants usually voted Republican; many powerful business leaders supported the Democrats.

The personalities of political leaders often dictated the voting patterns of individuals and groups. In 1884 the banker J. P. Morgan voted Democratic because he admired Grover Cleveland, while Irish-Americans, traditionally Democrats, cast thousands of ballots for Republican James G. Blaine. In 1892, when Cleveland defeated Benjamin Harrison, a prominent steel manufacturer wrote to his even more prominent competitor, Andrew Carnegie: "I am very sorry for President Harrison, but I cannot see that our interests are going to be affected one way or the other." And Carnegie replied: "We have nothing to fear. . . . Cleveland is [a] pretty good fellow. Off for Venice tomorrow."

The bulk of the people—farmers, laborers, shopkeepers, white-collar workers—distributed their ballots fairly evenly between the two parties in most elec-

tions; the balance of political power after 1876 was almost perfect—"the most spectacular degree of equilibrium in American history." Between 1856 and 1912 the Democrats elected a president only twice (1884 and 1892), but most contests were extremely close. Majorities in both the Senate and the House fluctuated continually. Between 1876 and 1896 the "dominant" Republican party controlled both houses of Congress and the presidency at the same time for only one 2-year period.

THE POLITICAL AFTERMATH OF WAR

Four questions obsessed politicians in these years. One was the "bloody shirt." The term, which became part of the language after a Massachusetts congressman dramatically displayed to his colleagues in the House the blood-stained shirt of an Ohio carpetbagger who had been flogged by terrorists in Mississippi, referred to the tactic of reminding the electorate of the northern states that the men who had taken the South out of the Union and precipitated the Civil War had been Democrats and that they and their descendants were still Democrats. Should their party regain power, former rebels would run the government and undo all the work accomplished at such sacrifice during the war. "Every man that endeavored to tear down the old flag," a Republican orator proclaimed in 1876, "was a Democrat. Every man that tried to destroy this nation was a Democrat. . . . The man that assassinated Abraham Lincoln was a Democrat. . . . Soldiers, every scar you have on your heroic bodies was given you by a Democrat."

Every scoundrel or incompetent who sought office under the Republican banner waved the bloody shirt in order to divert the attention of northern voters from his own shortcomings, and the technique worked so well that many decent candidates could not resist the temptation to employ it in close races. Nothing, of course, so effectively obscured the real issues of the day.

Waving the bloody shirt was related intimately to the issue of the rights of blacks. Throughout this period Republicans vacillated between trying to build up their organization in the South by appealing to black voters—which required them to make sure that blacks in the South could vote—and trying to win conservative white support by stressing economic issues such as the tariff. When the former strategy seemed wise, they waved the bloody shirt with vigor; in the latter case, they piously announced that the blacks' future was "as safe in the hands of one party as it is in the other."

The question of veterans' pensions also bore a close relationship to the bloody shirt. Following the

Civil War, Union soldiers founded the Grand Army of the Republic (GAR). By 1890 the organization had a membership of 409,000. The GAR put immense pressure on Congress, first for aid to veterans with service-connected disabilities, then for those with any disability, and eventually for all former Union soldiers. Republican politicians played on the emotions of the former soldiers by waving the bloody shirt, but the tough-minded leaders of the GAR demanded that they prove their sincerity by treating in open-handed fashion the warriors whose blood had stained the shirt.

The tariff was another perennial issue in post–Civil War politics. Despite considerable loose talk about free trade, almost no one in the United States except for a handful of professional economists, most of them college professors, believed in eliminating duties on imports. Manufacturers desired protective tariffs to keep out competing products, and a majority of their workers were convinced that wage levels would fall if goods produced by cheap foreign labor entered the United States untaxed. Many farmers supported protection, although almost no competing agricultural products were being imported. Congressman William McKinley of Ohio, who reputedly could make reciting a tariff schedule sound like poetry, stated the majority opinion in the clearest terms: high tariffs foster the growth of industry and thus create jobs. "Reduce the tariff and labor is the first to suffer," he said.

The tariff could have been a real political issue because American technology was advancing so rapidly that many industries no longer required protection from foreign competitors. A powerful argument could have been made for scientific rate making that would adjust duties to actual conditions and avoid overprotection. The Democrats professed to believe in moderation, yet whenever party leaders tried to revise the tariff downward, Democratic congressmen from Pennsylvania, New York, and other industrial states sided with the Republicans. Many Republicans endorsed tariff reform in principle, but when particular schedules came up for discussion, most of them demanded the highest rates for industries in their own districts and traded votes shamelessly with colleagues representing other interests in order to get what they wanted. Every new tariff bill became an occasion for logrolling, lobbying, and outrageous politicking rather than for sane discussion and careful evaluation of the public interest.

A third political question in this period was currency reform. During the Civil War, the government, faced with obligations it could not meet by taxing or borrowing, suspended specie payments and issued about $450 million in paper money. The greenbacks did not command the full confidence of a people accustomed to money readily convertible into gold or

▲ An 1887 cartoon indicting the Senate for closely attending to the Big (read, fat) Trusts rather than to the needs of the public (whose "entrance" to the Senate is "closed"). Drawn by Joseph Keppler, a caricaturist who was born and trained in Germany, this type of grotesque satire greatly influenced late nineteenth-century American comic arts.

silver. Greenbacks seemed to threaten inflation, for how could one trust the government not to issue them in wholesale lots to avoid passing unpopular tax laws? Thus, when the war ended, strong sentiment developed for withdrawing the greenbacks from circulation and returning to a bullion standard. "By a law resting on the concurring judgment . . . of mankind in all ages and countries, the precious metals have been the measure of value," one politician wrote. "That law can no more be repealed by act of Congress than the law of gravitation."

In fact, beginning during Reconstruction, prices declined sharply. The deflation increased the real income of bondholders and other creditors but injured debtors. Farmers were particularly hard hit, for many of them had borrowed heavily during the wartime boom to finance expansion.

Here was a question of real significance. Many groups supported some kind of currency inflation. A National Greenback party nominated Peter Cooper, an iron manufacturer, for president in 1876. Cooper received only 81,000 votes, but a new Greenback Labor party polled over a million in 1878, electing 14 congressmen. However, the major parties refused to

confront each other over the currency question. While Republicans professed to be the party of sound money, most western Republicans favored expansion of the currency. And while one wing of the Democrats flirted with the Greenbackers, the conservative, or "Bourbon," Democrats favored deflation as much as Republicans did. Under various administrations steps were taken to increase or decrease the amount of money in circulation, but the net effect on the economy was not significant.

The final major political issue of these years was civil service reform. That the federal bureaucracy needed overhauling nearly everyone agreed. As American society grew larger and more complex, the government necessarily took on more functions. The need for professional administration increased. The number of federal employees rose from 53,000 in 1871 to 256,000 at the end of the century. Corruption flourished; waste and inefficiency were the normal state of affairs. The collection of tariff duties offered perhaps the greatest opportunity for venality. The New York Custom House, one observer wrote in 1872, teemed with "corrupting merchants and their clerks and runners, who think that all men can be

bought, and . . . corrupt swarms [of clerks], who shamelessly seek their price."

With a succession of relatively ineffective presidents and a Congress that squandered its energies on private bills, pork-barrel projects, and other trivia, the administration of the government was strikingly inefficient.

Every honest observer could see the need for reform, but the politicians refused to surrender the power of dispensing government jobs to their lieutenants without regard for their qualifications. They argued that patronage was the lifeblood of politics, that parties could not function without armies of loyal political workers, and that the workers expected and deserved the rewards of office when their efforts were crowned with victory at the polls. Typical was the attitude of the New York assemblyman who, according to Theodore Roosevelt, had "the same idea about Public Life and the Civil Service that a vulture has of a dead sheep." When reformers suggested establishing the most modest kind of professional, nonpartisan civil service, politicians of both parties subjected them to every kind of insult and ridicule even though both the Democratic and Republican parties regularly wrote civil service reform planks into their platforms.

BLACKS AFTER RECONSTRUCTION

Minorities were treated with callousness and contempt in the postwar decades. That the South would deal harshly with the former slaves once federal control was relaxed probably should have been expected. Men like Governor Wade Hampton of South Carolina had promised to respect black civil rights. "We . . . will secure to every citizen, the lowest as well as the highest, black as well as white, full and equal protection in the enjoyment of all his rights under the Constitution," Hampton said in 1877. This pledge was not kept.

President Hayes had urged blacks to trust southern whites. A new Era of Good Feelings had dawned, he announced after making a goodwill tour of the South shortly after his inauguration. By December 1877 he had been sadly disillusioned. "By state legislation, by frauds, by intimidation, and by violence of the most atrocious character, colored citizens have been deprived of the right of suffrage," he wrote in his diary. However, he did nothing to remedy the situation. Frederick Douglass called Hayes's policy "sickly conciliation."

Hayes's successors in the 1880s did no better. "Time is the only cure," President Garfield said, thereby confessing that he had no policy at all. President Arthur gave federal patronage to antiblack groups in an effort to split the Democratic South. In

President Cleveland's day blacks had scarcely a friend in high places, North or South. In 1887 Cleveland explained to a correspondent why he opposed "mixed schools." Expert opinion, the president said, believed "that separate schools were of much more benefit for the colored people." Hayes, Garfield, and Arthur were Republicans, Cleveland a Democrat; party made little difference. Both parties subscribed to hypocritical statements about equality and constitutional rights, and neither did anything to implement them.

For a time blacks were not totally disenfranchised in the South. Rival white factions tried to manipulate them, and corruption flourished as widely as in the machine-dominated wards of the northern cities. In the 1890s, however, the southern states, led by Mississippi, began to deprive blacks of the vote despite the Fifteenth Amendment. Poll taxes raised a formidable economic barrier, one that also disenfranchised many poor whites. Literacy tests completed the work; a number of states provided a loophole for illiterate whites by including an "understanding" clause whereby an illiterate person could qualify by demonstrating an ability to explain the meaning of a section of the state constitution when an election official read it to him. Blacks who attempted to take the test were uniformly declared to have failed it.

In Louisiana, 130,000 blacks voted in the election of 1896. Then the law was changed. In 1900 only 5000 votes were cast by blacks. "We take away the Negroes' votes," a Louisiana politician explained, "to protect them just as we would protect a little child and prevent it from injuring itself with sharp-edged tools." Almost every Supreme Court decision after 1877 that affected blacks somehow nullified or curtailed their rights. In *Hall* v. *De Cuir* (1878) the Court even threw out a state law forbidding segregation on riverboats, arguing that it was an unjustifiable interference with interstate commerce. The *Civil Rights Cases* (1883) declared the Civil Rights Act of 1875 unconstitutional. Blacks who were refused equal accommodations or privileges by hotels, theaters, and other privately owned facilities had no recourse at law, the Court announced. The Fourteenth Amendment guaranteed their civil rights against invasion by the states, not by individuals.

Finally, in *Plessy* v. *Ferguson* (1896), the Court ruled that even in places of public accommodation, such as railroads and, by implication, schools, segregation was legal as long as facilities of equal quality were provided. "If one race be inferior to the other socially, the Constitution of the United States cannot put them upon the same plane." In a noble dissent in

Plessy v. Ferguson, 1896

the Plessy case, Justice John Marshall Harlan protested this line of argument. "Our Constitution is color-blind," he said. "The arbitrary separation of citizens, on the basis of race . . . is a badge of servitude wholly inconsistent with civil freedom. . . . The two races in this country are indissolubly linked together, and the interests of both require that the common government of all shall not permit the seeds of race hatred to be planted under the sanction of law."

More than half a century was to pass before the Court came around to Harlan's reasoning and reversed the *Plessy* decision. Meanwhile, total segregation was imposed throughout the South. Separate schools, prisons, hospitals, recreational facilities, and even cemeteries were provided for blacks, and these were almost never equal to those available to whites.

Most Northerners supported the government and the Court. Newspapers presented a stereotyped, derogatory picture of blacks, no matter what the circumstances. Northern magazines, even high-quality publications such as *Harper's, Scribner's,* and *The Century,* repeatedly made blacks the butt of crude jokes.

The restoration of white rule abruptly halted the progress in public education for blacks that the Reconstruction governments had made. Church groups and private foundations such as the Peabody Fund and the Slater Fund, financed chiefly by northern philanthropists, supported black schools after 1877, among them two important experiments in vocational training, Hampton Institute and Tuskegee Institute.

These schools had to overcome considerable resistance and suspicion in the white community; they survived only because they taught a docile, essentially subservient philosophy, preparing students to accept second-class citizenship and become farmers and craftsmen. Since proficiency in academic subjects might have given the lie to the southern belief that blacks were intellectually inferior to whites, such subjects were avoided.

The southern insistence on segregating the public schools, buttressed by the separate but equal decision of the Supreme Court in *Plessy* v. *Ferguson,* imposed a crushing financial burden on poor, sparsely settled communities, and the dominant opinion that blacks were not really educable did not encourage these communities to make special efforts in their behalf.

BOOKER T. WASHINGTON: A "REASONABLE" CHAMPION FOR BLACKS

Since nearly all contemporary biologists, physicians, and other supposed experts on race were convinced that blacks were inferior beings, educated Northerners

▲ Booker T. Washington's famous Atlanta address in 1895 received mixed reactions in the black community. His most fervent challenge came from W. E. B. Du Bois, a professor at Atlanta University, who rejected Washington's call for patience and accommodation as a means to end racial segregation.

generally accepted black inferiority as fact. The English observer James Bryce, who had a wide acquaintance among Americans of this type, contended that blacks had "no capacity for abstract thinking, for scientific inquiry, or for any kind of invention." Being "unspeakably inferior," they were "unfit to cope with a superior race."

Like Bryce, most Americans did not especially wish blacks ill; they simply refused to consider them quite human and consigned them complacently to oblivion, along with the Indians. A vicious circle was established. By denying blacks decent educational opportunities and good jobs, the dominant race could use the blacks' resultant ignorance and poverty to justify the inferior facilities offered them.

Southern blacks reacted to this deplorable situation in a variety of ways. Some sought redress in racial pride and what would later be called black nationalism. Some became so disaffected that they tried to revive the African colonization movement. "Africa is our home," insisted Bishop Henry M. Turner, a huge, plainspoken man who had served as an army chaplain during the war and as a member of the Georgia legislature during Reconstruction. "Every man that has the sense of an animal must see there is no future in this country for the Negro." Another militant, T. Thomas Fortune, editor of the New York *Age* and founder of the Afro-American League (1887), called on blacks to demand full civil rights, better

▲ Photograph of a 1902 history class at Tuskegee Institute, a coeducational school for African Americans in east-central Alabama. Booker T. Washington was its principal from its incorporation in 1881 until his death in 1915. It is now Tuskegee University.

schools, and fair wages and to fight against discrimination of every sort. "Let us stand up like men in our own organization," he urged. "If others use . . . violence to combat our peaceful arguments, it is not for us to run away from violence."

For a time, militancy and black separatism won few adherents among southern blacks. For one thing, life was better than it had been under slavery. Segregation actually helped southern blacks who became barbers, undertakers, restaurateurs, and shopkeepers because whites were reluctant to supply such services to blacks. Even when whites competed with black businesses, the resentment caused by segregation led blacks to patronize establishments run by people of their own race. According to the most conservative estimates, the living standard of the average southern black more than doubled between 1865 and 1900. But this only made many southern whites more angry and vindictive.

This helps explain the tactics of Booker T. Washington, one of the most extraordinary Americans of that generation. Washington had been born a slave in Virginia in 1856. Laboriously he obtained an education, supporting himself while a student by working as a janitor. In 1881, with the financial help of northern philanthropists, he founded Tuskegee Institute in Alabama. His experiences convinced Washington that blacks must lift themselves up by their own bootstraps but that they must also accommodate themselves to white prejudices. A persuasive speaker and a brilliant fund-raiser, he soon developed a national reputation as a "reasonable" champion of his race. (In 1891 Harvard awarded him an honorary degree.)

In 1895 Washington made a now-famous speech to a mixed audience at the Cotton States International Exposition in Atlanta. To the blacks he said: "Cast down your bucket where you are," by which he meant stop fighting segregation and second-class citizenship and concentrate on learning useful skills. "Dignify and glorify common labor," he urged. "Agitation of questions of racial equality is the extremest folly." Progress up the social and economic ladder would come not from "artificial forcing" but from self-improvement. "There is as much dignity in tilling a field as in writing a poem."

Washington asked the whites of what he called "our beloved South" to lend the blacks a hand in their efforts to advance themselves. If you will do so, he promised, you will be "surrounded by the most patient, faithful, law-abiding, and unresentful people that the world has seen."

This "Atlanta Compromise" delighted white Southerners and won Washington financial support in every section of the country. He became one of the most powerful men in the United States, consulted by presidents, in close touch with business and philanthropic leaders, and capable of influencing in countless unobtrusive ways the fate of millions of blacks.

Blacks responded to the compromise with mixed feelings. Accepting Washington's approach might relieve them of many burdens and dangers. Being obsequious might, like discretion, be the better part of valor. But Washington was asking them to give up specific rights in return for vague promises of future help. The cost was high in surrendered personal dignity and lost hopes of obtaining real justice.

Washington's career illustrates the terrible dilemma that American blacks have always faced: the choice between confrontation and accommodation. This choice was particularly difficult in the late nineteenth century.

Washington chose accommodation. It is easy to condemn him as a toady but difficult to see how, at that time, a more aggressive policy could have succeeded. One can even interpret the Atlanta Compromise as a subtle form of black nationalism; in a way, Washington was not urging blacks to accept inferiority and racial slurs but to ignore them. His own behavior lends force to this view, for his method of operating was indeed subtle, even devious. In public he minimized the importance of civil and political rights and accepted separate but equal facilities—if they were truly equal. Behind the scenes he lobbied against restrictive measures, marshaled large sums of money to fight test cases in the courts, and worked hard in northern states to organize the black vote and make sure that black political leaders got a share of the spoils of office. He may not have been an admirable man, but he was a useful one. His defects point up more the unlovely aspects of the age than those of his own character.

WHITE VIOLENCE AND VENGEANCE

By the time of the Atlanta Compromise, however, Washington's calls for "sagacious silence," as one black militant put it, could scarcely be heard over the anguished cries of black victims of white violence. For decades, some southern whites had tried to replace the legal subjugation of slavery with psychological subjugation through terror. "They had to have a license to kill anything but a nigger," a black Southerner recalled. "We was always in season." Each year from 1890 through 1910, nearly a hundred blacks were lynched.

These numbers, which omit those blacks who were executed after biased though nominally legal trials, fail to tell the whole story of the intensification of violence against blacks. An example was the lynching in 1899 of Sam Hose in a town outside Atlanta. Hose, a black laborer, killed his boss in self-defense. He was seized by a white mob and chained to a tree. His ears, fingers, toes, and genitals were cut off and his face was skinned. Then, while still alive, he was doused with kerosene and set on fire. A crowd numbering in the thousands watched, in the words of one newspaper account, "with unfeigning satisfaction." The dead man's body parts were auctioned: small bones went for 25 cents; his liver, "crisply cooked," for 10 cents.

White fears were excited by feverish rumors of black males as rapists and predators. "There is a black vampire hovering over our beloved North Carolina," Rebecca Strowd warned the White Government Leagues in 1898. Violence and violent rhetoric succeeded in disfranchising southern black men and driving them, often literally, out of public spaces. Ironically, this created an opportunity for black women to fill the leadership void, taking increasingly prominent roles as spokespersons in religious and reform associations.

The public activities of black women reformers and of white supremacists such as Rebecca Strowd contradicted ideals of feminine domesticity, but their arguments affirmed middle-class sensibilities. Thus black women insisted that whites uphold Christian brotherhood, while women such as Strowd called on white men to do their duty in protecting their womenfolk. By advancing middle-class ideology, however, these women distanced themselves from the working classes of both races. Few male sharecroppers or industrial workers could hope to earn enough to enable their wives to devote themselves exclusively to the home or to the cultivation of middle-class proprieties. And many working-class women, having sampled the independence of paid work, were unpersuaded of the appeal of domesticity.

THE WEST AFTER THE CIVIL WAR

Many parts of the region had as large a percentage of foreign-born residents as the populous eastern states—nearly a third of all Californians were foreign-born, as were more than 40 percent of Nevadans and over half the residents of Idaho and Arizona. There were, of course, large populations of Spanish-speaking Americans of Mexican origin all over the Southwest. Chinese and Irish laborers were pouring into California by the thousands, and there were substantial numbers of Germans in Texas. Germans, Scandinavians, and other Europeans were also numerous on the High Plains east of the Rockies.

Although the image of the West as the land of great open spaces is accurate enough, the region

DEBATING THE PAST

Was the frontier exceptionally violent? In 1882 the *New York Daily Graphic* described Jesse James *(left)* as "the most renowned murderer and robber of his age." Here he is shown with members of his gang, each holding a rifle and wearing a holster and pistol, a stereotypical expression of gun violence in the frontier West.

But several decades ago historians challenged the notion that the western frontier was exceptionally violent. Robert Dykstra observed that most of the frontier was devoted to agriculture, and that such communities were peaceable. John Unruh, Jr. and John Reid were struck by how few crimes occurred during the difficult, long months of the overland trail. Stuart N. Udall, former secretary of the interior, reflected the opinions of a panel at the Western History Association that rejected "the current contention that gun violence was a 'principal factor' in the history of the American west."

Some historians have approached the issue by compiling comparative statistics of homicides per 100,000 population (the standard way that federal crime statistics are now expressed). In 1985, when Miami had a homicide rate of 33, the highest in the nation, Roger D. McGrath found that a California mining camp had a rate of 116 in the 1870s and 1880s. John Boessenecker found that in 1851 Los Angeles County had a staggering rate of 1240. Clare McKenna, Jr., arrived at a similar conclusion based on statistics for rural California. Critics, however, rejected the methodology. They note that in a frontier town of 100 people, a single murder generates a fearful homicide rate of 1000. Little wonder that Jesse James was perceived as a one-gang crime wave.

Robert R. Dykstra, *The Cattle Towns* (1968), John Unruh, Jr., *The Plains Across* (1979), John Reid, *Law for the Elephant* (1980), Roger D. McGrath, *Gunfighters, Highwaymen & Vigilantes* (1985), John Boessenecker, *Gold Dust and Gunsmoke* (1999), Clare V. McKenna, Jr., *Race and Homicide in Nineteenth-Century California* (2002), David Courtwright, *Violent Land* (1996), David Peterson del Mar, *Beaten Down: A History of Interpersonal Violence in the West* (2002).

contained several bustling cities. San Francisco, with a population approaching 250,000 in the late 1870s, had long outgrown its role as a rickety boomtown where the forty-niners bought supplies and squandered whatever wealth they had sifted from the streams of the Sierras. Though still an important warehouse and supply center, it had become the commercial and financial heart of the Pacific Coast and a center of light manufacturing, food processing, and machine shops. Denver, San Antonio, and Salt Lake City were far smaller, but growing rapidly and equally "urban."

There was, in short, no one West, no typical Westerner. If the economy was predominantly agricultural and extractive, it was also commercial and entering the early stages of industrial development. The seeds of such large enterprises as Wells Fargo, Levi Strauss, and half a dozen important department store empires were sown in the immediate postwar decades.

Beginning in the mid-1850s a steady flow of Chinese migrated to the United States, most of them to the west coast. About four or five thousand a year came, until the negotiation of the Burlingame Treaty of 1868, the purpose of which was to provide cheap labor for railroad construction crews. Thereafter the annual influx more than doubled, although before 1882 it exceeded 20,000 only twice. When the railroads were completed and the Chinese began to compete with native workers, a great cry of resentment went up on the west coast. Riots broke out in San Francisco in 1877. Chinese workers were called "groveling worms," "more slavish and brutish than the beasts that roam the fields." The California constitution of 1879 denied the right to vote to any "native of China" along with idiots, the insane, and persons convicted of "any infamous crime."

When Chinese immigration increased in 1882 to nearly 40,000, the protests reached such a peak that Congress passed a law prohibiting all Chinese immigration for ten years. Later legislation extended the ban indefinitely.

The Plains Indians

For 250 years the Indians had been driven back steadily, yet on the eve of the Civil War they still inhabited roughly half the United States. By the time of Hayes's inauguration, however, the Indians had been shattered as independent peoples, and in another decade the survivors were penned up on reservations, the government committed to a policy of extinguishing their way of life.

In 1860 the survivors of most of the eastern tribes were living peacefully in Indian Territory, what is now Oklahoma. In California the forty-niners had made short work of the local tribes. Elsewhere in the

West—in the deserts of the Great Basin between the Sierras and the Rockies, in the mountains themselves, and on the semiarid, grass-covered plains between the Rockies and the edge of white civilization in eastern Kansas and Nebraska—nearly a quarter of a million Indians dominated the land.

By far the most important lived on the High Plains. From the Blackfoot of southwestern Canada and the Sioux of Minnesota and the Dakotas to the Cheyenne of Colorado and Wyoming and the Comanche of northern Texas, the Plains tribes possessed a generally uniform culture. All lived by hunting the hulking American bison, or buffalo, which ranged over the Plains by the millions. The buffalo provided the Indians with food, clothing, and even shelter, for the famous Indian tepee was covered with hides. On the treeless Plains, dried buffalo dung was used for fuel. The buffalo was also an important symbol in Indian religion.

Although they seemed the epitome of freedom, pride, and self-reliance, the Plains Indians had begun to fall under the sway of white power. They eagerly adopted the products of the more technically advanced culture—cloth, metal tools, weapons, cheap decorations. However, the most important thing the whites gave them had nothing to do with technology: It was the horse.

The horse was among the many large mammals that became extinct in the Western Hemisphere around 10,000 B.C.E. Cortés reintroduced the horse to America in the sixteenth century. Multiplying rapidly thereafter, the animals soon roamed wild from Texas to the Argentine. By the eighteenth century the Indians of the Plains had made them a vital part of their culture.

Horses thrived on the Plains and so did their masters. Mounted Indians could run down buffalo instead of stalking them on foot. They could move more easily over the country and fight more effectively too. They could acquire and transport more possessions and increase the size of their tepees, for horses could drag heavy loads heaped on A-shaped frames (called *travois* by the French), whereas earlier Indians had only dogs to depend on as pack animals. The frames of the *travois*, when disassembled, served as poles for tepees. The Indians also adopted modern weapons: the cavalry sword, which they particularly admired, and the rifle. Both added to their effectiveness as hunters and fighters. However, like the whites' liquor and diseases, horses and guns caused problems. The buffalo herds began to diminish, and warfare became bloodier and more frequent.

In a familiar and tragic pattern, the majority of the western tribes greeted the first whites to enter their domains in a friendly fashion. Lewis and Clark and their handful of companions crossed and recrossed the entire region without a single clash with the Indians they encountered. As late as the 1830s, white hunters

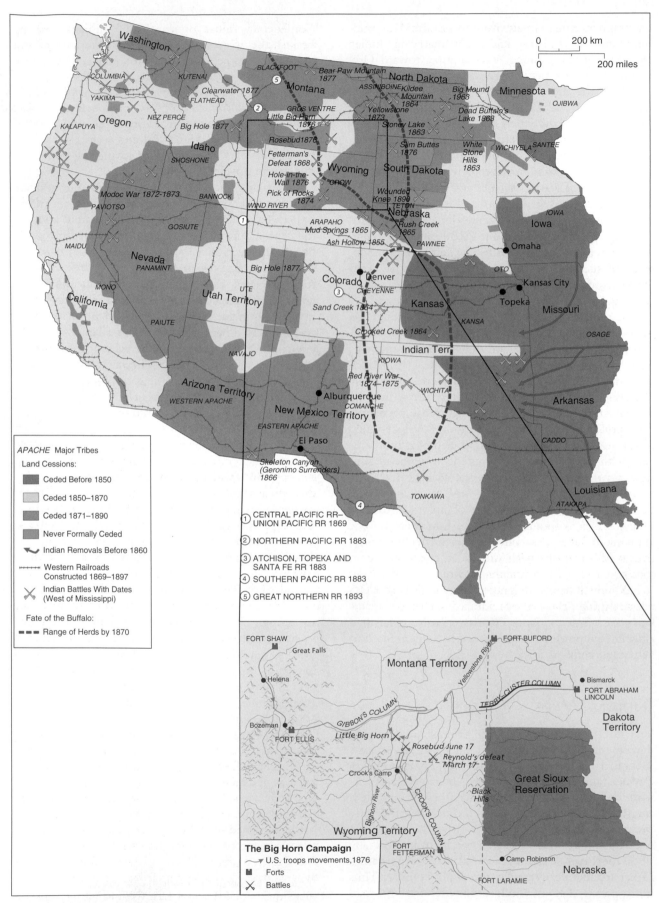

The map legend contains the following:

APACHE Major Tribes

Land Cessions:

- Ceded Before 1850
- Ceded 1850–1870
- Ceded 1871–1890
- Never Formally Ceded
- Indian Removals Before 1860
- Western Railroads Constructed 1869–1897
- Indian Battles With Dates (West of Mississippi)

Fate of the Buffalo:
- Range of Herds by 1870

① CENTRAL PACIFIC RR–UNION PACIFIC RR 1869
② NORTHERN PACIFIC RR 1883
③ ATCHISON, TOPEKA AND SANTA FE RR 1883
④ SOUTHERN PACIFIC RR 1883
⑤ GREAT NORTHERN RR 1893

Map labels (main map):

Washington, Columbia, Kutenai, Yakima, Oregon, Kalapuya, Nez Perce, Flathead, Blackfoot, Clearwater 1877, Montana, Bear Paw Mountain 1877, Assiniboine, North Dakota, Minnesota, Ojibwa, Gros Ventre, Kildee Mountain 1864, Big Mound 1963, Little Big Horn 1876, Yellowstone 1873, Idaho, Shoshone, Big Hole 1877, Rosebud1876, Stoney Lake 1863, Dead Buffalo's Lake 1868, Wichiyela, Santee, Fetterman's Defeat 1868, Slim Buttes 1876, White Stone Hills 1863, Wyoming, Crow, South Dakota, Hole-in-the-Wall 1876, Pick of Rocks 1874, Wounded Knee 1890, Teton, Wind River, Paviotso, Bannock, Gosiute, Maidu, Nevada, Panamint, Arapaho, Mud Springs 1865, Rush Creek 1865, Nebraska, Pawnee, Iowa, Omaha, Ash Hollow 1855, Mono, Ute, Big Hole 1877, Colorado, Denver, Cheyenne, Kansas, Oto, Kansas City, Topeka, Missouri, California, Paiute, Utah Territory, Sand Creek 1864, Kansa, Osage, Navajo, Crooked Creek 1864, Indian Terr, Arizona Territory, Kiowa, Red River War 1874–1875, Wichita, Arkansas, Western Apache, New Mexico Territory, Comanche, Alburquerque, Eastern Apache, Caddo, El Paso, Skeleton Canyon (Geronimo Surrenders) 1866, Tonkawa, Louisiana, Atakapa

Inset map — The Big Horn Campaign:

U.S. troops movements,1876
Forts
Battles

Fort Shaw, Great Falls, Helena, Bozeman, Fort Ellis, Gibbon's Column, Little Big Horn, Crook's Camp, Bighorn River, Crook's Column, Wyoming Territory, Fort Fetterman, Fort Laramie, Montana Territory, Yellowstone River, Terry Custer Column, Bismarck, Fort Buford, Fort Abraham Lincoln, Dakota Territory, Rosebud June 17, Reynold's defeat March 17, Black Hills, Great Sioux Reservation, Camp Robinson, Nebraska

▲ **Indian Wars, 1860–1890**

and trappers ranged freely over most of the West, trading with the Indians and often marrying Indian women. Settlers pushing cross-country toward Oregon in the 1840s met with relatively little trouble.

After the start of the gold rush the need to link the East with California meant that the tribes were pushed aside. Deliberately the government in Washington prepared the way. In 1851 Thomas Fitzpatrick—an experienced mountain man, a founder of the Rocky Mountain Fur Company, scout for the first large group of settlers to Oregon in 1841 and for American soldiers in California during the Mexican War, and now an Indian agent—summoned a great "council" of the tribes. About 10,000 Indians, representing nearly all the Plains tribes, gathered that September at Horse Creek, 37 miles east of Fort Laramie, in what is now Wyoming.

The Indians respected Fitzpatrick, who had recently married a woman who was half Indian. At Horse Creek he persuaded each tribe to accept definite limits to its hunting grounds. For example, the Sioux nations were to stay north of the Platte River, and the Cheyenne and Arapaho were to confine themselves to the Colorado foothills. In return the Indians were promised gifts and annual payments. This policy, known as "concentration," was designed to cut down on intertribal warfare and—far more important—to enable the government to negotiate separately with each tribe. It was the classic strategy of divide and conquer.

Although it made a mockery of diplomacy to treat Indian tribes as though they were European powers, the United States maintained that each tribe was a sovereign nation, to be dealt with as an equal in solemn treaties. Both sides knew that this was not the case. When Indians agreed to meet in council, they were tacitly admitting defeat. They seldom drove hard bargains or broke off negotiations. Moreover, tribal chiefs had only limited power; young braves frequently refused to respect agreements made by their elders.

Indian Wars

The government showed little interest in honoring agreements with Indians. No sooner had the Kansas-Nebraska bill become law than the Kansas, Omaha, Pawnee, and Yankton Sioux tribes began to feel pressure for further concessions of territory. A gold rush into Colorado in 1859 sent thousands of greedy prospectors across the Plains to drive the Cheyenne and Arapaho from land guaranteed them in 1851. By 1860 most of Kansas and Nebraska had been cleared. Other trouble developed in the Sioux country. Thus it happened that in 1862, after federal troops had been pulled out of the West for service against the

Confederacy, most of the Plains Indians rose up against the whites. For five years intermittent but bloody clashes kept the entire area in a state of alarm.

This was guerrilla warfare, with all its horror and treachery. In 1864 a party of Colorado militia fell on an unsuspecting Cheyenne community at Sand Creek and killed an estimated 450. "Kill and scalp all, big and little," Colonel J. M. Chivington, a minister in private life, told his men. A white observer described the scene: "They were scalped, their brains knocked out; the men used their knives, ripped open women, clubbed little children, knocked them in the head with their guns, beat their brains out, mutilated their bodies in every sense of the word." General Nelson A. Miles called this "Chivington massacre" the "foulest and most unjustifiable crime in the annals of America," but it was no worse than many incidents in earlier conflicts with Indians and not very different from what was later to occur in guerrilla wars involving American troops in the Philippines (which General Miles also found disturbing) and in Vietnam.

In turn the Indians slaughtered dozens of isolated white families, ambushed small parties, and fought many successful skirmishes against troops and militia. They achieved their most notable triumph in December 1866, when the Oglala Sioux, under their great chief Red Cloud, wiped out a party of 82 soldiers under Captain W. J. Fetterman. Red Cloud fought ruthlessly, but only when goaded by the construction of the Bozeman Trail, a road through the heart of the Sioux hunting grounds in southern Montana.[1]

In 1867 the government tried a new strategy. The "concentration" policy had evidently not gone far enough. All the Plains Indians would be confined to two small reservations, one in the Black Hills of the Dakota Territory, the other in Oklahoma, and forced to become farmers. At two great conclaves held in 1867 and 1868 at Medicine Lodge Creek and Fort Laramie, the principal chiefs yielded to the government's demands.

Many Indians refused to abide by these agreements. With their whole way of life at stake, they raged across the Plains like a prairie fire—and were almost as destructive.

That a relative handful of "savages," without central leadership, could hold off the cream of the army, battle-hardened in the Civil War, can be explained by the character of the vast, trackless country and the

DOCUMENT
Secretary of the Interior's Report on Indian Affairs

DOCUMENT
Red Cloud's Speech

---

[1]Fetterman had boasted that with 80 cavalrymen he could ride the entire length of the Bozeman Trail. When he tried, however, he blundered into an ambush.

ineptness of many American military commanders. Indian leadership was also poor in that few chiefs were capable of organizing a campaign or following up an advantage. But the Indians made superb guerrillas. Every observer called them the best cavalry soldiers in the world. Armed with stubby, powerful bows capable of driving an arrow clear through a bull buffalo, they were a fair match for troops equipped with carbines and Colt revolvers. Expertly they led pursuers into ambushes, swept down on unsuspecting supply details, stole up on small parties the way a mountain lion stalks a grazing lamb. They could sometimes be rounded up, as when General Philip Sheridan herded the tribes of the Southwest into Indian Territory in 1869. But once the troops withdrew, braves began to melt away into the emptiness of the surrounding grasslands. The distinction between "treaty" Indians, who had agreed to live on the new reservations, and the "nontreaty" variety shifted almost from day to day. Trouble flared here one week, next week somewhere else, perhaps 500 miles away. No less an authority than General William Tecumseh Sherman testified that a mere 50 Indians could often "checkmate" 3000 soldiers.

If one concedes that no one could reverse the direction of history or stop the invasion of Indian lands, then some version of the "small reservation" policy would probably have been best for the Indians. Had they been guaranteed a reasonable amount of land and adequate subsidies and allowed to maintain their way of life, they might have accepted the situation and ceased to harry the whites.

Whatever chance that policy had was weakened by the government's poor administration of Indian affairs. In dealing with Indians, nineteenth-century Americans displayed a grave insensitivity. After 1849 the Department of the Interior supposedly had charge of tribal affairs. Most of its agents systematically cheated the Indians. One, heavily involved in mining operations on the side, diverted goods intended for his charges to his private ventures. When an inspector looked into his records, he sold him shares in a mine. That worthy in turn protected himself by sharing some of the loot with the son of the commissioner of Indian affairs. Army officers squabbled frequently with Indian agents over policy, and an "Indian Ring" in the Department of the Interior system typically stole funds and supplies intended for the reservation Indians. "No branch of the national government is so spotted with fraud, so tainted with corruption . . . as this Indian Bureau," Congressman Garfield charged in 1869.

At about this time a Yale paleontologist, Othniel C. Marsh, who wished to dig for fossils on the Sioux reservation, asked Red Cloud for permission to enter his domain. The chief agreed on condition that Marsh, whom the Indians called Big Bone Chief, take

▲ An Oglala Sioux named Kills Two painted this portrayal of an Indian horse dance. Horses were vital to survival for the Sioux, as their inclusion in such ceremonies demonstrates.

back with him samples of the moldy flour and beef that government agents were supplying to his people. Appalled by what he saw on the reservation, Professor Marsh took the rotten supplies directly to President Grant and prepared a list of charges against the agents. General Sherman, in overall command of the Indian country, claimed in 1875: "We could settle Indian troubles in an hour, but Congress wants the patronage of the Indian bureau, and the bureau wants the appropriations without any of the trouble of the Indians themselves." General Sheridan was no lover of Indians. "The only good Indians I ever saw," he said in an oft-quoted remark, "were dead." But he understood why they behaved as they did. "We took away their country and their means of support, broke up their mode of living, their habits of life, introduced disease and decay among them, and it was for this and against this that they made war. Could anyone expect less?"

Grant wished to place the reservations under army control, but the Indians opposed this. They fared no better around army camps than on the reservations. In 1869 Congress created a nonpolitical Board of Indian Commissioners to oversee Indian affairs, but the bureaucrats in Washington stymied the commissioners at every turn.

In 1874 gold was discovered in the Black Hills Indian reservation. By the next winter thousands of

miners had invaded the reserved area. Already alarmed by the approach of crews building the Northern Pacific Railroad, the Sioux once again went on the warpath. Joining with nontreaty tribes to the west, they concentrated in the region of the Bighorn River, in southern Montana Territory.

The summer of 1876 saw three columns of troops in the field against them. The commander of one column, General Alfred H. Terry, sent ahead a small detachment of the Seventh Cavalry under Colonel George A. Custer with orders to locate the Indians' camp and then block their escape route into the inaccessible Bighorn Mountains. Custer was vain and rash, and vanity and rashness were grave handicaps when fighting Indians. Grossly underestimating the number of the Indians, he decided to attack directly with his tiny force of 264 men. At the Little Bighorn late in June he found himself surrounded by 2500 Sioux under Rain-in-the-Face, Crazy Horse, and Sitting Bull. He and all his men died on the field.

Because it was so one-sided, "Custer's Last Stand" was not a typical battle, although it may be taken as symbolic of the Indian warfare of the period in the sense that it was characterized by bravery, foolhardiness, and a tragic waste of life. The battle greatly heartened the Indians, but it did not gain them their cause. That autumn, short of rations and hard-pressed by overwhelming numbers of soldiers, they surrendered and returned to the reservation.

THE DESTRUCTION OF TRIBAL LIFE

Thereafter, the fighting slackened. For this the building of transcontinental railroads and the destruction of the buffalo were chiefly responsible. An estimated 13 to 15 million head had roamed the Plains in the mid-1860s. Then the slaughter began. Thousands were butchered to feed the gangs of laborers engaged in building the Union Pacific Railroad. Thousands

▲ Gathering the dead at Wounded Knee, where more than 200 Sioux men, women, and children were massacred by U.S. troops on December 29, 1890. The Teton Sioux, suffering from the reduction of their reservation, had been inspired by Wovoka, a prophet, who had said that the whites would disappear if the Sioux performed their "ghost dance" rituals. When the Ghost Dance movement spread, federal military authorities resolved to stamp it out. On December 14 Chief Sitting Bull was killed while being arrested; his people left their reservation at Pine Ridge and fled into the Badlands. The soldiers pursued them and the Indians surrendered. As they were being disarmed, however, a scuffle broke out and the troops opened fire. Thirty soldiers were also killed during the fighting at Wounded Knee.

more fell before the guns of sportsmen. Buffalo hunting became a fad, and a brisk demand developed for buffalo rugs and mounted buffalo heads. Railroads made the Army a far more efficient force. Troops and supplies could be moved swiftly when trouble with the tribes erupted. The lines also contributed to the decimation of the buffalo by running excursion trains for hunters; even the shameful practice of gunning down the beasts directly from the cars was allowed.

The discovery in 1871 of a way to make commercial use of buffalo hides completed the tragedy. In the next three years about 9 million head were killed; after another decade the animals were almost extinct. No more efficient way could have been found for destroying the Plains Indians. The disappearance of the bison left them starving and homeless.

By 1887 the tribes of the mountains and deserts beyond the Plains had also given up the fight. Typical of the heartlessness of the government's treatment of these peoples was that afforded the Nez Percé of Oregon and Idaho, who were led by the remarkable Chief Joseph. After outwitting federal troops in a campaign across more than a thousand miles of rough country, Joseph finally surrendered in October 1877. The Nez Percé were then settled on "the malarial bottoms of the Indian Territory" in far-off Oklahoma.

The last Indians to abandon the unequal battle were the relentless Apache of the Southwest, who finally yielded on the capture of their leader, Geronimo, in 1886.

By the 1880s, the advance of whites into the Plains had become, in the words of one congressman,

▲ A mound of buffalo skulls. In 1870 an estimated 30 million buffalo roamed the Plains; by 1900, there were fewer than 1000. During eight months from 1867–1868, William F. Cody (Buffalo Bill) killed 4280 buffalo, which fed construction crews for the Union Pacific railroad. Tourists also took up buffalo hunting, often shooting from trains. The depletion of the buffalo, which provided the Plains Indians with meat and hides, was a major source of conflict with whites.

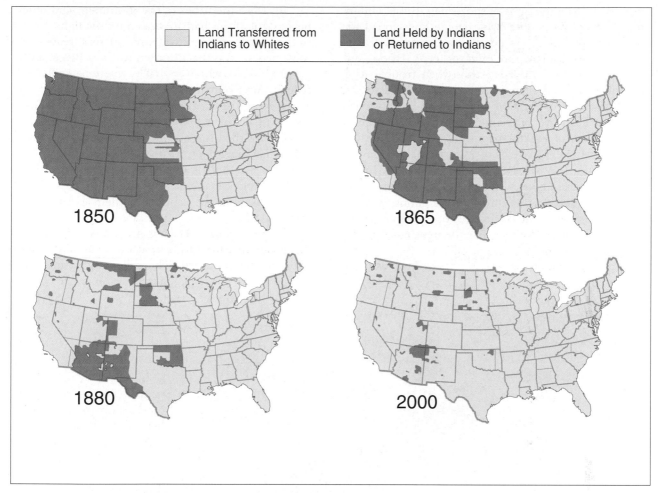

▲ **Loss of Indian Lands, 1850–2000**

as irresistible "as that of Sherman's to the sea." Greed for land lay behind the pressure, but large numbers of disinterested people, including most of those who deplored the way the Indians had been treated in the past, believed that the only practical way to solve the "Indian problem" was to persuade the Indians to abandon their tribal culture and live on family farms. The "wild" Indian must be changed into a "civilized" member of "American" society.

To accomplish this goal Congress passed the Dawes Severalty Act of 1887. Tribal lands were to be split up into individual allotments. To keep speculators from wresting the allotments from the Indians while they were adjusting to their new way of life, the land could not be disposed of for 25 years. Funds were to be appropriated for educating and training the Indians, and those who accepted allotments, took up residence "separate from any tribe," and "adopted the habits of civilized life" were to be granted United States citizenship.

The sponsors of the Severalty Act thought they were effecting a fine humanitarian reform. "We must

throw some protection over [the Indian]," Senator Henry L. Dawes declared. "We must hold up his hand." But no one expected all the Indians to accept allotments at once, and for some years little pressure was put on any to do so. The law was a statement of policy rather than a set of specific rules and orders. "Too great haste . . . should be avoided," Indian Commissioner John Atkins explained. "Character, habits, and antecedents cannot be changed by enactment."

The Dawes Act had disastrous results in the long run. It assumed that Indians could be transformed into small agricultural capitalists by an act of Congress. It shattered what was left of the Indians' culture without enabling them to adapt to white ways. Moreover, unscrupulous white men systematically tricked many Indians into leasing their allotments for a pittance, and local authorities often taxed Indian lands at excessive rates. In 1934, after about 86 million of the 138 million acres assigned under the Dawes Act had passed into white hands, the government returned to a policy of encouraging tribal ownership of Indian lands.

▲ An ad for Indian land, offered for sale by the U.S. Department of the Interior. In 1889 alone, white settlers claimed 2 million acres of Indian Territory. By 1892, they had acquired some 30 million acres. During the decade of the 1890s, the white population of Oklahoma Territory—as it was called in 1890—increased from 60,000 to 400,000.

THE LURE OF GOLD AND SILVER IN THE WEST

The natural resources of the nation were exploited in these decades even more ruthlessly and thoughtlessly than were its human resources. Americans had long regarded the West as a limitless treasure to be grasped as rapidly as possible, and after 1865 they engrossed its riches still faster and in a wider variety of ways. From the mid-1850s to the mid-1870s thousands of gold-crazed prospectors fanned out through the Rockies, panning every stream and hacking furiously at every likely outcropping from the Fraser River country of British Columbia to Tucson in southern Arizona, from the eastern slopes of the Sierras to the Great Plains.

Gold and silver were scattered throughout the area, though usually too thinly to make mining profitable. Whenever anyone made a "strike," prospectors, the vast majority utterly without previous experience but driven by what a mining journal of the period called an "unhealthy desire" for sudden wealth, flocked to the site, drawn by rumors of stream beds gleaming with gold-rich gravel and of nuggets the size of men's fists. For a few months the area teemed with activity. Towns of 5000 or more sprang up overnight; improvised roads were crowded with people and supply wagons. Claims were staked out along every stream and gully. Then, usually, expectations faded in the light of reality: high prices, low yields, hardship, violence, and deception. The boom collapsed and the towns died as quickly as they had risen. A few would have found wealth, the rest only backbreaking labor and disappointment—until tales of another strike sent them dashing feverishly across the land on another golden chase.

In the spring of 1858 it was on the Fraser River in Canada that the horde descended, 30,000 Californians in the vanguard. The following spring, Pikes Peak in Colorado attracted the pack, experienced California prospectors ("yonder siders") mixing with "greenhorns" from every corner of the globe. In June 1859 came the finds in Nevada, where the famous Comstock Lode yielded ores worth nearly $4000 a ton. In 1861, while men in the settled areas were laying down their tools to take up arms, the miners were racing to the Idaho panhandle, hoping to become millionaires overnight. The next year the rush was to the Snake River valley, then in 1863 and 1864 to Montana. In 1874 to 1876 the Black Hills in the heart of the Sioux lands were inundated.

In a sense the Denvers, Aurarias, Virginia Cities, Orofinos, and Gold Creeks of the West during the war years were harbingers of the attitudes that flourished in the East in the age of President Grant and his immediate successors. The miners enthusiastically adopted the get-rich-quick philosophy, willingly enduring privations and laboring hard, always with the object of striking it rich. The idea of reserving any part of the West for future generations never entered their heads.

The sudden prosperity of the mining towns attracted every kind of shady character—according to one forty-niner "rascals from Oregon, pickpockets from New York, accomplished gentlemen from Europe, interlopers from Lima and Chile, Mexican thieves, gamblers from no particular spot, and assassins manufactured in Hell." Gambling dens, dance halls, saloons, and brothels mushroomed wherever precious metal was found.

Law enforcement was a constant problem. Much of the difficulty lay in the antisocial attitudes of the miners themselves. Gold and silver dominated people's thoughts and dreams, and few paid much attention to the means employed in accumulating this wealth. Storekeepers charged outrageous prices; claim holders "salted" worthless properties with nuggets in order to swindle gullible investors.

▲ Creede, Colorado, circa 1890, a mining town whose inhospitability to women is suggested by their absence. One reason is indicated in information compiled for another Colorado mining town, Leadville, which, with a population of 20,000, had 250 saloons, 120 gambling establishments, 100 brothels, and only 4 churches.

Ostentation characterized the successful, braggadocio those who failed. During the administration of President Grant, Virginia City, Nevada, was at the peak of its vulgar prosperity, producing an average of $12 million a year in ore. Built on the richness of the Comstock Lode ($306 million in gold and silver was extracted from the Comstock in 20 years), it had 25 saloons before it had 4000 people. By the 1870s its mountainside site was disfigured by ugly, ornate mansions where successful mine operators ate from fine china and swilled champagne as though it were water.

Wild Bill Hickok

In 1873, after the discovery of the Big Bonanza, a seam of rich ore more than 50 feet thick, the future of Virginia City seemed boundless. Other discoveries shortly thereafter indicated to optimists that the mining boom in the West would continue indefinitely. The finds in the Black Hills district in 1875 and 1876, heralding deposits yielding eventually $100 million, led to the mushroom growth of Deadwood, home of Wild Bill Hickok, Deadwood Dick, Calamity Jane, and such lesser-known characters as California Jack and Poker Alice. The West continued to yield much gold and silver, especially silver, but big corporations produced nearly all of it. The mines around Deadwood were soon controlled by

one large company, Homestake Mining. Butte, Montana, was similarly dominated by Anaconda Mining.

This is the culminating irony of the history of the mining frontier: Shoestring prospectors, independent and enterprising, made the key discoveries. They established local institutions and supplied the West with much of its color and folklore. But the stockholders of large corporations, many of whom had never seen a mine, made off with the lion's share of the wealth. Those whose worship of gold was direct and incessant, the prospectors who peopled the mining towns and gave the frontier its character, mostly died poor, still seeking a prize as elusive if not as illusory as the pot of gold at the end of the rainbow.

For the mining of gold and silver is not essentially different from the mining of coal and iron. To operate profitably, large capital investments were required. Tunnels had to be blasted deep into the earth and miniature railroads laid out to transport the ore-bearing rock to the surface. Heavy machinery had to be purchased and transported to remote regions to extract the precious metal. To do this work, hundreds of skilled miners (mostly "deep" miners from Cornwall, in England) had to be imported and paid. Henry Comstock, the prospector who gave his name to the Comstock Lode, was luckier than most, but he sold his claims to the lode for a pittance, disposing of what

became one valuable mine for $40 and receiving only $10,000 for his share of the fabulous Ophir, the richest concentration of gold and silver ever found.

Though marked by violence, fraud, greed, and lost hopes, the gold rushes had valuable results. The most obvious was the new metal itself, which bolstered the financial position of the United States during and after the Civil War. Quantities of European goods needed for the war effort and for postwar economic development were paid for with the yield of the new mines. Gold and silver also caused a great increase of interest in the West. A valuable literature appeared, part imaginative, part reportorial, describing the mining camps and the life of the prospectors. These works fascinated contemporaries (as they have continued to fascinate succeeding generations when adapted to the motion picture and to television). Mark Twain's *Roughing It* (1872), based in part on his experiences in the Nevada mining country, is the most famous example of this literature.

Each new strike and rush, no matter how ephemeral, brought permanent settlers along with the prospectors: farmers, cattlemen, storekeepers, teamsters, lawyers, and ministers. The boomtowns had to import everything from bread, meat, and liquor to building materials and tools of every sort. Without the well-worn trails blazed by earlier hunters and migrants headed for Oregon and California, and of freighting companies equipped to haul heavy loads over long distances, the towns could not have existed. Some of the gold seekers saw from the start that a better living could be made supplying the needs of prospectors than looking for the elusive metal. Others, failing to find mineral wealth, took up whatever occupation they could rather than starve or return home empty-handed. In every mining town—along with the saloons and brothels—schools, churches, and newspaper offices sprang up.

The mines also speeded the political organization of the West. Colorado and Nevada became territories in 1861, Arizona and Idaho in 1863, Montana in 1864. Although Nevada was admitted before it had 60,000 residents (in 1864, to ratify the Thirteenth Amendment and help reelect Lincoln), most of these territories did not become states for decades. But because of the miners, the framework for future development was early established.

BIG BUSINESS AND THE LAND BONANZA

While the miners were engrossing the mineral wealth of the West, other interests were snapping up the region's choice farmland. Presumably the Homestead Act of 1862 had ended the reign of the speculator and the large landholder. An early amendment to the act even prevented husbands and wives from filing separate claims. The West, land reformers had assumed, would soon be dotted with 160-acre family farms.

They were doomed to disappointment. Most landless Americans were too poor to become farmers even when they could obtain land without cost. The expense of moving a family to the ever-receding frontier exceeded the means of many, and the cost of a plow, hoes and scythes, draft animals, a wagon, a well, fencing, and of building the simplest house, might come to $1000—a formidable barrier. As for the industrial workers for whom the free land was supposed to provide a "safety valve," they had neither the skills nor the inclination to become farmers. Homesteaders usually came from districts not far removed from frontier conditions. And despite the intent of the law, speculators often managed to obtain large tracts. They hired men to stake out claims, falsely swear that they had fulfilled the conditions laid down in the law for obtaining legal title, and then deed the land over to their employers.

Furthermore, 160 acres were not enough for raising livestock or for the kind of commercial agriculture that was developing west of the Mississippi. Congress made a feeble attempt to make larger holdings available to homesteaders by passing the Timber Culture Act of 1873, which permitted individuals to claim an additional 160 acres if they would agree to plant a quarter of it in trees within 10 years. This law proved helpful to some farmers in Kansas, Nebraska, and the Dakotas. Nevertheless, less than 25 percent of the 245,000 who took up land under it obtained final title to the property. Raising large numbers of seedling trees on the plains was a difficult task.

While futilely attempting to make a forest in parts of the treeless Plains, the government permitted private interests to gobble up and destroy many of the great forests that clothed the slopes of the Rockies and the Sierras. The Timber and Stone Act of 1878 allowed anyone to acquire a quarter section of forest land for $2.50 an acre if it was "unfit for civilization." This laxly drawn measure enabled lumber companies to obtain thousands of acres by hiring dummy entrymen, whom they marched in gangs to the land offices, paying them a few dollars for their time after they had signed over their claims.

Had the land laws been better drafted and more honestly enforced, it is still unlikely that the policy of granting free land to small homesteaders would have succeeded. Aside from the built-in difficulties faced by small-scale agriculturalists in the West, too many people in every section were eager to exploit the nation's land for their own profit. Immediately after the Civil War, Congress reserved 47.7 million acres of public land in the South for homesteaders, stopping all cash sales in the region. But in 1876 this policy was

reversed and the land thrown open. Speculators flocked to the feast in such numbers that the Illinois Central Railroad ran special trains from Chicago to Mississippi and Louisiana. Between 1877 and 1888 over 5.6 million acres were sold; much of the land was covered with valuable pine and cypress.

However they attained their acres, frontier farmers of the 1870s and 1880s grappled with novel problems as they pushed across the Plains with their families. The soil was rich, but the climate, especially in the semiarid regions beyond 98° longitude, made agriculture frequently difficult and often impossible. Blizzards, floods, grasshopper plagues, and prairie fires caused repeated heartaches, but periodic drought and searing summer heat were the worst hazards, destroying the hopes and fortunes of thousands.

At the same time, the flat immensity of the land, combined with newly available farm machinery and the development of rail connections with the East, encouraged the growth of enormous corporation-controlled "bonanza" farms. One such organization was the railroad-owned empire managed by Oliver Dalrymple in the Dakota Territory, which cultivated 25,000 acres of wheat in 1880. Dalrymple employed 200 pairs of harrows to prepare his soil, 125 seeders to sow his seed, and 155 binders to harvest his crop.

Bonanza farmers could buy supplies wholesale and obtain concessions from railroads and processors, but even the biggest organizations could not cope with prolonged drought, and most of the bonanza outfits failed in the dry years of the late 1880s. Those wise farmers who diversified their crops and cultivated their land intensively fared better in the long run, although even they could not hope to earn a profit in really dry years.

Despite the hazards of Plains agriculture, the region became the breadbasket of America in the decades following the Civil War. By 1889 Minnesota topped the nation in wheat production, and ten years later four of the five leading wheat states lay west of the Mississippi. The Plains also accounted for heavy percentages of the nation's other cereal crops, together with immense quantities of beef, pork, and mutton.

Like other exploiters of the nation's resources, farmers took whatever they could from the soil with little heed for preserving its fertility and preventing erosion. The consequent national loss was less apparent because it was diffuse and slow to assume drastic proportions, but it was nonetheless real.

WESTERN RAILROAD BUILDING

Further exploitation of land resources by private interests resulted from the government's policy of subsidizing western railroads. Here was a clear illustration of the conflict between the idea of the West as a national heritage to be disposed of to deserving citizens and the concept of the region as a cornucopia pouring forth riches to be gathered up and carted off by anyone powerful and determined enough to take them. When it came to a choice between giving a particular tract to railroads or to homesteaders, the homesteaders nearly always lost out. On the other hand, the swift development of western railroads was essential if farmers, miners, and cattle ranchers were to prosper.

Unless the government had been willing to build the transcontinental lines itself—and this was unthinkable in an age dominated by belief in individual exploitation—some system of subsidy was essential. Private investors would not hazard the huge sums needed to lay tracks across hundreds of miles of rugged, empty country when traffic over the road could not possibly profit for many years. It might appear that subsidizing construction by direct outlays of public funds would have been adopted, but that idea had few supporters. Most voters were wary of entrusting the dispensing of large sums to politicians. Grants of land seemed a sensible way of financing construction. The method avoided direct outlays of public funds, for the companies could pledge the land as security for bond issues or sell it directly for cash.

In many cases the value of the land granted might be recovered by the government when it sold other lands in the vicinity, for such properties would certainly be worth more after transportation facilities to eastern markets had been constructed. "Why," the governor of one eastern state asked in 1867, "should private individuals be called upon to make a useless sacrifice of their means, when railroads can be constructed by the unity of public and private interests, and made profitable to all?"

Federal land grants to railroads began in 1850 with those allotted to the Illinois Central. Over the next two decades about 49 million acres were given to various lines indirectly in the form of grants to the states, but the most lavish gifts of the public domain were those made directly to builders of intersectional trunk lines. These roads received more than 155 million acres, although about 25 million acres reverted to the government because some companies failed to lay the required miles of track. About 75 percent of this land went to aid the construction of four transcontinental railroads: the Union Pacific–Central Pacific line, running from Nebraska to San Francisco, completed in 1869; the Atchison, Topeka and Santa Fe, running from Kansas City to Los Angeles by way of Santa Fe and Albuquerque, completed in 1883; the Southern Pacific, running from San Francisco to New Orleans by way of Yuma and El Paso, completed in 1883; and the Northern Pacific, running

▲ Chinese workers building a railroad trestle in the Sierras (1877). "Without them," Leland Stanford, president of the Central Pacific Railroad said, "it would be impossible to complete the western portion of this great national highway." Some Chinese were drawn from the gold fields further north, and others were imported from China, under five-year contracts with the railroads in which they were paid $10 or $12 a month.

from Duluth, Minnesota, to Portland, Oregon, completed in 1883.

The Pacific Railway Act of 1862 established the pattern for these grants. It gave the builders of the Union Pacific and Central Pacific railroads 5 square miles of public land on each side of their right-of-way for each mile of track laid. The land was allotted in alternate sections, forming a pattern like a checkerboard, the squares of one color representing railroad property, the other government property. Presumably this arrangement benefited the entire nation since half the land close to the railroad remained in public hands.

However, whenever grants were made to railroads, the adjacent government lands were not opened to homesteaders—on the theory that free land in the immediate vicinity of a line would prevent the road from disposing of its properties at good prices. Since, in addition to the land granted the railroads, a wide zone of "indemnity" lands was reserved to allow the roads to choose alternative sites to make up for lands that settlers had already taken up within the checkerboard, homesteading was in fact prohibited near land-grant railroads. More than 20 years af-

ter receiving its immense grant, the Northern Pacific was still attempting to keep homesteaders from filing in the indemnity zone. President Cleveland finally put a stop to this in 1887, saying that he could find "no evidence" that "this vast tract is necessary for the fulfillment of the grant."

Historians have argued at length about the fairness of the land-grant system. No railroad corporation waxed fat directly from the sale of its lands, which were sold at prices averaging between $2 and $5 an acre. Collectively the roads took in between $400 million and $500 million from this source, but only over the course of a century. Land-grant lines encouraged the growth of the West by advertising their property widely and by providing cheap transportation for prospective settlers and efficient shipping services for farmers. They were required by law to carry troops and handle government business free or at reduced rates, which saved the government millions over the years. At the same time the system imposed no effective restraints on how the railroads used the funds raised with federal aid. Being able to lay track with money obtained from land grants, the operators tended to be extravagant and often downright corrupt.

The construction of the Central Pacific in the 1860s illustrates how the system encouraged extravagance. The line was controlled by four businessmen: Collis P. Huntington ("scrupulously dishonest" but an excellent manager); Leland Stanford, a Sacramento grocer and politician; Mark Hopkins, a hardware merchant; and Charles Crocker, a hulking, relentless driver of men who had come to California during the gold rush and made a small fortune as a merchant. The Central Pacific and the Union Pacific were given, in addition to their land grants, loans in the form of government bonds—from $16,000 to $48,000 for each mile of track laid, depending on the difficulty of the terrain. The two competed with each other for the subsidies, the Central Pacific building eastward from Sacramento, the Union Pacific westward from Nebraska. They put huge crews to work grading and laying track, bringing up supplies over the already completed road. The Union Pacific employed Civil War veterans and Irish immigrants; the Central, Chinese immigrants.

This plan favored the Union Pacific. While the Central Pacific was inching up the gorges and granite of the mighty Sierras, the Union Pacific was racing across the level plains laying 540 miles of track between 1865 and 1867. Once beyond the Sierras, the Central Pacific would have easy going across the Nevada–Utah plateau country, but by then it might be too late to prevent the Union Pacific from making off with most of the government aid.

Crocker managed the Central Pacific construction crews. He wasted huge sums by working

through the winter in the High Sierras. Often the men labored in tunnels dug through 40-foot snow-drifts to get at the frozen ground. To speed construction of the Summit Tunnel, Crocker had a shaft cut down from above so that crews could work out from the middle as well as in from each end. In 1866, over the most difficult terrain, he laid 28 miles of track, at a cost of more than $280,000 a mile. Experts later estimated that 70 percent of this sum could have been saved had speed not been a factor. Such prodigality made economic sense to Huntington, Stanford, Hopkins, and Crocker because of the profits they were making through its construction company and because of the gains they could count on once they reached the flat country beyond the Sierras, where costs would amount to only half the federal aid.

Crocker's herculean efforts paid off. The mountains were conquered, and then the crews raced across the Great Basin to Salt Lake City and beyond. The meeting of the rails—the occasion of a national celebration—took place at Promontory, north of Ogden, Utah, on May 10, 1869. Leland Stanford drove the final ceremonial golden spike with a silver hammer.[2] The Union Pacific had built 1086 miles of track, the Central 689 miles.

In the long run the wasteful way in which the Central Pacific was built hurt the road severely. It was ill constructed, over grades too steep and around curves too sharp, and burdened with debts that were too large. Steep grades meant that heavier, more expensive locomotives burning more coal were needed to pull lighter loads—a sure way to lower profits. Such was the fate of nearly all the railroads constructed with the help of government subsidies.

The only transcontinental railroad built without land grants was the Great Northern, running from St. Paul, Minnesota, to the Pacific. Spending private capital, its guiding genius, James J. Hill, was compelled to build economically and to plan carefully. As a result, his was the only transcontinental line to weather the depression of the 1890s without going into bankruptcy.

THE CATTLE KINGDOM

VIDEO
Cowboys and Cattle

While miners were digging out the mineral wealth of the West and railroaders were taking possession of much of its land, another group was exploiting endless acres of its grass. For 20 years after the Civil War cattlemen and sheep raisers dominated huge areas of the High Plains, making millions of dollars by grazing their herds on lands they did not own.

Columbus brought the first cattle to the New World in 1493, on his second voyage, and later conquistadores took them to every corner of Spain's American empire. Mexico proved to be so well suited to cattle raising that many were allowed to roam loose. They multiplied rapidly, and by the late eighteenth century what is now southern Texas harbored enormous herds. The beasts interbred with nondescript "English" cattle, brought into the area by settlers from the United States, to produce the Texas longhorn. Hardy, wiry, ill-tempered, and fleet, with horns often attaining a spread of 6 feet, these animals were far from ideal as beef cattle and almost as hard to capture as wild horses, but they existed in southern Texas by the millions, most of them unowned.

The lack of markets and transportation explains why Texas cattle were lightly regarded. But conditions were changing. Industrial growth in the East was causing an increase in the urban population and a consequent rise in the demand for food. At the same time, the expansion of the railroad network made it possible to move cattle cheaply over long distances. As the iron rails inched across the Plains, astute cattlemen began to do some elementary figuring. Longhorns could be had locally for $3 and $4 a head. In the northern cities they would bring ten times that much, perhaps even more. Why not round them up and herd them northward to the railroads, allowing them to feed along the way on the abundant grasses of the Plains? The land was unoccupied and owned by the federal government. Anyone could drive cattle across it without paying a fee or asking anyone's permission. The grass the cattle ate on the way swiftly renewed itself.

In 1866 a number of Texans drove large herds northward toward Sedalia, Missouri, railhead of the Missouri Pacific. This route took the herds through wooded and settled country and across Indian reservations, which provoked many difficulties. At the same time Charles Goodnight and Oliver Loving successfully drove 2000 head in a great arc west to the New Mexico Territory and then north to Colorado.

The next year the drovers, inspired by a clever young Illinois cattle dealer named Joseph G. McCoy and other entrepreneurs, led their herds north by a more westerly route, across unsettled grasslands, to the Kansas Pacific line at Abilene, Kansas, which McCoy described as "a very small, dead place, consisting of about one dozen log huts." They earned excellent profits, and during the next five years about 1.5 million head made the "long drive" over the Chisholm Trail to Abilene, where they were sold to

DOCUMENT
McCoy, Chisholm Trail

---

[2]A mysterious "San Francisco jeweler" passed among the onlookers, taking orders for souvenir watch chains that he proposed to make from the spike at $5 each.

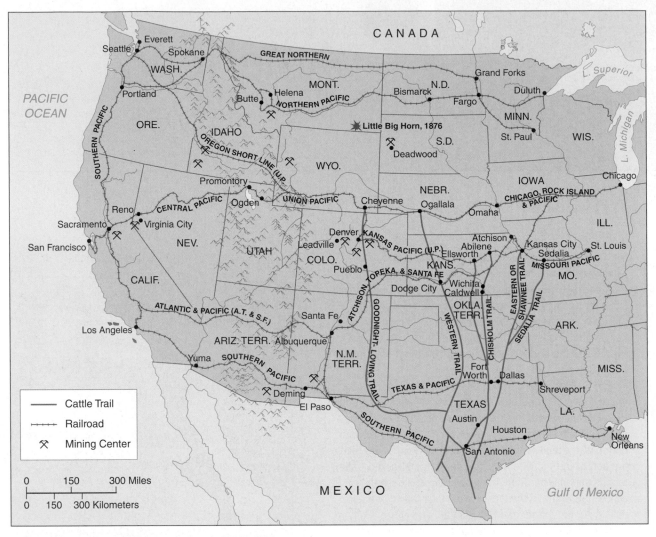

▲ **The West: Cattle, Railroads, and Mining, 1850–1893**

ranchers, feedlot operators, and the agents of eastern meatpackers. Other shipping points sprang up as the railroads pushed westward. According to the best estimates 10 million head were driven north before the practice ended in the mid-1880s. (For the story of one cowboy, see the American Lives essay on Nat Love, pp. 470–471.)

OPEN-RANGE RANCHING

Soon cattlemen discovered that the hardy Texas stock could survive the winters of the northern Plains. Attracted by the apparently limitless forage, they began to bring up herds to stock the vast regions where the buffalo had so recently roamed. Introducing pedigreed Hereford bulls, they improved the stock without weakening its resistance to harsh conditions. By 1880 some 4.5 million head had spread across the sea of grass that ran from Kansas to Montana and west to the Rockies.

The prairie grasses offered ranchers a bonanza almost as valuable as the gold mines. Open-range ranching required actual ownership of no more than a few acres along some watercourse. In this semiarid region, control of water enabled a rancher to dominate all the surrounding area back to the divide separating his range from the next stream without investing a cent in the purchase of land. His cattle, wandering freely on the public domain, fattened on grass owned by all the people, to be turned into beefsteak and leather for the profit of the rancher.

Theoretically, anyone could pasture stock on the open range, but without access to water it was impossible to do so. "I have 2 miles of running water," a cattleman said in testifying before the Public Land Commission. "That accounts for my ranch being where it is. The next water from me in one direction is 23 miles; now no man can have a ranch between

▶ *text continues on page 470*

American Lives

Nat Love

Nat Love, a slave, was born on a plantation in Davidson County, Tennessee in 1854. He never knew his exact birth date because his owner did not trouble to record such facts. Nat's father was a foreman on the plantation; his mother milked cows, cooked, and operated a loom. Although Love described his master as "kind and indulgent," his earliest memories were of begging for scraps "like a pet dog" from his master's table.

The Civil War changed plantation life. The master served in Lee's army, and wartime shortages were aggravated when Union troops helped themselves to provisions. But the presence of Union soldiers exhilarated Nat and his friends, who played war whenever they could. Because none would take the part of the Confederates, the slave boys attacked "rebel" rabbits and insects. Their victory over bumble bees they called "the Battle of the Wilderness," their taking of a hornet's nest, the "capture of Fort Sumter."

When Love's master returned after Appomattox, he did not tell the slaves that they were free. Word spread, of course, and Love's father eventually rented twenty acres from his former master. On Sundays, the only day without chores, Nat and his friends sneaked into the woods and fought "rock battles." After one of them was nearly killed, their parents put an end to this amusement. Nat then spent Sundays at a nearby horse farm, where he learned how to ride. Soon he was earning 10 cents for every colt he "broke."

But Nat's father died, and the family's circumstances were dire. None of the children had shoes; much of the time they were nearly naked. When they weren't working in the cornfield or garden, they collected nuts and berries. Nat grew restless with the drudgery of farm life and longed to see the world. His opportunity came when he won a horse in a raffle and sold it back to the man running the raffle. He bought clothing and food for his family, and, in February 1869, he set out for the frontier. He was fifteen years old.

Months later, he arrived in Dodge City, Kansas, "a typical frontier city, with a great many saloons, dance halls, and gambling houses, and very little of anything else." At a camp outside of town, he met a group of cowboys and asked for a

▲ Nat Love, posed here with the requisite implements, claimed to have been the "Deadwood Dick" on whom a series of novels was based.

job. Eager to have some fun with the black "tenderfoot," they agreed, provided that he could prove he could ride; then they put him on the wildest horse in camp. Love held desperately onto the bucking bronco, much to everyone's astonishment. The boss hired him at $30 a month. He also gave Nat a saddle, a Colt 45 pistol and a new name—"Love" being unsuitable for a cowboy. Nat was now "Red River Dick."

His outfit soon left Dodge and rode south to collect another herd in Texas. Three days later, they were attacked by nearly a hundred mounted Indians. "When I saw them coming after us and heard their blood curdling yell, I was too badly scared to run," Nat recalled. When the cowboys started shooting, he did, too. Before the Indians were driven away, they had killed one cowboy and made off with most of the horses and provisions. The cowboy was buried in a blanket beneath a pile of stones. Red River Dick and the others walked most of the way to Texas.

Over the next three years, Dick served with outfits that drove cattle to grazing ranges throughout the West or from the ranges to markets in Dodge City, Abilene, Wichita, Ellsworth, and Caldwell (see the map on p. 469). Every spring and fall the ranchers staged a great roundup, driving in all the cattle to a central place, separating them by the brands, culling steers for shipment to market, and branding new calves. Dick specialized as a brand reader. He "cut out" those belonging to his employer and drove them back to that herd.

Love's life was filled with adventure. Disputes over ownership often led to gunfights. On Christmas Day, 1872, an argument over a horse erupted into a gunfight in Holbrook, Arizona, and several of Dick's friends were killed. In 1876, while Dick was driving five hundred steers from the Rio Grande to a ranch in the Shoshone mountains of northern Wyoming, Indians attacked and stampeded the cattle. The battle raged through the night and the steers went wild. In the morning, several score Indians were dead, most of them trampled to death by the cattle. Several nights later, a buffalo stampede tore through the camp, scattering the cattle and killing another cowboy. Another time, Dick broke up a robbery of a Union Pacific railroad station. After he won a roping and riding competition in Deadwood, South Dakota, he was known as "Deadwood Dick." Shortly afterward, while hunting strays, he was shot by Indians and captured. When he recovered, the Indian chief offered him his daughter in marriage along with 100 ponies. Instead Dick stole a horse and escaped.

By the late 1880s, railroads were hauling cattle from the grazing ranges to slaughterhouses in Kansas City, Omaha, Chicago, and St. Louis. The heyday of the cowboy was over. In 1889, Dick went to Denver and got married. The following year he found a job as a porter on the Pullman Railroad cars. He died in 1921.

This account of the life of Nat Love is based largely on his 1907 autobiography. In that book, Love claimed that he was the inspiration for the popular "Deadwood Dick" dime novels by Edward L. Wheeler, first published in the 1870s. He also insisted that he had been shot fourteen times, could drink enormous volumes of whiskey without impairment, and was a friend of "Buffalo Bill" Cody, Kit Carson, and Jesse James. Perhaps the most dubious of his claims was that he never encountered racial prejudice. Actually, cowboys were a mixed lot: Mexican *vaqueros* and African Americans made up about a third of them, along with many Texans, Civil War veterans, former miners, and, in the words of Theodore Roosevelt, "wild spirits from every land." Love's life, like so much about the frontier west, was the stuff of legend. (Nat Love's autobiography is available online at http://docsouth.unc.edu/authors.html.)

these two places. I have control of the grass, the same as though I owned it." By having his cowhands take out homestead claims along watercourses in his region, a rancher could greatly expand the area he dominated. In the late 1870s one Colorado cattle baron controlled an area roughly the size of Connecticut and Rhode Island even though he owned only 105 small parcels that totaled about 15,500 acres.

With the demand for meat rising and transportation cheap, princely fortunes could be made in a few years. Capitalists from the East and from Europe began to pour funds into the business. Eastern "dudes" like Theodore Roosevelt, a young New York assemblyman who sank over $50,000 in his Elkhorn Ranch in the Dakota Territory in 1883, bought up cattle as a sort of profitable hobby. (Roosevelt, clad in buckskin and bearing a small armory of rifles and six-shooters, made quite a splash in Dakota, but not as a rancher.) Soon large outfits such as the Nebraska Land and Cattle Company, controlled by British investors, and the Union Cattle Company of Wyoming, a $3 million corporation, dominated the business, just as large companies had taken over most of the important gold and silver mines.

Unlike other exploiters of the West's resources, cattle ranchers did not at first injure or reduce any public resource. Grass eaten by their stock annually renewed itself; droppings from the animals enriched the soil. Furthermore, ranchers poached on the public domain because there was no reasonable way for them to obtain legal possession of the large areas necessary to raise cattle on the Plains. Federal land laws made no allowance for the special conditions of the semiarid West.

A system to take account for those conditions was soon devised by Major John Wesley Powell, later the director of the United States Geological Survey. His *Report on the Lands of the Arid Region of the United States* (1879) suggested that western lands be divided into three classes: irrigable lands, timber lands, and "pasturage" lands. On the pasturage lands the "farm unit" ought to be at least 2560 acres (four sections), Powell urged. Groups of these units should be organized into "pasturage districts" in which the ranchers "should have the right to make their own regulations for the division of lands, the use of the water . . . and for the pasturage of lands in common or in severalty."

BARBED-WIRE WARFARE

Congress refused to change the land laws in any basic way, and this had two harmful effects. First, it encouraged fraud: Those who could not get title to enough land honestly turned to subterfuge. The Desert Land Act (1877) allowed anyone to obtain 640 acres in the arid states for $1.25 an acre provided the owner irrigated part of it within three years. Since the original claimant could transfer the holding, the ranchers set their cowboys and other hands to filing claims, which were then signed over to them. Over 2.6 million acres were taken up under the act, and according to the best estimate, 95 percent of the claims were fraudulent—no sincere effort was made to irrigate the land.

Second, overcrowding became a problem that led to serious conflicts, even killings, because no one had uncontestable title to the land. The leading ranchers banded together in cattlemen's associations to deal with overcrowding and with such problems as quarantine regulations, water rights, and thievery. In most cases these associations devised effective and sensible rules, but their functions would better have been performed by the government, as such matters usually are.

To keep other ranchers' cattle from those sections of the public domain they considered their own, the associations and many individuals began to fence huge areas. This was possible only because of the invention in 1874 of barbed wire by Joseph F. Glidden, an Illinois farmer. By the 1880s thousands of miles of the new fencing had been strung across the Plains, often across roads and in a few cases around entire communities. "Barbed-wire wars" resulted, fought by rancher against rancher, cattleman against sheepman, herder against farmer. The associations tried to police their fences and to punish anyone who cut their wire. Posted signs gave dire warnings to trespassers. "The Son of a Bitch who opens this fence had better look out for his scalp," one such sign announced, another fine statement of the philosophy of the age.

By stringing so much wire the cattlemen were unwittingly destroying their own way of doing business. On a truly open range, cattle could fend for themselves, instinctively finding water during droughts, drifting safely downwind before blizzards. Barbed wire prevented their free movement. During winter storms these slender strands became as lethal as high-tension wires: the drifting cattle piled up against them and died by the thousands.

Resources and Conflict in the West

The boom times were ending. Overproduction was driving down the price of beef; expenses were on the rise; many sections of the range were badly overgrazed. The dry summer of 1886 left the stock in such poor condition as winter approached that the *Rocky Mountain Husbandman* urged its readers to sell their cattle despite the prevailing low prices rather than "endanger the whole herd by having the range overstocked."

Some ranchers took this advice; those who did not made a fatal error. Winter that year arrived early and with unparalleled fury. Blizzards raged and tem-

▲ In 1885 masked Nebraskans seeking access to water posed for photographer S. D. Butcher, who captioned the picture "Settlers taking the law into their own hands: Cutting 15 miles of the Brighton Ranch fence."

peratures plummeted far below zero. Cattle crowded into low places only to be engulfed in giant snow-drifts; barbed wire took a fearful toll. When spring finally came, the streams were choked with rotting carcasses. Between 80 and 90 percent of all cattle on the range were dead. "We have had a perfect smashup all through the cattle country," Theodore Roosevelt wrote sadly in April 1887 from Elkhorn Ranch.

That cruel winter finished open-range cattle-raising. The large companies were bankrupt; many independent operators, Roosevelt among them, became discouraged and sold out. When the industry revived, it was on a smaller, more efficiently organized scale. The fencing movement continued, but now ranchers enclosed only the land they actually owned. It then became possible to bring in pedigreed bulls to improve the breed. Cattle-raising, like mining before it, ceased to be an adventure in rollicking individualism and became a business.

By the late 1880s the bonanza days of the West were over. No previous frontier had caught the imagination of Americans so completely as the Great West,

with its heroic size, its awesome emptiness, its massive, sculptured beauty. Most of what Walter Prescott Webb, author of the classic study *The Great Plains* (1931) called the "primary windfalls" of the region—the furs, the precious metals, the forests, the cattle, and the grass—had been snatched up by first comers and by individuals already wealthy. Big companies were taking over all the West's resources. The frontier was no more.

But the frontier never existed except as an intellectual construction among white settlers and those who wrote about them. To the Indians, the land was simply home. The "conquest of the frontier" was thus an appealing evasion: it transformed the harmful actions and policies of the nation into an expression of human progress, the march westward of "civilization."

"Civilization," though, was changing. The nation was becoming more powerful, richer, and larger, and its economic structure more complex and diversified as the West yielded its treasures. But the East, and especially eastern industrialists and financiers, was increasingly dominating the economy of the entire nation.

MILESTONES

1859	Discovery of the Comstock Lode lures miners west		1879	Specie payments resume
1864	Chivington massacre of Cheyenne		1881	Booker T. Washington founds Tuskegee Institute for blacks
1869	Union Pacific Railroad completed		1883	Supreme Court overturns Civil Rights Act of 1875 in *Civil Rights Cases*
	Board of Indian Commissioners established		1886–1887	Blizzards end open-range ranching
1873	Timber Culture Act encourages western forestation		1887	Dawes Severalty Act splits tribal lands
1875	Civil Rights Act requires equal access to public accommodations		1888	Englishman James Bryce analyzes American political system in *The American Commonwealth*
1876	Sioux slaughter Custer's cavalry at Battle of Little Bighorn		1890–1900	Blacks are deprived of the vote in the South
1877	Desert Land Act favors ranchers		1895	Booker T. Washington urges self-improvement in Atlanta Compromise speech
	U.S troops capture Cheif Joseph of Nez Perce after 1000-mile retreat			
1878	Timber and Stone Act favors lumber companies		1896	Supreme Court upholds "separate but equal" in *Plessy* v. *Ferguson*
1879	Major Powell's *Report on the Lands of the Arid Region* suggests division of West			

SUPPLEMENTARY READING

Recent historians of the West do not regard it as a frontier to be settled, but as a region where white settlers and Native American peoples converged, to the destruction of the latter's way of life. For the older view, see Frederick Jackson Turner's *The Frontier in American History* (1920), which has been updated in R. A. Billington and Martin Ridge, *Westward Expansion* (1982). For a summary of the newer interpretation, see Gregory H. Nobles, *American Frontiers* (1997). See also Patricia Nelson Limerick, *The Legacy of Conquest* (1987), Richard White, *"It's Your Misfortune and None of My Own"* (1991), and Elliott West, *Contested Plains: Indians, Goldseekers, and the Rush to Colorado* (1998).

The economic, political, and legal ideas current in this period are covered in David M. Wrobel, *Promised Lands* (2002), Sidney Fine, *Laissez Faire and the General Welfare State* (1956), and James W. Hurst, *Law and the Conditions of Freedom in the Nineteenth Century United States* (1956).

On government policy and white attitudes toward Indians, see Robert F. Berkhofer, Jr., *The White Man's Indian* (1978), Robert Wooster, *The Military and U.S. Indian Policy* (1988), and Andrew C. Isenberg, *The Destruction of the Bison* (2000).

On race relations in the South, see Michael Perman, *Struggle for Mastery: Disfranchisement in the South, 1888-1908* (2001), Leon Litwack, *Trouble in Mind* (1998), Glenda E. Gilmore, *Gender and Jim Crow* (1996), Joel Williamson, *The Crucible of Race* (1984), C. Vann Woodward, *The Strange Career of Jim Crow* (1966), and Samuel Spencer, *Booker T. Washington* (1967). For a thoughtful study of the persistence of the black elite in Washington,

D.C., see Jacqueline M. Moore, *Leading the Race* (1999). On immigration, see Ronald Takaki, *Strangers from a Different Shore: A History of Asian Americans* (1989), and John Higham, *Strangers in the Land* (1955).

Two superb recent studies, in addition to Elliott West, cited above, have transformed our understanding of the California gold rush: Susan Lee Johnson, *Roaring Camp: The Social World of the California Gold Rush* (2000), and Malcolm J. Rohrbough, *Days of Gold: The California Gold Rush and the American Nation* (1997). Bonanza farming is described in H. M. Drache, *The Day of the Bonanza* (1964). For women on the frontier, see also Julie R. Jeffrey, *Frontier Women* (1979), John Mack Faragher, *Women and Men on the Overland Trail* (1979), Sandra L. Myres, *Westering Women and the Frontier Experience* (1982), and Paula Petric, *No Step Backward: Women and Family on the Rocky Mountain Frontier* (1987).

For a compelling account of the development of transcontinental railroads see David Haward Bain, *Empire Express: Building the First Transcontinental Railroad* (1999). See also David Lavender, *The Great Persuader* (1970), Albro Martin, *James J. Hill* (1976), and Robert G. Athearn, *Union Pacific Country* (1971).

On cattle ranching on the Plains, a good account is Lewis Atherton, *The Cattle Kings* (1961), but see also Don Worcester, *The Chisholm Trail* (1980). For the cowboy and his life, see Joe B. Frantz and Julian E. Choate, *The American Cowboy* (1955), and Robert R. Dykstra, *The Cattle Towns* (1968).

SUGGESTED WEBSITES

Indian Affairs: Laws and Treaties, Compiled and Edited by Charles J. Kappler (1904)
http://digital.library.okstate.edu/kappler/
This digitized text at Oklahoma State University includes pre-removal treaties with the five Civilized Tribes and other tribes.

The Northern Great Plains, 1880–1920: Photographs from the Fred Hulstrand and F. A. Pazandak Photograph Collections
http://memory.loc.gov/ammem/award97/ndfahtml/ngphome.html
This American Memory site from the Library of Congress contains "two collections from the Institute for Regional Studies at North Dakota State University" with "900 photographs of rural and small-town life at the turn of the century." Included are "images of sod homes and the people who built them; images of farms and the machinery that made them prosper; and images of one-room schools and the children who were educated in them."

The Transcontinental Railroad
http://www.sfmuseum.org/hist1/rail.html
The Museum of the City of San Francisco site has excellent information on the Transcontinental Railroad.

Geronimo
http://odur.let.rug.nl/~usa/B/geronimo/geronixx.htm
This site contains biographical and autobiographical information about the famous Native American who resisted European American domination.

National Museum of the American Indian
http://www.si.edu/
The Smithsonian Institution maintains this site, providing information about the museum. The museum is dedicated to everything about Native Americans.

African American Perspectives: Pamphlets from the Daniel A. P. Murry Collections, 1818–1907
http://memory.loc.gov/ammem/aap/aaphome.html
This collection includes writings of famous African Americans, including Frederick Douglass, Booker T. Washington, Ida B. Wells-Barnett, Benjamin W. Arnett, Alexander Crummel, and Emanuel Love.

An Industrial Giant

▼ A photograph by William Henry Jackson of Chicago, looking north on Wabash from Adams. Jackson, who specialized in western landscape photographs, was struck by the rectangular symmetry of the modern city.

When the Civil War began, the country's industrial output, while important and increasing, did not approach that of major European powers. By the end of the century the United States had become far and away the colossus among world manufacturers, dwarfing the production of Great Britain and Germany. The world had never seen such a remarkable example of rapid economic growth. The value of American manufactured products rose from $1.8 billion in 1859 to over $13 billion in 1899. Modern economists estimate that the output of goods and services in the country (the gross national product, or GNP) increased by 44 percent between 1874 and 1883 and continued to expand in succeeding years. This growth was not confined to the Northeast. Wisconsin, for example, underwent a major transformation between 1873 and 1893. An economy based on grain and lumber became a mainly urban-centered industrial economy. The consequences for the nation's political institutions, if less visible, were equally profound.

ESSENTIALS OF INDUSTRIAL GROWTH

American manufacturing flourished for many reasons. New natural resources were discovered and exploited steadily, thereby increasing opportunities. These opportunities, in turn, attracted the brightest and most energetic of a vigorous and expanding population. The growth of

the country added constantly to the size of the national market, and protective tariffs shielded that market from foreign competition. Foreign capital, however, entered the market freely, in part because tariffs kept out so many foreign goods.

The dominant spirit of the time encouraged businessmen to maximum effort by emphasizing progress, yet it also produced a generation of Robber Barons. The energetic search for wealth led to corrupt business practices such as stock manipulation, bribery, and cutthroat competition and ultimately to "combinations in restraint of trade," a kind of American euphemism for monopoly. European immigrants provided the additional labor needed by expanding industry; 2.5 million arrived in the 1870s, twice that number in the 1880s. These immigrants saw America as a land of opportunity, and for many, probably most, it was that indeed. But for others, emigrating to the United States meant a constant struggle for survival; dreary, often unhealthy living conditions; and grinding poverty.

It was a period of rapid advance in basic science, and technicians created a bountiful harvest of new machines, processes, and power sources that increased productivity in many industries and created new industries as well. In agriculture there were what one contemporary expert called "an endless variety of cultivators," better harvesters and binding machines, and combines capable of threshing and bagging 450 pounds of grain a minute. An 1886 report of the Illinois Bureau of Labor Statistics claimed that "new machinery has displaced fully 50 percent of the muscular labor formerly required to do a given amount of work in the manufacture of agricultural implements." Of course that also meant that many farm families were "displaced" from their homes and livelihoods, and it made farmers dependent on the vagaries of distant markets and powerful economic forces they could not control.

As a result of improvements in the milling of grain, packaged cereals appeared on the American breakfast table. The commercial canning of food, spurred by the "automatic line" canning factory, expanded so rapidly that by 1887 a writer in *Good Housekeeping* could say: "Housekeeping is getting to be ready made, as well as clothing." The Bonsack cigarette-rolling machine created a new industry that changed the habits of millions. George B. Eastman created still another with his development of mass-produced, roll photographic film and the simple but efficient Kodak camera. The perfection of the typewriter by the Remington company in the 1880s revolutionized the way office work was performed. But even some of these inventions were mixed blessings. The harm done by the popularity of cigarettes, for example, needs no explanation.

RAILROADS: THE FIRST BIG BUSINESS

In 1866, returning from his honeymoon in Europe, 30-year-old Charles Francis Adams, Jr., grandson and great-grandson of presidents, full of ambition and ready, as he put it, to confront the world "face to face," looked about in search of a career. "Surveying the whole field," he later explained, "I fixed on the railroad system as the most developing force and the largest field of the day, and determined to attach myself to it." Adams's judgment was acute: For the next 25 years the railroads were probably the most significant element in American economic development, railroad executives the most powerful people in the country.

Railroads were important first as an industry in themselves. Fewer than 35,000 miles of track existed when Lee laid down his sword at Appomattox. In 1875 railroad mileage exceeded 74,000 and the skeleton of the network was complete. Over the next two decades the skeleton was fleshed out. In 1890 the mature but still-growing system took in over $1 billion in passenger and freight revenues. (The federal government's income in 1890 was only $403 million.) The value of railroad properties and equipment was more than $8.7 billion. The national railroad debt of $5.1 billion was almost five times the national debt of $1.1 billion! By 1900 the nation had 193,000 miles of track.

The emphasis in railroad construction after 1865 was on organizing integrated systems. The lines had high fixed costs: taxes, interest on their bonds, maintenance of track and rolling stock, and salaries of office personnel. A short train with half-empty cars required almost as many workers and as much fuel to operate as a long one jammed with freight or passengers. To earn profits the railroads had to carry as much traffic as possible. They therefore spread out feeder lines to draw business to their main lines the way the root network of a tree draws water into its trunk.

Before the Civil War, passengers and freight could travel by rail from beyond Chicago and St. Louis to the Atlantic coast, but only after the war did true interregional trunk lines appear. In 1861, for example, the New York Central ran from Albany to Buffalo. One could proceed from Buffalo to Chicago, but on a different company's trains. In 1867 the New York Central passed into the hands of "Commodore" Cornelius Vanderbilt, who had made a large fortune in the shipping business. Vanderbilt already controlled lines running from Albany to New York City; now he merged these properties with the New York Central. In 1873 he integrated the Lake Shore and Michigan Southern into his empire and two years later the Michigan Central. At his death in 1877 the

▲ The daily passenger train of the Union Pacific on its transcontinental line, crossing the Rocky Mountains. In 1869, just after the transcontinental line was completed, travel from New York City to San Francisco took nearly a week. First class passengers, who rode in special cars such as those pictured above, paid a fare of $150. Second-class or immigrant passengers paid less than half as much, but they were crowded into cars that were attached to freight trains.

New York Central operated a network of over 4500 miles of track between New York City and most of the principal cities of the Midwest.

While Vanderbilt was putting together the New York Central complex, Thomas A. Scott was fusing roads to Cincinnati, Indianapolis, St. Louis, and Chicago to his Pennsylvania Railroad, which linked Pittsburgh and Philadelphia. In 1871 the Pennsylvania line obtained access to New York; soon it reached Baltimore and Washington. By 1869 another important system, the Erie, extended from New York to Cleveland, Cincinnati, and St. Louis. Soon thereafter it too tapped the markets of Chicago and other cities. In 1874 the Baltimore and Ohio rail line also obtained access to Chicago.

The transcontinentals were trunk lines from the start; the emptiness of the western country would have made short lines unprofitable, and builders quickly grasped the need for direct connections to eastern markets and thorough integration of feeder lines.

The dominant system builder of the Southwest was Jay Gould, a soft-spoken, unostentatious-looking man who was in fact ruthless, cynical, and aggressive. Another railroad president once called Gould a "perfect eel." Gould took over the Kansas Pacific, running from Denver to Kansas City, and consolidated it with the Union Pacific and the Missouri Pacific, a line from Kansas City to St. Louis. Often he put together such properties merely to unload them on other railroads at a profit, but his grasp of the importance of integration was sound.

In the Northwest, Henry Villard, a German-born former newspaperman, constructed another great complex based on his control of the Northern Pacific.

▲ The Union Railroad Station in Montgomery, Alabama, designed by Henry Hobson Richardson, the nation's foremost architect of the era. Richardson borrowed ideas from the past—the arches evoked the early Middle Ages—but adapted them to contemporary purposes. This building's massiveness and horizontal lines hinted at the power and reach of the railroads.

James J. Hill controlled the Great Northern system, still another western network.

The Civil War had highlighted the need for thorough railroad connections in the South. Shortly after the conflict the Chesapeake and Ohio opened a direct line from Norfolk, Virginia, to Cincinnati. By the late 1880s, the Richmond and West Point Terminal Company controlled an 8558-mile network. Like other southern trunk lines such as the Louisville and Nashville and the Atlantic Coast Line, this system was controlled by northern capitalists.

The trunk lines interconnected and thus had to standardize many of their activities. This, in turn, led to the standardization of other aspects of life. The present system of time zones was developed in 1883 by the railroads. The standard track gauge (4 feet 8½ inches) was established in 1886. Standardized car coupling and braking mechanisms, standard signal systems, even standard methods of accounting were essential to the effective functioning of the network.

The lines sought to work out fixed rates for carrying different types of freight, charging more for valuable manufactured goods than for bulky products like coal or wheat, and they agreed to permit rate concessions to shippers when necessary to avoid hauling empty cars. In other words, they charged what the traffic would bear. However, by the 1880s the men who ran the railroads had come to recognize the advantages of cooperating with one another to avoid "senseless" competition. Railroad management was becoming a kind of profession, with certain standard ways of doing things, even with its own professional journals and with regional organizations such as the Eastern Trunk Line Association and the Western Traffic Association.

Because of their voracious appetite for traffic, railroads in sparsely settled regions and in areas with undeveloped resources devoted much money and effort to stimulating local economic growth. The Louisville and Nashville railroad, for instance, was a prime mover in the expansion of the iron industry in Alabama in the 1880s.

To speed the settlement of new regions, the land-grant railroads sold land cheaply and on easy terms, for sales meant future business as well as current income. They offered reduced rates to travelers interested in buying farms and set up "bureaus of immigration" that distributed brochures describing the wonders of the new country. Their agents greeted immigrants at the eastern ports and tried to steer them to railroad property. They sent agents who were usually themselves immigrants—often ministers—all over Europe to recruit prospective settlers.

Technological advances in railroading accelerated economic development in complex ways. In 1869 George Westinghouse invented the air brake. By enabling an engineer to apply the brakes to all cars simultaneously (formerly each car had to be braked separately by its own conductor or brakeman), this invention made possible revolutionary increases in the size of trains and the speed at which they could safely operate. The sleeping car, invented in 1864 by George Pullman, now came into its own.

To pull the heavier trains, more powerful locomotives were needed. They in turn produced a call for stronger and more durable rails to bear the additional weight. Steel, itself reduced in cost because of technological developments, supplied the answer, for steel rails outlasted iron by many years despite the use of much heavier equipment.

A close tie developed between the railroads and the nation's telegraph network, dominated by the Western Union Company. Commonly the railroads allowed Western Union to string wires along their rights-of-way, and they transported telegraphers and their equipment without charge. In return they received free telegraphic service, important for efficiency and safety.

IRON, OIL, AND ELECTRICITY

The transformation of iron manufacturing affected the nation almost as much as railroad development. Output rose from 920,000 tons in 1860 to 10.3 million tons in 1900, but the big change came in the development of ways to mass-produce steel. In its pure form (wrought iron) the metal is tough but relatively soft. Ordinary cast iron, which contains large amounts of carbon and other impurities, is hard but brittle. Steel, which contains 1 or 2 percent carbon, combines the hardness of cast iron with the toughness of wrought iron. For nearly every purpose—structural girders for bridges and buildings, railroad track, machine tools, boiler plate, barbed wire—steel is immensely superior to other kinds of iron.

But steel was so expensive to manufacture that it could not be used for bulky products until the invention in the 1850s of the Bessemer process, perfected independently by Henry Bessemer, an Englishman, and William Kelly of Kentucky. Bessemer and Kelly discovered that a stream of air directed into a mass of molten iron caused the carbon and other impurities to combine with oxygen and burn off. When measured amounts of carbon, silicon, and manganese were then added, the brew became steel. What had been a rare metal could now be produced by the hundreds and thousands of tons. The Bessemer process and the open-hearth method, a slower but more precise technique that enabled producers to sample the molten mass and thus control quality closely, were introduced commercially in the 1860s. In 1870, 77,000 tons of steel were manufactured; by 1890, that had expanded to nearly 5 million tons. Such growth would have been impossible without the huge supplies of iron ore in the United States and the coal necessary to fire the furnaces that refined it. In the 1870s the great iron fields rimming Lake Superior began to yield their treasures. The enormous iron concentrations of the Mesabi region made a compass needle spin like a top. Mesabi ores could be mined with steam shovels, almost like gravel.

Pittsburgh, surrounded by vast coal deposits, became the iron and steel capital of the country, the Minnesota ores reaching it by way of steamers on the Great Lakes and rail lines from Cleveland. Other cities in Pennsylvania and Ohio were important producers, and a separate complex, centering on Birmingham, Alabama, developed to exploit local iron and coal fields.

The petroleum industry expanded even more spectacularly than iron and steel. Edwin L. Drake drilled the first successful well in Pennsylvania in 1859. During the Civil War, production ranged between 2 million and 3 million barrels a year. By 1890 the figure had leaped to about 50 million barrels.

Before the invention of the gasoline engine and the automobile, the most important petroleum product was kerosene, which was burned in lamps. Refiners heated crude oil in large kettles and, after the volatile elements had escaped, condensed the kerosene in coils cooled by water. The heavier petroleum tars were discarded.

Technological advances came rapidly. By the early 1870s, refiners had learned how to "crack" petroleum by applying high temperatures to the crude oil in order to rearrange its molecular structure, thereby increasing the percentage of kerosene yielded. By-products such as naphtha, gasoline (used in vaporized form as an illuminating gas), rhigolene (a local anesthetic), cymogene (a coolant for refrigerating machines), and many lubricants and waxes began to appear on the market. At the same time a great increase in the supply of crude oil—especially after the German-born chemist Herman Frasch perfected a method for removing sulfur from low-quality petroleum—drove prices down.

These circumstances put a premium on refining efficiency. Larger plants using expensive machinery and employing skilled technicians became more important. In the mid-1860s only three refineries in the country could process 2000 barrels of crude oil a week; a decade later plants capable of handling 1000 barrels a day were common.

Two other important new industries were the telephone and electric light businesses. Both were typical of the period, being products of technical advances and intimately related to the growth of a high-speed, urban civilization that put great stress on communication. The telephone was invented in 1876 by Alexander Graham Bell, who had been led to the study of acoustics through his interest in the education of the deaf. The invention soon proved its value. By 1900 there were almost 800,000 telephones in the country, twice the total for all Europe. The American Telephone and Telegraph Company, a consolidation of over 100 local systems, dominated the business.

▶ *text continues on page 484*

Mapping
the Past

Were the Railroads Indispensable to Economic Growth?

In 1891 financier Sidney Dillon credited the railroads for the nation's impressive economic growth during the previous half century. Without them, he claimed, most of the nation's natural resources would have remained untouched, civilization would have "crept slowly" on, and the immense spaces from the Appalachians to the Pacific would have remained "an unknown and unproductive wilderness."

That the railroads were indispensable to the nation's economy during the nineteenth century has long been a commonplace of historical writing. One of the main reasons for it is

summarized in the map below, "The railroads: Moving agricultural products to eastern markets, 1890."

This map shows that the urban areas of the nation, with a population density of over 90 people per square mile (shaded in purple), were chiefly located in New England, the Middle Atlantic seaboard, and the industrial regions surrounding Pittsburgh, Cleveland, Cincinnati, Detroit, and Chicago. The map also indicates that the main grain-growing regions were in the Midwest, the northern Plains, and the South. The nation's basic economic geography presumed a transporta-

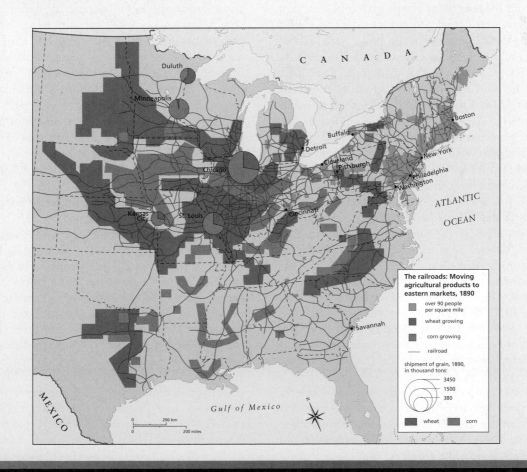

The railroads: Moving agricultural products to eastern markets, 1890

- over 90 people per square mile
- wheat growing
- corn growing
- railroad

shipment of grain, 1890, in thousand tons:
3450
1500
380

wheat   corn

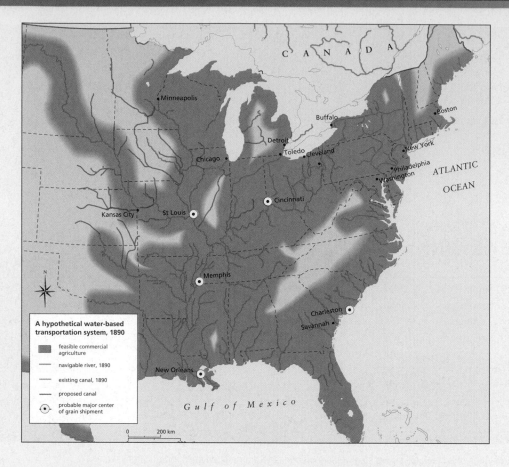

A hypothetical water-based transportation system, 1890

- feasible commercial agriculture
- navigable river, 1890
- existing canal, 1890
- proposed canal
- probable major center of grain shipment

0   200 km

tion system to ship grain from the Midwest and South to the urban consumption centers in the East.

By 1890, the map also suggests that the nation's railway system served this purpose. Railroads linked the major wheat markets of the upper Great Plains (principally Minneapolis and Duluth) and corn markets of the central Midwest (Chicago, St. Louis, and Kansas City) to the industrial cities of Ohio and Pennsylvania and the urban region along the Atlantic coast extending from Washington, D.C. to Maine. The dense web of competing railway lines should have kept freight charges low, and often did do so. Attempts to "pool" the available traffic and fix high rates usually collapsed. One reason the railways were the focus of much criticism was their centrality to the economy.

But in 1964, economic historian Robert Fogel challenged the assumption that the late nineteenth-century rail system was "indispensable" to economic growth. He asserted that if the nation had instead invested in building more canals and dredging more rivers, a water-based transportation system could have functioned nearly as effectively as the railways.

The map above entitled "A hypothetical water-based transportation system, 1890" shows how the nation's navigable rivers, supplemented by existing and new canals, could have collected cereals from agricultural regions and moved them to eastern markets. This map also suggests how a water-based transportation system would have altered the relationship

among regions. In the absence of the railroads, the dry upper Great Plains would have remained nearly undeveloped, while commercial agriculture would have been concentrated in the Mississippi, Ohio, and Missouri River valleys, and along the rivers that empty into the Gulf of Mexico and the Atlantic seaboard. The major centers of grain shipment would have been New Orleans, St. Louis, Cincinnati, Memphis, and Charleston. Minneapolis, Duluth, Chicago, and Kansas City would not have become major economic centers.

This "hypothetical" water-based transportation system would likely have been as efficient as the railroads. In 1890, the cost of shipping wheat from Chicago to New York City was 5.2 cents per ton-mile by rail, but only 1.4 cents by water. Fogel estimated that a water-based transportation system would have saved $38 million in carrying costs annually, though there would have been additional costs in warehouse construction and spoilage (boats are slower than trains). The railroads, in short, were not "indispensable" to move foodstuffs to eastern cities.

Yet the railroads stimulated economic development in other ways. Their demand for iron and steel jump-started the iron and steel industries, crucial for manufacturing and urban construction. The development of powerful locomotives gave rise to advances in steam and machine technology. Perhaps most important, the railroads promoted effective systems of corporate organization that stimulated economic development throughout the economy.

▲ This 1895 painting of a steel mill shows steelworkers preparing to pour molten steel, produced by the Bessemer converter, into ingot molds. Later the ingots would be rolled into various shapes. The hard, refined steel produced by the Bessemer process was ideal for railroad track.

When Western Union realized the importance of the telephone, it tried for a time to compete with Bell by developing a machine of its own. The man it commissioned to devise this machine was Thomas A. Edison, but Bell's patents proved unassailable. Edison had already made a number of contributions toward solving what he called the "mysteries of electrical force," including a multiplex telegraph capable of sending four messages over a single wire at the same time. At Menlo Park, New Jersey, he built the prototype of the modern research laboratory, where specific problems could be attacked on a mass scale by a team of trained specialists. During his lifetime he took out more than 1000 patents, dealing with machines as varied as the phonograph, the motion-picture projector, the storage battery, and the mimeograph.

Edison's most significant achievement was the incandescent lamp, or electric lightbulb. Others before him had experimented with the idea of producing light by passing electricity through a filament in a vacuum. Always, however, the filaments quickly burned out. Edison tried hundreds of fibers before producing, in 1879, a carbonized filament that would glow brightly in a vacuum tube for as long as 170 hours

without crumbling. At Christmastime he decorated the grounds about his laboratory with a few dozen of the new lights. People flocked by the thousands to see this miracle of the "Wizard of Menlo Park." The inventor boasted that soon he would be able to illuminate entire towns, even great cities like New York.

He was true to his promise. In 1882 his Edison Illuminating Company opened a power station in New York City and began to supply current for lighting to 85 consumers, including the *New York Times* and the banking house of J. P. Morgan and Company. Soon central stations were springing up everywhere until, by 1898, there were about 3000 in the country.

DOCUMENT

Edison, The Success of the Electric Light

The substitution of electric for steam power in factories was as liberating as that of steam for waterpower before the Civil War. Small, safe electric motors replaced dangerous and cumbersome mazes of belts and wheels. The electric power industry expanded rapidly. By the early years of the twentieth century almost 6 billion kilowatt-hours of electricity were being produced annually. Yet this was only the beginning.

▲ "A sneeze captured on film"—the first copyrighted movie (1894). In 1889 Thomas A. Edison conceived of a machine that would do for the eye what the phonograph did for the ear. Over the next two years, Edison invented two separate devices—a camera to take a rapid sequence of pictures and a machine to view them called a Kinetoscope. In 1893 he developed reliable film for his camera. The motion picture industry was born.

COMPETITION AND MONOPOLY: THE RAILROADS

During the post–Civil War era, expansion in industry went hand in hand with concentration. The principal cause of this trend, aside from the obvious economies resulting from large-scale production and the growing importance of expensive machinery, was the downward trend of prices after 1873. The deflation, which resulted mainly from the failure of the money supply to keep pace with the rapid increase in the volume of goods produced, affected agricultural goods as well as manufactures, and it lasted until 1896 or 1897.

Contemporaries believed that they were living through a "great depression." That label is misleading, for output expanded almost continuously, and at a rapid rate, until 1893, when production slumped and a true depression struck the country. Falling prices, however, kept a steady pressure on profit margins, and this led to increased production and thus to intense competition for markets.

According to the classical economists, competition advanced the public interest by keeping prices low and ensuring the most efficient producer the largest profit. Up to a point it accomplished these purposes in the years after 1865, but it also caused side effects that injured both the economy and society as a whole. Railroad managers, for instance, found it impossible to enforce "official" rate schedules and maintain their regional associations once competitive pressures mounted. In 1865 it had cost from 96 cents to $2.15 per 100 pounds, depending on the class of freight, to ship goods from New York to Chicago. In 1888 rates ranged from 35 cents to 75 cents.

Competition cut deeply into railroad profits, causing the lines to seek desperately to increase volume. They did so chiefly by reducing rates still more, on a selective basis. They gave rebates (secret reductions below the published rates) to large shippers in order to capture their business. Giving discounts to those who shipped in volume made economic sense: It was easier to handle freight in carload lots than in smaller units. So intense was the battle for business, however, that the roads often made concessions to big customers far beyond what the economics of bulk shipment justified. In the 1870s the New York Central regularly reduced the rates charged important shippers by 50 to 80 percent. One large Utica dry-goods merchant received a rate of 9 cents while others paid 33 cents. Two big New York City grain merchants paid so little that they soon controlled the grain business of the entire city.

Railroad officials disliked rebating but found no way to avoid the practice. "Notwithstanding my horror of rebates," the president of a New England trunk line told one of his executives in discussing the case of a brick manufacturer, "bill at the usual rate, and rebate Mr. Cole 25 cents a thousand." In extreme cases the railroads even gave large shippers drawbacks, which were rebates on the business of the shippers' competitors! Besides rebating, railroads issued passes to favored shippers, built sidings at the plants of important companies without charge, and gave freely of their landholdings to attract businesses to their territory. "The force of competition," a railroad man explained, "is one that no carrying corporation can withstand and before which the managing officers of a

corporation are helpless." James F. Joy of the Chicago, Burlington, and Quincy made the same point more bluntly: "Unless you prepare to defend yourselves," he advised the president of the Michigan Central, "you will be boarded by pirates in all quarters."

To make up for losses forced on them by competitive pressures, railroads charged higher rates at waypoints along their tracks where no competition existed. Frequently it cost more to ship a product a short distance than a longer one. Rochester, New York, was served only by the New York Central. In the 1870s it cost 30 cents to transport a barrel of flour from Rochester to New York City, a distance of 350 miles. At the same time flour could be shipped from Minneapolis to New York, a distance of well over 1000 miles, for only 20 cents a barrel. One Rochester businessman told a state investigating committee that he could save 18 cents a hundredweight by sending goods to St. Louis by way of New York, where several carriers competed for the traffic, even though, in fact, the goods might come back through Rochester over the same tracks on the way to St. Louis!

Although cheap transportation stimulated the economy, few people benefited from cutthroat competition. Small shippers—and all businessmen in cities and towns with limited rail outlets—suffered; railroad discrimination speeded the concentration of industry in large corporations located in major centers. The instability of rates even troubled interests like the Midwestern flour millers who benefited from the competitive situation, for it hampered planning. Nor could manufacturers who received rebates be entirely happy, since few could be sure that some other producer was not getting a larger reduction.

Probably the worst sufferers were the railroads themselves. The loss of revenue resulting from rate cutting, combined with inflated debts, put most of them in grave difficulty when faced with a downturn in the business cycle. In 1876 two-fifths of all railroad bonds were in default; three years later 65 lines were bankrupt. Wits called Samuel J. Tilden, the 1876 Democratic presidential candidate, "the Great Forecloser" because of his work reorganizing bankrupt railroads at this time.

Since the public would not countenance bankrupt railroads going out of business, these companies were placed in the hands of court-appointed receivers. The receivers, however, seldom provided efficient management and had no funds at their disposal for new equipment.

During the 1880s the major roads responded to these pressures by building or buying lines in order to create interregional systems. These were the first giant corporations, capitalized in the hundreds of millions of dollars. Their enormous cost led to another wave of bankruptcies when a true depression struck in the 1890s.

The consequent reorganizations brought most of the big systems under the control of financiers, notably J. Pierpont Morgan and such other private bankers as Kuhn, Loeb of New York and Lee, Higginson of Boston.

Critics called the reorganizations "Morganizations." Representatives of the bankers sat on the board of every line they saved and their influence was predominant. They consistently opposed rate wars, rebating, and other competitive practices. In effect, control of the railroad network became centralized, even though the companies maintained their separate existences and operated in a seemingly independent manner. When Morgan died in 1913, "Morgan men" dominated the boards of the New York Central; the Erie; the New York, New Haven, and Hartford; the Southern; the Pere Marquette; the Atchison, Topeka and Santa Fe; and many other lines.

COMPETITION AND MONOPOLY: STEEL

The iron and steel industry was also intensely competitive. Despite the trend toward higher production, demand varied erratically from year to year, even from month to month. In good times producers built new facilities, only to suffer heavy losses when demand declined. The forward rush of technology put a tremendous emphasis on efficiency; expensive plants quickly became obsolete. Improved transportation facilities allowed manufacturers in widely separated places to compete with one another.

The kingpin of the industry was Andrew Carnegie. Carnegie was born in Scotland and came to the United States in 1848 at the age of 12. His first job, as a bobbin boy in a cotton mill, brought him $1.20 a week, but his talents perfectly fitted the times and he rose rapidly: to Western Union messenger boy, to telegrapher, to private secretary, to railroad manager. He saved his money, made some shrewd investments, and by 1868 had an income of $50,000 a year.

At about this time he decided to specialize in the iron business. Carnegie possessed great talent as a salesman, boundless faith in the future of the country, an uncanny knack of choosing topflight subordinates, and enough ruthlessness to survive in the iron and steel jungle. Where other steelmen built new plants in good times, he preferred to expand in bad times, when it cost far less to do so. During the 1870s, he later recalled, "many of my friends needed money. . . . I bought out five or six of them. That is what gave me my leading interest in this steel business."

Carnegie grasped the importance of technological improvements. Slightly skeptical of the Bessemer

▲ Worker apartments envelop the Homestead Steel Works. During a strike in 1889, the county sheriff and his men had been chased away by the strikers, who had considerable political power in Homestead. In 1892 Henry Clay Frick took charge of the mills and nearly crushed the unions by bringing in outsiders— strikebreakers as well as the Pennsylvania National Guard.

process at first, once he became convinced of its practicality he adopted it enthusiastically. In 1875 he built the J. Edgar Thomson Steel Works, named after a president of the Pennsylvania Railroad, his biggest customer. He employed chemists and other specialists and was soon making steel from iron oxides that other manufacturers had discarded as waste. He was a merciless competitor. When a plant manager announced: "We broke all records for making steel last week," Carnegie replied: "Congratulations! Why not do it every week?" Carnegie sold rails by paying "commissions" to railroad purchasing agents, and he was not above reneging on a contract if he thought it profitable and safe to do so.

By 1890 the Carnegie Steel Company dominated the industry, and its output increased nearly tenfold during the next decade. Profits soared. Alarmed by his increasing control of the industry, the makers of finished steel products such as barbed wire and tubing considered pooling their resources and making steel themselves. Carnegie, his competitive temper aroused, threatened to manufacture wire, pipes and other finished products. A colossal steel war seemed imminent.

However, Carnegie longed to retire in order to devote himself to philanthropic work. He believed that great wealth entailed social responsibilities and that it was a disgrace to die rich. When J. P. Morgan approached him through an intermediary with an offer to buy him out, he assented readily. In 1901 Morgan put together United States Steel, the "world's first billion-dollar corporation." This combination included all the Carnegie properties, the Federal Steel Company (Carnegie's largest competitor), and such important fabricators of finished products as the American Steel and Wire Company, the American Tin Plate Company, and the National Tube Company. Vast reserves of Minnesota iron ore and a fleet of Great Lakes ore steamers were also included. U.S. Steel was capitalized at $1.4 billion, about twice the value of its component properties but not necessarily an overestimation of its profit-earning capacity. The owners of Carnegie Steel received $492 million, of which $250 million went to Carnegie himself.

COMPETITION AND MONOPOLY: OIL

The pattern of fierce competition leading to combination and monopoly is well illustrated by the history of the petroleum industry. Irresistible pressures pushed the refiners into a brutal struggle to dominate the business. Production of crude oil, subject to the uncertainties of prospecting and drilling, fluctuated constantly and without regard for need. In general, output surged far ahead of demand.

By the 1870s the chief oil-refining centers were Cleveland, Pittsburgh, Baltimore, and the New York City area. Of these Cleveland was the fastest growing, chiefly because the New York Central and Erie railroads competed fiercely for its oil trade and the Erie Canal offered an alternative route.

The Standard Oil Company of Cleveland, founded in 1870 by a 31-year-old merchant named John D. Rockefeller, emerged as the giant among the refiners. Rockefeller exploited every possible technical advance and employed fair means and foul to persuade competitors either to sell out or to join forces. By 1879 he controlled 90 percent of the nation's oil-refining capacity along with a network of oil pipelines and large reserves of petroleum in the ground.

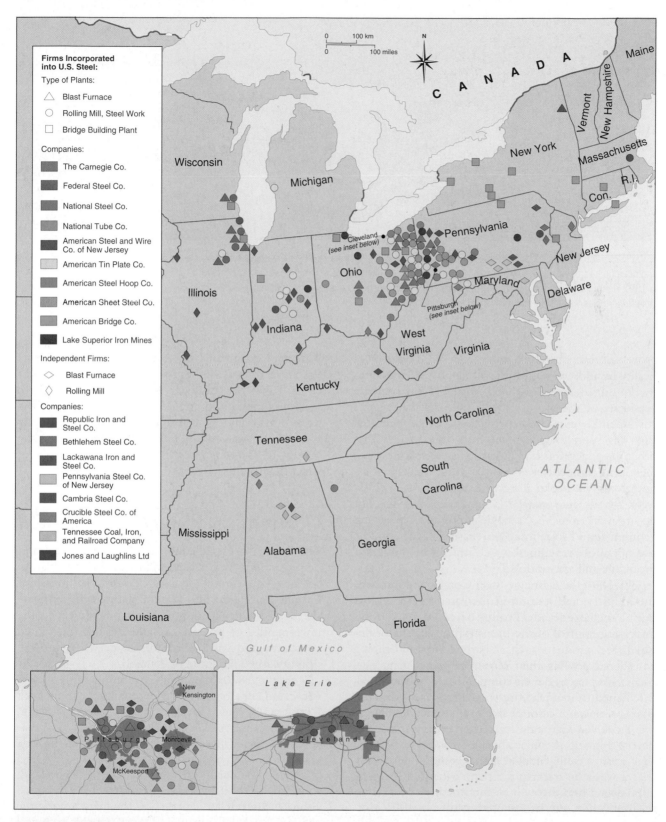

▲ The Forging of U.S. Steel

Standard Oil emerged victorious from the competitive wars because Rockefeller and his associates were the toughest and most imaginative fighters as well as the most efficient refiners in the business. In addition to obtaining from the railroads a 10 percent rebate and drawbacks on its competitors' shipments, Standard Oil cut prices locally to force small independents to sell out or face ruin. Since kerosene was sold in grocery stores, Standard supplied its own outlets with meat, sugar, and other products at artificially low prices to help crush the stores that handled other brands of kerosene. The company employed spies to track down the customers of independents and offer them oil at bargain prices. Bribery was also a Standard practice; the reformer Henry Demarest Lloyd quipped that the company had done everything to the Pennsylvania legislature except refine it.

Although a bold planner and a daring taker of necessary risks, Rockefeller was far too orderly and astute to enjoy the free-swinging battles that plagued his industry. Born in an upstate New York village in 1839, he settled in Cleveland in 1855 and became a produce merchant. During the Civil War he invested in a local refinery and by 1865 was engaged full time in the oil business.

Like Carnegie, Rockefeller was an organizer; he knew little about the technology of petroleum. His forte was meticulous attention to detail: stories are told of his ordering the number of drops of solder used to seal oil cans reduced from 40 to 39 and of his insisting that the manager of one of his refineries account for 750 missing barrel bungs. Not miserliness but a profound grasp of the economies of large-scale production explain this behavior.

Rockefeller competed ruthlessly not primarily to crush other refiners but to persuade them to join with him, to share the business peaceably and rationally so that all could profit. Competition was obsolescent, he argued, though no more effective competitor than he ever lived.

Having achieved his monopoly, Rockefeller stabilized and structured it by creating a new type of business organization, the trust. Standard Oil was an Ohio corporation, prohibited by local law from owning plants in other states or holding stock in out-of-state corporations. As Rockefeller and his associates took over dozens of companies with facilities scattered across the country, serious legal and managerial difficulties arose. How could these many organizations be integrated with Standard Oil of Ohio?

A rotund, genial little Pennsylvania lawyer named Samuel C. T. Dodd came up with an answer to this question in 1879.[1] The stock of Standard of Ohio and of all the other companies that the Rockefeller interests

had swallowed up was turned over to nine trustees, who were empowered to "exercise general supervision" over all the properties. In exchange, stockholders received trust certificates, on which dividends were paid. This seemingly simple device brought order to the petroleum business. Competition almost disappeared; prices steadied; profits skyrocketed. By 1892 John D. Rockefeller was worth over $800 million.

The Standard Oil Trust was not a corporation. It had no charter, indeed no legal existence at all. For many years few people outside the organization knew that it existed. The form they chose persuaded Rockefeller and other Standard Oil officials that without violating their consciences, they could deny under oath that Standard Oil of Ohio owned or controlled

▲ A regally attired John D. Rockefeller, astride a barrel from his Standard Oil refinery, his crown encircled by the railroads he controlled. His actual attire was considerably less conspicuous.

---

[1]The trust formula was not "perfected" until 1882.

other corporations "directly or indirectly through its officers or agents." The trustees controlled these organizations—and Standard of Ohio too!

After Standard Oil's duplicity was revealed during a New York investigation in 1888, the word *trust,* formerly signifying a fiduciary arrangement for the protection of the interests of individuals incompetent or unwilling to guard them themselves, became a synonym for monopoly. However, from the company's point of view, monopoly was not the purpose of the trust—that had been achieved before the device was invented. Centralization of the management of diverse and far-flung operations in the interest of efficiency was its chief function. Standard Oil headquarters in New York became the brain of a complex network where information from salaried managers in the field was collected and digested, where top managerial decisions were made, and whence orders went out to armies of drillers, refiners, scientists, and salesmen.

COMPETITION AND MONOPOLY: RETAILING AND UTILITIES

That utilities such as the telephone and electric lighting industries tended to form monopolies is not difficult to explain, for in such fields competition involved costly duplication of equipment and, particularly in the case of the telephone, loss of service efficiency. However, competitive pressures were strong in the early stages of their development. Since these industries depended on patents, Bell and Edison had to fight mighty battles in the courts with rivals seeking to infringe on their rights. When Edison first announced his electric light, capitalists, engineers, and inventors flocked to Menlo Park. He proudly revealed to them the secrets of his marvelous lamp. Many hurried away to turn this information to their own advantage, thinking the "Wizard" a naive fool. When they invaded the field, the law provided Edison with far less protection than he had expected. "My electric light inventions have brought me no profits, only forty years of litigation," Edison later complained. A patent, he said bitterly, was "simply an invitation to a lawsuit."

Competition in the electric lighting business raged for some years among Edison, Westinghouse, and another corporation, the Thomson-Houston Electric Company, which was operating 870 central lighting stations by 1890. In 1892 the Edison and Thomson-Houston companies merged, forming General Electric, a $35 million corporation. Thereafter, General Electric and Westinghouse maintained their dominance in the manufacture of bulbs and electrical equipment as well as in the distribution of electrical power.

The pattern of competition leading to dominance by a few great companies was repeated in many businesses. In life insurance an immense expansion took place after the Civil War, stimulated by the development of a new type of group policy, the "tontine," by Henry B. Hyde of the Equitable Life Company.[2] High-pressure salesmanship prevailed; agents gave rebates to customers by shaving their own commissions; companies stole crack agents from their rivals and raided new territories. They sometimes invested as much as 96 percent of the first year's premiums in obtaining new business. By 1900, after three decades of fierce competition, three giants dominated the industry—Equitable, New York Life, and Mutual Life, each with approximately $1 billion of insurance in force.

In retailing, the period saw the growth of urban department stores. In 1862 Alexander T. Stewart had built an eight-story emporium in New York City that covered an entire block and employed 2000 persons. John Wanamaker in Philadelphia and Marshall Field in Chicago headed similar establishments by the 1880s, and there were others. These department stores advertised heavily, stressing low prices, efficient service, and money-back guarantees. High volume made for large profits. Here is how one of Field's biographers described his methods:

> His was a one-price store, with the price plainly marked on the merchandise. Goods were not misrepresented, and a reputation for quality merchandise and for fair and honest dealing was built up. . . . Courtesy toward customers was an unfailing rule.

AMERICAN AMBIVALENCE TO BIG BUSINESS

The expansion of industry and its concentration in fewer and fewer hands changed the way many people felt about the role of government in economic and social affairs. On the one hand, they professed to believe strongly in a government policy of noninterference, or laissez-faire. "'Things regulate themselves' . . . means, of course, that God regulates them by his general laws," Professor Francis Bowen of Harvard wrote in his *American Political Economy* (1870).

Certain intellectual currents encouraged this type of thinking. Charles Darwin's *The Origin of Species* was published in 1859, and by the 1870s his theory of evolution was beginning to influence opinion in the

---

[2]A tontine policy paid no dividends for a stated period of years. The heirs of the policyholder who died received the face value but no dividends. At the end of the tontine period, survivors collected not only their own dividends but those of the unfortunates who had died or permitted their policies to lapse. This was psychologically appealing, since it stressed living rather than dying and added an element of gambling to insurance.

United States. That nature had ordained a kind of inevitable progress, governed by the natural selection of those individual organisms best adapted to survive in a particular environment, seemed eminently reasonable to most Americans, for it fitted well with their own experiences. "Let the buyer beware; that covers the whole business," the sugar magnate Henry O. Havemeyer explained to an investigating committee. "You cannot wet-nurse people from the time they are born until the time they die. They have to wade and get stuck, and that is the way men are educated."

This reasoning was similar to that of the classical economists and was thus at least as old as Adam Smith's *Wealth of Nations* (1776). But it appeared to supply a hard scientific substitute for Smith's somewhat vague "invisible hand" as an explanation of why free competition advanced the common good.

Yale professor William Graham Sumner sometimes used the survival-of-the-fittest analogy in teaching undergraduates. "Professor," one student asked Sumner, "don't you believe in any government aid to industries?" "No!" Sumner replied, "It's root, hog, or die." The student persisted: "Suppose some professor of political science came along and took your job away from you. Wouldn't you be sore?" "Any other professor is welcome to try," Sumner answered promptly. "If he gets my job, it is my fault. My business is to teach the subject so well that no one can take the job away from me." Sumner's argument described what came to be known as *social Darwinism,* the belief that the activities of people, that is, their business and social relationships, were governed by the Darwininan principle that "the fittest" will always "survive" if allowed to exercise their capacities without restriction.

But the fact that Americans disliked powerful governments in general and strict regulation of the economy in particular had never meant that they objected to all government activity in the economic sphere. Banking laws, tariffs, internal-improvement legislation, and the granting of public land to railroads are only the most obvious of the economic regulations enforced in the nineteenth century by both the federal government and the states. Americans saw no contradiction between government activities of this type and the free enterprise philosophy, for such laws were intended to release human energy and thus increase the area in which freedom could operate. Tariffs stimulated industry and created new jobs, railroad grants opened up new regions for development, and so on.

The growth of huge industrial and financial organizations and the increasing complexity of economic relations frightened people yet made them at the same time greedy for more of the goods and services the new society was turning out. To many, the great new corporations and trusts resembled Frankenstein's monster—marvelous and powerful but a grave threat to society. The astute James Bryce described the changes in *The American Commonwealth* (1888):

> Modern civilization . . . has become more exacting. It discerns more benefits which the organized power of government can secure, and grows more anxious to attain them. Men live fast, and are impatient of the slow working of natural laws. . . . Unlimited competition seems to press too hard on the weak. The power of groups of men organized by incorporation as joint-stock companies, or of small knots of rich men acting in combination, has developed with unexpected strength in unexpected ways, overshadowing individuals and even communities, and showing that the very freedom of association which men sought to secure by law . . . may, under the shelter of the law, ripen into a new form of tyranny.

To some extent public fear of the industrial giants reflected concern about monopoly. If Standard Oil dominated oil refining, it might raise prices inordinately at vast cost to consumers. Charles Francis Adams, Jr., expressed this feeling in the 1870s: "In the minds of the great majority, and not without reason, the idea of any industrial combination is closely connected with that of monopoly, and monopoly with extortion."

Although in isolated cases monopolists did raise prices unreasonably, generally they did not. On the contrary, prices tended to fall until by the 1890s a veritable "consumer's millennium" had arrived. Far more important in causing resentment was the fear that the monopolists were destroying economic opportunity and threatening democratic institutions. It was not the wealth of tycoons like Carnegie and Rockefeller and Morgan so much as their influence that worried people. In the face of the growing disparity between rich and poor, could republican institutions survive? "The belief is common," wrote Charles Francis Adams's brother Henry as early as 1870, "that the day is at hand when corporations . . . will ultimately succeed in directing government itself."

Some observers believed either autocracy or a form of revolutionary socialism to be almost inevitable. Campaigning for the governorship of Texas in 1890, James S. Hogg, a staunch conservative, said: "Within a few years, unless something is done, most of the wealth and talent of our country will be on one side, while arrayed on the other will be the great mass of the people, composing the bone and sinew of this government." John Boyle O'Reilly, a liberal Catholic journalist, wrote in 1886: "There is something worse than Anarchy, bad as that is; and it is irresponsible power in the hands of mere wealth."

As criticism mounted, business leaders rose to their own defense. Rockefeller described in graphic

DEBATING THE PAST

Were the industrialists "robber barons" or savvy entrepreneurs? The Biltmore mansion in Asheville, North Carolina *(left)*, was completed in 1895 by the Vanderbilts; its landscaping alone required 1000 workers.

Such wealth caused consternation at the time, and a later generation of historians picked up on the issue. In 1934 biographer Matthew Josephson, writing during the nation's worst depression, blamed the late nineteenth-century industrialists—robber barons, in his words—for the evident flaws in the economy. But in 1942, when the United States was at war and its industries were out-producing Nazi Germany and Japan, historians Thomas C. Cochran and William Miller, calling the period an "Age of Enterprise," contended that the industrialists had exhibited skill and daring.

Historians subsequently shifted focus from the character of the entrepreneurs to the systems they built. In the early 1960s Alfred D. Chandler, Jr. argued that the great industrialists, in response to the demands of burgeoning urban markets, created the requisite large-scale industrial enterprises.

Other historians countered that much of the nation's industrial growth was achieved not by the huge corporations and their famous owners, but by small firms (John N. Ingham, 1991) or by mid-level managers (Oliver Zunz, 1990).

Most historians concede that the industrialists often put their fortunes to good use. The critics of Andrew Carnegie, for example, may have studied in one of the scores of libraries he donated to communities, such as that in Tuskegee, Alabama *(right)*.

Matthew Josephson, *The Robber Barons* (1934), Thomas C. Cochran and William Miller, *The Age of Enterprise* (1942), Alfred D. Chandler, Jr., *Strategy and Structure* (1962), John N. Ingham, *Making Iron and Steel* (1991), Oliver Zunz, *Making America Corporate* (1990).

DOCUMENT

Carnegie, "Wealth"

terms the chaotic conditions that plagued the oil industry before the rise of Standard Oil: "It seemed absolutely necessary to extend the market for oil . . . and also greatly improve the process of refining so that oil could be made and sold cheaply, yet with a profit. We proceeded to buy the largest and best refining concerns and centralized the administration of them with a view to securing greater economy and efficiency." Carnegie, in an essay published in 1889, insisted that the concentration of wealth was necessary if humanity was to progress, softening this "Gospel of Wealth" by insisting that the rich must use their money "in the manner which . . . is best calculated to produce the

most beneficial results for the community." The rich man was merely a trustee for his "poorer brethren," Carnegie said, "bringing to their service his superior wisdom, experience, and ability to administer." Lesser tycoons echoed these arguments.

The voices of the critics were louder if not necessarily more influential. Many clergymen denounced unrestrained competition, which they considered un-Christian. The new class of professional economists (the American Economic Association was founded in 1885) tended to repudiate laissez-faire. State aid, Richard T. Ely of Johns Hopkins University wrote, "is an indispensable condition of human progress."

REFORMERS: GEORGE, BELLAMY, LLOYD

The popularity of a number of radical theorists reflects public feeling in the period. In 1879 Henry George, a California journalist, published *Progress and Poverty,* a forthright attack on the uneven distribution of wealth in the United States. George argued that labor was the true and only source of capital. Observing the speculative fever of the West, which enabled landowners to reap profits merely by holding property while population increased, George proposed a property tax that would confiscate this "unearned increment." The value of land depended on society and should belong to society; allowing individuals to keep this wealth was the major cause of the growing disparity between rich and poor, George believed.

George's "single tax," as others called it, would bring in so much money that no other taxes would be necessary, and the government would have plenty of funds to establish new schools, museums, theaters, and other badly needed social and cultural services. While the single tax on property was never adopted, George's ideas attracted enthusiastic attention. Single tax clubs sprang up throughout the nation, and *Progress and Poverty* became a best-seller.

DOCUMENT

Bellamy, from *Looking Backward*

Even more spectacular was the reception afforded *Looking Backward, 2000–1887,* a utopian novel written in 1888 by Edward Bellamy. This book, which sold over a million copies in its first few years, described a future America that was completely socialized, all economic activity carefully planned. Bellamy compared nineteenth-century society to a lumbering stagecoach upon which the favored few rode in comfort while the mass of the people hauled them along life's route. Occasionally one of the toilers managed to fight his way onto the coach; whenever a rider fell from it, he had to join the multitude dragging it along.

Such, Bellamy wrote, was the working of the vaunted American competitive system. He suggested that the ideal socialist state, in which all citizens shared equally, would arrive without revolution or violence. The trend toward consolidation would continue, he predicted, until one monster trust controlled all economic activity. At this point everyone would realize that nationalization was essential.

A third influential attack on monopoly was that of Henry Demarest Lloyd, whose *Wealth Against Commonwealth* appeared in 1894. Lloyd, a journalist of independent means, devoted years to preparing a denunciation of the Standard Oil Company. Marshaling masses of facts and vivid examples of Standard's evildoing, he assaulted the trust at every point. Although in his zeal Lloyd sometimes distorted and exaggerated the evidence to make his indictment more effective—"Every important man in the oil, coal and many other trusts ought today to be in some one of our penitentiaries," he wrote in a typical overstatement—as a polemic his book was peerless. His forceful but uncomplicated arguments and his copious references to official documents made *Wealth Against Commonwealth* utterly convincing to thousands. The book was more than an attack on Standard Oil. Lloyd denounced the application of Darwin's concept of survival of the fittest to economic and social affairs, and he condemned laissez-faire policies as leading directly to monopoly.

The popularity of these books indicates that the trend toward monopoly in the United States worried many. But despite the drastic changes suggested in their pages, none of these writers questioned the underlying values of the middle-class majority. They insisted that reform could be accomplished without serious inconvenience to any individual or class. In *Looking Backward* Bellamy pictured the socialists of the future gathered

▲ Edward Bellamy, author of the utopian novel, *Looking Backward* (1888). Bellamy's socialism, though genteel, unsettled many. *The Household Encyclopaedia* (1892) included this photograph of Bellamy in a section on phrenology, the "science" of ascertaining a person's character and intellectual traits from the shape of his or her cranium. Of Bellamy's, it concluded: "Large perceptive faculties; defective reasoning powers."

around a radiolike gadget in a well-furnished parlor listening to a minister delivering an inspiring sermon.

Nor did most of their millions of readers seriously consider trying to apply the reformers' ideas. Henry George ran for mayor of New York City in 1886 and lost narrowly to Abram S. Hewitt, a wealthy iron manufacturer, but even if he had won, he would have been powerless to apply the single tax to metropolitan property. The national discontent was apparently not as profound as the popularity of these works might suggest. If John D. Rockefeller became the bogeyman of American industry because of Lloyd's attack, no one prevented him from also becoming the richest man in the United States.

REFORMERS: THE MARXISTS

By the 1870s the ideas of European socialists were beginning to penetrate the United States, and in 1877 a Socialist Labor party was founded. The first serious attempt to explain the ideas of German political philosopher Karl Marx to Americans was Laurence Gronlund's *The Cooperative Commonwealth,* which was published in 1884, two years before Marx's *Das Kapital* was translated into English.

Capitalism, Gronlund claimed, contained the seeds of its own destruction. The state ought to own all the means of production. Competition was "Established Anarchy," middlemen were "parasites," speculators "vampires." "Capital and Labor," he wrote in one of the rare humorous lines in his book, "are just as harmonious as roast beef and a hungry stomach." Yet like other harsh critics of that day, Gronlund expected the millennium to arrive in a peaceful, indeed orderly manner. The red flag of socialism, he said, "has no relation to blood." The movement could accommodate "representatives of all classes," even "thoughtful" middleman parasites.

The leading voice of the Socialist Labor party, Daniel De Leon, editor of the party's weekly, *The People,* was a different type. He was born in the West Indies, son of a Dutch army doctor stationed in Curaçao, and educated in Europe. He emigrated to the United States in the 1870s, where he was progressively attracted by the ideas of Henry George, then Edward Bellamy and the Knights of Labor, and finally Marx. While personally mild-mannered and kindly, when he put pen to paper he became a doctrinaire revolutionary. He excoriated American labor unions in *The People,* insisting that industrial workers could improve their lot only by adopting socialism and joining the Socialist Labor party. He paid scant attention, however, to the practical needs or even to the opinions of rank-and-file working people. In 1891 he was the Socialist Labor party's candidate for governor of New York.

THE GOVERNMENT REACTS TO BIG BUSINESS: RAILROAD REGULATION

Political action related to the growth of big business came first on the state level and dealt chiefly with the regulation of railroads. Even before the Civil War, a number of New England states established railroad commissions to supervise lines within their borders; by the end of the century, 28 states had such boards.

Strict regulation was largely the result of agitation by the National Grange of the Patrons of Husbandry. The Grange, founded in 1867 by Oliver H. Kelley, was created to provide social and cultural benefits for isolated rural communities. As it spread and grew in influence—14 states had Granges by 1872 and membership reached 800,000 in 1874—the movement became political too. "Granger" candidates, often not themselves farmers (many local businessmen resented such railroad practices as rebating), won control of a number of state legislatures in the West and South. Granger-controlled legislatures established "reasonable" maximum rates and outlawed "unjust" discrimination. The legislature also set up a commission to enforce the laws and punish violators.

DOCUMENT

Grange 1879

The railroads protested, insisting that they were being deprived of property without due process of law. In *Munn* v. *Illinois* (1877), a case that involved a grain elevator whose owner had refused to comply with a state warehouse act, the Supreme Court upheld the constitutionality of this kind of act. Any business that served a public interest, such as a railroad or a grain warehouse, was subject to state control, the justices ruled. Legislatures might fix maximum charges; if the charges seemed unreasonable to the parties concerned, they should direct their complaints to the legislatures or to the voters, not to the courts.

Regulation of the railroad network by the individual states was inefficient, and in some cases the commissions were incompetent and even corrupt. When the Supreme Court, in the case of *Wabash, St. Louis & Pacific Railroad* v. *Illinois* (1886), declared unconstitutional an Illinois regulation outlawing the long-and-short-haul evil, federal action became necessary. The railroad had charged 25 cents per 100 pounds for shipping goods from Gilman, Illinois, to New York City but only 15 cents to ship goods from Peoria, which was 86 miles farther from New York. Illinois judges had held this to be illegal, but the Supreme Court decided that Illinois could not regulate interstate shipments.

Congress filled the gap created by the *Wabash* decision in 1887 by passing the Interstate Commerce Act. All charges made by railroads "shall be reasonable

and just," the act stated. Rebates, drawbacks, the long-and-short-haul evil, and other competitive practices were declared unlawful, and so were their monopolistic counterparts—pools and traffic-sharing agreements. Railroads were required to publish schedules of rates and forbidden to change them without due public notice. Most important, the law established an Interstate Commerce Commission (ICC), the first federal regulatory board, to supervise the affairs of railroads, investigate complaints, and issue cease and desist orders when the roads acted illegally.

The Interstate Commerce Act broke new ground, yet it was neither a radical nor a particularly effective measure. Its terms contradicted one another, some being designed to stimulate, others to penalize, competition. The chairman of the commission soon characterized the law as an "anomaly." It sought, he said, to "enforce competition" at the same time that it outlawed "the acts and inducements by which competition is ordinarily effected."

The new commission had less power than the law seemed to give it. It could not fix rates, only bring the roads to court when it considered rates unreasonably high. Such cases could be extremely complicated; applying the law "was like cutting a path through a jungle." With the truth so hard to determine and the burden of proof on the commission, the courts in nearly every instance decided in favor of the railroads.

Nevertheless, by describing so clearly the right of Congress to regulate private corporations engaged in interstate commerce, the Interstate Commerce Act challenged the philosophy of laissez-faire. Later legislation made the commission more effective. The commission also served as the model for a host of similar federal administrative authorities, such as the Federal Communications Commission (1934).

THE GOVERNMENT REACTS TO BIG BUSINESS: THE SHERMAN ANTITRUST ACT

As with railroad legislation, the first antitrust laws originated in the states, but they were southern and western states with relatively little industry, and most of the statutes were vaguely worded and ill-enforced. Federal action came in 1890 with the passage of the Sherman Antitrust Act. Any combination "in the form of trust or otherwise" that was "in restraint of trade or commerce among the several states, or with foreign nations" was declared illegal. Persons forming such combinations were subject to fines of $5000 and a year in jail. Individuals and businesses suffering losses because of actions that violated the law were authorized to sue in the federal courts for triple damages.

Where the Interstate Commerce Act sought to outlaw the excesses of competition, the Sherman Act was supposed to restore competition. If businessmen joined together to "restrain" (monopolize) trade in a particular field, they should be punished and their deeds undone. "The great thing this bill does," Senator George Frisbie Hoar of Massachusetts explained, "is to extend the common-law principle . . . to international and interstate commerce." This was important because the states ran into legal difficulties when they tried to use the common law to restrict corporations engaged in interstate activities.

But the Sherman Act was rather loosely worded—Thurman Arnold, a modern authority, once said that it made it "a crime to violate a vaguely stated economic policy." Critics have argued that the congressmen were more interested in quieting the public clamor for action against the trusts than in actually breaking up any of the new combinations. Quieting the clamor was certainly one of their objectives. However, they were trying to solve a new problem and were not sure how to proceed. A law with teeth too sharp might do more harm than good. Most Americans assumed that the courts would deal with the details, as they always had in common law matters.

In fact, the Supreme Court quickly emasculated the Sherman Act. In *United States* v. *E. C. Knight Company* (1895) it held that the American Sugar Refining Company had not violated the law by taking over a number of important competitors. Although the Sugar Trust now controlled about 98 percent of all sugar refining in the United States, it was not restraining trade. "Doubtless the power to control the manufacture of a given thing involves in a certain sense the control of its disposition," the Court said in one of the greatest feats of judicial understatement of all time. "Although the exercise of that power may result in bringing the operation of commerce into play, it does not control it, and affects it only incidentally and indirectly."

If the creation of the Sugar Trust did not violate the Sherman Act, it seemed unlikely that any other combination of manufacturers could be convicted under the law. However, in several cases in 1898 and 1899 the Supreme Court ruled that agreements to fix prices or divide markets did violate the Sherman Act. These decisions precipitated a wave of outright mergers in which a handful of large companies swallowed up hundreds of smaller ones. Presumably mergers were not illegal. When, some years after his retirement, Andrew Carnegie was asked by a committee of the House of Representatives to explain how he had dared participate in the formation of the U.S. Steel Corporation, he replied: "Nobody ever mentioned the Sherman Act to me, that I remember."

THE LABOR UNION MOVEMENT

Organizing
American Labor
in the Late 19th
Century

At the time of the Civil War only a small percentage of the American workforce was organized, and most union members were cigarmakers, printers, carpenters, and other skilled artisans, not factory hands. Aside from ironworkers, railroad workers, and miners, few industrial laborers belonged to unions. Nevertheless the union was the workers' response to the big corporation: a combination designed to eliminate competition for jobs and to provide efficient organization for labor.

After 1865 the growth of national craft unions, which had been stimulated by labor dissatisfaction during the Civil War, quickened perceptibly. In 1866 a federation of these organizations, the National Labor Union, was founded and by the early 1870s many new trades, notably in railroading, had been unionized.

Most of the leaders of these unions were visionaries who were out of touch with the practical needs and aspirations of workers. They opposed the wage system, strikes, and anything that increased the laborers' sense of being members of the working class. A major objective was the formation of worker-owned cooperatives.

Terence Powderly
at Knights of
Labor Convention

Far more remarkable was the Knights of Labor, a curious organization founded in 1869 by a group of Philadelphia garment workers headed by Uriah S. Stephens. Like so many labor organizers of the period, Stephens was a reformer of wide interests rather than a man dedicated to the specific problems of industrial workers. He, his successor Terence V. Powderly, and many other leaders of the Knights would have been thoroughly at home in the labor organizations of the Jacksonian era. Like the Jacksonians, they supported political objectives that had no direct connection with working conditions, such as currency reform and the curbing of land speculation. They rejected the idea that workers must resign themselves to remaining wage earners. By pooling their resources, working people could advance up the economic ladder and enter the capitalist class. "There is no good reason," Powderly wrote in his autobiography, *The Path I Trod,* "why labor cannot, through cooperation, own and operate mines, factories, and railroads." The leading Knights saw no contradiction between their denunciation of "soulless" monopolies and "drones" like bankers and lawyers and their talk of "combining all branches of trade in one common brotherhood." Such muddled thinking led the Knights to attack the wage system and to frown on strikes as "acts of private warfare."

If the Knights had one foot in the past, they also had one foot in the future. They supported some startlingly advanced ideas. Rejecting the traditional grouping of workers by crafts, they developed a concept closely resembling modern industrial unionism. They welcomed blacks (though mostly in segregated locals), women, and immigrants, and they accepted unskilled workers as well as artisans. The eight-hour day was one of their basic demands, their argument being that increased leisure would give workers time to develop more cultivated tastes and higher aspirations. Higher pay would inevitably follow.

The growth of the union, however, had little to do with ideology. Stephens had made the Knights a

▲ Here Jay Gould, perhaps the most vilified of the "robber barons," is depicted as a spider amidst a web of control bound by the telegraph lines of Western Union. Alfred Chandler, Jr., as noted in the feature Debating the Past on p. 492, took a more positive look at the nation's industrialists. He credited Gould with salvaging the Union Pacific Railroad, building his own railroad company (Missouri Pacific), and rationalizing the nation's communications system.

▲ This famous depiction of the Haymarket bombing (1886), which appeared in *Harper's Weekly*, suggests that the police were being fired on. In actuality, the bomb exploded after the crowd had begun to disperse. Then the police began firing into the crowd.

secret organization with an elaborate initiatory ritual. Under his leadership, as late as 1879 it had fewer than 10,000 members. Under Powderly, secrecy was discarded. Between 1882 and 1886 successful strikes by local "assemblies" against western railroads, including one against the hated Jay Gould's Missouri Pacific, brought recruits by the thousands. The membership passed 42,000 in 1882, 110,000 in 1885, and in 1886 it soared beyond the 700,000 mark. Alas, sudden prosperity was too much for the Knights. Its national leadership was unable to control local groups. A number of poorly planned strikes failed dismally, and the public was alienated by sporadic acts of violence and intimidation. Disillusioned recruits began to drift away.

Circumstances largely fortuitous caused the collapse of the organization. By 1886 the movement for the eight-hour day had gained wide support among workers, including many who did not belong to unions. Several hundred thousand (estimates vary) were on strike in various parts of the country by May of that year. In Chicago, a center of the eight-hour

movement, about 80,000 workers were involved, and a small group of anarchists was trying to take advantage of the excitement to win support.

When a striker was killed in a fracas at the McCormick Harvesting Machine Company, the anarchists called a protest meeting on May 4, at Haymarket Square. Police intervened to break up the meeting, and someone—his identity was never established—hurled a bomb into their ranks. Seven policemen were killed and many others injured.

DOCUMENT
Engel, Address by a Haymarket Anarchist

THE AMERICAN FEDERATION OF LABOR

Although the anarchists were the immediate victims of the resulting public indignation and hysteria—seven were condemned to death and four eventually executed—organized labor, especially the Knights, suffered heavily. No tie between the Knights and the bombing could be established, but the union had

been closely connected with the eight-hour agitation, and the public tended to associate it with violence and radicalism. Its membership declined as suddenly as it had risen, and soon it ceased to exist as a force in the labor movement.

The Knights' place was taken by the American Federation of Labor (AFL), a combination of national craft unions established in 1886. In a sense the AFL was a reactionary organization. Its principal leaders, Adolph Strasser and Samuel Gompers of the Cigarmakers Union, were, like the founders of the Knights of Labor, originally interested in utopian social reforms. They even toyed with the idea of forming a workers' political party. Experience, however, soon led them to concentrate on organizing skilled workers and fighting for "bread-and-butter" issues such as higher wages and shorter hours. "Our organization does not consist of idealists," Strasser explained to a congressional committee. "We do not control the production of the world. That is controlled by the employers. . . . I look first to cigars."

The AFL accepted the fact that most workers would remain wage earners all their lives and tried to develop in them a sense of common purpose and pride in their skills and station. Strasser and Gompers paid great attention to building a strong organization of dues-paying members committed to unionism as a way of improving their lot. Rank-and-file AFL members were naturally eager to win wage increases and other benefits, but most also valued their unions for the companionship they provided, the sense of belonging to a group. In other words, despite statements such as Strasser's, unions, in and out of the AFL, were a kind of club as well as a means of defending and advancing their members' material interests.

The chief weapon of the federation was the strike, which it used to win concessions from employers and to attract recruits. Gompers, president of the AFL almost continuously from 1886 until his death in 1924, encouraged workers to make "intelligent use of the ballot" in order to advance their interests. The federation worked for such things as eight-hour days, employers' liability, and mine-safety laws, but it avoided direct involvement in politics. "I have my own philosophy and my own dreams," Gompers once told a left-wing French politician, "but first and foremost I want to increase the workingman's welfare year by year. . . . The French workers waste their economic force by their political divisions."

Gompers's approach to labor problems produced solid, if unspectacular, growth for the AFL. Unions with a total of about 150,000 members formed the federation in 1886. By 1892 the membership had reached 250,000, and in 1901 it passed the million mark.

LABOR MILITANCY REBUFFED

The stress of the AFL on the strike weapon reflected rather than caused the increasing militancy of labor. Workers felt themselves threatened from all sides: the growing size and power of their corporate employers; the substitution of machines for human skills; the invasion of foreign workers willing to accept substandard wages. At the same time they had tasted some of the material benefits of industrialization and had learned the advantages of concerted action.

The average employer behaved like a tyrant when dealing with his workers. He discharged them arbitrarily when they tried to organize unions; he hired scabs to replace strikers; he frequently failed to provide the most rudimentary protection against injury on the job. Some employers, Carnegie for example, professed to approve of unions, but almost none would bargain with labor collectively. To do so, they argued, would be to deprive workers of their freedom to contract for their own labor in any way they saw fit.

The industrialists of the period were not all ogres; they were as alarmed by the rapid changes of the times as their workers, and since they had more at stake materially, they were probably more frightened by the uncertainties. Deflation, technological change, and intense competition kept even the most successful under constant pressure.

The thinking of most employers was remarkably confused. They considered workers who joined unions "disloyal," and at the same time they treated labor as a commodity to be purchased as cheaply as possible. "If I wanted boiler iron," Henry B. Stone, a railroad official, explained, "I would go out on the market and buy it where I could get it cheapest, and if I wanted to employ men, I would do the same." Yet Stone was furious when the men he had "bought" joined a union. When labor was scarce, employers resisted demands for higher wages by arguing that the price of labor was controlled by its productivity; when it was plentiful, they justified reducing wages by referring to the law of supply and demand.

Thus capital and labor were often spoiling for a fight, frequently without fully understanding why. When labor troubles developed, they tended to be bitter, even violent. In 1877 a great railroad strike convulsed much of the nation. It began on the Baltimore and Ohio system in response to a wage cut and spread to other eastern lines and then throughout the West until about two-thirds of the railroad mileage of the country had been shut down. Violence broke out, rail yards were put to the torch, dismayed and frightened businessmen formed militia companies to patrol the streets of Chicago and other cities. Eventually President Hayes sent federal troops to the trouble spots to restore order, and the strike collapsed. There

had been no real danger of revolution, but the violence and destruction of the strike had been without precedent in America.

The disturbances of 1877 were a response to a business slump, those of the next decade a response to good times. Twice as many strikes occurred in 1886 as in any previous year. Even before the Haymarket bombing centered the country's attention on labor problems, the situation had become so disturbing that President Grover Cleveland, in the first presidential message devoted to labor problems, had urged Congress to create a voluntary arbitration board to aid in settling labor disputes—a remarkable suggestion for a man of Cleveland's conservative, laissez-faire approach to economic issues.

In 1892 a violent strike broke out among silver miners at Coeur d'Alene, Idaho, and a far more important clash shook Andrew Carnegie's Homestead steel plant near Pittsburgh when strikers attacked 300 private guards brought in to protect strikebreakers. Seven guards were killed at Homestead and the rest forced to "surrender" and march off ignominiously. The Homestead affair was part of a struggle between capital and labor in the steel industry. Steel producers insisted that the workers were holding back progress by resisting technological advances, while the workers believed that the company was refusing to share the fruits of more efficient operation fairly. The strike was precipitated by the decision of company officials to crush the union at all costs. The final defeat, after a five-month walkout, of the 24,000-member Amalgamated Association of Iron and Steel Workers, one of the most important elements in the AFL, destroyed unionism as an effective force in the steel industry and set back the progress of organized labor all over the country.

As in the case of the Haymarket bombing, the activities of radicals on the fringe of the dispute turned the public against the steelworkers. The boss of Homestead was Henry Clay Frick, a tough-minded foe of unions who was determined to "teach our employees a lesson." Frick made the decision to bring in strikebreakers and to employ Pinkerton detectives to protect them. During the course of the strike, Alexander Berkman, an anarchist, burst into Frick's office and attempted to assassinate him. Frick was only slightly wounded, but the attack brought him much sympathy and unjustly discredited the strikers.

The most important strike of the period took place in 1894. It began when the workers at George Pullman's Palace Car factory outside Chicago walked out in protest against wage cuts. (While reducing wages, Pullman insisted on holding the line on rents in the company town of Pullman; when a delegation called on him to remonstrate, he refused to give in and had three of the leaders fired.) Some Pullman workers belonged to the American Railway Union, headed by Eugene V. Debs. After the strike had dragged along for weeks, the union voted to refuse to handle trains with Pullman cars. The union was perfectly willing to handle mail trains, but the owners refused to run trains unless they were made up of a full complement of cars.

When Pullman cars were added to mail trains, the workers refused to move them. The resulting railroad strike tied up trunk lines running in and out of Chicago. The railroad owners appealed to President Cleveland to send troops to preserve order. On the pretext that the soldiers were needed to ensure the movement of the mails, Cleveland agreed. When Debs defied a federal injunction to end the walkout, he was jailed for contempt and the strike was broken.

▲ Members of the American Railway Union trying to stop trains carrying Pullman cars out of Chicago, as depicted by an artist. The sheriff, with badge, is at the center of the scene. Both the rioting workers and the company's men carry guns.

WHITHER AMERICA, WHITHER DEMOCRACY?

Each year more of the nation's wealth and power seemed to fall into fewer hands. As with the railroads, other industries were being influenced, if not completely dominated, by bankers. The firm of J. P. Morgan and Company controlled many railroads; the largest steel, electrical, agricultural machinery, rubber, and shipping companies; two life insurance companies; and a number of banks. By 1913 Morgan and the Rockefeller National City Bank group between them could name 341 directors to 112 corporations worth over $22.2 billion. The "Money Trust," a loose but potent fraternity of financiers, seemed fated to become the ultimate monopoly.

Centralization unquestionably increased efficiency, at least in industries that used a great deal of expensive machinery to turn out goods for the mass market, and in those where close coordination of output, distribution, and sales was important. The public benefited immensely from the productive efficiency of the new empires. Living standards rose.

But the trend toward giantism raised doubts. With ownership falling into fewer hands, what would be the ultimate effect of big business on American democracy? What did it mean for ordinary people when a few tycoons possessed huge fortunes and commanded such influence even on Congress and the courts?

The crushing of the Pullman strike demonstrated the power of the courts to break strikes by issuing injunctions. And the courts seemed only concerned with protecting the interests of the rich and powerful. Particularly ominous for organized labor was the fact that the federal government based its request for the injunction that broke the strike on the Sherman Antitrust Act, arguing that the American Railway Union was a combination in restraint of trade. An indirect result of the Pullman strike was that while serving his sentence for contempt, Eugene Debs was visited by a number of prominent socialists who sought to convert him to their cause. One gave him a copy of Karl Marx's *Capital*, which he found too dull to finish, but he did read *Looking Backward* and *Wealth Against Commonwealth*. In 1897 he became a socialist.

MILESTONES

1859	First oil well is drilled in Pennsylvania
	Charles Darwin publishes *The Origin of Species*
1868	Carnegie Steel Company is formed
1869	George Westinghouse invents air brake
	Garment workers found Knights of Labor
1870–1890	Railroad trunk lines are completed
1876	Alexander Graham Bell invents telephone
1877	Great railroad strike convulses nation
	Munn v. *Illinois* upholds state regulatory laws
1879	Thomas Edison invents electric light bulb
	Reformer Henry George publishes *Progress and Poverty*
1884	Marxist Laurence Gronlund publishes *The Cooperative Commonwealth*
1886	Anarchists clash with police in Chicago's Haymarket bombing
	Craft unions found American Federation of Labor (AFL)
1887	Interstate Commerce Act regulates railroads
1888	Edward Bellamy publishes utopian *Looking Backward*
1889	Philanthropist Andrew Carnegie publishes "Gospel of Wealth"
1890	Sherman Antitrust Act outlaws monopolies
1892	Seven Pinkerton guards are killed in Homestead steel strike
	General Electric Company is formed
1894	Eugene V. Debs leads American Railway Union in Pullman strike
	Henry Demarest Lloyd condemns laissez-faire in *Wealth Against the Commonwealth*
1895	*U.S.* v. *E.C. Knight Company* weakens Sherman Act
1901	J. P. Morgan forms U.S. Steel, "world's first billion-dollar corporation"

SUPPLEMENTARY READING

In addition to the works cited in Debating the Past (p. 492), see John A. Garraty, *The New Commonwealth* (1968), Alfred D. Chandler, Jr., *Railroads: The Nation's First Big Business* (1965), and Thomas Cochran, *Railroad Leaders* (1953). On the ways that technology transformed the way people understood daily life, see David E. Nye, *Electrifying America* (1990), and Jill Jonnes, *Empires of Light* (2003). Sven Beckert, *The Monied Metropolis: New York City and the Consolidation of the American Bourgeoisie, 1850–1896* (2001) outlines the special significance of that city in the nation's economic development and cultural mores.

The nation's expansive economy in the 1990s sparked interest in the leading businessmen and inventors a century earlier. For a detailed study of the key investment figure, see Jean Strouse, *Morgan: American Financier* (1999). Other examples include Harold C. Livesay, *Andrew Carnegie and the Rise of Big Business* (2000); Michael P. Malone, *James J. Hill* (1996); Ron Chernow, *Titan* (1998), on John D. Rockefeller and the oil industry; James A. Mackey, *Alexander Graham Bell: A Life* (1997); and Neil Baldwin, *Edison: Inventing the Century* (2001).

For the radical critics, see John L. Thomas, *Alternative Americas: Henry George, Edward Bellamy, Henry Demarest Lloyd* (1983), Howard H. Quint, *The Forging of American Socialism* (1964), L. Glen Seretan, *Daniel De Leon: The Odyssey of an American Marxist* (1979), and also the radicals' own writings.

On the growth of unions see David Montgomery, *Beyond Equality* (1967), Leon Fink, *Workingmen's Democracy: The Knights of Labor and American Politics* (1983), and Nick Salvatore, *Eugene V. Debs* (1982). Jo Ann Argersinger, *Making the Amalgamated* (1999) describes the relation of gender and ethnicity in the rise of the clothing workers' union in Baltimore. Robert E. Weird, *Knights Unhorsed* (2000) blames internal dissension for the Knights' rapid decline. Lawrence Blickman, *A Living Wage* (1997) insists that labor radicalism persisted even after unionized workers won steady wages. The important strikes and labor violence of the period are covered in David O. Stowell, *Streets, Railroads, and the Great Strike of 1877* (1999), R. V. Bruce, *1877: Year of Violence* (1959), Paul Avrich, *The Haymarket Tragedy* (1984), Carl S. Smith, *Urban Disorder and the Shape of Belief* (1995), and Richard Schneirov, ed., *The Pullman Strike and the Crisis of the 1890s* (1999). On working-class culture, see Herbert G. Gutman, *Work, Culture, and Society in Industrializing America* (1976), and Roy Rosenzweig, *Eight Hours for What We Will* (1983). On the challenge confronting the unions, see David Montgomery, *The Fall of the House of Labor* (1987).

SUGGESTED WEBSITES

Alexander Graham Bell Family Papers at the Library of Congress

http://memory.loc.gov/ammem/bellhtml/bellhome.html

This site contains papers from 1862 to 1939, as well as a chronology, images, selected, selected documents, and interpretive essays about Bell.

Alexander Graham Bell Telephone Sketch

http://lcweb2.loc.gov/cgi-bin/query/D?mcc:1:./temp/~ammem_gqbY::

This Library of Congress site has the sketch Bell made of his invention, the telephone.

Anarchist Archives at Pitzer University

http://dwardmac.pitzer.edu/Anarchist_Archives/archivehome.html

This archives includes classic anarchist texts, especially information about and graphics of the Haymarket Riot.

John D. Rockefeller and the Standard Oil Company

http://www.micheloud.com/FXM/SO/

This study with accompanying images by François Micheloud tells of the rise of Rockefeller and his mammoth company.

National Refinery Company

http://www.enarco.com/

This positive history of the company reflects industrial changes of late-nineteenth-century America.

Labor–Management Conflict in American History

http://history.osu.edu/Projects/LaborConflict/Default.htm

This Ohio State University site includes primary accounts of some of the major events in the history of the labor–management conflict in the late-nineteenth and early-twentieth centuries.

Samuel Gompers Papers at the University of Maryland

http://www.history.umd.edu/Gompers/index.html

This site includes information about the papers project. It also has a photo gallery, selected documents, and a brief history of the first president of the American Federation of Labor.

American Society in the Industrial Age

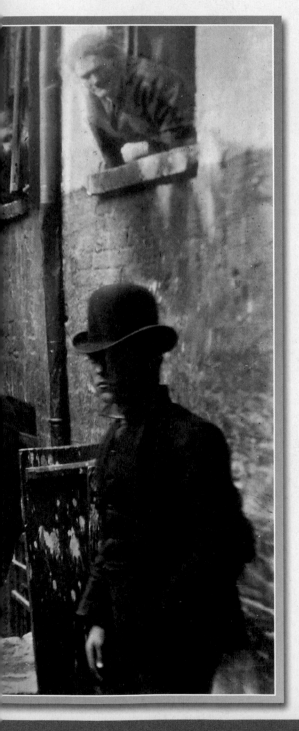

▼ Jacob Riis's photograph of the slums of lower Manhattan, from his classic *How the Other Half Lives* (1890)

CHAPTER CONTENTS

The industrialization that followed the Civil War profoundly affected every aspect of American life. New machines, improvements in transportation and communication, the appearance of the great corporation with its uncertain implications for the future—all made deep impressions on the shape and character of American society. The growth of cities and the influx of tens of thousands of immigrants who knew little about urban life and who neither spoke nor understood English transformed the immigrants and the world they inhabited.

The United States was fast becoming a modern nation. Some found this alarming. Physician George M. Beard contended that "modern civilization" overloaded the human nervous system the way burning too many of Thomas Edison's lightbulbs would overload an electrical circuit. On the other hand, Edward Bellamy saw the future as a "paradise of order, equity, and felicity." Most Americans took a more balanced view, believing that the modern world encompassed new possibilities as well as perils. The future beckoned, and yet it also menaced.

MIDDLE-CLASS LIFE

"This middle-class country had got a middle-class president, at last," Ralph Waldo Emerson had noted with satisfaction when Lincoln took office in 1861. Emerson did not endorse an economic class so much as a set of values that were, pointedly, antithetical to those of the antebellum South. Middle-class culture took the best aspects of romanticism—

the enshrinement of human potential, the restless striving for personal betterment, the zest for competition and excitement—and tempered them with a passion for self-control and regularity.

But the Civil War sapped middle-class culture of its reforming zeal. The vital energy that had spawned a host of antebellum reform movements became transmuted into greater mass; the fervor of the individual was channeled into institutions. American society and culture underwent a process of "incorporation," as the predominant form of the business world seeped deep into the American consciousness.

The middle-class family similarly lost some of its moral fervor and gained a new substantiality. The transition can be summarized by comparing the March family in Louisa May Alcott's *Little Women* (1868–1869) with William Dean Howell's Laphams (*The Rise of Silas Lapham*) (1885) and his Basil Marches (*Hazard of New Fortunes*) (1890). Where piety is the cornerstone of Alcott's family, epitomized by Marmee's unceasing attempts to teach the girls to accept God's will, the Laphams assert their middle-class pretensions by building an ostentatious home in the suburbs and the Marches, by impeccable mastery of etiquette. Social conventions checked wayward assertions of individualism.

Historians had long claimed that family relations were similarly stiff and, in matters pertaining to sexuality, downright prudish. One witless historian imagined that intercourse occurred "in a dark bedroom into which the husband would creep to create his offspring in silence while the wife endured the connection in a coma." But diaries and letters provide ample proof that many couples experienced emotionally intense and sexually fulfilling relationships. Elaborate and protracted courtship rituals, which doubtless proved frustrating, intensified the expression of love by delaying its gratification. Middle-class mothers at the end of the century had two or three children, four or five fewer than their grandmothers. Their families were smaller mostly because they married later in life and practiced abstinence, though during the last half of the century there was a "commercial explosion," as one scholar termed it, in the dissemination of contraceptive devices and the practice of abortion.

The children in middle-class families, while much treasured, were carefully supervised. Upwardly striving

▲ The glove counter at Rike's Department Store in Dayton, Ohio (1893). Shopping was an excuse for middle-class women to venture from the home into public. Rike's department store was decorated much like the Victorian home: potted ferns, stuffed animals, and carpeted stairways. The salesgirl *(far right)* was obliged to leave the home to work. She spent much of her income to "keep up appearances" to enable her to mix with middle-class shoppers.

parents were much concerned about the status and prospects of their children's marriage partners, but it was no longer considered proper to interfere with "the course of true love" for any materialistic or purely social reason.

While most women remained home to supervise their children, men worked away from home, in shops and offices. Members of the professions and the large and diffuse groups of shopkeepers, small manufacturers, skilled craftsmen, and established farmers that made up the middle class lived in varying degrees of comfort. A family with an annual income of $1000 in the 1880s would have no need to skimp on food, clothing, or shelter. When Professor Woodrow Wilson moved with his family to Wesleyan University in 1888, he was able to rent a large house and employ two full-time servants on his salary of $2500 a year. Indeed, at this time, about a quarter of all urban families employed at least one servant.

Middle-class family life was defined in terms of tangible goods: fashionable clothes and, especially, a large home crowded with furniture, books, lamps, and all manner of bibelots. Modern scholars have indicted the morality as well as the aesthetics of this incipient "culture of consumption," criticisms commonly aired by the people themselves. No attack on middle-class culture and its conspicuous consumption exceeds the venom of Thorstein Veblen's *Theory of the Leisure Class* (1899). Fashionable clothes, he observed,

Health Check at
Ellis Island

University, has left a moving description of what it was like. He arrived in 1874 on the Hamburg-American liner *Westphalia* amid a horde of other newcomers. Disembarking at Hoboken, he was taken by tug to the immigration reception center at Castle Garden on the southern tip of Manhattan Island. He confessed to the authorities that he had only 5 cents to his name and knew no Americans except—by reputation—Franklin, Lincoln, and Harriet Beecher Stowe. But he explained in eloquent phrases why he wanted to live in the land of liberty rather than in the Austro-Hungarian empire.

The officials conferred briefly, then admitted him. After a good breakfast, supplied by the immigration authorities, someone from the Castle Garden Labor Bureau offered him a job as a farmhand in Delaware. Within 24 hours of his arrival he had reached his destination, ready to go to work.

Before 1882, when—in addition to the Chinese—criminals, and persons adjudged mentally defective or liable to become public charges were excluded, entry into the United States was almost unrestricted. Indeed, until 1891 the Atlantic coast states, not the federal government, exercised whatever controls were imposed on newcomers. Even when federally imposed, medical inspection was perfunctory. Public health officials boasted that with "one glance" at each arrival, the inspectors could "take in six details, namely the scalp, face, neck, hands, gait and general condition, both mental and physical." Only those who failed this "test" were examined more closely. On average, only 1 immigrant in 50 was ultimately rejected.

Private agencies, philanthropic and commercial, served as a link between the new arrivals and employers looking for labor. Until the Foran Act of 1885 outlawed the practice, a few companies brought in skilled workers under contract, advancing them passage money and collecting it in installments from their paychecks, a system somewhat like the indentured servitude of colonial times. Numerous nationality groups assisted (and sometimes exploited) their compatriots by organizing "immigrant banks" that recruited labor in the old country, arranged transportation, and then housed the newcomers in boardinghouses in the United States while finding them jobs. The *padrone* system of the Italians and Greeks was typical. The *padrone,* a sort of contractor who agreed to supply gangs of unskilled workers to companies for a lump sum, usually signed on immigrants unfamiliar with American wage levels at rates that ensured him a healthy profit.

Beginning in the 1880s, the spreading effects of industrialization in Europe caused a shift in the sources of American immigration from northern and western to southern and eastern sections of the Continent. In 1882, 789,000 immigrants entered the United States; more than 350,000 came from Great Britain and Germany, only 32,000 from Italy, and fewer than 17,000 from Russia. In 1907—the all-time peak year, with 1,285,000 immigrants—Great Britain and Germany supplied fewer than half as many as they had 25 years earlier, while Russia and Italy were supplying eleven times as many as then. Up to 1880, only about 200,000 southern and eastern Europeans had migrated to America. Between 1880 and 1910, approximately 8.4 million arrived.

NEW IMMIGRANTS FACE NEW NATIVISM

The "new" immigrants, like the "old" Irish of the 1840s and 1850s, were mostly peasants. They also seemed more than ordinarily clannish; southern Italians typically called all people outside their families *forestieri,* "foreigners." Old-stock Americans thought them harder to assimilate, and in fact many were. Some Italian immigrants, for example, were unmarried men who had come to the United States to earn enough money to buy a farm back home. Such people made hard and willing workers but were not much concerned with being part of an American community.

These "birds of passage" were a substantial minority, but the immigrant who saved in order to bring his wife and children or his younger brothers and sisters to America was more typical. In addition, thousands of immigrants came as family groups and intended to remain. Some, like the eastern European Jewish migrants, were refugees who were almost desperately eager to become Americans, although of course they retained and nurtured much of their traditional culture.

VIDEO

Ellis Island
Immigrants, 1903

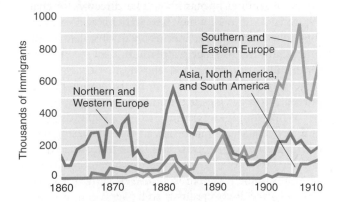

▲ **Immigration, 1860–1910**

In this graph, Germany is counted as a part of northern and western Europe. Note the new immigration from southern and eastern Europe in the early 1900s.

▲ An 1890s classroom with more than forty children, all about the same age and set to the same assignment by a woman teacher. The urban public school had arrived.

unskilled workers quickly grasped the possibilities. Science courses were taught in some of the new high schools, but secondary education was still assumed to be only for those with special abilities and youths whose families did not require that they immediately become breadwinners. As late as 1890 fewer than 300,000 of the 14.3 million children attending public and private schools had progressed beyond the eighth grade and nearly a third of these were attending private institutions.

In 1880 Calvin M. Woodward opened a Manual Training School in St. Louis, and soon a number of similar schools were offering courses in carpentry, metalwork, sewing, and other crafts. Woodward thought of vocational training as part of a broad general education rather than as preparation for a specific occupation, but by 1890, 36 cities had established purely vocational public high schools.

Because manual training attracted the backing of industrialists, organized labor was at first suspicious of the new trend. One union leader called trade schools "breeding schools for scabs and rats." Fortunately, the usefulness of such training soon became evident to the unions; by 1910 the AFL was lobbying side by side with the National Association of Manufacturers for more trade schools.

Education certainly helped young people to rise in the world, but progress from rags to real riches was far from common. Carnegies were rare. A study of the family backgrounds of 200 late-nineteenth-century business leaders revealed that nearly all of them grew up in well-to-do middle-class families. They were far better educated than the general run, and most were members of one or another Protestant church.

The unrealistic expectations inspired by the rags-to-riches myth more than the absence of real opportunity probably explains why so many workers, even when expressing dissatisfaction with life as it was, continued to subscribe to such middle-class values as hard work and thrift—that is, they continued to hope.

THE "NEW" IMMIGRATION

Industrial expansion increased the need for labor, and this in turn powerfully stimulated immigration. Between 1866 and 1915 about 25 million foreigners entered the United States. Industrial growth alone does not explain the influx. The launching in 1858 of the English liner *Great Eastern*, which was nearly 700 feet from stem to stern and weighed about 19,000 tons, opened a new era in transatlantic travel. Although most immigrants traveled in steerage, which was cramped and almost totally lacking in anything that could be considered an amenity, the Atlantic crossing, once so hazardous, became safe and speedy with the perfection of the steamship. Competition between the great packet lines such as Cunard, North German Lloyd, and Holland-America drove down the cost of the passage, and advertising by the lines further stimulated traffic.

"Push" pressures as well as these "pull" factors had much to do with this "new" immigration. Improvements in transportation produced unexpected and disruptive changes in the economies of many European countries. Cheap wheat from the United States, Russia, and other parts of the world poured into Europe, bringing disaster to farmers throughout Europe. The spreading industrial revolution and the increased use of farm machinery led to the collapse of the peasant economy of central and southern Europe. For rural inhabitants this meant the loss of self-sufficiency, the fragmentation of landholdings, unemployment, and for many the decision to make a new start in the New World.

Political and religious persecutions pushed still others into the migrating stream, but the main reason for immigration remained the desire for economic betterment. "In America," a British immigrant reported, "you get pies and puddings."

While immigrants continued to people the farms of America, industry absorbed an ever-increasing number of the newcomers. In 1870 one industrial worker in three was foreign-born. When congressional investigators examined 21 major industries early in the new century, they discovered that well over half of the labor force had not been born in the United States.

Most of the new millions entered the country by way of New York City. A Serbian immigrant, Michael Pupin, later a distinguished physicist at Columbia

Middle-class women did replace men as teachers in most of the nation's grade schools, and they also replaced men as clerks and secretaries and operators of the new typewriters in government departments and in business offices. Most men with the knowledge of spelling and grammar that these positions required had better opportunities and were uninterested in office work, so women high school graduates, of whom there was an increasing number, filled the gap.

Both department store clerks and "typewriters" (as they were called) earned more money than unskilled factory workers, and working conditions were more pleasant. Opportunities for promotion for women, however, were rare; managerial posts in these fields remained almost exclusively in the hands of men.

FARMERS

Long the backbone of American society, independent farmers and the agricultural way of life were rapidly being left behind in the race for wealth and status. The number of farmers and the volume of agricultural production continued to rise, but agriculture's relative place in the national economy was declining. Between 1860 and 1890 the number of farms rose from 2 million to 4.5 million; wheat output leaped from 173 million bushels to 449 million, cotton from 5.3 million bales to 8.5 million. The rural population increased from 25 million to 40.8 million. Yet industry was expanding far faster, and the urban population, quadrupling in the period, would soon overtake and pass that of the countryside.

Along with this relative decline, farmers suffered a decline in status. Compared to middle-class city dwellers, they seemed provincial and behind the times. People in the cities began to refer to farmers as "rubes," "hicks," and "hayseeds" and to view them with amused tolerance or even contempt.

This combination of circumstances angered and frustrated farmers. Waves of radicalism swept the agricultural regions, giving rise to demands for social and economic experiments that played a major role in breaking down rural laissez-faire prejudices. As we have seen, in the 1870s pressure from the Patrons of Husbandry produced legislation regulating railroads and warehouses. This Granger movement also led to many cooperative experiments in the marketing of farm products and in the purchase of machinery, fertilizers, and other goods.

DOCUMENT

Advice on
Keeping Children
on the Farm

Farmers were not all affected by economic developments in the same way. Because of the steady decline of the price level, those in newly settled regions were usually worse off than those in older areas since they had to borrow money to get started and were therefore burdened with fixed interest charges that became harder to meet each year. In the

IMAGE

The Purposes of
the Grange

▲ A sod house in North Dakota, 1896. Individual "bricks" of sod were hewn from the ground and stacked in layers to build such houses. The roof was made of timber packed with branches, twigs, straw, and more sod. This house was expanded with a room made of planed lumber (right). Sod houses were quite cool in summer and warm in winter, although excess moisture was always a problem.

induce "aesthetic nausea," prompting women to soon discard them; college athletics was equally wasteful, "since success as an athlete presumes, not only a waste of time, but also a waste of money." (Veblen, never popular on campus, had trouble holding a job.)

SKILLED AND UNSKILLED WORKERS

DOCUMENT

Massachusetts Bureau of Statistics of Labor

Wage earners felt the full force of the industrial tide, being affected in countless ways— some beneficial, others unfortunate. As manufacturing and mining became more important, the number of workers in these fields multiplied rapidly: from 885,000 in 1860 to more than 3.2 million in 1890. While workers lacked much sense of solidarity, they exerted a far larger influence on society at the turn of the century than they had in the years before the Civil War.

More efficient methods of production enabled them to increase their output, making possible a rise in their standard of living. The working day still tended to approximate the hours of daylight, but it was shortening perceptibly by the 1880s, at least in many occupations. In 1860 the average had been 11 hours, but by 1880 only one worker in four labored more than 10 hours and radicals were beginning to talk about 8 hours as a fair day's work.

This generalization, however, conceals some important differences. Skilled industrial workers—such types as railroad engineers and conductors, machinists, and iron molders—were quite well off in most cases. But it was still true that unskilled laborers could not earn enough to maintain a family decently by their own efforts alone.

Industrialization created problems for workers beyond the obvious one of earning enough money to support themselves. By and large, skilled workers, always better off than the unskilled, improved their positions relatively, despite the increased use of machinery. Furthermore, when machines took the place of human skills, jobs became monotonous. Mechanization undermined both the artisans' pride and their bargaining power vis-à-vis their employers. As expensive machinery became more important, the worker seemed of necessity less important. Machines more than workers controlled the pace of work and its duration. The time clock regulated the labor force more rigidly than the most exacting foreman. The length of the workday may have declined, but the pace of work and the danger involved in working around heavy, high-speed machinery increased accordingly.

As businesses grew larger, personal contact between employer and hired hand tended to disappear. Relations between them became less human, more businesslike, and ruthless. On the other hand, large enterprises usually employed a higher percentage of managerial and clerical workers than smaller companies, thus providing opportunities for more "blue-collar" workers to rise in the industrial hierarchy. But the trend toward bigness made it more difficult for workers to rise from the ranks of labor to become manufacturers themselves, as Andrew Carnegie, for example, had done during the Civil War era.

Another problem for workers was that industrialization tended to accentuate swings of the business cycle. On the upswing something approaching full employment existed, but in periods of depression unemployment became a problem that affected workers without regard for their individual abilities. It is significant that the word *unemployment* (though not, of course, the condition itself) was a late-nineteenth-century invention.

WORKING WOMEN

Women continued to supply a significant part of the industrial working force. But now many more of them were working outside their homes; the factory had almost completely replaced the household as the seat of manufacturing.[1] Textile mills and "the sewing trades" absorbed a large percentage of women, but in all fields women were paid substantially lower wages than men.

Women found many new types of work in these years, a fact commented on by the *New York Times* as early as 1869. They made up the overwhelming majority of salespersons and cashiers in the big new department stores. Store managers considered women more polite, easier to control, and more honest than male workers, all qualities especially valuable in the huge emporiums. Over half of the more than 1700 employees in A. T. Stewart's New York store were women.

Educated, middle-class women also dominated the new profession of nursing that developed alongside the expanding medical profession and the establishment of large urban hospitals. To nearly all doctors, to most men, and indeed to many women of that day, nursing seemed the perfect female profession since it required the same characteristics that women were thought to have by nature: selflessness, cleanliness, kindliness, tact, sensitivity, and submissiveness to male control. Typical was this remark of a contemporary authority: "Since God could not care for all the sick, he made women to nurse." Why it had not occurred to the Lord to make more women physicians, or for that matter members of other prestigious professions like law and the clergy, this man did not explain, probably because it had not occurred to him either.

---

[1] However, at least half of all working women were domestic servants.

1870s farmers in Illinois and Iowa suffered most—which accounts for the strength of the Granger movement in that region. Except as a purely social organization, the Grange had little importance in eastern states, where rapidly expanding urban markets made farmers relatively prosperous. A typical eastern farm family raising wheat and other grains and perhaps some livestock worked hard but made a good living. Such a family might employ a neighbor's daughter to help with housework, milking, and similar chores and a "hired hand" whose work was mainly in the fields.

By the late 1880s farmers in the old Middle West had also become better established. Even when prices dipped and a general depression gripped the country, they were able to weather the bad times nicely by taking advantage of lower transportation costs, better farm machinery, and new fertilizers and insecticides to increase output and by shifting from wheat to the production of corn, oats, hogs, and cattle, which had not declined so drastically in price.

On the agricultural frontier from Texas to the Dakotas, and through the states of the old Confederacy, farmers were less fortunate. The burdens of the crop-lien system kept thousands of southern farmers in penury, while on the Plains life was a succession of hardships. The first settlers in western Kansas, Nebraska, and the Dakotas took up land along the rivers and creeks, where they found enough timber for home building, fuel, and fencing. Later arrivals had to build houses of the tough prairie sod and depend on hay, sunflower stalks, and buffalo dung for fuel.

Frontier farm families had always had to work hard and endure the hazards of storm, drought, and insect plagues, along with isolation and loneliness. But all these burdens were magnified on the prairies and the High Plains. Life was particularly hard for farm women, who, in addition to childcare and housework, performed endless farm chores—milking cows, feeding livestock, raising vegetables, and so on. "I . . . am set and running every morning at half-past four o'clock, and run all day, often until half-past eleven P.M.," one farm woman explained. "Is it any wonder I have become slightly demoralized?"

WORKING-CLASS FAMILY LIFE

Early social workers who visited the homes of industrial laborers in this period reported enormous differences in the standard of living of people engaged in the same line of work, differences related to such variables as health, intelligence, the wife's ability as a homemaker and the degree of the family's commitment to middle-class values, and pure luck. Some families spent most of their income on food; others

saved substantial sums even when earning no more than $400 or $500 a year. Family incomes varied greatly among workers who received similar hourly wages, depending on the steadiness of employment and on the number of family members holding jobs.

Consider the cases of two Illinois coal miners, each a decent, hardworking union man with a large family, each earning $1.50 a day in 1883. One was out of work nearly half the year; his income in 1883 was only $250. He, his wife, and their five children, aged 3 to 19, lived in a two-room tenement. They existed almost exclusively on a diet of bread and salt meat. Nevertheless, as an investigator reported, their home was neat and clean and three of the children were attending school.

The other miner, father of four children, worked full time and brought home $420 in 1883. He owned a six-room house and an acre of land, where the family raised vegetables. Their food bill for the year was more than ten times that of the family just described: two admirable families, probably similar in social attitudes and perhaps in political loyalties but with very different standards of living.

The cases of two families headed by railroad brakemen provide a different variation. One man brought home only $360 to house and feed a wife and eight children. Here is the report of a state official who interviewed the family: "Clothes ragged, children half-dressed and dirty. They all sleep in one room regardless of sex. . . . The entire concern is as wretched as could be imagined. Father is shiftless. . . . Wife is without ambition or industry."

The other brakeman and his wife had only two children, and he earned $484 in 1883. They owned a well-furnished house, kept a cow, and raised vegetables for home consumption. Although they were far from rich, they managed to put aside enough for insurance, reading matter, and a few small luxuries.

WORKING-CLASS ATTITUDES

Social workers and government officials made many efforts in the 1880s and 1890s to find out how working people felt about all sorts of matters connected with their jobs. Their reports reveal a wide spectrum of opinion. To the question, asked of two Wisconsin carpenters, "What new laws, in your opinion, ought to be enacted?" one replied: "Keep down strikes and rioters. Let every man attend to his own business." But the other answered: "Complete nationalization of land and all ways of transportation. Burn all government bonds. A graduated income tax. . . . Abolish child labor and [pass] any other act that capitalists say is wrong."

Every variation of opinion between these extremes was expressed by working people in many sections and in many kinds of work. In 1881 a female

textile worker in Lawrence, Massachusetts, said to an interviewer: "If you will stand by the mill, and see the people coming out, you will be surprised to see the happy, contented look they all have."

Despite such remarks and the general improvement in living standards, it is clear, if only from the large number of bitter strikes of the period, that there was a considerable dissatisfaction among industrial workers. Writing in 1885, the labor leader Terence V. Powderly reported that "a deep-rooted feeling of discontent pervades the masses."

The discontent had many causes. For some, poverty was still the chief problem, but for others, rising aspirations triggered discontent. Workers were confused about their destiny; the tradition that no one of ability need remain a hired hand died hard. They wanted to believe their bosses and the politicians when those worthies voiced the old slogans about a classless society and the community of interest of capital and labor. "Our men," William Vanderbilt of the New York Central said in 1877, "feel that, although I . . . may have my millions and they the rewards of their daily toil, still we are about equal in the end. If they suffer, I suffer, and if I suffer, they cannot escape." "The poor," another conservative said a decade later, "are not poor because the rich are rich." Instead "the service of capital" softened their lot and gave them many benefits. Statements such as these, though self-serving, were essentially correct. The rich were growing richer and more people were growing rich, but ordinary workers were better off too. However, the gap between the very rich and the ordinary citizen was widening. "The tendency . . . is toward centralization and aggregation," the Illinois Bureau of Labor Statistics reported in 1886. "This involves a separation of the people into classes, and the permanently subordinate status of large numbers of them."

WORKING YOUR WAY UP

To study mobility in a large industrial country is extraordinarily difficult. Americans in the late nineteenth century believed their society offered great opportunities for individual advancement, and to prove it they pointed to men like Andrew Carnegie and to other poor boys who accumulated large fortunes. How general was the rise from rags to riches (or even to modest comfort) is another question.

Americans had been on the move, mostly, of course, in a westward direction, since the colonial period, but studies of census records show that there was considerable geographic mobility in urban areas throughout the last half of the nineteenth century and into the twentieth. Most investigations reveal that only about half the people recorded in one census

were still in the same place ten years later. The nation had a vast reservoir of rootless people. For many, the way to move up in the world was to move on.

In most of the cities studied, mobility was accompanied by some economic and social improvement. On the average, about a quarter of the manual laborers traced rose to middle-class status during their lifetimes, and the sons of manual laborers were still more likely to improve their place in society. In New York City about a third of the Italian and Jewish immigrants of the 1890s had risen from unskilled to skilled jobs a decade later. Even in Newburyport, Massachusetts, a town that was something of an economic backwater, most laborers made some progress, though far fewer rose to skilled or white-collar positions than in more prosperous cities.

Such progress was primarily the result of the economic growth the nation was experiencing and of the energy and ambition of the people, native-born and immigrant alike, who were pouring into the cities in such numbers. The public education system gave an additional boost to the upwardly mobile.

The history of American education after about 1870 reflects the impact of social and economic change. Although Horace Mann, Henry Barnard, and others had laid the foundations for state-supported school systems, most of these systems became compulsory only after the Civil War, when the growth of cities provided the concentration of population and financial resources necessary for economical mass education. In the 1860s about half the children in the country were getting some formal education, but this did not mean that half the children were attending school at any one time. Sessions were short, especially in rural areas, and many teachers were poorly trained. President Calvin Coolidge noted in his autobiography that the one-room school he attended in rural Vermont in the 1880s was open only in slack seasons when the twenty-odd students were not needed in the fields. "Few, if any, of my teachers reached the standard now required," he wrote, adding that his own younger sister had obtained a teaching certificate and actually taught a class when she was only 12.

Thereafter, steady growth and improvement took place. Attendance in the public schools increased from 6.8 million in 1870 to 15.5 million in 1900, a remarkable expansion even when allowance is made for the growth of the population. More remarkable still, during a time when prices were declining steadily, public expenditures for education nearly quadrupled. A typical elementary school graduate, at least in the cities, could count on having studied, besides the traditional "Three Rs," history, geography, a bit of science, drawing, and physical training.

Industrialization created many demands for vocational and technical training; both employers and

1870s farmers in Illinois and Iowa suffered most—which accounts for the strength of the Granger movement in that region. Except as a purely social organization, the Grange had little importance in eastern states, where rapidly expanding urban markets made farmers relatively prosperous. A typical eastern farm family raising wheat and other grains and perhaps some livestock worked hard but made a good living. Such a family might employ a neighbor's daughter to help with housework, milking, and similar chores and a "hired hand" whose work was mainly in the fields.

By the late 1880s farmers in the old Middle West had also become better established. Even when prices dipped and a general depression gripped the country, they were able to weather the bad times nicely by taking advantage of lower transportation costs, better farm machinery, and new fertilizers and insecticides to increase output and by shifting from wheat to the production of corn, oats, hogs, and cattle, which had not declined so drastically in price.

On the agricultural frontier from Texas to the Dakotas, and through the states of the old Confederacy, farmers were less fortunate. The burdens of the crop-lien system kept thousands of southern farmers in penury, while on the Plains life was a succession of hardships. The first settlers in western Kansas, Nebraska, and the Dakotas took up land along the rivers and creeks, where they found enough timber for home building, fuel, and fencing. Later arrivals had to build houses of the tough prairie sod and depend on hay, sunflower stalks, and buffalo dung for fuel.

Frontier farm families had always had to work hard and endure the hazards of storm, drought, and insect plagues, along with isolation and loneliness. But all these burdens were magnified on the prairies and the High Plains. Life was particularly hard for farm women, who, in addition to childcare and housework, performed endless farm chores—milking cows, feeding livestock, raising vegetables, and so on. "I . . . am set and running every morning at half-past four o'clock, and run all day, often until half-past eleven P.M.," one farm woman explained. "Is it any wonder I have become slightly demoralized?"

WORKING-CLASS FAMILY LIFE

Early social workers who visited the homes of industrial laborers in this period reported enormous differences in the standard of living of people engaged in the same line of work, differences related to such variables as health, intelligence, the wife's ability as a homemaker and the degree of the family's commitment to middle-class values, and pure luck. Some families spent most of their income on food; others

saved substantial sums even when earning no more than $400 or $500 a year. Family incomes varied greatly among workers who received similar hourly wages, depending on the steadiness of employment and on the number of family members holding jobs.

Consider the cases of two Illinois coal miners, each a decent, hardworking union man with a large family, each earning $1.50 a day in 1883. One was out of work nearly half the year; his income in 1883 was only $250. He, his wife, and their five children, aged 3 to 19, lived in a two-room tenement. They existed almost exclusively on a diet of bread and salt meat. Nevertheless, as an investigator reported, their home was neat and clean and three of the children were attending school.

The other miner, father of four children, worked full time and brought home $420 in 1883. He owned a six-room house and an acre of land, where the family raised vegetables. Their food bill for the year was more than ten times that of the family just described: two admirable families, probably similar in social attitudes and perhaps in political loyalties but with very different standards of living.

The cases of two families headed by railroad brakemen provide a different variation. One man brought home only $360 to house and feed a wife and eight children. Here is the report of a state official who interviewed the family: "Clothes ragged, children half-dressed and dirty. They all sleep in one room regardless of sex. . . . The entire concern is as wretched as could be imagined. Father is shiftless. . . . Wife is without ambition or industry."

The other brakeman and his wife had only two children, and he earned $484 in 1883. They owned a well-furnished house, kept a cow, and raised vegetables for home consumption. Although they were far from rich, they managed to put aside enough for insurance, reading matter, and a few small luxuries.

WORKING-CLASS ATTITUDES

Social workers and government officials made many efforts in the 1880s and 1890s to find out how working people felt about all sorts of matters connected with their jobs. Their reports reveal a wide spectrum of opinion. To the question, asked of two Wisconsin carpenters, "What new laws, in your opinion, ought to be enacted?" one replied: "Keep down strikes and rioters. Let every man attend to his own business." But the other answered: "Complete nationalization of land and all ways of transportation. Burn all government bonds. A graduated income tax. . . . Abolish child labor and [pass] any other act that capitalists say is wrong."

Every variation of opinion between these extremes was expressed by working people in many sections and in many kinds of work. In 1881 a female

textile worker in Lawrence, Massachusetts, said to an interviewer: "If you will stand by the mill, and see the people coming out, you will be surprised to see the happy, contented look they all have."

Despite such remarks and the general improvement in living standards, it is clear, if only from the large number of bitter strikes of the period, that there was a considerable dissatisfaction among industrial workers. Writing in 1885, the labor leader Terence V. Powderly reported that "a deep-rooted feeling of discontent pervades the masses."

The discontent had many causes. For some, poverty was still the chief problem, but for others, rising aspirations triggered discontent. Workers were confused about their destiny; the tradition that no one of ability need remain a hired hand died hard. They wanted to believe their bosses and the politicians when those worthies voiced the old slogans about a classless society and the community of interest of capital and labor. "Our men," William Vanderbilt of the New York Central said in 1877, "feel that, although I . . . may have my millions and they the rewards of their daily toil, still we are about equal in the end. If they suffer, I suffer, and if I suffer, they cannot escape." "The poor," another conservative said a decade later, "are not poor because the rich are rich." Instead "the service of capital" softened their lot and gave them many benefits. Statements such as these, though self-serving, were essentially correct. The rich were growing richer and more people were growing rich, but ordinary workers were better off too. However, the gap between the very rich and the ordinary citizen was widening. "The tendency . . . is toward centralization and aggregation," the Illinois Bureau of Labor Statistics reported in 1886. "This involves a separation of the people into classes, and the permanently subordinate status of large numbers of them."

Working Your Way Up

To study mobility in a large industrial country is extraordinarily difficult. Americans in the late nineteenth century believed their society offered great opportunities for individual advancement, and to prove it they pointed to men like Andrew Carnegie and to other poor boys who accumulated large fortunes. How general was the rise from rags to riches (or even to modest comfort) is another question.

Americans had been on the move, mostly, of course, in a westward direction, since the colonial period, but studies of census records show that there was considerable geographic mobility in urban areas throughout the last half of the nineteenth century and into the twentieth. Most investigations reveal that only about half the people recorded in one census were still in the same place ten years later. The nation had a vast reservoir of rootless people. For many, the way to move up in the world was to move on.

In most of the cities studied, mobility was accompanied by some economic and social improvement. On the average, about a quarter of the manual laborers traced rose to middle-class status during their lifetimes, and the sons of manual laborers were still more likely to improve their place in society. In New York City about a third of the Italian and Jewish immigrants of the 1890s had risen from unskilled to skilled jobs a decade later. Even in Newburyport, Massachusetts, a town that was something of an economic backwater, most laborers made some progress, though far fewer rose to skilled or white-collar positions than in more prosperous cities.

Such progress was primarily the result of the economic growth the nation was experiencing and of the energy and ambition of the people, native-born and immigrant alike, who were pouring into the cities in such numbers. The public education system gave an additional boost to the upwardly mobile.

The history of American education after about 1870 reflects the impact of social and economic change. Although Horace Mann, Henry Barnard, and others had laid the foundations for state-supported school systems, most of these systems became compulsory only after the Civil War, when the growth of cities provided the concentration of population and financial resources necessary for economical mass education. In the 1860s about half the children in the country were getting some formal education, but this did not mean that half the children were attending school at any one time. Sessions were short, especially in rural areas, and many teachers were poorly trained. President Calvin Coolidge noted in his autobiography that the one-room school he attended in rural Vermont in the 1880s was open only in slack seasons when the twenty-odd students were not needed in the fields. "Few, if any, of my teachers reached the standard now required," he wrote, adding that his own younger sister had obtained a teaching certificate and actually taught a class when she was only 12.

Thereafter, steady growth and improvement took place. Attendance in the public schools increased from 6.8 million in 1870 to 15.5 million in 1900, a remarkable expansion even when allowance is made for the growth of the population. More remarkable still, during a time when prices were declining steadily, public expenditures for education nearly quadrupled. A typical elementary school graduate, at least in the cities, could count on having studied, besides the traditional "Three Rs," history, geography, a bit of science, drawing, and physical training.

Industrialization created many demands for vocational and technical training; both employers and

▲ An 1890s classroom with more than forty children, all about the same age and set to the same assignment by a woman teacher. The urban public school had arrived.

unskilled workers quickly grasped the possibilities. Science courses were taught in some of the new high schools, but secondary education was still assumed to be only for those with special abilities and youths whose families did not require that they immediately become breadwinners. As late as 1890 fewer than 300,000 of the 14.3 million children attending public and private schools had progressed beyond the eighth grade and nearly a third of these were attending private institutions.

In 1880 Calvin M. Woodward opened a Manual Training School in St. Louis, and soon a number of similar schools were offering courses in carpentry, metalwork, sewing, and other crafts. Woodward thought of vocational training as part of a broad general education rather than as preparation for a specific occupation, but by 1890, 36 cities had established purely vocational public high schools.

Because manual training attracted the backing of industrialists, organized labor was at first suspicious of the new trend. One union leader called trade schools "breeding schools for scabs and rats." Fortunately, the usefulness of such training soon became evident to the unions; by 1910 the AFL was lobbying side by side with the National Association of Manufacturers for more trade schools.

Education certainly helped young people to rise in the world, but progress from rags to real riches was far from common. Carnegies were rare. A study of the family backgrounds of 200 late-nineteenth-century business leaders revealed that nearly all of them grew up in well-to-do middle-class families. They were far

better educated than the general run, and most were members of one or another Protestant church.

The unrealistic expectations inspired by the rags-to-riches myth more than the absence of real opportunity probably explains why so many workers, even when expressing dissatisfaction with life as it was, continued to subscribe to such middle-class values as hard work and thrift—that is, they continued to hope.

THE "NEW" IMMIGRATION

Industrial expansion increased the need for labor, and this in turn powerfully stimulated immigration. Between 1866 and 1915 about 25 million foreigners entered the United States. Industrial growth alone does not explain the influx. The launching in 1858 of the English liner *Great Eastern*, which was nearly 700 feet from stem to stern and weighed about 19,000 tons, opened a new era in transatlantic travel. Although most immigrants traveled in steerage, which was cramped and almost totally lacking in anything that could be considered an amenity, the Atlantic crossing, once so hazardous, became safe and speedy with the perfection of the steamship. Competition between the great packet lines such as Cunard, North German Lloyd, and Holland-America drove down the cost of the passage, and advertising by the lines further stimulated traffic.

"Push" pressures as well as these "pull" factors had much to do with this "new" immigration. Improvements in transportation produced unexpected and disruptive changes in the economies of many European countries. Cheap wheat from the United States, Russia, and other parts of the world poured into Europe, bringing disaster to farmers throughout Europe. The spreading industrial revolution and the increased use of farm machinery led to the collapse of the peasant economy of central and southern Europe. For rural inhabitants this meant the loss of self-sufficiency, the fragmentation of landholdings, unemployment, and for many the decision to make a new start in the New World.

Political and religious persecutions pushed still others into the migrating stream, but the main reason for immigration remained the desire for economic betterment. "In America," a British immigrant reported, "you get pies and puddings."

While immigrants continued to people the farms of America, industry absorbed an ever-increasing number of the newcomers. In 1870 one industrial worker in three was foreign-born. When congressional investigators examined 21 major industries early in the new century, they discovered that well over half of the labor force had not been born in the United States.

Most of the new millions entered the country by way of New York City. A Serbian immigrant, Michael Pupin, later a distinguished physicist at Columbia

Health Check at
Ellis Island

University, has left a moving description of what it was like. He arrived in 1874 on the Hamburg-American liner *Westphalia* amid a horde of other newcomers. Disembarking at Hoboken, he was taken by tug to the immigration reception center at Castle Garden on the southern tip of Manhattan Island. He confessed to the authorities that he had only 5 cents to his name and knew no Americans except—by reputation—Franklin, Lincoln, and Harriet Beecher Stowe. But he explained in eloquent phrases why he wanted to live in the land of liberty rather than in the Austro-Hungarian empire.

The officials conferred briefly, then admitted him. After a good breakfast, supplied by the immigration authorities, someone from the Castle Garden Labor Bureau offered him a job as a farmhand in Delaware. Within 24 hours of his arrival he had reached his destination, ready to go to work.

Before 1882, when—in addition to the Chinese—criminals, and persons adjudged mentally defective or liable to become public charges were excluded, entry into the United States was almost unrestricted. Indeed, until 1891 the Atlantic coast states, not the federal government, exercised whatever controls were imposed on newcomers. Even when federally imposed, medical inspection was perfunctory. Public health officials boasted that with "one glance" at each arrival, the inspectors could "take in six details, namely the scalp, face, neck, hands, gait and general condition, both mental and physical." Only those who failed this "test" were examined more closely. On average, only 1 immigrant in 50 was ultimately rejected.

Private agencies, philanthropic and commercial, served as a link between the new arrivals and employers looking for labor. Until the Foran Act of 1885 outlawed the practice, a few companies brought in skilled workers under contract, advancing them passage money and collecting it in installments from their paychecks, a system somewhat like the indentured servitude of colonial times. Numerous nationality groups assisted (and sometimes exploited) their compatriots by organizing "immigrant banks" that recruited labor in the old country, arranged transportation, and then housed the newcomers in boardinghouses in the United States while finding them jobs. The *padrone* system of the Italians and Greeks was typical. The *padrone,* a sort of contractor who agreed to supply gangs of unskilled workers to companies for a lump sum, usually signed on immigrants unfamiliar with American wage levels at rates that ensured him a healthy profit.

Beginning in the 1880s, the spreading effects of industrialization in Europe caused a shift in the sources of American immigration from northern and western to southern and eastern sections of the Continent. In 1882, 789,000 immigrants entered the United States; more than 350,000 came from Great Britain and Germany, only 32,000 from Italy, and fewer than 17,000 from Russia. In 1907—the all-time peak year, with 1,285,000 immigrants—Great Britain and Germany supplied fewer than half as many as they had 25 years earlier, while Russia and Italy were supplying eleven times as many as then. Up to 1880, only about 200,000 southern and eastern Europeans had migrated to America. Between 1880 and 1910, approximately 8.4 million arrived.

NEW IMMIGRANTS FACE NEW NATIVISM

The "new" immigrants, like the "old" Irish of the 1840s and 1850s, were mostly peasants. They also seemed more than ordinarily clannish; southern Italians typically called all people outside their families *forestieri,* "foreigners." Old-stock Americans thought them harder to assimilate, and in fact many were. Some Italian immigrants, for example, were unmarried men who had come to the United States to earn enough money to buy a farm back home. Such people made hard and willing workers but were not much concerned with being part of an American community.

These "birds of passage" were a substantial minority, but the immigrant who saved in order to bring his wife and children or his younger brothers and sisters to America was more typical. In addition, thousands of immigrants came as family groups and intended to remain. Some, like the eastern European Jewish migrants, were refugees who were almost desperately eager to become Americans, although of course they retained and nurtured much of their traditional culture.

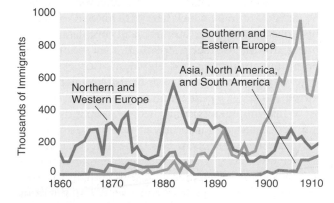

▲ **Immigration, 1860–1910**
In this graph, Germany is counted as a part of northern and western Europe. Note the new immigration from southern and eastern Europe in the early 1900s.

VIDEO

Ellis Island
Immigrants, 1903

▲ Contemporary cartoonists reflected the "new nativist" attitude against unrestricted immigration. Frank Beard's 1885 drawing shows anarchists, socialists, and members of the Mafia (indicated here as the Black Hand) arriving from the sewers of Europe and being resisted by Columbia and her watchdogs "Law" and "Order."

Cultural differences among immigrants were often large and had important effects on their relations with native-born Americans and with other immigrant groups. Italians who settled in the city of Buffalo, for example, adjusted relatively smoothly to urban industrial life because of their close family and kinship ties. Poverty, unemployment, females holding jobs outside the home, and other traumas that might have been expected to disrupt family relationships apparently had little effect. Polish immigrants in Buffalo, having different traditions, found adjustment more difficult.

German American and Irish American Catholics had different attitudes that caused them to clash over such matters as the policies of the Catholic University in Washington. Although (or perhaps because) the Haymarket anarchists were German-born, in 1887 one prominent German American denounced the Knights of Labor as a hotbed of radicalism—and was said to have claimed that it was dominated by "Irish ignoramuses." Controversies erupted between Catholic and Protestant German Americans, between Greek American groups supporting various political factions in their homeland, and so on.

Confused by such differences and conflicts, many "older" Americans concluded, wrongly but under-standably, that the new immigrants were incapable of becoming good citizens and should be kept out. During the 1880s, large numbers of social workers, economists, and church leaders, worried by the problems that arose when so many poor immigrants flocked into cities already bursting at the seams, began to believe that some restriction should be placed on the incoming human tide. The directors of charitable organizations, which bore the burden of aiding the most unfortunate immigrants, complained that their resources were being exhausted by the needs of the flood.

Social Darwinists and people obsessed with pseudoscientific ideas about "racial purity" also found the new immigration alarming. Misunderstanding the findings of the new science of genetics, they attributed the social problems associated with mass immigration to supposed physiological characteristics of the newcomers. Forgetting that earlier Americans had accused pre–Civil War Irish and German immigrants of similar deficiencies, they decided that the peoples of southern and eastern Europe were racially (and therefore permanently) inferior to "Nordic" and "Anglo-Saxon" types and ought to be kept out.

IMAGE

Looking Backward at Immigrant Origins

Workers, fearing the competition of people with low living standards and no bargaining power, spoke out against the "enticing of penniless and unapprised immigrants . . . to undermine our wages and social welfare." In 1883 the president of the Amalgamated Iron and Steel Workers told a Senate committee that Hungarian, Polish, Italian, and other immigrants "can live where I think a decent man would die; they can live on . . . food that other men would not touch." A Wisconsin iron worker put it this way: "Immigrants work for almost nothing and seem to be able to live on wind—something I can not do."

Employers were not disturbed by the influx of people with strong backs willing to work hard for low wages. Nevertheless, by the late 1880s many employers were alarmed about the supposed radicalism of the immigrants. The Haymarket bombing focused attention on the handful of foreign-born extremists in the country and loosed a flood of unjustified charges that "anarchists and communists" were dominating the labor movement. Nativism, which had waxed in the 1850s under the Know-Nothing banner and waned during the Civil War, now flared up again, and for similar reasons. Denunciations of "longhaired, wild-eyed, bad-smelling, atheistic, reckless foreign wretches," of "Europe's human and inhuman rubbish," of the "cutthroats of Beelzebub from the Rhine, the Danube, the Vistula and the Elbe" crowded the pages of the nation's press. The Grand Army of the Republic, an organization of Civil War veterans, grumbled about foreign-born radicals.

These nativists, again like the pre–Civil War variety, disliked Catholics and other minority groups more than immigrants as such. The largest nativist organization of the period, the American Protective Association, founded in 1887, existed primarily to resist what its members called "the Catholic menace." The Protestant majority treated "new" immigrants as underlings, tried to keep them out of the best jobs, and discouraged their efforts to climb the social ladder. This prejudice functioned only at the social and economic level. But nowhere in America did prejudice lead to interference with religious freedom in the narrow sense. And neither labor leaders nor important industrialists, despite their misgivings about immigration, took a broadly antiforeign position.

Foreign-Born Population, 1890

After the Exclusion Act of 1882 and the almost meaningless 1885 ban on importing contract labor, no further restrictions were imposed on immigration until the twentieth century. Strong support for a literacy test for admission developed in the 1890s, pushed by a new organization, the Immigration Restriction League. Since there was much more illiteracy in the southeastern quarter of Europe than in the northwestern, such a test would discriminate without seeming to do so on national or racial grounds. A literacy test bill passed both houses of Congress in 1897, but President Cleveland vetoed it. Such a "radical departure" from the "generous and free-handed policy" of the past, Cleveland said, was unjustified. He added, perhaps with tongue in cheek, that a literacy requirement would not keep out "unruly agitators," who were only too adept at reading and writing.

THE EXPANDING CITY AND ITS PROBLEMS

Americans who favored restricting immigration made much of the fact that so many of the newcomers crowded into the cities, aggravating problems of housing, public health, crime, and immorality. Immigrants concentrated in the cities because the jobs created by expanding industry were located there. So, of course, did native-born Americans; the proportion of urban dwellers had been steadily increasing since about 1820.

It is important to keep in mind that population density is not necessarily related to the existence of large cities. In the late nineteenth century there were areas in Asia as large as the United States that were as densely populated as Belgium and England yet overwhelmingly rural. The United States by any standard was sparsely populated, but well before the Civil War it had become one of the most urban nations in the world.

Industrialization does not entirely explain the growth of nineteenth-century cities. All the large American cities began as commercial centers, and the development of huge metropolises like New York and Chicago would have been impossible without the national transportation network. But by the final decades of the century, the expansion of industry had become the chief cause of city growth. Thus the urban concentration continued; in 1890 one person in three lived in a city, by 1910 nearly one in two.

A steadily increasing proportion of the urban population was made up of immigrants. In 1890 the foreign-born population of Chicago almost equaled the total population of Chicago in 1880; a third of all Bostonians and a quarter of all Philadelphians were immigrants; and four out of five residents of New York City were either foreign-born or the children of immigrants.

After 1890 the immigrant concentration became even more dense. The migrants from eastern and southern Europe lacked the resources to travel to the agriculturally developing regions (to say nothing of the sums necessary to acquire land and farm equipment). As the concentration progressed it fed upon

DEBATING THE PAST

Did immigrants assimilate? In this 1909 photograph, immigrant children at Ellis Island hold American flags as they share a ride in an "Uncle Sam" wagon. Did they and their parents readily adjust to life in the United States?

In 1951 historian Oscar Handlin thought not. He asserted that immigrants were "uprooted" from the lives they had known and "replanted" in "strange ground, among strangers, where strange manners prevailed." Many were shattered by the experience, which accounted for rampant crime, ruptured families, and social disorder in tenement districts.

But subsequent studies found that many immigrants adapted well. John Bodnar (1985) pointedly described immigrants as "transplanted" rather than "uprooted." When challenged by new situations, they "forged a culture, a constellation of behavioral and thought patterns which would offer them explanations, order, and a prescription for how to live with their lives." Sometimes they modified traditional institutions to serve new purposes; sometimes they created new ones, such as ethnic clubs and parochial schools. The diversity of immigrant experiences was reflected in the *Harvard Encyclopedia of American Ethnic Groups* (1980), edited by Handlin and Stephen Thernstrom. The trend toward specialized studies of different groups prompted Arthur M. Schlesinger, Jr. (1992) to bemoan his profession's role in the "disuniting of America."

In short, each child in "Uncle Sam's" wagon experienced life in his or her own way; but they were in for the ride together.

Oscar Handlin, *The Uprooted*, 1951, John Bodnar, *The Transplanted* (1985), Arthur M. Schlesinger, Jr., *The Disuniting of America* (1992). Other studies anticipating Bodnar's thesis are Francis G. Courvares, *The Remaking of Pittsburgh* (1984), Humbert S. Nelli, *Italians in Chicago* (1970), Alan Dawley, *Class and Community* (1976), and Virginia Yans-McLaughlin, *Family and Community: Italian Immigrants in Buffalo* (1977). Ronald Takaki, *A Different Mirror* (1993), endorses the multiculturalist approach. See also Roger Daniels, *Guarding the Golden Door: American Immigration Policy and Immigrants since 1882* (2004).

itself, for all the eastern cities developed many ethnic neighborhoods, in each of which immigrants of one nationality congregated. Lonely, confused, often unable to speak English, the Italians, the Greeks, the Polish and Russian Jews, and other immigrants tended to settle where their predecessors had settled.

Most newcomers intended to become United States citizens, to be absorbed in the famous American

"melting pot." But they also wanted to maintain their traditional culture. They supported "national" churches and schools. Newspapers in their native languages flourished, as did social organizations of all sorts. Each great American city became a Europe in microcosm. New York City, the great *entrepôt*, had a Little Italy; Polish, Greek, Jewish, and Bohemian quarters; and even a Chinatown.

Although ethnic neighborhoods were crowded, unhealthy, and crime-ridden, and many of the residents were desperately poor, they were not ghettos in the European sense, for those who lived there were not compelled by law to remain. Thousands "escaped" yearly to better districts. American ghettos were places where hopes and ambitions were fulfilled, where people worked hard and endured hardships in order to improve their own and their children's lot.

Observing the immigrants' attachment to "foreign" values and institutions, numbers of "natives" accused the newcomers of resisting Americanization and blamed them for urban problems. The immigrants were involved in these problems, but the rapidity of urban expansion explains the troubles associated with city life far more fully than the high percentage of foreigners.

TEEMING TENEMENTS

The cities were suffering from growing pains. Sewer and water facilities frequently could not keep pace with skyrocketing needs. By the 1890s the tremendous growth of Chicago had put such a strain on its sanitation system that the Chicago River had become virtually an open sewer, and the city's drinking water contained such a high concentration of germ-killing chemicals that it tasted like creosote. In the 1880s all the sewers of Baltimore emptied into the sluggish Back Basin, and according to the journalist H. L. Mencken, every summer the city smelled "like a billion polecats." Fire protection became less and less adequate; garbage piled up in the streets faster than it could be carted away; and the streets themselves crumbled beneath the pounding of heavy traffic. Urban growth proceeded with such speed that new streets were laid out more rapidly than they could be paved. Chicago had more than 1400 miles of dirt streets in 1890.

IMAGE

New York City Tenements

People poured into the great cities faster than housing could be built to accommodate them. The influx into areas already densely packed in the 1840s became unbearable as rising property values and the absence of zoning laws conspired to make builders use every possible foot of space, squeezing out light and air ruthlessly in order to wedge in a few additional family units.

Substandard living quarters aggravated other evils such as disease and the disintegration of family life, with its attendant mental anguish, crime, and juvenile delinquency. The bloody New York City riots of 1863, though sparked by dislike of the Civil War draft and of blacks, reflected the bitterness and frustration of thousands jammed together amid filth and threatened by disease. A citizens' committee seeking to discover the causes of the riots expressed its amazement after visiting the slums "that so much misery, disease, and wretchedness can be huddled together and hidden . . . unvisited and unthought of, so near our own abodes."

New York City created a Metropolitan Health Board in 1866, and a state tenement house law the following year made a feeble beginning at regulating city housing. Another law in 1879 placed a limit on the percentage of lot space that could be covered by new construction and established minimal standards of plumbing and ventilation. The magazine *Plumber and Sanitary Engineer* sponsored a contest to pick the best design for a tenement that met these specifications. The winner of the competition was James E. Ware, whose plan for a "dumbbell" apartment house managed to crowd from 24 to 32 four-room apartments on a plot of ground only 25 by 100 feet.

Despite these efforts in 1890 more than 1.4 million persons were living on Manhattan Island, and in some sections the population density exceeded 900 persons per acre. Jacob Riis, a reporter, captured the

▲ Impoverished immigrant families, like the one in this 1889 Jacob Riis photograph, often lived in tiny windowless rooms in crowded tenement districts. Riis devised a "flash bulb" for indoor photographs in poorly illuminated rooms like this one.

horror of the crowded warrens in his classic study of life in the slums, *How the Other Half Lives* (1890):

> Be a little careful, please! The hall is dark and you might stumble. . . . Here where the hall turns and dives into utter darkness is . . . a flight of stairs. You can feel your way, if you cannot see it. Close? Yes! What would you have? All the fresh air that enters these stairs comes from the hall-door that is forever slamming. . . . The sinks are in the hallway, that all the tenants may have access—and all be poisoned alike by their summer stenches. . . . Here is a door. Listen! That short, hacking cough, that tiny, helpless wail—what do they mean? . . . The child is dying of measles. With half a chance it might have lived; but it had none. That dark bedroom killed it.

The unhealthiness of the tenements was notorious. No one knows exactly, but as late as 1900 about three quarters of the residents of New York City's Lower East Side lacked indoor toilets and had to use backyard outhouses to relieve themselves. One noxious corner became known as the "lung block" because of the prevalence of tuberculosis among its inhabitants. In 1900 three out of five babies born in one poor district of Chicago died before their first birthday.

Equally frightening was the impact of overcrowding on the morals of tenement dwellers. The number of prison inmates in the United States increased by 50 percent in the 1880s, and the homicide rate nearly tripled, most of the rise occurring in cities. Driven into the streets by the squalor of their homes, slum youths formed gangs bearing names like Alley Gang, Rock Gang, and Hell's Kitchen Gang. From petty thievery and shoplifting they graduated to housebreaking, bank robbery, and murder. According to Jacob Riis, when the leader of the infamous Whyo Gang, convicted of murder, confessed his sins to a prison chaplain, "his father confessor turned pale . . . though many years of labor as chaplain of the Tombs had hardened him to such rehearsals."

Slums bred criminals—the wonder was that they bred so few. They also drove well-to-do residents into exclusive sections and to the suburbs. From Boston's Beacon Hill and Back Bay to San Francisco's Nob Hill, the rich retired into their cluttered mansions and ignored conditions in the poorer parts of town.

THE CITIES MODERNIZE

As American cities grew larger and more crowded, thereby aggravating a host of social problems, practical forces operated to bring about improvements. Once the relationship between polluted water and disease was fully understood, everyone saw the need for decent water and sewage systems. (See the essay, "Mapping the Past: Cholera: A New Disease Strikes the Nation," pp. 516–517.) While some businessmen profited from corrupt dealings with the city machines, more of them wanted efficient and honest government in order to reduce their tax bills. City dwellers of all classes resented dirt, noise, and ugliness, and in many communities public-spirited groups formed societies to plant trees, clean up littered areas, and develop recreational facilities. When one city undertook improvements, others tended to follow suit, spurred on by local pride and the booster spirit.

Gradually the basic facilities of urban living were improved. Streets were paved, first with cobblestones and wood blocks and then with smoother, quieter asphalt. Gaslight, then electric arc lights, and finally Edison's incandescent lamps brightened the cities after dark, making law enforcement easier, stimulating night life, and permitting factories and shops to operate after sunset.

Urban transportation underwent enormous changes. Until the 1880s, horse-drawn cars running on tracks set flush with the street were the main means of urban public transportation. In 1860 New York City's horsecars were carrying about 100,000 passengers a day. But horsecars had serious drawbacks. Enormous numbers of horses were needed, and feeding and stabling the animals was costly. Their droppings (10 pounds per day per horse) became a major source of urban pollution. That is why the invention of the electric trolley car in the 1880s put an end to horsecar transportation. Trolleys were cheaper and less unsightly than horsecars and quieter than steam-powered trains.

A retired naval officer, Frank J. Sprague, installed the first practical electric trolley line in Richmond, Virginia, in 1887–1888. At once other cities seized on the trolley. Lines soon radiated outward from the city centers, bringing commuters and shoppers from the residential districts to the business district. Without them the big-city department stores could not have flourished as they did. By 1895 some 850 lines were busily hauling city dwellers over 10,000 miles of track, and mileage tripled in the following decade. As with other new enterprises, ownership of street railways quickly became centralized until a few big operators controlled the trolleys of more than 100 eastern cities and towns.

Streetcars changed the character of big-city life. Before their introduction urban communities were limited by the distances people could conveniently walk to work. The "walking city" could not easily extend more than 2½ miles from its center. Streetcars

▶ *text continues on page 518*

Mapping
the Past

Cholera: A New Disease Strikes the Nation

Urbanization during the nineteenth century contributed to the modernization of the nation, but it also brought an ancient disease to the United States: cholera. Cholera did not kill as many people as malaria or tuberculosis, but it was probably the most terrifying disease of the century. Cholera was new to the United States, and its symptoms were gruesome. People were stricken, sometimes in mid-stride, with severe abdominal cramps. Unremitting diarrhea followed, often culminating in dehydration and kidney failure. About half of those who contracted the disease died.

The disease had centuries earlier originated on the overcrowded banks of the Ganges River in India. In early 1831 the disease appeared in eastern Europe and moved steadily westward. In January 1832 it surfaced in England. Health officials in the United States then braced for an onslaught. In June an outbreak of cholera in Montreal prompted wealthy New Yorkers to flee. On June 26 cases appeared in New York City. Soon afterward the disease spread westward along the Erie Canal and then into cities in the Great Lakes region and along the Ohio and Mississippi Rivers. Simultaneously it struck Charleston, South Carolina, and New Orleans, Louisiana.

During the next fifty years cholera outbreaks were fairly common during summer. In 1849 and 1866 it swept through the nation, taking tens of thousands of lives. Most people believed that cholera spread directly from one person to another by bodily contact. When it hit a city, neighboring communities would close the roads and governors called out militias to keep infected persons away. Because cholera outbreaks often appeared first in impoverished tenement districts, immigrants were often blamed for the disease.

But after a cholera epidemic killed nearly 14,000 people in London in 1849, John Snow, a physician, determined that most who contracted cholera drew their drinking water from the lower Thames River; people served by an upriver pumping station rarely fell ill from the disease. Snow concluded that infected people with diarrhea passed a "poison" into the Thames, which people downriver ingested. (In 1883 Robert Koch identified Snow's "poison": it was a comma-shaped bacterium.)

Physicians, meanwhile, struggled to treat the disease. Some prescribed opium or whiskey, others chloroform or strychnine. One physician claimed that a sick patient rallied

▶ In this cartoon, Boss Tweed welcomes Cholera—a skeletal figure of death carrying a handbag from "Asia"—into the rat-infested and filthy slums of New York. Fear of cholera and other diseases led to the creation of powerful public bodies, relatively free from political interference, to promote sanitation and clean water.

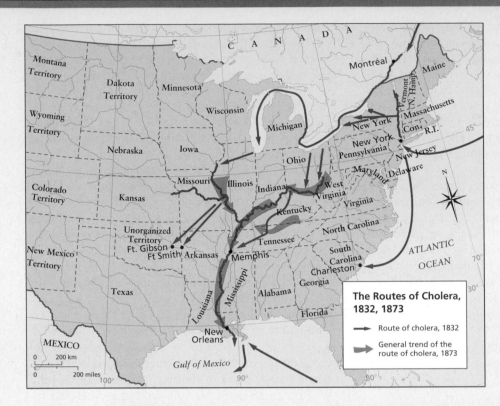

The Routes of Cholera, 1832, 1873

→ Route of cholera, 1832

⇒ General trend of the route of cholera, 1873

after drinking four or five glasses of champagne. But scholars now doubt that any treatment did much good. Prevention was the only way to fight cholera.

In 1866, in response to another cholera outbreak, New York City established a Metropolitan Board of Health to clean up cisterns and garbage. The success of these measures prompted the city to build an extensive network of aqueducts to bring clean water from distant reservoirs and watersheds. The city's clean water became one of its main assets.

Elsewhere, the situation was less encouraging. In February 1873 cholera hit New Orleans and spread up the Mississippi River, ravaging low-lying urban areas where drinking water had been contaminated with sewage.

Nashville was one such city. The city's pumping station was originally located upriver, far to the east of the city. But as the city rapidly filled out a forty-block region east of city hall and the state capitol, sewage seeped into the Cumberland River above the pumping station. In 1873 a cholera epidemic swept through the area. The prison was especially hard hit. The Capitol Hill district, on high ground to the west of Brown's Creek, had few cholera cases. In all, 647 people from Nashville died of cholera that summer.

The cholera epidemic in Nashville, 1873

☐ low-lying ground
■ chief site of cholera

increased this radius to 6 miles or more, which meant that the area of the city expanded enormously. Dramatic population shifts resulted as the better-off moved away from the center in search of air and space, abandoning the crumbling, jam-packed older neighborhoods to the poor. Thus economic segregation speeded the growth of ghettos. Older peripheral towns that had maintained some of the self-contained qualities of village life were swallowed up, becoming metropolitan centers.

As time passed, each new area, originally peopled by rising economic groups, tended to become crowded and then to deteriorate. By extending their tracks beyond the developed areas, the streetcar companies further speeded suburban growth because they assured developers, bankers, builders, and middle-class home buyers of efficient transport to the center of town. By keeping fares low (5 cents a ride was standard) the lines enabled poor people to "escape" to the countryside on holidays.

Advances in bridge design, notably the perfection of the steel-cable suspension bridge by John A.

▲ A tenement in Baltimore was also a community. Crowded conditions bred disease, but also forced people to learn to get along.

Roebling, aided the ebb and flow of metropolitan populations. The Brooklyn Bridge described by a poet as "a weird metallic Apparition . . . the cables, like divine messages from above . . . cutting and dividing into innumerable musical spaces the nude immensity of the sky," was Roebling's triumph. Completed in 1883 at a cost of $15 million, it was soon carrying more than 33 million passengers a year over the East River between Manhattan and Brooklyn.

Even the high cost of urban real estate, which spawned the tenement, produced some beneficial results in the long run. Instead of crowding squat structures cheek by jowl on 25-foot lots, architects began to build upward. Stone and brick apartment houses, sometimes elegantly known as "French flats," replaced many dumbbell tenements. The introduction of the iron-skeleton type of construction, which freed the walls from bearing the immense weight of a tall building, was the work of a group of Chicago architects who had been attracted to the metropolis of the Midwest by opportunities to be found amid the ashes of the great fire of 1871. The group included William Le Baron Jenney, John A. Holabird, Martin Roche, John W. Root, and Louis H. Sullivan. Jenney's Home Insurance Building, completed in 1885, was the first metal-frame edifice. Height alone, however, did not satisfy these innovators; they sought a form that would reflect the structure and purpose of their buildings.

Their leader was Louis Sullivan. Architects must discard "books, rules, precedents, or any such educational impediments" and design functional buildings, he argued. A tall building "must be every inch a proud and soaring thing, rising in sheer exultation . . . from bottom to top . . . a unit without a single dissenting line." Sullivan's Wainwright Building in St. Louis and his Prudential Building in Buffalo, both completed in the early 1890s, combined spare beauty, modest construction costs, and efficient use of space in path-breaking ways. Soon a "race to the skies" was on in the great cities of America, and the words *skyscraper* and *skyline* entered the language.

The "White City," a magnificent evocation of pseudo-classical structures, built for the Chicago World's Fair of 1893 by Daniel H. Burnham, with its broad vistas and acres of open space, led to a national "city beautiful" movement, the most lasting result of which was the development of many public parks. The landscape architect Frederick Law Olmsted, designer of New York's Central Park, was a leading figure in the movement.

But efforts to relieve the congestion in slum districts made little headway. In Brooklyn Alfred T. White established Home Buildings, a 40-family model tenement in 1877; eventually he expanded the

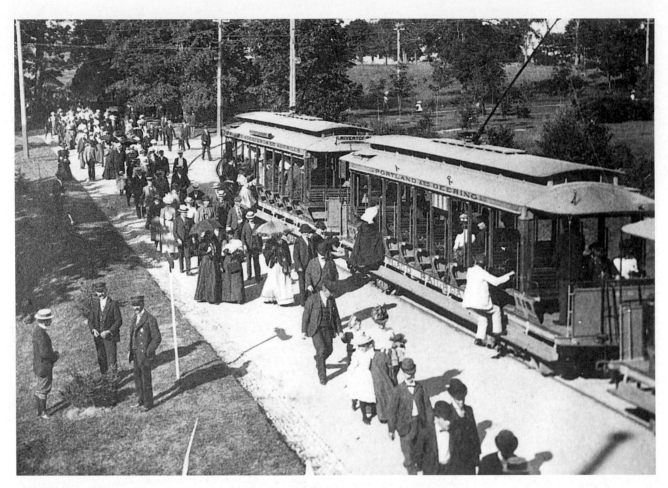

▲ On Sundays in the late nineteenth century, city people crowded into streetcars and thronged to the countryside. Enticed by this taste of bucolic splendor, many chose to live in the suburbs and take the streetcars to work downtown. Soon, the population density of the suburbs resembled that of the cities.

experiment to include 267 apartments. Each unit had plenty of light and air and contained its own sink and toilet. Ellen Collins developed a smaller project in Manhattan's Fourth Ward in the 1890s. These model tenements were self-sustaining, but of necessity they yielded only modest returns. The landlords were essentially philanthropists; their work had no significant impact on urban housing in the nineteenth century.

LEISURE ACTIVITIES: MORE FUN AND GAMES

By bringing together large numbers of people, cities made possible many kinds of social activity difficult or impossible to maintain in rural areas. Cities remained unsurpassed as centers of artistic and intellectual life. New York was the outstanding example, as seen in its many theaters and in the founding of the American Museum of Natural History (1870), the Metropolitan Museum of Art (1870), and the Metropolitan Opera (1883), but other cities were equally hospitable to such endeavors. Boston's Museum of Fine Arts, for example, was founded in 1870 and the Boston Symphony in 1881.

Of course less sophisticated forms of recreation also flourished in the urban environment. From 1865 to 1885 the number of breweries in Massachusetts quadrupled. It is only a slight exaggeration to say that in crowded urban centers there was a saloon on every corner; during the last third of the century the number of saloons in the country tripled. Saloons were strictly male working-class institutions, usually decorated with pictures and other mementos of sports heroes, the bar perhaps under the charge of a retired pugilist.

For workingmen the saloon was a kind of club, a place to meet friends, exchange news and gossip,

▲ Luna Park at Coney Island was a vast living theatre, in which the strollers were both spectators and actors. At night, a quarter million electric lights turned Luna Park into what its designer, Frederic Thompson, called "a different world—a dream world, perhaps a nightmare world—where all is bizarre and fantastic."

gamble, and eat, as well as to drink beer and whiskey. Saloons also flourished because factory owners and other employers of large numbers of workers tended to forbid the consumption of alcohol on their premises. In addition, the gradual reduction of the workday left men with more free time, which may explain why vaudeville and burlesques, the latter described by one straightlaced critic as a "disgraceful spectacle of padded legs juggling and tight-laced wriggling," also proliferated.

Calvinist-inspired opposition to sports as a frivolous waste of valuable time was steadily evaporating, replaced among the upper and middle classes by the realization that games like golf and tennis were "healthy occupation[s] for mind and body." Bicycling became a fad, both as a means of getting from place to place in the ever-expanding cities and as a form of exercise and recreation.

Many of the new streetcar companies built picnic grounds and amusement parks at their outer limits. In good weather thousands seeking to relax after a hard day's work flocked to these "trolley parks" to enjoy a fresh-air meal or patronize the shooting galleries, merry-go-rounds, and "freak shows."

DOCUMENT

Fox, from *Coney Island Frolics*

The postwar era also saw the first important development of spectator sports, again because cities provided the concentrations of population necessary to support them. Curious relationships developed between upper- and working-class interests and between competitive sports as pure enjoyment for players and spectators and sports as something to bet on. Horse racing had strictly upper-class origins, but racetracks attracted huge crowds of ordinary people more intent on picking a winner than on improving the breed.

Professional boxing offers an even better example. It was in a sense a hobby of the rich, who sponsored favorite gladiators, offered prizes, and often wagered large sums on the matches. But the audiences were made up overwhelmingly of young working-class males, from whose ranks most of the fighters emerged. The gambling and also the brutality of the bloody, bare-knuckle character of the fights caused many communities to outlaw boxing, a fact that added to the appeal of the sport for some.

The first widely popular pugilist was the legendary "Boston Strong Boy," John L. Sullivan, who became heavyweight champion in 1882 by disposing of one Paddy Ryan in nine rounds. Sullivan was an immensely powerful man whose idea of fighting, according to his biographer, "was simply to hammer his opponent into unconsciousness," something he did repeatedly during his ten-year reign. Sullivan became an international celebrity and made and lost large sums during this period. He was also the beneficiary of patronage in such forms as a diamond belt worth $10,000 presented to him by some of his admirers. Yet boxing remained a raffish, clandestine occupation. One of Sullivan's important fights took place in France, on the estate of Baron Rothchild, yet when it ended both he and his opponent were arrested.

Three major team games, baseball, football, and basketball, developed in something approaching their modern form during the last quarter of the century. Various forms of what became baseball were played long before that time. Organized teams, in most cases made up of upper-class amateurs, first emerged in the 1840s, but the game only became truly popular during the Civil War, when it was a major form of camp recreation for the troops.

After the war professional teams began to appear (the first, the Cincinnati Red Stockings, paid players between $800 and $1400 for the season), and in 1876 teams in eight cities formed the National League. The American League followed in 1901. After a brief period of rivalry, the two leagues made peace in 1903, the year of the first World Series.

Organized play led to codification of the rules and improvements in technique and strategy, for example, the development of "minor" leagues; impartial umpires calling balls and strikes and ruling on close plays; the use of catcher's masks and padded gloves; the invention of various kinds of curves and other erratic pitches (often enhanced by "doctoring" the ball). As early as the 1870s, baseball was being called "the national game" and losing all upper-class connotations. Important games attracted crowds in the tens of thousands; betting became a problem. Despite its urban origins, its broad green fields and dusty base

▲ Thomas Eakins's *Baseball Players Practicing,* painted in 1875, one year before the organization of the National League. The relative similarity of the batter's stance to that favored today suggests the timelessness of this national pastime.

paths gave the game a rural character that only recently has begun to fade away.

Nobody "invented" baseball, but both football and basketball owe their present form to individuals. James Naismith's invention of basketball is undisputed. In 1891, while a student at a YMCA school, he attached peach baskets to the edge of an elevated running track in the gymnasium and drew up what are still the basic rules of the game. The first basketball was a soccer ball. The game was popular from the start, but because it was played indoors it was not an important spectator sport until much later.

Football was not created by one person in the way that basketball was; it evolved out of English rugby. For many decades it remained almost entirely a college sport (and thus played almost entirely by upper- and middle-class types). Organized collegiate sports dated back to before the Civil War; the first intercollegiate matches were rowing races between Harvard and Yale students. The first intercollege football game occurred when Princeton defeated Rutgers in 1869, and by the 1880s college football had become extremely popular.

Much of the game's modern character, however, was the work of Walter Camp, the athletic director and football coach of Yale. Camp cut the size of teams

from 15 to 11, and he invented the scrimmage line, the four-down system, and the key position of quarterback. He publicized the game in a series of books, ranging from *How to Coach a Team* (1886) to *Jack Hall at Yale* (1909). Camp's prestige was such that when he named his first All-American team after the 1889 season, no one challenged his judgment. Well into the twentieth century, the players that Camp selected were *the* All-Americans.

Camp claimed that amateur sports like football taught the value of hard work, cooperation, and fair play. His practice was more questionable. He is known to have recruited players who could not meet Yale's academic standards and to have found means of putting money in his players' pockets. At Yale and elsewhere all the problems that emphasis on athletic achievement poses for modern institutions of higher education existed in microcosm well before 1900.

Spectator sports had little appeal to women at this time and indeed for decades thereafter. And few women participated in organized athletics. Sports were "manly" activities; a women might ride a bicycle, play croquet and perhaps a little tennis, but to display any concentrated interest in excelling in a sport was considered unfeminine.

CHRISTIANITY'S CONSCIENCE AND THE SOCIAL GOSPEL

The modernization of the great cities was not solving most of the social problems of the slums. As this fact became clear, a number of urban religious leaders began to take a hard look at the situation. Traditionally, American churchmen had insisted that where sin was concerned there were no extenuating circumstances. To the well-to-do they preached the virtues of thrift and hard work; to the poor they extended the possibility of a better existence in the next world; to all they stressed one's responsibility for one's own behavior—and thus for one's own salvation. Such a point of view brought meager comfort to residents of slums. Consequently, the churches lost influence in the poorer sections. Furthermore, as better-off citizens followed the streetcar lines out from the city centers, their church leaders followed them.

In New York, 17 Protestant congregations abandoned the depressed areas of Lower Manhattan between 1868 and 1888. Catering thereafter almost entirely to middle-class and upper-class worshipers, the pastors tended to become even more conservative. No more strident defender of reactionary ideas existed than the pastor of Brooklyn's fashionable Plymouth Congregational Church, Henry Ward Beecher. Beecher, a younger brother of Harriet Beecher Stowe, the author of *Uncle Tom's Cabin*, attributed poverty to the improvidence of laborers who, he claimed, squandered their wages on liquor and tobacco. "No man in this land suffers from poverty," he said, "unless it be more than his fault—unless it be his sin." The best check on labor unrest was a plentiful supply of cheap immigrant labor, he told President Hayes. Unions were "the worst form of despotism and tyranny in the history of Christendom."

An increasing proportion of the residents of the blighted districts were Catholics, and the Roman church devoted much effort to distributing alms, maintaining homes for orphans and old people, and other forms of social welfare. But church leaders seemed unconcerned with the social causes of the blight; they were deeply committed to the idea that sin and vice were personal, poverty an act of God. They deplored the rising tide of crime, disease, and destitution among their coreligionists, yet they failed to see the connection between these evils and the squalor of the slums. "Intemperance is the great evil we have to overcome," wrote the president of the leading Catholic charitable organization, the Society of St. Vincent de Paul. "It is the source of the misery for at least three-fourths of the families we are called upon to visit and relieve."

The conservatism of most Protestant and Catholic clergymen did not prevent some earnest preachers from working directly to improve the lot of the city poor. Some followed the path blazed by Dwight L. Moody, a lay evangelist who became famous throughout America and Great Britain in the 1870s. A gargantuan figure weighing nearly 300 pounds, Moody conducted a vigorous campaign to persuade the denizens of the slums to cast aside their sinful ways. He went among them full of enthusiasm and God's love and made an impact no less powerful than that of George Whitefield during the Great Awakening of the eighteenth century or Charles Grandison Finney in the first part of the nineteenth. The evangelists founded mission schools in the slums and tried to provide spiritual and recreational facilities for the unfortunate. They were prominent in the establishment of American branches of the YMCA (1851) and the Salvation Army (1880).

However, the evangelists paid little heed to the causes of urban poverty and vice, believing that faith in God would enable the poor to transcend the material difficulties of life. For a number of Protestant clergymen who had become familiar with the slums, a different approach seemed called for. Slum conditions caused the sins and crimes of the cities; the wretched human beings who committed them could not be blamed, these ministers argued. They began to preach a "Social Gospel" that focused on improving living conditions rather than on saving souls. If people were to lead pure lives, they must have enough to eat, de-

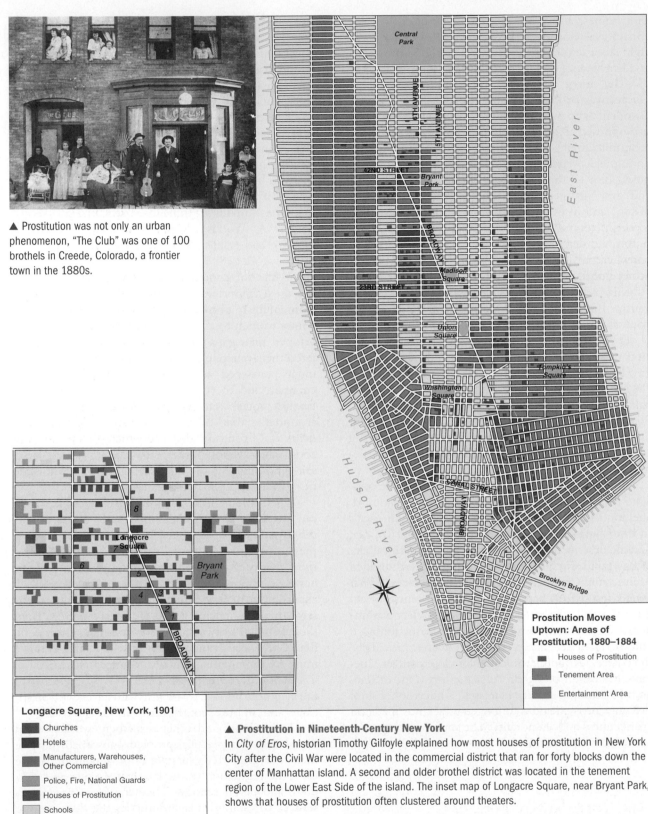

▲ Prostitution was not only an urban phenomenon, "The Club" was one of 100 brothels in Creede, Colorado, a frontier town in the 1880s.

Prostitution Moves Uptown: Areas of Prostitution, 1880–1884

◼ Houses of Prostitution

◼ Tenement Area

◼ Entertainment Area

Longacre Square, New York, 1901

◼ Churches

◼ Hotels

◼ Manufacturers, Warehouses, Other Commercial

◼ Police, Fire, National Guards

◼ Houses of Prostitution

◼ Schools

◼ Single Family

◼ Theaters, Music Halls

*1 Knickerbocker Theater   2 The Casino
3 Empire Theater   4 Metropolitan Opera House
5 Broadway Theater   6 American Theater
7 Hammerstein's Victoria Music Hall
8 Lyric Theater*

▲ Prostitution in Nineteenth-Century New York

In *City of Eros*, historian Timothy Gilfoyle explained how most houses of prostitution in New York City after the Civil War were located in the commercial district that ran for forty blocks down the center of Manhattan island. A second and older brothel district was located in the tenement region of the Lower East Side of the island. The inset map of Longacre Square, near Bryant Park, shows that houses of prostitution often clustered around theaters.

cent homes, and opportunities to develop their talents. Social Gospelers advocated civil service reform, child labor legislation, regulation of big corporations, and heavy taxes on incomes and inheritances.

The most influential preacher of the Social Gospel was probably Washington Gladden. At first, Gladden, who was raised on a Massachusetts farm, had opposed all government interference in social and economic affairs, but his experiences as a minister in Springfield, Massachusetts, and Columbus, Ohio, exposed him to the realities of life in industrial cities, and his views changed. In *Applied Christianity* (1886) and in other works he defended labor's right to organize and strike and denounced the idea that supply and demand should control wage rates. He favored factory inspection laws, strict regulation of public utilities, and other reforms.

Gladden never questioned the basic values of capitalism. But by the 1890s a number of ministers had gone all the way to socialism. The Reverend William D. P. Bliss of Boston, for example, believed in the kind of welfare state envisioned by Edward Bellamy in *Looking Backward*. He founded the Society of Christian Socialists (1889) and edited a radical journal, *The Dawn*. In addition to nationalizing industry, Bliss and other Christian Socialists advocated government unemployment relief programs, public housing and slum clearance projects, and other measures designed to aid the city poor.

Nothing so well reveals the receptivity of the public to the Social Gospel as the popularity of Charles M. Sheldon's novel *In His Steps* (1896), one of America's all-time best-sellers. Sheldon, a minister in Topeka, Kansas, described what happened in the mythical city of Raymond when a group of leading citizens decided to live truly Christian lives, asking themselves "What would Jesus do?" before adopting any course of action. Naturally the tone of Raymond's society was immensely improved, but basic social reforms followed quickly. The Rectangle, a terrible slum area, "too dirty, too coarse, too sinful, too awful for close contact," became the center of a great reform effort. One of Raymond's "leading society heiresses" undertook a slum clearance project, and a concerted attack was made on drunkenness and immorality. The moral regeneration of the entire community was soon accomplished.

The Settlement Houses

Although millions read *In His Steps,* its effect, and that of other Social Gospel literature, was merely inspirational. On the practical level, a number of earnest souls began to grapple with slum problems by organizing what were known as settlement houses. These were community centers located in poor districts that provided guidance and services to all who would use them. The settlement workers, most of them idealistic, well-to-do young people, lived in the houses and were active in neighborhood affairs.

The prototype of the settlement house was London's Toynbee Hall, founded in the early 1880s; the first American example was the Neighborhood Guild, opened on the Lower East Side of New York in 1886 by Dr. Stanton Coit. By the turn of the century 100 had been established, the most famous being Jane Addams's Hull House in Chicago (1889), Robert A. Woods's South End House in Boston (1892), and Lillian Wald's Henry Street Settlement in New York (1893).

While some men were active in the movement, the most important settlement house workers were women fresh from college—the first generation of young women to experience the trauma of having developed their capacities only to find that society offered them few opportunities to use them. The settlements provided an outlet for their hopes and energies, and they seized upon the work avidly. An English social reformer who visited Hull House around the turn of the century described the residents as "strong-minded energetic women, bustling about their various enterprises" and "earnest-faced self-subordinating and mild-mannered men who slide from room to room apologetically."

The settlement workers tried to interpret American ways to the new immigrants and to create a community spirit in order to teach, in the words of one of them, "right living through social relations." Unlike most charity workers, who acted out of a sense of upper-class responsibility toward the unfortunate, they expected to benefit morally and intellectually themselves by experiencing a way of life far different from their own and by obtaining "the first-hand knowledge the college classroom cannot give." Lillian Wald, a nurse by training, explained the concept succinctly in *The House on Henry Street* (1915): "We were to live in the neighborhood . . . identify ourselves with it socially, and, in brief, contribute to it our citizenship."

Lillian Wald and other settlement workers soon discovered that practical problems absorbed most of their energies. They agitated for tenement house laws, the regulation of the labor of women and children, and better schools. They employed private resources to establish playgrounds in the slums, along with libraries, classes in everything from child nutrition and home management to literature and arts and crafts, social clubs, and day-care centers. When they observed that many poor families were so occupied with the struggle to survive that they were neglecting

or even abandoning their children, they tried to place the children in foster homes in the country.

In Boston Robert A. Woods organized clubs to get the youngsters of the South End off the streets, helped establish a restaurant where a meal could be had for 5 cents, acted as an arbitrator in labor disputes, and lobbied for laws tightening up the franchises of public utility companies. In Chicago Jane Addams developed an outstanding cultural program that included classes in music and art and an excellent "little theater" group. Hull House soon boasted a gymnasium, a day nursery, and several social clubs. Addams also worked tirelessly and effectively for improved public services and for social legislation of all kinds. She even got herself appointed garbage inspector in her ward and hounded local landlords and the garbage contractor until something approaching decent service was established.

A few critics considered the settlement houses mere devices to socialize the unruly poor by teaching them the "punctilios of upper-class propriety," but almost everyone appreciated their virtues. By the end of the century the Catholics, laggard in entering the arena of practical social reform, were joining the movement, partly because they were losing many communicants to socially minded Protestant churches. The first Catholic-run settlement house was founded in 1898 in an Italian district of New York. Two years later Brownson House in Los Angeles, catering chiefly to Mexican immigrants, threw open its doors.

With all their accomplishments, the settlement houses seemed to be fighting a losing battle. "Private beneficence," Jane Addams wrote of Hull House, "is totally inadequate to deal with the vast numbers of the city's disinherited." As a tropical forest grows faster than a handful of men armed with machetes can cut it down, so the slums, fed by an annual influx of hundreds of thousands, blighted new areas more rapidly than the intrepid settlement house workers could clean up old ones. It became increasingly apparent that the wealth and authority of the state must be brought to bear in order to keep abreast of the problem.

CIVILIZATION AND ITS DISCONTENTS

As the nineteenth century died, the majority of the American people, especially those comfortably well-off, the residents of small towns, the shopkeepers, and some farmers and skilled workers, remained confirmed optimists and uncritical admirers of their civilization. However, blacks, immigrants, and others who failed to share equitably in the good things of life, along with a growing number of humanitarian

reformers, found little to cheer about and much to lament in their increasingly industrialized society. Giant monopolies flourished despite federal restrictions. The gap between rich and poor appeared to be widening, while the slum spread its poison and the materially successful made a god of their success. Human values seemed in grave danger of being crushed by impersonal forces typified by the great corporations.

In 1871 Walt Whitman, usually so full of extravagant praise for everything American, had called his fellow countrymen the "most materialistic and money-making people ever known":

> I say we had best look our times and lands searchingly in the face, like a physician diagnosing some deep disease. Never was there, perhaps, more hollowness of heart than at present, and here in the United States.

By the late 1880s a well-known journalist could write to a friend: "The wheel of progress is to be run over the whole human race and smash us all." Others noted an alarming jump in the national divorce rate and an increasing taste for all kinds of luxury. "People are made slaves by a desperate struggle to keep up appearances," a Massachusetts commentator declared, and the economist David A. Wells expressed concern over statistics showing that heart disease and mental illness were on the rise. These "diseases of civilization," Wells explained, were "one result of the continuous mental and nervous activity which modern high-tension methods of business have necessitated."

Wells was a prominent liberal, but pessimism was no monopoly of liberals. A little later, Senator Henry Cabot Lodge of Massachusetts, himself a millionaire, complained of the "lawlessness" of "the modern and recent plutocrat" and his "disregard of the rights of others." Lodge spoke of "the enormous contrast between the sanguine mental attitude prevalent in my youth and that, perhaps wiser, but certainly darker view, so general today." His one-time Harvard professor, Henry Adams, was still more critical of the way his contemporaries had become moneygrubbers. "All one's friends," he complained, along with church and university leaders and other educated people, "had joined the banks to force submission to capitalism."

Of course intellectuals often tend to be critical of the world they live in, whatever its nature; Thoreau denounced materialism and the worship of progress in the 1840s as vigorously as any late nineteenth-century prophet of gloom. But the voices of the dissatisfied were rising. Despite the many benefits that industrialization had made possible, it was by no means clear around 1900 that the American people were really better off under the new dispensation.

MILESTONES

1858	English launch transatlantic liner *Great Eastern*	1887	Nativists found American Protective Association
1870	Metropolitan Museum of Art and American Museum of Natural History open in New York City	1888	Richmond, Virginia opens first urban electric streetcar system
1876	Eight teams form National Baseball League	1889	Jane Addams founds Hull House
			Yale's Walter Camp names first All-American football team
1880	American branch of Salvation Army is founded	1890s	Louis Sullivan's skyscrapers rise
1880s	"New" immigration begins	1890	Jacob Riis publishes *How the Other Half Lives*
1882	John L. Sullivan wins heavyweight boxing championship		Calvin Woodward opens his Manual Training School
	Exclusion Act bans Chinese immigrants	1896	Charles M. Sheldon asks "What would Jesus do?" in best-selling *In His Steps*
1883	Roebling completes Brooklyn Bridge		
1885	Foran Act outlaws importing contract skilled labor	1897	Cleveland vetoes Congress's literacy test bill

SUPPLEMENTARY READING

Henry Adams, *The Education of Henry Adams* (1918), is a fascinating if highly personal view of the period, and James Bryce, *The American Commonwealth* (1888), while primarily a political analysis, contains a great deal of information about social conditions. For two classic accounts of the settlement house movement, see Jane Addams, *Twenty Years at Hull House* (1910), and Lillian Wald, *The House on Henry Street* (1915). Addams's own life is the subject of two recent biographies: Jean Bethke Elshtain, *Jane Addams and the Dream of American Democracy* (2002), and Victoria Bissel Brown, *The Education of Jane Addams* (2004).

An enormous number of books deal with the social history of late nineteenth-century America. John A. Garraty, *The New Commonwealth* (1968), treats most of the subjects covered in this chapter; Arthur M. Schlesinger's classic study, *The Rise of the City* (1933), provides a wealth of information about social trends. Robert Wiebe's *The Search for Order* (1967) shows how corporate and administrative bureaucracies overspread the nation, while Alan Trachtenberg, *The Incorporation of America* (1982), considers the cultural implications of Wiebe's insight. See also Gunther Barth, *City People* (1980).

On middle-class life and culture, see John Kasson, *Rudeness and Civility* (1990), Karen Halttunen, *Confidence Men and Painted Women* (1982), Burton Bledstein, *The Culture of Professionalism* (1976), and Mark C. Carnes, *Secret Ritual and Manhood in Victorian America* (1989). Karen Lystra, *Searching the Heart* (1989), emphasizes the close character of marriage, and Peter Gay, *The Bourgeois*

Experience (1984–1997), argues that the middle classes throughout the Western world were not prudes; the repressive hypothesis is outlined in Ronald Walter, *Primers for Prudery* (1974). On contraception see Janet F. Brodie, *Contraception and Abortion in Nineteenth-Century America* (1994). On the family generally, see Colleen McDannell, *The Christian Home in Victorian America* (1986), and Carl Degler, *At Odds* (1980). On prostitution, Marilyn Wood Hill, *Their Sisters' Keepers* (1993), and Timothy Gilfoyle, *City of Eros* (1992). On issues of consumption see Daniel Horowitz, *The Morality of Spending* (1985), William Leach, *Land of Desire: Merchants, Power, and the Rise of a New American Culture* (1993), and Elaine S. Abelson, *When Ladies' Go A-Thieving* (1989).

A broad survey on issues of disease is Gerald N. Grob, *The Deadly Truth: A History of Disease in America* (2002).

On working-class culture, Keith Peiss, *Cheap Amusements: Working Women and Leisure in Turn-of-the-Century New York* (1986), and Roy Rosenzweig, *Eight Hours for What We Will* (1983) are excellent. Roy Rosenzweig and Elizabeth Blackmar provide an interesting account of cultural tensions between middle and working classes in *The Park and the People: A History of Central Park* (1992).

A brief interpretive history of urban development is Charles N. Glaab and A. Theodore Brown, *A History of Urban America* (1967). Kenneth T. Jackson, *Crabgrass Frontier* (1985), is a pioneering history of suburban development, and Jon C. Teaford, *The Unheralded Triumph* (1984), gives weight to the accomplishments of the cities

as well as to their inadequacies. For the growing pains of American cities, consult Jacob Riis, *How the Other Half Lives* (1890). S. B. Warner, Jr., *Streetcar Suburbs* (1962) is an interesting study of Boston's development that is full of suggestive ideas about late nineteenth-century growth. See also Paul Boyer, *Urban Masses and Moral Order in America* (1978).

On the early development of intercollegiate sports, see Ronald A. Smith, *Sports and Freedom: The Rise of Big-Time College Athletics* (1988); on sports and modernization, see Melvin L. Adelman, *A Sporting Time* (1986), and Allen Guttmann, *From Ritual to Record* (1978). The response of religion to industrialism is discussed in Henry F. May, *Protestant Churches and Industrial America* (1949).

SUGGESTED WEBSITES

Coal Mining During the Gilded Age and Progressive Era
http://history.osu.edu/Projects/Gilded_Age/default.htm
This Ohio State University site examines the development of the coal industry, including the sometimes violent labor–management conflict.

Touring Turn-of-the-Century America: Photographs from the Detroit Publishing Company, 1880–1920
http://memory.loc.gov/ammem/detroit/dethome.html
This Library of Congress collection has thousands of photographs from turn-of-the-century America.

Inside an American Factory: The Westinghouse Works, 1904
http://lcweb2.loc.gov/ammem/papr/west/westhome.html
Part of the American Memory Project at the Library of Congress, this site provides a glimpse inside a turn-of-the-century factory.

Thorsten Veblen's *The Theory of the Leisure Class*
http://xroads.virginia.edu/~HYPER/VEBLEN/veb_toc.html
This University of Virginia site includes a picture of Veblen as well as the text of his influential book.

Intellectual and Cultural Trends

▼ Winslow Homer's ironically titled *Fox Hunt* (1893), in which crows harry the snow-bound fox. Darwin's concept of the "survival of the fittest" undermined the Victorian belief in a purposeful and benevolent God.

CHAPTER CONTENTS

Industrialization altered the way Americans thought at the same time that it transformed their ways of making a living. Technological advances revolutionized the communication of ideas more drastically than they did the transportation of goods or the manufacture of steel. The materialism that permeated American attitudes toward business also affected contemporary education and literature, while Charles Darwin's theory of evolution influenced American philosophers, lawyers, and historians profoundly.

New ideas about how children should be educated and what they should be taught emerged along with new methods of communicating information to adults. As society became more complex, the need for specialized training increased, with the result that higher education became more important. Americans began to make significant contributions both in the "hard" sciences, such as chemistry and physics, and in the relatively new "soft" social sciences, such as psychology, political science, and sociology. A new literary flowering comparable to the "renaissance" of the 1840s and 1850s occurred in the 1870s and 1880s. By the end of the century America had finally emerged intellectually from the shadow of Europe.

THE KNOWLEDGE REVOLUTION

Improvements in public education and the needs of an increasingly complex society for every type of intellectual skill caused a veritable revolution in how knowledge was discovered, disseminated, and put to use. Observing the effects of formal education on their children, many older people were eager to experience some of its benefits. Nothing so

▲ Photograph of the first Remington typewriter, 1874. The typewriter was the idea of Christopher Sholes, a tinkerer at a machine shop in Milwaukee, Wisconsin. He put printer's type at the end of little rods, which struck a flat plate on which had been placed a sheet of carbon paper. E. Remington, a gun manufacturer in Ilion, New York, decided to build Sholes's "type-writer."

well illustrates the desire for new information as the rise of the Chautauqua movement, founded by John H. Vincent, a Methodist minister, and Lewis Miller, an Ohio manufacturer of farm machinery. Vincent had charge of Sunday schools for the Methodist church. In 1874 he and Miller organized a two-week summer course for Sunday school teachers on the shores of Lake Chautauqua in New York. Besides instruction, they offered good meals, evening songfests around the campfire, and a relaxing atmosphere—all for $6 for the two weeks.

The 40 young teachers who attended were delighted with the program, and soon the leafy shore of Lake Chautauqua became a city of tents each summer as thousands poured into the region from all over the country. The founders expanded their offerings to include instruction in literature, science, government, and economics. Famous authorities, including, over the years, six presidents of the United States, came to lecture to open-air audiences on every subject imaginable. Eventually Chautauqua supplied speakers to reading circles throughout the country; it even offered correspondence courses leading over a four-year period to a diploma, the program designed, in Vincent's words, to give "the college outlook" to persons who had not had the opportunity to obtain a higher

education. Books were written specifically for the program, and a monthly magazine, the *Chautauquan,* was published.

Such success provoked imitation, and by 1900 there were about 200 Chautauqua-type organizations. Intellectual standards in these programs varied greatly; in general they were very low. Entertainment was as important an objective as enlightenment. Musicians (good and bad), homespun humorists, inspirational lecturers, and assorted quacks shared the platform with prominent preachers and scholars. Moneymaking undoubtedly motivated many of the entrepreneurs who operated the centers, all of which, including the original Chautauqua, reflected the prevailing tastes of the American people—diverse, enthusiastic, uncritical, and shallow. Nevertheless the movement provided opportunities for thousands seeking stimulation and intellectual improvement.

Still larger numbers profited from the proliferation of public libraries. By the end of the century nearly all the states supported libraries. Private donors, led by the steel industrialist Andrew Carnegie, contributed millions to the cause. In 1900 over 1700 libraries in the United States had collections of more than 5000 volumes.

Newspapers were an even more important means of disseminating information and educating the masses. Here new technology supplied the major incentive for change. The development by Richard Hoe and Stephen Tucker of the web press (1871), which printed simultaneously on both sides of paper fed into it from large rolls, and Ottmar Mergenthaler's linotype machine (1886), which cast rows of type as needed directly from molten metal, cut printing costs dramatically. Machines for making paper out of wood pulp reduced the cost of newsprint to a quarter of what it had been in the 1860s. By 1895 machines were printing, cutting, and folding 32-page newspapers at a rate of 24,000 an hour.

The telegraph and transoceanic cables wrought a similar transformation in the gathering of news. Press associations, led by the New York Associated Press, flourished; the syndicated article appeared; and a few publishers—Edward W. Scripps was the first—began to acquire chains of newspapers.

Population growth and better education created an ever-larger demand for printed matter. At the same time, the integration of the economy enabled manufacturers to sell their goods all over the country. Advertising became important, and sellers soon learned that newspapers and magazines were excellent means of placing their products before millions of eyes. Advertising revenues soared just when new machines and general expansion were making publishing an expensive business. The day of the journeyman printer-

editor ended. Rich men such as the railroad magnate Jay Gould and the mining tycoon George Hearst invested heavily in newspapers in the postwar decades.

Publishers tended to be conservative, but reaching the masses meant lowering intellectual and cultural standards, appealing to emotions, and adopting popular, sometimes radical, causes. Cheap, mass-circulation papers had first appeared in the 1830s and 1840s, the most successful being the *Sun*, the *Herald*, and the *Tribune* in New York, the *Philadelphia Public Ledger*, and the *Baltimore Sun*. None of them much exceeded a circulation of 50,000 before the Civil War. The first publisher to reach a truly massive audience was Joseph Pulitzer, a Hungarian-born immigrant who made a first-rate paper of the *St. Louis Post-Dispatch*. In 1883 Pulitzer bought the *New York World*, a sheet with a circulation of perhaps 20,000. Within a year he was selling 100,000 copies daily, and by the late 1890s the *World*'s circulation regularly exceeded 1 million.

Pulitzer achieved this brilliant success by casting a wide net. To the masses he offered bold, black headlines devoted to crime (ANOTHER MURDERER TO HANG), scandal (VICE ADMIRAL'S SON IN JAIL), catastrophe (TWENTY-FOUR MINERS KILLED), society and the theater (LILY LANGTRY'S NEW ADMIRER), together with feature stories, political cartoons, sports pages, comics, and pictures. For the educated and affluent he provided better political and financial coverage than the most respectable New York journals. Pulitzer made the *World* a crusader for civic improvement by attacking political corruption, monopoly, and slum problems. His energetic reporters literally made news, masquerading as criminals and poor workers in order to write graphic accounts of conditions in New York's jails and sweatshops.

"The *World* is the people's newspaper," Pulitzer boasted, and in the sense that it interested men and women of every sort, he was correct. Pulitzer's methods were quickly copied by competitors, especially William Randolph Hearst, who purchased the *New York Journal* in 1895 and soon outdid the *World* in sensationalism. But no other newspaperman of the era approached Pulitzer in originality, boldness, and the knack of reaching the masses without abandoning seriousness of purpose and basic integrity.

Magazine Journalism

Growth and ferment also characterized the magazine world. In 1865 there were about 700 magazines in the country, by the turn of the century more than 5000. Until the mid-1880s, few of the new magazines were in any way unusual. A handful of serious periodicals, such as the *Atlantic Monthly*, *Harper's*, and *The Century*, dominated the field. They were staid in tone and conservative in political caste. Articles on current affairs, a good deal of fiction and poetry, historical and biographical studies, and similar material filled their pages, and many of them justly prided themselves on the quality of their illustrations. Although they had great influence, none approached mass circulation because of the limited size of the upper-middle-class audience they aimed at. *The Century* reached a peak in the 1880s of about 250,000 when it published a series of articles on Civil War battles by famous commanders, but it could not sustain that level. A circulation of 100,000 was considered good for such magazines.

Magazines directed at the average citizen were of low quality. The leading publisher of this type in the 1860s and 1870s was Frank Leslie, whose periodicals bore such titles as *Frank Leslie's Chimney Corner*, *Frank Leslie's Illustrated Newspaper*, and *Frank Leslie's Jolly Joker*. Leslie specialized in illustrations of current events (he put as many as 34 engravers to work on a single picture in order to bring it out quickly) and on providing what he frankly admitted was "mental pabulum"—a combination of cheap romantic fiction, old-fashioned poetry, jokes, and advice columns. Some of his magazines sold as many as 300,000 copies per issue.

After about 1885 vast changes began to take place. New magazines such as *Forum* (1886) and *Arena* (1889) emphasized hard-hitting articles on controversial subjects by leading experts. The weekly *Literary Digest* (1890) offered summaries of press opinion on current events, and the *Review of Reviews* (1891) provided monthly commentary on the news.

Even more startling changes revolutionized the mass-circulation field. In 1889 Edward W. Bok became editor of the *Ladies' Home Journal*. Besides advice columns ("Ruth Ashmore's Side Talks with Girls"), he offered articles on childcare, gardening, and interior decorating, published fine contemporary novelists, and commissioned public figures, such as presidents Grover Cleveland and Benjamin Harrison, to discuss important questions. He printed colored reproductions of art masterpieces—the invention of cheap photoengraving was of enormous significance in the success of mass-circulation magazines—and crusaded for women's suffrage, conservation, and other reforms. Bok did more than cater to public tastes; he created new tastes. He even refused to accept patent medicine advertising, a major source of revenue for many popular magazines.

Bok and his many competitors reached millions of readers. Like Pulitzer in the newspaper field, they

found ways of interesting rich and poor, the cultivated and the ignorant. Utilizing the new printing technology to cut costs and drawing heavily on advertising revenues, they sold their magazines for 10 or 15 cents a copy and still made fortunes.

COLLEGES AND UNIVERSITIES

The same forces that were affecting the dissemination of information were also altering higher education and professional training. The number of colleges rose from about 350 to 500 between 1878 and 1898, and the student body roughly tripled. Despite this growth, less than 2 percent of the college-age population attended college, but the aspirations of the nation's youth were rising, and more and more parents had the financial means necessary for fulfilling them.

DOCUMENT

The Morrill Act

More significant than the expansion of the colleges were the alterations in their curricula and in the atmosphere permeating the average campus. In 1870 most colleges remained what they had been in the 1830s: small, limited in their offerings, intellectually stagnant. The ill-paid professors were seldom scholars of stature. Thereafter, change came like a flood tide. State universities proliferated; the federal government's land-grant program in support of training in "agriculture and the mechanic arts," established under the Morrill Act of 1862, came into its own; wealthy philanthropists poured fortunes into old institutions and founded new ones; educators introduced new courses and adopted new teaching methods; professional schools of law, medicine, education, business, journalism, and other specialties increased in number.

In the forefront of reform was Harvard, the oldest and most prestigious college in the country. In the 1860s it possessed an excellent faculty, but teaching methods were antiquated and the curriculum had remained almost unchanged since the colonial period. In 1869, however, a dynamic president, the chemist Charles W. Eliot, undertook a transformation of the college. Eliot introduced the elective system, gradually eliminating required courses and expanding offerings in such areas as modern languages, economics, and the laboratory sciences. For the first time, students were allowed to borrow books from the library!

Eliot also encouraged the faculty to experiment with new teaching methods, and he brought in professors with original minds and new ideas. One was Henry Adams, grandson of John Quincy Adams, who made the study of medieval history a truly intellectual

experience. "Mr. Adams roused the spirit of inquiry and controversy in me," one student later wrote.

Under Eliot's guidance the standards of the medical school were raised. In the law school, Christopher Columbus Langdell introduced the case method of study. In some respects Eliot went too far—the elective system encouraged superficiality and laxness in many students—but on balance he transformed Harvard from a college, "a place to which a young man is sent," to a university, a place "to which he goes."

An even more important development in higher education was the founding of Johns Hopkins in 1876. This university was one of many established in the period by wealthy industrialists; its benefactor, the Baltimore merchant Johns Hopkins, had made his fortune in the Baltimore and Ohio Railroad. Its distinctiveness, however, was due to the vision of Daniel Coit Gilman, its first president.

Gilman modeled Johns Hopkins on the German universities, where meticulous research and freedom of inquiry were the guiding principles. In staffing the institution, he sought scholars of the highest reputation, scouring Europe as well as America in his search for talent and offering outstanding men high salaries for that time—up to $5000 for a professor, roughly ten times the income of a skilled artisan. At the same time, he employed a number of relatively unknown but brilliant younger scholars, such as Herbert Baxter Adams, whom he made an associate in history on the strength of his excellent doctoral dissertation at the University of Heidelberg. Gilman promised his teachers good students and ample opportunity to pursue their own research (which explains why so many Hopkins professors repeatedly turned down attractive offers from other universities).

Johns Hopkins specialized in graduate education. In the generation after its founding, it turned out a remarkable percentage of the most important scholars in the nation, including Woodrow Wilson in political science, John Dewey in philosophy, Frederick Jackson Turner in history, and John R. Commons in economics. The seminar conducted by Herbert Baxter Adams was particularly productive: The Adams-edited *Johns Hopkins Studies in Historical and Political Science,* consisting of the doctoral dissertations of his students, was both voluminous and "the mother of similar studies in every part of the United States."

The success of Johns Hopkins did not stop the migration of American scholars to Europe; more than 2000 matriculated at German universities during the 1880s. But as Hopkins graduates took up professorships at other institutions and as scholars

▲ The earliest colleges were "vocational," their chief purpose being to furnish clergy for the colonists. The colonists, most of whom were farmers, would have been astonished by Cornell University's school of agriculture, whose purpose was to teach the vocation of farming. At the left of the picture are some of the school's experimental gardens.

trained elsewhere adopted the Hopkins methods, true graduate education became possible in most sections of the country.

The example of Johns Hopkins encouraged other wealthy individuals to endow universities offering advanced work. Clark University in Worcester, Massachusetts, founded by Jonas Clark, a merchant and real estate speculator, opened its doors in 1889. Its president, G. Stanley Hall, had been a professor of psychology at Hopkins, and he built the new university in that institution's image. More important was John D. Rockefeller's creation, the University of Chicago (1892). The president of the University of Chicago, William Rainey Harper, was a brilliant biblical scholar—he received his Ph.D. from Yale at the age of 18—and an imaginative administrator. The new university, he told Rockefeller, should be designed "with the example of Johns Hopkins before our eyes."

Like Daniel Coit Gilman, Harper sought topflight scholars for his faculty. He offered such high salaries that he was besieged with over 1000 applications. Armed with Rockefeller dollars, he "raided" the best institutions in the nation. He decimated the faculty of the new Clark University—"an act of wreckage," the indignant President Hall complained, "comparable to anything that the worst trust ever attempted against its competitors." Chicago offered first-class graduate and undergraduate education.

During its first year there were 120 instructors for fewer than 600 students, and despite fears that the mighty tycoon Rockefeller would enforce his social and economic views on the institution, academic freedom was the rule.

State and federal aid to higher education expanded rapidly. The Morrill Act, granting land to each state at a rate of 30,000 acres for each senator and representative, provided the endowments that gave many important modern universities, such as Illinois, Michigan State, and Ohio State, their start. While the federal assistance was earmarked for specific subjects, the land-grant colleges offered a full range of courses, and all received additional state funds. The land-grant universities adopted new ideas quickly. They were coeducational from the start, and most developed professional schools and experimented with extension work and summer programs.

Typical of the better state institutions was the University of Michigan, which reached the top rank among the nation's universities during the presidency of James B. Angell (1871–1909). Like Eliot at Harvard, Angell expanded the undergraduate curriculum and strengthened the law and medical schools. He encouraged graduate studies, seeking to make Michigan "part of the great world of scholars," and sought ways in which the university could serve the general community.

Important advances were made in women's higher education. Beginning with Vassar College,

which opened its doors to 300 women students in 1865, the opportunity for young women to pursue serious academic work gradually expanded. Wellesley and Smith, both founded in 1875, completed the so-called Big Three women's colleges. Together with the already established Mount Holyoke, and with Bryn Mawr (1885), Barnard (1889), and Radcliffe (1893), they became known as the Seven Sisters.

The only professional careers easily available to women were nursing, teaching, and the new area called social work. Nevertheless, the remarkable women that these institutions trained were conscious of their uniqueness and determined to demonstrate their capabilities. They provided most of the leaders of the early twentieth-century drive for equal rights for women.

Not all the changes in higher education were beneficial. The elective system led to superficiality; students gained a smattering of knowledge of many subjects and mastered none. For example, 55 percent of the Harvard class of 1898 took elementary courses and no others during their four years of study. Intensive graduate work often produced narrowness of outlook and research monographs on trivial subjects. Attempts to apply the scientific method in fields such as history and economics often enticed students into making smug (and preposterous) claims to objectivity and definitiveness.

The gifts of rich industrialists sometimes came with strings, and college boards of trustees tended to be dominated by businessmen who sometimes attempted to impose their own social and economic beliefs on faculty members. Although few professors lost their positions because their views offended trustees, at many institutions trustees exerted constant nagging pressures that limited academic freedom and scholarly objectivity. At state colleges, politicians often interfered in academic affairs, even treating professorships as part of the patronage system.

Thorstein Veblen pointed out in his caustic study of *The Higher Learning in America* (1918) that "the intrusion of businesslike ideals, aims and methods" harmed the universities in countless subtle ways. Size alone—the verbose Veblen called it "an executive weakness for spectacular magnitude"—became an end in itself, and the practical values of education were exalted over the humanistic. When universities grew bigger, administration became more complicated and the prestige of administrators rose inordinately. At many institutions professors came to be regarded as mere employees of the governing boards. In 1893 the members of the faculty of Stanford University were officially classified as personal servants of Mrs. Leland Stanford, widow of the founder. This was done in good cause—the Stanford estate was tied up in probate court and the ruling made it possible to pay professors out of Mrs. Stanford's allowance for household expenses—but that such a procedure was even conceivable must have appalled the scholarly world.

As the number of college graduates increased, and as colleges ceased being primarily training institutions for clergymen, the influence of alumni on educational policies began to make itself felt, not always happily. Campus social activities became more important. Fraternities proliferated. Interest in organized sports first appeared as a laudable outgrowth of the general expansion of the curriculum, but soon athletic contests were playing a role all out of proportion to their significance. After football evolved as the leading intercollegiate sport (over 50,000 attended the Yale-Princeton game in 1893), it became a source of revenue that many colleges dared not neglect. Since students, alumni, and the public demanded winning teams, college administrators stooped to subsidizing student athletes, in extreme cases employing players who were not students at all. One exasperated college president quipped that the B.A. degree was coming to mean Bachelor of Athletics.

Thus higher education reflected American values, with all their strengths and weaknesses. A complex society required a more professional and specialized education for its youth; the coarseness and the rampant materialism and competitiveness of the era inevitably found expression in the colleges and universities.

REVOLUTION IN THE SOCIAL SCIENCES

In the social sciences a close connection existed between the practical issues of the age and the achievements of the leading thinkers. The application of the theory of evolution to every aspect of human relations, the impact of industrialization on society—such topics were of intense concern to American economists, sociologists, and historians. An understanding of Darwin increased the already strong interest in studying the development of institutions and their interactions with one another. Controversies over trusts, slum conditions, and other problems drew scholars out of their towers and into practical affairs.

Social scientists were impressed by the progress being made in the physical and biological sciences. They eagerly applied the scientific method to their own

specialties, hoping thereby to arrive at objective truths in fields that by nature were essentially subjective.

Among the economists something approaching a revolution took place in the 1880s. The classical school, which maintained that immutable natural laws governed all human behavior and which used the insights of Darwin only to justify unrestrained competition and laissez-faire, was challenged by a group of young economists who argued that as times changed, economic theories and laws must be modified in order to remain relevant. Richard T. Ely, another of the scholars who made Johns Hopkins a font of new ideas in the 1880s, summarized the thinking of this group in 1885. "The state [is] an educational and ethical agency whose positive aid is an indispensable condition of human progress," Ely proclaimed. Laissez-faire was outmoded and dangerous. Economic problems were basically moral problems; their solution required "the united efforts of Church, state and science." The proper way to study these problems was by analyzing actual conditions, not by applying abstract laws or principles.

This approach produced the so-called institutionalist school of economics, whose members made detailed, on-the-spot investigations of labor unions, sweatshops, factories, and mines. The study of institutions would lead both to theoretical insights and to practical social reform, they believed. John R. Commons, one of Ely's students at Johns Hopkins and later professor of economics at the University of Wisconsin, was the outstanding member of this school. His ten-volume *Documentary History of American Industrial Society* (1910–1911) reveals the institutionalist approach at its best.

A similar revolution struck sociology in the mid-1880s. Prevailing opinion up to that time rejected the idea of government interference with the organization of society. The influence of the English social Darwinist, Herbert Spencer, who objected even to public schools and the postal system, was immense. Spencer and his American disciples, among them Edward L. Youmans, editor of *Popular Science Monthly*, twisted the ideas of Darwin to mean that society could be changed only by the force of evolution, which moved with cosmic slowness. "You and I can do nothing at all," Youmans told the reformer Henry George. "It's all a matter of evolution. Perhaps in four or five thousand years evolution may have carried men beyond this state of things."

Similar currents of thought influenced other social sciences. In *Systems of Consanguinity* (1871), the pioneer anthropologist Lewis Henry Morgan developed a theory of social evolution and showed how kinship relationships reflected and affected tribal

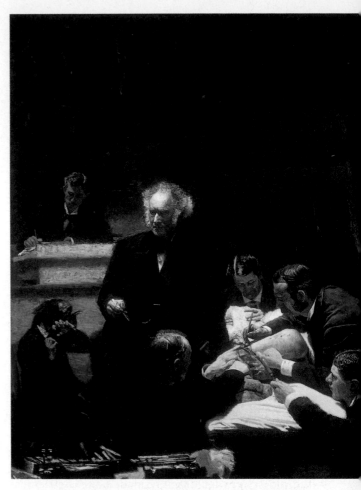

▲ Thomas Eakins's *The Gross Clinic* (1875). To better understand how to depict the body, Eakins resolved to study how it functioned. To that end, in 1873 he enrolled in anatomy classes at the Jefferson Medical College in Philadelphia. This painting is of Samuel Gross, lecturing while removing the dead bone from the thigh of a patient.

institutions. The new political scientists were also evolutionists and institutionalists. The Founding Fathers, living in a world dominated by Newton's concept of the universe as an immense, orderly machine, had conceived of the political system as an impersonal set of institutions and principles—a government of laws rather than of men. Nineteenth-century thinkers (John C. Calhoun is the best example) concerned themselves with abstractions, such as states' rights, and ignored the extralegal aspects of politics, such as parties and pressure groups. In the 1880s political scientists began to employ a different approach. In his doctoral dissertation at Johns Hopkins, *Congressional Government* (1885), Woodrow Wilson analyzed the American political system. He concluded that the real locus of authority lay in the committees of Congress, which had no

constitutional basis at all. Wilson was by no means a radical, but he viewed politics as a dynamic process and offered no theoretical objection to the expansion of state power. "Every means," he wrote in *The State* (1889), "by which society may be perfected through the instrumentality of government . . . ought certainly to be diligently sought."

PROGRESSIVE EDUCATION

Traditionally, American teachers had emphasized the three Rs and relied on strict discipline and rote learning. Typical of the pedagogues of the period was the Chicago teacher, described by a reformer in the 1890s, who told her students firmly: "Don't stop to think, tell me what you know!" Yet new ideas were attracting attention. According to a German educator, Johann Friedrich Herbart, teachers could best arouse the interest of their students by relating new information to what they already knew; good teaching called for professional training, psychological insight, enthusiasm, and imagination, not merely facts and a birch rod. At the same time, evolutionists were pressing for a kind of education that would help children to "survive" by adapting to the demands of their environment.

Forward-looking educators seized on these ideas because dynamic social changes were making the old system increasingly inadequate. Settlement house workers discovered that slum children needed training in handicrafts, good citizenship, and personal hygiene as much as in reading and writing. They were appalled by the local schools, which suffered from the same diseases—filth, overcrowding, rickety construction—that plagued the tenements, and by school systems that were controlled by machine politicians who doled out teaching positions to party hacks and other untrained persons. They argued that school playgrounds, nurseries, kindergartens, and adult education programs were essential in communities where most women worked and many people lacked much formal education. "We are impatient with the schools which lay all stress on reading and writing," Jane Addams declared. This type of education "fails to give the child any clew to the life about him." The philosopher who summarized and gave direction to these forces was John Dewey, a professor at the University of Chicago. Dewey was concerned with the implications of evolution—indeed, of all science—for education. Essentially his approach was ethical. Was the nation's youth being properly prepared for the tasks it faced in the modern world? He became interested in Francis W. Parker's

remarkable experimental school in Chicago, which was organized as "a model home, a complete community and embryonic democracy." In 1896, together with his wife, Dewey founded the Laboratory School to put his educational ideas to the test. Three years later he published *The School and Society,* describing and defending his theories.

"Education," Dewey insisted, was "the fundamental method of social progress and reform." To seek to improve conditions merely by passing laws was "futile." Moreover, in an industrial society the family no longer performed many of the educational functions it had carried out in an agrarian society. Farm children learn about nature, about work, about human character in countless ways denied to children in cities. The school can fill the gap by becoming "an embryonic community . . . with types of occupations that reflect the life of the larger society." At the same time, education should center on the child, and new information should be related to what the child already knows. Children's imagination, energy, and curiosity are tools for broadening their outlook and increasing their store of information. Finally, the school should become an instrument for social reform, "saturating [the child] with the spirit of service" and helping to produce a "society which is worthy, lovely, and harmonious." Education, in other words, ought to build character and teach good citizenship as well as transmit knowledge.

The School and Society created a stir, and Dewey immediately assumed leadership of what in the next generation was called progressive education. Although the gains made in public education before 1900 were more quantitative than qualitative and the philosophy dominant in most schools was not very different at the end of the century from that prevailing in Horace Mann's day, change was in the air. The best educators of the period were full of optimism, convinced that the future was theirs.

LAW AND HISTORY

Even jurisprudence, by its nature conservative and rooted in tradition, felt the pressure of evolutionary thought and the new emphasis on studying institutions as they actually are. In 1881 Oliver Wendell Holmes, Jr. published *The Common Law.* Rejecting the ideas that judges should limit themselves to the mechanical explication of statutes and that law consisted only of what was written in law books, Holmes argued that "the felt necessities of the time" rather than precedent should determine the rules by which people are governed. "The life of the law has not been logic; it has been experience," he wrote. "It is

DEBATING THE PAST

Did the frontier engender individualism and democracy? This 1887 photograph depicts a family in Custer County, Nebraska. Their optimism is indicated by the fact that they have begun to build a house *(center)*; yet their isolation suggests their vulnerability, as does the dugout *(upper left)* they now live in. Were such people self-reliant individualists or needy dependents?

In 1893 historian Frederick Jackson Turner argued that the boundless expanses of the frontier gave rise to democracy, individualism and "withal that buoyancy and exuberance which comes with freedom." Insofar as the frontier was then receding before the advance of urbanization and industrialization, Turner's readers had cause for alarm. Historians adopting the Turnerian analysis—and there were many—were generally pessimistic about the prospects for American democracy.

Philosopher John Dewey (1922) was among those who dissented. He argued that rather than promoting democracy, the frontier had a "depressing effect upon the free life of inquiry and criticism." Other scholars insisted that democracy flourished not in the West but in urban and industrial areas. In subsequent decades scholars challenged Turner's assertions that frontier peoples were self-sufficient and their democratic institutions vital.

Richard White (1991) insisted that the West, more so than any other region, had been "historically a dependency of the federal government." Donald Worster (1992) contended that its predominant economy—cattle raising and irrigation agriculture—was developed mostly by large corporations.

And even if the frontier promoted democratic sensibilities, this came at the cost of dispossessing the Indians—missing from the photograph—who had previously ranged over this land.

Donald Wurster, *Under Western Skies* (1992), Richard White, *"It's Your Misfortune and None of My Own"* (1991), Peggy Pascoe, *Relations of Rescue: The Search for Female Moral Authority in the American West, 1874–1939* (1990), Patricia Limerick, *Legacy of Conquest* (1988), and Elliot West, *The Contested Plains* (1998).

revolting," he added on another occasion, "to have no better reason for a rule of law than that so it was laid down in the time of Henry IV."

Holmes went on to a long and brilliant judicial career, during which he repeatedly stressed the right of the people, through their elected representatives, to deal with contemporary problems in any reasonable way, unfettered by outmoded conceptions of the proper limits of government authority. Like the societies they regulated, laws should evolve as times and conditions changed, he said.

This way of reasoning caused no sudden reversal of judicial practice. Holmes's most notable opinions as a judge tended to be dissents. But his philosophy reflected the advanced thinking of the late nineteenth century, and his influence grew with every decade of the twentieth.

The new approach to knowledge did not always advance the cause of liberal reform. Historians in the graduate schools became intensely interested in studying the origins and evolution of political institutions. They concluded, after much "scientific" study of old charters and law codes, that the roots of democracy were to be found in the customs of the ancient tribes of northern Europe. This theory of the "Teutonic origins" of democracy, which has since been thoroughly discredited, fitted well with the prejudices of people of British stock, and it provided ammunition for those who favored restricting immigration and for those who argued that blacks were inferior beings.

Out of this work, however, came an essentially democratic concept, the frontier thesis of Frederick Jackson Turner, still another scholar trained at Johns Hopkins. Turner's essay "The Significance of the Frontier in American History" (1893) argued that the frontier experience, through which every section of the country had passed, had affected the thinking of the people and the shape of American institutions. The isolation of the frontier and the need during each successive westward advance to create civilization anew, Turner wrote, account for the individualism of Americans and the democratic character of their society. Nearly everything unique in our culture could be traced to the existence of the frontier, he claimed.

Turner, and still more his many disciples, made too much of his basic insights. Life on the frontier was not as democratic as Turner believed, and it certainly does not "explain" American development as completely as he said it did. Nevertheless, his work showed how important it was to investigate the evolution of institutions, and it encouraged historians to study social and economic, as well as purely political, subjects. If the claims of the new historians to objectivity and definitiveness were absurdly overstated,

their emphasis on thoroughness, exactitude, and impartiality did much to raise standards in the profession. Perhaps the finest product of the new scientific school, a happy combination of meticulous scholarship and literary artistry, was Henry Adams's nine-volume *History of the United States During the Administrations of Jefferson and Madison.*

REALISM IN LITERATURE

When what Mark Twain called the Gilded Age began, American literature was dominated by the romantic mood. All the important writers of the 1840s and 1850s except Hawthorne, Thoreau, and Poe were still living. Longfellow stood at the height of his fame, and the lachrymose Susan Warner—"tears on almost every page"—continued to turn out stories in the style of her popular *The Wide, Wide World.* Romanticism, however, had lost its creative force; most writing in the decade after 1865 was sentimental trash pandering to the preconceptions of middle-class readers. Magazines like the *Atlantic Monthly* overflowed with stories about fair ladies worshiped from afar by stainless heroes, women coping selflessly with drunken husbands, and poor but honest youths rising through various combinations of virtue and diligence to positions of wealth and influence. Most writers of fiction tended to ignore the eternal conflicts inherent in human nature and the social problems of the age; polite entertainment and pious moralizing appeared to be their only objectives.

The patent unreality, even dishonesty, of contemporary fiction eventually caused a reaction. The most important forces giving rise to the Age of Realism were those that were transforming every other aspect of American life: industrialism, with its associated complexities and social problems; the theory of evolution, which made people more aware of the force of the environment and the basic conflicts of existence; the new science, which taught dispassionate, empirical observation. Novelists undertook the examination of social problems such as slum life, the conflict between capital and labor, and political corruption. They created multidimensional characters, depicted persons of every social class, used dialect and slang to capture the flavor of particular types, and fashioned painstaking descriptions of the surroundings into which they placed their subjects. The romantic novel did not disappear. General Lew Wallace's *Ben Hur* (1880) and Frances Hodgson Burnett's *Little Lord Fauntleroy* (1886) were best-sellers. But by 1880 realism was the point of view of the finest literary talents in the country.

MARK TWAIN

While it was easy to romanticize the West, that region lent itself to the realistic approach. Almost of necessity, novelists writing about the West described coarse characters from the lower levels of society and dealt with crime and violence. It would have been difficult indeed to write a genteel romance about a mining camp. The outstanding figure of western literature, the first great American realist, was Mark Twain.

Twain, whose real name was Samuel L. Clemens, was born in 1835. He grew up in Hannibal, Missouri, on the banks of the Mississippi. After mastering the printer's trade and working as a riverboat pilot, he went west to Nevada in 1861. The wild, rough life of Virginia City fascinated him, but prospecting got him nowhere, and he became a reporter for the

Territorial Enterprise. Soon he was publishing humorous stories about the local life under the nom de plume Mark Twain. In 1865, while working in California, he wrote "The Celebrated Jumping Frog of Calaveras County," a story that brought him national recognition. A tour of Europe and the Holy Land in 1867 to 1868 led to *The Innocents Abroad* (1869), which made him famous.

Twain's greatness stemmed from his keen reportorial eye and ear, his eagerness to live life to the full, his marvelous sense of humor, and his ability to be at once in society and outside it, to love humanity yet be repelled by human vanity and perversity. He epitomized the zest and adaptability of his age and also its materialism. No contemporary pursued the almighty dollar more zealously. An inveterate speculator, he made a fortune with his pen and lost it in

▲ A sidewheeler on the Mississippi. In 1856 Samuel Clemens became an apprentice to a steamboat pilot and spent the next four years—among the most carefree in his life—plying the waters of the Mississippi River. In his writings, the river was a metaphor for a journey of discovery; a century later, the highway would function in a similar way for many American novelists.

foolish business ventures. He wrote tirelessly and endlessly about America and Europe, his own times and the feudal past, about tourists, slaves, tycoons, cracker-barrel philosophers—and human destiny. He was equally at home and equally successful on the Great River of his childhood, in the mining camps, and in the eastern bourgeois society of his mature years. But every prize slipped through his fingers. Twain died a dark pessimist, surrounded by adulation yet alone, an alien and a stranger in the land he loved and knew so well.

Twain, from *The Gilded Age*

Twain excelled every contemporary in the portrayal of character. In his biting satire, *The Gilded Age* (1873), he created that magnificent mountebank Colonel Beriah Sellers, purveyor of eyewash ("the Infallible Imperial Oriental Optic Liniment") and false hopes, ridiculous, unscrupulous, but lovable. In *Huckleberry Finn* (1884), his masterpiece, his portrait of the slave Jim, loyal, patient, naive, yet withal a man, is unforgettable. When Huck takes advantage of Jim's credulity merely for his own amusement, the slave turns from him coldly and says: "Dat truck dah is trash; en trash is what people is dat puts dirt on de head er dey fren's en makes 'em ashamed." And there is Huck Finn himself, full of devilry, romantic, amoral—up to a point—and at bottom the complete realist. When Miss Watson tells him he can get anything he wants by praying for it, he makes the effort, is disillusioned, and concludes: "If a body can get anything they pray for, why don't Deacon Winn get back the money he lost on pork? . . . Why can't Miss Watson fat up? No, I says to myself, there ain't nothing in it."

Whether directly, as in *The Innocents Abroad* and in his fascinating account of the world of the river pilot, *Life on the Mississippi* (1883), or when transformed by his imagination in works of fiction such as *Tom Sawyer* (1876) and *A Connecticut Yankee in King Arthur's Court* (1889), Mark Twain always put much of his own experience and feeling into his work. "The truth is," he wrote in 1886, "my books are mainly autobiographies." A story, he told a fellow author, "must be written with the blood out of a man's heart." His innermost confusions, the clash between his recognition of the pretentiousness and meanness of human beings and his wish to be accepted by society, added depths and overtones to his writing that together with his comic genius give it lasting appeal. He could not rise above the sentimentality and prudery of his generation entirely, for these qualities were part of his nature. He never dealt effectively with sexual love, for example, and often—even in *Huckleberry Finn*—contrived to end his tales

on absurdly optimistic notes that ring false after so many brilliant pages portraying life as it is. On balance Twain's achievement was magnificent. Rough and uneven like the man himself, his works catch more of the spirit of the age he named than those of any other writer.

WILLIAM DEAN HOWELLS

Twain's realism was far less self-conscious than that of his longtime friend William Dean Howells. Like Twain, Howells, who was born in Ohio in 1837, had little formal education. He learned the printer's trade from his father and became a reporter for the *Ohio State Journal*. In 1860 he wrote a campaign biography of Lincoln and was rewarded with an appointment as consul in Venice. His sketches in *Venetian Life* (1866) were a product of this experience. After the Civil War he worked briefly for *The Nation* in New York and then moved to Boston, where he became editor of the *Atlantic Monthly*. In 1886 he returned to New York as editor of *Harper's*.

A long series of novels and much literary criticism poured from Howells's pen over the next 30 years. While he insisted on treating his material honestly, he was not at first a critic of society, being content to write about what he called "the smiling aspects" of life. Realism to Howells meant concern for the complexities of individual personalities and faithful description of the genteel, middle-class world he knew best.

Besides a sharp eye and an open mind, Howells had a real social conscience. Gradually he became aware of the problems that industrialization had created. In 1885, in *The Rise of Silas Lapham,* he dealt with some of the ethical conflicts faced by businessmen in a competitive society. The harsh public reaction to the Haymarket bombing in 1886 stirred him, and he threw himself into a futile campaign to prevent the execution of the anarchist suspects. Thereafter he moved rapidly toward the left; soon he was calling himself a socialist. "After fifty years of optimistic content with 'civilization' . . . I now abhor it, and feel that it is coming out all wrong in the end, unless it bases itself anew on a real equality," he wrote. But he added immediately: "Meanwhile I wear a fur-lined overcoat, and live in all the luxury my money can buy." In *A Hazard of New Fortunes* (1890), he attempted to portray the whole range of metropolitan life, weaving the destinies of a dozen interesting personalities from diverse sections and social classes. The book represents a triumph of realism in its careful descriptions of various sections of New

York and the ways of life of rich and poor, in the intricacy of its characters, and in its rejection of sentimentality and romantic love.

His own works were widely read, and Howells was also the most influential critic of his time. He helped bring the best contemporary foreign writers, including Tolstoy, Dostoevsky, Ibsen, and Zola, to the attention of readers in the United States, and he encouraged many important young American novelists, among them Stephen Crane, Theodore Dreiser, Frank Norris, and Hamlin Garland.

Some of these writers went far beyond Howells's realism to what they called naturalism. Many, like Twain and Howells, began as newspaper reporters. Working for a big-city daily in the 1890s was sure to teach anyone a great deal about the dark side of life. Naturalist writers believed that the human being was essentially an animal, a helpless creature whose fate was determined by environment. Their world was Darwin's world—mindless, without mercy or justice. They wrote chiefly about the most primitive emotions—lust, hate, greed. In *Maggie, A Girl of the Streets* (1893), Stephen Crane described the seduction, degradation, and eventual suicide of a young woman, all set against the background of a sordid slum; in *The Red Badge of Courage* (1895), he captured the pain and humor of war. In *McTeague* (1899), Frank Norris told the story of a brutal, dull-witted dentist who murdered his greed-crazed wife with his bare fists.

Such stuff was too strong for Howells, yet he recognized its importance and befriended the younger writers in many ways. He found a publisher for *Maggie* after it had been rejected several times, and he wrote appreciative reviews of the work of Garland and Norris. Even Theodore Dreiser, who was contemptuous of Howells's writings and considered him hopelessly middle class in point of view, appreciated his aid and praised his influence on American literature. Dreiser's first novel, *Sister Carrie* (1900), treated sex so forthrightly that it was withdrawn after publication.

HENRY JAMES

Henry James was very different in spirit and background from the tempestuous naturalists. Born to wealth, reared in a cosmopolitan atmosphere, twisted in some strange way while still a child and unable to achieve satisfactory relationships with women, James spent most of his mature life in Europe, writing novels, short stories, plays, and volumes of criticism. Although far removed from the world of practical affairs, he was preeminently a realist, determined, as he once said, "to leave a multitude of pictures of my time" for the future to contemplate. He admired the European realists and denounced the "floods of tepid soap and water which under the name of novels are being vomited forth" by the romancers. "All life belongs to you," he told his fellow novelists. "There is no impression of life, no manner of seeing it and feeling it, to which the plan of the novelist may not offer a place."

Although he preferred living in the cultivated surroundings of London high society, James yearned for the recognition of his fellow Americans almost as avidly as Mark Twain. However, he was incapable of modifying his rarefied, overly subtle manner of writing. Most serious writers of the time admired his books, and he received many honors, but he never achieved widespread popularity. His major theme was the clash of American and European cultures, his primary interest the close-up examination of wealthy, sensitive, yet often corrupt persons in a cultivated but far from polite society.

James dealt with social issues such as feminism and the difficulties faced by artists in the modern world, but he subordinated them to his interest in his subjects as individuals. *The American* (1877) told the story of the love of a wealthy American in Paris for a French noblewoman who rejected him because her family disapproved of his commercial background. *The Portrait of a Lady* (1881) described the disillusionment of an intelligent woman married to a charming but morally bankrupt man and her eventual decision to remain with him nonetheless. *The Bostonians* (1886) was a complicated and psychologically sensitive study of the varieties of female behavior in a seemingly uniform social situation.

James's reputation, greater today than in his lifetime, rests more on his highly refined accounts of the interactions of individuals and their environment and his masterful commentaries on the novel as a literary form than on his ability as a storyteller. Few major writers have been more long-winded, more prone to circumlocution. Yet few have been so dedicated to their art, possessed of such psychological penetration, or so successful in producing a large body of important work.

REALISM IN ART

American painters responded to the times as writers did, but with this difference: Despite the new concern for realism, the romantic tradition retained its vitality. Preeminent among the realists was Thomas Eakins,

▲ Thomas Eakins's interest in science was as great as his interest in art. In the early 1880s he collaborated with photographer Eadweard Muybridge in serial-action photographic experiments and later devised a special camera for his anatomical studies. The picture below was taken with the Marey wheel. The impact of Eakins's photographic experiments is evident in *The Swimming Hole*, painted in 1883 *(above)*. At that time Eakins was director of the art school at the Pennsylvania Academy of the Fine Arts.

who was born in Philadelphia in 1844. Eakins studied in Europe in the late 1860s and was influenced by the great realists of the seventeenth century, Velasquez and Rembrandt. Returning to America in 1870, he passed the remainder of his life teaching and painting in Philadelphia.

The scientific spirit of the age suited Eakins perfectly. He mastered human anatomy; some of his finest paintings, such as *The Gross Clinic* (1875), are graphic illustrations of surgical operations. He was an early experimenter with motion pictures, using the camera to capture exactly the attitudes of human beings and animals in action. Like his friend Walt Whitman, whose portrait is one of his greatest achievements, Eakins gloried in the ordinary. But he had none of Whitman's weakness for sham and self-delusion. His portraits are monuments to his integrity and craftsmanship: never would he touch up or soften a likeness to please his sitter. When the Union League of Philadelphia commissioned a canvas of Rutherford B. Hayes, Eakins showed the president working in his shirtsleeves, which scandalized the club fathers. His work was no mere mirror reflecting surface values. His study of six men bathing *(The Swimming Hole)* is a stark portrayal of nakedness; his surgical scenes catch the tenseness of a situation without descending into sensationalism.

Winslow Homer, a Boston-born painter best known for his brilliant watercolors, was also influenced by realist ideas. Homer was a lithographer as well as a master of the watercolor medium, yet he had had almost no formal training. Indeed, he had contempt for academicians and refused to go abroad to study. Aesthetics seemed not to concern him at all; he liked to shock people by referring to his profession as "the picture line." His concern for accuracy was so intense that in preparation for painting *The Life Line* (1884) he made a trip to Atlantic City to observe the handling of a breeches buoy. "When I have selected [a subject]," he said, "I paint it exactly as it appears."

During the Civil War, Homer worked as an artist-reporter for *Harper's Weekly*, and he continued to do magazine illustrations for some years thereafter. He roamed America, painting scenes of southern farm life, Adirondack campers, and, after about 1880, magnificent seascapes and studies of fishermen and sailors.

Homer's work contains romantic elements. His *Gulf Stream* (1899), showing a sailor on a small, broken boat menaced by an approaching waterspout and a school of sharks, and his *Fox Hunt* (1893) (see pp. 528–529), in which huge, ominous crows hover over a fox at bay, express his interest in the violence and drama of raw nature, a distinctly romantic theme.

However, his approach, even in these works, was utterly prosaic. When some viewers complained about the fate of the black sailor in *Gulf Stream*, Homer wrote his dealer sarcastically: "Tell these ladies that the unfortunate Negro . . . will be rescued and returned to his friends and home, and live happily ever after."

The careers of Eakins and Homer show that the late-nineteenth-century American environment was not uncongenial to first-rate artists. Nevertheless, at least two major American painters abandoned native shores for Europe. One was James A. McNeill Whistler, whose portrait of his mother, which he called *Arrangement in Grey and Black*, is probably the most famous canvas ever painted by an American. Whistler left the United States in 1855 when he was 21 and spent most of his life in Paris and London. "I shall come to America," he announced grandly, "when the duty on works of art is abolished!"

Whistler made a profession of eccentricity, but he was a talented and versatile artist. Some of his portraits are triumphs of realism, whereas his misty studies of the London waterfront—which the critic John Ruskin characterized as pots of paint flung in the face of the beholder and which Whistler conceived as visual expressions of poetry—are thoroughly romantic in conception. Paintings such as *Whistler's Mother* represent still another expression of his talent. Spare and muted in tone, they are more interesting as precise arrangements of color and space than as images of particular objects; they had considerable influence on the course of modern art.

The second important expatriate artist was Mary Cassatt, daughter of a wealthy Pittsburgh banker and sister of Alexander J. Cassatt, who was president of the Pennsylvania Railroad around the turn of the century. She went to Paris as a tourist and dabbled in art like many conventional young socialites, then was caught up in the impressionist movement and decided to become a serious painter. Her work is more French than American and was little appreciated in the United States before World War I. When once she returned to America for a visit, the *Philadelphia Public Ledger* reported: "Mary Cassatt, sister of Mr. Cassatt, president of the Pennsylvania Railroad, returned from Europe yesterday. She has been studying painting in Paris, and owns the smallest Pekinese dog in the world."

If Mary Cassatt was unappreciated and if Whistler had reasons for considering Americans uncultured, it remains true that interest in art was considerable. Museums and art schools increased in

▶ *text continues on page 546*

Re-Viewing the Past

Titanic

James Cameron's *Titanic* was a blockbuster. He made audiences feel what it was like to be on the ship. When the deck tilted to the right, viewers leaned to the left; many gasped as the ship plunged into the icy depths. What sent a shiver down the spine was the knowledge that real people had experienced what was being depicted on the screen.

Cameron well understood the audience's craving to relive a true story. By showing footage of the actual HMS *Titanic* on the floor of the Atlantic, fish gliding silently through its barnacle-encrusted wreckage, he reminded audiences that what they were seeing had actually happened. He spent scores of millions of dollars devising computer-enhanced techniques to ensure that his *Titanic* looked like the one that went down in the North Atlantic on the night of April 14–15, 1912.

But Cameron's *Titanic* was more than a disaster movie. It was also the story of two young people who fall in love. The romance begins when Jack (Leonardo DiCaprio), a struggling artist, spots Rose (Kate Winslet), a wealthy socialite, climbing over the railing and peering despondently into the water below. Obliged to marry a contemptuous (and contemptible) snob, she is miserable. Jack, from a lower deck, scrambles up and persuades her to forego the plunge.

As a reward for saving Rose, Jack is invited to dine with Rose's table. At dinner, Rose appraises Jack more carefully—and is impressed. He looks good in a tuxedo, displays plenty of moxie, and possesses artistic talent ("Jack, you see things!"). She proposes that she pose for him in the nude. A few hours later they venture below decks and, in anticipation of the courtship rituals of future decades, locate an automobile, climb inside, and rip off each other's clothes. Soon the car is bouncing. The windows steam up, and a hand leaves an imprint, fingers outstretched in ecstasy.

Minutes later they are cooled off when the ship has its close encounter of the icy kind. Jack—young, vital, alive—perishes in the frigid waters; but he has imparted to Rose a gift of love, and thus of life. This tale of young lovers, held apart by society, is a nautical "Romeo and Juliet," a brief, pure instant of love, tragically ended by death.

If Cameron's *Titanic* is a love story for the ages, it was also frozen in a particular place and in a particular time. Much as Cameron spent millions to show the ship as it really was, he took similar pains to give a convincing rendering of New York society, especially its clothing, silverware, and social conventions.

Of the latter, the most significant for the story are the elaborate rituals of Victorian courtship. Rose seeks to break free from her impending marriage partly because she despises her fiancé, but also because marriage to him constitutes the final, irreversible step into the gilded cage of a society lady. Jack's presence at dinner with the "best" of society underscores the shallow materialism of this upper crust and its preoccupation with wealth, its disdain for those who lack both, its absurd rules of etiquette, and its repressive attitudes toward sexuality. Viewers of the movie, looking through Rose's eyes, may wonder how such rituals ever came to be.

▼ Leonardo DiCaprio and Kate Winslet as lovers on the *Titanic*.

Some had existed for centuries. The idealization of courtly love and pure womanhood was commonplace in medieval literature; in the early nineteenth century novelist Jane Austen described the subtle interplay of money and romance in England. But the rituals of New York society in the Gilded Age were characterized by sumptuous and public displays of wealth—glittering balls, and extravagant "Grand Tours" of Europe.

This new mode of courtship was largely the creation of Mrs. John Jacob Astor, wife of one of New York's wealthiest businessmen, and her friends. After the Civil War, industrialization and urbanization were generating new wealth and destroying the old at a dizzying pace. While prominent businessmen and investment bankers were devising institutions to impose order on this creative industrial chaos, their wives were regularizing its social elite. They endeavored to determine who should be admitted to New York's "best" families—and who should not. They concluded that it was not enough to be rich; the elite of the nation must also adhere to high standards of etiquette and decorum.

By controlling entrance into society, women such as Mrs. Astor (and her imitators in nearly every city in the nation) also determined the disposition, through marriage and inheritance, of the nation's largest fortunes. Society women possessed power.

Although the system was created and supervised by mature women, it demanded the compliance of adolescent girls. The process began when a mother took her daughter on a round of visits to society women, to whom they would present their "calling cards." If mother and daughter were judged suitable, they would be invited in for tea; if the girl behaved with decorum (and if her father's assets proved sound), she would be invited to balls and other formal events. At or near her sixteenth birthday, her parents would hold a ball in her honor—in New York the event usually took place at Delmonico's restaurant—marking her "debut" into society. She wore a white gown symbolizing her virginity. A male relative presented her formally to the prominent women. Now she could accept male suitors.

This highly stylized—almost tribal—ritual brought young women to the threshold of womanhood. Marriage awaited beyond the door. Many eagerly anticipated the acquisition of adult status and the social power it entailed. Others regarded this rite with terror. (Novelist Edith Wharton remembered her debut as a "long cold agony of shyness.") In the early twentieth century, some young women began to rebel. Elsie Clews, daughter of a Wall Street banker, refused to wear corsets. When her mother wasn't looking, she took off her veil and white gloves. She subsequently scandalized Newport—the fashionable Rhode Island summer resort for society's wealthy—by going swimming with a young man without a chaperone (but not without a bathing suit). To her mother's dismay, Clews delayed marriage and went to Barnard College; eventually she became a respected anthropologist (Elsie Clews Parsons).

▲ A young society couple courting in New York, about 1914.

Kate Winslet's "Rose" was, like Elsie Clews, a prematurely "modern" woman. But Clews tore off only her veil and white gloves, not all her clothes; she dispensed with the rituals of courtship, not its substance. Even in the waning years of the Victorian era, few wealthy young women succumbed to impoverished men, however earnest and appealing.

Victorian courtship was necessarily protracted. Young women did not unburden themselves to strangers; and even to friends, especially of the opposite sex, the process of revealing one's inner feelings unfolded slowly, often after a series of tests and trials. One person's tentative disclosure invited a reciprocal response. Letters and diaries show that, over time, these personal revelations often led to sexual intimacies. Nowadays many people regard Victorian marriages as unfeeling and stiff; but many Victorians maintained that their personal intimacies were the more delicious for having been long delayed.

Cameron's *Titanic looked* like the past; but the heart of the movie is Jack and Rose's whirlwind romance. While Rose's story addresses some of the anxieties of young society women, it more closely resembles the courtship patterns of Hollywood today than the experiences of young people at the beginning of the last century.

▲ Now widely recognized as one of America's finest impressionist painters, Mary Cassatt found her talent ignored in this country during her lifetime. This 1878 painting was entitled, *Little Girl in a Blue Armchair*.

number, and settlement house workers put on exhibitions that attracted enthusiastic crowds. Wealthy patrons gave countless commissions to portrait painters and poured fortunes into collecting. Martin A. Ryerson, with money made in lumber, bought the works of the French impressionists when few Americans understood their importance. Charles L. Freer of the American Car and Foundry Company was a specialist in oriental art. John G. Johnson, a successful corporation lawyer, covered the walls of his Philadelphia mansion with Italian primitives, accumulated before anyone else appreciated them. Other enthusiasts, notably the banker J. P. Morgan, employed experts to help them put together their collections. Nor were the advanced painters of the day rejected by wealthy patrons. While Eakins's work was undervalued, he received many important commissions. Some of Homer's canvases commanded thousands of dollars, and so did those of the radical Whistler.

THE PRAGMATIC APPROACH

It would have been remarkable indeed if the intellectual ferment of the late nineteenth century had not affected contemporary ideas about the meaning of life, the truth of revealed religion, moral values, and similar fundamental problems. In particular the theory of evolution, so important in altering contemporary views of science, history, and social relations, produced significant changes in American thinking about religious and philosophical questions.

Evolution posed an immediate challenge to religion: If Darwin was correct, the biblical account of the creation was obviously untrue and the idea that the human race had been formed in God's image was highly unlikely. A bitter controversy erupted, described by President Andrew D. White of Cornell in *The Warfare of Science with Theology in Christendom* (1896). While millions continued to believe in the

literal truth of the Bible, among intellectuals, lay and clerical, victory went to the evolutionists because, in addition to the arguments of the geologists and the biologists, scholars were throwing light on the historical origins of the Bible, showing it to be of human rather than divine inspiration.

Evolution did not undermine the faith of any large percentage of the population. If the account of the creation in Genesis could not be taken literally, the Bible remained a repository of wisdom and inspiration. Such books as John Fiske's *The Outlines of Cosmic Philosophy* (1874) provided religious persons with the comforting thesis that evolution, while true, was merely God's way of ordering the universe—as the liberal preacher Washington Gladden put it, "a most impressive demonstration of the presence of God in the world."

The effects of Darwinism on philosophy were less dramatic but in the end more significant. Fixed systems and eternal truths were difficult to justify in a world that was constantly evolving. By the early 1870s a few philosophers had begun to reason that ideas and theories mattered little except when applied to specifics.

"Nothing justifies the development of abstract principles but their utility in enlarging our concrete knowledge of nature," wrote Chauncey Wright, secretary of the American Academy of Arts and Sciences. In "How to Make Our Ideas Clear" (1878), Wright's friend Charles S. Peirce, an amazingly versatile and talented albeit obscure thinker, argued that concepts could be fairly understood only in terms of their practical effects. Once the mind accepted the truth of evolution, Peirce believed, logic required that it accept the impermanence even of scientific laws. There was, he wrote, "an element of indeterminacy, spontaneity, or absolute chance in nature."

This startling philosophy, which Peirce called pragmatism, was presented in more understandable language by William James, brother of the novelist. James was one of the most remarkable persons of his generation. Educated in London, Paris, Bonn, and Geneva—as well as at Harvard—he studied painting, participated in a zoological expedition to South America, earned a medical degree, and was professor at Harvard successively of comparative anatomy, psychology, and finally philosophy. His *Principles of Psychology* (1890) may be said to have established that discipline as a modern science. His *Varieties of Religious Experience* (1902), which treated the subject from both psychological and philosophical points of view, helped thousands of readers reconcile their religious faith with their increasing knowledge of psychology and the physical universe.

Although he was less rigorous a logician than Peirce, James's wide range and his verve and imagination as a writer made him by far the most influential philosopher of his time. He rejected the deterministic interpretation of Darwinism and all other one-idea explanations of existence. Belief in free will was one of his axioms; environment might influence survival, but so did the *desire* to survive, which existed independent of surrounding circumstances. Even truth was relative; it did not exist in the abstract but *happened* under particular circumstances. What a person thought helped to make thought occur, or come true. The mind, James wrote in a typically vivid phrase, has "a vote" in determining truth. Religion was true, for example, because people were religious.

The pragmatic approach inspired much of the reform spirit of the late nineteenth century and even more of that of the early twentieth. James's hammer blows shattered the laissez-faire extremism of Herbert Spencer. In "Great Men and Their Environment" (1880) James argued that social changes were brought about by the actions of geniuses whom society had selected and raised to positions of power, rather than by the impersonal force of the environment. Such reasoning fitted the preconceptions of rugged individualists yet encouraged those dissatisfied with society to work for change. Educational reformers like John Dewey, the institutionalist school of economists, settlement house workers, and other reformers adopted pragmatism eagerly. James's philosophy did much to revive the buoyant optimism that had characterized the pre–Civil War reform movement.

Yet pragmatism brought Americans face-to-face with somber problems. While relativism made them optimistic, it also bred insecurity, for there could be no certainty, no comforting reliance on any eternal value in the absence of absolute truth. Pragmatism also seemed to suggest that the end justified the means, that what worked was more important than what ought to be. At the time of James's death in 1910, the *Commercial and Financial Chronicle* pointed out that the pragmatic philosophy was helpful to businessmen in making decisions. By emphasizing practice at the expense of theory, the new philosophy encouraged materialism, anti-intellectualism, and other unlovely aspects of the American character. And what place had conventional morality in such a system? Perhaps pragmatism placed too much reliance on the free will of human beings, ignoring their capacity for selfishness and self-delusion.

The people of the new century found pragmatism a heady wine. They would quaff it freely and enthusiastically—down to the bitter dregs.

MILESTONES

1862	Morrill Act establishes land-grant colleges	1886	Ottmar Mergenthaler invents linotype machine
1865	Vassar College is founded for women		William Dean Howells becomes editor of *Harper's*
1869	Charles W. Eliot becomes Harvard's president	1889	Edward W. Bok becomes editor of the *Ladies' Home Journal*
1874	Chautauqua movement begins	1890	William James publishes *Principles of Psychology*
1876	Johns Hopkins University is founded to specialize in graduate education	1893	Frederick Jackson Turner publishes "Significance of the Frontier in American History"
1881	Oliver Wendell Holmes, Jr. publishes *The Common Law*		
	Henry James publishes *The Portrait of a Lady*	1895	William Randolph Hearst purchases the *New York Journal*
1883	Joseph Pulitzer purchases *New York World*	1899	John Dewey publishes *The School and Society*
1884	Mark Twain publishes *Huckleberry Finn*		

SUPPLEMENTARY READING

All the surveys of American intellectual history deal extensively with this period. The modern classics include Louis Hartz, *The Liberal Tradition in America* (1955), Clinton Rossiter, *Conservatism in America* (1962), and Henry S. Commager, *The American Mind* (1950). Louis Menand, *The Metaphysical Club* (2001), John Patrick Diggins, *The Promise of Pragmatism* (1994), Jackson Lears, *No Place for Grace: Antimodernism and the Transformation of American Culture, 1880–1920* (1981), and Gail Bederman, *Manliness and Civilization* (1995) are also stimulating.

On the impact of Darwin on late nineteenth-century America, see Richard Hofstadter's *Social Darwinism in American Thought* (1955), though his view has been substantially modified by Robert C. Bannister, *Social Darwinism* (1979). See also Carl Degler, *In Search of Human Nature: The Decline and Revival of Darwinism in American Social Thought* (1991), and Paul Crook, *Darwinism, War and History* (1994). James Turner, *Without God Without Creed: The Origins of Unbelief in America* (1996), contends that Darwinism promoted skepticism.

A recent interpretation of the Chautauqua movement is John E. Tapia, *Circuit Chautauqua* (1997). On journalism, see especially David Nasaw, *The Chief: The Life of William Randolph Hearst* (2000), and George Juergens, *Joseph Pulitzer and the New York World* (1966).

On higher education, see George Marsden, *The Soul of the American University* (1994), and Laurence R. Veysey, *The Emergence of the American University* (1965).

Kim Townsend, *Manhood at Harvard* (1996), William McNeill, *Hutchins' University* (1992), on the University of Chicago, and Robert McCaughey, *Stand, Columbia* (2004) are especially stimulating. Thorstein Veblen, *The Higher Learning in America* (1918) is full of provocative opinions.

Good introductions to law and the social sciences during this period include, respectively, Morton Horwitz, *The Transformation of American Law, 1870–1960* (1992), and Dorothy Ross, *The Origins of American Social Science* (1991). See also Linda Simon, *Genuine Reality: A Life of William James* (1998). For trends in educational theory, see Lawrence A. Cremin, *American Education: The Metropolitan Experience* (1988).

On women, see Rosalind Rosenberg, *Beyond Separate Spheres: Intellectual Roots of Modern Feminism* (1982), and Regina Morantz-Sanchez, *Sympathy and Science: Women Physicians in American Medicine* (1985). See also Jane Hunter, *How Young Ladies Became Girls: The Victorian Origins of American Girlhood* (2003).

On Twain, see Everett Emerson, *Mark Twain: A Literary Life* (1999); on Henry Adams during this period, Edward Chalfant, *Better in Darkness* (1994); on Henry James, Leon Edel, *Henry James* (1953–1962). Interesting studies of art and society include Kathleen Pyne, *Art and the Higher Life: Painting and Evolutionary Thought in Late Nineteenth-Century America* (1996), and Barbara Novak, *Nature and Culture* (1995).

SUGGESTED WEBSITES

Touring Turn-of-the-Century America: Photographs from the Detroit Publishing Company, 1880–1920
http://memory.loc.gov/ammem/detroit/dethome.html
This Library of Congress collection has thousands of photographs from turn-of-the-century America.

American Authors
http://xroads.virginia.edu/~HYPER/hypertex.html
This University of Virginia site contains hypertexts of the works of many prominent American authors, including Mark Twain, Stephen Crane, and Theodore Dreiser.

I Hear America Singing
http://www.thirteen.org/cgi-bin/ihas.cgi
American music came into its own at the turn of the century, as this fascinating site demonstrates.

National Geographic and the *Titanic*
http://www.nationalgeographic.com/society/ngo/explorer/titanic/movie.html
This National Geographic site offers historical perspective and balanced coverage of the *Titanic* tragedy.

Politics: Local, State, and National

A folk-art poster celebrating the Grangers, a movement founded in 1867 to protect farmers from powerful corporations.

During the last third of the nineteenth century, American politics reflected changes in its economic and social institutions. The public spectacles of typical antebellum politics—parades down Main Street and debates in Court House squares—were being superseded by new institutions. Mass circulation newspapers, themselves a product of new machines and distribution systems, became increasingly effective in shaping public opinion. Exactly what the parties stood for, however, was often difficult to determine. American political parties have nearly always avoided clear-cut stands on controversial questions in order to appeal to as wide a segment of the electorate as possible, but in the last quarter of the nineteenth century, their equivocations assumed abnormal proportions. This was due in part to the precarious balance of power between them. None dared declare itself too clearly on any question lest it drive away more voters than it attracted.

POLITICAL STRATEGY AND TACTICS

The rapid pace of social and economic change militated against political decisiveness. No one in or out of politics had as yet devised effective solutions for many current problems. When party leaders tried to deal with the money question, they discovered that the bankers and the professional economists were as confused as the public at large. "We dabble in theories of our own and clutch convulsively at the doctrines of others," a Philadelphia banker confessed. "From the vast tract of mire by which the subject is surrounded, overlaid, and besmeared, it is almost impossible to arrive at anything like a fair estimate of its real nature." How could mere politicians act rationally or consistently in such circumstances?

Reformers could thunder self-righteously against the spoils system, but how could political parties exist without it? Young economists like Richard T. Ely and Henry Carter Adams were insisting that laissez-faire was outmoded, but no one had yet devised the techniques and instruments that would have to be used if the economy was to be measured and managed effectively by a central authority. The embryonic social sciences had not even collected the statistical information necessary for efficient direction of the economy. If the politicians steered clear of the "real" issues, they did so as much out of a healthy respect for their own ignorance as out of any desire to avoid controversy.

Voting Along Ethnic and Religious Lines

The major parties had national committees, and delegates met in national conventions every four years to select their presidential candidates and draft "platforms," but they remained essentially separate state organizations. Professionals spent far more time dealing with local people and local issues than they did thinking about tariffs and money policy and other matters of broad national concern. They had to understand how different kinds of people felt about such matters if they wanted to win their support. In many parts of the country, that meant entering a veritable maze of diverse and often conflicting interests. People's ethnic backgrounds, their religious affiliations, whether they lived in cities or on farms, how they felt about the Civil War, and countless aspects of their lives that had no apparent relationship to national political issues affected whether they voted Republican or Democratic.

The politicians of the period were not shy about explaining why people voted the way they did. Senator George Frisbie Hoar of Massachusetts, for example, offered such an analysis in an 1889 magazine article. The Republicans, he wrote, were "the men who do the work of piety and charity in our churches . . . who administer our school systems . . . who own and till their own farms . . . who perform skilled labor . . . who went to the war . . . who paid the debt, and kept the currency sound, and saved the nation's honor." The Democrats, he went on, were "the old slave-owner and slave-driver, the saloon-keeper, the ballot-box-stuffer, the Ku-Klux, the criminal class of the great cities, and men who cannot read or write."

Despite the partisan character of Hoar's analysis, it contained an element of truth; a more disinterested observer, James Bryce, wrote in *The American Commonwealth* that at least in the North "the best people" were Republicans, whereas a "vast ignorant fluctuating mass of people" were Democrats. But if Hoar or even Bryce were correct, the Republicans would have swept the northern states at every election, which they assuredly did not.

In any case, it was (and it remains) even more difficult to discover *why* people voted one way or the other in the decades after the Civil War. People of Irish descent tended to vote Democratic, but whether they did so because they lived in cities or because they were Roman Catholics was not always clear.

Plausible generalizations break down when examined closely. Northerners were Republicans; Southerners, Democrats; Catholics were Democrats; Protestants, Republicans; German-Americans voted Democratic, Americans of Scandinavian descent, Republican. All these statements and many others like them are subject to a multitude of exceptions. And of course they conflict one with another. They offer little guidance for predicting how, for example, a German Lutheran living in Tennessee would vote.

Local and state issues interacted with religious and ethnic backgrounds to affect political attitudes. Prohibition, public education, and other matters subject to state and local control that seemed to have little or no relation to religion were in fact questions on which voters split along religious and ethnic lines. All these tangles influenced the way political leaders devised their strategies and chose candidates for office. Moreover, how voters felt about local issues almost invariably affected how they voted in national elections.

City Bosses

City governments were influenced by the religious and ethnic character of the inhabitants and further complicated by the special problems of late-nineteenth-century urban life: rapid, helter-skelter growth; the influx of European immigrants; the need to develop costly transportation, sanitation, and other public utility systems; and the crime and corruption that the size, confusion, and anonymity incidental to urban existence fostered.

The movement to the suburbs of large numbers of middle-class city people who might have been expected to supply the political leadership needed to deal with these problems created a vacuum of sorts, a vacuum that was filled by political bosses, with their informal but powerful "machines."

The immigrants who flocked into American cities in the 1880s and early 1890s made up much of the "vast ignorant fluctuating mass" that Bryce was referring to in his description of party align-

ments. They were largely of peasant stock, and having come from societies unacquainted with democracy, they had no experience with representative government. The tendency of urban workers to move frequently in search of better jobs further lessened the likelihood that they would develop political influence independently.

Furthermore, the difficulties of life in the slums bewildered and often overwhelmed newcomers, both native- and foreign-born. Hopeful, but passive and naive, they could hardly be expected to take a broad view of social problems when so beset by personal ones. This enabled shrewd urban politicians—most of them in this period of Irish origin, the Irish being the first-comers among the migrants and, according to mobility studies, more likely to stay put—to take command of the city masses and march them in obedient phalanxes to the polls.

Most city machines were loose-knit neighborhood organizations headed by ward bosses, not tightly geared hierarchical bureaucracies ruled by a single leader. "Big Tim" Sullivan of New York's Lower East Side and "Hinky Dink" Kenna of Chicago were typical of the breed. Sullivan, Kenna, and others like them performed many useful services for people they liked to think of as their constituents. They found jobs for new arrivals and distributed food and other help to all in bad times. Anyone in trouble with the law could obtain at least a hearing from the ward boss, and often, if the crime was minor or due to ignorance, the difficulty was quietly "fixed" and the culprit was sent off with a word of caution. Sullivan provided turkey dinners for 5000 or more homeless people each Christmas, distributed new shoes to the poor children of his district on his birthday, and arranged summer boat rides and picnics for young and old alike. At any time of year the victim of some sudden disaster could turn to the local clubhouse for help. Informally, probably without consciously intending to do so, the bosses educated the immigrants in the complexities of American civilization, helping them to leap the gulf between the almost medieval society of their origins and the modern industrial world.

The price of such aid—the bosses were not altruists—was unquestioning political support, which the bosses converted into cash. In New York, Sullivan levied tribute on gambling, had a hand in the liquor business, and controlled the issuance of peddlers' licenses. When he died in 1913, he was reputedly worth $1 million. Yet he and others like him were immensely popular; 25,000 grieving constituents followed Big Tim's coffin on its way to the grave.

The more visible and better-known city bosses played even less socially justifiable roles than the ward bosses. Their principal technique for extracting

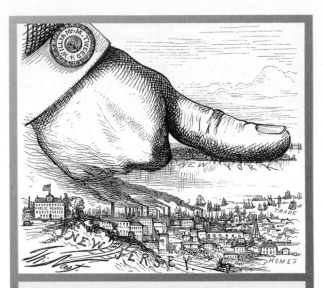

DEBATING THE PAST

Were city governments corrupt and incompetent?
This 1871 cartoon lampoons "Boss Tweed" for crushing a helpless New York City.

James Bryce (1888), a British observer, described municipal government as "the one conspicuous failure of the United States." Two years later Andrew D. White, president of Cornell, called American city governments "the worst in Christendom—the most expensive, the most inefficient, and the most corrupt." In 1904 journalist Lincoln Steffens's *The Shame of the Cities* offered a searing denunciation of municipal corruption throughout the nation, a view with which most historians long concurred. As late as 1974, Ernest S. Griffith characterized nineteenth-century municipal governments as cesspools of corruption and inefficiency.

But by then, the cities struggled merely to maintain the hospitals, museums, orphanages, waterworks, and sewage and transit systems that had been built during the Gilded Age. In *The Unheralded Triumph* (1984), Jon Teaford applauded municipal leaders of the late nineteenth century for building the complex infrastructure of rapidly growing cities. Historians such as John Buenker (1973) also observed that bosses provided essential services for needy immigrants.

Corrupt bosses like Tweed stuck their hands deep into city coffers; but their thumbs failed to keep down those who built the great cities.

James Bryce, *The American Commonwealth* (1888), Jon C. Teaford, *The Unheralded Triumph: City Government in America, 1860–1900* (1984), Ernest S. Griffith, *A History of American City Government* (1974), John Buenker, *Urban Liberalism and Progressive Reform* (1973).

money from the public till was the kickback. To get city contracts, suppliers were made to pad their bills and, when paid for their work with funds from the city treasury, turn over the excess to the politicians. Similarly, operators of streetcar lines, gas and electricity companies, and other public utilities were compelled to pay huge bribes to obtain favorable franchises.

The most notorious of the nineteenth-century city bosses was William Marcy Tweed, whose "Tweed Ring" extracted tens of millions of dollars from New York City during the brief period 1869 to 1871. Tweed was swiftly jailed. More typical was Richard Croker, who ruled New York's Tammany Hall organization from the mid-1880s to the end of the century. Croker held a number of local offices, but his power rested on his position as chairman of the Tammany Hall finance committee. Although more concerned than Tweed with the social and economic services that machines provided, Croker was primarily a corrupt political manipulator; he accumulated a large fortune and owned a mansion and a stable of racehorses, one of which was good enough to win the English Derby.

Despite their welfare work and their popularity, most bosses were essentially thieves. Efforts to romanticize them as the Robin Hoods of industrial society grossly distort the facts. However, the system developed and survived because too many middle-class city dwellers were indifferent to the fate of the poor. Except during occasional reform waves, few tried to check the rapaciousness of the politicos.

Many substantial citizens shared at least indirectly in the corruption. The owners of tenements were interested in crowding as many rent payers as possible into their buildings. Utility companies seeking franchises preferred a system that enabled them to buy favors. Honest citizens who had no selfish stake in the system and who were repelled by the sordidness of city government were seldom sufficiently concerned to do anything about it. When young Theodore Roosevelt decided to seek a political career in 1880, his New York socialite friends laughed in his face. They told him, Roosevelt wrote in his autobiography, "that politics were 'low'; that the organizations were not controlled by 'gentlemen'; that I would find them run by saloonkeepers, horse-car conductors, and the like."

Many so-called urban reformers resented the boss system mainly because it gave political power to people who were not "gentlemen" or, as one reformer put it, to a "proletarian mob" of "illiterate peasants, freshly raked from Irish bogs, or Bohemian mines, or Italian robber nests." A British visitor in Chicago struck at the root of the urban problem of the era. "Everybody is fighting to be rich," he said, "and nobody can attend to making the city fit to live in."

PARTY POLITICS: SIDESTEPPING THE ISSUE

As for national politics, with the Democrats invincible in the South and the Republicans predominant in New England and most of the states beyond the Mississippi, the outcome of presidential elections was usually determined in a handful of populous states: New York (together with its satellites, New Jersey and Connecticut), Ohio, Indiana, and Illinois. The fact that opinion in these states on important questions such as the tariff and monetary policy was divided and that every imaginable religious and ethnic interest was represented in the electorate goes far to explain why the parties hesitated to commit themselves on issues. In every presidential election, Democrats and Republicans concentrated their heaviest guns on these states. Of the eighteen Democrats and Republicans nominated for president in the nine elections between 1868 and 1900, only three were not from New York, Ohio, Indiana, or Illinois, and all three lost.

Partisanship was intense in these states. A story is told of a Democrat from a town in Illinois who was trying to persuade a doctor he knew to settle there. He admitted that the town already had five doctors, more than enough to care for the medical needs of the populace. But all five were Republicans. "If you come here you can commence all the Democratic practice," he assured the doctor. There are, he added sagely, "a set of public men here that will do what they can for you." Campaigns were conducted in a carnival atmosphere, entertainment being substituted for serious debate. Large sums were spent on brass bands, barbecues, uniforms, and banners. Speakers of national reputation were imported to attract crowds, and spellbinders noted for their leather lungs—this was before the day of the loudspeaker—and their ability to rouse popular emotions were brought in to address mass meetings.

With so much depending on so few, the level of political morality was abysmal. Mudslinging, character assassination, and plain lying were standard practice; bribery was routine. Drifters and other dissolute citizens were paid in cash—or more often in free drinks—to vote the party ticket. The names of persons long dead were solemnly inscribed in voting registers, their suffrages exercised by impostors.

During the 1880 campaign the Democratic national chairman, hearing that the Republicans were planning to transport Kentuckians into Indiana to vote illegally in that crucial state, urged Indiana Democrats to "check this outrageous fraud." Then, perhaps seeking an easier solution to the problem, he added: "If necessary . . . keep even with them." Since, as this incident demonstrates, both parties indulged in these tactics, their efforts often canceled each other's, yet presidents were sometimes made and unmade in this sordid fashion.

LACKLUSTER LEADERS

The leading statesmen of the period showed as little interest in important contemporary questions as the party hacks who made up the rank and file of their organizations. Consider the presidents.

Rutherford B. Hayes, president from 1877 to 1881, came to office with a distinguished record. He attended Kenyon College and Harvard Law School before settling down to practice in Cincinnati. Although he had a family to support, he volunteered for service in the Union army within weeks after the first shell fell on Fort Sumter. "A just and necessary war," he called it in his diary. "I would prefer to go into it if I knew I was to die . . . than to live through and after it without taking any part."

Hayes was wounded at South Mountain on the eve of Antietam and later served under Sheridan in the Shenandoah Valley campaign of 1864. Entering the army as a major, he emerged a major general. In 1864 he was elected to Congress; four years later he became governor of Ohio, serving three terms altogether. The Republicans nominated him for president in 1876 because of his reputation for honesty and moderation, and his election, made possible by the Compromise of 1877, seemed to presage an era of sectional harmony and political probity.

Outwardly Hayes had a sunny disposition; inwardly, in his own words, he was sometimes "nervous to the point of disaster." Despite his geniality, he was utterly without political glamour. He played down the tariff issue. On the money question he was conservative. He cheerfully approved the resumption of gold payments in 1879 and vetoed bills to expand the currency. He accounted himself a civil service reformer, being opposed to the collection of political contributions from federal officeholders.

Hayes complained about the South's failure to treat blacks decently after the withdrawal of federal troops, but he took no action. He worked harder for civil service reform, yet failed to achieve the "thorough, rapid, and complete" change he had promised.

In most matters, he was content to "let the record show that he had made the requests."

Hayes's successor, James A. Garfield, was cut down by an assassin's bullet four months after his inauguration. Even in that short time, however, his ineffectiveness had been demonstrated. During the war Garfield fought at Shiloh and later at Chickamauga. In two years he rose from lieutenant colonel to major general. In 1863 he won a seat in Congress, where his oratorical and managerial skills brought him to prominence in the affairs of the Republican party.

Garfield was studious and industrious and had wide-ranging interests. His weakness was indecisiveness—what an admirer described as a "want of certainty." He did not enjoy waving the bloody shirt, but when hard-pressed politically—as when his name was linked with the Crédit Mobilier railroad scandal—he would lash out at the South in an effort to distract the voters.

Although eager to improve the efficiency of the government and resentful of the "intellectual

▲ A former officer under General Philip Sheridan, Rutherford B. Hayes was sympathetic to the plight of southern blacks, but, like many northern politicians of his generation, took no action to stop the racist oppression.

dissipation" resulting from time wasted listening to the countless appeals of office seekers, he often wilted under pressure from the spoilsmen. Only on fiscal policy did he take a firm stand: He opposed categorically all inflationary schemes.

Political patronage proved to be Garfield's undoing. The Republican party in 1880 was split into two factions, the "Stalwarts" and the "Half-Breeds." The Stalwarts, led by New York Senator Roscoe Conkling, believed in the blatant pursuit of the spoils of office. The Half-Breeds did not disagree but behaved more circumspectly, hoping to attract the support of independents. Competition for office was the main reason for their rivalry.

Garfield had been a compromise choice at the 1880 Republican convention. His election precipitated a great battle over patronage, the new president standing in a sort of no-man's land between the factions. He did stand up to the most grasping politicians, resisting in particular the demands of Senator Conkling. By backing the investigation of a post office scandal and by appointing a Half-Breed the collector of the Port of New York, he infuriated the

▲ In this 1880 campaign lithograph by Currier & Ives, "Farmer Garfield" uses a scythe made of honesty, ability, and patriotism to cut a swath to the White House through brush infested by snakes like Falsehood and Malice. One snake bears the countenance of Garfield's predecessor, Hayes.

Stalwarts. In July 1881 an unbalanced Stalwart lawyer named Charles J. Guiteau shot Garfield in the Washington railroad station. After lingering for weeks, the president died on September 19.

The assassination of Garfield elevated Chester A. Arthur to the presidency. A New York lawyer and abolitionist, Arthur became an early convert to the Republican party and rose rapidly in its local councils. In 1871 Grant gave him the juiciest political plum in the country, the collectorship of the Port of New York, which he held until removed by Hayes in 1878 for refusing to keep his hands out of party politics.

The vice presidency was the only elective position that Arthur had ever held. Before Garfield's death, he had paid little attention to questions like the tariff and monetary policy, being content to take in fees ranging upward of $50,000 a year as collector of the port and to oversee the operations of the New York customs office, with its hordes of clerks and laborers. (During Arthur's tenure, the novelist Herman Melville was employed as an "outdoor inspector" by the custom house.) Of course, Arthur was an unblushing defender of the spoils system, though in fairness it must be said that he was personally honest and an excellent administrator.

The tragic circumstances of his elevation to the presidency sobered Arthur considerably. Although he was a genial, convivial man, perhaps overly fond of good food and flashy clothes, he comported himself with great dignity as president. He handled patronage matters with restraint, and he gave at least nominal support to the movement for civil service reform, which had been strengthened by the public's indignation at the assassination of Garfield. In 1883 Congress passed the Pendleton Act, "classifying" about 10 percent of all government jobs and creating the bipartisan Civil Service Commission to administer competitive examinations for these positions. The law made it illegal to force officeholders to make political contributions and empowered the president to expand the list of classified positions at his discretion.

DOCUMENT
Pendleton Civil
Service Act

As an administrator Arthur was systematic, thoughtful, businesslike, and at the same time cheerful and considerate. Just the same, he too was a political failure. He made relatively little effort to push his program through Congress. In any case, the Stalwarts would not forgive his "desertion," and the reform element could not forget his past. He did not seek a second term in 1884.

The election of 1884 brought the Democrat Grover Cleveland to the White House. Cleveland

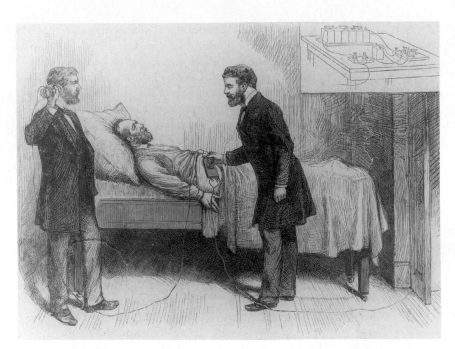

▲ James A. Garfield, mortally wounded. After failing to locate the bullet, surgeons called in Alexander Graham Bell, the famous inventor. Bell conceived of a device, pictured here, that anticipated the mine detector. Bell's machine failed to locate the bullet, however, perhaps because the metal bed springs interfered with its operation. Garfield died, either from the bullet or the surgeon's unsuccessful attempts to extricate it.

"Mulligan letters," which connected him with the corrupt granting of congressional favors to the Little Rock and Fort Smith Railroad. On the other hand, it came out during the campaign that Cleveland, a bachelor, had fathered an illegitimate child. Instead of debating public issues, the Republicans chanted the ditty

Ma! Ma! Where's my pa?
Gone to the White House,
Ha! Ha! Ha!

to which the Democrats countered

Blaine, Blaine, James G. Blaine,
The continental liar from the State of
Maine.

grew up in western New York. After studying law, he settled in Buffalo. Although somewhat lacking in the social graces and in intellectual pretensions, he had a basic integrity that everyone recognized; when a group of reformers sought a candidate for mayor in 1881, he was a natural choice. His success in Buffalo led to his election as governor of New York in 1882.

In the governor's chair his no-nonsense attitude toward public administration endeared him to civil service reformers at the same time that his basic conservatism pleased businessmen. When he vetoed a popular bill to force a reduction of the fares charged by the New York City elevated railway on the ground that it was an unconstitutional violation of the company's franchise, his reputation soared. Here was a man who cared more for principle than for the adulation of the multitude, a man who was courageous, honest, hardworking, and eminently sound. The Democrats nominated him for president in 1884.

The election revolved around personal issues, for the platforms of the parties were almost identical. On the one hand, the Republican candidate, the dynamic James G. Blaine, had an immense following, but his reputation had been soiled by the publication of the

Blaine lost more heavily in the mudslinging than Cleveland, whose quiet courage in saying, "Tell the truth" when his past was brought to light contrasted favorably with Blaine's glib and unconvincing denials. A significant group of eastern Republicans, known as mugwumps, campaigned for the Democrats.[1] However, Blaine ran a strong race against a general pro-Democratic trend; Cleveland won the election by fewer than 25,000 votes. The change of 600 ballots in New York would have given that state, and the presidency, to his opponent.

As a Democrat, Cleveland had no stomach for refighting the Civil War. Civil service reformers overestimated his commitment to their cause, for he believed in rotation in office. He would not summarily dismiss Republicans, but he thought that when they had served four years, they "should as a rule give way to good men of our party." He did, however, insist on honesty and efficiency regardless of party. As a result, he made few poor appointments.

Cleveland had little imagination and too narrow a conception of his powers and duties to be a successful president. His appearance perfectly reflected his character: A squat, burly man weighing well over 200

---

[1]The mugwumps considered themselves reformers, but on social and economic questions nearly all of them were very conservative. They were sound-money proponents and advocates of laissez-faire. Reform to them consisted almost entirely of doing away with corruption and making the government more efficient.

▲ President Grover Cleveland and Frances Folsom in 1888. The couple had married two years earlier; he was 48, and she, 21, the youngest First Lady. Her popularity blunted criticisms that Cleveland, a bachelor, had earlier fathered an illegitimate child. When he lost the 1888 election, his wife predicted that she would return as First Lady. Four years later, she did.

pounds, he could defend a position against heavy odds, yet he lacked flexibility. He took a fairly broad view of the powers of the federal government, but he thought it unseemly to put pressure on Congress, believing in "the entire independence of the executive and legislative branches."

Toward the end of his term Cleveland bestirred himself and tried to provide constructive leadership on the tariff question. The government was embarrassed by a large revenue surplus, which Cleveland hoped to reduce by cutting the duties on necessities and on raw materials used in manufacturing. He devoted his entire annual message of December 1887 to the tariff, thereby focusing public attention on the subject. When worried Democrats reminded

him that an election was coming up and that the tariff might cause a rift in the organization, he replied simply: "What is the use of being elected or re-elected, unless you stand for something?"

In that contest, Cleveland obtained a plurality of the popular vote, but his opponent, Benjamin Harrison, grandson of President William Henry Harrison, carried most of the key northeastern industrial states by narrow margins, thereby obtaining a comfortable majority in the electoral college, 233 to 168.

Harrison and Morton Campaign Ad

Although intelligent and able, Harrison was too reserved to make a good politician. One observer called him a "human iceberg." During the Civil War he fought under Sherman at Atlanta and won a reputation as a stern, effective disciplinarian. In 1876 he ran unsuccessfully for governor of Indiana, but in 1881 was elected to the Senate.

Harrison believed ardently in protective tariffs, stating firmly, if illogically, that he was against "cheaper costs" because cheaper costs seemed "necessarily to involve a cheaper man and woman under the coat." His approach to fiscal policy was conservative, though he was freehanded in the matter of veterans' pensions. He would not use "an apothecary's scale," he said, "to weigh the rewards of men who saved the country." No more flamboyant waver of the bloody shirt existed.

Harrison professed to favor civil service reform, but fashioned an unimpressive record on the question. He appointed the vigorous young reformer Theodore Roosevelt to the Civil Service Commission and then proceeded to undercut him systematically. Before long the frustrated Roosevelt was calling the president a "cold blooded, narrow minded, prejudiced, obstinate, timid old psalm singing Indianapolis politician."

Under Harrison, Congress distinguished itself by expending, for the first time in a period of peace, more than $1 billion in a single session. It raised the tariff to an all-time high. The Sherman Antitrust Act was also passed.

Harrison had little to do with the fate of any of these measures. By and large he failed, as one historian has said, to give the people "magnetic and responsive leadership." The Republicans lost control of Congress in 1890, and two years later Grover Cleveland swept back into power, defeating Harrison by more than 350,000 votes.

Congress was intermittently led by some capable leaders. One of the most outstanding was James G. Blaine of Maine, who served from 1863 to 1881, first in the House and then in the Senate. He

was essentially a reasonable man, a member of the moderate Republican faction during Reconstruction. He favored sound money without opposing inflexibly every suggestion for increasing the volume of the currency. He adopted a moderate and tolerant attitude toward the South. Almost alone among the politicians of his generation, he was deeply interested in foreign affairs. His personal warmth captivated thousands.

Dozens of other figures might be mentioned; the following are representative types. Congressman William McKinley of Ohio was the most personally attractive. He was a man of simple honesty, nobility of character, quiet warmth—and a politician to the core. The peak of his career still lay in the future in the early 1890s.

Another Ohioan, John Sherman, brother of the famous Civil War general, had a deserved reputation for expertise in financial matters. He gave his name (and not much else) to the Antitrust Act of 1890 and to other important legislation, but in retrospect he left little mark on the history of the country.

Thomas B. Reed, Republican congressman from Maine, was a witty, widely read man but ultraconser-vative and cursed with a sharp tongue that he could never curb. Reed coined the famous definition of a statesman: "a politician who is dead." When one pompous politico said in his presence that he would rather be right than president, Reed advised him not to worry since he would never be either. Reed had large ambitions and the courage of his convictions, but his vindictiveness kept him from exercising a constructive influence.

CROPS AND COMPLAINTS

The vacuity of American politics may well have stemmed from the complacency of the middle-class majority. The country was growing; no foreign enemy threatened it; the poor were mostly recent immigrants, blacks, and others with little influence, who were easily ignored by those in comfortable circumstances. However, one important group in society suffered increasingly as the years rolled by: the farmers. Out of their travail came the force that finally, in the 1890s, brought American politics face to face with the problems of the age.

▲ Photograph of a farm family in Custer, Nebraska in 1888, a region where Populist sentiment was strong.

After the Civil War, however, farmers did well. Harvests were bountiful and wheat prices high, with wheat at over a dollar a bushel in the early 1870s. Well into the 1880s farmers on the Plains experienced boom conditions. In that decade the population of Kansas increased by 43 percent, that of Nebraska by 134 percent, that of the Dakotas by 278 percent. Land prices rose and farmers borrowed money to expand their farms.

In the 1890s disaster struck. First came a succession of dry years and poor harvests. Then farmers in Australia, Canada, Russia, and Argentina took advantage of improvements in transportation to sell their produce in European markets that had relied on American foodstuffs. The price of wheat fell to about 60 cents a bushel. Cotton, the great southern staple, which sold for more than 30 cents a pound in 1866 and 15 cents in the early 1870s, at times in the 1890s fell below 6 cents.

The tariff on manufactured goods appeared to aggravate the farmers' predicament, and so did the domestic marketing system, which enabled a multitude of middlemen to gobble up a large share of the profits of agriculture. The shortage of credit, particularly in the South, was an additional burden.

The downward swing of the business cycle in the early 1890s completed the devastation. Settlers who had paid more for their lands than they were worth and borrowed money at high interest rates to do so found themselves squeezed relentlessly. Thousands lost their farms and returned eastward, penniless and dispirited. The population of Nebraska increased by fewer than 4000 persons in the entire decade of the 1890s.

THE POPULIST MOVEMENT

The agricultural depression triggered a new outburst of farm radicalism, the Alliance movement. Alliances were organizations of farmers' clubs, most of which had sprung up during the bad times of the late 1870s. The first Knights of Reliance group was founded in 1877 in Lampasas County, Texas. As the Farmers Alliance, this organization gradually expanded in northeastern Texas, and after 1885 it spread rapidly throughout the cotton states. Alliance leaders stressed cooperation. Their co-ops bought fertilizer and other supplies in bulk and sold them at fair prices to members. They sought to market their crops cooperatively but could not raise the necessary capital from banks, with the result that some of them began to question the workings of the American financial and monetary system. They became economic and social radicals in the

process. A similar though less influential Alliance movement developed in the North.

The alliances adopted somewhat differing policies, but all agreed that agricultural prices were too low, that transportation costs were too high, and that something was radically wrong with the nation's financial system. "There are three great crops raised in Nebraska," an angry rural editor proclaimed in 1890. "One is a crop of corn, one is a crop of freight rates, and one a crop of interest. One is produced by farmers who by sweat and toil farm the land. The other two are produced by men who sit in their offices and behind their bank counters and farm the farmers." All agreed on the need for political action if the lot of the agriculturalist was to be improved.

Although the state alliances of the Dakotas and Kansas joined the Southern Alliance in 1889, for a time local prejudices and conflicting interests prevented the formation of a single national organization. Northern farmers mostly voted Republican, Southerners Democratic, and resentments created during the Civil War lingered in all sections. Cotton-producing Southerners opposed the protective tariff; most Northerners, fearing the competition of foreign grain producers, favored it. Railroad regulation and federal land policy seemed vital questions to Northerners; financial reform loomed most important in southern eyes. Northerners were receptive to the idea of forming a third party, while Southerners, wedded to the one-party system, preferred working to capture local Democratic machines.

The farm groups entered local politics in the 1890 elections. Convinced of the righteousness of their cause, they campaigned with tremendous fervor. The results were encouraging. In the South, Alliance-sponsored gubernatorial candidates won in Georgia, Tennessee, South Carolina, and Texas; eight southern legislatures fell under Alliance control, and forty-four representatives and three senators committed to Alliance objectives were sent to Washington. In the West, Alliance candidates swept Kansas and captured a majority in the Nebraska legislature and enough seats in Minnesota and South Dakota to hold the balance of power between the major parties.

Such success, coupled with the reluctance of the Republicans and Democrats to make concessions to their demands, encouraged Alliance leaders to create a new national party. By uniting southern and western farmers, they succeeded in breaking the sectional barrier erected by the Civil War. If they could recruit industrial workers, perhaps a real political revolution could be accomplished. In February 1892, farm lead-

▲ A gathering of Grangers near Winchester, Illinois in 1873. Note the bandwagon (literally!) to the left, the women with parasols and bonnets *(right)*, and the American flags *(everywhere)*. This "radical" political movement had the feel of a county fair or religious revival; both had doubtless been held in the same spot.

ers, representatives of the Knights of Labor, and various professional reformers, some 800 in all, met at St. Louis. They organized the People's, or Populist, party, and issued a call for a national convention to meet at Omaha in July.

That convention nominated General James B. Weaver of Iowa for president (with a one-legged Confederate veteran as his running mate) and drafted a platform that called for a graduated income tax and national ownership of railroads and the telegraph and telephone systems. It also advocated a "subtreasury" plan that would permit farmers to keep nonperishable crops off the market when prices were low. Under this proposal the government would make loans in the form of greenbacks to farmers, secured by crops held in storage in federal warehouses. When prices rose, the farmers could sell their crops and repay the loans. To combat deflation further, the platform demanded the unlimited coinage of silver and an increase in the money supply "to no less than $50 per capita."

To make the government more responsive to public opinion, the Populists urged the adoption of the initiative and referendum procedures and the election of U.S. senators by popular vote. To win the support of industrial workers, their platform denounced the use of Pinkerton detectives in labor disputes and backed the eight-hour day and the restriction of "undesirable" immigration.

The Populists saw themselves not as a persecuted minority but as a victimized majority betrayed by what would a century later be called the establishment. They were at most ambivalent about the free enterprise system, and they tended to attribute social and economic injustices not to built-in inequities in the system but to nefarious conspiracies organized by selfish interests in order to subvert the system.

The appearance of the new party was the most exciting and significant aspect of the presidential campaign of 1892, which saw Harrison and Cleveland refighting the

DOCUMENT

Mary Elizabeth Lease, the Popular Crusader

▲ In Kansas in 1893 a Populist governor and a Populist-controlled Senate invalidated the election of some Republicans in the Kansas House of Representatives, giving the Populists control of that body, too. The displaced Republicans, denied seats, smashed their way into the capitol building with this sledgehammer and ousted the Populists, who decided to meet in a separate building. Each proclaimed itself to be the true legislature of Congress and passed its own laws. Eventually the Kansas Supreme Court decided in favor of the Republican legislature and disbanded the Populist gathering.

election of 1888. The Populists put forth a host of colorful spellbinders: Tom Watson, a Georgia congressman whose temper was such that on one occasion he administered a beating to a local planter with the man's own riding crop; William A. Peffer, a senator from Kansas whose long beard and grave demeanor gave him the look of a Hebrew prophet; "Sockless Jerry" Simpson of Kansas, unlettered but full of grassroots shrewdness and wit, a former Greenbacker, and an admirer of the single tax doctrine of Henry George; Ignatius Donnelly, the "Minnesota Sage," who claimed to be an authority

on science, economics, and Shakespeare (he believed that Francis Bacon wrote the plays) and whose widely read novel, *Caesar's Column* (1891), pictured an America of the future wherein a handful of plutocrats tyrannized masses of downtrodden workers and serfs.

In the one-party South, Populist strategists sought to wean black farmers away from the ruling Democratic organization. Southern black farmers had their own Colored Alliance, and even before 1892 their leaders had worked closely with the white alliances. Nearly 100 black delegates had attended the Populist convention at St. Louis. Of course, the blacks would be useless to the party if they could not vote; therefore, white Populist leaders opposed the southern trend toward disfranchising African Americans and called for full civil rights for all.

DOCUMENT

The People's Party Platform

In the Northwest, the Populists assailed the "bankers' conspiracy" in unbridled terms. Ignatius Donnelly, running for governor of Minnesota, wrote another futuristic political novel, *The Golden Bottle,* and made 150 speeches, vowing to make the campaign "the liveliest ever seen" in the state.

▲ Mary Elizabeth Lease was a prominent Populist, noted for her rallying cry to "raise less corn and more hell."

The results proved disappointing. Tom Watson lost his seat in Congress, and Donnelly ran a poor third in the Minnesota gubernatorial race. The Populists did sweep Kansas. They elected numbers of local officials in other western states and cast over a million votes for General Weaver. But the effort to unite white and black farmers in the South failed miserably. Conservative Democrats, while continuing with considerable success to attract black voters, played on racial fears cruelly, insisting that the Populists sought to undermine white supremacy. Since most white Populists saw the alliance with blacks as at best a marriage of convenience, this argument had a deadly effect. Elsewhere, even in the old centers of the Granger movement, the party made no significant impression. Urban workers remained aloof.

By standing firmly for conservative financial policies, Cleveland attracted considerable Republican support and won a solid victory over Harrison in the electoral college, 277 to 145. Weaver's electoral vote was 22.

SHOWDOWN ON SILVER

One conclusion that politicians reached after analyzing the 1892 election was that the money question, particularly the controversy over the coinage of silver, was of paramount interest to the voters. Despite the wide-ranging appeal of the Populist platform, most of Weaver's strength came from the silver-mining states.

In truth, the issue of gold versus silver was superficial; the important question was what, if anything, should be done to check the deflationary spiral. The declining price level benefited people with fixed incomes and injured most others. Industrial workers profited from deflation except when depression caused unemployment.

By the early 1890s, discussion of federal monetary policy revolved around the coinage of silver. Traditionally, the United States had been on a bimetallic standard. Both gold and silver were coined, the number of grains of each in the dollar being adjusted periodically to reflect the commercial value of the two metals. The discovery of numerous gold mines in California in the 1840s and 1850s depressed the price of gold relative to silver. By 1861, a silver dollar could be melted down and sold for $1.03. No miner took silver to the mint to be stamped into coin. In a short time, silver dollars were withdrawn and only gold dollars circulated. However, an avalanche of silver from the mines of Nevada and Colorado gradually depressed the price until, around 1874, it again be-

came profitable for miners to coin their bullion. Alas, when they tried to do so, they discovered that the Coinage Act of 1873, taking account of the fact that no silver had been presented to the mint in years, had demonetized the metal.

Silver miners denounced this "Crime of '73." Inflationists joined them in demanding a return to bimetallism. They knew that if more dollars were put into circulation, the value of each dollar would decline; that is, prices and wages would rise. Conservatives, still fighting the battle against inflationary greenback paper money, resisted strongly. The result was a series of compromises. In 1878 the Bland-Allison Act authorized the purchase of between $2 and $4 million of silver a month at the market price, but this had little inflationary effect because the government consistently purchased the minimum amount. The commercial price of silver continued to fall. In 1890 the Sherman Silver Purchase Act required the government to buy 4.5 million *ounces* of silver monthly, but in the face of increasing supplies the price of silver fell still further. By 1894, a silver coin weighed 32 times more than a gold one.

The compromises satisfied no one. Silver miners grumbled because their bullion brought in only half what it had in the early 1870s. Debtors noted angrily that because of the general decline in prices, the dollars they used to meet their obligations were worth more than twice as much as in 1865. Advocates of the gold standard feared that unlimited silver coinage would be authorized, "destroying the value of the dollar."

THE DEPRESSION OF 1893

Both the silverites and "gold bugs" warned of economic disaster if their policies were not followed. Then, in 1893, after the London banking house of Baring Brothers collapsed, a financial panic precipitated a worldwide industrial depression. In the United States hundreds of cotton mills and iron foundries closed, never to reopen. During the harsh winter of 1893–1894, millions were without jobs. Discontented industrial workers added their voices to the complaints of the Midwestern farmers.

President Cleveland believed that the controversy over silver had caused the depression by shaking the confidence of the business community and that all would be well if the country returned to a single gold standard. He summoned a special session of Congress, and by exerting immense political pressure he obtained the repeal of the Sherman Silver Purchase

▲ William Jennings Bryan's "Cross of Gold" speech inspired this cartoonist's caricature of it as "plagiarized from the Bible." Bryan's speech in favor of bimetallism was, in fact, studded with religious references. He described the unlimited coinage of silver and gold as a "holy cause" supported by those who built churches "where they praise their Creator."

Act in October 1893. All that this accomplished was to split the Democratic party, its southern and western wings deserting him almost to a man.

During 1894 and 1895, while the nation floundered in the worst depression it had ever experienced, a series of events further undermined public confidence. In the spring of 1894 several "armies" of the unemployed, the most imposing led by Jacob S. Coxey, an eccentric Ohio businessman, marched on Washington to demand relief. Coxey wanted the government to undertake a program of federal public works and to authorize local communities to exchange non-interest-bearing bonds with the Treasury for $500 million in paper money, the funds to be used to hire unemployed workers to build roads. The scheme, Coxey claimed, would pump money into the economy, provide work for the jobless, and benefit the entire nation by improving transportation facilities.

When Coxey's group of demonstrators, perhaps 500 in all, reached Washington, he and two other leaders were arrested for trespassing on the grounds of the Capitol. Their followers were dispersed by club-wielding policemen. This callous treatment convinced many Americans that the government had little interest in the suffering of the people, an opinion strengthened when Cleveland, in July 1894, used federal troops to crush the Pullman strike.

The next year the Supreme Court handed down several reactionary decisions. In *United States* v. *E. C. Knight Company* it refused to employ the Sherman Antitrust Act to break up the Sugar Trust. In *Pollock* v. *Farmers' Loan and Trust Company* it invalidated a federal income tax law despite the fact that a similar measure levied during the Civil War had been upheld by the Court in *Springer* v. *United States* (1881). Finally, the Court denied a writ of habeas corpus to Eugene V. Debs of the American Railway Union, who was languishing in prison for disobeying a federal injunction during the Pullman strike.

On top of these indications of official conservatism came a desperate financial crisis. Throughout 1894 the Treasury's supply of gold dwindled as worried citizens exchanged greenbacks (now convertible into gold) for hard money and foreign investors cashed in large amounts of American securities. The government tried to sell bonds for gold to bolster the reserve, but the gold reserve continued to melt away. Early in 1895 it touched a low point of $41 million.

At this juncture a syndicate of bankers headed by J. P. Morgan turned the tide by underwriting a $62 million bond issue, guaranteeing that half the gold would come from Europe. This caused a great public outcry; the spectacle of the nation being saved from bankruptcy by a private banker infuriated millions.

These events, together with the continuing depression, discredited the Cleveland administration. "I haven't got words to say what I think of that old bag of beef," Governor "Pitchfork Ben" Tillman of South Carolina, who had resolutely resisted the Populists in 1892, told a local audience two years later. "If you send me to the Senate, I promise I won't be bulldozed by him."

As the presidential election of 1896 approached, with the Populists demanding unlimited coinage of silver, the major parties found it impossible to continue straddling the money question. The

Populist vote had increased by 42 percent in the 1894 congressional elections. Southern and western Democratic leaders feared that they would lose their following unless Cleveland was repudiated. Western Republicans, led by Senator Henry M. Teller of Colorado, were threatening to bolt to the Populists unless their party came out for silver coinage. After a generation of political equivocation, the major parties had to face an important issue squarely.

The Republicans, meeting to choose a candidate at St. Louis in June 1896, announced for the gold standard. "We are unalterably opposed to every measure calculated to debase our currency or impair the credit of our country," the platform declared. "We are therefore opposed to the free coinage of silver. . . . The existing gold standard must be maintained." The party then nominated Ohio's William McKinley for president. McKinley, best known for his staunch advocacy of the protective tariff yet highly regarded by labor, was expected to run strongly in the Midwest and the East.

DOCUMENT

Bryan, "Cross of Gold" Speech

The Democratic convention met in July at Chicago. The pro-gold Cleveland element made a hard fight, but the silverites swept them aside. The high point came when a youthful Nebraskan named William Jennings Bryan spoke for silver against gold, for western farmers against the industrial East. Bryan's every sentence provoked ear-shattering applause.

> We have petitioned and our petitions have been scorned; we have entreated, and our entreaties have been disregarded; we have begged, and they have mocked when our calamity came. We beg no longer; we entreat no more; we petition no more. We defy them!

The crowd responded like a great choir to Bryan's oratorical cues. "Burn down your cities and leave our farms," he said, "and your cities will spring up again as if by magic; but destroy our farms and the grass will grow in the streets of every city in the country." He ended with a marvelous figure of speech that set the tone for the coming campaign. "You shall not press down upon the brow of labor this crown of thorns," he warned, bringing his hands down suggestively to his temples. "You shall not crucify mankind upon a cross of gold!" Dramatically, he extended his arms to the side, the very figure of the crucified Christ.

The convention promptly adopted a platform calling for "the free and unlimited coinage of both silver and gold at the present legal ratio of 16 to 1" and went on to nominate Bryan, who was barely 36, for president.

This action put tremendous pressure on the Populists. If they supported the Democrat Bryan, they risked losing their party identity; if they nominated another candidate, they would ensure McKinley's election. In part because the delegates could not find a person of stature willing to become a candidate against Bryan, the Populist convention nominated him, seeking to preserve the party identity by substituting Watson for the Democratic vice-presidential nominee, Arthur Sewall of Maine.

THE ELECTION OF 1896

Never did a presidential campaign raise such intense emotions. The Republicans from the silver-mining states swung solidly behind Bryan. But many solid-money Democrats, especially in the Northeast, refused to accept the decision of the Chicago convention. Cleveland professed to be "so dazed by the political situation that I am in no condition for speech or thought on the subject." Many others adopted the policy of Governor David B. Hill of New York, who said, "I am a Democrat still—very still." The extreme gold bugs, calling themselves National Democrats, nominated their own candidate, 79-year-old Senator John M. Palmer of Illinois. Palmer ran only to injure Bryan. "Fellow Democrats," he announced, "I will not consider it any great fault if you decide to cast your vote for William McKinley."

At the start the Republicans seemed to have everything in their favor. Bryan's youth and relative lack of political experience—two terms in the House—contrasted unfavorably with McKinley's distinguished war record, his long service in Congress and as governor of Ohio, and his reputation for honesty and good judgment. The severe depression operated in favor of the party out of power, although by repudiating Cleveland the Democrats escaped much of the burden of explaining away his errors. The newspapers came out almost unanimously for the Republicans. Important Democratic papers such as the *New York World*, the *Boston Herald*, the *Baltimore Sun*, the *Chicago Chronicle*, and the *Richmond Times* supported McKinley editorially and even slanted news stories against the Democrats. The *New York Times* accused Bryan of being insane, his affliction being variously classified as "paranoia querulenta,"

▶ *text continues on page 568*

Mapping the Past

The Election of 1896

Congressional Election of 1894

The depression of 1893, which lasted much of the decade, altered the geography of American politics. President Cleveland's defense of the gold standard fractured the Democrats. In the congressional election of 1894 (top, p. 567), Republicans seized control of both houses of Congress and increased their delegation in the House by 100 votes. Democratic candidates for the House of Representatives fared poorly throughout the North and East. The election, too, showed the strength of the pro-silver position. Populist candidates prevailed in Nebraska, Kansas, Colorado, Alabama, and North Carolina, and silverites in Nevada.

In the wake of this debacle, Democratic leaders from the West and South proposed that the party reach out to the Populists and abandon the gold standard. Their views prevailed during the 1896 Democratic convention, which adopted a platform that endorsed the free coinage of silver and that nominated William Jennings Bryan, a proponent of silver, for President. The Republicans nominated William McKinley, whose endorsement of the gold standard, though ambiguously worded, ensured that the election of 1896 would be the most sharply defined since the Civil War.

The Presidential Election of 1896

On election day, Bryan won in the South, the Plains states, and the Rocky Mountain region, but McKinley carried the East; the Midwest, including even Iowa, Minnesota, and North Dakota; and the Pacific Coast states of Oregon and California.

The sharp sectional division marked the failure of the Populist effort to unite northern and southern farmers and also the triumph of the industrial part of the country over the agricultural. Business and financial interests voted solidly for the Republicans, fearing that a Bryan victory would bring economic chaos. When one Nebraska landowner tried to float a mortgage during the campaign, a loan company official wrote him: "If McKinley is elected, we think we will be in the market, but we do not care to make any investments while there is an uncertainty as to what kind of money a person will be paid back in."

Other social and economic interests were far from being united. Many thousands of farmers voted for McKinley, as his success in states such as North Dakota, Iowa, and Minnesota proved. In the farm areas north of the Ohio and east of the Missouri Rivers, the agricultural depression was not severe, and farm radicalism was almost nonexistent.

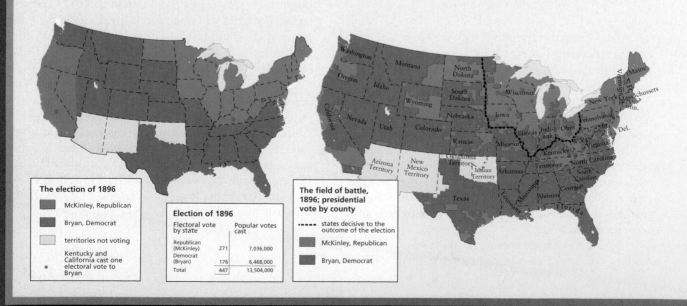

The election of 1896

- McKinley, Republican
- Bryan, Democrat
- territories not voting
- Kentucky and California cast one electoral vote to Bryan

Election of 1896

Electoral vote by state	Popular votes cast
Republican (McKinley) 271	7,036,000
Democrat (Bryan) 176	6,468,000
Total 447	13,504,000

The field of battle, 1896; presidential vote by county

- ----- states decisive to the outcome of the election
- McKinley, Republican
- Bryan, Democrat

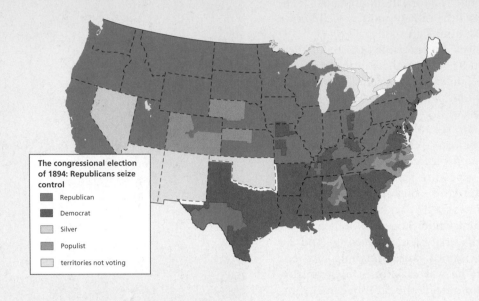

The congressional election of 1894: Republicans seize control

- Republican
- Democrat
- Silver
- Populist
- territories not voting

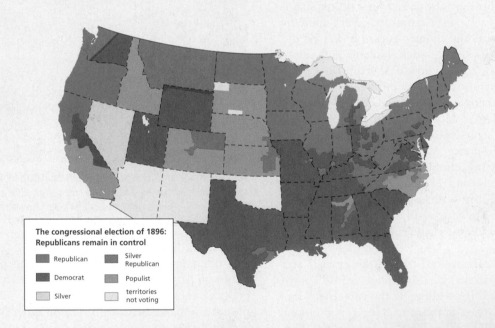

The congressional election of 1896: Republicans remain in control

- Republican
- Democrat
- Silver
- Silver Republican
- Populist
- territories not voting

A preponderance of the labor vote also went to the Republicans. In part this resulted from the tremendous pressures that many industrialists applied to their workers. "Men," one manufacturer announced, "vote as you please, but if Bryan is elected . . . the whistle will not blow Wednesday morning." Some companies placed orders for materials subject to cancellation if the Democrats won. Yet coercion was not a major factor, for McKinley was highly regarded in labor circles. While governor of Ohio, he had advocated the arbitration of industrial disputes and backed a law fining employers who refused to permit workers to join unions. He had invariably based his advocacy of high tariffs on the argument that American wage levels would be depressed if foreign goods could enter the country untaxed. The Republicans carried nearly all the large cities, and in closely contested states such as Illinois and Ohio this made the difference between victory and defeat.

"graphomania," and "oratorical monomania." The Democrats had very little money and few well-known speakers to fight the campaign.

But Bryan proved a formidable opponent. Casting aside tradition, he took to the stump personally, traveling 18,000 miles and making over 600 speeches. He was one of the greatest of orators. A big, handsome man with a voice capable of carrying without strain to the far corners of a great hall yet equally effective before a cluster of auditors at a rural crossroads, he projected an image of absolute sincerity without appearing fanatical or argumentative. At every major stop on his tour, huge crowds assembled. In Minnesota he packed the 10,000-seat St. Paul Auditorium, while thousands milled in the streets outside. His energy was amazing, and his charm and good humor were unfailing. At one whistle-stop, while he was shaving in his compartment, a small group outside the train began clamoring for a glimpse of him. Flinging open the window and beaming through the lather, he shook hands cheerfully with each of the admirers. Everywhere he hammered away at the money question. Yet he did not totally neglect other issues. He was defending, he said, "all the people who suffer from the operations of trusts, syndicates, and combines."

McKinley's campaign was managed by a new type of politician, Marcus Alonzo Hanna, an Ohio businessman. In a sense Hanna was a product of the Pendleton Civil Service Act. When deprived of the contributions of officeholders, the parties turned to business for funds, and Hanna was one of the first leaders with a foot in both camps. Politics fascinated him, and despite his wealth and wide interests, he was willing to labor endlessly at the routine work of political organization.

McKinley and Hobart Campaign Poster

Hanna aspired to be a kingmaker and early fastened on McKinley, whose charm he found irresistible, as the vehicle for satisfying his ambition. He spent about $100,000 of his own money on the preconvention campaign. His attitude toward the candidate, one mutual friend observed, was "that of a big, bashful boy toward the girl he loves."

Before most Republicans realized how effective Bryan was on the stump, Hanna perceived the danger and sprang into action. Since the late 1880s the character of political organization had been changing. The Civil Service Act was also cutting down on the number of jobs available to reward campaign workers. At the same time, the new mass circulation newspapers and the nationwide press associations were increasing the pressure on candidates to speak openly

▲ Poster of William McKinley, Republican candidate for President in 1896, upheld by workers and businessmen alike, while campaigning for "prosperity at home" and "prestige abroad." He also stood for "civilization," whatever that meant.

and often on national issues. This trend put a premium on party organization and consistency—the old political trick of speaking out of one side of the mouth to one audience and out the other to a different audience no longer worked very well. The old military metaphors of political discourse, the terms *campaign* and *spoils* and *standard bearer*, remained, but others more businesslike became popular: *boss*, *machine*, *lobbyist*. As the federal government became more involved in economic issues, business interests found more reason to be concerned about national elections and were more willing to spend money on behalf of candidates whose views they approved.

Hanna understood what was happening to politics. Certain that money was the key to political power, he raised an enormous campaign fund. When businessmen hesitated to contribute, he pried open their purses by a combination of persuasiveness and

intimidation. Banks and insurance companies were "assessed" a percentage of their assets, big corporations a share of their receipts, until some $3.5 million had been collected.

Hanna disbursed these funds with efficiency and imagination. He sent 1500 speakers into the doubtful districts and blanketed the land with 250 million pieces of campaign literature, printed in a dozen languages. "He has advertised McKinley as if he were a patent medicine," Theodore Roosevelt, never at a loss for words, exclaimed.

Incapable of competing with Bryan as a swayer of mass audiences, McKinley conducted a "front-porch campaign." This technique dated from the first Harrison-Cleveland election, when Harrison regularly delivered off-the-cuff speeches to groups of visitors representing special interests or regions in his hometown of Indianapolis. The system conserved the candidate's energies and enabled him to avoid the appearance of seeking the presidency too openly—which was still considered bad form—and at the same time allowed him to make headlines throughout the country.

Guided by the masterful Hanna, McKinley brought the front-porch method to perfection. Superficially the proceedings were delightfully informal. From every corner of the land, groups representing various regions, occupations, and interests descended on McKinley's unpretentious frame house in Canton, Ohio. Gathering on the lawn—the grass was soon reduced to mud, the fence stripped of pickets by souvenir hunters—the visitors paid their compliments to the candidate and heard him deliver a brief speech, while beside him on the porch his aged mother and adoring invalid wife listened with rapt attention. Then there was a small reception, during which the delegates were given an opportunity to shake their host's hand.

Despite the air of informality, these performances were carefully staged. The delegations arrived on a tightly coordinated schedule worked out by McKinley's staff and the railroads, which operated cut-rate excursion trains to Canton from all over the nation. McKinley was fully briefed on the special interests and attitudes of each group, and the speeches of delegation leaders were submitted in advance. Often his secretary amended these remarks, and on occasion McKinley wrote the visitors' speeches himself. His own talks were carefully prepared, each calculated to make a particular point. All were reported fully in the newspapers. Thus without moving from his doorstep, McKinley met thousands of people from every section of the country.

These tactics worked admirably. On election day McKinley collected 271 electoral votes to Bryan's 176, the popular vote being 7,036,000 to 6,468,000. (See the feature essay, Mapping the Past, "The Election of 1896," pp. 566–567.)

THE MEANING OF THE ELECTION

During the campaign, some frightened Republicans had laid plans for fleeing the country if Bryan were elected, and belligerent ones, such as Theodore Roosevelt, then police commissioner of New York City, readied themselves to meet the "social revolutionaries" on the battlefield. Victory sent such people into transports of joy. Most conservatives concluded that the way of life they so fervently admired had been saved for all time.

However heartfelt, such sentiments were not founded on fact. With workers standing beside capitalists and with the farm vote split, it cannot be said that the election divided the nation class against class or that McKinley's victory saved the country from revolution.

Far from representing a triumph for the status quo, the election marked the coming of age of modern America. The battle between gold and silver, which everyone had considered so vital, had little real significance. The inflationists seemed to have been beaten, but new discoveries of gold in Alaska and South Africa and improved methods of extracting gold from low-grade ores soon led to a great expansion of the money supply. In any case, within two decades the system of basing the volume of currency on bullion had been abandoned. Bryan and the "political" Populists who supported him, supposedly the advance agents of revolution, were oriented more toward the past than the future; their ideal was the rural America of Jefferson and Jackson.

McKinley, for all his innate conservatism, was capable of looking ahead toward the new century. His approach was national where Bryan's was basically parochial. Though never daring and seldom imaginative, McKinley was able to deal pragmatically with current problems. Before long, as the United States became increasingly an exporter of manufactures, he would even modify his position on the tariff. And no one better reflected the spirit of the age than Mark Hanna, the outstanding political realist of his generation. Far from preventing change, the outcome of the election of 1896 made possible still greater changes as the United States moved into the twentieth century.

MILESTONES

1872	Ulysses Grant is reelected president	1890	Sherman Silver Purchase Act requires government silver purchase
1873	Congress suspends the coining of silver ("Crime of '73")	1892	People's (Populist) Party is founded
1876	Rutherford B. Hayes is elected president		Cleveland is elected president a second time
1877	Farmers Alliance movement is founded	1893	Sherman Silver Purchase Act is repealed
1878	Bland-Allison Act authorizes government silver purchases	1893	Panic of 1893 causes industrial depression
1880	James Garfield is elected president	1894	Coxey's Army marches to Washington to demand relief
1881	Garfield is assassinated; Grover Cleveland becomes president	1895	Supreme Court declares federal income tax unconstitutional (*Pollock* v. *Farmers' Loan and Trust Company*)
1883	Pendleton Act creates Civil Service Commission		J. P. Morgan raises $62 million in gold for the U.S. Treasury
1884	Republicans support Democrats during Mugwump Movement	1896	William Jennings Bryan delivers "Cross of Gold" speech
	Grover Cleveland is elected president		William McKinley is elected president
1887	Interstate Commerce Act regulates railroad rates		
	Cleveland delivers tariff message		
1888	Benjamin Harrison is elected president		

SUPPLEMENTARY READING

There are several superb analyses of the political system of the period written by men who studied it firsthand: James Bryce, *The American Commonwealth* (1888), and Woodrow Wilson, *Congressional Government* (1886). On the evolution of political parties, see Paul Kleppner, *The Third Electoral System, 1853–1892* (1979), and Michael E. McGerr, *The Decline of Popular Politics* (1986).

C. Vann Woodward, *Origins of the New South* (1951) is an important regional study. Following in Woodward's path are Heather Cox Richardson, *The Death of Reconstruction* (2001), and Michael Perman, *Struggle for Mastery: Disfranchisement in the South, 1888–1908* (2001), who focus on the 1890s as the pivotal decade for the defeat of Reconstruction. Samuel C. Hyde, Jr., examines the tension between the old planting elite of the South and plain folk in *Pistols and Politics* (1996). Suzanne Lebsock, *A Murder in Virginia* (2003), provides a fascinating account of the intersection of race, politics, and economic factors in a murder trial. On lynching, see Christopher Waldrep, *The Many Faces of Judge Lynch: Extralegal Violence and Punishment in America* (2002).

See also Gretchen Ritter, *Goldbugs and Greenbacks* (1997), Ross Evans Paulson, *Liberty, Equality and Justice: Civil Rights, Women's Rights and the Regulation of Business, 1865–1932* (1997), Irwin Unger, *The Greenback Era*

(1964), Walter T. K. Nugent, *Money and American Society* (1968), Geoffrey Blodgett, *The Gentle Reformers* (1966), and Ari Hoogenboom, *Outlawing the Spoils* (1961).

Among biographies of political leaders, the following are especially worth consulting: Ari Hoogenboom, *Rutherford B. Hayes* (1995), Allan Peskin, *Garfield* (1999), Thomas C. Reeves, *Gentleman Boss: Chester A. Arthur* (1975), H. Paul Jeffers, *An Honest President* (2000); on Cleveland, Allan Nevins, *Grover Cleveland* (1932), Homer E. Socolovsky and Allan B. Spetter, *The Presidency of Benjamin Harrison* (1987), H. Wayne Morgan, *William McKinley and His America* (1963), and Stephen D. Kantrowitz, *Ben Tillman and the Reconstruction of White Supremacy* (2000).

Populism has been the subject of intensive study. Richard Hofstadter, *The Age of Reform* (1955), takes a dim view of populism as a reform movement; Lawrence Goodwyn, *Democratic Promise: The Populist Movement in America* (1976), calls it "a people's movement of mass democratic aspiration." Elizabeth Sanders, *Roots of Reform* (1999), champions the farmers' political efforts, a position amplified by Gene Clanton, *Congressional Populism and the Crisis of the 1890s* (1998). Peter Argersinger, *The Limits of Agrarian Radicalism: Western Populism and American Politics* (1995), Sheldon Hackney, *Populism to Progressivism in Alabama* (1969), and Steven Hahn, *The Roots of Southern*

Populism (1983), are more than local studies. Michael Kazin, *The Populist Persuasion* (1994), insists on the enduring legacy of the movement.

On the depression of the 1890s, consult Charles Hoffman, *The Depression of the Nineties* (1970), Carlos Schwantes, *Coxey's Army* (1985), Stanley Buder, *Pullman* (1967), and Nick Salvatore, *Eugene V. Debs* (1982). On Bryan and the election of 1896, see Paul E. Glad, *The Trumpet Soundeth* (1960), Robert W. Cherny, *A Righteous Cause: William Jennings Bryan* (1985), Stanley L. Jones, *The Presidential Election of 1896* (1964), and Robert F. Durden, *The Climax of Populism* (1965).

SUGGESTED WEBSITES

James Garfield
http://www.ipl.org/ref/POTUS/jagarfield.html
This site contains basic factual data about Garfield's election and presidency, speeches, and online bibliography.

Benjamin Harrison
http://www.ipl.org/ref/POTUS/bharrison.html
This site contains basic factual data about Harrison's election and presidency, speeches, and online bibliography.

Chester Arthur
http://www.ipl.org/ref/POTUS/caarthur.html
This site contains basic factual data about Arthur's election and presidency, speeches, and online bibliography.

William Jennings Bryan
http://ap.grolier.com/article?assetid=
0064310-00&templatename=/article/article.html
This site treats the career and ideas of the three-time presidential candidate.

William McKinley
http://www.ipl.org/ref/POTUS/wmckinley.html
This site contains basic factual data about McKinley's election and presidency, speeches, and online bibliography.

The Era of William McKinley
http://history.osu.edu/projects/mckinley/
This site contains numerous images from various stages of William McKinley's career along with a brief bibliographical essay. This Ohio State University site also has a section with an excellent collection of McKinley-era cartoons.

The Age of Reform

▼ "Boy Working in Glass Factory, Alexandria, Virginia, 1911," by Lewis Hine, part of a ten-year study of child labor. Hine pioneered photography as a means for social reform.

CHAPTER CONTENTS

AMERICAN LIVES **Emma Goldman**

DEBATING THE PAST **Were the progressives forward-looking?**

The period bounded roughly by the end of the nineteenth century and American entry into World War I is usually called the progressive era. Like all such generalizations about complex subjects, this title involves a great simplification. Whether *progressive* is taken to mean "tending toward change" or "improvement" or is merely used to suggest an attitude of mind, it was neither a unique nor a universal characteristic of the early years of the twentieth century. Progressive elements had existed in earlier periods and did not disappear when the first American soldiers took ship for France. In important ways the progressivism of the time was a continuation of the response to industrialism that began after the Civil War. Historians have scoured the sources trying to define and explain the progressive era, without satisfying everyone. Nevertheless the term *progressive* provides a useful description of this exciting and significant period of American history.

ROOTS OF PROGRESSIVISM

The progressives were never a single group seeking a single objective. The movement sprang from many sources. One was the fight against corruption and inefficiency in government, which began with the

▲ Orchard Street, a tenement district in lower Manhattan, New York. The unpaved street, ankle deep in mud, is lined with garbage. The sidewalks are packed with makeshift stalls and wagons, loaded with food, clothing, and other commodities for sale. Reformers worried that the congestion and filth of such streets constituted a health hazard. But many people who lived there enjoyed the sociability of the crowded streets; note that the man at the lower left is smiling.

Liberal Republicans of the Grant era and was continued by the mugwumps of the 1880s. The struggle for civil service reform was only the first skirmish in this battle; the continuing power of corrupt political machines and the growing influence of large corporations and their lobbyists on municipal and state governments outraged thousands of citizens and led them to seek ways of purifying politics and making the machinery of government at all levels responsive to the majority rather than to special-interest groups.

Progressivism also had roots in the effort to regulate and control big business, which characterized the Granger and Populist agitation of the 1870s and 1890s. The failure of the Interstate Commerce Act to end railroad abuses and of the Sherman Antitrust Act to check the growth of large corporations became increasingly apparent after 1900. The return of prosperity after the depression of the 1890s encouraged reformers by removing the inhibiting fear, so influential in the 1896 presidential campaign, that an assault on the industrial giants might lead to the collapse of the economy.

Between 1897 and 1904 the trend toward concentration in industry accelerated. Such new giants as Amalgamated Copper (1899), U.S. Steel (1901), and International Harvester (1902) attracted most of the attention, but even more alarming were the overall statistics. In a single year (1899) more than 1200 firms were absorbed in mergers, the resulting combinations being capitalized at $2.2 billion. By 1904 there were 318 industrial combinations in the country with an aggregate capital of $7.5 billion. People who considered bigness inherently evil demanded that the huge new "trusts" be broken up or at least strictly controlled.

Settlement house workers and other reformers concerned about the welfare of the urban poor made up a third battalion in the progressive army. This was an area in which women made the most important contributions. The working and living conditions of slum dwellers remained abominable, and the child labor problem was particularly acute; in 1900 about 1.7 million children under the age of 16 were working

full time—more than the membership of the American Federation of Labor. In addition, laws regulating the hours and working conditions of women in industry were far from adequate, and almost nothing had been done, despite the increased use of dangerous machinery in the factories, to enforce safety rules or to provide compensation or insurance for workers injured on the job. As the number of professionally competent social workers grew, the movement for social welfare legislation gained momentum.

America was becoming more urban, more industrial, more mechanized, more centralized—in short, more complex. This trend put a premium on efficiency and cooperation. It seemed obvious to the progressives that people must become more socially minded, the economy more carefully organized.

By attracting additional thousands of sympathizers to the general cause of reform, the return of prosperity after 1896 fueled the progressive movement. Good times made people more tolerant and generous. As long as profits were on the rise, the average employer did not object if labor improved its position too. Middle-class Americans who had been prepared to go to the barricades in the event of a Bryan victory in 1896 became conscience-stricken when they compared their own comfortable circumstances with those of the "huddled masses" of immigrants and native-born poor.

Giant industrial and commercial corporations undermined not so much the economic well-being as the ambitions and sense of importance of the middle class. What owner of a small mill or shop could now hope to rise to the heights attained by Carnegie or merchants like John Wanamaker and Marshall Field? The growth of large labor organizations worried such types. In general, character and moral values seemed less influential; organizations—cold, impersonal, heartless—were coming to control business, politics, and too many other aspects of life.

Protestant pastors accustomed to the respect and deference of their flocks found their moral leadership challenged by materialistic congregations who did not even pay them decent salaries. College professors worried about their institutions falling under the sway of wealthy trustees who had little interest in or respect for learning. Lawyers had been "the aristocracy of the United States," James Bryce recalled in 1905; they were now merely "a part of the great organized system of industrial and financial enterprise."

The middle classes could support reform measures without feeling that they were being very radical because they were resisting change and because the intellectual currents of the time harmonized with their ideas of social improvement and the welfare state. The new doctrines of the social scientists, the

Social Gospel religious leaders, and the philosophers of pragmatism provided a salubrious climate for progressivism. Many of the thinkers who had formulated these doctrines in the 1880s and 1890s turned to the task of putting them into practice in the new century. Their number included the economist Richard T. Ely, the philosopher John Dewey, and the Baptist clergyman Walter Rauschenbusch, who in addition to his many books extolling the Social Gospel was active in civic reform movements.

THE MUCKRAKERS

DOCUMENT

Steffens, from
*The Shame of
the Cities*

As the diffuse progressive army gradually formed its battalions, a new journalistic fad brought the movement into focus. For many years magazines had been publishing articles discussing current political, social, and economic problems. Henry Demarest Lloyd's first blast at the Standard Oil monopoly appeared in the *Atlantic Monthly* in 1881. Over the years the tempo and forcefulness of this type of literature increased. Then, in the fall of 1902, *McClure's* began two particularly hard-hitting series of articles, one on Standard Oil by Ida Tarbell, the other on big-city political machines by Lincoln Steffens. These articles provoked much comment. When the editor, S. S. McClure, decided to include in the January 1903 issue an attack on labor gangsterism in the coal fields along with installments of the Tarbell and Steffens series, he called attention to the circumstance in a striking editorial.

Something was radically wrong with the "American character," McClure wrote. These articles showed that large numbers of American employers, workers, and politicians were fundamentally immoral. Lawyers were becoming tools of big business, judges were permitting evildoers to escape justice, the churches were materialistic, educators seemed incapable of understanding what was happening. "There is no one left; none but all of us," McClure concluded. "We have to pay in the end."

McClure's editorial caused a sensation. The issue sold out quickly. Thousands of readers found their own vague apprehensions brought into focus. Some became active in progressive movements; still more lent passive support.

Other editors jumped to adopt the McClure formula. A small army of professional writers soon flooded the periodical press with denunciations of the insurance business, the drug business, college athletics, prostitution, sweatshop labor, political corruption, and dozens of other subjects. This type of article inspired Theodore Roosevelt, with his gift for vivid language, to compare the journalists to "the Man

with the Muck-Rake" in John Bunyan's *Pilgrim's Progress*, whose attention was so fixed on the filth at his feet that he could not notice the "celestial crown" that was offered him in exchange. Roosevelt's characterization grossly misrepresented the literature of exposure, but the label *muckraking* was thereafter affixed to the type. Despite its literal connotations, *muckraker* became a term of honor.

THE PROGRESSIVE MIND

Progressives sought to arouse the conscience of "the people" in order to "purify" American life. They were convinced that human beings were by nature decent, well intentioned, and kind. (After all, the words *human* and *humane* have the same root.) Unlike many earlier reformers, they believed that the source of society's evils lay in the structure of its institutions, not in the weaknesses or sinfulness of individuals. Therefore local, state, and national government must be made more responsive to the will of citizens who stood for the traditional virtues. In the South, many people who considered themselves progressives even argued that poll taxes and other measures designed to disfranchise blacks were reforms because they discouraged a class of people they considered unthinking and shiftless from voting.

When government had been thus reformed, then it must act; whatever its virtues, laissez-faire was obsolete. Businessmen, especially big businessmen, must be compelled to behave fairly, their acquisitive drives curbed in the interests of justice and equal opportunity for all. The weaker elements in society—women, children, the poor, the infirm—must be protected against unscrupulous power.

Despite its fervor and democratic rhetoric, progressivism was paternalistic, moderate, and often softheaded. Typical reformers of the period oversimplified complicated issues and treated their personal values as absolute standards of truth and morality. Thus progressives often acted at cross-purposes; at times some were even at war with themselves. This accounts for the diffuseness of the movement.

Many progressives who desired to improve the living standards of industrial workers rejected the proposition that workers could help themselves best by organizing powerful national unions. They found it difficult to cooperate with actual working people, who seemed to them unrefined and narrow-minded. Union leaders favored government action to outlaw child labor and restrict immigration but adopted a laissez-faire attitude toward wages-and-hours legislation; they preferred to win these objectives through collective bargaining, thereby justifying their own existence. Many who favored "municipal socialism" (public ownership of streetcar lines, waterworks, and other local utilities) adamantly opposed national ownership of railroads. Progressives stressed individual freedom yet gave strong backing to the drive to deprive the public of its right to drink alcoholic beverages. Few progressives worked more assiduously than Congressman George W. Norris of rural Nebraska for reforms that would increase the power of the ordinary voter, such as the direct primary and popular election of senators, yet Norris characterized the mass of urban voters as "the mob."

The progressives never challenged the fundamental principles of capitalism, nor did they attempt a basic reorganization of society. They would have little to do with the socialist brand of reform. Wisconsin was the most progressive of states, but its leaders never cooperated with the Socialist party of Milwaukee. When socialists threatened to win control of Los Angeles in 1911, California progressives made common cause with reactionary groups in order to defeat them. Many progressives were anti-immigrant, and only a handful had anything to offer blacks, surely the most exploited group in American society.

A good example of the relatively limited radicalism of most progressives is offered by the experiences of progressive artists. Early in the century a number of painters, including Robert Henri, John Sloan, and George Luks, tried to develop a distinctively American style. They turned to city streets and the people of the slums for their models, and they depended more on inspiration and inner conviction than on careful craftsmanship to achieve their effects.

These so-called ashcan artists were individualists, yet they supported political and social reform and were caught up in the progressive movement. Sloan was a socialist; Henri claimed to be an anarchist. Most saw themselves as rebels. But artistically the ashcan painters were not very advanced. Their idols were long-dead European masters such as Hogarth, Goya, and Daumier. They were uninfluenced by the outburst of postimpressionist activity then taking place in Europe. To their dismay, when they included canvases by Matisse, Picasso, and other European artists in a show of their own works at the Sixty-ninth Regiment Armory in New York City in 1913, the "advanced" Europeans got all the attention.

"RADICAL" PROGRESSIVES: THE WAVE OF THE FUTURE

Some people espoused more radical views. The hard times of the 1890s and the callous reactions of conservatives to the victims of that depression pushed many

toward Marxian socialism. In 1900 the labor leader Eugene V. Debs ran for president on the Socialist ticket. He polled fewer than 100,000 votes. When he ran again in 1904 he got more than 400,000, and in later elections still more. Labor leaders hoping to organize unskilled workers in heavy industry were increasingly frustrated by the craft orientation of the American Federation of Labor, and some saw in socialism a way to win rank-and-file backing.

In 1905 Debs, William "Big Bill" Haywood of the Western Federation of Miners, Mary Harris "Mother" Jones, a former organizer for the United Mine Workers, Daniel De Leon of the Socialist Labor party, and a few others organized a new union: the Industrial Workers of the World. The IWW was openly anticapitalist. The preamble to its constitution began: "The working class and the employing class have nothing in common."

But the IWW never attracted many ordinary workers. Haywood, its most prominent leader, was usually a general in search of an army. His forte was attracting attention to spontaneous strikes by unorganized workers, not the patient recruiting of workers and the pursuit of practical goals. Shortly after the founding of the IWW, he was charged with complicity in the murder of an antiunion governor of Idaho after an earlier strike but was acquitted. In 1912 he was closely involved in a bitter and at times bloody strike of textile workers in Lawrence, Massachusetts, which was settled with some benefit to the strikers, and in a strike the following winter and spring by silk workers in Paterson, New Jersey, which was a failure.

Other "advanced" European ideas affected the thinking and behavior of some important progressive intellectuals. Sigmund Freud's psychoanalytical theories attracted numbers of Americans, especially after G. Stanley Hall invited Freud and some of his disciples to lecture at Clark University in 1909. Not many progressives actually read *The Interpretation of Dreams* or any of Freud's other works, none of which was translated into English before 1909, but many picked up enough of the vocabulary of psychoanalysis to discourse impressively about the significance of slips of the tongue, sublimation, and infant sexuality.

Some saw in Freud's ideas reason to effect a "revolution of manners and morals" that would have shocked (or at least embarrassed) Freud, who was personally quite conventional. They advocated easy divorce, trial marriage, and doing away with the double standard in all matters relating to sex. They rejected Victorian reticence and what they incorrectly identified as "puritan" morality out of hand, and they called for programs of sex education, especially the dissemination of information about methods of birth control.

▲ The impact of *The Silent War*, a 1906 novel by John Ames Mitchell that dealt with the growing class struggle in America, was enhanced by William Balfour-Ker's graphic illustration *From the Depths*.

Most large cities boasted groups of these "bohemian" thinkers, by far the most famous being the one centered in New York City's Greenwich Village. The dancer Isadora Duncan, the photographer Alfred Stieglitz, the novelist Floyd Dell, several of the ashcan artists, and the playwright Eugene O'Neill rubbed shoulders with Big Bill Haywood of the IWW, the anarchist Emma Goldman, the psychoanalyst A. A. Brill, the militant feminist advocate of birth control, Margaret Sanger, Max Eastman, editor of their organ, *The Masses*, and John Reed, a young Harvard graduate who was soon to become famous for his eyewitness account of the Russian Revolution, *Ten Days That Shook the World*.

Goldman, Haywood, Sanger, and a few others in this group were genuine radicals who sought basic changes in bourgeois society, but most of the Greenwich Village intellectuals were as much concerned with

▶ *text continues on page 580*

American Lives

Emma Goldman

In January 1886 a sixteen-year-old Jewish girl named Emma Goldman arrived in New York City from St. Petersburg, Russia, where her parents ran a grocery store. As soon as immigration officials had examined her and approved her entry into the United States, she hurried on to Rochester, New York, where her half-sister lived. Emma was extremely independent-minded. Her father had tried to force her to marry when she was fifteen, saying when she protested that "all a Jewish daughter needs to know is how to prepare *gefülte* fish, cut noodles fine, and give the man plenty of children." Defying her father, Emma had flatly refused to marry. "I wanted to study, to know life, to travel," she explained years later. She had also found the harsh government of the Russian Czar unbearable. Like most immigrants she expected the United States, "the land of opportunity," to be a kind of paradise on earth.

Moving in with her half-sister's family, Emma got a job in a factory sewing coats and earning $2.50 a week. She paid her sister $1.50 a week for room and board and spent 60 cents a week on carfare to get to and from her job, leaving her only 40 cents for all her other needs. But when she asked her employer for more money he simply told her to "look for work elsewhere." This she did, finding a job at another factory that paid $4 a week.

In 1887 she married Jacob Kirshner, another Russian immigrant, but they did not get along and soon divorced. She moved to New Haven, Connecticut, where she worked in a corset factory. In 1889 she moved to New York City. There she took up with a group of radicals, most of them either socialists or anarchists. She herself was by this time an ardent anarchist, convinced by her experiences with the darker aspects of American capitalism that *all* governments repressed individual freedom and should simply be abolished.

In New York Emma fell in love with another Russian-born radical, Alexander Berkman. They started a kind of commune with another couple, sharing everything equally. Emma worked at home sewing shirts. Alexander found a job making cigars. They never married.

Next, the couple moved back to New Haven, where Emma started a cooperative dressmaking shop. Then they moved to Springfield, Massachusetts, where, with Berkman's cousin, an artist, they opened a photography studio. When this business failed, they borrowed $150 and opened an ice-cream parlor.

Nearly all immigrants of that period retained their faith in the promise of American life even after they discovered that the streets were not paved with gold and that the people and the government were not as perfect as they had expected when they arrived. But Emma was so disappointed by the United States that she became even more radical. The harsh punishment meted out to the anarchists who were accused of the Haymarket bombing of 1886 shocked her deeply.

In 1892 when she and Berkman learned of the bloody battle of Pinkertons and strikers during the Homestead steel strike, they closed the ice-cream parlor and went to New York. They formed a plan to assassinate Henry Clay Frick, the archvillain of the Homestead drama. First they tried to manufacture a bomb, but that proved to be beyond their powers. Berkman then went to Pittsburgh, where, posing as a representative of an agency that provided strikebreakers, he got into Frick's office. Pulling a pistol, Berkman aimed for Frick's head but the shot went wide and hit Frick in the shoulder. Berkman then stabbed Frick, but still the Homestead boss survived. Convicted of the attempt on Frick's life, Berkman was imprisoned for fourteen years.

The next year Goldman was herself arrested and sentenced to a year in jail for making an "incendiary" speech urging unemployed workers to distrust politicians and demand government relief. Upon her release, she was taken up by leading native-born radicals. She got to know Lillian Wald and other New York settlement workers, but while she respected their motives, she disparaged their methods. It did little good to teach good table manners to poor people who had no food, she believed. Leaving the United States, Goldman went to Vienna, where she trained as a nurse. When she returned to America, she worked as a midwife among the New York poor, an experience that made her an outspoken advocate of birth control. She also helped organize a theatrical group, managed a touring group of Russian actors, and lectured on theatrical topics.

In 1901, Goldman was arrested on charges of inspiring Leon Czolgosz to assassinate President McKinley. Czolgosz had attended one of Goldman's lectures, but there was no

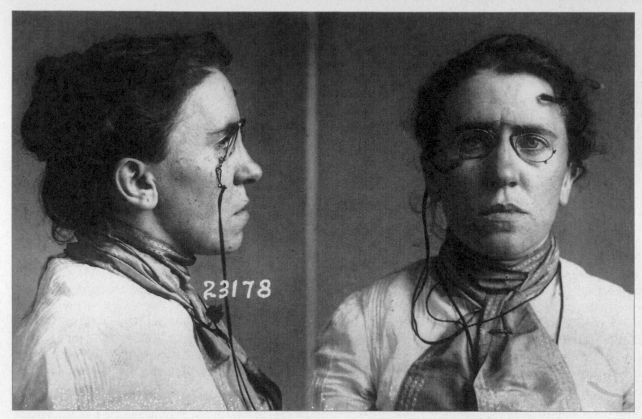

▲ A "mug shot" of Emma Goldman, 1901. She was arrested so often that she took to carrying a book with her everywhere so that she would have something to read in jail if she were arrested.

direct connection between the two, and the charges against her were dropped.

In 1906 Goldman founded *Mother Earth*, an anarchist journal. When Alexander Berkman was released from prison later that year, she made him its editor. *Mother Earth* denounced governments, organized religion, and private property. Goldman believed in a primitive form of communism in which all would share equally and no one would have power over anyone else.

By this time Goldman had become a celebrity. "Her name in those days was enough to produce a shudder," recalled Margaret Anderson, editor of a literary magazine. "She was considered a monster, an exponent of free love and bombs."

During the next decade Goldman campaigned for freedom of speech all over the United States and in Canada and lectured in support of birth control. She even developed a plan so that subscribers to *Mother Earth* could also get the *American Journal of Eugenics*, a magazine that advocated contraception. In 1915, after Margaret Sanger was arrested for disseminating information on birth control, Goldman did the same in public speeches. She was arrested and spent two weeks in jail.

Goldman regarded the Great War—and especially American entry in it—as a calamity beyond measure. When

Congress passed a conscription act, she, Berkman, and a few other radicals organized the No-Conscription League, not so much to persuade men to resist the draft as to provide aid and comfort to anyone who did so.

In 1917 Goldman and Berkman were convicted of conspiring to persuade men not to register for the draft. They served two years in federal prison. In 1919 they were deported to Russia. Two years later, disillusioned with the Bolsheviks, she left the Soviet Union.

"Red Emma" Goldman was not a typical American, but she was in many ways a typical American immigrant. She held on to the culture of the old country; most of her close friends in the United States were Russians. But at the same time she learned English and quickly became familiar with American ways. She worked hard and developed valuable skills. Gradually she moved up the economic ladder: from sweatshop laborer, to factory worker, to running a shop, to nursing, to lecturing, and to editing a magazine. And while she was critical of the government and economic system of the United States, she was a typical immigrant also in insisting that she was an American patriot. "The kind of patriotism we represent," she said during her trial in 1917, "is the kind of patriotism which loves America with open eyes."

aesthetic as social issues. *The Masses* described itself as "a revolutionary and not a reform magazine . . . a magazine whose final policy is to do as it pleases." Nearly all of them came from middle-class backgrounds. They found the far-different world of the Italian and Jewish immigrants of the Village and its surrounding neighborhoods charming. But they did not become involved in the immigrants' lives the way the settlement house workers did. Their influence on their own times, therefore, was limited. "Do as I say, not as I do" is not an effective way to change minds. They are historically important, however, because many of them were genuinely creative people and because many of the ideas and practices they advocated were adopted by later generations.

The creative writers of the era, applying the spirit of progressivism to the realism they had inherited from Howells and the naturalists, tended to adopt an optimistic tone. The poet Ezra Pound, for example, at this time talked grandly of an American renaissance and fashioned a new kind of poetry called imagism, which, while not appearing to be realistic, abjured all abstract generalizations and concentrated on concrete word pictures to convey meaning. "Little" magazines and experimental theatrical companies sprang to life by the dozen, each convinced that it would revolutionize its art. The poet Carl Sandburg, the best-known representative of the Chicago school, denounced the local plutocrats but sang the praises of the city they had made: "Hog Butcher for the World," "City of the Big Shoulders."

Most writers eagerly adopted Freudian psychology without understanding it. Freud's teachings seemed only to mean that they should cast off the restrictions of Victorian prudery; they ignored his essentially dark view of human nature. Theirs was an "innocent rebellion," exuberant and rather muddleheaded.

POLITICAL REFORM: CITIES FIRST

To most "ordinary" progressives, political corruption and inefficiency lay at the root of the evils plaguing American society, nowhere more obvious than in the nation's cities. Urban life's anonymity and complexity help explain why slavery did not flourish in cities, but also why the above-named vices did flourish. As the cities grew, their antiquated and boss-ridden administrations became more and more disgraceful. Consider the example of San Francisco. After 1901, a shrewd lawyer named Abe Ruef ruled one of the most powerful and dissolute political machines in the nation. Only one kind of paving material was used on San Francisco's streets, and Ruef was the lawyer for the company that supplied it. When the gas company asked for a rate increase of 10 cents per 100 cubic feet, Ruef, who was already collecting $1000 a month from the company as a "retainer," demanded and got an outright bribe of $20,000. A streetcar company needed city authorization to install overhead trolley wires; Ruef's approval cost the company $85,000. Prostitution flourished, with Ruef and his henchmen sharing in the profits. There was a brisk illegal trade in liquor licenses and other favors. Similar conditions existed in dozens of communities. For his famous muckraking series for *McClure's*, Lincoln Steffens visited St. Louis, Minneapolis, Pittsburgh, New York, Chicago, and Philadelphia and found them all riddled with corruption.

Beginning in the late 1890s progressives mounted a massive assault on dishonest and inefficient urban governments. In San Francisco a group headed by Fremont Older, a newspaperman, and Rudolph Spreckels, a wealthy sugar manufacturer, broke the machine and lodged Ruef in jail. In Toledo, Ohio, Samuel M. "Golden Rule" Jones won election as mayor in 1897 and succeeded in arousing the citizenry against the corrupt officials. Other important progressive mayors were Tom L. Johnson of Cleveland, whose administration Lincoln Steffens called the best in the United States; Seth Low and later John P. Mitchell of New York; and Hazen S. Pingree of Detroit.

City reformers could seldom destroy the machines without changing urban political institutions. Some cities obtained "home rule" charters that gave them greater freedom from state control in dealing with local matters. Many created research bureaus that investigated government problems in a scientific and nonpartisan manner. A number of middle-sized communities (Galveston, Texas, was the prototype) experimented with a system that integrated executive and legislative powers in the hands of a small elected commission, thereby concentrating responsibility and making it easier to coordinate complex activities. Out of this experiment came the city manager system, under which the commissioners appointed a professional manager to administer city affairs on a nonpartisan basis. Dayton, Ohio, which adopted the plan after a flood devastated the town in 1913, offers the best illustration of the city manager system in the progressive era.

Once the political system had been made responsive to the desires of the people, the progressives hoped to use it to improve society itself. Many cities experimented with "gas and water socialism," taking over public utility companies and operating them as departments of the municipal government. Under "Golden Rule" Jones, Toledo established a minimum wage for city employees, built playgrounds and golf

courses, and moderated its harsh penal code. Mayor Seth Low improved New York's public transportation system and obtained passage of the tenement house law of 1901. Mayor Tom Johnson forced a fare cut to 3 cents on the Cleveland street railways.

POLITICAL REFORM: THE STATES

To carry out this kind of change required the support of state legislatures since all municipal government depends on the authority of a sovereign state. Such approval was often difficult to obtain—local bosses were usually entrenched in powerful state machines, and rural majorities insensitive to urban needs controlled most legislatures. Therefore the progressives had to strike at inefficiency and corruption at the state level too.

During the first decade of the new century, Robert M. La Follette, one of the most remarkable figures of the age, transformed Wisconsin, the progressive state par excellence. La Follette was born in Primrose, Wisconsin, in 1855. He had served three terms as a Republican congressman (1885–1891) and developed a reputation as an uncompromising foe of corruption before being elected governor in 1900. That the people would always do the right thing if properly informed and inspired was the fundamental article of his political faith. "Machine control is based upon misrepresentation and ignorance," La Follette said. "Democracy is based upon knowledge." His own career seemed to prove his point, for in his repeated clashes with the conservative Wisconsin Republican machine, he won battle after battle by vigorous grassroots campaigning.

Despite the opposition of railroad and lumbering interests, Governor La Follette obtained a direct primary system for nominating candidates, a corrupt practices act, and laws limiting campaign expenditures and lobbying activities. In power he became something of a boss himself. He made ruthless use of patronage, demanded absolute loyalty of his subordinates, and often stretched, or at least oversimplified, the truth when presenting complex issues to the voters.

La Follette was a consummate showman who never rose entirely above rural prejudices. He was prone to scent a nefarious "conspiracy" organized by "the interests" behind even the mildest opposition to his proposals. But he was devoted to the cause of honest government. Realizing that some state functions called for specialized technical knowledge, he used commissions and agencies to handle such matters as railroad regulation, tax assessment, conservation, and highway construction. Wisconsin established a legislative reference library to assist lawmakers in drafting bills. For work of this kind, La Follette called on the faculty of the University of Wisconsin, enticing top-notch economists and political scientists into the public service and drawing freely on the advice of such outstanding social scientists as Richard T. Ely, John R. Commons, and E. A. Ross.

The success of these policies, which became known as the Wisconsin Idea, led other states to adopt similar programs. Reform administrations swept into office in Iowa and Arkansas (1901); Oregon (1902); Minnesota, Kansas, and Mississippi (1904); New York and Georgia (1906); Nebraska (1909); and New Jersey and Colorado (1910). In some cases the reformers were Republicans, in others Democrats, but in all the example of Wisconsin was influential. By 1910, fifteen states had established legislative reference services, most of them staffed by personnel trained in Wisconsin. The direct primary system became almost universal.

Some states went beyond Wisconsin in striving to make their governments responsive to the popular will. In 1902 Oregon began to experiment with the initiative, a system by which a bill could be forced on the attention of the legislature by popular petition, and the referendum, a method for allowing the electorate to approve measures rejected by their representatives and to repeal measures that the legislature had passed. Eleven states, most of them in the West, legalized these devices by 1914.

STATE SOCIAL LEGISLATION

The first state laws aimed at social problems long antedated the progressive era, but most were either so imprecise as to be unenforceable or, like the Georgia law "limiting" textile workers to eleven hours a day, so weak as to be ineffective. In 1874 Massachusetts restricted the working hours of women and children to ten per day, and by the 1890s many other states, mostly in the East and Midwest, had followed suit. Illinois passed an eight-hour law for women workers in 1893. A New York law of 1882 struck at the sweatshops of the slums by prohibiting the manufacture of cigars on premises "occupied as a house or residence."

As part of this trend, some states established special rules for workers in hazardous industries. In the 1890s several states limited the hours of railroad workers on the grounds that fatigue sometimes caused railroad accidents. Utah restricted miners to eight hours in 1896. In 1901 New York finally enacted an effective tenement house law, greatly increasing the area of open space on building lots and requiring toilets for each apartment, better ventilation systems, and more adequate fireproofing.

▲ Orphans on the steps of an orphanage, 1911. From 1854 to 1929, nearly 200,000 orphans or abandoned children from eastern cities were sent on "orphan trains" to live with farming families in the Midwest. Billy the Kid was one of the less successful "orphan train" placements.

Before 1900 the collective impact of such legislation was not impressive. Powerful manufacturers and landlords often succeeded in defeating the bills or rendering them innocuous. The federal system further complicated the task of obtaining effective legislation.

The Fourteenth Amendment to the Constitution, although enacted to protect the civil rights of blacks, imposed a revolutionary restriction on the states by forbidding them to "deprive any person of life, liberty, or property without due process of law." Since much state social legislation represented new uses of coercive power that conservative judges considered dangerous and unwise, the Fourteenth Amendment gave them an excuse to overturn the laws on the grounds that they deprived someone of liberty or property.

As stricter and more far-reaching laws were enacted, many judges, sensing what they took to be a trend toward socialism and regimentation, adopted an increasingly narrow interpretation of state authority to regulate business. In 1905 the United States Supreme Court declared in the case of *Lochner* v. *New York* that a New York ten-hour act for bakers deprived the bakers of the liberty of working as long as they wished and thus violated the Fourteenth Amendment. Justice Oliver Wendell Holmes, Jr., wrote a famous dissenting opinion in this case. If the people of New York believed that the public health was endangered by bakers working long hours, he reasoned, it was not the Court's job to overrule them.

Nevertheless, the progressives continued to battle for legislation to use state power against business. Women played a particularly important part in these struggles. Sparked by the National Child Labor Committee, organized in 1904, reformers over the next ten years obtained laws in nearly every state banning the employment of young children and limiting the hours of older ones. Many of these laws were poorly enforced, yet when Congress passed a federal child labor law in 1916, the Supreme Court, in *Hammer* v. *Dagenhart* (1918), declared it unconstitutional.[1]

Little Spinner in Globe Cotton Mill

By 1917 nearly all the states had placed limitations on the hours of women industrial workers, and about ten had set minimum wage standards for women. But once again federal action that would have extended such regulation to the entire country did not materialize. A minimum wage law for women in the District of Columbia was overturned by the Court in *Adkins* v. *Children's Hospital* (1923).

Laws protecting workers against on-the-job accidents were also enacted by many states. Disasters like the 1911 fire in New York City, in which nearly 150 women perished because the Triangle shirtwaist factory had no fire escapes, led to the passage of stricter

---

[1]A second child labor law, passed in 1919, was also thrown out by the Court, and a child labor amendment, submitted in 1924, failed to achieve ratification by the necessary three-quarters of the states.

municipal building codes and factory inspection acts. By 1910 most states had modified the common-law principle that a worker accepted the risk of accident as a condition of employment and was not entitled to compensation if injured unless it could be proved that the employer had been negligent. Gradually the states adopted accident insurance plans, and some began to grant pensions to widows with small children. Most manufacturers favored such measures, if for no other reason than that they regularized procedures and avoided costly lawsuits.

The passage of so much state social legislation sent conservatives scurrying to the Supreme Court for redress. Such persons believed that no government had the power to deprive either workers or employers of the right to negotiate any kind of labor contract they wished. The decision of the Supreme Court in *Lochner* v. *New York* seemed to indicate that the justices would adopt this point of view. When an Oregon law limiting women laundry workers to ten hours a day was challenged in *Muller* v. *Oregon* (1908), Florence Kelley and Josephine Goldmark of the Consumers' League persuaded Louis D. Brandeis to defend the statute before the Court.

The Consumers' League, whose slogan was "investigate, agitate, legislate," was probably the most effective of the many women's reform organizations of the period. With the aid of league researchers, Brandeis prepared a remarkable brief stuffed with economic and sociological evidence indicating that long hours damaged both the health of individual women and the health of society. This nonlegal evidence greatly impressed the justices, who upheld the constitutionality of the Oregon law. "Woman's physical structure, and the functions she performs in consequence thereof, justify special legislation," they concluded. After 1908 the right of states to protect women, children, and workers performing dangerous and unhealthy tasks by special legislation was widely accepted. The use of the "Brandeis brief" technique to demonstrate the need for such legislation became standard practice.

Progressives also launched a massive if ill-coordinated attack on problems related to monopoly. The variety of regulatory legislation passed by the states between 1900 and 1917 was almost infinite. Wisconsin enacted a graduated personal income tax, forced corporations to bear a larger share of the cost of government, created an industrial commission to enforce the state's labor and factory legislation, and established a conservation commission, headed by Charles R. Van Hise, president of the University of Wisconsin.

A similar spate of legislation characterized the brief reign of Woodrow Wilson as governor of New Jersey (1911–1913). Urged on by the relentless Wilson, the legislature created a commission to fix rates and set standards for railroad, gas, electric, and telephone corporations, enacted storage and food inspection laws, and passed seven bills (the "Seven Sisters" laws) tightening the state's loose controls over corporations. Economic reforms in other states were less spectacular but impressive in the mass. However, piecemeal state regulation failed to solve the problems of an ever more complex economy. The most significant battles for economic reform were fought in Congress.

POLITICAL REFORM: THE WOMAN SUFFRAGE MOVEMENT

On the national level the progressive era saw the culmination of the struggle for woman suffrage. The shock occasioned by the failure of the Fourteenth and Fifteenth Amendments to give women the vote after the Civil War continued to embitter most leaders of

▲ A banner in a 1911 woman's suffrage parade carries one of the longest-standing arguments in favor of women getting the vote.

the movement. But it resulted in a split among feminists. One group, the American Woman's Suffrage Association (AWSA), focused on the vote question alone. The more radical National Woman's Suffrage Association (NWSA), led by Elizabeth Cady Stanton and Susan B. Anthony, concerned itself with many issues of importance to women as well as suffrage. The NWSA put the immediate interests of women ahead of everything else. It was deeply involved in efforts to unionize women workers, yet it did not hesitate to urge women to be strikebreakers if they could get better jobs by doing so.

Aside from their lack of unity, feminists were handicapped in the late nineteenth century by Victorian sexual inhibitions, which most of their leaders shared. Even under the best of circumstances, dislike of male-dominated society is hard enough to separate from dislike of men. At a time when sex was an unmentionable topic in polite society, some of the most militant advocates of women's rights probably did not understand their own feelings. Most feminists, for example, opposed contraception, insisting that birth control by any means other than continence would encourage what they called masculine lust. The Victorian idealization of female "purity" and the popular image of women as the revered guardians of home and family further confused many reformers. And the trend of nineteenth-century scientific thinking influenced by the Darwinian concept of biological adaptation led to the conclusion that the female personality was different from that of the male and that the differences were inherent, not culturally determined.

These ideas and prejudices enticed feminists into a logical trap. If women were morally superior to men—a tempting conclusion—giving women the vote would improve the character of the electorate. Society would benefit because politics would become less corrupt, war a thing of the past. "City housekeeping has failed," said Jane Addams of Hull House in arguing for the reform of municipal government, "partly because women, the traditional housekeepers, have not been consulted."

Woman Suffrage
Before the
19th Century

The trouble with this argument (aside from the fact that opponents could easily demonstrate that in states where women did vote, governments were no better or worse than elsewhere) was that it surrendered the principle of equality. In the long run this was to have serious consequences for the women's movement, although the immediate effect of the purity argument was probably to advance the suffragists' cause.

By the early twentieth century there were signs of progress. In 1890 the two major women's groups combined as the National American Woman's Suffrage Association (NAWSA). Stanton and Anthony were the

▲ That women were intrinsically *better* than men was another argument in support of woman suffrage. Note that this woman in the turn-of-the-century poster has a halo, and her clothes are arranged in the shape of a cross.

first two presidents of the association, but new leaders were emerging, the most notable being Carrie Chapman Catt, a woman who combined superb organizing abilities and political skills with commitment to broad social reform. The NAWSA made winning the right to vote its main objective and concentrated on a state-by-state approach. Wyoming gave women the vote in 1869, and Utah, Colorado, and Idaho had been won over to women's suffrage by 1896.

The burgeoning of the progressive movement helped as middle-class recruits of both sexes adopted the suffrage cause. The 1911 election in California was crucial. Fifteen years earlier, California voters had rejected the measure. But in 1911, despite determined opposition from saloonkeepers, the proposal barely passed. Within three years, most other Western states fell into line. For the first time, large numbers of working-class women began to agitate for the vote. In 1917, bosses at New York City's Tammany Hall, who had engineered the defeat of woman suffrage in

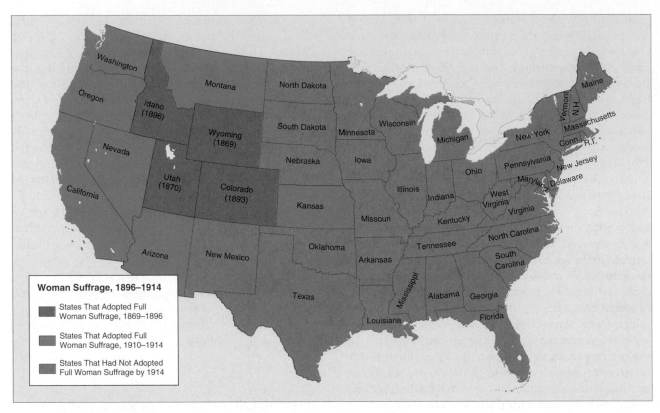

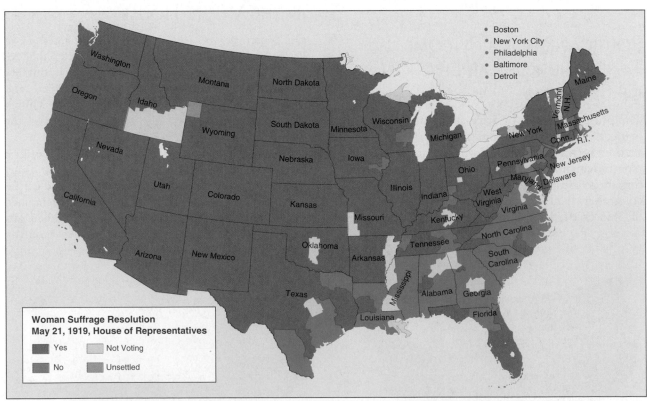

▲ The Advance of Woman Suffrage

In 1869 Wyoming, while still a territory, voted to give women the vote. The next year, after Mormon leader Brigham Young endorsed woman suffrage, Utah followed. Then came Colorado (1893) and Idaho (1896), frontier states that sought to attract women settlers. In 1911, by a margin of 3587 votes, California endorsed woman suffrage, and within three years the remainder of the western states had done so, too. World War I stimulated support for the Woman Suffrage (Nineteenth) Amendment. The May 21, 1919, vote in the House of Representatives shows that most of the opposing votes came from southern congressmen who believed that woman suffrage would be the first step securing the vote for blacks.

that state two years earlier, concluded that passage was inevitable and threw their support to the measure, which passed. The suffragists then shifted the campaign back to the national level, the lead taken by a new organization, the Congressional Union, headed by Alice Paul and the wealthy reformer Alva Belmont. When President Wilson refused to support the idea of a constitutional amendment granting women the vote, militant women picketed the White House. A number of them, including the daughter of Thomas Bayard, a former senator and secretary of state, were arrested and sentenced to sixty days in the workhouse. This roused a storm of criticism, and Wilson quickly pardoned the picketers. After some hesitation the NAWSA stopped concentrating on the state-by-state approach and began to campaign for a constitutional amendment. Pressure on Congress mounted steadily. Later, Vice President Thomas R. Marshall complained of the "everlasting clatter of the militant suffragettes" that (he said) was keeping Congress from transacting other business. This was an overstatement, but in any case the amendment finally won congressional approval in 1919. By 1920 the necessary three-quarters of the states had ratified the Nineteenth Amendment; the long fight was over.

POLITICAL REFORM: INCOME TAXES AND POPULAR ELECTION OF SENATORS

The progressive reform drive also found expression in the Sixteenth Amendment to the Constitution, authorizing federal income taxes, and the Seventeenth, which required the popular election of senators, both ratified in 1913. A group of "insurgent" congressmen also managed to reform the House of Representatives by limiting the power of the

Speaker. During the early years of the century, operating under the system established in the 1890s by "Czar" Thomas B. Reed, Speaker Joseph G. Cannon exercised tyrannical authority, appointing the members of all committees and controlling the course of legislation. Representatives could seldom obtain the floor without obtaining the Speaker's consent. In 1910 the insurgents, led by George W. Norris, stripped Cannon of his control over the House Rules Committee. Thereafter, appointments to committees were determined by the entire membership, acting through party caucuses. This change was thoroughly progressive. "We want the House to be representative of the people and each individual member to have his ideas presented and passed on," Norris explained.

No other important alterations of the national political system were made during the progressive era. Although some twenty states passed presidential primary laws, the cumbersome method of electing presidents was not changed.

THEODORE ROOSEVELT: COWBOY IN THE WHITE HOUSE

On September 6, 1901, an anarchist named Leon Czolgosz shot President McKinley during a public reception at the Pan-American Exposition at Buffalo, New York. Eight days later McKinley died and Theodore Roosevelt became president of the United States. His ascension to the presidency marked the beginning of a new era in national politics.

Although only forty-two, by far the youngest president in the nation's history up to that time, Roosevelt brought solid qualifications to the office. Son of a well-to-do New York merchant, he had graduated from Harvard in 1880 and studied law

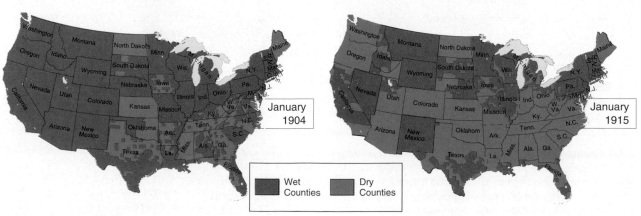

▲ **The Advance of Prohibition**

▲ Theodore Roosevelt in full oratorical flight.

▲ The original stuffed bear, introduced as a toy in 1903. About the same time president "Teddy" Roosevelt, a big game hunter, refrained from shooting a bear cub. A cartoon rendering of that cub resembled the new toy, which people began referring to as "Teddy's Bears"—soon shortened to "Teddy Bears."

briefly at Columbia, though he did not obtain a degree. In addition to political experience that included three terms in the New York assembly, six years on the United States Civil Service Commission, two years as police commissioner of New York City, another as assistant secretary of the navy, and a term as governor of New York, he had been a rancher in the Dakota Territory and a soldier in the Spanish-American War. He was also a well-known historian: His *Naval War of 1812* (1882), begun during his undergraduate days at Harvard, and his four-volume *Winning of the West* (1889–1896) were valuable works of scholarship, and he had written two popular biographies and other books as well. Politically, he had always been a loyal Republican. He rejected the mugwump heresy in 1884, despite his distaste for Blaine, and during the tempestuous 1890s he vigorously denounced populism, Bryanism, and "labor agitators."

Nevertheless, Roosevelt's elevation to the presidency alarmed many conservatives, and not without reason. He did not fit their conception, based on a composite image of the chief executives from Hayes to McKinley, of what a president should be like. He seemed too undignified, too energetic, too outspoken, too unconventional. It was one thing to have operated a cattle ranch, another to have captured a gang of rustlers at gunpoint; one thing to have run a metropolitan police force, another to have roamed New York slums in the small hours to catch patrolmen fraternizing with thieves and prostitutes; one thing to have commanded a regiment, another to have killed a Spaniard personally.

Roosevelt had been a sickly child, plagued by asthma and poor eyesight, and he seems to have spent much of his adult life compensating for the sense of inadequacy that these troubles bred in him. He repeatedly carried his displays of physical stamina

and personal courage and his love of athletics and big-game hunting to preternatural lengths. Henry Adams, who watched Roosevelt's development over the years with a mixture of fear and amusement, said that he was "pure act."

Once, while fox hunting, Roosevelt fell from his horse, cutting his face severely and breaking his left arm. Instead of waiting for help or struggling to some nearby house to summon a doctor, he clambered back on his horse and resumed the chase. "I was in at the death," he wrote next day. "I looked pretty gay, with one arm dangling, and my face and clothes like the walls of a slaughter house." That evening, after his arm had been set and put in splints, he attended a dinner party.

Roosevelt worshiped aggressiveness and was extremely sensitive to any threat to his honor as a gentleman. When another young man showed some slight interest in Roosevelt's fiancée, he sent for a set of French dueling pistols. His teachers found him an interesting student, for he was intelligent and imaginative, if annoyingly argumentative. "Now look here, Roosevelt," one Harvard professor finally said to him, "let me talk. I'm running this course."

Few individuals have rationalized or sublimated their feelings of inferiority as effectively as Roosevelt and to such good purpose. And few have been more genuinely warmhearted, more full of spontaneity, more committed to the ideals of public service and national greatness. As a political leader he was energetic and hard-driving. Conservatives and timid souls, sensing his aggressiveness even when he held it in check, distrusted Roosevelt's judgment, fearing he might go off half-cocked in some crisis. In fact his judgment was nearly always sound; responsibility usually tempered his aggressiveness.

When Roosevelt was first mentioned as a running mate for McKinley in 1900, he wrote: "The Vice Presidency is a most honorable office, but for a young man there is not much to do." As president it would have been unthinkable for him to preside over a caretaker administration devoted to maintaining the status quo. However, the reigning Republican politicos, basking in the sunshine of the prosperity that had contributed so much to their victory in 1900, distrusted anything suggestive of change.

Had Roosevelt been the impetuous hothead that conservatives feared, he would have plunged ahead without regard for their feelings and influence. Instead he moved slowly and often got what he wanted by using his executive power rather than by persuading Congress to pass new laws. His domestic program included some measure of control of big corporations, more power for the Interstate Commerce Commission (ICC), and the conservation of natural resources. By consulting congressional leaders and following their advice not to bring up controversial matters like the tariff and currency reform, he obtained a modest budget of new laws.

The Newlands Act (1902) funneled the proceeds from land sales in the West into federal irrigation projects. The Department of Commerce and Labor, which was to include a Bureau of Corporations with authority to investigate industrial combines and issue reports, was established. The Elkins Railroad Act of 1903 strengthened the ICC's hand against the railroads by making the receiving as well as the granting of rebates illegal and by forbidding the roads to deviate in any way from their published rates.

ROOSEVELT AND BIG BUSINESS

Roosevelt soon became known as a trustbuster, and in the sense that he considered the monopoly problem the most pressing issue of the times, this was accurate to an extent. But he did not believe in breaking up big corporations indiscriminately. Regulation seemed the best way to deal with large corporations because, he said, industrial giantism "could not be eliminated unless we were willing to turn back the wheels of modern progress."

With Congress unwilling to pass a stiff regulatory law, Roosevelt resorted to the Sherman Act to get at the problem. Although the Supreme Court decision in the Sugar Trust case seemed to have emasculated that law, in 1902 he ordered the Justice Department to bring suit against the Northern Securities Company.

He chose his target wisely. The Northern Securities Company controlled the Great Northern, the Northern Pacific, and the Chicago, Burlington and Quincy railroads. It had been created in 1901 after a titanic battle on the New York Stock Exchange between the forces of J. P. Morgan and James J. Hill and those of E. H. Harriman, who was associated with the Rockefeller interests. In their efforts to obtain control of the Northern Pacific, the rivals had forced its stock up to $1000 a share, ruining many speculators and threatening to cause a panic.

Neither side could win a clear-cut victory, so they decided to put the stock of all three railroads in a holding company owned by the two groups. Since Harriman already controlled the Union Pacific and the Southern Pacific, the plan resulted in a virtual monopoly of western railroads. The public had been alarmed, for the merger seemed to typify the rapaciousness of the tycoons.

The announcement of the suit caused consternation in the business world. Morgan rushed to the White House. "If we have done anything wrong," he said to the president, "send your man to my man and they can fix it up." Roosevelt was not fundamentally opposed to this sort of agreement, but it was too late to compromise in this instance. Attorney General Philander C. Knox pressed the case vigorously, and in 1904 the Supreme Court ordered the dissolution of the Northern Securities Company.

Roosevelt then ordered suits against the meat packers, the Standard Oil Trust, and the American Tobacco Company. His stock among progressives rose, yet he had not embarrassed the conservatives in Congress by demanding new antitrust legislation.

The president went out of his way to assure cooperative corporation magnates that he was not against size per se. At a White House conference in 1905, Roosevelt and Elbert H. Gary, chairman of the board of U.S. Steel, reached a "gentlemen's agreement" whereby Gary promised "to cooperate with the Government in every possible way." The Bureau of Corporations would conduct an investigation of U.S. Steel, Gary allowing it full access to company records. Roosevelt in turn promised that if the investigation revealed any corporate malpractices, he would allow Gary to set matters right voluntarily, thereby avoiding

DEBATING THE PAST

Were the progressives forward-looking?
"Jack and the Wall Street Giants" shows a diminutive Teddy Roosevelt taking on the titans of Wall Street, among them railroad barons James J. Hill and Jay Gould and financier J. P. Morgan. The cartoon anticipates the familiar argument—that the progressives

sought genuine change. But it also suggests that the prospects for victory were poor. Note that TR stands alone. By the 1930s, when the nation was mired in depression, many blamed the progressives. In 1932 John Chamberlain published a "Farewell to Reform" that excoriated progressive leaders for failing to check the power of the trusts. That failure, Richard Hofstadter (1955) declared, was rooted in their psychology. The progressives, mostly members of the middle class and the declining old elites, felt threatened by the increasing power and status of the new tycoons, many of them coarse, domineering, and fond of vulgar display. The antics of machine politicians who made a mockery of the traditions of duty, service, and patriotism associated with statesmanship also troubled them. They sought to restore "familiar and traditional ideals," and their nostrums were as old-fashioned as their goals. Revisionist historians such as Gabriel Kolko (1963) pushed Hofstadter's argument still further: the progressives never sought meaningful reform in the first place. They endorsed government regulation to prevent anarchic economic competition, and they hoped to ameliorate the plight of workers to forestall revolution. Their "progressivism" was in fact the "triumph of conservatism." Daniel Rodgers (1998) was among the many who insisted that this portrait was overdrawn. The progressives in the United States were not much different from reformers at that time in Europe. All shared a dynamic rhetoric; all sought to counteract the increasing concentration of industrial power; none met with great success. In the cartoon TR is armed only with the sword of "Public Service." Did he mean to preach to the giants or slay them?

John Chamberlain, *Farewell to Reform* (1932), Richard Hofstadter, *The Age of Reform* (1955), Gabriel Kolko, *The Triumph of Conservatism* (1963), Allen Weinstein, *The Decline of Socialism in America* (1967), Robert Wiebe, *The Search for Order* (1967), Daniel Rodgers, *Atlantic Crossings* (1998).

---

an antitrust suit. He reached a similar agreement with the International Harvester Company two years later.

There were limits to the effectiveness of such arrangements. Standard Oil agreed to a similar détente and then reneged, refusing to turn over vital records to the bureau. The Justice Department brought suit against the company under the Sherman Act, and eventually it was broken up at the order of the Supreme Court. Roosevelt would have preferred a more binding kind of regulation, but when he asked for laws giving the government supervisory authority over big combinations, Congress refused to act.

ROOSEVELT AND THE COAL STRIKE

Roosevelt made remarkable use of his executive power during the anthracite coal strike of 1902. In June the United Mine Workers (UMW), led by John Mitchell, laid down their picks and demanded higher wages, an eight-hour day, and recognition of the union. Most of the anthracite mines were owned by railroads. Two years earlier the miners had won a 10 percent wage increase in a similar strike, chiefly because the owners feared that labor unrest might endanger the election of McKinley. Now the coal

companies were dead set against further concessions; when the men walked out, they shut down the mines and prepared to starve the strikers into submission.

The strike dragged on through summer and early fall. The miners conducted themselves with great restraint, avoiding violence and offering to submit their claims to arbitration. As the price of anthracite soared with the approach of winter, sentiment in their behalf mounted.

The owners' spokesman, George F. Baer of the Reading Railroad, proved particularly inept at public relations. Baer stated categorically that God was on the side of management, but when someone suggested asking an important Roman Catholic prelate to arbitrate the dispute, he replied icily: "Anthracite mining is a business and not a religious, sentimental or academic proposition."

Roosevelt shared the public's sympathy for the miners, and the threat of a coal shortage alarmed him. Early in October he summoned both sides to a conference in Washington and urged them as patriotic Americans to sacrifice any "personal consideration" for the "general good." His action enraged the coal operators, for they believed he was trying to force them to recognize the union. They refused even to speak to the UMW representatives at the conference and demanded that Roosevelt end the strike by force and bring suit against the union under the Sherman Act. Mitchell, aware of the immense prestige that Roosevelt had conferred on the union by calling the conference, cooperated fully with the president.

The attitudes of management and of the union further strengthened public support for the miners. Even former president Grover Cleveland, who had used federal troops to break the Pullman strike, said that he was "disturbed and vexed by the tone and substance of the operators' deliverances." Encouraged by this state of affairs, Roosevelt took a bold step: He announced that unless a settlement was reached promptly, he would order federal troops into the anthracite regions, not to break the strike but to seize and operate the mines.

The threat of government intervention brought the owners to terms. A Cabinet member, Elihu Root, worked out the details with J. P. Morgan, whose firm had major interests in the Reading and other railroads, while cruising the Hudson River on Morgan's yacht. The miners would return to the pits and all issues between them and the coal companies would be submitted for settlement to a commission appointed by Roosevelt. Both sides accepted the arrangement, and the men went back to work. In March 1903 the commission granted the miners a 10 percent wage increase and a nine-hour workday.

To the public the incident seemed a perfect illustration of the progressive spirit—in Roosevelt's

words, everyone had received a "square deal." In fact the results were by no means so clear-cut. The miners gained relatively little and the companies lost still less, for they were not required to recognize the UMW and the commission also recommended a 10 percent increase in the price of coal, ample compensation for the increased wage costs. The president was the main winner. The public acclaimed him as a fearless, imaginative, public-spirited leader. Without calling on Congress for support, he had expanded his own authority and hence that of the federal government. His action marked a major forward step in the evolution of the modern presidency.

▲ Before the passage of the Pure Food and Drug Act in 1906, manufacturers were free to use any ingredients they chose. Many "tonics" kept their promises of increased vigor by delivering doses of cocaine, alcohol, or other narcotics.

TR's TRIUMPHS

By reviving the Sherman Act, settling the coal strike, and pushing moderate reforms through Congress, Roosevelt ensured that he would be reelected president in 1904. Progressives, if not captivated, were at least pleased by his performance. Conservative Republicans offered no serious objection. Sensing that Roosevelt had won over the liberals, the Democrats nominated a conservative, Judge Alton B. Parker of New York, and bid for the support of eastern industrialists.

This strategy failed, for businessmen continued to eye the party of Bryan with intense suspicion. They preferred, as the *New York Sun* put it, "the impulsive candidate of the party of conservatism to the conservative candidate of the party which the business interests regard as permanently and dangerously impulsive." Despite his resentment at Roosevelt's attack on the Northern Securities Company, J. P. Morgan contributed $150,000 to the Republican campaign. Other tycoons gave with equal generosity. Roosevelt swept the country, carrying even the normally Democratic border states of Maryland and Missouri.

Encouraged by the landslide and the increasing militancy of progressives, Roosevelt pressed for more reform legislation. His most imaginative proposal was a plan to make the District of Columbia a model progressive community. He suggested child labor and factory inspection laws and a slum clearance program, but Congress refused to act. Likewise, his request for a minimum wage for railroad workers was rejected.

He had greater success when he proposed still another increase in the power of the Interstate Commerce Commission. Rebating remained a serious problem. With progressive state governors demanding federal action and farmers and manufacturers, especially in the Midwest, clamoring for relief against discriminatory rates, Roosevelt was ready by 1905 to make railroad legislation his major objective. The ICC should be empowered to fix rates, not merely to challenge unreasonable ones. It should have the right to inspect the private records of the railroads since fair rates could not be determined unless the true financial condition of the roads was known.

Because these proposals struck at rights that businessmen considered sacrosanct, many congressmen balked. But Roosevelt applied presidential pressure, and in June 1906 the Hepburn bill became law. It gave the commission the power to inspect the books of railroad companies, to set maximum rates (once a complaint had been filed by a shipper), and to control sleeping car companies, owners of oil pipelines, and other firms engaged in transportation. Railroads could no longer issue passes freely—an important check on their political influence. In all, the Hepburn Act made the ICC a more powerful and more active body. Although it did not outlaw judicial review of ICC decisions, thereafter those decisions were seldom overturned by the courts.

Congress also passed meat inspection and pure food and drug legislation. In 1906 Upton Sinclair published *The Jungle*, a devastating exposé of the filthy conditions in the Chicago slaughterhouses. Sinclair was more interested in writing a socialist tract than he was in meat inspection, but his book, a bestseller, raised a storm against the packers. After Roosevelt read *The Jungle* he sent two officials to Chicago to investigate. Their report was so shocking, he said, that its publication would "be well-nigh ruinous to our export trade in meat." He threatened to release the report, however, unless Congress acted. After a hot fight, the meat inspection bill passed. The Pure Food and Drug Act, forbidding the manufacture and sale of adulterated and fraudulently labeled products, rode through Congress on the coattails of this measure.

Roosevelt has probably received more credit than he deserves for these laws. He had never been deeply interested in pure food legislation, and he considered Dr. Harvey W. Wiley, chief chemist of the Department of Agriculture and the leader of the fight for this reform, something of a crank. He compromised with opponents of meat inspection cheerfully, despite his loud denunciations of the evils under attack. "As now carried on the [meat-packing] business is both a menace to health and an outrage on decency," he said: "No legislation that is not drastic and thoroughgoing will be of avail." Yet he went along with the packers' demand that the government pay the costs of inspection, though he believed that "the only way to secure efficiency is by the imposition upon the packers of a fee." Nevertheless, the end results were positive and in line with his conception of the public good.

To advanced liberals Roosevelt's achievements seemed limited when placed beside his professed objectives and his smug evaluations of what he had done. How could he be a reformer and a defender of established interests at the same time? Roosevelt found no difficulty in holding such a position. As one historian has said: "He stood close to the center and bared his teeth at the conservatives of the right and the liberals of the extreme left."

ROOSEVELT TILTS LEFT

As the progressive movement advanced, Roosevelt advanced with it. He never accepted all the ideas of what he called its "lunatic fringe," but he took steadily more liberal positions. He always insisted that he was not hostile to business interests, but when those interests sought to exploit the national domain, they had no more implacable foe. Conservation of

natural resources was dear to his heart and probably his most significant achievement as president. He placed some 150 million acres of forest lands in federal reserves, and he strictly enforced the laws governing grazing, mining, and lumbering.

As Roosevelt became more liberal, conservative Republicans began to balk at following his lead. The sudden panic that struck the financial world in October 1907 speeded the trend. Government policies had no direct bearing on the panic, which began with a run on several important New York trust companies and spread to the Stock Exchange when speculators found themselves unable to borrow money to meet their obligations. In the emergency Roosevelt authorized the deposit of large amounts of government cash in New York banks. He informally agreed to the acquisition of the Tennessee Coal and Iron Company by U.S. Steel when the bankers told him that the purchase was necessary to end the panic. In spite of his efforts, conservatives insisted on referring to the financial collapse as "Roosevelt's panic," and they blamed the president for the depression that followed on its heels.

Roosevelt, however, turned left rather than right. In 1908 he came out in favor of federal income and inheritance taxes, stricter regulation of interstate corporations, and reforms designed to help industrial workers. He denounced "the speculative folly and the flagrant dishonesty" of "malefactors of great wealth," further alienating conservative, or Old Guard, Republicans, who resented the attacks on their integrity implicit in Roosevelt's statements. When the president began criticizing the courts, the last bastion of conservatism, he lost all chance of obtaining further reform legislation. As he said himself, during his last months in office "stagnation continued to rage with uninterrupted violence."

WILLIAM HOWARD TAFT: THE LISTLESS PROGRESSIVE, OR MORE IS LESS

But Roosevelt remained popular and politically powerful; before his term ended, he chose William Howard Taft, his secretary of war, to succeed him and easily obtained Taft's nomination. William Jennings Bryan was again the Democratic candidate. Campaigning on Roosevelt's record, Taft carried the country by well over a million votes, defeating Bryan 321 to 162 in the Electoral College.

Taft was intelligent, experienced, and public spirited; he seemed ideally suited to carry out Roosevelt's policies. Born in Cincinnati in 1857, educated at Yale, he had served as an Ohio judge, as solicitor general of the United States under Benjamin Harrison, and then

as a federal circuit court judge before accepting McKinley's assignment to head the Philippine Commission in 1900. His success as civil governor of the Philippines led Roosevelt to make him secretary of war in 1904.

Taft supported the Square Deal loyally. This, together with his mentor's ardent endorsement, won him the backing of most progressive Republicans. Yet the Old Guard liked him too; although outgoing, he had none of the Roosevelt impetuosity and aggressiveness. His genial personality and his obvious desire to avoid conflict appealed to moderates.

However, Taft lacked the physical and mental stamina required of a modern chief executive. Although not lazy, he weighed over 300 pounds and needed to rest this vast bulk more than the job allowed. He liked to eat in leisurely fashion, to idle away mornings on the golf course, to take an afternoon nap. Campaigning bored him; speech making seemed a useless chore. The judicial life was his real love; intense partisanship dismayed and confused him. He was too reasonable to control a coalition and not ambitious enough to impose his will on others. He found extremists irritating and persistent people (including his wife) difficult to resist. He supported many progressive measures, but he never absorbed the progressive spirit.

Taft honestly wanted to carry out most of Roosevelt's policies. He enforced the Sherman Act vigorously and continued to expand the national forest reserves. He signed the Mann-Elkins Act of 1910, which empowered the ICC to suspend rate increases without waiting for a shipper to complain and established the Commerce Court to speed the settlement of railroad rate cases. An eight-hour day for all persons engaged in work on government contracts, mine safety legislation, and several other reform measures received his approval. He even summoned Congress into special session specifically to reduce tariff duties—something that Roosevelt had not dared to attempt.

But Taft had been disturbed by Roosevelt's sweeping use of executive power. "We have got to work out our problems on the basis of law," he insisted. Whereas Roosevelt had excelled at maneuvering around congressional opposition and at finding ways to accomplish his objectives without waiting for Congress to act, Taft adamantly refused to use such tactics. His restraint was in many ways admirable, but it reduced his effectiveness.

In case after case, Taft's lack of vigor and his political ineptness led to trouble. In the matter of the tariff, he favored downward revision. When the special session met in 1909, the House promptly passed a bill that was in line with his desires. But Senate protectionists restored the high rates of the act of 1897 on most items. A group of insurgent senators, led by Robert La Follette of Wisconsin, fought these changes, producing masses of statistics to show that the proposed

schedules on cotton goods, woolens, and other products were unreasonably high. They were fighting the president's battle, yet Taft did little to help them. He signed the high Payne-Aldrich measure and called it "the best [tariff] bill that the Republican party ever passed." His attitude dumbfounded the progressives.

In 1910 Taft got into difficulty with the conservationists. Although he believed in husbanding natural resources carefully, he did not like the way Roosevelt had circumvented Congress in adding to the forest reserves. He demanded, and eventually obtained, specific legislation to accomplish this purpose. The issue that aroused the conservationists concerned the integrity of his secretary of the interior, Richard A. Ballinger. A less than ardent conservationist, Ballinger returned to the public domain certain waterpower sites that the Roosevelt administration had withdrawn on the legally questionable ground that they were to become ranger stations. Ballinger's action alarmed Chief Forester Gifford Pinchot, the darling of the conservationists. When Pinchot learned that Ballinger intended to validate the shaky claim of mining interests to a large tract of coal-rich land in Alaska, he launched an intemperate attack on the secretary.

In the Ballinger-Pinchot controversy Taft felt obliged to support his own man. The coal lands dispute was complex, and Pinchot's charges were exaggerated. It was certainly unfair to call Ballinger "the most effective opponent the conservation policies have yet had." When Pinchot, whose own motives were partly political, persisted in criticizing Ballinger, Taft dismissed him. He had no choice under the circumstances, but a more adept politician might have found some way of avoiding a showdown.

BREAKUP OF THE REPUBLICAN PARTY

One ominous aspect of the Ballinger-Pinchot affair was that Pinchot was a close friend of Theodore Roosevelt. After Taft's inauguration, Roosevelt had gone off to hunt big game in Africa, bearing in his baggage an autographed photograph of his protégé and a touching letter of appreciation, in which the new president said: "I can never forget that the power I now exercise was a voluntary transfer from you to me." For months, as he trudged across Africa, guns blazing, Roosevelt was out of touch with affairs in the United States. As soon as he emerged from the wilderness in March 1910, bearing more than 3000 trophies, including 9 lions, 5 elephants, and 13 rhinos, he was caught up in the squabble between the progressive members of his party and its titular head. Pinchot met him in Italy, laden with injured innocence and a packet of angry letters from various progressives. TR's intimate friend Senator Henry Cabot Lodge, essentially a conservative, barraged him with

messages, the gist of which was that Taft was lazy and inept and that Roosevelt should prepare to become the "Moses" who would guide the party "out of the wilderness of doubt and discontent" into which Taft had led it.

Roosevelt hoped to steer a middle course, but Pinchot's complaints impressed him. Taft had decided to strike out on his own, he concluded. "No man must render such a service as that I rendered Taft and expect the individual . . . not in the end to become uncomfortable and resentful," he wrote Lodge sadly. Taft sensed the former president's coolness and was offended. He was egged on by his ambitious wife, who wanted him to stand clear of Roosevelt's shadow and establish his own reputation.

Perhaps the resulting rupture was inevitable. The Republican party was dividing into two factions, the progressives and the Old Guard. Forced to choose between them, Taft threw in his lot with the Old Guard. Roosevelt backed the progressives. Speaking at Osawatomie, Kansas, in August 1910, he came out for a comprehensive program of social legislation, which he called the New Nationalism. Besides attacking "special privilege" and the "unfair money-getting" practices of "lawbreakers of great wealth," he called for a broad expansion of federal power. "The betterment we seek must be accomplished," he said, "mainly through the National Government."

The final break came in October 1911, when the president ordered an antitrust suit against U.S. Steel. Roosevelt, of course, opposed breaking up large corporations. "The effort at prohibiting all combination has substantially failed," Taft said. "The way out lies . . . in completely controlling them." He was prepared to enforce the Sherman Act "or die in the attempt." But what angered Roosevelt was Taft's emphasis in the suit on U.S. Steel's absorption of the Tennessee Coal and Iron Company, which Roosevelt had unofficially authorized during the panic of 1907. The government's antitrust brief made Roosevelt appear to have been either an abettor of monopoly or, far worse, a fool who had been duped by the steel corporation. Early in 1912 he declared himself a candidate for the Republican presidential nomination.

Roosevelt plunged into the preconvention campaign with typical energy. He was almost uniformly victorious in states that held presidential primaries, carrying even Ohio, Taft's home state. However, the president controlled the party machinery and entered the national convention with a small majority of the delegates. Since some Taft delegates had been chosen under questionable circumstances, the Roosevelt forces challenged the right of 254 of them to their seats. The Taft-controlled credentials committee, paying little attention to the evidence, gave all but a few of the disputed seats to the president, who then won the nomination on the first ballot.

Had Roosevelt swallowed his resentment and bided his time, Taft would almost certainly have been defeated in the election, and the 1916 Republican nomination would have been Roosevelt's for the asking. But he was understandably outraged by the ruthless manner in which the Taft "steamroller" had overridden his forces. When his leading supporters urged him to organize a third party, and when two of them, George W. Perkins, formerly a partner of the banker J. P. Morgan, and the publisher Frank Munsey, offered to finance the campaign, Roosevelt agreed to make the race.

VIDEO
Bull Moose Campaign Speech

In August, amid scenes of hysterical enthusiasm, the first convention of the Progressive party met at Chicago and nominated him for president. Announcing that he felt "as strong as a bull moose," Roosevelt delivered a stirring "confession of faith," calling for strict regulation of corporations, a tariff commission, national presidential primaries, minimum wage and workers' compensation laws, the elimination of child labor, and many other reforms.

THE ELECTION OF 1912

The Democrats made the most of the opportunity offered by the Republican schism. Had they nominated a conservative or allowed Bryan a fourth chance, they would probably have ensured Roosevelt's election. Instead, after battling through forty-six ballots at their convention in Baltimore, they nominated Woodrow Wilson, who had achieved a remarkable liberal record as governor of New Jersey. Incidentally, Wilson was one of three southern candidates for the nomination, further evidence that the sectional conflicts of Reconstruction had been forgotten.

Although as a political scientist Wilson had criticized the status quo and taken a pragmatic approach to the idea of government regulation of the economy, he had objected strongly to Bryan's brand of politics. In 1896 he voted for the Gold Democratic party candidate instead of Bryan. But by 1912, influenced partly by ambition and partly by the spirit of the times, he had been converted to progressivism. He called his brand of reform the New Freedom.

DOCUMENT
Roosevelt, "The New Nationalism"

The federal government could best advance the cause of social justice, Wilson reasoned, by eradicating the special privileges that enabled the "interests" to flourish. Where Roosevelt had lost faith in competition as a way of protecting the public against monopolies, Wilson insisted that competition could be restored. The government must break up the great trusts, establish fair rules for doing business, and subject violators to stiff punishments. Thereafter, the free enterprise system would protect the public from

exploitation without destroying individual initiative and opportunity. "If America is not to have free enterprise, then she can have freedom of no sort whatever," he said. Although rather vague, this argument appealed to thousands of voters who found the growing power of large corporations disturbing, but who hesitated to make the thoroughgoing commitment to government control of business that Roosevelt was advocating.

Roosevelt's reasoning was perhaps theoretically more sound. He called for a New Nationalism. Laissez-faire made less sense than it had in earlier times. The complexities of the modern world seemed to call for a positive approach, a plan, the close application of human intelligence to social and economic problems.

But being more in line with American experience than the New Nationalism, Wilson's New Freedom had much to recommend it. The danger that selfish individuals would use the power of the state for their own ends had certainly not disappeared, despite the efforts of progressives to make government more responsive to popular opinion. Any considerable expansion of national power, as Roosevelt proposed, would increase the danger and probably create new difficulties. Managing so complicated an enterprise as an industrialized nation was sure to be a formidable task for the federal government. Furthermore, individual freedom of opportunity merited the toleration of a certain amount of inefficiency.

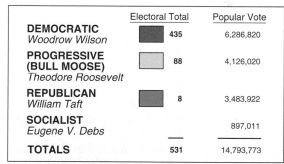

	Electoral Total	Popular Vote
DEMOCRATIC *Woodrow Wilson*	435	6,286,820
PROGRESSIVE (BULL MOOSE) *Theodore Roosevelt*	88	4,126,020
REPUBLICAN *William Taft*	8	3,483,922
SOCIALIST *Eugene V. Debs*		897,011
TOTALS	531	14,793,773

▲ **The Election of 1912**
The fourth-largest vote getter in the election of 1912 was Eugene V. Debs of the Socialist party, who gained about 900,000 popular votes (or approximately 6 percent of the total popular vote) but no electoral votes.

To choose between the New Nationalism and the New Freedom, between the dynamic Roosevelt and the idealistic Wilson, was indeed difficult. Thousands grappled with this problem before going to the polls, but partisan politics determined the outcome of the election. Taft got the hard-core Republican vote but lost the progressive wing of the GOP to Roosevelt. Wilson had the solid support of both conservative and liberal Democrats. As a result, Wilson won an easy victory in the Electoral College, receiving 435 votes to Roosevelt's 88 and Taft's 8. The popular vote was Wilson, 6,286,000; Roosevelt, 4,126,000; and Taft, 3,484,000.

If partisan politics had determined the winner, the election was nonetheless an overwhelming endorsement of progressivism. The temper of the times was shown by the 897,000 votes for Eugene Debs, who was again the Socialist candidate. Altogether, professed liberals amassed over 11 million of the 15 million ballots cast. Wilson was a minority president, but he took office with a clear mandate to press forward with further reforms.

WILSON: THE NEW FREEDOM

No one ever rose more suddenly or spectacularly in American politics than Woodrow Wilson. In the spring of 1910 he was president of Princeton University; he had never held or even run for public office. In the fall of 1912 he was president-elect of the United States. Yet if his rise was meteoric, in a very real sense he had devoted his life to preparing for it. He was born in Staunton, Virginia, in 1856, the son of a Presbyterian minister. As a student he became interested in political theory, dreaming of representing his state in the Senate. He studied law solely because he thought it the best avenue to public office, and when he discovered that he did not like legal work, he took a doctorate at Johns Hopkins in political science.

For years Wilson's political ambitions appeared doomed to frustration. He taught at Bryn Mawr, then at Wesleyan, finally at his alma mater, Princeton. He wrote several influential books, among them *Congressional Government* and *The State,* and achieved an outstanding reputation as a teacher and lecturer. In 1902 he was chosen president of Princeton and soon won a place among the nation's leading educators. He revised the curriculum, introducing many new subjects and insisting that students pursue an organized and integrated course of study. He instituted the preceptorial system, which placed the students in close intellectual and social contact with their teachers. He attracted outstanding young scholars to the Princeton faculty.

In time Wilson's educational ideas and his overbearing manner of applying them got him in trouble with some of Princeton's alumni and trustees. Al-

▲ Woodrow Wilson, presiding over the 1906 Princeton commencement, with steel magnate and educational philanthropist Andrew Carnegie firmly in tow.

though his university career was wrecked, the controversies, in which he appeared to be championing democracy and progress in the face of reactionary opponents, brought him at last to the attention of the politicians. Then, in a great rush, came power and fame.

Wilson was an immediate success as president. Since Roosevelt's last year in office Congress had been almost continually at war with the executive branch and with itself. Legislative achievements had been few. Now a small avalanche of important measures received the approval of the lawmakers. In October 1913 the Underwood Tariff brought the first significant reduction of duties since before the Civil War. To compensate for the expected loss of revenue, the act provided for a graduated tax on personal incomes.

Two months later the Federal Reserve Act gave the country a central banking system for the first time since Jackson destroyed the Bank of the United States. The measure divided the nation into twelve banking districts, each under the supervision of a Federal Reserve bank, a sort of bank for bankers. All national banks in each district and any state banks that wished to participate had to invest 6 percent of their capital and surplus in the reserve bank, which was empowered to exchange (the technical term is *rediscount*) paper money, called Federal Reserve notes, for the commercial and agricultural paper that

member banks took in as security from borrowers. The volume of currency was no longer at the mercy of the supply of gold or any other particular commodity.

The crown and nerve center of the system was the Federal Reserve Board in Washington, which appointed a majority of the directors of the Federal Reserve banks and had some control over rediscount rates (the commission charged by the reserve banks for performing the rediscounting function). The board provided a modicum of public control over the banks, but the effort to weaken the power of the great New York banks by decentralizing the system proved ineffective. Nevertheless, a true central banking system was created.

When inflation threatened, the reserve banks could raise the rediscount rate, discouraging borrowing and thus reducing the amount of money in circulation. In bad times it could lower the rate, making it easier to borrow and injecting new dollars into the economy. Much remained to be learned about the proper management of the money supply, but the nation finally had a flexible yet safe currency.

In 1914 Congress passed two important laws affecting corporations. One created the Federal Trade Commission (FTC) to replace Roosevelt's Bureau of Corporations. In addition to investigating corporations and publishing reports, this nonpartisan board could issue cease-and-desist orders against "unfair" trade practices brought to light through its research. The law did not define the term *unfair,* and the commission's rulings could be taken on appeal to the federal courts, but the FTC was nonetheless a powerful instrument for protecting the public against the trusts.

The second measure, the Clayton Antitrust Act, made certain specific business practices illegal, including price discrimination that tended to foster monopolies; "tying" agreements, which forbade retailers from handling the products of a firm's competitors; and the creation of interlocking directorates as a means of controlling competing companies. The act exempted labor unions and agricultural organizations from the antitrust laws and curtailed the use of injunctions in labor disputes. The officers of corporations could be held individually responsible if their companies violated the antitrust laws.

The Democrats controlled both houses of Congress for the first time since 1890 and were eager to make a good record, but Wilson's imaginative and aggressive use of presidential power was decisive. He called the legislators into special session in April 1913 and appeared before them to lay out his program; he was the first president to address Congress in person since John Adams. Then he followed the course of administration bills closely. He had a private telephone line installed between the Capitol and the White House. Administration representatives haunted the cloakrooms and lobbies of both houses. Cooperative

congressmen began to receive notes of praise and encouragement, recalcitrant ones stern demands for support, often pecked out on the president's own portable typewriter. When lobbyists tried to frustrate his plans for tariff reform by bringing pressure to bear on key senators, he made a dramatic appeal to the people. "The public ought to know the extraordinary exertions being made by the lobby in Washington," he told reporters. "Only public opinion can check and destroy it." The voters responded so strongly that the Senate passed the tariff bill substantially as Wilson desired it.

Wilson explained his success by saying, only half humorously, that running the government was child's play for anyone who had managed the faculty of a university. Responsible party government was his objective; he expected individual Democrats to support the decisions of the party majority, and his idealism never prevented him from awarding the spoils of office to city bosses and conservative congressmen, as long as they supported his program. Nor did his career as a political theorist make him rigid and doctrinaire. In practice the differences between his New Freedom and Roosevelt's New Nationalism tended to disappear. The Underwood Tariff and the Clayton Antitrust Act fitted the philosophy Wilson had expounded during the campaign, but the FTC represented a step toward the kind of regulated economy that Roosevelt advocated. So did the Federal Reserve system.

There were limits to Wilson's progressivism, limits imposed partly by his temperament and partly by his philosophy. He objected as strenuously to laws granting special favors to farmers and workers as to those benefiting the tycoons. When a bill was introduced in 1914 making low-interest loans available to farmers, he refused to support it. "It is unwise and unjustifiable to extend the credit of the Government to a single class of the community," he said. He considered the provision exempting unions from the antitrust laws equally unsound. Nor would he push for a federal law prohibiting child labor; such a measure would be unconstitutional, he believed. He also refused to back the constitutional amendment giving the vote to women.

By the end of 1914 Wilson's record, on balance, was positive but distinctly limited. The president believed that the major progressive goals had been achieved; he had no plans for further reform. Many other progressives thought that a great deal more remained to be done.

THE PROGRESSIVES AND MINORITY RIGHTS

On one important issue, race relations, Wilson was distinctly reactionary. With a mere handful of exceptions, the progressives exhibited strong prejudices against

▲ Although lynchings were common after the Civil War, by the 1890s they had become public spectacles. Sometimes special "excursion" trains were scheduled, employers released workers, and families would bring picnics to the event. This lynching, viewed by a crowd of 10,000, took place at Paris, Texas, in 1893.

nonwhite people and against certain categories of whites as well. Many were as unsympathetic to immigrants from Asia and eastern and southern Europe as any of the "conservative" opponents of immigration in the 1880s and 1890s. The Gentlemen's Agreement excluding Japanese immigrants was reached in 1907 at the height of the progressive movement. In the same year, Congress appointed a commission headed by Senator William Dillingham of Vermont to study the immigration question. The Dillingham Commission labored for more than two years and brought forth a 41-volume report that led in 1913 to a bill restricting the number of newcomers to be admitted and reducing especially the influx from eastern and southern Europe. Only the outbreak of war in Europe in 1914, which cut immigration to a trickle, prevented the passage of this measure.

American Indians were also affected by the progressives' racial attitudes. Where the sponsors of the Dawes Act (1887) had assumed that Indians were inherently capable of adopting the ways of "civilized" people, in the progressive period the tendency was to write Indians off as fundamentally inferior and to assume that they would make second-class citizens at best. Francis Leupp, Theodore Roosevelt's commissioner of Indian affairs, put it this way in a 1905 report: "If nature has set a different physical stamp upon different races of men it is fair to assume that the variation . . . is manifested in mental and moral traits as well. . . . Nothing is gained by trying to undo

nature's work." A leading muckraker, Ray Stannard Baker, who was far more sympathetic to blacks than most progressives, dismissed Indians as pathetic beings, "eating, sleeping, idling, with no more thought of the future than a white man's child."

In 1902 Congress passed the Dead Indian Land Act, which made it easier for Indians to sell allotments that they had inherited, and in 1906 another law further relaxed restrictions on land sales. Efforts to improve the education of Indian children continued, but most progressives assumed that only vocational training would help them. Theodore Roosevelt knew from his experiences as a rancher in the Dakota Territory that Indians could be as energetic and capable as whites, but he considered these "exceptional." As for the rest, it would be many generations before they could be expected to "move forward" enough to become "ordinary citizens," Roosevelt believed.

To say that African Americans did not fare well at the hands of progressives would be a gross understatement. Populist efforts to unite white and black farmers in the southern states had led to the imposition of further repressive measures. Segregation became more rigid, white opposition to black voting more monolithic. In 1900 the body of a Mississippi black was dug up by order of the state legislature and reburied in a segregated cemetery; in Virginia in 1902 the daughter of Robert E. Lee was arrested for riding in the black

DOCUMENT

"Events in Paris, Texas," from Ida B. Wells, *A Red Record*

section of a railroad car. "Insult is being added to injury continually," a black journalist in Alabama complained. "Have those in power forgotten that there is a God?"

Many progressive women, still smarting from the insult to their sex entailed in the Fourteenth and Fifteenth Amendments and eager to attract southern support for their campaign for the vote, adopted racist arguments. They contrasted the supposed corruption and incompetence of black voters with their own "purity" and intelligence. Southern progressives of both sexes argued that disfranchising blacks would reduce corruption by removing from unscrupulous white politicians the temptation to purchase black votes!

The typical southern attitude toward the education of blacks was summed up in a folk proverb: "When you educate a Negro, you spoil a good field hand." In 1910 only about 8000 black children in the entire South were attending high schools. Despite the almost total suppression of black rights, lynchings continued to occur; between 1900 and 1914 more than 1100 blacks were murdered by mobs, most (but not all) in the southern states. In the rare cases in which local prosecutors brought the lynchers to trial, juries almost without exception brought in verdicts of not guilty.

Booker T. Washington was shaken by this trend, but he could find no way to combat it. The times were passing him by. He appealed to his white southern "friends" for help but got nowhere. Increasingly he talked about the virtues of rural life, the evils of big cities, and the uselessness of higher education for black people. By the turn of the century a number of young, well-educated blacks, most of them Northerners, were breaking away from his accommodationist leadership.

BLACK MILITANCY

William E. B. Du Bois was the most prominent of the militants. Du Bois was born in Great Barrington, Massachusetts, in 1868. His father, a restless wanderer of Negro and French Huguenot stock, abandoned the family, and young William grew up on the edge of poverty. Neither accepted nor openly rejected by the overwhelmingly white community, he devoted himself to his studies, showing such brilliance that his future education was ensured by scholarships: to Fisk University, then to Harvard, then to the University of Berlin. In 1895 Du Bois became the first American black to earn a Ph.D. in history from Harvard; his dissertation, *The Suppression of the African Slave Trade* (1896), remains a standard reference.

Personal success and "acceptance" by whites did not make the proud and sensitive Du Bois complacent.

Outraged by white racism and the willingness of many blacks to settle for second-class citizenship, he set out to make American blacks proud of their color— "Beauty is black," he said—and of their African origins and culture.

Like Washington, Du Bois wanted blacks to lift themselves up by their own bootstraps. They must establish their own businesses, run their own newspapers and colleges, write their own literature; they must preserve their identity rather than seek to amalgamate themselves into a society that offered them only crumbs and contempt. At first he cooperated with Washington, but in 1903, in the essay "Of Mr. Booker T. Washington and Others," he subjected Washington's "attitude of adjustment and submission" to polite but searching criticism. Washington had asked blacks to give up political power, civil rights, and the hope of higher education, not realizing that "voting is necessary to modern manhood, that . . . discrimination is barbarism, and that black boys need education as well as white boys." Washington "apologizes for injustice," Du Bois charged. "He belittles the emasculating effects of caste distinctions, and opposes the higher training and ambitions of our brightest minds." Du Bois deemed this totally wrong. "The way for a people to gain their reasonable rights is not by voluntarily throwing them away."

Du Bois was not an uncritical admirer of the ordinary American black. He believed that "immorality, crime, and laziness" were common vices. Quite properly he blamed the weaknesses of blacks on the treatment afforded them by whites, but his approach to the solution of racial problems was frankly elitist. "The Negro race," he wrote, "is going to be saved by its exceptional men," what he called the "talented tenth" of the black population. After describing in vivid detail how white mistreatment had corrupted his people, Du Bois added loftily: "A saving remnant continually survives and persists, continually aspires, continually shows itself in thrift and ability and character." Du Bois, moreover, prided himself on being of mixed races.

Whatever his prejudices, Du Bois exposed both the weaknesses of Washington's strategy and the callousness of white American attitudes. Accommodation was not working. Washington was praised, even lionized by prominent southern whites, yet when Theodore Roosevelt invited him to a meal at the White House they exploded with indignation, and Roosevelt, although not personally prejudiced, meekly backtracked, never repeating his "mistake." He defended his record by saying, "I have stood as valiantly for the rights of the negro as any president since Lincoln." That, sad to relate, was true enough.

Not mere impatience but despair led Du Bois and a few like-minded blacks to meet at Niagara Falls in July 1905 and to issue a stirring list of demands: the unrestricted right to vote, an end to every kind of segregation, equality of economic opportunity, higher education for the talented, equal justice in the courts, and an end to trade-union discrimination. This Niagara movement did not attract mass support, but it did stir the consciences of some whites, many of them the descendants of abolitionists, who were also becoming disenchanted by the failure of accommodation to provide blacks with real opportunity.

In 1909, the centennial of the birth of Abraham Lincoln, a group of these liberals, including the newspaperman Oswald Garrison Villard (grandson of William Lloyd Garrison), the social worker Jane Addams, the philosopher John Dewey, and the novelist William Dean Howells, founded the National Association for the Advancement of Colored People (NAACP). The organization was dedicated to the eradication of racial discrimination. Its leadership was predominantly white in the early years, but Du Bois became a national officer and the editor of its journal, *The Crisis.*

A turning point had been reached. After 1909 virtually every important leader, white and black alike, rejected the Washington approach. More and more, blacks turned to the study of their past in an effort to stimulate pride in their heritage. In 1915 Carter G. Woodson founded the Association for the Study of Negro Life and History; the following year he began editing the *Journal of Negro History,* which became the major publishing organ for scholarly studies on the subject.

This militancy produced few results in the Progressive Era. Theodore Roosevelt behaved no differently than earlier Republican presidents; he courted blacks when he thought it advantageous, turned his back when he did not. When he ran for president on the Progressive ticket in 1912, he pursued a "lily-white" policy, hoping to break the Democrats' monopoly in the South. By trusting in "[white] men of justice and of vision," Roosevelt argued in the face of decades of experience to the contrary, "the colored men of the South will ultimately get justice."

The southern-born Wilson was actively antipathetic to blacks. During the 1912 campaign he appealed to them for support and promised to "assist in advancing the interest of their race" in every possible way. Once elected, he refused even to appoint a privately financed commission to study the race problem. Southerners dominated his administration and Congress; as a result, blacks were further degraded. No fewer than thirty-five blacks in the Atlanta post office lost their jobs. In Washington employees in many government offices were rigidly segregated, and those who objected were summarily discharged.

These actions stirred such a storm that Wilson backtracked a little, but he never abandoned his belief that segregation was in the best interests of both races. "Wilson . . . promised a 'new freedom,'" one newspaperman complained. "On the contrary we are given a stone instead of a loaf of bread." Even Booker T. Washington admitted that his people were more "discouraged and bitter" than at any time in his memory.

Du Bois, who had supported Wilson in 1912, attacked administration policy in *The Crisis.* In November 1914 the militant editor of the *Boston Guardian,* William Monroe Trotter, a classmate of Du Bois at Harvard and a far more caustic critic of the Washington approach, led a delegation to the White House to protest the segregation policy of the government. When Wilson accused him of blackmail, Trotter lost his temper, and an ugly confrontation resulted. The mood of black leaders had changed completely.

By this time the Great War had broken out in Europe. Soon every American would feel its effects, blacks perhaps more than any other group. In November 1915, a year almost to the day after Trotter's clash with Wilson, Booker T. Washington died. One era had ended; a new one was beginning.

▲ A striking likeness of W. E. B. Du Bois drawn by Winold Reiss when Du Bois was in his fifties.

MILESTONES

1890	National American Woman Suffrage Association is founded	1908	Theodore Roosevelt convenes National Conservation Conference
1900	Robert La Follette is elected governor of Wisconsin		*Muller* v. *Oregon* upholds law limiting women's work hours
	McKinley is reelected president		William Howard Taft is elected president
1901	McKinley is assassinated; Theodore Roosevelt becomes president	1909	NAACP is founded
1902	Roosevelt helps settle anthracite coal strike	1910	Ballinger-Pinchot Affair deepens Roosevelt-Taft rift
	Oregon adopts initiative system for proposing legislation	1911	Roosevelt gives New Nationalism speech
1904	Northern Securities case revives Sherman Antitrust Act	1912	Roosevelt runs for president on Progressive ticket
	National Child Labor Committee is established		Woodrow Wilson is elected president
	Theodore Roosevelt is elected president	1913	Sixteenth Amendment authorizes federal income taxes
1905	Anticapitalist Industrial Workers of the World (IWW) is founded		Seventeenth Amendment provides for direct election of U.S. senators
1906	Hepburn Act strengthens Interstate Commerce Commission		Underwood Tariff reduces duties
	Upton Sinclair exposes Chicago slaughterhouses in *The Jungle*		Federal Reserve Act gives the United States a central banking system again
1907	U.S. Steel absorbs Tennessee Coal and Iron Company	1914	Federal Trade Commission is created to protect against trusts
			Clayton Antitrust Act regulates business
		1920	Nineteenth Amendment guarantees women the right to vote

SUPPLEMENTARY READING

The Progressive Era is surveyed in A. S. Link, *Woodrow Wilson and the Progressive Era* (1954), Steven J. Diner, *A Very Different Age* (1997), and Michael McGerr, *A Fierce Discontent: The Rise and Fall of the Progressive Movement in America, 1870–1920* (2003). Two recent scholars examine American progressivism in the context of reform movements elsewhere: Daniel T. Rodgers, *Atlantic Crossings: Social Politics in a Progressive Age* (1998) and Alan Dawley, *Changing the World: American Progressives in War and Revolution* (2003). The works cited in the Debating the Past feature (p. 589) are also essential.

The role of muckraking journalism is explored in David Nasaw, *The Chief: The Life of William Randolph Hearst* (2000). See also D. M. Chalmers, *The Social and Political Ideas of the Muckrakers* (1964), and Peter Lyon, *Success Story: The Life and Times of S. S. McClure* (1963).

On workers and the radical intellectuals, see Leon Fink, *Progressive Intellectuals and the Dilemmas of Democratic Commitment* (1997), Leslie Fishbein, *Rebels in Bohemia* (1982), Thomas Bender, *New York Intellectuals* (1987), Henry F. May, *The End of American Innocence* (1964), and Nathan G. Hale, *Freud and the Americans* (1971).

Studies of the South include Dewey W. Grantham, *The South in Modern America* (1994), and George B. Tindall, *The Emergence of the New South* (1967). For particular states, consult, for Wisconsin, Nancy Unger, *Fighting Bob La Follette* (2000) and Bernard A. Weisberger, *The La Follettes of Wisconsin* (1994); also Hoyt L. Warner, *Progressivism in Ohio* (1964), Sheldon Hackney, *Populism to Progressivism in Alabama* (1969), and Zane L. Miller, *Boss Cox's Cincinnati* (1968). See also John D. Buenker, *Urban Liberalism and Progressive Reform* (1973). Kenneth Finegold, *Experts and Politicians* (1995) compares the struggles between urban machines and reformers in New York, Cleveland, and Chicago. James J. Connolly, *The Triumph of Ethnic Progressivism* (1998) examines the political dynamics in Boston. J. Anthony Lukas, *Big Trouble* (1997), provides a detailed account of labor strife in Idaho and Colorado.

On the woman suffrage campaign, see Ellen Carol DuBois, *Harriot Stanton Blanch and the Winning of Woman Suffrage* (1997), and Gayle Gullett, *Becoming Citizens: The Emergence and Development of the California Women's Movement, 1880–1911* (2000). Other useful works include Lynn D. Gordon, *Gender and Higher Education in the Progressive Era* (1990), Robyn Muncy, *Creating a Female*

Dominion in American Reform, 1890–1935 (1991), and Paula Baker, *The Moral Frameworks of Public Life: Gender, Politics and the State in Rural New York, 1870–1930* (1991). On the plight of orphans, see Linda Gordon, *The Great Arizona Orphan Abduction* (1999).

Books treating special aspects of progressivism include Edward A. Purcell, *Brandeis and the Progressive Constitution* (2000), and Samuel Haber, *Efficiency and Uplift* (1964). On the regulation of business, see Tony Freyer, *Regulating Big Business: Antitrust in Great Britain and America, 1880–1990* (1992), James Weinstein, *The Corporate Ideal and the Liberal State* (1981), Albro Martin, *Enterprise Denied: Origins of the Decline of American Railroads* (1971), and Naomi Lamoreaux, *The Great Merger Movement in American Business, 1895–1940* (1985).

On African Americans, see David Levering Lewis, *W. E. B. DuBois: Biography of a Race, 1868–1919* (1993), and *W. E. B. DuBois: The Fight for Equality, 1919–1963* (2000), Charles F. Kellogg, *NAACP: A History of the National Association for the Advancement of Colored People*

(1970). On the treatment of Indians, consult Frederick E. Hoxie, *A Final Promise: The Campaign to Assimilate the Indians* (1984).

H. W. Brands, *TR* (1997), and William H. Harbaugh, *Power and Responsibility* (1961) provide sound, scholarly treatments of Roosevelt's career. Edmund Morris's *Theodore Rex* (2001) is engaging. An interesting critique of Roosevelt's environmental policies can be found in Karl Jacoby, *Crimes Against Nature* (2001).

On Taft, see Donald F. Anderson, *William Howard Taft: A Conservative's Conception of the Presidency* (1973), and Paolo E. Coletta, *The Presidency of William Howard Taft* (1973). The Republican party breakup and the history of the Progressive party are discussed in John. A. Garraty, *Right-hand Man: The Life of George W. Perkins* (1960).

The standard multi-volume biography of Wilson is Arthur S. Link, *Wilson* (1947–1965). See also August Heckscher, *Woodrow Wilson* (1991), and John A. Garraty, *Woodrow Wilson* (1956).

SUGGESTED WEBSITES

History of the Suffrage Movement
http://www.rochester.edu/SBA
This site includes a chronology, important texts relating to woman suffrage, and bibliographical information about Susan B. Anthony and Elizabeth Cady Stanton.

The Conservation Movement, 1850–1920
http://memory.loc.gov/ammem/amrvhtml/
conshome.html
This American Memory site brings together scores of primary sources and photographs about "the historical formation and cultural foundations of the movement to conserve and protect America's natural heritage."

African American Perspectives: Pamphlets from the Daniel A. P. Murry Collections, 1818–1907
http://memory.loc.gov/ammem/aap/aaphome.html
This collection includes writings of famous African Americans, including Frederick Douglass, Booker T. Washington, Ida B. Wells-Barnett, Benjamin W. Arnett, Alexander Crummel, and Emanuel Love.

Coal Mining During the Gilded Age and Progressive Era
http://www.history.osu.edu/Projects/Gilded_Age/
default.htm
This Ohio State University site examines the development of the coal industry, including the sometimes violent labor–management conflict.

Theodore Roosevelt Association
http://www.theodoreroosevelt.org/
This site contains much bibliographical and research information about Theodore Roosevelt.

NAACP On-line
http://www.naacp.org/past_future/index.html
The National Association for the Advancement of Colored People's official website explains its mission and includes a primary document explaining the start of the NAACP.

The Triangle Shirtwaist Factory Fire, March 25, 1911
http://www.ilr.cornell.edu/trianglefire/
The Kheel Center for Labor–Management Documentation and Cornell University Archives put together this excellent site of oral histories, images, and essays.

Labor–Management Conflict in American History
http://www.history.osu.edu/Projects/Laborconflict/
default.htm
This Ohio State University site includes primary accounts of some of the major events in the history of the labor–management conflict.

Bill Haywood Trial (1907)
http://www.law.umkc.edu/faculty/projects/ftrials/
haywood/haywood.htm
This site contains images, chronology, court, and official documents maintained by Dr. Doug Linder at the University of Missouri—Kansas City Law School.

Theodore Roosevelt
http://www.ipl.org/dir/POTUS/troosevelt.html
This site contains basic factual data about Roosevelt's election and presidency, speeches, and online bibliography.

The 1906 San Francisco Earthquake
http://www-socal.wr.usgs.gov/wald/1906/1906.html
This site contains scholarly articles dealing with the earthquake, its source and history.

Federal Reserve Act of 1913
http://odur.let.rug.nl/~usa/E/usbank/bank13.htm
The federal government's role in U.S. banking was finally resolved in 1913.

William Howard Taft
http://www.ipl.org/dir/POTUS/whtaft.html
This site contains basic factual data about Taft's election and presidency, speeches, and online bibliography

From Isolation to Empire

▼ A fanciful contemporary rendering of the Battle of San Juan Hill, with soldiers in clean, crisp uniforms. Note the Spanish fleet at Santiago Bay in the distance.

CHAPTER CONTENTS

DEBATING THE PAST **Did the United States acquire an overseas empire for economic reasons?**

AMERICAN LIVES **Frederick Funston**

I n the decades following the Civil War, Americans were occupied with exploiting the West and building their great industrial machine. They gave little thought to foreign affairs. Even some American statesmen were curiously disinterested. In 1885 Secretary of State Thomas F. Bayard declared that he looked upon the political intrigues of Europe "with impatience and contempt." During the 1888 presidential campaign Benjamin Harrison reflected a widely held belief when he said that the United States was "an apart nation" and so it should remain. James Bryce made the same point in *The American Commonwealth.* "Happy America," he wrote, stood "apart in a world of her own . . . safe even from menace."

ISOLATION OR IMPERIALISM?

Yet if Americans had little concern for what was going on in Europe, their economic interest in Latin America was great and growing, and in East Asia only somewhat less so. Shifts in foreign commerce resulting from industrialization strengthened this interest with every passing year. Whether one sees isolation or expansion as the hallmark of American foreign policy after 1865 depends on what part of the world one looks at. (See Debating the Past, "Did the United States acquire an overseas empire for economic reasons?" p. 605.)

The disdain of the people of the United States for Europe rested on several historical foundations. Faith in the unique character of American civilization—and the converse of that belief, suspicion of Europe's

supposedly aristocratic and decadent society—formed the chief basis of this isolation. Bitter memories of indignities suffered during the Revolution and the Napoleonic Wars and anger at the hostile attitude of the great powers toward the United States during the Civil War strengthened it, as did the dislike of Americans for the pomp and punctilio of European monarchies. Also important was the undeniable truth that the United States, in an era before airplanes, was virtually invulnerable to European attack and at the same time incapable of mounting an offensive against any European power. In turning their backs on Europe, Americans were taking no risk and passing up few opportunities—hence their indifference.

When occasional conflicts with one or another of the great powers erupted, the United States pressed its claims hard. It insisted, for example, that Great Britain pay for the loss of some 100,000 tons of American shipping sunk by Confederate cruisers that had been built in British yards during the rebellion. Some politicians even demanded that the British pay for the entire cost of the war after the Battle of Gettysburg—some $2 billion—on the grounds that without British backing the Confederacy would have collapsed at about that point. However, the controversy never became critical, and in 1871 the two nations signed the Treaty of Washington, agreeing to arbitrate the so-called *Alabama* claims. The next year the judges awarded the United States $15.5 million for the ships and cargoes that had been destroyed. Such incidents never amounted to much.

ORIGINS OF THE LARGE POLICY: COVETING COLONIES

The nation's interests elsewhere in the world gradually increased. During the Civil War, France had established a protectorate over Mexico, installing the Archduke Maximilian of Austria as emperor. In 1866 Secretary of State William H. Seward demanded that the French withdraw, and the United States moved 50,000 soldiers to the Rio Grande. While fear of American intervention was only one of many reasons for their action, the French pulled their troops out of Mexico during the winter of 1866–1867. Mexican nationalists promptly seized and executed Maximilian. In 1867, at the instigation of Seward, the United States purchased Alaska from Russia for $7.2 million, thereby ridding the continent of another foreign power.

In 1867 the aggressive Seward acquired the Midway Islands in the western Pacific, which had been

discovered in 1859 by an American naval officer, N. C. Brooks. Seward also made overtures toward annexing the Hawaiian Islands, and he looked longingly at Cuba. In 1870 President Grant submitted to the Senate a treaty annexing the Dominican Republic. He applied tremendous pressure in an effort to obtain ratification, thus forcing a "great debate" on extracontinental expansion. Expansionists stressed the wealth and resources of the country, the markets it would provide, even its "salubrious climate." But the arguments of the opposition proved more persuasive. The distance of the Dominican Republic from the continent and its crowded, dark-skinned population of what one congressman called "semi-civilized, semi-barbarous men who cannot speak our language" made annexation unattractive. The treaty was rejected. Seward had to admit that there was no significant support in the country for his expansionist plans. Prevailing opinion was well summarized by a Philadelphia newspaper: "The true interests of the American people will be better served . . . by thorough and complete development of the immense resources of our existing territory than by any rash attempts to increase it."

The internal growth that preoccupied Americans eventually led them to look outward. By the late 1880s the country was exporting a steadily increasing share of its agricultural and industrial output. Exports, only $450 million in 1870, passed the billion-dollar mark early in the 1890s. Imports increased at a rate only slightly less spectacular.

"Uncle Sam Teaching the World"

The character of foreign trade was also changing: Manufactures loomed ever more important among exports until in 1898 the country shipped abroad more manufactured goods than it imported. By this time American steelmakers could compete with producers anywhere in the world. In 1900 one American firm received a large order for steel plates from a Glasgow shipbuilder, and another won contracts for structural steel to be used in constructing bridges for the Uganda Railroad in British East Africa. When a member of Parliament questioned the colonial secretary about the latter deal, the secretary replied: "Tenders [bids] were invited in the United Kingdom . . . [but] one of the American tenders was found to be considerably the lowest in every respect and was therefore accepted." When American industrialists became conscious of their ability to compete with Europeans in far-off markets, they took more interest in world affairs, particularly during periods of depression, when domestic consumption fell.

Shifting intellectual currents further altered the attitudes of Americans. Darwin's theories, applicable by

DEBATING THE PAST

Did the United States acquire an overseas empire for economic reasons? The American flag, second from left, flies over a warehouse in Guangzhou on the south coast of China in the late nineteenth century. The second photo, dated 1898, is of a family of Presbyterian missionaries in Beijing, attended by Chinese servants. In an influential work, diplomat and historian George F. Kennan (1951) contended that expansionist policies during these years were animated by excessive morality and idealism. McKinley went to war with Spain over the injustice of its colonial rule in Cuba, and he claimed to colonize the Philippines to "educate the Filipinos, and uplift and Christianize them." This idealism, Kennan maintained, did not serve the national interest.

During the 1960s and 1970s, however, revisionist historians argued that expansionist schemes were not in the least motivated by idealism. William A. Williams (1972) claimed that American policymakers sought profitable economic penetration of underdeveloped areas. Their subsidiary aim was to encourage these countries to "modernize," that is, to remake themselves in the image of the United States. The Open Door policy, in Williams's view, was not unrealistic and by no means a failure—indeed, it was too successful. He criticized American policy because of its harmful effects on underdeveloped countries. The policy, Williams contended, was "tragic" rather than evil, because its creators were not evil but only possessing limited vision. They did not recognize the contradictions in their ideas and values. They saw American expansion as beneficial to all concerned—and not exclusively in materialistic terms. They genuinely believed that they were exporting democracy along with capitalism and industrialization. Yet while U.S. statesmen abroad certainly sought to fill the warehouses, records show that they spent most of their time speaking with American missionaries and attending to their problems. Religions and moral considerations did matter.

George F. Kennan, *American Diplomacy* (1951), Walter LaFeber, *The New Empire* (1963), William Appleman Williams, *The Tragedy of American Diplomacy* (1972), Thomas J. McCormick, *China Market* (1967).

DOCUMENT

Strong, from
Our Country

analogy to international relations, gave the concept of manifest destiny a new plausibility. Darwinists like the historian John Fiske argued that the American democratic system of government was so clearly the world's "fittest" that it was destined to spread peacefully over "every land on the earth's surface." In *Our Country* (1885) Josiah Strong found racist and religious justifications for American expansionism, again based on the theory of evolution. The Anglo-Saxon race, centered now in the United States, possessed "an instinct or genius for colonization," Strong claimed. "God, with infinite wisdom and skill is training the Anglo-Saxon race for . . . the final competition of races." Soon American civilization would "move down upon" Mexico and all Latin America and "out upon the islands of the sea, over upon Africa and beyond." "Can anyone doubt," Strong asked, "that the result of this . . . will be 'the survival of the fittest'?"[1]

_____

[1]In later writings Strong insisted that by "fittest" he meant "social efficiency," not "mere strength."

The completion of the conquest of the American West encouraged Americans to consider expansion beyond the seas. "For nearly 300 years the dominant fact in American life has been expansion," declared Frederick Jackson Turner, propounder of the frontier thesis. "That these energies of expansion will no longer operate would be a rash prediction." Turner and writers who advanced other expansionist arguments were much influenced by foreign thinking. European liberals had tended to disapprove of colonial ventures, but in the 1870s and 1880s many of them were changing their minds. English liberals in particular began to talk and write about the "superiority" of English culture, to describe the virtues of the "Anglo-Saxon race," to stress a "duty" to spread Christianity among the heathen, and to advance economic arguments for overseas expansion.

European ideas were reinforced for Americans by their observation of the imperialist activities of the European powers in what would today be called underdeveloped areas. "While the great powers of Europe are steadily enlarging their colonial domination in Asia and Africa," James G. Blaine said in 1884, "it is the especial province of this country to improve and expand its trade with the nations of America." While Blaine emphasized commerce, the excitement and adventure of overseas enterprises appealed to many people even more than the economic possibilities or any sense of obligation to fulfill a supposed national, religious, or racial destiny.

Finally, military and strategic arguments were advanced to justify adopting a "large" policy. The powerful Union army had been demobilized rapidly after Appomattox; in the 1880s only about 25,000 men were under arms, their chief occupation fighting Indians in the West.

Half the navy, too, had been scrapped after the war, and the remaining ships were obsolete. While other nations were building steam-powered iron warships, the United States still depended on wooden sailing vessels. In 1867 a British naval publication accurately described the American fleet as "hapless, broken-down, tattered [and] forlorn."

Although no foreign power menaced the country, the decrepit state of the navy vexed many of its officers and led one of them, Captain Alfred Thayer Mahan, to develop a startling theory about the importance of sea power. He explained his theory in two important books, *The Influence of Sea Power Upon History* (1890) and *The Influence of Sea Power Upon the French Revolution and Empire* (1892). According to Mahan, history proved that a nation with a powerful navy and the overseas bases necessary to maintain

it would be invulnerable in war and prosperous in time of peace. Applied to the current American situation, this meant that in addition to building a modern fleet, the United States should obtain a string of coaling stations and bases in the Caribbean, annex the Hawaiian Islands, and cut a canal across Central America. A more extensive colonial empire might follow, but these bases and the canal they would protect were essential first steps to ensure America's future as a great power.

Writing at a time when the imperialist-minded European nations showed signs of extending their influence in South America and the Pacific islands, Mahan attracted many influential disciples. One was Congressman Henry Cabot Lodge of Massachusetts, a prominent member of the Naval Affairs Committee. Lodge had married into a navy family and was close with the head of the new Naval War College, Commodore Stephen B. Luce. In 1883 he helped push through Congress an act authorizing the building of three steel warships, and he consistently advocated expanding and modernizing the fleet. Elevated to the Senate in 1893, Lodge pressed for expansionist policies, basing his arguments on the strategic concepts of Mahan. "Sea power," he proclaimed, "is essential to the greatness of every splendid people." Lodge's friend Theodore Roosevelt was another ardent supporter of the "large" policy, but he had little influence until McKinley appointed him assistant secretary of the navy in 1897.

TOWARD AN EMPIRE IN THE PACIFIC

The interest of the United States in the Pacific and East Asia began in the late eighteenth century, when the first American merchant ship dropped anchor in Canton harbor. After the Treaty of Wanghia (1844), American merchants in China enjoyed many privileges and trade expanded rapidly. Missionaries began to flock into the country—in the late 1880s, over 500 were living there.

The Hawaiian Islands were an important way station on the route to China, and by 1820 merchants and missionaries were making contacts there. As early as 1854 a movement to annex the islands existed, although it foundered because Hawaii insisted on being admitted to the Union as a state. Commodore Perry's expedition to Japan led to the signing of a commercial treaty (1858) that opened several Japanese ports to American traders.

The United States pursued a policy of cooperating with the European powers in expanding commercial

opportunities in East Asia. In Hawaii the tendency was to claim a special position but to accept the fact that Europeans also had interests in the islands. This state of affairs did not change radically following the Civil War. Despite Chinese protests over the exclusion of their nationals from the United States after 1882, American commercial privileges in China were not disturbed.

American influence in Hawaii increased steadily; the descendants of missionary families, most of them engaged in raising sugar, dominated the Hawaiian monarchy. While they made no overt effort to make the islands an American colony, all the expansionist ideas of the era—manifest destiny, Darwinism, Josiah Strong's racist and religious assumptions, and the relentless force of American commercial interests—pointed them in that direction. In 1875 a reciprocity treaty admitted Hawaiian sugar to the United States free of duty in return for a promise to yield no territory to a foreign power. When this treaty was renewed in 1887, the United States obtained the right to establish a naval base at Pearl Harbor. In addition to occupying Midway, America obtained a foothold in the Samoan Islands in the South Pacific.

During the 1890s American interest in the Pacific area steadily intensified. Conditions in Hawaii had much to do with this. The McKinley Tariff Act of 1890, discontinuing the duty on raw sugar and compensating American producers of cane and beet sugar by granting them a bounty of 2 cents a pound, struck Hawaiian sugar growers hard, for it destroyed the advantage they had gained in the reciprocity treaty.

The following year the death of the complaisant King Kalakaua brought Queen Liliuokalani, a determined nationalist, to the throne. Placing herself at the head of a "Hawaii for the Hawaiians" movement, she abolished the existing constitution under which the white minority had pretty much controlled the islands and attempted to rule as an absolute monarch. The resident Americans then staged a coup. In January 1893, with the connivance of the U.S. minister, John L. Stevens, who ordered 150 marines from the cruiser *Boston* into Honolulu, they deposed Queen Liliuokalani and set up a provisional government. Stevens recognized their regime at once, and the new government sent a delegation to Washington to seek a treaty of annexation.

In the closing days of the Harrison administration such a treaty was negotiated and sent to the Senate, but when Cleveland took office in March, he withdrew it. The new president disapproved of the way American troops had been used to overthrow the monarchy. He sent a special commis-

▲ Sugar planters deposed Hawaii's Queen Liliuokalani, a determined nationalist, in 1893 and requested United States annexation. This 1887 portrait of Queen Liliuokalani was taken in London during Queen Victoria's jubilee.

sioner, James H. Blount, to Hawaii to investigate. When Blount reported that the Hawaiians opposed annexation, the president dismissed Stevens and attempted to restore Queen Liliuokalani. Since the provisional government was by that time firmly entrenched, this could not be accomplished peacefully. Because Cleveland was unwilling to use force against the Americans in the islands, however much he objected to their actions, he found himself unable to do anything. The revolutionary government of Hawaii remained in power, independent yet eager to be annexed.

The Hawaiian debate continued sporadically over the next four years. It provided a thorough airing of the question of overseas expansion. Fears that another power—Great Britain or perhaps Japan—might step into the void created by Cleveland's refusal to act alarmed those who favored annexation.

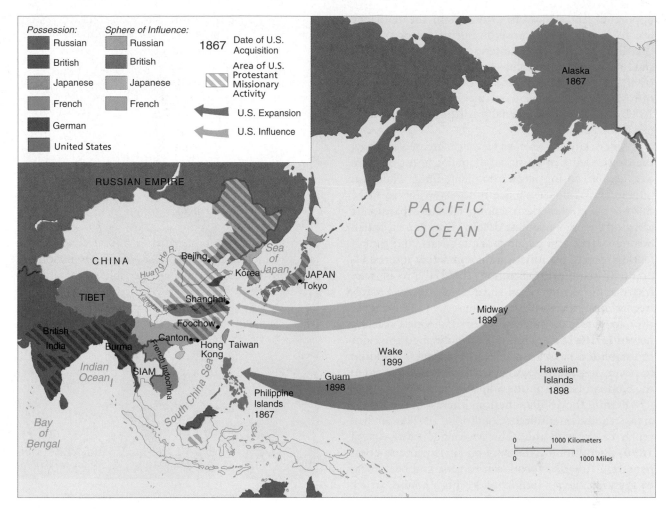

▲ **The Course of Empire, 1867–1901**

When the Republicans returned to power in 1897, a new annexation treaty was negotiated, but domestic sugar producers now threw their weight against it, and the McKinley administration could not obtain the necessary two-thirds majority in the Senate. Finally, in July 1898, after the outbreak of the Spanish-American War, Congress annexed the islands by joint resolution, a procedure requiring only a simple majority vote.

Toward an Empire in Latin America

Most of the arguments for extending American influence in the Pacific applied more strongly to Central and South America, where the United States had much larger economic interests and where the strategic importance of the region was clear. Furthermore, the Monroe Doctrine had long conditioned the American people to the idea of acting to protect national interests in the Western Hemisphere.

As early as 1869 President Grant had come out for an American-owned canal across the isthmus of Panama, in spite of the fact that the United States had agreed in the Clayton-Bulwer Treaty with Great Britain (1850) that neither nation would "obtain or maintain for itself any exclusive control" over an interoceanic canal. In 1880, when the French engineer Ferdinand de Lesseps organized a company to build a canal across the isthmus, President Hayes announced that the United States would not permit a European power to control such a waterway. "The policy of the country is a canal under American control," he announced, another blithe disregard of the Clayton-Bulwer agreement.

When Cleveland returned to power in 1893, the possibility of trouble in Latin America seemed remote, for he had always opposed imperialistic ventures. Yet scarcely two years later the United States was again on the verge of war in South America as a result of a crisis in Venezuela, and before this issue was settled Cleveland had made the most powerful claim to American hegemony in the hemisphere ever uttered. The tangled borderland between Venezuela and British Guiana had long been in dispute, Venezuela demanding more of the region than it was entitled to and Great Britain making exaggerated claims and imperiously refusing to submit the question to arbitration. What made a crisis of the controversy was the political situation in the United States. With his party rapidly deserting him because of his stand on the silver question, and with the election of 1896 approaching, President Cleveland desperately needed a popular issue.

There was considerable latent anti-British feeling in the United States. By taking the Venezuelan side in the boundary dispute, Cleveland would be defending a weak neighbor against a great power, a position certain to evoke a popular response. "Turn this Venezuela question up or down, North, South, East or West, and it is a winner" one Democrat advised the president.

Cleveland did not resist the temptation to intervene. In July 1895 he ordered Secretary of State Richard Olney to send a near ultimatum to the British. By occupying the disputed territory, Olney insisted, Great Britain was invading Venezuela and violating the Monroe Doctrine. Quite gratuitously, he went on to boast: "Today the United States is practically sovereign on this continent, and its fiat is law upon the subjects to which it confines its interposition." Unless Great Britain responded promptly by agreeing to arbitration, the president would call the question to the attention of Congress.

The note threatened war, but the British ignored it for months. They did not take the United States seriously as a world power, and with reason, for the American navy, although expanding, could not hope to stand up against the British, who had 50 battleships, 25 armored cruisers, and many smaller vessels. When Lord Salisbury, the prime minister and foreign secretary, finally replied, he rejected outright the argument that the Monroe Doctrine had any status under international law and refused to arbitrate what he called the "exaggerated pretensions" of the Venezuelans.

If Olney's note had been belligerent, this reply was supercilious and sharp to the point of asperity. Cleveland was furious. On December 17, 1895, he asked Congress for authority to appoint an American commission to determine the correct line between British Guiana and Venezuela. When that had been done, he added, the United States should "resist by every means in its power" the appropriation by Great Britain of any territory "we have determined of right belongs to Venezuela." Congress responded at once, unanimously appropriating $100,000 for the boundary commission. Popular approval was almost universal.

In Great Britain government and people suddenly awoke to the seriousness of the situation. No one wanted a war with the United States over a remote patch of tropical real estate. In Europe, Britain was concerned about German economic competition and the increased military power of that nation. In addition Canada would be terribly vulnerable to American attack in the event of war. The immense potential strength of the United States could no longer be ignored. Why make an enemy of a nation of 70 million, already the richest industrial power in the world? To fight with the United States, the British colonial secretary realized, "would be an absurdity as well as a crime."

Great Britain agreed to arbitrate the boundary. The war scare subsided; soon Olney was talking about "our inborn and instinctive English sympathies" and offering "to stand side by side and shoulder to shoulder with England in . . . the defense of human rights." When the boundary tribunal awarded nearly all the disputed region to Great Britain, whatever ill feeling the surrender may have occasioned in that country faded away. Instead of leading to war, the affair marked the beginning of an era of Anglo-American friendship. It had the unfortunate effect, however, of adding to the long-held American conviction that the nation could get what it wanted in international affairs by threat and bluster—a dangerous illusion.

THE CUBAN REVOLUTION

On February 10, 1896, scarcely a week after Venezuela and Great Britain had signed the treaty ending their dispute, General Valeriano Weyler arrived in Havana from Spain to take up his duties as governor of Cuba. His assignment to this post was occasioned by the guerrilla warfare that Cuban nationalist rebels had been waging for almost a year. Weyler, a tough and ruthless soldier, set out to administer Cuba with "a salutary rigor." He began herding the rural population into wretched "reconcentration" camps to

▲ Instability in Latin America led many to speculate that the United States would play an increasingly dominant role in the region. In Louis Dalrymple's 1895 cartoon, Uncle Sam wins the affection of the damsel Cuba as Spanish misrule and native insurgency lay waste to each other.

deprive the rebels of food and recruits. Resistance in Cuba hardened.

The United States had been interested in Cuba since the time of John Quincy Adams and, were it not for northern opposition to adding more slave territory, might well have obtained the island one way or another before 1860. When the Cubans revolted against Spain in 1868, considerable support for intervening on their behalf developed. Hamilton Fish, Grant's secretary of state, resisted this sentiment, and Spain managed to pacify the rebels in 1878 by promising reforms. But change was slow in coming—slavery was not abolished until 1886. The worldwide depression of the 1890s hit the Cuban economy hard, and when an American tariff act in 1894 jacked up the rate on Cuban sugar by 40 percent, thus cutting off Cuban growers from the American market, the resulting distress precipitated another revolt.

Public sympathy in the United States went to the Cubans, who seemed to be fighting for liberty and democracy against an autocratic Old World power. Most newspapers supported the rebels; labor unions, veterans' organizations, many Protestant clergymen, a great majority of American blacks, and important politicians in both major parties demanded that the United States aid their cause. Rapidly increasing American investments in Cuban sugar plantations, now approaching $50 million, were endangered by the fighting and by the social chaos sweeping across the island.

Cuban propagandists in the United States played on American sentiments cleverly. When reports, often exaggerated, of the cruelty of "Butcher" Weyler and the horrors of his reconcentration camps filtered into America, the cry for action intensified. In April 1896 Congress adopted a resolution suggesting that the revolutionaries be granted the rights of belligerents. Since this would have been akin to formal recognition, Cleveland would not go that far, but he did exert diplomatic pressure on Spain to remove the causes of the rebels' complaints, and he offered the services of his government as mediator. The Spanish rejected the suggestion. For a time the issue subsided. The election of 1896 deflected American attention from Cuba, and then McKinley refused to take any action that might disturb Spanish-American relations. Business interests—except

▲ The explosion of the *Maine* in Havana harbor, killing 260 men, caused much speculation in the newspapers and across the nation as to its cause. Many Americans pointed the finger at Spain, a reaction that typified American sentiment toward the Spanish in 1898. What really caused the explosion remains unknown. Each of the colors for this chromolithograph, by Louis Kurz and Alexander Allison, was produced from a different lithographer stone.

those with holdings in Cuba—backed McKinley, for they feared that a crisis would upset the economy, which was just beginning to pick up after the depression. In Cuba General Weyler made some progress toward stifling rebel resistance.

American expansionists, however, continued to demand intervention, and the press, especially Joseph Pulitzer's *New York World* and William Randolph Hearst's *New York Journal,* competing fiercely to increase circulation, kept resentment alive with tales of Spanish atrocities. McKinley remained adamant. Although he warned Spain that Cuba must be pacified, and soon, his tone was friendly and he issued no ultimatum. A new government in Spain relieved the situation by recalling Weyler and promising partial self-government to the Cubans. In a message to Congress in December 1897, McKinley urged that Spain be

given "a reasonable chance to realize her expectations" in the island. McKinley was not insensible to Cuba's plight—while far from being a rich man, he made an anonymous contribution of $5000 to the Red Cross Cuban relief fund—but he genuinely desired to avoid intervention.

His hopes were doomed, primarily because Spain failed to "realize her expectations." The fighting in Cuba continued. When riots broke out in Havana in January 1898, McKinley ordered the battleship *Maine* to Havana harbor to protect American citizens.

Shortly thereafter Hearst's *New York Journal* printed a letter written to a friend in Cuba by the Spanish minister in Washington, Dupuy de Lôme. The letter had been stolen by a spy. De Lôme, an experienced but arrogant diplomat, failed to appreciate McKinley's efforts to avoid intervening in Cuba. In

the letter he characterized the president as a *politicastro*, or "small-time politician," which was a gross error, and a "bidder for the admiration of the crowd," which was equally insulting though somewhat closer to the truth. Americans were outraged, and de Lôme's hasty resignation did little to soothe their feelings.

VIDEO
Burial of the *Maine* Victims

Then, on February 15, the *Maine* exploded and sank in Havana harbor, 260 of the crew perishing in the disaster. Interventionists in the United States accused Spain of having destroyed the ship and clamored for war. The willingness of Americans to blame Spain indicates the extent of anti-Spanish opinion in the United States by 1898. No one has ever discovered what actually happened. A naval court of inquiry decided that the vessel had been sunk by a submarine mine, but it now seems more likely that an internal explosion destroyed the *Maine*. The Spanish government could hardly have been foolish enough to commit an act that would probably bring American troops into Cuba.

With admirable courage, McKinley refused to panic; but he could not resist the wishes of millions of citizens that something be done to stop the fighting and allow the Cubans to determine their own fate. Spanish pride and Cuban patriotism had taken the issue of peace or war out of the president's hands. Spain could not put down the rebellion, and it would not yield to the nationalists' increasingly extreme demands. To have granted independence to Cuba might have caused the Madrid government to fall, might even have led to the collapse of the monarchy, for the Spanish public was in no mood to surrender. The Cubans, sensing that the continuing bloodshed aided their cause, refused to give the Spanish regime room to maneuver. After the *Maine* disaster, Spain might have agreed to an armistice had the rebels asked for one, and in the resulting negotiations it might well have given up the island. The rebels refused to make the first move. The fighting continued, bringing the United States every day closer to intervention.

The president faced a dilemma. Most of the business interests of the country, to which he was particularly sensitive, opposed intervention. His personal feelings were equally firm. "I have been through one war," he told a friend. "I have seen the dead piled up, and I do not want to see another." Congress, however, seemed determined to act. When he submitted a restrained report on the sinking of the *Maine*, the Democrats in Congress, even most of those who had supported Cleveland's policies, gleefully accused him of timidity. Vice President

Garret A. Hobart warned him that the Senate could not be held in check for long; should Congress declare war on its own, the administration would be discredited.

McKinley spent a succession of sleepless nights; sedatives brought him no repose. Finally, early in April, the president drafted a message asking for authority to use the armed forces "to secure a full and final termination of hostilities" in Cuba.

At the last moment the Spanish government seemed to yield; it ordered its troops in Cuba to cease hostilities. McKinley passed this information on to Congress along with his war message, but he gave it no emphasis and did not try to check the march toward war. To seek further delay would have been courageous but not necessarily wiser. Merely to stop fighting was not enough. The Cuban nationalists now insisted on full independence, and the Spanish politicians were unprepared to abandon the last remnant of their once-great American empire. If the United States took Cuba by force, the Spanish leaders might save their political skins; if they meekly surrendered the island, they were done for.

THE "SPLENDID LITTLE" SPANISH-AMERICAN WAR

On April 20, 1898, Congress, by joint resolution, recognized the independence of Cuba and authorized the use of the armed forces to drive out the Spanish. An amendment proposed by Senator Henry M. Teller disclaiming any intention of adding Cuban territory to the United States passed without opposition. Four days later Spain declared war on the United States.

The Spanish-American War was fought to free Cuba, but the first action took place on the other side of the globe, in the Philippine Islands. Weeks earlier, Theodore Roosevelt, at the time assistant secretary of the navy, had alerted Commodore George Dewey, who was in command of the United States Asiatic Squadron located at Hong Kong, to move against the Spanish base at Manila if war came. Dewey had acted promptly, drilling his gun crews, taking on supplies, giving his gleaming white ships a coat of battle-gray paint, and establishing secret contacts with the Filipino nationalist leader, Emilio Aguinaldo. When word of the declaration of war reached him, Dewey steamed from Hong Kong across the South China Sea with four cruisers and two gunboats. On the night of April 30 he entered

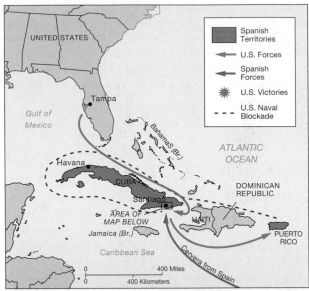

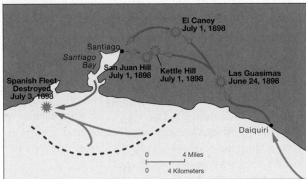

▲ Spanish-American War: Caribbean Theater

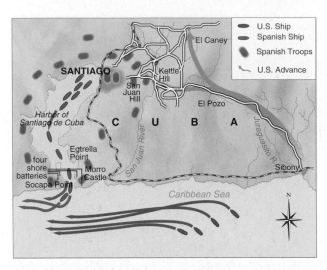

▲ Spanish Debacle at Santiago, June 3, 1898

VIDEO

Roosevelt's
Rough Riders

Manila Bay, and at daybreak he opened fire on the Spanish fleet at 5000 yards. His squadron made five passes, each time reducing the range; when the smoke had cleared, all ten of Admiral Montojo's ships had been destroyed. Not a single American was killed in the engagement.

Dewey immediately asked for troops to take and hold Manila, for now that war had been declared, he could not return to Hong Kong or put in at any other neutral port. McKinley took the fateful step of dispatching some 11,000 soldiers and additional naval support. On August 13 these forces, assisted by Filipino irregulars under Aguinaldo, captured Manila.

Meanwhile, in Cuba, the United States had won a swift and total victory, though more because of the weakness of the Spanish armed forces than because of the power or efficiency of the American. When the war began, the U.S. regular

army consisted of about 28,000 men. This tiny force was bolstered by 200,000 hastily enlisted volunteers. In May an expeditionary force gathered at Tampa, Florida. That hamlet was inundated by the masses of men and supplies that descended upon it. Entire regiments sat without uniforms or weapons while hundreds of freight cars jammed with equipment lay forgotten on sidings. Army management was abominable, rivalry between commanders a serious problem. Aggressive units like the regiment of "Rough Riders" raised by Theodore Roosevelt, who had resigned his navy department post to become a lieutenant colonel of volunteers, scrambled for space and supplies, shouldering aside other units to get what they needed. "No words could describe . . . the confusion and lack of system and the general mismanagement of affairs here," the angry Roosevelt complained.

Since a Spanish fleet under Admiral Pascual Cervera was known to be in Caribbean waters, no invading army could safely embark until the fleet could be located. On May 29 American ships found Cervera at Santiago harbor, on the eastern end of Cuba, and established a blockade. In June a 17,000-man expeditionary force commanded by General William Shafter landed at Daiquiri, east of Santiago, and pressed quickly toward the city, handicapped more by its own bad staff work than by the enemy, though the Spanish troops resisted bravely. The Americans sweated through Cuba's torrid summer in heavy wool winter uniforms, ate "embalmed beef" out of cans, and fought mostly with old-fashioned rifles using black powder cartridges that marked the position of each soldier with a puff of smoke whenever he pulled the

▲ Admiral Dewey aboard the *Olympia,* directing the attack on the Spanish fleet at Manila Bay, which Dewey suspected of being mined. Dewey's nephew, who commanded a supply ship with the fleet, proposed to lead the way into the bay. "Billy," responded Dewey, "mines or no mines, I am leading the squadron in myself." But Dewey's squadron had arrived before the harbor had been mined and it entered unharmed.

trigger. On July 1 they broke through undermanned Spanish defenses and stormed San Juan Hill, the intrepid Roosevelt in the van. ("Are you afraid to stand up while I am on horseback?" Roosevelt demanded of one soldier.)

With Santiago harbor in range of American artillery, Admiral Cervera had to run the blockade. On July 3 his black-hulled ships, flags proudly flying, steamed forth from the harbor and fled westward along the coast. Like hounds after rabbits, five American battleships and two cruisers, commanded by Rear Admiral William T. Sampson and Commodore Winfield Scott Schley, ran them down. In four hours the entire Spanish force was destroyed by a hail of 8-inch and 13-inch projectiles (the size of artillery shells refers to their diameter). Damage to the American ships was superficial; only one American seaman lost his life in the engagement.

The end then came abruptly. Santiago surrendered on July 17. A few days later, other U.S. troops completed the occupation of Puerto Rico. On August 12, one day before the fall of Manila, Spain agreed to get out of Cuba and to cede Puerto Rico and an island in the Marianas (Guam) to the United States. The future of the Philippines was to be settled at a formal peace conference, convening in Paris on October 1.

DEVELOPING A COLONIAL POLICY

Although the Spanish resisted surrendering the Philippines at Paris, they had been so thoroughly defeated that they had no choice. The decision hung rather on the outcome of a conflict over policy within the United States. The war, won at so little cost militarily, produced problems far larger than those it solved.[2] The nation had become a great power in the world's eyes. As a French diplomat wrote a few years later, "[The United States] is seated at the table where the great game is played, and it cannot leave it." European leaders had been impressed by the forcefulness of Cleveland's diplomacy in the Venezuela boundary dispute and by the efficiency displayed by the navy in the war. The annexation of Hawaii and other overseas bases intensified their conviction that the United States was determined to become a major force in international affairs.

But were the American people determined to exercise that force? The debate over taking the Philippine Islands throws much light on their attitudes. The imagination of Americans had been captured by the trappings of empire, not by its essence. It was titillating to think of a world map liberally sprinkled with American flags and of the economic benefits that colonies might bring, but most citizens were not prepared to join in a worldwide struggle for power and influence. They entered blithely on adventures in far-off regions without facing the implications of their decision.

Since the United States (in the Teller Amendment) had abjured any claim to Cuba, even though the island had long been desired by expansionists, logic dictated that a similar policy be applied to the Philippines, a remote land few Americans had ever thought about before 1898. But expansionists were eager to annex the entire archipelago. Even before he had learned to spell the name, Senator Lodge was saying that "the Phillipines [sic] mean a vast future trade

---

[2]More than 5000 Americans died as a result of the conflict, but fewer than 400 fell in combat. The others were mostly victims of yellow fever, typhoid, and other diseases.

and wealth and power," offering the nation a greater opportunity "than anything that has happened . . . since the annexation of Louisiana."

President McKinley adopted a more cautious stance, but he too favored "the general principle of holding on to what we can get." A speaking tour of the Midwest in October 1898, during which he experimented with varying degrees of commitment to expansionism, convinced him that the public wanted the islands. Business opinion had shifted dramatically during the war. Business leaders were now calling the Philippines the gateway to the markets of East Asia.

THE ANTI-IMPERIALISTS

The war had produced a wave of unifying patriotic feeling. It greatly furthered reconciliation between the North and the South; two major generals, for example, were Confederate veterans. But victory raised new divisive questions. An important minority objected strongly to the U.S. acquisition of overseas possessions. Persons as different in interest and philosophy as the tycoon Andrew Carnegie and the labor leader Samuel Gompers, as the venerable Republican Senator George Frisbie Hoar of Massachusetts and "Pitchfork Ben" Tillman, the southern Democratic firebrand, together with the writers Mark Twain and William Dean Howells, the reformers Lincoln Steffens and Jane Addams, and the educators Charles W. Eliot of Harvard and David Starr Jordan of Stanford united in opposing the annexation of the Philippines.

The anti-imperialists insisted that since no one would consider statehood for the Philippines, it would be unconstitutional to annex them. It was a violation of the spirit of the Declaration of Independence to govern a foreign territory without the consent of its inhabitants, Senator Hoar argued; by taking over "vassal states" in "barbarous archipelagoes" the United States was "trampling . . . on our own great Charter, which recognizes alike the liberty and the dignity of individual manhood."

McKinley was not insensitive to this appeal to idealism and tradition, which was the fundamental element in the anti-imperialist argument. But he rejected it for several reasons. Many people who opposed Philippine annexation were neither idealists nor constitutional purists. Partisanship led numbers of Democrats to object. Other anti-imperialists were governed by racial and ethnic prejudices, as Senator Hoar's statement indicates. They opposed

not expansion as such—Carnegie, for example, was eager to have Canada added to the Union—but expansion that brought under the American flag people whom they believed unfit for American citizenship. Labor leaders particularly feared the competition of "the Chinese, the Negritos, and the Malays" who presumably would flood into the United States if the Philippines were taken.

More compelling to McKinley was the absence of any practical alternative to annexation. Public opinion would not sanction restoring Spanish authority in the Philippines or allowing some other power to have them. That the Filipinos were sufficiently advanced and united socially to form a stable government if granted independence seemed unlikely. Senator Hoar believed that "for years and for generations, and perhaps for centuries, there would have been turbulence, disorder and revolution" in the islands if they were left to their own devices.

Strangely—for he was a kind and gentle man— Hoar faced this possibility with equanimity. McKinley was unable to do so. The president searched the depths of his soul and could find no solution but annexation. Of course the state of public feeling made the decision easier, and he probably found the idea of presiding over an empire appealing. Certainly the commercial possibilities did not escape him. In the end it was with a heavy sense of responsibility that he ordered the American peace commissioners to insist on acquiring the Philippines. To salve the feelings of the Spanish the United States agreed to pay $20 million for the archipelago, but it was a forced sale, accepted by Spain under duress.

The peace treaty faced a hard battle in the U.S. Senate, where a combination of partisan politics and anticolonialism made it difficult to amass the two-thirds majority necessary for ratification. McKinley had shrewdly appointed three senators, including one Democrat, to the peace commission. This predisposed many members of the upper house to approve the treaty, but the vote was close. William Jennings Bryan, titular head of the Democratic party, could probably have prevented ratification had he urged his supporters to vote nay. Although he was opposed to taking the Philippines, he did not do so. To reject the treaty would leave the United States technically at war with Spain and the fate of the Philippines undetermined; better to accept the islands and then grant them independence. The question should be decided, Bryan said, "not by a minority of the Senate but by a majority of the people" at the next presidential election. Perplexed by Bryan's stand, a number of Democrats allowed themselves to be persuaded by the expansionists'

arguments and by McKinley's judicious use of patronage; the treaty was ratified in February 1899 by a vote of 57 to 27.

THE PHILIPPINE INSURRECTION

DOCUMENT

Twain, "Incident in the Philippines"

The national referendum that Bryan had hoped for never materialized. Bryan himself confused the issue in 1900 by making free silver a major plank in his platform, thereby driving conservative anti-imperialists into McKinley's arms. Moreover, early in 1899 the Filipino nationalists under Aguinaldo, furious because the United States would not withdraw, took up arms. A savage guerrilla war resulted, one that cost far more in lives and money than the "splendid little" Spanish-American conflict.

IMAGE

Filipino Guerillas

Like all conflicts waged in tangled country chiefly by small, isolated units surrounded by a hostile civilian population, neither side displayed much regard for the "rules" of war. Goaded by sneak attacks and instances of cruelty to captives, American soldiers, most of whom had little respect for Filipinos to begin with, responded in kind. (See American Lives, "Frederick Funston," pp. 621–622.) Civilians were rounded up, prisoners tortured, property destroyed. Horrifying tales of rape, arson, and murder by U.S. troops filtered into the country, providing ammunition for the anti-imperialists. "You seem to have about finished your work of civilizing the Filipinos," Andrew Carnegie wrote angrily to one of the American peace commissioners. "About 8000 of them have been completely civilized and sent to Heaven. I hope you like it." In fact, far more than 8000 Filipinos lost their lives during the conflict, which raged for three years. More than 70,000 American soldiers had to be sent to the islands before the resistance was crushed, and about as many of them lost their lives as had perished in the Cuban conflict.

A commission that had been sent to the Philippines by McKinley in 1899 before the fighting started to study the problem attributed the insurrection to the ambitions of the nationalist leaders and recommended that the Philippines be granted independence at an indefinite future date. In 1900 McKinley sent another commission, this one headed by William Howard Taft, a federal judge, to establish a government. Taft, a warmhearted, affable man, took an instant liking to the Filipinos, and his policy of encouraging them to participate in the territorial

▲ Emilio Aguinaldo, shown here with his young son, commanded Filipino insurgents who worked with Commodore Dewey to help overthrow Spanish rule of the Philippines in 1898. He later took up arms against the United States in a brutal three-year struggle when President McKinley opposed granting independence to the islands.

government attracted many converts. In July 1901 he became the first civilian governor of the Philippines.

Actually, the reelection of McKinley in 1900 settled the Philippine question so far as most Americans were concerned. Anti-imperialists still claimed that it was unconstitutional to take over territories without the consent of the local population. Their reasoning, while certainly not unsound, was unhistorical. No American government had seriously considered the wishes of the American Indians, the French and Spanish settlers in Louisiana, the Eskimos of Alaska, or the people of Hawaii when it had seemed in the national interest to annex new lands.

CUBA AND THE UNITED STATES

Nevertheless, grave constitutional questions arose as a result of the acquisitions that followed the Spanish-American War. McKinley acted with remarkable independence in handling the problems involved in expansion. He set up military governments in Cuba,

Puerto Rico, and the Philippines without specific congressional authority. But eventually both Congress and the Supreme Court took a hand in shaping colonial policy. In 1900 Congress passed the Foraker Act, establishing a civil government for Puerto Rico. It did not give the Puerto Ricans either American citizenship or full local self-government, and it placed a tariff on Puerto Rican products imported into the United States.

The tariff provision was promptly challenged in the courts on the grounds that Puerto Rico was part of the United States, but in *Downes* v. *Bidwell* (1901) the Supreme Court upheld the legality of the duties. In this and other "insular cases" the reasoning of the judges was more than ordinarily difficult to follow. ("We suggest, without intending to decide, that there may be a distinction between certain natural rights enforced in the Constitution . . . and what may be termed artificial or remedial rights," the *Downes* opinion held.) The effect, however, was clear: the Constitution did not follow the flag; Congress could act toward the colonies almost as it pleased. A colony, one dissenting justice said, could be kept "like a disembodied shade, in an indeterminate state of ambiguous existence for an indefinite period."

While the most heated arguments raged over Philippine policy, the most difficult colonial problems concerned the relationship between the United States and Cuba, for their idealism and self-interest clashed painfully. Despite the desire of most Americans to get out of Cuba, an independent government could not easily be created. Order and prosperity did not automatically appear when the red and gold ensigns of Spain were hauled down from the flagstaffs of Havana and Santiago.

The insurgent government was feeble, corrupt, and oligarchic, the Cuban economy in a state of collapse, life chaotic. The first Americans entering Havana found the streets littered with garbage and the corpses of horses and dogs. All public services were at a standstill; it seemed essential for the United States, as McKinley said, to give "aid and direction" until "tranquillity" could be restored.

As soon as American troops landed in Cuba trouble broke out between them and the populace. Most American soldiers viewed the ragged, half-starved insurgents as "thieving dagoes" and displayed an unfortunate racial prejudice against their dark-skinned allies. The novelist Stephen Crane, who covered the war for Pulitzer's *World*, reported: "Both officers and privates have the most lively contempt for the Cubans. They despise them."

General Shafter did not help matters. He believed the Cubans "no more fit for self-government

than gunpowder is for hell," and he used the insurgents chiefly as labor troops. After the fall of Santiago, he refused to let rebel leaders participate in the formal surrender of the city. This infuriated the proud and idealistic Cuban commander, General Calixto Garcia.

When McKinley established a military government for Cuba late in 1898, it was soon embroiled with local leaders. Then an eager horde of American promoters descended on Cuba in search of profitable franchises and concessions. Congress put a stop to this exploitation by forbidding all such grants as long as the occupation continued.

The problems were indeed knotty, for no strong local leader capable of uniting Cuba appeared. Even Senator Teller, father of the Teller Amendment, expressed concern lest "unstable and unsafe" elements gain control of the country. European leaders expected that the United States would eventually annex Cuba; and many Americans, including General Leonard Wood, who became military governor in December 1899, considered this the best solution. The desperate state of the people, the heavy economic stake of Americans in the region, and its strategic importance militated against withdrawal.

In the end the United States did withdraw, after doing a great deal to modernize sugar production, improve sanitary conditions, establish schools, and restore orderly administration. In November 1900 a Cuban constitutional convention met at Havana and proceeded without substantial American interference or direction to draft a frame of government. The chief restrictions imposed by this document on Cuba's freedom concerned foreign relations; at the insistence of the United States, it authorized American intervention whenever necessary "for the preservation of Cuban independence" and "the maintenance of a government adequate for the protection of life, property, and individual liberty." Cuba had to promise to make no treaty with a foreign power compromising its independence and to grant naval bases on its soil to the United States.

The Cubans, after some grumbling, accepted this arrangement, known as the Platt Amendment. It had the support of most American opponents of imperialism. The amendment was a true compromise: it safeguarded American interests while granting to the Cubans real self-government on internal matters. In May 1902 the United States turned over the reins of government to the new republic. The next

DOCUMENT

The Platt Amendment

▶ *text continues on page 620*

American Lives

Frederick Funston

On the night of March 22, 1901, as rain battered his campsite in the wildest reaches of Luzon Island in the Philippines, Frederick Funston pondered what awaited him the next day. Ten miles to the north lay his prey, Emilio Aguinaldo, President of the Philippine Republic. For two years, the American army had been trying to capture Aguinaldo. But Aguinaldo and his men had slipped away repeatedly. This time Funston was close. His ruse was working.

Funston had had a wild idea, something out of a boy's adventure story. He conceived it after capturing a Filipino messenger carrying coded documents. Funston's interrogation of the courier had been successful. (It was later said that Funston had subjected him to the "water cure," an effective new aid to military intelligence whereby several gallons of water were forced down a suspect's throat; his painfully distended belly was then beaten with logs.) The courier confirmed that Aguinaldo's secret headquarters was located in a remote area of Luzon.

Funston had chosen eighty Filipino scouts from the Macabebes, a tribe hostile to Aguinaldo. He outfitted them in the uniforms of Aguinaldo's army and trained them to pretend to be Filipino nationalists escorting five American "prisoners" (including Funston) for presentation to Aguinaldo. When Funston outlined his scheme to his superior, General Arthur MacArthur had deep misgivings. "Funston, this is a desperate undertaking," he said as they parted. "I fear I shall never see you again."

The words pleased Funston, who longed to be a hero. Ever since he was a child, he worried that he failed to measure up to his father. Edward "Foghorn" Funston had been an artillery officer during the Civil War and a fiery Republican congressman afterward. At six feet two and 200 pounds, he was regarded by all as an exemplar of nineteenth-century manhood. But Frederick, born in 1864, was only five foot four and slightly built. As a boy, Frederick was always much smaller than his friends and effeminate in appearance. His schoolmates teased him. He compensated for his appearance with bravado displays of martial manliness. He read all that he could about war in dime novels and frontier tales. He craved a military career, but though his father was a congressman, West Point rejected him: his grades were mediocre, and he was too small.

In 1886 he went instead to the University of Kansas, but there proved something of a misfit. His energies were devoted to the wholly unsuccessful pursuit of the most desirable women on campus, all of whom spurned him. Increasingly he retreated from social situations, preferring to drink alone in his room, periodically bursting out in a drunken rage, screaming obscenities at the top of his lungs.

He dropped out of college and sought to avoid human contact. First, he explored an unmapped section of Death Valley in California. Then he volunteered to gather botanical samples in Alaska for the Department of Agriculture. When the department proposed that he command an entire expedition for the purpose, he flatly turned them down. "I do not need anybody to take care of me, and I do not want to take care of

▲ Frederick Funston: hero or antihero?

anybody." Alone, he trekked into the frigid wastes of northern Alaska and remained there for the better part of a year. When he ran out of food he ate his sled dogs.

During those long, hollow nights, Funston realized that he could hardly prove that he measured up if no one were around to take the measurements. He decided to become a soldier, not caring much against whom he fought. In 1895 he was offered—and accepted—a commission as an artillery officer with the Cuban rebels.

In Cuba he made up for his lack of gunnery skill by sneaking his Hotchkiss cannon absurdly close to Spanish fortifications at night, often within 400 yards. As the sun rose, the Spaniards, aghast at what was sitting on their doorstep, fired everything they had at Funston's cannon. Funston calmly adjusted the sights, pulled the lanyard, and climbed upon the parapet, shouting "Viva Cuba libre!" He was repeatedly wounded; once, a bullet pierced his lungs. When a severe hip wound became infected, he returned to the United States for medical assistance.

But he was not yet done with war. In 1898 Funston was given command of the Kansas regiments that had volunteered against Spain. To his dismay, they were sent to the Philippines, where the Spaniards had already ceased fighting. But after President McKinley decided to annex the Philippines, war broke out between the American army and the Filipino nationalists. Funston finally got what he craved: sweeping charges, glorious victories, and newspaper feature stories. Yet the jokes about his size persisted. Behind his back, his men called him the "Bantam General." The *New York Times,* in its coverage of a battle in which he won a Congressional Medal of Honor, ran the headline: "Daring Little Colonel Funston." The opening paragraph attributed Funston's courage to the fact that he was too small to hit.

But now, if he captured Aguinaldo, Funston, the little man, would become a great one.

The next day, Funston's Macabebes and their five American "prisoners" met up with a contingent of Aguinaldo's army, which escorted them into the town of Palanan where Aguinaldo maintained his headquarters. The Macabebes were led to a bandstand in the town square, where they were presented to an honor guard of the Filipino army. Aguinaldo watched from a window above. When shots rang out, thinking the troops were firing a salute, he shouted, "Stop that foolishness. Don't waste ammunition!"

Then Funston burst into Aguinaldo's compound:

"I am General Funston, commander of the expedition. You are a prisoner of war of the Army of the United States of America. You will be treated with due consideration and sent to Manila at the first opportunity in a steamer, which is coming to take us on board."

Dazed, Aguinaldo replied: "Is this not some joke?"

In Manila, after being subjected to intense pressure by American authorities, Aguinaldo renounced the Filipino revolution, swore allegiance to the United States, and called on his followers to do likewise. The Philippine-American conflict was virtually over. Frederick Funston had almost single-handedly won the war.

For a time, Funston was a sensation. He was promoted to brigadier general. Newspaper editors and politicians championed him for governor of Kansas or for vice president on a ticket headed by Theodore Roosevelt in 1904. But within a few years Funston all but vanished. Anti-imperialists pointed out that Funston and the Americans had surrendered and then fired their weapons, and that the Macabebes had been wearing enemy uniforms; both actions violated international law. Worse, several reporters and some of his soldiers noted that Funston had ordered the execution of Filipino prisoners. He was subsequently given inconsequential commands.

One hundred years after Funston's capture of Aguinaldo, U.S. troops would again be tracking a rebel fugitive: Osama bin Laden, mastermind of the September 11, 2001 attacks on the World Trade Center and Pentagon. That virtually no one recalled Funston's single-handed pursuit and capture of Aguinaldo was one measure of how completely he had slipped from view.

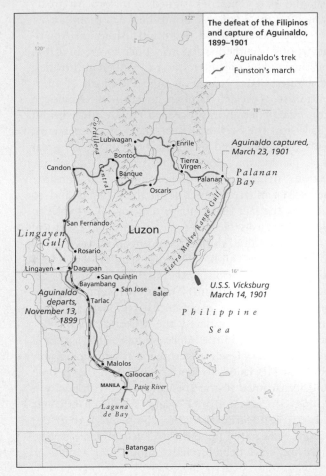

The defeat of the Filipinos and capture of Aguinaldo, 1899–1901

〰 Aguinaldo's trek
〰 Funston's march

year the two countries signed a reciprocity treaty tightening the economic bonds between them.

True friendship did not result. Although American troops occupied Cuba only once more, in 1906, and then at the specific request of Cuban authorities, the United States repeatedly used the threat of intervention to coerce the Cuban government. American economic penetration proceeded rapidly and without regard for the well-being of the Cuban peasants, many of whom lived in a state of peonage on great sugar plantations. Nor did the Americans' good intentions make up for their tendency to consider themselves innately superior to the Cubans and to overlook the fact that Cubans did not always wish to adopt American customs and culture. The reform program instituted during the occupation was marred by attempts to apply American standards at every step. The new schools used American textbooks that had been translated into Spanish without adapting the material to the experience of Cuban children. General Wood considered the Cubans "inert" because they showed little interest in his plans to grant a large measure of self-government to municipal authorities. He failed to understand that the people were accustomed to the Spanish system with decision making concentrated in Havana. Wood, an efficient and energetic administrator, complained that the Cubans were mired in "old ruts," yet the same charge might well have been leveled at him.

THE UNITED STATES IN THE CARIBBEAN AND CENTRAL AMERICA

If the purpose of the Spanish-American War had been to bring peace and order to Cuba, the Platt Amendment was a logical step. The same purpose soon necessitated a further extension of the principle, for once the United States accepted the role of protector and stabilizer in parts of the Caribbean and Central America, it seemed desirable, for the same economic, strategic, and humanitarian reasons, to supervise the entire region.

The Caribbean and Central American countries were economically underdeveloped, socially backward, politically unstable, and desperately poor. Everywhere a few families owned most of the land and dominated social and political life. Most of the people were uneducated peasants, many of whom were little better off than slaves. Rival cliques of wealthy families struggled for power, force being the usual method of effecting a change in government. Most of the meager income of the average Caribbean

state was swallowed up by the military or diverted into the pockets of the current rulers.

Cynicism and fraud poisoned the relations of most of these nations with the great powers. European merchants and bankers systematically cheated their Latin American customers, who in turn frequently refused to honor their obligations. Foreign bankers floated bond issues on outrageous terms, while revolutionary governments in the region annulled concessions and repudiated debts with equal disdain for honest business dealing.

Activities of the United States in the Caribbean

In 1902, shortly after the United States had pulled out of Cuba, trouble erupted in Venezuela, where a dictator, Cipriano Castro, was refusing to honor debts owed the citizens of European nations. To force Castro to pay up, Germany and Great Britain established a blockade of Venezuelan ports and destroyed a number of Venezuelan gunboats and harbor defenses. Under American pressure the Europeans agreed to arbitrate the dispute. For the first time, European powers had accepted the broad implications of the Monroe Doctrine. The British prime minister, Arthur Balfour, went so far as to state publicly that "it would be a great gain to civilization if the United States were more actively to interest themselves in making arrangements by which these constantly recurring difficulties . . . could be avoided."

By this time Theodore Roosevelt had become president of the United States, and he quickly capitalized on the new European attitude. In 1903 the Dominican Republic defaulted on bonds totaling some $40 million. When European investors urged their governments to intervene, Roosevelt announced that under the Monroe Doctrine the United States could not permit foreign nations to intervene in Latin America. But, he added, Latin American nations should not be allowed to escape their obligations. "If we intend to say 'Hands off' . . . sooner or later we must keep order ourselves," he told Secretary of War Elihu Root.

The president did not want to make a colony of the Dominican Republic. "I have about the same desire to annex it as a gorged boa constrictor might have to swallow a porcupine wrong-end-to," he said. He therefore arranged for the United States to take charge of the Dominican customs service—the one reliable source of revenue in that poverty-stricken country. Fifty-five percent of the customs duties would be devoted to debt payment, the remainder turned over to the Dominican government to care for its internal needs. Roosevelt defined his policy, known as the Roosevelt Corollary to the Monroe Doctrine, in a message to Congress in December 1904.

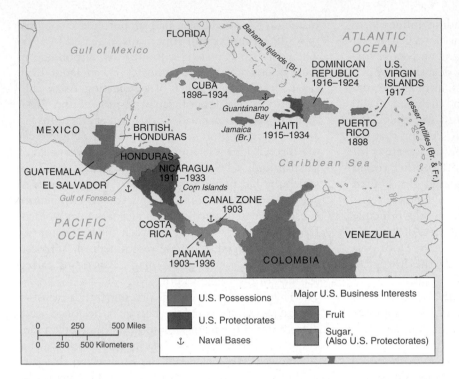

Puerto Rico was ceded by Spain to the United States after the Spanish-American War; the Virgin Islands were bought from Denmark; the Canal Zone was leased from Panama. The ranges of dates following Cuba, the Dominican Republic, Haiti, Nicaragua, and Panama cover those years during which the United States either had troops in occupation or in some other way (such as financial) had a protectorate relationship with that country.

"Chronic wrongdoing" in Latin America, he stated with his typical disregard for the subtleties of complex affairs, might require outside intervention. Since, under the Monroe Doctrine, no other nation could step in, the United States must "exercise . . . an international police power."

In the short run this policy worked admirably. Dominican customs were honestly collected for the first time and the country's finances put in order. The presence of American warships in the area provided a needed measure of political stability. In the long run, however, the Roosevelt Corollary caused a great deal of resentment in Latin America, for it added to nationalist fears that the United States wished to exploit the region for its own benefit.

THE OPEN DOOR POLICY

The insular cases, the Platt Amendment, and the Roosevelt Corollary established the framework for American policy both in Latin America and in East Asia. Coincidental with the Cuban rebellion of the 1890s, a far greater upheaval had convulsed the ancient empire of China. In 1894–1895 Japan easily defeated China in a war over Korea. Alarmed by Japan's aggressiveness, the European powers hastened to carve out for themselves new spheres of influence along China's coast. After the annexation of the Philippines, McKinley's secretary of state, John Hay, urged on by business leaders fearful of losing out in the scramble to exploit the Chinese market, tried to prevent the further absorption of China by the great powers.

For the United States to join in the dismemberment of China was politically impossible because of anti-imperialist feeling, so Hay sought to protect American interests by clever diplomacy. In a series of "Open Door" notes (1899) he asked the powers to agree to respect the trading rights of all countries and to impose no discriminatory duties within their spheres of influence. Chinese tariffs should continue to be collected in these areas and by Chinese officials.

The replies to the Open Door notes were at best noncommittal, yet Hay blandly announced in March 1900 that the powers had "accepted" his suggestions! Thus he could claim to have prevented the breakup of the empire and protected the right of Americans to do business freely in its territories. In reality nothing had been accomplished; the imperialist nations did not extend their political control of China only because they feared that by doing so they might precipitate a major war among themselves. Nevertheless, Hay's action marked a revolutionary departure from the traditional American policy of isolation, a bold advance into the complicated and dangerous world of international power politics.

Within a few months of Hay's announcement the Open Door policy was put to the test. Chinese

nationalists, angered by the spreading influence of foreign governments, launched the so-called Boxer Rebellion. They swarmed into Peking and drove foreigners behind the walls of their legations, which were placed under siege. For weeks, until an international rescue expedition (which included 2500 American soldiers) broke through to free them, the fate of the foreigners was unknown. Fearing that the Europeans would use the rebellion as a pretext for further expropriations, Hay sent off another round of Open Door notes announcing that the United States believed in the preservation of "Chinese territorial and administrative entity" and in "the principle of equal and impartial trade with all parts of the Chinese Empire." This broadened the Open Door policy to include all China, not merely the European spheres of influence.

Hay's diplomacy was superficially successful. Although the United States maintained no important military force in East Asia, American business and commercial interests there were free to develop and to compete with Europeans. But once again European jealousies and fears rather than American cleverness were responsible. When the Japanese, mistrusting Russian intentions in Manchuria, asked Hay how he intended to implement his policy, he replied meekly that the United States was "not prepared . . . to enforce these views on the east by any demonstration which could present a character of hostility to any other power." The United States was being caught up in the power struggle in East Asia without having faced the implications of its actions.

In time the country would pay a heavy price for this unrealistic attitude, but in the decade following 1900 its policy of diplomatic meddling unbacked by bayonets worked fairly well. Japan attacked Russia in a quarrel over Manchuria, smashing the Russian fleet in 1905 and winning a series of battles on the mainland. Japan was not prepared for a long war, however, and suggested to President Roosevelt that an American offer to mediate would be favorably received.

Eager to preserve the nice balance in East Asia, which enabled the United States to exert influence without any significant commitment of force, Roosevelt accepted the hint. In June 1905 he invited the belligerents to a conference at Portsmouth, New Hampshire. At the conference the Japanese won title to Russia's sphere around Port Arthur and a free hand in Korea, but when they demanded Sakhalin Island and a large money indemnity, the Russians balked. Unwilling to resume the war, the Japanese settled for half of Sakhalin and no money.

The Treaty of Portsmouth was unpopular in Japan, and the government managed to place the blame on Roosevelt, who had supported the compromise. Ill feeling against Americans increased in 1906 when the San Francisco school board, responding to local opposition to the influx of cheap labor from Japan, instituted a policy of segregating Asian children in a special school. Japan protested, and President Roosevelt persuaded the San Franciscans to abandon segregation in exchange for his pledge to cut off further Japanese immigration. He accomplished this through a "Gentlemen's Agreement" (1907) in which the Japanese promised not to issue passports to laborers seeking to come to America. Discriminatory legislation based specifically on race was thus avoided. However, the atmosphere between the two countries remained charged. Japanese resentment at American racial prejudice was great; many Americans talked fearfully of the "yellow peril."

Theodore Roosevelt was preeminently a realist in foreign relations. "Don't bluster," he once said. "Don't flourish a revolver, and never draw unless you intend to shoot." In East Asia he failed to follow his own advice. He considered the situation in that part of the world fraught with peril. The Philippines, he said, were "our heel of Achilles," indefensible in case of a Japanese attack. He suggested privately that the United States ought to "be prepared for giving the islands independence . . . much sooner than I think advisable from their own standpoint."

Yet while Roosevelt did not appreciably increase American naval and military strength in East Asia, neither did he stop trying to influence the course of events in the area, and he took no step toward withdrawing from the Philippines. He sent the fleet on a world cruise to demonstrate its might to Japan but knew well that this was mere bluff. "The 'Open Door' policy," he advised his successor, "completely disappears as soon as a powerful nation determines to disregard it." Nevertheless he allowed the belief to persist in the United States that the nation could influence the course of East Asian history without risk or real involvement.

THE PANAMA CANAL

In the Caribbean region American policy centered on building an interoceanic canal across Central America. Expanding interests in Latin America and East Asia made a canal necessary, a truth pointed up during the war with Spain by the two-month voyage of USS *Oregon* around South America from California waters to participate in the action against Admiral Cervera's fleet at Santiago. The first step was to get rid of the old Clayton-Bulwer Treaty with Great

▲ The mosquito that carried yellow fever, from an electron microscope photo. Major Walter Reed of the U.S. Army proved that yellow fever was not spread directly among humans, but from the bites of infected mosquitoes. The virus then multiplied in the human bloodstream. Headache, backache, fever, and vomiting ensued. Liver cells were destroyed, resulting in jaundice—thus the name "yellow fever." American surgeon William Crawford Gorgas worked to eliminate yellow fever by destroying the breeding grounds of these mosquitoes. The last yellow fever outbreak in the United States struck New Orleans and parts of the South in 1905.

the commission valued at only $40 million. Lacking another potential purchaser, the French company lowered its price to $40 million, and after a great deal of clever propagandizing by Philippe Bunau-Varilla, a French engineer with heavy investments in the company, President Roosevelt settled on the Panamanian route.

In January 1903 Secretary of State Hay negotiated a treaty with Tomás Herrán, the Colombian chargé d'affaires in Washington. In return for a 99-year lease on a zone across Panama 6 miles wide, the United States agreed to pay Colombia $10 million and an annual rent of $250,000. The Colombian senate, however, unanimously rejected this treaty, in part because it did not adequately protect Colombian sovereignty over Panama and in part because it hardly seemed fair that the New Panama Canal Company should receive $40 million for its frozen assets and Colombia only $10 million. The government demanded $15 million directly from the United States, plus $10 million of the company's share.

A little more patience might have produced a mutually satisfactory settlement, but Roosevelt looked on the Colombians as highwaymen who were "mad to get hold of the $40,000,000 of the Frenchmen." ("You could no more make an agreement with the Colombian rulers," Roosevelt later remarked, "than you could nail currant jelly to a wall.") When Panamanians, egged on by the French company, staged a revolution in November 1903, he ordered the cruiser *Nashville* to Panama. Colombian government forces found themselves looking down the barrels of the guns of the *Nashville* and shortly thereafter eight other American warships. The revolution succeeded.

Roosevelt instantly recognized the new Republic of Panama. Secretary Hay and the new "Panamanian" minister, Bunau-Varilla, then negotiated a treaty granting the United States a zone 10 miles wide in perpetuity, on the same terms as those rejected by

Britain, which barred the United States from building a canal on its own. In 1901 Lord Pauncefote, the British ambassador, and Secretary of State John Hay negotiated an agreement abrogating the Clayton-Bulwer pact and giving the United States the right to build and, by implication, fortify a transisthmian waterway. The United States agreed in turn to maintain any such canal "free and open to the vessels of commerce and of war of all nations."

One possible canal route lay across the Colombian province of Panama, where the French-controlled New Panama Canal Company had taken over the franchise of the old De Lesseps company. Only fifty miles separated the oceans in Panama. The terrain, however, was rugged and unhealthy. While the French company had sunk much money into the project, it had little to show for its efforts aside from some rough excavations. A second possible route ran across Nicaragua. This route was about 200 miles long but was relatively easy since much of it traversed Lake Nicaragua and other natural waterways.

President McKinley appointed a commission to study the alternatives. It reported that the Panamanian route was technically superior, but recommended building in Nicaragua because the New Panama Canal Company was asking $109 million for its assets, which

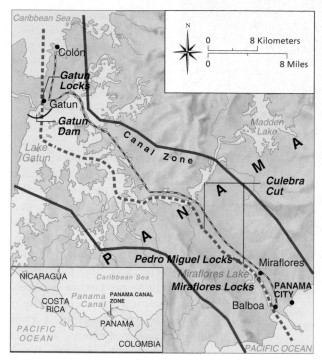

▲ **The U.S. Panama Canal**
Following many negotiations, construction on the Panama Canal
began in 1904. After many delays and hardships, it was completed
in 1914.

Colombia. Within the Canal Zone the United States
could act as "the sovereign of the territory . . . to the
entire exclusion of . . . the Republic of Panama." The
United States guaranteed the independence of the republic. The New Panama Canal Company then received its $40 million, including a substantial share
for Bunau-Varilla.

Historians have condemned Roosevelt for his
actions in this shabby affair, and with good reason.
It was not that he fomented the revolution, for he
did not. Separated from the government at Bogotá
by an impenetrable jungle, the people of Panama
province had long wanted to be free of Colombian
rule. Since an American-built canal would bring a
flood of dollars and jobs to the area, they were prepared to take any necessary steps to avoid having the
United States shift to the Nicaraguan route. Nor was
it that Roosevelt prevented Colombia from suppressing the revolution. He sinned, rather, in his disregard of Latin American sensibilities. He referred to
the Colombians as "dagoes" and insisted smugly
that he was defending "the interests of collective civilization" when he overrode their opposition to his
plans. "They cut their own throats," he said. "They
tried to hold us up; and too late they have discovered their criminal error."

If uncharitable, Roosevelt's analysis was not entirely inaccurate, yet it did not justify his haste in
taking Panama under his wing. "Have I defended
myself?" Roosevelt asked Secretary of War Root.
"You certainly have, Mr. President," Root retorted.
"You were accused of seduction and you have conclusively proved that you were guilty of rape."
Throughout Latin America, especially as nationalist
sentiments grew stronger, Roosevelt's intolerance
and aggressiveness in the canal incident bred resentment and fear.

In 1921 the United States made amends by giving Colombia $25 million. Colombia in turn recog-
nized the independence of the Republic of Panama,
but Panama was independent only in name because
the United States controlled the canal. Meanwhile,
the first vessels passed through the canal in 1914—
and American hegemony in the Caribbean expanded.
Yet even in that strategically vital area there was more
show than substance to American strength. The navy
ruled Caribbean waters largely by default, for it lacked
adequate bases in the region. In 1903, as authorized
by the Cuban constitution, the United States obtained an excellent site for a base at Guantanamo Bay,
but before 1914 Congress appropriated only $89,000
to develop it.

The tendency was to try to influence outlying areas without actually controlling them. Roosevelt's
successor, William Howard Taft, called this policy
"dollar diplomacy," his reasoning being that economic penetration would bring stability to underdeveloped areas and power and profit to the United
States without the government's having to commit
troops or spend public funds.

Under Taft the State Department won a place for
American bankers in an international syndicate engaged in financing railroads in Manchuria. When
Nicaragua defaulted on its foreign debt in 1911, the
department arranged for American bankers to reorganize Nicaraguan finances and manage the customs
service. Although the government truthfully insisted
that it did not "covet an inch of territory south of the
Rio Grande," dollar diplomacy provoked further apprehension in Latin America. Efforts to establish similar arrangements in Honduras, Costa Rica, and
Guatemala all failed. In Nicaragua orderly administration of the finances did not bring internal peace. In
1912, 2500 American marines and sailors had to be
landed to put down a revolution.

Economic penetration proceeded briskly. American investments in Cuba reached $500 million by
1920, and smaller but significant investments were
made in the Dominican Republic and in Haiti. In
Central America the United Fruit Company accumulated large holdings in banana plantations, railroads,

▲ The Culebra cut—a mountain containing some 100 million cubic yards of rock that had been removed for the Panama Canal.

and other ventures. Other firms plunged heavily into Mexico's rich mineral resources.

IMPERIALISM WITHOUT COLONIES

The United States deserves fair marks for effort in its foreign relations following the Spanish-American War, barely passable marks for performance, and failing marks for results. If one defines imperialism narrowly as a policy of occupying and governing foreign lands, American imperialism lasted for an extremely short time. With trivial exceptions, all the American colonies—Hawaii, the Philippines, Guam, Puerto Rico, the Guantanamo base, and the Canal Zone—were obtained between 1898 and 1903. In retrospect it seems clear that the urge to own colonies was only fleeting; the legitimate questions raised by the anti-imperialists and the headaches connected with the management of overseas possessions soon produced a change of policy.

The objections of protectionists to the lowering of tariff barriers, the shock of the Philippine insurrection, and a growing conviction that the costs of colonial administration outweighed the profits affected American thinking. Hay's Open Door notes (which anti-imperialists praised highly) marked the beginning of the retreat from imperialism as thus defined, while the Roosevelt Corollary and dollar diplomacy signaled the consolidation of a new policy. Elihu Root summarized this policy as it applied to the Caribbean nations (and by implication to the rest of the underdeveloped world) in 1905: "We do not want to take them for ourselves. We do not want any foreign nations to take them for themselves. We want to help them."

Yet imperialism can be given a broader definition. Although the United States did not seek colonies, it pursued a course that promoted American economic penetration of underdeveloped areas without the trouble of owning and controlling them. American statesmen regarded American expansion as beneficial to all concerned. They genuinely believed that they were exporting democracy along with capitalism and industrialization. But U.S. economic penetration has had many unfortunate results for the nonindustrial nations. Americans were particularly, though not uniquely, unimpressed by the different social and cultural patterns of people in far-off lands and insensitive to their wish to develop in their own way.

Both the U.S. government and American businessmen showed little interest in finding out what the people of Cuba wanted from life. They assumed that the Cubans wanted what everybody (read "Americans") wanted and, if by some strange chance this was not the case, that it was best to give it to them anyway. Dollar diplomacy had two main objectives, the avoidance of violence and the economic development of Latin America; it paid small heed to how peace was maintained and how the fruits of development were distributed. The policy was self-defeating, for in the long run stability depended on the support of local people, and this was seldom forthcoming.

By the eve of World War I the United States had become a world power and had assumed what it saw as a duty to guide the development of many countries with traditions far different from its own. The American people, however, did not understand what world power involved. While they stood ready to extend their influence into distant lands, they did so with little awareness of the implications of their behavior for themselves or for other peoples. The national psychology, if such a term has any meaning, remained fundamentally isolationist. Americans understood that their wealth and numbers made their nation strong and that geography made it virtually invulnerable. Thus they proceeded to do what they wanted to do in foreign affairs, limited more by their humanly flexible consciences than by any rational analysis of the probable consequences. This policy seemed safe enough—in 1914.

MILESTONES

1850	Britain and United States sign Clayton-Bulwer Treaty concerning interoceanic canal
1858	Commercial treaty with Japan opens several ports to American trade
1867	United States buys Alaska from Russia
1871	Treaty of Washington settles *Alabama* claims
1875	Reciprocity treaty increases U.S. influence in Hawaii
1885	Josiah Strong justifies expansionism in *Our Country*
1890	A. T. Mahan fuels American imperialism in *The Influence of Sea Power*
1893	United States helps sugar planters depose Queen Liliuokalani of Hawaii
1895	United States supports Venezuela in European border dispute over British Guiana
1898	*Maine* explodes in Havana harbor
	Spanish-American war breaks out
	Dewey defeats Spanish fleet at Battle of Manila Bay
	Theodore Roosevelt leads Rough Riders at the Battle of San Juan Hill
	United States annexes Hawaii

1899	Hays's Open Door notes safeguard United States access to China trade
1900	Platt Amendment gives United States naval stations and right to intervene in Cuba
1901	Hay-Pauncefote Treaty gives United States rights to build interoceanic canal
	Supreme Court's insular cases give Congress free reign over colonies
1902	Europeans accept Monroe Doctrine during Venezuela bond dispute
1904	Roosevelt Corollary to Monroe Doctrine gives United States "international police power"
1907	"Gentlemen's Agreement" curtails Japanese immigration

SUPPLEMENTARY READING

Contemporary attitudes are reflected in Josiah Strong, *Our Country* (1885), and Alfred T. Mahan, *The Influence of Sea Power Upon History* (1890), which provides the clearest presentation of Mahan's thesis.

For post–Civil War diplomatic history the works cited in Debating the Past (p. 605) are essential. See also Milton Plesur, *America's Outward Thrust* (1971), John A. S. Grenville and George B. Young, *Politics, Strategy, and American Diplomacy: Studies in Foreign Policy* (1966), Thomas D. Schoonover, *The United States in Central America* (1991), and David Healy, *U.S. Expansionism: The Imperialist Urge in the 1890's* (1970). Emily S. Rosenberg, *Financial Missionaries to the World: The Politics and Culture of Dollar Diplomacy, 1900–1930* (1999) shows how cultural and economic forces intersected to promote expansionism.

On Hawaiian annexation, see Merze Tate, *The United States and the Hawaiian Kingdom* (1965). On the Spanish-

American War, see John L. Offner, *An Unwanted War: The Diplomacy of the United States and Spain over Cuba, 1895–1898* (1992).

On the consequences of imperialism Robert L. Beisner, *Twelve Against Empire: The Anti-imperialists* (1968) contains lively and thoughtful sketches of leading foes of expansion. See also E. Berkeley Tompkins, *Anti-imperialism in the United States* (1970). For colonial problems in the Philippines, see Stuart Creighton Miller, *"Benevolent Assimilation": The American Conquest of the Philippines, 1899–1903* (1982), and H. W. Brands, *Bound to Empire: The United States and the Philippines* (1992). On the Caribbean, see Thomas O'Brien, *The Revolutionary Mission: American Enterprise in Latin America, 1900–1945* (1996). David McCullough, *The Path Between the Seas* (1977), is excellent on the history of the Panama Canal.

SUGGESTED WEBSITES

William McKinley

http://www.ipl.org/div/POTUS/wmckinley.html

This site contains basic factual data about McKinley's election and presidency, speeches, and online bibliography.

The Era of William McKinley

http://www.history.osu.edu/Projects/Mckinley/default.htm

This site contains numerous images from various stages of William McKinley's career along with a brief bibliographical essay. This Ohio State University site also has a section with an excellent collection of McKinley-era cartoons.

William McKinley and the Spanish-American War

http://www.history.osu.edu/Projects/Mckinley/SpanAmWar.html

Part of the Ohio State University site about William McKinley. This section highlights the Spanish-American War with an essay and photographs.

Sentenaryo/Centennial: The Philippine Revolution and the Philippine-American War

http://www.boondocksnet.com/centennial/index.html

Jim Zwick organizes primary documents, images, and essays focusing on U.S. involvement in the Philippines.

Selected Naval Documents: The Spanish-American War

http://www.history.navy.mil/wars/spanam/sn98-1.htm

The primary documents speak volumes to the activity of the U.S. Navy during the conflict with Spain.

The Spanish-American War

http://lcweb.loc.gov/rr/hispanic/1898/trask.html

This article by historian David Trask includes links to other related sites. The article is provided by the Library of Congress.

The First Open Door Note

http://odur.let.rug.nl/~usa/D/1876-1900/foreignpolicy/opendr.htm

The Open Door note played an important ideological role in U.S. foreign policy at the end of the nineteenth century. Read the text of that document on this site.

Imperialism Web Page

http://www.smplanet.com/imperialism/toc.html

Focusing on the period around 1900, this site puts much information about American imperialism in one place.

Theodore Roosevelt Association

http://www.theodoreroosevelt.org/

This site contains much bibliographical and research information about Theodore Roosevelt.

Woodrow Wilson and the Great War

▼ In *Gassed* (1918–1919) John Singer Sargent, who specialized in portraits of society ladies, shows soldiers blinded from poison gas staggering toward aid stations.

Woodrow Wilson's approach to foreign relations was well intentioned and idealistic but somewhat confused. He knew that the United States had no wish to injure any foreign state and assumed that all nations would recognize this fact and cooperate. He wanted to help the republics of Latin America achieve stable democratic governments and improve the living conditions of their people. Imperialism was, in his eyes, immoral. But he felt obliged to sustain and protect American interests abroad. The maintenance of the Open Door in China and the completion of the Panama Canal were as important to him as they had been to Theodore Roosevelt.

Wilson's view of foreign nations was shortsighted and provincial. Like nineteenth-century Christian missionaries, he wanted to spread the gospel of American democracy, to lift and enlighten the unfortunate and the ignorant—but in his own way. "I am going to teach the South American republics to elect good men!" he told one British diplomat.

WILSON'S "MORAL" DIPLOMACY

Wilson set out to raise the moral tone of American foreign policy by denouncing dollar diplomacy. Encouraging bankers to lend money to countries like China, he said, implied the possibility of "forcible interference"

if the loans were not repaid, and that would be "obnoxious to the principles upon which the government of our people rests." To seek special economic concessions in Latin America was "unfair" and "degrading." The United States would deal with Latin American nations "upon terms of equality and honor."

In certain small matters Wilson succeeded in conducting American diplomacy on this idealistic basis. When the Japanese attempted in the notorious Twenty-One Demands (1915) to reduce China almost to the status of a Japanese protectorate, he persuaded them to modify their conditions slightly.

Where more important interests were concerned, Wilson sometimes failed to live up to his promises. Because of the strategic importance of the Panama Canal, he was unwilling to tolerate "unrest" anywhere in the Caribbean. Within months of his inauguration he was pursuing the same tactics circumstances had forced on Roosevelt and Taft. The Bryan-Chamorro Treaty of 1914, which gave the United States an option to build a canal across Nicaragua, made that country virtually an American protectorate and served to maintain in power an unpopular dictator, Adolfo Díaz.

A much more serious example of missionary diplomacy occurred in Mexico. In 1911 a liberal coalition overthrew the dictator Porfirio Díaz, who had been exploiting the resources and people of Mexico for the benefit of a small class of wealthy landowners, clerics, and military men since the 1870s. Francisco Madero became president.

Madero, a wealthy landowner apparently influenced by the progressive movement in the United States, was committed to economic reform and the drafting of a democratic constitution. Unfortunately, he was weak-willed and a terrible administrator. Conditions in Mexico deteriorated rapidly, and less than a month before Wilson's inauguration, one of Madero's generals, Victoriano Huerta, seized power and had his former chief murdered. Huerta was an unabashed reactionary, but he was committed to maintaining the stability that foreign investors desired. Most of the European powers promptly recognized his government.

The American ambassador, together with important American financial and business interests in Mexico and in the United States, urged Wilson to do so too, but he refused. His sympathies were all with the government of Madero, whose murder had horrified him. "I will not recognize a government of butchers," he said. This was unconventional; nations do not ordinarily consider the means by which a foreign regime has come to power before deciding to establish diplomatic relations.

Wilson brought enormous pressure to bear against Huerta. He dragooned the British into withdrawing

recognition. He dickered with other Mexican factions. He demanded that Huerta hold free elections as the price of American mediation in the continuing civil war. Huerta would not yield an inch. Indeed, he drew strength from Wilson's effort to oust him, for even his enemies resented American interference in Mexican affairs. Frustration, added to his moral outrage, weakened Wilson's judgment. He subordinated his wish to let the Mexicans solve their own problems to his desire to destroy Huerta.

The tense situation exploded in April 1914, when a small party of American sailors was arrested in the port of Tampico, Mexico. When the Mexican government refused to supply the apology demanded by the sailors' commander, Wilson fastened on the affair as an excuse for sending troops into Mexico.

The invasion took place at Veracruz, whence Winfield Scott had launched the assault on Mexico City in 1847. Instead of meekly surrendering the city, the Mexicans resisted tenaciously, suffering 400 casualties before falling back. This bloodshed caused dismay throughout Latin America. Huerta, hard-pressed by Mexican opponents, abdicated. On August 20, 1914, General Venustiano Carranza entered Mexico City in triumph.

Carranza favored representative government, but he proved scarcely more successful than the tyrant Huerta in controlling the country. One of his own generals, Francisco "Pancho" Villa, rose against him and seized control of Mexico City.

Wilson now made a monumental blunder. Villa professed to be willing to cooperate with the United States, and Wilson, taking him at his word, gave him his support. However, Villa was little more than an ambitious bandit with no other objective than personal power. Carranza, though no radical, was committed to social reform. Fighting back, he drove the Villistas into the northern provinces.

Wilson finally realized the extent of Carranza's influence in Mexico, and in October 1915 he recognized the Carranza government. Still his Mexican troubles were not over. Early in 1916, Villa, seeking to undermine Carranza by forcing the United States to intervene, stopped a train in northern Mexico and killed sixteen American passengers in cold blood. Then he crossed into New Mexico and burned the town of Columbus, killing nineteen. Having learned his lesson, Wilson would have preferred to bear even this assault in silence, but public opinion forced him to send American troops under General John J. Pershing across the border in pursuit of Villa.

Villa proved impossible to catch. Cleverly he drew Pershing deeper and deeper into Mexico, and this alarmed Carranza, who insisted that the Americans withdraw. Several clashes occurred between Pershing's

men and Mexican regulars, and for a brief period in June 1916 war seemed imminent. Wilson now acted bravely and wisely. Early in 1917 he recalled Pershing's force, leaving the Mexicans to work out their own destiny.

Missionary diplomacy in Mexico had produced mixed but in the long run beneficial results. By opposing Huerta, Wilson had surrendered to his prejudices, yet he had also helped the real revolutionaries even though they opposed his acts. His bungling bred anti-Americanism in Mexico, but by his later restraint in the face of stinging provocations, he permitted the constitutionalists to consolidate their power.

EUROPE EXPLODES IN WAR

On June 28, 1914, in the Austro-Hungarian provincial capital of Sarajevo, Gavrilo Princip, a young student, assassinated the Archduke Franz Ferdinand,

heir to the imperial throne. Princip was a member of the Black Hand, a Serbian terrorist organization. He was seeking to further the cause of Serbian nationalism. Instead his rash act precipitated a general European war. Within little more than a month, following a complex series of diplomatic challenges and responses, two great coalitions, the Central Powers (chiefly Germany, Austria-Hungary, and Ottoman Turkey) and the Allied Powers (chiefly Great Britain, France, and Russia), were locked in a brutal struggle that brought one era in world history to a close and inaugurated another.

The outbreak of this Great War caught Americans psychologically unprepared; few understood its significance. President Wilson promptly issued a proclamation of neutrality and asked the nation to be "impartial in thought." Of course, not even the president had the superhuman self-control that this request called for, but the almost unanimous reaction of Americans, aside from dismay, was that the conflict

▲ During World War I, advancing armies unloosed ferocious artillery barrages to destroy deeply entrenched enemy positions. Before the Third Battle of Ypres, the British fired four and a half million shells at German defenses, pulverizing the landscape. But as the British moved forward they became mired in mud *(above);* they lost 300,000 men in the action. Few Americans perceived the special horrors of this type of warfare.

did not concern them. They were wrong, for this would become the first world war, and Americans would not escape its outcome.

There were good reasons, aside from a failure to understand the significance of the struggle, why the United States sought to remain neutral. Over a third of its 92 million inhabitants were either European-born or the children of European immigrants. Sentimental ties bound them to the lands of their ancestors. American involvement would create new internal stresses in a society already strained by the task of assimilating so many diverse groups. War was also an affront to the prevailing progressive spirit, which assumed that human beings were reasonable, high-minded, and capable of settling disputes peaceably. Along with the traditional American fear of entanglement in European affairs, these were ample reasons for remaining aloof.

Although most Americans hoped to keep out of the war, nearly everyone was partial to one side or the other. People of German or Austrian descent, about 8 million in number, and the nation's 4.5 million Irish Americans, motivated chiefly by hatred of the British, sympathized with the Central Powers. The majority of the people, however, influenced by bonds of language and culture, preferred an Allied victory, and when the Germans launched a mighty assault across neutral Belgium in an effort to outflank the French armies, many Americans were outraged.

As the war progressed, the Allies cleverly exploited American prejudices by such devices as publishing exaggerated tales of German atrocities against Belgian civilians. A supposedly impartial study of these charges by the widely respected James Bryce, author of *The American Commonwealth*, portrayed the Germans as ruthless barbarians. The Germans also conducted a propaganda campaign in the United States, but they labored under severe handicaps and won few converts.

FREEDOM OF THE SEAS

Propaganda did not basically alter American attitudes; far more important were questions arising out of trade and commerce. Under international law, neutrals could trade freely with any belligerent. Americans were prepared to do so, but because the British fleet dominated the North Atlantic, they could not. The situation was similar to the one that had prevailed during the Napoleonic Wars. The British declared nearly all commodities, even foodstuffs, to be contraband of war. They forced neutral merchant ships into British or French ports in order

to search them for goods headed for the enemy. Many cargoes were confiscated, often without payment. American firms that traded with the Central Powers were "blacklisted," which meant that no British subject could deal with them. When Americans protested, the British answered that in a battle for survival, they dared not adhere to old-fashioned rules of international law.

Had the United States insisted that Great Britain abandon these "illegal" practices, as the Germans demanded, no doubt it could have had its way. The British foreign secretary, Sir Edward Grey, later admitted: "The ill-will of the United States meant certain defeat. The object of diplomacy, therefore, was to secure the maximum of blockade that could be enforced without a rupture with the United States." It is ironic that an embargo, which failed so ignominiously in Jefferson's day, would have been almost instantly effective if applied at any time after 1914, for American supplies were vital to the Allies.

Although British tactics frequently exasperated Wilson, they did not result in the loss of innocent lives. He never considered taking as drastic a step as an embargo. He faced a dilemma. To allow the British to make the rules meant siding against the Central Powers. Yet to insist on the old rules (which had never been strictly obeyed in wartime) meant siding against the Allies because that would have deprived them of much of the value of their naval superiority. *Nothing* the United States might do would be truly impartial.

Wilson's own sentiments made it doubly difficult for him to object strenuously to British practices. No American admired British institutions and culture more extravagantly. "Everything I love most in the world is at stake," he confessed privately to the British ambassador. A German victory "would be fatal to our form of Government and American ideals."

In any event, the immense expansion of American trade with the Allies made an embargo unthinkable. While commerce with the Central Powers fell to a trickle, that with the Allies soared from $825 million in 1914 to over $3.2 billion in 1916. An attempt to limit this commerce would have raised a storm; to have eliminated it would have caused a catastrophe. Munitions makers and other businessmen did not want the United States to enter the war. Neutrality suited their purposes admirably.

Britain and France soon exhausted their ready cash, and by early 1917 they had borrowed well over $2 billion. Although these loans violated no principle of international law, they fastened the United States more closely to the Allies' cause.

NOTICE!

TRAVELLERS intending to embark on the Atlantic voyage are reminded that a state of war exists between Germany and her allies and Great Britain and her allies; that the zone of war includes the waters adjacent to the British Isles; that, in accordance with formal notice given by the Imperial German Government, vessels flying the flag of Great Britain, or of any of her allies, are liable to destruction in those waters and that travellers sailing in the war zone on ships of Great Britain or her allies do so at their own risk.

IMPERIAL GERMAN EMBASSY
WASHINGTON, D. C., APRIL 22, 1915.

▲ Three weeks before the *Lusitania* was torpedoed, this notice appeared in the classified sections of Washington newspapers.

During the first months of the Great War, the Germans were not especially concerned about neutral trade or American goods because they expected to crush the Allied armies quickly. When their first swift thrust into France was blunted along the Marne River, only twenty miles from Paris, and the war became a bloody stalemate, they began to challenge the Allies' control of the seas. Unwilling to risk their battleships and cruisers against the much larger British fleet, they resorted to a new weapon, the submarine, commonly known as the U-boat (for *Unterseeboot*). German submarines played a role in World War I not unlike that of American privateers in the Revolution and the War of 1812: They ranged the seas stealthily in search of merchant ships. However, submarines could not operate under the ordinary rules of war, which required that a raider stop its prey, examine its papers and cargo, and give the crew and passengers time to get off in lifeboats before sending it to the bottom. When surfaced, U-boats were vulnerable to the deck guns that many merchant ships carried; they could even be sunk by ramming, once they had stopped and put out a boarding party. Therefore, they commonly launched their torpedoes from below the surface without warning, often resulting in a heavy loss of life.

In February 1915 the Germans declared the waters surrounding the British Isles a zone of war and announced that they would sink without warning all enemy merchant ships encountered in the area. Since Allied vessels sometimes flew neutral flags to disguise their identity, neutral ships entering the zone would do so at their own risk. This statement was largely bluff, for the Germans had only a handful of submarines at sea; but they were feverishly building more.

Wilson—perhaps too hurriedly, considering the importance of the question—warned the Germans that he would hold them to "strict accountability" for any loss of American life or property resulting from violations of "acknowledged [neutral] rights on the high seas." He did not distinguish clearly between losses incurred through the destruction of *American* ships and those resulting from the sinking of other vessels. If he meant to hold the Germans responsible for injuries to Americans on *belligerent* vessels, he was changing international law as arbitrarily as the Germans were. Secretary of State Bryan, who opposed Wilson vigorously on this point, stood on sound legal ground when he said: "A ship carrying contraband should not rely upon passengers to protect her from attack—it would be like putting women and children in front of an army."

Correct or not, Wilson's position reflected the attitude of most Americans. It seemed barbaric to them that defenseless civilians should be killed without warning; Americans refused to surrender their "rights" as neutrals to cross the North Atlantic on any ship they wished. The depth of their feeling was demonstrated when, on May 7, 1915, the submarine *U–20* sank the British liner *Lusitania* off the Irish coast. Nearly 1200 persons, including 128 Americans, lost their lives.

The torpedoing of the *Lusitania* caused as profound and emotional a reaction in the United States as that following the destruction of the *Maine* in Havana harbor. Wilson, like McKinley in 1898, was

▲ This is an artist's rendering of the "Sinking of the *Lusitania*," which resulted in the loss of nearly 1200 people, including 128 Americans.

shocked, but he kept his head. He demanded that Germany disavow the sinking, indemnify the victims, and promise to stop attacking passenger vessels. When the Germans quibbled about these points, he responded with further diplomatic correspondence rather than with an ultimatum.

In one sense this was sound policy. The Germans pointed out that they had published warnings in American newspapers saying they considered the *Lusitania* subject to attack, that the liner was carrying munitions, and that on past voyages it had flown the American flag as a *ruse de guerre*. It would have been difficult politically for the German government to back down before an American ultimatum; however, after dragging the controversy out for nearly a year, it apologized and agreed to pay an indemnity. After the torpedoing of the French channel steamer *Sussex* in March 1916 had produced another stiff American protest, the Germans at last promised, in the *Sussex* pledge, to stop sinking merchant ships without warning.

Had Wilson forced a showdown in 1915, he would have alienated a large segment of American opinion. Even his relatively mild notes resulted in the resignation of Secretary of State Bryan, who believed it unneutral to treat German violations of international law differently from Allied violations—and Bryan reflected the feelings of thousands.[1]

Yet if Wilson had sought a declaration of war over the *Lusitania*, a majority of Congress and the country would probably have gone along, and in that event the dreadful carnage in Europe would have ended much sooner. This is the reasoning of hindsight, yet such a policy would have been logical, given Wilson's assumptions about the justice of the Allied cause and America's stake in an Allied victory.

In November 1915 Wilson at last began to press for increased military and naval expenditures. Nevertheless, he continued to vacillate. He dispatched a sharp note protesting Allied blacklisting of American firms, and to his confidant, Colonel Edward M. House, he called the British "poor boobs!"

THE ELECTION OF 1916

Part of Wilson's confusion in 1916 resulted from the political difficulties he faced in his fight for re-election. He had won the presidency in 1912 only

---

[1]Wilson appointed Robert Lansing, counselor of the State Department, to succeed Bryan.

because the Republican party had split in two. Now Theodore Roosevelt, the chief defector, had become so incensed by Wilson's refusal to commit the United States to the Allied cause that he was ready to support almost any Republican in order to guarantee the president's defeat. At the same time, many progressives were complaining about Wilson's unwillingness to work for further domestic reforms. Unless he could find additional support, he seemed likely to be defeated. He attacked the problem by wooing the progressives. In January 1916 he appointed Louis D. Brandeis to the Supreme Court. In addition to being an advanced progressive, Brandeis was the first Jewish American appointed to the Court. Wilson's action won him many friends among people who favored fair treatment for minority groups. In July he bid for the farm vote by signing the Farm Loan Act to provide low-cost loans based on agricultural credit. Shortly thereafter, he approved the Keating-Owen Child Labor Act barring goods manufactured by the labor of children under sixteen from interstate commerce, and a workers' compensation act for federal employees. He persuaded Congress to pass the Adamson Act, establishing an eight-hour day for railroad workers, and he modified his position on the tariff by approving the creation of a tariff commission.

Each of these actions represented a sharp reversal. In 1913 Wilson had considered Brandeis too radical even for a Cabinet post. The new farm, labor, and tariff laws were all examples of the kind of "class legislation" he had refused to countenance in 1913 and 1914. Wilson was putting into effect much of the Progressive platform of 1912. His actions paid spectacular political dividends when Roosevelt refused to run as a Progressive and came out for the Republican nominee, Associate Justice Charles Evans Hughes. The Progressive convention then endorsed Hughes, who had compiled a fine liberal record as governor of New York, but many of Roosevelt's 1912 supporters felt that he had betrayed them and voted for Wilson.

The key issue in the campaign was American policy toward the warring powers. Wilson intended to stress preparedness, which he was now wholeheartedly supporting. However, during the Democratic convention, the delegates shook the hall with cheers whenever orators referred to the president's success in keeping the country out of the war. One spellbinder, referring to the *Sussex* pledge, announced that the president had "wrung from the most militant spirit that ever brooded above a battlefield an acknowledgement of American rights and an agreement to American demands," and the convention erupted in a demonstration that lasted more than twenty minutes. Thus "He Kept Us Out of War" became the Democratic slogan.

To his credit, Wilson made no promises. "I can't keep the country out of war," he told one member of his Cabinet. "Any little German lieutenant can put us into the war at any time by some calculated outrage." His attitude undoubtedly cost him the votes of extremists on both sides, but it won the backing of thousands of moderates.

The combination of progressivism and the peace issue placed the Democrats on substantially equal terms with the Republicans; thereafter, personal factors probably tipped the balance. Hughes was very stiff (Theodore Roosevelt called him a bearded Woodrow Wilson) and an ineffective speaker; he offended a number of important politicians, especially in crucial California, where he inadvertently snubbed the popular progressive governor, Hiram Johnson; and he equivocated on a number of issues. Nevertheless, on election night he appeared to have won, having carried nearly all the East and Midwest. Late returns gave Wilson California, however, and with it victory by the narrow margin of 277 to 254 in the Electoral College. He led Hughes in the popular vote, 9.1 million to 8.5 million.

THE ROAD TO WAR

Encouraged by his triumph, appalled by the continuing slaughter on the battlefields, fearful that the United States would be dragged into the conflagration, Wilson made one last effort to end the war by negotiation. In 1915 and again in 1916 he had sent his friend Colonel House on secret missions to London, Paris, and Berlin to try to mediate among the belligerents. Each had proved fruitless, but after another long season of bloodshed, perhaps the powers would listen to reason.

Wilson's own feelings were more genuinely neutral than at any other time during the war, for the Germans had stopped sinking merchant ships without warning and the British had irritated him repeatedly by their arbitrary restrictions on neutral trade. He drafted a note to the belligerents asking them to state the terms on which they would agree to lay down their arms. Unless the fighting ended soon, he warned, neutrals and belligerents alike would be so ruined that peace would be meaningless.

When neither side responded encouragingly, Wilson, on January 22, 1917, delivered a moving speech aimed at "the people of the countries now at war" more than at their governments. Any settlement

imposed by a victor, he declared, would breed hatred and more wars. There must be "peace without victory," based on the principles that all nations were equal and that every nationality should determine its own form of government. He mentioned, albeit vaguely, disarmament and freedom of the seas, and he suggested the creation of some kind of international organization to preserve world peace. "There must be not a balance of power, but a community of power," he said, and he added, "I am speaking for the silent mass of mankind everywhere."

This noble appeal met a tragic fate. The Germans had already decided to renounce the *Sussex* pledge and unleash their submarines against all vessels headed for Allied ports. After February 1, any ship in the war zone would be attacked without warning. Possessed now of more than 100 U-boats, the German military leaders had convinced themselves that they could starve the British people into submission and reduce the Allied armies to impotence by cutting off the flow of American supplies. The United States would probably declare war, but the Germans believed that they could overwhelm the Allies before the Americans could get to the battlefields in force. In 1917, after the German military leaders had made this decision, events moved relentlessly, almost uninfluenced by the actors who presumably controlled the fate of the world:

> *February 3: Housatonic* torpedoed. Wilson announces to Congress that he has severed diplomatic relations with Germany.
>
> *February 24:* Walter Hines Page, United States ambassador to Great Britain, transmits to the State Department an intercepted German dispatch (the "Zimmermann telegram") revealing that Germany has proposed a secret alliance with Mexico; Mexico to receive, in the event of war with the United States, "the lost territory in Texas, New Mexico, and Arizona."
>
> *February 25:* Cunard liner *Laconia* torpedoed; two American women perish.
>
> *February 26:* Wilson asks Congress for authority to arm American merchant ships.
>
> *March 1:* Zimmermann telegram released to the press.
>
> *March 4:* President Wilson takes oath of office, beginning his second term. Congress adjourns without passing the armed ship bill, the measure having been filibustered to death by antiwar senators. Wilson characterizes the filibusterers, led by Senator Robert M. La Follette, as "a little group of willful men, representing no opinion but their own."
>
> *March 9:* Wilson, acting under his executive powers, orders the arming of American merchantmen.
>
> *March 12:* Revolutionary provisional government established in Russia. *Algonquin* torpedoed.
>
> *March 15:* Czar Nicholas II of Russia abdicates.
>
> *March 16: City of Memphis, Illinois, Vigilancia* torpedoed.
>
> *March 21: New York World,* a leading Democratic newspaper, calls for declaration of war on Germany. Wilson summons Congress to convene in a special session on April 2.
>
> *March 25:* Wilson calls up the National Guard.
>
> *April 2:* Wilson asks Congress to declare war. Germany is guilty of "throwing to the winds all scruples of humanity," he says. America must fight, not to conquer, but for "peace and justice. . . . The world must be made safe for democracy."
>
> *April 4, 6:* Congress declares war—the vote, 82–6 in the Senate, 373–50 in the House.

The bare record conceals Wilson's agonizing search for an honorable alternative to war. To admit that Germany posed a threat to the United States meant confessing that interventionists had been right all along. To go to war meant, besides sending innocent Americans to their deaths, allowing "the spirit of ruthless brutality [to] enter into the very fibre of our national life."

DOCUMENT

United States Declaration of War (1917)

The president's Presbyterian conscience tortured him relentlessly. He lost sleep, appeared gray and drawn. When someone asked him which side he hoped would win, he answered petulantly, "Neither." "He was resisting," Secretary of State Lansing recorded, "the irresistible logic of events." In the end Wilson could salve his conscience only by giving intervention an idealistic purpose: the war had become a threat to humanity. Unless the United States threw its weight into the balance, Western civilization itself might be destroyed. Out of the long bloodbath must come a new and better world. The war must be fought to end, for all time, war itself. Thus in the name not of vengeance and victory but of justice and humanity he sent his people into battle.

MOBILIZING THE ECONOMY

America's entry into the Great War determined its outcome. The Allies were running out of money and supplies; their troops, decimated by nearly three years in the trenches, were exhausted, disheartened, and rebellious. In February and March 1917, U-boats sent over a million tons of Allied shipping to the bottom of the Atlantic. The outbreak of the Russian Revolution in March 1917, at first lifting the spirits of the Western democracies, led to the

Bolshevik takeover under Lenin. The Russian armies collapsed; by December 1917 Russia was out of the war and the Germans were moving masses of men and equipment from the eastern front to France. Without the aid of the United States, it is likely that the war would have ended in 1918 on terms dictated from Berlin. Instead American men and supplies helped contain the Germans' last drives and then push them back to final defeat.

It was a close thing, for the United States entered the war little better prepared to fight than it had been in 1898. The conversion of American industry to war production had to be organized and carried out without prearrangement. Confusion and waste resulted. The hurriedly designed shipbuilding program was an almost total fiasco. The gigantic Hog Island yard in Maine, which employed at its peak over 34,000 workers, completed its first vessel only after the war ended. Airplane, tank, and artillery construction programs developed too slowly to affect the war. The big guns that backed up American soldiers in 1918 were made in France and Great Britain; of the 8.8 million rounds of artillery ammunition fired by American troops, a mere 8000 were manufactured in the United States. Congress authorized the manufacture of 20,000 airplanes, but only a handful, mostly British-designed planes made in America, got to France.

American pilots such as the great "ace" Captain Eddie Rickenbacker flew British Sopwiths and De Havillands or French Spads and Nieuports. Theodore Roosevelt's son Quentin was shot down while flying a Spad over Château Thierry in July 1918.

The problem of mobilization was complicated. It took Congress six weeks of hot debate merely to decide on conscription. Only in September 1917, nearly six months after the declaration of war, did the first draftees reach the training camps, and it is hard to see how Wilson could have speeded this process appreciably. He wisely supported the professional soldiers, who insisted that he resist the appeals of politicians who wanted to raise volunteer units, even rejecting, at considerable political cost, Theodore Roosevelt's offer to raise an entire army division.

Wilson was a forceful and inspiring war leader once he grasped what needed to be done. He displayed both determination and unfailing patience in the face of frustration and criticism. Raising an army was only a small part of the job. The Allies had to be supplied with food and munitions, and immense amounts of money had to be collected.

After several false starts, Wilson placed the task in the hands of the War Industries Board (WIB). The board was given almost dictatorial power to allocate scarce materials, standardize production, fix prices,

▲ U-Boat Campaign, 1914–1918

and coordinate American and Allied purchasing. Evaluating the mobilization effort raises interesting historical questions. The antitrust laws were suspended and producers were encouraged, even compelled, to cooperate with one another. Government regulation went far beyond what the New Nationalists had envisaged in 1912.

As for the New Freedom variety of laissez-faire, it had no place in a wartime economy. The nation's railroads, strained by immensely increased traffic, became progressively less efficient. A monumental tie-up in December and January 1917–1918 finally persuaded Wilson to appoint Secretary of the Treasury William G. McAdoo director-general of the railroads, with power to run the roads as a single system. McAdoo's Railroad Administration pooled all railroad equipment, centralized purchasing, standardized accounting practices, and raised wages and passenger rates.

Wilson accepted the kind of government-industry agreement developed under Theodore Roosevelt that he had denounced in 1912. Prices were set by the WIB at levels that allowed large profits—U.S. Steel, for example, despite high taxes, cleared over half a billion dollars in two years. It is at least arguable that producers would have turned out just as much even if compelled to charge lower prices.

At the start of the war, army procurement was decentralized and inefficient—as many as eight bureaus were purchasing material in competition with one another. One official bought 1200 typewriters, stacked them in the basement of a government building, and announced proudly to his superior: "There is going to be the greatest competition for typewriters around here, and I have them all."

► *text continues on page 640*

American
Lives

Harry S Truman

When the United States declared war on Germany in 1917, a Kansas farmer named Harry Truman, a former corporal in the National Guard, enlisted at once. He did so because he had been deeply impressed by President Wilson's talk about the need to make the world safe for democracy and because, as he explained later to his fiancée, Bess Wallace, "I wouldn't be left out of the greatest history-making epoch the world has ever seen." Being a former member of the National Guard, he was commissioned a first lieutenant of artillery.

In September Truman was sent for training to Camp Doniphan on the flat, treeless plains of Oklahoma. For six months he had scarcely a free moment, the training ranging from endless hours of drill, to learning how to fire a 3-inch artillery piece, to handling horses, to mastering the meaning and function of military terms like defilade and enfilade, to evening lectures about the war by Allied officers. In March 1918 he finally shipped out on the *George Washington* for France, accompanied by his unit and (he was extremely near-sighted) six pairs of glasses.

There, after a brief period living off the fat of the land in a hotel in the port of Brest, Truman was sent to an artillery school in Lorraine, where he learned to fire the famous French 75 cannons, the most important Allied artillery weapon. One practice maneuver, he wrote his fiancée, was witnessed by General Pershing himself, attended by a small army of staff officers and "more limousines than a January funeral."

In late August 1918, Truman, now a captain commanding a battery of the 2nd Battalion of the 129th Field Artillery, saw his first action, firing poison gas shells at German positions in the Vosges Mountains on the extreme eastern end of the front. When the Germans returned the fire, his inexperienced men broke in panic. Truman was knocked from his horse by the concussion of a shell and pinned to the ground when the horse fell on top of him, but he was uninjured and managed to stop the runaways and restore order. "The men think I am not much afraid of shells," he wrote later, "but they don't know I was too scared to run."

A month later the battalion was part of the great Allied attack in the Argonne Forest. H hour for his battery came

▲ Harry Truman as a captain during World War I.

▲ Harry and Bess Truman on wedding day on June 28, 1919. Eight years earlier, Truman had proposed to "Bessie" in a letter: "I've always had a sneakin' notion that some day maybe I'd amount to something. I doubt it now."

before dawn on September 26. "In three hours," Truman's biographer David McCullough writes, "more ammunition was expended than during the entire Civil War." Next day, following advancing infantry units, Truman and his men passed piles of American dead and they were harassed by a German aviator who swooped down low and lobbed hand grenades at them.

The Argonne fighting was long and exceptionally bloody, even for the western front. Luckily Truman's battery suffered only 3 casualties and the entire 129th Field Artillery only 129. Nevertheless, his service in France was "the most terrific experience" of Truman's life. Already a slight man, during the Argonne offensive he lost twenty pounds.

Two weeks after the armistice Truman found himself on leave in Paris. In a single day he did just about everything expected of a tourist—dining at Maxim's famous restaurant; catching a show at the Folies-Bergère, which he described as "what you'd expect at the Gaiety [in Kansas City] only more so"; getting his picture taken beside a captured German can-non; riding down the Champs-Elysées in a taxi; and taking in Notre Dame, the Arc de Triomphe, the Louvre museum, Napoleon's tomb, and all the other sights.

Back with his division at a camp in a muddy field near Ver-dun, life became a time of endless waiting, made worse rather than better by news from America, where a virulent influenza epidemic was killing thousands. "Every day nearly someone of my outfit will hear that his mother, sister or sweetheart is dead," Truman wrote. Much of his time was spent trying to keep the bored soldiers in his battery from get-ting in trouble. "It's some trick to keep 190 men out of devil-ment now," he wrote a cousin.

Finally, in March, orders came to break camp and head for home. After parading in triumph through Kansas City on horseback, Captain Harry Truman was honorably discharged on May 6 at Camp Funston, Kansas. On June 28, at Trinity Episcopal Church in Independence, Missouri, he and Bess Wallace were married.

▲ "Enlist"—a poster by Fred Spear, published in June 1915 by the Boston Committee of Public Safety, evoking the drowning deaths of women and children of the *Lusitania*.

Mobilization required close cooperation between business and the military. However, the army, suspicious of civilian institutions, resisted cooperating with them. Wilson finally compelled the War Department to place officers on WIB committees, laying the foundation for what was later to be known as the "industrial-military complex," an alliance between business and military leaders.

The history of industrial mobilization was the history of the entire home-front effort in microcosm: marvels were performed, but the task was so gigantic and unprecedented that a full year passed before an efficient system had been devised, and many unforeseen results occurred.

The problem of mobilizing agricultural resources was solved more quickly, and this was fortunate because in April 1917 the British had on hand only a six-week supply of food. As food administrator Wilson appointed Herbert Hoover, a mining engineer who had headed the Belgian Relief Commission earlier in the war. Acting under powers granted by the Lever Act of 1917, Hoover set the price of wheat at $2.20 a bushel in order to encourage production. He established a government corporation to purchase the entire American and Cuban sugar crop, which he then doled out to American and British refiners. To avoid rationing he organized a campaign to persuade consumers to conserve food voluntarily. One slogan ran "If U fast U beat U boats"; another, "Serve beans by all means."

"Wheatless Mondays" and "meatless Tuesdays" were the rule, and although no law compelled their observance, the public responded patriotically. Boy Scouts dug up backyards and vacant lots to plant vegetable gardens; chefs devised new recipes to save on scarce items; restaurants added horsemeat, rabbit, and whale steak to their menus and doled out butter and sugar to customers in minuscule amounts. Mothers pressured their children to "Hooverize" their plates. Chicago residents were so successful in making use of leftovers that the volume of raw garbage in the city declined from 12,862 tons to 8,386 tons per month.

Without subjecting its own citizens to serious inconvenience, the United States increased food exports from 12.3 million tons to 18.6 million tons. Farmers, of course, profited greatly. Their real income went up nearly 30 percent between 1915 and 1918.

WORKERS IN WARTIME

With the army siphoning so many men from the labor market and with immigration reduced to a trickle, unemployment disappeared and wages rose. Although the cost of living soared, imposing hardships on people with fixed incomes, the boom produced unprecedented opportunities.

Americans, always a mobile people, pulled up their roots in record numbers. Disadvantaged groups, especially blacks, were particularly attracted by jobs in big-city factories. Early in the conflict, the government began regulating the wages and hours of workers building army camps and manufacturing uniforms. In April 1918 Wilson created the National War Labor Board, headed by former president Taft and Frank P. Walsh, a prominent lawyer, to settle labor disputes. The board considered more than 1200 cases and prevented many strikes. The War Labor Policies Board, chaired by Felix Frankfurter of the Harvard Law School, set wages-and-hours standards for each major war industry. Since these were determined in consultation

with employers and representatives of labor, they speeded the unionization of workers by compelling management, even in antiunion industries like steel, to deal with labor leaders. Union membership rose by 2.3 million during the war.

However, the wartime emergency roused the public against strikers; some conservatives even demanded that war workers, like soldiers, be conscripted. While he opposed strikes that impeded the war effort, Wilson set great store in preserving the individual worker's freedom of action. It would be "most unfortunate . . . to relax the laws by which safeguards have been thrown about labor," he said. "We must accomplish the results we desire by organized effort rather than compulsion."

Trends in the steel industry reflected the improvement of wartime labor earnings. Wages of unskilled steelworkers more than doubled. Thousands of southern blacks flocked into the steel towns. Union organizers made inroads in many plants, and by the summer of 1918 they were preparing an all-out effort to unionize the industry. If the world was to be made safe for democracy, they argued, there must be "economic democracy [along] with political democracy."

PAYING FOR THE WAR

Wilson managed the task of financing the war effectively. The struggle cost the United States about $33.5 billion, not counting pensions and other postwar expenses. About $7 billion of this was lent to the Allies,[2] but since this money was spent largely in America, it contributed to the national prosperity.

Over two-thirds of the cost of the war was met by borrowing. Five Liberty and Victory Loan drives, spurred by advertising, parades, and other appeals to patriotism, persuaded people to open their purses. Industrialists, eager to instill in their employees a sense of personal involvement in the war effort, conducted campaigns in their plants. Some went so far as to threaten "A Bond or Your Job," but more typical was the appeal of the managers of the Gary, Indiana, plant of U.S. Steel, who published bond advertisements in six languages in order to reach their immigrant workers.

In addition to borrowing, the government collected about $10.5 billion in taxes during the war. A steeply graduated income tax took more than 75

---

[2]In 1914 Americans owed foreigners about $3.8 billion. By 1919 Americans *were owed* $12.5 billion by Europeans alone.

percent of the incomes of the wealthiest citizens. A 65 percent excess-profits tax and a 25 percent inheritance tax were also enacted. Thus although many individuals made fortunes from the war, its cost was distributed far more equitably than during the Civil War.

Americans also contributed generously to philanthropic agencies engaged in war work. Most notable, perhaps, was the great 1918 drive of the United War Work Council, an interfaith religious group, which raised over $200 million mainly to finance recreational programs for the troops overseas.

PROPAGANDA AND CIVIL LIBERTIES

Wilson was preeminently a teacher and preacher, a specialist in the transmission of ideas and ideals. He excelled at mobilizing public opinion and inspiring Americans to work for the better world he hoped would emerge from the war. In April 1917 he created the Committee on Public Information (CPI), headed by the journalist George Creel. Soon 75,000 speakers were deluging the country with propaganda prepared by hundreds of CPI writers. They pictured the war as a crusade for freedom and democracy, the Germans as a bestial people bent on world domination.

A large majority of the nation supported the war enthusiastically. But thousands of persons—German-Americans and Irish-Americans, for example; people of pacifist leanings such as Jane Addams, the founder of Hull House; and some who thought both sides in the war were wrong— still opposed American involvement. Creel's committee and a number of unofficial "patriotic" groups allowed their enthusiasm for the conversion of the hesitant to become suppression of dissent. People who refused to buy war bonds were often exposed to public ridicule and even assault. Those with German names were persecuted without regard for their views; some school boards outlawed the teaching of the German language; sauerkraut was renamed "liberty cabbage." Opponents of the war were subjected to coarse abuse. A cartoonist pictured Senator Robert La Follette, who had opposed entering the war, receiving an Iron Cross from the German militarists, and the faculty of his own University of Wisconsin voted to censure him.

Although Wilson spoke in defense of free speech, his actions opposed it. He signed the Espionage Act of 1917, which imposed fines of up to $10,000 and

DOCUMENT

Buffington, "Friendly Words to the Foreign Born"

▲ These members of the Woman's Peace party urge Wilson to find a way to stay out of the war in Europe. They are carrying fans to reinforce their message.

jail sentences ranging to twenty years on persons convicted of aiding the enemy or obstructing recruiting, and he authorized the postmaster general to ban from the mails any material that seemed treasonable or seditious.

In May 1918, again with Wilson's approval, Congress passed the Sedition Act, which made "saying anything" to discourage the purchase of war bonds a crime, with the proviso that investment counselors could still offer "bona fide and not disloyal advice" to clients. The law also made it illegal to "utter, print, write, or publish any disloyal, profane, scurrilous, or abusive language" about the government, the Constitution, or the uniform of the army or navy. Socialist periodicals such as *The Masses* were suppressed, and Eugene V. Debs was sentenced to ten years in prison for making an antiwar speech. Ricardo Flores Magón, an anarchist, was sentenced to twenty years in jail for publishing a statement criticizing Wilson's Mexican policy, an issue that had nothing to do with the war.

These laws went far beyond what was necessary to protect the national interest. Citizens were jailed for suggesting that the draft law was unconstitutional and for criticizing private organizations like the Red Cross and the YMCA. One woman was sent to prison for writing, "I am for the people, and the government is for the profiteers."

The Supreme Court upheld the constitutionality of the Espionage Act in *Schenck* v. *United States* (1919), a case involving a man who had mailed circulars to draftees urging them to refuse to report for induction into the army. Free speech has its limits, Justice Oliver Wendell Holmes, Jr., explained. No one has the right to cry, "Fire!" in a crowded theater. When there is a "clear and present danger" that a particular statement would threaten the national interest, it can be repressed by law. In peacetime Schenck's circulars would be permissible, but not in time of war.

The "clear and present danger" doctrine did not prevent judges and juries from interpreting the espionage and sedition acts broadly, and although in many instances higher courts overturned their decisions, this usually did not occur until after the war. The wartime repression far exceeded anything that happened in Great Britain and France. In 1916 the French novelist Henri Barbusse published *Le Feu (Under Fire)*, a graphic account of the horrors and purposelessness of trench warfare. In one chapter Barbusse described a pilot flying over the trenches on a Sunday, observing French and German soldiers at Mass in the open fields, each worshiping the same God. Yet *Le Feu* circulated freely in France and even won the coveted Prix Goncourt.

WARTIME REFORMS

The American mobilization experience was part and product of the progressive era. The work of the progressives at the national and state levels in expanding government functions in order to deal with social and economic problems provided precedents and conditioned the people for the all-out effort of 1917 and 1918. Social and economic planning and the management of huge business operations by public boards and committees got their first practical tests. College professors, technicians, and others with complex skills entered government service en masse. The federal government for the first time actively entered such fields as housing and labor relations.

Many progressives believed that the war was creating the sense of common purpose that would stimulate the people to act unselfishly to benefit the poor and to eradicate social evils. Patriotism and public service seemed at last united. Secretary of War Newton D. Baker, a prewar urban reformer, expressed this attitude in supporting a federal child labor law: "We cannot afford, when we are losing boys in France, to lose children in the United States."

Anti-VD Poster, WWI

Men and women of this sort worked for a dozen causes only remotely related to the war effort. The women's suffrage movement was brought to fruition, as was the campaign against alcohol. Both the Eighteenth Amendment, outlawing alcoholic beverages, and the Nineteenth, giving women the vote, were adopted at least in part because of the war. Reformers began to talk about health insurance. The progressive campaign against prostitution and venereal disease gained strength, winning the enthusiastic support both of persons worried about inexperienced local girls being seduced by the soldiers and of those concerned lest prostitutes lead innocent soldiers astray. One of the latter type claimed to have persuaded "over 1000 fallen women" to promise not to go near any army camps.

The effort to wipe out prostitution around military installations was a cause of some misunderstanding with the Allies, who provided licensed facilities for their troops as a matter of course. When the premier of France graciously offered to supply prostitutes for American units in his country, Secretary Baker is said to have remarked: "For God's sake . . . don't show this to the President or he'll stop the war." Apparently Baker had a rather peculiar sense of humor. After a tour of the front in France, he assured an American women's group that life in the trenches was "far less uncomfortable" than he had thought and that not a single American doughboy

was "living a life which he would not be willing to have [his] mother see him live."

WOMEN AND BLACKS IN WARTIME

Although a number of prominent feminists were pacifists, most supported the war enthusiastically, moved by patriotism and the belief that opposition to the war would doom their hopes of gaining the vote. They also expected that the war would open up many kinds of high-paying jobs to women. To some extent it did; about a million women replaced men in uniform, but the numbers actually engaged in war industries were small (about 6000 found jobs making airplanes, for example), and the gains were fleeting. When the war

▲ Women workers at the Dupont factory in Old Hickory, Tennessee, in 1917. They are forming smokeless gunpowder into long strips, which will then be cut to be used in artillery shells and other armaments.

▲ When manufacturers in East Saint Louis (Illinois) sought to weaken labor unions by hiring African American workers from Mississippi and western Tennessee, the white workers went on a rampage. When the dust had cleared, much of East Saint Louis had burned down and several dozen blacks and a few whites were dead. Here several National Guardsmen lead a black to safety.

materialize. Between 1870 and 1890 only about 80,000 blacks moved to northern cities. Compared with the influx from Europe and from northern farms, this number was inconsequential. The black proportion of the population of New York City, for example, fell from over 10 percent in 1800 to under 2 percent in 1900.

Around the turn of the century, as the first postslavery generation reached maturity and as southern repression increased, the northward movement quickened—about 200,000 blacks migrated between 1890 and 1910. Then, after 1914, the war boom drew blacks north in a flood. Agents of northern manufacturers flocked into the cotton belt to recruit them in wholesale lots. "Leave the benighted land," urged the *Chicago Defender,* a black-owned newspaper with a considerable circulation in southern states. "Get out of the South." Half a million made the move between 1914 and 1919. The African American population of New York City rose from 92,000 to 152,000; that of Chicago from 44,000 to 109,000; that of Detroit from 5700 to 41,000.

ended, most women who were engaged in industrial work either left their jobs voluntarily or were fired to make room for returning veterans. Some women went overseas as nurses, and a few served as ambulance drivers and YMCA workers.

Most unions were unsympathetic to the idea of enrolling women, and the government did little to encourage women to do more for the war effort than prepare bandages, knit warm clothing for soldiers, participate in food conservation programs, and encourage people to buy war bonds. There was a Women in Industry Service in the Department of Labor and a Woman's Committee of the Council of National Defense, but both served primarily as window dressing for the Wilson administration. The final report of another wartime agency, issued in 1919, admitted that few women war workers had been paid as much as men and that women had been promoted more slowly than men, were not accepted by unions, and were discharged promptly when the war ended.

The wartime "great migration" of southern blacks to northern cities where jobs were available brought them important economic benefits. Actually, the emigration of blacks from the former slave states began with emancipation, but the mass exodus that many people had expected was slow to

Life for the newcomers was difficult; many whites resented them; workers feared them as potential strikebreakers yet refused to admit them into their unions. In East St. Louis, Illinois, where employers had brought in large numbers of blacks in an attempt to discourage local unions from striking for higher wages, a bloody riot erupted during the summer of 1917 in which nine whites and an undetermined number of blacks were killed. As in peacetime, the Wilson administration was at worst antagonistic and at best indifferent to blacks' needs and aspirations.

Nevertheless, the blacks who moved north during the war were, as a group, infinitely better off, materially and psychologically, than those they left behind. Many earned good wages and were accorded at least some human rights. They were not treated by the whites as equals, or even in most cases entirely fairly, but they could vote, send their children to decent schools, and within reasonable limits do and say what they pleased without fear of humiliation or physical attack.

African American Population, 1910 and 1950

▲ A recruiting poster for the "True Sons of Freedom," which encouraged African Americans to enlist. In fact, some 350,000 black Americans served in segregated units during the Great War. Several such units fought alongside French units, and 171 African Americans were awarded the French Legion of Honor, an award for courageous military service.

killed seventeen white civilians, black recruits were dispersed among many camps for training to lessen the possibility of trouble.

In the military service, all blacks were placed in segregated units. Only a handful were commissioned officers. Despite the valor displayed by black soldiers in the Civil War and the large role they played in the Spanish-American War, where five blacks had won the Congressional Medal of Honor, most blacks, even those sent overseas, were assigned to labor battalions, working as stevedores and common laborers. But many fought and died for their country. Altogether about 200,000 served overseas. There were black Red Cross nurses in France, and some blacks held relatively high posts in government agencies in Washington, the most important being Emmett J. Scott, who was special assistant for Negro affairs in the War Department.

W. E. B. Du Bois supported the war wholeheartedly. He praised Wilson for making, at last, a strong statement against lynching, which had increased to a shocking extent during the previous decade. He even went along with the fact that the handful of black officer candidates were trained in a segregated camp. "Let us," he wrote in *The Crisis*, "while the war lasts, forget our special grievances and close ranks shoulder to shoulder with our fellow citizens and the allied nations that are fighting for democracy."

There were two black regiments in the regular army and a number of black national guard units when the war began, and once these outfits were brought up to combat strength, no more volunteers were accepted. Indeed, at first no blacks were conscripted; Southerners in particular found the thought of giving large numbers of guns to blacks and teaching them how to use them most disturbing. However, blacks were soon drafted, and once they were, a larger proportion of them than whites were taken. One Georgia draft board exempted more than 500 of 815 white registrants and only 6 of the 202 blacks in its jurisdiction before its members were relieved of their duties. After a riot in Texas in which black soldiers

Many blacks condemned Du Bois's accommodationism (which he promptly abandoned when the war ended), but most saw the war as an opportunity to demonstrate their patriotism and prove their worth. For the moment the prevailing mood was one of optimism. "We may expect to see the walls of prejudice gradually crumble"—this was the common attitude of blacks in 1917 and 1918. If winning the war would make the world safe for democracy, surely blacks in the United States would be better off when it was won. Whether or not this turned out to be so was (and still is) a matter of opinion.

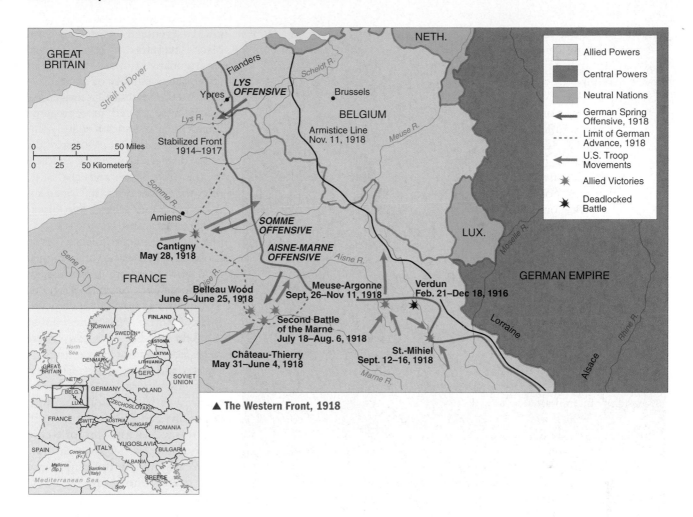

▲ The Western Front, 1918

AMERICANS: TO THE TRENCHES AND OVER THE TOP

All activity on the home front had one ultimate objective: defeating the Central Powers on the battlefield. This was accomplished. The navy performed with special distinction. In April 1917, German submarines sank more than 870,000 tons of Allied shipping; after April 1918, monthly losses never reached 300,000 tons. The decision to send merchant ships across the Atlantic in convoys screened by destroyers made the reduction possible. Checking the U-boats was essential because of the need to transport American troops to Europe. Slightly more than 2 million soldiers made the voyage safely. Those who crossed on fast ocean liners were in little danger as long as the vessel maintained high speed and followed a zigzag course, a lesson learned from the *Lusitania,* whose captain had neglected both precautions. Those who traveled on slower troop transports benefited from the protection of destroyers and also from the fact that the Germans concentrated on attacking

supply ships. They continued to believe that inexperienced American soldiers would not be a major factor in the war.

The first units of the American Expeditionary Force (AEF), elements of the regular army commanded by General John J. Pershing, reached Paris on Independence Day, 1917. They took up positions on the front near Verdun in October. Not until the spring of 1918, however, did the "doughboys" play a significant role in the fighting, though their mere presence boosted French and British morale.

AUDIO
"Over There"

Pershing insisted on maintaining his troops as independent units; he would not allow them to be filtered into the Allied armies as reinforcements. This was part of a perhaps unfortunate general policy that reflected America's isolationism. (Wilson always referred to the other nations fighting Germany as "associates," not as "allies.")

In March 1918 the Germans launched a great spring offensive, their armies strengthened by thousands of veterans from the Russian front. By late May

they had reached a point on the Marne River near the town of Château-Thierry, only fifty miles from Paris. Early in June the AEF fought its first major engagements, driving the Germans back from Château-Thierry and Belleau Wood.

In this fighting only about 27,500 Americans saw action, and they suffered appalling losses. Nevertheless, when the Germans advanced again in the direction of the Marne in mid July, 85,000 Americans were in the lines that withstood their charge. Then, in the major turning point of the war, the Allied armies counterattacked. Some 270,000 Americans participated, helping to flatten the German bulge between Reims and Soissons. By late August the American First Army, 500,000 strong, was poised before the Saint-Mihiel salient, a deep extension of the German lines southeast of Verdun. On September 12 this army, buttressed by French troops, struck and in two days wiped out the salient.

Late in September began the greatest American engagement of the war. No fewer than 1.2 million doughboys drove forward west of Verdun into the Argonne Forest. For over a month of indescribable horror they inched ahead through the tangle of the Argonne and the formidable defenses of the Hindenburg line, while to the west, French and British armies staged similar drives. In this one offensive the AEF suffered 120,000 casualties. Finally, on November 1, they broke the German center and raced toward the vital Sedan-Mézières railroad. On November 11, with Allied armies advancing on all fronts, the Germans signed the armistice, ending the fighting.

PREPARING FOR PEACE

The fighting ended on November 11, 1918, but the shape of the postwar world remained to be determined. European society had been shaken to its foundations. Confusion reigned. People wanted peace yet burned for revenge. Millions faced starvation. Other millions were disillusioned by the seemingly purposeless sacrifices of four years of horrible war. Communism—to some an idealistic promise of human betterment, to others a commitment to rational economic and social planning, to still others a danger to individual freedom, toleration, and democracy—having conquered Russia, threatened to envelop Germany and much of the defunct Austro-Hungarian Empire, perhaps even the victorious Allies. How could stability be restored? How could victory be made worth its enormous cost?

Woodrow Wilson had grasped the significance of the war while most statesmen still thought that triumph on the battlefield would settle everything automatically. As early as January 1917 he had realized that victory would be wasted if the winners permitted themselves the luxury of vengeance. Such a policy would disrupt the balance of power and lead to economic and social chaos. The victors must build a better society, not punish those they believed had destroyed the old.

In a speech to Congress on January 8, 1918, Wilson outlined a plan, known as the Fourteen Points, designed to make the world "fit and safe to live in." The peace treaty should be negotiated in full view of world opinion, not in secret. It should guarantee the freedom of the seas to all nations, in war as in peacetime. It should tear down barriers to international trade, provide for a drastic reduction of armaments, and establish a colonial system that would take proper account of the interests of the native peoples concerned. European boundaries should be redrawn so that no substantial group would have to live under a government not of its own choosing.

More specifically, captured Russian territory should be restored, Belgium evacuated, Alsace-Lorraine returned to France, the heterogeneous nationalities of Austria-Hungary accorded autonomy. Italy's frontiers should be adjusted "along clearly recognizable lines of nationality," the Balkans made free, Turkey divested of its subject peoples, an independent

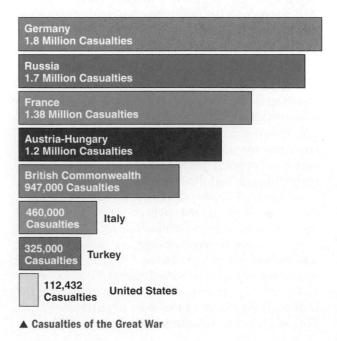

▲ Casualties of the Great War

▲ A street sweeper in New York wearing a mask to protect him from the Spanish influenza. Citizens of San Francisco were roused by the popular jingle: "Obey the Laws. Wear the gauze. Protect your jaws from septic paws." In fact, the Spanish influenza virus contained just eight strands of RNA, a piece of genetic code too small to be seen with a microscope. The masks were useless.

Polish state (with access to the Baltic Sea) created. To oversee the new system, Wilson insisted, "a general association of nations must be formed under specific covenants for the purpose of affording mutual guarantees of political independence and territorial integrity to great and small states alike."

Wilson's Fourteen Points for a fair peace lifted the hopes of people everywhere. After the guns fell silent, however, the vagueness and inconsistencies in his list became apparent. Complete national self-determination was impossible in Europe; there were too many regions of mixed population for every group to be satisfied. Self-determination, like the war itself, also fostered the spirit of nationalism that Wilson's dream of international organization, a

league of nations, was designed to de-emphasize. Furthermore, the Allies had made territorial commitments to one another in secret treaties that ran counter to the principle of self-determination, and they were not ready to give up all claims to Germany's colonies. Freedom of the seas in wartime posed another problem; the British flatly refused to accept the idea. In every Allied country, millions rejected the idea of a peace without indemnities. They expected to make the enemy pay for the war, hoping, as Sir Eric Geddes, first lord of the Admiralty, said, to squeeze Germany "as a lemon is squeezed—until the pips squeak."

Wilson assumed that the practical benefits of his program would compel opponents to fall in line. He had the immense advantage of seeking nothing for his own country and the additional strength of being leader of the one important nation to emerge from the war richer and more powerful than it had been in 1914.

Yet this combination of altruism, idealism, and power was his undoing; it intensified his tendency to be overbearing and undermined his judgment. He had never found it easy to compromise. Once, when he was president of Princeton, he got into an argument over some abstract question with a professor while shooting a game of pool. To avoid acrimony, the professor finally said: "Well, Doctor Wilson, there are two sides to every question." "Yes," Wilson answered, "a right side and a wrong side." Now, believing that the fate of humanity hung on his actions, he was unyielding. Always a preacher, he became in his own mind a prophet—almost, one fears, a kind of god.

In the last weeks of the war Wilson proved to be a brilliant diplomat, first dangling the Fourteen Points before the German people to encourage them to overthrow Kaiser Wilhelm II and sue for an armistice, then sending Colonel House to Paris to persuade Allied leaders to accept the Fourteen Points as the basis for the peace. When the Allies raised objections, House made small concessions, but by hinting that the United States might make a separate peace with Germany, he forced them to agree. Under the armistice, Germany had to withdraw behind the Rhine River and surrender its submarines, together with quantities of munitions and other materials. In return it received the assurance of the Allies that the Wilsonian principles would prevail at the Paris peace conference.

Wilson then came to a daring decision: He would personally attend the conference as a member of the United States Peace Commission. This was a precedent-shattering step, for no president

had ever left American territory while in office. (Taft, who had a summer home on the St. Lawrence River in Canada, never vacationed there during his term, believing that to do so would be unconstitutional.)

Wilson probably erred in going to Paris, but not because of the novelty or possible illegality of the act. By going, he was turning his back on obvious domestic problems. Western farmers believed that they had been discriminated against during the war, since wheat prices had been controlled while southern cotton had been allowed to rise unchecked from seven cents a pound in 1914 to thirty-five cents in 1919. The administration's drastic tax program had angered many businessmen. Labor, despite its gains, was restive in the face of reconversion to peacetime conditions.

Wilson had increased his political difficulties by making a partisan appeal for the election of a Democratic Congress in 1918. Republicans, who had in many instances supported his war program more loyally than the Democrats, considered the action a gross affront. The appeal failed; the Republicans won majorities in both houses. Wilson appeared to have been repudiated at home at the very moment that he set forth to represent the nation abroad. Most important, Wilson intended to break with the isolationist tradition and bring the United States into a league of nations. Such a revolutionary change would require explanation; he should have undertaken a major campaign to convince the American people of the wisdom of this step.

THE PARIS PEACE CONFERENCE AND THE VERSAILLES TREATY

Wilson arrived in Europe a world hero. He toured England, France, and Italy briefly and was greeted ecstatically almost everywhere. The reception tended to increase his sense of mission and to convince him, in the fashion of a typical progressive, that whatever the European politicians might say about it, "the people" were behind his program.

▲ The "Big Four" at the Hotel Crillon in Paris. First row, from the left: Orlando of Italy, Lloyd George of Great Britain, Clemenceau of France, and Wilson of the United States.

When the conference settled down to its work, control quickly fell into the hands of the so-called Big Four: Wilson, Prime Minister David Lloyd George of Great Britain, Premier Georges Clemenceau of France, and Prime Minister Vittorio Orlando of Italy. Wilson stood out in this group but did not dominate it. His principal advantage in the negotiations was his untiring industry. He alone of the leaders tried to master all the complex details of the task.

The 78-year-old Clemenceau cared only for one thing: French security. He viewed Wilson cynically, saying that since mankind had been unable to keep God's Ten Commandments, it was unlikely to do better with Wilson's Fourteen Points. Lloyd George's approach was pragmatic and almost cavalier. He sympathized with much that Wilson was trying to accomplish but found the president's frequent sermonettes about "right being more important than might, and justice being more eternal than force" incomprehensible. "If you want to succeed in politics," Lloyd George advised a British statesman, "you must keep your conscience well under control." Orlando, clever, cultured, a believer in international cooperation but inflexible where Italian national interests were concerned, was not the equal of his three colleagues in influence. He left the conference in a huff when they failed to meet all his demands.

The conference labored from January to May 1919 and finally brought forth the Versailles Treaty.

▲ **Europe Before World War I**

▲ **Europe After World War I**

American liberals whose hopes had soared at the thought of a peace based on the Fourteen Points found the document abysmally disappointing.

The peace settlement failed to carry out the principle of self-determination completely. It gave Italy a large section of the Austrian Tyrol, though the area contained 200,000 people who considered themselves Austrians. Other German-speaking groups were incorporated into the new states of Poland and Czechoslovakia.

The victors forced Germany to accept responsibility for having caused the war—an act of senseless vindictiveness as well as a gross oversimplification—and to sign a "blank check," agreeing to pay for all damage to civilian properties and even future pensions and other indirect war costs. This reparations bill, as finally determined, amounted to $33 billion. Instead of attacking imperialism, the treaty attacked German imperialism; instead of seeking a new international social order based on liberty and democracy, it created a great-power entente designed to crush Germany and to exclude Bolshevik Russia from the family of nations. It said nothing about freedom of the seas, the reduction of tariffs, or disarmament.

Wilson himself backtracked on his pledge to honor the right of self-determination. For example, Point 12 of the Fourteen Points called for the "autonomous development" of Arab peoples who had lived under Ottoman rule. But Wilson had second thoughts about their self-determination. Secretary of State Lansing worried about the "danger of putting such ideas into the minds of certain races," particularly the "Mohammedans of Syria and Palestine." Wilson reluctantly deleted explicit references to self-determination from the postwar settlements. Arab leaders seethed. Similarly, Ho Chi Minh, a young Vietnamese nationalist, was embittered by the failure at Versailles to deliver his people from French colonial rule. He decided to become a communist revolutionary. The repercussions of Arab and Vietnamese discontent, though far removed from American interests at the time, would be felt in full force much later.

To those who had taken Wilson's "peace without victory" speech and the Fourteen Points literally, the Versailles Treaty seemed an abomination. The complaints of the critics were individually reasonable, yet their conclusions were not entirely fair. The new map of Europe left fewer people on "foreign" soil than in any earlier period of history. Although the Allies seized the German colonies, they were required, under the mandate system, to render the League of Nations annual accounts of their stewardship and to prepare the inhabitants for eventual independence. Above all, Wilson had persuaded the powers to incorporate the League of Nations in the treaty.

Wilson expected the League of Nations to make up for all the inadequacies of the Versailles Treaty.

Once the League had begun to function, problems like freedom of the seas and disarmament would solve themselves, he argued, and the relaxation of trade barriers would surely follow. The League would arbitrate international disputes, act as a central body for registering treaties, and employ military and economic sanctions against aggressor nations. Each member promised (Article 10) to protect the "territorial integrity" and "political independence" of all other members. No nation could be made to go to war against its will, but Wilson emphasized that all were *morally* obligated to carry out League decisions. By any standard, Wilson had achieved a remarkably moderate peace, one full of hope for the future. Except for the war guilt clause and the heavy reparations imposed on Germany, he could be justly proud of his work.

THE SENATE REJECTS THE LEAGUE OF NATIONS

When Wilson returned from France, he finally directed his attention to the task of winning public approval of his handiwork. A large majority of the people probably favored the League of Nations in principle, though few understood all its implications or were entirely happy with every detail. Wilson had persuaded the Allies to accept certain changes in the original draft to mollify American opposition. No nation could be forced to accept a colonial mandate, and "domestic questions" such as tariffs and the control of immigration and the Monroe Doctrine were excluded from League control.

Many senators found these modifications insufficient. Even before the peace conference ended, thirty-seven Republican senators signed a manifesto, devised by Henry Cabot Lodge of Massachusetts, opposing Wilson's League and demanding that the question of an international organization be put off until "the urgent business of negotiating peace terms with Germany" had been completed. Wilson rejected this suggestion icily. Further alterations were out of the question. "Anyone who opposes me . . . I'll crush!" he told one Democratic senator. "I shall consent to nothing. The Senate must take its medicine." Thus the stage was set for a monumental test of strength between the president and the Republican majority in the Senate.

Partisanship, principle, and prejudice clashed mightily in this contest. A presidential election loomed. Should the League prove a success, the Republicans wanted to be able to claim a share of the credit, but Wilson had refused to allow them to participate in drafting the document. This predisposed all of them to favor changes. Politics aside, genuine alarm at the possible sacrifice of American sovereignty to an international authority led many Republicans to urge modification of the League covenant, or constitution. Personal dislike of Wilson and his high-handed methods motivated others. Yet the noble purpose of the League made many reluctant to reject it entirely. The intense desire of the people to have an end to the long war made GOP leaders hesitate before voting down the Versailles Treaty, and they could not reject the League without rejecting the treaty.

Wilson could count on the Democratic senators almost to a man, but he had to win over many Republicans to obtain the two-thirds majority necessary for ratification. Republican opinion divided roughly into three segments. At one extreme were some dozen "irreconcilables," led by the shaggy-browed William E. Borah of Idaho, an able and kindly person of progressive leanings but an uncompromising isolationist. Borah claimed that he would vote against the League even if Jesus Christ returned to earth to argue in its behalf, and most of his followers were equally inflexible. At the other extreme stood another dozen "mild" reservationists who were in favor of the League but who hoped to alter it in minor ways, chiefly for political purposes. In the middle were the "strong" reservationists, senators willing to go along with the League only if American sovereignty were fully protected and if it were made clear that their party had played a major role in fashioning the final document.

Senator Lodge, the leader of the Republican opposition, was a haughty, rather cynical, intensely partisan individual. He possessed a keen intelligence, a mastery of parliamentary procedure, and, as chairman of the Senate Foreign Relations Committee, a great deal of power. Although not an isolationist, he had little faith in the League. He also had a profound distrust of Democrats, especially Wilson, whom he considered a hypocrite and a coward. The president's pious idealism left him cold. While perfectly ready to see the country participate actively in world affairs, Lodge insisted that its right to determine its own best interests in every situation be preserved. He had been a senator since 1893 and an admirer of senatorial independence since early manhood. When a Democratic president tried to ram the Versailles Treaty down the Senate's throat, he fought him with every weapon he could muster.

DOCUMENT

Henry Cabot Lodge's Objections to Treaty of Versailles

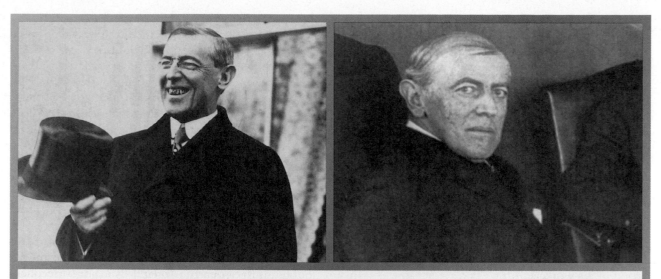

DEBATING THE PAST

Did a stroke sway Wilson's judgment? Wilson's refusal to accept some of Lodge's reservations to the League of Nations ensured its defeat; and without the participation of the young new superpower, the League was likely doomed to failure. Was Wilson's refusal motivated by principle or personal pique?

Historians such as Arthur Link (1957) maintained that Lodge's reservations would have emasculated the League. Because "half a League" was worse than none at all, Wilson was right to have stood firm. Wilson's critics described his actions as little more than a temper tantrum, like a child who destroys a favorite toy. George Kennan (1951) thought Wilson's judgment was beclouded by foolish and impractical moral imperatives.

These pictures suggest another interpretation. The first shows Wilson at his inauguration in 1912; the second, at his last cabinet meeting in 1919, after he had suffered a major stroke. Edwin Weinstein (1981), a physician, found that Wilson's stroke had been more debilitating than had been reported. His impaired physical condition had probably contributed to Wilson's obdurate refusal to compromise.

Arthur Link, *Wilson the Diplomatist* (1957), George Kennan, *American Diplomacy* (1951), Edwin Weinstein, *A Medical and Psychological Biography* (1981).

Lodge belonged to the strong reservationist faction. His own proposals, known as the Lodge Reservations, fourteen in number to match Wilson's Fourteen Points, limited U.S. obligations to the League and stated in unmistakable terms the right of Congress to decide when to honor these obligations. Some of the reservations were mere quibbles. Others, such as the provision that the United States would not endorse Japan's seizure of Chinese territory, were included mainly to embarrass Wilson by pointing up compromises he had made at Versailles. The most important reservation applied to Article 10 of the League covenant, which committed signatories to protect the political independence and territorial integrity of all member nations. Wilson had rightly called Article 10 "the heart of the Covenant." One of Lodge's reservations made it inoperable so far as the United States was concerned

"unless in any particular case the Congress . . . shall by act or joint resolution so provide."

Lodge performed brilliantly, if somewhat unscrupulously, in uniting the three Republican factions behind his reservations. He got the irreconcilables to agree to them by conceding their right to vote against the final version in any event, and he held the mild reservationists in line by modifying some of his demands and stressing the importance of party unity. Reservations—as distinct from amendments—would not have to win the formal approval of other League members. In addition, the Lodge proposals dealt forthrightly with the problem of reconciling traditional concepts of national sovereignty with the new idea of world cooperation. Supporters of the League could accept them without sacrifice of principle. Wilson, however, refused to agree. "Accept the Treaty with the Lodge reservations?" the president snorted

when a friendly senator warned him that he must accept a compromise. "Never! Never!"

This foolish intransigence seems almost incomprehensible in a man of Wilson's intelligence and political experience. In part his hatred of Lodge accounts for it, in part his faith in his League. His physical condition in 1919 also played a role. At Paris he had suffered a violent attack of indigestion that was probably a symptom of a minor stroke. Thereafter, many observers noted small changes in his personality, particularly increased stubbornness and a loss of good judgment. Instead of making concessions, the president set out early in September on a nationwide speaking crusade to rally support for the League. In three weeks, Wilson traveled some 10,000 miles by train and gave forty speeches, some of them brilliant. But they had little effect on senatorial opinion, and the effort drained his last physical reserves. On September 25, after an address in Pueblo, Colorado, he collapsed. The rest of the trip had to be canceled. A few days later, in Washington, he suffered a severe stroke that partially paralyzed his left side.

For nearly two months the president was almost totally cut off from affairs of state, leaving supporters of the League leaderless while Lodge maneuvered the reservations through the Senate. Gradually, popular attitudes toward the League shifted. Organized groups of Italian-, Irish-, and German-Americans, angered by what they considered unfair treatment of their native lands in the Versailles Treaty, clamored for outright rejection. The arguments of the irreconcilables persuaded many citizens that Wilson had made too sharp a break with America's isolationist past and that the Lodge Reservations were therefore necessary. Other issues connected with the reconversion of society to a peacetime basis increasingly occupied the public mind.

A coalition of Democratic and moderate Republican senators could easily have carried the treaty. That no such coalition was organized was Wilson's fault. Lodge obtained the simple majority necessary to add his reservations to the treaty merely by keeping his own party united. When the time came for the final roll call on November 19, Wilson, bitter and emotionally distraught, urged the Democrats to vote for rejection. "Better a thousand times to go down fighting than to dip your colors to dishonorable compromise," he explained to his wife. Thus the amended treaty failed, thirty-five to fifty-five, the irreconcilables and the Democrats voting against it. Lodge then allowed the original draft without his reservations to come to a vote. Again the result was defeat, thirty-eight to fifty-three. Only one Republican cast a ballot for ratification.

Dismayed but not yet crushed, friends of the League in both parties forced reconsideration of the treaty early in 1920. Neither Lodge nor Wilson would yield an inch. Lodge, who had little confidence in the effectiveness of any league of nations, was under no compulsion to compromise. Wilson, who believed that the League was the world's best hope, did have such a compulsion. Yet he would not compromise either, and this ensured the Treaty's defeat.

Wilson's behavior is further evidence of his physical and mental decline. (See Debating the Past," Did a stroke sway Wilson's judgment?" p. 652.) Had he died or stepped down, the treaty, with reservations, would almost certainly have been ratified. When the Senate balloted again in March, half the Democrats voted for the treaty with the Lodge Reservations. The others, mostly southern party regulars, joined the irreconcilables. Together they mustered thirty-five votes, seven more than the one-third that meant defeat.

DEMOBILIZATION

To win the war, the nation had accepted drastic regulation of the economy in order to increase production and improve social efficiency. When the war ended, the government, in Wilson's words, "took the harness off" at once, blithely assuming that the economy could readjust itself without direction. The army was hastily demobilized, pouring millions of veterans into the job market without plan. All society seemed in flux. When the War Department sent letters to the next of kin of 30,000 soldiers buried in France, 12,000 of the letters were returned as undeliverable. No person of the name on the envelope lived at the indicated address. Nearly all controls established by the War Industries Board and other agencies were dropped overnight. Billions of dollars' worth of war contracts were canceled.

Business boomed in 1919 as consumers spent wartime savings on cars, homes, and other goods that had been in short supply during the conflict. But temporary shortages caused inflation; by 1920 the cost of living stood at more than twice the level of 1913.

Inflation in turn produced labor trouble. The unions, grown strong during the war, struck for wage increases. Over 4 million workers, one out of five in the labor force, were on strike at some time during 1919. Work stoppages aggravated shortages, triggering further inflation and more strikes. Then came one of the most precipitous economic declines in American history. Between July 1920 and March 1922 prices, especially agricultural prices, plummeted.

Unemployment soared. Thus the unrealistic attitude of the Wilson government toward the complexities of economic readjustment caused considerable strife.

THE RED SCARE

Far more serious than the economic losses were the social effects of these difficulties. Everyone wanted peace, but wartime tensions did not subside; apparently people continued to need some release for the aggressive drives they had formerly focused on the Germans. Most Americans found strikes frustrating and drew invidious comparisons between the lot of the unemployed soldier who had risked his life for a dollar a day and that of the striker who had drawn fat wages during the war in perfect safety.

The activities of radicals in the labor movement led millions of citizens to associate unionism and strikes with the new threat of communist world revolution. Although there were only a relative handful of communists in the United States, Russia's experience persuaded many people that a tiny minority of ruthless revolutionaries could take over a nation of millions if conditions were right. Communists appointed themselves the champions of workers; labor unrest attracted them magnetically. When strikes broke out, some accompanied by violence, many people interpreted them as communist-inspired preludes to revolution. Louis Wiley, an experienced *New York Times* reporter, told a friend at this time that anarchists, socialists, and radical labor leaders were "joining together with the object of overthrowing the American Government through a bloody revolution and establishing a Bolshevist republic."

Organized labor in America had seldom been truly radical. The Industrial Workers of the World (IWW) had made little impression in most industries. But some labor leaders had been attracted to socialism, and many Americans failed to distinguish between the common ends sought by communists and socialists and the entirely different methods by which they proposed to achieve those ends. When a general strike paralyzed Seattle in February 1919, the fact that a procommunist had helped organize it sent shivers down countless conservative spines. When the radical William Z. Foster began a drive to organize the steel industry at about this time, the fears became more intense. In September 1919 a total of 343,000 steelworkers walked off their jobs, and in the same month the Boston police went on strike. Violence marked the steel strike, and the suspension of police protection in Boston led to looting and fighting that

ended only when Governor Calvin Coolidge (who might have prevented the strike had he acted earlier) called out the National Guard.

During the same period a handful of terrorists caused widespread alarm by attempting to murder various prominent persons, including John D. Rockefeller, Justice Oliver Wendell Holmes, Jr., and Attorney General A. Mitchell Palmer. Although the terrorists were anarchists and anarchism had little in common with communism, many citizens lumped all extremists together and associated them with a monstrous assault on society.

What aroused the public even more was the fact that most radicals were not American citizens. Wartime fear of alien saboteurs easily transformed itself into peacetime terror of foreign radicals. In place of Germany, the enemy became the lowly immigrant, usually an Italian or a Jew or a Slav and usually an industrial worker. In this muddled way, radicalism, unionism, and questions of racial and national origins combined to make many Americans believe that their way of life was in imminent danger. That few immigrants were radicals, that most workers had no interest in communism, and that the extremists themselves were faction-ridden and irresolute did not affect conservative thinking. From all over the country came demands that radicals be ruthlessly suppressed. Thus the "red scare" was born.

Attorney General Palmer was the key figure in the resulting purge. He had been a typical progressive, a supporter of the League of Nations and such reforms as woman suffrage and child labor legislation. But pressure from Congress and his growing conviction that the communists really were a menace led him to join the "red hunt." Soon he was saying of the radicals: "Out of the sly and crafty eyes of many of them leap cupidity, cruelty, insanity, and crime; from their lopsided faces, sloping brows, and misshapen features may be recognized the unmistakable criminal type."

In August 1919, Palmer established within the Department of Justice the General Intelligence Division, headed by J. Edgar Hoover, to collect information about clandestine radical activities. In November, Justice Department agents in a dozen cities swooped down on the meeting places of an anarchist organization known as the Union of Russian Workers. More than 650 persons, many of them unconnected with the union, were arrested but in only 43 cases could evidence be found to justify deportation.

Nevertheless, the public reacted so favorably that Palmer, thinking now of winning the 1920 Democratic presidential nomination, planned an immense roundup of communists. He obtained 3000 warrants,

▲ The "red scare" that followed the Great War caused panic and new racial violence throughout the nation. Paranoid delusions of "dangerous aliens" and "foreign subversives" were prevalent, as this cartoon demonstrates.

and on January 2, 1920, his agents, reinforced by local police and self-appointed vigilantes, struck simultaneously in 33 cities.

About 6000 persons were taken into custody, many of them citizens and therefore not subject to the deportation laws, many others unconnected with any radical cause. Some were held incommunicado for weeks while the authorities searched for evidence against them. In a number of cases, individuals who went to visit prisoners were themselves thrown behind bars on the theory that they too must be communists. Hundreds of suspects were jammed into filthy "bullpens," beaten, and forced to sign "confessions."

The public tolerated these wholesale violations of civil liberties because of the supposed menace of communism. Gradually, however, protests began to be heard, first from lawyers and liberal magazines, then from a wider segment of the population. No revolutionary outbreak had taken place. Of 6000 seized in the Palmer raids, only 556 proved liable to deportation. The widespread ransacking of communists' homes and meeting places produced mountains of inflammatory literature but only three pistols.

Palmer, attempting to maintain the crusade, announced that the radicals planned a gigantic terrorist demonstration for May Day, 1920. In New York and other cities thousands of police were placed on round-the-clock duty; federal troops stood by anxiously. But the day passed without even a rowdy meeting. Suddenly Palmer appeared ridiculous. The red scare swiftly subsided.

THE ELECTION OF 1920

Wilson still hoped for vindication at the polls in the presidential election, which he sought to make a "great and solemn referendum" on the League. He would have liked to run for a third term, but in his enfeebled condition he attracted no support among Democratic leaders. The party nominated James M. Cox of Ohio.

Cox favored joining the League, but the election did not produce the referendum on the new organization that Wilson desired. The Republicans, whose candidate was another Ohioan, Senator Warren G. Harding, equivocated shamelessly on the issue. The election turned on other matters, largely emotional. Disillusioned by the results of the war, many Americans had had their fill of idealism. They wanted, apparently, to end the long period of moral uplift and reform agitation that had begun under Theodore Roosevelt and return to what Harding called "normalcy."

To the extent that the voters were expressing opinions on Wilson's League, their response was overwhelmingly negative. Senator Harding, a strong reservationist, swept the country, winning over 16.1 million votes to Cox's 9.1 million. In July 1921, Congress formally ended the war with the Central Powers by passing a joint resolution.

The defeat of the League was a tragedy both for Wilson, whose crusade for a world order based on peace and justice ended in failure, and for the world, which was condemned to endure another, still more horrible and costly war. Perhaps this dreadful outcome could not have been avoided. Had Wilson compromised and Lodge behaved like a statesman instead of a politician, the United States would have joined the League, but it might well have failed to respond when called on to meet its obligations. As events soon demonstrated, the League powers acted timidly and even dishonorably when challenged by aggressor nations.

Yet it might have been different had the Senate ratified the Versailles Treaty. What was lost when the treaty failed was not peace but the possibility of peace, a tragic loss indeed.

MILESTONES

1914	United States invades Veracruz, Mexico
	Great War begins in Europe
1915	German U-boat torpedoes *Lusitania*
	United States recognizes Carranza government in Mexico
1916	Wilson appoints Louis D. Brandeis to Supreme Court
	Adamson Act gives railroad workers 8-hour day
	"Pancho" Villa burns Columbus, New Mexico
	Wilson is reelected president
1917	Germany resumes unrestricted submarine warfare
	Russian Revolution begins
	United States declares war on Central Powers
	Herbert Hoover is named food administrator
	Bernard Baruch heads War Industries Board
	Former President Taft heads War Labor Board

1918	Sedition Act limits freedom of speech
	Wilson announces Fourteen Points
	Republicans gain control of both houses of Congress
	Armistice ends the Great War
1918–1919	Flu epidemic kills 600,000 Americans
1919	Steel workers strike
	Red Scare culminates in Palmer raids
	Big Four meet at Paris Peace Conference
	Senate rejects Versailles Treaty and League of Nations
	Wilson wins Nobel Peace Prize, suffers massive stroke
1920	Senate again rejects Versailles Treaty and League of Nations
	Warren Harding is elected president

SUPPLEMENTARY READING

The war on the home front is covered in David M. Kennedy, *Over Here: The First World War and American Society* (1980). Paul A. C. Koistinen, *Mobilizing for Modern War* (1997) examines the emergence of business and military ties during the war. Other useful volumes include Robert D. Cuff, *The War Industries Board* (1973), Stephen L. Vaughn, *Holding Fast the Inner Lines* (1980), which deals with the Committee on Public Information, Donald Johnson, *The Challenge to American Freedoms* (1963), and David Brody, *Steelworkers in America* (1960).

On American military participation, see Mark Meigs, *Optimism at Armageddon* (1997), and Frank E. Vandiver, *Black Jack: The Life and Times of John J. Pershing* (1977). On blacks in the army, see Arthur E. Barbeau and Florette Henri, *The Unknown Soldiers* (1974). See also Herbert A. Johnson, *Wingless Eagle: U.S. Army Aviation through World War* (2001). Women's role with the AEF is examined in Susan Zeiger, *In Uncle Sam's Service* (1999).

On the peace settlement, in addition to the biographies of Wilson, consult Thomas J. Knock, *The War to End All Wars: Woodrow Wilson and the Quest for a New World Order*

(1992), A. J. Mayer, *Politics and Diplomacy of Peacemaking* (1967), John M. Cooper, *Breaking the Heart of the World* (2001), focusing on Wilson, John A. Garraty, *Henry Cabot Lodge* (1953), and Ralph Stone, *The Irreconcilables* (1970).

On labor, see David Montgomery, *The Fall of the House of Labor: The Workplace, the State, and American Labor Activism, 1865–1921* (1987). For a detailed study of organized labor in the South, see Bryant Simon, *A Fabric of Defeat* (1998). Kathleen Kennedy, *Disloyal Mothers and Scurrilous Citizens* (1999), examines the intersection of war, gender, and free speech. On radicalism and the red scare, see R. K. Murray, *The Red Scare* (1955), Stanley Coben, *A. Mitchell Palmer* (1963), David Brody, *The Steel Strike of 1919* (1965), and E. Anthony Lukas, *Big Trouble* (1997), on labor disturbances in the Far West. On the election of 1920, see Wesley Bagby, *The Road to Normalcy* (1962), Burl Noggle, *Into the Twenties* (1974), and Robert K. Murray, *The Harding Era* (1969). On the Spanish influenza epidemic see John Barry, *Great Influenza* (2004), and Gina Kolata, *Flu: The Story of the Great Influenza Pandemic of 1918 and the Search for the Virus That Caused It* (1999).

Wilson's handling of foreign relations is discussed in several volumes by Arthur S. Link: *Woodrow Wilson and the Progressive Era* (1954), and *Wilson the Diplomatist* (1957). See also N. Gordon Levin, Jr., *Woodrow Wilson and World Politics* (1968), Lloyd Ambrosius, *Woodrow Wilson and the American Diplomatic Tradition* (1987), and Manfred Jonas, *The United States and Germany* (1984). Latin American affairs under Wilson are treated in Dana G. Munro, *Intervention and Dollar Diplomacy in the Caribbean* (1964).

SUGGESTED WEBSITES

Woodrow Wilson

http://www.ipl/org/div/POTUS/wwilson.html

This site contains basic factual data about Wilson's election and presidency, speeches, and online bibliography.

The Flu Epidemic of 1918

http://www.pbs.org/wgbh/amex/influenza/

Today, the flu is an annoyance for most people. Yet in 1918, a major flu epidemic swept the United States, killing 600,000 people.

American Leaders Speak: Recordings from World War I and the 1920 Election

http://memory.loc.gov/ammem/nfhtml/

This Library of Congress site contains fifty-nine recordings from American leaders at the turn of the century.

The Great Migration in Chicago

http://lcweb.loc.gov/exhibits/african/afam011.html

This site looks at the black experience in the great migration to one prominent destination.

World War I Document Archives

http://www.lib.byu.edu/~rdh/wwi/

This archive contains sources about World War I in general, not just America's involvement.

World War I: Trenches on the Web

http://www.worldwar1.com

This site provides a mass of data concerning the prosecution of the world's first global war.

Postwar Society and Culture: Change and Adjustment

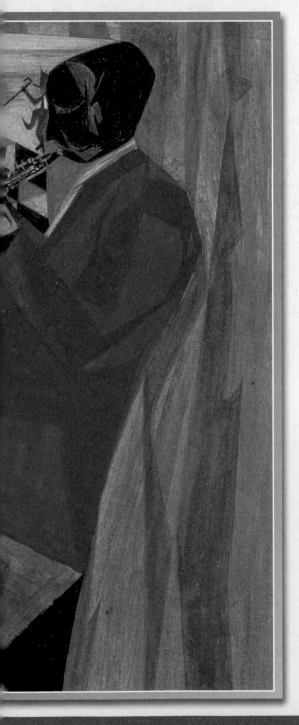

▼ Artist Jacob Lawrence described his style as "dynamic cubism" and owed much to Henri Matisse and other modernists. But he said his core "artistic sensibility" came from the colors and sights of the tenements of Harlem.

CHAPTER CONTENTS

The Great War seemed to many of those who lived through it a turning point in history, the real division separating the nineteenth from the new twentieth century. Actually most of what seemed new to the people of the 1920s had begun to appear well before 1917, and the changes they noticed were still going on. They were in the midst of adjusting to new social, cultural, and economic forces, forces that were to shape their lives and those of their children and grandchildren.

CLOSING THE GATES TO NEW IMMIGRANTS

The ending of the red scare did not herald the disappearance of xenophobia. It was perhaps inevitable and possibly wise that some limitation be placed on the entry of immigrants into the United States after the war. An immense backlog of prospective migrants had piled up during the conflict, and the desperate postwar economic condition of Europe led hundreds of thousands to seek better circumstances in the United States. Immigration increased from 110,000 in 1919 to 430,000 in 1920 and to 805,000 in 1921, with every prospect of continuing to rise.

In 1921 Congress, reflecting a widespread prejudice against eastern and southern Europeans, passed an emergency act establishing a quota system. Each year 3 percent of the number of foreign-born residents of the United States in 1910 (about 350,000 persons) might enter the

country. Each country's quota was based on the number of its nationals in the United States in 1910. This meant that only a relative handful of the total would be from southern and eastern Europe. In 1924 the quota was reduced to 2 percent and the base year shifted to 1890, thereby lowering further the proportion of southern and eastern Europeans admitted.

In 1929 Congress established a system that allowed only 150,000 immigrants a year to enter the country. (In recent years, that annual number of legal immigrants has been increased to 700,000.) Each national quota was based on the supposed origins of the entire white population of the United States in 1920, not merely on the foreign-born. Here is an example of how the system worked:

$$\frac{\text{Italian quota}}{150,000} = \frac{\text{Italian-origin population, 1920}}{\text{White population, 1920}}$$

$$\frac{\text{Italian quota}}{150,000} = \frac{3,800,000}{95,500,000}$$

Italian quota = 6000 (approximately)

▲ "Give me your tired, your poor, your huddled masses yearning to breathe free, the wretched refuse of your teeming shore"—these words of Emma Lazarus, inscribed at the base of the Statue of Liberty, tell only part of the story. Most immigrants were young and hopeful, like this family at Ellis Island; many were resolute and ambitious. The restriction of immigration during the 1920s, conceived to exclude misfits, also deprived the nation of such as these.

The system was complicated and unscientific, for no one could determine with accuracy the "origins" of millions of citizens. More seriously, it ignored America's long history of constantly changing ethnic heterogeneity. The motto *E Pluribus Unum*, conceived to represent the unity of the original 13 states, applied even more appropriately to the blending of different cultures into one nationality. The new law sought to freeze the mix, to turn the American melting pot into a kind of gigantic ice cube.

The law reduced actual immigration to far below 150,000 a year. Between 1931 and 1939, for example, only 23,000 British immigrants came to the United States, far below Britain's annual quota of 65,000. Meanwhile, hundreds of thousands of southern and eastern Europeans waited for admission.

The United States had closed the gates. The National Origins Act caused the foreign-born percentage of the population to fall from about 13 percent in 1920 to 4.7 percent in 1970. (In comparison, in 2005 over 11 percent of the population was foreign born.) Instead of an open, cosmopolitan society eager to accept, in Emma Lazarus's stirring line, the "huddled masses yearning to breathe free," America now became committed to preserving a homogeneous, "Anglo-Saxon" population.

Distaste for the "new" immigrants from eastern Europe, many of whom were Jewish, expanded into a more general antisemitism in the 1920s. American Jews, whether foreign-born or native, were subjected to increasing discrimination, not because they were slow in adopting American ways but because (being ambitious and hardworking, as immigrants were supposed to be) many of them were getting ahead in the world somewhat more rapidly than expected. Prestigious colleges like Harvard, Yale, and Columbia that had in the past admitted Jews based on their academic records now imposed unofficial but effective quotas. Medical schools also established quotas, and no matter how talented, most young Jewish lawyers and bankers could find places only in so-called "Jewish" firms.

New Urban Social Patterns

The census of 1920 revealed that for the first time a majority of Americans (54 million in a population of 106 million) lived in "urban" rather than "rural" places. These figures are somewhat misleading when applied to the study of social attitudes because the census classified anyone in a community of 2500 or more as urban. Of the 54 million "urban" residents in 1920, over 16 million lived in villages and towns of fewer than 25,000 persons and the evidence suggests strongly that a large majority of them held

ideas and values more like those of rural citizens than like those of city dwellers. But the truly urban Americans, the one person in four who lived in a city of 100,000 or more—and particularly the nearly 16.4 million who lived in metropolises of at least half a million—were increasing steadily in number and influence. More than 19 million persons moved from farms to cities in the 1920s, and the population living in centers of 100,000 or more increased by about a third.

The urban environment transformed family structure, educational opportunities, and dozens of other aspects of human existence. Indeed, since most of the changes in the relations of husbands, wives, and children that had occurred in the nineteenth century were related to the fact that people were leaving farms to work in towns and cities, these trends continued and were intensified in the early twentieth century as more and more people settled in urban centers. In addition, couples continued to marry more because of love and physical attraction than because of social position or economic advantage or because of the wishes of their parents. In each decade, people married slightly later in life and had fewer children.

Earlier differences between working-class and middle-class family structures persisted. In 1920 about a quarter of the American women who were working were married, but less than 10 percent of all married women were working. Middle-class married women who worked were nearly all either childless or highly paid professionals who were able to employ servants. Most male skilled workers now earned enough to support a family in modest comfort so long as they could work steadily, but an unskilled laborer still could not. Wives in most such families helped out, usually by taking in laundry or doing piecework sewing for jobbers.

By the 1920s the idea of intrafamily democracy had emerged. In such families, husbands and wives would deal with each other as equals, which given existing conditions meant sharing housework and childcare, downplaying male authority, and stressing mutual satisfaction in sexual and other matters. On the one hand, they should be friends and lovers, not merely housekeepers, earners of money, and producers of children. On the other hand, advocates of these companionate relationships believed that there was nothing particularly sacred about marriage; divorce should be made easier for couples that did not get along, provided they did not have children.

In *The Companionate Marriage* (1927), Benjamin B. Lindsey, a juvenile court judge, suggested a kind of trial marriage, a period during which a young couple could get used to each other before undertaking to raise a family. By practicing contraception such couples could separate without doing serious damage to anyone if they decided to end the relationship. If the relationship remained firm and loving, it would become a traditional marriage and their children would grow up in a loving environment that would help them to become warm, well-adjusted adults.

Much attention was given to "scientific" child-rearing. Childcare experts (a new breed) agreed that routine medical examinations and good nutrition were of central importance, but they were divided about how the socialization and psychological development of the young should be handled. One school stressed rigid training. Children could be "spoiled" by indulgence; toilet training should begin early in infancy; thumb sucking should be suppressed; too much kissing could turn male youngsters into "mama's boys." "Children are made not born," John B. Watson, a former president of the American Psychological Association who was also a vice president of the important J. Walter Thompson advertising agency, explained in *The Psychological Care of Infant and Child* (1928). "Never hug and kiss them, never let them sit in your lap. If you must, kiss them once on the forehead when they say good night."

Another school favored a more permissive approach. Toilet training could wait; parents should pay attention to their children's expressed needs, not impose a generalized set of rules on them.

The growth of large cities further loosened social constraints on sexuality. Amidst the sea of people that surged down the streets or into the subways, the solitary individual acquired a freedom derived from anonymity. (For further perspective on urban life, see the Re-Viewing the Past essay "*Chicago,*" pp. 662–663.) Homosexuals, in particular, developed a set of identifying signals and fashioned a distinctive culture in parks, cafeterias, nightclubs, and rooming houses of big cities. Because most others wrongly assumed that male homosexuality was characterized by effeminacy, they were unaware of the extent of the emerging gay culture. But by the late 1920s and early 1930s homosexual parades, dances, and nightclub acts had become public events.

THE YOUNGER GENERATION

The Great War profoundly affected the generation born around the turn of the century. It had raised, and its outcome dashed, their hopes for the future. Now the narrowness and prudery of so many of their

▶ *text continues on page 664*

Re-Viewing the Past

Chicago

Chicago (2003) is a tale of illicit sex, booze, and "all that jazz." The characters played by Renée Zellweger and Catherine Zeta-Jones aspire to cabaret stardom. Each is married, each is having an affair, each is jilted, and each shoots her wayward lover because "he had it coming." The newspapers gleefully promote their stories. From prison, while awaiting trial for murder, the women compete to garner the most headlines, courting the fame that will boost their careers. Richard Gere, who plays their celebrity lawyer, "razzle dazzles" all Chicago (including both juries) and gets the women acquitted. *Chicago* is a musical. It does not claim to be history. Trial lawyers do not tap dance upon the judge's bench, nor do prisoners tango on death row. The movie, however, is based on a true story; and both the movie and the story illuminate important aspects of the Roaring Twenties.

On March 11, 1924 Walter Law, an automobile salesman, was found slumped against the steering wheel of a car in downtown Chicago. He was dead from a gunshot wound to the head. A pistol and an empty bottle of gin were on the floor. The car was registered to Belva Gaertner, a twice-divorced cabaret singer known as Belle Brown. Police hurried to her rooming house and peppered her with questions.

"We went driving, Mr. Law and I," she told them. The couple stopped at the Bingham "café," bought a bottle of gin (illegally, since this was during Prohibition), and drove around town. "I don't know what happened next," she declared. During the interrogation Gaertner paced nervously, perhaps for good reason: Her clothes were soaked with blood. She was charged with murder.

On April 3, police received a phone call that a man had attempted to rape a young married woman and that she had shot him. The woman was Beulah Annan, who worked at a laundry. At her apartment, police found Harry Kalstedt dead from a gunshot wound. Mrs. Annan insisted that she had acted in self-defense, and her husband supported her story. But police hammered away at the fact that Kalstedt had worked at the same laundry as Mrs. Annan, and that he had been shot in the back. Mrs. Annan eventually confessed that

▼ Catherine Zeta-Jones and Renée Zellweger.

▲ Beulah Annan and Belva Gaertner, "lady murderesses."

the two had been having an affair and that, when he threatened to dump her, she shot him. For two hours, as he lay dying, she drank cocktails and listened to a recording of "Hula Lou," a foxtrot about a Hawaiian girl "with more sweeties than a dog has fleas."

Maurine Watkins, a young reporter, covered both stories for the Chicago *Tribune*. Murder had long been a staple of local journalism, but Watkins recognized the extraordinary appeal of this story: jazz, booze, and two comely "lady murderesses," as Watkins termed them. While awaiting trial in prison, the women provided Watkins with splendid quotes.

Gaertner told Watkins that she was innocent. "No woman can love a man enough to kill him," she explained. "There are always plenty more." She added: "Gin and guns—either one is bad enough, but together they get you in a dickens of a mess." When the grand jury ruled that she could be tried for murder, Gaertner was irritated. "That was bum," she snapped. She called the jurors "narrow-minded old birds—bet they never heard a jazz band in their lives. Now, if I'm tried, I want worldly men, broad-minded men, men who know what it is to get out a bit. Why, no one like that would convict me!"

Watkins described Gaertner as "stylish" and "classy" but called Annan the "prettiest woman ever accused of murder in Chicago"—"young, slender, with bobbed auburn hair; wide set, appealing blue eyes, upturned nose; translucent skin, faintly, very faintly, rouged, an ingenuous smile. Refined features, intelligent expression—an 'awfully nice girl.'" This account appeared on the front page.

During the trial, Annan's attorney pointed to "this frail little girl, struggling with a drunken brute." On May 25, after deliberating less than two hours, the all-male jury acquitted her of the crime. (Justice in those days was swift; in Illinois, too, it was devoid of women, who did not gain the right to serve on juries until 1939.) Two weeks after Annan's trial, Gaertner was also found not guilty. "Another pretty woman gone free," muttered the prosecutor. Watkins noted that four other women remained on death row, but none were as "stylish" or "pretty" as Gaertner and Annan.

Unlike the movie's "lady murderesses," Annan and Gaertner did not team up in a cabaret act. Annan had a nervous breakdown, was institutionalized, and died in 1928. Of Gaertner's subsequent life, little is known. Watkins abandoned journalism and entered Yale drama school. In 1926 she wrote *Chicago,* a comedy derived from the Gaertner and Annan trials, and it ran on Broadway for 172 performances. The next year Cecil B. De Mille adapted the play as a silent movie. In 1975 director Bob Fosse bought the rights to *Chicago* and created the Broadway musical on which the 2003 movie was based.

The "lady murderesses" became part of the lore of the Roaring Twenties; the story seemed to confirm the fears of traditionalists. One minister warned about jazz's "wriggling movement and sensuous stimulation" of the body's "sensory center." Short, bobbed, or marcelled hair was similarly worrisome, because it signified a young woman's break from convention. Silk stockings, skirts that exposed the knees, and straight dresses that de-emphasized the waist further suggested that women's bodies were not meant solely for childbirth. The movie makes all of these points with suitable salaciousness.

The movie also echoes widespread concerns about city life. Several months after the acquittal of Gaertner and Annan, *Literary Digest* warned "country girls" of the moral dangers of large cities. Such criticisms of the modern city echoed the judgments of sociologists, especially those of "the Chicago school" of urban sociology, headed by Robert Park of the University of Chicago. The Chicago sociologists contended that large cities shattered traditional bonds of family and community and fostered crime and deviance. In *The Gold Coast and the Slum* (1929), sociologist Harvey Zorbaugh maintained that life in much of downtown Chicago was "the direct antithesis of all we are accustomed to think of as normal in society." Big-city life was characterized by a "laxity of conventional standards, and of personal and social disorganization."

Scholars now recognize that the portrait of urban city life as propounded by "the Chicago school"—and by movies such as *Chicago*—was overdrawn. Urbanization did not shatter family and ethnic ties. Neighborliness and community persisted even in blighted tenement districts. Few people cast off social conventions, much less succumbed to murderous impulses. In short, Belva Gaertner and Beulah Annan were good copy, and stories such as theirs helped make that celebrated decade roar, but most folks painted the town less vividly, if at all.

▲ A couple demonstrating the Charleston, characterized by toes-in jabs and heel-twisting steps. Originally a black folk dance common in the South—thus its name—the Charleston became a national craze after 1923 when it was featured in *Runnin' Wild*, a black musical.

elders and the stuffy conservatism of nearly all politicians seemed not merely old-fashioned but ludicrous. The actions of red-baiters and reactionaries led them to exaggerate the importance of their right to express themselves in bizarre ways. Their models and indeed some of their leaders were the prewar Greenwich Village bohemians.

The 1920s has been described as the Jazz Age, the era of "flaming youth," when young people danced to syncopated "African" rhythms, careened about the countryside in automobiles in search of pleasure and forgetfulness, and made gods of movie stars and professional athletes. This view of the period bears a superficial resemblance to reality. "Younger people," one observer noted in 1922, were attempting "to create a way of life free from the bondage of an authority that has lost all meaning." But if they differed from their parents and

grandparents, it was primarily because young people were adjusting to more profound and more rapid changes in their world than their grandparents could have imagined.

Beliefs that only the avant-garde had held before the war became commonplace. Put differently, trends that were barely perceptible during the progressive era now reached avalanche proportions. This was particularly noticeable in relationships between the sexes. Courtship, for example, was transformed. In the late nineteenth century, a typical young man "paid a call" on a female friend. He met and conversed with her parents, perhaps over coffee and cookies. The couple remained at home, the parents nearby if not actually participating in what was essentially a social (one might say, public) event held in a private place.

By the 1920s paying calls was being replaced by *dating*; the young man called only to "pick up" his "date," the two to go off, free of parental supervision, to whatever diversion they wished.

Many dating conventions counteracted the trend toward freedom in sexual matters. A man asked a woman "for a date" because dating meant going somewhere and spending money, and the man was expected to do the transporting and pay the bill. This made the woman doubly dependent; under the old system, *she* provided the refreshments, and there was no taboo against her doing the inviting.

But there is no question that for the young people of the 1920s, relations between the sexes were becoming more relaxed and uninhibited. Respectable young women smoked cigarettes, something previously done in public only by prostitutes and bohemian types. They cast off heavy corsets, wore lipstick and "exotic" perfumes, and shortened both their hair and their skirts, the latter rising steadily from instep to ankle to calf to knee and beyond as the decade progressed. For decades female dressmakers and beauty salon proprietors had sold their own beauty products and potions. By 1920, however, new cosmetic corporations, managed primarily by men, appropriated the products and marketing strategies of local women entrepreneurs and catered to national mass markets.

Freudian psychology and the more accessible ideas of the British "sexologist" Havelock Ellis reached steadily deeper into the popular psyche. According to A. A. Brill, the chief American popularizer of Freud's theories, the sex drive was irrepressible. "Love and sex are the same thing," he wrote. "The urge is there, and whether the individual desires it or no, it always manifests itself." Since sex was "the central function of life," Ellis argued, it must be "simple and natural and pure and good." Bombarded by

these exciting ideas, to say nothing of their own inclinations, young people found casting off their inhibitions more and more tempting.

Conservatives bemoaned what they described as the breakdown of moral standards, the fragmentation of the family, and the decline of parental authority—all with some reason. Nevertheless, society was not collapsing. Much of the rebelliousness of the young, like their particular style of dress, was faddish in nature, in a sense a kind of youthful conformity. This was particularly true of college students. Elaborate rituals governed every aspect of their extracurricular life, which was consuming a steadily larger share of most students' time and energy. Fraternity and sorority initiations, "proms," attendance at Saturday afternoon football games, styles of dress, and college slang, seemingly aspects of independence and free choice, were nearly everywhere shaped and controlled by peer pressure.

But young people's new ways of relating to one another, while influenced by the desire to conform, were not mere fads and were not confined to people under 30. This can be seen most clearly in the birth control movement, the drive to legalize the use of contraceptives.

THE "NEW" WOMAN

The young people of the 1920s were more open about sex and perhaps more sexually precocious than the young had been before the war. This does not mean that most of them engaged in sexual intercourse before marriage or that they tended to marry earlier. Single young people might "believe in" birth control, but relatively few (at least by modern standards) had occasion to practice it. Contraception was a concern of married people, and particularly of married women.

Margaret Sanger, "Happiness in Marriage"

The leading American proponent of birth control in the 1920s, actually the person who coined the term, was Margaret Sanger, one of the less self-centered Greenwich Village bohemians. Before the war she was a political radical, a friend of Eugene Debs, "Big Bill" Haywood, and the anarchist Emma Goldman. Gradually, however, her attention focused on the plight of the poor women she encountered while working as a nurse; many of these women, burdened by large numbers of children, knew nothing about contraception. Sanger began to write articles and pamphlets designed to enlighten them, but when she did so she ran afoul of the Comstock Act of 1873, an antiobscenity law that banned the distribution of informa-

▲ This photograph of Margaret Sanger was taken during her trial in January 1917. Having opened the nation's first birth control clinic in Brooklyn, New York, she was convicted of disseminating information on contraception and served 30 days in prison. Friends had advised Sanger to dress conservatively and affect a "Madonna type" persona, much as she appeared here, with her son. Despite her demure clothing, her eyes express her characteristic assertiveness.

tion about contraception from the mails. She was frequently in trouble with the law, but she was persistent to the edge of fanaticism. In 1921 she founded the American Birth Control League and two years later a research center.

The medical profession, though wary of the issue, gave some support to the birth control movement, as did the eugenicists, who claimed that unless the fecundity of "unfit" types (people others might describe simply as poor) was curbed, "race suicide" would result. Sanger accepted support wherever it could be found; by the end of the decade she was no longer on the cutting edge of the movement or even a very radical feminist. But by that time resistance to

the use of contraception was crumbling. However, the Supreme Court did not determine that the right to use contraceptives was guaranteed by the Constitution until the 1960s.

Other gender-based restrictions and limitations of particular importance to women also seemed to be breaking down. The divorce laws had been modified in most states. More women were taking jobs, attracted by the expanding demand for clerks, typists, salespeople, receptionists, telephone operators, and similar service-oriented occupations. Over 10.6 million women were working by the end of the decade, in contrast with 8.4 million in 1920. The Department of Labor's Women's Bureau, outgrowth of a wartime agency, was founded in 1920 and was soon conducting investigations of the working conditions women faced in different industries and how various laws affected them.

But most of these gains were illusory. Relaxation of the strict standards of sexual morality did not eliminate the double standard. More women worked, but most of the jobs they held were still menial or of a kind that few men wanted: domestic service, elementary school teaching, clerical work, selling behind a counter. One of the worst blows fell in 1923 when in the case of *Adkins* v. *Children's Hospital*, the Supreme Court declared a federal law that limited the hours of work for women in the District of Columbia unconstitutional.

When they competed for jobs with men, women usually received much lower wages. Women's Bureau studies demonstrated this repeatedly; yet when the head of the bureau, Mary Anderson, tried to get employers to raise women's wages, most of them first claimed that the men had families to support, and when she reminded them that many female employees also had family responsibilities, they told her that there was a "tacit understanding" that women were to make less than men. "If I paid them the same," one employer said, "there would be a revolution." Efforts to get the American Federation of Labor to take up the issue failed; few of the unions in the federation admitted women.

More women graduated from college, but the colleges placed more emphasis on subjects like home economics that seemed designed to make them better housewives rather than professional nutritionists or business executives. As one Vassar College administrator (a woman!) said, colleges should provide "education for women along the lines of their chief interests and responsibilities, motherhood and the home."

The 1920s proved disillusioning to feminists, who now paid a price for their single-minded pursuit of the right to vote in the progressive era. After the ratification of the Nineteenth Amendment, Carrie Chapman Catt was exultant: "We are no longer petitioners," she announced, "but free and equal citizens." Many activists, assuming the battle won, lost interest in agitating for change. They believed that the suffrage amendment had given them the one weapon needed to achieve whatever women still lacked. In fact, it soon became apparent that women did not vote as a bloc. Many married women voted for the candidates their husbands supported.

When radical feminists discovered that voting did not automatically bring true equality, they founded the Women's party and began campaigning for an equal rights amendment. Their dynamic leader, Alice Paul, disdained specific goals such as disarmament, ending child labor, and liberalized birth control. Total equality for women was the one objective. The party considered protective legislation governing the hours and working conditions of women discriminatory. This caused the so-called social feminists, who believed that children and working women needed the protection provided by such laws, to break away.

The Women's party never attracted a wide following, but only partly because of the split with the social feminists. Many of the younger radical women, like the bohemians of the progressive era, were primarily concerned with their personal freedom to behave as they wished; politics did not interest them. But a more important reason was that nearly all the radicals failed to see that questions of gender—the attitudes that men and women *were taught* to take toward each other, not immutable physical or psychological differences—stood in the way of sexual equality. Many more women joined the more moderate League of Women Voters, which attempted to mobilize support for a broad spectrum of reforms, some of which had no specific connection to the interests of women as such. The entire women's movement lost momentum. The battle for the equal rights amendment persisted through the 1930s, but it was lost. By the end of that decade the movement was moribund.

POPULAR CULTURE: MOVIES AND RADIO

The postwar decade saw immense changes in popular culture. Unlike the literary flowering of the era (see page 675), these changes seemed in tune with the times, not a reaction against them. This was true in part because they were products as much of technology as of human imagination.

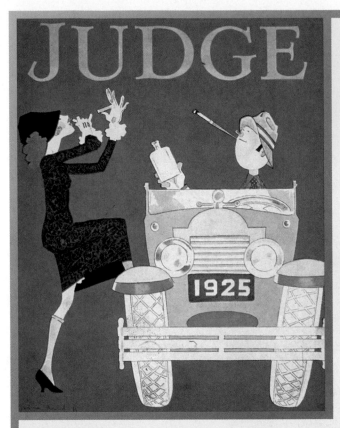

DEBATING THE PAST

Was the decade of the 1920s one of self-absorption?
This magazine cover is a stereotypical expression of the
Roaring Twenties: a chic young woman, knee exposed,
smoking, drinking, and cavorting with a gin-toting cad in
a roadster.

The decade was scarcely over when Frederick Lewis
Allen indicted it in *Only Yesterday* (1931), an immediate
bestseller. In his view young people believed that "life
was futile and nothing much mattered." So they
occupied themselves with "tremendous trifles" such as
mah-jongg, jazz, and illicit booze. Of the wider world, they
cared little. In 1937 Samuel Eliot Morison and Henry

Steele Commager added a political gloss to Allen's
cultural pessimism. Because people were "weary of
reform and disillusioned by the crusade of democracy,"
they drifted toward conservatism.

Two important works were published in 1955. John
Higham referred to the "tribal twenties" as a time when
Americans attempted to "close the gates" of immigration,
and Richard Hofstadter derided the decade as an
insignificant "*entr'acte*" bracketed by the more
consequential eras of progressivism and New Deal reform.

William Leuchtenburg (1958) sought to balance these
assessments: there was much more to the decade than
"raccoon coats and bathtub gin." While conceding that
politicians had failed to solve problems of state authority,
industrial concentration, and mass culture, they had not
done much worse than the progressives. (Recall Debating
the Past in Chapter 22, p. 589).

In later decades leftist scholars such as Roland
Marchand (1985) associated the 1920s with the triumph
of advertising and consumption, part of a "cultural
hegemony" that promoted sales to ensure corporate
profits. On the other hand, Kathy Peiss (1998) was
among a group of scholars who insisted that
consumption could add depth and richness to life. She
found, for example, that in purchasing cosmetics women
partook of the "pleasures of fantasy and desire."

George Chauncey (1994) championed the self-
absorption—self-expression?—of gays who, left mostly to
themselves, exulted in a remarkably open homosexual
culture in the big cities.

Frederick Lewis Allen, *Only Yesterday* (1931), Samuel Eliot
Morison and Henry Steele Commager, *The Growth of the
American Republic* (1937), John Higham, *Strangers in the Land*
(1955), Richard Hofstadter, *The Age of Reform* (1955), William
Leuchtenburg, *The Perils of Prosperity* (1958), Roland
Marchand, *Advertising the American Dream* (1985), T. J.
Jackson Lears, *Fables of Abundance* (1995), Warren I. Susman,
Culture as History (1984), Kathy Peiss, *Hope in a Jar* (1998),
George Chauncey, *Gay New York* (1994).

The first motion pictures were made around
1900, but the medium only came into its own after
the Great War. The early films, such as the eight-
minute epic *The Great Train Robbery* (1903), were
brief, action-packed, and unpretentious. Professional
actors and most educated people viewed them with
amused contempt. But their success was instantaneous with recent immigrants and many other slum
dwellers. In 1912 there were nearly 13,000 movie
houses in the United States, more than 500 in New
York City alone. Many of these places were converted
stores called nickelodeons because the admission
charge was only 5 cents.

In the beginning the mere recording of movement seemed to satisfy the public, but success led to
rapid technical and artistic improvements and consequently to more cultivated audiences. D. W. Griffith's 12-reel *Birth of a Nation* (1915) was a particularly important breakthrough in both areas,
although Griffith's sympathetic treatment of the Ku
Klux Klan of Reconstruction days angered blacks
and white liberals.

FREE —*Send coupon for 8 x 10 Art Print of this beautiful painting—the Kissproof Girl. Printed in 12 colors, mailed flat for framing.*

NEW

Kissproof
the waterproof rouge . . . . in a startling jade green case

50¢

New! Different! Exquisitely modern! Daintily thin! Never before has a Compact Rouge been offered in such a strikingly original case! Luxurious gold and brilliant jade green! An Exclusive Compact Rouge for Particular Women —yet costs but 50¢! And its genuine Kissproof!

Waterproof
it stays on!

Kissproof— the modern rouge — stays on no matter WHAT one does! A single application lasts all day! The youthful NATURAL Kissproof color will make your cheeks temptingly kissable—blushingly red—pulsating with the very spirit of reckless, irrepressible youth! Your first application of Kissproof will delight you!

Your dealer, if up to date, has this striking new rouge. Get it today! Look for the rich gold and jade green case—and be sure it's stamped Kissproof! If your dealer cannot yet supply you, send direct or

Send for Kissproof Beauty Box

It contains a week's supply of this new, natural Kissproof Compact Rouge, a dainty miniature Kissproof Lipstick, a whole month's supply of Delica-Brow, the original liquid dressing for the lashes and brows, and a week's supply of Kissproof, the Extra Hour Face Powder. Send the coupon now—you'll be glad Kissproof is what it IS after you start using it!

Kissproof, Inc., Dept. 1902
3012 Clybourn Ave., Chicago
Send me the Kissproof Beauty Box. I enclose 20c to cover cost of packing and mailing. Also send art print of the Kissproof Girl FREE. Check shade of powder
☐ Flesh   ☐ White
☐ Brunette   ☐ Ivory
Name..................
Address.................

Kissproof *is waterproof ...it stays on!*

Kissproof Lipstick 50¢

Kissproof Compact Rouge 50¢

Kissproof Face Powder $1.00

▲ Would women believe the claims of cosmetics advertisements? "Kissproof" promised to make a woman's lips "pulsate with the very spirit of reckless, irrepressible youth." In a 1927 survey of housewives in Columbus, Ohio, Pond's Company found that two-thirds of the women could not even recall the company's advertisements. Younger women, however, were more impressionable. When the J. Walter Thompson advertising agency asked Vassar students to describe cosmetics, they unconsciously used the exact phrases from advertising copy—proof of its power.

By the mid–1920s the industry, centered in Hollywood, California, was the fourth largest in the nation in capital investment. Films moved from the nickelodeons to converted theaters. So large was the audience that movie "palaces" seating several thousand people sprang up in the major cities. *Daily* ticket sales averaged more than 10 million. With the introduction of talking movies, *The Jazz Singer* (1927) being the first of significance, and color films a few years later, the motion picture reached technological maturity. Costs and profits mounted; by the 1930s million-dollar productions were common.

Many movies were still tasteless trash catering to the prejudices of the multitude. Sex, crime, war, romantic adventure, broad comedy, and luxurious living were the main themes, endlessly repeated in predictable patterns. Popular actors and actresses tended to be either handsome, talentless sticks or so-called character actors who were typecast over and over again as heroes, villains, or comedians. The stars attracted armies of adoring fans and received thousands of dollars a week for their services. Critics charged that the movies were destroying the legitimate stage (which underwent a sharp decline), corrupting the morals of youth, and glorifying the materialistic aspects of life.

Nevertheless the motion picture made positive contributions to American culture. Beginning with the work of Griffith, filmmakers created an entirely new theatrical art, using close-ups to portray character and heighten tension and broad, panoramic shots to transcend the limits of the stage. They employed, with remarkable results, special lighting effects, the fadeout, and other techniques impossible in the live theater. Movies enabled dozens of established actors to reach wider audiences and developed many first-rate new ones. As the medium matured, it produced many dramatic works of high quality. At its best the motion picture offered a breadth and power of impact superior to anything on the traditional stage.

Charlie Chaplin was the greatest film star of the era. His characterization of the sad-eyed little tramp with his toothbrush moustache and his cane, tight frock coat, and baggy trousers became famous throughout the world. Chaplin's films were superficially unpretentious; they seemed even in the 1920s

old-fashioned, aimed at the lower-class audiences that had first found the movies magical. But his work proved both universally popular and enduring; he was perhaps the greatest comic artist of all time. The animated cartoon, perfected by Walt Disney in the 1930s, was a lesser but significant cinematic achievement; Mickey Mouse, Donald Duck, and other Disney cartoon characters gave endless delight to millions of children.

Even more pervasive than the movies in its effects on the American people was radio. Wireless transmission of sound was developed in the late nineteenth century by many scientists in Europe and the United States. During the war radio was put to important military uses and was strictly controlled, but immediately thereafter the airwaves were thrown open to everybody.

Radio was briefly the domain of hobbyists, thousands of "hams" broadcasting in indiscriminate fashion. Even under these conditions, the manufacture of radio equipment became a big business. In 1920 the first commercial station (KDKA in Pittsburgh) began broadcasting, and by the end of 1922 over 500 stations were in operation. In 1926 the National Broadcasting Company, the first continentwide network, was created.

It took little time for broadcasters to discover the power of the new medium. When one pioneer interrupted a music program to ask listeners to phone in requests, the station received 3000 calls in an hour. The immediacy of radio explained its tremendous impact. As a means of communicating the latest news, it had no peer; beginning with the broadcast of the 1924 presidential nominating conventions, all major public events were covered live. Advertisers seized on radio too; it proved to be as effective a way to sell soap as to transmit news.

DOCUMENT

Advertisements from 1925 and 1927

Advertising had mixed effects on broadcasting. The sums paid by businesses for airtime made possible elaborate entertainments performed by the finest actors and musicians, all without cost to listeners. However, advertisers hungered for mass markets. They preferred to sponsor programs of little intellectual content, aimed at the lowest tastes and utterly uncontroversial. And good and bad alike, programs were constantly interrupted by irritating pronouncements extolling the supposed virtues of one commercial product or another.

In 1927 Congress limited the number of stations and parceled out wavelengths to prevent interference. Further legislation in 1934 established the Federal Communications Commission (FCC), with power to revoke the licenses of stations that failed to operate in the public interest. But the FCC placed no effective controls on programming or on advertising practices.

THE GOLDEN AGE OF SPORTS

The extraordinary popularity of sports in the postwar period can be explained in a number of ways. People had more money to spend and more free time to fill. Radio was bringing suspenseful, play-by-play accounts of sports contests into millions of homes, thus encouraging tens of thousands to want to see similar events with their own eyes. New means of persuasion developed by advertisers to sell lipstick, breakfast cereal, and refrigerators were applied with equal success to sporting events and to the athletes who participated in them.

There had been great athletes before; indeed probably the greatest all-around athlete of the twentieth century was Jim Thorpe, a Sac and Fox Indian who won both the pentathlon and the decathlon at the 1912 Olympic Games, made Walter Camp's All-American football team in 1912 and 1913, then played major league baseball for several years before becoming a pioneer founder and player in the National Football League. But what truly made the 1920s a golden age was a coincidence—the emergence in a few short years of a remarkable collection of what today would be called superstars.

In football there was the University of Illinois's Harold "Red" Grange, who averaged over 10 yards a carry during his college career and who in one incredible quarter during the 1924 game between Illinois and Michigan carried the ball four times and scored a touchdown each time, gaining in the process 263 yards. In prize fighting, heavyweight champion Jack Dempsey, the "Manassas Mauler," knocked out a succession of challengers in bloody battles only to be deposed in 1927 by "Gentleman Gene" Tunney, who gave him a 15-round boxing lesson and then, according to Tunney's own account, celebrated by consuming "several pots of tea."

During the same years William "Big Bill" Tilden dominated tennis, winning the national singles title every year from 1920 to 1925 along with nearly every other tournament he entered. Beginning in 1923, Robert T. "Bobby" Jones ruled over the world of golf with equal authority, his climactic achievement being his capture of the amateur and open championships of both the United States and Great Britain in 1930.

A few women athletes dominated their sports during this Golden Age in similar fashion. In tennis Helen Wills was three times United States singles champion and the winner of the women's singles at Wimbledon eight times in the late 1920s and early 1930s. The swimmer Gertrude Ederle, holder of 18 world records by the time she was 17, swam the English Channel on her second attempt, in 1926. She was not only the first woman to do so, but she did it faster than any of the four men who had previously made it across.

▲ Newly built Yankee Stadium, on opening day of the 1923 baseball season. Babe Ruth hit his first home run and soon Yankee Stadium was dubbed "the House that Ruth Built." That year, perhaps his best, Ruth hit 41 home runs, batted .393, and drew 170 walks. He got on base more than half the times he appeared at the plate. Ruth's feats matched the colossal appearance of Yankee Stadium, whose arches evoked the imperial grandeur of ancient Rome.

However, the sports star among stars was "the Sultan of Swat," baseball's Babe Ruth.[1] Ruth not only dominated baseball, he changed it from a game ruled by pitchers and low scores to one in which hitting was more greatly admired. Originally himself a brilliant pitcher, his incredible hitting ability made him more valuable in the outfield, where he could play every day. Before Ruth, John "Home Run" Baker was the most famous slugger; his greatest annual home run total was 12, achieved shortly before the Great War. Ruth hit 29 in 1919 and 54 in 1920, his first year with the New York Yankees. By 1923 he was so feared that pitchers intentionally walked him more than half the times he appeared at the plate.

The achievements of these and other outstanding athletes had a cumulative effect. New stadiums were built, and they were filled by "the largest crowds that ever witnessed athletic sports since the fall of Rome." Record crowds paying unprecedented sums attended all sorts of events.

Football was the preeminent school sport. At many colleges football afternoons came to resemble religious rites both in their formality, with their cheerleaders and marching bands, and in the fervor of the crowds. A national magazine entitled a 1928 article "The Great God Football," and the editor of a college newspaper denounced "disloyal" students who took seats in the grandstand where they could see what was happening on the field, rather than encouraging the team by doing their bit in the student cheering section in the end zone.

Tens of thousands of men and women took up tennis, golf, swimming, and calisthenics. Social dancing became more energetic. The turkey trot, a popular prewar dance, led in the next decade to the Charleston and what one historian called "an imitative swarm of hops, wriggles, squirms, glides and gallops named after all the animals in the menagerie."

URBAN–RURAL CONFLICTS: FUNDAMENTALISM

These were buoyant times for people in tune with the times—the young, the devil-may-care, factory workers with money in their pockets, many different types. But nearly all of them were city people. However, the tensions and hostilities of the 1920s exaggerated an

---

[1] His full name was George Herman Ruth, but the nickname, Babe, given to him early in his career, was what everyone called him.

▲ At the Scopes Monkey trial, this open-air stall offers anti-evolution books, such as those by William Jennings Bryan and another title, "Hell & the High School."

older rift in American society—the conflict between urban and rural ways of life. To many among the scattered millions who tilled the soil and among the millions who lived in towns and small cities, the new city-oriented culture seemed sinful, overly materialistic, and unhealthy. To them change was something to be resented and resisted.

Yet there was no denying its fascination. Made even more aware of the appeal of the city by radio and the automobile, farmers and townspeople coveted the comfort and excitement of city life at the same time that they condemned its vices. Rural society proclaimed the superiority of its ways at least in part to protect itself from temptation. Change, omnipresent in the postwar world, must be resisted even at the cost of individualism and freedom.

One expression of this resistance was a resurgence of religious fundamentalism. Although it was especially prevalent among Baptists and Methodists, fundamentalism was primarily an attitude of mind, profoundly conservative, rather than a religious

idea. Fundamentalists rejected the theory of evolution as well as advanced hypotheses on the origins of the universe.

Urban sophisticates tended to dismiss fundamentalists as boors and hayseed fanatics, yet the persistence of old-fashioned ideas was understandable. In rural areas where educational standards were low and culture relatively static, old ideas remained unchallenged. The power of reason, so obvious in a technologically advanced society, seemed much less obvious to rural people. Farmers, living in close contact with the capricious, elemental power of nature, tended to have more respect for the force of divine providence than did city people. Beyond this, the majesty and beauty of the King James translation of the Bible, the only book in countless rural homes, made it extraordinarily difficult for many persons to abandon their belief in its literal truth.

What made crusaders of the fundamentalists, however, was their resentment of modern urban culture. Although in some cases they harassed liberal

ministers, their religious attitudes had little public significance; their efforts to impose their views on public education were another matter. The teaching of evolution must be prohibited, they insisted. Throughout the 1920s they campaigned vigorously for laws banning discussion of Darwin's theory in textbooks and classrooms. By 1929 five southern states had passed laws prohibiting the teaching of evolution in the public schools.

Their greatest asset in this unfortunate crusade was William Jennings Bryan. Age had not improved the "Peerless Leader." After leaving Wilson's Cabinet in 1915 he devoted much time to religious and moral issues, but without applying himself conscientiously to the study of these difficult questions. He went about the country charging that "they"—meaning the mass of educated Americans—had "taken the Lord away from the schools." He denounced the use of public money to undermine Christian principles, and he offered $100 to anyone who would admit to being descended from an ape. His immense popularity in rural areas assured him a wide audience, and no one came forward to take his money.

The fundamentalists won a minor victory in 1925, when Tennessee passed a law forbidding instructors in the state's schools and colleges to teach "any theory that denies the story of the Divine Creation of man as taught in the Bible." Although the bill passed both houses by big majorities, most legislators voted aye only because they dared not expose themselves to charges that they disbelieved the Bible. Educators in the state, hoping to obtain larger school appropriations from the legislature, hesitated to protest. Governor Austin Peay, an intelligent and liberal-minded man, feared to veto the bill lest he jeopardize other measures he was backing. "Probably the law will never be applied," he predicted when he signed it. Even Bryan, who used his influence to obtain passage of the measure, urged—unsuccessfully—that it include no penalties.

On learning of the passage of this act, the American Civil Liberties Union announced that it would finance a test case challenging its constitutionality if a Tennessee teacher would deliberately violate the statute. Urged on by friends, John T. Scopes, a young biology teacher in Dayton, reluctantly agreed to do so. He was arrested. A battery of nationally known lawyers came forward to defend him, and the state obtained the services of Bryan himself. The "Monkey Trial" became an overnight sensation.

Clarence Darrow, chief counsel for the defendant, stated the issue clearly. "Scopes isn't on trial," he said, "civilization is on trial. The prosecution is opening the doors for a reign of bigotry equal to any-

thing in the Middle Ages. No man's belief will be safe if they win." The comic aspects of the trial obscured this issue. Big-city reporters like H. L. Mencken of the *Baltimore Evening Sun* flocked to Dayton to make sport of the fundamentalists. Scopes's conviction was a foregone conclusion; after the jury rendered its verdict, the judge fined him $100.

Nevertheless the trial exposed both the stupidity and the danger of the fundamentalist position. The high point came when Bryan agreed to testify as an expert witness on the Bible. In a sweltering courtroom, both men in shirtsleeves, the lanky, rough-hewn Darrow cross-examined the aging champion of fundamentalism, exposing his childlike faith and his scientific ignorance. Bryan admitted to believing that Eve had been created from Adam's rib and that a whale had swallowed Jonah. "I believe in a God that can make a whale and can make a man and make both do what He pleases," he explained.

The Monkey Trial ended badly for nearly everyone concerned. Scopes moved away from Dayton; the judge, John Raulston, was defeated when he sought reelection; Bryan died in his sleep a few days after the trial. But fundamentalism continued to flourish, not only in the nation's backwaters but also in many cities, brought there by rural people in search of work. In retrospect, even the heroes of the Scopes trial—science and freedom of thought—seem somewhat less stainless than they did to liberals at the time. The account of evolution in the textbook used by Scopes was far from satisfactory, yet it was advanced as unassailable fact. The book also contained statements that to the modern mind seem at least as bigoted as anything that Bryan said at Dayton. In a section on the "Races of Man," for example, it described Caucasians as "the highest type of all . . . represented by the civilized white inhabitants of Europe and America."

URBAN–RURAL CONFLICTS: PROHIBITION

The conflict between the countryside and the city was fought on many fronts, and in one sector the rural forces achieved a quick victory. This was the Eighteenth Amendment, ratified in 1919, which prohibited the manufacture, transportation, and sale of alcoholic beverages. Although there were some big-city advocates of prohibition, the Eighteenth Amendment, in the words of one historian marked a triumph of the "Corn Belt over the conveyor belt."

The temperance movement had been important since the age of Jackson; it was a major issue in many

states during the Gilded Age, and by the progressive era powerful organizations like the Anti-Saloon League and the Women's Christian Temperance Union were seeking to have drinking outlawed entirely. Indeed, prohibition was a typical progressive reform, moralistic, backed by the middle class, and aimed at frustrating "the interests"—in this case the distillers.

World War I aided the prohibitionists by increasing the need for food. The Lever Act of 1917 outlawed the use of grain in the manufacture of alcoholic beverages, primarily as a conservation measure. The prevailing dislike of foreigners helped the dry cause still more: Beer drinking was associated with Germans. State and local laws had made a large part of

▲ During Prohibition, rival gangs in many big cities contended for control of the lucrative (and illegal) sale of liquor. On Valentine's Day, 1929, Al Capone's gangsters, in police uniforms, barged into a garage at 2122 North Clark Street, Chicago, lined up the members of the George "Bugs" Moran gang, and shot them *(above)*. Three months later Capone spent a year in prison for carrying a concealed weapon. He was later sentenced to 11 years in prison for income tax fraud, though he attained early release for good behavior.

the country dry by 1917. National prohibition became official in January 1920.

AUDIO

"Prohibition Is a Failure"

This "experiment noble in purpose," as Herbert Hoover called it, achieved a number of socially desirable results. It reduced the national consumption of alcohol from 2.6 gallons per capita in the period just before the war to less than 1 gallon in the early 1930s. Arrests for drunkenness fell off sharply, as did deaths from alcoholism. Fewer workers squandered their wages on drink. If the drys had been willing to legalize beer and wine, the experiment might have worked. Instead, by insisting on total abstinence, they drove thousands of moderates to violate the law. Strict enforcement became impossible, especially in the cities.

In areas where sentiment favored prohibition strongly, liquor remained difficult to find. Elsewhere, anyone with sufficient money could obtain it easily. Smuggling became a major business, *bootlegger* a household word. Private individuals busied themselves learning how to manufacture "bathtub gin." Many druggists issued prescriptions for alcohol with a free hand. The manufacture of wine for religious ceremonies was legal, and consumption of sacramental wine jumped by 800,000 gallons during the first two years of prohibition. The saloon disappeared, replaced by the speakeasy, a supposedly secret bar or club, operating under the benevolent eye of the local police.

That the law was often violated does not mean that it was ineffective, any more than violations of laws against theft and murder mean that those laws are ineffective. Although gangsters such as Alphonse "Scarface Al" Capone of Chicago were engaged in the liquor traffic, their "organizations" existed before the passage of the Eighteenth Amendment. But prohibition widened already serious rifts in the social fabric of the country. Besides undermining public morality by encouraging hypocrisy, it almost destroyed the Democratic party as a national organization. Democratic immigrants in the cities hated it, but southern Democrats sang its praises, often while continuing to drink (the humorist Will Rogers quipped that Mississippi would vote dry "as long as the voters could stagger to the polls").

The hypocrisy of prohibition had a particularly deleterious effect on politicians, a class seldom famous for candor. Members of Congress catered to the demands of the powerful lobby of the Anti-Saloon League yet failed to grant adequate funds to the Prohibition Bureau. Nearly all the prominent leaders, Democrat and Republican, from Wilson and La Follette to Hoover and Franklin D. Roosevelt, equivocated shamelessly on the liquor question. By the end

of the decade almost every competent observer recognized that prohibition at least needed to be overhauled, but the well-organized and powerful dry forces rejected all proposals for modifying it.

THE KU KLUX KLAN

DOCUMENT

"Creed of Klanswomen"

The most horrible manifestation of the social malaise of the 1920s was the revival of the Ku Klux Klan. This new Klan, founded in 1915 by William J. Simmons, a former preacher, admitted only native-born white Protestants. The distrust of foreigners, blacks, Catholics, and Jews implicit in this regulation explains why it flourished in the social climate that spawned religious fundamentalism, immigration restriction, and prohibition. In 1920 two unscrupulous publicity agents, Edward Y. Clarke and Elizabeth Tyler, got control of the movement and organized a massive membership drive, diverting a major share of the initiation fees into their own pockets. In a little over a year they enrolled 100,000 recruits, and by 1923 they claimed the astonishing total of 5 million.

Simmons gave his society trappings and mystery calculated to attract gullible and bigoted people who yearned to express their frustrations and hostilities without personal risk. Klansmen masked themselves in white robes and hoods and enjoyed a childish mumbo jumbo of magnificent-sounding titles and dogmas (kleagle, klaliff, kludd, kloxology, kloran). They burned crosses in the night, organized mass demonstrations to intimidate people they disliked, and put pressure on businessmen to fire black workers from better-paying jobs.

The Klan had relatively little appeal in the Northeast or in metropolitan centers in other parts of the country, but it found many members in middle-sized cities and in the small towns and villages of midwestern and western states like Indiana and Oregon. The scapegoats in such regions were immigrants, Jews, and especially Catholics. The rationale was an urge to return to an older, supposedly finer America and to stamp out all varieties of nonconformity. Klansmen "watched everybody," themselves safe from observation behind their masks and robes. They persecuted gamblers, "loose" women, violators of the prohibition laws, and anyone who happened to differ from them on religious questions or who belonged to a "foreign race."

The very success of the Klan led to its undoing. Factionalism sprang up, and rival leaders squabbled over the large sums that had been collected from the membership. The cruel and outrageous behavior of the organization roused both liberals and conservatives in every part of the country. And of course its

▲ A Ku Klux Klan initiation ceremony photographed in Kansas in the 1920s. During its peak influence at mid-decade, Klan endorsement was essential to political candidates in many areas of the West and Midwest. Campaigning for reelection in 1934, an Indiana congressman testified, "I was told to join the Klan, or else."

victims joined forces against their tormentors. When the powerful leader of the Indiana Klan, a middle-aged reprobate named David C. Stephenson, was convicted of assaulting and causing the death of a young woman, the rank and file abandoned the organization in droves. The Klan remained influential for a number of years, contributing to the defeat of the Catholic Alfred E. Smith in the 1928 presidential election, but it ceased to be a dynamic force after 1924. By 1930 it had only some 9000 members.

SACCO AND VANZETTI

The excesses of the fundamentalists, the xenophobes, the Klan, the red-baiters, and the prohibitionists disturbed American intellectuals profoundly. More and more they became alienated, bitter, and contemptuous of those who appeared to control the country. Yet their alienation came at the very time that society was subjected to complex economic, political, and technological challenges that required the attention of people with brains and sophistication. This compounded the confusion and disillusionment characteristic of the period.

Nothing demonstrates this fact as clearly as the Sacco-Vanzetti case. In April 1920 two men in South Braintree, Massachusetts, killed a paymaster and a guard in a daring daylight robbery of a shoe factory. Shortly thereafter Nicola Sacco and Bartolomeo Vanzetti were charged with the crime, and in 1921 they were convicted of murder. Sacco and Vanzetti were anarchists and Italian immigrants. Their trial was a travesty of justice. The presiding judge, Webster Thayer, conducted the proceedings like a prosecuting attorney; privately he referred to the defendants as "those anarchist bastards."

DOCUMENT

Bartolomeo Vanzetti, Court Statement

The case became a cause célèbre. Prominent persons throughout the world protested, and for years Sacco and Vanzetti were kept alive by efforts to obtain a new trial. Vanzetti's quiet dignity and courage in the face of death wrung the hearts of millions. "You see me before you, not trembling," he told the court. "I never commit a crime in my life. . . . I am so convinced to be right that if you could execute me two times, and if I could be reborn two other times, I would live again and do what I have done already." When, in August 1927, the two were at last electrocuted, the disillusionment of American intellectuals with prevailing values was profound. Some historians, impressed by modern ballistic studies of Sacco's gun, now suspect that he, at least, may have been guilty. Nevertheless,

the truth and the shame remain: Sacco and Vanzetti paid with their lives for being radicals and aliens, not for any crime.

LITERARY TRENDS

The literature of the 1920s reflects the disillusionment of the intellectuals. The prewar period had been an age of hopeful experimentation in the world of letters. But the progressive era writers, along with most other intellectuals, were beginning to abandon this view by about 1912. The wasteful horrors of the Great War and then the antics of the fundamentalists and the cruelty of the red-baiters and the Klan turned them into critics of society. Among the many writers shaken by the execution of Sacco and Vanzetti were the poet Edna St. Vincent Millay, the playwright Maxwell Anderson, and the novelists Upton Sinclair and John Dos Passos. After the war the poet Ezra Pound dropped his talk of an American Renaissance and wrote instead of a "botched civilization." The soldiers of the Great War, he said,

> *walked eye-deep in hell*
> *believing in old men's lies, then unbelieving*
> *came home, home to a lie,*
> *home to deceits,*
> *home to old lies and new infamy . . .*

Yet out of this negativism came a literary flowering of major importance. The herald of the new day was Henry Adams, whose autobiography, *The Education of Henry Adams,* was published posthumously in 1918. Adams's disillusionment long antedated the war, but his description of late-nineteenth-century corruption and materialism and his warning that industrialism was crushing the human spirit beneath the weight of its machines appealed powerfully to newborn pessimists. Soon hundreds of bright young men and women were referring to themselves, with a self-pity almost maudlin, as the "lost generation."

The symbol of the lost generation, in his own mind as well as to his contemporaries and to later critics, was F. Scott Fitzgerald. Born to modest wealth in St. Paul, Minnesota, in 1896, Fitzgerald attended Princeton and served in the army during the Great War. He rose to sudden fame in 1920 when he published *This Side of Paradise,* a somewhat sophomoric novel that appealed powerfully to college students and captured the fears and confusions of the lost generation. In *The Great Gatsby* (1925), a more mature work, Fitzgerald dissected a modern millionaire—coarse, unscrupulous, jaded, in love with another

man's wife. Gatsby's tragedy lay in his dedication to a woman who, Fitzgerald made clear, did not merit his passion. He lived in "the service of a vast, vulgar, meretricious beauty," and in the end he understood this himself.

The tragedy of *The Great Gatsby* was related to Fitzgerald's own. Pleasure-loving and extravagant, he squandered the money earned by *This Side of Paradise*. When *The Great Gatsby* failed to sell as well, he turned to writing potboilers. "I really worked hard as hell last winter," he told the critic Edmund Wilson, "but it was all trash and it nearly broke my heart." While some of his later work, particularly *Tender Is the Night* (1934), is first-class, he descended into the despair of alcoholism and ended his days as a Hollywood scriptwriter.

Many young American writers and artists became expatriates in the 1920s. They flocked to Rome, Berlin, and especially Paris, where they could live cheaply and escape what seemed to them the "conspiracy against the individual" prevalent in their own country. The *quartier latin* along the left bank of the Seine was a large-scale Greenwich Village in those days. Writers, artists, and eccentrics of every sort lived there. Some made meager livings as journalists, translators, and editors, perhaps turning an extra dollar from time to time by selling a story or a poem to an American magazine or a painting to a tourist.

Ernest Hemingway was the most talented of the expatriates. He had served in the Italian army during the war and been grievously wounded (in spirit as well as in body). He settled in Paris in 1922 to write. His first novel, *The Sun Also Rises* (1926), portrayed the café world of the expatriate and the rootless desperation, amorality, and sense of outrage at life's meaninglessness that obsessed so many in those years. In *A Farewell to Arms* (1929) he drew on his military experiences to describe the confusion and horror of war.

Hemingway's books were best-sellers and he became a legend in his own time, but his style rather than his ideas explains his towering reputation. Few novelists have been as capable of suggesting powerful emotions and action in so few words. Mark Twain and Stephen Crane were his models; Gertrude Stein, a writer and revolutionary genius, his teacher. But his style was his own, direct, simple, taut, sparse:

> I went out the door and down the hall to the room where Catherine was to be after the baby came. I sat in a chair there and looked at the room. I had the paper in my coat that I had bought when I went out for lunch and I read it. . . . After a while I stopped reading and turned off the light and watched it get dark outside. *(A Farewell to Arms)*

▲ Zelda and Scott Fitzgerald on the steps of their Riviera villa, where both indulged in lavish and well-liquored parties. Many reviewers regarded F. Scott Fitzgerald's novel *The Beautiful and the Damned* (1922), which describes a wealthy if listless young couple's penchant for parties and booze, as a portrait of their own marriage.

This kind of writing, evoking rather than describing emotion, fascinated readers and inspired hundreds of imitators; it has made a permanent mark on world literature. What Hemingway had to say was of less universal interest—he was an unabashed, rather muddled romantic, an adolescent emotionally. He wrote about bullfights, hunting and fishing, violence; while he did so with masterful penetration, these themes placed limits on his work that he never transcended. The critic Alfred Kazin summed up Hemingway in a sentence: "He brought a major art to a minor vision of life."

Edith Wharton, like Adams, was of the New York aristocracy. She was educated by tutors and governesses and never went to college. To counteract what she called "the creeping darkness of neurasthenia," she traveled frequently to Europe, eventually chose to live there, and took up writing. After co-authoring a book

on home decoration, she wrote novels on marriage and manners in some ways reminiscent of Henry James. In Paris at the outset of the Great War, she threw herself into war-related charities. But while the shock of the war jolted Fitzgerald and Hemingway into the vanguard of innovation, she retreated from the jangling energy of postwar life and culture. "I am steeping myself in the nineteenth century," she explained to a friend, "like taking refuge in a mighty temple." The product of her retreat, *The Age of Innocence* (1920), offered a penetrating portrait of an unsettlingly serene if vanished world. *The Nation* remarked that Wharton had described the wealthy of old New York "as familiarly as if she loved them and as lucidly as if she hated them." Though the younger novelists of the decade often dismissed her work as uninventive and dowdy, and she theirs as unformed and thin, her judgment has proven the more enduring.

Although neither was the equal of Hemingway, Fitzgerald or Wharton, two other writers of the 1920s deserve mention: H. L. Mencken and Sinclair Lewis. Each reflected the distaste of intellectuals for the climate of the times. Mencken, a Baltimore newspaperman and founder of one of the great magazines of the era, the *American Mercury,* was a thoroughgoing cynic. He coined the world *booboisie* to define the complacent, middle-class majority, and he fired superbly witty broadsides at fundamentalists, prohibitionists, and "Puritans." "Puritanism," he once said, "is the haunting fear that someone, somewhere, may be happy."

But Mencken was never indifferent to the many aspects of American life that roused his contempt. Politics at once fascinated and repelled him, and he assailed the statesmen of his generation with magnificent impartiality:

BRYAN: "If the fellow was sincere, then so was P. T. Barnum. . . . He was, in fact, a charlatan, a mountebank, a zany without sense or dignity."

WILSON: "The bogus Liberal. . . . A pedagogue thrown up to 1,000 diameters by a magic lantern."

COOLIDGE: "A cheap and trashy fellow, deficient in sense and almost devoid of any notion of honor—in brief, a dreadful little cad."

HOOVER: "Lord Hoover is no more than a pious old woman, a fat Coolidge. . . . He would have made a good bishop."

As these examples demonstrate, Mencken's diatribes, while amusing, were not profound. In perspective he seems more a professional iconoclast than a constructive critic; like both Fitzgerald and Hemingway, he was something of a perennial adolescent. However, he consistently supported freedom of expression of every sort.

Sinclair Lewis was probably the most popular American novelist of the 1920s. Like Fitzgerald, his first major work brought him instant fame and notoriety—and for the same reason. *Main Street* (1920) portrayed the smug ignorance and bigotry of the American small town so accurately that even Lewis's victims recognized themselves; his title became a symbol for provinciality and middle-class meanness of spirit. In *Babbitt* (1922), he created what many people considered the typical businessman of the 1920s, gregarious, a "booster," blindly orthodox in his political and social opinions, a slave to every cliché, and full of loud self-confidence but under the surface a bumbling, rather timid fellow who would have liked to be better than he was but dared not try.

Lewis went on to dissect the medical profession in *Arrowsmith* (1925), religion in *Elmer Gantry* (1927), and fascism in *It Can't Happen Here* (1935). Although his indictment of contemporary society rivaled Mencken's in savagery, Lewis was not a cynic. Superficially as objective as an anthropologist, he remained at heart committed to the way of life he was assaulting. His remarkable powers of observation depended on his identification with the society he described. He was frustrated by the fact that his victims, recognizing themselves in his pages, accepted his criticisms with remarkable good temper and, displaying the very absence of intellectual rigor that he decried, cheerfully sought to reform.

Lacking Mencken's ability to remain aloof, Lewis tended to value his own work in terms of its popular reception. He craved the good opinion and praise of his fellows. When he was awarded the Pulitzer Prize for *Arrowsmith* (1925), he petulantly refused it because it had not been offered earlier. (The Pulitzer jury for 1921 had selected his *Main Street,* but the trustees of Columbia University, who supervised the award, overruled the jury because the book had offended some prominent Midwesterners.) He politicked shamelessly for a Nobel Prize, which he received in 1930, the first American author to win this honor.

Lewis was preeminently a product of the 1920s. When times changed, he could no longer portray society with such striking verisimilitude; none of his later novels approached the level of *Main Street* and *Babbitt*. When critics noticed this, Lewis became bewildered, almost disoriented. He died in 1951 a desperately unhappy man.

As significant as the creation of new literature was the innovation in its distribution. In 1926 a New York advertising man founded the Book-of-the-Month Club. As originally conceived, subscribers to the "club" agreed to buy one new book each month, none costing more than $3, to be chosen by a jury of five prominent writers. The idea caught fire and by the end of the decade it had over 110,000 members. The club introduced thousands to new writers, especially women, including Edna Ferber, Gertrude Stein, and Pearl Buck. But it otherwise tended to hold to familiar formulas. The omission of Hemingway, Faulkner, and Fitzgerald from the club's offerings is striking. With good reason critics complained that the club imposed a "literary dictatorship" on the middle-brow masses.

THE "NEW NEGRO"

The postwar reaction brought despair for many blacks. Aside from the barbarities of the Klan, they suffered from the postwar middle-class hostility to labor (and from the persistent reluctance of organized labor to admit black workers into its ranks). The increasing presence of southern blacks in northern cities also caused conflict. Some 393,000 settled in New York, Pennsylvania, and Illinois in the 1920s, most of them in New York City, Philadelphia, and Chicago. The black population of New York City more than doubled between 1920 and 1930.

In earlier periods blacks in northern cities had tended to live together, but in small neighborhoods scattered over large areas. Now the tendency was toward concentration in what came to be called ghettos.

Even in small northern cities where they made up only a tiny proportion of the population, blacks were badly treated. When Robert S. and Helen M. Lynd made their classic sociological analysis of "Middletown" (Muncie, Indiana), they discovered that although black and white children attended the same schools, the churches, the larger movie houses, and other places of public accommodation were segregated. The local YMCA had a gymnasium where high school basketball was played, but the secretary refused to allow any team with a black player to use it. Even the news in Muncie was segregated. Local papers chronicled the affairs of the black community—roughly 5 percent of the population—under the heading "In Colored Circles."

Coming after the hopes inspired by wartime gains, the disappointments of the 1920s produced a new militancy among many blacks. In 1919 W. E. B. Du Bois wrote in *The Crisis*: "We are cowards

▲ Black separatist Marcus Garvey and his followers were one of many factions of the black movement during the 1920s and 1930s. Other groups, such as the NAACP, worked to bring blacks and whites together, rather than segregating them further.

and jackasses if . . . we do not marshal every ounce of our brain and brawn to fight . . . against the forces of hell in our own land." He increased his commitment to black nationalism, organizing a series of Pan African Conferences in an effort—futile, as it turned out—to create an international black movement.

Du Bois never made up his mind whether to work for integration or black separatism. Such ambivalence never troubled Marcus Garvey, a West Indian whose Universal Negro Improvement Association attracted hundreds of thousands of followers in the early 1920s. Garvey had nothing but contempt for whites, for light-skinned blacks like Du Bois, and for organizations such as the NAACP, which sought to bring whites and blacks together to fight segregation and other forms of prejudice. "Back to Africa" was his slogan; the black man must "work out his salvation in his motherland." (Paradoxically, Garvey's ideas won the enthusiastic support of the Ku Klux Klan and other white racist groups.)

Garvey's message was naive, but it served to build racial pride among the masses of poor and unschooled blacks. He dressed in elaborate braided uniforms, wore a plumed hat, drove about in a limousine. Both God and Christ were black, he insisted. He organized black businesses of many sorts, including a company that manufactured black dolls. He established a corps of Black Cross nurses and a Black Star Line Steamship Company to transport blacks back to Africa.

More sophisticated black leaders like Du Bois detested Garvey, whom they thought something of a charlatan. Garvey's motives are at this distance unclear, and part of his troubles resulted only from his being a terrible businessman. In 1923 his steamship line went into bankruptcy. He was convicted of defrauding the thousands of his supporters who had invested in its stock and was sent to prison. Nevertheless, his message, if not his methods, helped to create the "New Negro," proud of being black and prepared to resist both mistreatment and white ideas. "Up you mighty race, you can accomplish what you will!"

The ghettos produced compensating advantages for blacks. One effect, not fully utilized until later, was to increase their political power by enabling them to elect representatives to state legislatures and to Congress and to exert considerable influence in closely contested elections. More immediately, city life stimulated self-confidence; despite their horrors, the ghettos offered economic opportunity, political rights, and freedom from the everyday debasements of life in the South. The ghetto was a black world where black men and women could be themselves.

Black writers, musicians, and artists found in the ghettos both an audience and the "spiritual emancipation" that unleashed their capacities. Jazz, the great popular music of the age, was largely the creation of black musicians working in New Orleans before the

▲ Zora Neale Hurston, a major figure of the Harlem Renaissance, wrote eighteen novels—many of which were made into movies.

turn of the century. By the 1920s it had spread throughout the country and to most of the rest of the world. White musicians and white audiences took it up—in a way it became a force for racial tolerance and understanding.

Jazz meant improvisation, and both players and audiences experienced in it a kind of liberation. Jazz was the music of the 1920s in part because it expressed the desire of so many people to break with tradition and throw off conventional restraints. Surely this helps to explain why it was so important to blacks.

Harlem, the largest black community in the world, became in the 1920s a cultural capital, center of the "Harlem Renaissance." Black newspapers and magazines flourished along with theatrical companies and libraries. Du Bois opened *The Crisis* to young writers and artists, and a dozen "little" magazines sprang up. Langston Hughes, one of the best poets of the era, described the exhilaration of his first arrival in this city within a city, a magnet for every black intellectual and artist. "Harlem! I . . . dropped my bags, took a deep breath, and felt happy again."

With some exceptions, African American writers like Hughes did not share in the disillusionment that afflicted so many white intellectuals. The persistence of prejudice angered them and made them militant.

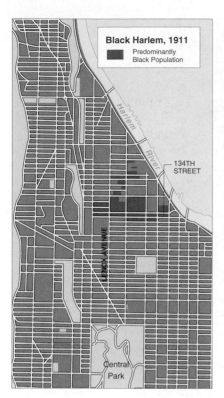
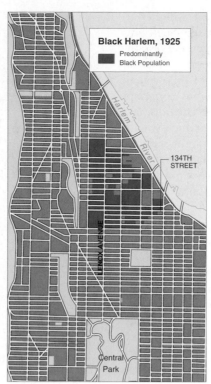
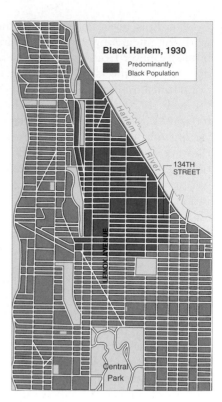

▲ **The Making of Black Harlem, 1911, 1925, 1930**

But to be militant, one must be at some level hopeful. Sociologists and psychologists (for whom the ghettos were indispensable social laboratories) were demonstrating that environment rather than heredity was preventing black economic progress. Together with the achievements of creative blacks, which for the first time were being appreciated by large numbers of white intellectuals, these discoveries seemed to herald the eventual disappearance of racial prejudice. The black, Alain Locke wrote in *The New Negro* (1925), "lays aside the status of beneficiary and ward for that of a collaborator and participant in American civilization." Alas, as Locke and other black intellectuals were soon to discover, this prediction, like so many made in the 1920s, did not come to pass.

ECONOMIC EXPANSION

Despite the turmoil of the times and the dissatisfactions expressed by some of the nation's best minds, the 1920s was an exceptionally prosperous decade. Business boomed, real wages rose, unemployment declined. The United States was as rich as all Europe; perhaps 40 percent of the world's total wealth lay in American hands. Little wonder that business leaders

and other conservatives described the period as a "new era."

The prosperity rested on many bases, one of which was the friendly, hands-off attitude of the federal government, which bolstered the confidence of the business community. The Federal Reserve Board kept interest rates low, a further stimulus to economic growth. Pent-up wartime demand helped to power the boom; the construction business in particular profited from a series of extremely busy years. The continuing mechanization and rationalization of industry provided a more fundamental stimulus to the economy. From heavy road-grading equipment and concrete mixers to devices for making cigars and glass tubes, from pneumatic tools to the dial telephone, machinery was replacing human hands at an ever more rapid rate. Industrial output almost doubled between 1921 and 1929 without any substantial increase in the industrial labor force. Greater use of power, especially of electricity, also encouraged expansion—by 1929 the United States was producing more electricity than the rest of the world combined.

Most important, American manufacturing was experiencing a remarkable improvement in efficiency. The method of breaking down the complex processes

The Human Desire to Own the Best ◆ Suggests *the Cadillac*

Own the Car You Long Have Wanted

Value more remarkable than that of this fine Cadillac Coach is simply not to be had in the motor car market.

For Cadillac has built—not merely a closed car at open car price—but a closed car in which outstanding value, quality and beauty go hand in hand.

Those who have viewed the Coach, who have observed the elegance and

comfort of its large five-passenger body and experienced the powerful, vibrationless performance of the V-63 eight-cylinder chassis, tell us that the car confers new meaning upon Coach design.

And so, in steadily increasing numbers, discriminating purchasers are acquiring this fine Cadillac Coach, fulfilling their desire to own the best.

$3185
f. o. b. Detroit

CADILLAC MOTOR CAR COMPANY, DETROIT, MICHIGAN
Division of General Motors Corporation

C A D I L L A C   C O A C H
STANDARD OF THE WORLD

▲ This 1925 magazine advertisement for a Cadillac Coach shows how twentieth-century businesses sought to link nineteenth-century symbols of wealth (horseback riding, the coat-of-arms of nobility, flower gardens) with symbolic expressions of modernity, encapsulated by the independence of short-haired, fashionably dressed young women.

of production into many simple operations and the use of interchangeable parts were nineteenth-century innovations; in the 1920s they were adopted on an almost universal scale. The moving assembly line, which carried the product to the worker, first devised by Henry Ford in his automobile plant in the decade before World War I, speeded production and reduced costs. In ten years the hourly output of Ford workers quadrupled. The time-and-motion studies of Frederick W. Taylor, developed early in the century, were applied in hundreds of factories after the war. Taylor's method was to make careful analyses of each step and movement in the manufacturing process. Then workers would be taught exactly how best to perform each function. Taylor described his system as "enforced standardization" made possible by the "enforced cooperation" of workers. "Taylorism" alarmed some union leaders, but no one could deny the effectiveness of "scientific shop management" methods.

THE AGE OF THE CONSUMER

The growing ability of manufacturers to produce goods meant that great effort had to be made to create new consumer demands. Advertising and salesmanship were raised almost to the status of fine arts. Bruce Barton, one of the advertising "geniuses" of the era, wrote a best-selling book, *The Man Nobody Knows* (1925), in which he described Jesus as the "founder of modern business," the man who "picked up twelve men from the bottom ranks . . . and forged them into an organization that conquered the world." In 1930 no less a personage than Eleanor Roosevelt, wife of the governor of New York, gave a testimonial for a leading breakfast cereal, which had, she said, "undoubtedly played its part" in building the "robust physique" of her teenage son, John.

Producers concentrated on making their goods more attractive and on changing models frequently to entice buyers into the market. The practice of selling goods on the installment plan helped bring expensive items within the reach of the masses. Inventions and technological advances created new or improved products: radios, automobiles, electric appliances such as vacuum cleaners and refrigerators, gadgets like cigarette lighters, and new forms of entertainment like motion pictures. These influences interacted much as the textile industry in the early nineteenth century and the railroad industry after the Civil War had been the "multipliers" of their times.

Undoubtedly the automobile had the single most important impact on the nation's economy in the 1920s. Although well over a million cars a year were being regularly produced by 1916, the real expansion of the industry came after 1921. Output reached 3.6 million in 1923 and fell below that figure only twice during the remainder of the decade. By 1929, 23 million private cars clogged the highways, an average of nearly one per family.

The auto industry created industries that manufactured tires and spark plugs and other products. It consumed immense quantities of rubber, paint, glass, nickel, and petroleum products. It triggered a gigantic road-building program: there were 387,000 miles of paved roads in the United States in 1921, 662,000 miles in 1929. Thousands of persons found employment in filling stations, roadside stands, and other businesses catering to the motoring public. The tourist industry profited, and the shift of population from the cities to the suburbs was accelerated.

Downtown Scene with Cars, 1911

The automobile made life more mobile yet also more encapsulated. It changed recreational patterns and family life. It created a generation of tinkerers

and amateur mechanics and explorers. In addition, it profoundly affected the way Americans thought. It gave them a freedom never before imagined. The owner of the most rickety jalopy could travel further, faster, and far more comfortably than a monarch of old with his pureblooded steeds and gilded coaches.

These benefits were real and priceless. But cars became important symbols. They gave their owners the feeling of power and status that a horse gave to a medieval knight. According to some authorities the typical American cared more about owning an automobile than a house.

In time there were undesirable, even dangerous results of the automotive revolution: roadside scenery disfigured by billboards, gas stations, and other enterprises aimed at satisfying the traveler's needs; horrendous traffic jams; soaring accident rates; air pollution; the neglect of public transportation, which was an important cause of the deterioration of inner cities. All these disadvantages were noticed during the 1920s, but in the springtime of the new industry they were discounted. The automobile seemed an unalloyed blessing—part toy, part tool, part symbol of American freedom, prosperity, and individualism.

HENRY FORD

The person most responsible for the growth of the automobile industry was Henry Ford, a self-taught mechanic from Greenfield, Michigan. Ford was neither a great inventor nor one of the true automobile pioneers. He was not even the first person to manufacture a good low-priced car (that being the achievement of Ransom E. Olds, producer of the "Merry Oldsmobile"). Ford's first brilliant insight was to "get the prices down to the buying power." Through mass production, cars could be made cheaply enough to put them within reach of the ordinary citizen. In 1908 he designed the Model T Ford, a simple, tough box on wheels. In a year he proved his point by selling 11,000 Model T's. Relentlessly cutting costs and increasing efficiency with the assembly line system, he expanded production at an unbelievable rate. By 1925 he was turning out more than 9000 cars a day, one approximately every 10 seconds, and the price of the Model T had been reduced below $300.

Ford's second insight was the importance of high wages in stimulating output (and selling more automobiles). The assembly line simplified the laborer's task and increased the pace of work; at the same time it made each worker much more productive. Jobs became boring and fatiguing, absenteeism and labor turnover serious problems. To combat this difficulty, in 1914 Ford established the $5 day, an increase of about $2 over prevailing wages. The rate of turnover in his plant fell 90 percent, and although critics charged that he recaptured his additional labor costs by speeding up the line, his policy had a revolutionary effect on wage rates. Later he raised the minimum to $6 and then to $7 a day.

Ford's profits soared along with sales; since he owned the entire company, he became a billionaire. He also became an authentic folk hero: his homespun style, his dislike of bankers and sophisticated society, and his intense individualism endeared him to millions. He stood as a symbol of the wonders of the American system—he had given the nation a marvelous convenience at a low price, at the same time enriching himself and raising the living standards of his thousands of employees.

Unfortunately, Ford had the defects of his virtues in full measure. He paid high wages but refused to deal with any union and he employed spies to investigate the private lives of his workers, and gangsters and thugs to enforce plant discipline. When he discovered a worker driving any car but a Ford, he had him dismissed. So close was the supervision in the factory that workers devised the "Ford whisper," a means of talking without moving one's lips.

Success made Ford stubborn. The Model T remained essentially unchanged for nearly 20 years. Other companies, notably General Motors, were soon turning out better vehicles for very little more money. Customers, increasingly affluent and style-conscious, began to shift to Chevrolets and Chryslers. Finally, in 1927, Ford shut down all operations for 18 months in order to retool for the Model A. His competitors rushed in during this period to fill the vacuum. Although his company continued to make a great deal of money, Ford never regained the dominant position he had held for so long.

Ford was enormously uninformed, yet—because of his success and the praise the world heaped on him—he did not hesitate to speak out on subjects far outside his area of competence, from the evils of drink and tobacco to medicine and international affairs. He developed political ambitions and published virulent anti-Semitic propaganda. He said he would not give 5 cents for all the art in the world.

While praising his talents as a manufacturer, historians have not dealt kindly with Ford the man, in part no doubt because he once said, "History is more or less the bunk."

THE AIRPLANE

Henry Ford was also an early manufacturer of airplanes, and while the airplane industry was not economically important in the 1920s, its development

in that decade laid the basis for changes in lifestyles and attitudes at least as momentous as those produced by the automobile. The invention of the internal combustion gasoline engine, with its extremely high ratio of power to weight, made the airplane possible, which explains why the early experiments with "flying machines" took place at about the same time that the prototypes of the modern automobile were being manufactured. Wilbur and Orville Wright made their famous flight at Kitty Hawk, North Carolina, in 1903, five years before Ford produced his Model T. Another pair of brothers, Malcolm and Haimes Lockheed, built their Model G, one of the earliest commercial planes (commercial in the sense that they used it to take passengers up at $5 a ride) in 1913.

The Great War speeded the advance of airplane technology, and most of the planes built in the 1920s were intended for military use. Practical commercial air travel was long delayed. Aerial acrobats, parachute jumpers, wing walkers, and other daredevils who put on shows at county fairs and similar places where crowds gathered were the principal civilian aviators of the 1920s. They "barnstormed" from town to town, living the same kind of inbred, encapsulated lives that circus people did, their chief rewards being the sense of independence and pride that the successful performance of their highly skilled but risky trade provided.

The great event of the decade for aviation, still an achievement that must strike awe in the hearts of reflective persons, was Charles A. Lindbergh's non-stop flight from New York to Paris in May 1927. It took more than 33 hours for Lindbergh's single-engine *Spirit of St. Louis* to cross the Atlantic, a formidable physical achievement for the pilot as well as an example of skill and courage. When the public learned that the intrepid "Lucky Lindy" was handsome, modest, uninterested in converting his new fame into cash, and a model of propriety (he neither drank nor smoked), his role as American hero was ensured. It was a role Lindbergh detested—one biographer has described him as "by nature solitary"—but could not avoid.

Lindbergh's flight enormously increased public interest in flying, but it was a landmark in aviation technology as well. The day of routine passenger flights was at last about to dawn. In July 1927, a mere two months after the *Spirit of St. Louis* touched down at Le Bourget Field in France, William E. Boeing of Boeing Air Transport began flying passengers and mail between San Francisco and Chicago, using the M–40, a plane of his own design and manufacture. Early in 1928 he changed the company name to United Aircraft and Trans-

▲ Wilbur Wright gliding at Kitty Hawk, 1903, ushering in a century where airplanes would become the basis for military power as well as the preferred means of long distance travel. Wilbur and his brother Orville realized that any airborne vehicle would need to move on three axes: to climb or descend, to steer to either side, and to bank in either direction. This resulted in a bi-wing design with a steering rudder.

port. Two years later Boeing produced the first all-metal low-wing plane and, in 1933, the twin-engine 247, a prototype for many others.

In retrospect the postwar era seems even more a period of transition than it appeared to most people at the time. Rarely had change come so swiftly, and rarely had old and new existed side by side in such profusion. Creativity and reaction, hope and despair, freedom and repression—the modern world in all its unfathomable complexity was emerging.

MILESTONES

1903	Wright brothers fly at Kitty Hawk, N.C.
1908	Henry Ford designs Model T automobile
1914	Ford establishes $5 day for autoworkers
1919	Eighteenth Amendment outlaws alcoholic beverages (Prohibition)
	Nineteenth Amendment gives women right to vote
1920	Sinclair Lewis publishes *Main Street*
	First commercial radio station, KDKA, begins broadcasting
1920s	Black culture flourishes in Harlem Renaissance
1921	Margaret Sanger founds American Birth Control League
1923	Supreme Court overturns law limiting women's work hours (*Adkins* v. *Children's Hospital*)
1924	Ku Klux Klan membership peaks
1925	Scopes is convicted for teaching evolution
	F. Scott Fitzgerald publishes *The Great Gatsby*
1926	Gertrude Ederle swims English Channel
	Ernest Hemingway publishes *The Sun Also Rises*
1927	Charles Lindbergh flies solo across Atlantic
	Sacco and Vanzetti are executed
	The Jazz Singer is first motion picture with sound
	Jack Dempsey loses heavyweight boxing title to Gene Tunney
	Babe Ruth hits 60 home runs
1928	John B. Watson publishes *The Psychological Care of Infant and Child*
1929	Capone's gang kills Moran's in Valentine's Day Massacre

SUPPLEMENTARY READING

In addition to the summaries outlined in Debating the Past (p. 667), Ann Douglas, *Terrible Honesty: Mongrel Manhattan in the 1920s* (1995), emphasizes the positive aspects of urban life, and Stanley Coben, *Rebellion Against Victorianism* (1991), emphasizes its elements of change. David Goldberg's survey, *Discontented America* (1999), focuses on divisions of race, ethnicity, and class. See also the volumes mentioned in previous chapters.

Nativism and immigration restriction are covered in Desmond King, *Making Americans* (2000), and John Higham, *Strangers in the Land* (1955). On changes in the family, see Steven Mintz and Susan Kellogg, *Domestic Revolutions* (1988); on other social trends, John D'Emilio and Estelle Freedman, *Intimate Matters* (1988), and Paula Fass, *The Damned and the Beautiful* (1977).

The "new" woman is discussed in Nancy F. Cott, *The Grounding of Modern Feminism* (1987), William Chafe, *The American Woman* (1972), Ellen Chesler, *Woman of Valor* (1992) (on Margaret Sanger and the birth control movement), Dorothy M. Brown, *Setting a Course: American Women in the 1920s* (1987), and Nancy Woloch, *Women and the American Experience* (1971). Women workers are dealt with in Winifred D. Wandersee, *Women's Work and Family Values* (1981). Peter N. Stearns, *Anxious Parents* (2003) is a survey of childrearing advice, with special emphasis on the early twentieth century.

On the evolution of celebrity in popular culture, see Charles L. Ponce de Leon, *Self-Exposure: Human-Interest Journalism and the Emergence of Celebrity in America, 1890–1940* (2002). On Hollywood, see Steven J. Ross, *Working-Class Hollywood: Silent Film and the Shaping of Class in America* (1998), and Robert Sklar, *Movie-Made America* (1976). On radio, see Susan J. Douglas, *Inventing American Broadcasting* (1987), Philip T. Rosen, *The Modern Stentors: Radio Broadcasting and the Federal Government* (1980), and Hugh R. Slotten, *Radio and Television Regulation: Broadcast Technology in the United States* (2000). Tona J. Hangen, *Redeeming the Dial: Radio, Religion, and Popular Culture in America* (2002), examines the intersection of popular culture and religion. On the rise of consumer credit, see Lendol Calder, *Financing the American Dream* (1999).

Fundamentalism is treated in Joel A. Carpenter, *Revive Us Again: The Reawakening of American Fundamentalism* (1997); the Scopes trial in Edward J. Larson, *Summer for the Gods: The Scopes Trial and America's Continuing Debate over Science and Religion* (1997), and Paul Conkin, *When All the Gods Trembled* (1998). On prohibition see Andrew Sinclair, *Prohibition: The Era of Excess* (1962), and Stanley Walker, *The Night Club Era* (1999), which focuses on New York. On the Klan, consult Nancy MacLean, *Behind the Mask of Chivalry: The Making of the Second Ku Klux Klan*

(1994), Jim Ruiz, *The Black Hood of the Ku Klux Klan* (1998), Kathleen Blee, *Women of the Klan* (1991), and Richard K. Tucker, *The Dragon and the Cross: The Rise and Fall of the Ku Klux Klan in Middle America* (1991).

Francis Russell, *Tragedy in Dedham* (1962), casts doubt on the innocence of Sacco and Vanzetti; see also Paul Avrich, *Sacco and Vanzetti: The Anarchist Background* (1991).

Milton C. Sernetet, *Bound for the Promised Land* (1997), emphasizes the religious dimensions of the black migration to the North. Alfred L. Brophy, *Reconstructing the Dreamland: The Tulsa Riot of 1921* (2002) is useful on that important episode. On blacks in Harlem, see Gilbert Osofsky, *Harlem: The Making of a Ghetto* (1965). The Harlem Renaissance is the subject of Steven Watson, *The Harlem Renaissance* (1995), and J. Martin Favor, *Authentic Blackness* (1999). Eric Porter, *What Is This Thing Called Jazz?* (2002) explores the connections between music and intellectual life.

The literature of the period is analyzed in Alfred Kazin, *On Native Grounds* (1942), Malcolm Cowley, *Exiles Return* (1934), and Edmund Wilson, *The Twenties* (1975). *See* Jeffrey Meyers, *Scott Fitzgerald: A Biography* (1994) and also his *Hemingway: A Biography* (1999); also Carlos H. Baker, *Hemingway* (1956); on Mencken, William R. Manchester, *Disturber of the Peace* (1951); on Lewis, Mark Schorer, *Sinclair Lewis* (1961); on Wharton, R. W. B. Lewis, *Edith Wharton* (1975), and Shari Benstock, *No Gifts from Chance* (1994). On the popularization of literature, see Joan Shelley Rubin, *The Making of Middlebrow Culture* (1992).

On Henry Ford, see Douglas Brinkley, *Wheels for the World* (2004); Clarence Hooker, *Life in the Shadows of the Crystal Palace 1910–1927* (1997), illuminates the role of labor at Ford. On the early history of General Motors, see David Farber, *Sloan Rules: Alfred P. Sloan and the Triumph of General Motors* (2002). On women and cars, see Virginia Scharff, *Taking the Wheel* (1991). Beth Bailey, *From Front Porch to Back Seat* (1988), considers the ramifications of the automobile on courtship.

SUGGESTED WEBSITES

Margaret Sanger Papers Projects
http://www.nyu.edu/projects/sanger/
This site at New York University contains information about Margaret Sanger and digital versions of several of her works.

Harlem: The Mecca of the New Negro
http://etext.lib.virginia.edu/harlem/
This site is the online text of the March 1925 Survey Graphic Harlem Number; the journal was the premier social work journal of the decade.

Harlem 1900–1940: An African American Community
http://www.si.umich.edu/CHICO/Harlem/
The New York Public Library's Schomburg Center for Research in Black Culture hosts this site that includes a database, a timeline, and an exhibit.

William P. Gottlieb Photographs of the Golden Age of Jazz
http://memory.loc.gov/ammem/wghtml/wghome.html
The Music Division of the Library of Congress has numerous images, audio, and scanned articles from the 1940s.

The Scopes Trial
http://xroads.virginia.edu/~UG97/inherit/1925home.html
This site gives general descriptions of the trial and the issues surrounding the landmark case.

Temperance and Prohibition
http://prohibition.osu.edu/
This site looks at the temperance movement over time and contains many informative links.

National Arts and Crafts Archives
http://arts-crafts.com/index.html
This site serves as a guide to materials on the Arts and Crafts movement, which lasted roughly from 1890 to 1929.

CHAPTER 26 The New Era: 1921–1933

▼ In Howard Thain's 1925 painting of New York's Times Square, the people are inconsequential grey blurs beneath the luminous wonders of consumption and pleasure.

CHAPTER CONTENTS

The men who presided over the government of the United States from 1921 to 1933 were Warren G. Harding, Calvin Coolidge, and Herbert Hoover. Harding was a newspaperman by trade, publisher of the *Marion Star*, with previous political experience as a legislator and lieutenant governor in his home state, Ohio, and as a United States senator. No president, before or since, looked more like a statesman; few were less suited for running the country.

Coolidge was a taciturn, extremely conservative New Englander with a long record in Massachusetts politics climaxed by his inept but much admired suppression of the Boston police strike while governor. Harding referred to him as "that little fellow from Massachusetts." Coolidge preferred to follow public opinion and hope for the best. "Mr. Coolidge's genius for inactivity is developed to a very high point," the correspondent Walter Lippmann wrote. "It is a grim, determined, alert inactivity, which keeps Mr. Coolidge occupied constantly."[1] Hoover was best known for his work as food administrator during the Great War and for his many speeches about "progressive individualism" delivered while serving as secretary of commerce under Harding and Coolidge.

---

[1]Coolidge was physically delicate, being plagued by chronic stomach trouble. He required 10 or 11 hours of sleep a day.

HARDING AND "NORMALCY"

Harding won the 1920 Republican nomination because the party convention could not decide between General Leonard Wood, who represented the Theodore Roosevelt progressives, and Frank Lowden, governor of Illinois. Harding's genial nature and lack of strong convictions made him attractive to many of the politicos after eight years of the headstrong Wilson. During the campaign he exasperated sophisticates by his ignorance and imprecision. He coined the famous vulgarism *normalcy* as a substitute for the word *normality*; referred, during a speech before a group of actors, to Shakespeare's play "Charles the Fifth," and committed numerous other blunders. "Why does he not get a private secretary who can clothe . . . his 'ideas' in the language customarily used by educated men?" one Boston gentleman demanded of Senator Lodge, who was strongly supporting Harding. Lodge, ordinarily a stickler for linguistic exactitude, replied acidly that he found Harding a paragon by comparison with Wilson, "a man who wrote English very well without ever saying

▲ Warren G. Harding looked presidential, and his voice was suitably deep and resonant. Yet he lacked mental agility and discipline. Republican Senator Frank Brandegee explained Harding's nomination by proclaiming him "the best of the second-raters," and thus the natural compromise between contending factions in the party.

anything." A large majority of the voters, untroubled by the candidate's lack of erudition, shared Lodge's confidence that Harding would be a vast improvement over Wilson.

Harding has often been characterized as lazy and incompetent. In fact, he was hardworking and politically shrewd; his major weaknesses were indecisiveness and an unwillingness to offend. He turned the most important government departments over to efficient administrators of impeccable reputation: Charles Evans Hughes, the secretary of state; Herbert Hoover in the Commerce Department; Andrew Mellon in the Treasury; and Henry C. Wallace in Agriculture. He kept track of what these men did but seldom initiated policy in their areas. However, Harding gave many lesser offices, and a few of major importance, to the unsavory "Ohio Gang" headed by Harry M. Daugherty, whom he made attorney general.

The president was too kindly, too well-intentioned, and too unambitious to be dishonest. He appointed corrupt officials like Daugherty, Secretary of the Interior Albert B. Fall, Director of the Mint "Ed" Scobey, and Charles R. Forbes, head of the new Veterans Bureau, out of a sense of personal obligation or because they were old friends who shared his taste for poker and liquor. Before 1921 he had enjoyed officeholding; he was adept at mouthing platitudes, a loyal party man who seldom questioned the decisions of his superiors. In the lonely eminence of the White House, whence, as President Harry Truman later said, the buck cannot be passed, he found only misery. "The White House is a prison," he complained. "I can't get away from the men who dog my footsteps. I am in jail."

"THE BUSINESS OF THE UNITED STATES IS BUSINESS"

Secretary of the Treasury Mellon, multimillionaire banker and master of the aluminum industry, dominated the administration's domestic policy. Mellon set out to lower the taxes of the rich, reverse the low-tariff policies of the Wilson period, return to the laissez-faire philosophy of McKinley, and reduce the national debt by cutting expenses and administrating the government more efficiently.

In principle his program had considerable merit. Tax rates designed to check consumer spending in time of war and to raise the huge sum needed to defeat the Central Powers were undoubtedly hampering economic expansion in the early 1920s. Certain

Purinton, "Big Ideas from Big Business"

industries that had sprung up in the United States during the Great War were suffering from German and Japanese competition now that the fighting had ended. Rigid regulation necessary during a national crisis could well be dispensed with in peacetime. And efficiency and economy in government are always desirable.

Yet Mellon carried his policies to unreasonable extremes. He proposed eliminating inheritance taxes and reducing the tax on high incomes by two-thirds, but he opposed lower rates for taxpayers earning less than $66,000 a year, apparently not realizing that economic expansion required greater mass consumption as well. Freeing the rich from "oppressive" taxation, he argued, would enable them to invest more in potentially productive enterprises, the success of which would create jobs for ordinary people. Little wonder that Mellon's admirers called him the greatest secretary of the treasury since Alexander Hamilton.

But Mellon's tax and tariff program ran into stiff opposition from midwestern Republicans and southern Democrats, who combined to form the so-called farm bloc. The revival of European agriculture after the World War cut the demand for American farm produce just when the increased use of fertilizers and machinery was boosting output. As in the era after the Civil War, farmers found themselves burdened with heavy debts while their income dwindled. In the decade after 1919 their share of the national income fell by nearly 50 percent. The farm bloc represented a kind of conservative populism, economic grievances combining with a general prejudice against "Wall Street financiers" and rich industrialists to unite agriculture against "the interests." Mellon epitomized everything the farm bloc disliked and their representatives in Congress pared back most of his proposals.

Mellon nevertheless succeeded in balancing the budget and reducing the national debt by an average of over $500 million a year. So committed were the Republican leaders to retrenchment that they even resisted the demands of veterans, organized in the politically potent American Legion, for an "adjusted compensation" bonus.

That the business community heartily approved the policies of Harding and Coolidge is not surprising. Both presidents were uncritical advocates of the business point of view. "We want less government in business and more business in government," Harding pontificated, to which Coolidge added, "The business of the United States is business." Harding and Coolidge used their power of appointment to convert regulatory bodies like the Interstate Commerce Commission (ICC) and the Federal Reserve Board into probusiness agencies that ceased almost entirely to restrict the activities of the industries they were supposed to be controlling. The ICC became almost the reverse of what it had been in the progressive era. The Federal Trade Commission, in the words of one bemused academic, seemed to be trying to commit hara-kiri.

THE HARDING SCANDALS

At least Mellon was honest. The Ohio gang used its power in the most corrupt way imaginable. Jesse Smith, a crony of Attorney General Daugherty, was what today would be called an influence peddler. When he was exposed in 1923, he committed suicide. Charles R. Forbes of the Veterans Bureau siphoned millions of dollars appropriated for the construction of hospitals into his own pocket. When he was found out, he fled to Europe. Later he returned, stood trial, and was sentenced to two years in prison. His assistant, Charles F. Cramer, committed suicide. Daugherty himself was implicated in the fraudulent return of German assets seized by the alien property custodian to their original owners. He escaped imprisonment only by refusing to testify on the ground that he might incriminate himself.

The worst scandal involved Secretary of the Interior Albert B. Fall, a former senator. In 1921 Fall arranged with the complaisant Secretary of the Navy Edwin Denby for the transfer to the Interior Department of government oil reserves being held for the future use of the navy. He then leased these properties to private oil companies. Edward L. Doheny's Pan-American Petroleum Company got the Elk Hills reserve in California; the Teapot Dome reserve in Wyoming was turned over to Harry F. Sinclair's Mammoth Oil Company. When critics protested, Fall explained that it was necessary to develop the Elk Hills and Teapot Dome properties because adjoining private drillers were draining off the navy's oil. Nevertheless, in 1923 the Senate ordered a full-scale investigation, conducted by Senator Thomas J. Walsh of Montana. It soon came out that Doheny had "lent" Fall $100,000 in hard cash, handed over secretly in a "little black bag." Sinclair had given Fall over $300,000 in cash and negotiable securities.

Although the three culprits escaped conviction on the charge of conspiring to defraud the government, Sinclair was sentenced to nine months in jail for

contempt of the Senate and for tampering with a jury, and Fall was fined $100,000 and given a year in prison for accepting a bribe. In 1927 the Supreme Court revoked the leases and the two reserves were returned to the government.

The public still knew little of the scandals when, in June 1923, Harding left Washington on a speaking tour that included a visit to Alaska. His health was poor and his spirits low, for he had begun to understand how his "Goddamn friends" had betrayed him. On the return trip from Alaska, he came down with what his physician, an incompetent crony whom he had made surgeon general of the United States, diagnosed as ptomaine poisoning resulting from his having eaten a tainted Japanese crab. In fact the president had suffered a heart attack. He died in San Francisco on August 2.

Few presidents have been more deeply mourned by the people at the moment of their passing. Harding's kindly nature, his very ordinariness, increased his human appeal. Three million people viewed his coffin as it passed across the country. When the scandals came to light, sadness turned to scorn and contempt. The poet e. e. cummings came closer to catching the final judgment of Harding's contemporaries than has any historian:

> *the first president to be loved by his*
> *"bitterest enemies" is dead*
> *the only man woman or child who wrote*
> *a simple declarative sentence with seven grammatical*
> *errors "is dead"*
> *beautiful Warren Gamaliel Harding*
> *"is" dead*
> *he's*
> *"dead"*
> *if he wouldn't have eaten them Yapanese Craps*
> *somebody might hardly never not have been*
> *unsorry, perhaps*

COOLIDGE PROSPERITY

Had he lived, Harding might well have been defeated in 1924 because of the scandals. Vice President Coolidge, unconnected with the troubles and not the type to surround himself with cronies of any kind, seemed the ideal person to clean out the corrupt officials. After he had replaced Attorney General Daugherty with Harlan Fiske Stone, dean of the Columbia University Law School, the scandals ceased to be a serious political handicap for the Republicans.

Coolidge soon became the darling of the conservatives. His admiration for businessmen and his

▲ Calvin Coolidge's quiet presidential style was a sharp contrast to the outspoken Warren Harding. When Coolidge died in 1933, humorist Dorothy Parker remarked, "How could they tell?"

devotion to laissez-faire knew no limit. "The man who builds a factory builds a temple," he said in all seriousness. "The Government can do more to remedy the economic ills of the people by a system of rigid economy in public expenditures than can be accomplished through any other action." Andrew Mellon, whom he kept on as secretary of the treasury, became his mentor in economic affairs.

Coolidge won the 1924 Republican nomination easily. The Democrats, badly split, required 103 ballots to choose a candidate. The southern wing, dry, anti-immigrant, pro-Klan, had fixed on William G. McAdoo, Wilson's secretary of the treasury. The eastern, urban, wet element supported Governor Alfred E. Smith of New York, child of the slums, a Catholic who had compiled a distinguished record in social welfare legislation. After days of futile politicking, the

▲ Because of hyperinflation, German bank notes were worth little more than the paper they were printed on. These German boys use them to make a kite.

party compromised on John W. Davis, a conservative corporation lawyer closely allied with the Morgan banking interests.

Dismayed by the conservatism of Coolidge and Davis, Robert M. La Follette, backed by the farm bloc, the Socialist party, the American Federation of Labor, and numbers of intellectuals, entered the race as the candidate of a new Progressive party. The Progressives adopted a neopopulist platform calling for the nationalization of railroads, the direct election of the president, the protection of labor's right to bargain collectively, and other reforms.

The situation was almost exactly the opposite of 1912, when one conservative had run against two liberals and had been swamped. Coolidge received 15.7 million votes, Davis 8.4 million, La Follette 4.8 million. In the Electoral College La Follette won only his native Wisconsin; Coolidge defeated Davis, 382 to 136. Conservatism was clearly the dominant mood of the country.

While Coolidge reigned, complacency was the order of the day. "The country," the president reported to Congress in 1928, "can regard the present with satisfaction, and anticipate the future with optimism."

Peace Without a Sword

Presidents Harding and Coolidge handled foreign relations in much the same way they managed domestic affairs. Harding deferred to senatorial prejudice against executive domination in the area and let Secretary of State Charles Evans Hughes make policy. Coolidge adopted a similar course. In directing foreign relations, they faced the obstacle of a resurgent isolationism. The bloodiness and apparent senselessness of the Great War convinced millions that the only way to be sure it would not happen again was to "steer clear" of "entanglements." That

these famous words had been used by Washington and Jefferson in vastly different contexts did not deter the isolationists of the 1920s from attributing to them the same authority they gave to Scripture. On the other hand, far-flung American economic interests, the need for both raw materials for industry and foreign markets for America's growing surpluses of agricultural and manufactured goods, made close attention to and involvement in developments all over the world unavoidable.

Isolationist sentiments, therefore, did not deter the government from seeking to advance American interests abroad. The Open Door concept remained predominant; the State Department worked to obtain opportunities in underdeveloped countries for exporters and investors, hoping both to stimulate the American economy and to bring stability to "backward" nations. Although this policy sometimes roused local resentments because of the tendency of the United States to support entrenched elites while the mass of peasants and city workers lived in poverty, it also resulted in a further retreat from active interventionism.

The first important diplomatic event of the period revealed a great deal about American foreign policy after the World War. During the war, Japan had greatly increased its influence in the Far East, especially in Manchuria, the northeastern province of warlord-dominated China. To maintain the Open Door in China, it would be necessary to check Japanese expansion. But there was little hope of restoring the old spheres of influence, which the mass of Chinese people bitterly resented. In addition, Japan, the United States, and Great Britain were engaged in expensive naval building programs, a competition none of them really wanted but from which all dared not withdraw unilaterally.

In November 1921, hoping to reach a general agreement with China, Japan, and the Europeans that would keep China open to the commerce of all and slow the armaments race, Secretary of State Hughes convened a conference in Washington. By the following February the Washington Conference had drafted three major treaties and a number of lesser agreements.

In the Five-Power Treaty, the United States, Great Britain, France, Japan, and Italy agreed to stop building battleships for ten years and to reduce their fleets of capital ships to a fixed ratio, with Great Britain and the United States limited to 525,000 tons, Japan to 315,000 tons, and France and Italy to 175,000 tons. The new ratio was expected to produce a balance of forces in the Pacific.

The Four-Power Treaty, signed by the United States, Great Britain, Japan, and France, committed these nations to respect one another's interests in the islands of the Pacific and to confer in the event that any other country launched an attack in the area.

All the conferees signed the Nine-Power Treaty, agreeing to respect China's independence and to maintain the Open Door. On the surface, this was of monumental importance to the United States since it seemed to mean that Japan had given up its territorial ambitions on the Asian mainland and that both the Japanese and the Europeans had formally endorsed the Open Door concept.

By taking the lead in drafting these agreements, the United States regained some of the moral influence it had lost by not joining the League of Nations. The treaties, however, were uniformly toothless. The signers of the Four-Power Treaty agreed only to consult in case of aggression in the Pacific; they made no promises to help one another or to restrict their own freedom of action. As President Harding assured the Senate, "there [was] no commitment to armed force, no alliance, no written or moral obligation to join in defense."

The naval disarmament treaty said nothing about the number of other warships that the powers might build, about the far more important question of land and air forces, or about the underlying industrial and financial structures that controlled the ability of the nations to make war. In addition, the 5:5:3 ratio actually enabled the Japanese to dominate the western Pacific. It made the Philippine Islands indefensible and exposed Hawaii to possible attack. In a sense these American bases became hostages of Japan. Yet Congress was so unconcerned about Japanese sensibilities that it refused to grant any immigration quota to Japan under the National Origins Act of 1924, even though the formula applied to other nations would have allowed only 100 Japanese a year to enter the country. The law, Secretary Hughes warned, produced in Japan "a sense of injury and antagonism instead of friendship and cooperation."

Hughes did not think war a likely result, but Japanese resentment of "white imperialism" played into the hands of the military party in that nation. Many Japanese army and navy officers considered war with the United States inevitable.

As for the key Nine-Power Treaty, Japan did not abandon its territorial ambitions in China, and China remained so riven by conflict among the warlords and so resentful of the "imperialists" that the economic advantages of the Open Door turned out to be small indeed.

The United States entered into all these agreements without realizing their full implications and not

really prepared to play an active part in Far Eastern affairs. "We have no favorites in the present dog fight in China," the head of the Far Eastern division of the State Department wrote of the civil war going on there in 1924. "They all look alike to us." The Japanese soon realized that the United States would not do much to defend its interests in China.

THE PEACE MOVEMENT

The Americans of the 1920s wanted peace but would neither surrender their prejudices and dislikes nor build the defenses necessary to make it safe to indulge these passions. "The people have had all the war, all the taxation, and all the military service that they want," President Coolidge announced in 1925.

Peace societies flourished, among them the Carnegie Endowment for International Peace, designed "to hasten the abolition of war, the foulest blot upon our civilization," and the Woodrow Wilson Foundation, aimed at helping "the liberal forces of mankind throughout the world . . . who intend to promote peace by the means of justice." In 1923 Edward W. Bok, retired editor of the *Ladies' Home Journal,* offered a prize of $100,000 for the best workable plan for preserving international peace. He was flooded with suggestions. Former Assistant Secretary of the Navy Franklin D. Roosevelt drafted one while recovering from an attack of polio. Such was the temper of the times that he felt constrained to include in the preamble this statement:

> We seek not to become involved as a nation in the purely regional affairs of groups of other nations, nor to give to the representatives of other peoples the right to compel us to enter upon undertakings calling for a leading up to the use of armed force without our full and free consent, given through our constitutional procedure.

So great was the opposition to international cooperation that the United States refused to accept membership on the World Court, although this tribunal could settle disputes only when the nations involved agreed. Too many peace lovers believed that their goal could be attained simply by pointing out the moral and practical disadvantages of war.

The culmination of this illusory faith in preventing war by criticizing it came with the signing of the Kellogg-Briand Pact in 1928. The treaty was born in the fertile brain of French Foreign Minister Aristide Briand, who was eager to collect allies

against possible attack by a resurgent Germany. In 1927 Briand proposed to Secretary of State Frank B. Kellogg that their countries agree never to go to war with each other. Kellogg found the idea as repugnant as any conventional alliance, but American isolationists and pacifists found the suggestion fascinating. They plagued Kellogg with demands that he negotiate such a treaty.

To extricate himself from this situation, Kellogg suggested that the pact be broadened to include all nations. Now Briand was angry. Like Kellogg, he saw how meaningless such a treaty would be, especially when Kellogg insisted that it be hedged with a proviso that "every nation is free at all times . . . to defend its territory from attack and it alone is competent to decide when circumstances require war in self-defense." Nevertheless, Briand too found public pressures irresistible. In August 1928, at Paris, diplomats from 15 nations bestowed upon one another an "international kiss," condemning "recourse to war for the solution of international controversies" and renouncing war "as an instrument of national policy." Seldom has so unrealistic a promise been made by so many intelligent people. Yet most Americans considered the Kellogg-Briand Pact a milestone in the history of civilization: The Senate, habitually so suspicious of international commitments, ratified it 85 to 1.

THE GOOD NEIGHBOR POLICY

The conflict between the desire to avoid foreign entanglements and the desire to advance American economic interests is well illustrated by events in Latin America. In dealing with this part of the world, Harding and Coolidge performed neither better nor worse than Wilson had. In the face of continued radicalism and instability in Mexico, which caused Americans with interests in land and oil rights to suffer heavy losses, President Coolidge acted with forbearance. His appointment of Dwight W. Morrow, a patient, sympathetic ambassador, resulted in an improvement in Mexican-American relations. The Mexicans were able to complete their social and economic revolution in the 1920s without significant interference by the United States.

Under Coolidge's successor, Herbert Hoover, the United States began at last to treat Latin American nations as equals. Hoover reversed Wilson's policy of trying to teach them "to elect good men." The Clark Memorandum (1930), written by Undersecretary of State J. Reuben Clark, disassociated

the right of intervention in Latin America from the Roosevelt Corollary. The corollary had been an improper extension of the Monroe Doctrine, Clark declared. The right of the United States to intervene depended rather on "the doctrine of self-preservation."

The distinction seemed slight to Latin Americans, but since it seemed unlikely that the existence of the United States could be threatened in the area, it was important. By 1934 the marines who had been occupying Nicaragua, Haiti, and the Dominican Republic had all been withdrawn and the United States had renounced the right to intervene in Cuban affairs, thereby abrogating the Platt Amendment to the Cuban constitution. Unfortunately, the United States did little to try to improve social and economic conditions in the Caribbean region, so the underlying envy and resentment of "rich Uncle Sam" did not disappear.

THE TOTALITARIAN CHALLENGE

The futility and danger of isolationism were exposed in September 1931 when the Japanese, long dominant in Chinese Manchuria, marched in an army and converted the province into a puppet state named Manchukuo. This violated both the Kellogg-Briand and Nine-Power pacts. China, now controlled by General Chiang Kai-shek, appealed to the League of Nations and to the United States for help. Neither would intervene. When League officials asked about the possibility of American cooperation in some kind of police action, President Hoover refused to consider either economic or military reprisals. The United States was not a world policeman, he said. The Nine-Power and Kellogg-Briand treaties were "solely moral instruments."

The League sent a commission to Manchuria to investigate. Henry L. Stimson, Hoover's secretary of state, announced (the Stimson Doctrine) that the United States would never recognize the legality of seizures made in violation of American treaty rights. This served only to irritate the Japanese.

In January 1932 Japan attacked Shanghai, the bloody battle marked by the indiscriminate bombing of residential districts. When the League at last officially condemned their aggressions, the Japanese withdrew from the organization and extended their control of northern China. The lesson of Manchuria was not lost on Adolf Hitler, who became chancellor of Germany on January 30, 1933.

It is easy, in surveying the diplomatic events of 1920–1929, to condemn the United States and the European democracies for their unwillingness to stand up for principles, their refusal to resist when Japan and later Germany and Italy embarked on the

▲ Japanese troops advance through the ruins of the Chinese city of Shanghai in March, 1932, a year after Japan had seized Manchuria. Five years later, Japan embarked on the conquest of all China.

aggressions that led to World War II. It is also proper to place some of the blame for the troubles of the era on the United States and the European democracies, which controlled much of the world's resources and were primarily interested in holding on to what they had.

WAR DEBTS AND REPARATIONS

The democracies did not take a strong stand against Japan in part because they were quarreling about other matters. Particularly divisive was the controversy over war debts—those of Germany to the Allies and those of the Allies to the United States. The United States had lent more than $10 billion to its comrades in arms. Since most of this money had been spent on weapons and other supplies in the United States, it might well have been considered part of America's contribution to the war effort. The public, however, demanded full repayment—with interest. "These were loans, not contributions," Secretary of the Treasury Mellon firmly declared. Even when the Foreign Debt Commission scaled down the interest rate from 5 percent to about 2 percent, the total, to be repaid over a period of 62 years, amounted to more than $22 billion.

Repayment of such a sum was virtually impossible. In the first place, the money had not been put to productive use. Dollars lent to build factories or roads might be expected to earn profits for the borrower, but those devoted to the purchase of shells only destroyed wealth. Furthermore, the American protective tariff reduced the ability of the Allies to earn the dollars needed to pay the debts.

The Allies tried to load their obligations to the United States, along with the other costs of the war, on the backs of the Germans. They demanded that the Germans pay reparations amounting to $33 billion. If this sum were collected, they declared, they could rebuild their economies and obtain the international exchange needed to pay their debts to the United States. But Germany was reluctant even to try to pay such huge reparations, and when Germany defaulted, so did the Allies.

Everyone was bitterly resentful: the Germans because they felt they were being bled white; the Americans, as Senator Hiram Johnson of California would have it, because the wily Europeans were treating the United States as "an international sucker"; the Allies because, as the French said, *"l'oncle Shylock"* (a play on the names Uncle Sam and Shylock, the moneylender in Shakespeare's *Merchant of Venice)* was

demanding his pound of flesh with interest. "If nations were only business firms," Clemenceau wrote President Coolidge in 1926, "bank notes would determine the fate of the world. . . . Come see the endless lists of dead in our villages."

Everyone shared the blame: the Germans because they resorted to a runaway inflation that reduced the mark to less than one trillionth of its prewar value, at least in part in hopes of avoiding their international obligations; the Americans because they refused to recognize the connection between the tariff and the debt question; the Allies because they made little effort to pay even a reasonable proportion of their obligations.

In 1924 an international agreement, the Dawes Plan, provided Germany with a $200 million loan designed to stabilize its currency. Germany agreed to pay about $250 million a year in reparations. In 1929 the Young Plan further scaled down the reparations bill. In practice, the Allies paid the United States about what they collected from Germany. Since Germany got the money largely from private American loans, the United States would have served itself and the rest of the world far better had it written off the war debts at the start. In any case, in the late 1920s Americans stopped lending money to Germany, the Great Depression struck, Germany defaulted on its reparations payments, and the Allies then gave up all pretense of meeting their obligations to the United States. The last token payments were made in 1933. All that remained was a heritage of mistrust and hostility.

THE ELECTION OF 1928

Meanwhile, dramatic changes had occurred in the United States. The climax of Coolidge prosperity came in 1928. The president—somewhat cryptically, as was his wont—decided not to run again, and Secretary of Commerce Hoover, whom he detested, easily won the Republican nomination. Hoover was the intellectual leader, almost the philosopher, of the New Era. American capitalists, he believed, had learned to curb their selfish instincts. Voluntary trade associations could create "codes of business practice and ethics that would eliminate abuses and make for higher standards."

Although stiff and uncommunicative and entirely without experience in elective office, Hoover made an admirable candidate in 1928. His roots in

► *text continues on page 698*

Mapping
the Past

FDR's Political Revolution

The 1932 election marked the beginning of a profound political upheaval. During most of the previous presidential elections of the twentieth century, Republicans generally carried New England, the mid-Atlantic, the industrial Midwest, and the North Central farm belt. The Democrats consistently swept the South and some border states. (The major exception to this pattern was in 1912, when the Republican vote was divided between William H. Taft and Theodore Roosevelt, who ran as a Progressive.)

But in 1932 Franklin D. Roosevelt shattered the political patterns of the preceding half-century. The geographic dimensions of his victory are summarized by the statewide results comparing 1928 and 1932.

In 1928 Hoover swept to a huge victory by carrying every state outside the Deep South except Massachusetts. Hoover received 21 million votes; his Democratic opponent, Alfred E. Smith, only 15 million. Hoover's Electoral College margin was 444 to 87, the greatest to that time.

Four years later Roosevelt carried every state in the nation except Pennsylvania, Delaware, Connecticut, Vermont, New Hampshire and Maine.

A more precise indicator of the geographical breadth of Roosevelt's support can be found by examining results at the county level within particular states. Such information for Ohio and Montana is included in the map sequence, "FDR's political revolution: Ohio and Montana, 1928–1932." Ohio is significant because it had long been a Republican bastion, carried by that party in 18 of the previous 20 elections. Montana reflected a western constituency not commonly associated with FDR's voting block, immigrant and urban voters.

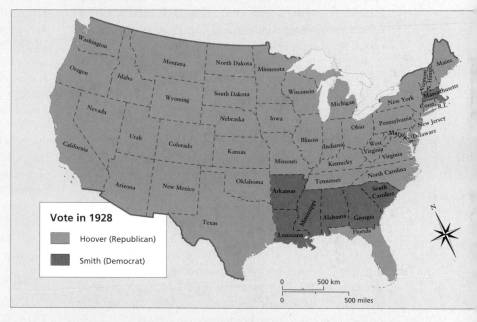

Vote in 1928

Hoover (Republican)

Smith (Democrat)

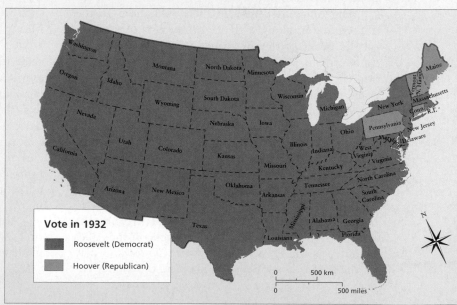

Vote in 1932

Roosevelt (Democrat)

Hoover (Republican)

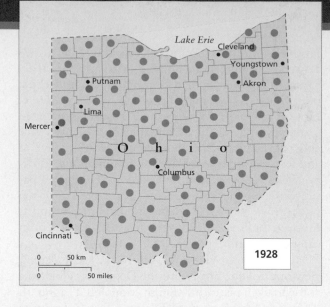

Ohio, 1928–1932

In 1928 Herbert Hoover, the Republican, ran well throughout the state, carrying 82 of 84 counties. Al Smith, the Democratic candidate, carried only Mercer and Putnam counties. Hoover won the remaining agricultural areas of the state, the industrial centers in Akron, Youngstown, and Cleveland, and the cities of Columbus and Cincinnati.

But in 1932, FDR carried Ohio, taking 60 counties. He prevailed in much of the farming country, the northeastern industrial areas, as well as Cincinnati and Columbus. The Republican hold on the state had been weakened nearly everywhere.

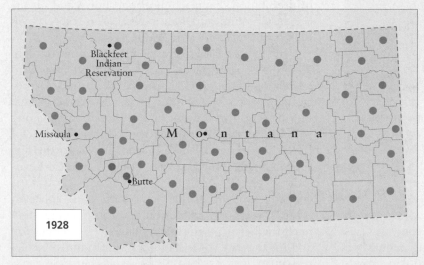

Montana, 1928–1932

A similar pattern was evident in Montana, whose economy was based on mining and agriculture. In 1928 it went for Hoover by a vote of 113,000 to 79,000. Smith, the Democrat, carried only Silver Bow and Deer Lodge counties, containing the industrial city of Butte and its environs, and the Blackfoot Indian Reservation in the north.

In 1932 FDR carried Montana, winning every county in the state except Sweet Grass, a farming and logging community that Hoover carried by 784 to 761 votes. In subsequent elections, FDR would sweep to even greater electoral victories. The electoral earthquake of 1932 transformed the political landscape for decades.

▲ Herbert Hoover relaxes during the 1928 presidential campaign. "That man has been offering me advice for the last five years," President Coolidge said of his secretary of commerce, "all of it bad."

the Midwest and West (Iowa-born, he was raised in Oregon and educated at Stanford University in California) neatly balanced his outstanding reputation among eastern business tycoons. He took a "modern" approach to both capital and labor; businessmen should cooperate with one another and with their workers too. He opposed both union busting and trustbusting. His career as a mining engineer had given him a wide knowledge of the world, yet he had become highly critical of Europe—which disarmed the isolationists, who might otherwise have suspected that his long years abroad had made him an effete cosmopolite.

The Democrats, having had their fill of factionalism in 1924, could no longer deny the nomination to Governor Al Smith. Superficially, Smith was

Hoover's antithesis. Born and raised in New York's Lower East Side slums, affable, witty, determinedly casual of manner, he had been schooled in machine politics by Tammany Hall. He was a Catholic, Hoover a Quaker, a wet where Hoover supported prohibition; he dealt easily with people of every race and nationality, while Hoover had little interest in and less knowledge of blacks and immigrants. However, like Hoover, Smith managed to combine a basic conservatism with humanitarian concern for the underprivileged. As adept in administration as Hoover, he was equally uncritical of the American capitalist system.

Unwilling to challenge the public's complacent view of Coolidge prosperity, the Democrats adopted a conservative platform. Smith appointed John J. Raskob, a wealthy automobile executive, to manage his campaign. Franklin D. Roosevelt, who ran for governor of New York at Smith's urging in 1928, charged that Hoover's expansion of the functions of the Department of Commerce had been at least mildly socialistic. This strategy failed miserably. Nothing Smith could do or say was capable of convincing many businessmen that he was a better choice than Hoover. His Catholicism, his brashness, his criticism of prohibition, his machine connections, and his urban background hurt him in rural areas, especially in the normally Democratic South.

In the election Hoover won a smashing triumph, 444 to 87 in the Electoral College, 21.4 million to 14 million in the popular vote. All the usually Democratic border states and even North Carolina, Florida, and Texas went to the Republicans, along with the entire West and the Northeast save for Massachusetts and Rhode Island. (See also the feature essay Mapping the Past, "FDR's Political Revolution," pp. 696–697.)

After this defeat the Democratic party appeared on the verge of extinction. Nothing could have been further from the truth. The religious question and his big-city roots had hurt Smith, but the chief reason he lost was prosperity—and the good times were soon to end. Hoover's overwhelming victory also concealed a political realignment that was taking place. Working-class voters in the cities, largely Catholic and unimpressed by Coolidge prosperity, had swung heavily to the Democrats. In 1924 the 12 largest cities had been solidly Republican; in 1928 all went Democratic. In agricultural states like Iowa, Smith ran far better than Davis had in 1924, for Coolidge's vetoes of bills designed to raise farm prices had caused considerable resentment. A new coalition of urban workers and dissatisfied farmers was in the making.

ECONOMIC PROBLEMS

The American economic system of the 1920s had grave flaws. Certain industries did not share in the good times. The coal business, suffering from the competition of petroleum, entered a period of decline. Cotton and woolen textiles also lagged because of the competition of new synthetics, principally rayon. Industry began to be plagued by falling profit margins and chronic unemployment.

The movement toward consolidation in industry, somewhat checked during the latter part of the progressive era, resumed; by 1929, 200 corporations controlled nearly half the nation's corporate assets. General Motors, Ford, and Chrysler turned out nearly 90 percent of all American cars and trucks. Four tobacco companies produced over 90 percent of the cigarettes. One percent of all financial institutions controlled 46 percent of the nation's banking business. Even retail merchandising, traditionally the domain of the small shopkeeper, reflected the trend. The A & P food chain expanded from 400 stores in 1912 to 17,500 in 1928. The Woolworth chain of five-and-ten-cent stores experienced similar growth.

Most large manufacturers, aware that bad public relations resulting from the unbridled use of monopolistic power outweighed any immediate economic gain, sought stability and "fair" prices rather than the maximum profit possible at the moment. "Regulated" competition was the order of the day, oligopoly the typical situation. The trade association movement flourished; producers formed voluntary organizations to exchange information, discuss policies toward government and the public, and "administer" prices in their industry. Usually the largest corporation, such as U.S. Steel in the iron and steel business, became the "price leader," its competitors, some themselves giants, following slavishly.

The success of the trade associations depended in part on the attitude of the federal government, for such organizations might well have been attacked under the antitrust laws. Their defenders, including President Harding, argued that the associations made business more efficient and prevented violent gyrations of prices and production. Secretary of Commerce Hoover put the facilities of his department at the disposal of the associations. "We are passing from a period of extremely individualistic action into a period of associational activities," Hoover stated. After Coolidge became president, the Antitrust Division of the Justice Department itself encouraged the trade associations to cooperate in ways that had previously been considered violations of the Sherman Act.

Even more important to the trade associations were the good times. With profits high and markets expanding, the most powerful producers could afford to share the bounty with smaller, less efficient competitors.

The weakest element in the economy was agriculture. Farm prices slumped and farmers' costs mounted. Besides having to purchase expensive machinery in order to compete, farmers were confronted by high foreign tariffs and in some cases quotas on the importation of foodstuffs. As crop yields per acre rose, chiefly because of the increased use of chemical fertilizers, agricultural prices fell further.

Despite the efforts of the farm bloc, the government did little to improve the situation. President Harding opposed direct aid to agriculture as a matter of principle. "Every farmer is a captain of industry," he declared. "The elimination of competition among them would be impossible without sacrificing that fine individualism that still keeps the farm the real reservoir from which the nation draws so many of the finest elements of its citizenship." During his administration Congress strengthened the laws regulating railroad rates and grain exchanges and made it easier for farmers to borrow money, but it did nothing directly to increase agricultural income. Nor did the high tariffs on agricultural produce have much effect. Being forced to sell their surpluses abroad, farmers found that world prices depressed domestic prices despite the tariff wall.

Thus the unprecedented prosperity rested on unstable foundations. The problem was mainly one of maldistribution of resources. Productive capacity raced ahead of buying power. Too large a share of the profits was going into too few pockets. The 27,000 families with the highest annual incomes in 1929 received as much money as the 11 million with annual incomes of under $1500, the minimum sum required at that time to maintain a family decently. High earnings and low taxes permitted huge sums to pile up in the hands of individuals who did not invest the money productively. A good deal of it went into stock market speculation, which led to the "big bull market" and eventually to the Great Depression.

THE STOCK MARKET CRASH OF 1929

In the spring of 1928, prices on the New York Stock Exchange, already at a historic high, began to surge ahead. As the presidential campaign gathered momentum, the market increased its upward pace,

stimulated by the candidates' efforts to outdo each other in praising the marvels of the American economic system. "Glamour" stocks skyrocketed—Radio Corporation of America rose from under 100 to 400 between March and November. A few conservative brokers expressed alarm, warning that most stocks were grossly overpriced. The majority scoffed at such talk. "Be a bull on America," they urged. "Never sell the United States short."

During the first half of 1929 stock prices climbed still higher. A mania for speculation swept the country, thousands of small investors putting their savings in common stocks. Then, in September the market wavered. Amid volatile fluctuations stock averages eased downward. Most analysts contended that the stock exchange was "digesting" previous gains. A Harvard economist expressed the prevailing view when he said that stock prices had reached a "permanently high plateau" and would soon resume their advance.

On October 24 a wave of selling sent prices spinning. Nearly 13 million shares changed hands—a record. Bankers and politicians rallied to check the decline, as they had during the Panic of 1907 (see p. 591). J. P. Morgan, Jr. rivaled the efforts of his father in that earlier crisis. President Hoover assured the people that "the business of the country . . . is on a sound and prosperous basis." But on October 29, the bottom seemed to drop out. More than 16 million shares were sold, prices plummeting. The boom was over.

HOOVER AND THE DEPRESSION

VIDEO

Prosperity of the 1920s and the Great Depression

The collapse of the stock market did not cause the Depression; stocks rallied late in the year, and business activity did not begin to decline significantly until the spring of 1930. The Great Depression was a worldwide phenomenon caused chiefly by economic imbalances resulting from the chaos of the Great War. In the United States too much wealth had fallen into too few hands, with the result that consumers were unable to buy all the goods produced. The trouble came to a head mainly because of the easy-credit policies of the Federal Reserve Board and the Mellon tax structure, which favored the rich. Its effects were so profound and prolonged because the politicians (and for that matter the professional economists) did not fully understand what was happening or what to do about it.

The chronic problem of underconsumption operated to speed the downward spiral. Unable to rid themselves of mounting inventories, manufacturers closed plants and laid off workers, thereby causing demand to

shrink further. Automobile output fell from 4.5 million units in 1929 to 1.1 million in 1932. When Ford closed his Detroit plants in 1931, some 75,000 workers lost their jobs, and the decline in auto production affected a host of suppliers and middlemen as well.

The financial system cracked under the strain. More than 1300 banks closed their doors in 1930, 3700 more during the next two years. Each failure deprived thousands of persons of funds that might have been used to buy goods; when the Bank of the United States in New York City became insolvent in December 1930, 400,000 depositors found their savings immobilized. And of course the industrial depression worsened the depression in agriculture by further reducing the demand for American foodstuffs. Every economic indicator reflected the collapse. New investments declined from $10 billion in 1929 to $1 billion in 1932, and the national income fell from over $80 billion to under $50 billion in the same brief period. Unemployment, under 1 million at the height of the boom, rose to at least 13 million.

President Hoover was an intelligent man, experienced in business matters and knowledgeable in economics. Secretary of the Treasury Mellon believed that the economy should be allowed to slide unchecked until the cycle had found its bottom. "Let the slump liquidate itself," Mellon urged. "Liquidate labor, liquidate stocks, liquidate the farmers. . . . People will work harder, live a more moral life. Values will be adjusted, and enterprising people will pick up the wrecks from less competent people." Hoover realized that such a policy would cause unbearable hardship for millions. He rejected Mellon's advice to let the Depression run its course.

Hoover's program for ending the Depression evolved gradually. At first he called on businessmen to maintain prices and wages. The government should cut taxes in order to increase consumers' spendable income, institute public works programs to stimulate production and create jobs for the unemployed, lower interest rates to make it easier for businesses to borrow in order to expand, and make loans to banks and industrial corporations threatened with collapse and to homeowners unable to meet mortgage payments. The president also proposed measures making it easier for farmers to borrow money, and he suggested that the government should support cooperative farm marketing schemes designed to solve the problem of overproduction. He called for an expansion of state and local relief programs and urged all who could afford it to give more to charity. Above all he tried to restore public confidence. The economy was basically healthy; the Depression was only a minor downturn; prosperity was "just around the corner."

▲ With the collapse of the stock market, Walter Thornton's assets evaporated but his debts remained. To help cover them he sold this snappy roadster for $100, a fraction of its original cost.

Although Hoover's plans were theoretically sound, they failed to check the economic slide, in part because of curious limitations in his conception of how they should be implemented. He placed far too much reliance on his powers of persuasion and the willingness of citizens to act in the public interest without legal compulsion. He urged manufacturers to maintain wages and keep their factories in operation, but the manufacturers, under the harsh pressure of economic realities, soon slashed wages and curtailed output sharply. He permitted the Federal Farm Board (created under the Agricultural Marketing Act of 1929) to establish semipublic stabilization corporations with authority to buy up surplus wheat and cotton, but he refused to countenance crop or acreage controls. The stabilization corporations poured out hundreds of millions of dollars without checking falling agricultural prices because farmers increased production faster than the corporations could buy up the excess for disposal abroad.

Hoover resisted proposals to shift responsibility from state and local agencies to the federal government, despite the fact—soon obvious—that they lacked the resources to cope with the emergency. By 1932 the federal government, with Hoover's approval, was spending $500 million a year on public works projects, but because of the decline in state and municipal construction, the total public outlay fell nearly $1 billion below what it had been in 1930. More serious was his refusal, on constitutional grounds, to allow federal funds to be used for the relief of individuals. State and municipal agencies and private charities must take care of the needy.

▲ Evicted from their homes, many unemployed gravitated to vacant industrial property, where they erected hovels from scraps of lumber, tarpaper, and cardboard. This shantytown is on the outskirts of Seattle.

Unfortunately the Depression was drying up the sources of private charities just as the demands on these organizations were expanding. State and municipal agencies were swamped just when their capacities to tax and borrow were shrinking. By 1932 more than 40,600 Boston families were on relief (compared with 7400 families in 1929); in Chicago 700,000 persons—40 percent of the workforce—were unemployed. Only the national government possessed the power and the credit to deal adequately with the crisis.

Yet Hoover would not act. He set up a committee to coordinate local relief activities but insisted on preserving what he called "the principles of individual and local responsibility." For the federal government to take over relief would "lead to the super-state where every man becomes the servant of the state and real liberty is lost."

Federal loans to commercial enterprises were constitutional, he believed, because the money could be put to productive use and eventually repaid. When drought destroyed the crops of farmers in the South and Southwest in 1930, the government lent them money to buy seed and even food for their livestock, but Hoover would permit no direct relief for the farmers themselves. In 1932 he approved the creation of the Reconstruction Finance Corporation (RFC) to lend money to banks, railroads, and insurance companies. The RFC represented an important extension of national authority, yet it was thoroughly in line with Hoover's philosophy. Its loans, secured by solid collateral, were commercial transactions, not gifts; the agency did almost nothing for individuals in need of relief. The same could be said of the Glass-Steagall Banking Act of 1932, which eased the tight credit situation

by permitting Federal Reserve banks to accept a wider variety of commercial paper as security for loans. The public grew increasingly resentful of the president's doctrinaire adherence to principle while breadlines lengthened and millions of willing workers searched fruitlessly for jobs.

As time passed and the Depression worsened, Hoover put more stress on the importance of balancing the federal budget, reasoning that since citizens had to live within their limited means in hard times, the government should set a good example. This policy was counterproductive; by reducing its expenditures the government made the Depression worse, which reduced federal revenue further. By June 1931 the budget was nearly $500 million in the red.

Hoover understood the value of pumping money into a stagnant economy. He might have made a virtue of necessity. The difficulty lay in the fact that nearly all "informed" opinion believed that a balanced budget was essential to recovery. The most prestigious economists insisted on it; so did business leaders, labor leaders, and even most socialists. In 1932, when the House of Representatives refused to vote a tax increase, the Democratic Speaker compelled reconsideration of the bill by asking those "who do not want to balance the budget to rise." Not a single member did so. As late as 1939 a public opinion poll revealed that over 60 percent of the people (even 57.5 percent of the unemployed) favored reducing government expenditures to balance the budget. When Hoover said, "prosperity cannot be restored by raids on the public Treasury," he was mistaken, but it is equally wrong to criticize him for failing to understand what almost no one understood in the 1930s.

Hoover can, however, be faulted for allowing his anti-European prejudices to interfere with the implementation of his program. In 1930 Congress passed the Hawley-Smoot Tariff Act, which raised duties on most manufactured products to prohibitive levels. Hoover signed it cheerfully. The new tariff made it impossible for European nations to earn the dollars they needed to continue making payments on their Great War debts to the United States, and it helped bring on a financial collapse in Europe in 1931. When that happened, Hoover wisely proposed a one-year moratorium on all international obligations. But the efforts of Great Britain and many other countries to save their own skins by devaluing their currencies in order to encourage foreigners to buy their goods led him to blame them for the Depression itself. He seemed unable to grasp what should have been obvious to a person of his intelligence: that high American tariffs made

DEBATING THE PAST

What caused the Great Depression? Here some 20,000 "bonus army" marchers camped outside the U.S. Capitol seeking assistance. Most were unemployed. What had caused the depression that threw so many out of work?

The first historian of the Depression wrote about it before it happened, or so some claimed. In the *Communist Manifesto* (1848) Karl Marx and Friedrich Engels had predicted that industrial capitalism would lead to overproduction, wars of expansion, and economic depressions. The Great Depression after 1929 lent credibility to the Marxist explanation.

But the economic revival following World War II indicated that either Marx was wrong or that capitalistic industrialism had not yet matured. Most historians now looked elsewhere for the cause of the Depression.

In 1954 economist John K. Galbraith focused on a mania for speculative investment in stocks, aggravated by easy credit policies. Other historians blamed federal policies, such as the high Smoot-Hawley tariff and the Federal Reserve's untimely constriction of credit immediately after the crash. But such measures alone could not have plunged the nation into a depression. Robert Sobel (1968) saw "no causal relationship between the events of late October 1929 and the great depression."

John Garraty (1986) showed that the Great Depression affected much of the world simultaneously. No one nation or policy caused it.

John K. Galbraith, *The Great Crash* (1954), Robert Sobel, *The Great Bull Market* (1968), Peter Temin, *Did Monetary Forces Cause the Great Depression?* (1976), John A. Garraty, *The Great Depression* (1986).

currency devaluation almost inevitable in Europe and that the curtailment of American investment on the Continent as a result of the Depression had dealt a staggering blow to the economies of all the European nations.

Much of the contemporary criticism of Hoover and a good deal of that heaped on him by later historians was unfair. Yet his record as president shows that he was too rigidly wedded to a particular theory of government to cope effectively with the problems of the day. Since these problems were in a sense insoluble—no one possessed enough knowledge to understand entirely what was wrong or enough authority to enforce corrective measures—flexibility and a willingness to experiment were essential to any program aimed at restoring prosperity. Hoover lacked these qualities. He was his own worst enemy, being too uncompromising to get on well with the politicians and too aloof to win the confidence and affection of ordinary people. He had too much faith in himself and his plans. When he failed to achieve the results he anticipated, he attracted, despite his devotion to duty and his concern for the welfare of the country, not sympathy but scorn.

THE ECONOMY HITS BOTTOM

During the spring of 1932, as the economy sounded the depths, thousands of Americans faced starvation. In Philadelphia during an 11-day period when no relief funds were available, hundreds of families existed on stale bread, thin soup, and garbage. In the nation as a whole, only about one-quarter of the unemployed were receiving any public aid. In Birmingham, Alabama, landlords in poor districts gave up trying to collect rents, preferring, one Alabama congressman told a Senate committee, "to have somebody living there free of charge rather than to have the house . . . burned up for fuel [by scavengers]." Many people were evicted, and they often gathered in ramshackle communities constructed of packing boxes, rusty sheet metal, and similar refuse on swamps, garbage dumps, and other wasteland. People began to call these places "Hoovervilles."

Thousands of tramps roamed the countryside begging and scavenging for food. At the same time, food prices fell so low that farmers burned corn for fuel. In Iowa and Nebraska farmers organized "farm holiday" movements, refusing to ship their crops to market in protest against the 31-cent-a-bushel corn and 38-cent wheat. They blocked roads and rail lines, dumped milk, overturned trucks, and established picket lines to enforce their boycott. The world seemed to have been turned upside down. Professor Felix Frankfurter of the Harvard Law School remarked only half humorously that henceforth the terms B.C. and A.D. would mean "Before Crash" and "After Depression."

The national mood ranged from apathy to resentment. In 1931 federal immigration agents and

Depression Breadlines in New York City

▲ Father and son lean into the wind as a sea of dust engulfs their farm in Cimarron County, Oklahoma, April 1936.

local groups in the Southwest began rounding up Mexican-Americans and deporting them. Some of those returned to Mexico had entered the United States illegally; others had come in properly. Unemployed Mexicans were ejected because they might become public charges, those with jobs because they were presumably taking bread from the mouths of citizens. "Capitalism is dying," the socialist theologian Reinhold Niebuhr remarked in 1932, "and . . . it ought to die."

Burning Bonus Army Shacks, 1932

In June and July 1932, 20,000 World War veterans marched on Washington to demand immediate payment of their "adjusted compensation" bonuses. When Congress rejected their appeal, some 2000 refused to leave, settling in a jerrybuilt camp of shacks and tents at Anacostia Flats, a swamp bordering the Potomac. President Hoover, alarmed, charged incorrectly that the "Bonus Army" was largely composed of criminals and radicals and sent troops into the Flats to disperse it with bayonets, tear gas, and tanks. The task was accomplished amid much confusion; fortunately no one was killed. The protest had been aimless and not entirely justified, yet the spectacle of the United States government chasing unarmed veterans with tanks appalled the nation.

The unprecedented severity of the Depression led some persons to favor radical economic and political changes. The disparity between the lots of the rich and the poor, always a challenge to democracy, became more striking and engendered considerable bitterness. "Unless something is done to provide employment," two labor leaders warned Hoover, "disorder . . . is sure to arise. . . . There is a growing demand that the entire business and social structure be changed because of the general dissatisfaction with the present system."

The Communist party gained few converts among farmers and industrial workers, but a considerable number of intellectuals, alienated by the trends of the 1920s, responded positively to the communists' emphasis on economic planning and the total

mobilization of the state to achieve social goals. Even the cracker-barrel humorist Will Rogers was impressed by reports of the absence of serious unemployment in Russia. "All roads lead to Moscow," the former muckraker Lincoln Steffens wrote.

THE DEPRESSION AND ITS VICTIMS

Depression is a word used by economists but also by psychologists, and the depression of the 1930s had profound psychological effects on its victims as well as the obvious economic ones. Almost without exception people who lost their jobs first searched energetically for new ones, but when they remained unemployed for more than a few months they sank gradually into apathy. E. Wight Bakke, a Yale sociologist who interviewed hundreds of unemployed men in the United States and England during the Depression, described the final stage of decline as "permanent readjustment," by which he meant that the long-term jobless simply gave up. The

VIDEO

Interview About Life in a Government Relief Camp

▲ Two boys, barefoot, at a clinic in Arkansas. In 1914 a Rockefeller Foundation study determined that hookworm, which caused debilitating anemia in the rural South, commonly entered the body through the feet. Although Arkansas legislators denounced the study as a plot to make its children buy northern shoes, the Rockefeller Foundation persisted in the campaign, which was backed by federal health officials in the 1930s.

▲ This photograph by Dorothea Lange captures the despair of a typical migrant California family during the depression. Many women had no other choice but to stay in tent cities or makeshift shelters with their children while their husbands searched for work.

settlement house worker Lillian Wald came to a similar conclusion. Unemployed people at her famous Henry Street settlement, she noticed, had lost both "ambition and pride."

Simple discouragement alone does not explain why so many of the jobless reacted this way. People who had worked all their adult lives often became ashamed of themselves when they could not find a job. Professor Bakke reported that half the unemployed people in New Haven that he interviewed never applied for public assistance no matter how desperate their circumstances. A purely physiological factor was often involved as well. When money ran low, people had to cut down on relatively expensive foods like fruit, meat, and dairy products. In New York City, for example, milk consumption fell by a million quarts a day. In nutritional terms people consumed

more carbohydrates and less food rich in energy-building vitamins and proteins. Listlessness (another word for apathy) often resulted.

The Depression affected the families of the jobless in many ways. It caused a dramatic drop in the birthrate, from 27.7 per thousand population in 1920 to 18.4 per thousand in the early 1930s, the lowest in American history. Sometimes it strengthened family ties. Some unemployed men spent more time with their children and helped their wives with cooking and housework. Others, however, became impatient when their children demanded attention, refused to help around the house, sulked, or took to drink.

The influence of wives in families struck by unemployment tended to increase, and in this respect women suffered less psychologically from the Depression. They were usually too busy trying to make ends meet to become apathetic. But the way they used this influence varied. Some wives were sympathetic, others scornful, when the "breadwinner" came home with empty hands. When the wife of an unemployed man managed to find a job, the result could be either gratitude and pride or bitter resentment on the man's part, resentment or a sense of liberation on the woman's.

Children often caused strains in families. Parental authority declined when there was less money available to supply children's needs. Some youngsters became angry when their allowance was cut or when told they could not have something they particularly wanted. Some adolescents found part-time jobs to help out. Others refused to go to school. If there is any generalization about the effects of the Depression on family relations it is probably an obvious one—where relationships were close and loving they became stronger, where they were not, the results could be disastrous.

THE ELECTION OF 1932

As the end of his term approached, President Hoover seemed to grow daily more petulant and pessimistic. The Depression, coming after 12 years of Republican rule, probably ensured a Democratic victory in any case, but his attitude as the election neared alienated many voters and turned defeat into rout.

Confident of victory, the Democrats chose Governor Franklin Delano Roosevelt of New York as their presidential candidate. Roosevelt owed his nomination chiefly to his success as governor. Under his administration, New York had led the

DOCUMENT

Hoover, New York Campaign Speech

nation in providing relief for the needy and had enacted an impressive program of old-age pensions, unemployment insurance, and conservation and public power projects. In 1928, while Hoover was carrying New York against Smith by a wide margin, Roosevelt won election by 25,000 votes. In 1930 he swept the state by a 700,000-vote majority, double the previous record. He also had the advantage of the Roosevelt name (he was a distant cousin of the inimitable TR), and his sunny, magnetic personality contrasted favorably with that of the glum and colorless Hoover.

Roosevelt was far from being a radical. Although he had supported the League of Nations while campaigning for the vice presidency in 1920, during the 1920s he had not seriously challenged the basic tenets of Coolidge prosperity. He never had much difficulty adjusting his views to prevailing attitudes. For a time he even served as head of the American Construction Council, a trade association. Indeed, his life before the Depression gave little indication that he understood the aspirations of ordinary people or had any deep commitment to social reform.

Roosevelt was born to wealth and social status in Dutchess County, New York, in 1882. Pampered in childhood by a doting yet domineering mother, he was educated at the exclusive Groton School and then at Harvard. Ambition as much as the desire to render public service motivated his career in politics; even after an attack of polio in 1921 left him badly crippled in both legs, he refused to abandon his hopes for high office. During the 1920s he was a hardworking member of the liberal wing of his party. He supported Smith for president in 1924 and 1928.

To some observers Roosevelt seemed rather a lightweight intellectually. When he ran for the vice presidency, the *Chicago Tribune* commented: "If he is Theodore Roosevelt, Elihu Root is Gene Debs, and Bryan is a brewer." Twelve years later many critics judged him too irresolute, too amiable, too eager to please all factions to be a forceful leader. Herbert Hoover thought he was "ignorant but well-meaning," and the political analyst Walter Lippmann, in a now-famous observation, called him "a pleasant man who, without any important qualifications for the job, would very much like to be President."

Despite his physical handicap—he could walk only a few steps, and then only with the aid of steel braces and two canes—Roosevelt was a marvelous campaigner. He traveled back and forth across the country, radiating confidence and good humor even when directing his sharpest barbs at the Republicans. Like every great political leader, he took as much from

▲ A vigorous-looking Franklin D. Roosevelt campaigning for the presidency in 1932. His vice-presidential running mate, John N. Garner, and the conveniently placed post allowed the handicapped candidate to stand when greeting voters along the way.

the people as he gave them, understanding the causes of their confusion and sensing their needs. "I have looked into the faces of thousands of Americans," he told a friend. "They have the frightened look of lost children. . . . They are saying: 'We're caught in something we don't understand; perhaps this fellow can help us out.'"

Voters responded in a similar manner. "The people," one member of the Hoover administration noted, "seem to be lifting eager faces to Franklin Roosevelt, having the impression that he is talking intimately to them." But this man then added: "I am glad of his enthusiasm and buoyance but it cannot escape the sense that he really does not understand the full meaning of his own recitations."

Roosevelt soaked up information and ideas from a thousand sources—from professors like Raymond Moley and Rexford Tugwell of Columbia, from politicians like the Texan vice-presidential candidate, John N. Garner, from social workers, businessmen, and lawyers. To those seeking specific answers to the questions of the

day, he was seldom satisfying. On such vital matters as farm policy, the tariff, and government spending, he equivocated, contradicted himself, or remained silent.

Aided by hindsight, historians have discovered portents of much of his later program in his campaign speeches. These pronouncements, buried among dozens of conflicting generalities, often passed unnoticed at the time. He said, for example, "if starvation and dire need on the part of any of our citizens make necessary the appropriation of additional funds which would keep the budget out of balance, I shall not hesitate to . . . ask the people to authorize the expenditure of that additional amount." In the same speech, however, he called for steep cuts in federal spending and a balanced budget, and he castigated Hoover for presiding over "the greatest spending administration in peace time in our history."

Nevertheless Roosevelt's basic position was unmistakable. There must be a "re-appraisal of values," a "New Deal." Instead of adhering to conventional limits on the extent of federal power, the government should do whatever was necessary to protect the unfortunate and advance the public good. Lacking concrete answers, Roosevelt advocated a point of view rather than a plan: "The country needs bold, persis-

tent experimentation. It is common sense to take a method and try it. If it fails, admit it frankly and try another. But above all, try something."

The popularity of this approach was demonstrated in November. Hoover, who had lost only eight states in 1928, won only six, all in the Northeast, in 1932. Roosevelt amassed 22.8 million votes to Hoover's 15.8 million and carried the Electoral College, 472 to 59. (See the feature essay Mapping the Past, "FDR's Political Revolution," pp. 696–697.)

During the interval between the election and Roosevelt's inauguration in March 1933, the Great Depression reached its nadir. The holdover "lame duck" Congress, last of its kind, proved incapable of effective action.[2] President Hoover, perhaps understandably, hesitated to institute changes without the cooperation of his successor. Roosevelt, for equally plausible reasons, refused to accept responsibility before assuming power officially. The nation, curiously apathetic in the face of so much suffering, drifted aimlessly, like a sailboat in a flat calm.

---

[2]The Twentieth Amendment (1933) provided for convening new Congresses in January instead of the following December. It also advanced the date of the president's inauguration from March 4 to January 20.

MILESTONES

1921–1922	Washington Conference tries to slow arms race	**1930**	Clark Memorandum renounces Roosevelt Corollary to Monroe Doctrine
1923	President Harding dies; Coolidge becomes president		Hawley-Smoot tariff raises duties on foreign manufactures
	Teapot Dome and other Harding scandals are exposed		Ten-year Dust Bowl begins in South and Midwest
1924	Dawes Plan restructures German reparations payments	**1931**	Japan invades Manchuria
	National Origins Act establishes immigration quotas		Hoover imposes moratorium on war debts
	Coolidge is elected president	**1932**	Federal troops disperse Bonus Marchers in Washington, D.C.
1928	Fifteen nations sign Kellogg-Briand Pact to "outlaw" war		Reconstruction Finance Corporation (RFC) lends to banks, railroads, insurance companies
	Herbert Hoover is elected president		Franklin Delano Roosevelt is elected president
1929	New York Stock Exchange crash ends big bull market; Great Depression begins	**1933**	Japan withdraws from League of Nations
	Young Plan further reduces German reparations		

SUPPLEMENTARY READING

The political history of the 1920s is surveyed in Robert K. Murray, *The Politics of Normalcy* (1973), Ellis W. Hawley, *The Great War and the Search for a Modern Order* (1979), Michael Parrish, *Anxious Decades: America in Prosperity and Depression, 1920–1941* (1992) and Geoffrey Parret, *America in the Twenties* (1982).

On the labor history of the postwar decade, see Robert H. Zieger, *Republicans and Labor* (1969). The best brief biography of Harding is Andrew Sinclair, *The Available Man* (1965). Robert Ferrell, *The Presidency of Calvin Coolidge* (1998), is the best study of Coolidge in the White House. On Hoover, see Martin L. Fausold, *The Presidency of Herbert Hoover* (1985), and a narrower monograph, Kendrick A. Clements, *Hoover, Conservatives and Consumerism* (2000).

David Burner, *The Politics of Provincialism* (1968), deals with the Democratic party in the 1920s. On the trade association movement, see Robert F. Himmelberg, *The Origins of the National Recovery Act* (1976).

Diplomatic developments are summarized in Selig Adler, *The Uncertain Giant* (1965), Akira Iriye, *After Imperialism* (1965), and *Across the Pacific* (1967), Stephen Kneeshaw, *The Pursuit of Peace* (1991), on the Kellogg-Briand pact, Thomas H. Buckley, *The United States and the Washington Conference* (1970), Charles De Benedetti, *Origins of the Modern Peace Movement* (1978), and John H. Wilson, *American Business and Foreign Policy* (1971).

On farm problems, see John D. Hicks, *Twentieth-Century Populism* (1951), and Gilbert C. Fite, *George N. Peek and the Fight for Farm Parity* (1954). On the election of 1928, see Oscar Handlin, *Al Smith and His America* (1958).

On isolationism, see Robert A. Divine, *The Reluctant Belligerent* (1965), and *The Illusion of Neutrality* (1962). On Latin American relations, see Irwin F. Gellman, *Good Neighbor Diplomacy* (1979).

SUGGESTED WEBSITE

America from the Great Depression to World War II: Photographs from the FSA and OWI, c. 1935–1945

http://memory.loc.gov/ammem/fsowhome.html

These images in the Farm Security Administration and Office of War Information Collection show Americans from all over the nation experiencing everything from despair to triumph in the 1930s and 1940s.

The New Deal: 1933–1941

▼ Isaac Soyer's *Employment Agency* (1937) captured the isolation and loss of self-esteem that accompanied joblessness.

CHAPTER CONTENTS

As the date of Franklin Roosevelt's inauguration approached, the banking system completely disintegrated. Starting in the rural West and spreading to major cities like Detroit and Baltimore, a financial panic swept the land. Depositors lined up before the doors of even the soundest institutions, desperate to withdraw their savings. Hundreds of banks were forced to close. In February, to check the panic, the governor of Michigan declared a "bank holiday," shutting every bank in the state for eight days. Maryland, Kentucky, California, and a number of other states followed suit; by inauguration day four-fifths of the states had suspended all banking operations. Other issues loomed, especially war clouds over Europe and east Asia, but few Americans could look much beyond their own immediate, and increasingly dire, economic prospects.

THE HUNDRED DAYS

Something drastic had to be done. The most conservative business leaders were as ready for government intervention as the most advanced radicals. Partisanship, while not disappearing, was for once

▲ A miner greets the president. Franklin's "first-class temperament" compensated for his "second-class intellect," Justice Oliver Wendell Holmes famously observed.

subordinated to broad national needs. A sign of this change came in February, even before Roosevelt took office, when Congress submitted to the states the Twenty-first Amendment, putting an end to prohibition. Before the end of the year the necessary three-quarters of the states had ratified it, and the prohibition era was over.

But it was unquestionably Franklin D. Roosevelt who provided the spark that reenergized the American people. His inaugural address reassured the country and at the same time stirred it to action. "The only thing we have to fear is fear itself. . . . This Nation asks for action, and action now. . . . I assume unhesitatingly the leadership of this great army of our people. . . ." Many such lines punctuated the brief address, which concluded with a stern pledge: "In the event that Congress shall fail . . . I shall not evade the clear course of duty that will then confront me. I shall ask the Congress for the one remaining instrument to meet the crisis—broad Executive power to wage a war against the emergency."

The inaugural captured the heart of the country; almost half a million letters of congratulation poured into the White House. When Roosevelt summoned Congress into special session on March 9, the legislators outdid one another to enact his proposals into law. "I had as soon start a mutiny in the face of a foreign foe as . . . against the program of the President," one representative declared. In the following "Hundred Days" serious opposition, in the sense of an organized group committed to resisting the administration, simply did not exist.

Roosevelt had the power and the will to act but no comprehensive plan of action. He and his eager congressional collaborators proceeded in a dozen directions at once, sometimes wisely, sometimes not, often at cross-purposes with themselves and one another. One of the first administration measures was the Economy Act, which reduced the salaries of federal employees by 15 percent and cut various veterans' benefits. Such belt-tightening measures could

VIDEO

FDR's
Inauguration

only make the Depression worse. But most New Deal programs were designed to stimulate the economy. All in all, an impressive body of new legislation was placed on the statute books.

On March 5 Roosevelt declared a nationwide bank holiday and placed an embargo on the exportation of gold. To explain the complexities of the banking problem to the public, Roosevelt delivered the first of his "fireside chats" over a national radio network. "I want to talk for a few minutes with the people of the United States about banking," he explained. His warmth and steadiness reassured millions. A plan for reopening the banks under Treasury Department licenses was devised, and soon most of them were functioning again, public confidence in their solvency restored. This solved the problem, but it also determined that banks would remain private institutions. Reform, not revolutionary change, had been decided upon at the very start of Roosevelt's presidency.

In April Roosevelt took the country off the gold standard, hoping thereby to cause prices to rise. Before the session ended, Congress established the Federal Deposit Insurance Corporation (FDIC) to guarantee bank deposits. It also forced the separation of investment banking and commercial banking concerns while extending the power of the Federal Reserve Board over both types of institutions, and it created the Home Owners Loan Corporation (HOLC) to refinance mortgages and prevent foreclosures. It passed the Federal Securities Act requiring promoters to make public full financial information about new stock issues and giving the Federal Trade Commission the right to regulate such transactions.[1]

THE NATIONAL RECOVERY ADMINISTRATION (NRA)

PWA in Action
Poster

Problems of unemployment and industrial stagnation had high priority during the Hundred Days. Congress appropriated $500 million for relief of the needy, and it created the Civilian Conservation Corps to provide jobs for men between the ages of 18 and 25 in reforestation and other conservation projects. To stimulate industry, Congress passed one of its most controversial measures, the National Industrial Recovery Act (NIRA). Besides establishing the Public Works Administration with authority to

spend $3.3 billion, this law permitted manufacturers to draw up industrywide codes of "fair business practices." Under the law producers could agree to raise prices and limit production without violating the antitrust laws. The law gave workers the protection of minimum wage and maximum hours regulations and guaranteed them the right "to organize and bargain collectively through representatives of their own choosing," an immense stimulus to the union movement.

The NIRA was a variant on the idea of the corporate state. This concept envisaged a system of industrywide organizations of capitalists and workers (supervised by the government) that would resolve conflicts internally, thereby avoiding wasteful economic competition and dangerous social clashes. It was an outgrowth of the trade association idea, although Hoover, who had supported voluntary associations, denounced it because of its compulsory aspects. It was also similar to experiments being carried out by the fascist dictator Benito Mussolini in Italy and by the Nazis in Adolf Hitler's Germany. It did not, of course, turn America into a fascist state, but it did herald an increasing concentration of economic power in the hands of interest groups, both industrialists' organizations and labor unions.

The act created a government agency, the National Recovery Administration (NRA), to supervise the drafting and operation of the business codes. Drafting posed difficult problems, first because each industry insisted on tailoring the agreements to its special needs and second because most manufacturers were unwilling to accept all the provisions of Section 7a of the law, which guaranteed workers the right to unionize and bargain collectively. While thousands of employers agreed to the pledge "We Do Our Part" in order to receive the Blue Eagle symbol of NRA, many were more interested in the monopolistic aspects of the act than in boosting wages and encouraging unionization. In practice, the largest manufacturers in each industry drew up the codes.

The effects of the NIRA were both more and less than the designers of the system had intended. In a sense it tried to accomplish the impossible—to change the very nature of business ethics and control the everyday activities of millions of individual enterprises. At the practical level, it did not end the Depression. There was a brief upturn in the spring of 1933, but the expected revival of industry did not take place; in nearly every case the dominant producers in each industry used their power to raise prices and limit production rather than to hire more workers and increase output.

Beginning with the cotton textile code, however, the agreements succeeded in doing away with the

---

[1]In 1934 this task was transferred to the new Securities and Exchange Commission, which was given broad authority over the activities of stock exchanges.

centuries-old problem of child labor in industry. They established the principle of federal regulation of wages and hours and led to the organization of thousands of workers, even in industries where unions had seldom been significant. Within a year John L. Lewis's United Mine Workers expanded from 150,000 members to half a million. About 100,000 automobile workers joined unions, as did a comparable number of steelworkers.

Labor leaders used the NIRA to persuade workers that Roosevelt wanted them to join unions—which was something of an overstatement. In 1935, because the craft-oriented AFL had displayed little enthusiasm for enrolling unskilled workers on an industrywide basis, John L. Lewis, together with officials of the garment trade unions, formed the Committee for Industrial Organization (CIO) and set out to rally workers in each of these mass-production industries into one union without regard for craft lines. Since a union containing all the workers in a factory was easier to organize and direct than separate craft unions, this was a far more effective way of unionizing factory labor. The AFL expelled these unions, however, and in 1938 the CIO became the Congress of Industrial Organizations. Soon it rivaled the AFL in size and importance.

THE AGRICULTURAL ADJUSTMENT ADMINISTRATION (AAA)

Roosevelt was more concerned about the plight of the farmers than that of any other group because he believed that the nation was becoming overcommitted to industry. The Agricultural Adjustment Act of May 1933 combined compulsory restrictions on production with government subsidies to growers of wheat, cotton, tobacco, pork, and a few other staple crops. The money for these payments was raised by levying processing taxes on middlemen such as flour millers. The object was to lift agricultural prices to "parity" with industrial prices, the ratio in most cases being based on the levels of 1909–1914, when farmers had been reasonably prosperous. In return for withdrawing part of their land from cultivation, farmers received "rental" payments from the Agricultural Adjustment Administration (AAA).

Since the 1933 crops were growing when the law was passed, Secretary of Agriculture Henry A. Wallace, son of Harding's secretary of agriculture and himself an experienced farmer and plant geneticist, decided to pay farmers to destroy the crops in the field. Cotton planters plowed up 10 million

acres, receiving $100 million in return. Six million baby pigs and 200,000 pregnant sows were slaughtered. Such ruthlessness appalled observers, particularly when they thought of the millions of hungry Americans who could have eaten all that pork.

Thereafter, limitation of acreage proved sufficient to raise some agricultural prices considerably. Tobacco growers benefited, and so did those who raised corn and hogs. The price of wheat also rose, though more because of bad harvests than because of the AAA program. But dairy farmers and cattlemen were hurt by the law, as were the railroads (which had less freight to haul) and, of course, consumers. Many farmers insisted that the NRA was raising the cost of manufactured goods more than the AAA was raising the prices they received for their crops. "While the farmer is losing his pants to his creditors," one Iowan complained, "NRA is rolling up his shirt. [Soon] we'll have a nudist colony."

DOCUMENT
An Attack on New Deal Farm Policies

A far more serious weakness of the program was its effect on tenant farmers and sharecroppers, many of whom lost their livelihoods when owners took land out of production to obtain AAA payments. In addition many landowners substituted machinery for labor. In the Cotton Belt farmers purchased more than 100,000 tractors during the 1930s. Each could do the work of several tenant or sharecropping families. Yet acreage restrictions and mortgage relief helped thousands of others. The law was a remarkable attempt to bring order to the chaotic agricultural economy. One New Deal official called it "the greatest single experiment in economic planning under capitalist conditions ever attempted by a democracy in times of peace." This was an overstatement. The AAA was a drastic change of American policy, but foreign producers of coffee, sugar, tea, rubber, and other staples had adopted the same techniques of restricting output and subsidizing growers well before the United States did.

THE TENNESSEE VALLEY AUTHORITY (TVA)

Another achievement of the Hundred Days was the creation of the Tennessee Valley Authority (TVA). During the Great War the government had constructed a hydroelectric plant at Muscle Shoals, Alabama, to provide power for factories manufacturing synthetic nitrate explosives. After 1920 farm groups and public power enthusiasts, led by Senator George W. Norris of Nebraska, had blocked administration

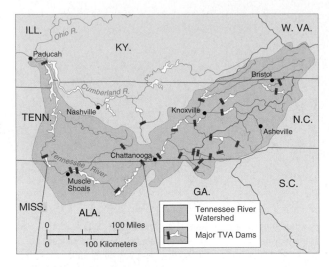

▲ **The Tennessee Valley Authority**

Although the Tennessee Valley Authority (TVA) never fully became the regional planning organization its sponsors had anticipated, the TVA nevertheless was able to expand the hydroelectric plants at Muscle Shoals, Alabama, and build dams, power plants, and transmission lines to service the surrounding area.

plans to turn these facilities over to private capitalists, but their efforts to have the site operated by the government had been defeated by presidential vetoes.

The Tennessee Valley Authority

Roosevelt wanted to make the Tennessee Valley area a broad experiment in social planning. Besides expanding the hydroelectric plants at Muscle Shoals and developing nitrate manufacturing in order to produce cheap fertilizers, he envisioned a coordinated program of soil conservation, reforestation, and industrialization.

Over the objections of private power companies, led by Wendell L. Willkie of the Commonwealth and Southern Corporation, Congress passed the TVA Act in May 1933. This law created a board authorized to build dams, power plants, and transmission lines and to sell fertilizers and electricity to individuals and local communities. The board could undertake flood control, soil conservation, and reforestation projects and improve the navigation of the river. Although the TVA never became the comprehensive regional planning organization some of its sponsors had anticipated, it improved the standard of living of millions of inhabitants of the valley. In addition to producing electricity and fertilizers and providing a "yardstick" whereby the efficiency—and thus the rates—of private power companies could be tested, it took on other functions ranging from the eradication of malaria to the development of recreational facilities.

THE NEW DEAL SPIRIT

By the end of the Hundred Days the country had made up its mind about Roosevelt's New Deal, and despite the vicissitudes of the next decade, it never changed it. A large majority labeled the New Deal a solid success. Considerable recovery had taken place, but more basic was the fact that Roosevelt, recruiting an army of officials to staff the new government agencies, had infused his administration with a spirit of bustle and optimism. The director of the presidential Secret Service unit, returning to the White House on inauguration day after escorting Herbert Hoover to the railroad station, found the executive mansion "transformed during my absence into a gay place, full of people who oozed confidence."

Dozens of people who lived through those stirring times have left records that reveal the New Deal spirit. "Come at once to Washington," Senator Robert La Follette, Jr., son of "Fighting Bob," telegraphed Donald Richberg, an old Theodore Roosevelt progressive. "Great things are under way." "I have been in a constant spin of activity," another New Dealer wrote a friend. "I feel as if I were alive all over, and that this cockeyed world is taking us somewhere." Justice Harlan Fiske Stone of the Supreme Court recorded: "Never was there such a change in the transfer of government."

Although Roosevelt was not much of an intellectual, his openness to suggestion made him eager to draw on the ideas and energies of experts of all sorts. New Deal agencies soon teemed with college professors and young lawyers without political experience.

The New Deal lacked any consistent ideological base. While the so-called Brain Trust (a group headed by Raymond Moley, a Columbia political scientist, which included Columbia economists Rexford G. Tugwell and Adolf A. Berle, Jr., and a number of others) attracted a great deal of attention, theorists never impressed Roosevelt much. His New Deal drew on the old populist tradition, as seen in its antipathy to bankers and its willingness to adopt schemes for inflating the currency; on the New Nationalism of Theodore Roosevelt, in its dislike of competition and its deemphasis of the antitrust laws; and on the ideas of social workers trained in the Progressive Era. Techniques developed by the Wilsonians also found a place in the system: Louis D. Brandeis had considerable influence on Roosevelt's financial reforms, and New Deal labor policy was an outgrowth of the experience of the War Labor Board of 1917–1918.

Within the administrative maze that Roosevelt created, rival bureaucrats battled to enforce their views. The "spenders," led by Tugwell, clashed with

those favoring strict economy, who gathered around Lewis Douglas, director of the budget. Roosevelt mediated between the factions. Washington became a battleground for dozens of special interest groups: the Farm Bureau Federation, the unions, the trade associations, and the silver miners. While the system was superior to that of Roosevelt's predecessors—who had allowed one interest, big business, to predominate—it slighted the unorganized majority. The NRA aimed frankly at raising the prices paid by consumers of manufactured goods; the AAA processing tax came ultimately from the pocketbooks of ordinary citizens.

THE UNEMPLOYED

At least 9 million persons were still without work in 1934 and hundreds of thousands of them were in real need. Malcolm Little, later famous as the radical black leader, Malcolm X, recalled:

> By 1934, we really began to suffer. This was about the worst depression year, and no one we knew had enough to eat or live on. . . . There was a bakery where, for a nickel, a couple of us children would buy a tall flour sack of day-old bread and cookies. . . . But there were times when there wasn't even a nickel and we would be so hungry we were dizzy. My mother would boil a big pot of dandelion greens and we would eat that.

Yet the Democrats confounded the political experts, including their own, by increasing their already large majorities in both houses of Congress in the 1934 elections. All the evidence indicates that most of the jobless continued to support the administration. Their loyalty can best be explained by Roosevelt's unemployment policies.

In May 1933 Congress had established the Federal Emergency Relief Administration (FERA) and given it $500 million to be dispensed through state relief organizations. Roosevelt appointed Harry L. Hopkins, an eccentric but brilliant and dedicated social worker, to direct the FERA. Hopkins insisted that the unemployed needed jobs, not handouts. In November he persuaded Roosevelt to create the Civil Works Administration (CWA) and swiftly put 4 million people to work building and repairing roads and public buildings, teaching, decorating the walls of post offices with murals, and utilizing their special skills in dozens of other ways.

The cost of this program frightened Roosevelt—Hopkins spent about $1 billion in less than five

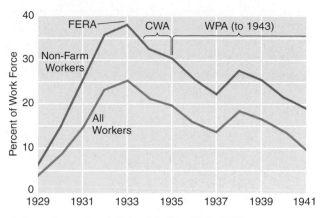

▲ **Unemployment and Federal Action, 1929–1941**
Unemployment of non-farm workers reached nearly 40 percent by early 1933. The Federal Emergency Relief Act (FERA) of May 1933 was followed by the Civil Works Administration (CWA) later that year, and then by the Works Progress Administration (WPA) in April 1935.

months—and he soon abolished the CWA. But an extensive public works program was continued through-out 1934 under the FERA. Despite charges that many of the projects were "boondoggles," thousands of roads, bridges, schools, and other structures were built or refurbished.

In May 1935 Roosevelt put Hopkins in charge of the Works Progress Administration (WPA). By the time this agency was disbanded in 1943 it had found employment for 8.5 million people. Besides building public works, the WPA made important cultural contributions. It developed the Federal Theatre Project, which put actors, directors, and stagehands to work; the Federal Writers' Project, which turned out valuable guidebooks, collected local lore, and published about 1000 books and pamphlets; and the Federal Art Project, which employed painters and sculptors. In addition, the National Youth Administration created part-time jobs for more than 2 million high school and college students.

At no time during the New Deal years did unemployment fall below 10 percent of the workforce, and in some places it was much higher. Unemployment in Boston, for instance, ranged between 20 and 30 percent throughout the 1930s. WPA did not go far enough, chiefly because Roosevelt could not escape his fear of drastically unbalancing the budget. Halfway measures did not stimulate the economy. The president also hesitated to undertake projects that might compete with private enterprises. Yet his caution did him no good politically; the business interests he sought to placate were becoming increasingly hostile to the New Deal.

LITERATURE IN THE DEPRESSION

Some American novelists found Soviet communism attractive and wrote "proletarian" novels in which ordinary workers were the heroes, and stylistic niceties gave way to the rough language of the street and the factory. Most of these books are of little artistic merit, and none achieved great commercial success. The best of the Depression writers avoided the party line, although they were critical of many aspects of American life. One was John Dos Passos, author of the trilogy *U.S.A.* (1930–1936).

Dos Passos came from a well-to-do family of Portuguese descent. He was educated at Harvard and drove an ambulance in France during the Great War. *U.S.A.* was a massive, intricately constructed work with an anticapitalist and deeply pessimistic point of view. It portrayed American society between 1900 and 1930 in broad perspective, interweaving the stories of five major characters and a galaxy of lesser figures. Throughout the narrative Dos Passos scattered capsule sketches of famous people, ranging from Andrew Carnegie and William Jennings Bryan to the movie idol Rudolph Valentino and the architect Frank Lloyd Wright. He included "newsreel" sections recounting events of the period and "camera eye" sections in which he revealed his personal reactions to the passing parade.

Dos Passos's method was relentless, cold, and methodical—utterly realistic. He displayed no sympathy for his characters or their world. *U.S.A.* was a monument to the despair and anger of liberals confronted with the Depression. After the Depression, however, Dos Passos rapidly abandoned his radical views.

The novel that best portrayed the desperate plight of the millions impoverished by the Depression was John Steinbeck's *The Grapes of Wrath* (1939), which described the fate of the Joads, an Oklahoma farm family driven by drought and bad times to abandon their land and become migratory laborers in California. Steinbeck captured the patient bewilderment of the downtrodden, the brutality bred of fear that characterized their exploiters, and the furious resentments of the radicals of the 1930s. He depicted the parching blackness of the Oklahoma dust bowl, the grandeur of California, the backbreaking toil of the migrant fruit pickers, and the ultimate indignation of a people repeatedly degraded. "In the eyes of the hungry there is a growing wrath. In the souls of the people the grapes of wrath are filling and growing heavy, growing heavy for the vintage."

Like so many other writers of the 1930s, Steinbeck was an angry man. "There is a crime here that goes beyond denunciation," he wrote. He had the compassion that Dos Passos lacked, and this quality raised *The Grapes of Wrath* to the level of great tragedy. In other works, such as *Tortilla Flat* (1935) and *The Long Valley* (1938), Steinbeck described the life of California cannery workers and ranchers with moving warmth without becoming overly sentimental.

Although his work was less political than that of Dos Passos or Steinbeck, Thomas Wolfe, a passionate, intensely troubled young man of vast but undisciplined talents, sought to describe the kaleidoscopic character of American life, the limitless variety of the nation. "I will know this country when I am through as I know the palm of my hand, and I will put it on paper and make it true and beautiful," he boasted.

During the last ten years of his short life, Wolfe wrote four novels: *Look Homeward, Angel* (1929), *Of Time and the River* (1935), and two published

▲ The original cover of Steinbeck's *Grapes of Wrath* (1939). "I am completely partisan," Steinbeck wrote. "Every effort I can bring to bear is . . . at the call of the common working people."

posthumously, *The Web and the Rock* (1939) and *You Can't Go Home Again* (1940). All were autobiographical and to some extent repetitious, for he was an unabashed egoist. Nevertheless he was a superb interpreter of contemporary society. He crammed his pages with unforgettable vignettes—a train hurtling across the Jersey meadows in the dark, a young woman clutching her skirt on a windswept corner, a group of derelicts huddled for shelter in a public toilet on a frigid night. And no writer caught more clearly the frantic pace and confusion of the great cities, the despair of the Depression, the divided nature of human beings, their fears and hopes, their undirected, uncontrollable energy.

William Faulkner, probably the finest of modern American novelists, responded to the era in still another way. Born in 1897, within a year of Fitzgerald and Hemingway, like Wolfe he attained literary maturity only in the 1930s. After service in the Canadian air force in the Great War, he returned to his native Mississippi, working at a series of odd jobs and publishing relatively inconsequential poetry and fiction. Suddenly, between 1929 and 1932, he burst into prominence with four major novels: *The Sound and the Fury, As I Lay Dying, Sanctuary,* and *Light in August.*

Faulkner created a local world, Yoknapatawpha County, and peopled it with some of the most remarkable characters in American fiction—the Sartoris family, typical of the old southern aristocracy worn down at the heels; the Snopes clan, shrewd, unscrupulous, boorish representatives of the new day; and many others. He pictured vividly the South's poverty and its pride, its dreadful racial problem, the guilt and obscure passions plaguing white and black alike. No contemporary excelled him as a commentator on the multiple dilemmas of modern life. His characters are possessed, driven to pursue high ideals yet weighted down with awareness of their inadequacies and their sinfulness. They are imprisoned in their surroundings however they may strive to escape them. The French novelist Simone de Beauvoir caught this aspect of Faulkner's work when she wrote that he "offered us a glimpse of fascinating depths . . . in those secret, shameful fires that rage in the bellies of men and women alike."

Faulkner was essentially a pessimist. His characters continually experience emotions too intense to be bearable, often too profound and too subtle for the natures he had given them. Nevertheless his stature was beyond question, and unlike so many other novelists of the period he maintained a high level in his later years. He was awarded the 1949 Nobel Prize for Literature.

THREE EXTREMISTS: LONG, COUGHLIN, AND TOWNSEND

Roosevelt's moderation and the desperation of the poor roused extremists both on the left and on the right. The most formidable was Louisiana's Senator Huey Long, the "Kingfish." Raised on a farm in northern Louisiana, Long was successively a traveling salesman, a lawyer, state railroad commissioner, governor, and, after 1930, United States senator. By 1933 his rule in Louisiana was absolute. Long was certainly a demagogue—yet the plight of all poor people concerned him deeply. More important, he tried to do something about it.

Long did not question segregation or white supremacy, nor did he suggest that Louisiana blacks should be allowed to vote. He used the word *nigger* with total un–self-consciousness, even when addressing northern black leaders. But he treated black-baiters with scathing contempt. When Hiram W. Evans, imperial wizard of the Ku Klux Klan, announced his intention to campaign against him in Louisiana, Long told reporters: "Quote me as saying

▲ Although Louisiana Senator Huey Long supported FDR in 1932, "the Kingfish" had changed his mind two years later, when this picture was taken. He opposed Roosevelt's large government bureaucracies, such as the National Recovery Administration (NRA), and sought more aggressive income redistribution. Also, he wanted to be president.

that that Imperial bastard will never set foot in Louisiana, and that when I call him a sonofabitch I am not using profanity, but am referring to the circumstances of his birth."

As a reformer, Long stood in the populist tradition; he hated bankers and "the interests." He believed that poor people, regardless of color, should have a chance to earn a decent living and get an education. His arguments were simplistic, patronizing, possibly insincere, but effective. "Don't say I'm working for niggers," he told one northern journalist. "I'm for the poor man—all poor men. Black and white, they all gotta have a chance. . . . 'Every Man a King'—that's my slogan."

Raffish, totally unrestrained, yet shrewd—a fellow southern politician called him "the smartest lunatic I ever saw"—Long had supported the New Deal at the start. But partly because he thought Roosevelt too conservative and partly because of his own ambition, he soon broke with the administration. While Roosevelt was probably more hostile to the big financiers than to any other interest, Long denounced him as "a phoney" and a stooge of Wall Street. "I can take him," he boasted in a typical sally. "His mother's watching him, and she won't let him go too far, but I ain't got no mother left, and if I had, she'd think anything I said was all right."

By 1935 Long's "Share Our Wealth" movement had a membership of over 4.6 million. His program called for the confiscation of family fortunes of more than $5 million and a tax of 100 percent on incomes over $1 million a year, the money to be used to buy every family a "homestead" (a house, a car, and other necessities) and provide an annual family income of $2000 to $3000, plus old-age pensions, educational benefits, and veterans' pensions. As the 1936 election approached, he planned to organize a third party to split the liberal vote. He assumed that the Republicans would win the election and so botch the job of fighting the Depression that he could sweep the country in 1940.

Less powerful than Long but more widely influential was Father Charles E. Coughlin, the "Radio Priest." A genial Canadian of Irish lineage, Coughlin in 1926 began broadcasting a weekly religious message over station WJR in Detroit. His mellifluous voice and orotund rhetoric attracted a huge national audience, and the Depression gave him a secular cause. In 1933 he had been an eager New Dealer, but his dislike of New Deal financial policies—he believed that inflating the currency would end the Depression—and his need for ever more sensational ideas to hold his radio audience led him to turn against the New Deal. By 1935 he was calling Roosevelt a "great betrayer and liar."

▲ Father Charles Coughlin, the "Radio Priest," whose weekly program reached 30 to 45 million listeners nationwide, photographed in Detroit as he promoted his National Union for Social Justice.

Although Coughlin's National Union for Social Justice was especially appealing to Catholics, it attracted people of every faith, particularly in the lower-middle-class districts of the big cities. Some of his talks caused more than a million people to send him messages of congratulation; contributions amounting to $500,000 a year flooded his headquarters. Coughlin attacked bankers, New Deal planners, Roosevelt's farm program, and the alleged sympathy of the administration for communists and Jews, both of which Coughlin denounced in his weekly talks. His program resembled fascism more than any leftist philosophy, but he posed a threat, especially in combination with Long, to the continuation of Democratic rule.

DOCUMENT

Coughlin, "A Third Party" (1936)

Another rapidly growing movement alarmed the Democrats in 1934–1935: Dr. Francis E. Townsend's campaign for "old-age revolving pensions." Townsend, a retired California physician, colorless and low-keyed, had an oversimplified and therefore appealing "solution" to the nation's troubles. The pitiful state of thousands of elderly persons, whose job prospects were even dimmer than those of the mass of the unemployed, he found shocking. He

advocated paying every person aged 60 years and over a pension of $200 a month, the only conditions being that the pensioners not hold jobs and that they spend the entire sum within 30 days. Their purchases, he argued, would stimulate production, thereby creating new jobs and revitalizing the economy. A stiff transactions tax, collected whenever any commodity changed hands, would pay for the program.

Economists quickly pointed out that with about 10 million persons eligible for the Townsend pensions, the cost would amount to $24 billion a year—roughly half the national income. But among the elderly the scheme proved extremely popular. Townsend Clubs, their proceedings conducted in the spirit of revivalist camp meetings, flourished everywhere, and the *Townsend National Weekly* reached a circulation of over 200,000. Although most Townsendites were anything but radical politically, their plan, like Long's Share Our Wealth scheme, would have revolutionized the distribution of wealth in the country. The movement marked the emergence of a new force in American society. With medical advances lengthening the average life span, the percentage of old people in the population was rising. The breakdown of close family ties in an increasingly mobile society now caused many of these citizens to be cast adrift to live out their last years poor, sick, idle, and alone.

With the possible exception of Long, the extremists had little understanding of practical affairs. (It could be said that Townsend knew what to do with money but not how to get it, and Coughlin knew how to get money but not what to do with it.) Collectively they represented a threat to Roosevelt; their success helped to make the president see that he must move boldly to restore good times or face serious political trouble in 1936.

Political imperatives had much to do with Roosevelt's decisions, and the influence of Justice Brandeis and his disciples, notably Felix Frankfurter, was great. They urged Roosevelt to abandon his probusiness programs, especially the NRA, and stress restoring competition and taxing corporations more heavily. The fact that most businessmen were turning away from him encouraged the president to accept this advice; so did the Supreme Court's decision in *Schecter* v. *United States* (May 1935), which declared the National Industrial Recovery Act unconstitutional. (The case involved the provisions of the NRA Live Poultry Code; the Court voided the act on the grounds that Congress had delegated too much legislative power to the code authorities and that the defendants, four brothers engaged in slaughtering chickens in New York City, were not engaged in interstate commerce.)

THE SECOND NEW DEAL

Existing laws had failed to end the Depression. Conservatives roundly denounced Roosevelt, and extremists were luring away some of his supporters. Voters, heartened by the partial success of early New Deal measures, were clamoring for further reforms. But the Supreme Court had declared many key New Deal measures unconstitutional. For these many reasons, Roosevelt, in June 1935, launched what historians call the Second New Deal.

There followed the "Second Hundred Days," one of the most productive periods in the history of American legislation. The National Labor Relations Act—commonly known as the Wagner Act—restored the labor guarantees wiped out by the *Schechter* decision. It gave workers the right to bargain collectively and prohibited employers from interfering with union organizational activities in their factories. A National Labor Relations Board (NLRB) was established to supervise plant elections and designate successful unions as official bargaining agents when a majority of the workers approved. It was difficult to force some big corporations to bargain "in good faith," as the law required, but the NLRB could conduct investigations of employer practices and issue cease and desist orders when "unfair" activities came to light.

The Social Security Act of August 1935 set up a system of old-age insurance, financed partly by a tax on wages (paid by workers) and partly by a tax on payrolls (paid by employers). It created a state-federal system of unemployment insurance, similarly financed. Liberal critics considered this social security system inadequate because it did not cover agricultural workers, domestics, self-employed persons, and some other groups particularly in need of its benefits. Health insurance was not included, and because the size of pensions depended on the amount earned, the lowest-paid workers could not count on much support after reaching 65. Yet the law was of major significance. Over the years the pension payments were increased and the classes of workers covered expanded. (The system, though substantially modified, remains in place today.)

The Rural Electrification Administration (REA), created by executive order, also began to function during this remarkable period. The REA lent money at low interest rates to utility companies and to farmer cooperatives interested in bringing electricity to rural areas. When the REA went into operation, only one farm in ten had electricity; by 1950 only one in ten did not.

Another important measure was the Wealth Tax Act of August 1935, which, while not the "soak the

▲ A vigorous Roosevelt has lassoed the Supreme Court, which now must gallop in tandem with his (second) New Deal. Roosevelt's image, even among critics, is that of a powerful leader; all but forgotten is the fact that Roosevelt's legs had atrophied from polio.

rich" measure both its supporters and its opponents claimed, raised taxes on large incomes considerably. Estate and gift taxes were also increased. Stiffer taxes on corporate profits reflected the Brandeis group's desire to penalize corporate giantism. Much of the opposition to other New Deal legislation arose from the fact that after these changes in the tax laws were made, the well-to-do had to bear a larger share of the cost of *all* government activities.

Whether the Second New Deal was more radical than the first depends largely on the vantage point from which it is considered. Measures like the Social Security Act had greater long-range effect on American life than the legislation of the First Hundred Days but were fundamentally less revolutionary than laws like the National Industrial Recovery Act and the Agricultural Adjustment Act, which attempted to establish a planned economy.

Herbert Hoover epitomized the attitude of conservatives when he called the New Deal "the most stupendous invasion of the whole spirit of Liberty that the nation has witnessed." Undoubtedly many opponents of the New Deal sincerely believed that it was undermining the foundations of American freedom. The cost of the New Deal also alarmed them. By 1936 some members of the administration had fallen under the influence of the British economist John Maynard Keynes, who argued that the world

Depression could be conquered if governments would deliberately unbalance their budgets by reducing interest rates and taxes and by increasing expenditures to stimulate consumption and investment.

Roosevelt never accepted Keynes's theories; he conferred with the economist in 1934 but could not grasp the "rigmarole of figures" with which Keynes deluged him. Nevertheless the imperatives of the Depression forced him to spend more than the government was collecting in taxes; thus he adopted in part the Keynesian approach. Conservative businessmen considered him financially irresponsible, and the fact that deficit spending seemed to be good politics made them seethe with rage.

THE ELECTION OF 1936

The election of 1936 loomed as a showdown. "America is in peril," the Republican platform declared. The GOP candidate, Governor Alfred M. Landon of Kansas, was a former follower of Theodore Roosevelt, a foe of the Ku Klux Klan in the 1920s, and a believer in government regulation of business. But he was a poor speaker, colorless, and handicapped by the reactionary views of many of his backers. Against the charm and political astuteness of Roosevelt, Landon's arguments—chiefly that he could administer the government more efficiently than the president—made little impression. He won the support of some anti–New Deal Democrats, among them two former presidential candidates, Al Smith and John W. Davis, but this was not enough.

DOCUMENT

FDR, Fireside Chat

The radical fringe put a third candidate in the field, Congressman William Lemke of North Dakota, who ran on the Union party ticket. Father Coughlin, denouncing Roosevelt as the "dumbest man ever to occupy the White House," rallied his National Union for Social Justice behind Lemke; Dr. Townsend also supported him. However, the extremists were losing ground by 1936. Huey Long had fallen victim to an assassin in September 1935, and his organization was taken over by a blatantly demagogic rightist, Gerald L. K. Smith. The New Deal, Smith said in 1936, was led by "a slimy group of men culled from the pink campuses of America," a reference to the increasingly popularity of Marxist principles among Depression-era intellectuals. The Townsendites fell under a cloud because of rumors that some of their leaders had their fingers in the organization's treasury. Father Coughlin's slanderous assaults on Roosevelt caused a backlash; a number of American Catholic prelates denounced him, and the Vatican issued an unofficial rebuke. Lemke got only 892,000 votes.

On election day the country gave the president a tremendous vote of confidence. He carried every state but Maine and Vermont. The Republicans elected only 89 members of the House of Representatives and their strength in the Senate fell to 16, an all-time low. In dozens of city and state elections, Democratic candidates also made large gains. Both Roosevelt's personality and his program had captivated the land. He seemed irresistible, the most powerfully entrenched president in the history of the United States.

Roosevelt did not win in 1936 because of the inadequacies of his foes. Having abandoned his efforts to hold the businessmen, whom he now denounced as "economic royalists," he appealed for the votes of workers and the underprivileged. The new labor unions gratefully poured thousands of dollars into the campaign to reelect him. Black voters switched to the Democrats in record numbers. Farmers liked Roosevelt because of his evident concern for their welfare: When the Supreme Court declared the Agricultural Adjustment Act unconstitutional (*United States* v. *Butler*, 1936), he immediately rushed through a new law, the Soil Conservation and Domestic Allotment Act, which accomplished the same objective by paying farmers to divert land from commercial crops to soil-building plants like clover and soybeans. Countless elderly persons backed Roosevelt out of gratitude for the Social Security Act. Homeowners were grateful for his program guaranteeing mortgages—eventually about 20 percent of all urban private dwellings were refinanced by the Home Owners Loan Corporation—and for the Federal Housing Administration, which, beginning in 1934, made available low-cost, long-term loans for modernizing old buildings and constructing new ones.

ROOSEVELT TRIES TO UNDERMINE THE SUPREME COURT

On January 20, in his second inaugural address, Roosevelt spoke of the plight of millions of citizens "denied the greater part of what the very lowest standards of today call the necessities of life." A third of the nation, he added without exaggeration, was "ill-housed, ill-clad, ill-nourished." He interpreted his landslide victory as a mandate for further reforms, and with his prestige and his immense congressional majorities, nothing appeared to stand in his way. Nothing, that is, except the Supreme Court.

Throughout Roosevelt's first term the Court had stood almost immovable against increasing the scope of federal authority and broadening the general power of government, state as well as national, to cope with the exigencies of the Depression. Of the nine justices, only Louis Brandeis, Benjamin N. Cardozo, and Harlan Fiske Stone viewed the New Deal sympathetically. Four others—James C. McReynolds, Willis Van Devanter, Pierce Butler, and George Sutherland—were intransigent reactionaries. Chief Justice Charles Evans Hughes and Justice Owen J. Roberts, while more open-minded, tended to side with the reactionaries on many questions.

Much of the early New Deal legislation, pushed through Congress at top speed during the Hundred Days, had been drafted without proper regard for the Constitution. Even the liberal justices considered the National Industrial Recovery Act unconstitutional (the *Schechter* decision was unanimous).

The reactionaries on the Court seemed governed by no consistent constitutional philosophy; they tended to limit the police power of the states when wages-and-hours laws came before them and to interpret it broadly when state laws restricting civil liberties were under consideration. In 1937 all the major measures of the Second Hundred Days appeared doomed. The Wagner Act had little chance of winning approval, experts predicted. Lawyers were advising employers to ignore the Social Security Act, so confident were they that the Court would declare it unconstitutional.

Faced with this situation, Roosevelt decided to ask Congress to shift the balance on the Court by increasing the number of justices, thinly disguising the purpose of his plan by making it part of a general reorganization of the judiciary. A member of the Court who reached the age of 70 would have the option of retiring at full pay. Should such a justice choose not to retire, the president was to appoint an additional justice, up to a maximum of six, to ease the burden of work for the aged jurists who remained on the bench.

Roosevelt knew that this measure would run into resistance, but he expected that the huge Democratic majorities in Congress could override any opposition and that the public would back him solidly. No astute politician had erred so badly in estimating the effects of an action since Stephen A. Douglas introduced the Kansas-Nebraska bill in 1854.

Although polls showed the public fairly evenly divided on the "Court-packing" bill, the opposition was vocal and influential. To the expected denunciations of conservatives were added the complaints of liberals fearful that the principle of court packing might in the future be used to subvert civil liberties. What, Senator Norris asked, would have been the reaction if a man like Harding had proposed such a measure? Opposition in Congress was immediate and intense; many who had cheerfully supported every

New Deal bill came out against the plan. The press denounced it, and so did most local bar associations. Chief Justice Hughes released a devastating critique; even the liberal Brandeis—the oldest judge on the court—rejected the bill out of hand. And many voters felt that Roosevelt had tried to trick them. The 1936 Democratic platform had spoken only of a possible amendment "clarifying" the Court's power, and Roosevelt had studiously avoided the issue during the campaign.

For months Roosevelt stubbornly refused to concede defeat, but in July 1937, he had to yield. Minor administrative reforms of the judiciary were enacted, but the size of the Court remained unchanged.

The struggle did result in saving the legislation of the Second New Deal. Alarmed by the threat to the Court, Justices Hughes and Roberts, never entirely committed to the conservative position, beat a strategic retreat on a series of specific issues. While the debate was raging in Congress, they sided with the liberals in upholding first a minimum wage law of the state of Washington that was little different from a New York act the Court had recently rejected, then the Wagner Act, then the Social Security Act. In May, Justice Van Devanter retired and Roosevelt replaced him with Senator Hugo Black of Alabama, a New Dealer. The conservative justices thereupon gave up the fight, and soon Roosevelt was able to appoint enough new judges to give the Court a large pro–New Deal majority. No further measure of significance was declared unconstitutional during his presidency. The Court fight hurt Roosevelt severely. His prestige never fully recovered. Conservative Democrats who had feared to oppose him because of his supposedly invulnerable popularity took heart and began to join with the Republicans on key issues. When the president summoned a special session of Congress in November 1937 and submitted a program of "must" legislation, not one of his bills was passed.

THE NEW DEAL WINDS DOWN

The Court fight marked the beginning of the end of the New Deal. Social and economic developments contributed to its decline, and the final blow originated in the area of foreign affairs. With unemployment high, wages low, and workers relatively powerless against their employers, most Americans had liked New Deal labor legislation and sympathized with the industrial unions whose growth it stimulated. The NRA, the Wagner Act, and the CIO's organization of industries like steel and automobiles changed the power structure within the economy. What amounted to a revolution in the lives of wage earners had occurred. Aside from the obvious changes—higher wages, shorter hours, paid vacations, insurance of various kinds—unionization had meant fair methods of settling disputes about work practices and a measure of job security based on seniority for tens of thousands of workers. The CIO in particular had done much to increase the influence of labor in politics and to bring blacks and other minorities into the labor movement.

In 1937 a series of "sit-down strikes" broke out, beginning at the General Motors plant in Flint, Michigan. Striking workers barricaded themselves inside the factories; when police and strikebreakers tried to dislodge them, they drove them off with barrages of soda bottles, tools, spare parts, and crockery. The tolerant attitude of the Roosevelt administration ensured the strikers against government intervention. "It is illegal," Roosevelt said of the General Motors strike, "but shooting it out . . . [is not] the answer. . . . Why can't those fellows in General Motors meet with the committee of workers?" Fearful that all-out efforts to clear their plants would result in the destruction of expensive machinery, most employers capitulated to the workers' demands. All the automobile manufacturers but Henry Ford quickly came to terms with the United Automobile Workers.

The major steel companies, led by U.S. Steel, recognized the CIO and granted higher wages and a 40-hour week. The auto and steel unions alone boasted more than 725,000 members by late 1937; other CIO units conquered the rubber industry, the electrical industry, the textile industry, and many more.

These gains and the aggressive way in which the unions pursued their objectives gave many members of the middle class second thoughts concerning the justice of labor's demands. Sit-down strikes, the disregard of unions for the "rights" of nonunion workers, and the violence that accompanied some strikes seemed to many not merely unreasonable but also a threat to social order. The enthusiasm of such people for all reform cooled rapidly.

While the sit-down strikes and the Court fight were going on, the New Deal suffered another heavy blow. Business conditions had been gradually improving since 1933. Heartened by the trend, Roosevelt, who had never fully grasped the importance of government spending in stimulating recovery, cut back sharply on the relief program in June 1937, with disastrous results. Between August and October the economy slipped downward like sand through a chute. Stock prices plummeted; unemployment rose by 2 million; industrial production slumped. This "Roosevelt recession" further damaged the president's reputation, and for many months he aggravated the situation by adopting an

DEBATING THE PAST

Did the New Deal succeed? A swimming pool such as this one in Carbon Hill, Alabama, built with federal "New Deal" funds, can be found in many cities and in most towns and villages in the United States. The New Deal visibly changed the nation; but did it succeed?

Few issues have been more controversial. At the time and for decades afterwards conservative historians such as Edgar E. Robinson denounced the New Deal as an economic failure that infringed on individual rights. Most liberals—foremost among them Arthur M. Schlesinger, Jr. (1957–1960)—acknowledged that the New Deal did not end the Depression but it did restrain corporations and address the needs of most workers, farmers, and consumers. That such people benefited from its actions was proven by how many of them voted for FDR, time and again.

William Leuchtenburg (1963) approved of much of the New Deal, but claimed that it left share croppers, slum dwellers, and most blacks "outside of the new equilibrium." It was but a "halfway revolution." A few years later Barton Bernstein (1968) led the far left in a blistering attack: "The New Deal failed to solve the problem of depression, it failed to raise the impoverished, it failed to redistribute income, it failed to extend equality and generally countenanced racial discrimination and segregation." The New Deal, in short, was no revolution at all.

In subsequent decades historians were more inclined to assess the New Deal in light of what was possible at the time. David Kennedy (1999), while acknowledging the New Deal's many failures, was struck by the "the boldness of its vision." Its achievements were as tangible as the city halls and high schools it had built, the people it had put to work, and the democratic nation it had preserved in time of crisis.

Edgar E. Robinson, *The Roosevelt Leadership* (1955), Arthur M. Schlesinger, Jr., *The Age of Roosevelt*, 3 volumes (1957–1960), William Leuchtenburg, *Franklin D. Roosevelt and the New Deal, 1932–1940* (1963), Barton Bernstein, *Towards a New Past* (1968), David M. Kennedy, *Freedom from Fear* (1999).

almost Hoover-like attitude. "Everything will work out all right if we just sit tight and keep quiet," he actually said.

While the president hesitated, rival theorists within his administration warred. The Keynesians, led by WPA head Harry Hopkins, Marriner Eccles of the Federal Reserve, and Secretary of the Interior Harold Ickes, clamored for stepped-up government spending. The conservatives, led by Treasury Secretary Henry Morgenthau, Jr., advocated retrenchment.

Perhaps confused by the conflict, Roosevelt seemed incapable of decisive action. When Keynes offered him "some bird's eye impressions" of the recession in February 1938, urging "large scale recourse to . . . public works and other investments aided by Government funds," Roosevelt sent him only a routine acknowledgment drafted by Morgenthau.

In April 1938 Roosevelt finally committed himself to heavy deficit spending. At his urging Congress passed a $3.75 billion public works bill. Two major pieces of legislation were also enacted at about this time. A new AAA program (February 1938) set marketing quotas and acreage limitations for growers of staples like wheat, cotton, and tobacco and authorized the Commodity Credit Corporation to lend money to farmers on their surplus crops.

The second measure, the Fair Labor Standards Act, abolished child labor and established a national minimum wage of 40 cents an hour and a maximum workweek of 40 hours, with time and a half for overtime. Although the law failed to cover many of the poorest-paid types of labor, its passage meant wage increases for 750,000 workers. In later years many more classes of workers were brought within its protection, and the minimum wage was repeatedly increased.

These measures further alienated conservatives without dramatically improving economic conditions. The resistance of many Democratic members of Congress to additional economic and social "experiments" hardened. As the 1938 elections approached, Roosevelt decided to go to the voters in an effort to strengthen party discipline and reenergize the New Deal. He singled out a number of conservative Democratic senators, notably Walter F. George of Georgia, Millard F. Tydings of Maryland, and "Cotton Ed" Smith of South Carolina, and tried to "purge" them by backing other Democrats in the primaries.

The purge failed. Southern voters liked Roosevelt but resented his interference in local politics. Smith dodged the issue of liberalism by stressing the question of white supremacy. Tydings emphasized Roosevelt's "invasion" of Maryland. In Georgia the president's enemies compared his campaign against George to General Sherman's march across the state during the Civil War. All three senators were easily renominated and then reelected in November. In the nation at large the Republicans made important gains for the first time since Roosevelt had taken office. The Democrats maintained nominal control of both houses of Congress, but the conservative coalition, while unable to muster the votes to do away with accomplished reforms, succeeded in blocking additional legislation.[2]

---

[2]The so-called conservative coalition was never a well-organized group. Its membership shifted from issue to issue; it had no real leaders and certainly no long-range plans.

SIGNIFICANCE OF THE NEW DEAL

After World War II broke out in 1939, the Great Depression was swept away on a wave of orders from the beleaguered European democracies. For this prosperity, Roosevelt received much undeserved credit. His New Deal had not returned the country to full employment. Despite the aid given to the jobless, the generation of workers born between 1900 and 1910 who entered the 1930s as unskilled laborers had their careers permanently stunted by the Depression. Far fewer rose to middle-class status than at any time since the 1830s and 1840s.

Roosevelt's willingness to experiment with different means of combating the Depression made sense because no one really knew what to do; however, his uncertainty about the ultimate objectives of the New Deal was counterproductive. He vacillated between seeking to stimulate the economy by deficit spending and trying to balance the budget; between a narrow "America first" economic nationalism and a broad-gauged international approach; between regulating monopolies and trustbusting; between helping the underprivileged and bolstering those already strong. At times he acted on the assumptions that the United States had a "mature" economy and that the major problem was overproduction. At other times he appeared to think that the answer to the Depression was more production. He could never make up his mind whether to try to rally liberals to his cause without regard for party or to run the government as a partisan leader, conciliating the conservative Democrats.

Roosevelt's fondness for establishing new agencies to deal with specific problems vastly increased the federal bureaucracy, indirectly added to the influence of lobbyists, and made it more difficult to monitor government activities. His cavalier attitude toward constitutional limitations on executive power, which he justified as being necessary in a national emergency, set in motion trends that so increased the prestige and authority of the presidency that the balance among the executive, legislative, and judicial branches was threatened.

Yet these are criticisms after the fact; they ignore what one historian has called the "sense of urgency and haste" that made the New Deal "a mixture of accomplishment, frustration, and misdirected effort." On balance, the New Deal had a constructive impact. By 1939 the country was committed to the idea that the federal government should accept responsibility for the national welfare and act to meet specific problems in every necessary way. What was most significant was not the proliferation of new agencies or the expansion of federal power. These were continuations of trends already a century old when the New Deal

▲ The proliferation of federal agencies during the New Deal inspired cartoonists. In this example, Swift's Gulliver—the United States—is tied down by the Lilliputian Brain Trusters.

the giant Bonneville and Grand Coulee dams in the West, were only the most spectacular part of a comprehensive New Deal program to develop the natural resources of the country. Exploitation of the natural resources of the West was checked, and a start was made toward the proper national management of the land and water of the region, along with its petroleum, lumber, and other resources. The NIRA and later labor legislation forced employers to reexamine their role in American life and to become more socially conscious. The WPA art and theater programs widened the horizons of millions. All in all, the spirit of the New Deal heightened the people's sense of community, revitalized national energies, and stimulated the imagination and creative instincts of countless citizens.

began. The importance of the "Roosevelt revolution" was that it removed the issue from politics. "Never again," the Republican presidential candidate was to say in 1952, "shall we allow a depression in the United States."

Because of New Deal decisions, many formerly unregulated areas of American life became subject to federal authority: the stock exchange, agricultural prices and production, labor relations, old-age pensions, relief of the needy. If the New Deal failed to end the Depression, it effected changes that have—so far, at least—prevented later economic declines from becoming catastrophes. By encouraging the growth of unions, the New Deal probably helped workers obtain a larger share of the profits of industry. By putting a floor under the income of many farmers, it checked the decline of agricultural living standards, though not that of the agricultural population. The social security program, with all its inadequacies, lessened the impact of bad times on an increasingly large proportion of the population and provided immense psychological benefits to all.

Among other important social changes, the TVA and the New Deal rural electrification program made farm life literally more civilized. Urban public housing, while never undertaken on a massive scale, helped rehabilitate some of the nation's worst slums. Government public power projects, such as

WOMEN AS NEW DEALERS: THE NETWORK

Largely because of the influence of Eleanor Roosevelt and Molly Dewson, head of the Women's Division of the Democratic National Committee, the Roosevelt administration employed far more women in positions of importance than any earlier one. Secretary of Labor Frances Perkins, the first woman appointed to a Cabinet post, had been active in labor relations for more than 20 years, as secretary of the Consumers' League during the progressive period, as a factory inspector immediately after the war, and as chair of the New York State Industrial Commission. As secretary of labor she helped draft New Deal labor legislation and kept Roosevelt informed on various labor problems outside the government.

In addition to Perkins, there were dozens of other women New Dealers. Dewson and Eleanor Roosevelt headed an informal but effective "network"—women in key posts who were always seeking to place reform-minded women in government jobs.

Through her newspaper column "My Day" and as a speaker on public issues, Eleanor Roosevelt became a major political force, especially in the area of civil rights, where the administration needed constant prodding.

▲ Eleanor Roosevelt dispensing soup to the needy. As a wealthy young socialite, she exhibited little interest in public matters. But after Eleanor discovered that Franklin was having an affair with her own social secretary, Lucy Mercer, Eleanor began to change. Her marriage, she confided to a friend, ceased to have any "fundamental love to draw on." Liberated and energized, she threw herself into social and political reform.

She particularly identified with efforts to obtain better treatment for blacks, in and out of government. Her best-known action occurred in 1939 after the Daughters of the American Revolution (DAR) refused to permit the use of their Washington auditorium for a concert by the black contralto Marian Anderson. Eleanor Roosevelt resigned from the DAR in protest, and after the President arranged for Anderson to sing at the Lincoln Memorial, she persuaded a small army of dignitaries to sponsor the concert. An interracial crowd of 75,000 people attended the performance. The *Chicago Defender,* an influential black newspaper, noted that the First Lady "stood like the Rock of Gibraltar against pernicious encroachments on the rights of minorities." (A disgruntled white Southerner made the same point differently: "She goes round telling the Negroes they are as good as anyone else.")

BLACKS DURING THE NEW DEAL

The shift of black voters from the Republican to the Democratic party during the New Deal years was one of the most significant political turnarounds in American history. In 1932 when things were at their worst, fewer African Americans defected from the Republican party than the members of any other traditionally Republican group. Four years later, however, blacks voted for Roosevelt in overwhelming numbers.

Blacks supported the New Deal for the same reasons that whites did, but how the New Deal affected blacks in general and racial attitudes specifically are more complicated questions. Claiming that he dared not antagonize southern congressmen, whose votes he needed for his recovery programs, Roosevelt did nothing about civil rights before 1941 and relatively little thereafter. For the same reason, many southern white liberals hesitated to support racial integration for fear that other liberal causes could be injured as a result.

Many of the early New Deal programs treated blacks as second-class citizens. Blacks were often paid at lower rates than whites under NRA codes (and so joked that NRA stood for "Negro Run Around" and "Negroes Ruined Again"). The early farm programs shortchanged black tenants and sharecroppers. Blacks in the Civilian Conservation Corps were assigned to

▲ Black sharecroppers evicted from their tenant farms were photographed by Arthur Rothstein along a Missouri road in 1939. Rothstein was one of a group of outstanding photographers who created a unique "sociological and economic survey" of the nation between 1936 and 1942 under the aegis of the Farm Security Administration.

all-black camps. TVA developments were rigidly segregated, and almost no blacks got jobs in TVA offices. New Deal urban housing projects inadvertently but nonetheless effectively increased the concentration of blacks in particular neighborhoods. Because the Social Security Act excluded agricultural laborers and domestic servants, it did nothing for hundreds of thousands of poor black workers or for Mexican-American farmhands in the Southwest. In 1939 unemployment was twice as high among blacks as among whites, and whites' wages were double the level of blacks' wages.

The fact that members of racial minorities got less than they deserved did not keep most of them from becoming New Dealers: Half a loaf was more than any American government had given blacks since the time of Ulysses S. Grant. As one black minister explained, "[Negroes] have never been so crazy as to wait for things to be perfect."

Aside from the direct benefits, blacks profited in other ways. Secretary of the Interior Harold L. Ickes appointed Charles Forman as a special assistant assigned "to keep the government honest when it came to race." In 1936 Roosevelt appointed Mary McLeod Bethune, founder of Bethune-Cookman College, as head of the Division of Negro Affairs in the National Youth Administration (NYA). She developed educational and occupational training programs for disadvantaged African American youths. Bethune, along with Forman, William Hastie, another black lawyer in Ickes's department, and a few others made up an informal "Black Cabinet" that lobbied throughout the Washington bureaucracy on behalf of better opportunities for blacks.

In the labor movement the new CIO unions accepted black members, and this was particularly significant because these unions were organizing industries—steel, automobiles, and mining among others—that employed large numbers of blacks. Thus, while black Americans suffered horribly during the Depression, New Deal efforts to counteract its effects brought them some relief and a measure of hope. And this became increasingly true with the passage of time. During Roosevelt's second term, blacks found far less to criticize than had been the case earlier.

A New Deal for Indians

New Deal policy toward American Indians built on earlier trends but carried them further. During the Harding and Coolidge administrations more Indian land had passed into the hands of whites, and agents of the Bureau of Indian Affairs had tried to suppress elements of Indian culture that they considered "pagan" or "lascivious." In 1924 Congress finally granted citizenship to all Indians, but it was still generally agreed by whites that Indians should be treated as wards of the state. Assimilation had failed; Indian languages and religious practices, patterns of family life, Indian arts and crafts had all resisted generations of efforts to "civilize" the tribes.

Government policy took a new direction in 1933 when President Roosevelt named John Collier commissioner of Indian affairs. In the 1920s Collier had studied the Indians of the Southwest and been appalled by what he learned. He became executive secretary of the American Indian Defense Association and, in 1925, editor of a reform-oriented magazine, *American Indian Life*. By the time he was appointed commissioner, the Depression had reduced perhaps a third of the 320,000 Indians living on reservations to penury.

Collier tried to revive the spirits of these people. He favored a pluralistic approach, seeking to help the Indians preserve their ancient cultures but also (somewhat contradictorily) to help them earn more money and make use of modern medical advances and modern techniques of soil conservation. He was particularly eager to encourage the revival of tribal governments that could represent the Indians in dealings with the United States government and function as community service centers.

In part because of Collier's urging, Congress passed the Indian Reorganization Act of 1934. This law did away with the Dawes Act allotment system

and enabled Indians to establish tribal governments with powers like those of cities, and it encouraged Indians to return individually owned lands to tribal control. About 4 million of the 90 million acres of Indian land lost under the allotment system were returned to the tribes.

New Deal Indian policy was controversial—among Indians as well as among white groups. Some critics charged Collier with trying to turn back the clock. Others attacked him as a segregationist and claimed that he was trying to restore "pagan" religious practices and convert the Indians to communism.

In truth the problem was more complicated than Collier had imagined. Indians who owned profitable allotments, such as those in Oklahoma who held valuable oil and mineral rights, did not relish turning over their land to tribal control. In New Mexico the Navajos, whose lands had relatively little commercial value, nonetheless voted decisively against going back to the communal system. All told, 77 of 269 tribes voted against communal holdings.

Collier resigned in 1945, and in the 1950s Congress "terminated" most government efforts aimed at preserving Indian cultures. Nevertheless, like so many of its programs, the New Deal's Indian policy was a bold effort to deal constructively with a long-standing national problem.

THE ROLE OF ROOSEVELT

How much of the credit for New Deal policies belongs personally to Franklin D. Roosevelt is debatable. He had little to do with many of the details and some of the broad principles behind the New Deal. His knowledge of economics was skimpy, his understanding of many social problems superficial, his political philosophy distressingly vague. The British leader Anthony Eden described him as "a conjurer, skillfully juggling with balls of dynamite, whose nature he failed to understand."

Nevertheless, every aspect of the New Deal bears the brand of Roosevelt's remarkable personality. Rexford Tugwell has left one of the best-balanced judgments of the president. "Roosevelt was not really very much at home with ideas," Tugwell explained. But he was always open to new facts, and something within him "forbade inaction when there was something to be done." Roosevelt constructed the coalition that made the program possible; his humanitarianism made it a reform movement of major significance. Although considered by many a terrible administrator because he encouraged rivalry among

▲ A 1935 cartoon entitled, "No Foreign Entanglements," in which Senate isolationism is frustrated by the global reach of American businesses.

his subordinates, assigned different agencies overlapping responsibilities, failed to discharge many incompetents, and frequently put off making difficult decisions, he was in fact one of the most effective chief executives in the nation's history. His seemingly haphazard practice of dividing authority among competing administrators unleashed the energies and sparked the imaginations of his aides.

Like Andrew Jackson, Roosevelt maximized his role as leader of all the people. His informal biweekly press conferences kept the public in touch with developments and himself in tune with popular thinking. His "fireside chats" convinced millions that he was personally interested in each citizen's life and welfare, as in a way he was. At a time when the size and complexity of the government made it impossible for any one person to direct the nation's destiny, Roosevelt managed the minor miracle of personifying that government to 130 million people. Under Hoover, a single clerk was able to handle the routine mail that flowed into the office of the president from ordinary citizens. Under Roosevelt, the task required a staff of 50.

While the New Deal was still evolving, contemporaries recognized Roosevelt's right to a place beside Washington, Jefferson, and Lincoln among the great presidents. Yet as his second term drew toward its close, some of his most important work still lay in the future.

THE TRIUMPH OF ISOLATIONISM

Franklin Roosevelt was at heart an internationalist, but like most world leaders in the 1930s, he placed revival of his own country's limping economy ahead of general world recovery. In April 1933 he took the United States off the gold standard, hoping that devaluing the dollar would make it easier to sell American goods abroad. The following month the World Economic Conference met in London. Delegates from 64 nations sought ways to increase world trade, perhaps by a general reduction of tariffs and the stabilization of currencies. After flirting with the idea of currency stabilization, Roosevelt threw a bombshell into the conference by announcing that the United States would not return to the gold standard. His decision increased international ill feeling, and the conference collapsed. The German financier Hjalmar Schacht announced smugly that Roosevelt was adopting the maxim of the great *Führer*, Adolf Hitler: "Take your economic fate in your own hands."

Against this background, vital changes in American foreign policy took place. Unable to persuade the country to take positive action against aggressors, internationalists like Secretary of State Stimson had begun in 1931 to work for a discretionary arms embargo law to be applied by the president in time of war against whichever side had broken the peace. By early 1933 Stimson had obtained Hoover's backing for an embargo bill, as well as the support of President-elect Roosevelt. First the munitions manufacturers and then the isolationists pounced on it, and in the resulting debate it was amended to make the embargo apply to *all* belligerents.

Instead of providing an effective if essentially negative tool for influencing international affairs, a blanket embargo would intensify America's ostrich-like isolationism. Stimson's policy would have permitted arms shipments to China but not to Japan, which might have discouraged the Japanese from attacking. As amended, the embargo would have automatically applied to both sides, thus removing the United States as an influence in the conflict. Although Roosevelt accepted the change, the internationalists in Congress did not, and when they withdrew their support the measure died.

The attitude of the munitions makers, who opposed both forms of the embargo, led to a series of studies of the industry. The most important was a Senate investigation (1934–1936) headed by Gerald P. Nye of North Dakota. Nye was convinced that "the interests" had conspired to drag America into World War I; his investigation was more an inquisition than an honest effort to discover what American bankers

"... and the Wolf chewed up the children and spit out their bones ... But those were <u>Foreign Children</u> and it really didn't matter."

▲ For a time Dr. Seuss—Theodor Seuss Geisel—did political cartoons. This one, published in October, 1941, makes fun of isolationists. The woman, wearing an "America First" sweater, is oblivious to the threat of Hitler, "Adolf the Wolf." Dr. Seuss's 1958 children's story—"Yertle the Turtle"—denounces tyranny. "You stay in your place while I sit here and rule," declares Yertle, atop a pile of turtles.

and munitions makers had been doing between 1914 and 1918. The committee's staff, ferreting into subpoenaed records, uncovered sensational facts about the lobbying activities and profits of various concerns. The Du Pont company's earnings, for example, had soared from $5 million in 1914 to $82 million in 1916. When one senator suggested to Irénée Du Pont that he was displaying a somewhat different attitude toward war than most citizens, Du Pont replied coolly: "Yes; perhaps. You were not in the game, or you might have a different viewpoint."

Munitions makers had profited far more from neutrality than from American participation in the war, but the Nye report convinced millions of citizens that the bankers who had lent the Allies money and the "merchants of death" who had sold them arms had tricked the country into war and that the "mistake" of 1917 must never be repeated.

While the Nye committee labored, Walter Millis published *The Road to War: America, 1914–1917*

(1935). In this best-seller Millis advanced the thesis that British propaganda, the heavy purchases of American supplies by the Allies, and Wilson's differing reactions to violations of neutral rights by Germany and Great Britain had drawn the United States into a war it could and should have steered clear of. Thousands found Millis's logic convincing, and isolationist sentiment increased.

The danger of another world war mounted steadily as Germany, Italy, and Japan repeatedly resorted to force to achieve their expansionist aims. In March 1935 Hitler instituted universal military training and denounced the settlement at Versailles. In May Mussolini massed troops in Italian Somaliland, using a trivial border clash as a pretext for threatening the ancient kingdom of Ethiopia.

Congress responded by passing the Neutrality Act of 1935, which forbade the sale of munitions to all belligerents whenever the president should proclaim that a state of war existed. Americans who took passage on belligerent ships after such a proclamation had been issued would do so at their own risk. Roosevelt would have preferred a discretionary embargo or no new legislation at all, but he dared not rouse the ire of the isolationists by vetoing the bill.

In October 1935 Italy invaded Ethiopia and Roosevelt invoked the new neutrality law. Secretary of State Cordell Hull asked American exporters to support a "moral embargo" on the sale of oil and other products not covered by the act. His plea was ignored; oil shipments to Italy tripled between October and January. Italy quickly overran and annexed Ethiopia. In February 1936 Congress passed a second neutrality act forbidding all loans to belligerents.

Then, in the summer of 1936, civil war broke out in Spain. The rebels, led by the reactionary General Francisco Franco and strongly backed by Italy and Germany, sought to overthrow the somewhat leftist Spanish Republic. Here, clearly, was a clash between democracy and fascism, and the neutrality laws did not apply to civil wars. However, Roosevelt now became more fearful of involvement than some isolationists. The president believed that American interference might cause the conflict in Spain to become a global war, and he was wary of antagonizing the substantial number of American Catholics who were sympathetic to the Franco regime. At his urging Congress passed another neutrality act broadening the arms embargo to cover civil wars.

Isolationism now reached its peak. A public opinion poll revealed in March 1937 that 94 percent of the people thought American policy should be directed at keeping out of all foreign wars rather than trying to prevent wars from breaking out. In April Congress passed still another neutrality law. It continued the embargo on munitions and loans, forbade Americans to travel on belligerent ships, and gave the president discretionary authority to place the sale of other goods to belligerents on a cash-and-carry basis. This played into the hands of the aggressors. While German planes and cannons were turning the tide in Spain, the United States was denying the hard-pressed Spanish loyalists even a case of cartridges.

In January, 1938 the House narrowly defeated the Ludlow amendment, which would have prohibited Congress from declaring war without the prior approval of the nation's voters. (See the feature essay Mapping the Past, "Isolationism in the 1930s," pp. 732–733.)

"With every surrender the prospects of a European war grow darker," Claude G. Bowers, the American ambassador to Spain, warned. The *New York Herald Tribune* pointed out that the neutrality legislation was literally reactionary—designed to keep the United States out of the war of 1914–1918, not the conflict looming on the horizon. President Roosevelt, in part because of domestic problems such as the Supreme Court packing struggle and the wave of sit-down strikes, and in part because of his own vacillation, seemed to have lost control over the formulation of American foreign policy. The American people, like wild creatures before a forest fire, were rushing in blind panic from the conflagration.

WAR AGAIN IN EUROPE

There were limits beyond which Americans would not go. In July 1937 the Japanese resumed their conquest of China, pressing ahead on a broad front. Roosevelt believed that invoking the neutrality law would only help the well-armed Japanese. Taking advantage of the fact that neither side had formally declared war, he allowed the shipment of arms and supplies to both sides.

Then the president went further. Speaking in Chicago in October, he condemned nations—he mentioned none by name—who were "creating a state of international anarchy and instability from which there is no escape through mere isolation or neutrality." The way to deal with "the epidemic of world lawlessness" was to "quarantine" it. Evidently Roosevelt had no specific plan in mind; nevertheless the "quarantine speech" produced a windy burst of isolationist rhetoric that forced him to back down.

▶ *text continues on page 734*

Mapping
the Past

Isolationism in the 1930s

Japan's Empire in the Pacific

In the early twentieth century the Chinese empire was crumbling, having long been undermined by outside powers. At the same time Japan was becoming a military and industrial dynamo. To sustain its growing population, which had nearly doubled since the 1860s, Japan sought to incorporate most of East Asia into its economic "co-prosperity sphere"—a euphemism for empire. Japan especially coveted China.

In 1910, following a brutal war against Korean guerrillas, Japan annexed Korea. During World War I, Japan seized German possessions in China and sent troops into part of Manchuria. In September 1931, ultranationalist Japanese officers at Mukden in Manchuria claimed that their forces had been attacked and used this is a pretext for occupying the entire province. In February, Japan installed a puppet government in Manchuria, which it called Manchukuo. On May 27, 1933 Japan withdrew from the League of Nations; four days later it invaded the Jehol province of China north of Beijing. In July, 1937, following a clash between Japanese and Chinese troops near Beijing, Japan seized the city and launched a full-scale offensive. By the end of the year, it had occupied Shanghai and Nanking. Tens of thousands of civilians died. President Roosevelt called for vague "positive endeavors" against Japan. His words had little effect.

Hitler and the Third Reich

In January 1933, following an electoral impasse, Adolf Hitler, head of the National Socialist (Nazi) party, was named chancellor of Germany. Hitler, an extremist who had been imprisoned in the 1920s for attempting to overthrow the Bavarian government, denounced the Versailles settlement and called for the establishment of a third German "reich"—a far-flung empire of German-speaking peoples. Within weeks of coming to power, he suspended the constitution, clamped down on the press, and encouraged the Nazi party's "storm troopers" to harass Jews, intellectuals, and Communists. Later that year, Hitler withdrew Germany from the League of Nations and built up its armed forces.

In March 1936 Germany reoccupied the Rhineland, in violation of the Versailles settlement. In March 1938, Germany annexed Austria, adding some 6 million people to Hitler's Third Reich. In September he also demanded annexation of the largely German-speaking Sudetenland of western Czechoslovakia; at a conference in Munich, France and Britain acceded to most of Hitler's demands; six months later, in violation of the Munich agreement, Germany gobbled up the remainder of Czechoslovakia. Then Hitler's armies moved to the Polish border.

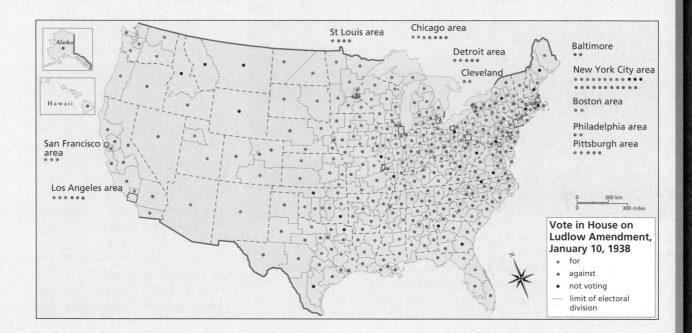

Vote in House on Ludlow Amendment, January 10, 1938
- for
- against
- not voting
— limit of electoral division

Isolationism in the United States

President Roosevelt denounced Japanese and Nazi aggression but was powerless to do much about it because of isolationism in the United States. One measure of the depth of opposition to American participation in another world war is indicated by the response of Congress to the Ludlow Amendment.

In 1935, Louis Ludlow, a Democratic representative from Indiana, proposed a constitutional amendment "to keep Americans out of slaughter pens in foreign countries." The bill provided that before Congress could declare war, it must first submit the matter to voters of the entire nation. Roosevelt was appalled by the bill, which he contended would "cripple" any president from conducting foreign affairs. For several years he managed to keep the legislation bottled up in committee by throwing his weight against the measure. But the renewal of the Japanese offensive against China in 1937 prompted representatives to bring the matter to a vote.

On January 10, 1938 the Ludlow Amendment was defeated in the House, as Roosevelt wished. But the margin, 209–188, was very narrow. The delegations from Kansas, North and South Dakota, and Wisconsin voted unanimously against FDR and in support of the amendment, as did all but a few representatives from Minnesota, Indiana, Nebraska, Michigan, and Ohio. The Far West and New England were evenly divided. Opposition to isolationism came chiefly from the South, where four out of five congressmen voted against the amendment, and in the northern cities, where Roosevelt's political clout was enormous.

Some historians assert that isolationism was especially strong among German-speaking Americans who did not wish to go to war against Germany. This map provides some confirmation for this judgment: Wisconsin, Minnesota, and Michigan, with large German American populations, were strongly isolationist. Farm states, too, were generally isolationist. Partly this may reflect the position, advanced by Senator Gerald P. Nye of North Dakota, that American participation in the Great War had been chiefly the work of eastern bankers and industrialists.

Yet despite the widespread support of isolationism, Roosevelt prevailed. His strongest base of support—the South and the large cities of the North and East, provided him with victory. It was, perhaps, the first small step toward American involvement in the Second World War.

▲ Prime Minister Winston Churchill inspects the ruins of the Coventral Cathedral, nearly demolished by German bombers in August, 1940 during the Battle of Britain. Germany claimed that the raid was a reprisal for British bombing of Munich. In all, 87,000 British civilians were killed and 2 million homes destroyed by German bombers.

"It's a terrible thing," he said, "to look over your shoulder when you are trying to lead—and to find no one there."

Roosevelt came gradually to the conclusion that resisting aggression was more important than keeping out of war, but when he did, the need to keep the country united led him at times to be less than candid in his public statements. Hitler's annexation of Austria in March 1938 caused him deep concern. The Nazis' vicious anti-Semitism had caused many of Germany's 500,000 Jewish citizens to seek refuge abroad. Now 190,000 Austrian Jews were under Nazi control. When Roosevelt learned that the Germans were burning synagogues, expelling Jewish children from schools, and otherwise mistreating innocent people, he said that he "could scarcely believe that such things could occur." But public opinion opposed changing the immigration law so that more refugees could be admitted, and the president did nothing.

In September 1938 Hitler demanded that Czechoslovakia cede the German-speaking Sudetenland to the Reich. British Prime Minister Neville Chamberlain and French Premier Edouard Daladier, in a conference with Hitler at Munich, yielded to Hitler's threats and promises and persuaded the Czechs to surrender the region. Roosevelt failed again to speak out. But when the Nazis seized the rest of Czechoslovakia in March 1939, Roosevelt called for "methods short of war" to demonstrate America's determination to check the fascists.

When Hitler threatened Poland in the spring of 1939, demanding the free city of Danzig and the Polish Corridor separating East Prussia from the rest of Germany, and when Mussolini invaded Albania, Roosevelt urged Congress to repeal the 1937 neutrality act so that the United States could sell arms to Britain and France in the event of war. Congress refused. "Captain," Vice President Garner told Roosevelt after counting noses in the Senate, "you haven't got the votes," and the president, perhaps unwisely, did not press the issue.

In August 1939 Germany and the Soviet Union signed a nonaggression pact, prelude to their joint assault on Poland. On September 1 Hitler's troops invaded Poland, at last provoking Great Britain and France to declare war. Roosevelt immediately asked Congress to repeal the arms embargo. In November, in a vote that followed party lines closely, the Democratic majority pushed through a law permitting the sale of arms and other contraband on a cash-and-carry basis. Short-term loans were authorized, but American vessels were forbidden to carry any products to the belligerents. Since the Allies controlled the seas, cash-and-carry gave them a tremendous advantage.

The German attack on Poland effected a basic change in American thinking. Keeping out of the war remained an almost universal hope, but preventing a Nazi victory became the ultimate, if not always conscious, objective of many citizens. In Roosevelt's case it was perfectly conscious, although he dared not express his feelings candidly because of isolationist strength in Congress and the country. He moved slowly, responding to rather than directing the course of events.

Cash-and-carry did not stop the Nazis. Poland fell in less than a month; then, after a winter lull that cynics called the "phony war," Hitler loosed his armored divisions. Between April 9 and June 22 he

taught the world the awful meaning of *Blitzkrieg*—lightning war. Denmark, Norway, the Netherlands, Belgium, and France were successively overwhelmed. The British army, pinned against the sea at Dunkirk, saved itself from annihilation only by fleeing across the English Channel. After the French submitted to his harsh terms on June 22, Hitler controlled nearly all of western Europe.

Roosevelt responded to these disasters in a number of ways. In the fall of 1939, reacting to warnings from Albert Einstein and other scientists that the Germans were trying to develop an atomic bomb, he committed federal funds to a top-secret atomic bomb program, which came to be known as the Manhattan Project. Even as the British and French were falling back, he sold them, without legal authority, surplus government arms. When Italy entered the war against France, the president called the invasion a stab in the back. During the first five months of 1940 he asked Congress to appropriate over $4 billion for national defense. To strengthen national unity he named Henry L. Stimson secretary of war[3] and another Republican, Frank Knox, secretary of the navy.

After the fall of France, Hitler attempted to bomb and starve the British into submission. The epic air battles over England during the summer of 1940 ended in a decisive defeat for the Nazis, but the Royal Navy, which had only about 100 destroyers, could not control German submarine attacks on shipping. Far more destroyers were needed. In this desperate hour, Prime Minister Winston Churchill, who had replaced Chamberlain in May 1940, asked Roosevelt for 50 old American destroyers to fill the gap.

The navy had 240 destroyers in commission and more than 50 under construction. But direct loan or sale of the vessels would have violated both international and American laws. Any attempt to obtain new legislation would have roused fears that the United States was going down the path that had led it into World War I. Long delay if not outright defeat would have resulted. Roosevelt therefore arranged to "trade" the destroyers for six British naval bases in the Caribbean. In addition, Great Britain leased bases in Bermuda and Newfoundland to the United States.

The destroyers-for-bases deal was a masterful achievement. It helped save Great Britain, and at the same time it circumvented isolationist prejudices since the president could present it as a shrewd bargain that bolstered America's defenses. A string of island bastions in the Atlantic was more valuable than 50 old destroyers.

Lines were hardening throughout the world. In September 1940, despite last-ditch isolationist resistance, Congress enacted the first peacetime draft in American history. Some 1.2 million draftees were summoned for one year of service, and 800,000 reservists were called to active duty. That same month Japan signed a mutual-assistance pact with Germany and Italy. This Rome-Berlin-Tokyo axis fused the conflicts in Europe and Asia, turning the struggle into a global war.

A Third Term for FDR

In the midst of these events the 1940 presidential election took place. Why Roosevelt decided to run for a third term is a much-debated question. Partisanship had something to do with it, for no other Democrat seemed so likely to carry the country. Nor would the president have been human had he not been tempted to hold on to power, especially in such critical times. His conviction that no one else could keep a rein on the isolationists was probably decisive. In any case, he was easily renominated. Vice President Garner, who had become disenchanted with Roosevelt and the New Deal, did not seek a third term; at Roosevelt's dictation, the party chose Secretary of Agriculture Henry A. Wallace to replace him.

By using concern about the European war to justify running for a tradition-breaking third term, Roosevelt brought down on his head the hatred of conservative Republicans and the isolationists of both major parties, just when they thought they would be rid of him. The leading Republican presidential candidates were Senator Robert A. Taft of Ohio, son of the former president, and District Attorney Thomas E. Dewey of New York, who had won fame as a "racket buster" and political reformer. Taft was considered conservative and lacking in political glamour; Dewey, barely 38, seemed too young and inexperienced. Instead the Republicans nominated the darkest of dark horses, Wendell L. Willkie of Indiana, the utility magnate who had led the fight against the TVA in 1933.

Despite his political inexperience and Wall Street connections, Willkie made an appealing candidate. He was an energetic, charming, openhearted man. His rough-hewn, rural manner (one Democrat called him "a simple, barefoot Wall Street lawyer") won him wide support in farm districts. Willkie had difficulty, however, finding issues on which to oppose Roosevelt. Good times were at last returning. The New Deal reforms were too popular and too much in line with his own thinking to invite attack. He believed as

---

[3]Stimson had held this post from 1911 to 1913 in the Taft Cabinet!

strongly as the president that America could no longer ignore the Nazi threat.

In the end Willkie focused his campaign on Roosevelt's conduct of foreign relations. A preponderance of the Democrats favored all-out aid to Britain, while most Republicans still wished to avoid foreign "entanglements." But the crisis was causing many persons to shift sides. Among interventionists, organizations like the Committee to Defend America by Aiding the Allies, headed by Republican William Allen White, and the small but influential Century Group contained members of both parties. So did the isolationist America First Committee, led by Robert E. Wood of Sears Roebuck and the famous aviator Charles A. Lindbergh.

While rejecting the isolationist position, Willkie charged that Roosevelt intended to make the United States a participant in the war. "If you re-elect him," he told one audience, "you may expect war in April 1941," to which Roosevelt retorted (disingenuously, since he knew he was not a free agent in the situation), "I have said this before, but I shall say it again and again and again: Your boys are not going to be sent into any foreign wars." In November Roosevelt carried the country handily, though by a smaller majority than in 1932 or 1936. The popular vote was 27 million to 22 million, the electoral count 449 to 82.

THE UNDECLARED WAR

The election encouraged Roosevelt to act more boldly. When Prime Minister Churchill informed him that the cash-and-carry system would no longer suffice because Great Britain was rapidly exhausting its financial resources, he decided at once to provide the British with whatever they needed. Instead of proposing to lend them money, a step certain to rouse memories of the vexatious war debt controversies, he devised the lend-lease program, one of his most ingenious and imaginative creations.

First he delivered a "fireside chat" that stressed the evil intentions of the Nazis and the dangers that a German victory would create for America. Aiding Britain should be looked at simply as a form of self-defense. "As planes and ships and guns and shells are produced," he said, American defense experts would decide "how much shall be sent abroad and how much shall remain at home." When the radio talk provoked a favorable public response, Roosevelt went to Congress in January 1941 with a plan calling for the expenditure of $7 billion for war materials that the president could sell, lend, lease, exchange, or transfer to any country whose defense he deemed

vital to that of the United States. After two months of debate, Congress gave him what he had asked for.

Although the wording of the Lend-Lease Act obscured its immediate purpose, the saving of Great Britain, the president was frank in explaining his plan. He did not minimize the dangers involved, yet his mastery of practical politics was never more in evidence. To counter Irish-American prejudices against the English, he pointed out that the Irish Republic would surely fall under Nazi domination if Hitler won the war. He coupled his demand for heavy military expenditures with his enunciation of the idealistic "Four Freedoms"—freedom of speech, freedom of religion, freedom from want, and freedom from fear—for which, he said, the war was being fought.

After the enactment of lend-lease, aid short of war was no longer seriously debated. The American navy began to patrol the North Atlantic, shadowing German submarines and radioing their locations to British warships and planes. In April 1941 United States forces occupied Greenland; in May the president declared a state of unlimited national emergency. After Hitler invaded the Soviet Union in June, Roosevelt moved slowly, for anti-Soviet feeling in the United States was intense.[4] But it was obviously to the nation's advantage to help any country that was resisting Hitler's armies. In November, $1 billion in lend-lease aid was put at the disposal of the Soviet Union.

Meanwhile, Iceland was occupied in July 1941, and the draft law was extended in August—by the margin of a single vote in the House of Representatives. In September the German submarine *U–652* fired a torpedo at the destroyer *Greer* in the North Atlantic. The *Greer,* which had provoked the attack by tracking *U–652* and flashing its position to a British plane, avoided the torpedo and dropped 19 depth charges in an effort to sink the submarine.

Roosevelt (nothing he ever did provided more ammunition for his critics) announced that the *Greer* had been innocently "carrying mail to Iceland." He called the U-boats "the rattlesnakes of the Atlantic" and ordered the navy to "shoot on sight" any German craft in the waters south and west of Iceland and to convoy merchant vessels as far as that island. After the sinking of the destroyer *Reuben James* on October 30, Congress voted to allow the arming of American merchant ships and to permit them to carry cargoes to Allied ports. For all practical purposes, though not yet officially, the United States had gone to war.

---

[4]During the 1930s the Soviet Union took a far firmer stand against the fascists than any other power, but after joining Hitler in swallowing up Poland, it attacked and defeated Finland during the winter of 1939–1940 and annexed the Baltic states. These acts virtually destroyed the small communist movement in the United States.

MILESTONES

1933 FDR becomes president

Hitler is elected German chancellor

FDR proclaims Good Neighbor Policy

Banking Act gives FDR broad powers

Civilian Conservation Corps (CCC) employs 250,000 young men

Federal Emergency Relief Act (FERA) funds relief programs

Agricultural Adjustment Act (AAA) seeks relief for farmers

Tennessee Valley Authority (TVA) plans dams and power plants

National Industrial Recovery Act (NIRA) establishes Public Works Administration (PWA) and National Recovery Administration (NRA)

Banking Act establishes Federal Deposit Insurance Corporation (FDIC)

Civil Works Administration puts 4 million to work

Twenty-first Amendment ends Prohibition

1934 Indian Reorganization Act gives tribes more autonomy

Securities and Exchange Commission (SEC) regulates stocks and bonds

Federal Communications Commission (FCC) regulates interstate and foreign communication

Federal Housing Administration (FHA) gives housing loans

1935 Emergency Relief Appropriation Act creates Works Project Administration (WPA)

Rural Electrification Administration brings electricity to farms

Supreme Court rules NIRA unconstitutional in *Schechter* v. *United States*

National Labor Relations Act (Wagner-Connery) encourages unionization

Social Security Act guarantees pensions and other benefits

Neutrality Act forbids wartime arms sales to belligerents

Italy invades and annexes Ethiopia

Walter Millis publishes isolationist *The Road to War: America, 1914–1917*

1936 FDR is reelected president in record landslide

Supreme Court declares AAA unconstitutional

1937 Roosevelt tries to pack Supreme Court

Japanese in China seize Beijing, Shanghai, Nanking

1938 Fair Labor Standards Act abolishes child labor, sets minimum wage

House of Representatives defeats Ludlow (isolationist) Amendment

Britain and France appease Hitler at Munich

1939 Germany invades Poland; World War II begins

1940 Hitler conquers Denmark, Norway, the Netherlands, Belgium, France

FDR is reelected to third term

Axis powers sign Rome-Berlin-Tokyo pact

Isolationists form America First Committee

1941 Lend-Lease Act helps Britain

SUPPLEMENTARY READING

The most important surveys of the New Deal are listed in the Debating the Past (p. 724). Analytical studies include Maxwell Bloomfield, *Peaceful Revolution* (2000), Ronald Edsforth, *The New Deal* (2000), Alan Brinkley, *Liberalism and Its Discontents* (1998), and Mark Leff, *The Limits of Symbolic Reform* (1984).

Of the many biographies of Roosevelt, see especially Frank Freidel, *Franklin D. Roosevelt* (1952–1973), James M. Burns, *Roosevelt: The Lion and the Fox* (1956), Geoffrey Ward, *Before the Trumpet: Young Franklin Roosevelt* (1985), and *A First-Class Temperament: The Emergence of Franklin Roosevelt* (1989). On Eleanor Roosevelt, see Blanche W. Cook, *Eleanor Roosevelt* (1992–1999), and Lois Scharf, *Eleanor Roosevelt: First Lady of American Liberalism* (1987). On Roosevelt's team of advisers, see Elliot A. Rosen, *Hoover, Roosevelt, and the Brains Trust* (1977).

For regional studies, see Bruce Shulman, *From Cotton Belt to Sunbelt* (1991), Charles H. Trout, *Boston, the Great Depression, and the New Deal* (1977), and Richard Lowitt, *The New Deal in the West* (1984).

On the New Deal and agriculture, see *From New Day to New Deal: American Farm Policy from Hoover to Roosevelt, 1928–1933* (1991); on the problems of the Dust Bowl, see James N. Gregory, *American Exodus: The Dust Bowl Migration and Okie Culture in California* (1989).

On the New Deal and business, see Ellis W. Hawley, *The New Deal and the Problem of Monopoly* (1966), Morton Keller, *Regulating the New Economy: Public Policy and Economic Change in America* (1990) and *Regulating a New Society: Public Policy and Social Change in America, 1900–1933* (1994).

On workers and the New Deal, see Edwin Amenta, *Bold Relief: Institutional Politics and the Origins of Modern Social Policy* (1998), Gery Gerstle, *Working-Class Americanism: The Politics of Labor in a Textile City 1914–1960* (1989), Vicki Ruiz, *Cannery Women, Cannery Lives: Mexican Women, Unionization, and the California Food Processing Industry, 1930–1950* (1987), Lizabeth Cohen, *Making a New Deal: Industrial Workers in Chicago, 1919–1939* (1990), and Melvyn Dubofsky, *The State and Labor in Modern America* (1994). Bruce Nelson,

Divided We Stand: American Workers and the Struggle for Black Equality (2001), describes a cleavage within the labor movement over racial issues. On the relation of private pensions and social security, see Jennifer Klein, *For All These Rights: Business, Labor, and the Shaping of America's Public-Private Welfare State* (2003).

On constitutional questions, see William E. Leuchtenburg, *The Supreme Court Reborn: The Constitutional Revolution in the Age of Roosevelt* (1995), and Paul L. Murphy, *The Constitution in Crisis Times* (1972).

For the activities of the radical fringe, consult Michael Denning, *The Cultural Front: The Laboring of American Culture in the Twentieth Century* (1996), Donald R. McCoy, *Angry Voices: Left-of-Center Politics in the New Deal Era* (1958), and D. H. Bennett, *Demagogues in the Depression* (1969). On blacks during the 1930s, see Raymond Wolters, *Negroes and the Great Depression* (1970), Nancy J. Weiss, *Farewell to the Party of Lincoln* (1983), and Harvard Sitkoff, *A New Deal for Blacks* (1978).

On women and gender, apart from the works cited above, see Suzanne Mettler, *Dividing Citizens* (1998), Landon Storrs, *Civilizing Capitalism* (2000), Susan Ware, *Beyond Suffrage: Women in the New Deal* (1981), and *Partner and I* (1987), a life of Molly Dewson. Also Linda Gordon, *Pitied But Not Entitled: Single Mothers and the History of Welfare* (1994), and Susan Ware, *Holding Their Own: American Women in the 1930s* (1982). On New Deal Indian policy, see Kenneth R. Philip, *John Collier's Crusade for Indian Reform* (1977). A chronologically broader but perceptive study is Kenneth R. Philp, *Termination Revisited: American Indians on the Trail to Self-Determination, 1933–1953* (1999).

A provocative analysis of modern art and the New Deal appears in Michael Szalay, *New Deal Modernism* (2000).

On isolationism and the events leading to Pearl Harbor, see Justus D. Doenecke, *Storm on the Horizon: The Challenge to American Intervention, 1939–1941* (2000), and David Reynolds, *From Munich to Pearl Harbor: Roosevelt's America and the Origins of the Second World War* (2001).

SUGGESTED WEBSITES

Voices from the Dust Bowl: The Charles L. Todd and Robert Sonkin Migrant Worker Collection, 1940–1941

http://memory.loc.gov/ammem/afctshtml/tshome.html

Farm Security Administration (FSA) studies of migrant work camps in central California in 1940 and 1941 are the bulk of this site. The collections include audio recordings, photographs, manuscript material, and publications.

The New Deal Network

http://newdeal.feri.org

This database includes photographs, political cartoons, and texts—including speeches, letters, and other historic documents—from the New Deal period.

Franklin Delano Roosevelt

http://www.ipl.org/div/POTUS/fdroosevelt.html

This site provides information about Roosevelt, the only president to serve more than two terms.

A New Deal for the Arts

http://www.archives.gov/exhibit_hall/
new_deal_for_the_arts/work_pays_america.html

Artwork, documents, and photographs recount the federal government's efforts to fund artists in the 1930s in the National Archives site.

Eleanor Roosevelt

http://ap.grolier.com/assetid=0336050-00&template=/
article/article.html

This site provides both information about the first lady and links to other relevant sites.

America from the Great Depression to World War II: Photographs from the FSA and OWI, c. 1935–1945

http://memory.loc.gov/ammem/fsowhome.html

These images in the Farm Security Administration—Office of War Information Collection show Americas from all over the nation experiencing everything from despair to triumph in the 1930s and 1940s.

American Life Histories: Manuscripts from the Federal Writers Project, 1936–1940

http://memory.loc.gov/ammem/wpaintro/
wpahome.html

The staff of the Folklore Project of the Federal Writers Project wrote these histories. Typically between 2000–15,000 words, the manuscripts provide a wonderful glimpse into American life.

▼ In 1944 painter Ben Shahn completed this poster for the political action group of the Congress of Industrial Organization (CIO), a major labor organization.

CHAPTER CONTENTS

By December 1941 the United States was at the brink of war, but public opinion would not have supported a formal declaration had it not been for Japan. Relations between Japan and the United States had worsened steadily after Japan resumed its war on China in 1937. As they extended their control, the invaders systematically froze out American and other foreign business interests. They declared that the Open Door policy was obsolete. Roosevelt retaliated by lending money to China and asking American manufacturers not to sell airplanes to Japan. In September 1940, Congress prohibited all sales of scrap iron to Japan. Japan immediately signed a treaty of alliance with Germany and Italy, which prompted Roosevelt to extend the embargo to include machine tools and other items. Despite these economic measures, Japan pushed ahead relentlessly to expand its economic empire in the Pacific.

THE ROAD TO PEARL HARBOR

Neither the United States nor Japan wanted war. Roosevelt considered Germany by far the more dangerous enemy and was alarmed by the possibility of engaging in a two-front war. In the spring of 1941 Secretary of State Hull conferred in Washington with the Japanese ambassador, Kichisaburo Nomura, in an effort to resolve their differences.

▲ Japan's surprise attack on Pearl Harbor on December 7, 1941, killed more than 2400 American servicemen and thrust the United States into World War II. President Roosevelt asked Congress for a declaration of war the next day, calling the attack "a date that will live in infamy."

Hull showed little appreciation of the political and military situation in East Asia. He demanded that Japan withdraw from China and promise not to attack the Dutch and French colonies in Southeast Asia.

Japan might well have accepted limited annexations in the area in return for the removal of American trade restrictions, but Hull seemed bent on converting the Japanese to pacifism by exhortation. He insisted on total withdrawal, to which even the moderates in Japan would not agree. When Hitler invaded the Soviet Union, thereby removing the threat of Russian intervention in East Asia, Japan decided to occupy French Indochina even at the risk of war with the United States. Roosevelt retaliated (July 1941) by freezing Japanese assets in the United States and clamping an embargo on oil. He hoped that the Japanese war machine, deprived of American oil, would grind to a halt.

Now the ultranationalist war party in Japan assumed control. Nomura was instructed to tell Hull that Japan would refrain from further expansion if the United States and Great Britain would cut off all aid to China and lift the economic blockade. Japan promised to pull out of Indochina once "a just peace" had been established with China. When the United States rejected these demands, the Japanese prepared to assault the Dutch East Indies, British Malaya, and the Philippines. To immobilize the United States

Pacific fleet, they planned a surprise aerial raid on the Hawaiian naval base at Pearl Harbor.

An American cryptanalyst, Colonel William F. Friedman, had cracked the Japanese diplomatic code: the Japanese were making plans to attack in early December. But in the hectic rush of events, both military and civilian authorities failed to make effective use of the information collected. They expected the blow to fall somewhere in East Asia, possibly the Philippines.

The garrison at Pearl Harbor was alerted against "a surprise aggressive move in any direction." The commanders there, Admiral Husband E. Kimmel and General Walter C. Short, believing an attack impossible, took precautions only against Japanese sabotage. Thus when planes from Japanese aircraft carriers swooped down upon Pearl Harbor on the morning of December 7, they found easy targets. In less than two hours they reduced the Pacific fleet to a smoking ruin: two battleships destroyed, six others heavily battered, nearly a dozen lesser vessels put out of action. More than 150 planes were wrecked; over 2300 soldiers and sailors were killed and 1100 wounded.

Never had American armed forces suffered a more devastating or shameful defeat. The official blame was placed chiefly on Admiral Kimmel and General Short. They might well have been more alert, but responsibility for the disaster was widespread. Military and civilian officials in Washington had failed

to pass on all that they knew to Hawaii or even to one another. On the other hand, the crucial intelligence about the coming attack that the code breakers provided was mixed with masses of other information and was extremely difficult to evaluate.

On December 8 Congress declared war on Japan. Formal war with Germany and Italy was still not inevitable—isolationists were far more ready to resist the "yellow peril" in Asia than to fight in Europe. The Axis powers, however, honored their treaty obligations to Japan and on December 11 declared war on the United States. America was now fully engaged in another great war, World War II. (The Great War fought by the previous generation was now identified as World War I.)

MOBILIZING THE HOME FRONT

World War II placed immense strains on the American economy and produced immense results. About 15 million men and women entered the armed services; they, and in part the millions more in Allied uniforms, had to be fed, clothed, housed, and supplied with equipment ranging from typewriters and paper clips to rifles and grenades, tanks, and airplanes. Congress granted wide emergency powers to the president. It refrained from excessive meddling in administrative problems and in military strategy. However, while the Democrats retained control of both houses throughout the war, their margins were relatively narrow. A coalition of conservatives in both parties frequently prevented the president from having his way and exercised close control over expenditures.

Roosevelt was an inspiring war leader but not a very good administrator. Any honest account of the war on the home front must reveal glaring examples of confusion, inefficiency, and pointless bickering. The squabbling and waste characteristic of the early New Deal period made relatively little difference—what mattered then was raising the nation's spirits and keeping people occupied; efficiency was less than essential, however desirable. But in wartime, the nation's fate, perhaps that of the entire free world, depended on delivering weapons and supplies to the battlefronts.

The confusion attending economic mobilization can easily be overstressed. Nearly all of Roosevelt's basic decisions were sensible and humane: to pay a large part of the cost of the war by collecting taxes rather than by borrowing and to base taxation on ability to pay; to ration scarce raw materials and consumer goods; to regulate prices and wages. If these decisions were not always translated into action with perfect effectiveness, they operated in the direction of efficiency and the public good.

Roosevelt's greatest accomplishment was his inspiring of industrialists, workers, and farmers with a sense of national purpose. In this respect his function duplicated his earlier role in fighting the Depression, and he performed it with even greater success.

The tremendous economic expansion can be seen in the official production statistics. In 1939 the United States was still mired in the Great Depression. The gross national product amounted to about $91.3 billion. In 1945, after allowing for changes in the price level, it was $166.6 billion. More specifically, manufacturing output nearly doubled and agricultural output rose 22 percent. In 1939 the United States turned out fewer than 6000 airplanes, in 1944 more than 96,000. Shipyards produced 237,000 tons of vessels in 1939, 10 million tons in 1943.

This growth was especially notable in the South and Southwest. This region got a preponderance of the new army camps built for the war as well as a large share of the new defense plants. Southern productive capacity increased by about 50 percent, and southern per capita output, while still low, crept closer to the national average.

Wartime experience proved that the Keynesian economists were correct in saying that government spending would spark economic growth. About 8 million people were unemployed in June 1940. After Pearl Harbor, unemployment virtually disappeared, and by 1945 the civilian workforce had increased by nearly 7 million. Military mobilization had begun well before December 1941, by which time 1.6 million men were already under arms. Economic mobilization proceeded much more slowly, mainly because the president refused to centralize authority. For months after Pearl Harbor various civilian agencies squabbled with the military over everything from the allocation of scarce raw materials to the technical specifications of weapons. Roosevelt refused to settle these conflicts.

THE WAR ECONOMY

Yet by early 1943 the nation's economic machinery had been converted to a wartime footing and was functioning effectively. Supreme Court Justice James F. Byrnes resigned from the Court to become a sort of "economic czar." His Office of War Mobilization had complete control over priorities and prices. Rents, food prices, and wages were strictly regulated, and items in short supply were rationed to consumers. While wages and prices had soared during 1942, after April 1943 they leveled off. Thereafter the cost of living scarcely changed until controls were lifted after the war.

Expanded industrial production together with conscription caused a labor shortage that increased the bargaining power of workers. At the same time, the national emergency required some limitation on the workers' right to take advantage of this power.

After Pearl Harbor Roosevelt created a National War Labor Board (NWLB) to arbitrate disputes and stabilize wage rates, and he banned all changes in wages without NWLB approval.

Prosperity and stiffer government controls added significantly to the strength of organized labor; indeed, the war had more to do with institutionalizing industrywide collective bargaining than the New Deal. As workers recognized the benefits of union membership, they flocked into the organizations. Strikes declined sharply, but some crippling work stoppages did occur. In May 1943, after John L. Lewis's United Mine Workers walked out of the pits, the government seized the coal mines. This strike led Congress to pass, over Roosevelt's veto, the Smith-Connally War Labor Disputes Act, which gave the president the power to take over any war plant threatened by a strike and outlawed strikes against seized plants. Although strikes continued to occur—the loss in hours of labor zoomed to 38 million in 1945—when Roosevelt asked for a labor draft law, Congress refused to go along.

Ration Stamps WWII

Wages and prices remained in fair balance. Overtime work fattened paychecks, and a new stress in labor contracts on paid vacations, premium pay for night work, and various forms of employer-subsidized health insurance were added benefits. The war effort had almost no adverse effect on the standard of living of the average citizen, a vivid demonstration of the productivity of the American economy. The manufacture of automobiles ceased and pleasure driving became next to impossible because of gasoline rationing, but most civilian activities went on much as they had before Pearl Harbor. Because of the need to conserve cloth, skirts were shortened, cuffs disappeared from men's trousers, and the vest passed out of style. Plastics replaced metals in toys, containers, and other products. While items such as meat, sugar, and shoes were rationed, they were doled out in amounts adequate for the needs of most persons. Americans had both guns and butter; belt-tightening of the type experienced by the other belligerents was unheard of.

The federal government spent twice as much money between 1941 and 1945 as in its entire previous history. This made heavy borrowing necessary. The national debt, which stood at less than $49 billion in 1941, increased by more than that amount each year between 1942 and 1945 and totaled nearly $260 billion when the war ended. However, more than 40 percent of the total was met by taxation, a far larger proportion than in any earlier war.

This policy helped to check inflation by siphoning off money that would otherwise have competed for scarce consumer goods. Heavy excise taxes on amusements and luxuries further discouraged spending, as

BUY WAR BONDS

▲ N. C. Wyeth, perhaps the foremost illustrator of the 1930s and 1940s, completed this war bonds poster early in the war.

did the government's war bond campaigns, which persuaded patriotic citizens to lend part of their income to Uncle Sam. High taxes on incomes (up to 94 percent) and on excess profits (95 percent), together with a limit of $25,000 a year after taxes on salaries, convinced people that no one was profiting inordinately from the war effort.

The income tax, which had never before touched the mass of white-collar and industrial workers, was extended downward until nearly everyone had to pay it. To collect efficiently the relatively small sums paid by most persons, Congress adopted the payroll-deduction system proposed by Beardsley Ruml, chairman of the Federal Reserve Bank of New York. Employers withheld the taxes owed by workers from their paychecks and turned the money over to the government.

The steeply graduated tax rates, combined with a general increase in the income of workers and farmers, effected a substantial shift in the distribution of wealth in the United States. The poor became richer, while the rich, if not actually poorer, collected a smaller proportion of the national income. The wealthiest 1 percent of the population had received 13.4 percent of the national income in 1935 and 11.5 percent in 1941. In 1944 this group received 6.7 percent.

WAR AND SOCIAL CHANGE

Enormous social effects stemmed from this shift, but World War II altered the patterns of American life in so many ways that it would be wrong to ascribe the transformations to any single source. Never was the population more fluid. The millions who put on uniforms found themselves transported first to training camps in every section of the country and then to battlefields scattered from Europe and Africa to the far reaches of the Pacific. Burgeoning new defense plants, influenced by a government policy of locating them in "uncongested areas," drew other millions to places like Hanford, Washington, and Oak Ridge, Tennessee, where great atomic energy installations were constructed, and to the aircraft factories of California and other states. As in earlier periods the trend was from east to west and from the rural south to northern cities. The population of California increased by more than 50 percent in the 1940s, that of other far western states almost as much.

During the war the marriage rate rose steeply, from 75 per thousand adult women in 1939 to 118 in 1946. A kind of backlog existed because many people had been forced to put off marrying and having children for financial reasons during the Great Depression. Now wartime prosperity put an end to that problem at the same time that large numbers of young couples were feeling the need to put down roots before the husbands went off to risk death in distant lands. The population of the United States had increased by only 3 million during the Depression decade of the 1930s; during the next *five* years it rose by 6.5 million.

MINORITIES IN TIME OF WAR: BLACKS, HISPANICS, AND INDIANS

The war affected black Americans in many ways. Several factors operated to improve their lot. One was their own growing tendency to demand fair treatment. Another was the reaction of Americans to Hitler's barbaric treatment of millions of Jews, an outgrowth of his doctrine of "Aryan" superiority. These barbarities compelled millions of white citizens to reexamine their views about race. If the nation expected African Americans to risk their lives for the common good, how could it continue to treat them as second-class citizens? Black leaders pointed out the inconsistency between fighting for democracy abroad and ignoring it at home. "We want democracy in Alabama," the NAACP announced, and this argument too had some effect on white thinking.

Blacks in the armed forces were treated more fairly than they had been in World War I. They were enlisted for the first time in the air force and the marines, and they were given more responsible positions in the army and navy. The army commissioned its first black general. Some 600 black pilots won their wings. Altogether about a million served, about half of them overseas. The extensive and honorable performance of these units could not be ignored by the white majority.

However, segregation in the armed services was maintained. Especially in and around army camps in the southern states, rigid segregation proved shocking to many northern white soldiers. In some cases German prisoners of war were seated in front of black American soldiers at camp movies. Such practices led frequently to rioting and even to local mutinies among black recruits.

The navy continued to confine black and Hispanic sailors to demeaning, noncombat tasks, and black soldiers were often provided with inferior recreational facilities and otherwise mistreated in and around army camps, especially those in the South. In 1943 William Hastie, a former New Dealer who was

▲ A poster commemorating Doris "Dorie" Miller, a mess attendant aboard the USS *West Virginia* at Pearl Harbor. Before the ship sank, Miller manned an antiaircraft machine gun and shot down several Japanese planes. He won the Navy Cross for courage, the first awarded to an African American.

serving as an adviser on racial matters to Secretary of War Stimson, resigned in protest because of the "reactionary policies and discriminatory practices of the Army and Air Forces in matters affecting Negroes."

However, economic realities operated significantly to the advantage of black civilians. More of them had been unemployed in proportion to their numbers than any other group; now the labor shortage brought employment for all. More than 5 million blacks moved from rural areas to cities between 1940 and 1945 in search of work. At least a million of them found defense jobs in the North and on the west coast, often developing valuable skills that had been difficult for blacks to acquire before the war because of the discriminatory policies of trade unions and many employers. The black population of Los Angeles, San Francisco, Denver, Buffalo, Milwaukee, and half a dozen other large industrial cities more than doubled in that brief period. The migrants were mostly forced to live in dreadful urban ghettoes, but their very concentration (and the fact that outside the South blacks could vote freely) made them important politically.

DOCUMENT

Randolph, "Why Should We March"

These gains failed to satisfy black leaders. The NAACP, which increased its membership from 50,000 in 1940 to almost 405,000 in 1946, adopted a more militant stance than in World War I. Discrimination in defense plants seemed far less tolerable than it had in 1917–1918. A. Philip Randolph, president of the Brotherhood of Sleeping Car Porters, organized a march of blacks on Washington in 1941 to demand equal opportunity for black workers. Fearing possible violence and the wrath of southern congressmen, Roosevelt tried to persuade Randolph to call off the march. "It would make the country look bad" and "help the Germans," he claimed. But Randolph persisted, and Roosevelt finally agreed to issue an order prohibiting discrimination in plants with defense contracts.

Prejudice and mistreatment did not cease. In areas around defense plants white resentment of the black "invasion" mounted. By 1943, 50,000 new blacks had crowded into Detroit. A wave of strikes disrupted production at U.S. Rubber and several former automobile plants where white workers laid down their tools to protest the hiring of blacks. In June a race riot marked by looting and bloody fighting raged for three days. By the time federal troops restored order, 25 blacks and 9 whites had been killed. Rioting also erupted in New York and many other cities.

In Los Angeles the attacks were upon Hispanic residents. Wartime employment needs resulted in a reversal of the Depression policy of forcing Mexicans out of the Southwest, and many thousands flocked north in search of work. Most had to accept menial jobs. But work was plentiful, and they, as well as resident Spanish-speaking Americans, experienced rising living standards.

A larger proportion of Mexican American men served in the armed forces than the national average, but some young civilian Hispanics in the Los Angeles region adopted a kind of civilian dress known as a zoot suit. These "uniforms" consisted of broad-brimmed fedoras, long coats, and pegged trousers. "Zoot suiters" tended to have money in their pockets, and their behavior (like their costume) was not always as circumspect as many local residents would have preferred. A grand jury undertook an investigation, and the Los Angeles City Council even debated banning the wearing of zoot suits. In 1943 rioting broke out when sailors on shore

▲ In World War II the U.S. government adopted the Navajo Indian language as a radio code. Navajos (who became known as "Code Talkers") were recruited, trained, and sent to Marine combat units already deployed. As the enemy was unable to break the code, confidential information was able to flow between the various units. Here two Navajos operate a portable radio set in the Bougainville jungle in 1943.

leave, apparently resenting these prosperous-appearing "foreign" civilians, began roaming the area attacking anyone they could find in a zoot suit.

The willingness of white leaders to tolerate attacks on blacks and Hispanics at a time when national unity was so necessary was particularly frustrating. For example, blood plasma from blacks and whites was kept separately even though the two "varieties" were indistinguishable and the process of storing plasma had been devised by a black doctor, Charles Drew.

Blacks became increasingly embittered. Roy Wilkins, head of the NAACP, put it this way in 1942: "No Negro leader with a constituency can face his members today and ask full support for the war in the light of the atmosphere the government has created." Many black newspaper editors were so critical of the administration that conservatives demanded they be indicted for sedition.

Roosevelt would have none of that, but the militants annoyed him; he felt that they should hold their demands in abeyance until the war had been won. Apparently he failed to realize the depth of black anger, and in this he was no different from the majority of whites. A revolution was in the making, yet in 1942 a poll revealed that a solid majority of whites still believed that black Americans were satisfied with their place in society. The riots of 1943 undoubtedly disabused some of them of this illusion.

Concern about national unity did lead to a reaction against the New Deal policy of encouraging Indians to preserve their ancient cultures and develop self-governing communities. There was even talk of going back to the allotment system and trying to assimilate Indians into the larger society. John Collier resigned as commissioner of Indian affairs in disgust in 1945. In fact, the war encouraged assimilation in several ways. More than 24,000 Indians served in the armed forces, an experience that brought them in contact with new people, new places, and new ideas. Many thousands more left the reservations to work in defense industries in cities all over the country.

THE TREATMENT OF GERMAN AND ITALIAN AMERICANS

Although World War II affected the American people far more drastically than had World War I, it produced much less intolerance and fewer examples of the repression of individual freedom of opinion. People seemed able to distinguish between Italian fascism and Italian Americans and between the government of Nazi Germany and Americans of German descent in a way that had escaped their parents. The fact that few Italian Americans admired Mussolini and that nearly all

German Americans were vigorously anti-Nazi helps explain this. So does the fact that both groups were well organized and prepared to use their considerable political power if necessary to protect themselves from abuse.

But the underlying public attitude was more important. Americans went to war in 1941 without illusions and without enthusiasm, determined to win but expecting only to preserve what they had. They therefore found it easier to tolerate dissent, to view the dangers they faced realistically, and to concentrate on the real foreign enemy without venting their feelings on domestic scapegoats. The nation's 100,000 conscientious objectors met with little hostility.

INTERNMENT OF THE JAPANESE

The relatively tolerant treatment accorded most people makes the nation's policies toward American citizens of Japanese extraction all the more difficult to comprehend. Generals on the west coast were understandably unnerved by the Japanese attack on Pearl Harbor and warned that people of Japanese descent might engage in sabotage or espionage for Japan. "The Japanese race is an enemy race," General John L. Dewitt claimed. The 112,000 Americans of Japanese

▲ A Japanese girl in California, tagged and awaiting deportation.

◄ **Japanese Relocation from the West Coast, 1942–1945**

Military Area West Coast

● Assembly Center

● Relocation Center

▫ Justice Department Internment Camp

■ Citizen Isolation Camp

ancestry, the majority of them native-born citizens, were "potential enemies." "The very fact that no sabotage has taken place to date," Dewitt observed, "is a disturbing and confirming indication that such action will be taken." This is like arguing that the driver with a perfect record is all the more likely to career into a tree at any moment. Secretary of War Stimson proposed the relocation of the west coast people of Japanese extraction, including American citizens, to internment camps in Wyoming, Arizona, and other interior states. President Roosevelt concurred but weakly suggested: "Be as responsible as you can."

The Japanese were properly indignant but also baffled, in some cases hurt more than angry. "We didn't feel Japanese. We felt American," one woman, the mother of three small children, recalled many years later. Some Japanese Americans refused to submit to military authorities. Gordon Hirabayashi, an American citizen and senior at the University of Washington, refused to report for transportation to an internment camp. After being convicted and sentenced to prison, he decided to appeal. Previous Supreme Courts had ruled that the government could deprive Americans of their freedoms during war only when the "military necessity" was compelling. By the time

the Supreme Court ruled on his and similar cases, the Japanese military had been thrown back in the Pacific; no invasion was even conceivable. Yet the justices worried that if they declared the internment policy to be unconstitutional, they would appear, "out of step" with the nation, as Justice Felix Frankfurter put it. In June 1943, the Court upheld the conviction of Hirabayashi. Finally, in *Ex parte Endo,* it forbade the internment of loyal Japanese American citizens. Unfortunately the latter decision was not handed down until December 1944.

WOMEN'S CONTRIBUTION TO THE WAR EFFORT

With economic activity on the rise and millions of men going off to war, a sudden need for more women workers developed. The trends of the 1920s—more women workers and more of them married—soon accelerated. By 1944, 6.5 million additional women had entered the workforce, and at the peak of war production in 1945, more than 19 million women were employed, many of them in well-

paying industrial jobs. Additional thousands were serving in the armed forces: 100,000 in the Women's Auxiliary Army Corps, others in navy, marine, and air corps auxiliaries.

Rosie the Riveter

At first there was considerable resistance to what was happening. About one husband in three objected in principle to his wife taking a job. Many employers in so-called heavy industry and in other fields traditionally dominated by men doubted that women could handle such tasks.

Unions frequently made the same point, usually without much evidence. A Seattle official of the International Brotherhood of Boilermakers and Iron Shipbuilders said of women job applicants: "They don't understand. . . . If one of these girls pressed the trigger on the yard rivet guns, she'd be going one way and the rivet the other." Actually, many women were soon doing "men's work" in the shipyards. The Seattle taxicab union objected to women drivers on the ground that "drivers are forced to do things and go places that would be embarrassing for a woman to do."

These male attitudes lost force in the face of the escalating demand for labor. That employers usually did not have to pay women as much as men made them attractive, as did the fact that they were not subject to the draft. A breakthrough occurred when the big Detroit automobile manufacturers agreed to employ women on their wartime production lines. Soon women were working not only as riveters and cab drivers but also as welders, as machine tool operators, and in dozens of other occupations formerly the exclusive domain of men.

Women took wartime jobs for many reasons other than the obvious economic ones. Patriotism, of course, was important, but so were the excitement of entering an entirely new world, the desire for independence, even loneliness. "It's thrilling work, and exciting, and something women have never done before," one woman reported. She was talking about driving a taxi.

▲ Posters such as this one helped persuade two million women to take jobs in defense plants. It suggests that although defense work required determination and strength, women who undertook such jobs would not lose their femininity (note the lipstick and mascara). In fact, most young women were given monotonous work on assembly lines; less than one in twenty were assigned to skilled jobs.

Black women workers had a particularly difficult time, employers often hesitating to hire them because they were black, black men looking down on them because they were women. But the need for willing hands was infinite. Sybil Lewis of Sapula, Oklahoma, went to Los Angeles and found a job as a waitress in a black restaurant. Then she responded to a notice of a training program at Lockheed Aircraft, took the course, and became a riveter making airplane gas tanks. When an unfriendly foreman gave her a less attractive assignment, she moved on to Douglas Aircraft. By 1943 she was working as a welder in a shipyard.

Few wartime jobs were easy, and for women there were special burdens, not the least of which was the prejudice of many of the men they worked with. For married women there was housework to do after a long day. One War Manpower Commission bureaucrat figured out that Detroit defense plants were losing 100,000 woman-hours a month because of employees taking a day off to do the family laundry. Although the government made some effort to provide day-care facilities, there were never nearly enough; this was one reason why relatively few women with small children entered the labor market during the war.

The war also affected the lives of women who did not take jobs. Families by the tens and hundreds of thousands pulled up stakes and moved to the centers of war production, such as Detroit and southern California. Housing was always in short supply in these areas, and while the men went off to the familiar surroundings of yard and factory, their wives had to cope with cramped quarters, ration books, the absence of friends and relatives, the problems encountered by their children in strange schools and playgrounds, in some situations even with outdoor toilets. With so many people living among strangers and in unstable circumstances it is not surprising that crime, juvenile delinquency, and prostitution increased, as indeed they did in other parts of the country too.

Newly married wives of soldiers and sailors (known generally as "war brides") often followed their husbands to training camps, where life was often as difficult as it was around defense plants. Those who did not faced other problems—adjusting to being married without having had much experience of marriage, loneliness, and worry. Whatever their own behavior, war brides quickly learned that society applied a double standard to infidelity, especially when it involved a man presumably risking his life in some far-off land. There was a general relaxation of sexual inhibitions, part of a decades-long trend but accelerated by the war. So many hasty marriages, followed by long periods of separation, also brought a rise in divorces, from about 170 per thousand marriages in 1941 to 310 per thousand in 1945.

Of course "ordinary" housewives also had to deal with shortages, ration books, and other inconveniences during the war. In addition most took on other duties and bore other burdens, such as tending "victory gardens" and preserving their harvests, using crowded public transportation when there was no gas for the family car, mending and patching old clothes when new ones were unavailable, participating in salvage drives, and doing volunteer work for hospitals, the Red Cross, or various civil defense and servicemen's centers.

ALLIED STRATEGY: EUROPE FIRST

Only days after Pearl Harbor, Prime Minister Churchill and his military chiefs met in Washington with Roosevelt and his advisers. In every quarter of the globe, disaster threatened. The Japanese were gobbling up East Asia. Hitler's armies, checked outside Leningrad and Moscow, were preparing for a massive attack in the direction of Stalingrad, on the Volga River. German divisions under General Erwin Rommel were beginning a drive across North Africa toward the Suez Canal. U-boats were taking a heavy toll in the North Atlantic. British and American leaders believed that eventually they could muster enough force to smash their enemies, but whether or not the troops already in action could hold out until this force arrived was an open question.

▲ "Marines call it that '2000-yard stare'," Tom Lee's 1944 portrait of a soldier.

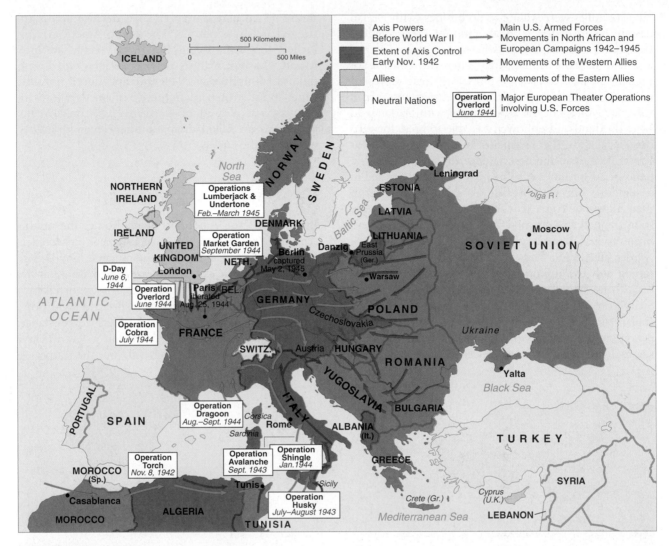

Map Legend:

- Axis Powers Before World War II
- Extent of Axis Control Early Nov. 1942
- Allies
- Neutral Nations
- → Main U.S. Armed Forces Movements in North African and European Campaigns 1942–1945
- → Movements of the Western Allies
- → Movements of the Eastern Allies
- Operation Overlord June 1944 — Major European Theater Operations involving U.S. Forces

Operations Lumberjack & Undertone *Feb.–March 1945*

Operation Market Garden *September 1944*

D-Day *June 6, 1944*

Operation Overlord *June 1944*

Operation Cobra *July 1944*

Berlin captured May 2, 1945

Paris liberated Aug. 25, 1944

Operation Dragoon *Aug.–Sept. 1944*

Operation Torch *Nov. 8, 1942*

Operation Avalanche *Sept. 1943*

Operation Shingle *Jan. 1944*

Operation Husky *July–August 1943*

▲ **The Liberation of Europe**

The decision of the strategists was to concentrate first against the Germans. Japan's conquests were in remote and, from the Allied point of view, relatively unimportant regions. If the Soviet Union surrendered, Hitler could throw all of German might against Great Britain. If it were defeated, Hitler's position in Europe might prove impregnable.

But how to strike at Hitler? American leaders wanted a second front in France, at least by 1943, and the Soviets, with their backs to the wall and bearing the full weight of the German war machine, heartily agreed. Churchill, however, was more concerned with protecting Britain's overseas possessions than with easing the pressure on the Soviet Union. He advocated instead air bombardment of German industry combined with an attempt to drive the Germans out of North Africa, and his argument carried the day.

During the summer of 1942 Allied planes began to bomb German cities. In a crescendo through 1943 and 1944, British and American bombers pulverized

the centers of Nazi might. While air attacks did not destroy the German army's capacity to fight, they hampered war production, tangled communications, and brought the war home to the German people in awesome fashion. Humanitarians deplored the heavy loss of life among the civilian population, but the response of the realists was that Hitler had begun indiscriminate bombing, and victory depended on smashing the German war machine.

World War II in Europe

In November 1942 an Allied army commanded by General Dwight D. Eisenhower struck at French North Africa. After the fall of France, the Nazis had set up a puppet regime in those parts of France not occupied by their troops, with headquarters at Vichy in central France. This collaborationist Vichy government controlled French North Africa. But the North African commandant, Admiral Jean Darlan, promptly switched sides when Eisenhower's forces landed. After a brief show of resistance, the French surrendered.

The Allies were willing to do business with Darlan despite his record as a collaborationist. This angered General Charles de Gaulle, who had organized a government in exile immediately after the collapse of France and who considered himself the true representative of the French people. Many Americans agreed with de Gaulle, but the arrangement with Darlan paid large dividends. Eisenhower was able to press forward quickly against the Germans. In February 1943 at Kasserine Pass in the desert south of Tunis, American tanks met Rommel's Afrika Korps. The battle ended in a standoff, but with British troops closing in from their Egyptian bases to the east, the Germans were soon trapped and crushed. In May, after Rommel had been recalled to Germany, his army surrendered.

In July 1943, while air attacks on Germany continued and the Russians slowly pushed the Germans back from the gates of Stalingrad, the Allies invaded Sicily from Africa. In September they advanced to the Italian mainland. Mussolini had already fallen from power and his successor, Marshal Pietro Badoglio, surrendered. However, the German troops in Italy threw up an almost impregnable defense across the rugged Italian peninsula. The Anglo American army inched forward, paying heavily for every advance. Monte Cassino, halfway between Naples and Rome, did not fall until May 1944, the capital itself not until June; months of hard fighting remained before the country was cleared of Germans. The Italian campaign was an Allied disappointment even though it weakened the enemy.

GERMANY OVERWHELMED

By the time the Allies had taken Rome, the mighty army needed to invade France had been collected in England under Eisenhower's command. On D-Day, June 6, 1944, the assault forces stormed ashore at five points along the coast of Normandy, supported by a great armada and thousands of planes and paratroops. Against fierce but ill-coordinated German resistance, they established a beachhead: Within a few weeks a million troops were on French soil. (See the feature es-

▲ On February 13 and 14, 1945, British and American incendiary bombs razed Dresden, the cultural capital of Germany. Some 35,000 perished. The purpose of the raid was to terrorize and demoralize the German people; the city's few war industries were not even targeted. This picture was taken more than a year after the bombing.

say, Re-Viewing the Past, "*Saving Private Ryan,*" pp. 754–755.)

Thereafter victory was assured, though nearly a year of hard fighting lay ahead. In August the American Third Army under General George S. Patton, an eccentric but brilliant field commander, erupted southward into Brittany and then veered east toward Paris. Another Allied army invaded France from the Mediterranean in mid-August and advanced rapidly north. Free French troops were given the honor of liberating Paris on August 25. Belgium was cleared by British and Canadian units a few days later. By mid-September the Allies were fighting on the edge of Germany itself.

The front now stretched from the Netherlands along the borders of Belgium, Luxembourg, and France all the way to Switzerland. If the Allies had mounted a massive assault at any one point, as the British commander, Field Marshal Bernard Montgomery, urged, the struggle might have been brought

▲ Once into Germany the Third Army advanced so quickly in the spring of 1945 that it came upon military installations almost without warning. The photograph here is of General Dwight D. Eisenhower inspecting the condition of the concentration camp at Gotha, Germany, where slain inmates had been left unburied by their fleeing captors.

to a quick conclusion. Although the two armies were roughly equal in size, the Allies had complete control of the air and 20 times as many tanks as the foe. The pressure of the advancing Russians on the eastern front made it difficult for the Germans to reinforce their troops in the west. But General Eisenhower believed a concentrated attack too risky. He prepared instead for a general advance.

While he was regrouping, the Germans on December 16 launched a counterattack, planned by Hitler himself, against the Allied center in the Ardennes Forest. The Germans hoped to break through to the Belgian port of Antwerp, thereby splitting the Allied armies in two. The plan was foolhardy and therefore unexpected, and it almost succeeded. The Germans drove a salient ("the bulge") about 50 miles into Belgium. But once the element of surprise had been overcome, their chance of breaking through to the sea was lost. Eisenhower concentrated first on preventing them from broadening the break in his lines and then on blunting the point of their advance. By late January 1945 the old line had been reestablished.

The Battle of the Bulge cost the United States 77,000 casualties and delayed Eisenhower's offensive, but it exhausted the Germans' last reserves. The Allies then pressed forward to the Rhine, winning a bridgehead on the far bank of the river on March 7. There-

after, one German city fell almost daily. With the Soviets racing westward against crumbling resistance, the end could not be long delayed. In April, American and Soviet forces made contact at the Elbe River. A few days later, with Soviet shells reducing his capital to rubble, Hitler, by then probably insane, took his own life in his Berlin air raid shelter. On May 8 Germany surrendered.

As the Americans drove swiftly forward in the late stages of the war, they began to overrun Nazi concentration camps where millions of Jews had been murdered. The Americans were horrified by what they discovered, but they should not have been surprised. Word of this holocaust, in which no less than 6 million people were slaughtered, had reached the United States much earlier. At first the news had been dismissed as propaganda, then discounted as grossly exaggerated. Hitler was known to hate Jews and to have persecuted them, but that he could order the murder of millions of innocent people, even children, seemed beyond belief. By 1943, however, the truth could not be denied.

Little could be done about those already in the camps, but there were thousands of refugees in

Nazi Murder Mills
WARNING:
This clip is very
graphic

► *text continues on page 756*

Re-Viewing the Past

Saving Private Ryan

Steven Spielberg's *Saving Private Ryan* (1998), starring Tom Hanks, has been widely praised as the most realistic combat movie ever made. This judgment is based chiefly on its re-creation of the June 6, 1944, Allied assault on Omaha Beach during the invasion of Normandy. The camera focuses on Hanks, rain dripping from helmet, huddled in a crowded landing vessel. Explosions rumble in the distance. The ship plows through heavy seas toward a blackened brow of land (see photograph below). Around him, men vomit. Explosions become louder and sharper. Nearby ships strike mines and blow up; others are obliterated by shellfire. Hanks's landing craft lurches to avoid the mayhem. Like hail against a tin roof, gunfire riddles the landing craft. Some of the men are hit, and the others hunch lower, still vomiting. A deafening din envelops the ship as its bow opens. A curtain of bullets instantly cuts down the men in front. Hanks and several others leap into the sea. They sink. The ship has stopped far short of the beach. As bullets tear through the water, ripping into those still submerged, Hanks struggles to the surface. He swims, weaponless, toward the beach.

He has crossed the threshold of hell, and over the next 15 minutes viewers descend with him the rest of the way.

Saving Private Ryan differs from other combat films not in the graphic horror of the bloodshed, but in its randomness. The audience expects Hanks to survive the opening scenes of the movie in which he stars, and he does. But all other bets are off: a valiant exploit, a kind gesture, a handsome face—none influences the grim lottery of battle. A medic frenziedly works on a severely wounded man, injecting morphine, compressing arteries, and binding wounds. Then more bullets splatter him beyond recognition. "Why can't you bastards give us a chance!" the medic screams. That is the point: When huge armies converge, hurling high explosives and steel at each other, one's chances of survival are unaffected by ethics or aesthetics.

▶ Actual photograph of Americam troops approaching code-named Omaha Beach at Normandy.

But having made this point with heart-pounding emphasis, the movie subverts it. Hanks, unnerved and dispirited, for a time hunkers down in the relative safety of the seawall. Then he begins to do his job and others rally around him. They blast a hole through obstacles, crawl toward the concrete fortifications above, penetrate trench defenses, blow up bunkers, and seize the hill. Many perish in the effort; Hanks, an infantry captain, is among the survivors.

Then comes a new mission, which occupies the remainder of the movie. George C. Marshall, U.S. Army Chief of Staff, has learned of a Mrs. Ryan who has been notified on a single day that three of her sons were killed in action. Her fourth son, James, a private in the 101st Airborne, has just parachuted into Normandy behind German lines. Marshall orders that he be returned to safety. This mission is given to Hanks and the eight surviving members of his platoon. They march inland, encounter snipers, ambushes, and, in the final scenes, a large detachment of German armored vehicles. But they also find Private Ryan (played by Matt Damon).

Along the way, the movie asks many provocative questions, such as whether war improves those who fight. "I think this is all good for me, sir," one earnest soldier confides to Hanks. "Really," Hanks says with a faint smile, "how is that?" The soldier cites Ralph Waldo Emerson: "War educates the senses. Calls into action the will. Perfects the physical constitution." "Emerson had a way of finding the bright side," Hanks deadpans, and the movie endorses his cynicism. Delirious and catatonic soldiers stumble across the battlefield. Others, terri-

▲ Tom Hanks, Matt Damon, and Edward Burns in *Saving Private Ryan*.

fied and jittery, shoot enemy soldiers who have surrendered. A sniper, intoning Old Testament verses, takes aim at unsuspecting enemies. Hanks's hand twitches uncontrollably, a physical manifestation of a disordered soul. War, demonstrably, has not made men better.

Except in one sense, and that may be all that matters: Hanks and his men have repeatedly demonstrated a willingness to give up their lives for others. Indeed, the movie's central dilemma concerns the moral arithmetic of sacrifice. Is it right to risk eight men to save one? To send a thousand men to near certain death in an initial assault to improve the chances of those that follow? To make one generation endure hell so that another may have freedom? The movie provides no ready answers. But in nearly the final scene it does issue a challenge. Hanks, mortally wounded, is lying amidst the corpses of his platoon, and he beckons to Ryan, who is unhurt. "Earn this," Hanks says, vaguely gesturing to the others.

Saving Private Ryan was part of a wave of nostalgic appreciation during the 1990s for the generation that had won World War II. A spate of books, movies, and TV documentaries were other expressions of this phenomenon. On accepting the Oscar for his film, Spielberg thanked his father, a World War II vet, "for showing me that there is honor in looking back and respecting the past."

But respect for the past entails getting it right, and the movie makes some significant errors and omissions. For one, it suggests that the men huddled at the base of the seawall blew up the concrete bunkers on their own. This was not possible. In fact, commanders of destroyers took their ships close to the beaches and fired countless heavy shells into the fortifications, allowing the infantry to move up the hills.

The movie also shows the German soldiers as uniformly expert and professional. But the German army had been decimated by losses in the Soviet Union. The army manning the Normandy defenses included many units composed mostly of old men, boys, or conscripted soldiers from Poland or the Soviet Union. Many surrendered as soon as they encountered American soldiers.

Of the movie's implausible elements, the premise that the U.S. Army high command ordered a special mission to pluck a grieving mother's son from danger was based on fact. A real Mrs. Niland received telegrams on the same day that three of her sons had been killed in action. Her fourth son, "Fritz," had parachuted into Normandy with the 101st Airborne. The Army did in fact snatch him from the front line and return him to safety.

The movie provides a fair rendering of many other elements of the battle: the inaccuracy of aerial bombing, which missed most of the beach fortifications; the confusion caused when hundreds of landing craft failed to reach their destination; the destruction of scores of gliders, which crashed into high hedgerows while attempting to land behind German lines.

Saving Private Ryan captures the effect of war on soldiers. Many men at Omaha Beach, like those depicted in the movie, were shattered by the experience. One private, nearly hit by a shell, recalled that he burst into tears. "My buddies got me behind a burned-out craft, where I cried for what seemed like hours. I cried until tears would no longer come. To this day I've never shed another." Other men confessed that, after the terror of a firefight, they shot Germans who had raised their arms in surrender. "In my opinion any enemy shot during this intense action had waited too long to surrender," one G.I. declared.

Yet through it all, some men, like the captain portrayed by Hanks, drew heroism from some unfathomed depths of the soul. One real soldier at Omaha Beach remembered "a captain and two lieutenants who demonstrated courage beyond belief as they struggled to bring order to the chaos around them."

Saving Private Ryan is not a fully accurate representation of the attack on Omaha Beach, but it depicts—realistically and memorably—how soldiers conferred meaning on the heedless calculus of modern warfare.

▲ **Nazi Concentration Camps**

occupied Europe who might have been spirited to safety. President Roosevelt declined to make the effort; he refused to bomb the Auschwitz death camp in Poland or the rail lines used to bring victims to its gas chambers on the grounds that the destruction of German soldiers and military equipment took precedence over any other objective. Thus, when American journalists entered the camps with the advancing troops, saw the heaps of still-unburied corpses, and talked with the emaciated survivors, their reports caused a storm of protest in America.

THE NAVAL WAR IN THE PACIFIC

Defeating Germany first had not meant abandoning the Pacific region entirely to the Japanese. While armies were being trained and matériel accumulated for the European struggle, much of the available American strength was diverted to maintaining vital communications in East Asia and preventing further Japanese expansion.

World War II in the Pacific

The navy's aircraft carriers had escaped destruction at Pearl Harbor, a stroke of immense good for-

▲ Midway, a tiny Pacific island that mattered only because of its airfield. The Japanese sent a naval task force to invade the island, but in June 1942 U.S. warplanes, some stationed at Midway though most were from aircraft carriers, sank several of the Japanese aircraft carriers accompanying the invasion force. Without air cover, the invasion was called off and Midway marked a turning point in the war in the Pacific.

tune because, without most tacticians realizing it, the airplane had revolutionized naval warfare. Commanders discovered that carrier-based planes were far more effective against warships than the heaviest naval artillery because of their greater range and more concentrated firepower. Battleships made excellent gun platforms from which to pound shore installations and support land operations, but against other vessels aircraft were of prime importance.

This truth was demonstrated in May 1942 in the Battle of the Coral Sea. Having captured an empire in a few months without the loss of any warship larger than a destroyer, the Japanese believed the war already won. This led them to overextend themselves.

The Coral Sea lies northeast of Australia and south of New Guinea and the Solomon Islands. Japanese mastery of these waters would cut Australia off from Hawaii and thus from American aid. Admiral Isoroku Yamamoto had dispatched a large fleet of troopships screened by many warships to attack Port Moresby, on the southern New Guinea coast. On May 7–8 planes from the American carriers *Lexington* and *Yorktown* struck the convoy's screen, sinking a small carrier and damaging a large one. Superficially, the battle seemed a victory for the Japanese, for their planes mortally wounded the *Lexington* and sank two other ships, but the troop transports had been forced to turn back—Port Moresby was saved. Although large numbers of cruisers and destroyers took part in the action, none came within sight or gun range of an enemy ship. All the destruction was wrought by carrier aircraft.

Encouraged by the Coral Sea "victory," Yamamoto decided to force the American fleet into a showdown battle by assaulting the Midway Islands, west of Hawaii. His armada never reached its destination. Between June 4 and 7 control of the central Pacific was decided entirely by airpower. American dive bombers sent four large Japanese carriers to the bottom. About 300 Japanese planes were destroyed. The United States lost only the *Yorktown* and a destroyer. Thereafter the initiative in the Pacific war shifted to the Americans, but victory came slowly and at painful cost.

American land forces were under the command of Douglas MacArthur, a brilliant but egocentric general whose judgment was sometimes distorted by his intense concern for his own reputation. MacArthur was in command of American troops in the Philippine Islands when the Japanese struck in December 1941. After his heroic but hopeless defense of Manila and the Bataan peninsula, President Roosevelt had him evacuated by PT boat to escape capture; those under MacArthur's command endured horrific conditions as prisoners of Japan.

Thereafter MacArthur was obsessed with the idea of personally leading an American army back to the Philippines. Although many strategists believed that the islands should be bypassed in the drive on the Japanese homeland, in the end MacArthur convinced the Joint Chiefs of Staff, who determined strategy. Two separate drives were undertaken, one from New Guinea toward the Philippines under MacArthur, the other through the central Pacific toward Tokyo under Admiral Chester W. Nimitz.

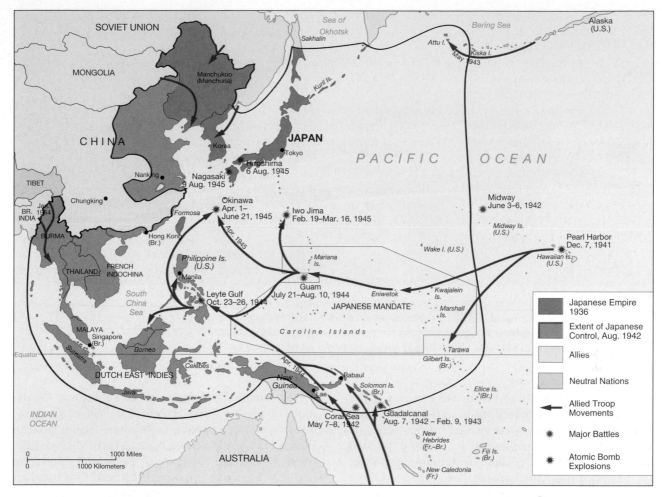

▲ **World War II, Pacific Theater**

ISLAND HOPPING

Before commencing this two-pronged advance, the Americans had to eject the Japanese from the Solomon Islands in order to protect Australia from a flank attack. Beginning in August 1942, a series of land, sea, and air battles raged around Guadalcanal Island in this archipelago. Once again American airpower was decisive, although the bravery and skill of the ground forces that actually won the island must not be underemphasized. American pilots, better trained and with tougher planes than the Japanese, had a relatively easier task. They inflicted losses five to six times heavier on the enemy than they sustained themselves. Japanese airpower disintegrated progressively during the long battle, and this in turn helped the fleet to take a heavy toll on the Japanese navy. By February 1943 Guadalcanal had been secured.

In the autumn of 1943 the American drives toward Japan and the Philippines got under way at last.

In the central Pacific campaign the Guadalcanal action was repeated on a smaller but equally bloody scale from Tarawa in the Gilbert Islands to Kwajalein and Eniwetok in the Marshalls. The Japanese soldiers on these islands fought for every foot of ground. They had to be blasted and burned from tunnels and concrete pillboxes with hand grenades, flamethrowers, and dynamite. They almost never surrendered. But Admiral Nimitz's forces were in every case victorious. By midsummer of 1944 this arm of the American advance had taken Saipan and Guam in the Marianas. Now land-based bombers were within range of Tokyo.

Meanwhile, MacArthur was leapfrogging along the New Guinea coast toward the Philippines. In October 1944 he made good his promise to return to the islands, landing on Leyte, south of Luzon. Two great naval clashes in Philippine waters, the Battle of the Philippine Sea (June 1944) and the Battle for Leyte Gulf (October 1944), completed the destruc-

tion of Japan's sea power and reduced its air force to a band of fanatical suicide pilots called *kamikazes,* who tried to crash bomb-laden planes into American warships and airstrips. The *kamikazes* caused much damage but could not turn the tide. In February 1945 MacArthur liberated Manila.

The end was now inevitable. B-29 Superfortress bombers from the Marianas rained high explosives and firebombs on Japan. The islands of Iwo Jima and Okinawa, only a few hundred miles from Tokyo, fell to the Americans in March and June 1945. But such was the tenacity of the Japanese soldiers that it seemed possible that it would take another year of fighting and a million more American casualties to subdue the main Japanese islands.

BUILDING THE ATOM BOMB

At this point came the most controversial decision of the entire war, and it was made by a newcomer on the world scene. In November 1944 Roosevelt had been elected to a fourth term, easily defeating Thomas E. Dewey. Instead of renominating Henry A. Wallace for vice president, whom conservatives considered too radical, the Democratic convention had nominated Senator Harry S Truman of Missouri, a reliable party man well liked by professional politicians. Then, in April 1945, President Roosevelt died of a cerebral hemorrhage. Thus it was Truman, a man painfully conscious of his limitations yet equally aware of the power and responsibility of his office, who had to decide what to do when, in July 1945, American scientists placed in his hands a new and awful weapon, the atomic bomb.

DOCUMENT

Einstein, Letter to President Roosevelt

After Roosevelt had responded to Albert Einstein's warning in 1939, government-sponsored atomic research had proceeded rapidly, especially after the establishment of the so-called Manhattan Project in May 1943. The manufacture of the element plutonium at Hanford, Washington, and of uranium 235 at Oak Ridge, Tennessee, continued, along with the design and construction of a transportable atomic bomb at Los Alamos, New Mexico, under the direction of J. Robert Oppenheimer. Almost $2 billion was spent before a successful bomb was exploded at Alamogordo, in the New Mexican desert, on July 16, 1945. As that first mushroom cloud formed over the desert, Oppenheimer recalled the prophetic words of the *Bhagavad Gita:* "I am become death, the shatterer of worlds."

Should a bomb with the destructive force of 20,000 tons of TNT be employed against Japan? By striking a major city, its dreadful power could be demonstrated convincingly, yet doing so would bring death to tens of thousands of Japanese civilians. Many of the scientists who had made the bomb now argued against its use. Others suggested alerting the Japanese and then staging a demonstration explosion at sea, but that idea was discarded because of concern that the bomb might fail to explode.

Truman was torn between his awareness that the bomb was "the most terrible thing ever discovered" and his hope that using it "would bring the war to an end." The bomb might cause a revolution in Japan, might lead the emperor to intervene, might even persuade the military to give up. Considering the thousands of Americans who would surely die in any conventional invasion of Japan and, on a less humane level, influenced by a desire to end the Pacific war before the Soviet Union could intervene effectively and thus claim a role in the peacemaking, the president chose to go ahead.

The moral soundness of Truman's decision has been debated ever since. (See Debating the Past, p. 760.) There is no doubt that hatred of the Japanese had something to do with the decision. What is often forgotten by those who deplore it is the fact that while the immediate result was the death of many thousands of innocent Japanese civilians, far more Japanese would have died—many more than the Americans who would have perished—if Japan had had to be invaded.

On August 6 the Superfortress *Enola Gay* dropped an atomic bomb on Hiroshima, killing about 78,000 persons (including 20 American prisoners of war) and injuring nearly 100,000 more out of a population of 344,000. Over 96 percent of the buildings in the city were destroyed or damaged. Three days later, while the stunned Japanese still hesitated, a second atomic bomb, the only other one that had so far been assembled, blasted Nagasaki. This second drop was less defensible morally, but it had the desired result. On August 15 Japan surrendered.

Thus ended the greatest war in history. Its cost was beyond calculation. No accurate count could be made even of the dead; we know only that the total was in the neighborhood of 20 million. As in World War I, American casualties—291,000 battle deaths and 671,000 wounded—were smaller than those of the other major belligerents. About 7.5 million Soviets died in battle, 3.5 million Germans, 1.2 million Japanese, and 2.2 million Chinese; Britain and France, despite much smaller populations, suffered losses almost as large as did the United States. And far more than in World War I, American resources, human and material, had made victory possible.

No one could account the war a benefit to humanity, but in the late summer of 1945 the future looked bright. Fascism was dead. The successful wartime

Debating the Past

Should the United States have used atom bombs against Japan? This photograph shows the ruins of Hiroshima after it had been destroyed by an atomic bomb.

Robert J. C. Butow's (1954) analysis of Japanese sources proved that the devastation of Hiroshima and Nagasaki had led to Japan's surrender. If there had been no atom bomb, the United States would probably have been forced to invade the islands. According to military estimates cited at the time, an invasion would have resulted in a half million American casualties. Biographers such as David McCullough (1992) and Alonzo L. Hamby (1995) agreed that, given public and congressional opinion, Truman had little choice but to end the war as quickly as possible and with the fewest American casualties.

But Gar Alperovitz (1965), writing when the United States was mired in a global struggle against the Soviet Union, proposed that Truman had been influenced more by a desire to intimidate Stalin than to force the surrender of Japan. This position was strengthened by subsequently declassified documents indicating that few U.S. military analysts anticipated losses as high as those reported in Butow and other sources. John Dower (1986) discovered evidence in Japanese sources that the Soviet declaration of war, which came in the wake of Hiroshima, shattered the confidence of the Japanese high command as much as the atomic bombs. Soviet entry alone might have ended the war. The American rush to use atomic weapons against Japan was due to "sheer visceral hatred" of the Japanese, Dower insisted.

The revisionist hypothesis—that Japan might have surrendered without the atomic bombs—is belied by exhaustive last-ditch Japanese preparations for defending the home islands. Whether this information justifies this first—and to date, only—use of nuclear weapons will forever remain a source of debate.

Robert J. C. Butow, *Japan's Decision to Surrender* (1954), Alonzo L. Hamby, *Man of the People* (1995), David McCullough, *Truman* (1992), Gar Alperovitz, *Atomic Diplomacy* (1965), and *The Decision to Use the Atomic Bomb and the Architecture of an American Myth* (1995), John W. Dower, *War Without Mercy* (1986), and Martin J. Sherwin, *A World Destroyed* (1975).

diplomatic dealings of Roosevelt, Churchill, and the Soviet dictator, Joseph Stalin, encouraged many to hope that the communists were ready to cooperate in rebuilding Europe. In the United States isolationism had disappeared; the message of Wendell Willkie's bestselling *One World*, written after a globe-circling tour made by the 1940 Republican presidential candidate at the behest of President Roosevelt in 1942, appeared to have been absorbed by the majority of the people.

Out of the death and destruction had come technological developments that seemed to herald a better world as well as a peaceful one. Enormous advances in the design of airplanes and the development of radar (which some authorities think was more important than any weapons system in winning the war) were about to revolutionize travel and the transportation of goods. Improvements in surgery and other medical advances gave promise of saving millions of lives, and

the development of penicillin and other antibiotics, which had greatly reduced the death rate among troops, would perhaps banish all infectious diseases.

Above all, there was the power of the atom. The force that seared Hiroshima and Nagasaki could be harnessed to serve peaceful needs, the scientists promised, with results that might free humanity forever from poverty and toil. The period of reconstruction would be prolonged, but with all the great powers adhering to the new United Nations charter, drafted at San Francisco in June 1945, international cooperation could be counted on to ease the burdens of the victims of war and help the poor and underdeveloped parts of the world toward economic and political independence. Such at least was the hope of millions in the victorious summer of 1945.

WARTIME DIPLOMACY

That hope was not to be realized, in large part because of a conflict that developed between the Soviet Union and the western Allies. During the course of World War II every instrument of mass persuasion in the country had been directed toward convincing the people that the Soviets were fighting America's battle as well as their own. Even before Pearl Harbor, former Ambassador Joseph E. Davies wrote in his best-selling *Mission to Moscow* (1941) that the communist leaders were "a group of able, strong men" with "honest convictions and integrity of purposes" who were "devoted to the cause of peace for both ideological and practical reasons." Communism was based "on the same principle of the 'brotherhood of man' which Jesus preached." Stalin possessed great dignity and charm, combined with much wisdom and strength of character, Davies said. "His brown eye is exceedingly kind and gentle. A child would like to sit in his lap and a dog would sidle up to him." In another book published in 1941 the journalist Walter Duranty described Stalin (who had ruthlessly executed hundreds of his former comrades) as "remarkably long-suffering in his treatment of various oppositions."

During the war Americans with as different points of view as General Douglas MacArthur and Vice President Henry A. Wallace took strongly pro-Soviet positions, and American newspapers and magazines published many laudatory articles about Russia. (Most refused to identify that nation by its communist name of Soviet Union.) *Life* reported that Russians "think like Americans." In 1943 *Time* named Stalin its Man of the Year. The film *Mission to Moscow,* a whitewash of the dreadful Moscow treason trials of the 1930s based on Ambassador Davies's book, portrayed Stalin as a wise, grandfatherly type, puffing comfortably on an old pipe. In *One World* (1943) Wendell Willkie wrote glowingly of the Russian people, their "effective society," and their simple, warmhearted leader. When Willkie suggested jokingly to Stalin that if he continued to make progress in improving the education of his people he might educate himself out of a job, the dictator "threw his head back and laughed and laughed," Willkie recorded. "Mr. Willkie, you know I grew up a Georgian peasant. I am unschooled in pretty talk. All I can say is I like you very much."

These views of the character of Joseph Stalin were naive, to say the least, but the United States and the Soviet Union agreed emphatically on the need to defeat Hitler. The Soviets repeatedly expressed a willingness to cooperate with the Allies in dealing with postwar problems. The Soviet Union was one of the 26 signers of the Declaration of the United Nations (January 1942), in which the Allies promised to eschew territorial aggrandizement after the war, to respect the right of all peoples to determine their own form of government, to work for freer trade and international economic cooperation, and to force the disarmament of the aggressor nations.[1]

VIDEO

The Big Three Conference at Yalta

In May 1943 the Soviet Union dissolved the Comintern, its official agency for the promulgation of world revolution. The following October, during a conference in Moscow with the Allies, Soviet Foreign Minister V. M. Molotov joined in setting up a European Advisory Commission to divide Germany into occupation zones after the war. That December, at a conference held in Teheran, Iran, Roosevelt, Churchill, and Stalin discussed plans for a new league of nations. When Roosevelt described the kind of world organization he envisaged, the Soviet dictator offered a number of constructive suggestions.

Between August and October 1944, Allied representatives met at Dumbarton Oaks, outside Washington. The chief Soviet delegate, Andrei A. Gromyko, opposed limiting the use of the veto by the great powers on the future United Nations (UN) Security Council, but he did not take a deliberately obstructionist position. At a conference held at Yalta in the Crimea in February 1945 Stalin joined Roosevelt and Churchill in the call for a meeting in April at San Francisco to draft a charter for the UN. "We argued freely and frankly across the table," Roosevelt reported later. "But at the end, on every point, unanimous agreement was reached. I may say we achieved a unity of thought

---

[1]These were the principles first laid down in the so-called Atlantic Charter, drafted by Roosevelt and Churchill at a meeting on the USS *Augusta* off Newfoundland in August 1941.

and a way of getting along together." Privately Roosevelt characterized Stalin as "a very interesting man" whose rough exterior clothed an "old-fashioned elegant European manner." He referred to him almost affectionately as "that old buzzard" and on one occasion called him "Uncle Joe" to his face. At Yalta, Stalin gave Roosevelt a portrait photograph, with a long Cyrillic inscription in his small, tightly written hand.

The UN charter drafted at the 50-nation San Francisco Conference gave each UN member a seat in the General Assembly, a body designed for discussion rather than action. The locus of authority in the new organization resided in the Security Council, "the castle of the great powers." This consisted of five permanent members (the United States, the Soviet Union, Great Britain, France, and China) and six others elected for two-year terms.

The Security Council was charged with responsibility for maintaining world peace, but any great power could block UN action whenever it wished to do so. The United States insisted on this veto power as strongly as the Soviet Union did. In effect the charter paid lip service to the Wilsonian ideal of a powerful international police force, but it incorporated the limitations that Henry Cabot Lodge had proposed in his 1919 reservation to Article X of the League Covenant, which relieved the United States from the obligation of enforcing collective security without the approval of Congress.

ALLIED SUSPICION OF STALIN

Long before the war in Europe ended, however, the Allies had clashed over important policy matters. Since later world tensions developed from decisions made at this time, an understanding of the disagreements is essential for evaluating several decades of history.

Much depends on one's view of the postwar Soviet system. If the Soviet government under Stalin was bent on world domination, events fall readily into one pattern of interpretation. If, having at enormous cost endured an unprovoked assault by the Nazis, it was seeking only to protect itself against the possibility of another invasion, these events are best explained differently. Because the United States has opened nearly all its diplomatic records, we know a great deal about how American foreign policy was formulated and about the mixed motives and mistaken judgments of American leaders. This helps explain why many scholars have been critical of American policy and the "cold warriors" who made and directed it. The Soviet Union, for many years, did not let even its own historians into its archives.

It is clear, however, that the Soviets resented the British-American delay in opening up a second front. They were fighting for survival against the full power of the German armies; any invasion, even an unsuccessful one, would have relieved some of the pressure. Roosevelt and Churchill would not move until they were ready, and Stalin had to accept their decision. At the same time, Stalin never concealed his determination to protect his country from future attack by extending its western frontier after the war. He warned the Allies repeatedly that he would not tolerate any unfriendly government along the western boundary of the Soviet Union.

Most Allied leaders, including Roosevelt, admitted privately during the war that the Soviet Union would annex territory and possess preponderant power in Eastern Europe after the defeat of Germany, but they never said this publicly. They believed that free governments could somehow be created in countries like Poland and Bulgaria that the Soviets would trust enough to leave to their own devices. "The Poles," Winston Churchill said early in 1945, "will have their future in their own hands, with the single limitation that they must honestly follow . . . a policy friendly to Russia. This is surely reasonable."

However reasonable, Churchill's statement was impractical. The Polish question was a terribly difficult one. The war, after all, had been triggered by the German attack on Poland; the British in particular felt a moral obligation to restore that nation to its prewar independence. During the war a Polish government in exile was set up in London, and its leaders were determined—especially after the discovery in 1943 of the murder of some 5000 Polish officers several years earlier at Katyn, in Russia, presumably by the Soviet secret police—to make no concessions to Soviet territorial demands. Public opinion in Poland (and indeed in all the states along Russia's western frontier) was not so much anti-Soviet as anti-Russian. Yet the Soviet Union's legitimate interests (to say nothing of its power in the area) could not be ignored.

YALTA AND POTSDAM

At the Yalta Conference, Roosevelt and Churchill agreed to Soviet annexation of large sections of eastern Poland. In return they demanded that free elections be held in Poland itself. "I want this election to be . . . beyond question," Roosevelt told Stalin. "It should be like Caesar's wife." In a feeble attempt at a joke he added: "I did not know her but they said she was pure." Stalin agreed, almost certainly with-

out intending to keep his promise. The elections were never held; Poland was run by a pro-Soviet puppet regime.

Stalin apparently could not understand why the Allies were so concerned about the fate of a small country remote from their strategic spheres. That they professed to be concerned seemed to him an indication that they had some secret, devious purpose. He could see no difference (and "revisionist" American historians agree with him) between the Soviet Union's dominating Poland and maintaining a government there that did not reflect the wishes of a majority of the Polish people and the United States's dominating many Latin American nations and supporting unpopular regimes within them. Roosevelt, however, was worried about the political effects that Soviet control of Poland might have in the United States. Polish-Americans would be furious if the United States allowed the Soviets to control their homeland.

But had Roosevelt described the difficulties to the Poles and the rest of the American people more frankly, their reaction might have been less angry. In any case, when he realized that Stalin was going to act as he pleased, Roosevelt was furious. "We can't do business with Stalin," he said shortly before his death in April 1945. "He has broken every one of the promises he made at Yalta." In July 1945, following the surrender of Germany, the new president, Harry Truman, met with Stalin and Churchill at Potsdam, outside Berlin.[2] They agreed to try the Nazi leaders as war criminals, made plans for exacting reparations from Germany, and confirmed the division of the country into four zones to be occupied separately by American, Soviet, British, and French troops. Berlin, deep in the Soviet zone, had itself been split into four sectors. Stalin rejected all arguments that he loosen his hold on Eastern Europe, and Truman (who received news of the successful testing of the atom bomb while at Potsdam) made no concessions. But he was impressed by Stalin. The dictator was "smart as hell," he wrote in his diary. "Stalin was an SOB," the plainspoken president explained to some officers

▲ Churchill, Roosevelt, and Stalin photographed at the week-long Yalta conference in February 1945. By April 1945, Roosevelt was dead.

while returning to the United States from Potsdam on the cruiser *Augusta*. Then he added: "Of course he thinks I'm one too."

On both sides suspicions were mounting, positions hardening. Yet all the advantages seemed to be with the United States. Was this not, as Henry Luce, the publisher of *Time* had declared, "the American century," an era when American power and American ideals would shape the course of events the world over? Besides its army, navy, and air force and its immense industrial potential, alone among the nations the United States possessed the atomic bomb. When Stalin's actions made it clear that he intended to control Eastern Europe and to exert influence elsewhere in the world, most Americans first reacted somewhat in the manner of a mastiff being worried by a yapping terrier: Their resentment was tempered by amazement. It took time for them to realize that the war had caused a fundamental change in international politics. The United States might be the strongest country in the world, but the western European nations, victor and vanquished alike, were reduced to their own and America's surprise to the status of second-class powers. The Soviet Union, on the other hand, had gained more influence than it had held under the czars and regained the territory it had lost as a result of World War I and the communist revolution.

----

[2]Clement R. Attlee replaced Churchill during the conference after his Labour party won the British elections.

MILESTONES

1941	Roosevelt prohibits discrimination in defense plants (Fair Employment Practices Committee)
	Japan attacks Pearl Harbor
	Roosevelt and Churchill draft Atlantic Charter
1942	Executive Order 9066 sends Japanese Americans to relocation camps
	Japanese take Philippines
	Carrier-based planes dominate Battle of Coral Sea
	U.S. airpower takes control of central Pacific at Battle of Midway
	U.S. troops invade North Africa
1943	Oppenheimer directs Manhattan Project to make atom bomb
	Race riots rage in Detroit and Los Angeles
	Allies invade Italy
	Roosevelt, Churchill, Stalin meet at Tehran, Iran

1944	Allies invade Normandy, France (D-Day)
	Battle of the Bulge exhausts German reserves
1945	Big Three meet at Yalta Conference
	Fifty nations draft UN Charter at San Francisco
	Roosevelt dies; Truman becomes president
	Germany surrenders (V-E Day)
	United States tests atom bomb at Alamogordo, New Mexico
	Truman, Churchill, Stalin meet at Potsdam
	United States drops atom bombs on Hiroshima and Nagasaki, Japan
	Japan surrenders (V-J Day)

SUPPLEMENTARY READING

On prewar relations between the United States and Japan, see Akira Iriye, *After Imperialism* (1965). The best history of the worldwide events leading to the Japanese attack on Pearl Harbor is Waldo Heinrichs, *Threshold of War* (1988), but for more detail see Gordon W. Prange, *At Dawn We Slept* (1981), and Michael S. Stackman, *Target: Pearl Harbor* (1990). Charles C. Tansill, *Back Door to War* (1952), and Charles A. Beard, *President Roosevelt and the Coming of the War* (1948), are interesting interpretations by isolationists. Useful overviews include David M. Kennedy, *Freedom from Fear: The American People in Depression and War* (1999), Murray Williamson and Allan R. Millett, *A War to Be Won* (2000), and Warren F. Kimball, *Forged in War: Roosevelt, Churchill and the Second World War* (1997). Mark A. Stoler, *Allies and Adversaries* (2000) focuses on the Joint Chiefs of Staff. Thomas S. Fleming, *The New Dealers' War* (2001) is critical of Roosevelt. See also Michael S. Sherry, *The Rise of American Airpower* (1987).

A recent, sober assessment of Pearl Harbor is Akira Iriye, *Pearl Harbor and the Coming of the Pacific War* (1999). On aerial warfare, see Williamson Murray, *War in the Air, 1914–1945* (1999) and Geoffrey Peret, *Winged Victory* (1993). Paul Fussell, *Wartime: Understanding and Behavior in the Second World War* (1989), provides a realistic

rendering of the carnage and chaos of modern warfare; Gerald F. Linderman, *The World Within War: America's Combat Experience in World War II* (1997), contends that the spectacle of war offers little sustenance to soldiers. The term "the greatest generation" is from Tom Brokaw's 1998 book by that title.

For a general, brief overview of the home front, see Lewis A. Erenberg and Susan E. Hirsch, *The War in American Culture: Society and Consciousness During World War II* (1996), John Morton Blum, *V Was for Victory* (1976), Doris Kearns Goodwin, *No Ordinary Time* (1995), and Steven Mintz and Susan Kellogg, *Domestic Revolutions* (1988). The effects of the war on women are described in D'Ann Campbell, *Women at War with America* (1984), Karen Anderson, *Wartime Women* (1981), and Susan M. Hartmann, *The Home Front and Beyond* (1982). William M. Tuttle, Jr., *"Daddy's Gone To War": The Second World War in the Lives of America's Children* (1993) offers an interesting perspective. The impact of the war on radical politics is examined in Bill V. Mullen, *Popular Fronts: Chicago and African-American Cultural Politics, 1935–46* (1999).

African American participation is the subject of Nat Brandt, *Harlem at War* (1996), Neil A. Wynn, *The Afro-American and the Second World War* (1993), Dominic J.

Capeci, Jr., *Race Relations in Wartime Detroit* (1984), and A. Russell Buchanan, *Black Americans in World War II* (1977). On the Japanese internment, see Greg Robinson, *By Order of the President: FDR and the Internment of Japanese Americans* (2001), and Roger Daniels, *Concentration Camps USA: Japanese Americans and World War II* (1971).

Major biographies include Geoffrey Perret, *Eisenhower* (1999), Stephen Ambrose, *Eisenhower* (1983), and Ed Cray, *General of the Army: George C. Marshall* (1990).

Richard Rhodes, *The Making of the Atom Bomb* (1986), is superb. On Leslie Groves, see Robert S. Norris, *Racing for the Bomb* (2002). For the relationship of the key scientists, see Gregg Herken, *Brotherhood of the Bomb* (2002).

SUGGESTED WEBSITES

Franklin Delano Roosevelt

http://www.ipl.org/div/POTUS/fdroosevelt.html

This site provides information about Roosevelt, the only president to serve more than two terms.

America from the Great Depression to World War II: Photographs from the FSA and OWI, c. 1935–1945

http://memory.loc.gov/ammem/fsowhome.html

These images in the Farm Security Administration—Office of War Information Collection show Americans from all over the nation experiencing everything from despair to triumph in the 1930s and 1940s.

A People at War

http://www.archives.gov/exhibit_hall/a_people_at_war/a_people_at_war.html

This National Archives exhibit takes a close look at the contributions millions of Americans made to the war effort.

Powers of Persuasion—Poster Art of World War II

http://www.archives.gov/publications/posters/original_posters.html

These powerful posters at the National Archives were part of the battle for the hearts and minds of the American people.

A-Bomb WWW Museum

http://www.csi.ad.jp/ABOMB/

This site offers information about the impact of the first atomic bomb as well as the background and context of weapons of total destruction.

The United States Holocaust Memorial Museum

http://www.ushmm.org/

This is the official Website of the Holocaust Museum in Washington, D.C.

The Seabees During World War II

http://www.seabeecook.com/history/

The Seabees are a U.S. Navy support unit best known for their construction projects. This site provides articles, pictures, and reminiscences of Seabees during the war. This site looks at the war behind the lines.

Tuskegee Airmen

http://www.wpafb.af.mil/museum/history/prewwii/ta.htm

The Air Force Museum at Wright-Patterson Air Force Base maintains this site about the African American pilots of World War II.

George C. Marshall

http://www.marshallfoundation.org/

This site, maintained by the George C. Marshall Foundation at the Virginia Military Institute, Lexington, Virginia, provides information on the values and career of U.S. Army Chief of Staff George C. Marshall.

The American Century

▼ Harsh yellow light, rimmed by green neon, illuminates a quartet of solitary figures in Edward Hopper's *Nighthawks* (1942). Hopper's painting anticipated the clean, critical edge of much postwar art.

CHAPTER CONTENTS

In late 1945 most Americans were probably more concerned with what was happening at home than with foreign developments, and no one was more aware of this than Harry Truman. When he received the news of Roosevelt's death, he claimed that he felt as though "the moon, the stars, and all the planets" had suddenly fallen upon him. Although he could not have been quite as surprised as he indicated (Roosevelt was known to have been in extremely poor health), he was acutely conscious of his own limitations.

Truman was born in Missouri in 1884. After his service in a World War I artillery unit, he opened a men's clothing store in Kansas City. The store failed in the postwar depression. Truman then became a minor cog in the political machine of Democratic boss Tom Pendergast. In 1934 Truman was elected to the U.S. Senate, where he proved to be a loyal but obscure New Dealer. He first attracted national attention during World War II when his "watchdog" committee on defense spending, working with devotion and efficiency, saved the government immense sums. This led to his nomination and election as vice president.

As president, Truman sought to carry on in the Roosevelt tradition. Curiously, he was at the same time humble and cocky, even brash—both idealistic and cold-bloodedly political. He adopted liberal objectives only to pursue them sometimes by rash, even repressive means. Too often he insulted opponents instead of convincing or appeasing them. Complications tended to confuse him, in which case he either dug in his heels or struck out blindly, usually with unfortunate results. On balance, however, he was a strong and in many ways a successful president.

THE POSTWAR ECONOMY

Nearly all the postwar leaders were worried by the possibility of a serious depression, and nearly all accepted the necessity of employing federal authority to stabilize the economy and speed national development. The Great Depression and the huge government expenditures made necessary by the war had proven the theories of John Maynard Keynes. Democrats and Republicans alike were convinced that it was possible to prevent sharp swings in the business cycle and therefore to do away with serious unemployment by monetary and fiscal manipulation.

Population Shifts, 1940-1950

When World War II ended, nearly everyone wanted to demobilize the armed forces, remove wartime controls, and reduce taxes. Yet everyone also hoped to prevent any sudden economic dislocation, to check inflation, and to make sure that goods in short supply were fairly distributed. Neither the politicians nor the public could reconcile these conflicting objectives. Labor wanted price controls retained but wage controls lifted; industrialists wished to raise prices and keep the lid on wages. Farmers wanted subsidies but opposed price controls and the extension of social security benefits to agricultural workers.

In this difficult situation President Truman failed to win either the confidence of the people or the support of Congress. On the one hand, he proposed a comprehensive program of new legislation that included a public housing scheme, aid to education, medical insurance, civil rights guarantees, a higher minimum wage, broader social security coverage, additional conservation and public powerprojects patterned after the TVA, increased aid to agriculture, and the retention of anti-inflationary controls. On the other hand, he ended rationing and other controls and signed a bill cutting taxes by some $6 billion. Whenever opposition to his plans developed, he vacillated between compromise and inflexibility.

Yet the country weathered the reconversion period with remarkable ease. The pent-up demand for houses, automobiles, clothing, washing machines, and countless other products, backed by the war-enforced savings of millions, kept factories operating at capacity. Economists had feared that the flood of millions of veterans into the job market would cause serious unemployment. But when the veterans returned (more than 60,000 of them accompanied by foreign brides), few went without work for long. Because of the boom, the demand for labor was large and growing. In addition, the government made an unprecedented educational opportunity available to veterans. Instead of a general bonus, which would have stimulated consumption and inflation, in 1944 Congress passed the GI Bill of Rights, which made subsidies available to veterans so they could continue their educations, learn new trades, or start new businesses. Nearly 8 million veterans took advantage of the education and training grants, greatly to their long-term advantage, and thus to the country's.

Cutting taxes and removing price controls did cause a period of rapid inflation. Food prices rose more than 25 percent between 1945 and 1947, which led to demands for higher wages and a wave of strikes—nearly 5000 in 1946 alone. Inflation and labor unrest helped the Republicans to win control of both houses of Congress in 1946 for the first time since the 1920s.

High on the Republican agenda was the passage of a new labor relations act. Labor leaders tended to support the Democrats, for they remembered gratefully the Wagner Act and other help given to them by the Roosevelt administration during the labor-management struggles of the 1930s. In 1943 the CIO had created a Political Action Committee to mobilize the labor vote. But the strikes of 1946 had alienated many citizens because they delayed the satisfaction of the demand for consumer goods.

This was the climate when in June 1947 the new Congress passed the Taft-Hartley Act over the veto of President Truman. The measure outlawed the closed shop (a provision written into many labor contracts requiring new workers to join the union before they could be employed). Most important, it authorized the president to seek court injunctions to prevent strikes that in his opinion endangered the national interest. The injunctions would hold for 80 days—a "cooling-off" period during which a presidential fact-finding board could investigate and make recommendations. If the dispute remained unresolved after 80 days, the president was to recommend "appropriate action" to Congress.

The Taft-Hartley Act made the task of unionizing unorganized industries more difficult, but it did not

seriously hamper existing unions. Although it outlawed the closed shop, it permitted union shop contracts, which forced new workers to join the union after accepting employment.

THE CONTAINMENT POLICY

Although postwar economic recovery went more smoothly than most expected, foreign policy issues vexed the Truman presidency. Repeatedly Stalin made it clear that he had no intention of even consulting with Western leaders about his domination of Eastern Europe, and he seemed intent on extending his power deep into war-devastated central Europe. The Soviet Union also controlled Outer Mongolia, parts of Manchuria, and northern Korea, and it had annexed the Kurile Islands and regained the southern half of Sakhalin Island from Japan. It was fomenting trouble in Iran. By January 1946 Truman had decided to stop "babying" the Russians. "Only one language do they understand," he noted in a memorandum. "How many divisions have you?"

Truman's problem—and it would bedevil American policymakers for years—was that Stalin had far more divisions than anyone else. Truman, a seasoned politician, had swiftly responded to the postwar clamor to "bring the boys home." In the two years following the surrender of Japan, the armed forces of the United States had dwindled from 6 million to 1.5 million. Stalin, who kept domestic foes out of office by having them shot, ignored domestic pressure to demobilize the Red Army, estimated by U.S. intelligence at twice the size of the American army.

Stalin and the Red Army evoked the image of Hitler's troops pouring across the north European plains. Like Hitler, Stalin was a cruel dictator who championed an ideology of world conquest. Averill Harriman, American ambassador to the Soviet Union, warned that communist ideology exerted an "outward thrust" more dangerous than Nazism. George Kennan, a scholarly foreign officer who also had served in Moscow, thought that ideology was more symptom than cause. Marxism, he wrote, merely provided the intellectual "fig-leaf of morality and respectability" for naked Soviet aggression. In an influential article, "The Sources of Soviet Conduct," published anonymously in the July 1947 issue of *Foreign Affairs,* Kennan argued that the instability and illegitimacy of the Soviet regime generated explosive internal pressures. These forces, vented outward, would cause the USSR to expand "constantly, wherever it is permitted to move" until it filled "every nook and cranny available to it in the basin of world power." A policy of "long-term, patient but firm and vigilant containment" was the best means of dealing with the Soviet Union.

"The Sources of Soviet Conduct" was powerfully argued, but the article was ambiguous and imprecise in crucial aspects. Exactly how the Soviets were to be "contained" and in what parts of the world the policy should be applied were not spelled out. At the outset containment was less a plan of action than a plea for the resolve to act. It did not look to the future so much as cringe from the past.

THE ATOM BOMB: A "WINNING" WEAPON?

Although Truman authorized use of the atom bomb to force the surrender of Japan, he had hoped that a demonstration of the weapon's power also would inhibit Stalin and serve as a counterweight to the

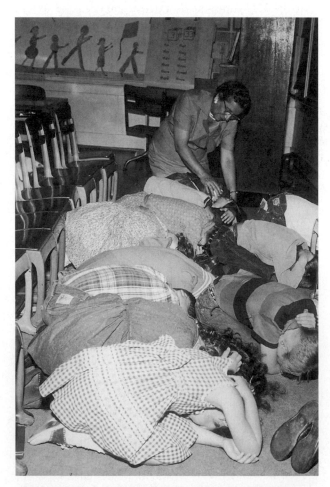

▲ "Duck and cover" drill in St. Petersburg, Florida, 1962. Such drills functioned more to allay public anxieties about nuclear war than to provide real protection from thermonuclear weapons.

numerically superior Red Army. Stalin, however, refused to be intimidated. "Atomic bombs are meant to frighten those with weak nerves," he told his advisers. His resolve had been stiffened as a result of Soviet espionage. Stalin knew that the American atomic arsenal—slightly more than a dozen bombs in 1947—was insufficient to destroy the Soviet Union's military machine.

The atomic bomb was a doubtful deterrent for another reason. Sobering accounts of the devastation of Hiroshima and Nagasaki and the suffering of the victims of radiation poisoning left many Americans uneasy. J. Robert Oppenheimer, director of the atom bomb design team, informed government officials that most scientists in the Manhattan Project would not continue such work. "I feel we have blood on our hands," he told President Truman. "Never mind," Truman snapped. "It'll all come out in the wash." Yet even Truman came to doubt whether the American people would again "permit" their president to use atomic weapons for aggressive purposes.

In November 1945 the United States suggested that the UN supervise all nuclear energy production, and the General Assembly created an Atomic Energy Commission to study the question. In June 1946 Commissioner Bernard Baruch offered a plan for the eventual outlawing of atomic weapons. Under this proposal UN inspectors operating without restriction anywhere in the world would ensure that no country made bombs clandestinely. When, at an unspecified date, the system was established successfully, the United States would destroy its stockpile of bombs.

Most Americans thought the Baruch plan magnanimous, and some considered it positively foolhardy, but the Soviets rejected it. They would neither permit UN inspectors in the Soviet Union nor surrender the Soviet Union's veto power over Security Council actions dealing with atomic energy. They demanded that the United States destroy its bombs at once. American leaders did not comply; they believed that the atom bomb would be, in Baruch's words, their "winning weapon" for years to come. Exactly how it would be used, they could not say.

A Turning Point in Greece

The strategy of containment began to take shape early in 1947 as a result of a crisis in Greece. Greek communists, waging a guerrilla war against the monarchy, were receiving aid from communist Yugoslavia and Bulgaria. Great Britain had been assisting the monarchists but could no longer afford this drain on its resources. In February 1947 the British informed President Truman that they would cut off aid to Greece.

The British predicament forced American policymakers to confront the fact that their European allies had not been able to rebuild their war-weakened economies. The communist "Iron Curtain" (a phrase coined by Winston Churchill) seemed about to close down on another nation. That the Soviet Union was actually discouraging the rebels out of fear of American intervention in the area the policymakers ignored. As Undersecretary of State Dean Acheson put it, the "corruption" of Greece might "infect" the entire Middle East and then spread through Asia Minor and Egypt and to Italy and France.

Truman therefore asked Congress to approve what became known as the Truman Doctrine. If Greece or Turkey fell to the communists, he said, all of the Middle East might be lost. To prevent this "unspeakable tragedy," he asked for $400 million in military and economic aid to Greece and Turkey. "It must be the policy of the United States to support free peoples who are resisting attempted subjugation by armed minorities or by outside pressures," he said.

DOCUMENT
Truman Doctrine
1947

By exaggerating the consequences of inaction and by justifying his request on ideological grounds, Truman obtained his objective. The result was the establishment of a right-wing, military-dominated government in Greece. In addition, by not limiting his request to the specific problem posed by the situation in Greece, Truman caused considerable concern in many countries.

The threat to Western Europe certainly loomed large in 1947. With the region, in the words of Winston Churchill (the great phrase-maker of the era), "a rubble-heap, a charnel house, a breeding-ground of pestilence and hate," the entire continent seemed in danger of falling into communist hands without the Soviet Union raising a finger.

The Marshall Plan and the Lesson of History

In a 1946 speech entitled "The Lesson of History," George C. Marshall, army chief of staff during World War II, reminded Americans that their isolationism had contributed to Hitler's unchecked early aggression. This time, Marshall noted, the people of the United States must be prepared to act against foreign aggressors. In 1947 Marshall was named secretary of state. He outlined an extraordinary plan by which the United States would finance the reconstruction of the European economy. "Hunger, poverty, desperation, and chaos" were the real enemies of freedom and democracy, Marshall said. The need was to restore

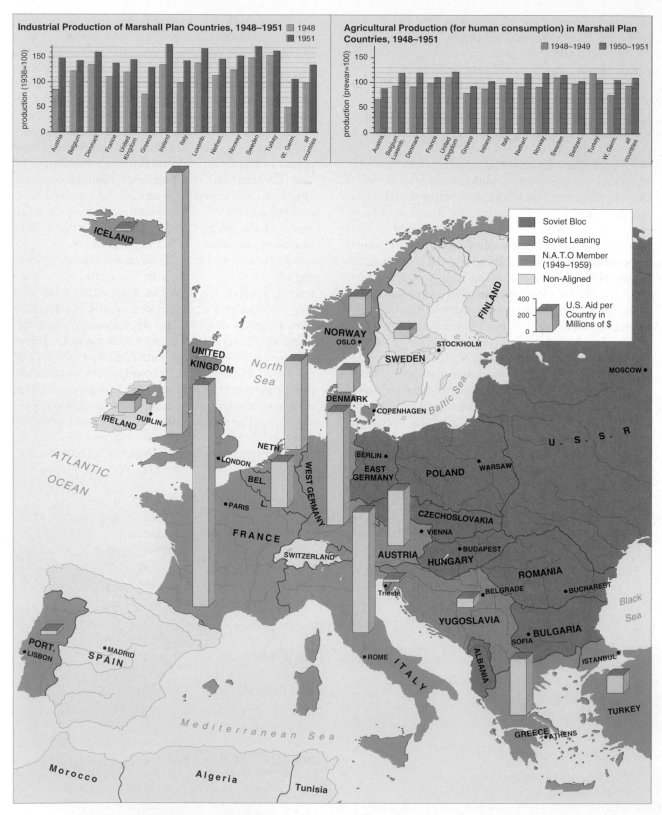

Industrial Production of Marshall Plan Countries, 1948–1951 ■ 1948 ■ 1951

production (1938=100)

Austria, Belgium, Denmark, France, United Kingdom, Greece, Ireland, Italy, Luxemb., Netherl., Norway, Sweden, Turkey, W. Germ., all countries

Agricultural Production (for human consumption) in Marshall Plan Countries, 1948–1951 ■ 1948–1949 ■ 1950–1951

production (prewar=100)

Austria, Belgium, Luxemb., Denmark, France, United Kingdom, Greece, Ireland, Italy, Netherl., Norway, Sweden, Switzerl., Turkey, W. Germ., all countries

Legend:
- Soviet Bloc
- Soviet Leaning
- N.A.T.O Member (1949–1959)
- Non-Aligned

U.S. Aid per Country in Millions of $
0 – 200 – 400

ICELAND

NORWAY — OSLO

SWEDEN — STOCKHOLM

FINLAND

North Sea

Baltic Sea

MOSCOW

U. S. S. R

UNITED KINGDOM

IRELAND — DUBLIN

LONDON

NETH.

BEL.

L.

PARIS

FRANCE

DENMARK — COPENHAGEN

BERLIN

EAST GERMANY

WEST GERMANY

POLAND — WARSAW

CZECHOSLOVAKIA

VIENNA

AUSTRIA

BUDAPEST

HUNGARY

ROMANIA — BUCHAREST

SWITZERLAND

Trieste

BELGRADE

YUGOSLAVIA

ATLANTIC OCEAN

PORT. — LISBON

SPAIN — MADRID

ROME

ITALY

ALBANIA

BULGARIA — SOFIA

Black Sea

ISTANBUL

TURKEY

GREECE — ATHENS

Mediterranean Sea

Morocco

Algeria

Tunisia

▲ **European Recipients of Marshall Plan, 1948–1952**

"the confidence of the European people in the economic future of their own countries." Even the Soviet Union and Soviet-bloc nations would be eligible for American aid.

The European powers eagerly seized upon Marshall's suggestion. They set up a 16-nation Committee for European Economic Cooperation, which soon submitted plans calling for up to $22.4 billion in American assistance.

The Soviet Union and its European satellites were tempted by the offer of aid and sent representatives to the initial planning meetings. But Stalin grew anxious that his satellite states, attracted by American money, would be drawn into the American orbit. He recalled his delegates and demanded that Eastern European nations do likewise. Those who hesitated were ordered to report to the Kremlin. "I went to Moscow as the Foreign Minister of an independent sovereign state," Jan Masaryk of Czechoslovakia commented bitterly. "I returned as a lackey of the Soviet government."

In February 1948 a communist coup took over the Czechoslovak government; Masaryk fell (or more likely was pushed) out a window to his death. These strong-arm tactics brought to mind the Nazi takeover of Czechoslovakia a decade earlier and helped persuade Congress to appropriate over $13 billion for the Marshall aid program. Results exceeded all expectations. By 1951 Western Europe was booming.

But Europe was now divided in two. In the West, where American-influenced governments were elected, private property was respected if often taxed heavily, and corporations gained influence and power. In the East, where the Soviet Union imposed its will and political system on client states, deep-seated resentment festered among subject peoples.

In March 1948 Great Britain, France, Belgium, the Netherlands, and Luxembourg signed an alliance aimed at social, cultural, and economic collaboration. The Western nations abandoned their understandable but counterproductive policy of crushing Germany economically. They announced plans for creating a single West German Republic with a large degree of autonomy.

In June 1948 the Soviet Union retaliated by closing off surface access to Berlin from the west. For a time it seemed that the Allies must either fight their way into the city or abandon it to the communists. Unwilling to adopt either alternative, Truman decided to fly supplies to the capital from Frankfurt, Hanover, and Hamburg. American C-47 and C-54 transports shuttled back and forth in fair weather and foul, carrying enough food, fuel, and other goods necessary to maintain more than 2 million West Berliners. The Berlin airlift put the Soviets in an uncomfortable position; if they were determined to keep supplies from West Berlin, they would have to start

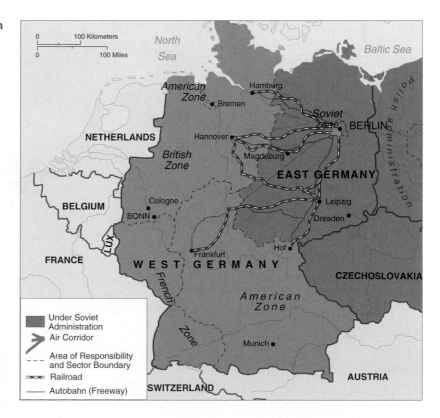

▶ **Air Relief to Berlin**

▲ In June 1948 the Soviet Union cut off all water and road traffic into West Berlin. Truman's plan to airlift food and fuel to provision 2.5 million people seemed impossible, but during the fifteen months of the Berlin crisis, planes such as this one, landing every four minutes, delivered nearly 2.5 million tons of supplies.

the fighting. They were not prepared to do so. In May 1949 they lifted the blockade.

But American generals intensified preparation of contingency plans for a Soviet attack. (See the feature essay Mapping the Past, "Planning Nuclear War," pp. 774–775.)

DEALING WITH JAPAN AND CHINA

Containment worked well in Europe, at least in the short run; in East Asia, where the United States lacked powerful allies, it was more expensive, less effective, and in most instances less justified. V-J Day found East Asia a shambles. Much of Japan was a smoking ruin. In China chaos reigned: Nationalists under Chiang Kai-shek (sometimes spelled Jiang Jieshi) dominated the south, communists under Mao Zedong controlled the northern countryside, and Japanese troops still held most northern cities. President Truman acted decisively and effectively with regard to Japan, unsurely and with unfortunate results where China was concerned. Even before the Japanese surrendered, he had decided not to allow the Soviet Union any significant role in the occupation of Japan. A four-power Allied Control Council was established, but American troops commanded by General Douglas MacArthur governed the country.

MacArthur displayed exactly the proper combination of imperiousness, tact, and intelligence needed to accomplish his purposes. The Japanese, revealing the same remarkable adaptability that had made possible their swift westernization in the latter half of the nineteenth century, accepted political and social changes that involved universal suffrage and parliamentary government, disbanding of its armed forces, the encouragement of labor unions, the breakup of some large estates and industrial combines, and the deemphasis of the emperor. Japan lost its far-flung island empire and all claim to Korea and the Chinese mainland but emerged economically strong, politically stable, and firmly allied with the United States.

The difficulties in China were probably insurmountable. Truman tried to bring Chiang's Nationalists and Mao's communists together. He sent General Marshall to China to seek a settlement, but neither Chiang nor Mao would make significant concessions. Mao was convinced—correctly, as time soon proved—that he could win all China by force, while Chiang, presiding over a corrupt and incompetent regime, grossly exaggerated his popularity among the Chinese people. In January 1947 Truman recalled Marshall and named him secretary of state. Soon thereafter civil war, suspended during the Japanese occupation, erupted in China.

THE ELECTION OF 1948

In the spring of 1948 President Truman's fortunes were at low ebb. Public opinion polls suggested that a majority of the people considered him incompetent or worse. The Republicans seemed so sure to win the 1948 presidential election that many prominent Democrats began to talk of denying Truman the nomination. Two of FDR's sons came out for General Eisenhower as the Democratic candidate. Governor Dewey, who again won the Republican nomination, ran confidently (even complacently), certain that he would carry the country.

Truman's position seemed hopeless because he had alienated both southern conservatives and northern liberals. The Southerners were particularly distressed because in 1946 the president had established a Committee on Civil Rights, which had recommended antilynching and anti–poll tax legislation and the creation of a permanent Fair Employment Practices Commission. When the Democratic convention adopted a strong civil rights plank, the southern delegates walked out. Southern conservatives then founded the States' Rights ("Dixiecrat") party and nominated J. Strom Thurmond of South Carolina for president.

► *text continues on page 776*

Mapping the Past

Planning Nuclear War

After World War II the United States sought to "contain" the Soviet Union. By 1949, President Truman's most visible strategy was to build up the nations of Europe to enable them to resist a Soviet invasion. To that end, the United States provided money for the defense of Greece and Turkey (Truman Doctrine, 1947) and for rebuilding the economic infrastructure of Europe (Marshall Plan, 1948). The United States also joined a military alliance (North Atlantic Treaty Organization) to provide a collective military response to a Soviet attack.

But American policy makers doubted that the European states, even with American support, could do much to block a major Soviet offensive in Western Europe. These doubts were reflected in secret U.S. war plans. One of the most comprehensive of these was Dropshot, prepared by the Joint Chiefs of Staff in 1949.

Operation Dropshot: Phase I—Defeat in Europe and Asia

Dropshot assumed that the Soviets would spend the early 1950s strengthening their armed forces. It further assumed that a Soviet attack would come around 1957. At that time,

without warning, Soviet armored divisions in East Germany would strike across the border into West Germany. West German armies on the border would likely collapse; their function was to delay the attack as long as possible while NATO troops regrouped along stronger defensive positions behind the Rhine River in an arc from the Netherlands to the Alps. But American planners assumed that even these troops would fall within a month to the vastly larger Red Army. NATO resistance in Europe would then evaporate and Soviet armies would occupy all of continental Europe. Only the British Isles, protected by British and American fleets, would remain outside of Soviet control. Dropshot further presumed that Soviet armies would seize Middle Eastern oil deposits and prevail in East Asia. NATO and the United States, according to Dropshot, would lose the first battles of World War III. But the war would not be over.

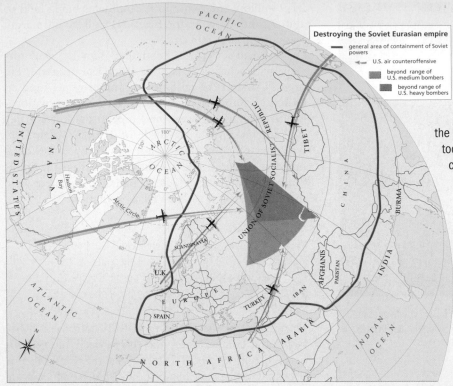

States would win World War III because of the superiority of its nuclear weapons.

The American nuclear plan assumed that the Soviet Union, even if it developed atomic bombs, could not deliver them to the United States. Soviet bases were too distant from American population centers. The attackers would have to fly great distances over NATO-controlled air space. Yet some Soviet bombers might get through, and to that end the Joint Chiefs prepared a list of "vital" and "critical" military and economic facilities that must be protected. The list, mapped below, included most of the major population centers of the nation.

Whether Soviet generals knew the details of Dropshot is unclear, but they well understood that the United States was prepared to use its growing arsenal of atomic bombs.

Operation Dropshot: Phase II—Nuclear Counterattack

Dropshot envisioned a second phase waged mostly by strategic bombers. ("Strategic" refers to military forces aimed at weakening the enemy generally rather than in tactical support of troops.) Nearly all of the Soviet Union west of Moscow was within range of American bombers based in Great Britain and the northeastern United States (flying over the North Pole), while all of the Soviet Union except the Urals could be hit by medium bombers from Alaska, North Africa, and Okinawa. These planes would drop some 300 atomic bombs on Soviet military targets and population centers. This nuclear attack would be "of such staggering effectiveness" that the Soviet Union would no longer be capable of waging war. In the last phase of World War III, American and British troops stationed in Britain would mount an amphibious invasion across the English Channel and liberate Western Europe. A second United States army would strike the underbelly of the Soviet Union from North Africa through the Bosporus and into the Black Sea basin.

But the Soviets, too, looked for a technological solution to their vulnerability to heavy American bombers with atomic weapons. They worked feverishly to build long distance guided rockets, which were known as intercontinental ballistic missiles—ICBMS. In 1957 the Soviets shocked most Americans, and war planners in the Pentagon, by launching the first man-made satellite, *Sputnik*, into outer space. *Sputnik* was propelled by a rocket capable of delivering atomic bombs from Soviet bases into outer space and then to the United States in less than thirty minutes. *Sputnik* rendered Dropshot obsolete. (The plan was declassified in 1977.)

For the next three decades, American and Soviet war planners worked incessantly to devise new weapons and technologies to win World War III.

Prospects

Generals, it is said, always prepare for the war they just fought. Dropshot outlines a scenario that in many respects resembles the course of World War II, with the Soviet Union replacing Hitler's war machine: a sudden and crushing strike westward; occupation of continental Europe; and a two-pronged American invasion, staged from Great Britain and North Africa, to defeat the foe. The difference was technological: the United

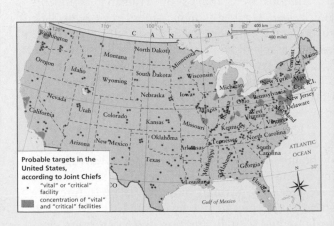

▲ In 1948 the strongly Republican *Chicago Daily Tribune* guessed its postelection editions before all the returns were in. For Truman, it was the perfect climax to his hard-won victory.

As for the liberals, in 1947 a group that believed Truman's containment policy a threat to world peace organized a new Progressive party and nominated former Vice President Henry A. Wallace. With two minor candidates sure to cut into the Democratic vote, the president's chances seemed minuscule.

Promising to "give 'em hell," Truman launched an aggressive whistle-stop campaign. Traveling by rail, he made several hundred informal but hard-hitting speeches. He excoriated the "do-nothing" Republican Congress, which had rejected his program and passed the Taft-Hartley Act, and he warned labor, farmers, and consumers that if Dewey won, Republican "gluttons of privilege" would do away with all the gains of the New Deal years.

Millions were moved by Truman's arguments and by his courageous fight against great odds. The success of the Berlin airlift during the presidential campaign helped him considerably, as did disaffection among normally Republican midwestern farmers. The Progressive party fell increasingly into the hands of communist sympathizers, driving away many liberals who might otherwise have supported Wallace.

Dewey's smug, lackluster speeches failed to attract independents. One party satirized his campaign by boiling it down to four platitudes: "Agriculture is important." "Our rivers are full of fish." "You cannot have freedom without liberty." "The future lies ahead." The president reinvigorated the New Deal coalition and won an amazing upset victory on election day. He collected 24.1 million votes to Dewey's

21.9 million, the two minor candidates being held to about 2.3 million. In the Electoral College his margin was a thumping 303 to 189.

Truman's victory encouraged him to press forward with what he called his Fair Deal program. He urged Congress to raise the minimum wage, fund an ambitious public housing program, develop a national health insurance system, and repeal the Taft-Hartley Act. However, relatively little of Truman's Fair Deal was enacted into law. Congress approved a federal housing program and measures increasing the minimum wage and social security benefits, but these were merely extensions of New Deal legislation.

CONTAINING COMMUNISM ABROAD

During Truman's second term the confrontation between the United States and the Soviet Union dominated the headlines. To strengthen ties with the European democracies, in April 1949 the North Atlantic Treaty was signed in Washington. The United States, Great Britain, France, Italy, Belgium, the Netherlands, Luxembourg, Denmark, Norway, Portugal, Iceland, and Canada[1] agreed "that an armed attack against one or more of them in Europe or North America shall be considered an attack against them all" and that in the event of such an attack each would take "individually and in concert with the other Parties, such action as it deems necessary, including the use of armed force." The pact established the North Atlantic Treaty Organization (NATO).

In September 1949 the Soviet Union detonated an atomic bomb. Truman had expressed doubts that the Soviets could build such sophisticated weapons. But when the explosion was confirmed, he called for rapid expansion of the American nuclear arsenal. He also asked his advisers to determine whether the United States should develop a new weapon thousands of times more destructive than atomic bombs. The "super" or hydrogen bomb would replicate the fusion process on the surface of the sun. The Atomic Energy Commission argued that there was no military use for hydrogen bombs, which would destroy hundreds of square miles as well as precipitate a dangerous arms race with the Soviet Union. The Joint Chiefs of Staff disagreed. Even if the hydrogen bomb could not be used in battle, they argued, its mere existence would intimidate enemies; and, the military

---

[1]In 1952, Greece and Turkey joined the alliance, and in 1954 West Germany.

men added, the Soviets would themselves build a hydrogen bomb whether or not the United States did so. (Unbeknownst to American leaders, Stalin was already developing a hydrogen bomb.) On January 31, 1950, Truman publicly announced that "though none wants to use it" he had no choice but to proceed with a hydrogen bomb.

In Asia the effort to contain communism in China had failed utterly. By the end of 1949 communist armies had administered a crushing defeat to the nationalists. The remnants of Chiang Kai-shek's forces fled to the island of Formosa, now called Taiwan. The "loss" of China to communism strengthened right-wing elements in the Republican party. They charged that Truman had not backed the Nationalists strongly enough and that he had stupidly underestimated Mao's dedication to the cause of world revolution.

Despite a superficial plausibility, neither charge made much sense. American opinion would not have supported military intervention, and such intervention unquestionably would have alienated the Chinese people. That *any* American action could have changed the outcome in China is unlikely. The United States probably gave the Nationalists too much aid rather than too little.

Containment had relied on American money, materials, and know-how, but not on American soldiers. In early 1950, Truman proposed to pare the budget by further reducing the nation's armed forces. Truman also called for a thorough review of the concept of containment. Dean Acheson, who recently had succeeded George Marshall as secretary of state, supervised the study. In March, it was submitted to the National Security Council, assigned a numerical designation (NSC-68), classified top secret, and sent to the nation's military and diplomatic leaders for review.

NSC-68 called for an enormous military expansion. The Soviet Union, it declared, was engaged in a worldwide assault on freedom: "A defeat of free institutions anywhere is a defeat everywhere." Instead of relying on other nations, the United States itself must develop sufficient military forces to stop communism from spreading *anywhere in the world*. Military spending therefore had to be increased by a staggering 350 percent to nearly $50 billion. If the Soviet Union failed to keep up with the American armed forces, it would no longer pose a threat, and if it attempted to match the high levels of American military spending, its less efficient economic system would collapse from the strain.

The document was submitted to Truman on April 7, 1950. He was initially cool to the idea and appalled by its cost. He had planned to cut $1 billion from the $14 billion military budget. Within a few months, however, events in Korea changed his mind.

DEBATING THE PAST

Did Truman needlessly exacerbate relations with the Soviet Union? Here Stalin applauds Soviet military might. Historian Thomas A. Bailey (1950), like most Americans at the time, blamed Stalin's takeover of Eastern Europe for the onset of the Cold War. In his view, Truman was right to contain Stalin.

But as the Cold War intensified and its costs mounted, historians looked more critically at Truman's actions. William Appleman Williams (1959) proposed that Truman had promoted worldwide containment of the Soviet Union chiefly to advance American interests abroad. Michael Hogan (1987) more subtly argued that the Marshall Plan put corporations at the center of the reconstruction of Europe. Walter La Feber (1967) and other revisionists found Truman's actions and rhetoric needlessly provocative.

John Lewis Gaddis (1972, 1982) rejected the contention that Truman was motivated by economic considerations. Truman's goal, rather, was to cobble together a military coalition capable of containing the Soviet Union militarily.

Historians focused on Truman because little was known of Stalin's thinking. But as Soviet archives opened up following the collapse of the Soviet Union, Gaddis revised his views. In *Now We Know* (1997), he emphasized Stalin's commitment to communist ideology. Truman had not goaded him into these beliefs. Thomas Mastny (1996) attributed the despot's behavior to his insecurity rather than his belief in communist ideology.

Thomas A. Bailey, *America Faces Russia* (1950), William Appleman Williams, *The Tragedy of American Diplomacy* (1959), Walter La Feber, *America, Russia and the Cold War* (1967), Michael Hogan, *Marshall Plan* (1987), John Lewis Gaddis, *The United States and the Origins of the Cold War* (1972), *Strategies of Containment* (1982), and *Now We Know* (1997), and Thomas Mastny, *The Cold War and Soviet Insecurity* (1996).

HOT WAR IN KOREA

After the Second World War the province of Korea was taken from Japan and divided at 38° north latitude into the Democratic People's Republic in the north, backed by the Soviet Union, and the Republic of Korea in the south, backed by the United States and the UN. Both powers withdrew their troops from the peninsula. The Soviets left behind a well-armed local force, but the Republic of Korea's army was small and ill trained.

American strategists, while seeking to "contain" communism in East Asia, had decided that military involvement on the Asian mainland was impracticable. America's first line of defense was to be its island bases in Japan and the Philippines. In a speech in January 1950 Acheson deliberately excluded Korea from what he described as the "defensive perimeter" of the United States in Asia. It was up to the South Koreans, backed by the UN, to protect themselves, Acheson said. This encouraged the North Koreans to attack.

In June 1950, when their armored divisions, led by 150 Soviet-made tanks, rumbled across the 38th parallel, the South Koreans were unable to stop them.

Truman was at his family home in Independence, Missouri, when Acheson telephoned with the news of the North Korean attack. "Dean," Truman explained, "we've got to stop the sons of bitches no matter what." Truman hastened to Washington. On the flight, he recalled how the communists in Korea were acting "just as Hitler, Mussolini, and the Japanese had acted ten, fifteen, and twenty years earlier." "If this were allowed to go unchallenged," he concluded, "it would mean a third world war, just as similar incidents had brought on the Second World War." With the backing of the UN Security Council (but without asking Congress to declare war), he sent American planes into battle.[2] Ground troops soon followed.

---

[2]The Soviet Union, which could have vetoed this action, was at the moment boycotting the Security Council because the UN had refused to give the Mao Zedong regime China's seat on that body.

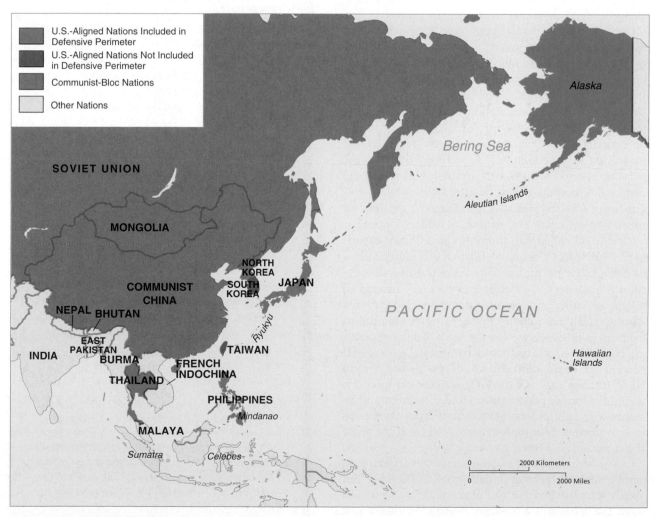

▲ **U.S. Defensive Perimeter in the Pacific, January 1950**

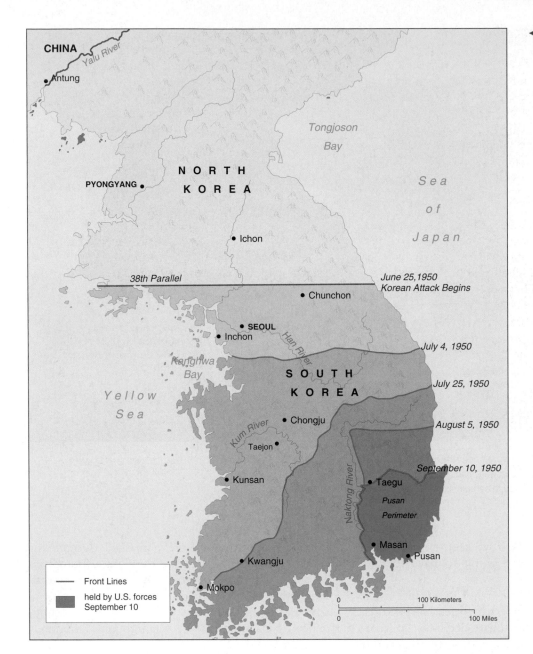

◄ **North Korean Offensive,
June–August 1950**

CHINA
Yalu River
Antung

NORTH KOREA

PYONGYANG

Tongjoson Bay

Sea of Japan

Ichon

38th Parallel

June 25, 1950
Korean Attack Begins

Chunchon

SEOUL
Inchon

Han River

Kanghwa Bay

July 4, 1950

SOUTH KOREA

July 25, 1950

Yellow Sea

Kum River

Chongju

August 5, 1950

Taejon

Naktong River

September 10, 1950

Kunsan

Taegu

Pusan Perimeter

Masan
Pusan

Kwangju

— Front Lines

held by U.S. forces
September 10

Mokpo

0   100 Kilometers

0   100 Miles

Truman also ordered the adoption of NSC-68 "as soon as feasible."

The Korean War, 1950-1953

Nominally the Korean War was a struggle between the invaders and the United Nations. General MacArthur, placed in command, flew the blue UN flag over his headquarters, and 16 nations supplied troops for his army. However, more than 90 percent of the forces were American. At first the North Koreans pushed them back rapidly, but in September a front was stabilized around the port of Pusan, at the southern tip of Korea. Then MacArthur executed a brilliant amphibious maneuver, striking at the west coast city of Inchon, about 50 miles south of

the 38th parallel. Outflanked, the North Koreans retreated in disorder. By October the battlefront had moved north of the 1945 boundary.

General MacArthur now proposed the conquest of North Korea, even if it meant bombing "privileged sanctuaries" on the Chinese side of the Korean border. Less sanguine military officials balked at taking on China but urged occupying North Korea to protect the future security of the south. A few of Truman's civilian advisers, the most important being George Kennan, opposed advancing beyond the 38th parallel, fearing intervention not only by the Red Chinese but also by the Soviets. "When we start walking inland from the tip of Korea, we have

▲ The Chinese counteroffensive of November 1950 caught the Americans by surprise and cut off many units. Here, U.S. Marines retreat southward, harassed by communist Chinese soldiers in the hills. American bombers blast a way through communist defenses to help the Americans escape.

about a 10,000 mile walk if we keep going," Kennan pointed out. "We are going to have to stop somewhere."

Truman authorized MacArthur to advance as far as the Yalu River, the boundary between North Korea and China. It was an unfortunate decision, an example of how power, once unleashed, so often gets out of hand. As the advance progressed, ominous reports came from north of the Yalu. Foreign Minister Chou En-lai warned that the Chinese would not "supinely" tolerate seeing their neighbors being "savagely invaded by imperialists." Chinese "volunteers" began to turn up among the captives taken by UN units.

Alarmed, Truman flew to Wake Island, in the Pacific, to confer with MacArthur, but the general, who had a low opinion of Asian soldiers, assured him that the Chinese would not dare to intervene. If they did, he added, his army would crush them easily; the war would be over by Christmas.

Seldom has a general miscalculated so badly. Ignoring intelligence reports and dividing his advancing units recklessly, he drove toward the Yalu. Suddenly, on November 26, 33 Chinese divisions, hidden in the interior mountains of Korea, smashed through the center of MacArthur's lines. Overnight a triumphant advance became a bloody, disorganized retreat. MacArthur now spoke of the "bottomless well of Chinese manpower" and justified his earlier confidence by claiming that he was fighting "an entirely new war."

The UN army rallied south of the 38th parallel, and MacArthur then urged that he be permitted to bomb Chinese installations north of the Yalu. He also suggested a naval blockade of the coast of China and the use of Chinese Nationalist troops. When Truman rejected these proposals on the ground that they would lead to a third world war, MacArthur, who tended to ignore the larger political aspects of the conflict, attempted to rouse Congress and the public against the president by openly criticizing administration policy. Truman ordered him to be silent, and when the general persisted, he removed him from command.

At first the Korean "police action" had been popular in the United States, but as the months passed and the casualties mounted, many citizens became

disillusioned and angry. To Americans accustomed to triumph and fond of oversimplifying complex questions, containment seemed, as its costs in blood and dollars mounted, a monumentally frustrating policy. Military men backed the president almost unanimously. General Omar N. Bradley, chairman of the Joint Chiefs of Staff, said that a showdown with communist China "would involve us in the wrong war, at the wrong place, at the wrong time and with the wrong enemy." In June 1951 the communists agreed to discuss an armistice in Korea, although the negotiations dragged on interminably. The war was unresolved when Truman left office: by the time it was over, it had produced 157,000 American casualties, including 54,200 dead.

If the Korean War persuaded Truman to adopt NSC-68, it also exposed the failings of the policy. By conceiving of communism as a monolithic force it tended to make it so, driving Red China and the Soviet Union into each other's arms. By committing American military forces to potential trouble spots throughout the world, it increased the likelihood they would prevail in none.

THE COMMUNIST ISSUE AT HOME

The Korean War highlighted the paradox that, at the pinnacle of its power, the influence of the United States in world affairs was declining. Its monopoly on nuclear weapons had been lost. China had passed into the communist orbit. Elsewhere in Asia and throughout Africa, new nations, formerly colonial possessions of the Western powers, were adopting a "neutralist" position in the Cold War. Despite the billions poured into armaments and foreign aid, national security seemed far from ensured.

Internal as well as external dangers loomed. Alarming examples of communist espionage in Canada, in Great Britain, and in the United States itself convinced many citizens that clever conspirators were everywhere at work undermining American security. Both the Republicans and conservative Democratic critics of Truman's domestic policies were charging that he was "soft" on communists.

There were never more than 100,000 communists in the United States, and party membership plummeted after the start of the Cold War. However, the possibility that a handful of spies could do enormous damage fueled a kind of panic that could be used for partisan purposes. In 1947, hoping to defuse the communists-in-government issue by being more zealous in pursuit of spies than his critics, Truman established a Loyalty Review Board to check up on government employees. The program made even sympathy for a long list of vaguely defined "totalitarian" or "subversive" organizations grounds for dismissal. During the following 10 years about 2700 government workers were discharged, only a relative handful of them for legitimate reasons. A much larger number resigned.

In 1948 Whittaker Chambers, an editor of *Time* who had formerly been a communist, charged that Alger Hiss, president of the Carnegie Endowment for International Peace and a former State Department official, had been a communist in the 1930s. Hiss denied the charge and sued Chambers for libel. Chambers then produced microfilms purporting to show that Hiss had copied classified documents for dispatch to Moscow. Hiss could not be indicted for espionage because of the statute of limitations; instead he was charged with perjury. His first trial resulted in a hung jury; his second, ending in January 1950, in conviction and a five-year jail term.

If a distinguished official such as Hiss had been disloyal, anything seemed possible. The case fed the fears of those who believed in the existence of a powerful communist underground in the United States. The disclosure in February 1950 that a British scientist, Klaus Fuchs, had betrayed atomic secrets to the Soviets heightened these fears, as did the arrest and conviction of his American associate, Harry Gold, and two other Americans, Julius and Ethel Rosenberg, on the same charge.

Although they were not major spies and the information they revealed was not important, the Rosenbergs were executed, to the consternation of many liberals in the United States and elsewhere. However, information gathered by other spies had speeded the Soviet development of nuclear weapons. This fact encouraged some Republicans to press the communists-in-government issue hard.

McCARTHYISM

In February 1950 an obscure senator, Joseph R. McCarthy of Wisconsin, introduced this theme in a speech to the even less well known Ohio County Republican Women's Club of Wheeling, West Virginia. "The reason we find ourselves in a position of impotency," he stated, "is not because our only powerful potential enemy has sent men to invade our shores, but rather because of the traitorous actions of those who have been treated so well by this nation." The State Department, he added, was "infested" with communists. "I have here in my hand a list of 205—a

DOCUMENT

McCarthy, Wheeling, West Virginia Speech

▲ Senator Joseph McCarthy's unsubstantiated charges of communist infiltration of the army led finally to his downfall.

part of a "conspiracy so immense and an infamy so black as to dwarf any previous venture in the history of man."

McCarthy was totally unscrupulous. The "big lie" was his most effective weapon: The enormity of his charges and the status of his targets convinced thousands that there must be some truth in what he was saying. Nevertheless, his crude tactics would have failed if the public had not been so worried about communism. The worries were caused by the reality of Soviet military power, the attack on Korea, the loss of the nuclear monopoly, and the stories about spies, some of them true.

list of names that were known to the Secretary of State as being members of the Communist Party and who nevertheless are still working and shaping . . . policy."[3]

Why this speech caused a sensation has never been satisfactorily explained. McCarthy had no shred of evidence to back up these statements, as a Senate committee headed by the conservative Democrat Millard Tydings of Maryland soon demonstrated. He never exposed a single spy or secret American communist. One reporter quipped that McCarthy could not tell Karl Marx from Groucho Marx.

But because of the government loyalty program, the Hiss case, and other recent events, thousands of people were too eager to believe McCarthy to listen to reason. Within a few weeks he was the most talked of person in Congress. Inhibited neither by scruples nor by logic, he lashed out in every direction, attacking international experts like Professor Owen Lattimore of Johns Hopkins University and diplomats such as John S. Service and John Carter Vincent, who were already under attack for having courageously pointed out the deficiencies of the Chiang Kai-shek regime during the Chinese civil war.

When McCarthy's victims indignantly denied his charges, he distracted the public with still more sensational accusations directed at other innocents. Even General Marshall, whose patriotism was beyond question, was subjected to McCarthy's abuse. The general, he said, was "steeped in falsehood,"

DWIGHT D. EISENHOWER

As the 1952 presidential election approached, Truman's popularity was again at low ebb. Senator McCarthy attacked him relentlessly for his handling of the Korean conflict and his "mistreatment" of General MacArthur. In choosing their candidate, the Republicans passed over the twice-defeated Dewey and their most prominent leader, Senator Robert A. Taft of Ohio, an outspoken conservative, and nominated General Dwight D. Eisenhower.

Eisenhower's popularity did not grow merely out of his achievements in World War II. Although a West Pointer (class of 1915), he struck most persons as anything but warlike. After the bristly, combative Truman, his genial personality and evident desire to avoid controversy proved widely appealing. In his reluctance to seek political office, Eisenhower reminded the country of George Washington, whereas his seeming ignorance of current political issues was no more a handicap to his campaign than the similar ignorance of Jackson and Grant in their times. People "liked Ike" because his management of the Allied armies suggested that he would be equally competent as head of the complex federal government. His promise during the campaign to go to Korea if elected to try to bring the war to an end was a political masterstroke.

The Democrats nominated Governor Adlai E. Stevenson of Illinois, whose grandfather had been vice president under Grover Cleveland. Stevenson's unpretentiousness was appealing, and his witty, urbane speeches captivated intellectuals. In retrospect,

---

[3]McCarthy was speaking from rough notes, and no one made an accurate record of his words. The exact number mentioned has long been in dispute. On other occasions he said there were 57 and 81 "card-carrying" communists in the State Department.

▲ Many critics lampooned Eisenhower for his banal amusements. A popular bumper sticker read: "BEN HOGAN [a famous golfer] FOR PRESIDENT. IF WE'RE GOING TO HAVE A GOLFER FOR PRESIDENT, LET'S HAVE A GOOD ONE." Others have viewed Eisenhower's passion for golf as characteristic of his presidential style: methodical, prudent, and, when in the rough, disarmingly shrewd.

however, it is clear that he had not the remotest chance of defeating the popular Eisenhower. His foes turned his strongest assets against him, denouncing his humor as frivolity, characterizing his appreciation of the complexities of life as self-doubt, and tagging his intellectual followers "eggheads," an appellation that effectively caricatured the balding, slope-shouldered, somewhat endomorphic candidate. The result was a Republican landslide: Eisenhower received almost 34 million votes to Stevenson's 27 million, and in the Electoral College his margin was 442 to 89.

On the surface, Eisenhower seemed the antithesis of Truman. The Republicans had charged the Democratic administration with being wasteful and extravagant, and Eisenhower planned to run his administration on sound business principles. He spoke scornfully of "creeping socialism," called for more local control of government affairs, and promised to reduce federal spending to balance the budget and cut taxes. He believed that by battling with Congress and pressure groups over the details of legislation, his immediate predecessors had sacrificed part of their status as chief representative of the American people. Like Washington, he tried to avoid being caught up in narrow partisan conflicts. Like Washington, he was not always able to do so.

Eisenhower was neither a reactionary nor a fool. He was unwilling to do away with existing social and economic legislation or to cut back on military expenditures. Some economists claimed that he reacted too slowly in dealing with business recessions and that he showed insufficient concern for speeding the rate of national economic growth. Yet he adopted an almost Keynesian approach to economic problems; that is, he tried to check downturns in the business cycle by stimulating the economy.

Eisenhower approved the extension of social security to an additional 10 million persons; created a new Department of Health, Education, and Welfare; began the St. Lawrence Seaway project; and in 1955 came out for federal support of education and a highway construction act that eventually produced a 40,000-mile network of superhighways covering every state in the Union. His somewhat doctrinaire belief in decentralization and private enterprise reduced the effectiveness of his social welfare measures, but on balance, he proved to be an excellent politician. He knew how to be flexible without compromising his basic values. His "conservatism" became first "dynamic conservatism" and then "progressive moderation." He summarized his attitude by saying that he was liberal in dealing with individuals but conservative "when talking about . . . the individual's pocketbook." He hoped to strengthen the moderate faction of his party, but despite his extraordinary popularity, he did not succeed in persuading many rightwing Republicans that this was a good idea.

THE EISENHOWER-DULLES FOREIGN POLICY

The American people, troubled and uncertain over the stalemate in Korea, counted on Eisenhower to find a way to employ the nation's immense strength constructively. The new president shared the general feeling that a change of tactics in foreign affairs was needed. He counted on his secretary of state to solve the practical problems.

His choice, John Foster Dulles, was a lawyer with considerable diplomatic experience. He had been an

▲ Detonation of 11-megaton hydrogen bomb over Bikini atoll in March, 1954. One megaton had the explosive power of one million tons of TNT. (The bomb that destroyed Hiroshima had the equivalent of 12,500 tons of TNT.)

outspoken critic of Truman's foreign policy. In a May 1952 article in *Life* entitled "A Policy of Boldness," he argued that global military containment was both expensive and ineffective: "We cannot build a 20,000-mile Maginot Line or match the Red armies man for man, gun for gun, and tank for tank at any particular time or place their general staff selects." Instead of waiting for the communist powers to make a move and then "containing" them, the United States should put more emphasis on nuclear bombs and less on conventional weapons. Such a "new look" military would be cheaper to maintain than a force of conventional weapons and a large standing army, and it would prevent the United States from being caught up in "local" conflicts like the Korean War. The nation's military

forces, spearheaded by its formidable nuclear arsenal, would serve as "a deterrent of war instead of a mere means of waging war after we got into it."

Korea offered the first test of his views. After Eisenhower's postelection trip to Korea failed to bring an end to the war, Dulles signaled his willingness to use tactical nuclear weapons in Korea by showily transferring nuclear warheads from the United States mainland to bomber units stationed in East Asia. He also issued a calculatedly vague warning about tough new measures. Several weeks later, in July 1953, the Chinese signed an armistice that ended hostilities but left Korea divided. The administration interpreted the softening of the Chinese position as proof that the nuclear threat had worked. (Dulles was apparently mistaken about the effectiveness of his Korean gambit. In recent years, Chinese officials have said that they were unaware at the time of the American nuclear threats.)

Emboldened by his evident triumph, Dulles again brandished the nuclear threat. Chiang Kai-shek had stationed 90,000 soldiers—one-third of his army—in Quemoy and Matsu, two small islands located a few miles from mainland China. In 1954 the Chinese communists began shelling the islands, presumably in preparation to invade them. Chiang appealed for American protection, warning that loss of the islands would bring about the collapse of Nationalist China. Dulles concurred that the consequences throughout East Asia would be "catastrophic." At a press conference in 1955 Eisenhower announced his willingness to use nuclear weapons to defend the islands, "just exactly as you would use a bullet or anything else." The Chinese communists backed down.

Massive retaliation succeeded, further, in reducing the defense budget. The reliance on a nuclear threat allowed Eisenhower to pare another half million men from the armed forces, saving $4 billion annually. On balance, however, Dulles's strategy was flawed, and many of his schemes were preposterous. Above all, massive retaliation made little sense when the Soviet Union possessed nuclear weapons as powerful as those of the United States.

VIDEO
"Duck and Cover"

McCarthy Self-Destructs

Although the State Department was now controlled by Dulles, a Republican and hard-line anticommunist, Senator McCarthy moderated his attacks on the department not a jot. In 1953 its overseas information program received his special attention.

AUDIO
Joseph P. McCarthy Speech

But McCarthy finally overreached himself. Early in 1954 he turned his guns on the army, accusing

▲ Senator Joe McCarthy and his aide Roy Cohn listen to testimony on communism in government in April, 1954. Cohn, a tough, young lawyer who had made a reputation prosecuting suspected communists in Manhattan, intimidated some people by threatening to make public their homosexuality; yet he was himself a homosexual who steadfastly denied it; in 1986 he died of AIDS. His story was symbolized in Tony Kushner's Pulitzer Prize–winning play *Angels in America* (1993).

Pentagon officials of trying to blackmail his committee. The resulting Army-McCarthy hearings, televised before the country, proved the senator's undoing. For weeks his dark scowl, his blind combativeness, and his disregard for every human value stood exposed for millions to see. When the hearings ended in June 1954 after some million words of testimony, his spell had been broken.

The Senate, with President Eisenhower, who despised McCarthy but who considered it beneath his dignity as president to "get into the gutter with that guy," applying pressure behind the scenes, at last moved to censure him in December 1954. This reproof completed the destruction of his influence. Although he continued to issue statements and wild charges, the country no longer listened. In 1957 he died of cirrhosis of the liver.

ASIAN POLICY AFTER KOREA

Shortly after an armistice was finally arranged in Korea in July 1953, new trouble erupted far to the south in the former French colony of Indochina. Nationalist rebels led by the communist Ho Chi Minh had been harassing the French in Vietnam, one of the three puppet kingdoms (the others were Laos and Cambodia) fashioned by France in Indochina after the defeat of the Japanese. When China recognized the rebels, who were known as the Vietminh, and supplied them with arms, President Truman countered with economic and military assistance to the French, and President Eisenhower continued and expanded this assistance.

Early in 1954 Ho Chi Minh's troops trapped and besieged a French army in the remote stronghold of Dien Bien Phu. Faced with the loss of 20,000 soldiers, France asked the United States to commit its air force to the battle.

By this time the United States was paying about three-quarters of France's expenses in Vietnam, but Eisenhower refused to send in planes. Although the likelihood of communist control of Vietnam worried him, his military judgment warned against such action. The idea of using American air strikes, he believed, was "just silly." The communists were "secreted all around in the jungle. How are we, in a few air strikes, to defeat them?"

In May the French garrison at Dien Bien Phu surrendered. In July France, Great Britain, the Soviet Union, and China signed an agreement dividing Vietnam along the 17th parallel. France withdrew from the area. The northern sector became the Democratic Republic of Vietnam, controlled by Ho Chi Minh; the southern remained in the hands of the emperor, Bao Dai. An election to settle the future of all Vietnam was scheduled for 1956.

When it seemed likely that the communists would win that election, Ngo Dinh Diem, a conservative anticommunist, overthrew Bao Dai and became president of South Vietnam. The United States supplied his government liberally with aid. The planned election was never held, and Vietnam remained divided.

Dulles responded to the diplomatic setback in Vietnam by establishing the Southeast Asia Treaty Organization (SEATO), but only three Asian nations—the Philippine Republic, which was granted independence in 1947, Thailand, and Pakistan—joined this alliance.[4]

ISRAEL AND THE MIDDLE EAST

The extermination of six million European Jews by the Nazis strengthened Jewish claims to a homeland and intensified pressure to allow hundreds of thousands of Jewish refugees to immigrate to Palestine, which was governed by Great Britain according to a

---

[4]The other signatories were Great Britain, France, the United States, Australia, and New Zealand.

League of Nations mandate. But the influx of Jewish settlers, and their calls for creation of a Jewish state (Israel), provoked Palestinian and Arab leaders. Fighting broke out. President Truman angered Arab leaders by endorsing the partition of the region into Israel and a Palestinian state. In 1947, the United Nations voted for partition and on May 14, 1948, the State of Israel was established. Within hours, Truman recognized its sovereignty.

Then Arab armies from Egypt, Jordan, Iraq, Syria, and Lebanon attacked Israel. Although badly outnumbered, the Israelis were better organized and better armed than the Arabs and drove them off with relative ease. With them departed nearly a million local Arabs, thereby creating a desperate refugee problem in nearby countries.

President Truman had consistently placed support for Israel before other considerations in the Middle East, partly because of the conviction that survivors of the Nazi holocaust were entitled to a country of their own and partly because of the political importance of the Jewish vote in the United States. Dulles and Eisenhower tried to restore balance by deemphasizing American support of Israel. They hoped to mollify the Arabs. Of increasing importance to the United States were the seas of oil that lay beneath the Middle East's deserts. Iran, Iraq, Kuwait, and Saudi Arabia sat upon nearly 60 percent of the world's known reserves. Gas-hungry Americans could ill-afford to alienate the Arab world.

In 1952 a revolution in Egypt had overthrown the dissolute King Farouk. Colonel Gamal Abdel Nasser emerged as the strongman of Egypt. The United States was prepared to lend Nasser money to build a huge dam on the Nile at Aswan. The dam was to be the key to an Egyptian irrigation program and a vast source of electric power. However, Eisenhower would not sell Egypt arms. The communists would.

For this reason Nasser drifted toward the communist orbit. When Eisenhower then decided not to finance the Aswan Dam, Nasser responded by nationalizing the Suez Canal. This move galvanized the British and French. Influenced by Dulles's argument that Egypt could be made an ally by cajolery, the British had acceded in 1954 to Nasser's demand that they evacuate their military base at Suez. Now their traditional lifeline to South Asia was at Egypt's mercy. In conjunction with the French, and without consulting the United States, the British in 1956 decided to take back the canal by force. The Israelis, alarmed by repeated Arab hit-and-run raids, also attacked Egypt.

Events moved swiftly. Israeli armored columns crushed the Egyptian army in the Sinai Peninsula in a matter of days. France and Britain occupied Port Said, at the northern end of the canal. Nasser sank ships to block the channel. In the UN the Soviet Union and the United States introduced resolutions calling for a cease-fire. Both were vetoed by Britain and France.

Then Nikita Khrushchev, who had become First Secretary of the Communist party of the Soviet Union following Stalin's death in 1953, threatened to send "volunteers" to Egypt and launch atomic missiles against France and Great Britain if they did not withdraw. Eisenhower also demanded that the invaders pull out of Egypt. In London large crowds demonstrated against their own government. On November 6, only nine days after the first Israeli units invaded Egypt, Prime Minister Anthony Eden, haggard and shaken, announced a cease-fire. Israel withdrew its troops. The crisis subsided as rapidly as it had arisen.

The United States had won a measure of respect in the Arab countries, but at what cost? Its major allies had been humiliated. Their ill-timed attack had enabled the Soviet Union to recover much of the prestige it had lost as a result of its brutal suppression of a Hungarian revolt that had broken out a week before the Suez fiasco.

When the Soviet Union seemed likely to profit from its "defense" of Egypt in the crisis, the president announced the Eisenhower Doctrine (January 1957), which stated that the United States was "prepared to use armed force" anywhere in the Middle East against "aggression from any country controlled by international communism." In practice, the Eisenhower Doctrine amounted to little more than a restatement of the containment policy.

EISENHOWER AND KHRUSHCHEV

In 1956 Eisenhower was reelected, defeating Adlai Stevenson even more decisively than he had in 1952. Despite evident satisfaction with their leader, however, the American people were in a sober mood. Hopes of pushing back the Soviet Union with clever stratagems and moral fervor were fading. Although the United States detonated the first hydrogen bomb in November 1952, the Soviets followed suit within six months. The Cold War between the superpowers had become yet more chilling.

Stalin died in March 1953, and after a period of internal conflict within the Kremlin, Nikita Khrushchev emerged as the new master of the Soviet Union. Khrushchev was perhaps the most confusing (and, arguably, confused) figure of the Cold War. Crude and bibulous, prone to violent tantrums and tearful histrionics, he delighted in shocking people with words and gestures. In the most famous of these, he pounded his shoe on the table during a debate at

the United Nations. He appealed to the anti-Western prejudices of countries just emerging from the yoke of colonialism, offering them economic aid and pointing to Soviet achievements in science and technology as proof that communism would vanquish the capitalist system without troubling to destroy it by force. Although a product of the Soviet system, Khrushchev recognized its deep failings and resolved to purge it of Stalinism. He released political prisoners from Stalin's gulags, or political prison camps, and told wide-eyed party functionaries that Stalin had committed monstrous crimes.

Eisenhower, a seasoned analyst of military capabilities, understood that Khrushchev's antics were meant to conceal the Soviet Union's many weaknesses: the bitter opposition to Soviet rule among peoples of Eastern Europe; the deficiencies of the overcentralized Soviet economy, especially agriculture; and the bureaucratic ossification of its armed forces. The Soviet Union had kept up a good pace in the nuclear arms race but had not attained nuclear parity. Thousands of American airplanes were based in Europe, northern Africa, and Turkey, placing most Soviet targets within easy range. Heavy Soviet bombers, on the other hand, faced the daunting prospect of lumbering thousands of miles over the Arctic and Pacific Oceans to reach American targets, harried all the while by lightning-fast fighter planes. The United States would win (whatever that meant) any nuclear war.

But this advantage disappeared in the exhaust cloud of a Soviet rocket, launched on October 4, 1957, that carried a 184-pound capsule named *Sputnik* far above the atmosphere into earth orbit. Soon, American policymakers knew, Soviet missiles capable of reaching American soil would be tipped with nuclear warheads. The nation's far-flung network of bomber defenses had become obsolete, and with it the strategy of massive retaliation.

Several weeks later Khrushchev rubbed hard at the rawest sore in the American psyche: the anguished memory of Pearl Harbor. In an interview with publisher William Randolph Hearst, Jr., Khrushchev blustered that the Soviet Union could launch 10 or 20 intercontinental missiles with nuclear warheads "tomorrow." He boasted that the American military was no match for the Soviet military behemoth. This was nonsense and Eisenhower knew it. Yet to point out the weaknesses of the Soviet military—to call Khrushchev's bluff—was potentially to goad the unstable Soviet leader to rash action. While critics at home flayed Eisenhower for allowing a "missile gap" with the Soviet Union, the president testily reassured the American people that they had little to fear, but otherwise remained silent.

▲ Vice President Richard M. Nixon and Soviet leader Nikita Khrushchev engaged in their "kitchen debate" over the future of capitalism at a Moscow trade fair in 1959. Although this encounter did little to advance United States–Soviet relations, it established Nixon's credentials as a tough negotiator.

In 1957 Dulles underwent surgery for abdominal cancer, and in April 1959 he had to resign. The next month he was dead. Eisenhower never had avoided making decisions in foreign policy, but now he personally took over much of the actual conduct of diplomacy. The key to his approach was restraint; he exercised commendable caution in every crisis. Like U. S. Grant, he was a soldier who hated war. From Korea through the crises over Indochina, Hungary, and Suez, he avoided risky new commitments. His behavior, like his temperament, contrasted sharply with that of the aggressive, oratorically overwrought Dulles.

World opinion was insistent that the great powers stop making and testing nuclear weapons, for every test explosion was contaminating the atmosphere with radioactive debris that threatened the future of all life. Unresolved controversies, especially the argument over divided Germany, might erupt at any moment into a globe-shattering war.

Neither the United States nor the Soviet Union dared ignore these dangers; each therefore adopted a more accommodating attitude. In the summer of 1959 Vice President Richard M. Nixon visited the Soviet Union, and his counterpart, Vice Premier Anastas I. Mikoyan, toured the United States. Although Nixon's visit was marred by a heated argument with Khrushchev about the virtues of their respective systems, conducted before a gaping crowd in the kitchen of a model American home that had been set up at a Moscow fair, these visits were encouraging.

In September Khrushchev came to America. His cross-country tour had its full share of comic contretemps—when denied permission to visit Disneyland

because authorities feared they could not protect him properly on the grounds, the heavy-handed Khrushchev accused the United States, only half humorously, of concealing rocket-launching pads there. But the general effect of his visit seemed beneficial. At the end of his stay, he and President Eisenhower agreed to convene a new four-power summit conference.

The meeting never took place. On May 1, 1960, high over Sverdlovsk, an industrial center deep in the Soviet Union, an American U–2 spy plane was shot down by antiaircraft fire. The pilot of the plane survived the crash, and he confessed to being a spy. His cameras contained aerial photographs of Soviet military installations. When Eisenhower assumed full responsibility for the mission, Khrushchev accused the United States of "piratical" and "cowardly" acts of aggression. The summit conference was canceled. In September, Khrushchev told the United Nations that the Soviet Union was turning out nuclear missiles "like sausages from an automatic machine."

LATIN AMERICA AROUSED

Events in Latin America compounded Eisenhower's difficulties. During World War II the United States, needing Latin American raw materials, had supplied its southern neighbors liberally with economic aid. In the period following victory a hemispheric mutual defense pact was signed at Rio de Janeiro in September 1947, and the following year the Organization of American States (OAS) came into being. In the OAS, decisions were reached by a two-thirds vote; the United States had neither a veto nor any special position.

But as the Cold War progressed, the United States neglected Latin American questions. Economic problems plagued the region, and in most nations reactionary governments reigned. Radical Latin Americans accused the United States of supporting cliques of wealthy tyrants, whereas conservatives blamed insufficient American economic aid for the plight of the poor.

Eisenhower, eager to improve relations, stepped up economic assistance. Resistance to communism nonetheless continued to receive first priority. In 1954 the government of Jacobo Arbenz Guzman in Guatemala began to import Soviet weapons. The United States promptly dispatched arms to neighboring Honduras. Within a month an army led by an exiled Guatemalan officer marched into the country from Honduras and overthrew Arbenz. Elsewhere in Latin America, Eisenhower, as Truman had before him, continued to support regimes that were kept in power by the local military.

The depth of Latin American resentment of the United States became clear in the spring of 1958,

when Vice President Nixon made what was supposed to be a goodwill tour of South America. Everywhere he was met with hostility. In Lima, Peru, he was mobbed; in Caracas, Venezuela, students pelted him with eggs and stones. He had to abandon the remainder of his trip. For the first time the American people gained some inkling of Latin American opinion and the social and economic troubles that lay behind it.

Events in Cuba demonstrated that there was no easy solution to Latin American problems. In 1959 a revolutionary movement headed by Fidel Castro overthrew Fulgencio Batista, one of the most noxious of the Latin American dictators. Eisenhower recognized the Castro government at once, but the Cuban leader soon began to criticize the United States in highly colored speeches. Castro confiscated American property without providing adequate compensation, suppressed civil liberties, and entered into close relations with the Soviet Union. After he negotiated a trade agreement with the Soviet Union in February 1960, which enabled the Russians to obtain Cuban sugar at bargain rates, the United States retaliated by prohibiting the importation of Cuban sugar into America.

Khrushchev then announced that if the United States intervened in Cuba, he would defend the country with atomic weapons. "The Monroe Doctrine has outlived its time," Khrushchev warned. Shortly before the end of his second term, Eisenhower broke off diplomatic relations with Cuba.

THE POLITICS OF CIVIL RIGHTS

During Eisenhower's presidency a major change occurred in the legal status of American blacks. Eisenhower had relatively little to do with this change, which was part of a broad shift in attitudes toward the rights of minorities in democracies. After 1945 the question of racial equality took on special importance because of the ideological competition with communism. Evidence of color prejudice in the United States damaged the nation's image, particularly in Asia and Africa, where the United States and the Soviet Union were competing for influence. An awareness of foreign criticism of American racial attitudes, along with resentment that almost a century after the Emancipation Proclamation they were still second-class citizens, produced a growing militancy among American blacks. At the same time, fears of communist subversion in the United States led to the repression of the rights of many white citizens. Even before McCarthy's fateful Wheeling speech, Congress contemplated a crackdown on suspected communists. In 1950, over Truman's veto, it passed an Internal Security Act (better known as the McCarran Act), which required every

"communist-front organization" to register with the attorney general. Members of such organizations were barred from defense work and from traveling abroad. The law even provided for construction of internment camps in the event of a national emergency.

Under Eisenhower, while the McCarthy hysteria reached its peak and declined, the government compiled a spotty record on civil rights. The search for subversive federal employees continued. The refusal to grant security clearance to Oppenheimer, one of the fathers of the atomic bomb, on the grounds that he had associated with communists and communist sympathizers, was the most glaring instance of the administration's catering to anticommunist extremists, for it was based on the supposition that Oppenheimer could be denied access to discoveries he had helped to make possible. Eisenhower completed the integration of the armed forces begun by Truman, but he was temperamentally incapable of a frontal assault on the racial problem. This was done by the Supreme Court, which interjected itself into the civil rights controversy in dramatic fashion in 1954.

Under pressure of litigation sponsored by the NAACP, the Court had been gradually undermining the "separate but equal" principle laid down in *Plessy* v. *Ferguson* in 1896, at least insofar as it applied to higher education. In 1938 it ordered the University of Missouri law school admit a black student because no law school for blacks existed in the state. This decision gradually forced some southern states to admit blacks to advanced programs. "You can't build a cyclotron for one student," the president of the University of Oklahoma confessed when the Court, in 1948, ordered Oklahoma to provide equal facilities. Two years later, when Texas actually attempted to create a separate law school for a single black applicant, the Court ruled that truly equal education could not be provided under such circumstances.

Brown v. Board of Education of Topeka, Kansas

In 1953 President Eisenhower appointed California's Governor Earl Warren chief justice of the United States Supreme Court. Convinced that the Court must take the offensive in the cause of civil rights, Warren succeeded in welding his associates into a unit on this question. In 1954 an NAACP-sponsored case, *Brown* v. *Board of Education of Topeka*, came up for decision. The NAACP lawyer,

▲ Angry jeers from whites rain down on Elizabeth Eckford, one of the first black students to arrive for registration at Little Rock's Central High School in 1957. State troops turned black students away from the school until President Eisenhower overruled the state decision and called in the National Guard to enforce integration.

Thurgood Marshall, challenging the "separate but equal" doctrine, submitted a mass of sociological evidence to show that the mere fact of segregation made equal education impossible and did serious psychological damage to both black and white children. Speaking for a unanimous Court, Warren reversed the *Plessy* decision. "In the field of public education, the doctrine of 'separate but equal' has no place," he declared. "Separate educational facilities are inherently unequal." The next year the Court ordered the states to end segregation "with all deliberate speed."

Despite these decisions, few districts in the southern and border states tried to integrate their schools. Many white Southerners who deplored the way blacks were treated in the region nonetheless opposed integrating the schools. As late as September 1956, barely 700 of the South's 10,000 school districts had been desegregated. The region became more alienated from the rest of the nation than at any time since Reconstruction.

White citizens' councils dedicated to all-out opposition sprang up throughout the South. When the school board of Clinton, Tennessee, integrated the local high school in September 1956, a mob rioted in protest, shouting "Kill the niggers!" and destroying the property of blacks. The school was kept open with the help of the National Guard until segregationists blew up the building with dynamite. In Virginia the governor announced a plan for "massive resistance" to integration that denied state aid to local school systems that wished to desegregate. When the University of Alabama admitted a single black woman in 1956, riots

broke out. University officials forced the student to withdraw temporarily and then expelled her when she complained more forcefully than they deemed proper.

President Eisenhower thought equality for blacks could not be obtained by government edict. He said that the Court's ruling must be obeyed, but he did little to discourage southern resistance to desegregation. "I am convinced that the Supreme Court decision set back progress in the South at least fifteen years," he remarked to one of his advisers. "The fellow who tries to tell me you can do these things by force is just plain nuts."

However, in 1957 events compelled him to act. When the school board of Little Rock, Arkansas, opened Central High School to a handful of black students, the governor of the state, Orval M. Faubus, called out the National Guard to prevent them from attending. Unruly crowds taunted the students and their parents. Eisenhower could not ignore the direct flouting of federal authority. After the mayor of Little Rock sent him a telegram saying, in part, "situation is out of control and police cannot disperse the mob," he dispatched 1000 paratroopers to Little Rock and summoned 10,000 National Guardsmen to federal duty, thus removing them from Faubus's control. The black students then began to attend class. A token force of soldiers was stationed at Central High for the entire school year to protect them.

Resistance strengthened the determination of blacks and many northern whites to make the South comply with the desegregation decision. Besides pressing cases in the federal courts, leaders of the movement organized a voter registration drive among southern blacks. As a result, the administration introduced what became the Civil Rights Act of 1957. It authorized the attorney general to obtain injunctions to stop election officials from interfering with blacks' efforts to register and vote. The law also established a Civil Rights Commission with broad investigative powers and a Civil Rights Division in the Department of Justice. Enforcing this Civil Rights Act was another matter. A later study of a typical county in Alabama revealed that between 1957 and 1960 more than 700 blacks with high school diplomas were rejected as unqualified by white election officials when they sought to register.

THE ELECTION OF 1960

As the end of his second term approached, Eisenhower somewhat reluctantly endorsed Vice President Richard Nixon as the Republican candidate to succeed him. Nixon had originally skyrocketed to national prominence by exploiting the public fear of communist subversion. "Traitors in the high councils of our government," he charged in 1950, "have made sure that the deck is stacked on the Soviet side of the diplomatic tables." In 1947 he was an obscure young congressman from California; in 1950 he won a seat in the Senate; two years later Eisenhower chose him as his running mate.

Whether Nixon believed what he was saying at this period of his career is unclear. He seemed wedded to the theory that politicians should slavishly represent their constituents' opinions rather than hold to their own views. He projected an image of almost frantic earnestness, yet he pursued a flexible course more suggestive of calculation than sincerity. Reporters generally had a low opinion of Nixon, and independent voters seldom found him attractive. He was always controversial, distrusted by liberals even when he supported liberal measures.

The Democrats nominated Senator John F. Kennedy of Massachusetts. His chief rival for the nomination, Lyndon B. Johnson of Texas, the Senate majority leader, became his running mate. Kennedy was the son of Joseph P. Kennedy, a wealthy businessman who had served as ambassador to Great Britain under Franklin Roosevelt. An indifferent student at Harvard, Kennedy in his junior year—1939—traveled with his father to Europe. When Hitler attacked Poland a few months later, Kennedy had the topic for his senior thesis: "Appeasement at Munich," in which he chastised British and American leaders in the 1920s and 1930s for a lack of foresight and resolve. Published in 1940 as *Why England Slept*, the book received favorable reviews and was briefly a best seller. During World War II, Kennedy served in the Pacific, captaining a torpedo boat. When the boat was sliced in two by a Japanese destroyer, Kennedy showed personal courage in rescuing his men. Besides wealth, intelligence, good looks, and charm, Kennedy had the advantage of his Irish-Catholic ancestry, a particularly valuable asset in heavily Catholic Massachusetts. After three terms in the House, he moved on to the Senate in 1952.

After his landslide reelection in 1958, only Kennedy's religion seemed to limit his political future. No Catholic had ever been elected president, and the defeat of Alfred E. Smith in 1928 had convinced most students of politics (including Smith) that none ever would be elected. Nevertheless, influenced by Kennedy's victories in the Wisconsin and West Virginia primaries—the latter establishing him as an effective campaigner in a predominantly Protestant region—the Democratic convention nominated him.

Kennedy had not been a particularly liberal congressman. He was not involved in the civil rights movement (which was not a major issue in the presidential campaign). He enthusiastically endorsed the Cold War and indicted the Eisenhower administration

for falling behind the Soviet Union in the race to build missiles. He admitted frankly that he liked Senator Joseph McCarthy and thought that "he may have something" in his campaign against supposed communists in government. However, as a presidential candidate, he sought to appear more forward-looking. He stressed his youth and "vigor" (a favorite word) and promised to open a "New Frontier" for the country. Nixon ran on the Eisenhower record, which he promised to extend in liberal directions.

A series of television debates between the candidates helped Kennedy by enabling him to demonstrate his maturity and mastery of the issues. Although both candidates laudably avoided it, the religious issue was important. His Catholicism helped Kennedy in eastern urban areas but injured him in many farm districts and throughout the West. Kennedy's victory, 303 to 219 in the Electoral College, was paper-thin in the popular vote, 34,227,000 to 34,109,000.

Although Kennedy was rich, white, and a member of the upper crust by any definition, his was a victory of minority groups (Jews, blacks, and blue-collar "ethnics" as well as Catholics gave him overwhelming support) over the traditional white Protestant majority, which went as heavily for Nixon as it had four years earlier for Eisenhower.

VIDEO

Kennedy-Nixon Debate

MILESTONES

1944	Congress provides subsidies to veterans in GI Bill of Rights	**1952**	Dwight D. Eisenhower is elected president
1946	UN creates Atomic Energy Commission	**1953**	John Foster Dulles institutes "New Look" nuclear-based foreign policy
1947	Taft-Hartley Act regulates unions and labor disputes		Korean War ends with armistice
1947	Truman announces Truman Doctrine to stop communism's spread	**1954**	Senate holds Army-McCarthy hearings
	George Kennan ("X") urges containment policy in *Sources of Soviet Conduct*		United States helps overthrow Arbenz in Guatemala
1948	Marshall Plan provides funds to rebuild Europe		French are defeated after siege of Dien Bien Phu
	Harry S Truman is elected president		Supreme Court orders school desegregation in *Brown* v. *Board of Education of Topeka*
	State of Israel is created as Jewish homeland; Arabs declare war	**1956**	Egypt nationalizes Suez Canal in Suez Crisis
1948–1949	United States supplies West Berlin during Berlin airlift		Eisenhower is reelected president
1949	United States and eleven other nations form North Atlantic Treaty Organization (NATO)	**1957**	National Guard enforces desegregation of Central High School in Little Rock, Arkansas
	USSR explodes atom bomb	**1959**	Fidel Castro overthrows Fulgencio Batista, takes power in Cuba
1950	North Korea invades South Korea	**1960**	John F. Kennedy is first Roman Catholic to be elected president
	NSC-68 calls for massive military buildup		
	Alger Hiss is convicted of perjury		
	McCarran Act restricts "subversive" activity		
	Senator Joseph McCarthy charges that the State Department is riddled with communists		
	UN counterattack in Korea is driven back by Red Chinese army		

SUPPLEMENTARY READING

General surveys include William Chafe, *The Unfinished Journey* (1986), James T. Patterson, *Grand Expectations: Postwar America, 1945–1974* (1996), David Halberstam, *The Fifties* (1993), H. W. Brands, *The Devil We Knew: Americans and the Cold War* (1993), John Patrick Diggins, *The Proud Decades, 1941–1960* (1989), and Michael S. Sherry, *In the Shadow of War* (1995). Older but influential interpretive works include Arthur M. Schlesinger Jr., *The Vital Center* (1949), Richard E. Neustadt, *Presidential Power* (1960), and James M. Burns, *The Deadlock of Democracy* (1964).

The evolution of American policy toward nuclear weapons is debated in Gar Alperovitz, *Atomic Diplomacy: Hiroshima and Potsdam* (1985), Gregg Herken, *The Winning Weapon: The Atomic Bomb in the Cold War* (1982), and Melvyn P. Leffler, *A Preponderance of Power: National Security, the Truman Administration, and the Cold War* (1992). An accessible overview is Richard Rhodes, *Dark Sun: The Making of the Hydrogen Bomb* (1995).

The 1948 election is described in Gary Donaldson, *Truman Defeats Dewey* (1999). On the origins of the shift of the South away from the Democrats, see Kari Frederickson, *The Dixiecrat Revolt and the End of the Solid South, 1932–1968* (2001). Postwar domestic politics are also treated in William L. O'Neill, *Riding High* (1986), and Alonzo L. Hamby, *The Imperial Years* (1976). On the cultural effects of the Cold War, see Elaine Tyler May, *Homeward Bound: American Families in the Cold War* (1988), and Paul Boyer, *By the Bomb's Early Light* (1986).

In addition to works cited in the previous chapter, see Donald R. McCoy, *The Presidency of Harry S Truman* (1984). David McCullough's, *Truman* (1992), is accessible and sympathetic; Alonzo L. Hamby's *Man of the People: A Life of Harry S Truman* (1995) is scholarly and analytical.

Among many analyses and evaluations of American foreign policy, George F. Kennan's writings stand out, both as primary sources and as interpretations. See his *Memoirs* (1969, 1972), *Realities of American Foreign Policy* (1954), and *Russia and the West Under Lenin and Stalin* (1961).

On Truman's foreign policy, see Paul G. Pierpaoli, Jr., *Truman and Korea* (1999), and Michael J. Hogan, *The Marshall Plan* (1987). Roger C. Miller, *To Save a City: The Berlin Airlift* (2000) is a succinct account.

The origins of the Korean War are now becoming clearer. In two volumes Bruce Cummings, *The Origins of the Korean War* (1981, 1990) emphasizes that the struggle was, at the outset, a civil war; William Stueck, *The Korean War: An International History* (1995) focuses on miscalculations by Stalin and Mao Zedong. On the war itself, see Stanley Sandler, *The Korean War* (1999). On MacArthur, see Geoffrey Perret, *Old Soldiers Never Die* (1996).

On McCarthyism, Ellen Schrecker, *Many Are the Crimes: McCarthyism in America* (1998) argues that the phenomenon was broader than McCarthy and became institutionalized in the FBI under J. Edgar Hoover. David Caute, *The Great Fear* (1978) is sharply critical. For different views of McCarthy himself, see Thomas C. Reeves, *Life and Times of Joe McCarthy* (1997), and Arthur Herman, *Joseph McCarthy* (2000). On the Hiss case see Allen Weinsten, *Perjury: The Hiss-Chambers Case* (1978), and Sam Tanenhaus, *Whittaker Chambers* (1997).

On the early history of the Civil Rights movement, see Mark Tushnet, *Making Civil Rights Law* (1994), and *Making Constitutional Law: Thurgood Marshall and the Supreme Court* (1997). See also Richard Kluger, *Simple Justice* (1976), and Harvard Sitkoff, *The Struggle for Black Equality* (1993). The writings of Martin Luther King, Jr., especially *Stride Toward Freedom* (1958) are also useful. The first volume of Taylor Branch's superb biography of Martin Luther King, Jr., *Parting the Waters* (1988), covers 1959 through 1963. Thomas Borstelmann, *The Cold War and the Color Line* (2001), and Mary Dudziak, *Cold War Civil Rights* (2000), show how the civil rights movement became embroiled in foreign policy issues, especially with respect to African nations.

Eisenhower's own view of his presidency can be found in Dwight D. Eisenhower, *Mandate for Change* (1963) and *Waging Peace* (1965). Recent (and increasingly positive) assessments include Robert Bowie and Richard Immerman, *Waging Peace: How Eisenhower Shaped an Enduring Cold War Strategy* (1998), Craig Campbell, *Destroying the Village: Eisenhower and Thermonuclear War* (1998), and Ray Takeyh, *The Origins of the Eisenhower Doctrine* (2000) on Suez.

Biographies on the central figures, in addition to those cited in the previous chapter, include James Chace, *Acheson* (1998), and Richard H. Immerman, *John Foster Dulles* (1999).

SUGGESTED WEBSITES

Harry S Truman
http://www.ipl.org/div/POTUS/hstruman.html
This site contains basic factual data about Truman's election, presidency, and speeches.

Cold War
http://cnn.com/SPECIALS/cold.war/
This is the companion site to the CNN Perspectives series on the Cold War. It contains information including interactive timelines and a quiz.

The Marshall Plan
http://www.archives.gov/exhibit_hall/
featured_documents/marshall_plan/
The National Archives site contains useful information on the Marshall Plan.

Korean War Project
http://www.koreanwar.org/
This site has information about the Korean War and is a guide to resources on that conflict.

NATO at 50
  http://www.cnn.com/SPECIALS/1999/nato/
This CNN site has an excellent timeline and images that tell the history of the North Atlantic Treaty Organization.

Senator Joe McCarthy—A Multimedia Celebration
  http://webcorp.com/mccarthy/
This Webcorp site includes audio and visual excerpts of McCarthy's speeches.

Harry S Truman Library and Museum
  http://www.trumanlibrary.org
This presidential library site has numerous photos and important documents relating to Truman.

Dwight David Eisenhower
  http://www.ipl.org/div/POTUS/ddeisenhower.html
This site contains an online bibliography covering Eisenhower's election, presidency, and speeches.

1950s America
  http://www.writing.upenn.edu/~afilreis/50s/home.html
This site by University of Pennsylvania Professor Al Filreis contains a large array of 1950s literature and images in an alphabetical index.

Hollywood and the Movies During the 1950s
  http://lib.berkeley.edu/MRC/50sbib.html
This site proves information on cinema and film during the 1950s.

The Dwight D. Eisenhower Library and Museum
  http://www.eisenhower.utexas.edu/
This site contains mainly photographs of the presidents.

From Camelot to Watergate

- This doesn't mean that you don't need to study right before a test, but you shouldn't have to stay up all night to prepare for it, and you should feel more confident when you take the test.

Do You Suffer From Test Anxiety?

- Do you do great on homework assignments, but you dread test days?
- Do you forget everything you know when you sit down to take a test?
- Does it seem like what you studied has nothing to do with the test you are taking?

Once you are sitting in the hot spot with your pencil in hand, use the DETER strategy for taking tests as described at http://www.how-to-study.com/A%20Strategy%20for%20Taking%20Tests.htm.

Directions: Read and understand the test directions.

Examine: Examine the entire test to see what is required.

Time: Determine how much time to allow for each item.

Easiest: Answer the easiest items first.

Review: Allow time to review the test to check your answers for accuracy and completeness.

Again, practice makes perfect. There are several web sites for taking practice tests. Here are a few:

- http://www.actstudent.org/testprep/index.html
- http://4tests.com/
- http://www.collegeboard.com/
- http://www.ets.org/

COMPUTER BASICS

For many classes, you need to know the basics about using a computer and possibly even surfing the Internet in order to complete certain assignments. If you are taking a distance learning class, you MUST have some basic knowledge of computers and the Internet.

You must be able to

- prepare, save, and retrieve files
- send and receive emails with attachments
- deposit files in an electronic drop box
- locate and navigate web sites
- download software and plug ins
- participate in discussion boards.

A good resource for learning about these items is http://www.learnthenet.com/english/index.html.

- Once you have reached this site, note the "How To" list at the left side of the screen.
- If you are a novice, you might want to start with "How to Use this Site."
- Otherwise, start with "Master the Basics" and then work your way down the list.

You will find information ranging from making the connection to the Internet to building your own web site.

- Click on each underlined word or title to access the information.
- This information is also available as the "Animated Internet."

Jan's Illustrated Computer Literacy 101 at http://www.jegsworks.com/Lessons/index.html includes lessons on the topics listed on the next screens, and the approach is very detailed yet easy to understand. Even if you have never touched a mouse before, you should be able to follow along.

Do you want to learn about specific items; i.e., WindowsXP or MSWord2003?

- These are Microsoft products.
- You can go to http://www.microsoft.com/ and find training on just about every product produced by Microsoft—even older versions.

The information above is just a teaser. We have included only a few websites because websites come and go. To learn more, check out the Internet and use a search engine, such as GOOGLE (www.google.com), to find sites on the topics we have referenced.

▼ "President Elect," a portrait of John Fitzgerald Kennedy, by James Rosenquist, a billboard painter who became a Pop-artist. Rosenquist liked to juxtapose familiar if dissimilar objects.

CHAPTER CONTENTS

Having lampooned the Eisenhower administration as stodgy and unimaginative, President Kennedy made a show of his style and wit. He flouted convention by naming his younger brother Robert attorney general. "I can't see that it's wrong to give him a little legal experience before he goes out to practice law," the president quipped. Kennedy also prided himself on being a man of letters, winner of a Pulitzer Prize for *Profiles in Courage*. He quoted Robert Frost and Dante. He played and replayed recordings of Winston Churchill, hoping to imprint the great orator's sonorous cadences on his own flat Bostonian vowels. At the instigation of his elegant wife, Jacqueline, Kennedy surrounded himself with the finest intellects at glittering White House galas to honor Nobel Prize winners and celebrated artists.

Kennedy's youthful senior staff boasted impressive scholarly credentials. His national security adviser, McGeorge Bundy, had been dean of the faculty at Harvard (and the first undergraduate at Yale to receive perfect scores in three college entrance examinations). Secretary of Defense Robert McNamara also had taught at Harvard before becoming the first non–family member to head the Ford Motor Company. The administration constituted, as journalist David Halberstam observed later, and somewhat ruefully, "the best and the brightest."

Kennedy's campaign slogan—"Let's get this country moving again"—was embodied in his own active life. He played rugged games of touch football with the press corps and romped with his young children in the Oval Office. In an article for *Sports Illustrated* entitled "The Soft American" and published just after the election, Kennedy complained that television, movies, and a comfortable lifestyle had made too many young people flabby. His earliest presidential initiative was a physical fitness campaign in the schools.

Kennedy's image of youthful vigor ("vigah," as he pronounced the word) was enhanced by the beauty and presence of Jacqueline, whose wide-eyed diffidence was commonly misunderstood and universally admired as regal bearing. The image was enhanced by Lerner and Loewe's musical *Camelot,* which opened a few weeks before the inauguration. Its evocation of King Arthur, who sought to lead his virile young knights in challenges great and good, suggested the Kennedy White House. (The musical became a favorite of the president; he often listened to cast recordings before going to sleep.) All Washington seemed aglow with excitement and energy. In the words of the administration's chief chronicler, Arthur M. Schlesinger, Jr. (another former Harvard professor): "Never had girls seemed so pretty, tunes so melodious, and evenings so blithe and unconstrained."

John F. Kennedy

Never, too, had the substance of an administration been so closely identified with the style of its president. But the dazzle was misleading. Although quick-witted and intelligent, Kennedy was no intellectual. His favorite reading was the James Bond spy novels of Ian Fleming. He never admitted it publicly, but most of *Profiles in Courage* had been ghostwritten by paid writers.

Nor did the president embody physical fitness. Congenital back problems, aggravated by war injuries, forced Kennedy to use crutches or a cane in private and to take heavy doses of painkillers and amphetamines. The president's permanent "tan" did not result from outdoor exercise, as the public assumed, but from Addison's disease, an often fatal failure of the adrenal glands for which Kennedy gave himself daily injections of cortisone. Though he publicly denied it, Kennedy was chronically ill throughout his presidency.

The president nevertheless engaged in many extramarital sexual affairs. Reporters covering the White House were aware of his often brazen indiscretions, but chose not to intrude on what they regarded as the president's private life.

THE CUBAN CRISES

"The torch has been passed to a new generation of Americans," Kennedy declared in his inaugural address. Their chief task was to stop the spread of communism. Whereas Eisenhower had relied on the nation's nuclear arsenal to intimidate the Kremlin, Kennedy proposed to challenge communist aggression whenever and wherever it occurred. "We shall pay any price, bear any burden, meet any hardship, support any friend, oppose any foe to assure the survival and the success of liberty," Kennedy intoned. A new breed of cold warrior, Kennedy called on young men and women to serve in the Peace Corps, an organization that he created to mobilize American idealism and technical skills to help developing nations. His was a call for commitment—and action.

▲ Fidel Castro *(right)* celebrates in Havana on May 1, 1961, several weeks after the debacle at the Bay of Pigs. Stung by this humiliating defeat, President Kennedy resolved to destroy Castro by other means. "My idea," Robert Kennedy said privately in November, "is to stir things up on the island with espionage, sabotage, general disorder." This CIA program, code-named MONGOOSE, included dozens of schemes to assassinate Castro. Pop-art then imitated life, as weekly television shows such as *I Spy* and *Mission: Impossible* featured daffy escapades much like those hatched by MONGOOSE.

Perhaps seduced by his own rhetoric, Kennedy blundered almost immediately. Anti-Castro exiles were eager to organize an invasion of their homeland, reasoning that the Cuban people would rise up against Castro and communism as soon as "democratic" forces provided the necessary leadership. Under Eisenhower the CIA had begun training some 2000 Cuban exiles in Nicaragua. Kennedy was of two minds about the proposed invasion. Some in his administration opposed it strongly, but his closest advisers, including his brother Robert, urged him to give his approval. In the end he did.

The invaders, 1400 strong, struck in April 1961. They landed at the Bay of Pigs, on Cuba's southern coast. But the Cuban people failed to flock to their lines, and soon Castro's army pinned the invaders down and forced them to surrender. Because American involvement could not be disguised, the affair exposed the United States to all the criticism that a straightforward assault would have produced, without accomplishing the overthrow of Castro. Worse, it made Kennedy appear impulsive as well as unprincipled. Castro tightened his connections with the Soviet Union.

In June, Kennedy met with Soviet Premier Khrushchev in Vienna. Furious over the invasion of Cuba, Khrushchev blustered about grabbing West Berlin. In August, he abruptly closed the border between East and West Berlin and erected a wall of concrete blocks and barbed wire across the city to stop the flow of East Germans into the noncommunist zone. At the same time, the Soviets resumed nuclear testing. Khrushchev ordered detonation of a series of gigantic hydrogen bombs, including one with a power 3000 times that of the bomb that had devastated Hiroshima.

Kennedy followed suit: He announced plans to build thousands of nuclear missiles, known as Minutemen, capable of hitting targets on the other side of the world. He expanded the American space program, vowing that an American would land on the moon within ten years. The president called on Congress to pass a large increase in military spending.

In secret, Kennedy resolved to destroy Castro. He ordered military leaders to plan for a full-scale invasion of Cuba. (One of the training maneuvers was code-named ORTSAC—Castro spelled backward.) He also instructed the CIA to undertake "massive activity" against Castro's regime. The CIA devised Operation Mongoose (named for an animal that devours poisonous snakes), a plan to slip spies, saboteurs, and assassins into Cuba. Although never officially endorsed by the president, Mongoose operated under the oversight of Robert Kennedy. Its attempts to assassinate Castro failed.

▲ "I am a Berliner," Kennedy declared from a balcony in West Berlin in June, 1961, and his words brought a roar of approval from the West Berliners. Gesturing toward the Berlin wall, he called it "the most obvious and vivid demonstration of the failures of the Communist system."

In 1962 Khrushchev precipitated the most dangerous confrontation of the Cold War. To forestall the anticipated American invasion of Cuba, he moved tanks, heavy bombers, and 42,000 Soviet troops and technicians to the island. But his most fateful step was to sneak several dozen guided nuclear missiles into the country and begin constructing launching pads for them. Although the range of these missiles was far less than that of the American Minutemen, if fired from Cuba the Soviet missiles could have delivered nuclear warheads to most of the eastern United States.

On October 14 American spy planes spotted the launching pads and missiles. The president faced a dreadful decision. After the Bay of Pigs fiasco, he

▲ This photograph, taken by an American U–2 spy plane and released during the Cuban missile crisis, shows the installation of liquid-fueled Soviet missiles. Khrushchev had assumed that the missiles could be kept secret. "Our military specialists informed us that strategic missiles can be reliably concealed in the palm forests of Cuba," one of Khrushchev's advisers recalled. Khrushchev, who assumed that the missiles would be harder to spot if they were in a horizontal position, ordered that the missiles be placed in an upright position only at night. This was a mistake: The U–2's easily detected the missiles in their horizontal position.

could not again appear to back down to the communists. But if he invaded Cuba or bombed the Soviet bases and missile sites, Khrushchev would likely seize West Berlin or bomb United States missile sites in Turkey. Either action might lead to a full-scale nuclear war and millions of deaths.

On October 22 Kennedy went on television to address the nation. The Soviet buildup was "a deliberately provocative and unjustified change in the status quo." He ordered the American navy to stop and search all vessels headed for Cuba and to turn back any containing "offensive" weapons. Kennedy called on Khrushchev to dismantle the missile bases and remove from the island all weapons capable of striking the United States. Any Cuban-based nuclear attack would result, he warned, in "a full retaliatory response upon the Soviet Union."

For days, while the world held its breath, Soviet ships steamed toward Cuba and work on the missile bases continued. Then Khrushchev backed down. He recalled the ships, withdrew the missiles, and reduced his military establishment in Cuba to modest proportions. Kennedy then lifted the blockade. He also promised not to invade Cuba, thus ensuring Castro's survival; Kennedy also agreed to withdraw U.S. missiles from Turkey, though this latter concession was not made public at the time.

Immediately the president was hailed for his steady nerve and consummate statesmanship; the Cuban missile crisis was widely regarded as his finest hour. Yet in retrospect it appears that he may have overreacted to the missiles in Cuba. The Soviet nuclear threat had been exaggerated. After *Sputnik*, the Soviet long-range missile program flopped, though this was not known at the time. By the summer of 1962 a "missile gap" existed, but it was overwhelmingly in favor of the United States, whose nuclear forces outnumbered those of the Soviet Union by a ratio of 17 to 1. Khrushchev's decision to put medium-range missiles in Cuba signified Soviet weakness rather than impending aggression.

Both Kennedy and Khrushchev were sobered by the missile crisis; afterward neither spoke so glibly about superpower confrontation. They agreed to the installation of a telephone "hot line" between the White House and the Kremlin, so that in any future crisis leaders of the two nations could communicate instantly. They also signed a treaty outlawing nuclear testing in the atmosphere. But Khrushchev's bluff had been called—a public humiliation from which he would never recover. Within two years, hard-liners in the Kremlin forced him out of office. His successor, Leonid Brezhnev, was an old-style Stalinist who inaugurated an intensive program of long-range missile development. The nuclear arms race moved to new terrain, uncertain and unimaginably dangerous.

THE VIETNAM WAR

After the French withdrew from Vietnam in 1954, the Vietnamese people were supposed to determine their own future. But Ngo Dinh Diem, the U.S.-backed leader in the south, feared that he would be defeated by Ho Chi Minh, a well-known nationalist and leader of the communist Viet Minh. Diem canceled the election scheduled for 1956. With Eisenhower's help, he attempted to build a new nation in the south. The United States sent weapons and a handful of American military "advisers" to help Diem equip and train a South Vietnamese army. Ho decided to ignore Diem and consolidate his rule in the north. Those Viet Minh units that remained in the south—they soon came to be known as Vietcong—were instructed to form secret cells and bide their time. During the late 1950s they gained in strength and militancy.

In May 1959 Ho decided that the time had come to overthrow Diem. Vietcong guerrillas infiltrated thousands of villages, ambushed South Vietnamese convoys, and assassinated government officials. Soon the Vietcong controlled large sections of the countryside, some almost within sight of the capital city of Saigon.

By the time Kennedy took office, Diem's government was tottering. As a senator, Kennedy had endorsed Diem and the attempt to build a noncommunist South Vietnam. He called it the "cornerstone of the Free World in Southeast Asia, the keystone in the arch, the finger in the dike." After the Bay of Pigs debacle, furthermore, Kennedy worried that his credibility with Khrushchev had been damaged. "If he thinks I'm inexperienced and have no guts," he told an aide, "we won't get anywhere with him. So we have to act." Vietnam, he added, "looks like the place."

Kennedy sharply increased the American military and economic commitment to South Vietnam. At the end of 1961 there were 3200 American military personnel in the country; within two years, there were more than 16,000, and 120 American soldiers had been killed. Despite the expanded effort, by the summer of 1963 Diem's regime was in ruins. An ardent Catholic, he cracked down on the Buddhists, who, joined by students, protested his repression. Thousands were arrested, and some were shot. In protest, several Buddhist monks became martyrs by setting themselves on fire in public.

Unable to persuade Diem to moderate his policies, Kennedy sent word to dissident Vietnamese generals of his willingness to support them if they ousted Diem. On November 1 several of these generals surrounded the presidential palace with troops and tanks, seized Diem, and killed him. Kennedy, though appalled by Diem's death, recognized the new junta.

"WE SHALL OVERCOME": THE CIVIL RIGHTS MOVEMENT

Kennedy initially approached the race question with exceeding caution. His razor-thin victory had depended on the votes both of African Americans in northern cities and white Democrats in the Deep South. As president, his visible support for one group would alienate the other. So Kennedy temporized, urging leaders on both sides to show restraint. This proved impossible.

During and after World War II, like a glacier, slowly but with massive force, a demand for change had developed in the South. Its roots lay in southern industrialization; in the shift from small sharecropping holdings to large commercial farms; in the vast wartime expenditures of the federal government on aircraft factories and army bases in the region; in the impact of the GI Bill on southern colleges and universities; and in the gradual development of a southern black middle class.

This change first came to national attention during the Eisenhower administration in the rigidly segregated city of Montgomery, Alabama. On Friday, December 1, 1955, Rosa Parks, a seamstress at the Montgomery Fair department store, boarded a bus on her way home from her job. She dutifully took a seat toward the rear as custom and law required. As white workers and shoppers filled the forward section, the driver ordered her to give up her place to a white passenger. Parks, who was also secretary of the Montgomery NAACP chapter, refused. She had decided, she later recalled, that "I would have to know once and for all what rights I had as a human being and a citizen."

She was arrested. Over the weekend, Montgomery's black leaders organized a boycott. "Don't ride the bus . . . Monday," their mimeographed notice ran. "If you work, take a cab, or share a ride, or walk." Monday dawned bitterly cold, but the boycott was a total success.

Most Montgomery blacks could not afford to miss a single day's wages, so the protracted struggle to get to work was difficult to maintain. Black-owned taxis reduced their rates sharply, and when the city declared this illegal, car pools were quickly organized. Few African Americans owned cars. Although nearly everyone who did volunteered, there were never more than 350 cars available to the more than 10,000 people who needed rides to their jobs and back every day. Nevertheless, the boycott went on.

Late in February the Montgomery authorities obtained indictments of 115 leaders of the boycott, but this move backfired because it focused national attention on the situation. A young clergyman, the Rev. Dr. Martin Luther King, Jr., was emerging as the leader of the boycott. A gifted speaker, he became an overnight celebrity. Money poured in from all over the country to support the movement. The boycott lasted for over a year. Finally the Supreme Court declared the local law enforcing racial separation unconstitutional: Montgomery had to desegregate its public transportation system.

This success encouraged blacks elsewhere in the South to band together against segregation. A new organization founded in 1957, the Southern Christian Leadership Conference (SCLC), headed by King, moved to the forefront of the civil rights movement. Other organizations joined the struggle, notably the Congress of Racial Equality (CORE), which had been founded in 1942.

In February 1960 four African American college students in Greensboro, North Carolina, sat down at a lunch counter at a Woolworth's store. "We do not serve Negroes," they were told. They returned with more and more demonstrators. By the end of the week over a thousand protesters descended on Woolworth's, led by a phalanx of football players from the nearby black college who cleared the way through a throng of Confederate flag-wavers. "Who do you think you are?" a white demanded. "We the Union army," a football player retorted.

This "sit-in" tactic was not new. CORE had staged sit-ins in Chicago restaurants back in 1943. But the Greensboro students sparked a national movement; students in dozens of other southern towns and cities copied their example. Within a fortnight more than 50 sit-ins were in progress in southern cities. By the end of 1961 over 70,000 people had participated in such demonstrations. Still another new organization, the Student Nonviolent Coordinating Committee (SNCC), was founded by black college students in 1960 to provide a focus for the sit-in movement and to conduct voter registration drives in the South, actions that more than any other roused the fury of southern segregationists.

In May 1961 black and white foes of segregation organized a "freedom ride" to test the effectiveness of federal regulations prohibiting discrimination in interstate transportation. Boarding two buses in Washington, an integrated group of 13 volunteers took off across the South toward New Orleans. In Alabama they ran into trouble. At Anniston racists set fire to one of the buses, and in Birmingham they were assaulted by a mob. But violence did not stop the freedom riders. Other groups followed, many deliberately seeking arrest to test local segregation ordinances. The resultant court cases repeatedly broke down legal racial barriers throughout the South.

This protracted struggle eventually yielded practical and moral benefits for southern whites as well as blacks. Gradually all but the most unwavering defenders of segregation changed their attitudes. But this took time, and many blacks were unwilling to wait.

Some blacks, contemptuous of white prejudices, were urging their fellows to reject "American" society and all it stood for. In the North, black nationalism became a potent force. Elijah Muhammad, leader of the Black Muslim movement, loathed whites so intensely that he demanded that a part of the United States be set aside exclusively for blacks. He urged his followers to be industrious, thrifty, and abstemious—and to view all whites with suspicion and hatred.

"This white government has ruled us and given us plenty hell, but the time has arrived that you taste a little of your own hell," Muhammad said. "There are many of my poor black ignorant brothers . . . preaching the ignorant and lying stuff that you should love your enemy. What fool can love his enemy?" Another important Black Muslim, Malcolm X, put it this way in a 1960 speech: "For the white man

▲ This Greyhound bus carried Freedom Riders—whites and blacks who fought segregation by intentionally violating segregation policies. When a mob of whites from Anniston, Alabama learned of this, they descended on the bus, slashed its tires, and piled into dozens of cars to chase it as it pulled away. As the bus was racing along Highway 78, the tires went flat. After the bus stopped, someone tossed a firebomb through the back window. As the riders got out of the bus, they were beaten. This photograph was shown that evening on wire services throughout the world.

to ask the black man if he hates him is just like the rapist asking the raped, or the wolf asking the sheep, 'Do you hate me?'" "If someone puts a hand on you," he advised blacks on another occasion, "send him to the cemetery."

Ordinary southern blacks became increasingly impatient. In the face of brutal repression by local police, many began to question Martin Luther King's tactic of nonviolent protest. After leading a series of demonstrations in Birmingham, Alabama, in 1963, King was thrown in jail. When local white clergymen, professing themselves sympathetic to the blacks' objectives, nonetheless urged an end to "untimely" protests, which (they claimed) "incite hatred and violence," King wrote his now-famous "Letter from Birmingham Jail," which contained this moving explanation of why he and his followers were unwilling to wait any longer for justice.

> [W]hen you take a cross-country drive and find it necessary to sleep night after night in the uncomfortable corners of your automobile because no motel will accept you; when you are humiliated day in and day out by nagging signs reading "white" and "colored"; when your first name becomes "nigger" and your middle name becomes "boy" . . . then you will understand why we find it so difficult to wait.

Civil Rights March on Washington

The brutal repression of the Birmingham demonstrations, captured in newspaper photos and on television broadcasts, brought a flood of recruits and money to the protesters' cause. Pushed by all these developments, President Kennedy reluctantly began to change his policy. His administration had from the start given lip service to desegregation and encouraged activists' efforts to register black voters in the South, but when confrontations arose the president hesitated, arguing that it was up to local officials to enforce the law. After Birmingham, however, Kennedy did give his support to a modest civil rights bill.

When this measure ran into stiff opposition in Congress, blacks organized a demonstration in Washington, attended by 200,000 people. At this gathering, King delivered his "I Have a Dream" address, looking forward to a time when racial prejudice no longer existed and people of all religions and colors could join hands and say, "Free at last! Free at last!" Kennedy sympathized with the Washington gathering but feared it would make passage of the civil rights bill more difficult rather than easier. As in other areas, he was not a forceful advocate of his own proposals.

TRAGEDY IN DALLAS: JFK ASSASSINATED

Through it all, Kennedy retained his hold on public opinion. In the fall of 1963 most observers believed he easily would win a second term. Then, while visiting Dallas, Texas, on November 22, he was shot in the head by an assassin, Lee Harvey Oswald, and died almost instantly. One measure of Kennedy's hold on the public imagination was the outpouring of grief that attended his death. Kennedy had given hope to people who had none. Young black civil rights activist Anne Moody, who later wrote *Coming of Age in Mississippi*, was working as a waitress in a segregated restaurant. "Tears were burning my cheeks," she recalled. Her boss, a Greek immigrant, gently suggested she take the rest of the day off. When she looked up, there were tears in his eyes too.

Kennedy's assassination precipitated an extraordinary series of events. Oswald had fired on the president with a rifle from an upper story of a warehouse. No one saw him pull the trigger. He was apprehended largely because he panicked and killed a policeman across town later in the day. He denied his guilt, but a mass of evidence connected him with the assassination of the president. Before he could be brought to trial, however, he was himself murdered by Jack Ruby, the owner of a Dallas nightclub. The incident took place in full view of television cameras, while Oswald was being transferred from one place of detention to another.

Each day brought new revelations. Oswald had defected briefly to the Soviet Union in 1959, then had returned to the United States and formed a pro-Castro organization in New Orleans. Many concluded that some nefarious conspiracy lay at the root of the tragedy. Oswald, the argument ran, was a pawn—either of communists or anticommunists (the conspiracy theories lost none of their appeal for being contradictory)—whose murder was designed to shield from exposure the masterminds who had engineered the assassination. A special commission headed by Chief Justice Earl Warren was convened to analyze the evidence. After a lengthy investigation, it concluded that Oswald had acted alone.

Instead of dampening charges of conspiracy, the report of the Warren Commission provoked new doubts. As word leaked out about the earlier CIA assassination attempts against Castro, the failure of the Warren Report even to mention Operation Mongoose made the commission suspect, all the more so since several members, including Allen Dulles, former director of the CIA, had known of the operation. (On the day of Kennedy's assassination, a CIA agent in Paris

▲ JFK and Jacqueline Kennedy in a motorcade in Dallas, November 22, 1963. Several minutes later, he was shot and killed.

met with a Cuban who had volunteered to assassinate Castro and gave the would-be assassin a ballpoint pen containing a poisoned hypodermic needle.) In fact, there is little solid evidence to suggest that Oswald was part of a wider conspiracy. But the decision of Dulles and other commissioners to protect CIA secrets engendered skepticism toward the Warren Commission—and the United States government.

LYNDON BAINES JOHNSON

John F. Kennedy's death made Lyndon B. Johnson president. From 1949 until his election as vice president Johnson had been a senator from Texas and, for most of that time, Senate Democratic leader. He could be heavy-handed or subtle, and also devious, domineering, persistent, and obliging. Many people swore

by him; few had the fortitude to swear at him. Above all he knew what to do with political power. "Some men," he said, "want power so they can strut around to 'Hail to the Chief'. . . . I wanted it to use it."

Johnson, who had consciously modeled his career after that of Franklin D. Roosevelt, considered social welfare legislation his specialty. The contrast with Kennedy could not have been sharper. In his inaugural address, Kennedy had made no mention of domestic issues. Kennedy's plans for federal aid for education, urban renewal, a higher minimum wage, and medical care for the aged were blocked in Congress by Republicans and southern Democrats. The same coalition also defeated his chief economic initiative—a broad tax cut to stimulate the economy. But Kennedy had reacted to these defeats mildly, almost wistfully. He thought the machinery of the federal government was cumbersome and ineffective.

▲ LBJ as Texas cowboy, a masculine image he assiduously cultivated. Biographers have suggested that Johnson was torn between the expectations of his father, a crude local politician who flouted polite society, and those of his mother, a refined woman who insisted that her son read poetry and practice the violin. Johnson later told biographer Doris Kearns Goodwin that he persisted in Vietnam because he worried that critics would accuse him of being "an unmanly man. A man without a spine."

Lyndon Johnson

Johnson knew how to make it work. On becoming president, he pushed hard for Kennedy's programs. Early in his career Johnson had voted against a bill making lynching a federal crime, and he also had opposed bills outlawing state poll taxes and establishing the federal Fair Employment Practices Commission. But after he became an important figure in national affairs, he consistently championed racial equality. Now he made it the centerpiece of his domestic policy. "Civil righters are going to have to wear sneakers to keep up with me," he boasted. Bills long buried in committee sailed through Congress. Early in 1964 Kennedy's tax cut was passed. A few months later, an expanded version of another Kennedy proposal became law as the Civil Rights Act of 1964.

THE GREAT SOCIETY

The much-strengthened Civil Rights Act outlawed discrimination by employers against blacks and also against women. It broke down legal barriers to black voting in the southern states and outlawed racial segregation of all sorts in places of public accommodation, such as movie theaters, hotels, and restaurants. In addition, unlike presidents Eisenhower and Kennedy, Johnson made sure that the government enforced civil rights legislation.

Johnson's success in steering the Civil Rights Act through Congress confirmed his belief that he could be a reformer in the tradition of Franklin Roosevelt. He declared war on poverty and set out to create a "great society" in which poverty no longer would exist. The primary objective of Johnson's war on poverty was to give poor people the opportunity to improve themselves.

In 1937 Roosevelt had been accused of exaggeration for claiming that one-third of the nation was "ill-housed, ill-clad, ill-nourished." In fact Roosevelt had underestimated the extent of poverty. Wartime economic growth reduced the percentage of poor people in the country substantially, but in 1960 between 20 and 25 percent of all American families—about 40 million people—were living below the poverty line, a government standard of minimum subsistence based on income and family size.

The presence of so many poor people in an "affluent" society was deplorable but not difficult to explain. In any community a certain number of people cannot support themselves because of physical, mental, or emotional problems. The United States also included entire regions, the best known being the Appalachian area, that had been bypassed by economic development and no longer provided their inhabitants with adequate economic opportunities.

Moreover, prosperity and advancing technology had changed the definition of poverty. Telephones, radios and electric refrigerators, and other goods unimaginable to the most affluent Americans of the 1860s, were necessities a hundred years later. But as living standards rose, so did job requirements. A strong back and a willingness to work no longer guaranteed a decent living. Technology was changing the labor market. Educated workers with special skills and good verbal abilities easily found well-paid jobs. Those who had no special skills or were poorly educated went without work.

The Economic Opportunity Act of 1964 created a mixture of programs, among them a Job Corps similar to the New Deal Civilian Conservation Corps; a community action program to finance local antipoverty efforts; and a system for training the unskilled unemployed and for lending money to small businesses in poor areas. The programs combined the progressive concept of government aid for those in need with the conservative idea of individual responsibility.

Buttressed by his legislative triumphs, Johnson sought election as president in his own right in 1964. He achieved this ambition in unparalleled fashion. His championing of civil rights won him the almost unanimous support of blacks; his tax policy attracted the well-to-do and the business interests; his war on poverty held the allegiance of labor and other traditionally Democratic groups. His down-home southern antecedents counterbalanced his liberalism on the race question in the eyes of many white Southerners.

The Republicans played into his hands by nominating the conservative Senator Barry M. Goldwater of Arizona, whose objective in Congress had been "not to pass laws but to repeal them." As a presidential candidate he favored such laissez-faire policies as cutting back on the social security system and doing away with the Tennessee Valley Authority. A large majority of voters found Goldwater out-of-date on economic questions and dangerously aggressive on foreign affairs.

In November, Johnson won a sweeping victory, collecting over 61 percent of the popular vote and carrying the whole country except Goldwater's Arizona and five states in the Deep South, where many conservatives were voting more against Johnson's civil rights policies than in favor of Goldwater. While not personally a racist, Goldwater had voted against the Civil Rights Act of 1964 and was opposed to government-mandated school integration.

Quickly Johnson pressed ahead with his Great Society program. In January 1965 he proposed a compulsory hospital insurance system, known as Medicare, for all persons over the age of 65. As amended by Congress, the Medicare Act consisted of Part A, hospital insurance for the retired (funded by increased Social Security taxes), and a voluntary plan, Part B, covering doctors' bills (paid for in part by the government). The law also provided for grants to the states to help pay the medical expenses of poor people, even those below the retirement age of 65. This part of the system was called Medicaid. Before the passage of the Medicare Act, about half of Americans over 65 years old had had no medical insurance.

Next, Congress passed the Elementary and Secondary Education Act in 1965, which supplied federal funds to school districts. Head Start, a program for poor preschoolers, was designed to prepare them for elementary school. It also incidentally improved the children's health by providing medical examinations and nutritious meals.

Impact of the Voting Rights Act of 1965

Still another important reform was the Voting Rights Act of 1965, pressed through Congress by President Johnson after more brutal repressions of civil rights demonstrators in the South. This law provided for federal intervention to protect black registration and voting in six southern states. It applied to state and local as well as federal elections.

Other laws passed at Johnson's urging in 1965 and 1966 included the creation of the National Endowment for the Arts and the National Endowment for the Humanities and measures supporting scientific research, highway safety, crime control, slum clearance, clean air, and the preservation of historic sites. Of particular significance was the Immigration Act of 1965, which did away with most provisions of the national-origin system of admitting newcomers. Instead, 290,000 persons a year were to be admitted on the basis of such priorities as job skills and need for political asylum. The law also placed a limit of 120,000 immigrants a year from countries in the Western Hemisphere. Previously, immigration from these countries had been unrestricted.

The Great Society program was one of the most remarkable outpourings of important legislation in American history. The results, however, were mixed. Head Start and a related program to help students in secondary schools prepare for college were regarded as successes. But the 1965 Education Act proved a disappointment. Too many local school districts found ways of using the federal money to cover their ordinary expenses, and the sums actually devoted to programs for the poor failed to improve most students' performances significantly.

Medicare and Medicaid certainly provided good medical treatment for millions of people, but because the patients no longer paid most of the bills, doctors, hospitals, and drug companies were able to raise fees and prices without fear of losing business. Medical costs escalated far more rapidly than the rate of inflation.

The Job Corps, which was designed to help poor people get better-paying jobs by providing them with vocational training, was an almost total failure. The cost of the training was high, relatively few trainees completed the courses, and of those who did, few found jobs in which they could make use of their new skills.

On balance, the achievements of the Great Society were far below what President Johnson had promised and his supporters had envisioned. The same, of course, can be said of most ambitious reform programs—of Reconstruction; of the Progressive movement; certainly of the New Deal, to which Johnson had contributed as a young man. Despite his long political experience, Johnson tried to accomplish too many things too quickly. He relied too heavily on the techniques of political manipulation. Perhaps he was carried away by his good fortune—that he would ever become president must have seemed to a man of his political acumen most unlikely after he failed to win the nomination in 1960. He seized too avidly this unexpected opportunity to make history. Without the crisis atmosphere that had appeared to justify hasty experimentation during the New Deal years, the public judged the results of the Great Society and the president who had shaped it skeptically.

JOHNSON ESCALATES THE WAR

After Diem's assassination, the situation in South Vietnam continued to deteriorate. One military coup followed another, and political instability aggravated military incapacity. President Johnson nevertheless felt that he had no choice but to prop up the South Vietnamese regime. "If I don't go in now," he told an adviser, "they'll be all over me in Congress. They won't be talking about my civil rights bill, or education, or beautification. No sir, they'll push Vietnam up my ass every time."

DOCUMENT

The Tonkin Gulf Resolution Message

Johnson decided to punish North Vietnam directly for prosecuting the war in the south. In early 1964 he secretly ordered American warships to escort the South Vietnamese navy on missions far into the Gulf of Tonkin; the South Vietnamese attacked North Vietnamese ships and port facilities and landed commandos in North Vietnam. After one such mission, American destroyers were fired on by North Vietnamese gunboats. Several nights later during a heavy storm, American ships reported that they were being fired on, though the enemy was never spotted. Using this Tonkin "incident" as pretext, Johnson demanded, and in an air of crisis obtained, an authorization from Congress to "repel any armed attack against the forces of the United States and to prevent further aggression." With this blank check, known as the Gulf of Tonkin Resolution, and buttressed by his sweeping defeat of Goldwater in the 1964 presidential election, Johnson authorized air attacks in North Vietnam. By the summer of 1965, American bombers were conducting some 5000 raids each month.

But the hail of bombs on North Vietnam had little effect on the struggle in the south. American intelligence officers concluded that the bombing campaign in the North actually strengthened the people's identification with Ho Chi Minh's government. Worse, the Vietcong expanded the areas under their control. After a fact-finding mission in the war zone, McGeorge Bundy concluded that the prospects were grim for South Vietnam. "The energy and persistence of the Vietcong are astonishing," he reported. "They

▲ **Southeast Asia, 1954–1975**

have accepted extraordinary losses and they come back for more. They show skill in their sneak attacks and ferocity when cornered." If the war was to be won, American soldiers—lots of them—would have to do much of the fighting themselves.

▶ *text continues on page 808*

Mapping
the Past

School Segregation After the *Brown* Decision

The 1954 *Brown* v. *Board of Education* decision prohibited racial segregation in the nation's public schools. But many states and school districts ignored federal court orders to comply with the desegregation order. President Eisenhower put down Arkansas Governor Orval Faubus's public challenge to federal authority in 1957, but he did little else to ensure compliance with *Brown*. President Kennedy, similarly, was reluctant to alienate white Southern voters. He named to the federal judiciary staunch supporters of school segregation. One of his appointees, E. Gordon West of Louisiana, called the *Brown* ruling "one of the truly regrettable decisions of all time."

The maps at right show the slow progress of school desegregation in the South. In 1954, 3870 school districts in the South had both white and black students. (South here includes Alabama, Arkansas, Florida, Georgia, Kentucky, Oklahoma, Louisiana, Mississippi, North Carolina, South Carolina, Tennessee, Texas, and Virginia.) In only three of these districts did any white and black students attend school together: Arkansas (2) and Texas (1). One of the 23 school districts in Maryland was desegregated. The percentage of African American students attending schools with whites in the South was slightly above zero.

In 1964 compliance with the Supreme Court's ruling had improved somewhat in the border states, but little in the Deep South. Of the 2586 school districts in the South that now had black and white students (the number of school districts had declined as a result of consolidation), 1150 reported that they were desegregated. Only 3 of Louisiana's 67 districts were desegregated, 4 of Mississippi's 150 districts, and 9 of Alabama's 118 districts.

But these figures were deceptive. Many southern districts allowed a few blacks into a single, formerly all-white, school but left the remainder of the schools segregated; thus they claimed that such districts were technically desegregated when in fact very few blacks attended schools with whites. Such evasions of *Brown* persisted for years. In Alabama,

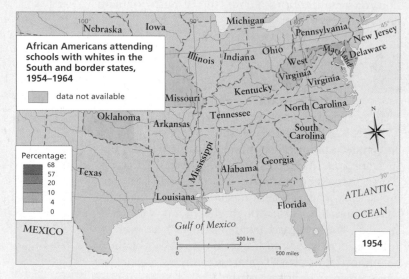

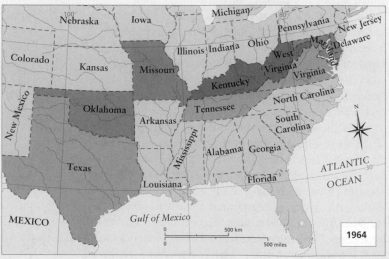